The Best Books for Academic Libraries

The Best Books for Academic Libraries
10 Volumes (ISBN 0-7222-0014-5)

The Best Books for
Academic Libraries

Religion & Philosophy

Volume 8

First Edition

The Best Books, Inc.
P. O. Box 893520
Temecula, CA. 92589-3520

ISBN 0-7222-0010-2 (10 Volume Set)
ISBN 0-7222-0018-8 (Volume 8)

```
Library of Congress Cataloging-in-Publication Data

The best books for academic libraries.-- 1st ed.
     v. cm.
Includes indexes.
Contents: v. 1. Science, technology, and agriculture -- v. 2. Medicine
-- v. 3. Language and literature -- v. 4. History of the Americas -- v.
5. World history -- v. 6. Social sciences -- v. 7. Political science,
law, education - v. 8. Religion and philosophy -- v. 9. Music & fine
arts -- v. 10. General works, military & naval, library science.
    ISBN 0-7222-0020-21-0.(set : alk. paper) -- ISBN 0-7222-0011-0 (v. 1 :
alk. paper. ISBN 0-7222-0012-9 (v. 2 : alk. paper) -- ISBN 0-7222-
0013-7 (v.3 : alk. paper) -- ISBN 0-7222-0014-5 (v. 4 : alk.
paper) -- ISBN 0-7222-0015-3 (v. 5 : alk. paper) ISBN 0-7222-0016-1
(v. 6 : alk. paper) -- ISBN 0-7222-0017-X (v. 7 : alk. paper) -- ISBN
0-7222-0018-8 (v. 8 : alk. paper) -- ISBN 0-7222-0019-6 (v. 9 : alk.
paper) -- ISBN 0-7222-0020-X (v. 10 : alk. paper).
    1.   Academic libraries--United States--Book lists.  I.  Best Books,
Inc.

Z1035 .B545 2002
011'.67—dc21   2002013790
```

For further information, contact:

The Best Books, Inc.
P.O. Box 893520
Temecula, CA 92589-3520
(Voice) 888-265-3531
(Fax) 888-265-3540

For product information/customer service, e-mail: customerservice@thebbooks.net

Visit our Web site: www.bestbooksfor.com

Table of Contents

Introduction

ABOUT THE PROJECT:

The Best Books for Academic Libraries was created to fill a need that has been growing in collection development for undergraduate and college libraries since the late 1980's. Our editorial department organized *The Best Books Database* (designed as a resource for university libraries) by consulting the leading book review journals, bibliographies, and reference books with subject bibliographies. It was compiled based upon the bibliographic standard from the Library of Congress (LC) MARC records. Each section was arranged by Library of Congress Classification Numbers.

PROCESSES FOR SUBJECT SELECTION AND COMPILATION:

To create *The Best Books for Academic Libraries,* the Editor conducted a comprehensive search of prominent Subject Librarians and Subject Specialists, experts in their area(s), to participate as Subject Advisors. The editorial processes utilized by The Best Books editorial staff are as follows:

1. Subject Advisors were asked to select the best books recommended for undergraduate and college libraries. Those who volunteered selected approximately one-third from over 170,000 books in *The Best Books Database* that they felt were essential to undergraduate work in their area(s) of expertise. Each Subject Advisor made their selections from subject surveys that were arranged by LC Classification Number. They added their choices of titles that were omitted from the surveys, and updated titles to the latest editions.

2. The Best Books editorial staff tabulated the returned surveys, and added the omissions into the database, following the LC MARC record standard, to arrive at a consensus of approximately the best 80,000 books.

3. Senior Subject Advisors were selected to conduct a final review of the surveys. They added any other titles they felt were essential to undergraduate work in their area(s) of expertise.

4. The final results were tabulated to create the First Edition of the 10 Volume set – *The Best Books for Academic Libraries.*

The actual title selection was left to the Subject Advisors. Each Advisor used the bibliographic resources available to them in their subject areas to make the best possible recommendations for undergraduate and college libraries. In order to achieve results that were well rounded, two to three Subject Advisors reviewed each section.

When there were discrepancies in the LC sorting and/or the description of any titles, The Best Books editorial staff defaulted to the information available on the LC MARC records.

The intention of this project, and The Best Books editorial staff, was to include only books in this listing. However, other titles may have been included, based upon recommendations by Subject Advisors and Senior Subject Advisors. In some cases, the Advisors did select annual reviews and multi-volume sets for inclusion in this work.

The editorial department has made every attempt to list the most recent publications for each title in this work. In the interest of maintaining a current core-collection bibliographic list, our Advisors were asked to note the most recent publications available, especially with regards to series and publishers that regularly produce new editions. Books were listed as the original edition (or latest reprint) when no information of a recent publication was available.

ARRANGEMENT BY LC CLASSIFICATION SCHEDULE:

Each section of this work was arranged by Library of Congress Classification Numbers (LCCN), using the Library of Congress Classification Schedule for ready reference. For the purposes of this project, we have organized a system of varying font sizes and the incorporation of Em-dashes (—) to identify whether the subject headings herein are **primary** (Main Class), **secondary** (Sub-Class), or **tertiary** (Sub-Sub-Class) in the LC Classification Schedule outline. The primary heading is presented in 14 point Times New Roman, the secondary in 12 point, and the tertiary in 10 point. This distinction can be viewed in the examples that follow:

Primary Classification:
(14 Point Times New Roman)

P49 Addresses, essays, lectures

P49.J35 1985
Jakobson, Roman,
   Verbal art, verbal sign, verbal time / Roman Jakobson ; Krystyna Pomorska and Stephen Rudy, editors ; with the assistance of Brent Vine. Minneapolis : University of Minnesota Press, c1985. xiv, 208 p. :
84-007268 808/.00141 0816613583
   Philology. Semiotics. Space and time in language.

Secondary Classification:
(12 Point Times New Roman)

P51 Study and teaching. Research — General

P51.L39 1998
   Learning foreign and second languages : perspectives in research and scholarship / edited by Heidi Byrnes. New York : Modern Language Association of America, 1998. viii, 322 p.
98-039497 418/.007 087352800X
   Language and languages -- Study and teaching. Second language acquisition.

Tertiary Classification:
(10 Point Times New Roman)

P92 Communication. Mass media — By region or country — Individual regions or countries, A-Z

P92.C5.C52 2000
   Chinese perspectives in rhetoric and communication / edited by D. Ray Heisey. Stamford, Conn. : Ablex Pub. Corp., 2000. xx, 297 p. ;
99-053426 302.2/0951 1567504949
   Communication and culture -- China. Rhetoric -- Political aspects -- China.

ERRORS, LACUNAE, AND OMISSIONS:

The Subject Advisors and Senior Subject Advisors were the sole source for recommending titles to include in the completed work, and no titles were intentionally added or omitted other than those that the Subject Advisors and Senior Subject Advisors recommended. There is no expressed or implied warranty or guarantee on this product.

The Best Books editorial department requests that any suggestions or errors be sent, via e-mail or regular mail, to be corrected in future editions of this project.

BEST BOOKS EDITORIAL STAFF:

This work is the ongoing product and group effort of a number of enthusiastic individuals: The Best Books editorial staff includes: Assistant Editor, Annette Wiles; Database Administrator, Richelle Tague; and Editor, Ashley Ludwig.

This volume would not be possible without the dedicated work of our Subject Advisors and Senior Subject Advisors who donated their time, resources and knowledge towards creating this Best Books list. To them, we are truly grateful. *(Denotes Senior Subject Advisors for *Volume 8 – Philosophy & Religion*.)

SUBJECT ADVISORS:

Chris Africa,* *Collection Management – Classics, University of Iowa Libraries, University of Iowa, Iowa City, Iowa*
Subject Advisor for: BL-BX – Religion

Marti Alt,* *Reference Librarian and General Humanities Bibliographer, The Ohio State University Libraries, Ohio State University, Columbus, Ohio*
Subject Advisor for: BL-BX – Religion

Robert Behlke, *Reference Librarian, SI Tanka/Huron (Cheyenne River Community College) University, Huron, South Dakota*
Subject Advisor for: B-BX – Philosophy & Religion

Su Chen, *Head, East Asian Library, University of Minnesota Libraries - Twin Cities, Minneapolis, Minnesota*
Subject Advisor for: B-BL – East Asian Philosophy

Laurie Cohen,* *Collection Services Librarian for Jewish Studies, Hillman Library, University of Pittsburgh, Pittsburgh, Pennsylvania*
Subject Advisor for: BL-BX – Religion

Sara Heitshu,* *Librarian, Social Sciences Team – Philosophy University of Arizona Main Library, University of Arizona, Tucson, Arizona.*
Subject Advisor for: B-BX – Philosophy & Religion

Olivia Olivares,* *Librarian, Social Sciences Team - Latin American Studies, University of Arizona Main Library, University of Arizona, Tucson, Arizona.*
Subject Advisor for: BL-BX – Religion

Dr. Dona Straley, *Middle East Studies Librarian, Ohio State University Libraries, Ohio State University*
Subject Advisor for: BM, BP – Middle Eastern Religion

Brent Roberts, *Reference & Instruction Librarian, Montana State University – Billings, Montana*
Subject Advisor for: B-BL – East Asian Philosophy

SENIOR SUBJECT ADVISORS:

Christine Africa,* *History and Social Sciences Bibliographer, University of Iowa Libraries, University of Iowa, Iowa City, Iowa.* Ms. Africa earned her Bachelor of Arts degree in history at Smith College, and her Ph.D. in History at the State University of New York at Binghamton. Christine subsequently earned her Masters of Library Science from the State University of New York at Albany. She was previously employed as a Reference Librarian at Miami University at Oxford, Ohio. Christine Africa is currently serving as the History and Social Sciences Bibliographer at the University of Iowa Libraries in Iowa City.

Senior Subject Advisor for: BL-BX – Religion

Laurie Cohen,* *Collection Services Librarian for Jewish Studies, Hillman Library, University of Pittsburgh.* Laurie Cohen earned her Masters in Library and Information Science at Indiana University, Bloomington, where she had an Association of Jewish Libraries Scholarship. She received her Bachelor of Arts degree in Sociology and Jewish Studies from Kent State University. Laurie currently serves at the University of Pittsburgh Hillman Library as the Collections Services Librarian for Education, Hispanic Languages & Literatures, Jewish Studies, Religious Studies, and Women's Studies. She also serves as a Reference Consultant, providing editorial and verification services for authors. Previously, Ms. Cohen served as a Bibliographer and Reference Librarian at the Hillman Library. She has worked as Adjunct Instructor at Wright State University in Dayton, Ohio where she also served as a Humanities Reference Librarian. While serving at the Hillman Library, Cohen has worked on many committees to evaluate and recommend changes in operations, patron services, and facilities, including: the Acquisitions Budget Committee, the Oakland Library Consortium Task Force on Shared Databases, the Strategic Planning Steering Committee, and the Networked Resources Committee.

Senior Subject Advisor for: BL-BX – Religion

Sara C. Heitshu,* *Librarian, Liaison for Philosophy & Linguistics, University of Arizona Main Library, University of Arizona, Tucson, Arizona.* Sara C. Heitshu earned her Bachelors Degree from St. Lawrence University, Phi Beta Kappa, and her AMLS at the University of Michigan, Beta Phi Mu. Currently, Ms. Heitshu is working at the University of Arizona Main Library, serving on the Social Sciences Team, as the liaison with the Philosophy and Linguistics departments, as well as the Department of American Indian Studies. Previously, she worked as Acting Assistant to the Dean for Planning and Special Projects, Assistant to University Librarian for Technical Services, and Acting University Librarian at the University of Arizona. Sara has also worked as Librarian at the University of Michigan Library, and the University of Connecticut Library. Sara has written reviews and articles for several professional publications, including *Technical Services Quarterly, Wilson Library Bulletin, Technicla Library Services, Library Quarterly,* as well as several others. She has often been a consultant or speaker for events such as Arizona State Library Association Conferences, and the University of Arizona Library. Ms. Heitshu is involved in many professional organizations, including the American Library Association, the Arizona State Library Association, the Acquisitions Librarian Editorial Board, and the Society for Scholarly Publishing. She has also been a member of the University of Michigan School of Library and Information Science Board Member, and the Universal Serials and Book Exchange Board.

Senior Subject Advisor for: B-BX – Philosophy and Religion

Olivia Olivares, * *Librarian, Social Sciences Team, University of Arizona Main Library, University of Arizona, Tucson, Arizona.* Olivia Olivares earned her Masters in Library Science from the University of Arizona. She received her Bachelor of Science in Political Science from Northern Arizona University. Ms. Olivares currently works as an Assistant Librarian on the Social Sciences Team at the University of Arizona Main Library. There, she works as the liaison to the Latin American Studies Department, the Mexican American Studies Department, the Anthropologizy Department & the College of Business. Olivia previously worked as a Reference Librarian for the Cline Library at Northern Arizona University. Olivia has worked as a contributing editor to the Hispanic American Periodicals Index, as well as has coordinated a book donation project with the U.S. Information Service office in La Paz, Bolivia through the Cline Library at NAU. Ms. Olivares' has written and co-written for numerous publications, including Magazines for Libraries, infotoday.com and has presented at the Arizona State Library Association Annual Conference. She has worked to continue her education in Library Science through the American Libraries Association and the University of Arizona. Her memberships to professional organizations include: The Arizona State Libraries Association – member of the ARLIRT (Reference Services) Roundtable, SSSS (Services to the Spanish-Speaking) Roundtable; and the Association of College & Research Libraries.

Senior Subject Advisor for: BL-BX – Titles relating to Religion

B Philosophy (General)

B20 Congresses

B20.E2 1959
Philosophy and culture--East and West; East-West philosophy in practical perspective, Charles A. Moore, editor. Honolulu, University of Hawaii Press, 1962. viii, 832 p.
61-017921   108.2
Philosophy -- Congresses. East and West.

B21 Collected works (nonserial) — English and American

B21.A5
Philosophy and analysis;   New   York, Philosophical Library, 1954. viii, 296 p.
55-014290
Analysis   (Philosophy)   Semantics (Philosophy)

B21.B56 2003
The Blackwell companion to philosophy/ edited by Nicholas Bunnin and E.P. Tsui-James. 2nd ed. Oxford, UK; Blackwell, 2003.
2002-023053   100 21   0631219080
Philosophy.

B21.B7 1955
Bronstein, Daniel J.,
Basic problems of philosophy; selected readings, with   introductions,   edited   by   Daniel J. Bronstein, Yervant H. Krikorian [and] Philip P. Wiener. 2d ed. Englewood Cliffs [N.J.] Prentice-Hall, 1955. 592 p.
55-009608   108.2
Philosophy.

B21.C25 vol. 26
Mates, Benson, 1919-
Stoic logic. Berkeley, University of California Press, 1953. 148 p.
53-009918
Logic. Stoics.

B21.C557 2003
Classics of philosophy/ [edited by] Louis P. Pojman. 2nd ed. New York: Oxford University Press, 2003. xvi, 1272 p.
2002-025254   100 21   0195148932
Philosophy.

B21.R273 1996
Radest, Howard B.,
Humanism with a human face: intimacy and the Enlightenment/ Howard B. Radest. Westport, Conn.: Praeger, 1996. xi, 212 p.
95-043764   144 20   0275949699
Humanism.   Intimacy   (Psychology) Enlightenment. Transcendentalism.

B21.S78 vol. 18
Edmund Husserl and the phenomenological tradition: essays in phenomenology/ edited by Robert Sokolowski. Washington, D.C.: Catholic University of America Press, c1988. xi, 267 p.
87-038181   100 s 142/.7 19   0813206561
Husserl,   Edmund,   1859-1938 Phenomenology.

B21.S78 vol. 20
Veatch, Henry Babcock.
Swimming against the current in contemporary philosophy: occasional essays and papers/ by Henry B. Veatch. Washington, D.C.: Catholic University of America Press, c1990. x, 337 p.
88-018940   100 s 149 19   0813206812
Philosophy, Modern -- 20th century. Ethics, Modern -- 20th century. Humanities -- History -- 20th century. Natural law -- History -- 20th century.

B21.S78 vol. 24
Revolution and continuity: essays in the history and philosophy of early modern science/ edited by Peter Barker and Roger Ariew. Washington, D.C.: Catholic University of America Press, c1991. v, 222 p.
90-019633   100 s 501 20   081320738X
Science -- History. Science -- History -- 17th century. Science -- Philosophy -- History. Continuity.

B21.S78 vol. 27
Aristotle in late antiquity/ edited by Lawrence P. Schrenk. Washington, D.C.: Catholic University of America Press, c1994. ix, 207 p.
93-006867   185   0813207819
Aristotle -- Influence.Philosophy, Ancient. Philosophy, Medieval. Philosophy -- Byzantine Empire.

B29 Collected works (nonserial) — Addresses, essays, lectures

B29.A73
Arendt, Hannah.
The life of the mind/ Hannah Arendt. New York: Harcourt Brace Jovanovich, c1978. 2 v.
77-001162   110   0151518955
Philosophy.

B29.A94
Ayer, A. J.
Philosophical   essays.   London,   Macmillan; 1954. 289 p.
54-004542   192
Philosophy.

B29.B4465 1991
Berlin, Isaiah,
The crooked timber of humanity: chapters in the history of ideas/ Isaiah Berlin; edited by Henry Hardy. 1st American ed. New York: Knopf: 1991. xi, 277 p.
90-053426   190 20   0679401318
Philosophy. Civilization, Modern.

B29.B54
Black, Max,
Models and metaphors; studies in language and philosophy.   Ithaca, N.Y., Cornell University Press 1962. 267 p.
62-009128   149.94
Philosophy. Language and languages -- Philosophy.

B29.B542 1990
Black, Max,
Perplexities: rational choice, the prisoner's dilemma, metaphor, poetic ambiguity, and other puzzles/ Max Black. Ithaca: Cornell University Press, 1990. ix, 201 p.
89-034777   100 20   0801422302
Philosophy.

B29.B7442 1992
Bromberger, Sylvain.
On what we know we don't know: explanation, theory, linguistics, and how questions shape them/ Sylvain Bromberger. Chicago: University of Chicago Press; vii, 231 p.
92-010906   121 20   0226075400
Philosophy. Science -- Philosophy. Language and languages -- Philosophy.

B29.C2785 1987
Cartwright, Richard.
Philosophical   essays/   Richard   Cartwright. Cambridge, Mass.: MIT Press, c1987. xxiii, 266 p.
87-002608   191 19   0262031302
Philosophy.

B29.C536 2002
Classics of Western philosophy/ edited by Steven M. Cahn. 6th ed. Indianapolis, IN: Hackett Pub., c2002. x, 1198 p.
2002-024067   190 21   0872206378
Philosophy.

B29.D62 1988
Doing philosophy historically/ edited by Peter H. Hare. Buffalo, N.Y.: Prometheus Books, 1988. 352 p.
87-032812   109 19   0879754265
Philosophy -- History. History -- Philosophy.

B29.D85
Dummett, Michael A. E.
Truth and other enigmas/ Michael Dummett. Cambridge: Harvard University Press, 1978. lviii, 470 p.
77-012777   192   0674910753
Frege, Gottlob, 1848-1925 -- Addresses, essays, lectures. Philosophy -- Addresses, essays, lectures. Logic -- Addresses, essays, lectures. Time -- Addresses, essays, lectures.

B29.E9 1968
Ewing, A. C.
Non-linguistic philosophy, by A. C. Ewing.
London, Allen & Unwin; 1968. 279 p.
68-028331   192   004100017X
Philosophy. Semantics (Philosophy)

B29.G17 1982
Gadamer, Hans Georg,
Reason in the age of science/ Hans-Georg
Gadamer; translated by Frederick G. Lawrence.
Cambridge, Mass.: MIT Press, 1982, c1981.
xxxiii, 179 p.
81-020911   100 19   0262070855
Philosophy.

B29.G253 1983
Gardner, Martin,
The whys of a philosophical scrivener/ Martin
Gardner. 1st ed. New York: W. Morrow, 1983.
453 p.
83-005395   191 19   068802064X
Philosophy.

B29.G619 1984
Goodman, Nelson.
Of mind and other matters/ Nelson Goodman.
Cambridge, Mass.: Harvard University Press,
1984. 210 p.
83-012868   191 19   0674631250
Philosophy.

B29.I54 2000
Inglis, Laura Lyn,
Old dead white men's philosophy/ Laura Lyn
Inglis and Peter K. Steinfeld. Amherst, N.Y.:
Humanity Books , 2000. xvii, 221 p.
00-025097   108/.2 21   1573928232
Feminist theory. Philosophy. Religion.

B29.K388 1989
Key themes in philosophy/ edited by A. Phillips
Griffiths. Cambridge [England]; Cambridge
University Press, c1989. v, 228 p.
89-036878   100 20   0521375797
Philosophy.

B29.M3673 1984
Margolis, Joseph,
Culture and cultural entities: toward a new unity
of science/ Joseph Margolis. Dordrecht; D.
Reidel Pub.Co.; xiii, 170 p.
83-004635   110 19   9027715742
Philosophy.

B29.M36774 1989
Marquard, Odo.
Farewell to matters of principle: philosophical
studies/ Odo Marquard; translated by Robert M.
Wallace with the assistance of Susan Bernstein
and James I. Porter. New York: Oxford
University Press, 1989. 147 p.
89-032850   100 20   0195051149
Philosophy.

B29.M453 1985
Mehta, J. L.
India and the West, the problem of
understanding: selected essays/ of J.L. Mehta;
[with an introduction by Wilfred Cantwell
Smith]. Chico, Calif.: Scholars Press, c1985.
xvii, 268 p.
85-002050   100 19   0891308261
Philosophy.

B29.M533 1978
Miller, John William.
The paradox of cause and other essays/ John
William Miller. New York: Norton, c1978.
192 p.
78-005998   191   0393011720
Philosophy -- Addresses, essays, lectures.

B29.M88 1979
Muirhead, John H. 1855-1940.
The use of philosophy: Californian addresses/ by
John H. Muirhead. Westport, Conn.: Greenwood
Press, 1979. 208 p.
78-024161   100   0313206627
Philosophy -- Addresses, essays, lectures.

B29.P88 1992
Putnam, Hilary.
Renewing philosophy/ Hilary Putnam.
Cambridge, Mass.: Harvard University Press,
1992. xii, 234 p.
92-010854   100 20   067476093X
Philosophy. Philosophy and science.

B29.R628 1999
Roshwald, Mordecai,
The transient and the absolute: an interpretation
of the human condition and of human endeavor/
Mordecai Roshwald.   Westport,   Conn.:
Greenwood Press, 1999. 198 p.
98-044217   128 21   0313309361
Philosophy. Will. Absolute, The.

B29.S43
Schwarz, Balduin V 1902-
The human person and the world of values; a
tribute to Dietrich Von Hildebrand by his friends
in philosophy. New York, Fordham University
Press [1960] xiii, 210 p.
60-010736
*Von   Hildebrand,   Dietrich,   --   1889-
Philosophy.*

B29.S53
Smart, J. J. C. 1920-
Philosophy and scientific realism. New York,
Humanities Press [1963] viii, 160 p.
63-021827   108.1
Philosophy

B29.S815 1991
Stove, D. C.
The Plato cult and other philosophical follies/
David Stove. Oxford, UK; B. Blackwell, 1991.
xiii, 209 p.
90-042130   100   0631177094
Philosophy.

B29.V55 1998
The   virtual   embodied:
resence/practice/technology/ edited by John
Wood. London; Routledge, 1998. xi, 226 p.
97-038905   128   041516026X
*Philosophy. Virtual reality. Body, Human
(Philosophy)*

B29.W4145
Weinberg, Julius R. 1908-1971.
Ockham, Descartes, and Hume: self-knowledge,
substance, and causality/ Julius R. Weinberg.
Madison: University of Wisconsin Press, 1977.
ix, 179 p.
76-011315   190   0299071200
*William, -- of Ockham, -- ca. 1285-ca. 1349 --
Addresses, essays, lectures. Descartes, Rene, --
1596-1650 -- Addresses, essays, lectures. Hume,
David, -- 1711-1776 -- Addresses, essays,
lectures. Philosophy -- Addresses, essays,
lectures.*

B29.W45 2001
What is philosophy?/ edited by C.P. Ragland and
Sarah Heidt. New Haven: Yale University Press,
c2001. vii, 196 p.
00-012597   100 21   0300087942
Philosophy.

B29.W48 1982
White, Morton Gabriel, 1917-
Religion, politics, and the higher learning: a
collection of essays/ Morton White. Westport,
Conn.: Greenwood, 1982, c1959. x, 140 p.
82-001013   190/.9/04   0313234809
Philosophy.

B29.W68 1982
World philosophy: essay-reviews of 225 major
works/ edited by Frank N. Magill; associate
editor, Ian P. McGreal. Englewood Cliffs, N.J.:
Salem Press, c1982. 5 v.
82-060268   100 19
Philosophy. Philosophers.

B29.W69 2003
The world's great philosophers/ edited by Robert
L. Arrington. Malden, MA: Blackwell Pub.,
2003. xiii, 361 p.
2002-004264   109/.2 21   0631231463
Philosophers. Philosophy.

B35 Directories

B35.I55
International   directory   of   philosophy   and
philosophers.   Bowling Green, Ohio [etc.]
Philosophy Documentation Center, Bowling
66-018830   102.5
Philosophy -- Directories.

B35.P48
The philosopher's phone book. Bowling Green, OH: Philosophy Documentation Center, Bowling Green
95-657650   102/.5/73 21
Philosophers -- United States -- Directories. Philosophers -- Canada -- Directories. Philosophy -- Directories.

B41 Dictionaries — International (Polyglot)

B41.B3 vol. 3
Rand, Benjamin,
Bibliography of philosophy, psychology, and cognate subjects, comp. by Benjamin Rand. New York, The Macmillan company; 2 v.
06-008773
Philosophy -- Bibliography. Psychology -- Bibliography.

B41.B3 1940
Baldwin, James Mark,
Dictionary of philosophy and psychology, including many of the principal conceptions of ethics, logic, aesthetics, philosophy of religion, mental pathology, anthropology, biology, neurology, physiology, economics, political and social philosophy, philo written by many hands and edited by James Mark Baldwin ... with the co-operation and assistance of an international board of consulting editors ... with ... extensive bibliographies. New ed., with corrections. New York, P. Smith, 1940-
40-027299   103
Philosophy -- Dictionaries. Philosophy -- Bibliography. Psychology -- Dictionaries. Psychology -- Bibliography.

B41.C35 1999
The Cambridge dictionary of philosophy/ edited by Robert Audi. Cambridge; Cambridge University Press, 1999. xxxv, 1001 p.
99-012920   103   052163136X
Philosophy -- Dictionaries.

B41.C66 1991
The concise encyclopedia of western philosophy and philosophers/ edited by J.O. Urmson and Jonathan Reé. New ed., completely rev. London; Routledge, 1991. xii, 331 p.
91-039858   190/.3 20   0415078830
Philosophy -- Encyclopedias. Philosophers -- Biography -- Encyclopedias.

B41.E5 1996
The encyclopedia of philosophy. Donald M. Borchert, editor in chief. New York: Macmillan Reference USA, Simon & Schuster Macmillan; xxxii, 775 p.
95-047988   103 20   0028646290
Philosophy -- Encyclopedias.

B41.I26 2001
Iannone, A. Pablo.
Dictionary of world philosophy/ A. Pablo Iannone. New York: Routledge, 2001.
00-042471   103 21   0415179955
Philosophy -- Dictionaries.

B41.K48 1995
Key ideas in human thought/ edited by Kenneth McLeish. Rocklin, CA: Prima Pub., 1995. x, 789 p.
94-034096   103 20   1559586508
Philosophy -- Dictionaries. Humanities -- Dictionaries. Science -- Dictionaries. Social sciences -- Dictionaries.

B41.L32 1986
Lacey, A. R.
A dictionary of philosophy/ A.R. Lacey. 2nd ed. London: Routledge & Kegan Paul, 1986. viii, 266 p.
87-146826   103/.21 19   0710209916
Philosophy -- Dictionaries.

B41.M38 1996
Mautner, Thomas.
A dictionary of philosophy/ Thomas Mautner. Cambridge, Mass.: Blackwell Publishers, c1996. xiii, 482 p.
95-021625   103 20   0631184597
Philosophy -- Dictionaries.

B41.R43 1999
Reese, William L.
Dictionary of philosophy and religion: Eastern and Western thought/ William L. Reese. Expanded ed. Amherst, N.Y.: Humanity Books, 1999. xiv, 856 p.
98-050459   103 21   1573924261
Philosophy -- Dictionaries. Religion -- Dictionaries.

B42 Dictionaries — French and Belgian

B42.V6 1924
Voltaire, 1694-1778.
Voltaire's Philosophical dictionary, selected and translated by H. I. Woolf. New York, A. A. Knopf, 1924. 316 p.
25-005224
Philosophy -- Dictionaries.

B43 Dictionaries — German

B43.W29 1997
Waibl, Elmar.
German dictionary of philosophical terms = Wörterbuch philosophischer Fachbegriffe Englisch/ Elmar Waibl, Philip Herdina. Müchen: K.G. Saur; 1997. 2 v.
98-133753   103 21   3598113412
Philosophy -- Dictionaries -- German.

B49 Terminology. Nomenclature — General works

B49.S63 1990
Sparkes, A. W.
Talking philosophy: a wordbook/ A.W. Sparkes. London; Routledge, 1991. 307 p.
89-048900   101/.4   0415042224
Philosophy -- Terminology.

B51 Encyclopedias

B51.C58 2000
Concise Routledge encyclopedia of philosophy. London; Routledge, 2000. xxxiv, 1030 p.
99-052692   100   0415223644
Philosophy -- Encyclopedias.

B51.O94 1995
The Oxford companion to philosophy/ edited by Ted Honderich. Oxford; Oxford University Press, 1995. xviii, 1009 p.
94-036914   100 20   0198661320
Philosophy -- History. Philosophers.

B51.R68 1998
Routledge encyclopedia of philosophy/ general editor, Edward Craig. London; Routledge, 1998. 10 v.
97-004549   100 21   041518715X
Philosophy -- Encyclopedias.

B51.4 Historiography — General works

B51.4.G72 1992
Gracia, Jorge J. E.
Philosophy and its history: issues in philosophical historiography/ Jorge J.E. Gracia. Albany: State University of New York Press, c1992. xxi, 387 p.
90-024213   109 20   0791408183
Philosophy -- Historiography.

B51.8 Pictorial works

B51.8.R8
Runes, Dagobert D. 1902-
Pictorial history of philosophy. New York, Philosophical Library [1959] x, 406 p.
59-016451   109
Philosophy -- Pictorial works.

B52 Study and teaching. Research — General works

B52.G5
Gilson, Etienne, 1884-1978.
History of philosophy and philosophical education; under the auspices of the Aristotelian Society of Marquette University. Milwaukee, Marquette Univ. Press, 1948. 49 p.
48-001955 107
   Thomas, -- Aquinas, Saint, -- 1225?-1274.Philosophy -- Study and teaching.

B52.G74 1999
Greene, Robert,
The death and life of philosophy/ Robert Greene. South Bend, Ind.: St. Augustine's Press, 1999. x, 306 p.
99-019015 101 21 1890318191
   Aristotle. Philosophy -- Study and teaching.

B52.H25 1992
Hamlyn, D. W.,
Being a philosopher: the history of a practice/ D.W. Hamlyn. London; Routledge, 1992. x, 187 p.
91-040390 100 20 0415029686
   Philosophy -- Study and teaching -- History. Philosophers.

B52.I56 1998
In the Socratic tradition: essays on teaching philosophy/ edited by Tziporah Kasachkoff. Lanham, Md.: Rowman & Littlefield, c1998. xxiii, 280 p.
97-036934 107/.1 21 0847684792
   Philosophy -- Study and teaching.

B52.L559 1988
Lipman, Matthew.
Philosophy goes to school/ Matthew Lipman. Philadelphia: Temple University Press, 1988. ix, 228 p.
87-018071 372.8 0877225370
   Philosophy -- Study and teaching (Elementary) -- United States.

B52.R25
Randall, John Herman, 1899-
How philosophy uses its past. New York, Columbia University Press, 1963. xiv, 106 p.
63-020464 109
   Philosophy -- History -- Study and teaching.

B52.7 Authorship

B52.7.K37 1997
Kastely, James L.,
Rethinking the rhetorical tradition: from Plato to postmodernism/ James L. Kastely. New Haven, Conn.: Yale University Press, c1997. viii, 293 p.
96-026861 190 20 0300068387
   Plato. Philosophy -- Authorship. Rhetoric -- Philosophy. Postmodernism.

B52.7.S44 2000
Seech, Zachary.
Writing philosophy papers/ Zachary Seech. 3rd ed. Belmont: Wadsworth Pub., c2000. x, 148 p.
99-034365 808/.0661 21 0534520960
   Philosophy -- Authorship. Philosophy -- Study and teaching.

B53 Philosophy. Methodology. Relation to other topics — General works

B53.A23
Abel, Reuben, 1911-
Man is the measure: a cordial invitation to the central problems of philosophy/ Reuben Abel. New York: Free Press, c1976. xxiv, 296 p.
75-016646 128 0029001404
   Philosophy. Human beings. Cosmology.

B53.A9 1946
Ayer, A. J. 1910-
Language, truth, and logic.   London, V. Gollancz, 1946. 160 p.
46-008544 101
   Experience.   Language   and   languages. Philosophy.

B53.B56
Boas, George, 1891-
The limits of reason. New York, Harper [1961] 162 p.
61-005255 111
   Philosophy.

B53.D4613 1982
Derrida, Jacques.
Margins of philosophy/ Jacques Derrida; translated, with additional notes, by Alan Bass. Chicago: University of Chicago Press, 1982. xxix, 330 p.
82-011137 190 19 0226143260
   Heidegger, Martin, 1889-1976. Sein und Zeit. Valéry, Paul, 1871-1945. Philosophy. Language and languages -- Philosophy. Ontology. Space and time.

B53.K38
Kekes, John.
The nature of philosophy/ John Kekes. Totowa, N.J.: Rowman and Littlefield, 1980. xiv, 226 p.
80-111351 100 0847662470
   Philosophy. Ideology.

B53.L29 1982
Lacey, A. R.
Modern philosophy, an introduction/ A.R. Lacey. Boston: Routledge & K. Paul, 1982. 246 p.
81-008710 190 0710009356
   Philosophy. Philosophy, Modern -- 20th century.

B53.L333 1991
Langan, Thomas.
Tradition and authenticity in the search for ecumenic wisdom/ Thomas Langan. Columbia: University of Missouri Press, c1992. 239 p.
91-032300 140 20 0826208002
   Methodology. Truth. Cultural relativism. Authenticity (Philosophy) History -- Philosophy. Tradition (Philosophy) Civilization, Modern -- 20th century. Wisdom.

B53.M36 1993
Masters, Roger D.
Beyond relativism: science and human values/ Roger D. Masters. Hanover, NH: University Press of New England, c1993. ix, 248 p.
93-016925 001 20 087451634X
   Methodology. Science -- Philosophy. Social sciences -- Philosophy. Ethics. Humanities. Relativity.

B53.R682 1990
Reading Rorty: critical responses to Philosophy and the mirror of nature (and beyond)/ edited by Alan R. Malachowski; associate editor Jo Burrows. Oxford, UK; B. Blackwell, 1990. xii, 384 p.
89-027035 191 20 063116149X
   Rorty, Richard. Philosophy and the mirror of nature. Philosophy. Philosophy, Modern. Representation (Philosophy) Analysis (Philosophy) Civilization -- Philosophy.

B53.W35 1992
Warnock, Mary.
The uses of philosophy/ Mary Warnock. Oxford, OX, UK; Cambridge, Mass., USA: Blackwell, 1992. 243 p.
91-043916 101 0631180389
   Philosophy. Ethics. Education -- Philosophy.

B54 Philosophy. Methodology. Relation to other topics — Electronic data processing

B54.D54 1998
The digital phoenix: how computers are changing philosophy/ edited by Terrell Ward Bynum and James H. Moor. Oxford; Blackwell Publishers, 1998. 412 p.
98-005373 102/.85 0631203524
   Philosophy -- Data processing. Philosophy -- Study and teaching -- Data processing.

B54.G75 1998
Grim, Patrick.
The philosophical computer: exploratory essays in philosophical computer modeling/ Patrick Grim, Gary Mar, and Paul St. Denis, with the Group for Logic and Formal Semantics. Cambridge, Mass.: MIT Press, c1998. viii, 321 p.
97-039498 101/.13 21 0262071851
   Philosophy -- Computer simulation. Logic -- Computer simulation. Philosophy -- Data processing. Logic -- Data processing.

B56 Philosophy. Methodology. Relation to other topics — Relation to theology and religion

B56.K47 1997
Kerr, Fergus.
Immortal longings: versions of transcending humanity/ Fergus Kerr. Notre Dame, Ind.: University of Notre Dame Press, 1997. x, 213 p.
97-001799   210 21   026801180X
Philosophy and religion. Transcendence (Philosophy)

B56.S8
Stace, W. T. 1886-
Mysticism and philosophy.   Philadelphia, Lippincott [1960] 349 p.
60-013581   149.3
Mysticism. Philosophy. Philosophy and religion.

B56.T73 2003
Transcendence in philosophy and religion/ edited by James E. Faulconer. Bloomington, IN: Indiana University Press, c2003. v, 151 p.
2002-012401   111/.6 21   0253215757
Philosophy and religion. Transcendence (Philosophy) Hermeneutics.

B56.V75 1999
Vries, Hent de.
Philosophy and the turn to religion/ Hent de Vries.   Baltimore,   Md.:   Johns   Hopkins University Press, 1999. xviii, 475 p.
99-010359   291.1/75 21   0801859956
Philosophy and religion -- History.

B59 Philosophy. Methodology. Relation to other topics — Relation to civilization

B59.C84 1991
Culture and modernity: East-West philosophic perspectives/   edited   by   Eliot   Deutsch. Honolulu: University of Hawaii Press, c1991. xvii, 641 p.
91-019107   100 20   0824813707
Philosophy and civilization -- Congresses. Civilization, Modern -- Congresses. East and West -- Congresses. Philosophy, Modern -- Congresses. Philosophy, Asian -- Congresses.

B63 Philosophy. Methodology. Relation to other topics — Relation to social sciences. Relation to sociology

B63.A3
Addis, Laird.
The logic of society: a philosophical study/ by Laird   Addis.   Minneapolis: University   of Minnesota Press, [1975] ix, 226 p.
74-083131   146/.4 0816607338
Philosophy. Social sciences -- Philosophy. History -- Philosophy.

B63.M45 1996
McIntyre, Lee C.
Laws and explanation in the social sciences: defending a science of human behavior/ by Lee C. McIntyre. Boulder, Colo.: Westview Press, c1996. x, 197 p.
95-049746   300/.1 20   0813328284
Philosophy and social sciences. Social sciences -- Philosophy. Psychology and philosophy.

B63.P6 1950
Popper, Karl Raimund, 1902-
The open society and its enemies.   Princeton, Princeton University Press, 1950. xii, 732 p.
50-058301   301
Social sciences. Philosophy.

B63.P62 1999
Popper's Open society after fifty years: the continuing relevance of Karl Popper/ edited by Ian Jarvie and Sandra Pralong. London; Routledge, 1999. x, 217 p.
98-047993   301   0415165024
Popper, Karl Raimund, -- Sir, -- 1902- -- Open society and its enemies -- Congresses.Philosophy -- Congresses. Social sciences -- Philosophy -- Congresses.

B63.W4213 1998
Wellmer, Albrecht.
Endgames: the   irreconcilable   nature   of modernity: essays   and   lectures/   Albrecht Wellmer;   translated   by   David   Midgley. Cambridge, Mass.: MIT Press, c1998. xv, 349 p.
98-002667   300/.1 0262231972
Philosophy   and   social   sciences. Postmodernism. Metaphysics.

B65 Philosophy. Methodology. Relation to other topics — Relation to law and political science

B65.P43 1996
Peterson, Richard T.
Democratic philosophy and the politics of knowledge/ Richard T.   Peterson. University Park, Pa.: Pennsylvania State University Press, c1996. 344 p.
95-023637   101 20   0271015454
Philosophy.   Democracy.   Liberalism. Postmodernism. Political science -- Philosophy.

B65.S8
Strauss, Leo.
Persecution and the art of writing/ by Leo Strauss. Glencoe, Ill.: Free Press, c1952. 204 p.
52-008158   104
Maimonides, Moses, -- 1135-1204. -- Dalalat al-hairin. Judah, -- ha-Levi, -- 12th cent. -- Kitab al-hujjah. Spinoza, Benedictus de, -- 1632-1677.   --   Tractatus   theologico-politicus. Philosophy. Political science. Persecution.

B67 Philosophy. Methodology. Relation to other topics — Relation to science

B67.B8 1954
Burtt, Edwin A. 1892-
The metaphysical foundations of modern physical science.   Garden   City,   N.Y., Doubleday, 1954. 352 p.
54-004532   500.2/01
Metaphysics -- History. Physical sciences -- Philosophy.

B67.S69 1991
Sorell, Tom.
Scientism: philosophy and the infatuation with science/ Tom Sorell. London; Routledge, 1991. xi, 206 p.
90-047550   149 20   0415033993
Scientism. Philosophy and science. Scientism -- History. Philosophy and science -- History.

B67.W55 1995
Wilson, Catherine, 1951-
The invisible world: early modern philosophy and the invention of the microscope/ Catherine Wilson. Princeton, N.J.: Princeton University Press, c1995. x, 280 p.
94-024556   113 0691034184
Philosophy and science -- Europe -- History -- 17th century. Philosophy, Modern -- 17th century. Microscopes -- Europe -- History -- 17th century. Europe -- Intellectual life -- 17th century.

B68 Curiosa. Miscellanea

B68.S55 2001
The Simpsons and philosophy: the d'oh! of Homer/ edited by William Irwin, Mark T. Conard, and Aeon J. Skoble. Chicago, Ill.: Open Court, c2001. ix, 303 p.
00-069897   100 21   0812694333
Philosophy -- Miscellanea.

B72 General works — English and American — 1801-

B72.C593 1999
The Columbia history of Western philosophy/ edited by Richard H. Popkin. New York: Columbia University Press, c1999. xxvi, 836 p.
98-015219   190   0231101287
Philosophy -- History.

B72.D4
De Selincourt, Aubrey, 1894-1962.
Six great thinkers: Socrates, St. Augustine, Lord Bacon, Rousseau, Coleridge, John Stuart Mill. London, H. Hamilton [1958] 180 p.
58-004282   921
Philosophers.

B72.D7
Dunham, Barrows, 1905-
Heroes & heretics; a political history of Western thought. New York, Knopf, 1964. ix, 484 p.
63-009141   109
Dissenters. Philosophy -- History.

B72.D8 1949
Durant, Will, 1885-
The story of philosophy; the lives and opinions of the greater philosophers. New York, Simon and Schuster, 1949 [c1933] xvi, 412 p.
50-001258   109
Philosophy. Philosophers.

B72.G68 2000
Gottlieb, Anthony.
The dream of reason: a history of western philosophy from the Greeks to the Renaissance/ Anthony Gottlieb. New York: W.W. Norton, 2000. ix, 468 p.
00-049012   180   0393049515
Philosophy -- History.

B72.G74 1992
Great thinkers of the Western world: the major ideas and classic works of more than 100 outstanding Western philosophers, physical and social scientists, psychologists, religious writers, and theol edited by Ian P. McGreal. New York, NY: HarperCollinsPublishers, c1992. xiii, 572 p.
91-038362   190   006270026X
Philosophy. Theology. Science.

B72.H317 2000
Harre, Rom.
One thousand years of philosophy: from Ramanuja to Wittgenstein/ Rom Harre. Malden, Mass.: Blackwell Publishers, 2000. xix, 362 p.
00-033743   109   0631219005
Philosophy -- History.

B72.J65
Jones, W. T. 1910-
A history of Western philosophy.   New York, Harcourt, Brace [1952] 1036 p.
52-001836   109
Philosophy -- History.

B72.K44 1998
Kenny, Anthony John Patrick.
A brief history of western philosophy/ Anthony Kenny. Malden, Mass.: Blackwell Publishers, 1998.
98-020921   190 21   0631201327
Philosophy -- History.

B72.L3
Lamprecht, Sterling Power, 1890-
Our philosophical traditions; a brief history of philosophy in Western civilization.   New York, Appleton-Century-Crofts [1955] 523 p.
55-009432   109
Philosophy -- History.

B72.M87 1993
Murdoch, Iris.
Metaphysics as a guide to morals/ Iris Murdoch. 1st American ed. New York, N.Y., U.S.A.: Allen Lane, Penguin Press, 1993. 520 p.
92-053533   100 20   0713991003
Philosophy. Ethics. Religion.

B72.O5 1954
Onians, Richard Broxton.
The origins of European thought about the body, the mind, the soul, the world, time, and fate; new interpretations of Greek, Roman, and kindred evidence, also of some basic Jewish and Christian beli   Cambridge [Eng.] University Press, 1954. xviii, 583 p.
54-003849   110
Philosophy. Civilization, Western.

B72.O8 1997
The Oxford illustrated history of Western philosophy/ edited by Anthony Kenny. Oxford; Oxford University Press, 1997. xii, 407 p.
96-041967   190 20   019285335X
Philosophy -- History.

B72.P33 2000
A parliament of minds: philosophy for a new millennium/ edited by   Michael Tobias, J. Patrick Fitzgerald, David Rothenberg. Albany, N.Y.: State University of New York Press, c2000. xix, 309 p.
99-043557   100 21   0791444848
Philosophy. Philosophers -- Interviews.

B72.R8
Russell, Bertrand, 1872-1970.
A history of western philosophy, and its connection with political and social circumstances from the earliest times to the present day.   New York, Simon and Schuster [1945] xxiii, 895 p.
45-008884   109
Philosophy -- History.

B72.R83 1959a
Russell, Bertrand, 1872-1970.
Wisdom of the West; a historical survey of Western philosophy in its social and political setting. Editor: Paul Foulkes. Designer: Edward Wright. With ten compositions by John Piper. Garden City, N.Y., Doubleday [1959] 320 p.
59-011326   190
Philosophy -- History. Philosophy -- Pictorial works.

B72.S64 1999
Smart, Ninian, 1927-
World philosophies/ Ninian Smart. London; Routledge, 1999. vii, 454 p.
98-007426   109   0415184665
Philosophy -- History. Religions.

B72.S654 1999
Solomon, Robert C.
The joy of philosophy: thinking thin versus the passionate life/ Robert C. Solomon. New York: Oxford University Press, 1999. xiii, 269 p.
98-050825   100 21   0195067592
Philosophy.

B72.S66 1996
Solomon, Robert C.
A short history of philosophy/ Robert C. Solomon, Kathleen M. Higgins. New York: Oxford University Press, 1996. xvii, 329 p.
95-012578   109 20   0195101960
Philosophy -- History.

B72.T43 1968
Tomlin, E. W. F.
The Western philosophers: an introduction [by] E.W.F. Tomlin. [1st ed. reprinted]. London, Hutchinson, 1968. 288 p.
68-141524   100   0090868005
Philosophers. Philosophy -- History.

B72.T8 1953
Tsanoff, Radoslav Andrea, 1887-
The great philosophers.   New York, Harper [1953] ix, 653 p.
52-010674   109
Philosophy -- History. Philosophers.

B72.W54 1998
Wilson, Edward Osborne, 1929-
Consilience: the unity of knowledge/ Edward O. Wilson. New York: Knopf: 1998. 332 p.
97-002816   121   0679450777
Philosophy. Order (Philosophy) Philosophy and science.

B73 General works — English and American — Addresses, essays, lectures

B73.F76 1993
From Africa to Zen: an invitation to world philosophy/ edited by Robert C. Solomon, Kathleen M. Higgins. Lanham, Md.: Rowman & Littlefield Publishers, c1993. xix, 298 p.
92-028469 109 0847677745
Philosophy -- History.

B73.R67 1988
Rosen, Stanley, 1929-
The quarrel between philosophy and poetry: studies in ancient thought/ Stanley Rosen. New York: Routledge, 1988. xiii, 223 p.
87-028628 101 0415001846
Philosophy. Philosophy, Ancient. Poetics.

B74 General works — English and American — Elementary textbooks

B74.C56
Clark, Gordon Haddon.
Thales to Dewey; a history of philosophy. Boston, Houghton Mifflin [1957] 548 p.
57-013630 109
Philosophy -- History.

B74.D68 1999
Double, Richard.
Beginning philosophy/ Richard Double. New York: Oxford University Press, 1999. xiii, 347 p.
97-040510 100 0195117816
Philosophy.

B74.G59 1992
Glymour, Clark N.
Thinking things through: an introduction to philosophical issues and achievements/ Clark Glymour. Cambridge, Mass.: MIT Press, c1992. xi, 382 p.
91-045667 121 20 026207141X
Philosophy. Evidence. Knowledge, Theory of. Philosophy of mind.

B75 General works — English and American — Outlines, syllabi, etc.

B75.M37 1990
Masterpieces of world philosophy/ edited by Frank N. Magill; selection by John K. Roth; with an introduction by John K. Roth. 1st ed. New York, NY: HarperCollins Publishers, c1990. xi, 684 p.
89-046545 100 20 0060164301
Philosophy. Philosophy -- Bibliography.

B82 General works — German — 1801-

B82.H5613 1976b
Hirschberger, Johannes.
A short history of Western philosophy/ by Johannes Hirschberger; translated from the German by Jeremy Moiser. Boulder, Colo.: Westview Press, 1977, c1976. xi, 218 p.
76-025125 190 0891586423
Philosophy -- History.

B99 General works — Other. By language, A-Z

B99.S82.W413 1982
Wedberg, Anders, 1913-1978.
A history of philosophy/ Anders Wedberg. Oxford: Clarendon Press, 1982-1984. 3 v.
81-022418 190 0198246390
Philosophy -- History.

B104 Collective biography

B104.B56 1996
Biographical dictionary of twentieth-century philosophers/ edited by Stuart Brown, Diané Collinson, Robert Wilkinson. London; Routledge, 1996 xx, 947 p.
97-185841 109/.2 B 21 0415060435
Philosophers -- Biography -- Dictionaries. Philosophy, Modern -- 20th century -- Dictionaries.

B104.W67 2000
World philosophers and their works/ editor, John K. Roth; managing editor, Christina J. Moose; project editor, Rowena Wildin. Pasadena, Calif.: Salem Press, c2000. 3 v.
99-055143 109 0893568783
Philosophers -- Biography -- Encyclopedias.

B105 Special topics, A-Z

B105.A35 A839 1993
Audi, Robert,
Action, intention, and reason/ Robert Audi. Ithaca, N.Y.: Cornell University Press, 1993. xi, 362 p.
93-022578 128/.4 20 0801481058
Act (Philosophy) Intentionality (Philosophy) Will. Free will and determinism. Responsibility. Reason.

B105.A35.A93 1989
Audi, Robert, 1941-
Practical reasoning/ Robert Audi. London; Routledge, 1989. 214 p.
88-026357 128/.4 0415033748
Act (Philosophy) Will. Ethics.

B105.A35 B3413 1993
Bakhtin, M. M.
Toward a philosophy of the act/ M.M. Bakhtin; translation and notes by Vadim Liapunov; edited by Michael Holquist & Vadim Liapunov. 1st ed. Austin: University of Texas Press, 1993. xxiv, 106 p.
93-007557 128/.4 20 029270805X
Act (Philosophy) Ethics. Communication -- Moral and ethical aspects. Literature -- Philosophy.

B105.A35 B55 2001
Bittner, Rüdiger,
Doing things for reasons/ Rüdiger Bittner. Oxford; Oxford University Press, 2001. xi, 204 p.
00-058440 128/.4 21 0195143647
Act (Philosophy)

B105.A35 D37 2001
Davidson, Donald,
Essays on actions and events/ Donald Davidson. 2nd ed. Oxford: Clarendon Press; xxi, 324 p.
2002-278425 128/.4 21 0199246270
Act (Philosophy) Events (Philosophy)

B105.A35 D3734 1985
Essays on Davidson: actions and events/ edited by Bruce Vermazen and Merrill B. Hintikka. Oxford: Clarendon Press; viii, 257 p.
84-018923 128/.4 19 0198247494
Davidson, Donald, 1917-Essays on actions and events. Act (Philosophy) Events (Philosophy)

B105.A35.D66 1987
Donagan, Alan.
Choice, the essential element in human action/ by Alan Donagan. London; Routledge & Kegan Paul, 1987. x, 197 p.
86-033895 128/.3 0710211686
Act (Philosophy) Choice (Psychology) Will.

B105.A35 J83 1999
Juarrero, Alicia.
Dynamics in action: intentional behavior as a complex system/ Alicia Juarrero. Cambridge, Mass.: MIT Press, c1999. x, 288 p.
99-023910 128/.4 21 0262100819
Act (Philosophy) Action theory.

B105.A35.M44 1992
Mele, Alfred R., 1951-
Springs of action: understanding intentional behavior/ Alfred R. Mele. New York: Oxford University Press, 1992. ix, 272 p.
91-017924 128/.4 019507114X
Act (Philosophy) Intentionality (Philosophy) Intentionalism.

B105.A35 P49 1997
The philosophy of action/ edited by Alfred R. Mele. Oxford; Oxford University Press, 1997. vi, 314 p.
96-008682 128/.4 20 0198751753
Act (Philosophy)

B105.A35 S44 1991
Segal, Jerome M.,
Agency and alienatiion: a theory of human presence/ Jerome M. Segal. Savage, Md.: Rowan & Littlefield, c1991. xii, 259 p.
91-011954 126 20 0847676285
Act (Philosophy) Action theory. Agent (Philosophy) Self. Self (Philosophy)

B105.A35.W33 1999
Wagner, Valeria.
Bound to act: models of action, dramas of inaction/ Valeria Wagner. Stanford, Calif.: Stanford University Press, c1999. vii, 275 p.
99-017526 128/.4 0804733309
Act (Philosophy)

B105.A35.W34 1989
Walton, Douglas N.
Practical reasoning: goal-driven, knowledge-based, action-guiding argumentation/ Douglas N. Walton. Savage, Md.: Rowman & Littlefield, c1990. xvi, 395 p.
88-026393 128/.3 0847676056
Act (Philosophy) Agent (Philosophy) Ethics.

B105.A55 A55 1999
Animal others: on ethics, ontology, and animal life/ edited by H. Peter Steeves; foreword by Tom Regan. Albany, N.Y.: State University of New York Press, c1999. xii, 294 p.
99-017303 179/.3 21 0791443108
Animals (Philosophy) Philosophy, European.

B105.A8.G65 1995
Golomb, Jacob.
In search of authenticity: from Kierkegaard to Camus/ Jacob Golomb. London; Routledge, 1995. 219 p.
94-043130 179/.9 0415119464
Authenticity (Philosophy) Existential ethics.

B105.B64 B35 2000
Baker, Lynne Rudder,
Persons and bodies: a constitution view/ Lynne Rudder Baker. Cambridge, U.K.; Cambridge University Press, 2000. xii, 233 p.
99-024024 128/.6 21 0521597196
Body, Human (Philosophy) Agent (Philosophy) Mind and body.

B105.B64 B64 1999
The body: classic and contemporary readings/ edited and introduced by Donn Welton. Malden, Mass.: Blackwell, 1999. xi, 375 p.
98-031144 128/.6 21 0631211853
Body, Human (Philosophy)

B105.B64 S45 1993
Self as body in Asian theory and practice/ edited by Thomas P. Kasulis with Roger T. Ames and Wimal Dissanayake. Albany: State University of New York Press, c1993. xx, 383 p.
91-026009 128 20 0791410803
Body, Human (Philosophy) -- Asia -- History. Self (Philosophy) -- Asia -- History. Mind and body -- Asia -- History.

B105.B64 S48 1994
Sheets-Johnstone, Maxine.
The roots of power: animate form and gendered bodies/ Maxine Sheets-Johnstone. Chicago: Open Court, c1994. x, 438 p.
94-027553 303.3 20 0812692586
Body, Human (Philosophy) Power (Philosophy) Feminist theory. Sex role. Postmodernism. Sexism in sociobiology. Evolution (Biology) -- Philosophy.

B105.B64 S85 2001
Sullivan, Shannon, 1967-
Living across and through skins: transactional bodies, pragmatism, and feminism/ Shannon Sullivan. Bloomington: Indiana University Press, c2001. vi, 204 p.
00-058159 128/.6 0253338530
Body, Human (Philosophy) Ecology. Pragmatism.

B105.C45.K1513 2000
K., Nora.
The Dead Philosophers' Cafe: an exchange of letters for children and adults/ Nora K. and Vittorio Hosle; translated by Steven Rendall. Notre Dame, Ind.: University of Notre Dame Press, c2000. vii, 166 p.
99-088246 108/.3 0268008949
Children and philosophy. Philosophy. Letters.

B105.C45.P44 1998
The philosopher's child: critical perspectives in the Western tradition/ edited by Susan M. Turner and Gareth B. Matthews. Rochester, NY: University of Rochester Press, 1998. x, 238 p.
98-016003 108/.3 1580460216
Children and philosophy.

B105.C45 R44 1999
Reed, Ronald F.
Friendship and moral education: twin pillars of philosophy for children/ Ronald F. Reed and Tony W. Johnson. New York: P. Lang, c1999. 227 p.
98-038610 108/.3 21 082043776X
Children and philosophy. Philosophy -- Study and teaching (Elementary) -- United States. Education -- Philosophy.

B105.C45 S78 1992
Studies in philosophy for children: Harry Stottlemeier's discovery/ edited by Ann Margaret Sharp and Ronald F. Reed; with sources and references by Matthew Lipman. Philadelphia: Temple University Press, 1992. xvii, 268 p.
91-003903 100 20 0877228736
Lipman, Matthew. Harry Stottlemeier's discovery. Children and philosophy. Philosophy -- Study and teaching (Elementary) -- United States.

B105.C455.H37 1988
Hardin, C. L., 1932-
Color for philosophers: unweaving the rainbow/ C.L. Hardin. Indianapolis: Hackett Pub. Co., c1988. xxii, 243 p.
87-015160 535.6/01 0872200396
Color (Philosophy)

B105.C46 D58 2002
Diversity and community: an interdisciplinary reader/ Philip Alperson [editor]. Malden, MA: Blackwell Pub., 2002.
2002-066431 307 21 0631219471
Community -- Philosophy. Multiculturalism. Identity (Psychology) Social structure.

B105.C46 I5 1996
In the company of others: perspectives on community, family, and culture/ edited by Nancy E. Snow. Lanham, Md.: Rowman & Littlefield, c1996. xx, 227 p.
95-043169 306/.01 20 0847681459
Community -- Philosophy. Culture -- Philosophy. Family -- Philosophy. Social structure. Feminist theory.

B105.C477 S42 1992
Seager, William,
Metaphysics of consciousness/ William Seager. London; New York: 1991. viii, 262 p.
91-016739 126 20 0415063574
Consciousness. Logical positivism.

B105.D4 S77 1998
Stroll, Avrum,
Sketches of landscapes: philosophy by example/ Avrum Stroll. Cambridge, Mass.: MIT Press, c1998. xiv, 282 p.
97-018852 191 21 0262193914
Philosophy. Description (Philosophy)

B105.D47 M37 1992
Martine, Brian J.
Indeterminacy and intelligibility/ Brian John Martine. Albany: State University Press of New York Press, c1992. xvi, 119 p.
91-038674 123 20 0791411745
Determinacy (Philosophy) Ontology. Relation (Philosophy)

B105.E46 S67 2000
Sorabji, Richard.
Emotion and peace of mind: from Stoic agitation to Christian temptation/ Richard Sorabji. Oxford; Oxford University Press, 2000. x, 499 p.
00-712281 128/.37/09 0198250053
Emotions (Philosophy) -- History. Peace of mind. Stoics -- History.

B105.E46.Y37 1999
Yanal, Robert J.
Paradoxes of emotion and fiction/ Robert J. Yanal. University Park, Pa.: Pennsylvania State University Press, c1999. xi, 164 p.
98-043075 128/.37 0271018933
Emotions (Philosophy) Fiction.

B105.E65.E45 2001
Ellis, B. D. 1929-
Scientific essentialism/ Brian Ellis. Cambridge; Cambridge University Press, 2001. xiv, 309 p.
00-063094 149 0521800943
Essence (Philosophy) Science -- Philosophy.

B105.E7.T47
Thomson, Judith Jarvis.
Acts and other events/ Judith Jarvis Thomson. Ithaca, N.Y.: Cornell University Press, 1977. 274 p.
77-004791   122   0801410509
Events (Philosophy) Act (Philosophy) Agent (Philosophy)

B105.F66 K67 1999
Korsmeyer, Carolyn.
Making sense of taste: food & philosophy/ Carolyn Korsmeyer. Ithaca, NY: Cornell University Press, 1999. xii, 232 p.
99-016165   664/.07 21   0801436982
Food -- Philosophy. Food -- Sensory evaluation. Food -- Aesthetics.

B105.I49 B72 1990
Brann, Eva T. H.
The world of the imagination: sum and substance/ by Eva T.H. Brann. Savage, Md.: Rowman & Littlefield, c1991. xiv, 810 p.
90-048616   153.3 20   0847676501
Imagination (Philosophy) Imagination (Philosophy) -- History. Imagination. Imagery (Psychology) Imagination in literature.

B105.I533 S33 1993
Scharfstein, Ben-Ami,
Ineffability: the failure of words in philosophy and religion/ Ben-Ami Scharfstein. Albany: State University of New York Press, c1993. xix, 291 p.
92-007544   121/.68 20   0791413489
Ineffable, The. Language and languages -- Philosophy.

B105.I56 B55 1992
Bilgrami, Akeel,
Belief and meaning: the unity and locality of mental content/ Akeel Bilgrami. Oxford, UK; Blackwell, 1992. ix, 301 p.
91-022287   121/.6 20   0631177760
Intentionality (Philosophy) Meaning (Philosophy)

B105.I56 D46 1987
Dennett, Daniel Clement.
The intentional stance/ Daniel C. Dennett. Cambridge, Mass.: MIT Press, c1987. xi, 388 p.
87-003018   128/.3 19   026204093X
Intentionality (Philosophy)

B105.I56 D464 1996
Dennett, Daniel Clement.
Kinds of minds: toward an understanding of consciousness/ Daniel C. Dennett. 1st ed. New York, NY: Basic Books, c1996. vii, 184 p.
96-164655   128/.2 21   0465073506
Intentionality (Philosophy) Consciousness. Thought and thinking.

B105.I56 L86 1995
Lyons, William E.
Approaches to intentionality/ William Lyons. Oxford: Clarendon Press; xiii, 261 p.
95-020275   128/.2 20   0198235267
Intentionality (Philosophy)

B105.I56 S37 1995
Schueler, G. F.
Desire: its role in practical reason and the explanation of action/ G. F. Schueler. Cambridge, Mass.: MIT Press, c1995. xi, 223 p.
94-018922   128/.4 20   0262193558
Intentionality (Philosophy) Desire (Philosophy) Practical reason.

B105.J87.C38 1998
Cave, Eric M.
Preferring justice: rationality, self-transformation, and the sense of justice/ Eric M. Cave. Boulder, Colo.: Westview Press, c1998. xiv, 183 p.
98-119238   172/.2   081332808X
Justice (Philosophy)

B105.J87.O54 1996
O'Neill, Onora, 1941-
Towards justice and virtue: a constructive account of practical reasoning/ Onora O'Neill. Cambridge; Cambridge University Press, 1996. x, 230 p.
95-049161   170   0521480957
Justice (Philosophy) Justice. Virtue.

B105.J87.S54 1987
Sher, George.
Desert/ George Sher. Princeton, N.J.: Princeton University Press, c1987. xiii, 215 p.
87-002823   170   0691077452
Justice (Philosophy)

B105.L45.A3
Adler, Mortimer Jerome, 1902-
The idea of freedom, by Mortimer J. Adler, for the Institute for Philosophical Research. Garden City, N. Y., Doubleday, 1958-61. 2 v.
58-007348   323.44
Liberty.

B105.M4 J64 1987
Johnson, Mark,
The body in the mind: the bodily basis of meaning, imagination, and reason/ Mark Johnson. Chicago: University of Chicago Press, 1987. xxxviii, 233 p.
86-025102   121/.68 19   0226403173
Meaning (Philosophy) Imagination (Philosophy) Reason. Metaphor.

B105.P53.M35 1999
Malpas, J. E.
Place and experience: a philosophical topography/ J.E. Malpas. Cambridge; Cambridge University Press, 1999. vii, 218 p.
98-039069   128/.4   0521642175
Place (Philosophy)

B105.P7.F57 1999
Fish, Stanley Eugene.
The trouble with principle/ Stanley Fish. Cambridge, Mass.: Harvard University Press, 1999. vi, 328 p.
99-035759   323/.01   0674910125
Principle (Philosophy) Political science -- Philosophy. Law and politics.

B105.R3S34 1970
Schutz, Alfred, 1899-1959.
Reflections on the problem of relevance. Edited, annotated, and with an introd. by Richard M. Zaner. New Haven, Yale University Press, 1970. xxiv, 186 p.
78-099840   111   0300012217
Carneades, -- 2nd cent. B.C. Husserl, Edmund, -- 1859-1938. Relevance (Philosophy)

B105.S43.H67 1998
Horowitz, Maryanne Cline, 1945-
Seeds of virtue and knowledge/ Maryanne Cline Horowitz. Princeton, N.J.: Princeton University Press, c1998. xviii, 373 p.
97-018580   128/.09   0691044635
Seeds (Philosophy) Seeds -- Religious aspects -- History of doctrines. Ethics -- Europe -- History. Europe -- Intellectual life.

B105.S55.M47 1998
Merrell, Floyd, 1937-
Simplicity and complexity: pondering literature, science, and painting/ Floyd Merrell. Ann Arbor: University of Michigan Press, c1998. x, 370 p.
97-040774   117   0472108603
Simplicity (Philosophy) Complexity (Philosophy) Simplicity in literature.

B105.S66.H3313 1995
Hadot, Pierre.
Philosophy as a way of life: spiritual exercises from Socrates to Foucault/ Pierre Hadot; edited by Arnold Davidson; translated by Michael Chase. Oxford; Blackwell, 1995.
94-028788   100   063118032X
Philosophy. Spiritual exercises -- History.

B105.S79 C5613 1995
Cioran, E. M.
Tears and saints/ E.M. Cioran; translated and with an introduction by Ilinca Zarifopol-Johnston. Chicago: University of Chicago Press, c1995. xxvi, 128 p.
95-013187   235/.2 20   0226106721
Suffering. Christian saints -- Miscellanea.

B105.T54.L86 1999
Luntley, Michael, 1953-
Contemporary philosophy of thought: truth, world, content/ Michael Luntley. Malden, Ma.: Blackwell Publishers, 1999. xii, 398 p.
98-008525   121/.68   0631190767
Thought and thinking. Language and languages -- Philosophy. Truth.

B105.U5 A15 1967
Aaron, Richard Ithamar,
The theory of universals, by Richard I. Aaron. 2nd ed. London, Clarendon P., 1967. viii, 246 p.
67-109306
Universals (Philosophy) [from old catalog]

B105.U5.L35
Landesman, Charles,
The problem of universals. Edited and with an introd. by Charles Landesman. New York, Basic Books [1971] vi, 314 p.
72-158443   101   0465063616
Universals (Philosophy)

B105.W3.D38 1992
Davis, Grady Scott.
Warcraft and the fragility of virtue: an essay in Aristotelian ethics/ Grady Scott Davis. Moscow, Idaho: University of Idaho Press, 1992. ix, 196 p.
91-020166   172/.42   0893011541
Aristotle -- Ethics.Just war doctrine. War (Philosophy) Justice.

B105.W3.E53 1996
An encyclopedia of war and ethics/ edited by Donald A. Wells. Westport, Conn.: Greenwood Press, 1996. ix, 539 p.
95-023647   172/.42/03   0313291160
War -- Moral and ethical aspects -- Encyclopedias. Just war doctrine -- Encyclopedias.

B105.W3.M55 1991
Miller, Richard Brian, 1953-
Interpretations of conflict: ethics, pacifism, and the just-war tradition/ Richard B. Miller. Chicago: University of Chicago Press, c1991. x, 294 p.
91-003044   172/.42   0226527956
War -- Moral and ethical aspects. Pacifism. Just war doctrine.

B105.W3.V37 1993
Vasquez, John A., 1945-
The war puzzle/ John A. Vasquez. Cambridge; Cambridge University Press, 1993. xiii, 378 p.
92-025775   172/.42   0521366739
War (Philosophy)

B105.W3 W37 2003
War after September 11/ edited by Verna V. Gehring. Lanham, Md.: Rowman & Littlefield Publishers, c2003. vii, 99 p.
2002-014864   172/.42 21   0742514684
War (Philosophy) Terrorism.

B105.W6 A53 1987
Ancient women philosophers, 600 B.C.-500 A.D./ edited by Mary Ellen Waithe. Dordrecht; M. Nijhoff; xxiv, 229 p.
86-008675   180/.88042 19   9024733685
Women philosophers. Philosophy, Ancient.

B105.W6 W64 2000
Women of color and philosophy: a critical reader/ edited by Naomi Zack. Malden, MA: Blackwell Publishers, 2000.
99-056766   191/.082 21   0631218661
Philosophy, Modern -- 20th century. Women philosophers -- United States. Philosophers -- United States.

B105.W6 W65 1996
Women philosophers/ edited by Mary Warnock. London: Dent, 1996 xlvii, 301 p.
97-173905   0460877380
Women philosophers.

B113 Ancient (600 B.C.-430 A.D.) — General works — German

B113.W613 1956
Windelband, W. 1848-1915.
History of ancient philosophy. Translated by Herbert Ernest Cushman. [New York] Dover Publications [1956] xv, 393 p.
57-014418   180
Philosophy, Ancient.

B115 Ancient (600 B.C.-430 A.D.) — General works — Other. By language, A-Z

B115.D36.F7513 1998
Friis Johansen, K. 1930-
A history of ancient philosophy: from the beginnings to Augustine/ Karsten Friis Johansen; translated by Henrik Rosenmeier. London; Routledge, 1998. xii, 685 p.
97-045072   180   0415127386
Philosophy, Ancient -- History.

B118 Ancient (600 B.C.-430 A.D.) — Nature philosophy of the ancients

B118.S36
Schrodinger, Erwin, 1887-1961.
Nature and the Greeks.   Cambridge [Eng.] University Press, 1954. 97 p.
54-002592   182
Philosophy, Ancient Science -- Philosophy.

B121 Ancient (600 B.C.-430 A.D.) — Orient — General special

B121.B55 1997
Billington, Ray.
Understanding Eastern philosophy/ Ray Billington. London; Routledge, 1997. x, 197 p.
97-224463   181 21   0415129656
Philosophy, Asian. Philosophy and religion.

B121.C66 1997
Companion encyclopedia of Asian philosophy/ edited by Brian Carr and Indira Mahalingam. London; Routledge, 1997. xxiii, 1136 p.
96-029027   181   041503535X
Philosophy, Asian -- Encyclopedias.

B121.E53 2001
Encyclopedia of Asian philosophy/ edited by Oliver Leaman. New York: Routledge , 2001.
00-032836   181/.003   0415172810
Philosophy, Asian -- Encyclopedias.Asia -- Religion -- Encyclopedias.

B121.K56 1985
Koller, John M.
Oriental philosophies/ John M. Koller. New York: Scribner, c1985. xi, 369 p.
84-020300   181   0684181452
Philosophy, Asian.

B121.K85 2001
Kupperman, Joel.
Classic Asian philosophy: a guide to the essential texts/ Joel J. Kupperman. Oxford [England]; Oxford University Press, 2001. x, 164 p.
00-020488   181 21   0195133358
Philosophy, Asian. Asia -- Religion.

B121.K86 1999
Kupperman, Joel.
Learning from Asian philosophy/ Joel J. Kupperman. New York: Oxford University Press, 1999. viii, 208 p.
98-032349   181   0195128311
Philosophy, Asian. Philosophy, Comparative.

B121.L43 2000
Leaman, Oliver,
Eastern philosophy: key readings/ Oliver Leaman. London: Routledge, 2000. xvi, 305 p.
00-710872   181 21   0415173582
Philosophy, Asian.

B121.R46 1984
Reyna, Ruth.
Dictionary of oriental philosophy/ edited and collated by Ruth Reyna; with a foreword by Moni Bagchi. New Delhi: Munshiram Manoharlal, 1984. xx, 419 p.
84-902365   181/.003/21
Philosophy, Asian -- Dictionaries -- Polyglot. Dictionaries, Polyglot.

B125-141 Ancient (600 B.C.-430 A.D.) — Orient — By region or country

B125.C45
Chan, Wing-tsit, 1901-
A source book in Chinese philosophy. Princeton, N.J., Princeton University Press, 1963. xxv, 856 p.
62-007398   181.11082
Philosophy, Chinese. Philosophy -- China -- History -- Sources.

B125.C513
Chu, Hsi, 1130-1200.
Reflections on things at hand; the Neo-Confucian anthology. Compiled by Chu Hsi and Lu Tsu-ch'ien. Translated, with notes, by Wing-tsit Chan. New York, Columbia University Press, 1967. xli, 441 p.
65-022548   180/.11
Neo-Confucianism.

B125.Y8 1982
Yüan thought: Chinese thought and religion under the Mongols/ Hok-lam Chan and Wm. Theodore de Bary, editors. New York: Columbia University Press, 1982. xiii, 545 p.
82-001259   181/.11/09022 19   023105324X
Philosophy, Chinese -- Congresses. China -- Religion -- Congresses.

B126.A44 1991
Allan, Sarah.
The shape of the turtle: myth, art, and cosmos in early China/ Sarah Allan. Albany, NY: State University of New York Press, c1991. xi, 230 p.
90-030424   299/.51/0931   0791404595
Philosophy, Chinese -- To 221 B.C. Mythology, Chinese. Cosmology, Chinese. China -- History -- Shang dynasty, 1766-1122 B.C. China -- Civilization -- To 221 B.C.

B126.A45 1997
Allan, Sarah.
The way of water and sprouts of virtue/ Sarah Allan. Albany: State University of New York Press, c1997. xiv, 181 p.
96-036341   181/.11 20   0791433862
Philosophy, Chinese. Philosophy of nature.

B126.C43 1975
Chai, Chu.
The story of Chinese philosophy/ Chu Chai, with Winberg Chai. Westport, Conn.: Greenwood Press, 1975, c1961. xxxiii, 252 p.
75-017196   181/.11   0837182891
Philosophy, Chinese.

B126.C44
Chan, Wing-tsit, 1901-
Historical charts of Chinese philosophy. New Haven, Far Eastern Publications, [1970, c1955]
55-001821
Philosophy, Chinese.

B126.C4466 1998
Chang, Ch un,
The four political treatises of the Yellow Emperor: original Mawangdui texts with complete English translations and an introduction/ Leo S. Chang and Yu Feng; with a foreword by Benjamin I. Schwartz. Honolulu: University of Hawai i Press, c1998. 230 p.
97-048960   181/.112 21   0824820088
Philosophy, Chinese -- To 221 B.C. China -- Politics and government -- To 221 B.C.

B126.C67
Creel, Herrlee Glessner, 1905-
Chinese thought, from Confucius to Mao Tse-tung. [Chicago] University of Chicago Press [1953] ix, 292 p.
53-010054   181.1
Philosophy, Chinese.

B126.C7 1975
Creel, Herrlee Glessner, 1905-
Sinism: a study of the evolution of the Chinese world-view/ by Herrlee Glessner Creel. Westport, Conn.: Hyperion Press, 1975, c1929. vii, 127 p.
74-002904   181/.11   0883551659
Philosophy, Chinese.China -- Religion.

B126.F42 1948
Feng, Yu-lan, 1895-
A short history of Chinese philosophy/ ed. by Derk Bodde. New York, Macmillan Co., 1948. xx, 368 p.
48-009573
Philosophy, Chinese.

B126.F43
Feng, Yu-lan, 1895-
The spirit of Chinese philosophy. Tr. by E. R. Hughes. London, K. Paul, Trench, Trubner [1947] xiv, 224 p.
48-001083
Philosophy, Chinese.

B126.G72 1990
Graham, A. C.
Studies in Chinese philosophy and philosophical literature/ A.C. Graham. Albany, N.Y.: State University of New York Press, c1990. 435 p.
90-030958   181/.11 20   0791404501
Philosophy, Chinese. Philosophical literature -- China.

B126.H255 1998
Hall, David L.
Thinking from the Han: self, truth, and transcendence in Chinese and Western culture/ David L. Hall and Roger T. Ames. Albany, N.Y.: State University of New York Press, c1998. xix, 336 p.
97-024491   181/.11 21   0791436144
Philosophy, Chinese. Philosophy. Philosophy, Comparative. East and West.

B126.H277 1992
Hansen, Chad, 1942-
A Daoist theory of Chinese thought: a philosophical interpretation/ Chad Hansen. New York: Oxford University Press, 1992. xv, 448 p.
91-003645   181/.114   0195067290
Philosophy, Chinese. Philosophy, Taoist. Chinese language -- Philosophy.

B126.H8 1963
Hu, Shih, 1891-1962.
The development of the logical method in ancient China. New York, Paragon Book Reprint Corp., 1963. 187 p.
63-021053   181.11
Logic -- History. Philosophy, Chinese.

B126.H84 1954
Hughes, E. R. 1883-1956.
Chinese philosophy in classical times. London, Dent; [1954] xiv, 336 p.
54-003630   181.1
Philosophy, Chinese.

B126.M34 1994
Makeham, John,
Name and actuality in early Chinese thought/ John Makeham. Albany: State University of New York Press, c1994. xviii, 286 p.
93-031922   181/.112 20   0791419843
Xu, Gan, 171-218 -- Criticism and interpretation. Philosophy, Chinese -- 221 B.C.-960 A.D.

B126.P38 1993
Peerenboom, R. P. 1958-
Law and morality in ancient China: the silk manuscripts of Huang-Lao/ R.P. Peerenboom. Albany: State University of New York Press, c1993. xvi, 380 p.
91-047541   181/.11   0791412377
Philosophy, Chinese -- To 221 B.C. Law (Philosophy) -- Early works to 1800. Taoism -- China -- Early works to 1800.

B126.W3
Waley, Arthur.
Three ways of thought in ancient China. Garden City, N.Y., Doubleday, 1956. 216 p.
56-005973   181.1
Philosophy, Chinese.

B126.W335 1946
Wang, Gung-hsing, 1909-
The Chinese mind ... New York, The John Day Company [1946] viii, 192 p.
46-004685   181.1
Philosophy, Chinese. Philosophy, Confucian.

B126.W7
Wright, Arthur F., 1913-1976,
Studies in Chinese thought. With contributions by Derk Bodde [and others. Chicago] University of Chicago Press [1953] xiv, 317 p.
53-013533   181.1
Philosophy, Chinese. Chinese language -- Translating. China -- Civilization.

B127.C49 Y83 1993
Yuasa, Yasuo.
The body, self-cultivation, and ki-energy/ Yuasa Yasuo; translated by Shigenori Nagatomo and Monte S. Hull. Albany: State University of New York Press, c1993. xxxvi, 229 p.
92-036569   128 20   0791416240
Qi (Chinese philosophy) Body, Human (Philosophy) Self-actualization (Psychology) Philosophy and science. Philosophy, Comparative.

B127.C65.B47 1998
Berthrong, John H., 1946-
Transformations of the Confucian way/ John H.
Berthrong. Boulder, Colo: Westview Press,
1998. xiv, 250 p.
98-010945   181/.112   0813328055
*Philosophy, Confucian -- History.
Confucianism -- History. Confucianism -- East
Asia -- History.*

B127.C65.C495 1990
Cheng, Chung-ying, 1935-
New dimensions of Confucian and Neo-
Confucian philosophy/ by Chung-ying Cheng.
Albany, N.Y.: State University of New York
Press, c1991. xi, 619 p.
89-019655   181/.112   0791402835
Philosophy, Confucian. Neo-Confucianism.

B127.C65.C64 1998
Confucianism and ecology: the interrelation of
heaven, earth, and humans/ edited by Mary
Evelyn Tucker and John Berthrong. Cambridge,
Mass.: Distributed by Harvard University Press,
c1998. xlv, 378 p.
98-018767   179/.1/0951   0945454155
*Philosophy, Confucian. Ecology -- China --
Philosophy. Environmental ethics -- China.*

B127.C65.E56 1990
Eno, Robert, 1949-
The Confucian creation of heaven: philosophy
and the defense of ritual mastery/ Robert Eno.
Albany: State University of New York Press,
c1990. xi, 349 p.
89-031194   181/.112   0791401901
*Philosophy, Confucian -- China -- History.
Confucianism -- China -- History. Heaven --
Confucianism -- History of doctrines.*

B127.C65.L495 1999
Li, Chenyang, 1956-
The Tao encounters the West: explorations in
comparative philosophy/ Chenyang Li. Albany:
State University of New York Press, c1999. xi,
234 p.
98-031714   181/.11   0791441350
*Philosophy,   Confucian.   Philosophy.
Philosophy, Comparative.*

B127.C65.L59 1998
Liu, Shu-hsien, 1934-
Understanding Confucian philosophy: classical
and Sung-Ming/ Shu-hsien Liu. Westport,
Conn.: Greenwood Press, 1998. xii, 273 p.
97-052294   181/.112   0313301549
Confucianism.

B127.C65 M44 1997
Meeting of minds: intellectual and religious
interaction in East Asian traditions of thought:
essays in honor of Wing-tsit Chan and William
Theodore de Bary/ edited by Irene Bloom and
Joshua A. Fogel. New York: Columbia
University Press, 1997. vi, 391 p.
95-020957   181 20   0231103530
*Philosophy, Confucian. Philosophy, Asian.
East Asia -- Religion.*

B127.C65 T55 1992
Tillman, Hoyt Cleveland.
Confucian discourse and Chu Hsi's ascendancy/
Hoyt Cleveland Tillman. Honolulu: University
of Hawaii Press, c1992. xv, 328 p.
92-009630   181/.112/09021 20   0824814169
*Chu, Hsi, 1130-1200. Philosophy, Confucian
-- History. Confucianism -- History. China --
Intellectual life -- 960-1644.*

B127.J4 Y4 1996
Yao, Xinzhong.
Confucianism and Christianity: a comparative
study of Jen and Agape/ Xinzhong Yao.
Brighton, U.K.: Sussex Academic Press;   viii,
263 p.
96-148018   299/.512172 21   1898723761
*Ren. Agape. Love -- Religious aspects --
Comparative studies. Confucianism -- Relations
-- Christianity. Christianity and other religions -
- Confucianism.*

B127.K66 E65 1993
Epistemological issues in classical Chinese
philosophy/ edited by Hans Lenk and Gregor
Paul. Albany: State University of New York
Press, c1993. ix, 194 p.
92-017185   121/.0951 20   0791414507
*Philosophy, Chinese -- To 221 B.C.
Knowledge, Theory of.*

B127.N4.C46 1977
Chang, Chun-mai, 1886-1969.
The development of Neo-Confucian thought/ by
Carsun Chang. Westport, Conn.: Greenwood
Press, 1977, c1957. 376 p.
77-008338   181/.11   0837196930
Neo-Confucianism.

B127.N4.C66 1970
The unfolding of Neo-Confucianism, by Wm.
Theodore de Bary and the Conference on
Seventeenth-Century Chinese Thought. New
York, Columbia University Press, 1975. xiv,
593 p.
74-010929   181/.09/512   0231038283
*Neo-Confucianism   --   Congresses.
Confucianism -- Relations -- Buddhism --
Congresses.   Buddhism   --   Relations   --
Confucianism -- Congresses.*

B127.N4.D397 1991
De Bary, William Theodore, 1919-
Learning for one's self: essays on the individual
in Neo-Confucian thought/ Wm. Theodore de
Bary. New York: Columbia University Press,
c1991. xiii, 461 p.
90-044575   126/.0951   0231074263
Neo-Confucianism. Self (Philosophy)

B127.N4.D399 1989
De Bary, William Theodore, 1919-
The message of the mind in Neo-Confucianism/
Wm. Theodore de Bary. New York: Columbia
University Press, c1989. xv, 292 p.
88-018740   181/.09512   0231068085
Neo-Confucianism -- China.

B127.N4 D4
De Bary, William Theodore,
Neo-Confucian orthodoxy and the learning of
the mind-and-heart/ Wm. Theodore de Bary.
New York: Columbia University Press, 1981.
xviii, 267 p.
81-003809   181/.09512 19   0231052286
*Neo-Confucianism.   Neo-Confucianism   --
Japan. Philosophy, Chinese. China -- Religion.*

B127.N4 H86 1999
Huang, Siu-chi,
Essentials of Neo-Confucianism: eight major
philosophers of the Song and Ming periods/
Siu-chi Huang. Westport, Conn.: Greenwood
Press, 1999. xii, 261 p.
99-010657   181/.112 21   031326449X
Neo-Confucianism. Philosophers -- China.

B127.N4.P74
Principle and practicality: essays in Neo-
Confucianism and practical learning/ Wm.
Theodore de Bary and Irene Bloom, editors.
New York: Columbia University Press, 1979.
xvi, 543 p.
78-011530   181/.09/512   023104612X
*Neo-Confucianism.   Practice   (Philosophy)
China -- History -- Ming dynasty, 1368-1644.
Japan -- History -- Tokugawa period, 1600-
1868.*

B127.T3 D36 2002
Daoist identity: history, lineage, and ritual/
edited by Livia Kohn and Harold D. Roth.
Honolulu: University of Hawai'i Press, c2002. x,
333 p.
2001-053064   181/.114 21   0824825047
Tao.

B127.T3 T43 1997
Teachings of the Tao: readings from the Taoist
spiritual tradition/ selected and translated by Eva
Wong. Boston: Shambhala; vii, 152 p.
96-009728   299/.5144 20   1570622450
Tao. Taoism. Spiritual life -- Taoism.

B128.C3474 T55 1994
Tillman, Hoyt Cleveland.
Ch'en Liang on public interest and the law/ Hoyt
Cleveland Tillman. Honolulu: University of
Hawaii Press, c1994. xxi, 150 p.
94-020450   181/.112 20   0824816102
*Ch en, Liang, 1143-1194 -- Contributions in
philosophy of law. Law -- China -- Philosophy.*

B128.C364 G73 1992
Graham, A. C.
Two Chinese philosophers: the metaphysics of
the brothers Ch êng/ A.C. Graham; foreword by
Irene Bloom. La Salle, Ill.: Open Court, c1992.
xxiii, 201 p.
92-022626   181/.112 20   0812692152
*Ch eng, I, 1033-1107. Ch eng, Hao, 1032-
1085.*

B128.C52.E5 1990
Chu, Hsi, 1130-1200.
Learning to be a sage: selections from the Conversations of Master Chu, arranged topically/ by Chu Hsi; translated with a commentary by Daniel K. Gardner. Berkeley: University of California Press, c1990. xii, 218 p.
89-039348   181/.11   0520065255
Philosophy -- Early works to 1800.

B128.C53 H7513 1991
Chu, Hsi,
Further reflections on things at hand: a reader/ Chu Hsi; translation and commentary by Allen Wittenborn. Lanham: University Press of America, c1991. xiii, 312 p.
91-023770   181/.112 20   0819183733
Philosophy, Confucian. Neo-Confucianism.

B128.C54.B78 1973
Bruce, J. Percy 1861-
Chu Hsi and his masters; an introduction to Chu Hsi and the Sung School of Chinese Philosophy, by J. Percy Bruce. London, Probsthain, 1923. [New York, AMS Press, 1973] xvi, 336 p.
78-038050   181/.11   0404569048
Chu, Hsi, -- 1130-1200.Philosophy, Chinese.

B128.C54.C42 1989
Chan, Wing-tsit, 1901-
Chu Hsi: new studies/ Wing-tsit Chan. Honolulu: University of Hawaii Press, c1989. viii, 628 p.
89-004799   181/.11   0824812018
Chu, Hsi, -- 1130-1200.

B128.C54 C465 2000
Ching, Julia.
The religious thought of Chu Hsi/ Julia Ching. New York: Oxford University Press, c2000. x, 348 p.
99-019667   181/.112 21   0195091892
Chu, Hsi, 1130-1200 -- Views on religion.

B128.C7.L5 1943
Confucius.
The wisdom of Confucius, edited and translated with notes by Lin Yutang; illustrated by Jeanyee Wong. New York, The Modern Library [1943] xvii, 265 p.
43-051329   181.1
Ethics, Chinese. Philosophy, Chinese.

B128.C8.C65 1972
Creel, Herrlee Glessner, 1905-
Confucius, the man and the myth [by] H. G. Creel. Westport, Conn., Greenwood Press [1972, c1949] xi, 363 p.
72-007816   299/.5126/4   0837165318
Confucius.

B128.C8.H35 1987
Hall, David L.
Thinking through Confucius/ David L. Hall, Roger T. Ames. Albany: State University of New York Press, c1987. xxii, 393 p.
87-006454   181/.09512   0887063764
Confucius.

B128.C8.L58 1979
Liu, Wu-chi, 1907-
A short history of Confucian philosophy/ Liu Wu-chi. Westport, Ct.: Hyperion Press, 1979. 229 p.
78-020480   181/.09/512   0883558572
Philosophy, Confucian.

B128.H66.E5 1988
Hsun-tzu, 340-245 B.C.1
Xunzi: a translation and study of the complete works/ John Knoblock. Stanford, Calif.: Stanford University Press, [c1988-   ] v. 1
87-033578   181/.09512   0804714517

B128.H7 G64 1999
Goldin, Paul Rakita,
Rituals of the way: the philosophy of Xunzi/ Paul Rakita Goldin. Chicago, Ill.: Open Court, c1999. xvi, 182 p.
99-010654   181/.112 21   0812694007
Xunzi, 340-245 B.C. Xunzi. Philosophy, Chinese -- To 221 B.C.

B128.H74 M33 1993
Machle, Edward J.,
Nature and heaven in the Xunzi: a study of the Tian lun/ by Edward J. Machle. Albany: State University of New York Press, c1993. xiii, 224 p.
92-031573   181/.112 20   0791415546
Xunzi, 340-245 B.C. Xunzi. Philosophy of nature.

B128.L83.H8 1944
Huang, Hsiu-chi, 1913-
Lu Hsiang shan ... a twelfth century Chinese idealist philosopher, by Siu chi Huang. New Haven, Conn., American Oriental Society, 1944. 116 p.
45-005004   181.1
Lu, Chiu-yuan, -- 1139-1193.Philosophy, Chinese.

B128.M324 H83 2001
Huang, Junjie,
Mencian hermeneutics: a history of interpretations in China/ Chün-chieh Huang. New Brunswick, N.J.: Transaction Publishers, c2001. viii, 317 p.
2001-037708   181/.112 21   0765801078
Mencius. Mengzi. Philosophy, Chinese -- To 221 B.C.

B128.M324.S48 1997
Shun, Kwong-loi, 1953-
Mencius and early Chinese thought/ Kwong-loi Shun. Stanford, Calif.: Stanford University Press, 1997. xii, 295 p.
96-012393   181/.112   0804727880
Mencius.Philosophy, Chinese -- To 221 B.C.

B128.M7.E5
Mo, Ti, fl. 400 B.C.-
The ethical and political works of Motse, translated from the original Chinese text by Yi-Pao Mei, PH. D. London, A. Probsthain, 1929. xiv, 275 p.
30-004133

B128.S514.W93 1996
Wyatt, Don J.
The recluse of Loyang: Shao Yung and the moral evolution of early Sung thought/ Don J. Wyatt. Honolulu, Hawaii: University of Hawai'i Press, c1996. xii, 340 p.
96-012396   181/.112   0824817559
Shao, Yung, -- 1011-1077.Philosophy, Chinese -- 960-1644.

B128.W4.E47
Wang, Shou-jen, 1472-1528.
Instructions for practical living, and other Neo-Confucian writing, by Wang Yang-ming. Translated, with notes, by Wing-tsit Chan. New York, Columbia University Press, 1963. xii, 358 p.
62-016688   181.11   0231024843

B130.R3
Radhakrishnan, S. 1888-1975,
A source book in Indian philosophy, edited by Sarvepalli Radhakrishnan and Charles A. Moore. Princeton, N.J., Princeton University Press, 1957. xxix, 683 p.
55-006698   181.4
Philosophy, Hindu.

B131.B45
Bernard, Theos, 1908-
Hindu philosophy. New York, Philosophical Library [1947] xi, 207 p.
47-011335   181.4
Philosophy, Hindu.

B131.E5
The Encyclopedia of Indian philosophies/ Sibajiban Bhattacharya ... [et al.]. Delhi, Motilal Banarsidass, 1970-1999 v. 1-8
70-911664   181/.4
Philosophy, Indic -- Dictionaries. Philosophy, Indic -- Bibliography.

B131.G635 1998
Gotshalk, Richard.
The beginnings of philosophy in India/ Richard Gotshalk. Lanham, Md.: University Press of America, c1998. xxiii, 448 p.
98-005354   181/.4   0761810536
Philosophy, Hindu.

B131.G67 1989
Grimes, John A., 1948-
A concise dictionary of Indian philosophy: Sanskrit terms defined in English/ John Grimes. Albany, N.Y.: State University of New York Press, c1989. 440 p.
88-036717   181/.4/03   0791401006
Philosophy, Indic -- Dictionaries -- Sanskrit. Sanskrit language -- Dictionaries -- English.

B131.I48 1982
Indian philosophy: past and future/ edited by S.S. Rama Rao Pappu and R. Puligandla. Delhi: Motila Banarsidass, 1982. xvii, 434 p.
82-901541   181/.4   0836406702
Philosophy, Indic.

B131.K49 1999
King, Richard, 1966-
Indian philosophy: an introduction to Hindu and Buddhist thought/ Richard King. Washington, D. C.: Georgetown University Press, 1999.
99-025986   181/.4   0878407561
Philosophy, Indic.

B131.M54.M64 2000
Mohanty, Jitendranath, 1928-
Classical Indian philosophy/ J.N. Mohanty. Lanham, Md.: Rowman & Littlefield Publishers, c2000. vii, 181 p.
99-036603   181/.4   0847689328
Philosophy, Indic. Jaina philosophy. Philosophy, Hindu.

B131.O73
Organ, Troy Wilson.
Western approaches to eastern philosophy/ Troy Wilson Organ. Athens: Ohio University Press, c1975. 282 p.
75-014554   181   0821401947
Philosophy, Indic. Philosophy, Comparative.

B131.R25 1952
Radhakrishnan, S. 1888-1975.
Contemporary Indian philosophy, by M. K. Gandhi [and others] edited by S. Radhakrishnan and J. H. Muirhead. London, G. Allen & Unwin [1952] 648 p.
52-010717   181.4
Philosophy, Hindu.

B131.Z52
Zimmer, Heinrich Robert, 1890-1943.
Philosophies of India; edited by Joseph Campbell. [New York] Pantheon Books [1951] xvii, 687 p.
51-013167   181.4
Philosophy, Indic.

B132.V3.B2 1960
Badarayana.
The Brahma sutra, the philosophy of spiritual life. Translated with an introd. and notes by S. Radhakrishnan. New York, Harper [1960] 606 p.
60-001206   181.48
Philosophy, Hindu. Vedanta.

B132.V3.D542
Deutsch, Eliot.
A source book of Advaita Vedanta [by] Eliot Deutsch [and] J. A. B. van Buitenen. Honolulu, University Press of Hawaii, 1971. ix, 335 p.
75-148944   181/.482   0870221892
Vedanta. Advaita.

B132.V3.L62 1980
Lott, Eric J.
Vedantic approaches to God/ Eric Lott; foreword by John Hick. Totowa, N.J.: Barnes & Noble, 1980. xii, 214 p.
78-017886   181/.48   0064943658
Sankaracarya. Ramanuja, -- 1017-1137. Madhva, -- 13th cent. Vedanta.

B132.Y6.D27 1973
Dasgupta, Surendranath, 1885-1952.
Yoga as philosophy and religion/ Surendranath Dasgupta. Delhi: Motilal Banarsidass, 1973, 1978. x, 200 p.
78-913009   181/.452
Yoga. Philosophy, Hindu. Patanjali.

B132.Y6.F46 1990
Feuerstein, Georg.
Encyclopedic dictionary of Yoga/ Georg Feuerstein. New York: Paragon House, 1990. xxix, 430 p.
89-023068   181/.45/03   155778244X
Yoga -- Dictionaries.

B132.Y6.M5
Mishra, Rammurti S.
Fundamentals of yoga; a handbook of theory, practice, and application. Drawings by Oscar Weinland. New York, Julian Press, 1959. 255 p.
59-010065   181.45
Yoga.

B132.Y6.V2913
Varenne, Jean.
Yoga and the Hindu tradition/ Jean Varenne; translated from the French by Derek Coltman. Chicago: University of Chicago Press, 1976. x, 253 p.
75-019506   181/.45   0226851141
Yoga.

B133.G4.A3
Gandhi, 1869-1948.
All men are brothers; life and thoughts of Mahatma Gandhi as told in his own words. Comp. and ed. by Krishna Kripalani; introd. by Sarvepalli Radhakrishnan. [Paris] UNESCO [1969,c1958] xvi, 196 p.
59-000426   923.254
Gandhi, -- Mahatma, -- 1869-1948.

B133.G4 G78 2001
Gruzalski, Bart.
On Gandhi/ Bart Gruzalski. Australia; Wadsworth/Thomson Learning, c2001. 86 p.
2001-271644   181/.4 21   0534583741
Gandhi, Mahatma, 1869-1948.

B136.F83 1971
Fujisawa, Chikao, 1893-
Zen and Shinto; the story of Japanese philosophy. Westport, Conn., Greenwood Press [1971, c1959] 92 p.
78-139133   181/.12   0837157498
Philosophy, Japanese. Zen Buddhism -- Japan. Shinto.

B141.H6713 1992
Hornung, Erik.
Idea into image: essays on ancient Egyptian thought/ Erik Hornung; translated by Elizabeth Bredeck. [New York]: Timken: c1992. 209 p.
91-046855   181/.2   0943221110
Philosophy, Egyptian.

B157-162.5 Ancient (600 B.C. -430 A.D.) — Orient — By religion

B157.C65.S25 1994
Samuelson, Norbert Max, 1936-
Judaism and the doctrine of creation/ Norbert M. Samuelson. Cambridge; Cambridge University Press, 1994. xi, 362 p.
93-046180   296.3/4   0521452147
Jewish cosmology. Philosophy, Jewish. Creation -- History of doctrines.

B162.J32 1988
Jacobson, Nolan Pliny.
The heart of Buddhist philosophy/ Nolan Pliny Jacobson. Carbondale: Southern Illinois University Press, c1988. xiv, 189 p.
87-017376   181/.043   0809313960
Philosophy, Buddhist.

B162.5.B483
Bhattacharyya, Narendra Nath, 1934-
Jain philosophy: historical outline/ by Narendra Nath Bhattacharyya. New Delhi: Munshiram Manoharlal Publishers, 1976. xix, 220 p.
76-902152   181/.04/4
Jaina philosophy.

B162.9 Ancient (600 B.C.-430 A.D.) — Occident — General works

B162.9.M34 1998
Marietta, Don E.
Introduction to ancient philosophy/ Don E. Marietta, Jr. Armonk, N.Y.: M.E. Sharpe, c1998. xiii, 219 p.
97-046373   180   0765602156
Philosophy, Ancient.

B163 Ancient (600 B.C.-430 A.D.) — Occident — Dictionaries. Encyclopedias

B163.E53 1997
Encyclopedia of classical philosophy/ edited by Donald J. Zeyl; associate editors, Daniel T. Devereux and Phillip T. Mitsis. Westport, Conn.: Greenwood Press, 1997. xv, 614 p.
96-002562   180/.3   0313287759
Philosophy, Ancient -- Encyclopedias. Philosophers, Ancient -- Biography -- Encyclopedias.

B165-491 Ancient (600 B.C.-430 A.D.) — Occident — Greece

B165.M22 2002
McEvilley, Thomas,
The shape of ancient thought: comparative studies in Greek and Indian philosophies/ Thomas McEvilley. New York: Allworth Press: c2002. xxxvi, 732 p.
2001-005510   180 21   1581152035
Philosophy, Ancient. Philosophy, Indic. Philosophy, Comparative.

B171.A56
Essays in ancient Greek philosophy/ edited by John P. Anton with George L. Kustas. Albany: State University of New York Press, [1971-c1992 v. 1-5
69-014648   180   087395050X
Plato -- Congresses.Philosophy, Ancient -- Congresses.

B171.A78 1966
Armstrong, A. H.
An introduction to ancient philosophy, by A.H. Armstrong. London, Methuen, 1965 xviii, 242 p.
66-070051   180.9
Philosophy, Ancient.

B171.B68
Boas, George, 1891-
Rationalism in Greek philosophy. Baltimore, Johns Hopkins Press [1961] 488 p.
61-015638   182
Philosophy, Ancient.

B171.B85 1950
Burnet, John, 1863-1928.
Greek philosophy, Thales to Plato, by John Burnet. London, Macmillan and co., limited, 1950. x, 360 p.
39-007819
Philosophy, Ancient.

B171.C36 1999
The Cambridge history of Hellenistic philosophy/ edited by Keimpe Algra ... [et al.]. Cambridge, U.K.; Cambridge University Press, 1999. xix, 916 p.
98-036033   180   0521250285
Philosophy, Ancient.

B171.C7
Cornford, Francis Macdonald, 1874-1943.
Before and after Socrates. Cambridge [Eng.] University Press, 1932. x, 113 p.
33-009379   180   0521091136
Plato. Socrates. Aristotle. Philosophy, Ancient.

B171.G55 1995
Gill, Christopher,
Greek thought/ by Christopher Gill. Oxford; Oxford University Press, 1995. 103 p.
96-127092   180 20   0199220743
Philosophy, Ancient. Greece -- Civilization -- To 146 B.C.

B171.G84
Guthrie, W. K. C. 1906-
In the beginning; some Greek views on the origins of life and the early state of man. Ithaca, N.Y., Cornell University Press [1957] 151 p.
58-002176   182
Philosophy, Ancient.

B171.I77 1989
Irwin, Terence.
Classical thought/ Terence Irwin. Oxford, [England]; Oxford University Press, 1989. xii, 266 p.
88-012616   180   0192191969
Philosophy, Ancient.

B171.L83 1992
Luce, John Victor,
An introduction to Greek philosophy/ J.V. Luce. London: Thames and Hudson, c1992. 174 p.
92-205519   180 20   0500276552
Philosophy, Ancient.

B172.H33513 2002
Hadot, Pierre.
What is ancient philosophy?/ Pierre Hadot; translated by Michael Chase. Cambridge, Mass.: Harvard University Press, 2002. xii, 362 p.
2002-017193   180 21   0674007336
Philosophy, Ancient.

B172.R63
Robin, Leon, 1866-1947.
Greek thought and the origins of the scientific spirit/ by Leon Robin. London: K. Paul, Trench, Trubner & Co. ltd.; 1928. xx, 409 p.
29-004655
Philosophy, Ancient.

B177.M47 1998
Method in ancient philosophy/ edited by Jyl Gentzler. Oxford: Clarendon Press; 1998. viii, 398 p.
97-024353   180   0198235712
Philosophy, Ancient. Methodology -- History.

B178.J67 1990
Jordan, William, 1954-
Ancient concepts of philosophy/ William Jordan. London; Routledge, 1990. xiii, 207 p.
90-031959   180   0415048346
Philosophy, Ancient. Methodology -- History.

B181.M59 1993
Modern thinkers and ancient thinkers: the Stanley Victor Keeling memorial lectures at University College London, 1981-1991/ edited by Robert W. Sharples. Boulder: Westview Press, 1993. vi, 201 p.
93-242141   180 20   0813319471
Philosophy, Ancient.

B181.S6
Snell, Bruno, 1896-
The discovery of the mind; the Greek origins of European thought. Translated by T. G. Rosenmeyer. Cambridge, Harvard University Press, 1953. xii, 323 p.
53-005261
Philosophy, Ancient. Greek literature -- History and criticism. Thought and thinking. Greece -- Intellectual life. Greece -- Religion.

B187.C38 H36 1998
Hankinson, R. J.
Cause and explanation in ancient Greek thought/ R.J. Hankinson. Oxford: Clarendon Press; xvi, 499 p.
98-026743   122/.0938 21   0198237456
Causation -- History. Explanation -- History. Philosophy, Ancient.

B187.C7.V55
Vlastos, Gregory.
Plato's universe/ Gregory Vlastos. Seattle: University of Washington Press, [1975] xiii, 130 p.
75-004548   113   0295953888
Plato.Cosmology -- History. Philosophy, Ancient.

B187.M25 S2713 2001
Sassi, Maria Michela, 1955-
The science of man in ancient Greece/ Maria Michela Sassi; translated by Paul Tucker; with a foreword by Sir Geoffrey Lloyd. Chicago: University of Chicago Press, c2001. xxx, 224 p.
00-009177   128/.0938   0226735303
Philosophical anthropology -- Greece -- History. Philosophy, Ancient.

B187.M55.S67 1993
Sorabji, Richard.
Animal minds and human morals: the origins of the Western debate/ Richard Sorabji. Ithaca, N.Y.: Cornell University Press, 1993. 267 p.
93-025811   179/.3   080142948X
Philosophy of mind -- History. Animal intelligence -- Philosophy -- History. Animal welfare -- Philosophy -- History.

B187.S7.A54 1994
Algra, Keimpe, 1959-
Concepts of space in Greek thought/ by Keimpe Algra. Leiden; E.J. Brill, 1995. 365 p.
94-033784   114/.0938   9004101721
Philosophy, Ancient. Space and time.

B187.T55.C3
Callahan, John Francis, 1912-
Four views of time in ancient philosophy. Cambridge, Harvard Univ. Press, 1948. ix, 209 p.
48-009013   115
Philosophy, Ancient. Space and time.

B187.T7.D39 1990
Denyer, Nicholas.
Language, thought, and falsehood in ancient Greek philosophy/ Nicholas Denyer. London; Routledge, 1991. xi, 222 p.
90-008367　121/.0938　0415022193
Truthfulness and falsehood -- History. Thought and thinking -- History. Language and languages -- Philosophy -- History.

B187.5.G3313 1998
Gadamer, Hans Georg, 1900-
The beginning of philosophy/ Hans-Georg Gadamer; translated by Rod Coltman. New York: Continuum, c1998. 132 p.
98-034594　182　0826411096
Pre-Socratic philosophers.

B187.5.N5413 2001
Nietzsche, Friedrich Wilhelm, 1844-1900.
The pre-Platonic philosophers/ Friedrich Nietzsche; translated from the German and edited, with an introduction and commentary, by Greg Whitlock. Urbana: University of Illinois Press, c2001. xlvi, 287 p.
99-056820　182　0252025598
Socrates. Pre-Socratic philosophers. Philosophy, Ancient.

B187.5.P66 1998
Popper, Karl Raimund, 1902-
The world of Parmenides: essays on the Presocratic enlightenment/ Karl R. Popper; edited by Arne F. Petersen, with the assistance of Jorgen Mejer. London; Routledge, 1998. x, 328 p.
97-017466　182　0415173019
Parmenides. Pre-Socratic philosophers.

B188.B34 1982
Barnes, Jonathan.
The Presocratic philosophers/ Jonathan Barnes. London; Routledge & Kegan Paul, 1982. xxiii, 703 p.
81-023465　182　0710092008
Pre-Socratic philosophers.

B188.C35 1999
The Cambridge companion to early Greek philosophy/ edited by A.A. Long. Cambridge; Cambridge University Press, 1999. xxx, 427 p.
98-038077　182 21　0521441226
Philosophy, Ancient.

B188.C6 1957
Cornford, Francis Macdonald, 1874-1943.
From religion to philosophy; a study in the origins of western speculation. New York, Harper [1957] 275 p.
57-010120　180
Philosophy, Ancient. Greece -- Religion.

B188.K5 1983
Kirk, G. S. 1921-
The presocratic philosophers: a critical history with a selection of texts. Cambridge [Cambridgeshire]; Cambridge University Press, 1983. xiii, 501 p.
82-023505　182　0521254442
Pre-Socratic philosophers.

B188.N513
Nietzsche, Friedrich Wilhelm, 1844-1900.
Philosophy in the tragic age of the Greeks. Translated, with an introd., by Marianne Cowan. Chicago, Regnery [c1962] 117 p.
63-001322　180
Philosophy, Ancient.

B188.R58
Robinson, John Mansley.
An introduction to early Greek philosophy; the chief fragments and ancient testimony, with connecting commentary. Boston, Houghton Mifflin [1968] x, 339 p.
68-001065　182
Philosophy, Ancient.

B193.B3 1964
Bailey, Cyril, 1871-1957.
The Greek atomists and Epicurus, a study. New York, Russell & Russell, 1964. viii, 619 p.
64-011844　187
Epicurus. Atomism.

B205.Z7.S36
Schofield, Malcolm.
An essay on Anaxagoras/ Malcolm Schofield. Cambridge [Eng.]; Cambridge University Press, 1980. xi, 187 p.
79-010348　182/.8　0521227224
Anaxagoras. Aristotle.

B208.Z7 C68 2003
Couprie, Dirk L.,
Anaximander in context: new studies in the origins of Greek philosophy/ Dirk L. Couprie, Robert Hahn, and Gerard Naddaf. Albany: State University of New York Press, c2003. xiii, 290 p.
2002-070713　182 21　0791455386
Anaximander. Philosophy, Ancient.

B223.K48
Heraclitus,
The cosmic fragments. Edited with an introd. and commentary by G. S. Kirk. Cambridge [Eng.] University Press, 1954. xv, 423 p.
54-002967　182.4

B235.P24.K56 1999
Kingsley, Peter.
In the dark places of wisdom / Peter Kingsley. Inverness, Calif.: Golden Sufi Center, 1999. 255 p.
98-012389　182/.3　189035001X
Parmenides.

B243.G88 1987
Guthrie, Kenneth Sylvan, 1871-1940.
The Pythagorean sourcebook and library: an anthology of ancient writings which relate to Pythagoras and Pythagorean philosophy/ compiled and translated by Kenneth Sylvan Guthrie; with additional translations by Thomas Taylor and Arthur Fairbanks, Jr.; introduced and edited by David R. Fideler; with a foreword by Joscelyn Godwin. Grand Rapids: Phanes Press, 1987. 361 p.
87-060459　182/.2　0933999518
Pythagoras and Pythagorean school.

B243.P45
Philip, James A.
Pythagoras and early Pythagoreanism [by] J. A. Philip. [Toronto] University of Toronto Press [1966] x, 222 p.
66-009226　182.2
Pythagoras and Pythagorean school.

B265.Z413 1962
Zeller, Eduard, 1814-1908.
Socrates and the Socratic schools. Newly translated from the 3d German ed. of E. Zeller by Oswald J. Reichel. New York, Russell & Russell, 1962. xii, 410 p.
62-010700　183.2
Socrates. Philosophy, Ancient.

B288.R5513 1991
Romilly, Jacqueline de.
The great Sophists in Periclean Athens/ Jacqueline de Romilly; translated by Janet Lloyd. Oxford [England]: Clarendon Press; 1992. xv, 260 p.
91-004759　183/.1/09385　0198242344
Sophists (Greek philosophy)

B288.W56 1996
Winter, Bruce W.
Philo and Paul among the Sophists/ Bruce W. Winter. Cambridge, U.K.; Cambridge University Press, 1997. xvi, 289 p.
96-044600　183/.1　0521591082
Philo, -- of Alexandria. Paul, -- the Apostle, Saint. Rhetoric in the Bible. Sophists (Greek philosophy) Rhetoric, Ancient. Alexandria (Egypt) -- Intellectual life. Corinth (Greece) -- Intellectual life.

B293.A34
Navia, Luis E.
Antisthenes of Athens: setting the world aright/ Luis E. Navia. Westport, Conn.: Greenwood Press, 2001. xii, 176 p.
00-069516　183/.2　0313316724
Antisthenes, -- ca. 445-ca. 360 B.C.

B305.D44.N38 1998
Navia, Luis E.
Diogenes of Sinope: the man in the tub/ Luis E. Navia. Westport, Conn.: Greenwood Press, 1998. x, 208 p.
98-015322　183/.4　0313306729
Diogenes, -- d. ca. 323 B.C. Cynics (Greek philosophy)

B316.P8 1963
Plato.
The trial and death of Socrates. Translated out of the Greek with introductory analyses by Benjamin Jowett. With a pref. by Huntington Cairns and illus. by Hans Erni. New York, Heritage Press [1963] xi, 274 p.
63-005438   888
Socrates.Philosophers -- Greece -- Biography.

B316.T33 1951
Taylor, A. E. 1869-1945.
Socrates. Boston, Beacon Press, 1951. 192 p.
51-012869   921.9
Socrates.

B317.G66 1996
Gooch, Paul W.
Reflections on Jesus and Socrates: word and silence/ Paul W. Gooch. New Haven: Yale University Press, c1996. xii, 308 p.
96-015792   128   0300066953
Jesus Christ. Socrates. Socrates -- Death and burial.

B317.H37 1994
Harrison, Paul R., 1955-
The disenchantment of reason: the problem of Socrates in modernity/ Paul R. Harrison. Albany, N.Y.: State University of New York Press, c1994. v, 258 p.
93-007295   183/.2   0791418375
Socrates. Hegel, Georg Wilhelm Friedrich, -- 1770-1831 -- Contributions in interpretation of Socrates. Kierkegaard, Soren, -- 1813-1855 -- Contributions in interpretation of Socrates. Reason. Philosophy, Modern -- 19th century.

B317.K6413 1998
Kofman, Sarah.
Socrates: fictions of a philosopher/ Sarah Kofman; translated by Catherine Porter. Ithaca, NY: Cornell University Press, 1998. vii, 296 p.
98-009840   183/.2   080143551X
Socrates.

B317.L34 2001
Lane, M. S.
Plato's progeny: how Socrates and Plato still captivate the modern   mind/ Melissa Lane. London: Duckworth, 2001. x, 165 p.
2003-427783   184 21   0715628925
Socrates -- Influence. Plato -- Influence.

B317.P68 2000
Brickhouse, Thomas C., 1947-
The philosophy of Socrates/ Thomas C. Brickhouse, Nicholas D. Smith. Boulder, Colo.: Westview Press, 2000. x, 290 p.
99-036572   183/.2   0813320844
Socrates.

B317.S645 1992
Socratic questions: new essays on the philosophy of Socrates and its significance/ edited by Barry S. Gower and Michael C. Stokes. London; Routledge, 1992. viii, 228 p.
91-039860   183/.2   0415069319
Socrates.

B317.S76 1988
Stone, I. F. 1907-
The trial of Socrates/ I.F. Stone. Boston: Little, Brown, c1988. xi, 282 p.
87-022855   183/.2   0316817589
Socrates. Socrates -- Trials, litigation, etc.

B317.V55
Vlastos, Gregory,
The philosophy of Socrates; a collection of critical essays. [1st ed.] Garden City, N.Y., Anchor Books, 1971. 354 p.
73-131115   183/.2
Socrates -- Addresses, essays, lectures.

B318.E8.R83 1999
Rudebusch, George, 1957-
Socrates, pleasure, and value/ George Rudebusch. New York: Oxford University Press, 1999. xiii, 169 p.
98-036534   183/.2   0195128559
Socrates.Ethics, Ancient. Pleasure. Hedonism.

B318.R45.M38 1996
McPherran, Mark L., 1949-
The religion of Socrates/ Mark L. McPherran. University Park, Pa.: Pennsylvania State University Press, c1996. xii, 353 p.
95-045059   292/.0092   0271015810
Socrates -- Religion.Greece -- Religion.

B338.Z413 1962
Zeller, Eduard, 1814-1908.
Plato and the older Academy. Translated with the author's sanction from the German of Eduard Zeller by Sarah Frances Alleyne and Alfred Goodwin. New York, Russell & Russell, 1962. xiii, 629 p.
62-010699   184
Plato.Philosophy, Ancient.

B358.A44 1984 vol. 2.385
Plato.
The symposium/ translated with comment by R.E. Allen. New Haven: Yale University Press, c1991. xi, 178 p.
90-026725   184 20   0300048742
Socrates.Love--Early   works   to   1800. Imaginary conversations--Early works to 1800.

B358.C57
Plato.
The collected dialogues of Plato, including the letters. Edited by Edith Hamilton and Huntington Cairns. With introd. and prefatory notes. [Translators: Lane Cooper and others. New York] Pantheon Books [1961] xxv, 1743 p.
61-011758   184

B358.N54 1999
Plato.
Plato on rhetoric and language: four key dialogues/ introduction by Jean Nienkamp. Mahwah, NJ: Hermagoras Press, c1999. ix, 220 p.
98-046510   184   1880393336
Rhetoric, Ancient. Language and languages -- Philosophy.

B365.B74 1989
Brickhouse, Thomas C.,
Socrates on trial/ Thomas C. Brickhouse and Nicholas D. Smith. Princeton, N.J.: Princeton University Press, c1989. xiv, 337 p.
88-017971   184 19   0691073325
Plato. Apology. Socrates -- Trials, litigation, etc.

B365.R44 1989
Reeve, C. D. C., 1948-
Socrates in the Apology: an essay on Plato's Apology   of   Socrates/   C.D.C.   Reeve. Indianapolis: Hackett, c1989. xv, 207 p.
89-033069   184   0872200892
Plato.   --   Apology.   Socrates   --   Trials, litigation, etc.

B366.S35 1998
Schmid, Walter T.
Plato's Charmides and the Socratic ideal of rationality/ W. Thomas Schmid. Albany, N.Y.: State University of New York Press, c1998. xv, 225 p.
97-027154   184   0791437639
Plato. -- Charmides.

B368.W45 1998
Weiss, Roslyn.
Socrates dissatisfied: an analysis of Plato's Crito/ Roslyn Weiss. New York: Oxford University Press, 1998. xii, 187 p.
97-012126   184   0195116844
Plato. -- Crito. Socrates. Obedience. Law -- Philosophy.

B371.A5.I78
Plato.
Gorgias/ Plato; translated with notes by Terence Irwin. Oxford: Clarendon Press; 1979. ix, 268 p.
79-040477   170   0198720874
Ethics. Political science -- Early works to 1800.

B377.W45 2001
Weiss, Roslyn.
Virtue in the cave: moral inquiry in Plato's Meno/ Roslyn Weiss. New York: Oxford University Press, 2001. x, 229 p.
00-061155   170   0195140761
Plato. -- Meno.Virtue.

B379.A2.B8
Plato.
Plato's Phaedo, edited with introduction and notes by John Burnet. Oxford, Clarendon Press [1967, c1911]
12-024501
Plato.Immortality.

B379.A5 G34 1993
Plato.
Phaedo/ Plato; translated and edited by David Gallop. Oxford; Oxford University Press, 1993.
92-029711   184 20   0192830902
Immortality (Philosophy) -- Early works to 1800.

B379.A87 1995
Ahrensdorf, Peter J., 1958-
The death of Socrates and the life of philosophy:
an interpretation of Plato's Phaedo/ Peter J.
Ahrensdorf. Albany: State University of New
York Press, c1995. x, 238 p.
94-040812 184 0791426335
*Plato. -- Phaedo.Rationalism. Philosophy and
religion.*

B380.A5 H3
Plato.
Phaedrus; translated with introd. and
commentary by R. Hackforth. New York:
Bobbs-Merrill, [1952]. 172 p.
52-008203 888.4

B380.N53 1999
Nicholson, Graeme.
Plato's Phaedrus: the philosophy of love/
Graeme Nicholson. West Lafayette, Ind.: Purdue
University Press, c1999. x, 231 p.
97-046404 184 1557531188
Plato. -- Phaedrus.Love.

B381.A5.T35
Plato.
Philebus and Epinomis. Translation and introd.
by A.E. Taylor. Edited by Raymond Klibansky
with the co-operation of Guido Calogero and
A.C. Lloyd. London, Nelson, 1956. vi, 271 p.
57-004421 888.4

B381.G3313 1991
Gadamer, Hans Georg, 1900-
Plato's dialectical ethics: phenomenological
interpretations relating to the Philebus/ Hans-
Georg Gadamer; translated and with an
introduction by Robert M. Wallace. New Haven:
Yale University Press, c1991. xxxv, 240 p.
91-007212 171/.4 0300048076
Plato. -- Philebus.Dialectic.

B382.A5 T39 1996
Plato.
Protagoras/ Plato; translated by C.C.W. Taylor.
New York: Oxford University Press, 1996. xxix,
92 p.
96-007901 170 20 0192823302
*Protagoras. Socrates. Sophists (Greek
philosophy) Ethics -- Early works to 1800.*

B382.H82 1982
Hubbard, B. A. F.
Plato's Protagoras: a Socratic commentary/
B.A.F. Hubbard & E.S. Karnofsky; with a
foreword by M.F. Burnyeat. London:
Duckworth, 1982. xvi, 171 p.
82-154079 170 19 0715616404
*Plato. Protagoras. Protagoras. Socrates.
Sophists (Greek philosophy) Ethics.*

B384.A5 1990
Plato.
Plato's sophist/ translated by William S. Cobb
with an introduction and endnotes. Savage, Md.:
Rowan & Littlefield, c1990. 126 p.
90-035225 184 0847676528
*Sophists (Greek philosophy) -- Early works to
1800. Methodology -- Early works to 1800.
Ontology -- Early works to 1800.*

B385.A5.C63 1993
Plato.
The Symposium; and, The Phaedrus: Plato's
erotic dialogues/ translated with introduction and
commentaries by William S. Cobb. Albany:
State University of New York Press, c1993. vii,
214 p.
92-035391 184 0791416178
*Socrates.Soul -- Early works to 1800. Love --
Early works to 1800. Rhetoric, Ancient.*

B385.A5.G68 1989
Plato.
Symposium of Plato = [Platonos Symposion]/
translated by Tom Griffith; engraved by Peter
Forster. Berkeley: University of California
Press, 1989. 1 v.
89-004878 184 0520066944
Socrates.Love -- Early works to 1800.

B386.A5.C6
Plato.
Plato's theory of knowledge; the Theaetetus and
the Sophist of Plato, translated with a running
commentary by Francis Macdonald Cornford.
New York, Liberal Arts Press [1957] 336 p.
57-004254 184.1
Knowledge, Theory of. Philosophy, Ancient.

B387.A96 1988
Ashbaugh, A. Freire.
Plato's theory of explanation: a study of the
cosmological account in the Timaeus/ Anne
Freire Ashbaugh. Albany, N.Y.: State University
of New York Press, c1988. vii, 195 p.
87-010256 110 0887066070
*Plato. -- Timaeus.Explanation -- History.
Cosmology -- History.*

B387.B7313 1995
Brisson, Luc.
Inventing the universe: Plato's Timaeus, the big
bang, and the problem of scientific knowledge/
Luc Brisson and F. Walter Meyerstein. Albany:
State University of New York Press, c1995.
193 p.
95-018054 113 0791426912
*Plato. -- Timaeus.Cosmology, Ancient. Big
bang theory. Cosmology.*

B391.E8.M6 1962
Plato.
Plato's epistles; a translation, with critical essays
and notes, by Glenn R. Morrow. Indianapolis,
Bobbs-Merrill, [1962] 282 p.
61-018063
Sicily (Italy) -- History -- To 800.

B393.R9
Ryle, Gilbert, 1900-1976.
Plato's progress. Cambridge, Cambridge U.P.,
1966. viii, 311 p.
66-015278 184
Plato.

B395.A29 1997
Ackrill, J. L.
Essays on Plato and Aristotle/ J.L. Ackrill.
Oxford: Clarendon Press; viii, 229 p.
96-041722 184 20 0198236417
Plato. Aristotle.

B395.A72 1991
Arieti, James A.
Interpreting Plato: the dialogues as drama/ James
A. Arieti. Savage, Md.: Rowman & Littlefield
Publishers, c1991. x, 270 p.
90-021190 184 0847676625
*Plato. -- Dialogues. Plato -- Literary art.
Philosophy.*

B395.B445 2000
Beversluis, John, 1934-
Cross-examining Socrates: a defense of the
interlocutors in Plato's early dialogues/ John
Beversluis. Cambridge, U.K.; Cambridge
University Press, 2000. xii, 416 p.
99-011232 184 0521550580
*Plato. -- Dialogues. Socrates. Sophists
(Greek philosophy)*

B395.C28 1992
The Cambridge companion to Plato/ edited by
Richard Kraut. Cambridge; Cambridge
University Press, 1992. xiv, 560 p.
92-004991 184 0521430186
Plato.

B395.C525 1980
Cherniss, Harold F. 1904-1987.
The riddle of the early Academy/ Harold
Cherniss; with an index for the Garland edition
by Leonardo Taran. New York, N.Y.: Garland
Pub., 1980. 121 p.
78-066594 184 0824096045
*Plato -- Addresses, essays, lectures. Aristotle
-- Addresses, essays, lectures.*

B395.C57 2000
Clay, Diskin.
Platonic questions: dialogues with the silent
philosopher/ Diskin Clay. University Park, Pa.:
Pennsylvania State University Press, c2000.
xxiii, 309 p.
99-056918 184 0271020431
Plato. -- Dialogues.

B395.C72
Crombie, I. M.
Plato, the midwifes apprentice, by I. M.
Crombie. New York, Barnes & Noble [1965,
c1964] viii, 195 p.
65-007748 184
Plato.

B395.G455 1999
Gordon, Jill, 1962-
Turning toward philosophy: literary device and dramatic structure in Plato's Dialogues/ Jill Gordon. University Park, Pa.: Pennsylvania State University Press, c1999. x, 182 p.
99-034786   184   0271019255
Plato. -- Dialogues.

B395.H85 1998
Howland, Jacob.
The paradox of political philosophy: Socrates' philosophic trial/ Jacob Howland. Lanham, Md.: Rowman & Littlefield Publishers, c1998. x, 342 p.
97-041428   184   0847689751
Plato. Socrates.

B395.K24 1996
Kahn, Charles H.
Plato and the Socratic dialogue: the philosophical use of a literary form/ Charles H. Kahn. Cambridge; Cambridge University Press, 1996. xxi, 431 p.
95-048307   184   0521433258
Plato. Socrates. Imaginary conversations.

B395.L38
Levinson, Ronald Bartlett, 1896-
In defense of Plato [by] Ronald B. Levinson. Cambridge, Harvard University Press, 1953. xii, 674 p.
53-005070   184.1
Plato.

B395.M275 1999
Marback, Richard.
Plato's dream of sophistry/ Richard Marback. Columbia: University of South Carolina Press, c1999. vi, 163 p.
97-045431   184   1570032408
Plato -- Influence. Plato -- Views on sophists. Plato -- Views on rhethoric. Philosophy -- History. Sophists (Greek philosophy) Rhetoric, Ancient.

B395.M79 1992
Moravcsik, J. M. E.
Plato and Platonism: Plato's conception of appearance and reality in ontology, epistemology, and ethics, and its modern echoes/ Julius Moravcsik. Oxford, UK; Blackwell, 1992. x, 342 p.
92-007543   184   1557862028
Plato.

B395.N54 1996
Nightingale, Andrea Wilson.
Genres in dialogue: Plato and the construct of philosophy/ Andrea Wilson Nightingale. Cambridge; Cambridge University Press, 1995. xiv, 222 p.
95-005879   184   052148264X
Plato.Greek literature -- History and criticism. Literary form. Rhetoric, Ancient.

B395.P166 1999
Palmer, John Anderson, 1965-
Plato's reception of Parmenides/ John A. Palmer. Oxford; Oxford University Press, 1999. xiii, 294 p.
98-046615   184   0198238002
Plato. Parmenides -- Influence.   Sophists (Greek philosophy)

B395.P54 1988
Platonic writings/Platonic readings/ edited by Charles L. Griswold, Jr. New York: Routledge, 1988. 321 p.
87-028635   184   0415001862
Plato. -- Dialogues.Dialogue.

B395.S23 1996
Sallis, John,1938-
Being and logos: reading the Platonic dialogues/ John Sallis. 3rd ed. Bloomington: Indiana University Press, c1996. xviii, 544 p.
95-050382   184 20   0253210712
Plato. Dialogues. Socrates.

B395.S28 1995
Sayre, Kenneth M., 1928-
Plato's literary garden: how to read a Platonic dialogue/ Kenneth M. Sayre. Notre Dame: University of Notre Dame Press, c1995. xxiii, 292 p.
95-016521   184   0268038082
Plato.Imaginary conversations.

B395.S48
Shorey, Paul, 1857-1934.
Platonism: ancient and modern/ by Paul Shorey. Berkeley, Calif.: University of California Press, 1938. 259 p.
38-028565   184.1
Plato.Platonists.

B395.S545 2000
Slaatte, Howard Alexander.
Plato's Dialogues and ethics/ Howard Alexander Slaatte. Lanham; University Press of America, c2000. iii, 146 p.
99-041509   184 21   0761815007
Plato. Dialogues. Ethics, Ancient.

B395.T22 2000
Tarrant, Harold.
Plato's first interpreters/ Harold Tarrant. Ithaca, N.Y.: Cornell University Press, 2000. viii, 263 p.
00-037677   184   080143792X
Plato.Platonists.

B395.T25 1956
Taylor, A. E.
Plato: the man and his work.   New York, Meridian Books, 1956. xi, 562 p.
56-010023   184.1
Plato.

B395.V58 1981
Vlastos, Gregory.
Platonic studies/ Gregory Vlastos. 2nd print., with corrections. [Princeton, N.J.]: Princeton University Press, c1981. xx, 478 p.
80-008732   184 19   0691100217
Plato -- Addresses, essays, lectures.

B395.W67 1964
Wild, John Daniel, 1902-1972.
Plato's theory of man; an introduction to the realistic philosophy of culture.   New York, Octagon Books, 1964 [c1946] x, 320 p.
64-016385   184
Plato.

B398.A4.L6
Lodge, Rupert Clendon, 1886-
Plato's theory of art.   London, Routledge & Paul [1953] viii, 316 p.
53-012709
Plato.Art -- Philosophy.

B398.A4.M87
Murdoch, Iris.
The fire & the sun: why Plato banished the artists/ Iris Murdoch. Oxford [Eng.]: Clarendon Press, 1977. 89 p.
77-005827   111.8/5   0198245807
Plato -- Aesthetics.Aesthetics, Ancient.

B398.D5.G66 1998
Gonzalez, Francisco J.
Dialectic and dialogue: Plato's practice of philosophical inquiry/ Francisco J. Gonzalez. Evanston, Ill.: Northwestern University Press, 1998. x, 418 p.
98-027564   184   0810115298
Plato.Dialectic -- History.

B398.E8.A56 1999
Annas, Julia.
Platonic ethics, old and new/ Julia Annas. Ithaca, NY: Cornell University Press, 1999. viii, 196 p.
98-030418   170/.92   0801485177
Plato -- Ethics.Platonists. Ethics, Ancient.

B398.E8 G2913 1986
Gadamer, Hans Georg,
The idea of the good in Platonic-Aristotelian philosophy/ Hans-Georg Gadamer; translated and with an introduction and annotation by P. Christopher Smith. New Haven: Yale University Press, c1986. xxxi, 182 p.
85-022710   170 19   0300034636
Plato -- Contributions in ethics. Aristotle -- Contributions in ethics. Ethics, Ancient.

B398.E8.G6 1972
Gould, John, 1927-
The development of Plato's ethics. New York, Russell & Russell [1972] xiii, 240 p.
70-180609   184
Plato -- Ethics.Ethics, Ancient.

B398.E8.M3 1981
Mackenzie, Mary Margaret.
Plato on punishment/ Mary Margaret Mackenzie. Berkeley: University of California Press, c1981. 278 p.
80-006065   364.6/01   0520041690
Plato -- Ethics.Punishment. Values. Ethics, Ancient.

B398.E8.W5
Wild, John Daniel, 1902-1972.
Plato's modern enemies and the theory of natural law.   [Chicago] University of Chicago Press [1953] xi, 259 p.
53-002434   184.1
Plato.Ethics. Natural law.

B398.G6 G47 1994
Gerson, Lloyd P.
God and Greek philosophy: studies in the early history of natural   theology/ L.P. Gerson. London; Routledge, 1994. xi, 340 p.
94-012758   210/.938 20   0415113059
God (Greek religion) Philosophy, Ancient. Natural theology -- History of doctrines.

B398.I3 R6
Ross, W. D.
Plato's theory of ideas.   Oxford, Clarendon Press, 1951. 250 p.
52-001984
Plato.

B398.K7.M64
Moline, Jon, 1937-
Plato's theory of understanding/ Jon Moline. Madison, Wis.: University of Wisconsin Press, 1981. xv, 255 p.
81-050826   121   0299086607
Plato -- Contributions in theory of knowledge.Knowledge,   Theory   of. Comprehension.

B398.K7 W48
White, Nicholas P.,
Plato on knowledge and reality/ Nicholas P. White. Indianapolis: Hackett Pub. Co., c1976. xvii, 254 p.
76-010993   121   0915144220
Plato -- Contributions in theory of knowledge.

B398.L3 S36 1995
Scott, Dominic.
Recollection and experience: Plato's theory of learning and its   successors/ Dominic Scott. Cambridge; Cambridge University Press, 1995. x, 289 p.
94-032443   121/.3 20   0521474558
Plato. Learning -- History. Innate ideas (Philosophy) -- History.

B398.L9.S26 1988
Santas, Gerasimos Xenophon.
Plato and Freud: two theories of love/ Gerasimos Santas. Oxford, England; B. Blackwell, 1988. xi, 195 p.
87-020823   128/.4   0631159142
Plato -- Contributions in concept of love. Freud, Sigmund, -- 1856-1939 -- Contributions in psychology of love. Love.

B398.M4.O26 1997
O'Connell, Robert J.
Plato on the human paradox/ by Robert J. O'Connell. New York: Fordham University Press, 1997. xviii, 162 p.
96-052170   110/.92   0823217574
Plato   --   Contributions   in metaphysics.Metaphysics -- History.

B398.R4.F4
Feibleman, James Kern, 1904-
Religious Platonism; the influence of religion on Plato and the influence of Plato on religion. London, Allen & Unwin [1959] 236 p.
60-001560   201
Plato -- Religion. Plato -- Influence.

B398.W5 F46 1994
Feminist interpretations of Plato/ edited by Nancy Tuana.   University Park, Pa.: Pennsylvania State University Press, c1994. xiv, 286 p.
93-030521   184 20   0271010444
Plato. Woman (Philosophy) Feminist theory.

B407.A26 1996
Aristotle.
Aristotle: introductory readings/ translated with introduction,   notes, and glossary by Terence Irwin and Gail Fine. Indianapolis, Ind.: Hackett Pub., c1996. xvii, 359 p.
96-009317   185 20   0872203395
Philosophy -- Early works to 1800.

B407.M2
Aristoteles.
The basic works of Aristotle, edited and with an introduction by Richard McKeon. New York, Random House [c1941] xxxix, 1487 p.
41-051734   888.5

B407.S6 1984
Aristotle.
The complete works of Aristotle: the revised Oxford translation/ edited by Jonathan Barnes. Princeton, N.J.: Princeton University Press, 1984. 2 v.
82-005317   185   0691099502
Philosophy.

B415.A5.C48 1991
Philoponus, John, 6th cent.
On Aristotle on the intellect (De anima 3.4-8)/ Philoponus; translated by William Charlton with the assistance of Fernand Bossier. Ithaca: Cornell University Press, 1991. vii, 183 p.
91-008806   128/.2   0801426812
Aristotle. -- De intellectu.Philosophy of mind -- Early works to 1800. Psychology -- Early works to 1850.

B415.E87 1991
Essays on Aristotle's De anima/ edited by Martha C. Nussbaum and   Amélie Oksenberg Rorty. Oxford [England]: Clarendon Press; viii, 439 p.
91-022833   128 20   0198244614
Aristotle. De anima. Psychology.

B430.A5.C5 1950
Aristotle.
Ethics. Introd. by J.A. Smith. Translated by D.P. Chase. New York, Dutton, 1950 xxxi, 310 p.
50-007336   170
Ethics.

B430.A5 R68 2002
Aristotle.
Nicomachean ethics/ Aristotle; translation (with historical introduction) by Christopher Rowe; philosophical introduction and   commentary by Sarah Broadie. Oxford; Oxford University Press, 2002. x, 468 p.
2002-283430   171/.3 21   0198752717
Ethics.

B430.A5.T4
Aristotle.
Ethics of Aristotle. The Nicomachean ethics, translated [by] J.A.K. Thomson. London Allen & Unwin [1953] 289 p.
53-013553
Ethics.

B430.T47 1996
Tessitore, Aristide.
Reading Aristotle's Ethics: virtue, rhetoric, and political philosophy/ Aristide Tessitore. Albany: State University of New York Press, c1996. xi, 155 p.
96-012731   171/.3   0791430472
Aristotle. -- Nicomachean ethics. Aristotle -- Ethics. Virtue. Political science -- Philosophy. Rhetoric, Ancient.

B430.U76 1988
Urmson, J. O.
Aristotle's ethics/ J.O. Urmson. Oxford; B. Blackwell, 1988 130 p.
87-029367   0631156739
Aristotle. Nicomachean ethics. Aristotle -- Contributions in ethics. Ethics.

B434.A5.A66
Aristotle.
Aristotle's Metaphysics: Books [mu] and [nu]/ translated with introd. and notes by Julia Annas. Oxford [Eng.]: Clarendon Press, 1976. 227 p.
77-353536   110   0198720858
Metaphysics -- Early works to 1800.

B434.A5.S2 1999
Aristotle.
Aristotle's Metaphysics/ a new translation by Joe Sachs. Santa Fe, N.M.: Green Lion Press, c1999. lx, 303 p.
98-083157   1888009020
Metaphysics -- Early works to 1800.

B434.S32 1994
Scaltsas, T.
Substances and universals in Aristotle's Metaphysics/ Theodore Scaltsas. Ithaca: Cornell University Press, 1994. ix, 292 p.
94-008911   111/.1   0801430038
Aristotle. -- Metaphysics.Substance (Philosophy) Universals (Philosophy)

B434.W58 1989
Witt, Charlotte,
Substance and essence in Aristotle: an interpretation of Metaphysics VII-IX/ Charlotte Witt. Ithaca: Cornell University Press, 1989. viii, 201 p.
88-024043   111/.1 19   0801421268
Aristotle. Metaphysics. Aristotle -- Contributions in essentialism. Metaphysics. Essence (Philosophy)

B434.W59 2003
Witt, Charlotte,
Ways of being: potentiality and actuality in Aristotle's Metaphysics / Charlotte Witt. Ithaca, N.Y.: Cornell University Press, 2003. x, 161 p.
2002-011975   110 21   0801440327
Aristotle. Metaphysics. Metaphysics. Ontology.

B438.A9513 1991
Ammonius,
On Aristotle's Categories/ Ammonius; translated by S. Marc Cohen and Gareth B. Matthews. Ithaca, N.Y.: Cornell University Press, 1991. 170 p.
91-055258   160   080142688X
Aristotle. -- Categoriae.Categories (Philosophy) -- Early works to 1800.

B441.A5 B37 1994
Aristotle.
Posterior analytics/ Aristotle; translated with a commentary by   Jonathan Barnes. 2nd ed. Oxford: Clarendon Press; xxv, 298 p.
93-017516   160 20   0198240880
Logic -- Early works to 1800. Knowledge, Theory of -- Early works to 1800. Definition (Logic) -- Early works to 1800. Science -- Methodology -- Early works to 1800.

B441.M525 1992
McKirahan, Richard D.
Principles and proofs: Aristotle's theory of demonstrative science/ Richard D. McKirahan, Jr. Princeton, N.J.: Princeton University Press, c1992. xiv, 340 p.
91-036774   160   0691073635
Aristotle. -- Posterior analytics. Aristotle -- Contributions in concept of demonstrative science. Science -- Philosophy. Knowledge, Theory of. Logic.

B481.A3
Adler, Mortimer Jerome,
Aristotle for everybody: difficult thought made easy/ by Mortimer   J. Adler. New York: Macmillan, c1978. xiv, 206 p.
78-000853   185   0025031007
Aristotle.

B485.A655 1990
Aristotle transformed: the ancient commentators and their influence/ edited by Richard Sorabji. Ithaca, N.Y.: Cornell University Press, 1990. ix, 545 p.
89-037190   185   0801424321
Aristotle -- Influence.Philosophy, Ancient.

B485.C35 1995
The Cambridge companion to Aristotle/ edited by Jonathan Barnes. Cambridge; Cambridge University Press, 1995. xxv, 404 p.
94-000516   185   0521411335
Aristotle.

B485.C48 1962
Cherniss, Harold F. 1904-1987.
Aristotle's criticism of Plato and the Academy. New York, Russell & Russell, 1962 [c1944] 610 p.
62-013831   185
Aristotle. Plato.

B485.F3 1969
Farrington, Benjamin,
Aristotle: founder of scientific philosophy. New York, Praeger [1969, c1965] vii, 118 p.
68-016211   185
Aristotle.

B485.F46 1998
Feminist interpretations of Aristotle/ edited by Cynthia A. Freeland. University Park, Pa.: Pennsylvania State University Press, c1998. xiv, 369 p.
97-019442   185   0271017295
Aristotle.Feminist theory.

B485.G595
Grene, Marjorie Glicksman, 1910-
A portrait of Aristotle/ Marjorie Grene. Chicago: University of Chicago Press, 1963. 271 p.
63-005556
Aristotle.

B485.I74 1988
Irwin, Terence.
Aristotle's first principles/ Terence Irwin. Oxford: Clarendon Press; 1988. xviii, 702 p.
88-012507   185   0198247176
Aristotle.Methodology -- History.

B485.M24 1991
Madigan, Patrick, 1945-
Aristotle and his modern critics: the use of tragedy in the nontragic vision/ Patrick Madigan. Scranton [Pa.]: University of Scranton Press; c1992. 120 p.
90-072044   808.2   0940866137
Aristotle. Aristotle. Tragedy.

B485.M8 1964
Mure, G. R. G. 1893-
Aristotle. New York, Oxford University Press, 1964. vii, 280 p.
64-001534   185
Aristotle.

B485.R6 1995
Ross, W. D.
Aristotle/ Sir David Ross; with a new introduction by John L. Ackrill. 6th ed. London; Routledge, 1995. xvi, 316 p.
94-043265   185 20   0415120683
Aristotle.

B485.W6
Woodbridge, Frederick James Eugene, 1867-1940.
Aristotle's vision of nature. Edited with an introd. by John Herman Randall, Jr. with the assistance of Charles H. Kahn and Harold A. Larrabee. New York, Columbia University Press, [1965] xxii, 169 p.
65-019446   185
Aristotle.

B491.A27.C43 1984
Charles, David
Aristotle's philosophy of action/ David Charles. Ithaca, N.Y.: Cornell University Press, 1984. xi, 282 p.
83-073068   128/.4   0801417082
Aristotle.Act (Philosophy) -- History.

B491.E7.A53 1994
Anagnostopoulos, Georgios.
Aristotle on the goals and exactness of ethics/ Georgios Anagnostopoulos. Berkeley: University of California Press, c1994. xiii, 468 p.
93-006063   170/.42/092   0520081250
Aristotle -- Ethics.Exact (Philosophy) Ethics, Ancient.

B491.E7.A76 1999
Aristotle's Ethics: critical essays/ edited by Nancy Sherman. Lanham, Md.: Rowman & Littlefield, c1999. xviii, 331 p.
98-041164   171/.3   084768914X
Aristotle -- Ethics.Ethics, Ancient.

B491.E7.H3 1980
Hardie, William Francis Ross.
Aristotle's ethical theory/ by W. F. R. Hardie.
Oxford; Oxford University Press, 1980. x, 448 p.
79-041243   171/.3   0198246323
Aristotle -- Ethics.Ethics, Ancient.

B491.E7.K47
Kenny, Anthony John Patrick.
Aristotle's theory of the will/ Anthony Kenny.
New Haven: Yale University Press, 1979. x,
181 p.
79-000426   171/.3   0300023952
*Aristotle -- Ethics.Ethics, Ancient. Free will
and determinism. Will.*

B491.E7 S44 1997
Sherman, Nancy,
Making a necessity of virtue: Aristotle and Kant
on virtue/ Nancy Sherman. Cambridge;
Cambridge University Press, 1997. xvii, 387 p.
96-026314   179/.9 20   0521564875
*Aristotle -- Ethics. Kant, Immanuel, 1724-
1804 -- Ethics.*

B491.E7.W3
Walsh, James J. 1924-
Aristotle's conception of moral weakness. New
York, Columbia University Press, 1963 [c1960]
199 p.
62-017695   184
Aristotle.Ethics, Greek.

B491.H36.W45 1992
White, Stephen A.
Sovereign virtue: Aristotle on the relation
between happiness and prosperity/ Stephen A.
White. Stanford, Calif.: Stanford University
Press, 1992. xiv, 337 p.
91-026348   171/.3   0804716943
Aristotle -- Ethics.Happiness.

B491.L8.L38 1980
Lear, Jonathan.
Aristotle and logical theory/ Jonathan Lear.
Cambridge; Cambridge University Press, 1980.
xi, 123 p.
79-020273   160/.92/4   0521230314
*Aristotle -- Contributions in logic.Logic --
History.*

B491.N3.B43 1995
Bechler, Z.
Aristotle's theory of actuality/ Zev Bechler.
Albany: State University of New York Press,
c1995. x, 270 p.
94-001045   185   0791422399
Aristotle.Philosophy of nature.

B491.P8.W33 1988
Wedin, Michael V. 1943-
Mind and imagination in Aristotle/ Michael V.
Wedin. New Haven: Yale University Press,
1988. xiv, 292 p.
88-011092   128/.2/0924   0300042310
*Aristotle -- Contributions in philosophy of
psychology. Aristotle -- Contributions in
philosophy of imagination.   Psychology --
History. Imagination (Philosophy) -- History.*

B491.S8.F74 1995
Freudenthal, Gad.
Aristotle's theory of material substance: heat and
pneuma, form and soul/ Gad Freudenthal.
Oxford: Clarendon Press; 1995. xi, 235 p.
94-048637   111/.1   0198240937
*Aristotle -- Contributions in philosophy of
substance. Aristotle -- Contributions in
philosophy of four elements.   Substance
(Philosophy) Four elements (Philosophy)*

B491.W6.O2
Oates, Whitney Jennings, 1904-
Aristotle and the problem of value. Princeton,
N.J., Princeton University Press, 1963. x, 387 p.
62-021106   121.8
Aristotle.Values.

B505-623 Ancient
(600 B.C.-430 A.D.) — Occident
— Greco-Roman philosophy

B505.C58 1968
Clarke, M. L.
The Roman mind; studies in the history of
thought from Cicero to Marcus Aurelius, by M.
L. Clarke. New York, Norton [1968] 172 p.
68-007693   187
Philosophy, Ancient.

B505.H75
Hyde, William De Witt, 1858-1917.
The five great philosophies of life/ by William
De Witt Hyde. New York: Macmillan, c1911. x,
296 p.
11-026974
Ethics.

B505.Z413 1962
Zeller, Eduard, 1814-1908.
The Stoics, Epicureans, and Sceptics. Translated
from the German of E. Zeller by Oswald J.
Reichel. New York, Russell & Russell, 1962.
xvi, 585 p.
62-010701   188
*Epicurus.Stoics. Philosophy, Ancient. Skeptics
(Greek philosophy)*

B508.C94 1996
The Cynics: the cynic movement in antiquity
and its legacy/ edited by R. Bracht Branham and
Marie-Odile Goulet-Caze. Berkeley: University
of California Press, c1996. ix, 456 p.
96-020375   183/.4   0520204492
Cynics (Greek philosophy)

B517.M4
Merlan, Philip, 1897-1968.
From Platonism to Neoplatonism.   The Hague,
M. Nijhoff, 1953. xv, 210 p.
53-007980
Platonists. Neoplatonism.

B517.N456 1992
Neoplatonism and Jewish thought/ edited by
Lenn E. Goodman. Albany: State University of
New York Press, c1992. xiii, 454 p.
92-008369   181/.06   079141339X
*Neoplatonism -- Congresses. Philosophy,
Jewish -- Congresses. Judaism and philosophy --
Congresses.*

B517.R36 1999
Rappe, Sara, 1960-
Reading neoplatonism: non-discursive thinking
in the texts of Plotinus, Proclus, and Damascius/
Sara Rappe. Cambridge; Cambridge University
Press, 1999.
99-011395   186/.4   0521651581
*Neoplatonism.   Reasoning   --   History.
Methodology -- History.*

B525.G66 1990
Groarke, Leo, 1953-
Greek scepticism: anti-realist trends in ancient
thought/ Leo Groarke. Montreal; McGill-
Queen's University Press, c1990. xv, 176 p.
91-172089   186   0773507566
*Skeptics (Greek philosophy) Philosophy,
Ancient.*

B525.H26 1995
Hankinson, R. J.
The sceptics/ R. J. Hankinson. London;
Routledge, 1995. viii, 376 p.
94-004592   186 20   0415047722
Skeptics (Greek philosophy)

B528.H3
Hadas, Moses,
Essential works of Stoicism. New York, Bantam
Books [1961] xvii, 205 p.
61-019353   188
Stoics.

B528.I59 1985
Inwood, Brad.
Ethics and human action in early Stoicism/ Brad
Inwood. Oxford [Oxfordshire]: Clarendon Press;
348 p.
84-020673   128/.4 19   0198247397
*Stoics. Philosophical anthropology -- History.
Ethics, Ancient.*

B528.R44 1989
Reesor, Margaret E.
The nature of man in early Stoic philosophy/
Margaret E. Reesor. London: G. Duckworth,
c1989. ix, 179 p.
89-037509   128/.0938   0312035799
*Stoics.   Human   beings.   Philosophical
anthropology.*

B528.S25
Sambursky, Samuel, 1900-
Physics of the Stoics.   London, Routledge and
Paul [1959] 153 p.
59-002293   530.938
Physics -- History -- Greece. Stoics.

B528.S68
The Stoics/ edited by John M. Rist. Berkeley: University of California Press, c1978. viii, 295 p.
75-027932   188   0520031350
Stoics -- Addresses, essays, lectures.

B528.V4 1983
Verbeke, Gerard.
The presence of Stoicism in medieval thought/ by Gerard Verbeke. Washington, D.C.: Catholic University of America Press, [1983] viii, 101 p.
82-004134   188   0813205735
Stoics -- History. Philosophy, Medieval.

B553.M33 1989
MacKendrick, Paul Lachlan, 1914-
The philosophical books of Cicero/ Paul MacKendrick; with the collaboration of Karen Lee Singh. New York: St. Martin's Press, 1989. vii, 429 p.
89-034979   186   031203623X
Cicero, Marcus Tullius.

B561.M52 E5 1995
Epictetus.
The art of living: the classic manual on virtue, happiness, and effectiveness/ Epictetus; a new interpretation by Sharon Lebell. 1st ed. [San Francisco]: HarperSanFrancisco, c1995. xiii, 113 p.
95-014398   188 20   006251346X
Ethics, Ancient. Conduct of life -- Early works to 1800.

B570.E5 I582 1994
Epicurus.
The Epicurus reader: selected writings and testimonia/ translated and edited, with notes, by Brad Inwood and L.P. Gerson; introduction by D.S. Hutchinson. Indianapolis: Hackett, c1994. xvi, 111 p.
93-044073   187 20   0872202410

B570.E5.S8
Epicurus.
The philosophy of Epicurus; letters, doctrines, and parallel passages from Lucretius. Translated with commentary and an introductory essay on ancient materialism by George K. Strodach. [Evanston, Ill.] Northwestern University Press, 1963. x, 262 p.
63-002787   187

B572.K64 1995
Koen, Avraam, 1949-
Atoms, pleasure, virtue: the philosophy of Epicurus/ Avraam Koen. New York: P. Lang, c1995. 161 p.
94-011510   187   0820422347
Epicurus.

B573.J57 1989
Jones, Howard,
The Epicurean tradition/ Howard Jones. London; Routledge, 1989. 276 p.
89-006226   187   0415020697
Epicurus -- Influence.

B577.L64.W5
Winspear, Alban Dewes, 1899-1973.
Lucretius and scientific thought.   Montreal, Harvest House [1963] 156 p.
63-017242   187
Lucretius Carus, Titus.

B580.H53 M3713 2002
Marcus Aurelius,
The emperor's handbook: a new translation of The meditations/ Marcus Aurelius; C. Scot Hicks and David V. Hicks. New York: Scribner, c2002. 148 p.
2002-075232   188 21   0743233832
Ethics. Stoics. Life.

B583.H3313 1998
Hadot, Pierre.
The inner citadel: the Meditations of Marcus Aurelius/ Pierre Hadot; translated by Michael Chase. Cambridge, Mass.: Harvard University Press, 1998. x, 351 p.
97-046971   188   0674461711
Marcus Aurelius, -- Emperor of Rome, -- 121-180. -- Meditations.Ethics. Stoics. Life.

B583.R88 1989
Rutherford, R. B.
The Meditations of Marcus Aurelius: a study/ R.B. Rutherford. Oxford: Clarendon Press; 1989. xviii, 282 p.
88-020834   188   0198148798
Marcus Aurelius, -- Emperor of Rome, -- 121-180. -- Meditations.Ethics. Stoics. Life.

B623.B37 1990
Barnes, Jonathan.
The toils of scepticism/ Jonathan Barnes. Cambridge; Cambridge University Press, 1990. xiii, 161 p.
89-027951   186/.1   0521383390
Sextus, -- Empiricus.Skepticism -- History.

B655-693 Ancient (600 B.C.-430 A.D.) — Occident — Alexandrian and early Christian philosophy

B655.Z69.A84 1999
Augustine through the ages: an encyclopedia/ general editor, Allan D. Fitzgerald; associate editors, John Cavadini ... [et al.]. Grand Rapids, Mich.: W.B. Eerdmans, c1999. il, 902 p.
99-012518   270.2/092   080283843X
Augustine, -- Saint, Bishop of Hippo -- Encyclopedias.

B655.Z7.A95 1999
The Augustinian tradition/ edited by Gareth B. Matthews. Berkeley: University of California Press, c1999. xix, 398 p.
97-035854   189/.2   0520209990
Augustine, -- Saint, Bishop of Hippo.

B655.Z7.B85 1996
Burt, Donald X.
Augustine's world: an introduction to his speculative philosophy/ Donald X. Burt. Lanham: University Press of America, c1996. xxvii, 277 p.
96-010254   189/.2   0761802940
Augustine, -- Saint, Bishop of Hippo.

B655.Z7.G52
Gilson, Etienne, 1884-1978.
The Christian philosophy of Saint Augustine. Translated by L. E. M. Lynch. New York, Random House [1960] xii, 398 p.
60-012121   189.2
Augustine, -- Saint, Bishop of Hippo.God -- Knowableness -- History of doctrines -- Early church, ca. 30-600.

B655.Z7 K29 2001
Kaye, Sharon M.
On Augustine/ Sharon M. Kaye, Paul Thomson. Australia; Wadsworth/Thomson Learning, c2001 83 p.
2001-267512   189/.2 21   0534583628
Augustine, Saint, Bishop of Hippo.

B659.D472 E5 1999
Boethius,
The consolation of philosophy/ Boethius; translated with introduction and explanatory notes by P.G. Walsh. Oxford: Clarendon Press; lvii, 171 p.
98-030457   100 21   0198152280
Philosophy and religion. Happiness.

B659.Z7.C45
Chadwick, Henry, 1920-
Boethius, the consolations of music, logic, theology, and philosophy/ Henry Chadwick. Oxford: Clarendon Press; 1981. xv, 313 p.
82-115955   189   019826447X
Boethius, -- d. 524.Theology, Doctrinal -- History -- Early church, ca. 30-600. Music -- Theory -- 500-1400. Philosophy, Medieval.

B659.Z7.D8 1980
Durr, Karl, 1888-
The propositional logic of Boethius / Karl Durr. Westport, Conn.: Greenwood Press, 1980. x, 79 p.
80-018931   160   0313211027
Boethius, -- d. 524 -- Logic.Proposition (Logic) Logic, Medieval. Syllogism.

B689.A4.E5 1981
Philo,
The contemplative life; The giants; and, Selections/ Philo of Alexandria; translation and introduction by David Winston; preface by John Dillon; [cover art, Liam Roberts]. New York: Paulist Press, c1981. xxi, 425 p.
80-084499   296.3   0809123339
Philosophy.

B689.Z7 S28
Sandmel, Samuel.
Philo of Alexandria: an introduction/ Samuel
Sandmel. New York: Oxford University Press,
1979. xii, 204 p.
78-010630 181/.3 0195025156
Philo, of Alexandria.

B689.Z7.W54 1989
Williamson, Ronald.
Jews in the Hellenistic world: Philo/ Ronald
Williamson. Cambridge [Cambridgeshire];
Cambridge University Press, 1989. xii, 314 p.
88-023432 181/.06 052130511X
Philo, -- of Alexandria.

B689.Z7.W83
Wolfson, Harry Austryn, 1887-1974.
Philo: foundations of religious philosophy in
Judaism, Christianity, and Islam/ by Harry
Austryn Wolfson. Cambridge: Harvard
University Press, 1948 [c1947]. 2 v.
47-030635 181.3
Philo, -- of Alexandria.

B693.E59 E5 1992
Plotinus.
The enneads: a new, definitive edition with
comparisons to other translations on hundreds
of key passages/ Plotinus; translated by Stephen
Mackenna. Burdett, New York: Published for the
Paul Brunton Philosophic Foundation by Larson
Publications, xx, 747 p.
91-077117 186/.4 20 0943914590
Philosophy -- Early works to 1800.

B693.Z7 C36 1996
The Cambridge companion to Plotinus/ edited by
Lloyd P. Gerson. Cambridge [England];
Cambridge University Press, xiii, 462 p.
95-045305 186/.4 20 0521476763
Plotinus.

B693.Z7 H2813 1993
Hadot, Pierre.
Plotinus, or, The simplicity of vision/ Pierre
Hadot; translated by Michael Chase; with an
introduction by Arnold I. Davidson. Chicago:
University of Chicago Press, 1993. xiii, 138 p.
93-025166 186/.4 20 0226311937
Plotinus.

B693.Z7.K3
Katz, Joseph, 1920-
Plotinus' search for the good. New York, King's
Crown Press, 1950. ix, 106 p.
50-011020
Plotinus.

B693.Z7.P5
Pistorius, Philippus Villiers.
Plotinus and neoplatonism; an introductory
study. Cambridge [Eng] Bowes & Bowes
[1952] 175 p.
52-003945 186.4
Plotinus. -- InNeoplatonism.

B720 Medieval (430-1450) — Collected works (nonserial)

B720.F7 1970
Fremantle, Anne Jackson, 1909-
The age of belief; the medieval philosophers.
Selected, with introd. and interpretive
commentary by Anne Fremantle. Freeport, N.Y.,
Books for Libraries Press [1970, c1954] 218 p.
75-117793 189 0836918290
Philosophy, Medieval.

B720.R43 1996
Readings in medieval philosophy/ [edited by]
Andrew B. Schoedinger. New York: Oxford
University Press, 1996. ix, 853 p.
95-014118 189 20 0195092937
Philosophy, Medieval.

B721 Medieval (430-1450) — General works

B721.B8 1971
Burch, George Bosworth, 1902-
Early medieval philosophy. Freeport, N.Y.,
Books for Libraries Press [1971, c1951] viii,
142 p.
70-148207 189/.4 0836980549
Philosophers, Medieval. Philosophy, Medieval.

B721.C54 2003
A companion to philosophy in the middle ages/
edited by Jorge J.E. Gracia and Timothy B.
Noone. Malden, MA: Blackwell Pub., 2003. xxi,
739 p.
2002-066421 189 21 0631216723
Philosophy, Medieval.

B721.E86 1993
Evans, G. R.
Philosophy and theology in the Middle Ages/
G.R. Evans. London; Routledge, 1993. x, 139 p.
92-014375 189 0415089085
*Philosophy, Medieval. Theology, Doctrinal --
History -- Middle Ages, 600-1500.*

B721.G5714 1991
Gilson, Etienne,
The spirit of mediaeval philosophy/ by Etienne
Gilson; translated by A.H.C. Downes. Notre
Dame: University of Notre Dame Press, 1991.
ix, 490 p.
90-050958 189 20 0268017409
*Philosophy, Medieval. Christianity --
Philosophy. Philosophy and religion.
Scholasticism. Thomists.*

B721.H34 1992
Haren, Michael.
Medieval thought: the western intellectual
tradition from antiquity to the thirteenth
century/ Michael Haren. 2nd ed. Toronto;
University of Toronto Press, 1992. ix, 315 p.
93-119427 189 20 0802077587
Philosophy, Medieval. Philosophy, Ancient.

B721.H36 1947
Hawkins, Denis John Bernard, 1906-
A sketch of mediaeval philosophy, by D. J. B.
Hawkins. New York, Sheed & Ward, 1947. vii,
174 p.
47-003881 189.4
Philosophy, Medieval.

B721.L4 1960
Leff, Gordon.
Medieval thought: St. Augustine to Ockham/ by
Gordon Leff. Chicago: Quadrangle Books, 1958.
317 p.
59-015208 189
Philosophy, Medieval.

B721.L87 1997
Luscombe, D. E.
Medieval thought/ David Luscombe. Oxford;
Oxford University Press, 1997. 248 p.
96-029604 189 0192891790
Philosophy, Medieval.

B721.V513 1959
Vignaux, Paul.
Philosophy in the Middle Ages, an introduction.
Translated from the French by E. C. Hall. New
York, Meridian Books [1959] 223 p.
59-012915 189
*Philosophy, Medieval. Religious thought --
Middle Ages, 600-1500.*

B731 Medieval (430-1450) — Special topics — Nominalism and realism

B731.R63 2002
Rodríguez Pereyra, Gonzalo.
Resemblance nominalism: a solution to the
problem of universals/ Gonzalo Rodriguez
Pereyra. Oxford; Clarendon Press, 2002. xii,
238 p.
2001-058834 111/.2 21 0199243778
*Nominalism. Universals (Philosophy)
Resemblance (Philosophy)*

B734 Medieval (430-1450) — Special topics — Scholasticism

B734.F3
Fairweather, Eugene Rathbone.
A scholastic miscellany: Anselm to Ockham.
Philadelphia, Westminster Press [1956] 457 p.
56-005104
Scholasticism.

B734.W8 1959
Wulf, Maurice Marie Charles Joseph de, 1867-1947.
The system of Thomas Aquinas. Formerly titled: Mediaeval philosophy illustrated from the system of Thomas Aquinas. New York, Dover Publications [1959] 151 p.
59-065175 189.4
Thomas -- Aquinas, Saint, -- 1225?-1274 -- Philosophy.Philosophy, Medieval.

B738 Medieval (430-1450) — Special topics — Other special topics, A-Z

B738.C65.C66
Conscience in medieval philosophy/ [edited by] Timothy C. Potts. Cambridge; Cambridge University Press, 1980. xiii, 152 p.
80-040380 170 0521232872
Conscience -- Religious aspects -- Christianity. Conscience -- Addresses, essays, lectures. Philosophy, Medieval -- Addresses, essays, lectures.

B738.M47.H4513 1994
Heimsoeth, Heinz, 1886-1975.
The six great themes of western metaphysics and the end of the Middle Ages/ Heinz Heimsoeth; translated with a critical introduction by Ramon J. Betanzos. Detroit: Wayne State University Press, c1994. 272 p.
93-033894 190 0814324770
Metaphysics -- History. Philosophy, Medieval.

B741 Medieval (430-1450) — Arabian and Moorish philosophers. Islamic philosophers — General works

B741.B7 1983
Boer, T. J. de
The history of philosophy in Islam/ T.J. de Boer; translated by Edward R. Jones. New Delhi: Cosmo, 1983. xiii, 216 p.
84-900402 181/.07 19
Philosophy, Islamic -- History.

B741.F265 1997
Fakhry, Majid.
A short introduction to Islamic philosophy, theology and mysticism/ Majid Fakhry. Oxford, England; Oneworld, c1997. x, 151 p.
98-187145 181/.07 21 1851681345
Philosophy, Islamic. Philosophy, Islamic -- History. Sufism -- History.

B741.L42 2001
Leaman, Oliver, 1950-
A brief introduction to Islamic philosophy/ Oliver Leaman. Malden, Mass.: Blackwell Pub., 2001. x, 199 p.
99-026650 181/.07 0745619606
Philosophy, Islamic.

B741.L43 2002
Leaman, Oliver,
An introduction to classical Islamic philosophy/ Oliver Leaman. 2nd ed. Cambridge,UK; Cambridge University Press, 2002. xv, 253 p.
2001-037349 181/.07 21 0521797578
Philosophy, Islamic. Philosophy, Medieval.

B741.O4 1939
O'Leary, De Lacy, b. 1872.
Arabic thought and its place in history, by De Lacy OLeary ... London, K. Paul, Trench, Trubner & Co., ltd.; 1939. 327 p.
40-031752 139.3
Philosophy, Arabic.

B741.W3
Walzer, Richard, 1900-
Greek into Arabic; essays on Islamic philosophy. Cambridge, Harvard University Press, 1962. 256 p.
62-005796 181.947
Philosophy, Islamic. Philosophy, Ancient. Philosophy, Comparative.

B745 Medieval (430-1450) — Arabian and Moorish philosophers. Islamic philosophers — Special topics, A-Z

B745.C6.N3 1993
Nasr, Seyyed Hossein.
An introduction to Islamic cosmological doctrines: conceptions of nature and methods used for its study by the Ikhwan al-Safa, al-Biruni, and Ibn Sina/ Seyyed Hossein Nasr. Albany: State University of New York Press, c1993. xxv, 322 p.
92-025842 113/.0917/671 0791415155
Biruni, Muhammad ibn Ahmad, -- 973?-1048. Avicenna, -- 980-1037. Islamic cosmology.

B745.K53.N48 1992
Netton, Ian Richard.
Al-Farabi and his school/ Ian Richard Netton. London; Routledge, 1992. xii, 128 p.
91-042233 181/.6 0415035945
Farabi -- Contributions in theory of knowledge.Knowledge, Theory of (Islam)

B745.K53.N485 1996
Netton, Ian Richard.
Seek knowledge: thought and travel in the house of Islam/ Ian Richard Netton. Richmond, Surrey [England]: Curzon Press, 1996. xiv, 162 p.
96-111198 297/.2 070070339X
Knowledge, Theory of (Islam) Thought and thinking. Travel -- Religious aspects -- Islam.

B746 Medieval (430-1450) — Arabian and Moorish philosophers. Islamic philosophers — Ikhwan al-Safa, Basra (Brothers of Purity or Sincerity)

B746.N47 1982
Netton, Ian Richard.
Muslim neoplatonists: an introduction to the thought of the Brethren of Purity, Ikhwan al-Safa/ Ian Richard Netton. London; G. Allen & Unwin, 1982. x, 146 p.
83-131009 181/.9 0042970431
Ikhwān al- òSafā.

B749-753 Medieval (430-1450) — Arabian and Moorish philosophers. Islamic philosophers — Individual philosophers

B749.Z7 L43 1998
Leaman, Oliver,
Averroes and his philosophy/ Oliver Leaman. Rev. ed. Richmond, Surrey [England]: Curzon, 1998. xvi, 204 p.
98-216926 181/.92 21 0700706755
Averroës, 1126-1198. Philosophy, Medieval.

B751.A5 S5 1974
Avicenna,
The life of Ibn Sina; a critical edition and annotated translation, by William E. Gohlman. [1st ed.] Albany, State University of New York Press, 1974. 163 p.
73-006793 189/.5 087395226X
Avicenna, 980-1037. Muslim philosophers -- Biography. Philosophy, Islamic.

B751.Z7.A6
Afnan, Soheil Muhsin.
Avicenna, his life and works/ Soheil M. Afnan. London, G. Allen & Unwin 1958. 298 p.
58-003795 189.3
Avicenna, -- 980-1037.Philosophy, Medieval.

B751.Z7 G66 1992
Goodman, Lenn Evan,
Avicenna/ Lenn E. Goodman. London; Routledge, 1992. xv, 240 p.
91-040142 181/.5 20 0415074096
Avicenna, 980-1037.

B753.F32 E5 2001
Fārābī.
Alfarabi, the political writings: selected aphorisms and other texts / translated and annotated by Charles E. Butterworth. Ithaca: Cornell University Press, 2001. xiii, 179 p.
00-012887 181/.6 21 0801438578
Philosophy, Islamic -- Early works to 1800.

B753.F33 A25 2001
F⁻ar⁻ab⁻i.
Alfarabi: philosophy of Plato and Aristotle/
translated, with an introduction, by Muhsin
Mahdi; with a foreword by Charles E.
Butterworth and Thomas L. Pangle. Rev. ed.
Ithaca, N.Y.: Cornell University Press, c2001.
xxxv, 158 p.
2001-047329 181/.6 21 0801487161
*Plato -- Contributions in concept of
happiness. Aristotle -- Contributions in concept
of happiness. Happiness. Philosophy, Ancient.*

B753.F33.P53
Farabi.
Philosophy of Plato and Aristotle. Translated
with an introd. by Muhsin Mahdi. [New York]
Free Press of Glencoe [1962] 158 p.
62-011856 180
Philosophy, Ancient.

B753.F34 G35 1990
Galston, Miriam,
Politics and excellence: the political philosophy
of Alfarabi/ Miriam Galston. Princeton, N.J.:
Princeton University Press, c1990. viii, 240 p.
90-032877 320/.01 20 0691078084
*F⁻ar⁻ab⁻i -- Contributions in political
science.*

B753.I24 C58 2002
Coates, Peter.
Ibn 'Arabi and modern thought: the history of
taking metaphysics seriously/ Peter Coates.
Oxford: Anqa, 2002. viii, 203 p.
2002-421180 181/.92 21 0953451372
*Ibn al-Arab⁻i, 1165-1240. Philosophy,
Modern.*

B755 Medieval (430-1450) — Jewish philosophers — General works

B755.C54 1996
Cohn-Sherbok, Dan.
Medieval Jewish philosophy: an introduction/
Dan Cohn-Sherbok. Richmond, Surrey: Curzon,
1996. x, 196 p.
97-140822 181/.06 0700704140
Philosophy, Jewish. Philosophy, Medieval.

B755.G66 1999
Goodman, Lenn Evan, 1944-
Jewish and Islamic philosophy: crosspollinations
in the classic age/ Lenn E. Goodman. New
Brunswick, N.J.: Rutgers University Press, 1999.
xv, 256 p.
99-027868 181/.06 0813527600
*Philosophy, Jewish. Philosophy, Islamic.
Philosophy, Medieval.*

B757 Medieval (430-1450) — Jewish philosophers — Special topics, A-Z

B757.L38.S7613 1995
Strauss, Leo.
Philosophy and law: contributions to the
understanding of Maimonides and his
predecessors/ Leo Strauss; translated by Eve
Adler. Albany: State University of New York
Press, c1995. v, 157 p.
93-034046 181/.06 0791419754
*Maimonides, Moses, -- 1135-1204. -- Dalalat
al-hairin.Law (Theology) Philosophy, Jewish.*

B759 Medieval (430-1450) — Jewish philosophers — Individual philosophers, A-Z

B759.M34 D62 1995
Dobbs-Weinstein, Idit,
Maimonides and St. Thomas on the limits of
reason/ Idit Dobbs-Weinstein. Albany: State
University of New York Press, c1995. x, 278 p.
94-003369 181/.06 20 0791424162
*Maimonides, Moses, 1135-1204. Thomas,
Aquinas, Saint, 1225?-1274. Philosophy,
Medieval. Faith and reason.*

B759.M34.K44 1991
Kellner, Menachem Marc, 1946-
Maimonides on Judaism and the Jewish people/
Menachem Kellner. Albany, N.Y.: State
University of New York Press, c1991. xii, 168 p.
90-044128 296.1/72 0791406911
*Maimonides, Moses, -- 1135-
1204.Philosophy, Jewish. Philosophy, Medieval.*

B759.M34.W45 1991
Weiss, Raymond L.
Maimonides' ethics: the encounter of
philosophic and religious morality/ Raymond L.
Weiss. Chicago: University of Chicago Press,
1991. ix, 224 p.
91-013921 296.3/85/092 0226891526
*Maimonides, Moses, -- 1135-1204 --
Ethics.Ethics, Jewish -- History.*

B765 Medieval (430-1450) — European philosophers

B765.A23.E82 1971
Abailard, Pierre, 1079-1142.
Peter Abelard's Ethics: an edition with
introduction, English translation and notes by
D.E. Luscombe. Oxford, Clarendon Press, 1971.
lxi, 144 p.
70-885574 241/.04/2
Christian ethics.

B765.A24 G73 1970b
Grane, Leif.
Peter Abelard; philosophy and Christianity in the
Middle Ages. Translated by Frederick and
Christine Crowley. Bibliography and notes
edited by Derek Baker. [1st American ed.] New
York, Harcourt, Brace & World [1970] 190 p.
74-013929 189/.4 B 0151717109
*Abelard, Peter, 1079-1142. Christianity --
Philosophy. Philosophy, Medieval.*

B765.A24 M37 1997
Marenbon, John.
The philosophy of Peter Abelard/ John
Marenbon. Cambridge; Cambridge University
Press, 1997. xx, 373 p.
96-011872 189/.4 20 0521553970
*Abelard, Peter, 1079-1142. Philosophy,
Medieval.*

B765.A81.A2513 2002
Anselm,
Three philosophical dialogues/ Anselm;
translated, with introduction and notes, by
Thomas Williams. Indianapolis, IN: Hackett
Pub., c2002. xiv, 110 p.
2001-051549 189/.4 21 0872206114
*Free will and determinism. Truth. Devil --
Christianity. Philosophy, Medieval.*

B765.A84.B46 1993
Bencivenga, Ermanno, 1950-
Logic and other nonsense: the case of Anselm
and his God/ Ermanno Bencivenga. Princeton,
N.J.: Princeton University Press, c1993. xii,
132 p.
93-018278 189/.4 0691074275
*Anselm, -- Saint, Archbishop of Canterbury, --
1033-1109.Logic, Medieval. God -- Proof,
Ontological.*

B765.B24.E28 1970
Easton, Stewart Copinger, 1907-
Roger Bacon and his search for a universal
science; a reconsideration of the life and work of
Roger Bacon in the light of his own stated
purposes [by] Stewart C. Easton. Westport,
Conn., Greenwood Press [1970, c1952] vii,
255 p.
70-100159 189 0837133998
*Bacon, Roger, -- 1214?-1294.Philosophers --
England -- Biography. Scientists -- England --
Biography. Occultists -- England -- Biography.*

B765.B24.W4 1974
Westacott, Evalyn, 1888-
Roger Bacon in life and legend, by E. Westacott.
[Folcroft, Pa.] Folcroft Library Editions, 1974
[c1953] 140 p.
74-014623 189 0841495475
*Bacon, Roger, -- 1214?-1294.Philosophers --
England -- Biography. Scientists -- England --
Biography. Occultists -- England -- Biography.*

B765.B74.D4
De Benedictis, Matthew M., 1914-
The social thought of Saint Bonaventure; a study in social philosophy, by Matthew M. De Benedictis. Washington, D.C., The Catholic university of America Press, 1946. xv, 276 p.
47-003395
Bonaventure, -- Saint, Cardinal, -- ca. 1217-1274.Social ethics. Sociology, Christian -- Catholic authors.

B765.J34.C33 2000
Carabine, Deirdre.
John Scottus Eriugena/ Deirdre Carabine. New York: Oxford University Press, 2000. xi, 131 p.
99-029192   189   0195113616
Erigena, Johannes Scotus, -- ca. 810-ca. 877.Philosophy, Medieval.

B765.L84.J64 1987
Johnston, Mark D. 1952-
The spiritual logic of Ramon Llull/ Mark D. Johnston. Oxford [Oxfordshire]: Clarendon Press; 1987. x, 336 p.
86-021857   160   0198249209
Llull, Ramon, -- 1232?-1316 -- Contributions in logic.Logic, Medieval.

B765.N53 D63 1981
Nicholas,
Nicholas of Cusa On learned ignorance: a translation and an appraisal of De docta ignorantia/ by Jasper Hopkins. Minneapolis: A.J. Benning Press, c1981. viii, 205 p.
80-082907   189/.5 19   0938060236
Mysticism -- Early works to 1800.

B765.O32 E5 1990
William,
Philosophical writings: a selection/ William of Ockham;   translated, with introduction and notes, by Philotheus Boehner; Latin texts and English translation revised by Stephen F. Brown, 1989; new foreword and bibliography by Stephen F. Brown. Indianapolis: Hackett Pub. Co., c1990. lxix, 167 p.
89-048587   189/.4 20   0872200795
Philosophy.

B765.O34.C36 1999
The Cambridge companion to Ockham/ edited by Paul Vincent Spade. Cambridge, U.K.; Cambridge University Press, 1999. xvii, 420 p.
98-038076   189/.4   052158244X
William, -- of Ockham, -- ca. 1285-ca. 1349.Philosophy, Medieval.

B765.T5.D43E
Thomas Aquinas, 1225?-1274.
Concerning being and essence   (De ente et essentia) Translated from the Latin with the addition of a preface by George G. Leckie. New York, Appleton-Century [c1937] xliv, 47 p.
37-002104
Ontology. Substance (Philosophy)

B765.T53 S8166 2002
Pasnau, Robert.
Thomas   Aquinas   on   human   nature: a philosophical study of Summa theologiae 1a, 75-89/ Robert Pasnau. Cambridge, UK; Cambridge University Press, 2002. xi, 500 p.
2001-025403   128 21   0521001897
Thomas,   Aquinas,   Saint,   1225?-1274. Summa   theologica.   Pars   1.   Philosophical anthropology. Man (Christian theology)

B765.T54 C29 1993
The Cambridge companion to Aquinas/ edited by Norman Kretzmann and   Eleonore Stump. Cambridge; Cambridge University Press, 1993. viii, 302 p.
92-031977   189/.4 20   0521431956
Thomas, Aquinas, Saint, 1225?-1274.

B765.T54 C64 1976
Copleston, Frederick Charles.
Thomas Aquinas/ by Frederick Copleston. London: Search Press; 1976. 272 p.
78-310121   230/.2/0924   0064912779
Thomas, Aquinas, Saint, 1225?-1274.

B765.T54.D35 1992
Davies, Brian, 1951-
The thought of Thomas Aquinas/ Brian Davies. Oxford: Clarendon Press; 1992. xv, 391 p.
91-035671   230/.2/092   0198264585
Thomas, -- Aquinas, Saint, -- 1225?-1274.Theology, Doctrinal -- History -- Middle Ages, 600-1500.

B765.T54.G47
Gilson, Etienne, 1884-1978.
Elements of Christian philosophy. Garden City, N.Y., Doubleday, Catholic Textbook Division [1960] 358 p.
60-006405   189.4
Thomas, -- Aquinas, Saint, -- 1225?-1274 -- Contributions in theology.Theology -- History -- Middle Ages, 600-1500. Philosophy, Medieval.

B765.T54 G5 1971
Gilson, Etienne,
The philosophy of St. Thomas Aquinas. Authorised translation from the 3d rev. and enl. ed. of 'Le thomisme', by Étienne Gilson. Translated by Edward Bullough. Edited by G. A. Elrington. Freeport, N.Y., Books for Libraries Press [1971] xv, 372 p.
70-157337   189/.4   0836957970
Thomas,   Aquinas,   Saint,   1225?-1274. Philosophy, Medieval.

B765.T54.K44 1993
Kenny, Anthony John Patrick.
Aquinas on mind/ Anthony Kenny. London; Routledge, 1993. 182 p.
92-012224   128/.2/092   0415044154
Thomas, -- Aquinas, Saint, -- 1225?-1274.Philosophy of mind -- History. Mind and body -- History. Philosophy, Medieval.

B775 Renaissance — General works

B775.C313 1964
Cassirer, Ernst, 1874-1945.
The individual and the cosmos in Renaissance philosophy. Translated with an introd. by Mario Domandi. New York, Barnes & Noble [1964, c1963] xv, 199 p.
64-002094   190
Individualism.   Knowledge,   Theory   of. Cosmology.

B775.K73
Kristeller, Paul Oskar,
Renaissance thought and its sources/ Paul Oskar Kristeller; edited   by Michael Mooney. New York: Columbia University Press, 1979. xiv, 347 p.
79-015521   190/.9/024   0231045123
Philosophy,   Renaissance.   Humanism   -- History. Science, Renaissance. Art, Renaissance. Literature, Medieval -- History and criticism. Renaissance -- Sources.

B776 Renaissance — By region or country, A-Z

B776.E5.W5 1976
Winny, James,
The frame of order: an outline of Elizabethan belief taken from treatises of the late sixteenth century/ edited by James Winny. Folcroft, Pa.: Folcroft Library Editions, 1976. 224 p.
76-025156   192   0841485424
Philosophy, English -- 16th century.Great Britain -- History -- Elizabeth, 1558-1603.

B776.S7.H57 1997
Hispanic philosophy in the age of discovery/ edited by Kevin White. Washington, D.C.: Catholic University of America Press, c1997. xv, 326 p.
96-014797   196/.1   0813208742
Philosophy, Spanish.Spain -- Intellectual life -- 1516-1700.

B778 Renaissance — Special topics — Humanism

B778.H3
Hadas, Moses, 1900-1966.
Humanism: the Greek ideal and its survival. New York, Harper [1960] 132 p.
60-007525   144   0844540115
Humanism.

B778.J3
Jaeger, Werner Wilhelm, 1888-1961.
Humanism and theology, under the auspices of the Aristotelian society of Marquette university, by Werner Jaeger. Milwaukee, Marquette university press, 1943. 87 p.
43-017104   144
Philosophy and religion. Humanism.

B778.K74 1961
Kristeller, Paul Oskar, 1905-
Renaissance thought: the classic, scholastic, and humanistic strains. New York, Harper [1961]
173 p.
62-005609   940.21
Humanism. Renaissance.

B779 Renaissance —
Special topics — Skepticism

B779.P65 2003
Popkin, Richard Henry,
The history of scepticism: from Savonarola to Bayle/ Richard Popkin. Rev. and expanded ed. Oxford; Oxford University Press, 2003. xxiv, 415 p.
2002-025769   149/.73 21   0195107683
Skepticism -- History.

B780 Renaissance —
Special topics —
Other special topics, A-Z

B780.W5.R5 1973
Rice, Eugene F.
The Renaissance idea of wisdom, by Eugene F. Rice, Jr. Westport, Conn., Greenwood Press [1973, c1958] ix, 220 p.
72-012117   190   0837167124
Wisdom. Philosophy, Renaissance.

B783 Renaissance —
Individual philosophers —
Bruno, Giordano

B783.D43.E6 1976
Bruno, Giordano, 1548-1600.
Cause, principle, and unity: five dialogues/ by Giordano Bruno; translated with an introduction by Jack Lindsay. Westport, Conn.: Greenwood Press, 1976, c1962. vii, 177 p.
76-028448   110   0837190401
Metaphysics -- Early works to 1800.

B785 Renaissance —
Individual philosophers — C - Z

B785.C24 H43 1997
Headley, John M.
Tommaso Campanella and the transformation of the world/ John M. Headley. Princeton, N.J.: Princeton University Press, c1997. xxv, 399 p.
96-037931   195 21   0691026793
Campanella, Tommaso, 1568-1639.

B785.F44 F52 1986
Ficino and Renaissance Neoplatonism/ edited by Konrad Eisenbichler and Olga Zorzi Pugliese. Ottawa, Canada: Dovehouse Editions Canada, 1986. 202 p.
86-235547   186/.4 19   0919473598
Ficino, Marsilio, 1433-1499. Philosophy, Italian. Renaissance -- Italy. Neoplatonism.

B785.M24.A48 1999
Althusser, Louis.
Machiavelli and us/ Louis Althusser; edited by Francois Matheron; translated by G.M. Goshgarian. New York: Verso, 1999. xxii, 136 p.
99-013811   320.1/092   1859847110
Machiavelli, Niccolo, -- 1469-1527.

B785.M24.D36 1997
Danel, Adam D., 1964-
A case for freedom: Machiavellian humanism/ Adam D. Danel. Lanham, Md.: University Press of America, c1997. xviii, 280 p.
96-041721   320.1/092   0761805575
Machiavelli, Niccolo, -- 1469-1527 -- Ethics.Free will and determinism. Liberty. Humanism.

B785.V63.D4713 2000
Vives, Juan Luis, 1492-1540.
The education of a Christian woman: a sixteenth-century manual/ Juan Luis Vives; edited and translated by Charles Fantazzi. Chicago: University of Chicago Press, c2000. xxx, 343 p.
99-030671   371.822   0226858146
Christian women -- Conduct of life -- Early works to 1800. Christian women -- Education -- Early works to 1800.

B790 Modern
(1450/1660-   ) —
Collected works (nonserial)

B790.B4
Beardsley, Monroe C.,
The European philosophers from Descartes to Nietzsche. New York, Modern Library [1960] 870 p.
60-010004   190
Philosophers, Modern. Philosophy, Modern.

B791 Modern (1450/1660-   ) —
General works — English

B791.B57 2000
The Blackwell guide to the modern philosophers: from Descartes to Nietzsche/ edited by Steven M. Emmanuel. Oxford, UK; Blackwell, 2000. xii, 423 p.
00-022954   190   0631210164
Philosophers, Modern -- Europe. Philosophy, Modern.

B791.B765 2003
Bunge, Mario Augusto.
Philosophical dictionary/ Mario Bunge. Enl. ed. Amherst, N.Y.: Prometheus Books, 2003. 315 p.
2002-031911   190/.3 21   1591020379
Philosophy, Modern -- Dictionaries.

B791.C582
Collins, James Daniel.
Interpreting modern philosophy, by James Collins. Princeton, N.J., Princeton University Press, 1972. xii, 463 p.
70-160259   190   0691071799
Kant, Immanuel, -- 1724-1804.Philosophy, Modern. Teleology.

B791.C73 1987
Craig, Edward.
The mind of God and the works of man/ Edward Craig. Oxford [Oxfordshire]: Clarendon Press, 1987. x, 353 p.
87-001514   190   0198249330
Philosophy, Modern.

B791.K535 2002
Kimball, Roger,
Lives of the mind: the use and abuse of intelligence from Hegel to Wodehouse/ Roger Kimball. Chicago: Ivan R. Dee, 2002. viii, 375 p.
2002-073681   190 21   1566634792
Philosophy, Modern.

B791.R77 1989
Rosen, Stanley, 1929-
The ancients and the moderns: rethinking modernity/ Stanley Rosen. New Haven: Yale University Press, c1989. x, 236 p.
88-026155   190   0300043317
Philosophy, Modern.

B791.S29 2001
Scruton, Roger.
A short history of modern philosophy: from Descartes to Wittgenstein / Roger Scruton. 2nd ed., [rev.]. London; Routledge, 2001.
2001-034885   190 21   0415267633
Philosophy, Modern.

B791.S39 2001
Sedgwick, Peter R.
Descartes to Derrida: an introduction to European philosophy/ Peter Sedgwick. Malden, Mass.: Blackwell Publishers, 2001. 310 p.
00-057917   190 21   0631201432
Philosophy, Modern. Philosophy, European.

B792 Modern (1450/1660-   ) —
General works — French

B792.M33
Maritain, Jacques, 1882-1973.
Three reformers: Luther--Descartes--Rousseau, by Jacques Maritain. London, Sheed & Ward [1928]
29-008562
Rousseau, Jean-Jacques, -- 1712-1778. Luther, Martin, -- 1483-1546. Descartes, Rene, -- 1596-1650.

B799 Modern (1450/1660-) — Comparative philosophy

B799.B34 1995
Bahm, Archie J.
Comparative philosophy: Western, Indian, and Chinese philosophies compared/ Archie J. Bahm. Rev. ed. Albuquerque, N.M.: World Books, c1995. xii, 103 p.
95-061792   100 20   0911714227
Philosophy, Comparative.

B799.B46 1997
Benesch, Walter, 1933-
An introduction to comparative philosophy: a travel guide to philosophical space/ Walter Benesch. New York: St. Martin's Press, 1997. ix, 229 p.
96-034793   100   033367832X
Philosophy, Comparative.

B799.I53 1988
Interpreting across boundaries: new essays in comparative philosophy/ edited by Gerald James Larson and Eliot Deutsch. Princeton, N.J.: Princeton University Press, c1988. ix, 316 p.
87-020611   100   0691073198
Philosophy, Comparative -- Congresses.

B799.N29 1986
Nakamura, Hajime,
A comparative history of ideas/ by Hajime Nakamura. Rev. ed. London; KPI; xx, 572 p.
86-176807   109 19   0710301227
Philosophy, Comparative. Religion. Religions.

B799.S32 1970
Saher, P. J.
Eastern wisdom and Western thought; a comparative study in the modern philosophy of religion, by P. J. Saher. New York, N.Y., Barnes and Noble [1970] 292 p.
73-016605   200/.1
Philosophy, Comparative. Religion -- Philosophy.

B799.S37 1998
Scharfstein, Ben-Ami, 1919-
A comparative history of world philosophy: from the Upanishads to Kant/ Ben-Ami Scharfstein. Albany: State University of New York Press, c1998. xiv, 685 p.
97-019489   109   0791436837
Philosophy, Comparative.

B799.W34 1995
Watts, Alan,
The Tao of philosophy: the edited transcripts/ Alan Watts. 1st ed. Boston: C.E. Tuttle, 1995. xv, 96 p.
95-022261   191 20   0804830525
Philosophy, Comparative. East and West. Philosophy.

B801 Modern (1450/1660-) — By period — 17th century

B801.C35 1998
The Cambridge history of seventeenth-century philosophy/ edited by Daniel Garber, Michael Ayers, with the assistance of Roger Ariew and Alan Gabbey. Cambridge; Cambridge University Press, 1998. 2 v.
96-025475   190/.9/032   0521588642
Philosophy, Modern -- 17th century.

B801.D57 1992
Discovering China: European interpretations in the Enlightenment/ edited by Julia Ching and Willard G. Oxtoby. Rochester, N.Y., USA: University of Rochester Press, 1992. xxxi, 211 p.
92-024272   303.48/24051 20   1878822144
Philosophy, Modern -- 17th century. Enlightenment -- Europe. Philosophers -- Europe -- Attitudes. Philosophy, Chinese. China -- Civilization. Europe -- Civilization -- Chinese influences.

B801.L63
Loeb, Louis E.
From Descartes to Hume: continental metaphysics and the development of modern philosophy/ Louis E. Loeb. Ithaca, N.Y.: Cornell University Press, c1981. 382 p.
80-069826   110/.9/032 19   0801412897
Philosophy, Modern -- 17th century. Metaphysics -- History -- 17th century.

B801.L67 2001
Losonsky, Michael.
Enlightenment and action from Descartes to Kant: passionate thought/ Michael Losonsky. Cambridge; Cambridge University Press, 2001. xvii, 221 p.
2001-025467   128/.09/032 21   0521806127
Enlightenment. Philosophy -- History -- 17th century. Reason -- Social aspects -- History -- 17th century.

B801.R57 1993
The Rise of modern philosophy: the tension between the new and traditional philosophies from Machiavelli to Leibniz/ edited by Tom Sorell. Oxford [England]: Clarendon Press; 1993. viii, 352 p.
92-024022   190/.9/032   019823953X
Philosophy, Modern -- 17th century. Philosophy, European.

B802 Modern (1450/1660-) — By period — 18th century. Philosophy of the enlightenment. Die Aufklarung (Germany)

B802.B45 1970
Berlin, Isaiah,
The Age of Enlightenment; the eighteenth century philosophers. Selected, with introd. and interpretive commentary by Isaiah Berlin. Freeport, N.Y., Books for Libraries Press [1970, c1956] 282 p.
72-117760   190   0836918223
Enlightenment. Philosophy, Modern -- 18th century.

B802.B7
Brinton, Crane, 1898-1968,
The portable age of reason reader. New York, Viking Press, 1956. 628 p.
56-009223   808.8
Enlightenment. Philosophy, Modern -- 18th century.

B802.C6 1960a
Cobban, Alfred.
In search of humanity; the role of the Enlightenment in modern history.   G. Braziller, 1960. 254 p.
60-013305
Enlightenment. Eighteenth century. Europe -- Intellectual life.

B802.E53 2003
Encyclopedia of the Enlightenment/ Alan Charles Kors, editor in chief. Oxford; Oxford University Press, 2003. 4 v.
2002-003766   940.2/5 21   019510434X
Enlightenment -- Encyclopedias. Enlightenment -- United States -- Encyclopedias. Philosophy -- Encyclopedias. Europe -- Intellectual life -- 18th century. United States -- Intellectual life -- 18th century.

B802.I87 2001
Israel, Jonathan Irvine.
Radical enlightenment: philosophy and the making of modernity, 1650-1750/ Jonathan I. Israel. Oxford; Oxford University Press, 2001. xvi, 810 p.
00-044086   940.2/5 21   0198206089
Spinoza, Benedictus de, 1632-1677. Enlightenment -- Europe. Europe -- Civilization -- 17th century. Europe -- Civilization -- 18th century.

B802.S34
Schlereth, Thomas J.
The cosmopolitan ideal in Enlightenment thought, its form and function in the ideas of Franklin, Hume, and Voltaire, 1694-1790/ Thomas J. Schlereth. Notre Dame, Ind.: University of Notre Dame Press, c1977. xxv, 230 p.
76-022405   190/.9/033   0268007209
Franklin, Benjamin, -- 1706-1790. Hume, David, -- 1711-1776. Voltaire, -- 1694-1778. Enlightenment. Philosophy, Modern -- 18th century. Internationalism.

B803 Modern (1450/1660-   ) — By period — 19th century

B803.B3813 1991
Bergman, Samuel Hugo, 1883-1975.
Dialogical philosophy from Kierkegaard to Buber/ Shmuel Hugo Bergman; translated from Hebrew by Arnold A. Gerstein. Albany, N.Y.: State University of New York Press, c1991. xvi, 257 p.
90-038138   190   0791406237
Kierkegaard, Soren, -- 1813-1855. Rosenzweig, Franz, -- 1886-1929. Buber, Martin, -- 1878-1965. Dialogue. Philosophy, Modern -- 19th century. Philosophy, Modern -- 20th century.

B803.C66 1998
A companion to continental philosophy/ edited by Simon Critchley and William Schroeder. Oxford, UK; Blackwell, 1998. xv, 680 p.
97-010146   190   0631190139
Philosophy, European. Philosophy, European -- 20th century. Philosophy, Modern -- 19th century.

B803.H33 1952
Hawton, Hector, 1901-
The feast of unreason. London, Watts [1952] 235 p.
53-015583   111   083713742X
Philosophy, Modern. Existentialism.

B803.I55 1995
Intersections: nineteenth-century philosophy and contemporary theory / edited with a critical introduction by Tilottama Rajan and David L. Clark. Albany: State University of New York Press, c1995. vii, 386 p.
94-015204   190/.9/034 20   0791422585
Philosophy, Modern -- 19th century. Literature -- Philosophy. Criticism.

B803.P4
Peckham, Morse.
Beyond the tragic vision; the quest for identity in the nineteenth century. New York, G. Braziller, 1962. 380 p.
62-009932   171.3
Philosophy, Modern. Civilization, Modern -- 19th century. Self.

B803.P57 1999
Pippin, Robert B.,
Modernism as a philosophical problem: on the dissatisfactions of European high culture/ Robert B. Pippin. 2nd ed. Malden, Mass.: Blackwell, 1999. xx, 234 p.
99-017513   190 21   0631214143
Philosophy, Modern -- 19th century. Civilization, Modern -- 19th century. Philosophy, Modern -- 20th century. Civilization, Modern -- 20th century. Europe -- Intellectual life -- 19th century. Europe -- Intellectual life -- 20th century.

B803.R25
Randall, John Herman, 1899-
Philosophy after Darwin: chapters for The career of philosophy, volume III, and other essays/ John Herman Randall, Jr.; edited by Beth J. Singer. New York: Columbia University Press, 1977. x, 352 p.
76-030897   190/.9   0231041144
Philosophy, Modern -- 19th century.

B803.S54 1993
Skorupski, John, 1946-
English-language philosophy, 1750 to 1945/ John Skorupski. Oxford; Oxford University Press, 1993. xiv, 233 p.
92-027017   190   0192192116
Philosophy, Modern -- 18th century. Philosophy, Modern -- 19th century. Philosophy, Modern -- 20th century.

B804 Modern (1450/1660-   ) — By period — 20th century

B804.A1.H36
Handbook of world philosophy: contemporary developments since 1945/ edited by John R. Burr. Westport, Conn.: Greenwood Press, 1980. xxii, 641 p.
80-000539   190/.904   0313223815
Philosophy, Modern -- 20th century -- Addresses, essays, lectures.

B804.A818 1982
Ayer, A. J. 1910-
Philosophy in the twentieth century/ A.J. Ayer. New York: Random House, c1982. x, 283 p.
82-040131   190/.9/04   0394504542
Philosophy, Modern -- 20th century.

B804.B46 1991b
Bernstein, Richard J.
The new constellation: the ethical-political horizons of modernity/postmodernity/ Richard J. Bernstein. Cambridge, UK: Polity Press, 1991. vii, 358 p.
92-196942   0745609201
Heidegger, Martin, 1889-1976. Philosophy, Modern -- 20th century. Philosophy, French -- 20th century. Postmodernism. Ethics, Modern -- 20th century. Political science -- Philosophy -- History -- 20th century.

B804.B48 1989
Bhaskar, Roy, 1944-
Reclaiming reality: a critical introduction to contemporary philosophy/ Roy Bhaskar. London; Verso, 1989. ix, 218 p.
89-005684   149/.2   086091951X
Philosophy, Modern -- 20th century.

B804.C573
Contemporary philosophy, a new survey/ edited by Guttorm Floistad. The Hague; M. Nijhoff; 1981-1993 v. 1-7; in 8
81-003972   190/.9/047   9024724368
Philosophy, Modern -- 20th century -- Addresses, essays, lectures.

B804.D28 1998
D'Amico, Robert.
Contemporary continental philosophy/ Robert D'Amico. Boulder, Colo.: Westview Press, 1998. xi, 267 p.
98-037834   190/.9/04   0813332214
Philosophy, Modern -- 20th century. Philosophy, European -- 20th century.

B804.D3713 1999
Delacampagne, Christian, 1949-
A history of philosophy in the twentieth century/ Christian Delacampagne; translated by M.B. DeBevoise. Baltimore, Md.: Johns Hopkins University Press, 1999. xviii, 330 p.
99-011237   190/.9/04   0801860164
Philosophy -- History -- 20th century.

B804.E43 1999
The Edinburgh encyclopedia of Continental philosophy/ general editor, Simon Glendinning. Edinburgh: University Press, c1999. xiii, 685 p.
99-488294   190 21   0748607838
Philosophy, European.

B804.G59 1990
Goldstein, Laurence, 1947-
The philosopher's habitat: an introduction to investigations in, and applications of, modern philosophy/ Laurence Goldstein. London; Routledge, 1990. xvii, 215 p.
89-006344   190/.9/04   0415042240
Philosophy, Modern -- 20th century.

B804.J2 1977
James, William, 1842-1910.
A pluralistic universe/ William James. Cambridge, Mass.: Harvard University Press, 1977. xxix, 488 p.
76-045464   191   0674673913
Philosophy, Modern -- Addresses, essays, lectures.

B804.K363 1994
Kearney, Richard.
Modern movements in European philosophy/ Richard Kearney. 2nd ed. Manchester; Manchester University Press, c1994. 367 p.
94-026467   142 20   0719042488
Philosophy, Modern -- 20th century. Philosophy, European -- 20th century.

B804.K68
Krutch, Joseph Wood, 1893-
The measure of man: on freedom, human values, survival, and the modern temper. Indianapolis, Bobbs-Merrill [1954] 261 p.
54-006504   190
Philosophy, Modern. Civilization, Modern -- 20th century.

B804.L37 1994
Lechte, John.
Fifty key contemporary thinkers: from structuralism to postmodernity / John Lechte. London; Routledge, 1994. xi, 251 p.
94-000996   190/.9/04 20   0415074088
Philosophy, Modern -- 20th century. Structuralism. Semiotics. Feminist theory. Philosophy, Marxist.

B804.M257 1979
Magee, Bryan.
Men of ideas/ Bryan Magee. New York: Viking Press, 1979, c1978. 314 p.
78-027263   190   0670468886
Philosophy, Modern -- 20th century. Philosophers -- Interviews.

B804.M284 1995
Margolis, Joseph,
Historied thought, constructed world: conceptual primer for the turn of the millennium/ Joseph Margolis. Berkeley: University of California Press, c1995. x, 377 p.
95-012639   190 20   0520201132
Philosophy, Modern -- Forecasting. Twenty-first century -- Forecasts. History -- Philosophy. Philosophy.

B804.M355 2001
McGinn, Colin,
The making of a philosopher: my insider's journey through twentieth century philosophy/ Colin McGinn. 1st ed. New York: HarperCollins, 2002.
2001-039502   192 21   0060197927
Philosophy, Modern -- 20th century.

B804.O55 1998
One hundred twentieth-century philosophers/ edited by Stuart Brown, Diané Collinson, Robert Wilkinson. London; Routledge, 1998. ix, 241 p.
97-030846   190/.9/04 B 21   0415179963
Philosophers -- Biography. Philosophy, Modern -- 20th century.

B804.P3 1955
Perry, Ralph Barton, 1876-1957.
Present philosophical tendencies; a critical survey of naturalism, idealism, pragmatism, and realism, together with a synopsis of the philosophy of William James. New York, G. Braziller, 1955. 383 p.
56-001839   190
Philosophy, Modern.

B804.P538 1997
Philosophy of meaning, knowledge, and value in the twentieth century/ edited by John V. Canfield. London; Routledge, 1997. xxxi, 466 p.
96-011902   190/.9/04 20   0415056055
Philosophy, Modern -- 20th century. Philosophy, British. Philosophy, American -- 20th century.

B804.U7
Urmson, J. O.
Philosophical analysis; its development between the two World Wars. Oxford, Clarendon Press, 1956. 202 p.
56-013682   190
Analysis (Philosophy)

B804.W389 1996
West, David,
An introduction to continental philosophy/ David West. Cambridge [England]; Polity Press, 1996. viii, 278 p.
96-038820   190 20   0745611850
Philosophy, European -- 20th century. Philosophy, Modern -- 18th century. Philosophy, Modern -- 19th century. Philosophy, European.

B804.W52
Who's who in philosophy. Dagobert D. Runes, editor. Lester E. Denonn, Ralph B. Winn, associate editors. New York, Greenwood Press [1969-]
79-088971   190   0837120950
Philosophy, Modern -- 20th century -- Bio-bibliography. Philosophers -- United States -- Directories. Philosophers, English -- Directories.

B808.2 Modern (1450/1660-) — Special topics and schools of philosophy — Alienation

B808.2.C48 1990
Churchich, Nicholas, 1919-
Marxism and alienation/ Nicholas Churchich. Rutherford [N.J.]: Fairleigh Dickinson University Press; c1990. 365 p.
88-046151   302.5/44   0838633722
Alienation (Philosophy) -- History. Philosophy, Marxist.

B808.5 Modern (1450/1660-) — Special topics and schools of philosophy — Analysis

B808.5.A532 1990
The Analytic tradition: meaning, thought, and knowledge/ edited by David Bell and Neil Cooper. Oxford, UK; B. Blackwell, 1991. xi, 225 p.
90-038301   146/.4   0631176861
Frege, Gottlob, -- 1848-1925. Analysis (Philosophy)

B808.5.B53 1963
Black, Max, 1909-
Philosophical analysis; a collection of essays. Englewood Cliffs, N.J., Prentice-Hall, 1963 [c1950] 401 p.
63-013299   108.2
Analysis (Philosophy)

B808.5.F76 2000
Friedman, Michael, 1947-
A parting of the ways: Carnap, Cassirer, and Heidegger/ Michael Friedman. Chicago: Open Court, c2000. xv, 175 p.
00-060658   193   0812694252
Carnap, Rudolf, -- 1891-1970. Cassirer, Ernst, -- 1874-1945. Heidegger, Martin, -- 1889-1976. Philosophy, European -- 20th century. Analysis (Philosophy)

B808.5.J33 1998
Jackson, Frank, 1943-
From metaphysics to ethics: a defence of conceptual analysis/ Frank Jackson. Oxford: Clarendon Press; 1998. ix, 174 p.
98-179225   146/.4   0198236182
Analysis (Philosophy)

B808.5.P3
Pap, Arthur, 1921-1959.
Elements of analytic philosophy. New York, Macmillan Co., 1949. xv, 526 p.
49-006863
Philosophy.

B808.5.A52 2001
Analytic philosophy: an anthology/ edited by A.P. Martinich and David Sosa. Malden, Mass.: Blackwell, 2001. ix, 517 p.
00-069789   146/.4 21   0631216472
Analysis (Philosophy)

B808.5.C555 2001
A companion to analytic philosophy/ edited by A.P. Martinich and David Sosa. Malden, Mass.: Blackwell, 2001. x, 497 p.
00-050770   146/.4 21   0631214151
Analysis (Philosophy) Philosophy, Modern -- 19th century. Philosophy, Modern -- 20th century.

B808.5.D86 1994
Dummett, Michael A. E.
Origins of analytical philosophy/ Michael Dummett. Cambridge, Mass.: Harvard University Press, 1994. xi, 199 p.
93-003772   146/.4 20   0674644727
Analysis (Philosophy) Phenomenology.

B808.5.H6 1997
Hospers, John,
An introduction to philosophical analysis/ John Hospers. 4th ed. Upper Saddle River, N.J.: Prentice Hall, c1997. vi, 282 p.
96-022937   100 20   0132663058
Analysis (Philosophy)

B808.5.S667 1993
Sorensen, Roy A.
Pseudo-problems: how analytic philosophy gets done/ Roy A. Sorensen. London; Routledge, 1993. 291 p.
93-015543   146/.4   041509464X
Analysis (Philosophy)

B808.5.W36 1986
Wang, Hao,
Beyond analytic philosophy: doing justice to what we know/ Hao Wang. Cambridge, Mass.: MIT Press, c1986. xii, 273 p.
85-000070   146/.4 19   0262231247
Analysis (Philosophy) Logic. Knowledge, Theory of. Philosophy, Modern -- 20th century.

B808.67 Modern (1450/1660-) — Special topics and schools of philosophy — Autonomy

B808.67.I56 1989
The Inner citadel: essays on individual autonomy/ edited by John Christman. New York: Oxford University Press, 1989. x, 267 p.
88-033280   126 19   0195058623
Autonomy (Philosophy) Individuality.

B808.67.W35 1998
Waller, Bruce N., 1946-
The natural selection of autonomy/ Bruce N. Waller. Albany, N.Y.: State University of New York Press, c1998. x, 193 p.
97-037753   128   0791438198
Autonomy (Philosophy) Responsibility. Biology -- Philosophy.

B808.9 Modern (1450/1660-) — Special topics and schools of philosophy — Consciousness

B808.9.C38 2000
Catalano, Joseph S.
Thinking matter: consciousness from Aristotle to Putnam and Sartre/ Joseph S. Catalano. New York: Routledge, 2000. vii, 224 p.
99-049935   110   0415926645
Consciousness. Matter.

B808.9.F57 1992
Flanagan, Owen J.
Consciousness reconsidered/ Owen Flanagan. Cambridge, Mass.: MIT Press, c1992. xiv, 234 p.
92-010057   126   0262061481
Consciousness. Mind and body.

B808.9.H47 1993
Herbert, Nick.
Elemental mind: human consciousness and the new physics/ Nick Herbert. New York, N.Y.: Dutton, 1993. xi, 308 p.
93-015700   128/.2   0525935061
Consciousness. Quantum theory.

B808.9.H87 1998
Hurley, S. L.
Consciousness in action/ S.L. Hurley. Cambridge, Mass.: Harvard University Press, 1998. xii, 506 p.
98-012790   126   0674164202
Consciousness. Act (Philosophy)

B808.9.K49 1999
Keyes, C. D.
Brain mystery light and dark: the rhythm and harmony of consciousness/ Charles Don Keyes. London; Routledge, 1999. xvi, 164 p.
98-016983   126 21   0415180511
Consciousness. Brain.

B808.9.N37 1996
The nature of consciousness: philosophical debates/ edited by Ned Block, Owen Flanagan, and Guven Guzeldere. Cambridge, Mass.: MIT Press, c1997. xxix, 843 p.
96-017500   126   0262023997
Consciousness. Philosophy of mind.

B808.9.S54 1998
Siewert, Charles P.,
The significance of consciousness/ Charles P. Siewert. Princeton, N.J.: Princeton University Press, c1998. x, 374 p.
97-032848   126 21   0691027242
Consciousness.

B808.9.S73 1994
Strawson, Galen.
Mental reality/ Galen Strawson. Cambridge, Mass.: MIT Press, 1994. xiv, 337 p.
93-047905   128/.2   0262193523
Consciousness. Behaviorism (Psychology) Mind and body.

B808.9.T935 2003
Tye, Michael.
Consciousness and persons: unity and identity/ Michael Tye. Cambridge, Mass.: MIT Press, 2003.
2002-040999   126 21   026220147X
Consciousness. Whole and parts (Philosophy)

B809.14 Modern (1450/1660-) — Special topics and schools of philosophy — Contextualism

B809.14.H34 2001
Hahn, Lewis Edwin, 1908-
A contextualistic worldview: essays/ by Lewis E. Hahn. Carbondale: Southern Illinois University Press, c2001. xviii, 187 p.
00-039504   146   0809323311
Contextualism (Philosophy) Philosophy, American -- 20th century.

B809.15 Modern (1450/1660-) — Special topics and schools of philosophy — Convention

B809.15.S56 1989
Sidelle, Alan, 1960-
Necessity, essence, and individuation: a defense of conventionalism/ Alan Sidelle. Ithaca: Cornell University Press, 1989. xv, 216 p.
89-007122   146/.44   0801421667
Convention (Philosophy) Necessity (Philosophy) Realism.

B809.2 Modern (1450/1660-) — Special topics and schools of philosophy — Critical thinking

B809.2.W75 2001
Wright, Larry,
Critical thinking: an introduction to analytical reading and reasoning/ Larry Wright. New York: Oxford University Press, 2001. x, 390 p.
00-051500   160 21   0195130332
Critical thinking.

B809.3 Modern (1450/1660-) — Special topics and schools of philosophy — Criticism

B809.3.B76 2002
Bronner, Stephen Eric,
Of critical theory and its theorists/ Stephen Eric Bonner. 2nd ed. New York: Routledge, 2002.
2001-058917   142 21   0415932637
Critical theory.

B809.3.M33 1991
McCarthy, Thomas A.
Ideals and illusions: on reconstruction and deconstruction in contemporary critical theory/ Thomas McCarthy. Cambridge, Mass.: MIT Press, c1991. x, 254 p.
90-047776   142   0262132680
Critical theory. Deconstruction.

B809.3.N67 1994
Norris, Christopher, 1947-
Truth and the ethics of criticism/ Christopher Norris. Manchester; Manchester University Press; c1994. 148 p.
94-016682   190/.9/04   0719044529
Critical theory. Postmodernism. Meaning (Philosophy)

B809.3.P49 2000
Phillips, John, 1956-
Contested knowledge: a guide to critical theory/ John Phillips. London; Zed Books, 2000. ix, 240 p.
00-033416   142   1856495574
Critical theory.

B809.6 Modern (1450/1660-) — Special topics and schools of philosophy — Deconstruction

B809.6.D46 1997
Derrida, Jacques.
Deconstruction in a nutshell: a conversation with Jacques Derrida/ edited with a commentary by John D. Caputo. New York: Fordham University Press, 1997. xv, 215 p.
96-045189 194 082321754X
Derrida, Jacques -- Interviews.Philosophers - - France -- Interviews. Deconstruction.

B809.7 Modern (1450/1660-) — Special topics and schools of philosophy — Dialectic

B809.7.D48 1993
Dialectic and narrative/ edited by Thomas R. Flynn and Dalia Judovitz. Albany: State University of New York Press, c1993. xxi, 382 p.
92-025668 101 20 0791414566
Heidegger, Martin, 1889-1976. Dialectic. Literature -- Philosophy. Postmodernism. Philosophy, Modern -- 20th century.

B809.7.N67 1980
Norman, Richard
Hegel, Marx, and dialectic: a debate/ Richard Norman and Sean Sayers. Brighton, Sussex: Harvester Press; viii, 188 p.
86-157651 0391017799
Hegel, Georg Wilhelm Friedrich, 1770-1831. Marx, Karl, 1818-1883. Dialectic.

B809.8-809.82 Modern (1450/1660-) — Special topics and schools of philosophy — Dialectic materialism. Marxist philosophy

B809.8.A32 1957
Acton, H. B. 1908-
The illusion of the epoch; Marxism-Leninism as a philosophical creed. Boston, Beacon Press [1957] 278 p.
57-003627
Dialectical materialism.

B809.8.A3273 1987
Afanas§ev, Viktor Grigor§evich.
Dialectical materialism/ V.G. Afansayev. Rev. ed. New York: International Publishers, 1987. v, 152 p.
87-003419 146/.32 19 0717806561
Dialectical materialism. Philosophy, Marxist.

B809.8.C68
Cornforth, Maurice Campbell.
The theory of knowledge. New York, International Publishers [1955] 240 p.
55-001818 121
Knowledge, Theory of.

B809.8.G29913 1970b
Garaudy, Roger.
Marxism in the twentieth century. Translated by Rene Hague. New York, Scribner [1970] 224 p.
70-106527 146/.3
Marx, Karl, -- 1818-1883.Dialectical materialism.

B809.8.L4734 2001
Lee, Wendy Lynne.
On Marx/ Wendy Lynne Lee. Belmont, Calif.: Wadsworth, 2001. 96 p.
2001-279196 0534576028
Marx, Karl, 1818-1883. Philosophy, Marxist. Communism -- Philosophy. Socialism -- Philosophy.

B809.8.L48 1955
Lewis, John, 1889-
Marxism and the irrationalists. London: Lawrence & Wishart, 1955 141 p.
55-025502 146
Dialectical materialism.

B809.8.L499
Lichtheim, George, 1912-
From Marx to Hegel. [New York] Herder and Herder [1971] viii, 248 p.
70-167871 146/.3
Marx, Karl, -- 1818-1883. Hegel, Georg Wilhelm Friedrich, -- 1770-1831. Adorno, Theodor W., -- 1903-1969. Dialectical materialism -- Addresses, essays, lectures.

B809.8.S39
Selsam, Howard, 1903-
Philosophy in revolution. New York, International Publishers [1957] 160 p.
56-012946
Dialectical materialism.

B809.8.S5745 1985
Sowell, Thomas,
Marxism: philosophy and economics/ by Thomas Sowell. 1st ed. New York: Morrow, c1985. 281 p.
84-062438 335.4 19 0688029639
Philosophy, Marxist. Marxian economics.

B809.8.S8575 2001
Sullivan, Stefan,
Marx for a post-communist era: on poverty, corruption, and banality/ Stefan Sullivan. New York: Routledge, 2001.
2001-041844 335.4/092 21 0415201934
Philosophy, Marxist.

B809.82.C5 K65 1996
Knight, Nick.
Li Da and Marxist philosophy in China/ Nick Knight. Boulder, Colo.: Westview Press, 1996. x, 326 p.
96-013928 181/.11 20 0813389933
Li, Da, 1890-1966. Philosophy, Marxist -- China. Communism -- China.

B809.9 Modern (1450/1660-) — Special topics and schools of philosophy — Difference

B809.9.S54 1991
Writing the politics of difference/ edited by Hugh J. Silverman. Albany: State University of New York Press, c1991. xvi, 372 p.
90-032126 190 20 0791404986
Difference (Philosophy) Philosophy, Modern - - 19th century. Philosophy, Modern -- 20th century. Philosophy, European. Existentialism. Phenomenology.

B812 Modern (1450/1660-) — Special topics and schools of philosophy — Dualism

B812.H37 1988
Hart, W. D. 1943-
The engines of the soul/ W.D. Hart. Cambridge; Cambridge University Press, 1988. xi, 190 p.
87-032648 128/.2 0521342902
Dualism. Mind and body. Causation.

B812.P77 1999
Prokhovnik, Raia.
Rational woman: a feminist critique of dichotomy/ Raia Prokhovnik. London; Routledge, 1999. x, 197 p.
98-047963 305.4/01 0415146186
Dualism. Reason. Emotion.

B815 Modern (1450/1660-) — Special topics and schools of philosophy — Emotions

B815.D4 1987
De Sousa, Ronald.
The rationality of emotion/ Ronald de Sousa. Cambridge, Mass.: MIT Press, c1987. xix, 373 p.
87-007761 128/.3 0262040921
Emotions. Rationalism. Objectivity.

B815.G67 1987
Gordon, Robert M.
The structure of emotions: investigations in cognitive philosophy/ Robert M. Gordon. Cambridge [Cambridgeshire]; Cambridge University Press, 1987. xiv, 161 p.
86-028397 152.4 0521331641
Emotions.

B816 Modern (1450/1660-) — Special topics and schools of philosophy — Empiricism (Associationalism)

B816.E53 1997
Encyclopedia of empiricism/ edited by Don Garrett and Edward Barbanell. Westport, Conn.: Greenwood Press, 1997. xvii, 455 p.
96-050212　146/.44/03　0313289328
Empiricism -- Encyclopedias.

B816.V36 2002
Van Fraassen, Bas C.,
The empirical stance/ Bas C. van Fraassen. New Haven, CT: Yale University Press, c2002. xix, 282 p.
2001-046649　146/.44 21　0300088744
Empiricism.

B818 Modern (1450/1660-) — Special topics and schools of philosophy — Evolution. Holism

B818.E82 1998
Evolution: society, science, and the universe/ edited by A.C. Fabian. Cambridge, U.K.; Cambridge University Press, 1998. v, 177 p.
97-023260　116　0521572088
Evolution.

B818.F66 1992
Fodor, Jerry A.
Holism: a shopper's guide/ Jerry Fodor and Ernest Lepore. Oxford; Blackwell, 1992. xiv, 274 p.
91-029538　149　063118192X
Holism. Meaning (Philosophy)

B818.R32 1990
Rachels, James, 1941-
Created from animals: the moral implications of Darwinism/ James Rachels. Oxford [England]; Oxford University Press, 1990. 245 p.
89-038670　171/.7　0192177753
Evolution -- Moral and ethical aspects.

B818.W95 1996
Wyller, Arne A.
The planetary mind/ Arne A. Wyller. Aspen, Colo.: MacMurray & Beck, c1996. 268 p.
95-018014　213　1878448641
Evolution. Philosophy of mind. Philosophy of nature.

B819 Modern (1450/1660-) — Special topics and schools of philosophy — Existential phenomenology

B819.C62 1990
Cooper, David Edward.
Existentialism: a reconstruction/ David E. Cooper. Oxford, UK; Blackwell, 1990. ix, 201 p.
89-018534　142/.78　0631161910
Existentialism.

B819.D455 1999
Dictionary of existentialism/ edited by Haim Gordon. Westport, Conn.: Greenwood Press, 1999. xii, 539 p.
98-030495　142/.78/03 21　0313274045
Existentialism -- Dictionaries.

B819.E86 1990
Raymond, Diane Christine,
Existentialism and the philosophical tradition/ Diane Barsoum Raymond. Englewood Cliffs, N.J.: Prentice Hall, c1991. xiii, 512 p.
90-033746　142/.78 20　0132957752
Existentialism.

B819.E865 1995
Existentialism: basic writings/ edited, with introductions, by Charles Guignon and Derk Pereboom. Indianapolis: Hackett, c1995. xxxviii, 340 p.
94-048670　142/.78 20　0872202143
Existentialism.

B819.E87 1980z
Existentialism: from Dostoevsky to Sartre/ edited, with an introduction, prefaces, and new translations by Walter Kaufmann. Rev. and expanded. New York: New American Library, [198-], c1975. 384 p.
88-039280　142/.78 19　0452009308
Existentialism. Existentialism in literature.

B819.G67
Greene, Maxine,
Existential encounters for teachers. New York, Random House [1967] xiii, 174 p.
67-013103　142/.7
Existentialism -- Addresses, essays, lectures.

B819.G68 1959
Grene, Marjorie Glicksman,
Introduction to existentialism. [Chicago] University of Chicago Press [1959] 149 p.
59-001934　111.1
Sartre, Jean Paul, 1905- Heidegger, Martin, 1889-1976. Kierkegaard, Søren, 1813-1855. Marcel, Gabriel, 1889-1973. Jaspers, Karl, 1883-1969. Existentialism.

B819.K32
Kaufmann, Walter Arnold.
Existentialism, religion, and death: thirteen essays/ by Walter Kaufmann. New York: New American Library, c1976. xix, 248 p.
76-018417　142/.7
Existentialism. Death. Jews -- Identity.

B819.M39 1992
McLachlan, James M.,
The desire to be God: freedom and the other in Sartre and Berdyaev/ James M. McLachlan. New York: P. Lang, c1992. x, 215 p.
91-031770　142/.78 20　0820417114
Sartre, Jean Paul, 1905- Berdëiìaev, Nikolaæi, 1874-1948. Existentialism. Liberty.

B819.R35
Read, Herbert Edward, 1893-1968.
Existentialism, Marxism, and anarchism; chains of freedom. London, Freedom Press [1949] 56 p.
50-037395
Sartre, Jean Paul, -- 1905-Liberty. Dialectic (Economics) Existentialism.

B819.R57
Roberts, David Everett, 1911-1955.
Existentialism and religious belief. Roger Hazelton, editor. New York, Oxford University Press, 1957. 344 p.
57-005176　111
Christianity -- Philosophy. Existentialism.

B819.S32
Sartre, Jean Paul, 1905-
Existentialism and humanism; translation and introduction by Philip Mairet. London, Methuen [1948] 70 p.
49-000061　111
Existentialism.

B819.S37
Schrag, Calvin O.
Existence and freedom; towards an ontology of human finitude. [Evanston, Ill.] Northwestern University Press [1961] 250 p.
61-014317
Existentialism.

B819.W3313
Wahl, Jean André,
Philosophies of existence: an introduction to the basic thought of Kierkegaard, Heidegger, Jaspers, Marcel, Sartre, by Jean Wahl; translated from the French by F. M. Lory. London, Routledge & K. Paul, 1969. vii, 126 p.
73-381259　142/.7　071006229X
Existentialism. Ontology.

B819.W5
Wild, John Daniel, 1902-1972.
The challenge of existentialism. Bloomington, Indiana University Press, 1955. vii, 297 p.
55-006272　142/.7
Existentialism.

B820-820.3 Modern (1450/1660-   ) — Special topics and schools of philosophy — General semantics

B820.H3
Hayakawa, S. I. 1906-
Symbol, status, and personality. New York, Harcourt, Brace & World [1963] vii, 188 p.
63-017772   149.94
General semantics.

B820.P58 1984
Pollock, John L.
The foundations of philosophical semantics/ John L. Pollock. Princeton, N.J.: Princeton University Press, c1984. x, 240 p.
83-043088   149/.946 19   0691072833
Semantics (Philosophy)

B820.R4 1971
Rapoport, Anatol, 1911-
Science and the goals of man; a study in semantic orientation. Foreword by S. I. Hayakawa. Westport, Conn., Greenwood Press [1971, c1950] xxxii, 262 p.
70-138126   149/.94   0837141427
General semantics.

B820.3.G37 1988
Gärdenfors, Peter.
Knowledge in flux: modeling the dynamics of epistemic states/ Peter Gärdenfors. Cambridge, Mass.: MIT Press, c1988. xi, 262 p.
87-031505   121/.6 19   0262071096
Epistemics. Knowledge, Theory of.

B821 Modern (1450/1660-   ) — Special topics and schools of philosophy — Humanism. Neo-humanism

B821.A36 1991
African-American humanism: an anthology/ edited by Norm R. Allen, Jr. Buffalo, N.Y.: Prometheus Books, 1991. 286 p.
91-003642   144/.08996073 20   0879756586
Humanism. Humanists. African Americans.

B821.A425 1991
Adams, E. M. 1919-
The metaphysics of self and world: toward a humanistic philosophy/ E.M. Adams. Philadelphia: Temple University Press, 1991. xv, 325 p.
90-039479   144   0877227845
Humanism. Metaphysics. Humanities.

B821.E35
Ehrenfeld, David W.
The arrogance of humanism/ David Ehrenfeld. New York: Oxford University Press, 1978. ix, 286 p.
78-001664   144   019502415X
Humanism -- 20th century.

B821.J627
Jones, Howard Mumford, 1892-
American humanism: its meaning for world survival. New York, Harper [1957] 108 p.
57-009586   144
Humanism.

B821.L3 1949a
Lamont, Corliss, 1902-
Humanism as a philosophy. New York, Philosophical Library [1949] 368 p.
49-007777
Humanism.

B821.S3 1912
Schiller, F. C. S. 1864-1937.
Humanism; philosophical essays, by F. C. S. Schiller. London, Macmillan and co., limited, 1903. xxxii, 297 p.
13-035193   144
Philosophy. Humanism. Humanism.

B822 Modern (1450/1660-) — Special topics and schools of philosophy — Idea

B822.B48 1999
Bevir, Mark.
The logic of the history of ideas/ Mark Bevir. Cambridge, U.K.; Cambridge University Press, c1999. xii, 337 p.
98-038079   190 21   0521640342
Idea (Philosophy) -- History.

B823 Modern (1450/1660-   ) — Special topics and schools of philosophy — Idealism. Transcendentalism

B823.E8 1974
Ewing, A. C. 1899-
Idealism: a critical survey/ by A. C. Ewing. London: Methuen; 1974. viii, 454 p.
74-193281   141   0064720284
Idealism.

B823.P55 1997
Pippin, Robert B.,
Idealism as modernism: Hegelian variations/ Robert B. Pippin. Cambridge; Cambridge University Press, 1997. xiii, 466 p.
96-008627   190 20   0521568730
Hegel, Georg Wilhelm Friedrich, 1770-1831. Idealism. Philosophy, Modern.

B823.T69 1997
Transcendental philosophy and everyday experience/ edited by Tom Rockmore and Vladimir Zeman. Atlantic Highlands, N.J.: Humanities Press, 1997. viii, 192 p.
96-037869   141/.3 21   0391040243
Transcendentalism.

B823.3-823.5 Modern (1450/1660-   ) — Special topics and schools of philosophy — Idealogy

B823.3.B25 1998
Balkin, J. M.
Cultural software: a theory of ideology/ J.M. Balkin. New Haven: Yale University Press, c1998. xii, 335 p.
97-037011   140   0300072880
Ideology. Culture. Social values.

B823.3.I285 1988
Ideological dilemmas: a social psychology of everyday thinking/ Michael Billig ... [et al.]. London; Sage Publications, 1988. 180 p.
88-061484   145   0803980957
Ideology. Thought and thinking. Social psychology.

B823.3.K613 1999
Kofman, Sarah.
Camera obscura: of ideology/ Sarah Kofman; translated by Will Straw. Ithaca, N.Y.: Cornell University Press, 1999. 100 p.
98-039015   140   0801436419
Ideology -- History.

B823.3.S56 1997
Sire, James W.
The universe next door: a basic worldview catalog/ James W. Sire. 3rd ed. Downers Grove, Ill: InterVarsity Press, c1997. 237 p.
97-010670   140 21   0830818995
Ideology. Theism. Naturalism. Nihilism (Philosophy) New Age movement.

B823.5.D78
Drucker, H. M.
The political uses of ideology [by] H. M. Drucker. [London] Macmillan: [1974] xiii, 170 p.
74-164485   301.5/92   0333154819
Marx, Karl, -- 1818-1883.Ideology. Political sociology.

B824 Modern (1450/1660-   ) — Special topics and schools of philosophy — Individualism

B824.B76 1996
Brown, R. Philip.
Authentic individualism: a guide for reclaiming the best of America's heritage/ R. Philip Brown. Lanham, Md.: University Press of America, c1996. xxii, 240 p.
95-039964   141/.4/0973 20   0761801529
Individualism. United States -- Civilization -- Philosophy.

B824.D4 1976
Devane, Richard S.
The failure of individualism: a documented essay/ by R. S. Devane. Westport, Conn.: Greenwood Press, 1976. xvii, 342 p.
75-028664 141/.4 0837184843
Individualism.

B824.E2 1964c
The status of the individual in East and West. Edited by Charles A. Moore with the assistance of Aldyth V. Morris. Honolulu, University of Hawaii Press, 1968. xxi, 606 p.
67-014717 141/.4
Individualism -- Addresses, essays, lectures.

B824.6 Modern (1450/1660-   ) — Special topics and schools of philosophy — Logical positivism

B824.6.B398
Bergmann, Gustav, 1906-
Meaning and existence. Madison, University of Wisconsin Press, 1960 [c1959] 274 p.
60-005036 111.1
Analysis (Philosophy) Logical positivism.

B824.6.F45
Ferre,
Language, logic, and God/ Frederick Ferre. -- New York: Harper, 1969. 184 p.
61-005259 149.94
Language and languages -- Philosophy. Theology. Logical positivism.

B824.6.L4
The Legacy of logical positivism; studies in the philosophy of science. Edited by Peter Achinstein and Stephen F. Barker. Baltimore, Johns Hopkins Press [1969] x, 300 p.
69-015396 146/.4 0801810140
Logical positivism -- Addresses, essays, lectures. Science -- Philosophy -- Addresses, essays, lectures.

B824.6.L6225 2003
Logical empiricism: historical & contemporary perspectives/ edited by Paolo Parrini, Wesley C. Salmon, Merrilee H. Salmon. Pittsburgh: University of Pittsburgh Press, c2003. ix, 396 p.
2002-155566 146/.42 21 0822941945
Logical positivism.

B825 Modern (1450/1660-   ) — Special topics and schools of philosophy — Materialism

B825.O24 1993
Objections to physicalism/ edited by Howard Robinson. Oxford: Clarendon Press; 1993. vi, 326 p.
92-028443 146/.3 0198242565
Materialism.

B828 Modern (1450/1660-   ) — Special topics and schools of philosophy — Mysticism

B828.C46 1989
Chapman, Tobias.
In defense of mystical ideas: support for mystical beliefs from a purely theoretical viewpoint/ Tobias Chapman. Lewiston, NY: E. Mellen Press, c1989. 115 p.
88-032655 210 0889463409
Mysticism. Meaning (Philosophy)

B828.2 Modern (1450/1660-   ) — Special topics and schools of philosophy — Naturalism

B828.2.B44 1998
Bhaskar, Roy,
The possibility of naturalism: a philosophical critique of the contemporary human sciences/ Roy Bhaskar. 3rd ed. London; Routledge, 1998. x, 194 p.
98-035442 149/.2 21 0415198747
Naturalism. Science -- Philosophy. Social sciences -- Philosophy.

B828.2.D4 1960
Dennes, William Ray, 1898-1982.
Some dilemmas of naturalism. New York, Columbia University Press, 1960. 151 p.
60-006029 146
Naturalism.

B828.2.N37 1993
Naturalism: a critical appraisal/ Steven J. Wagner and Richard Warner, editors. Notre Dame, Ind.: University of Notre Dame Press, c1993. 342 p.
91-051119 146 0268014728
Naturalism.

B828.2.R66 2000
Rosenberg, Alexander, 1946-
Darwinism in philosophy, social science, and policy/ Alexander Rosenberg. Cambridge; Cambridge University Press, 2000. ix, 257 p.
99-038044 146 0521662974
Naturalism. Social Darwinism.

B828.3 Modern (1450/1660-   ) — Special topics and schools of philosophy — Nihilism

B828.3.C76 1988
Crosby, Donald A.
The specter of the absurd: sources and criticisms of modern nihilism/ by Donald A. Crosby. Albany: State University of New York Press, c1988. viii, 456 p.
87-020917 149/.8 0887067190
Nihilism (Philosophy)

B828.3.G55 1995
Gillespie, Michael Allen.
Nihilism before Nietzsche/ Michael Allen Gillespie. Chicago: University of Chicago Press, 1995. xxiv, 311 p.
94-012205 149/.8 20 0226293475
Nietzsche, Friedrich Wilhelm, 1844-1900. Descartes, René, 1596-1650. Nihilism (Philosophy)

B828.3.L39 1988
Levin, David Michael,
The opening of vision: nihilism and the postmodern situation/ David Michael Levin. New York: Routledge, 1988. xii, 560 p.
87-020623 149/.8 19 0415004128
Nihilism (Philosophy) Civilization, Modern -- 1950-

B828.3.M27 1989
Martin, Glen T.,
From Nietzsche to Wittgenstein: the problem of truth and nihilism in the modern world/ Glen T. Martin. New York: P. Lang, c1989. xv, 401 p.
88-027200 149/.8 19 0820409170
Nietzsche, Friedrich Wilhelm, 1844-1900. Wittgenstein, Ludwig, 1889-1951. Nihilism (Philosophy) Truth. Philosophy, Modern -- 19th century. Philosophy, Modern -- 20th century.

B828.3.T66 1998
Toole, David, 1962-
Waiting for Godot in Sarajevo: theological reflections on nihilism, tragedy, and apocalypse/ David Toole. Boulder, Colo.: Westview Press, 1998. xix, 332 p.
98-011336 909.82 0813335035
Nihilism -- Religious aspects -- Christianity. Tragic, The -- Religious aspects -- Christianity. Christianity and politics.

B828.45 Modern (1450/1660-   ) — Special topics and schools of philosophy — Perception

B828.45.C66 1992
The Contents of experience: essays on perception/ edited by Tim Crane. Cambridge [England]; Cambridge University Press, 1992. xi, 275 p.
91-034041 121/.3 20 0521417279
Perception (Philosophy) Experience.

B828.45.F67 2000
Foster, John, 1941 May 5-
The nature of perception/ John Foster. Oxford; Oxford University Press, 2000. viii, 289 p.
00-703265 121/.34 0198237693
Perception (Philosophy)

B828.45.O55 2001
Oliver, Kelly, 1958-
Witnessing: beyond recognition/ Kelly Oliver. Minneapolis, MN: University of Minnesota Press, c2001. ix, 251 p.
00-009646 128 0816636273
Recognition (Philosophy) Perception (Philosophy) Social perception.

B828.45.P48 1988
Perceptual knowledge/ edited by Jonathan Dancy. Oxford; Oxford University Press, 1988. 226 p.
87-035216   121/.3 19   0198750749
Perception (Philosophy) Knowledge, Theory of.

B828.45.R62 1994
Robinson, Howard.
Perception/ Howard Robinson. London; Routledge, 1994. xii, 260 p.
93-049381   121/.3 20   0415033640
Perception (Philosophy)

B828.45.V565 2002
Vision and mind: selected readings in the philosophy of perception/ edited by Alva Noë and Evan Thompson. Cambridge, Mass.: MIT Press, c2002. x, 627 p.
2002-023533   121/.34 21   0262140780
Perception (Philosophy)

B828.5 Modern (1450/1660-   ) — Special topics and schools of philosophy — Personalism

B828.5.G73 1996
Grant, Patrick.
Personalism and the politics of culture: readings in literature and religion from the New Testament to the poetry of Northern Ireland/ Patrick Grant. New York: St. Martin's Press, 1996. x, 211 p.
96-011589   141/.5   031216176X
Personalism. Personalism in literature. Religion and literature.

B829.5 Modern (1450/1660-   ) — Special topics and schools of philosophy — Phenomenology

B829.5.B63 2001
Bodies of resistance: new phenomenologies of politics, agency, and culture/ edited by Laura Doyle. Evanston, Ill.: Northwestern University Press, c2001. xxxiv, 305 p.
2001-003577   142/.7 21   0810118475
Phenomenology.

B829.5.C74 1987
Critical and dialectical phenomenology/ edited by Donn Welton and Hugh J. Silverman. Albany: State University of New York Press, c1987. xxiii, 300 p.
86-030922   121   0887064744
Phenomenology.

B829.5.E53 1997
Encyclopedia of phenomenology/ edited by Lester Embree ... [et al.]. Dordrecht; Kluwer Academic Publishers, c1997. xiv, 764 p.
96-051040   142/.7/03 21   0792329562
Phenomenology -- Encyclopedias. Philosophers -- Biography -- Encyclopedias.

B829.5.G6 1966
Goodman, Nelson.
The structure of appearance.   Indianapolis, Bobbs-Merrill [c1966] xix, 392 p.
65-026543   142/.7
Phenomenology. Structuralism. System theory.

B829.5.L8132
Luijpen, W. 1922-
A first introduction to Existential phenomenology. by William A. Luijpen and Henry J. Koren. Pittsburgh, Duquesne University Press [1969] 243 p.
79-075975   142/.7
Phenomenology. Existentialism.

B829.5.M647 2000
Moran, Dermot.
Introduction to phenomenology/ Dermot Moran. London; Routledge, 2000. xx, 568 p.
99-042071   142/.7   0415183723
Phenomenology.

B829.5.N38 1999
Naturalizing phenomenology: issues in contemporary phenomenology and cognitive science/ edited by Jean Petitot ... [et al.]. Stanford, Calif.: Stanford University Press, c1999. xxi, 641 p.
99-028716   142/.7 21   0804736103
Phenomenology. Cognitive science.

B829.5.P393 1972
Peursen, Cornelis Anthonie van, 1920-
Phenomenology and analytical philosophy, by Cornelis A. van Peursen. Pittsburgh, Duquesne University Press [1972] 190 p.
79-176037   142/.7   0820701394
Phenomenology. Analysis (Philosophy) Logical positivism.

B829.5.S38 1970
Schutz, Alfred,
On phenomenology and social relations; selected writings. Edited and with an introd. by Helmut R. Wagner. Chicago, University of Chicago Press [1970] vii, 327 p.
73-102072   301/.045   0226741524
Husserl, Edmund, 1859-1938. Weber, Max, 1864-1920. Phenomenology. Social psychology.

B829.5.S576 2000
Sokolowski, Robert.
Introduction to phenomenology/ Robert Sokolowski. Cambridge, UK; Cambridge University Press, 2000. ix, 238 p.
99-021499   142/.7   0521660998
Phenomenology.

B829.5.S642
Spiegelberg, Herbert.
The phenomenological movement; a historical introduction. 2d ed. The Hague, M. Nijhoff, [1965-   ]
66-004960   142.7
Phenomenology -- History.

B829.5.T4
Thevenaz,
What is phenomenology?: And other essays/ Pierre Therenaz; Edited with an introd. by James M. Edie, pref. by John Wild, translated by James M. Edie, Charles Courtney [and] Paul Brockelman. -- Chicago: Quadrangle Books, [1962] 191 p.
62-012189   142.7
Phenomenology.

B831 Modern (1450/1660-   ) — Special topics and schools of philosophy — Positivism

B831.S5
Simon, Walter Michael, 1922-
European positivism in the nineteenth century, an essay in intellectual history.   Ithaca, N.Y., Cornell University Press [1963] xi, 384 p.
63-016446   146.4
Comte, Auguste, -- 1798-1857. Positivism. Philosophy, Modern -- 19th century.

B831.2 Modern (1450/1660-   ) — Special topics and schools of philosophy — Postmodernism

B831.2.B47 1995
Bertens, Johannes Willem.
The idea of the postmodern: a history/ Hans Bertens. London; Routledge, 1995. ix, 284 p.
94-014352   149 20   0415060125
Postmodernism.

B831.2.D48 1997
Devaney, M. J., 1964-
"Since at least Plato--" and other postmodernist myths/ M.J. Devaney. New York: St. Martin's Press, 1997. ix, 245 p.
97-007781   149/.97   0312175116
Postmodernism.

B831.2.E55 1996
Elliott, Anthony.
Subject to ourselves: social theory, psychoanalysis, and postmodernity/ Anthony Elliott. Cambridge, Mass.: Polity Press, 1996.
95-053959   150.19/5   0745614221
Postmodernism. Psychoanalysis and culture.

B831.2.E63 2000
Encyclopedia of postmodernism/ edited by Charles E. Winquist and Victor E. Taylor. New York: Routledge, 2000.
00-028239   149/.97/03   0415152941
Postmodernism -- Encyclopedias.

B831.2.F56 1996
Finn, Geraldine.
Why Althusser killed his wife: essays on discourse and violence/ Geraldine Finn. Atlantic Highland, N.J.: Humanities Press, 1996. xii, 203 p.
95-008841   190/.9/04   0391039075
Postmodernism. Feminist theory.

B831.2.M46 1996
Mensch, James R.
Knowing and being: a postmodern reversal/
James Richard Mensch. University Park, Pa.:
Pennsylvania State University Press, c1996.
232 p.
95-040442　149/.9　0271015543
*Postmodernism.　Subjectivity.　Object
(Philosophy)*

B831.2.M48 1999
Meynell, Hugo Anthony.
Postmodernism and the New Enlightenment/ by
Hugo A. Meynell. Washington, D.C.: Catholic
University of America Press, 1999. xii, 198 p.
99-017999　149/.97　0813209463
Postmodernism.

B831.2.N66 1993
Norris, Christopher, 1947-
The truth about postmodernism/ Christopher
Norris. Oxford, UK; Blackwell, 1993. 333 p.
92-033828　149/.9　0631187170
*Kant,　Immanuel,　--　1724-
1804.Postmodernism.*

B831.2.N68 1992
Norris, Christopher,
Uncritical theory: postmodernism, intellectuals
& the Gulf War/ Christopher Norris. Amherst:
University of Massachusetts Press, c1992. 218 p.
92-012147　190/.9/04 20　0870238183
Postmodernism. Persian Gulf War, 1991.

B831.2.P53 1995
Picturing　cultural　values　in　postmodern
America/ edited by William G. Doty.
Tuscaloosa: University of Alabama Press,
c1995. xiii, 252 p.
94-013361　149 20　0817307338
*Postmodernism -- United States. Aesthetics,
Modern -- 20th century. Religion and culture --
United States.*

B831.2.P675 1993
Postmodernism: a reader/ edited and introduced
by Thomas Docherty. New York: Columbia
University Press, c1993. xiv, 528 p.
92-028779　190/.9/04 20　0231082215
Postmodernism.

B831.2.P683 2002
Postmodernism: the key figures/ edited by Hans
Bertens and Joseph Natoli. Malden, Mass.:
Blackwell Publishers, 2002. xvi, 384 p.
2001-043233　149/.97 21　0631217975
Postmodernism.

B831.2.S27 1993
Sarup, Madan.
An introductory guide to post-structuralism and
postmodernism/ Madan Sarup. 2nd ed. Athens:
University of Georgia Press, 1993. xii, 206 p.
93-000056　149/.96 20　0820315311
*Postmodernism.　　　　　Poststructuralism.
Philosophy, Modern -- 20th century.*

B831.2.S35 1999
Schiralli, Martin, 1947-
Constructive postmodernism: toward renewal in
cultural and literary studies/ Martin Schiralli.
Westport, Conn.: Bergin & Garvey, 1999. 163 p.
99-022081　149/.97　0897896955
*Postmodernism.　　　　　　Deconstruction.
Postmodernism (Literature)*

B831.2.V3813 1992
Vattimo, Gianni, 1936-
The transparent society/ Gianni Vattimo;
translated by David Webb. Baltimore: Johns
Hopkins University Press, 1992. v, 129 p.
92-010839　306　0801845270
Postmodernism.

B831.3 Modern (1450/1660-　) — Special topics and schools of philosophy — Practice

B831.3.M332 2001
May, Todd, 1955-
Our practices, our selves, or, What it means to
be human/ Todd May. University Park, Pa.:
Pennsylvania State University Press, c2001. x,
206 p.
00-032367　128　0271020857
*Practice　(Philosophy)　Philosophical
anthropology.*

B831.5 Modern (1450/1660-　) — Special topics and schools of philosophy — Pragmatics

B831.5.H33 1998
Habermas, Jurgen.
On the pragmatics of communication/ Jurgen
Habermas; edited by Maeve Cooke. Cambridge,
Mass.: MIT Press, c1998. viii, 454 p.
98-018171　193　0262082659
Pragmatics.

B831.5.M3
Martin, R. M. 1916-
Toward a systematic pragmatics. Amsterdam,
North-Holland Pub. Co., 1959. xv, 107 p.
60-001429　149.9
Pragmatics.

B831.5.S73 1999
Stalnaker, Robert.
Context and content: essays on intentionality in
speech and thought/ Robert C. Stalnaker.
Oxford; Oxford University Press, 1999. 283 p.
98-049339　121 21　0198237073
Pragmatics. Intentionality (Philosophy)

B832 Modern (1450/1660-　) — Special topics and schools of philosophy — Prgmatism

B832.A34 2000
The agrarian roots of pragmatism/ edited by Paul
B. Thompson and Thomas C. Hilde. Nashville:
Vanderbilt University Press, 2000. ix, 342 p.
00-008775　144/.3/0973　0826513395
*Pragmatism -- History. Agriculture --
Philosophy -- History.*

B832.B36 1997
Bauerlein, Mark.
The pragmatic mind: explorations in the
psychology of belief/ Mark Bauerlein. Durham,
NC: Duke University Press, 1997. xix, 136 p.
97-006289　144/.3/0973　0822320045
*Emerson, Ralph Waldo, -- 1803-1882. Peirce,
Charles S. -- (Charles Sanders), -- 1839-1914.
James, William, -- 1842-1910. Psychology --
United States -- Philosophy -- History.
Pragmatism -- History.*

B832.J2 1955
James, William, 1842-1910.
Pragmatism, and four essays from The meaning
of truth. New York, Meridian Books, 1955.
269 p.
55-009701　144
Pragmatism.

B832.J2 1978
James, William,
Pragmatism, a new name for some old ways of
thinking; The meaning of truth, a sequel to
Pragmatism/ William James. Cambridge, Mass.:
Harvard University Press, 1978. xxx, 369 p.
77-028535　144/.3　0674697367
Pragmatism. Truth.

B832.K6
Konvitz, Milton Ridvas, 1908-
The American pragmatists; selected writings.
Edited by Milton R. Konvitz and Gail Kennedy.
New York, Meridian Books [1960] 413 p.
60-012329　144.3
Pragmatism.

B832.M85
Muirhead, John H. 1855-1940.
The Platonic tradition in Anglo-Saxon
philosophy; studies in the history of idealism in
England and America, by John H. Muirhead ...
London, G. Allen & Unwin ltd.; [1931] 446 p.
31-010962　141
*Plato.Idealism.　　Philosophy,　English.
Philosophy, American.*

B832.R42 2000
Rescher, Nicholas.
Realistic pragmatism: an introduction to
pragmatic philosophy/ Nicholas Rescher.
Albany, N.Y.: State University of New York
Press, c2000. xiv, 254 p.
99-015030　144/.3　0791444074
Pragmatism.

B832.R45 1995
Rhetoric, sophistry, pragmatism/ edited by Steven Mailloux. Cambridge; Cambridge University Press, 1995. xii, 251 p.
94-019820   144/.3 20   0521467802
Pragmatism. Rhetoric -- Philosophy. Philosophy and social sciences.

B832.S45 1996
Seigfried, Charlene Haddock,
Pragmatism and feminism: reweaving the social fabric/ Charlene Haddock Seigfried. Chicago: University of Chicago Press, c1996. x, 342 p.
95-046879   144/.3/082 20   0226745589
James, William, 1842-1910. Dewey, John, 1859-1952. Pragmatism. Feminist theory.

B833.N48 1999
New essays on the rationalists/ edited by Rocco J. Gennaro and Charles Huenemann. New York: Oxford University Press, 1999. xvii, 391 p.
98-030454   149/.7/09032 21   019512488X
Descartes, René, 1596-1650. Spinoza, Benedictus de, 1632-1677. Leibniz, Gottfried Wilhelm, Freiherr von, 1646-1716. Rationalism -- History -- 17th century. Rationalism -- History -- 18th century.

B835 Modern (1450/1660-) — Special topics and schools of philosophy — Realism

B835.C75 1998
Critical realism: essential readings/ edited by Margaret Archer ... [et al.]. London; Routledge, 1998. xxiv, 756 p.
98-018861   149/.2   0415196310
Critical realism.

B835.D48 1991
Devitt, Michael,
Realism and truth/ Michael Devitt. 2nd ed. Oxford, UK; B. Blackwell, 1991. xii, 327 p.
91-003062   149/.2 20   0631175512
Realism. Truth. Science -- Philosophy.

B835.P88 1988
Putnam, Hilary.
Representation and reality/ Hilary Putnam. Cambridge, Mass.: MIT Press, c1988. xv, 136 p.
87-035279   128/.2 19   0262161087
Realism. Mind-brain identity theory. Functionalism (Psychology) Truth. Reference (Philosophy) Mathematics -- Philosophy. Computers.

B835.W5
Wild, John Daniel, 1902-1972.
Introduction to realistic philosophy. New York, Harper [1948] xi, 516 p.
48-009434   149.2   006047100x
Philosophy. Realism.

B837 Modern (1450/1660-) — Special topics and schools of philosophy — Scepticism (Skepticism)

B837.A55 1985
Annas, Julia.
The modes of scepticism: ancient texts and modern interpretations/ Julia Annas and Jonathan Barnes. Cambridge; Cambridge University Press, 1985. 203 p.
84-020053   186 19   0521276446
Skepticism.

B837.H55 1988
Hiley, David R.
Philosophy in question: essays on a Pyrrhonian theme/ David R. Hiley. Chicago: University of Chicago Press, 1988. ix, 207 p.
87-019986   149/.73   0226334333
Skepticism. Life. Philosophy.

B837.K87 1992
Kurtz, Paul, 1925-
The new skepticism: inquiry and reliable knowledge/ Paul Kurtz. Buffalo, N.Y.: Prometheus Books, 1992. 371 p.
92-028358   149/.73   0879757663
Skepticism.

B837.L38 1992
Laursen, John Christian.
The politics of skepticism in the ancients, Montaigne, Hume, and Kant/ by John Christian Laursen. Leiden; E.J. Brill, 1992. 253 p.
92-028512   149/.73   9004094598
Skepticism -- Political aspects. Knowledge, Theory of. Philosophy, Comparative.

B837.S566 1999
Skepticism: a contemporary reader/ edited by Keith DeRose and Ted A. Warfield. New York: Oxford University Press, 1999. v, 314 p.
98-022393   149/.73 21   0195118278
Skepticism.

B840 Modern (1450/1660-) — Special topics and schools of philosophy — Semantics. Meaning

B840.B37 1999
Barwise, Jon.
Situations and attitudes/ Jon Barwise & John Perry. Stanford, Calif.: CSLI Publications, c1999. lxxxviii, 352 p.
99-014053   121/.68 21   1575861933
Semantics (Philosophy)

B840.C6 1963
Cohen, L. Jonathan
The diversity of meaning. [New York] Herder and Herder [1963] 340 p.
62-020961   149.94
Semantics (Philosophy)

B840.H5 1998
Hi-fives: a trip to semiotics/ edited by Roberta Kevelson. New York: Peter Lang, c1998. 249 p.
98-025588   302.2   0820438421
Semiotics. Semantics (Philosophy)

B840.L4
Lehrer, Adrienne,
Theory of meaning, edited by Adrienne and Keith Lehrer. Englewood Cliffs, N.J., Prentice-Hall [1970] viii, 216 p.
72-117011   149/.94   0139145982
Semantics (Philosophy)

B840.L46
Lewis, Hywel David
Clarity is not enough; essays in criticism of linguistic philosophy. New York, Humanities Press, 1963. 447 p.
63-024283
Semantics (Philosophy) Analysis (Philosophy)

B840.M36 1958a
Martin, R. M. 1916-
Truth & denotation; a study in semantical theory. [Chicago] University of Chicago Press [1958] xii, 304 p.
57-012813
Semantics (Philosophy)

B840.M455 1990
Meaning and truth: essential readings in modern semantics/ Jay L. Garfield & Murray Kiteley [editors]. 1st ed. New York: Paragon House, 1991. xxviii, 637 p.
90-031315   121/.68 20   1557783004
Semantics (Philosophy) Meaning (Philosophy) Truth.

B840.M6 1955
Morris, Charles William, 1901-
Signs, language, and behavior. New York, G. Braziller, 1955 [c1946] xii, 365 p.
56-001550   422
Semantics (Philosophy)

B840.N64 1999
Nogales, Patti D., 1961-
Metaphorically speaking/ Patti D. Nogales. Stanford, Calif.: CSLI Publications, 1999. 241 p.
98-054375   121/.68   1575861593
Metaphor. Semantics (Philosophy) Concepts.

B840.O7
Osgood, Charles Egerton.
The measurement of meaning [by] Charles E. Osgood, George J. Suci [and] Percy H. Tannenbaum. Urbana, University of Illinois Press, 1957. 342 p.
56-005684   153.1
Semantics (Philosophy) Meaning (Psychology)

B840.Q5
Quine, W. V.
Word and object. [Cambridge] Technology Press of the Massachusetts Institute, [1960] 294 p.
60-009621　149.94
Semantics (Philosophy) Logic, Symbolic and mathematical. Language and languages -- Philosophy.

B840.S4
Searle, John R.
Speech acts: an essay in the philosophy of language [by] John R. Searle. London, Cambridge U.P., 1969. vii, 203 p.
68-024484　401　0521071844
Speech acts (Linguistics) Semantics (Philosophy)

B840.S82
Steinberg, Danny D.,
Semantics; an interdisciplinary reader in philosophy, linguistics and psychology. Edited by Danny D. Steinberg & Leon A. Jakobovits. Cambridge [Eng.] University Press, 1971. x, 603 p.
78-123675　149/.94　0521078229
Semantics (Philosophy) Semantics.

B840.T8 1970
Turbayne, Colin Murray.
The myth of metaphor. With forewords by Morse Peckham and Foster Tait, and an appendix by Rolf Eberle. Rev. ed. Columbia, University of South Carolina Press [1970] xv, 241 p.
77-119332　149/.94　0872491714
Descartes, René, 1596-1650. Newton, Isaac, Sir, 1642-1727. Semantics (Philosophy) Science -- Methodology. Metaphor.

B840.W65 1993
Wright, Crispin,
Realism, meaning, and truth/ Crispin Wright. 2nd ed. Oxford, UK; Blackwell, 1993. xvi, 509 p.
92-019114　121/.6 20　0631171185
Semantics (Philosophy) Meaning (Philosophy) Realism.

B841.4 Modern (1450/1660-) — Special topics and schools of philosophy — Structuralism

B841.4.D49 1987
Dews, Peter.
Logics of disintegration: post-structuralist thought and the claims of critical theory/ Peter Dews. London; Verso, 1987. xvii, 268 p.
87-021623　149/.96　0860918130
Poststructuralism. Frankfurt school of sociology. Philosophy, French -- 20th century.

B841.4.G37 1981
Gardner, Howard.
The quest for mind: Piaget, Lévi-Strauss, and the structuralist movement/ Howard Gardner. 2nd ed. Chicago: University of Chicago Press, 1981. xiii, 303 p.
81-011391　300/.1 19　0226283321
Piaget, Jean, 1896- Lévi-Strauss, Claude. Structuralism.

B841.4.P513
Piaget, Jean,
Structuralism. Translated and edited by Chaninah Maschler. New York, Basic Books [1970] vi, 153 p.
76-130191　149/.9　0465082386
Structuralism.

B841.4.S853
Structuralism and since: from Lévi Strauss to Derrida/ edited, with an introd., by John Sturrock. Oxford; Oxford University Press, 1979. 190 p.
79-040746　149/.9　0192891057
Structuralism -- Addresses, essays, lectures.

B841.6 Modern (1450/1660-) — Special topics and schools of philosophy — Subjectivity

B841.6.C37 1992
Cascardi, Anthony J., 1953-
The subject of modernity/ Anthony J. Cascardi. Cambridge [England]; Cambridge University Press, 1992. x, 316 p.
91-012689　126　0521412870
Subjectivity. Philosophy, Modern. Civilization, Modern.

B843 Modern (1450/1660-) — Special topics and schools of philosophy — Utilitarianism

B843.G66 1995
Goodin, Robert E.
Utilitarianism as a public philosophy/ Robert E. Goodin. Cambridge; Cambridge University press, 1995. xii, 352 p.
94-003385　171/.5 20　052146806X
Utilitarianism. Political science -- Philosophy.

B843.M23 1993
Maclean, Anne, 1947-
The elimination of morality: reflections on utilitarianism and bioethics/ Anne Maclean. London; Routledge, 1993. x, 219 p.
93-020281　171/.5　0415010810
Utilitarianism. Bioethics.

B844 Modern (1450/1660-) — Special topics and schools of philosophy — Violence

B844.H65 1989
Hoffman, Piotr.
Violence in modern philosophy/ Piotr Hoffman. Chicago: University of Chicago Press, 1989. ix, 163 p.
88-034125　128/.4　0226347958
Violence. Philosophy, Modern. Knowledge, Theory of.

B846 Modern (1450/1660-) — Special topics and schools of philosophy — Vision

B846.L48 1999
Levin, David Michael, 1939-
The philosopher's gaze: modernity in the shadows of enlightenment/ David Michael Levin. Berkeley: University of California Press, 1999. ix, 493 p.
98-043812　190　0520217802
Philosophy, Modern. Appearance (Philosophy)

B846.M63 1993
Modernity and the hegemony of vision/ edited by David Michael Levin. Berkeley: University of California Press, c1993. xii, 408 p.
93-001523　128/.3 20　0520079736
Philosophy, Modern. Vision.

B851-945 Modern (1450/1660-) — By region or country — United States

B851.A44 2002
American philosophies: an anthology/ edited by Leonard Harris, Scott L. Pratt, and Anne Waters. Malden, MA: Blackwell Publishers, 2002. viii, 456 p.
2001-035009　191 21　0631210024
Philosophy, American.

B851.A48 1978
Ames, Van Meter, 1898-
Zen and American thought/ Van Meter Ames. Westport, Conn.: Greenwood Press, [1978] c1962. viii, 293 p.
77-018523　181/.04/3927　0313200661
Philosophy, American. Religious thought -- United States. Zen Buddhism.

B851.F35 1993
Falling in love with wisdom: American philosophers talk about their calling/ edited by David D. Karnos, Robert G. Shoemaker. New York: Oxford University Press, 1993. ix, 261 p.
92-021965　191　0195072014
Philosophers -- United States. Philosophy.

B851.K85 2001
Kuklick, Bruce,
A history of philosophy in America, 1720-2000/ Bruce Kuklick. Oxford; Clarendon Press, 2001. xiii, 326 p.
2001-036594   191 21   0198250312

B851.N6
Novak, Michael.
American philosophy and the future; essays for a new generation. New York, Scribner [1968] x, 367 p.
68-027795   191
Philosophy, American

B851.R93 1999
Ryder, John, 1951-
Interpreting America: Russian and Soviet studies of the history of American thought/ John Ryder. Nashville: Vanderbilt University Press, 1999. xxxiii, 326 p.
98-058118   191   0826513344
Philosophy, American -- History.

B851.S37
Schlesinger, Arthur Meier, 1917-
Paths of American thought. Edited by Arthur M. Schlesinger, Jr. and Morton White. Boston, Houghton Mifflin, 1963. 614 p.
63-014184   191.09
Philosophy, American -- History. United States -- Intellectual life -- Addresses, essays, lectures.

B851.S48
Smith, John Edwin.
The spirit of American philosophy. New York, Oxford University Press, 1963. 219 p.
63-012553   191
Philosophy, American.

B858.T6
Townsend, Harvey Gates, 1885-
Philosophical ideas in the United States [by] Harvey Gates Townsend ... New York, American book company [c1934] v, 293 p.
34-018313   191
Philosophy, American. Philosophy -- History -- United States.

B865.R5 1958
Riley, Woodbridge, 1869-1933.
American philosophy: the early schools. New York, Russell & Russell [1958?] 595 p.
58-013298   191
Philosophy, American.

B870.A5 1972
Edwards, Jonathan,
The philosophy of Jonathan Edwards from his private notebooks. Edited   by Harvey G. Townsend. Westport, Conn., Greenwood Press [1972] xxii, 270 p.
72-007503   191   0837165113
Edwards, Jonathan, 1703-1758 -- Notebooks, sketchbooks, etc. Philosophy.

B878.B6 1993
Boorstin, Daniel J. 1914-
The lost world of Thomas Jefferson: with a new preface/ Daniel J. Boorstin. Chicago: University of Chicago Press, c1993. xiii, 306 p.
93-017196   101   0226064972
Jefferson, Thomas, -- 1743-1865.Philosophy, American -- 18th century. Philosophy, American -- 19th century. United States -- Intellectual life -- 1783-1865.

B893.R4 1964
Reck, Andrew J., 1927-
Recent American philosophy; studies of ten representative thinkers, by Andrew J. Reck. New York, Pantheon Books [1964] xxiii, 343 p.
64-013268   191.0904
Philosophy, American -- 20th century. Philosophers, American.

B893.W55 2000
Wilshire, Bruce W.
The primal roots of American philosophy: pragmatism,   phenomenology,   and   Native American thought/ Bruce Wilshire. University Park, Pa.: Pennsylvania State University Press, c2000. xi, 241 p.
99-047237   191   0271020253
Philosophy, American -- 19th century. Philosophy, American -- 20th century.

B905.B56 1996
Biographical dictionary of transcendentalism/ edited by Wesley T. Mott. Westport, Conn.: Greenwood Press, 1996. xvi, 315 p.
95-045187   810.9/384 B 20   0313288364
Transcendentalists (New England) -- Biography -- Dictionaries. Authors, American -- 19th century -- Biography -- Dictionaries. Authors, American -- Homes and haunts -- New England -- Dictionaries.

B905.E4 1842a
Ellis, Charles M. 1818-1878.
An   essay   on   transcendentalism,   1842. Gainesville, Fla., Scholars' Facsimiles & Reprints, 1954.
54-010045
Transcendentalism (New England)

B905.M5
Miller, Perry, 1905-1963.
The   transcendentalists,   an   anthology. Cambridge, Harvard University Press, 1950. xvii, 521 p.
50-007360   141
Transcendentalism (New England)

B905.P6 1970
Pochmann, Henry A.
New England transcendentalism and St. Louis Hegelianism; phases in the history of American idealism, by Henry A. Pochmann. New York, Haskell House, 1970. 144 p.
68-055163   141   0838306101
Alcott,   Amos   Bronson,   1799-1888. Brokmeyer,   Henry   Conrad,   1826-1906. Emerson,   Ralph   Waldo,   1803-1882   -- Philosophy. Harris, William Torrey, 1835-1909. Hegel, Georg Wilhelm Friedrich, 1770-1831. Transcendentalism (New England) Philosophy -- Missouri -- Saint Louis -- History.

B905.S65 1988
The   Spirituality   of   the   American transcendentalists: selected   writings of Ralph Waldo   Emerson,   Amos   Bronson   Alcott, Theodore Parker, and   Henry David Thoreau/ edited with introductions and notes by Catherine L.   Albanese. Macon, Ga.: Mercer University Press, c1988. viii, 360 p.
87-034730   810/.8/0382 19   0865542589
Transcendentalism   (New   England) Spirituality.

B905.V47 1993
Versluis, Arthur, 1959-
American   transcendentalism   and   Asian religions/ Arthur Versluis. New York: Oxford University Press, 1993. viii, 355 p.
92-024770   303.48/27305   0195076583
Transcendentalism (New England)Asia -- Religion -- Influence.

B921.J24 H23 1994
Habegger, Alfred.
The father: a life of Henry James, Sr./ Alfred Habegger. 1st ed. New York: Farrar, Straus, and Giroux, 1994. viii, 578 p.
93-041823   191 B 20   0374153833
James,   Henry,   1811-1882. James family. Intellectuals -- United States -- Biography. Religious thought -- United States -- 19th century.

B921.J24.W3
Warren, Austin, 1899-
The elder Henry James.   New York, The Macmillan company, 1934. xvi, 269 p.
34-010686   921.1
James, Henry, -- 1811-1882.

B931.T44 B46 1994
Bennett, Jane,
Thoreau's nature: ethics, politics, and the wild/ Jane Bennett. Thousand Oaks, Calif.: Sage Publications, c1994. xxvii, 141 p.
94-029570   818/.309 20   0803938691
Thoreau,   Henry   David,   1817-1862   -- Knowledge -- Natural history. Thoreau, Henry David, 1817-1862 -- Political and social views. Thoreau, Henry David, 1817-1862 -- Ethics.

B931.T44 H37
Harding, Walter Roy,
Henry David Thoreau; a profile. Edited by
Walter Harding. [1st ed.] New York, Hill and
Wang [1971] xxiii, 260 p.
74-163577 818/.3/09 B 0809093515
　Thoreau, Henry David, 1817-1862 --
Philosophy.

B934.F7
Frankel, Charles, 1917-
The golden age of American philosophy. New
York, G. Braziller, c1960. 534 p.
60-005612 191.082
　Philosophy, American.

B934.K8 1966
Kurtz, Paul, 1925-
American philosophy in the twentieth century; a
sourcebook from pragmatism to philosophical
analysis, edited, with an introductory survey,
notes, and bibliographies, by Paul Kurtz. New
York, Macmillan [1966] 573 p.
65-024107 191.08
　Philosophy, American -- 20th century.

B935.D5
Directory of American philosophers. Bowling
Green, Ohio: Philosophy Documentation Center,
[1963-]
62-004947
　Philosophers -- United States -- Directories.
Philosophy -- Directories.

B935.K84
Kuklick, Bruce,
The rise of American philosophy, Cambridge,
Massachusetts, 1860-1930/ Bruce Kuklick. New
Haven: Yale University Press, 1977. xxvii,
674 p.
76-049912 191 0300020392
　Philosophy, American -- 19th century.
Philosophy, American -- 20th century.

B935.P66 1999
Portraits of American continental philosophers/
edited with photographs by James R. Watson/
Bloomington, Ind.: Indiana University Press,
1999. viii, 228 p.
99-035079 191 0253335930
　Philosophers -- United States. Philosophy,
European.

B935.T45 1996
Tejera, V.
American modern: the path not taken: aesthetics,
metaphysics, and intellectual history in classic
American philosophy/ Victorino Tejera.
Lanham, Md.: Rowman & Littlefield, c1996. ix,
223 p.
96-009045 191 0847683095
　Peirce, C. H. -- (Charles Henry), -- 1814-
1855. Dewey, John, -- 1859-1952. Santayana,
George, -- 1863-1952. Philosophy, American --
20th century. Philosophy, American -- 19th
century.

B936.E85 1997
Existence in Black: an anthology of Black
existential philosophy/ edited and with an
introduction by Lewis R. Gordon. New York:
Routledge, 1997. xviii, 328 p.
96-024896 191/.089/96073 20 0415914507
　Afro-American philosophy. Existentialism.
Liberty -- Philosophy.

B936.W55 2000
McCumber, John.
Time in the ditch: American philosophy and the
McCarthy era/ John McCumber. Evanston, Ill.:
Northwestern University Press, c2001. xxiii,
213 p.
00-010668 191 0810118092
　McCarthy, Joseph, -- 1908-1957 --
Influence.Philosophy, American -- 20th century.

B944.A37.A37 1998
African-American philosophers: 17
conversations/ edited by George Yancy. New
York: Routledge, 1998. x, 358 p.
98-015201 191/.089/96073 041592099X
　Afro-American philosophy. Afro-American
philosophers -- Interviews. Philosophers --
United States -- Interviews.

B944.A37.G67 2000
Gordon, Lewis R. 1962-
Existentia Africana: understanding Africana
existential thought/ Lewis R. Gordon. New
York: Routledge, 2000. xii, 228 p.
99-047909 142/.78/08996 0415926432
　Afro-American philosophy. Existentialism.

B944.E94 F85 1999
Fulton, Ann.
Apostles of Sartre: existentialism in America,
1945-1963/ Ann Fulton. Evanston, Ill.:
Northwestern University Press, 1999. vii, 170 p.
99-018175 142/.78/0973 21 0810112906
　Sartre, Jean Paul, 1905- -- Influence.
Existentialism -- United States -- History -- 20th
century. Philosophy, American -- 20th century.

B944.P67.L38 1999
Lawler, Peter Augustine.
Postmodernism rightly understood: the return to
realism in American thought/ Peter Augustine
Lawler. Lanham, Md.: Rowman & Littlefield,
1999. vii, 195 p.
99-013633 149/.97 0847694259
　Postmodernism -- United States. Philosophy,
American -- 20th century. United States --
Intellectual lifle -- 20th century.

B944.P72.R68 1998
Roth, Robert J.
Radical pragmatism: an alternative/ by Robert J.
Roth. New York: Fordham University Press,
1998. xviii, 168 p.
98-037297 144/.3 0823218511
　Teilhard de Chardin, Pierre.Philosophy and
religion. Pragmatism.

B944.P72.W47 1989
West, Cornel.
The American evasion of philosophy: a
genealogy of pragmatism/ Cornel West.
Madison, Wis.: University of Wisconsin Press,
c1989. 279 p.
88-040446 144/.3/0973 0299119602
　Pragmatism -- History. Philosophy, American
-- History.

B945.A2864.A35
Adler, Mortimer Jerome, 1902-
Philosopher at large: an intellectual
autobiography/ by Mortimer J. Adler. New
York: Macmillan, c1977. xii, 349 p.
77-001383 191 0025004905
　Adler, Mortimer Jerome, -- 1902-
Philosophers -- United States -- Biography.

B945.B473.N48 1991
Bergmann, Gustav, 1906-
New foundations of ontology/ Gustav
Bergmann; edited by William Heald; foreword
by Edwin B. Allaire. Madison, Wis.: University
of Wisconsin Press, c1992. xx, 372 p.
91-031693 111 0299131300
　Ontology.

B945.B773 P4 1984
Burke, Kenneth,
Permanence and change: an anatomy of purpose/
Kenneth Burke. 3rd ed., with a new afterword.
Berkeley: University of California Press, [1984],
c1954. lix, 336 p.
83-018021 191 19 0520041461
　Ethics, Evolutionary. Motivation (Psychology)
Change.

B945.B774 B94 1993
Bygrave, Stephen,
Kenneth Burke: rhetoric and ideology/ Stephen
Bygrave. London; Routledge, 1993. xii, 123 p.
92-028019 191 20 0415022118
　Burke, Kenneth, 1897- Rhetoric --
Philosophy. Ideology.

B945.C163.L6336 1998
Richardson, Alan W.
Carnap's construction of the world: the Aufbau
and the emergence of logical empiricism/ Alan
W. Richardson. Cambridge, U.K.; Cambridge
University Press, 1998. x, 242 p.
97-008814 121 0521430089
　Carnap, Rudolf, -- 1891-1970. -- Logische
Aufbau der Welt.Knowledge, Theory of --
History -- 20th century. Logical positivism --
History -- 20th century.

B945.C164 M39 2002
Mayhall, C. Wayne.
On Carnap/ C. Wayne Mayhall. Australia;
Wadsworth/Thomson Learning, c2002. 99 p.
2002-282317 0534604714
　Carnap, Rudolf, 1891-1970. Logical
positivism. Science -- Philosophy.

B945.C271 2002
Cavell, Stanley,
Must we mean what we say?: a book of essays/
Stanley Cavell. Updated ed. Cambridge, UK;
Cambridge University Press, 2002. xlii, 365 p.
2002-071642   190 21   0521529190
Philosophy, Modern.

B945.C273.P58 1994
Cavell, Stanley, 1926-
A pitch of philosophy: autobiographical
exercises/ Stanley Cavell. Cambridge, Mass.:
Harvard University Press, 1994. xv, 196 p.
93-047642   191   0674669800
*Cavell, Stanley, -- 1926-Philosophy,
American. Philosophy.*

B945.C274.G68 1998
Gould, Timothy.
Hearing things: voice and method in the writing
of Stanley Cavell/ Timothy Gould. Chicago:
University of Chicago Press, c1998. xxii, 230 p.
98-023109   191   0226305627
*Cavell, Stanley, -- 1926-Language and
languages -- Philosophy. Methodology.*

B945.C53F3 1970
Cohen, Morris Raphael, 1880-1947.
The faith of a liberal; selected essays. Freeport,
N.Y., Books for Libraries Press [1970, c1946]
ix, 497 p.
76-111820   191   0836915984
Liberalism.

B945.C54.A3 1975
Cohen, Morris Raphael, 1880-1947.
A dreamer's journey: the autobiography of
Morris Raphael Cohen. New York: Arno Press,
1955, c1949. xiii, 318 p.
74-027972   191   040506702X
*Cohen, Morris Raphael, -- 1880-1947. Cohen,
Morris Raphael, -- 1880-1947 -- Bibliography.
Philosophers -- United States -- Biography. Jews
-- United States.*

B945.C54 H64
Hollinger, David A.
Morris R. Cohen and the scientific ideal/ David
A. Hollinger. Cambridge: MIT Press, [1975] xvi,
262 p.
75-012850   191   0262080842
Cohen, Morris Raphael, 1880-1947.

B945.D4.B65 1998
Boisvert, Raymond D.
John Dewey: rethinking our time/ Raymond D.
Boisvert. Albany, N.Y.: State University of New
York Press, c1998. xii, 189 p.
96-052291   191   0791435296
Dewey, John, -- 1859-1952.

B945.D4.C36 1995
Campbell, James, 1948-
Understanding John Dewey: nature and
cooperative intelligence/ James Campbell.
Chicago, Ill.: Open Court, c1995. xii, 310 p.
95-001492   191   0812692845
Dewey, John, -- 1859-1952.

B945.D4.J33 1998
Jackson, Philip W. 1928-
John Dewey and the lessons of art/ Philip W.
Jackson. New Haven: Yale University Press,
c1998. xvi, 204 p.
97-034861   700/.1   0300072139
*Dewey, John, -- 1859-1952 --
Aesthetics.Aesthetics, American. Aesthetics,
Modern -- 19th century. Aesthetics, Modern --
20th century.*

B945.D41.B4
Dewey, John, 1859-1952.
On experience, nature, and freedom;
representative selections. Edited, with an introd.
by Richard J. Bernstein. New York, Liberal Arts
Press [1960] 293 p.
59-015784   191

B945.D41 G68 1994
Dewey, John,
The moral writings of John Dewey/ edited by
James Gouinlock. Rev. ed. Amherst, N.Y.:
Prometheus Books, c1994. liv, 282 p.
94-004482   171/.2 20   0879758821
Ethics.

B945.D41.H53 1998
Dewey, John, 1859-1952.
The essential Dewey/ edited by Larry A.
Hickman and Thomas M. Alexander.
Bloomington: Indiana University Press, c1998.
2 v.
97-043936   191   0253333903
Philosophy.

B945.D41 1967
Dewey, John, 1859-1952.
The early works, 1882-1898. Carbondale,
Southern Illinois University Press [1967-72. v.]
5 v.
67-013938   150   0809304961
Philosophy. Ethics.

B945.D41 1976
Dewey, John, 1859-1952.
The middle works, 1899-1924/ John Dewey;
edited by Jo Ann Boydston; with an introd. by
Joe R. Burnett ... [et al.]. Carbondale: Southern
Illinois University Press, c1976-c1983. 15 v.
76-007231   370.1/092/4   0809307537
Education -- Philosophy. Philosophy.

B945.D41 1981
Dewey, John, 1859-1952.
The later works, 1925-1953/ John Dewey; edited
by Jo Ann Boydston, associate textual editors,
Patricia Baysinger, Barbara Levine; with an
introd. by Sidney Hook, with a new introd. by
John Dewey, edited by Joseph Ratner.
Carbondale: Southern Illinois University Press;
c1981-c1990. 17 v.
80-027285   191   0809309866
Philosophy.

B945.D43.I5
Dewey, John, 1859-1952.
The influence of Darwin on philosophy, and
other essays in contemporary thought, by John
Dewey. New York, P. Smith, 1951 [c1910] vi,
309 p.
52-009803
Evolution. Philosophy.

B945.D43.P5
Dewey, John, 1859-1952.
Philosophy and civilization, by John Dewey.
New York, Minton, Balch & Company, 1931.
vii, 334 p.
31-028147   191.9
Philosophy. Civilization.

B945.D43 P7 1975
Dewey, John, 1859-1952.
Philosophy of education (Problems of men).
Totowa, N.J., Littlefield, Adams c1946. 311 p.
56-013732   0822601265
Philosophy. Education.

B945.D44.A43
Dewey, John, 1859-1952.
John Dewey and Arthur F. Bentley: a
philosophical correspondence, 1932-1951.
Selected and edited by Sidney Ratner and Jules
Altman, with James E. Wheeler as associated
editor. With an introd. by Sidney Ratner. New
Brunswick, N.J., Rutgers University Press
[1964] vii, 737 p.
64-017674   191.082

B945.D44.B65 1988
Boisvert, Raymond D.
Dewey's metaphysics/ Raymond D. Boisvert.
New York: Fordham University Press, 1988. xii,
227 p.
88-080074   110/.92   0823211967
*Dewey, John, -- 1859-1952.Metaphysics --
History -- 20th century.*

B945.D44 D495 1999
Dewey reconfigured: essays on Deweyan
pragmatism/ edited by Casey Haskins and
David I. Seiple. Albany, N.Y.: State University
of New York Press, c1999. xvi, 254 p.
99-013704   191 21   0791443205
Dewey, John, 1859-1952. Pragmatism.

B945.D44.E43 1998
Eldridge, Michael.
Transforming experience: John Dewey's cultural
instrumentalism/ Michael Eldridge. Nashville:
Vanderbilt University Press, 1998. xii, 236 p.
97-045427   191   0826513190
*Dewey, John, -- 1859-1952.Instrumentalism
(Philosophy)*

B945.D44.G4
Geiger, George Raymond, 1903-
John Dewey in perspective. New York, Oxford
University Press, 1958. 248 p.
58-009463
Dewey, John, -- 1859-1952.

B945.D44.H47 1971
Hook, Sidney, 1902-
John Dewey, an intellectual portrait. New York, The John Day Co., [c1939] ix, 242 p.
39-027986   191   0837139511
Dewey, John, -- 1859-1952.

B945.D44.P5
The Philosopher of the common man; essays in honor of John Dewey to celebrate his eightieth birthday. New York, G. P. Putnam's Sons [c1940] 228 p.
40-008301   191.9
Dewey, John, -- 1859-1952 -- cn

B945.D44.R43 1998
Reading Dewey: interpretations for a postmodern generation/ edited by Larry A. Hickman. Bloomington: Indiana University Press, c1998. xxi, 271 p.
97-040911   191   0253333849
Dewey, John, -- 1859-1952.

B945.D44.R6 1963
Roth, Robert J.
John Dewey and self-realization. Englewood Cliffs, N.J., Prentice-Hall [1963,c1962] 152 p.
63-013272   171.3
Dewey, John, -- 1850-1952.Self-realization.

B945.E33.P5
Edman, Irwin, 1896-1954.
Philosopher's quest [by] Irwin Edman. New York, The Viking Press, 1947. 275 p.
47-001408   191.9
Philosophy.

B945.F24.A36 1983
Feibleman, James Kern, 1904-
Philosophers lead sheltered lives; a first volume of memoirs. London, Allen & Unwin [1952] 321 p.
53-002465   921.1

B945.F634 C35 2002
Cain, M. J.
Fodor: language, mind, and philosophy/ M.J. Cain. Cambridge, UK; Polity, 2002. 240 p.
2001-040618   191 21   0745624731
Fodor, Jerry A.

B945.F634.M4 1991
Meaning in mind: Fodor and his critics/ edited by Barry Loewer and Georges Rey. Oxford, UK; Blackwell, 1991. xxxvii, 343 p.
90-046105   128/.2/092   0631171037
Fodor, Jerry A.Philosophy of mind -- History -- 20th century. Content (Psychology) -- History -- 20th century. Semantics (Philosophy) -- History -- 20th century.

B945.F634 P74 2001
Preti, Consuelo.
On Fodor/ Consuelo Preti, Victor Velarde-Mayol. Belmont, CA, USA: Wadsworth/Thomson Learning, c2001. 90 p.
2001-268478   191 21   0534583652
Fodor, Jerry A.

B945.G593.L52 1991
Goldman, Alvin I., 1938-
Liaisons: philosophy meets the cognitive and social sciences/ Alvin I. Goldman. Cambridge, Mass.: MIT Press, c1992. viii, 336 p.
91-018905   120   0262071355
Philosophy and cognitive science. Knowledge, Theory of. Knowledge, Sociology of.

B945.G63.S8
Gotshalk, Dilman Walter, 1901-
Structure and reality; a study of first principles [by] D. W. Gotshalk. New York, Dial Press [c1937] xiv, 292 p.
37-031473

B945.G83.B6
Guerard, Albert Leon, 1880-1959.
Bottle in the sea [by] Albert Guerard. Cambridge, Harvard University Press, 1954. 159 p.
54-005019   194.9
Philosophy.

B945.H354.A3 1990
Hartshorne, Charles, 1897-
The darkness and the light: a philosopher reflects upon his fortunate career and those who made it possible/ Charles Hartshorne. Albany: State University of New York Press, 1990. xv, 426 p.
89-029354   191   0791403378
Hartshorne, Charles, -- 1897-Philosophers -- United States -- Biography.

B945.H354.A4 2001
Hartshorne and Brightman on God, process, and persons: the correspondence, 1922-1945/ edited by Randall E. Auxier and Mark Y.A. Davies. Nashville: Vanderbilt University Press, 2001. 184 p.
00-010467   191   082651376X
Hartshorne, Charles, -- 1897- -- Correspondence. Brightman, Edgar Sheffield, -- 1884-1953 -- Correspondence.

B945.H354.D65 1988
Dombrowski, Daniel A.
Hartshorne and the metaphysics of animal rights/ Daniel A. Dombrowski. Albany, N.Y.: State University of New York Press, c1988. 159 p.
87-016591   179/.3   0887067042
Hartshorne, Charles, -- 1897-God. Animals. Vegetarianism.

B945.H451 2001
Hempel, Carl Gustav,
The philosophy of Carl G. Hempel: studies in science, explanation, and rationality/ Carl G. Hempel; edited by James H. Fetzer. Oxford; Oxford University Press, 2001. xxxiii, 423 p.
99-087203   191 21   019514158X
Knowledge, Theory of. Science -- Philosophy.

B945.H68 1971
Hook, Sidney, 1902-
The quest for being, and other studies in naturalism and humanism. Westport, Conn., Greenwood Press [1971] 254 p.
79-139136   191   0837157528
Philosophy, Modern -- Addresses, essays, lectures.

B945.J21.P4 1962
James, William, 1842-1910.
Essays on faith and morals. Selected by Ralph Barton Perry. Cleveland, World Pub. Co. [1962] ix, 341 p.
62-010170   191
Ethics.

B945.J21.P87 1997
The Cambridge companion to William James/ edited by Ruth Anna Putnam. Cambridge; Cambridge University Press, 1997. xii, 406 p.
96-029099   191   0521452783
James, William, -- 1842-1910.

B945.J21 1984
James, William,
William James: the essential writings/ [edited by] Bruce W. Wilshire; with a preface by James M. Edie. Albany: State University of New York Press, c1984. lxv, 369 p.
84-008848   191 19   0873959345
Philosophy.

B945.J21 2000
James, William,
Pragmatism and other writings/ William James; edited with an introduction and notes by Giles Gunn. New York: Penguin Books, 2000. xxxix, 358 p.
99-036952   191 21   0140437355
Philosophy. Pragmatism. Psychology.

B945.J23.E66
James, William, 1842-1910.
Essays in philosophy/ William James; [edited by Frederick H. Burkhardt, Fredson Bowers, Ignas K. Skrupskelis; introd. by John J. McDermott]. Cambridge, Mass.: Harvard University Press, 1978. xxxv, 410 p.
77-027361   100   0674267125
Philosophy -- Addresses, essays, lectures.

B945.J23 M47 2002
James, William,
The meaning of truth/ William James. Mineola, N.Y.: Dover Publications, 2002. xxi, 297 p.
2002-019434   144/.3 21   0486421406
Truth. Pragmatism.

B945 .J24 B39 1999
Bird, Graham,
William James/ Graham Bird. London; Routledge, 1999. vi, 221 p.
00-687930   191 21   0415203813
James, William, 1842-1910.

B945.J24B7
Brennan, Bernard P.
The ethics of William James. New York: Bookman Associates, 1961. 183 p.
61-015677
Ethics.

B945.J24.B762000
Brown, Hunter.
William James on radical empiricism and religion/ Hunter Brown. Toronto; University of Toronto Press, c2000. 185 p.
00-710300   210/.92   0802047343
James, William, -- 1842-1910 -- Contributions in philosophy of religion.Religion -- Philosophy. Empiricism. Pragmatism.

B945.J24 F67 1982
Ford, Marcus Peter,
William James's philosophy: a new perspective/ Marcus Peter Ford. Amherst: University of Massachusetts Press, c1982. x, 124 p.
81-016314   191 19   0870233661
James, William, 1842-1910.

B945.J24.G35 1999
Gale, Richard M., 1932-
The divided self of William James/ Richard M. Gale. Cambridge; Cambridge University Press, c1999. x, 364 p.
98-030477   191
James, William, -- 1842-1910.

B945.J24.O55 2001
Oliver, Phil, 1957-
William James's "Springs of delight": the return to life/ Phil Oliver. Nashville: Vanderbilt University Press, 2001. xvi, 256 p.
00-010464   191   0826513662
James, William, -- 1842-1910.Perception (Philosophy)

B945.J24.S84 1996
Suckiel, Ellen Kappy.
Heaven's champion: William James's philosophy of religion/ Ellen Kappy Suckiel. Notre Dame, Ind.: University of Notre Dame Press, c1996. xvi, 184 p.
95-050814   201   0268038147
James, William, -- 1842-1910 -- Religion.Religion -- Philosophy. Pragmatism.

B945.K393.R43 1996
Kearns, John T., 1936-
Reconceiving experience: a solution to a problem inherited from Descartes/ John T. Kearns. Albany: State University of New York Press, c1996. 474 p.
96-001082   128/.4   0791430715
Descartes, Rene, -- 1596-1650 -- Contributions in philosophy of experience.Experience. Language and logic. Language and languages -- Philosophy.

B945.K794 P74 2003
Preti, Consuelo.
On Kripke/ Consuelo Preti. [Belmont, Calif.]: Thomson/Wadsworth, c2003. 96 p.
2003-275709   0534583660
Kripke, Saul A., 1940-

B945.L273.P45
Langer, Susanne Katherina (Knauth) 1895-
Philosophical sketches. [Baltimore] Johns Hopkins Press [1962] 190 p.
62-012570   191

B945.L451G6
Lewis, Clarence Irving, 1883-1964.
Collected papers. Edited by John D. Goheen and John L. Mothershead, Jr. Stanford, Calif., Stanford University Press, 1970. x, 444 p.
73-097913   108   0804707170
Philosophy.

B945.L454.P5
The Philosophy of C. I. Lewis. Edited by Paul Arthur Schilpp. La Salle, Ill., Open Court [1968] xiv, 709 p.
67-010007   191
Lewis, Clarence Irving, -- 1883-1964 -- Addresses, essays, lectures.

B945.L583 R48 1996
Lovejoy, Arthur O.
The revolt against dualism: an inquiry concerning the existence of ideas/ Arthur O. Lovejoy; with a new introduction by Jonathan B. Imber. New Brunswick, N.J., U.S.A.: Transaction Publishers, c1996. xlv, 405 p.
95-020118   121/.4 20   1560008474
Dualism. Knowledge, Theory of. Mind and body. Idea (Philosophy)

B945.M298 1998 vol. 1
Marcuse, Herbert, 1898-
Technology, war, and fascism/ Herbert Marcuse; edited by Douglas Kellner. London; Routledge, 1998. xvi, 278 p.
97-014885   191   0415137802
Technology -- Philosophy. War (Philosophy) Fascism.

B945.M2983 S86 1972
Marcuse, Herbert,
Studies in critical philosophy; translated [from the German and French] by Joris de Bres. London, NLB, 1972. 227 p.
72-196064   146/.3   090230853X
Sartre, Jean Paul, 1905- Popper, Karl Raimund, Sir, 1902- Dialectical materialism. Authority.

B945.M461.R4
Mead, George Herbert, 1863-1931.
Selected writings. Edited, with an introd. by Andrew J. Reck. Indianapolis, Bobbs-Merrill [c1964] lxxii, 416 p.
64-016708   191
Philosophy

B945.M464 D48 2002
De Waal, Cornelis.
On Mead/ Cornelis de Waal. Australia; Wadsworth/Thomson Learning, c2002. 89 p.
2002-277592   191 21   0534583962
Mead, George Herbert, 1863-1931.

B945.M54.J6 1948a
Jones, Marc Edmund, 1888-
George Sylvester Morris: his philosophical career and theistic idealism. Philadelphia, D. McKay Co., 1948. xvi, 430 p.
49-007314
Morris, George Sylvester, -- 1840-1889.

B945.M82A3
Muller, Gustav Emil, 1898-
Instead of a biography. New York, Philosophical Library [1970] viii, 237 p.
79-097936   191   0802223214
Muller, Gustav Emil, -- 1898-

B945.N333 O74 1995
Nagel, Thomas,
Other minds: critical essays, 1969-1994/ Thomas Nagel. New York: Oxford University Press, 1995. viii, 229 p.
94-031621   128/.2 20   019509008X
Philosophy of mind. Ethics. Ethics, Modern -- 20th century. Political science -- Philosophy.

B945.N533.O6 1995
Nielsen, Kai, 1926-
On transforming philosophy: a metaphilosophical inquiry/ Kai Nielsen. Boulder, Colo.: Westview Press, 1995. xiv, 289 p.
95-019899   101   0813306663
Philosophy. Methodology.

B945.N683 S63 1997
Nozick, Robert.
Socratic puzzles/ Robert Nozick. Cambridge, Mass.: Harvard University Press, 1997. viii, 400 p.
96-039221   191 21   0674816536
Socrates. Methodology. Philosophy. Political science -- Philosophy. Ethics.

B945.N684 R63 2002
Robert Nozick/ edited by David Schmidtz. Cambridge, UK; Cambridge University Press, 2002. x, 230 p.
2001-035263   191 21   0521006716
Nozick, Robert.

B945.P43.C5 1968
Peirce, Charles S. 1839-1914.
Chance, love, and logic; philosophical essays. Edited with an introd. by Morris R. Cohen. With a supplementary essay on the pragmatism of Peirce by John Dewey. New York, Barnes & Noble [1968, c1923] xxxiii, 318 p.
68-023762   191
Pragmatism. Science -- Philosophy. Metaphysics.

B945.P44.A3 1998
Peirce, Charles S. 1839-1914.
His glassy essence: an autobiography of Charles Sanders Peirce/ Kenneth Laine Ketner. Nashville: Vanderbilt University Press, c1998. xiii, 416 p.
98-008886   181   0826513131
Peirce, Charles S. -- (Charles Sanders), -- 1839-1914.Philosophers -- United States -- Biography.

B945.P44 B74 1998
Brent, Joseph.
Charles Sanders Peirce: a life/ Joseph Brent. Rev. and enl. ed. Bloomington, Ind.: Indiana University Press, c1998. xx, 412 p.
98-023868   191 B 21   0253211611
Peirce, Charles S. (Charles Sanders), 1839-1914. Philosophers -- United States -- Biography.

B945.P44.B8 1939
Buchler, Justus, 1914-
Charles Peirce's empiricism, by Justus Buchler ... with a foreword by Professor Ernest Nagel ... New York, Harcourt, Brace and company; 1939. xvii, 275 p.
40-004294   146.44
Peirce, Charles S. -- (Charles Sanders), -- 1839-1914.

B945.P44 D434 2000
Deledalle, Gerard.
Charles S. Peirce's philosophy of signs: essays in comparative semiotics/ Gerard Deledalle. Bloomington: Indiana University Press, c2000. xii, 199 p.
00-024320   121/.68   0253337364
Peirce, Charles S. -- (Charles Sanders), -- 1839-1914.Semiotics.

B945.P44.G68 1969
Goudge, Thomas A., 1910-
The thought of C. S. Peirce [by] Thomas A. Goudge. New York, Dover Publications [1969, c1950] xii, 360 p.
72-094324   191   0486222160
Peirce, Charles S. -- (Charles Sanders), -- 1839-1914.

B945.P44 H67 2000
Hookway, Christopher.
Truth, rationality, and pragmatism: themes from Peirce/ Christopher Hookway. Oxford: Clarendon Press; vi, 313 p.
99-089742   191 21   0198238363
Peirce, Charles S. (Charles Sanders), 1839-1914.

B945.P44.M465 1997
Merrell, Floyd, 1937-
Peirce, signs, and meaning/ Floyd Merrell. Toronto; University of Toronto Press, c1997. xvii, 384 p.
97-160381   121/.68   0802041353
Peirce, Charles S. -- (Charles Sanders), -- 1839-1914.Meaning (Philosophy) -- History. Semiotics -- History.

B945.P44.S47 1994
Sheriff, John K., 1944-
Charles Peirce's guess at the riddle: grounds for human significance/ John K. Sheriff. Bloomington: Indiana University Press, c1994. xxiii, 100 p.
93-033835   191   0253352045
Peirce, Charles S. -- (Charles Sanders), -- 1839-1914.

B945.P583 S63 1997
Polanyi, Michael,
Society, economics & philosophy: selected papers/ Michael Polanyi;   edited with an introduction by R.T. Allen. New Brunswick, N.J.: Transaction Publishers, c1997. viii, 395 p.
96-042469   192 20   1560002786
Philosophy. Political science -- Philosophy. Economics -- Philosophy.

B945.Q51 1976
Quine, W. V.
The ways of paradox, and other essays/ W. V. Quine. Cambridge, Mass.: Harvard University Press, 1976. x, 335 p.
76-004200   191   0674948351
Philosophy.

B945.Q53 P87 1992
Quine, W. V.
Pursuit of truth/ W.V. Quine. Rev. ed. Cambridge, Mass.: Harvard University Press, 1992. x, 114 p.
92-005606   121 20   0674739515
Meaning (Philosophy) Reference (Philosophy) Knowledge, Theory of. Semantics (Philosophy)

B945.Q53.Q54 1987
Quine, W. V.
Quiddities: an   intermittently   philosophical dictionary/ W.V. Quine. Cambridge, Mass.: Belknap Press of Harvard University Press, 1987. 249 p.
87-011974   103/.2   0674743512
Philosophy -- Dictionaries.

B945.Q54.G5 1982
Gibson, Roger F.
The philosophy of W.V. Quine: an expository essay/ Roger F. Gibson, Jr.; with a foreword by W.V. Quine. Tampa: University Presses of Florida, c1982. xx, 218 p.
81-016338   191   0813007070
Quine, W. V. -- (Willard Van Orman)

B945.Q54 N45 2000
Nelson, Lynn Hankinson,
On Quine/ Lynn Hankinson Nelson, Jack Nelson.   Australia;   Wadsworth/Thomson Learning, c2000. 98 p.
00-700017   191 21   0534576222
Quine, W. V. (Willard Van Orman)

B945.R233 I67 1990
Rand, Ayn.
Introduction to objectivist epistemology/ Ayn Rand; with an   additonal essay by Leonard Peikoff; edited by Harry Binswanger and Leonard Peikoff. Expanded 2nd ed. New York, N.Y.: New American Library, 1990. 314 p.
89-039565   121 20   0452010306
Philosophy. Objectivism (Philosophy)

B945.R234 P44 1991
Peikoff, Leonard.
Objectivism: the philosophy of Ayn Rand/ Leonard Peikoff. New York, N.Y., U.S.A.: Dutton, c1991. xv, 493 p.
91-000638   191 20   0525933808
Rand, Ayn. Objectivism (Philosophy)

B945.R234.S35 1995
Sciabarra, Chris Matthew, 1960-
Ayn Rand: the Russian radical/ Chris Matthew Sciabarra. University Park, Pa.: Pennsylvania State University Press, c1995. xiii, 477 p.
94-034071   191   0271014407
Rand,   Ayn.Objectivism   (Philosophy) Dialectic. Philosophers -- Russia.

B945.R454 R37 1994
Rescher, Nicholas.
American   philosophy   today,   and   other philosophical   studies/   Nicholas   Rescher. Lanham, Md.: Rowman & Littlefield,c 1994. xii, 175 p.
94-016451   191 20   0847679365
Philosophy, American -- 20th century. Ethics. Philosophy.

B945.R52 1991 Vol.3
Rorty, Richard.
Truth and progress/ Richard Rorty. Cambridge; Cambridge University Press, c1998. viii, 355 p.
97-037618   191 21   0521553474
Truth. Progress. Ethics.

B945.R52 1991 vol. 1
Rorty, Richard.
Objectivity, relativism, and truth/ Richard Rorty. Cambridge; Cambridge University Press, 1991. x, 226 p.
90-041632   191 s   0521353696
Representation   (Philosophy)   Truth. Objectivity.

B945.R524.N54 1991
Nielsen, Kai, 1926-
After the demise of the tradition: Rorty, critical theory, and the fate of philosophy/ Kai Nielsen. Boulder: Westview Press, 1991. x, 278 p.
90-023123   191   0813380448
Rorty,   Richard.Methodology.   Philosophy, Modern -- 20th century. Postmodernism.

B945.R524.P73 2000
A pragmatist's progress?: Richard Rorty and American intellectual history/ edited by John Pettegrew. Lanham, Md.: Rowman & Littlefield, c2000. vii, 222 p.
99-087950 144/.3/0973 084769061X
Rorty, Richard.Pragmatism -- History -- 20th century.United States -- Intellectual life -- 20th century.

B945.R524 R673 2000
Rorty and his critics/ edited by Robert B. Brandom. Malden, Mass.: Blackwell Publishers, 2000. xx, 410 p.
99-086000 191 21 0631209824
Rorty, Richard.

B945.R524.R68 1999
Rothleder, Dianne, 1964-
The work of friendship: Rorty, his critics, and the project of solidarity/ Dianne Rothleder. Albany: State University of New York Press, c1999. xvii, 163 p.
98-008132 191 079144127X
Rorty, Richard.Friendship.

B945.R61 1988
Royce, Josiah,
Josiah Royce: selected writings/ edited by John E. Smith and William Kluback. New York: Paulist Press, c1988. x, 342 p.
88-019494 191 19 0809104105
Royce, Josiah, 1855-1916 -- Religion. Religion -- Philosophy.

B945.R63.L6
Royce, Josiah, 1855-1916.
Logical essays. Edited by Daniel S. Robinson. Dubuque, Iowa, W. C. Brown Co. [1951] xvi, 447 p.
51-008059 160.4
Logic.

B945.R63.M48 1998
Royce, Josiah, 1855-1916.
Metaphysics/ Josiah Royce; William Ernest Hocking, initial editor; co-edited by Richard Hocking and Frank Oppenheim. Albany, NY: State University of New York Press, c1998. xxi, 346 p.
97-047449 110 0791438651
Metaphysics.

B945.R63.R3 1958
Royce, Josiah, 1855-1916.
The religious aspect of philosophy: a critique of the bases of conduct and of faith. New York: Harper, [1958] 484 p.
58-005303 191.9
Philosophy and religion.

B945.R64 C54 1999
Clendenning, John,
The life and thought of Josiah Royce/ John Clendenning . Rev. and expanded ed. Nashville: Vanderbilt University Press, 1999. xvii, 446 p.
98-025325 191 B 21 0826513220
Royce, Josiah, 1855-1916. Philosophers -- United States -- Biography.

B945.R64.C6
Cotton, James Harry, 1898-
Royce on the human self. Cambridge, Harvard University Press, 1954. xiv, 347 p.
54-008622 191.9
Royce, Josiah, -- 1855-1916.

B945.R64.K44 1997
Kegley, Jacquelyn Ann K.
Genuine individuals and genuine communities: a Roycean public philosophy/ Jacquelyn Ann K. Kegley. Nashville, Tenn.: Vanderbilt University Press, 1997. x, 260 p.
96-035640 320/.092 0826512860
Royce, Josiah, -- 1855-1916 -- Political and social views.Political science -- Philosophy. Individuation (Philosophy) Community.

B945.R64 O657 1987
Oppenheim, Frank M.,
Royce's mature philosophy of religion/ Frank M. Oppenheim. Notre Dame, Ind.: University of Notre Dame Press, c1987. xviii, 403 p.
87-012458 200/.1 19 026801633X
Royce, Josiah, 1855-1916 -- Contributions in philosophy of religion. Royce, Josiah, 1855-1916. Problem of Christianity.

B945.S21 C59 1995
Santayana, George,
The birth of reason & other essays/ by George Santayana; edited by Daniel Cory. New York: Columbia University Press, [1995] xxxii, 186 p.
95-017688 191 20 0231102771
Philosophy.

B945.S21.C6
Santayana, George, 1863-1952.
The idler and his works, and other essays. Edited and with a pref. by Daniel Cory. New York, G. Braziller, 1957. ix, 209 p.
57-001165 104
Philosophy.

B945.S21 E3 1936
Santayana, George,
The philosophy of Santayana; selections from the works of George Santayana, edited, with an introductory essay, by Irwin Edman. New York, C. Scribner's sons; lvi, 587 p.
36-024974 191.9

B945.S2 1986 vol. 1
Santayana, George,
Persons and places: fragments of autobiography/ George Santayana; edited by William G. Holzberger and Herman J. Saatkamp, Jr.; with an introduction by Richard C. Lyon. Critical ed. Cambridge, Mass.: MIT Press, c1986. xl, 761 p.
86-027765 191 s 191 B 19 0262691140
Santayana, George, 1863-1952. Philosophers -- United States -- Biography.

B945.S2 1986 vol. 5
Santayana, George,
The letters of George Santayana/ G. Santayana; edited and with an introduction by William G. Holzberger. Santayana ed. Cambridge, Mass.: MIT Press, 2001-<2002 > v. <1-2 >
00-048978 191 21 0262194570
Santayana, George, 1863-1952 -- Correspondence. Philosophers -- United States -- Correspondence.

B945.S23.D5 1957
Santayana, George, 1863-1952.
Dialogues in limbo, with three new dialogues/ by George Santayana. Ann Arbor: University of Michigan Press, 1957, c1948. 248 p.
57-000687 191.9
United States -- Description and travel.

B945.S23 L7 1998
Santayana, George,
The life of reason/ George Santayana. Amherst, N.Y.: Prometheus Books, 1998.
98-015125 191 21 1573922102
Reason. Philosophy. Progress.

B945.S23.R38
Santayana, George, 1863-1952.
The realm of spirit. Book fourth of Realms of being. New York, C. Scribner's sons, 1940. xiii, 302 p.
40-027664 126
Consciousness.

B945.S23.R4
Santayana, George, 1863-1952.
The realm of truth. Book third of Realms of being, by George Santayana. London, Constable & company ltd., 1937. xiv, 142 p.
38-005347 111.83
Truth.

B945.S23.R42 1972
Santayana, George, 1863-1952.
Realms of being. New York, Cooper Square Publishers, 1972 [c1942] xxxii, 862 p.
72-079638 111 0815404255
Ontology. Matter. Truth.

B945.S24.A8
Arnett, Willard Eugene, 1921-
Santayana and the sense of beauty [by] Willard E. Arnett. Bloomington, Indiana University Press 1955 xv, 252 p.
55-008448 191.9
Santayana, George, -- 1863-1952.Aesthetics.

B945.S24 L48 1992
Levinson, Henry S.
Santayana, pragmatism, and the spiritual life/ Henry Samuel Levinson. Chapel Hill: University of North Carolina Press, c1992. xvi, 348 p.
91-050785 191 20 0807820318
Santayana, George, 1863-1952. Pragmatism. Spiritual life.

B945.S24 S56 2000
Singer, Irving.
George Santayana, literary philosopher/ Irving Singer. New Haven: Yale University Press, c2000. xiii, 217 p.
99-053686   191 21   0300080379
Santayana, George, 1863-1952.

B945.S24 S65
Sprigge, Timothy L. S.
Santayana: an examination of his philosophy [by] Timothy L. S. Sprigge. London, Routledge & K. Paul [1974] xii, 247 p.
73-091038   191   0710077211
Santayana, George, 1863-1952.

B945.S354.A4 1989
Schutz, Alfred, 1899-1959.
Philosophers in exile: the correspondence of Alfred Schutz and Aron Gurwitsch, 1939-1959/ edited by Richard Grathoff; translated by J. Claude Evans; foreword by Maurice Natanson. Bloomington: Indiana University Press, c1989. xxxviii, 341 p.
88-046037   193   0253326273
Schutz, Alfred, -- 1899-1959 -- Correspondence. Gurwitsch, Aron -- Correspondence. Husserl, Edmund, -- 1859-1938. Phenomenology. Philosophers -- United States -- Biography.

B945.V54.A36
Vivas, Eliseo.
Two roads to ignorance: a quasi biography/ by Eliseo Vivas. Carbondale: Southern Illinois University Press, c1979. xiii, 304 p.
79-000757   191   0809309165
Vivas, Eliseo. Philosophers -- United States -- Biography.

B945.W396 B48
Weiss, Paul,
Beyond all appearances. Carbondale, Southern Illinois University Press [1974] xx, 393 p.
74-005484   191   0809306174
Human beings. Reality. Phenomenology. Ideals (Philosophy) Knowledge, Theory of.

B945.W396.P5
Weiss, Paul, 1901-
Philosophy in process. Carbondale, Southern Illinois University Press [1966-c1989] v. 1-8
63-014293   191   0809304015
Philosophy.

B945.W396 P54 1996
Weiss, Paul,
The philosophy of Paul Weiss/ edited by Lewis Edwin Hahn. Chicago: Open Court, c1995. xix, 705 p.
95-043059   191 20   0812692993
Weiss, Paul, 1901- Philosophy.

B945.W474.A3 1999
White, Morton Gabriel, 1917-
A philosopher's story/ Morton White. University Park, Penn.: Pennsylvania State University Press, c1999. viii, 363 p.
98-039334   191   0271018747
White, Morton Gabriel, -- 1917-Philosophers -- United States -- Biography.

B995 Modern (1450/1660-) — By region or country — Canada. British America

B995.G724 G45 1996
George Grant and the subversion of modernity: art, philosophy, politics, religion, and education/ edited by Arthur Davis. Toronto; University of Toronto Press, 1996. xv, 346 p.
97-123090   191 21   080207622X
Grant, George Parkin, 1918- -- Congresses. Philosophy and civilization -- Congresses. Philosophy, Canadian -- 20th century -- Congresses.

B1001-1046 Modern (1450/1660-) — By region or country — Latin America

B1001.L38 2003
Latin American philosophy: currents, issues, debates/ edited by Eduardo Mendieta. Bloomington, IN: Indiana University Press, 2003. vi, 218 p.
2002-008760   199/.8 21   0253215633
Philosophy, Latin American.

B1001.Z423
Zea, Leopoldo, 1912-
The Latin-American mind. Translated from the Spanish by James H. Abbott and Lowell Dunham. Norman, University of Oklahoma Press [1963] 308 p.
63-009955   199.8
Philosophy, Spanish American. Positivism.

B1008.L53.S24 1999
Saenz, Mario, 1956-
The identity of liberation in Latin American thought: Latin American historicism and the phenomenology of Leopoldo Zea/ Mario Saenz. Lanham, MD: Lexington Books, c1999. x, 372 p.
98-045632   199/.72   073910019X
Zea, Leopoldo, -- 1912-Liberty. Philosophy, Latin American. Phenomenology.

B1008.P6 W66
Woodward, Ralph Lee,
Positivism in Latin America, 1850-1900: Are order and progress reconcilable? Edited and with an introd. by Ralph Lee Woodward, Jr. Lexington, Mass., Heath [1971] xviii, 130 p.
72-152809   146/.4
Positivism. Philosophy, Latin American.

B1016.M413
Major trends in Mexican philosophy. Notre Dame, University of Notre Dame Press [1966] 328 p.
66-014624
Philosophy, Mexican.

B1019.V34 H3
Haddox, John H.
Vasconcelos of Mexico, philosopher and prophet, by John H. Haddox. Austin, University of Texas Press [1967] ix, 103 p.
67-065612   199/.72
Vasconcelos, José, 1881-1959.

B1028.P34 2000
Henry, Paget.
Caliban's reason: introducing Afro-Carribean philosophy/ Paget Henry. New York: Routledge, c2000. xiii, 304 p.
99-047426   199/.729/08996   0415926459
Philosophy, Black -- West Indies.

B1034.D874 T45 2000
Thinking from the underside of history: Enrique Dussel's Philosophy of liberation/ edited by Linda Martín Alcoff and Eduardo Mendieta. Lanham, Md.: Rowman & Littlefield Publishers , c2000. ix, 300 p.
00-024820   199/.82 21   0847696510
Dussel, Enrique D.

B1046.J35 1989
Jaksic, Ivan, 1954-
Academic rebels in Chile: the role of philosophy in higher education and politics/ Ivan Jaksic. Albany: State University of New York Press, c1989. xiii, 259 p.
88-012675   199/.83   0887068782
Philosophy, Chilean -- History. Education, Higher -- Chile -- History. Political science -- Chile -- Philosophy -- History. Chile -- Intellectual life.

B1111 Modern (1450/1660-) — By region or country — England. Ireland. Scotland. Wales — General works

B1111.M4
Mehta, Ved, 1934-
Fly and the fly-bottle; encounters with British intellectuals. Boston, Little, Brown [1962] 269 p.
63-012097   192
Philosophers, British. Historians, British.

B1131-1299 Modern (1450/1660-) — By region or country — England. Ireland. Scotland. Wales — 17th century

B1131.J3
James, David Gwilym, 1905-1968.
The life of reason; Hobbes, Locke, Bolingbroke. London, Longmans, Green [1949] xiii, 272 p.
49-048438   192
Hobbes, Thomas, -- 1588-1679. Locke, John, -- 1632-1704. Bolingbroke, Henry St. John, -- Viscount, -- 1678-1751.

B1131.S65 1994
Snider, Alvin Martin,
Origin and authority in seventeenth-century England: Bacon, Milton, Butler/ Alvin Snider. Toronto; University of Toronto Press, c1994. viii, 286 p.
95-106754   820.9/384 20   0802028659
Bacon, Francis, 1561-1626. Novum organum. Milton, John, 1608-1674. Paradise lost. Butler, Samuel, 1612-1680. Hudibras. Philosophy, English -- 17th century. Beginning -- History -- 17th century. English poetry -- Early modern, 1500-1700 -- History and criticism.

B1133.C2.C353
Cassirer, Ernst, 1874-1945.
The Platonic renaissance in England. Translated by James P. Pettegrove. Austin, University of Texas Press, 1953. vii, 207 p.
53-010835   192   087752128X
Cambridge Platonists.

B1133.C2 P6 1971
Powicke, Frederick James,
The Cambridge Platonists; a study. [Hamden, Conn.] Archon Books, 1971. x, 219 p.
79-151196   141   0208010882
Cambridge Platonists.

B1133.K56 B37 2002
Barnaby, Andrew Thomas.
Literate experience: the work of knowing in seventeenth-century English writing/ Andrew Barnaby and Lisa J. Schnell. 1st ed. New York: Palgrave Macmillan, 2002. x, 243 p.
2002-020075   820.9/38 21   0312293518
Bacon, Francis, 1561-1626 -- Influence. Knowledge, Theory of -- England -- History -- 17th century. Knowledge, Theory of, in literature. English literature -- Early modern, 1500-1700 -- History and criticism.

B1133.S4.W54 1968
Wiley, Margaret Lenore, 1908-
The subtle knot; creative scepticism in seventeenth-century England, by Margaret L. Wiley. New York, Greenwood Press, 1968. 303 p.
68-054994   149/.73
Skepticism. Philosophy, English -- 17th century. Religious thought -- England.

B1153. 1857
Bacon, Francis, 1561-1626.
The works of Francis Bacon, Baron of Verulam ... Collected and edited by James Spedding, Robert Leslie Ellis, and Douglas Denon Heath. London, Longman, 1857-74. 14 v.
12-030732

B1155.B3313 1999
Bacon, Francis,
Selected philosophical works/ Francis Bacon; edited, with introduction, by Rose-Mary Sargent. Indianapolis, IN: Hackett Pub., c1999. xxxviii, 290 p.
99-028713   192 21   0872204715
Philosophy. Science -- Philosophy. Natural history.

B1168.E5 J3713 2000
Bacon, Francis,
The new organon/ Francis Bacon; edited by Lisa Jardine, Michael Silverthorne. Cambridge [U.K.]; Cambridge University Press, 2000. xxxv, 252 p.
99-023266   160 21   0521564832
Induction (Logic) -- Early works to 1800. Science -- Methodology -- Early works to 1800.

B1190. 1975
Bacon, Francis, 1561-1626.
The advancement of learning: book 1/ [by] Francis Bacon; edited by William A. Armstrong. London: Athlone Press, 1975. 153 p.
79-322749   121   0485136058
Science -- Methodology. Logic -- Early works to 1800.

B1191.K54 B33 2000
Bacon, Francis,
The advancement of learning/ edited with introduction, notes, and commentary by Michael Kiernan. Oxford [England]; Clarendon Press; lxxxv, 420 p.
00-699911   121 21   0198123485
Logic -- Early works to 1800. Knowledge, Theory of -- Early works to 1800. Learning -- Philosophy -- Early works to 1800. Science -- Methodology -- Early works to 1800.

B1197.B45
Bevan, Bryan.
The real Francis Bacon, a biography. London, Centaur Press, 1960 303 p.
61-000320   921.2
Bacon, Francis, -- 1561-1626.Philosophers, British.

B1197.M47 1996
Mathews, Nieves.
Francis Bacon: the history of a character assassination/ Nieves Mathews. New Haven: Yale University Press, c1996. xiii, 592 p.
96-060105   192   0300064411
Bacon, Francis, -- 1561-1626.Philosophers -- Great Britain -- Biography. Statesmen -- Great Britain -- Biography. Lawyers -- Great Britain -- Biography.

B1197.Z34 1998
Zagorin, Perez.
Francis Bacon/ by Perez Zagorin. Princeton, N.J.: Princeton University Press, c1998. xvi, 286 p.
97-041404   192   0691059284
Bacon, Francis, -- 1561-1626.Philosophers -- Great Britain -- Biography.

B1198.C7
Crowther, J. G. 1899-
Francis Bacon, the first statesman of science. London, Cresset Press, 1960. 362 p.
60-004102   192
Bacon, Francis, -- 1561-1626 -- cn

B1198.P44 1988
Perez-Ramos, Antonio.
Francis Bacon's idea of science and the maker's knowledge tradition/ Antonio Perez-Ramos. Oxford [England]: Clarendon Press; 1988. xi, 334 p.
88-009835   121/.092/4   0198249799
Bacon, Francis, -- 1561-1626 -- Contributions in philosophy of science.Science -- Philosophy -- History -- 17th century.

B1246.M38 1999
Martinich, Aloysius.
Hobbes a biography/ A.P. Martinich. Cambridge, UK; Cambridge University Press, c1999. xvi, 390 p.
98-036567   192   0521495830
Hobbes, Thomas, -- 1588-1679.Philosophers -- England -- Biography.

B1247.C26 1996
The Cambridge companion to Hobbes/ edited by Tom Sorell. Cambridge; Cambridge University Press, 1996. xii, 404 p.
95-008796   192   0521410193
Hobbes, Thomas, -- 1588-1679.

B1247.C66 2000
Condren, Conal.
Thomas Hobbes/ Conal Condren. New York: Twayne Publishers, c2000. xix, 183 p.
99-054906   192   0805716971
Hobbes, Thomas, -- 1588-1679.

B1247.P42 1988
Perspectives on Thomas Hobbes/ edited by G.A.J. Rogers and Alan Ryan. Oxford: Clarendon Press; 1988. 209 p.
88-023466   192   0198249985
Hobbes, Thomas, -- 1588-1679.Philosophy, English -- 17th century.

B1247.S63 1986
Sorell, Tom.
Hobbes/ Tom Sorell. London; Routledge & Kegan Paul, 1986. xii, 163 p.
86-000499   192 19   0710098456
Hobbes, Thomas, 1588-1679.

B1247.T8 1989
Tuck, Richard,
Hobbes/ Richard Tuck. Oxford [England];
Oxford University Press, 1989. viii, 127 p.
88-029148   192 19   0192876686
Hobbes, Thomas, 1588-1679.

B1248.E7 B66 1994
Boonin, David.
Thomas Hobbes and the science of moral virtue/
David Boonin-Vail. Cambridge; Cambridge
University Press, 1994. xi, 219 p.
93-048754   171/.2 20   0521462096
Hobbes, Thomas, 1588-1679 -- Ethics.

B1248.E7 S54 1992
Shelton, George,
Morality and sovereignty in the philosophy of
Hobbes/ George Shelton. New York: St.
Martin's Press, c1992. x, 324 p.
92-006301   171/.2 20   0312080948
*Hobbes, Thomas, 1588-1679. Ethics, Modern
-- 17th century.*

B1248.F74 H63 1999
Hobbes and Bramhall: on liberty and necessity/
edited by Vere Chappell. Cambridge, U.K.;
Cambridge University Press, c1999. xxxiv,
104 p.
98-038086   123/.5 21   0521596688
*Hobbes, Thomas, 1588-1679 -- Contributions
in concept of free will and Bramhall, John,
1594-1663 -- Contributions in concept of free
will and Free will and determinism.*

B1248.M36.J64 1993
Johnson, Laurie M.
Thucydides, Hobbes, and the interpretation of
realism/ Laurie M. Johnson. DeKalb, Ill.:
Northern Illinois University Press, 1993. xiv,
259 p.
92-034016   320/.092/2   0875801757
*Hobbes, Thomas, -- 1588-1679. Thucydides.
Human beings. Philosophical anthropology.
Justice (Philosophy)*

B1253. 1990
Locke, John, 1632-1704.
Drafts for the Essay concerning human
understanding, and other philosophical writings/
John Locke; edited by Peter H. Nidditch and
G.A.J. Rogers. Oxford: Clarendon Press, [1990-
] v. 1
90-033167   121   0198245459
*Knowledge, Theory of -- Early works to 1800.
Philosophy -- Early works to 1800.*

B1294.J46 1983
Jenkins, John J.
Understanding Locke: an introduction to
philosophy through John Locke's Essay/ John J.
Jenkins. Edinburgh: University Press, c1983.
xviii, 256 p.
83-151780   121   0852244495
*Locke, John, -- 1632-1704. -- Essay
concerning human understanding.Knowledge,
Theory of -- Early works to 1800.*

B1294.M18
Mackie, J. L.
Problems from Locke/ by J. L. Mackie. Oxford
[Eng.]: Clarendon Press, 1976. ix, 237 p.
76-365002   121   0198245556
*Locke, John, -- 1632-1704. -- Essay
concerning human understanding.Knowledge,
Theory of. Perception. Substance (Philosophy)*

B1296.T46 2001
Thomson, Garrett.
On Locke/ Garrett Thomson. Australia;
Wadsworth/Thomson Learning, c2001. 86 p.
2001-267510   192 21   0534576281
Locke, John, 1632-1704.

B1297.Y6 1968
Yolton, John W.
John Locke and the way of ideas, by John W.
Yolton. Oxford, Clarendon Press, 1968. x,
235 p.
76-389586   121   0198243316
Locke, John, -- 1632-1704.

B1297.Y64 1993
Yolton, John W.
A Locke dictionary/ John W. Yolton. Oxford,
UK; Blackwell, 1993. 348 p.
92-035261   192   0631175474
Locke, John, -- 1632-1704 -- Dictionaries.

B1298.R4.W65 1996
Wolterstorff, Nicholas.
John Locke and the ethics of belief/ Nicholas
Wolterstorff. Cambridge; Cambridge University
Press, 1996. xxi, 248 p.
95-007256   121   0521551188
*Locke, John, -- 1632-1704. -- Essay
concerning human understanding. Locke, John, -
- 1632-1704 -- Religion.*

B1299.N34 M37 1995
McGuire, J. E.
Tradition and innovation: Newton's metaphysics
of nature/ J.E. McGuire. Dordrecht; Kluwer
Academic Publishers, c1995. xvi, 290 p.
95-030104   113/.092 20   0792336178
*Newton, Isaac, Sir, 1642-1727 --
Contributions in philosophy of Philosophy of
nature -- History -- 17th century. Philosophy of
nature -- History -- 18th century.*

B1301-1349 Modern (1450/1660-) — By region or country — England. Ireland. Scotland. Wales — 18th century

B1301.D53 1999
The dictionary of eighteenth-century British
philosophers/ general editors: John W. Yolton,
John Valdimir Price, and John Stephens. Bristol,
England; Thoemmes, 1999. 2 v.
00-361775   192 B 21   1855061236
*Philosophy, British -- 18th century --
Dictionaries. Philosophers -- Great Britain --
18th century -- Dictionaries. Philosophy, British
-- 18th century -- Dictionaries.*

B1301.W5 1972
Willey, Basil,
The eighteenth-century background: studies on
the idea of nature in the thought of the period.
Harmondsworth, Penguin, 1972. 284 p.
73-156254   113/.2   0140214887
*Eighteenth century. Natural theology. Natural
law. Naturalism in literature. English literature
-- 18th century -- History and criticism.*

B1302.E6 E46 1999
The empiricists: critical essays on Locke,
Berkeley, and Hume/ edited by Margaret
Atherton. Lanham, Md.: Rowman & Littlefield
Publishers, c1999. xx, 258 p.
98-039077   146/.44 21   0847689131
*Locke, John, 1632-1704. Berkeley, George,
1685-1753 Hume, David, 1711-1776.
Empiricism -- History. Philosophy, British --
History.*

B1302.E65 P67 2000
Porter, Roy, 1946-
The creation of the modern world: the untold
story of the British Enlightenment/ Roy Porter.
New York: W.W. Norton, 2000. xxiv, 727 p.
00-049632   940.2/53   0393048721
Enlightenment -- Great Britain.

B1326.D36 1998
Berkeley, George,
Three dialogues between Hylas and Philonous/
George Berkeley; edited by Jonathan Dancy.
Oxford; Oxford University Press, 1998. v, 186 p.
97-012129   192 21   0198751486
Idealism. Soul.

B1331.D38 1998
Berkeley, George,
A treatise concerning the principles of human
knowledge/ George Berkeley; edited by
Jonathan Dancy. Oxford; Oxford University
Press, 1998. vi, 237 p.
97-012131   121 21   0198751613
Knowledge, Theory of.

B1331.T8 1963
Berkeley, George, 1685-1753.
The principles of human knowledge, and Three
dialogues between Hylas and Philonous. Introd.
by G. J. Warnock. Cleveland, World Pub. Co.
[1963] 288 p.
63-008797   121
Knowledge, Theory of. Idealism. Soul.

B1334.B47 2000
Berkeley's Principles and Dialogues: background
source materials/ edited by C.J. McCracken, I.C.
Tipton. Cambridge, U.K.; Cambridge University
Press, 2000. x, 300 p.
99-059435   192   0521496810
*Berkeley, George, -- 1685-1753. -- Treatise
concerning the principles of human knowledge.
Berkeley, George, -- 1685-1753. -- Three
dialogues between Hylas and Philonous.
Knowledge, Theory of. Idealism. Soul.*

B1334.F64 2001
Fogelin, Robert J.
Routledge philosophy guidebook to Berkeley and the Principles of human knowledge/ Robert J. Fogelin. New York: Routledge, 2001.
00-054869   121 21   0415250110
Berkeley, George, 1685-1753. Treatise concerning the principles of Knowledge, Theory of. Idealism.

B1339.A7 1988
Armstrong, D. M. 1926-
Berkeley's theory of vision: a critical examination of Bishop Berkeley's Essay towards a new theory of vision/ D.M. Armstrong. New York: Garland Pub., 1988. 106 p.
88-021471   121/.3   0824024486
Berkeley, George, -- 1685-1753. -- Essay towards a new theory of vision.Vision. Immaterialism (Philosophy)

B1339.S38 1994
Schwartz, Robert, 1940-
Vision: variations on some Berkeleian themes/ Robert Schwartz. Oxford, UK; Blackwell, 1994. vii, 162 p.
93-019417   121/.3   1557862206
Berkeley, George, -- 1685-1753. -- Essay towards a new theory of vision.Vision -- Research. Philosophy of mind.

B1348.B44 1982
Berkeley: critical and interpretive essays/ Colin M. Turbayne, editor. Minneapolis: University of Minnesota Press, c1982. xii, 340 p.
82-001967   192   0816610657
Berkeley, George, -- 1685-1753 -- Addresses, essays, lectures.

B1348.P36 2000
Pappas, George Sotiros, 1942-
Berkeley's thought/ George S. Pappas Ithaca, N.Y.: Cornell University Press, 2000. xi, 261 p.
99-088432   192   0801437008
Berkeley, George, -- 1685-1753.

B1348.W56 1989
Winkler, Kenneth P.
Berkeley: an interpretation/ Kenneth P. Winkler. Oxford [England]: Clarendon Press; c1989. xiv, 317 p.
88-025116   192   0198249071
Berkeley, George, -- 1685-1753.

B1349.M35.M65 1988
Moked, Gabriel.
Particles and ideas: Bishop Berkeley's corpuscularian philosophy/ Gabriel Moked. Oxford [England]: Clarendon Press; 1988. viii, 245 p.
87-035579   117   019824990X
Berkeley, George, -- 1685-1753 -- Contributions in corpuscularian philosophy of matter. Berkeley, George, -- 1685-1753. -- Siris. Matter -- History -- 18th century.

B1401-1545 Modern (1450/1660-) — By region or country — England. Ireland. Scotland. Wales — Scottish philosophers, 18th and early 19th centuries

B1401.R6 1979
Robinson, Daniel Sommer, b. 1888.
The story of Scottish philosophy: a compendium of selections from the writings of nine pre-eminent Scottish philosophers, with biobibliographical essays/ compiled and edited, and with an introd. and a supplementary essay by Daniel Sommer Robinson; foreword by Perry E. Gresham. Westport, Conn.: Greenwood Press, 1979, c1961. 290 p.
78-012114   192   0313210829
Philosophy, Scottish. Philosophy, Scottish -- Bio-bibliography.

B1455.A5 1975
Hume, David, 1711-1776.
Enquiries concerning human understanding and concerning the principles of morals/ by David Hume; reprinted from the posthumous edition of 1777 and edited with introd., comparative table of contents, and analytical index by L. A. Selby-Bigge. Oxford: Clarendon Press, 1975. xl, 417 p.
75-327338   192   0198245351
Knowledge, Theory of. Ethics.

B1485. 1978
Hume, David, 1711-1776.
A treatise of human nature/ by David Hume; edited with an analytical index by L. A. Selby-Bigge. Oxford: Clarendon Press; 1978. xix, 743 p.
77-030415   128   0198245874
Knowledge, Theory of.

B1489.P43 1990
Pears, David Francis.
Hume's system: an examination of the first book of his Treatise/ David Pears. Oxford; Oxford University Press, 1990. ix, 204 p.
90-035855   128   0198751001
Hume, David, -- 1711-1776. -- Treatise of human nature. -- Book 1.Knowledge, Theory of. Philosophy of mind.

B1497.A25
Hume, David, 1711-1776.
The letters of David Hume. Edited by J. Y. T. Greig. Oxford, Clarendon Press [1932] 2 v.
32-021313
Hume, David, -- 1711-1776.Philosophers -- Great Britain -- Correspondence.

B1497.M65 1980
Mossner, Ernest Campbell, 1907-
The life of David Hume/ Ernest Campbell Mossner. Oxford: Clarendon Press; 1980. xx, 709 p.
78-041137   192   0198243812
Hume, David, -- 1711-1776.Philosophers -- Scotland -- Biography.

B1498.F46 2000
Feminist interpretations of David Hume/ edited by Anne Jaap Jacobson. University Park, Pa.: Pennsylvania State University Press, c2000. xi, 323 p.
99-037479   192   0271019700
Hume, David, -- 1711-1776.Feminist theory.

B1498.H4 1983
Hendel, Charles William, 1890-
Studies in the philosophy of David Hume/ Charles W. Hendel. New York: Garland Pub., 1983, c1963. li, 516 p.
82-048334   192   0824054067
Hume, David, -- 1711-1776.

B1498.S8
Stewart, John B. 1924-
The moral and political philosophy of David Hume. New York, Columbia University Press, 1963. viii, 422 p.
63-020701   192
Hume, David, -- 1711-1776.

B1498.U53 1992
Jenkins, John J.
Understanding Hume/ by John J. Jenkins; and edited by Peter Lewis and Geoffrey Madell. Edinburgh: Edinburgh University Press; 1992. 216 p.
92-001118   192   0389209864
Hume, David, -- 1711-1776.

B1498.Z3
Zabeeh, Farhang.
Hume, precursor of modern empiricism: an analysis of his opinions on meaning, metaphysics, logic, and mathematics. The Hague, M. Nijhoff, 1960. vii, 166 p.
61-004735
Hume, David, -- 1711-1776. -- cn

B1499.C38.S38 1989
Schwerin, Alan, 1953-
The reluctant revolutionary: an essay on David Hume's account of necessary connection/ Alan Schwerin. New York: P. Lang, c1989. 150 p.
88-013216   122/.092/4   0820407577
Hume, David, -- 1711-1776 -- Contributions in theory of causation.Causation -- History -- 18th century.

B1499.E8.H855
Mackie, J. L.
Hume's moral theory/ J.L. Mackie. London; Routledge & K. Paul, 1980. viii, 166 p.
79-041565   170/.92/4   0710005245
Hume, David, -- 1711-1776 -- Ethics.Ethics.

B1499.K7.W45 1998
White, Jeremy J.
A Humean critique of David Hume's theory of knowledge/ Jeremy Joyner White; edited by John A. Gueguen. Lanham, Md.: University Press of America, c1998. xi, 180 p.
98-014349   121/.092   0761810897
Hume, David, -- 1711-1776 -- Contributions in theory of knowledge.Knowledge, Theory of.

B1499.M47.F55 1990
Flage, Daniel E., 1951-
David Hume's theory of mind/ Daniel E. Flage.
London; Routledge, 1990. ix, 197 p.
89-027518　128/.2/092　0415021383
Hume, David, -- 1711-1776 -- Contributions in philosophy of mind.Philosophy of mind.

B1499.M5.J64 1999
Johnson, David, 1952-
Hume, holism, and miracles/ David Johnson.
Ithaca, N.Y.: Cornell University Press, 1999.
106 p.
99-037179　212　080143663X
Hume, David, -- 1711-1776 -- Views on miracles.Miracles -- History of doctrines -- 18th century.

B1499.R4.D35 1990
Danford, John W.
David Hume and the problem of reason: recovering the human sciences/ John W. Danford. New Haven: Yale University Press, c1990. xii, 228 p.
89-029104　121　0300046677
Hume, David, -- 1711-1776 -- Contributions in concept of reason.Reason.

B1153 1996
Bacon, Francis,
Philosophical studies, c. 1611-c. 1619/ Francis Bacon; edited with introduction, notes, and commentaries by Graham Rees; with facing-page translations by Graham Rees and Michael Edwards. Oxford [England]; Clarendon Press; cxvi, 503 p.
95-038755　192 20　019812290X
Philosophy. Science. Science -- Philosophy.

B1533.I2 1997
Reid, Thomas, 1710-1796.
Thomas Reid, an inquiry into the human mind: on the principles of common sense/ edited by Derek R. Brookes. University Park, Pa.: Pennsylvania State University Press, 1997. xxv, 345 p.
97-016293　128/.2　0271017414
Philosophy of mind. Senses and sensation. Common sense.

B1545.Z7.G74 1999
Griswold, Charles L., 1951-
Adam Smith and the virtues of enlightenment/ Charles L. Griswold, Jr. Cambridge, U.K.; Cambridge University Press, c1999. xiv, 412 p.
98-012845　192　0521621275
Smith, Adam, -- 1723-1790 -- Ethics.Ethics, Modern -- 18th century.

B1561-1674 Modern (1450/1660-) — By region or country — England. Ireland. Scotland. Wales — 19th and 20th centuries

B1561.W55
Willey, Basil, 1897-
More nineteenth century studies; a group of honest doubters. New York, Columbia University Press, 1956. 304 p.
57-013564　192
Nineteenth century. Philosophy, Modern -- History. English literature -- 19th century. -- History and criticism.

B1571.H33 1955
Halevy, Elie, 1870-1937.
The growth of philosophic radicalism. Translated by Mary Morris. With a pref. by A. D. Lindsay. Boston, Beacon Press [1955] xix, 554 p.
55-013792　144
Bentham, Jeremy, -- 1748-1832.Utilitarianism.France -- History -- Revolution -- Causes.

B1574.B34.C75 1990
Crimmins, James E., 1953-
Secular utilitarianism: social science and the critique of religion in the thought of Jeremy Bentham/ James E. Crimmins. Oxford [England]: Clarendon Press; 1990. viii, 348 p.
89-049126　171/.5　0198277415
Bentham, Jeremy, -- 1748-1832 -- Religion.Utilitarianism. Religion and the social sciences -- History. Christianity and the social sciences -- History. Great Britain -- Religion -- 18th century. Great Britain -- Religion -- 19th century.

B1574.B34.M5 1951
Mill, John Stuart, 1806-1873.
On Bentham and Coleridge. With an introd. by F. R. Leavis. New York, G. W. Stewart [1951] 168 p.
51-001842　192.9
Coleridge, Samuel Taylor, -- 1772-1834. Bentham, Jeremy, -- 1748-1832.

B1602.A2 1963
Mill, John Stuart, 1806-1873.
Collected works. [Toronto, University of Toronto Press, 1963-c1991. v. 1-30...
63-025976　192
Philosophy. Political science. Economics.

B1606.A2 1961
Mill, John Stuart, 1806-1873.
The early draft of John Stuart Mill's autobiography. Edited by Jack Stillinger. Urbana, University of Illinois Press, 1961. 218 p.
61-062769　921.2

B1606.P3
Packe, Michael St. John.
The life of John Stuart Mill. With a pref. by F. A. Hayek. New York, Macmillan, 1954. xvi, 567 p.
54-004589　921.2
Mill, John Stuart, -- 1806-1873.

B1607.A53 2000
Anderson, Susan Leigh.
On Mill/ Susan Leigh Anderson. Australia; Wadsworth/Thomson Learning, c2000. 90 p.
00-268267　192 21　0534576001
Mill, John Stuart, 1806-1873.

B1607.A55 1969
Anschutz, Richard Paul, 1902-
The philosophy of J. S. Mill. Oxford, Clarendon Press [1963] 196 p.
53-008183　192.7
Mill, John Stuart, -- 1806-1873.

B1607.A95
August, Eugene R., 1935-
John Stuart Mill: a mind at large/ Eugene August. New York: Scribner, [1975] xii, 276 p.
75-012649　192　0684142325
Mill, John Stuart, -- 1806-1873.

B1607.C25 1998
The Cambridge companion to Mill/ edited by John Skorupski. Cambridge; Cambridge University Press, 1998. xiii, 591 p.
97-002968　192　0521419875
Mill, John Stuart, -- 1806-1873.

B1607.D58 1991
Donner, Wendy, 1948-
The liberal self: John Stuart Mill's moral and political philosophy/ Wendy Donner. Ithaca, N.Y.: Cornell University Press, c1991. x, 229 p.
91-055065　171/.5/092　0801426294
Mill, John Stuart, -- 1806-1873.Ethics, Modern -- 19th century. Political science -- Philosophy -- History -- 19th century.

B1607.W65
Woods, Thomas.
Poetry and philosophy; a study in the thought of John Stuart Mill. London, Hutchinson [1961] 207 p.
61-002911　192
Mill, John Stuart, -- 1806-1873.

B1615.C62 1924
Contemporary British philosophy; personal statements. 1st-2d ser. By J. B. Baillie [and others] Edited by J. H. Muirhead. London, Allen & Unwin; [1924-25] 2 v.
24-026491　192
Philosophy, English -- 20th century.

B1618.A8 1970
Austin, J. L. 1911-1960.
Philosophical papers. Edited by J. O. Urmson and G. J. Warnock. Oxford, Clarendon Press, 1970. vii, 290 p.
70-019274　192　0198243464
Philosophy -- Addresses, essays, lectures.

B1618.A83.H6
Austin, J. L. 1911-1960.
How to do things with words/ [by] J.L. Austin. Cambridge: Harvard University Press, 1962. vii, 166 p.
62-052034   149.94
Language and languages -- Philosophy. Semantics.

B1618.A91 1974
Ayer, A. J. 1910-
The central questions of philosophy/ A. J. Ayer. New York: Holt, Rinehart and Winston, 1974, c1973. x, 243 p.
74-004407   192   0030131162
Philosophy.

B1618.B73.E7 1914
Bradley, F. H. 1846-1924.
Essays on truth and reality, by F.H. Bradley. Oxford, Clarendon press, 1914. xvi, 480 p.
14-010755
Truth. Reality.

B1618.B74.A67 1998
Appearance versus reality: new essays on Bradley's metaphysics/ edited by Guy Stock. Oxford: Clarendon Press; 1998. x, 236 p.
97-036679   192   019823659X
Bradley, F. H. -- (Francis Herbert), -- 1846-1924.Metaphysics.

B1618.B75.R4 1969
Broad, C. D. 1887-1971.
Religion, philosophy, and psychical research: selected essays/ Charlie Broad.   New York: Humanities Press, 1969, [1953] 308 p.
53-005653   133.072
Philosophy. Psychical research -- Addresses, essays, lectures. Religion.

B1618.C57
Dombrowski, Daniel A.
Not even a sparrow falls: the philosophy of Stephen R.L. Clark/ Daniel A. Dombrowski. East Lansing, Mich.: Michigan State University Press, c2000. xvi, 366 p.
99-050947   192   087013549X
Clark, Stephen R. L.

B1618.C73.E86 2000
Collingwood, R. G. 1889-1943.
An essay on philosophical method/ R.G. Collingwood. South Bend, Ind.: St. Augustine's Press, 2000.
99-056513   101   1890318167
Methodology.

B1618.C73.S6 1982
Collingwood, R. G. 1889-1943.
Speculum mentis, or, The map of knowledge/ by R.G. Collingwood. Westport, Conn.: Greenwood Press, 1982. 327 p.
82-015552   192   0313237018
Art. Religion. Science.

B1618.C763.U5
Cornford, Francis Macdonald, 1874-1943.
The unwritten philosophy and other essays. Edited with an introductory memoir by W.K.C. Guthrie. Cambridge [Eng.] University Press, 1950. xix, 138 p.
50-013598   108
Philosophy

B1626.F573.P48 1998
Flew, Antony, 1923-
Philosophical essays/ Antony Flew; edited by John Shosky. Lanham, Md.: Rowman & Littlefield Publishers, c1998. 213 p.
97-027642   192   0847685780
Philosophy. Analysis (Philosophy)

B1645.H4.H8 1970b
Haldane, R. B. Haldane 1856-1928.
Human experience; a study of its structure. Westport, Conn., Greenwood Press [1970] xxiii, 229 p.
75-098226   121   0837136849
Experience. Philosophy.

B1646.H764
Honderich, Ted.
Philosopher: a kind of life/ Ted Honderich. London; Routledge, 2000.
00-042213   192   0415236975
Honderich, Ted.Philosophers -- England -- Biography.

B1646.J73.R4 1936a
Joad, C. E. M. 1891-1953.
Return to philosophy: being a defence of reason, an affirmation of values, and a plea for philosophy/ by C. E. M. Joad. London: Faber and Faber, [1935]. 279 p.
36-010372
Huxley, Aldous, -- 1894-1963.Philosophy. Reason. Truth.

B1646.K77.I55
Koestler, Arthur, 1905-
Insight and outlook: an inquiry into the common foundations of science, art, and social ethics/ Arthur Koestler. New York: Macmillan, 1949. 442 p.
49-007339   192.9
Philosophy.

B1647.M124.B45 2000
Bellantoni, Lisa, 1969-
Moral progress: a process critique of MacIntyre/ Lisa Bellantoni. Albany, N.Y.: State University of New York Press, c2000. xii, 126 p.
99-030969   170/.92   0791444430
MacIntyre, Alasdair C.Process philosophy. Ethics.

B1647.M186.A3 1998
Magee, Bryan.
Confessions of a philosopher/ Bryan Magee. New York: Random House, 1998.
97-026479   192   0375500286
Magee, Bryan.Philosophy -- Introductions. Philosophers -- Great Britain -- Biography.

B1647.M73.C6 1962
Moore, G. E. 1873-1958.
Commonplace book, 1919-1953. Edited by Casimir Lewy. London, Allen & Unwin; [1962] 411 p.
63-005709   192

B1647.M73.P4 1959
Moore, G. E. 1873-1958.
Philosophical studies.   Paterson,   N. J., Littlefield, Adams, 1959. 342 p.
59-003192   190
Philosophy, Modern.

B1647.M74.B35 1990
Baldwin, Thomas, 1947-
G.E. Moore/ Thomas Baldwin. London; Routledge, 1990. xviii, 337 p.
89-010324   192   0415009049
Moore, G. E. -- (George Edward), -- 1873-1958.

B1649.P633.A9413 1992
Popper, Karl Raimund, 1902-
In search of a better world: lectures and essays from thirty years/ Karl Popper; translated by Laura J. Bennett, with additional material by Melitta Mew. London; Routledge, 1992. x, 245 p.
92-005394   192   0415087740
Philosophy.

B1649.P64.H33 2000
Hacohen, Malachi Haim, 1957-
Karl Popper, the formative years, 1902-1945: politics and philosophy in interwar Vienna/ Malachi Haim Hacohen. Cambridge, U.K.; Cambridge University Press, 2000. xiii, 610 p.
99-047921   192   0521470536
Popper, Karl Raimund, -- Sir, -- 1902-Philosophers -- England -- Biography. Philosophers -- Austria -- Biography.

B1649.R91.C37
Russell, Bertrand, 1872-1970.
Bertrand Russell: an introduction/ edited selections from his writings [by] Brian Carr. London: Allen and Unwin, 1975. 149 p.
75-327863   192   0041920325
Philosophy.

B1649.R91.E38
Russell, Bertrand, 1872-1970.
Basic writings, 1903-1959. Edited by Robert E. Egner and Lester E. Denonn. New York, Simon and Schuster [1961] 736 p.
61-003396   192

B1649.R91 1983
Russell, Bertrand, 1872-1970.
The collected papers of Bertrand Russell/ edited by Kenneth Blackwell ... [et al.]. London; G. Allen & Unwin, 1983-1997 v. 1-4
83-015865   192   004920095X
Philosophy.

B1649.R93.B4
Russell, Bertrand, 1872-1970.
Bertrand Russell speaks his mind. Cleveland, World Publishing Co. [1960] 173 p.
60-006689   192

B1649.R93.E8
Russell, Bertrand, 1872-1970.
Essays in skepticism. New York, Philosophical Library, [1962] 90 p.
62-018547

B1649.R93.L6
Russell, Bertrand, 1872-1970.
Logic and knowledge; essays, 1901-1950./ Edited by Robert Charles Marsh. London: G. Allen & Unwin, 1956. xi, 382 p.
56-014393   192.9   0041640012
Philosophy. Logic, Symbolic and mathematical -- Addresses, esssays, lectures.

B1649.R93.O9 1927a
Russell, Bertrand, 1872-1970.
Philosophy/ by Bertrand Russell. W. W. Norton & Company, Inc., c1927. 307 p.
27-023824
Philosophy. Physics -- Philosophy. Psychology.

B1649.R93.U49
Russell, Bertrand, 1872-1970.
Understanding history, and other essays. New York, Philosophical Library [1957] 122 p.
58-000291   104
History -- Philosophy. Philosophy.

B1649.R94.B33
Bertrand Russell; a collection of critical essays. Edited by D. F. Pears. Garden City, N.Y., Anchor Books, 1972. x, 387 p.
76-171339   192
Russell, Bertrand, -- 1872-1970 -- Addresses, essays, lectures.

B1649.R94.C55 1976
Clark, Ronald William.
The life of Bertrand Russell/ Ronald W. Clark. New York: Knopf, 1976, c1975. 766 p.
75-008226   192   0394490592
Russell, Bertrand, -- 1872-1970.

B1649.R94 O34 2000
Odell, S. Jack,
On Russell/ S. Jack Odell. Belmont, CA: Wadsworth/Thomson Learning, c2000. 90 p.
00-551605   192 21   0534576168
Russell, Bertrand, 1872-1970.

B1649.R94.R93 1988
Ryan, Alan.
Bertrand Russell: a political life/ Alan Ryan. New York: Hill and Wang, 1988. xi, 226 p.
88-006461   320/.092   0809028972
Russell, Bertrand, -- 1872-1970. Russell, Bertrand, -- 1872-1970 -- Views on political science. Political science -- History -- 20th century.

B1649.R94.S35 1952
Schilpp, Paul Arthur, 1897-
The philosophy of Bertrand Russell. New York, Tudor Pub. Co. [1952] xv, 829 p.
53-002059   192.9
Russell, Bertrand, -- 1872-1970.

B1649.R96.O8 1929
Russell, Bertrand, 1872-1970.
Our knowledge of the external world, by Bertrand Russell. New York, W. W. Norton & Company, inc. [c1929]
29-007231
Philosophy.

B1649.S234.W5 1940
White, Stephen Solomon, 1890-
A comparison of the philosophies of F. C. S. Schiller and John Dewey ... by Stephen Solomon White. [Chicago] 1940.
41-007152   144
Schiller, Frederick Canning Scott, -- 1864-1937. Dewey, John, -- 1859-1952. Pragmatism.

B1649.S863.M5
Stout, George Frederick, 1860-1944.
Mind & matter, by G. F. Stout. The first of two volumes based on the Gifford lectures delivered in the University of Edinburgh in 1919 and 1921. Cambridge [Eng.] The University press, 1931. xiv, 325 p.
31-031950   111
Mind and body. Philosophy, Modern. Science -- Philosophy.

B1652.A2 1966
Spencer, Herbert, 1820-1903.
The works of Herbert Spencer. [Osnabruck, Zeller, [1966] 21 v.
68-109116   192
Philosophy.

B1667.S384.P47 1998
The philosophy of P.F. Strawson/ edited by Lewis Edwin Hahn. Chicago, Ill.: Open Court, 1998. xviii, 428 p.
98-022805   192   0812693779
Strawson, P. F.

B1674.W351.N6
Whitehead, Alfred North, 1861-1947.
Alfred North Whitehead: an anthology/ selected by F.S.C. Northrop and Mason W. Gross; introductions and a note on Whitehead's terminology by Mason W. Gross. New York: Macmillan, 1953. 928 p.
53-012112   192.9
Philosophy.

B1674.W354.B47 1998
Berthrong, John H., 1946-
Concerning creativity: a comparison of Chu Hsi, Whitehead, and Neville/ John H. Berthrong. Albany, NY: State University of New York Press, c1998. xvii, 254 p.
98-022840   100   0791439437
Whitehead, Alfred North, -- 1861-1947 -- Contributions in philosophy of creativity. Chu, Hsi, -- 1130-1200 -- Contributions in philosophy of creativity. Neville, Robert C. -- Contributions in philosophy of creativity. Creative ability. Philosophy, Comparative. Process philosophy.

B1674.W354.C5
Christian, William A., 1905-
An interpretation of Whitehead's metaphysics, by William A. Christian. New Haven, Yale University Press, 1959. 419 p.
59-006794   110
Whitehead, Alfred North, -- 1861-1947 -- Contributions in metaphysics.Metaphysics -- History -- 20th century.

B1674.W354F68 2000
Ford, Lewis S.
Transforming process theism/ Lewis S. Ford. Albany: State University of New York Press, c2000. xxii, 380 p.
99-047128   211/.3   0791445356
Whitehead, Alfred North, -- 1861-1947 -- Contributions in concept of God.God -- History of doctrines -- 20th century. Theism. Process theology.

B1674.W354.F7 1990
Franklin, Stephen T.
Speaking from the depths: Alfred North Whitehead's hermeneutical metaphysics of propositions, experience, symbolism, language, and religion/ Stephen T. Franklin. Grand Rapids, Mich.: W.B. Eerdmans Pub. Co., c1990. xiv, 410 p.
89-001204   192   0802803709
Whitehead, Alfred North, -- 1861-1947.

B1674.W354.H67 1993
Hosinski, Thomas E., 1946-
Stubborn fact and creative advance: an introduction to the metaphysics of Alfred North Whitehead/ Thomas E. Hosinski. Lanham, Md.: Rowman & Littlefield, c1993. xix, 263 p.
92-046864   110/.92   084767827X
Whitehead, Alfred North, -- 1861-1947.Metaphysics. Philosophy and religion.

B1674.W354.J6 1962
Johnson, A. H. 1910-
Whitehead's theory of reality. New York, Dover Publications [1962] 267 p.
62-006841   192
Whitehead, Alfred North, -- 1861-1947.Reality.

B1674.W354.K5
Kline, George Louis, 1921-
Alfred North Whitehead, essays on his philosophy. Englewood Cliffs, N.J., Prentice-Hall [1963] x, 214 p.
63-013849   192
Whitehead, Alfred North, -- 1861-1947.

B1674.W354.L38 1961
Leclerc, Ivor.
The relevance of Whitehead; philosophical essays in commemoration of the centenary of the birth of Alfred North Whitehead. London, Allen & Unwin; [1961] 383 p.
61-003432   0391002481
Whitehead, Alfred North, -- 1861-1947.Philosophy

B1674.W354.S45 1970
Sherburne, Donald W.
A Whiteheadian aesthetic; some implications of Whitehead's metaphysical speculation, by Donald W. Sherburne. With a foreword by F. S. C. Northrop. [Hamden, Conn.] Archon Books, 1970 [c1961] xxix, 219 p.
70-103997   111.8/5   0208008195
Whitehead, Alfred North, -- 1861-1947 -- Aesthetics.Aesthetics, Modern -- 20th century.

B1674.W354.W53 1990
Whitehead's metaphysics of creativity/ edited by Friedrich Rapp and Reiner Wiehl. Albany: State University of New York Press, c1990. x, 223 p.
89-004479   192   0791402029
Whitehead, Alfred North, -- 1861-1947.

B1674.W37.M6
Whitehead, Alfred North, 1861-1947.
Modes of thought, by Alfred North Whitehead. Six lectures delivered in Wellesley college, Massachusetts, and two lectures in the University of Chicago. New York, The Macmillan company, 1938.
38-033184   192.9
Philosophy.

B1674.W38.S5 1950
Shahan, Ewing Pope.
Whitehead's theory of experience. New York, King's Crown Press, 1950. viii, 140 p.
50-009059   192.9
Whitehead, Alfred North, -- 1861-1947.Experience.

B1809-2430 Modern (1450/1660-)
— By region or country —
France

B1809.S85 W55 2001
Williams, Caroline,
Contemporary French philosophy: modernity and the persistence of the subject/ Caroline Williams. London; Athlone Press, 2001.
00-067642   194 21   0485006324
Philosophy, French. Subject (Philosophy) -- History. Philosophy, Modern. Philosophy, French -- 20th century. Subject (Philosophy) -- History -- 20th century. Philosophy, Modern -- 20th century.

B1815.S68 1969
Spink, John Stephenson.
French free-thought from Gassendi to Voltaire, by J. S. Spink. New York, Greenwood Press [1969, c1960] ix, 345 p.
69-014089   211/.4/0944
Philosophy, French. Philosophy -- France -- History. Free thought -- History.

B1837.C67 1988
Descartes, Rene, 1596-1650.
Descartes: selected philosophical writings/ translated by John Cottingham, Robert Stoothoff, Dugald Murdoch; with an introduction by John Cottingham. Cambridge; Cambridge University Press, 1988. xii, 249 p.
87-026799   194   0521358124
Philosophy.

B1837.S55 1958
Descartes, Rene, 1596-1650.
Descartes philosophical writings, selected and translated by Norman Kemp Smith. New York, Modern Library [1958] 300 p.
58-006362   194.1
Philosophy.

B1848.E5 C73 1998b
Descartes, René,
Discourse on method; and, Meditations on first philosophy/ René Descartes; translated by Donald A. Cress. 4th ed. Indianapolis: Hackett Pub., c1998. xv, 103 p.
98-038149   194 21   0872204200
Methodology. Science--Methodology. First philosophy.

B1849.R6
Roth, Leon, 1896-1963.
Descartes' Discourse on method, by Leon Roth. Oxford, The Clarendon press, 1937. viii, 142 p.
38-007723   194.1
Descartes, Rene, -- 1596-1650. -- Discours de la methode.

B1854.B4
Beck, L. J.
The metaphysics of Descartes; a study of the Meditations, by L.J. Beck. Oxford, Clarendon Press, 1965. xi, 307 p.
66-001407   194
Descartes, Rene, -- 1596-1650. -- Meditationes de prima philosophia.

B1868.R43.J6
Joachim, Harold H. 1868-1938.
Descartes's Rules for the direction of the mind, London, Allen & Unwin [1957] 122 p.
57-005261
Descartes, Rene, -- 1596-1650. -- Regulae ad directionem ingenii.

B1873.N93 1999
Nye, Andrea, 1939-
The princess and the philosopher: letters of Elisabeth of the Palatine to Rene Descartes/ Andrea Nye. Lanham, Md.: Rowman & Littlefield Publishers, c1999. xiii, 187 p.
98-044821   193   0847692655
Descartes, Rene, -- 1596-1650 -- Correspondence. Elisabeth, -- Countess Palatine, -- 1618-1680 -- Correspondence. Philosophy, Modern -- 17th century.

B1873.R6313 1998
Rodis-Lewis, Genevieve
Descartes: his life and thought/ Genevieve Rodis-Lewis; translated by Jane Marie Todd. Ithaca: Cornell University Press, 1998. xvii, 263 p.
97-038681   194   080143372X
Descartes, Rene, -- 1596-1650.Philosophers -- France -- Biography.

B1873.V7 1970
Vrooman, Jack Rochford.
Rene Descartes; a biography.   New York, Putnam [1970] 308 p.
68-025463   194
Descartes, Rene, -- 1596-1650.

B1875.G33 2001
Garber, Daniel, 1949-
Descartes embodied: reading Cartesian philosophy through Cartesian science/ Daniel Garber. Cambridge; Cambridge University Press, 2001. xii, 337 p.
00-036288   194   0521783534
Descartes, Rene, -- 1596-1650. Descartes, Rene, -- 1596-1650 -- Knowledge -- Science. Science -- Philosophy -- History -- 17th century.

B1875.M342
Maritain, Jacques, 1882-1973.
The dream of Descartes, together with some other essays, translated by Mabelle L. Andison. New York, Philosophical library [c1944] 220 p.
45-002003   194.1   0804603006
Descartes, Rene, -- 1596-1650.

B1875.S368 2000
Schouls, Peter A.
Descartes and the possibility of science/ Peter A. Schouls. Ithaca: Cornell University Press, 2000. x, 171 p.
00-024021　194　080143775X
Descartes, Rene, -- 1596-1650.Science -- Philosophy.

B1875.W56 1978
Williams, Bernard Arthur Owen.
Descartes: the project of pure enquiry/ Bernard Williams. Atlantic Highlands, N.J.: Humanities Press, 1978. 320 p.
78-005023　194　0391005634
Descartes, Rene, -- 1596-1650.

B1878.M55.R68 1998
Rozemond, Marleen.
Descartes's dualism/ Marleen Rozemond. Cambridge, Mass.: Harvard University Press, 1998. xviii, 279 p.
97-042399　128/.2　0674198409
Descartes, Rene, -- 1596-1650 -- Contributions in dualist doctrine of mind and body.Mind and body -- History -- 17th century.

B1878.S55.C87
Curley, E. M. 1937-
Descartes against the skeptics/ E. M. Curley. Cambridge: Harvard University Press, 1978. xvii, 242 p.
77-014366　194　0674198263
Descartes, Rene, -- 1596-1650.Skepticism.

B1897.S368 2000
The Cambridge companion to Malebranche/ edited by Steven Nadler. Cambridge [England]; Cambridge University Press, 2000. xi, 319 p.
00-022060　194　0521622123
Malebranche, Nicolas, -- 1638-1715.

B1900.E5.C3
Pascal, Blaise, 1623-1662.
Great shorter works of Pascal. Translated with an introd. by Emile Cailliet and John C. Blankenagel. Philadelphia, The Westminster Press [1948] 231 p.
48-016776　194　0837160723
Philosophy Philosophers -- France -- Correspondence, reminiscences, etc.

B1901.P42 E5 1986
Pascal, Blaise,
Selections from the Thoughts/ Blaise Pascal; translated and edited by Arthur H. Beattie. Arlington Heights, Ill.: Harlan Davidson, [1986], c1965. xiv, 124 p.
86-002215　230/.2 19　0882950657
Apologetics--Early works to 1800.

B1901.P44.H8
Hubert, Marie Louise,
Pascal's unfinished Apology, a study of his plan. New Haven, Yale University Press, 1952. ix, 165 p.
52-009266　239
Pascal, Blaise, -- 1623-1662. -- Pensees.Apologetics -- 17th century.

B1903.B43 1968
Bishop, Morris, 1893-1973.
Pascal; the life of genius. New York, Greenwood Press, 1968 [c1964] x, 398 p.
68-009538　194
Pascal, Blaise, -- 1623-1662.

B1903.M63 1976
Mortimer, Ernest.
Blaise Pascal: the life and work of a realist/ Ernest Mortimer. New York: Harper, [1959?] 249 p.
59-007155　194
Pascal, Blaise, -- 1623-1662.

B1911.M3
Manuel, Frank Edward.
The prophets of Paris. Cambridge, Harvard University Press, 1962. x, 349 p.
62-008182　194
Philosophers, French.

B1925.M25.Y64 1991
Yolton, John W.
Locke and French materialism/ John W. Yolton. Oxford: Clarendon Press; 1991. 239 p.
90-039833　146/.3/094109032　0198242743
Locke, John, -- 1632-1704 -- Influence.Materialism -- France -- History. Philosophy, French -- 17th century. Philosophy, French -- 18th century.

B2016.C68 1966
Crocker, Lester G.
Diderot, the embattled philosopher [by] Lester G. Crocker. New York, Free Press [1966] 420 p.
66-022213　194
Diderot, Denis, -- 1713-1784.

B2137.B7 1963
Broome, J. H.
Rousseau, a study of his thought. New York, Barnes & Noble. [1963] 231 p.
63-003455　848.5
Rousseau, Jean Jacques.

B2137.S34 2001
Scholz, Sally J.
On Rousseau/ Sally Scholz. Australia; Wadsworth/Thomson Learning, c2001. 92 p.
2001-267511　848/.509 21　0534583687
Rousseau, Jean-Jacques, 1712-1778.

B2137.W7 1963
Wright, Ernest Hunter, 1882-
The meaning of Rousseau. New York, Russell & Russell, 1963. 168 p.
63-009326　194
Rousseau, Jean-Jacques, -- 1712-1778.

B2247.S6
Sokoloff, Boris, 1893-
The "mad" philosopher, Auguste Comte. New York, Vantage Press [1961] 186 p.
61-016280　921.4
Comte, Auguste, -- 1798-1857.

B2421.G88 2001
Gutting, Gary.
French philosophy in the twentieth century/ Gary Gutting. Cambridge, U.K.; Cambridge University Press, 2001. xiv, 419 p.
00-050241　194　0521662125
Philosophy, French -- 20th century.

B2421.L3713 2001
Lecourt, Dominique.
The mediocracy: French philosophy since the mid-1970s/ Dominique Lecourt; translated by Gregory Elliott. London; Verso, 2001. xv, 240 p.
00-063393　194　1859847935
Philosophy, French -- 20th century.

B2421.S6
Smith, Colin, 1914-
Contemporary French philosophy; a study in norms and values. New York, Barnes & Noble [1964] 266 p.
64-003599　194.0904
Philosophy, French -- 20th century.

B2430.B254.T55 1984
Tiles, Mary.
Bachelard, science and objectivity/ Mary Tiles. Cambridge [Cambridgeshire]; Cambridge University Press, 1984. xxii, 242 p.
84-005001　121　0521248035
Bachelard, Gaston, -- 1884-1962.

B2430.B344.P55 1999
Pilardi, Jo-Ann, 1941-
Simone de Beauvoir writing the self: philosophy becomes autobiography/ Jo-Ann Pilardi. Westport, Conn.: Greenwood Press, c1999. 133 p.
97-044836　194　0313302537
Beauvoir, Simone de, -- 1908-Self (Philosophy)

B2430.B344 S36 2000
Scholz, Sally J.
On de Beauvoir/ Sally J. Scholz. Australia; Wadsworth Thomson Learning, c2000. 89 p.
00-265254　194 21　0534576036
Beauvoir, Simone de, 1908-

B2430.B4.M313 1988
Bergson, Henri, 1859-1941.
Matter and memory/ Henri Bergson; authorized translation by Nancy Margaret Paul and W. Scott Palmer. New York: Zone Books, 1988. 284 p.
87-037124　128/.3　0942299043
Mind and body. Matter.

B2430.B4.P362
Bergson, Henri, 1859-1941.
The creative mind, by Henri Bergson...translated by Mabelle L. Andison. New York, Philosophical library [1946] 307 p.
46-002618　104　0806504218
Bernard, Claude, -- 1813-1878. James, William, -- 1842-1910. Ravaisson, Felix, -- 1813-1900. Philosophy Metaphysics Creativeness

B2430.B43.H33
Hanna, Thomas, 1928-
The Bergsonian heritage. New York, Columbia University Press, 1962. viii, 170 p.
62-016690   194
Bergson, Henri, -- 1859-1941.

B2430.D453.Q4713 1994
Deleuze, Gilles.
What is philosophy?/ Gilles Deleuze & Felix Guattari; translated by Hugh Tomlinson and Graham Burchell. New York: Columbia University Press, c1994. x, 253 p.
93-040801   100   0231079885
Philosophy. Science. Logic.

B2430.D454.B78 1997
Brusseau, James, 1964-
Isolated experiences: Gilles Deleuze and the solitudes of reversed Platonism/ James Brusseau. Albany, N.Y.: State University of New York Press, c1998. 223 p.
97-012980   194   0791436713
Deleuze, Gilles.

B2430.D454.B83 2000
Buchanan, Ian, 1969-
Deleuzism: a metacommentary/ Ian Buchanan. Durham, NC: Duke University Press, 2000. 209 p.
99-056849   194   0822325489
Deleuze, Gilles.

B2430.D454.M35 1998
Marks, John, 1964-
Gilles Deleuze: vitalism and multiplicity/ John Marks. Chicago, Ill.: Pluto Press, 1998. viii, 204 p.
97-050567   194   0745308732
Deleuze, Gilles.

B2430.D483.D6613 1995
Derrida, Jacques.
The gift of death/ Jacques Derrida; translated by David Wills. Chicago: University of Chicago Press, c1995. viii, 115 p.
94-028893   194   0226143058
Generosity. Gifts. Responsibility.

B2430.D483.P6613 1997
Derrida, Jacques.
Politics of friendship/ Jacques Derrida; translated by George Collins. London; Verso, c1997. xii, 308 p.
97-011930   177/.62   185984913X
Friendship.

B2430.D484.B457 2000
Bennington, Geoffrey.
Interrupting Derrida/ Geoffrey Bennington. London; Routledge, 2000. xiv, 235 p.
99-056919   194   0415224268
Derrida, Jacques.

B2430.D484.D477 1992
Derrida: a critical reader/ edited by David Wood. Oxford, UK; Blackwell, 1992. ix, 297 p.
91-046355   194   0631161023
Derrida, Jacques.

B2430.D484 H34 2002
Hahn, Stephen,
On Derrida/ Stephen Hahn. Australia; Wadsworth/Thomson Learning, c2002. 90 p.
2002-265894   194 21   0534576311
Derrida, Jacques.

B2430.D484.H69 1998
Howells, Christina.
Derrida: deconstruction from phenomenology to ethics/ Christina Howells. Malden, MA: Polity Press, 1998. 175 p.
98-040809   194   0745611672
Derrida, Jacques.Deconstruction.

B2430.D484.K74 2000
Krell, David Farrell.
The purest of bastards: works of mourning, art, and affirmation in the thought of Jacques Derrida/ David Farrell Krell. University Park, Pa.: Pennsylvania State University Press, c2000. xiii, 237 p.
99-032685   194   0271019913
Derrida, Jacques.

B2430.D484.W475 2000
Wheeler, Samuel C.
Deconstruction as analytic philosophy/ Samuel C. Wheeler III. Stanford, Calif.: Stanford University Press, 2000. viii, 294 p.
99-086425   149   0804737525
Derrida, Jacques. Davidson, Donald, -- 1917- Deconstruction.

B2430.F722.E5 1997
Foucault, Michel.
The essential works of Foucault, 1954-1988/ Paul Rabinow, series editor. New York: New Press, 1997-1999. 3 v.
96-031819   194   1565843525
Philosophy, French -- 20th century.

B2430.F724.A64 1988
After Foucault: humanistic knowledge, postmodern challenges/ edited by Jonathan Arac. New Brunswick: Rutgers University Press, c1988. x, 208 p.
88-006455   194   0813513294
Foucault, Michel.

B2430.F724.B47 1990
Bernauer, James William.
Michel Foucault's force of flight: toward an ethics for thought/ James W. Bernauer. Atlantic Highlands, NJ: Humanities Press International, 1990. xii, 261 p.
89-031526   194   0391036351
Foucault, Michel. Foucault, Michel -- Ethics. Ethics, Modern -- 20th century.

B2430.F724.C365 1999
Carrette, Jeremy R.
Foucault and religion: spiritual corporality and political spirituality/ Jeremy R. Carrette. London; Routledge, 2000. xv, 215 p.
99-031682   210/.92   0415202590
Foucault, Michel -- Contributions in philosophy of religion.Religion -- Philosophy.

B2430.F724.C37 1987
Carroll, David, 1944-
Paraesthetics: Foucault, Lyotard, Derrida/ David Carroll. New York: Methuen, 1987. xviii, 219 p.
87-011296   111/.85/0922   0416017312
Foucault, Michel. Lyotard, Jean Francois. Derrida, Jacques. Aesthetics, Modern -- 20th century.

B2430.F724.E7513 1991
Eribon, Didier.
Michel Foucault/ Didier Eribon; translated by Betsy Wing. Cambridge, Mass.: Harvard University Press, 1991. xiii, 374 p.
91-007186   194   0674572874
Philosophers -- France -- Biography.

B2430.F724.F5713 1992
Fink-Eitel, Hinrich.
Foucault: an introduction/ Hinrich Fink-Eitel; translated from the German by Edward Dixon. Philadelphia: Pennbridge Books, 1992. viii, 101 p.
92-060242   194   1880055023
Foucault, Michel.

B2430.F724.M327 1993
Macey, David, 1949-
The lives of Michel Foucault: a biography/ David Macey. New York: Pantheon Books, c1993. xxiii, 599 p.
93-028220   194   0679430741
Foucault, Michel.Philosophers -- France -- Biography.

B2430.F724.N55 1998
Nilson, Herman, 1965-
Michel Foucault and the games of truth/ Herman Nilson; translated by Rachel Clark. New York: St. Martin's Press, 1998. xv, 159 p.
97-038831   194   0312212976
Foucault, Michel -- Contributions in philosophy of life. Nietzsche, Friedrich Wilhelm, -- 1844-1900 -- Influence. Foucault, Michel. -- Histoire de la sexualite. Sex customs -- History. Ethics, Ancient. Life.

B2430.F724.O43 1989
O'Farrell, Clare.
Foucault: historian or philosopher?/ Clare O'Farrell. New York: St. Martin's Press, 1989. xii, 188 p.
89-033424   194   0312034636
Foucault, Michel.

B2430.F724.P73 1995
Prado, C. G.
Starting with Foucault: an introduction to genealogy/ C.G. Prado. Boulder: Westview Press, 1995. ix, 181 p.
95-002425   194   0813317908
Foucault, Michel.Genealogy (Philosophy)

B2430.J283.P8513 1994
Janicaud, Dominique, 1937-
Powers of the rational: science, technology, and the future of thought/ Dominique Janicaud; translated by Peg Birmingham and Elizabeth Birmingham. Bloomington: Indiana University Press, c1994. xiv, 286 p.
94-006693   128/.4   0253331080
Power (Philosophy) Reason. Science -- Philosophy.

B2430.L146.B6713 1991
Borch-Jacobsen, Mikkel.
Lacan: the absolute master/ Mikkel Borch-Jacobsen; translated by Douglas Brick. Stanford, Calif.: Stanford University Press, 1991. xi, 295 p.
90-043813   150.19/5/092   0804715564
Lacan, Jacques, -- 1901-Psychoanalysis and philosophy.

B2430.L483 D5413 2000
Levinas, Emmanuel.
God, death, and time/ Emmanuel Levinas; translated by Bettina Bergo. Stanford, Calif.: Stanford University Press, c2000. xii, 296 p.
00-059523   194   0804736650
Philosophy. Death. Time.

B2430.L484.D4513 1999
Derrida, Jacques.
Adieu to Emmanuel Levinas/ Jacques Derrida; translated by Pascale-Anne Brault and Michael Naas. Stanford, Calif.: Stanford University Press, c1999. ix, 152 p.
99-021519   194   0804732671
Levinas, Emmanuel.

B2430.L484.R63 1999
Robbins, Jill.
Altered reading: Levinas and literature/ Jill Robbins. Chicago: University of Chicago Press, c1999. xxiv 185 p.
98-037917   194   0226721124
Levinas, Emmanuel.Literature -- Philosophy -- History -- 20th century.

B2430.L484.W35 1999
Wall, Thomas Carl, 1954-
Radical passivity: Levinas, Blanchot, and Agamben/ Thomas Carl Wall; with a foreword by William Flesch. New York: State University of New York Press, c1999. xv, 192 p.
98-027843   111   0791440478
Levinas, Emmanuel. Blanchot, Maurice. Agamben, Giorgio, -- 1942-

B2430.L964.B46 1988
Bennington, Geoffrey.
Lyotard: writing the event/ Geoffrey Bennington. New York: Columbia University Press, 1988. 189 p.
87-072758   194   0231067585
Lyotard, Jean-Francois.

B2430.L964W55 1998
Williams, James.
Lyotard: towards a postmodern philosophy/ James Williams. Cambridge, U.K.; Polity Press, 1998. viii, 150 p.
98-023964   194   0745610994
Lyotard, Jean Francois.

B2430.M253.A93
Marcel, Gabriel, 1889-1973.
Searchings. New York, Newman Press [1967] 118 p.
67-015716   194
Philosophy.

B2430.M253.E85 1965
Marcel, Gabriel, 1889-1973.
Being and having; an existentialist diary. New York, Harper & Row [1965] xvii, 236 p.
65-009149   110
Consciousness. Ontology. Faith.

B2430.M254.P47 1984
The Philosophy of Gabriel Marcel/ edited by Paul Arthur Schilpp and Lewis Edwin Hahn. La Salle, Ill.: Open Court Pub. Co., c1984. xviii, 624 p.
83-004063   194   0875483690
Marcel, Gabriel, -- 1889-1973 -- Addresses, essays, lectures.

B2430.M33.R32
Maritain, Jacques, 1882-1973.
The range of reason. New York, Scribner, 1952. 227 p.
52-014464   104
Philosophy. Christianity and politics.

B2430.M3763.T49 1991
Merleau-Ponty, Maurice, 1908-1961.
Texts and dialogues/ Maurice Merleau-Ponty; edited and with an introduction by Hugh J. Silverman and James Barry, Jr.; translated by Michael B. Smith, et al. New Jersey: Humanities Press, 1992. xxi, 207 p.
90-046082   194   0391037021
Merleau-Ponty, Maurice, -- 1908-1961.Philosophy. Philosophy, Modern -- 20th century. Philosophers -- France -- Interviews.

B2430.M378.E5 1964
Merleau-Ponty, Maurice, 1908-1961.
The primacy of perception, and other essays on phenomenological psychology, the philosophy of art, history, and politics. Edited, with an introd. by James M. Edie. [Evanston, Ill.] Northwestern University Press, 1964. xix, 228 p.
64-022712   194
Phenomenology.

B2430.M379.S43
Merleau-Ponty, Maurice, 1908-1961.
Sense and non-sense. Translated, with a pref., by Hubert L. Dreyfus & Patricia Allen Dreyfus. [Evanston, Ill.] Northwestern University Press, 1964. xxvii, 193 p.
64-023443   194   0810101661
Phenomenology.

B2430.M379.V513
Merleau-Ponty, Maurice, 1908-1961.
The visible and the invisible; followed by working notes. Edited by Claude Lefort. Translated by Alphonso Lingis. Evanston [Ill.] Northwestern University Press, 1968. lvi, 282 p.
68-031025   111
Ontology. Knowledge, Theory of.

B2430.M44.B6 1970
Boas, George, 1891-
A critical analysis of the philosophy of Emile Meyerson. Freeport, N.Y., Books for Libraries Press [1970] v, 146 p.
70-109616   194   0836952243
Meyerson, Emile, -- 1859-1933.

B2430.N363.E8713 2000
Nancy, Jean-Luc.
Being singular plural/ Jean-Luc Nancy; translated by Robert D. Richardson and Anne E. O'Byrne. Stanford, Calif.: Stanford University Press, 2000. xvi, 207 p.
00-057326   194   0804739749
Ontology. Philosophical anthropology.

B2430.R553.C7513 1998
Ricoeur, Paul.
Critique and conviction: conversations with Francois Azouvi and   Marc de Launay/ Paul Ricoeur; translated by Kathleen Blamey. New York: Columbia University Press, c1998. 194 p.
97-027567   194   023110734X
Ricoeur, Paul -- Interviews.Philosophers -- France -- Interviews.

B2430.R553.D813 1991
Ricoeur, Paul.
From text to action/ Paul Ricoeur; translated by Kathleen Blamey and John B. Thompson. Evanston, Ill.: Northwestern University Press, 1991. xvi, 346 p.
91-013556   194   0810109786
Ideology. Hermeneutics. Criticism.

B2430.R553.J8713 2000
Ricoeur, Paul.
The just/ Paul Ricoeur; translated by David Pellauer. Chicago: University of Chicago Press, c2000. xxiv, 161 p.
99-040311   172/.2   0226713393
Justice (Philosophy) Law -- Philosophy.

B2430.R554 M85 2002
Muldoon, Mark.
On Ricoeur/ Mark Muldoon. Australia; Wadsworth/Thomson Learning, c2002. 99 p.
2002-282316   194 21   0534583997
Ricœur, Paul.

B2430.R554.V37 1990
Vanhoozer, Kevin J.
Biblical narrative in the philosophy of Paul Ricoeur: a study in hermeneutics and theology/ Kevin J. Vanhoozer. Cambridge [England]; Cambridge University Press, 1990. xiii, 308 p.
89-007288 220.6/01 0521344255
Ricoeur, Paul.Narration in the Bible -- History -- 20th century. Bible -- Philosophy -- History -- 20th century. Hermeneutics -- History -- 20th century.

B2430.S32.E53
Sartre, Jean Paul, 1905-
The philosophy of Jean-Paul Sartre. Edited by Robert Denoon Cumming. New York, Random House [1965] xii, 491 p.
65-011282 194
Philosophy.

B2430.S33.C3213 1992
Sartre, Jean Paul, 1905-
Notebooks for an ethics/ Jean-Paul Sartre; translated by David Pellauer. Chicago: University of Chicago Press, 1992. xxiv, 583 p.
92-005030 170 0226735117
Ethics.

B2430.S33 C713 1991
Sartre, Jean-Paul,
Critique of dialectical reason/ Jean-Paul Sartre. London; Verso, < -1991> v. <2 >
90-077272 142/.78 20 0860913112
History -- Philosophy. Existentialism. Dialectical materialism.

B2430.S33.V4713 1992
Sartre, Jean Paul, 1905-
Truth and existence/ Jean-Paul Sartre; original text established and annotated by Arlette Elkaim-Sartre; translated by Adrian van den Hoven; edited and with an introduction by Ronald Aronson. Chicago: University of Chicago Press, 1992. xlix, 94 p.
92-005889 121 0226735222
Knowledge, Theory of.

B2430.S34.A753 1993
Anderson, Thomas C., 1935-
Sartre's two ethics: from authenticity to integral humanity/ Thomas C. Anderson. Chicago, Ill.: Open Court, c1993. xiv, 215 p.
93-023370 171/.2 0812692322
Sartre, Jean Paul, -- 1905- -- Ethics.Ethics, Modern -- 20th century.

B2430.S34.B87 1990
Busch, Thomas W., 1937-
The power of consciousness and the force of circumstances in Sartre's philosophy/ Thomas W. Busch. Bloomington: Indiana University Press, c1990. xiv, 112 p.
89-045191 194 0253312833
Sartre, Jean Paul, -- 1905-

B2430.S34.C5248 1991
Charme, Stuart L.
Vulgarity and authenticity: dimensions of otherness in the world of Jean-Paul Sartre/ Stuart Zane Charme. Amherst: University of Massachusetts Press, c1991. x, 255 p.
90-023296 194 0870237403
Sartre, Jean Paul, -- 1905-Marginality, Social -- Philosophy -- History -- 20th century. Interpersonal relations -- Philosophy -- History -- 20th century. Difference (Philosophy)

B2430.S34.C5413 1987
Cohen-Solal, Annie, 1948-
Sartre: a life/ Annie Cohen-Solal; translated by Anna Cancogni; edited by Norman MacAfee. New York: Pantheon Books, c1987. xiii, 591 p.
86-042615 848/.91409 0394525256
Sartre, Jean Paul, -- 1905-Philosophers -- France -- Biography. Authors, French -- 20th century -- Biography.

B2430.S34.D63 1993
Dobson, Andrew.
Jean-Paul Sartre and the politics of reason: a theory of history/ Andrew Dobson. Cambridge [England]; Cambridge University Press, 1993. xii, 199 p.
92-042301 194 0521434491
Sartre, Jean-Paul, -- 1905-History -- Philosophy. Existentialism. Dialectical materialism.

B2430.S34.F42 1999
Feminist interpretations of Jean-Paul Sartre/ edited by Julien S. Murphy. University Park, Pa.: Pennsylvania State University Press, c1999. xiv, 346 p.
98-037145 194 0271018844
Sartre, Jean Paul, -- 1905-Feminist theory.

B2430.S34.G63 1995
Gordon, Hayim.
Sartre and evil: guidelines for a struggle/ Haim Gordon and Rivca Gordon. Westport, Conn.: Greenwood Press, 1995. xxiii, 235 p.
94-030930 170 031327861X
Sartre, Jean Paul, -- 1905- -- Views on good and evil.Good and evil.

B2430.S34.G7
Greene, Norman Nathaniel, 1926-
Jean-Paul Sartre: the existentialist ethic. Ann Arbor, University of Michigan Press [1960] 213 p.
60-009975 111.1
Sartre, Jean Paul, -- 1905-Existentialism.

B2430.S34 K337 2000
Kamber, Richard.
On Sartre/ Richard Kamber. Australia; Wadsworth/Thomson Learning, c2000. 98 p.
00-269506 194 21 0534576249
Sartre, Jean Paul, 1905- Existentialism.

B2430.S34.L24
LaCapra, Dominick, 1939-
A preface to Sartre/ Dominick La Capra. Ithaca: Cornell University Press, 1978. 250 p.
78-058022 848/.9/1409 0801411750
Sartre, Jean Paul, -- 1905-

B2430.S34.M8
Murdoch, Iris.
Sartre, romantic rationalist. New Haven, Yale University Press, 1953. 78 p.
53-005267 194.9
Sartre, Jean Paul, -- 1905-Existentialism.

B2430.S34.S3
Salvan, Jacques Leon, 1898-
To be and not to be; an analysis of Jean-Paul Sartre's ontology. Detroit, Wayne State University Press, 1962. 155 p.
61-012269
Sartre, Jean Paul, -- 1905-Ontology.

B2430.S34.S369 1999
Scriven, Michael, 1947-
Jean-Paul Sartre: politics and culture in Postwar France/ Michael Scriven. New York: St. Martin's Press, 1999. xv, 193 p.
98-055201 320/.092 0312221940
Sartre, Jean Paul, -- 1905- -- Political and social views.Politics and culture -- France.

B2430.S34.T52 1984
Thompson, Kenneth, 1937-
Sartre, life and works/ Kenneth and Margaret Thompson. New York, N.Y.; Facts on File, c1984. xv, 227 p.
82-015585 848/.91409 0871967197
Sartre, Jean Paul, -- 1905-Philosophers -- France -- Biography. Authors, French -- 20th century -- Biography.

B2430.T373.P5613 1999
Teilhard de Chardin, Pierre.
The human phenomenon/ Pierre Teilhard de Chardin; a new edition and translation of Le phenomene humain by Sarah Appleton-Weber; with a foreword by Brian Swimme. Brighton [UK]; Sussex Academic Press, c1999. xxxi, 281 p.
99-032883 113 1902210298
Cosmology. Evolution. Philosophical anthropology.

B2430.W473.L3513
Weil, Simone, 1909-1943.
Lectures on philosophy/ Simone Weil; translated by Hugh Price; with an introd. by Peter Winch. Cambridge [Eng.]; Cambridge University Press, 1978. vii, 232 p.
77-026735 194 052122005X
Philosophy -- Addresses, essays, lectures.

B2430.W473.L43
Weil, Simone, 1909-1943.
Letter to a priest. [Translated by A. F. Wills] New York, Putnam [1954] 85 p.
52-013660 194.9

B2430.W474.B434 1998
Bell, Richard H.
Simone Weil: the way of justice as compassion/ Richard H. Bell. Lanham: Rowman & Littlefield Publishers, c1998. xviii, 259 p.
98-017453   194   0847690792
Weil, Simone, -- 1909-1943.

B2430.W474.F54 1999
Finch, Henry Le Roy.
imone Weil and the intellect of grace/ by Henry Leroy Finch; edited by Martin Andic; foreword by Annie Finch. New York: Continuum, 1999. xii, 177 p.
99-032607   194   0826411908
Weil, Simone, -- 1909-1943.

B2430.W474.N48 1991
Nevin, Thomas R., 1944-
Simone Weil: portrait of a self-exiled Jew/ by Thomas R. Nevin. Chapel Hill: University of North Carolina Press, c1991. xiv, 488 p.
91-009784   194   0807819999
Weil, Simone, -- 1909-1943. Weil, Simone, -- 1909-1943 -- Religion. Philosophers -- France -- Biography.

B2430.W474.P4613
Petrement, Simone.
Simone Weil: a life/ Simone P_etrement; translated from the French by Raymond Rosenthal. New York: Pantheon Books, c1976. xiv, 576 p.
76-009576   194   0394498151
Weil, Simone, -- 1909-1943.Philosophers -- France -- Biography.

B2521-3376 Modern (1450/1660-) — By region or country — Germany. Austria (German)

B2521.R63 1988
Roberts, Julian, 1950-
German philosophy: an introduction/ Julian Roberts. Atlantic Highlands, NJ: Humanities Press International, 1988. viii, 296 p.
87-021445   193   0391035673
Philosophy, German.

B2528.E3.S3
Santayana, George, 1863-1952.
Egotism in German philosophy, by George Santayana. London, J. M. Dent & sons ltd. [1939] xii, 177 p.
40-030212
Philosophy, German. Egoism.

B2598.B74 1984
Brown, Stuart C.
Leibniz/ Stuart Brown. Minneapolis: University of Minnesota Press, c1984. xii, 223 p.
84-013205   193   0816613907
Leibniz, Gottfried Wilhelm, -- Freiherr von, -- 1646-1716.

B2598.R46
Rescher, Nicholas.
The philosophy of Leibniz. Englewood Cliffs, N.J., Prentice-Hall [1967] viii, 168 p.
66-029698   193
Leibniz, Gottfried Wilhelm, -- Freiherr von, -- 1646-1716.

B2621.B68
Bredvold, Louis I. b. 1888.
The brave new world of the enlightenment, by Louis I. Bredvold. Ann Arbor, University of Michigan Press [c1961] 164 p.
61-010987   193
Enlightenment.

B2741.D5
Dewey, John, 1859-1952.
German philosophy and politics. New York, H. Holt, 1915. 134 p.
15-013173
Philosophy, German.

B2745.C36 2000
The Cambridge companion to German idealism/ edited by Karl Ameriks. Cambridge, U.K.; Cambridge University Press, 2000. xiii, 306 p.
00-020469   193   0521651786
Idealism, German. Philosophy, German -- 18th century. Philosophy, German -- 19th century.

B2758 .B5
Kant, Immanuel, 1724-1804.
An Immanuel Kant reader. New York, Harper [1960] 290 p.
60-007962   193
Philosophy, German.

B2758.F7
Kant, Immanuel, 1724-1804.
The philosophy of Kant; Immanuel Kant's moral and political writings. Edited, with an introd., by Carl J. Friedrich. New York, Modern Library [1949] l, 476 p.
50-000267   193.2

B2758.1992
Kant, Immanuel, 1724-1804.
Lectures on logic/ Immanuel Kant; translated and edited by J. Michael Young. Cambridge; Cambridge University Press, 1992. xxxii, 695 p.
91-034583   160   0521360137
Logic, Modern -- 18th century.

B2766.E6.G7 1998
Kant, Immanuel, 1724-1804.
Groundwork of the metaphysics of morals/ Immanuel Kant; translated and edited by Mary Gregor; with an introduction by Christine M. Korsgaard. Cambridge, U.K.; Cambridge University Press, 1998. xxxvi, 76 p.
97-030153   170   0521622352
Ethics -- Early works to 1800.

B2766.E6.P3 1967
Kant, Immanuel, 1724-1804.
The moral law; Kant's Groundwork of the metaphysic of morals. Translated and analysed by H. J. Paton. New York, Barnes & Noble [1967] 142 p.
67-004642   171
Ethics.

B2773.E5.B4
Kant, Immanuel, 1724-1804.
Critique of practical reason; translated, with an introd., by Lewis White Beck. New York, Liberal Arts Press [1956] 168 p.
56-002993   193.2
Ethics.

B2774.B4
Beck, Lewis White.
A commentary on Kant's Critique of practical reason/ Lewis White Beck. Chicago: University of Chicago Press, 1984, c1960. xiv, 306 p.
60-005464   121   0226040763
Kant, Immanuel, -- 1724-1804. -- Kritik der praktischen Vernunft.Reason.

B2779.B44 1987
Bencivenga, Ermanno, 1950-
Kant's Copernican revolution/ Ermanno Bencivenga. New York: Oxford University Press, 1987. x, 262 p.
86-023607   121   0195049578
Kant, Immanuel, -- 1724-1804. -- Kritik der reinen Vernunft.Knowledge, Theory of. Causation. Reason.

B2779.C54 1999
Collins, Arthur W.
Possible experience: understanding Kant's Critique of pure reason/ Arthur W. Collins. Berkeley: University of California Press, c1999. xix, 200 p.
98-033670   121   0520214986
Kant, Immanuel, -- 1724-1804. -- Kritik der reinen Vernunft.Knowledge, Theory of. Causation. Reason.

B2779.G74 2001
Greenberg, Robert, 1934-
Kant's theory of a priori knowledge/ Robert Greenberg. University Park, PA: Pennsylvania State University Press, 2001. ix, 278 p.
00-037453   121   0271020830
Kant, Immanuel, -- 1724-1804. -- Kritik der reinen Vernunft.A priori -- History -- 18th century.

B2779.S26 2000
Kant's early critics: the empiricist critique of the theoretical philosophy/ translated and edited by Brigitte Sassen. Cambridge; Cambridge University Press, 2000. ix, 331 p.
99-059882   193   0521781671
Kant, Immanuel, -- 1724-1804. -- Kritik der reinen Vernunft.Empiricism. Knowled, Theory of. Reason.

B2779.W4 1958
Weldon, T. D.
Kant's Critique of pure reason.   Oxford,
Clarendon Press, 1958. 331 p.
58-004404   121
Kant, Immanuel, -- 1724-1804. -- Kritik der reinen Vernunft.

B2791.E5.G7 1960a
Kant, Immanuel, 1724-1804.
Religion within the limits of reason alone.
Translated, with an introd. and notes, by
Theodore M. Greene and Hoyt H. Hudson. With
a new essay, The ethical significance of Kant's
Religion, by John R. Silber. La Salle, Ill., Open
Court Pub. Co., 1960. cliv, 190 p.
61-001013   193
Philosophy and religion.

B2797.C313
Cassirer, Ernst, 1874-1945.
Kant's life and thought/ Ernst Cassirer;
translated by James Haden; introduction by
Stephan Korner. New Haven: Yale University
Press, c1981. xxiii, 429 p.
81-003354   193   0300023588
Kant, Immanuel, -- 1724-1804.

B2797.K86 2001
Kuehn, Manfred.
Kant: a biography/ Manfred Kuehn. New York:
Cambridge University Press, 2001. xxii, 544 p.
00-033671   193   0521497043
Kant, Immanuel, -- 1724-1804.Philosophers -- Germany -- Biography.

B2798.H43
Hendel, Charles William, 1890-
The philosophy of Kant and our modern world;
four lectures delivered at Yale University
commemorating the 150th anniversary of the
death of Immanual Kant.   New York, Liberal
Arts Press [1957] 132 p.
57-014773   193.2
Kant, Immanuel, -- 1724-1804.

B2798.S315 2000
Schonfeld, Martin,
The philosophy of the young Kant: the
precritical project/ Martin Schonfeld. New York:
Oxford University Press, 2000. xv, 348 p.
99-030602   193   0195132181
Kant, Immanuel, -- 1724-1804.

B2799.A4.E87
Essays in Kant's aesthetics/ edited and
introduced by Ted Cohen & Paul Guyer.
Chicago: University of Chicago Press, c1982. x,
323 p.
81-013091   111/.85/0924   0226112268
Kant, Immanuel, -- 1724-1804 -- Aesthetics -- Addresses, essays, lectures.Aesthetics -- Addresses, essays, lectures.

B2799.E8.B28 1995
Baron, Marcia.
Kantian ethics almost without apology/ Marcia
W. Baron. Ithaca: Cornell University Press,
1995. xiii, 244 p.
95-009555   170/.92   0801428297
Kant, Immanuel, -- 1724-1804 -- Ethics.Ethics.

B2799.E8.M85 1970
Murphy, Jeffrie G.
Kant: the philosophy of right [by] Jeffrie G.
Murphy. London, Macmillan; 1970. 186 p.
75-108406   170/.924   0333074602
Kant, Immanuel, -- 1724-1804 -- Ethics.Law - - Philosophy.

B2799.E8.S53 1994
Seung, T. K., 1930-
Kant's Platonic revolution in moral and political
philosophy/ T.K. Seung. Baltimore: Johns
Hopkins University Press, 1994. xv, 268 p.
94-007529   170/.92   0801848504
Kant, Immanuel, -- 1724-1804.Ethics. Political science -- Philosophy.

B2799.E8.S83 1989
Sullivan, Roger J., 1928-
Immanuel Kant's moral theory/ Roger J.
Sullivan. Cambridge [England]; Cambridge
University Press, 1989. 413 p.
88-010225   170/.92/4   0521360110
Kant, Immanuel, -- 1724-1804 -- Ethics.Ethics -- History -- 18th century.

B2799.E8.W59 1999
Wood, Allen W.
Kant's ethical thought/ Allen W. Wood.
Cambridge; Cambridge University Press, 1999.
xxiv, 436 p.
98-032168   170/.92   0521640563
Kant, Immanuel, -- 1724-1804 -- Contributions in ethics.

B2799.F8.A44 1990
Allison, Henry E.
Kant's theory of freedom/ Henry E. Allison.
Cambridge [England]; Cambridge University
Press, 1990. xii, 304 p.
89-077710   123/.5/092   052138270X
Kant, Immanuel, -- 1724-1804 -- Contributions in concept of free will and determinism.Free will and determinism.

B2799.H7.B43
Kant, Immanuel, 1724-1804.
On history. Edited, with an introd. by Lewis
White Beck. Translated by Lewis White Beck,
Robert E. Anchor and Emil L. Fackenheim.
Indianapolis, Bobbs-Merrill [1963] xxxi, 154 p.
62-022315   901
History -- Philosophy.

B2799.M5.H43
Heidegger, Martin, 1889-1976.
Kant and the problem of metaphysics. Translated
by James S. Churchill. Foreword by Thomas
Langan. Bloomington, Indiana University Press
[1962] xxv, 255 p.
62-008974   110
Kant, Immanuel, -- 1724-1804.Metaphysics.

B2799.M52.B76 1994
Brook, Andrew.
Kant and the mind/ Andrew Brook. Cambridge
[England]; Cambridge University Press, 1994.
xii, 327 p.
93-022703   128/.2/092   0521450365
Kant, Immanuel, -- 1724-1804 -- Contributions in philosophy of mind.Philosophy of mind -- History -- 19th century.

B2799.S37.K45 1998
Keller, Pierre, 1956-
Kant and the demands of self-consciousness/
Pierre Keller. Cambridge, UK; Cambridge
University Press, 1998. vii, 286 p.
99-211605   126/.092   0521630770
Kant, Immanuel, -- 1724-1804 -- Contributions in philosophy of self.Self-consciousness. Self (Philosophy)

B2808. 1988
Fichte, Johann Gottlieb, 1762-1814.
Fichte, early philosophical writings/ translated
and edited by Daniel Breazeale. Ithaca, N.Y.:
Cornell University Press, 1988. xx, 455 p.
87-047871   193   0801417791
Philosophy.

B2844.B52.E5 1987
Fichte, Johann Gottlieb, 1762-1814.
The vocation of man/ Johann Gottlieb Fichte;
translated, with introduction and notes, by Peter
Preuss. Indianapolis: Hackett Pub. Co., c1987.
xvi, 123 p.
87-003610   128   0872200388
Human beings. Faith.

B2894.W42.Z5 1997
Zizek, Slavoj.
The abyss of freedom/ Slavoj Zizek. Ages of the
world/ F.W.J. von Schelling. Ann Arbor, Mich.:
University of Michigan Press, c1997. 182 p.
96-051746   111   0472096524
Schelling, Friedrich Wilhelm Joseph von, -- 1775-1854. -- Weltalter. Lacan, Jacques, -- 1901- Absolute, The. Free will and determinism. History -- Philosophy.

B2901.B87 2001
Burbidge, John W., 1936-
Historical dictionary of Hegelian philosophy/
John W. Burbidge. Lanham, MD: Scarecrow
Press, 2001. xvii, 205 p.
00-041285   193   0810838788
Hegel, Georg Wilhelm Friedrich, -- 1770-1831 -- Dictionaries.

B2901.I58 1992
Inwood, M. J., 1944-
A Hegel dictionary/ Michael Inwood. Oxford, OX, UK; Cambridge, Mass., USA: 1992. vii, 347 p.
92-013463   193   0631175326
Hegel, Georg Wilhelm Friedrich, -- 1770-1831 -- Dictionaries.

B2908.E5.L6
Hegel, Georg Wilhelm Friedrich, 1770-1831.
--Selections, edited by J. Loewenberg. New York, C. Scribner's sons [c1929]
29-008405
Hegel, Georg Wilhelm Friedrich, -- 1770-1831 -- Philosophy.

B2923.Z7.M313 1970
Marx, Karl, 1818-1883.
Critique of Hegel's 'Philosophy of right'. Translated from the German by Annette Jolin and Joseph O'Malley. Edited with an introd. and notes by Joseph O'Malley. Cambridge [Eng.] University Press, 1970. lxvii, 151 p.
74-112471   320.1/1   0521078369
Hegel, Georg Wilhelm Friedrich, -- 1770-1831. -- Grundlinien der Philosophie des Rechts.

B2929.K613
Kojeve, Alexandre, 1902-1968.
Introduction to the reading of Hegel, by Alexandre Kojeve. Lectures on the phenomenology of spirit assembled by Raymond Queneau. Edited by Allan Bloom. Translated from the French by James H. Nichols, Jr. New York, Basic Books [1969] xiv, 287 p.
70-078467   193
Hegel, Georg Wilhelm Friedrich, -- 1770-1831. -- Phanomenologie des Geistes.

B2929.L6
Loewenberg, Jacob.
Hegel's Phenomenology: dialogues on The life of mind/ J. Loewenberg. La Salle, Ill.: Open Court Pub. Co., 1965. xv, 377 p.
65-015621   193
Hegel, Georg Wilhelm Friedrich, -- 1770-1831. -- Phanomenologie des Geistes.

B2936.Z7.L37
Lauer, Quentin.
Hegel's idea of philosophy. With a new translation of Hegel's Introduction to the history of philosophy. New York, Fordham University Press, 1971. x, 159 p.
74-152244   193   0823209253
Philosophy -- History.

B2942.A313
Hegel, Georg Wilhelm Friedrich, 1770-1831.
Hegel's Science of logic; translated [from the German] by A. V. Miller, foreword by J. N. Findlay. London, Allen & Unwin; 1969. 845 p.
75-390294   160   0041930134
Logic.

B2942.E5.H288 1991
Hegel, Georg Wilhelm Friedrich, 1770-1831.
The encyclopaedia logic, with the Zusatze: Part I of the Encyclopaedia of philosophical sciences with the Zusatze/ G.W.F. Hegel; a new translation with introduction and notes by T.F. Geraets, W.A. Suchting, and H.S. Harris. Indianapolis: Hackett, c1991. xlviii, 381 p.
90-029023   160   087220071X
Logic.

B2947.A67 2000
Althaus, Horst.
Hegel: an intellectual biography/ Horst Althaus; translated by Michael Tarse. Malden, Mass.: Polity Press, 2000. vii, 292 p.
00-039957   193   0745617816
Hegel, Georg Wilhelm Friedrich, -- 1770-1831.Philosophers -- Germany -- Biography.

B2947.P56 2000
Pinkard, Terry P.
Hegel: a biography/ Terry Pinkard. Cambridge; Cambridge University Press, 2000. xx, 780 p.
99-034812   193   0521496799
Hegel, Georg Wilhelm Friedrich, -- 1770-1831.Philosophers -- Germany -- Biography.

B2948.C28 1993
The Cambridge companion to Hegel/ edited by Frederick C. Beiser. Cambridge [England]; Cambridge University Press, 1993. viii, 518 p.
92-015572   193   0521382742
Hegel, Georg Wilhelm Friedrich, -- 1770-1831.

B2948.H3178 1987
Hegel and modern philosophy/ edited by David Lamb. London; Croom Helm, c1987. ix, 262 p.
87-021727   193   0709941684
Hegel, Georg Wilhelm Friedrich, -- 1770-1831.Philosophy, Modern.

B2948.K3
Kaufmann, Walter Arnold.
Hegel; reinterpretation, texts, and commentary [by] Walter Kaufmann. Garden City, N.Y., Doubleday, 1965. 498 p.
65-013982   193
Hegel, Georg Wilhelm Friedrich, -- 1770-1831.

B2948.M48 1998
Miklowitz, Paul S.
Metaphysics to metafictions: Hegel, Nietzsche, and the end of philosophy/ Paul S. Miklowitz. Albany, N.Y.: State University of New York Press, c1998. xxv, 221 p.
97-035112   193   0791438775
Hegel, Georg Wilhelm Friedrich, -- 1770-1831. Nietzsche, Friedrich Wilhelm, -- 1844-1900. Metaphysics -- History.

B2948.R62513 1993
Rockmore, Tom, 1942-
Before and after Hegel: a historical introduction to Hegel's thought/ Tom Rockmore. Berkeley: University of California Press, c1993. xi, 211 p.
93-009719   193   0520082052
Hegel, Georg Wilhelm Friedrich, -- 1770-1831.Philosophy, Modern -- 19th century.

B2949.D5.P56 1988
Pinkard, Terry P.
Hegel's dialectic: the explanation of possibility/ Terry Pinkard. Philadelphia: Temple University Press, 1988. xi, 236 p.
88-022677   193   0877225702
Hegel, Georg Wilhelm Friedrich, -- 1770-1831 -- Contributions in dialectic.Dialectic -- History -- 19th century.

B2949.H5P54 1956
Hegel, Georg Wilhelm Friedrich, 1770-1831.
The philosophy of history/ Georg Wilhelm Friedrich Hegel; prefaces by Charles Hegel; and the translator, J. Sibree; a new introduction by C. J. Friedrich. New York: Dover Publications, Inc., 1956. xvi, 457 p.
57-000401   193   0486201120
History -- Philosophy.

B2949.J84.Y68 1998
Yovel, Yirmiahu.
Dark riddle: Hegel, Nietzsche, and the Jews/ by Yirmiyahu Yovel. University Park, Pa.: Pennsylvania State University Press, 1998. xx, 235 p.
97-049192   296/.0943   0271017813
Hegel, Georg Wilhelm Friedrich, -- 1770-1831 -- Views on Judaism. Nietzsche, Friedrich Wilhelm, -- 1844-1900 -- Views on Judaism. Judaism and philosophy -- History -- 19th century.

B2949.L8.E77 1990
Essays on Hegel's logic/ edited by George di Giovanni. Albany: State University of New York Press, c1990. xi, 218 p.
89-029183   160   0791402916
Hegel, Georg Wilhelm Friedrich, -- 1770-1831 -- Contributions in logic -- Congresses.Logic, Modern -- 20th century -- Congresses.

B2949.R3.C73 1998
Crites, Stephen.
Dialectic and gospel in the development of Hegel's thinking/ Stephen Crites. University Park, Pa.: Pennsylvania State University Press, c1998. xvii, 572 p.
97-039499   193   0271017597
Hegel, Georg Wilhelm Friedrich, -- 1770-1831 -- Religion. Hegel, Georg Wilhelm Friedrich, -- 1770-1831 -- Views on Christianity. Hegel, Georg Wilhelm Friedrich, -- 1770-1831. -- Phanomenologie des Geistes. Theology, Doctrinal -- Germany -- History -- 19th century. Philosophy and religion -- History -- 19th century. Dialectic -- History -- 19th century.

B2949.R3.K8313 1987
Kung, Hans, 1928-
The Incarnation of God: an introduction to Hegel's theological thought as prolegomena to a future christology/ Hans Kung; translated by J.R. Stephenson. New York: Crossroad, c1987. xv, 601 p.
86-023262   230/.092/4   0824507932
Hegel, Georg Wilhelm Friedrich, -- 1770-1831 -- Contributions in theology. Jesus Christ -- History of doctrines -- 19th century. God -- History of doctrines -- 19th century.

B2949.S54.F67 1989
Forster, Michael N.
Hegel and skepticism/ Michael N. Forster. Cambridge, Mass.: Harvard University Press, 1989. 256 p.
88-024294   149/.73/09   0674387074
Hegel, Georg Wilhelm Friedrich, -- 1770-1831 -- Views on skepticism.Skepticism -- History -- 19th century.

B2971.G7.E52
Feuerbach, Ludwig, 1804-1872.
Principles of the philosophy of the future/ Ludwig Feuerbach; translated, with an introd., by Manfred H. Vogel. Indianapolis, Ind.: Bobbs-Merrill, c1966. lxxxiii, 85 p.
64-066068   193
Philosophy. Religion -- Philosophy.

B2973.E5 1934a
Engels, Friedrich, 1820-1895.
Ludwig Feuerbach and the outcome of classical German philosophy, by Frederick Engels; with an appendix of other material of Marx and Engels relating to dialectical materialism. New York: International publishers, [1934] 101 p.
35-014077
Feuerbach, Ludwig, -- 1804-1872.Materialism. Socialism.

B3114.E5.P3
Schopenhauer, Arthur, 1788-1860.
On the basis of morality/ Arthur Schopenhauer; translated by E. F. J. Payne; with an introd. by Richard Taylor. Indianapolis: Bobbs-Merrill, 1981, c1965. xxviii, 226 p.
65-026525   0672604450
Ethics.

B3118.E5.S38 1960
Schopenhauer, Arthur, 1788-1860.
The Art of literature/ by Arthur Schopenhauer; translated by T. Bailey Saunders. [Ann Arbor]: University of Michigan Press, 1960. 114 p.
61-066074   193
Literature

B3148.C36 1999
The Cambridge companion to Schopenhauer/ edited by Christopher Janaway. Cambridge, U.K.; Cambridge University Press, 1999. xiv, 478 p.
99-011396   193   0521621062
Schopenhauer, Arthur, -- 1788-1860.

B3148.J36 1989
Janaway, Christopher.
Self and world in Schopenhauer's philosophy/ Christopher Janaway. Oxford [England]: Clarendon Press; 1989. xii, 378 p.
88-028631   193   0198249691
Schopenhauer, Arthur, -- 1788-1860.

B3148.M27 1983
Magee, Bryan.
The philosophy of Schopenhauer/ by Bryan Magee. Oxford: Clarendon Press; 1983. 400 p.
82-022523   193   0198246730
Schopenhauer, Arthur, -- 1788-1860.

B3199.A33.M4813 2000
Adorno, Theodor W., 1903-1969.
Metaphysics: concept and problems/ Theodor W. Adorno; edited by Rolf Tiedemann; translated by Edmund Jephcott. Stanford, Calif.: Stanford University Press, 2000.
00-058765   110   0804742472
Metaphysics. Philosophy.

B3199.A33.P76 2000
Adorno, Theodor W., 1903-1969.
Problems of moral philosophy/ Theodor W. Adorno; edited by Thomas Schroder; translated by Rodney Livingstone. Stanford, Calif.: Stanford University Press, 2000. viii, 224 p.
99-066706   170   0804739366
Ethics.

B3199.A34.A4213 1999
Adorno, Theodor W., 1903-1969.
The complete correspondence, 1928-1940/ Theodor W. Adorno and Walter Benjamin; edited by Henri Lonitz; translated by Nicholas Walker. Cambridge, Mass.: Harvard University Press, 1999. viii, 383 p.
99-010988   193   0674154274
Adorno, Theodor W., -- 1903-1969 -- Correspondence. Benjamin, Walter, -- 1892-1940 -- Correspondence. Philosophers, Modern -- Germany -- Correspondence. Authors, German -- 20th century -- Correspondence.

B3199.A34.M4413 1998
Menke-Eggers, Christoph, 1958-
The sovereignty of art: aesthetic negativity in Adorno and Derrida/ Christoph Menke; translated by Neil Solomon. Cambridge, Mass.: MIT Press, c1998. xiii, 310 p.
97-046401   111/.85   0262133407
Adorno, Theodor W., -- 1903-1969 -- Aesthetics. Derrida, Jacques -- Aesthetics. Negativity (Philosophy) -- History -- 20th century. Aesthetics, Modern -- 20th century. Deconstruction.

B3199.A34.N53 1997
Nicholsen, Shierry Weber.
Exact imagination, late work: on Adorno's Aesthetics/ Shierry Weber Nicholsen. Cambridge, Mass.: MIT Press, c1997. 270 p.
97-009398   111/.85/092   0262140624
Adorno, Theodor W., -- 1903-1969. Adorno, Theodor W., -- 1903-1969. -- Asthetische Theorie. Aesthetics, Modern -- 20th century.

B3209.B584.R6313 1996
Rochlitz, Rainer.
The disenchantment of art: the philosophy of Walter Benjamin/ Rainer Rochlitz; translated by Jane Marie Todd. New York: Guilford Press, 1996. vi, 298 p.
96-000026   111/.85/092   0898624088
Benjamin, Walter, -- 1892-1940 -- Aesthetics.Aesthetics, Modern -- 20th century. Art -- Philosophy.

B3209.B751.J67213 1998
Bloch, Ernst, 1885-1977.
Literary essays/ Ernst Bloch; translated by Andrew Joron and others. Stanford, Calif.: Stanford University Press, 1998. xiv, 538 p.
98-011401   834/.912   0804727066
Bloch, Ernst, -- 1885-1977 -- Aesthetics.Aesthetics, Modern -- 20th century. Literature -- Philosophy. Arts -- Philosophy.

B3212.Z7 V45 2000
Velarde-Mayol, Victor.
On Brentano/ Victor Velarde-Mayol. Australia; Wadsworth/Thomson Learning, c2000. 92 p.
00-268270   193 21   0534576117
Brentano, Franz Clemens, 1838-1917.

B3213.B82.E5
Buber, Martin, 1878-1965.
The knowledge of man; selected essays. Edited, with an introductory essay, by Maurice Friedman. Translated by Maurice Friedman and Ronald Gregor Smith. New York, Harper & Row [1965] 184 p.
66-000181   128.08
Philosophical anthropology. Interpersonal relations -- Philosophy.

B3213.B82 E52 2002
Buber, Martin,
The Martin Buber reader: essential writings/ edited by Asher Biemann. 1st ed. New York: Palgrave Macmillan, 2002. vi, 303 p.
2002-016924   296.3 21   0312292902
Philosophy. Judaism. Hasidism. Relationism. Philosophy and religion. Community -- Philosophy. Zionism.

B3213.B82.E53
Buber, Martin, 1878-1965.
Writings. Selected, edited, and introduced by Will Herberg. New York, Meridian Books, 1956. 351 p.
56-006573   181.3
Philosophy.

B3213.B83I213 1970
Buber, Martin, 1878-1965.
I and Thou. A new translation with a prologue "I and You" and notes by Walter Kaufmann. New York, Scribner [1970] 185 p.
72-123845   181/.3
Life. Relationism. God -- Knowableness.

B3213.B84.D48
Diamond, Malcolm Luria.
Martin Buber, Jewish existentialist. New York, Oxford University Press, 1960. 240 p.
60-007059   181.3
Buber, Martin, -- 1878-1965.

B3213.B84.F726 1991
Friedman, Maurice S.
Encounter on the narrow ridge: a life of Martin Buber/ Maurice Friedman. New York: Paragon House, 1991. xi, 496 p.
90-044502   296.3/092   1557784531
Buber, Martin, -- 1878-1965.Jewish philosophers -- Germany -- Biography. Jewish philosophers -- Israel -- Biography. Zionists -- Biography.

B3216.C34.S3 1958
Schilpp, Paul Arthur, 1897-
The philosophy of Ernst Cassirer. New York, Tudor Pub. Co. [1958, c1949] xviii, 936 p.
58-009554   193
Cassirer, Ernst, -- 1874-1945. -- cn

B3240.F483.C66 1999
Feyerabend, Paul K., 1924-
Conquest of abundance: a tale of abstraction versus the richness of being/ Paul Feyerabend; edited by Bert Terpstra. Chicago: University of Chicago Press, c1999. xviii, 285 p.
99-032398   110   0226245330
Reality. Abstraction.

B3240.F484.W67 2000
The worst enemy of science?: essays in memory of Paul Feyerabend/ edited by John Preston, Gonzalo Munevar, & David Lamb. New York: Oxford University Press, 2000. xvii, 171 p.
99-013710   193   0195128745
Feyerabend, Paul K., -- 1924-

B3240.F493.F8713 1998
Figal, Gunter, 1949-
For a philosophy of freedom and strife: politics, aesthetics, metaphysics/ Gunter Figal; translated with notes by Wayne Klein. Albany: State University of New York Press, c1998. xi, 226 p.
97-019141   193   0791436977
Metaphysics. Political science -- Philosophy. Aesthetics.

B3245.F24.N66 2001
Noonan, Harold W.
Frege: a critical introduction/ Harold W. Noonan. Cambridge: Polity; 2001. viii, 244 p.
0745616720
Frege, Gottlob, -- 1848-1925.

B3245.F24 S24 2001
Salerno, Joseph.
On Frege/ Joseph Salerno. Australia; Wadsworth/Thomson Learning, c2001. 98 p.
2001-267104   193 21   0534583679
Frege, Gottlob, 1848-1925.

B3245.F24.S7
Sternfeld, Robert.
Frege's logical theory. Foreword by George Kimball Plochmann. Carbondale, Southern Illinois University Press [1966] xii, 200 p.
65-012392   160.924
Frege, Gottlob, -- 1848-1925 -- Logic.

B3248.G33.H47 1999
Gadamer, Hans Georg, 1900-
Hermeneutics, religion, and ethics/ Hans-Georg Gadamer; translated by Joel Weinsheimer. New Haven: Yale University Press, c1999. xiv, 172 p.
99-013088   121/.686   0300074077
Hermeneutics. Religion. Ethics.

B3248.G34.C64 1998
Coltman, Rodney R., 1957-
The language of hermeneutics: Gadamer and Heidegger in dialogue/ Rod Coltman. Albany: State University of New York Press, c1998. xviii, 187 p.
97-042842   121/.686/0922   0791438996
Gadamer, Hans Georg, -- 1900- -- Contributions in hermeneutics. Heidegger, Martin, -- 1889-1976 -- Contributions in hermeneutics. Hermeneutics -- History -- 20th century.

B3248.G343.L6313 1998
Gadamer, Hans Georg, 1900-
Praise of theory: speeches and essays/ Hans-Georg Gadamer; translated by Chris Dawson. New Haven, Conn.: Yale University Press, c1998. xxxviii, 185 p.
98-007115   193   0300073100
Philosophy.   Theory   (Philosophy) Hermeneutics.

B3258.H323.P5513 1987
Habermas, Jurgen.
The philosophical discourse of modernity: twelve lectures/ Jurgen Habermas; translated by Frederick Lawrence. Cambridge, Mass.: MIT Press, c1987. xx, 430 p.
87-012397   190   0262081636
Philosophy, Modern -- 20th century. Philosophy, Modern -- 19th century. Civilization, Modern -- Philosophy.

B3273.P53.E7 1972
Hartmann, Eduard von, 1842-1906.
Philosophy of the unconscious; speculative results according to the inductive method of physical science. With a pref. by C. K. Ogden. Westport, Conn., Greenwood Press [1972] xxxviii, 372 p.
76-108843   154   0837137322
Subconsciousness. Consciousness.

B3279.H285 2000
Hatab, Lawrence J., 1946-
Ethics and finitude: Heideggerian contributions to moral philosophy/ Lawrence J. Hatab. Lanham, Md.: Rowman & Littlefield, c2000. xvi, 223 p.
99-086407   171/.2   0847696820
Heidegger, Martin, -- 1889-1976 -- Ethics.

B3279.H48.B44513 1999
Heidegger, Martin, 1889-1976.
Contributions to philosophy: from enowning/ Martin Heidegger; translated by Parvis Emad and Kenneth Maly. Bloomington, Ind.: Indiana University Press, c1999. xliv, 369 p.
99-034597   193   0253336066
Philosophy.

B3279.H48.F7313 1967
Heidegger, Martin, 1889-1976.
What is a thing? Translated by W. B. Barton, Jr., and Vera Deutsch, with an analysis by Eugene T. Gendlin. Chicago, H. Regnery Co. [1968, c1967] vii, 310 p.
67-031050   141/.3
Kant, Immanuel, -- 1724-1804 -- Addresses, essays, lectures.Ding an sich -- Addresses, essays, lectures. Metaphysics -- Addresses, essays, lectures.

B3279.H48.G7713 1994
Heidegger, Martin, 1889-1976.
Basic questions of philosophy: selected "problems" of "logic"/ Martin Heidegger; translated by Richard Rojcewicz and Andre Schuwer. Bloomington: Indiana University Press, c1994. xx, 192 p.
93-030513   111/.8   0253326850
Truth.

B3279.H48.S43 1996
Heidegger, Martin, 1889-1976.
Being and time; : a translation of Sein und Zeit/ Martin Heidegger; translated by Joan Stambaugh. Albany, NY: State University of New York Press, c1996. xix, 487 p.
96-000476   111   0791426777
Ontology. Space and time.

B3279.H48.S489 1994
Vogel, Lawrence.
The fragile "we": ethical implications of Heidegger's Being and Time/ Lawrence Vogel. Evanston, Ill.: Northwestern University Press, 1994. x, 138 p.
94-013274   111   081011139X
Heidegger, Martin, -- 1889-1976. -- Sein und Zeit. Heidegger, Martin, -- 1889-1976 -- Ethics. Ethics, Modern -- 20th century. Ethics, German -- History -- 20th century.

B3279.H48.W413 1998
Heidegger, Martin, 1889-1976.
Pathmarks/ Martin Heidegger; edited by William McNeill. Cambridge; Cambridge University Press, 1998. xiii, 385 p.
97-022565   193   0521433622
Philosophy. Ontology.

B3279.H48.Z44 1999
Inwood, M. J., 1944-
A Heidegger dictionary/ Michael Inwood. Malden, Mass.: Blackwell Publishers, 1999.
99-017512   193   0631190945
Heidegger, Martin, -- 1889-1976 -- Dictionaries.

B3279.H48V63
Heidegger, Martin, 1889-1976.
The essence of reasons. Translated by Terrence Malick. Evanston [Ill.] Northwestern University Press, 1969. xviii, 144 p.
69-012849   193
Ontology. Reason. Cosmology.

B3279.H49.B63313 2000
Boer, Karin de.
Thinking in the light of time: Heidegger's encounter with Hegel/ Karin de Boer. Albany, NY: State University of New York Press, c2000. xii, 406 p.
99-038489   193   0791445054
Heidegger, Martin, -- 1889-1976 -- Contributions in concept of the finite. Hegel, Georg Wilhelm Friedrich, -- 1770-1831. Finite, The -- History -- 20th century.

B3279.H49.C25 1993
The Cambridge companion to Heidegger/ edited by Charles Guignon. Cambridge [England]; Cambridge University Press, 1993. xx, 389 p.
92-022753   193   0521385709
Heidegger, Martin, -- 1889-1976.

B3279.H49.C273 1993
Caputo, John D.
Demythologizing Heidegger/ John D. Caputo. Bloomington: Indiana University Press, c1993. xiii, 234 p.
93-000461   193   0253313066
Heidegger, Martin, -- 1889-1976. Heidegger, Martin, -- 1889-1976 -- Political and social views. Philosophy and religion -- History -- 20th century. Justice -- Biblical teaching. Philosophy, Ancient.

B3279.H49.D33 1998
Dastur, Francoise, 1942-
Heidegger and the question of time/ Francoise Dastur; translated by Francois Raffoul and David Pettigrew. Atlantic Highlands, N.J.: Humanities Press, 1998. xxxi, 79 p.
96-040852   115/.092   0391040324
Heidegger, Martin, -- 1889-1976 -- Contributions in philosophy of time.Time -- History -- 20th century.

B3279.H49.D455 2000
Denker, Alfred, 1960-
Historical dictionary of Heidegger's philosophy/ Alfred Denker. Lanham, Md.: Scarecrow Press, 2000. xxviii, 378 p.
99-054067   193   0810837374
Heidegger, Martin, -- 1889-1976 -- Dictionaries.

B3279.H49.F3413 1989
Farias, Victor, 1940-
Heidegger and nazism/ Victor Farias; edited, with a foreword by Joseph Margolis and Tom Rockmore; French materials translated by Paul Burrell with the advice of Dominic Di Bernardi; German materials translated by Gabriel R. Ricci. Philadelphia: Temple University Press, 1989. xxi, 349 p.
89-032963   193   0877226407
Heidegger, Martin, -- 1889-1976 -- Views on national socialism.National socialism.

B3279.H49.G57 2000
Glazebrook, Trish.
Heidegger's philosophy of science/ Trish Glazebrook. New York: Fordham University Press, 2000. xii, 278 p.
00-025802   193   0823220370
Heidegger, Martin, -- 1889-1976 -- Contributions in philosophy of science.Science -- Philosophy -- History -- 20th century.

B3279.H49.H33 1992
Heidegger: a critical reader/ edited by Hubert Dreyfus and Harrison Hall. Oxford, UK; B. Blackwell, 1992. 303 p.
91-029540   193   0631163417
Heidegger, Martin, -- 1889-1976.

B3279.H49.I7513 1999
Irigaray, Luce.
The forgetting of air in Martin Heidegger/ Luce Irigaray; translated by Mary Beth Mader. Austin: University of Texas Press, 1999. viii, 198 p.
98-058123   193   0292738714
Heidegger, Martin, -- 1889-1976.

B3279.H49 J34 2000
Johnson, Patricia Altenbernd,
On Heidegger/ Patricia Altenbernd Johnson. Belmont, CA: Wadsworth/Thomson Learning, c2000. 92 p.
00-551601   193 21   0534575978
Heidegger, Martin, 1889-1976.

B3279.H49.L9613 1990
Lyotard, Jean Francois.
Heidegger and "the jews"/ Jean-Francois Lyotard; translation by Andreas Michel and Mark S. Roberts; foreword by David Carroll. Minneapolis: University of Minnesota Press, c1990. xxix, 106 p.
90-034234   193   0816618569
Heidegger, Martin, -- 1889-1976 -- Views on Jews.Holocaust, Jewish (1939-1945) Deconstruction. Marginality, social.

B3279.H49.M27413 1998
Marion, Jean-Luc, 1946-
Reduction and givenness: investigations of Husserl, Heidegger, and phenomenology/ Jean-Luc Marion; translated by Thomas A. Carlson. Evanston, Ill.: Northwestern University Press, c1998. xvii, 261 p.
97-052350   142/.7   0810112167
Heidegger, Martin, -- 1889-1976. Husserl, Edmund, -- 1859-1938. Phenomenology -- History.

B3279.H49.M3754 1999
McCumber, John.
Metaphysics and oppression: Heidegger's challenge to Western philosophy/ John McCumber. Bloomington, Ind.: Indiana University Press, c1999. xiv, 338 p.
98-045926   193   025333473X
Heidegger, Martin, -- 1889-1976.Metaphysics -- History. Political persecution -- History.

B3279.H49.N33
Naess, Arne.
Four modern philosophers: Carnap, Wittgenstein, Heidegger, Sartre. Translated by Alastair Hannay. Chicago, University of Chicago Press [1968] xiii, 367 p.
68-014011   190
Wittgenstein, Ludwig, -- 1889-1951. -- cn Sartre, Jean Paul, -- 1905- -- dn Carnap, Rudolf, -- 1891-1970.

B3279.H49.P65 1999
Polt, Richard F. H., 1964-
Heidegger: an introduction/ Richard Polt. Ithaca, N.Y.: Cornell University Press, 1999. xi, 197 p.
98-030460   193   0801435846
Heidegger, Martin, -- 1889-1976.

B3279.H49.R36 1993
Reading Heidegger: commemorations/ edited by John Sallis. Bloomington: Indiana University Press, c1993. xi, 418 p.
91-027080   193   0253350530
Heidegger, Martin, -- 1889-1976.

B3279.H49.Y68 1997
Young, Julian.
Heidegger, philosophy, Nazism/ Julian Young. Cambridge, U.K.; Cambridge University Press, 1997. xv, 232 p.
96-029115   193   0521582768
Heidegger, Martin, -- 1889-1976.National socialism.

B3279.H94.A129 Vol.59,etc
Life-- scientific philosophy: phenomenology of life and the sciences of life/ edited by Anna-Teresa Tymieniecka. Dordrecht; Kluwer Academic Publishers, c1999. 2 v.
98-008187   142/.7   079235141X
Life. Phenomenology.

B3279.H94.C28 1995
The Cambridge companion to Husserl/ edited by Barry Smith and David Woodruff Smith. Cambridge; Cambridge University Press, 1995. viii, 518 p.
95-003957   193   0521430232
Husserl, Edmund, -- 1859-1938.

B3279.H94.K64
Kolakowski, Leszek.
Husserl and the search for certitude/ Leszek Kolakowski. New Haven: Yale University Press, 1975. 85 p.
74-029724   193   0300018584
Husserl, Edmund, -- 1859-1938 -- Addresses, essays, lectures.Certainty -- Addresses, essays, lectures.

B3279.H94.L395 1998
Levinas, Emmanuel.
Discovering existence with Husserl/ Emmanuel Levinas; [translated and edited by Richard A. Cohen and Michael B. Smith]. Evanston, Ill.: Northwestern University Press, 1998. xxii, 198 p.
98-003984   193   0810113600
Husserl, Edmund, -- 1859-1938.Phenomenology.

B3279.H94 V45 2000
Velarde-Mayol, Victor.
On Husserl/ Victor Velarde-Mayol. Belmont, CA: Wadsworth/Thomson Learning, c2000. 85 p.
00-551606   193 21   0534576109
Husserl, Edmund, 1859-1938.

B3279.H94W453 2000
Welton, Donn.
The other Husserl: the horizons of transcendental phenomenology/ Donn Welton. Bloomington: Indiana University Press, c2000. xvi, 496 p.
00-038906   193   025333795X
Husserl, Edmund, -- 1859-1938.Phenomenology.

B3279.H972i
Husserl, Edmund, 1859-1938.
Ideas: general introduction to pure phenomenology. Translated by W. R. Boyce Gibson. London, Allen & Unwin; [1952] 465 p.
54-008950
Phenomenology.

B3279.J33.P533 1968
Jaspers, Karl, 1883-1969.
The perennial scope of philosophy. Translated by Ralph Manheim. [Hamden, Conn.] Archon Books, 1968. 188 p.
68-012525   193
Philosophy.

B3279.J33.V453
Jaspers, Karl, 1883-1969.
Reason and anti-reason in our time. Translated by Stanley Godman. New Haven, Yale University Press, 1952. 96 p.
52-013037   193   0208011145

B3279.J33P513
Jaspers, Karl, 1883-1969.
Philosophy. Translated by E. B. Ashton. Chicago, University of Chicago Press [1969-71] 3 v.
69-019922   193   0226394913
Philosophy.

B3305.M74.B21513 1995
Balibar, Etienne, 1942-
The philosophy of Marx/ Etienne Balibar; translated by Chris Turner. London; Verso, 1995. iv, 139 p.
95-020985   193   1859849512
Marx, Karl, -- 1818-1883.

B3305.M74.B78 1998
Brudney, Daniel.
Marx's attempt to leave philosophy/ Daniel Brudney. Cambridge, Mass.: Harvard University Press, 1998. xviii, 425 p.
97-038497   193   0674551338
Marx, Karl, -- 1818-1883. Feuerbach, Ludwig, -- 1804-1872. Philosophy, German -- 19th century.

B3305.M74.H333 2000
Harries, Martin.
Scare quotes from Shakespeare: Marx, Keynes, and the language of reenchantment/ Martin Harries. Stanford, Calif. Stanford University Press, 2000. viii, 209 p.
00-020696   001.1   0804736219
Marx, Karl, -- 1818-1883. Keynes, John Maynard, -- 1883-1946. Shakespeare, William, -- 1564-1616 -- Influence.

B3305.M74.H6 1994
Hook, Sidney, 1902-
From Hegel to Marx: studies in the intellectual development of Karl Marx/ by Sydney Hook. New York: Columbia University Press, c1994. xxx, 335 p.
93-046389   335.4/092   023109664X
Marx, Karl, -- 1818-1883. Hegel, Georg Wilhelm Friedrich, -- 1770-1831. History -- Philosophy.

B3305.M74.K3 1972
Kamenka, Eugene.
The ethical foundations of Marxism. London, Routledge and Kegan Paul, 1972. xxii, 208 p.
73-157233   172   0710073607
Marx, Karl, -- 1818-1883.Communist ethics.

B3305.M74.M326 1987
Mah, Harold.
The end of philosophy, the origin of "ideology": Karl Marx and the crisis of the young Hegelians/ Harold Mah. Berkeley: University of California Press, c1987. ix, 305 p.
86-011418   193   0520058488
Marx, Karl, -- 1818-1883. Bauer, Bruno, -- 1809-1882. Ruge, Arnold, -- 1802-1880. Philosophy, German -- 19th century.

B3305.M74.M3755 1992
Marx and Aristotle: nineteenth-century German social theory and classical antiquity/ edited by George E. McCarthy. Savage, Md.: Rowman & Littlefield Publishers, c1992. x, 379 p.
91-037536   193   0847677133
Marx, Karl, -- 1818-1883. Aristotle. Philosophy, Ancient -- Influence.Germany -- Civilization -- Greek influenbces.

B3305.M74.M3915 1990
McCarthy, George E.
Marx and the ancients: classical ethics, social justice, and nineteenth-century political economy/ George E. McCarthy. Savage, Md.: Rowman & Littlefield, c1990. xi, 342 p.
90-036564   193   0847676412
Marx, Karl, -- 1818-1883.Philosophy, Ancient. Social ethics -- History. Social justice -- History.

B3305.M74.T8 1972
Tucker, Robert C.
Philosophy and myth in Karl Marx, by Robert C. Tucker. Cambridge [Eng.] University Press, 1972. 263 p.
70-180022   193   0521084555
Marx, Karl, -- 1818-1883.

B3305.M74.W4746 1998
Wilde, Lawrence.
Ethical Marxism and its radical critics/ Lawrence Wilde. New York: St. Martin's Press, c1998. viii, 189 p.
98-015611   171/.7   0312216165
Marx, Karl, -- 1818-1883. -- Ethics.Communist ethics. Ethics, Modern -- 19th century. Ethics, Modern -- 20th century.

B3311.D54 1999
Diethe, Carol, 1943-
Historical dictionary of Nietzscheanism/ Carol Diethe. Lanham, Md.: Scarecrow Press, 1999. xvii, 265 p.
98-026822   193   0810835126
Nietzsche, Friedrich Wilhelm, -- 1844-1900 -- Dictionaries.

B3312.E52.K3
Nietzsche, Friedrich Wilhelm, 1844-1900.
The portable Nietzsche; selected and translated, with an introd., prefaces, and notes, by Walter Kaufmann. New York, Viking Press, 1954. 687 p.
54-007985   193.9

B3312.E52.W67
Nietzsche, Friedrich Wilhelm, 1844-1900.
The philosophy of Nietzsche ... New York, The Modern library [1937] 1146 p.
37-027408   193.9

B3313.A4 1998
Cauchi, Francesca.
Zarathustra contra Zarathustra: the tragic buffoon/ Francesca Cauchi. Aldershot, Hants, England; Ashgate, c1998. x, 185 p.
97-076930   193   1840143517
Nietzsche, Friedrich Wilhelm, -- 1844-1900. -- Also sprach Zarathustra.

B3313.A43 E5 1999
Nietzsche, Friedrich Wilhelm,
Thus spake Zarathustra/ Friedrich Nietzsche; translated by Thomas Common. Mineola, NY: Dover Publications, 1999. x, 270 p.
99-013580   193 21   0486406636
Superman (Philosophical concept) Philosophy.

B3313.A44.R67 1995
Rosen, Stanley, 1929-
The mask of enlightenment: Nietzsche's Zarathustra/ Stanley Rosen. Cambridge; Cambridge University Press, 1995. xviii, 264 p.
94-045502   131   0521495466
Nietzsche, Friedrich Wilhelm, -- 1844-1900. -- Also sprach Zarathustra.

B3313.G43.P67 2000
Porter, James I., 1954-
The invention of Dionysus: an essay on The birth of tragedy/ James I. Porter. Stanford, Calif.: Stanford University Press, 2000. xiii, 224 p.
00-022875   111/.85   0804736995
Nietzsche, Friedrich Wilhelm, -- 1844-1900. -- Geburt der Tragodie. Plato. Metaphysics -- History -- 19th century. Dionysus (Greek deity)

B3313.G43.S24 1991
Sallis, John, 1938-
Crossings: Nietzsche and the space of tragedy/ John Sallis. Chicago: University of Chicago Press, 1991. x, 158 p.
90-043060   193   0226734366
Nietzsche, Friedrich Wilhelm, -- 1844-1900. -- Geburt der Tragodie. Socrates. Tragic, The. Music -- Philosophy and aesthetics. Dionysus (Greek deity)

B3313.J43 E5 2002
Nietzsche, Friedrich Wilhelm,
Beyond good and evil: prelude to a philosophy of the future/ Friedrich Nietzsche; edited by Rolf-Peter Horstmann, Judith Norman; translated by Judith Norman. Cambridge; Cambridge University Press, 2002. xxxiv, 193 p.
2001-035672   193 21   0521779138
Philosophy.

B3313.M52.E5 1984
Nietzsche, Friedrich Wilhelm, 1844-1900.
Human, all too human: a book for free spirits/ Friedrich Nietzsche; translated by Marion Faber, with Stephen Lehmann; introduction and notes by Marion Faber. Lincoln: University of Nebraska Press, c1984. xxvii, 275 p.
83-025955   128   0803283539
Human beings.

B3316.J313
Jaspers, Karl, 1883-1969.
Nietzsche: an introduction to the understanding of his philosophical activity/ Karl Jaspers; translated by Charles F. Wallraff and Frederick J. Schmitz. Chicago: H. Regnery, 1969, c1965. xiv, 496 p.
65-012660   193
Nietzsche, Friedrich Wilhelm, -- 1844-1900.

B3317.B41513 1992
Bataille, Georges, 1897-1962.
On Nietzsche/ by Georges Bataille; translated by Bruce Boone; introduction by Sylvere Lotringer. New York: Paragon House, 1992. xxxiv, 199 p.
91-026664   193   155778325X
Nietzsche, Friedrich Wilhelm, -- 1844-1900.

B3317.H38 1998
Heilke, Thomas W., 1960-
Nietzsche's tragic regime: culture, aesthetics, and political education/ Thomas Heilke. Dekalb: Northern Illinois University Press, 1998. xv, 215 p.
97-024737   193   0875802338
Nietzsche, Friedrich Wilhelm, -- 1844-1900 -- Political and social views. Nietzsche, Friedrich Wilhelm, -- 1844-1900 -- Aesthetics. Nietzsche, Friedrich Wilhelm, -- 1844-1900 -- Views on education. Europe -- Civilization -- 19th century.

B3317.H43 1988
Heller, Erich, 1911-
The importance of Nietzsche: ten essays/ Erich Heller. Chicago: University of Chicago Press, 1988. xi, 199 p.
88-018649   193   0226326373
Nietzsche, Friedrich Wilhelm, -- 1844-1900.

B3317.L37
Lea, F. A. 1915-1977.
The tragic philosopher; a study of Friedrich Nietzsche.   New York, Philosophical Library [1957] 354 p.
57-013831   193.9
Nietzsche, Friedrich Wilhelm, -- 1844-1900.

B3317.M29
Manthey-Zorn, Otto, 1879-
Dionysus: the tragedy of Nietzsche/ By Otto Manthey-Zorn. Amherst: Amherst College Press, 1956. 210 p.
56-011510   193.9
Nietzsche, Friedrich Wilhelm, -- 1844-1900.

B3317.M65
Morgan, George Allen, 1905-
What Nietzsche means, by George Allen Morgan, jr. Cambridge, Mass., Harvard university press, 1941. xviii, 408 p.
41-002572   196.9
Nietzsche, Friedrich Wilhelm, -- 1844-1900. -- cn

B3317.N492 1998
Nietzsche: critical assessments/ edited by Daniel W. Conway. London; Routledge, 1998.
97-029031   193   0415135621
Nietzsche, Friedrich Wilhelm, -- 1844-1900.

B3317.T39 1997
Taylor, Quentin P., 1964-
The republic of genius: a reconstruction of Nietzsche's early thought/ Quentin P. Taylor. Rochester, NY: University of Rochester Press, 1997.
97-018439   193   1878822942
Nietzsche, Friedrich Wilhelm, -- 1844-1900.

B3317.W456 2000
Why Nietzsche still?: reflections on drama, culture, politics/ edited by Alan D. Schrift. Berkeley, Calif.: University of California Press, c2000. xv, 309 p.
99-031466   193   0520218515
Nietzsche, Friedrich Wilhelm, -- 1844-1900.

B3318.A4.Y67 1992
Young, Julian.
Nietzsche's philosophy of art/ Julian Young. Cambridge; Cambridge University Press, 1992. xiii, 170 p.
91-003022   111/.85/092   0521411246
Nietzsche, Friedrich Wilhelm, -- 1844-1900 -- Aesthetics.Aesthetics, Modern -- 19th century.

B3318.C56 P67 2000
Porter, James I., 1954-
Nietzsche and the philology of the future/ James I. Porter. Stanford, Calif.: Stanford University Press, c2000. xiii, 449 p.
00-041055   193   0804736677
Nietzsche, Friedrich Wilhelm, -- 1844-1900 -- Contributions in classicism.Classicism -- History and criticism.

B3318.E9.B47 1987
Bernstein, John Andrew, 1944-
Nietzsche's moral philosophy/ John Andrew Bernstein. Rutherford [N.J.]: Fairleigh Dickinson University Press; c1987. 214 p.
85-046001   170/.92/4   0838632831
Nietzsche, Friedrich Wilhelm, -- 1844-1900 -- Contributions in ethics.Ethics, Modern -- 19th century.

B3318.O75.N54 1991
Nietzsche and Asian thought/ edited by Graham Parkes. Chicago: University of Chicago Press, c1991. xii, 253 p.
90-024809   193   0226646831
Nietzsche, Friedrich Wilhelm, -- 1844-1900 -- Knowledge -- Philosophy, Oriental. Nietzsche, Friedrich Wilhelm, -- 1844-1900 -- Influence. Philosophy, Asian. Philosophy, Modern -- 19th century. Philosophy, Modern -- 20th century.

B3318.R4.J33
Jaspers, Karl, 1883-1969.
Nietzsche and Christianity. [Translated from the German by E.B. Ashton. [Chicago] H. Regnery Co. [1961] ix, 111 p.
61-017371   193
Nietzsche, Friedrich Wilhelm, -- 1844-1900.Christianity -- Philosophy.

B3319.E9.H85 1990
Hunt, Lester H., 1946-
Nietzsche and the origin of virtue/ Lester H. Hunt. London; Routledge, 1991. xxiii, 200 p.
90-032305   170/.92   0415040531
Nietzsche, Friedrich Wilhelm, -- 1844-1900 -- Ethics. Nietzsche, Friedrich Wilhelm, -- 1844-1900 -- Political and social views. Ethics, Modern -- 19th century. Political science -- Philosophy.

B3329.S52.E5 1949
Schweitzer, Albert, 1875-
The wit and wisdom of Albert Schweitzer; edited, with an introd., by Charles R. Joy. Boston, Beacon Press, 1949. vii, 104 p.
49-011511   208.1
Schweitzer, Albert, 1875-1965.

B3329.S52.E5 1965
Schweitzer, Albert.
Albert Schweitzer: an anthology.　Beacon Pr.,
1965. 367 p.
65-012499　193
　Civilization -- Philosophy.

B3332.S674 C6813 2000
Courtine-Denamy, Sylvie.
Three women in dark times: Edith Stein, Hannah
Arendt, Simone Weil, or Amor fati, amor mundi
/ Sylvie Courtine-Denamy; translated from the
French by G.M. Goshgarian. Ithaca, N.Y.:
Cornell University Press, 2000. xi, 272 p.
00-010475　181/.06　0801435722
　Stein, Edith, -- Saint, -- 1891-1942. Arendt,
Hannah. Weil, Simone, -- 1909-1943. Women
philosophers -- Europe -- Biography. Jewish
philosophers -- Europe -- Biography.

B3354.V5.P6 1965
Vaihinger, Hans, 1852-1933.
The philosophy of as if: a system of the
theoretical, practical and religious fictions of
mankind, by H. Vaihinger; translated [from the
6th German ed.] by C. K. Ogden. London,
Routledge & K. Paul, [1965] xlviii, 368 p.
67-079188
　Nietzsche, Friedrich Wilhelm, -- 1844-1900.
Kant, Immanuel, -- 1724-1804. Positivism.
Pragmatism. Fiction, Theory of.

B3354.V884.H84 1993
Hughes, Glenn, 1951-
Mystery and myth in the philosophy of Eric
Voegelin/ Glenn Hughes. Columbia: University
of Missouri Press, c1993. viii, 131 p.
92-034192　193　0826208754
　Voegelin, Eric, -- 1901-Consciousness --
History -- 20th century. Mysticism.

B3361.Z7.S336 1996
Schluchter, Wolfgang, 1938-
Paradoxes of modernity: culture and conduct in
the theory of Max Weber/ Wolfgang Schluchter;
translated by Neil Solomon. Stanford, Calif.:
Stanford University Press, 1996. 389 p.
95-016141　301/.092　0804724555
　Weber, Max, -- 1864-1920.

B3376.W563.P637 1992
Werhane, Patricia Hogue.
Skepticism, rules, and private languages/
Patricia H. Werhane. Atlantic Highlands, N.J.:
Humanities Press, 1992. xi, 196 p.
91-038783　401　0391037501
　Wittgenstein, Ludwig, -- 1889-1951. --
Philosophische Untersuchungen.Language and
languages -- Philosophy. Semantics
(Philosophy)

B3376.W563.T7356 1990
Peterson, Donald, 1956-
Wittgenstein's early philosophy: three sides of
the mirror/ Donald Peterson. Toronto; University
of Toronto Press, c1990. xii, 204 p.
92-217224　192　0802027709
　Wittgenstein, Ludwig, -- 1889-1951. --
Tractatus logico-philosophicus.Language and
languages -- Philosophy. Logic, Symbolic and
mathematical.

B3376.W564.A64 1988
Ackermann, Robert John, 1933-
Wittgenstein's city/ Robert John Ackermann.
Amherst: University of Massachusetts Press,
1988. xiii, 267 p.
87-010895　192　0870235893
　Wittgenstein, Ludwig, -- 1889-1951.

B3376.W564.C345 1996
The Cambridge companion to Wittgenstein/
edited by Hans Sluga, David G. Stern.
Cambridge; Cambridge University Press, 1996.
ix, 509 p.
96-005300　192　0521460255
　Wittgenstein, Ludwig, -- 1889-1951.

B3376.W564.C57 1999
Clack, Brian R.
Wittgenstein, Frazer, and religion/ Brian R.
Clack. New York, N.Y.: St. Martin's Press,
1999. x, 200 p.
98-021471　200/.92　0312216424
　Wittgenstein, Ludwig, -- 1889-1951 --
Religion. Frazer, James George, -- Sir, -- 1854-
1941. -- Golden bough. Wittgenstein, Ludwig, --
1889-1951. -- Bemerkungen uber Frazers
Golden bough. Magic. Religion. Mythology.

B3376.W564.C65 2000
Cook, John W. 1930-
Wittgenstein, empiricism, and language/ John
W. Cook. New York: Oxford University Press,
2000. xv, 224 p.
99-010740　192　019513298X
　Wittgenstein, Ludwig, -- 1889-
1951.Reductionism. Language and languages --
Philosophy.

B3376.W564.C74 1989
Creegan, Charles L., 1959-
Wittgenstein and Kierkegaard: religion,
individuality, and philosophical method/ Charles
L. Creegan. London; Routledge, 1989. v, 158 p.
88-023633　192　0415000661
　Wittgenstein, Ludwig, -- 1889-1951 --
Contributions in methodology. Wittgenstein,
Ludwig, -- 1889-1951 -- Religion. Wittgenstein,
Ludwig, -- 1889-1951 -- Contributions in
concept of individuality. Religion -- Philosophy.
Methodology. Individuality.

B3376.W564.H244 1999
Hacker, P. M. S.
Wittgenstein/ P.M.S. Hacker. New York:
Routledge, 1999.
99-014479　192　041592376X
　Wittgenstein, Ludwig, -- 1889-1951.

B3376.W564.H295 1989
Hanfling, Oswald.
Wittgenstein's later philosophy/ Oswald
Hanfling. Albany, NY: State University of New
York Press, c1989. viii, 193 p.
88-027979　192　0791400700
　Wittgenstein, Ludwig, -- 1889-1951.

B3376.W564 H56 2000
Hintikka, Jaakko,
On Wittgenstein/ Jaakko Hintikka. Australia;
Wadsworth/Thomson Learning, c2000. 65 p.
00-269010　192 21　0534575943
　Wittgenstein, Ludwig, 1889-1951.

B3376.W564.H63 2000
Hodges, Michael P.
Thinking in the ruins: Wittgenstein and
Santayana on contingency/ Michael Hodges and
John Lachs. Nashville: Vanderbilt University
Press, 2000. xiii, 128 p.
99-006700　191　0826513417
　Wittgenstein, Ludwig, -- 1889-1951.
Santayana, George, -- 1863-1952.

B3376.W564.J33 1998
Jacquette, Dale.
Wittgenstein's thought in transition/ Dale
Jacquette. West Lafayette, Ind.: Purdue
University Press, c1998. x, 356 p.
97-009813　192　155753103X
　Wittgenstein, Ludwig, -- 1889-1951.

B3376.W564.J364 2001
Janik, Allan.
Wittgenstein's Vienna revisited/ Allan Janik.
New Brunswick, USA:　Transaction Publishers,
c2001. xv, 287 p.
00-054383　943.6/13044　0765800500
　Wittgenstein, Ludwig, -- 1889-1951.Logical
positivism -- History.Vienna (Austria) --
Intellectual life -- 20th century.

B3376.W564.M2 1958
Malcolm, Norman, 1911-
Ludwig Wittgenstein, a memoir. With a
biographical sketch by Georg Henrik von
Wright. London, Oxford University Press, 1958.
99 p.
58-004281　921.3
　Wittgenstein, Ludwig, -- 1889-1951.

B3376.W564.N49 2000
The new Wittgenstein/ edited by Alice Crary and
Rupert Read. London; Routledge, 2000. ix,
403 p.
99-048803　192　0415173183
　Wittgenstein, Ludwig, -- 1889-1951.

B3376.W564.P5
Pitcher, George.
The philosophy of Wittgenstein.　Englewood
Cliffs, N.J., Prentice-Hall [1964] xi, 340 p.
64-012550　193
　Wittgenstein, Ludwig, -- 1889-1951.

B3376.W564.W5556 1989
Wittgenstein: attention to particulars: essays in honour of Rush Rhees (1905-89)/ edited by D.Z. Phillips and Peter Winch. New York: St. Martin's Press, c1989. vii, 205 p.
89-034718   192   0312034997
Wittgenstein, Ludwig, -- 1889-1951. Rhees, Rush.

B3581-3614 Modern (1450/1660-) — By region or country — Italy

B3581.P73.M35 1992
Mali, Joseph.
The rehabilitation of myth: Vico's New science/ Joseph Mali. Cambridge; Cambridge University Press, 1992. xv, 275 p.
91-041975   195   0521419522
Vico, Giambattista, -- 1668-1744. -- Principi di una scienza nuova.Myth. Philosophy. Social sciences.

B3581.P74.P65
Pompa, Leon.
Vico: a study of the new science/ Leon Pompa. London; Cambridge University Press, 1975. xii, 194 p.
74-079140   195   0521205840
Vico, Giambattista, -- 1668-1744. -- Principi di una scienza nuova.

B3583.A3
Adams, H. P.
The life and writings of Giambattista Vico, by H. P. Adams. London, G. Allen & Unwin, ltd. [1935] 236 p.
35-013423
Vico, Giambattista, -- 1668-1744.

B3614.C74.A5
Croce, Benedetto, 1866-1952.
An autobiography, translated from the Italian by R.G. Collingwood, with a preface by J.A. Smith. Oxford, The Clarendon Press, 1927. 116 p.
27-024040
Croce, Benedetto, 1866-1952. Philosophers -- Italy -- Biography.

B3614.C74.S6 1952a
Sprigge, Cecil J. S. 1896-
Benedetto Croce: man and thinker. New Haven, Yale University Press, 1952. 64 p.
52-010461   921.5
Croce, Benedetto, -- 1866-1952.

B3958-3999 Modern (1450/1660-) — By region or country — Netherlands (Low Countries)

B3958.R3
Spinoza, Benedictus de, 1632-1677.
The philosophy of Spinoza, selected from his chief works, with a life of Spinoza and an introduction, by Joseph Ratner. New York, The Modern library [c1927] lxx, 376 p.
27-006162

B3973.E5.E38
Spinoza, Benedictus de, 1632-1677.
Ethics/ by Benedict de Spinoza; translated by George Eliot; edited by Thomas Deegan. Salzburg: Institut fur Anglistik und Amerikanistik, 1981. xi, 259 p.
81-169614   170
Ethics.

B3997.N33 1999
Nadler, Steven M., 1958-
Spinoza: a life/ Steven Nadler. Cambridge, U.K.; Cambridge University Press, 1999. xiii, 407 p.
98-036034   199/.492   0521552109
Spinoza, Benedictus de, -- 1632-1677.Philosophers -- Netherlands -- Biography.

B3998.F43
Feuer, Lewis Samuel, 1912-
Spinoza and the rise of liberalism.   Boston, Beacon Press [1958] x, 323 p.
58-006235   199.492
Spinoza, Benedictus de, -- 1632-1677.Liberalism.

B3998.H275 1992
Harris, Errol E.
Spinoza's philosophy, an outline/ Errol E. Harris. Atlantic Highlands, N.J.: Humanities Press, 1992. x, 125 p.
91-035694   199/.492   0391037366
Spinoza, Benedictus de, -- 1632-1677.

B3998.R6 1963
Roth, Leon, 1896-1963.
Spinoza, Descartes, & Maimonides. New York, Russell & Russell [1963, c1924] 148 p.
63-015176   190
Spinoza, Benedictus de, -- 1632-1677. Descartes, Rene, -- 1596-1650. Maimonides, Moses, -- 1135-1204.

B3999.F8.K37 1987
Kashap, S. Paul.
Spinoza and moral freedom/ S. Paul Kashap. Albany: State University of New York Press, c1987. xvi, 198 p.
86-030210   170   0887065295
Spinoza, Benedictus de, -- 1632-1677.Free will and determinism -- History -- 17th century. Ethics, Modern -- 17th century.

B4201 Modern (1450/1660-) — By region or country — Russia — General works

B4201.E3
Edie, James M.,
Russian philosophy. Edited by James M. Edie, James P. Scanlan [and] Mary-Barbara Zeldin, with the collaboration of George L. Kline. Chicago, Quadrangle Books [1965] 3 v.
64-010928   197.2
Philosophy, Russian. Philosophers -- Soviet Union -- Biography. Slavophilism.

B4238-4262 Modern (1450/1660-) — By region or country — Russia — By period

B4238.B43.S314 1950a
Berdiaev, Nikolai, 1874-1948.
Dream and reality; an essay in autobiography. [Translated by Katherine Lampert] New York, Macmillan, 1951 [c1950] xv, 332 p.
51-001608   921.7
Berdiaev, Nikolai, -- 1874-1948.

B4238.B43.T83 1953
Berdiaev, Nikolai, 1874-1948.
The realm of spirit and the realm of Caesar; translated by Donald A. Lowrie. New York, Harper [1953, c1952] 182 p.
53-005002   197
Socialism. Spirituality. Civilization Philosophy.

B4249.L384.A69 1972
Althusser, Louis.
Lenin and philosophy, and other essays. Translated from the French by Ben Brewster. New York, Monthly Review Press [1972, c1971] 253 p.
78-178710   335.43   085345213X
Lenin, Vladimir Ilich, -- 1870-1924. Marx, Karl, -- 1818-1883. -- Kapital.

B4262.E5.W69 2000
Solovyov, Vladimir Sergeyevich, 1853-1900.
Politics, law, and morality: essays/ by V.S. Soloviev; edited and translated by Vladimir Wozniuk; foreword by Gary Saul Morson. New Haven: Yale University Press, c2000. xxix, 330 p.
99-041463   197   0300079958
Philosophy.

B4351-4378 Modern (1450/1660-) — By region or country — Scandinavia

B4351.A34.K5
Kierkegaard, Soren, 1813-1855.
On authority and revelation: The book on Adler, or A Cycle of ethico-religious essays. Translated, with an introduction and notes by Walter Lowrie. Princeton, Princeton University Press, 1955. xxvii, 205 p.
55-006246   198.9
Adler, Adolph Peter, -- 1812-1869.

B4371.W38 2001
Watkin, Julia.
Historical dictionary of Kierkegaard's philosophy/ Julia Watkin. Lanham, Md.: Scarecrow Press, 2001. xx, 411 p.
00-038762   198/.9   0810838176
Kierkegaard, Soren, -- 1813-1855 -- Dictionaries.

B4372.E5.A8
Kierkegaard, Soren, 1813-1855.
The living thoughts of Kierkegaard/ presented
by W.H. Auden. New York: D. McKay, c1952.
225 p.
52-013506   198.9
Philosophy.

B4372.E5 2000
Kierkegaard, Soren, 1813-1855.
The essential Kierkegaard/ edited by Howard V.
Hong and Edna H. Hong. Princeton, N.J.:
Princeton University Press, 2000.
99-039031   198/.9   0691033099
Philosophy.

B4373.A4723.W47 1996
Westphal, Merold.
Becoming a self: a reading of Kierkegaard's
concluding unscientific postscript/ Merold
Westphal. West Lafayette, Ind.: Purdue
University Press, c1996. xiii, 261 p.
96-008604   201   1557530890
*Kierkegaard, Soren, -- 1813-1855. --
Afsluttende   uvidenskabelig
efterskrift.Christianity   --   Philosophy.
Apologetics. Self (Philosophy)*

B4373.O42.E5 1989
Kierkegaard, Soren, 1813-1855.
The concept of irony, with continual reference to
Socrates: together with notes of Schelling's
Berlin lectures/ by Soren Kierkegaard; edited
and translated with introduction and notes by
Howard V. Hong and Edna H. Hong. Princeton,
N.J.: Princeton University Press, c1989. xxv,
633 p.
89-003642   190   0691073546
*Schelling, Friedrich Wilhelm Joseph von, --
1775-1854.Irony. Socrates.*

B4373.S83.E55 1967
Kierkegaard, Soren, 1813-1855.
Stages on life's way. Translated by Walter
Lowrie. Introd. by Paul Sponheim. New York,
Schocken Books [1967] 472 p.
66-014875   198.9

B4375.K54 2000
Hong, Nathaniel J.
Cumulative index to Kierkegaard's writings/
prepared by Nathaniel J. Hong, Kathryn Hong,
Regine Prenzel-Guthrie. Princeton, N.J.:
Princeton University Press, 2000.
99-058557   198/.9   0691032254
Kierkegaard, Soren, -- 1813-1855 -- Indexes.

B4376.S6713 1996
Encounters with Kierkegaard: a life as seen by
his contemporaries/ collected, edited, and
annotated by Bruce H. Kirmmse; translated by
Bruce H. Kirmmse and Virginia R. Laursen.
Princeton, N.J.; Princeton University Press,
c1996. xx, 358 p.
95-043183   198/.9   0691011060
*Kierkegaard,   Soren,   --   1813-
1855.Philosophers -- Denmark -- Biography.
Authors, Danish -- Denmark -- Biography.
Theologians -- Denmark -- Biography.*

B4377.G715 1992
Green, Ronald Michael.
Kierkegaard and Kant: the hidden debt/ Ronald
M. Green. Albany: State University of New
York Press, c1992. xviii, 301 p.
91-030775   198/.9   0791411079
*Kierkegaard, Soren, -- 1813-1855. Kant,
Immanuel, -- 1724-1804.*

B4377.K45 1998
Kierkegaard: a critical reader/ edited by
Jonathan Ree and Jane Chamberlain. Oxford,
UK; Blackwell, 1998. x, 186 p.
97-022299   193   063120198X
Kierkegaard, Soren, -- 1813-1855.

B4377.L35
Lawson, Lewis A.,
Kierkegaard's   presence   in   contemporary
American life: essays from various disciplines.
Edited, with an introd. and bibliography, by
Lewis A. Lawson. Metuchen, N.J., Scarecrow
Press, 1970 [c1971] 299 p.
76-142237   198/.9   0810803585
*Kierkegaard,   Soren,   --   1813-1855   --
Addresses, essays, lectures.*

B4377.T514
Thompson, Josiah,
Kierkegaard: a collection of critical essays.
Edited by Josiah Thompson. Garden City, N.Y.,
Anchor Books, 1972. xv, 464 p.
78-175420   198/.9   0385019785
*Kierkegaard,   Soren,   --   1813-1855   --
Addresses, essays, lectures.*

B4378.E8.F68 1992
Foundations   of   Kierkegaard's   vision   of
community: religion, ethics, and politics in
Kierkegaard/ edited by George B. Connell and
C. Stephen Evans. Atlantic Highlands, N.J.:
Humanities   Press   International,   c1992.   xxii,
245 p.
91-009137   198.9   0391037242
*Kierkegaard, Soren, -- 1813-1855 -- Ethics.
Kierkegaard, Soren, -- 1813-1855 -- Political
and social views. Self (Philosophy) Philosophy
and religion. Political science -- Philosophy.*

B4378.S4.K54 1998
Kierkegaard: the self in society/ edited by
George Pattison and Steven Shakespeare. New
York: St. Martin's Press, 1998. xii, 225 p.
97-040506   198/.9   031221166X
*Kierkegaard,   Soren,   --   1813-
1855.Interpersonal relations. Self (Philosophy)*

B4378.S4.T38 2000
Taylor, Mark C., 1945-
Journeys to selfhood: Hegel and Kierkegaard/
Mark C. Taylor. New York: Fordham University
Press, 2000. xxi, 298 p.
00-025099   126/.092/2   0823220583
*Kierkegaard, Soren, -- 1813-1855. Hegel,
Georg Wilhelm Friedrich, -- 1770-1831. Self
(Philosophy)*

B4568 Modern (1450/1660-   ) —
By region or country —
Spain and Portugal

B4568.O73.Q4313 1961
Ortega Y Gasset, Jose, 1883-1955.
What is philosophy? Translated from the
Spanish by Mildred Adams. New York, Norton
[1961, c1960] 252 p.
61-005621   101
Philosophy -- Addresses, essays, lectures.

B4568.O74.H63
Holmes, Oliver W., 1938-
Human reality and the social world: Ortega's
philosophy of history/ Oliver W. Holmes.
Amherst: University of Massachusetts Press,
1975. xi, 175 p.
74-021238   901   0870231731
*Ortega y Gasset, Jose, -- 1883-1955.History -
- Philosophy.*

B4568.U53.D5 1954
Unamuno, Miguel de, 1864-1936.
Tragic sense of life. Translator: J. E. Crawford
Flitch. [New York] Dover Publications [1954]
xxxv, 332 p.
54-004730   196
*Immortality.   Philosophy   and   religion.
Pessimism.*

B4695 Modern (1450/1600-) —
By region or country —
Eastern Europe

B4695.H63 S8
Hoernle, Reinhold Friedrich Alfred, 1880-
1943.
Studies in philosophy. Edited and with a memoir
by Daniel S. Robinson. Cambridge, Harvard
University Press [1952] xvii, 333 p.
53-009922
Philosophy. -- cm

B5005-5241 Modern (1450/1600-)
— By region or country — Asia

B5005.G74 1995
Great thinkers of the Eastern world: the major
thinkers and the philosophical and religious
classics of China, India, Japan, Korea, and the
world of Islam/ edited by Ian P. McGreal. New
York: HarperCollins Publishers, c1995. xvii,
505 p.
94-019418   181   0062700855
*Philosophy, Asian. Philosophers -- Asia.
Religious biography -- Asia. Asia -- Religion.*

B5131.I5
Indian philosophy today/ edited by N. K.
Devaraja. Delhi: Macmillan Co. of India, 1975.
xxiii, 286 p.
75-908522   181/.4
*Philosophy, Indic -- 20th century --
Addresses, essays, lectures.*

B5134.B483.P57 1994
Bhaskar, Roy, 1944-
Plato etc.: the problems of philosophy and their resolution/ Roy Bhaskar. London; Verso, 1994. xii, 267 p.
94-021159   100   0860914992
Philosophy. Critical realism.

B5134.G42 G46 1998
Ghose, Aurobindo, 1872-1950.
The essential writings of Sri Aurobindo/ edited by Peter Heehs. Delhi; Oxford University Press, 1998. xxx, 388 p.
98-902992   0195642848

B5231.C523 2002
Contemporary chinese philosophy/ edited by Chung-Ying Cheng and Nicholas Bunnin Malden, Mass.: Blackwell Publishers, 2002. xiv, 429 p.
2001-043245   181/.11 21   0631217258
Philosophy, Chinese -- 20th century.

B5231.R37 1992
Raphals, Lisa Ann,
Knowing words: wisdom and cunning in the classical traditions of China and Greece/ Lisa Raphals. Ithaca, N.Y.: Cornell University Press, 1992. xviii, 273 p.
91-055554   181/.11 20   0801426197
Philosophy, Chinese. Philosophy, Ancient.

B5231.T46 1990
Thought and law in Qin and Han China: studies dedicated to Anthony Hulsewé on the occasion of his eightieth birthday/ edited by W.L. Idema and E. Zürcher. Leiden; E.J. Brill, 1990. ix, 244 p.
90-042393   931/.04 20   9004092692
Philosophy, Chinese. Law -- China -- History.

B5231.W846 1997
Wu, Kuang-ming.
On Chinese body thinking: a cultural hermeneutic/ by Kuang-ming Wu. Leiden; Brill, 1997. xvi, 492 p.
97-183418   181/.11 21   9004101500
Philosophy, Chinese. Philosophy, Comparative. Body, Human (Philosophy) East and West.

B5233.C6 C66 1991
Confucianism and the modernization of China/ Silke Krieger, Rolf Trauzettel ed. Mainz: V. Hase & Koehler Verlag, c1991. xiv, 474 p.
94-202352   181/.112 20   3775812423
Philosophy, Confucian -- Congresses. Confucian ethics -- Congresses.

B5233.C6 E45 1990
Elman, Benjamin A.,
Classicism, politics, and kinship: the Ch ang-chou school of new text Confucianism in late imperial China/ Benjamin A. Elman. Berkeley: University of California Press, c1990. xxxiii, 409 p.
89-034636   181/.112 20   0520066731
Philosophy, Confucian -- China -- Changzhou (Jiangsu Sheng, China) Political science -- China -- History -- 18th century. Changzhou (Jiangsu Sheng, China) -- Intellectual life.

B5233.C6 W55 1995
Wilson, Thomas A.,
Genealogy of the way: the construction and uses of the Confucian tradition in late imperial China/ Thomas A. Wilson. Stanford, Calif.: Stanford University Press, 1995. x, 376 p.
94-022077   181/.112 20   0804724253
Philosophy, Confucian. Learning and scholarship -- China -- History.

B5234.F44.A3713 2000
Feng, Yu-lan, 1895-
The hall of three pines: an account of my life/ Feng Youlan; translated by Denis C. Mair. Honolulu: University of Hawai'i Press, c2000. xii, 409 p.
99-035524   181/.11   0824814282
Feng, Yu-lan, -- 1895-Philosophers -- China -- Biography.

B5234.L485 H83 1995
Huang, Chin-hsing.
Philosophy, philology, and politics in eighteenth-century China: Li Fu and the Lu-Wang school under the Ch ing/ Chin-shing Huang. Cambridge; Cambridge University Press, 1995. xviii, 204 p.
95-013358   181/.112 20   0521482259
Li, Fu, 1673-1750. Philosophy, Chinese -- 1644-1912. Neo-Confucianism. Political science -- China -- Philosophy.

B5234.M35.M3413 1990
Mao, Tse-tung, 1893-1976.
Mao Zedong on dialectical materialism: writings on philosophy, 1937/ edited by Nick Knight. Armonk, N.Y.: M.E. Sharpe, c1990. 295 p.
89-049016   181/.11   0873326822
Dialectical materialism.

B5241.E2
The Japanese mind; essentials of Japanese philosophy and culture. Charles A. Moore, editor, with the assistance of Aldyth V. Morris. Honolulu, East-West Center Press [1967] x, 357 p.
67-016704   199/.52
Philosophy, Japanese.Japan -- Intellectual life.

B5305-5377 Modern (1450/1600-) — By region or country — Africa

B5305.A373 2000
African philosophy as cultural inquiry/ edited by Ivan Karp and D.A. Masolo. Bloomington: Indiana University Press, c2000. vii, 270 p.
00-038870   199/.6   0253214173
Philosophy, African.

B5305.A375 1998
The African philosophy reader/ edited by P.H. Coetzee and A.P.J. Roux. London; Routledge, 1998. xiii, 467 p.
98-033970   199/.6   0415189055
Philosophy, African.

B5305.I43 1998
Imbo, Samuel Oluoch, 1961-
An introduction to African philosophy/ Samuel Oluoch Imbo. Lanham, Md.: Rowman & Littlefield, c1998. xvii, 157 p.
97-048810   199/.6   0847688402
Philosophy, African.

B5377.S24 1990
Sage philosophy: indigenous thinkers and modern debate on African philosophy/ edited by H. Odera Oruka. Leiden; E.J. Brill, 1990. xxxi, 281 p.
90-045039   199/.6   9004092838
Philosophy -- Africa, Sub-Saharan. Philosophy, African. Wisdom.

B5704 Modern (1450/1600-) — By region or country — Oceania

B5704.S554.S56 1999
Singer and his critics/ edited by Dale Jamieson. Oxford, UK; Blackwell Publishers, 1999. ix, 368 p.
98-042231   170/.92   1557869081
Singer, Peter, -- 1946- -- Ethics.

B5800-5802 Modern (1450/1600-) — By religion — Judaism

B5800.O77 1997
Oppenheim, Michael D., 1946-
Speaking/writing of God: Jewish philosophical reflections on the life with others/ Michael Oppenheim. Albany, NY: State University of New York Press, c1997. x, 201 p.
96-041186   296.3/092/2   0791434575
Rosenzweig, Franz, -- 1886-1929. Levinas, Emmanuel. Philosophy, Jewish. Holocaust (Jewish theology) Feminism -- Religious aspects -- Judaism.

B5802.P67.K46 1998
Kepnes, Steven, 1952-
Reasoning after revelation: dialogues in postmodern Jewish philosophy/ Steven Kepnes, Peter Ochs, and Robert Gibbs. Boulder, Colo: Westview Press, 1998. ix, 163 p.
98-020348   181/.06   081333506X
Philosophy, Jewish. Postmodernism -- Religious aspects -- Judaism. Judaism -- 20th century.

BC Logic

BC6 Collected works (nonserial)

BC6.B8
Butler, R. J.
Analytical philosophy.   New York, Barnes & Noble, 1962
63-002583   108.2
Logic.

BC6.I8
Iseminger, Gary,
Logic and philosophy; selected readings. New York, Appleton-Century-Crofts [1968] viii, 248 p.
68-015407   160/.8
Logic -- Addresses, essays, lectures.

BC6.J3
Jager, Ronald.
Essays in logic from Aristotle to Russell. Englewood Cliffs, N.J., Prentice-Hall, 1963. viii, 180 p.
63-007922   160.82
Logic

BC6.S8
Strawson, P. F.
Philosophical logic, edited by P. F. Strawson. London, Oxford U.P., 1967. 177 p.
68-072121   160/.8
Logic.

BC15 History — General works — 1801-

BC15.B643 1970
Bochenski, Joseph M., 1902-
A history of formal logic, by I. M. Bochenski. Translated and edited by Ivo Thomas. New York, Chelsea Pub. Co. [1970] xxii, 567 p.
72-113118   160/.9   0828402388
Logic -- History.

BC15.K55
Kneale, W. C.
The development of logic/ by William Kneale and Martha Kneale. Oxford [Eng.]: Clarendon Press, c1962, 1978. viii, 783 p.
62-001892   160.9   0198241836
Logic -- History.

BC21 History — Special topics, A-Z

BC21.E64 B65 1993
Boh, Ivan,
Epistemic logic in the later Middle Ages/ Ivan Boh. London; Routledge, 1993. xv, 189 p.
93-018490   160/.9/02 20   0415057264
Epistemics -- History. Logic, Medieval.

BC25-28 History — By period — Ancient

BC25.S76 1988
Staal, Frits.
Universals: studies in Indian logic and linguistics/ Frits Staal. Chicago: University of Chicago Press, 1988. x, 267 p.
87-023187   160/.954 19   0226770001
Hindu logic. Language and logic. Universals (Philosophy)

BC28.B58
Bochenski, Joseph M., 1902-
Ancient formal logic.   Amsterdam, North-Holland Pub. Co., 1951. vi, 122 p.
52-002552
Logic.

BC34 History — By period — Medieval

BC34.B76 1993
Broadie, Alexander.
Introduction to medieval logic/ Alexander Broadie. 2nd ed. Oxford: Clarendon Press; viii, 219 p.
92-033382   160/.9/023 20   0198240260
Logic, Medieval.

BC38 History — By period — Modern

BC38.E33 1989
Edgar, William J.
The elements of logic: for use in computer science, mathematics, and philosophy/ William J. Edgar. Chicago: Science Research Associates, c1989. ix, 149 p.
88-023402   160 19   0574187553
Logic, Modern. Logic, Symbolic and mathematical.

BC38.H6 1961
Howell, Wilbur Samuel, 1904-
Logic and rhetoric in England, 1500-1700. New York, Russell & Russell [1961, c1956] vii, 411 p.
61-019959   160
Logic -- History. Rhetoric -- 1500-1800.

BC50 Philosophy. Methodology. Relation to other topics

BC50.D42
Dewey, John, 1859-1952.
Essays in experimental logic. New York, Dover Publications [n.d.] 444 p.
54-010017   160.4
Thought and thinking. Realism. Logic.

BC50.D43
Dewey, John, 1859-1952.
Logic, the theory of inquiry, by John Dewey. New York, H. Holt and Company [c1938] viii, 546 p.
38-027918   160
Logic. Thought and thinking. Logic

BC50.G4 1956
Geach, P. T.
Mental acts, their content and their objects. London, Routledge & Paul, [n.d.] 136 p.
58-000966   160
Logic.

BC50.M36 2000
Mason, Richard.
Before logic/ Richard Mason. Albany: State University of New York Press, c2000. 153 p.
99-059365   160   0791445313
Logic.

BC50.N23
Nagel, Ernest, 1901-
Logic without metaphysics, and other essays in the philosophy of science. Glencoe, Ill., Free Press [1957, c1956] 433 p.
56-010582   160
Logic.

BC51 Philosophy. Methodology. Relation to other topics — Relation to speculative philosophy

BC51.B58 1998
Boolos, George.
Logic, logic, and logic/ George Boolos; with introductions and afterword by John P. Burgess; edited by Richard Jeffrey. Cambridge, Mass: Harvard University Press, 1998. ix, 443 p.
97-037668   160 21   0674537661
Logic.

BC51.B664 1993
Brenner, William H.,
Logic and philosophy: an integrated introduction/ William H. Brenner. Notre Dame: University of Notre Dame Press, c1993. x, 217 p.
92-056865   160 20   0268012997
Logic. Philosophy.

BC51.D85 1991
Dummett, Michael A. E.
The logical basis of metaphysics/ Michael Dummett. Cambridge, Mass.: Harvard University Press, 1991. xi, 355 p.
90-039999   121/.68
Metaphysics. Logic.

BC51.P88 1971
Putnam, Hilary.
Philosophy of logic. New York, Harper & Row [1971] 76 p.
71-149364   160   0061360422
Logic.

BC51.Q5 1986
Quine, W. V.
Philosophy of logic/ W.V. Quine. Cambridge, Mass.: Harvard University Press, 1986. ix, 109 p.
85-024734   160   0674665635
Logic. Philosophy.

BC55 Philosophy. Methodology. Relation to other topics — Relation to ethics

BC55.L4
Leys, Wayne A. R.
Ethics for policy decisions; the art of asking deliberative questions. New York, Prentice-Hall, 1952. 428 p.
52-008388   171
Ethics. Logic.

BC57 Philosophy. Methodology. Relation to other topics — Other

BC57.N94 1990
Nye, Andrea, 1939-
Words of power: a feminist reading of the history of logic/ Andrea Nye. New York: Routledge, 1990. xiii, 190 p.
89-028195   160/.82   0415901995
Logic -- History. Feminist theory.

BC60-63 General works, treatises, and advanced textbooks — Deductive logic — Early works through 1800

BC60.L64 1988
Logic and the philosophy of language/ editors, Norman Kretzmann, Eleonore Stump. Cambridge [Cambridgeshire]; Cambridge University Press, 1988. viii, 531 p.
87-030542   160   0521236002
Logic -- Early works to 1800. Language and languages -- Philosophy -- Early works to 1800. Logic, Medieval -- Sources.

BC63.K3 1972
Kant, Immanuel, 1724-1804.
Kant's Introduction to logic and his Essay on the mistaken subtilty of the four figures. Translated by Thomas Kingsmill Abbott, with a few notes by Coleridge. Westport, Conn., Greenwood Press [1972, c1963] 100 p.
77-156197   160   0837161487
Logic.

BC71 General works, treatises, and advanced textbooks — Deductive logic — 1801-

BC71.B3
Beardsley, Monroe C.
Practical logic. New York, Prentice-Hall, 1950. xxviii, 580 p.
50-008820   160
Logic.

BC71.B32 1966
Beardsley, Monroe C.
Thinking straight; principles of reasoning for readers and writers [by] Monroe C. Beardsley. 3d ed. Englewood Cliffs, N.J., Prentice-Hall [1966] ix, 292 p.
66-016388   160
Logic.

BC71.C6 1938
Coffey, Peter, 1876-
The science of logic; an inquiry into the principles of accurate thought and scientific method, by P. Coffey. New York, P. Smith, 1938. 2 v.
39-015569   160b
Logic. Science -- Methodology. Thought and thinking.

BC71.C63 1977
Cohen, Morris Raphael,
A preface to logic/ by Morris R. Cohen. New York: Dover Publications, 1977, c1944. xi, 209 p.
77-075235   160   0486235173
Logic.

BC71.C65 2002
A companion to philosophical logic/ edited by Dale Jacquette. Malden, Mass.: Blackwell, 2002. xiii, 816 p.
2001-043236   160 21   0631216715
Logic.

BC71.D25 1981
Davies, Martin, 1950-
Meaning, quantification, necessity: themes in philosophical logic/ Martin Davies. London; Routledge & Kegan Paul, 1981. xii, 282 p.
81-201700   160   0710007590
Logic.

BC71.E57 1994
Epstein, Richard L.,
The semantic foundations of logic/ Richard L. Epstein. New York: Oxford University Press, [1994-] v. <1 >
94-013517   160 20   0195087607
Logic. Logic, Symbolic and mathematical. Semantics.

BC71.E67 1978
Logic and language (first series): essays/ by Gilbert Ryle ... [et al.]; edited with an introduction by Antony Flew. Oxford: B. Blackwell, 1978, c1960. vii, 206 p.
86-182070   149/.94 19   063103420X
Logic. Language and languages.

BC71.G34 1980
Geach, P. T.
Reference and generality: an examination of some medieval and modern theories/ by Peter T. Geach. 3d ed. Ithaca, N.Y.: Cornell University Press, 1980. 231 p.
80-010977   160   080141315X
Logic. Language and languages -- Philosophy. Reference (Philosophy) Logic, Medieval.

BC71.G7 1997
Grayling, A. C.
An introduction to philosophical logic/ A.C. Grayling. 3rd ed. Oxford, UK; Blackwell Publishers, 1997. vii, 343 p.
97-003849   160 21   0631299289
Logic. Language and languages -- Philosophy.

BC71.H15
Haack, Susan.
Philosophy of logics/ Susan Haack. Cambridge [Eng.]; Cambridge University Press, 1978. xvi, 276 p.
77-017071   160   0521219884
Logic.

BC71.J38 1981
Jeffrey, Richard C.
Formal logic: its scope and limits/ Richard Jeffrey. 2d ed. New York: McGraw-Hill, c1981. xiv, 198 p.
80-023655   160 19   0070323216
First-order logic.

BC71.J53 1991
Johnson-Laird, P. N. 1936-
Deduction/ P.N. Johnson-Laird, Ruth M.J. Byrne. Hove, UK; L. Erlbaum Associates, c1991. xii, 243 p.
91-188872 153.4/33 0863771483
Logic. Reasoning.

BC71.J7 1916
Joseph, H. W. B. 1867-1943.
An introduction to logic, by H.W.B. Joseph ... Oxford, Clarendon Press, 1916. xii, 608 p.
19-005069
Logic.

BC71.M36 2000
McGinn, Colin,
Logical properties: identity, existence, predication, necessity, truth/ Colin McGinn. Oxford: Clarendon Press; vi, 114 p.
00-056653 160 21 0199241813
Logic.

BC71.N6
Northrop, F. S. C. 1893-
The logic of the sciences and the humanities. New York, Macmillan Co., 1947. xiv, 402 p.
48-005077 160
Logic. Methodology. Knowledge, Theory of.

BC71.P377 1991
Parry, William T.
Aristotelian logic/ William T. Parry and Edward A. Hacker. Albany: State University of New York Press, c1991. x, 545 p.
90-044126 160 20 0791406903
Logic.

BC71.P38 2000
Paulos, John Allen.
I think, therefore I laugh: the flip side of philosophy/ John Allen Paulos. [2nd ed.]. New York: Columbia University Press, c2000. x, 178 p.
99-034799 190/.207 21 0231119151
Logic. Philosophy -- Humor.

BC71.P7 1972
Prazak, Milos.
Language and logic. Westport, Conn., Greenwood Press [1972, c1963] 154 p.
76-141264 160 0837158605
Logic. Language and languages -- Philosophy.

BC71.Q48 1963
Quine, W. V.
From a logical point of view; 9 logico-philosophical essays. New York, Harper & Row [1963, c1961] viii, 184 p.
61-015277
Logic.

BC71.Q5 1982
Quine, W. V.
Methods of logic/ W.V. Quine. Cambridge, Mass.: Harvard University Press, 1982. x, 333 p.
81-022929 160 0674571754
Logic.

BC71.R43 1994
Read, Stephen, 1947-
Thinking about logic: an introduction to the philosophy of logic/ Stephen Read. Oxford; Oxford University Press, 1994. viii, 262 p.
94-005697 160 019289238X
Logic.

BC71.S25 1995
Salmon, Merrilee H.
Introduction to logic and critical thinking/ Merrilee H. Salmon. 3rd ed. Fort Worth: Harcourt Brace College Publishers, c1995. xvii, 471 p.
94-072861 160 20 0155430645
Logic. Reasoning.

BC71.S47 1991
Sher, Gila.
The bounds of logic: a generalized viewpoint/ Gila Sher. Cambridge, Mass.: MIT Press, c1991. xv, 178 p.
91-009580 160 0262193116
Logic.

BC71.W65 1989
Wolfram, Sybil, 1931-
Philosophical logic: an introduction/ Sybil Wolfram. London; Routledge, 1989. xiv, 290 p.
88-023963 160 0415023181
Logic.

BC91-99 General works, treatises, and advanced textbooks — Inductive and empirical logic — 1801-

BC91.B25 1992
Baird, Davis.
Inductive logic: probability and statistics/ Davis Baird. Englewood Cliffs, N.J.: Prentice Hall, c1992. xvi, 384 p.
91-027074 161 20 0135396859
Induction (Logic) Statistics.

BC91.C6 1989
Cohen, L. Jonathan
An introduction to the philosophy of induction and probability/ L. Jonathan Cohen. Oxford: Clarendon Press; 1989. x, 217 p.
88-021674 161 019875079X
Induction (Logic) Probabilities.

BC91.C63
Cohen, L. Jonathan
The implications of induction, by L. Jonathan Cohen. London, Methuen, 1970. vii, 248 p.
76-489330 161 041616000X
Induction (Logic) Probabilities.

BC91.M6 1930
Mill, John Stuart, 1806-1873.
A system of logic, ratiocinative and inductive; being a connected view of the principles of evidence and the methods of scientific investigation/ by John Stuart Mill. London, Longmans, Green, 1930. xvi, 622 p.
10-007122
Knowledge, Theory of. Logic. Science -- Methodology.

BC91.S5 1986
Skyrms, Brian.
Choice and chance: an introduction to inductive logic/ Brian Skyrms. Belmont, Calif: Wadsworth Pub. Co., c1986. vi, 218 p.
85-007137 161 0534051901
Induction (Logic) Probabilities.

BC91.S96
Swinburne, Richard,
The justification of induction. [London, Oxford University Press, 1974. 179 p.
74-158460 161 0198570293
Induction (Logic)

BC99.P65.M6713 1988
Mortimer, Halina.
The logic of induction/ Halina Mortimer, with additional material by I. Craig; translator Ewa Such-Klimontowicz, translation editors I. Craig and A. Cohn. Chichester [England]; Halsted Press, 1988. 182 p.
88-022962 161 0470212349
Induction (Logic)

BC108 Elementary textbooks. Outlines, syllabi, etc. — 1801- — English

BC108.A543 2001
Allen, Colin.
Logic primer/ Colin Allen and Michael Hand. 2nd ed. Cambridge, Mass.: MIT Press, c2001. xvii, 191 p.
00-048960 160 21 0262511266
Logic.

BC108.B27 1998
Soccio, Douglas J.
Practical logic: an antidote for uncritical thinking/ Douglas J. Soccio and Vincent E. Barry. 5th ed. Fort Worth: Harcourt Brace College Publishers, c1998. xviii, 505 p.
97-073101 160 21 0155030361
Logic.

BC108.B72 1961
Brennan, Joseph Gerard, 1910-
A handbook of logic. New York, Harper [1961] 250 p.
61-008557 160
Logic.

BC108.C52
Chase, Stuart, 1888-
Guides to straight thinking, with 13 common fallacies. New York, Harper [1956] 212 p.
56-008747   160
Logic. Fallacies (Logic)

BC108.C67
Cohen, Morris Raphael, 1880-1947.
An introduction to logic and scientific method, by Morris R. Cohen and Ernest Nagel. New York, Harcourt, Brace and company [c1934] xii, 467 p.
34-002513   160
Logic. Methodology.

BC108.C69 1986
Copi, Irving M.
Introduction to logic/ Irving M. Copi. New York: Macmillan; c1986. xiv, 617 p.
85-013751   160   0023250208
Logic.

BC108.H18 1999
Haight, M. R.
The snake and the fox: an introduction to logic/ Mary Haight. London; Routledge, 1999. xi, 495 p.
98-034515   170   0415166934
Logic.

BC108.H36 1993
Henry, Granville C.
The mechanism and freedom of logic/ Granville C. Henry. Lanham: University Press of America, c1993. ix, 232 p.
92-035172   160   0819189634
Logic. Prolog (Computer program language)

BC108.K59 1993
Kosko, Bart.
Fuzzy thinking: the new science of fuzzy logic/ Bart Kosko. New York: Hyperion, c1993. xvi, 318 p.
92-042019   160   1562828398
Logic. Philosophy and science. Fuzzy systems.

BC108.L44 2000
LePore, Ernest, 1950-
Meaning and argument: an introduction to logic through language/ Ernest Lepore. Malden, Mass.: Blackwell, 2000. xvi, 418 p.
99-033936   160   0631205810
Logic. Language and logic.

BC108.P8 1962
Prior, Arthur N.
Formal logic. Oxford, Clarendon Press, 1962. 341 p.
62-003329   160
Logic.

BC108.P89
Purtill, Richard L., 1931-
Logical thinking [by] Richard L. Purtill. New York, Harper & Row [1972] xiii, 157 p.
70-174532   160   0060452978
Logic. Logic -- Problems, exercises, etc.

BC108.R77
Ruby, Lionel.
The art of making sense: a guide to logical thinking/ by Lionel Ruby. Philadelphia: Lippincott, c1954. 286 p.
54-006108   160
Logic.

BC108.S2 1984
Salmon, Wesley C.
Logic/ Wesley C. Salmon. Englewood Cliffs, N.J.: Prentice-Hall, c1984. xii, 180 p.
83-013924   160   013540021X
Logic.

BC108.S9 1955
Swabey, Marie Taylor (Collins), 1891-
Logic and nature. New York, New York University Press, 1955. 199 p.
55-005979
Logic.

BC108.Z35 2000
Zalabardo, Jose L.
Introduction to the theory of logic/ Jose L. Zalabardo. Boulder, Colo.: Westview Press, c2000. xiii, 330 p.
99-045588   160   0813390613
Logic.

BC126 Many-valued logic

BC126.R4
Rescher, Nicholas.
Many-valued logic. New York, McGraw-Hill [1969] xv, 359 p.
69-011708   164
Many-valued logic.

BC128 First-order logic

BC128.B37 1993
Barwise, Jon.
The language of first-order logic: including the Mackintosh version of Tarski's world 4.0/ Jon Barwise & John Etchemendy. 3rd ed., rev. & expanded. Stanford, Calif.: Center for the Study of Language and Information, xiv, 313 p.
93-000419   160 20   0937073997
First-order logic.

BC135 Symbolic and mathematical logic — 1801-

BC135.B435
Bergmann, Merrie.
The logic book/ Merrie Bergmann, James Moor, Jack Nelson. New York: Random House, c1980. ix, 459 p.
79-016459   160   0394323238
Logic, Symbolic and mathematical. Predicate (Logic)

BC135.B45
Beth, Evert Willem.
Formal methods; an introduction to symbolic logic and to the study of effective operations in arithmetic and logic. Dordrecht, D. Reidel Pub. Co.; [1962] 170 p.
62-003731   164
Logic, Symbolic and mathematical.

BC135.B7 1940
Boole, George, 1815-1864.
The laws of thought (1854) Chicago, The Open court publishing company, 1940. xvi, 448 p.
41-008050   164
Logic, Symbolic and mathematical. Thought and thinking. Probabilities.

BC135.C312
Carnap, Rudolf, 1891-1970.
The continuum of inductive methods. [Chicago] University of Chicago Press [1952] v, 92 p.
52-007477   161
Logic, Symbolic and mathematical.

BC135.C316 1959
Carnap, Rudolf, 1891-1970.
Introduction to semantics, and Formalization of logic. Cambridge, Harvard University Press, 1959. xiv, 159 p.
58-013846   149.94
Semantics (Philosophy) Logic, Symbolic and mathematical.

BC135.C323
Carnap, Rudolf, 1891-1970.
The logical syntax of language, by Rudolf Carnap ... London, Rutledge and K. Paul, [1964,c1937] xvi, 352 p.
37-007689   164
Logical positivism. Logic, Symbolic and mathematical.

BC135.C33
Carnap, Rudolf, 1891-1970.
Philosophy and logical syntax, by Rudolf Carnap... London, K. Paul, Trench, Trubner & Co., ltd., 1935. 100 p.
35-008828   164
Logic, Symbolic and mathematical. Language and languages. Philosophy.

BC135.C42
Church, Alonzo, 1903-
Introduction to mathematical logic. Princeton, Princeton University Press, [1956-   ]
53-010150   164
Logic, Symbolic and mathematical.

BC135.C58 1979
Copi, Irving M.
Symbolic logic/ by Irving M. Copi. New York: Macmillan, c1979. xiii, 398 p.
78-015671   511/.3   0023249803
Logic, Symbolic and mathematical.

BC135.E83 1990
Etchemendy, John, 1952-
The concept of logical consequence/ John Etchemendy. Cambridge, Mass.: Harvard University Press, 1990. 174 p.
89-028866 160 0674156420
Tarski, Alfred.Logic, Symbolic and mathematical.

BC135.F6813 1964
Frege, Gottlob, 1848-1925.
The basic laws of arithmetic; exposition of the system. Translated and edited, with an introd., by Montgomery Furth. Berkeley, University of California Press, 1964. lxiii, 142 p.
64-023479 164
Logic, Symbolic and mathematical.

BC135.F7 1980
Frege, Gottlob, 1848-1925.
Translations from the philosophical writings of Gottlob Frege/ edited Peter Geach and Max Black; index prepared by E.D. Klemke. Oxford, England: Blackwell, 1980. x, 228 p.
82-124415 160 0631129014
Logic, Symbolic and mathematical -- Addresses, essays, lectures. Mathematics -- Philosophy -- Addresses, essays, lectures.

BC135.G39 1990
Gensler, Harry J.,
Symbolic logic: classical and advanced systems/ Harry J. Gensler. Englewood Cliffs, N.J.: Prentice Hall, c1990. vi, 329 p.
89-048288 160 20 0138799415
Logic, Symbolic and mathematical.

BC135.G7
Grandy, Richard E.
Advanced logic for applications/ Richard E. Grandy. Dordrecht, Holland; D. Reidel Pub. Co., c1977. xi, 167 p.
77-003046 511/.3 9027707812
Logic, Symbolic and mathematical.

BC135.H35
Henle, Paul
Structure, method, and meaning; essays in honor of Henry M. Sheffer, with a foreword by Felix Frankfurter. Edited by Paul Henle, Horace M. Kallen [and] Susanne K. Langer. New York, Liberal Arts Press, 1951. xvi, 306 p.
51-002957 160.4
Sheffer, Henry Maurice.Logic, Symbolic and mathematical.

BC135.H514
Hilbert, David, 1862-1943.
Principles of mathematical logic, by D. Hilbert and W. Ackermann; translated from the German by Lewis M. Hammond, George G. Leckie [and] F. Steinhardt. Edited and with notes by Robert E. Luce. New York, Chelsea Pub. Co., 1950. xii, 172 p.
50-004784 164
Logic, Symbolic and mathematical.

BC135.H68 1997
Howson, Colin.
Logic with trees: an introduction to symbolic logic/ Colin Howson. London; Routledge, 1997. xiii, 197 p.
96-007315 160 20 0415133416
Logic, Symbolic and mathematical.

BC135.K53 2002
Klenk, Virginia,
Understanding symbolic logic/ Virginia Klenk. 4th ed. Upper Saddle River, N.J.: Prentice Hall, c2002. xv, 447 p.
2001-036244 160 21 0130201421
Logic, Symbolic and mathematical.

BC135.K67 1992
Koslow, Arnold.
A structuralist theory of logic/ Arnold Koslow. Cambridge [England]; Cambridge University Press, 1992. xi, 418 p.
91-023787 160 0521412676
Logic, Symbolic and mathematical. Implication (Logic) Structuralism.

BC135.L5 1960
Lieber, Lillian Rosanoff, 1886-
Mits, wits, and logic. Drawings by Hugh Gray Lieber. New York, Norton [1960] 240 p.
60-012023 164
Logic, Symbolic and mathematical. Science -- Philosophy.

BC135.M35
Massey, Gerald J.
Understanding symbolic logic [by] Gerald J. Massey. New York, Harper & Row [1970] xix, 428 p.
75-101535 164
Logic, Symbolic and mathematical.

BC135.M37 1972
Mates, Benson, 1919-
Elementary logic. New York, Oxford University Press, 1972. xii, 237 p.
74-166004 511/.3 019501491X
Logic, Symbolic and mathematical.

BC135.P683 1990
Pollock, John L.
Technical methods in philosophy/ John L. Pollock. Boulder: Westview Press, 1990. x, 126 p.
89-038216 160 0813378710
Logic, Symbolic and mathematical. Set theory. Predicate calculus.

BC135.P775
Prior, Arthur N.
Past, present and future, by Arthur Prior. Oxford, Clarendon P., 1967. x, 217 p.
67-091521 164
Logic, Symbolic and mathematical. Time. Modality (Logic)

BC135.P78
Prior, Arthur N.
Time and modality. Oxford, Clarendon Press, 1957. viii, 148 p.
57-002267 164
Logic, Symbolic and mathematical.

BC135.Q48 1951
Quine, W. V.
Mathematical logic. Cambridge, Harvard University Press, 1951. 346 p.
51-007541 164
Logic, Symbolic and mathematical.

BC135.R4
Reichenbach, Hans, 1891-1953.
Elements of symbolic logic. New York, Macmillan Co., 1947. xiii, 444 p.
47-005338 164
Logic, Symbolic and mathematical.

BC135.R58 1978
Rosser, J. Barkley 1907-
Logic for mathematicians/ J. Barkley Rosser. New York: Chelsea Pub. Co., c1978. xv, 574 p.
77-007663 511/.3 0828402949
Logic, Symbolic and mathematical.

BC135.S14 1991
Sainsbury, R. M.
Logical forms: an introduction to philosophical logic/ Mark Sainsbury. Oxford, UK; B. Blackwell, 1991. vii, 398 p.
90-040876 160 0631177779
Logic, Symbolic and mathematical.

BC135.T35 1983
Tarski, Alfred.
Logic, semantics, metamathematics: papers from 1923 to 1938/ by Alfred Tarski; translated by J.H. Woodger. Indianapolis, Ind.: Hackett Pub. Co., c1983. xxx, 506 p.
83-010850 160 0915144751
Logic, Symbolic and mathematical. Semantics (Philosophy)

BC135.T48
Thomason, Richmond H.
Symbolic logic; an introduction [by] Richmond H. Thomason. [New York] Macmillan [1969, c1970] xiii, 367 p.
72-083069 164
Logic, Symbolic and mathematical.

BC135.W5 1971
Wittgenstein, Ludwig, 1889-1951.
Prototractatus; an early version of Tractatus logico-philosophicus. Edited by B. F. McGuinness, T. Nyberg [and] G. H. von Wright, with a translation by D. F. Pears [and] B. F. McGuinness. An historical introd. by G. H. von Wright and a facsim. of the author's manuscript. Ithaca, N.Y., Cornell University Press [1971] 256 p.
79-136737 192 0801406102
Logic, Symbolic and mathematical. Language and languages -- Philosophy.

BC135.W52 A5 1971
Anscombe, G. E. M.
An introduction to Wittgenstein's Tractatus [by] G. E. M. Anscombe. 4th ed. London, Hutchinson, 1971. 179 p.
72-181122   192   0090511301
Wittgenstein, Ludwig, 1889-1951. Tractatus logico-philosophicus. Logic, Symbolic and mathematical. Language and languages -- Philosophy.

BC135.W52.S8 1981
Stenius, Erik.
Wittgenstein's Tractatus: a critical exposition of its main lines of thought/ by Erik Stenius. Westport, Conn.: Greenwood Press, 1981, c1960. xi, 241 p.
81-013222   192   0313232466
Wittgenstein, Ludwig, -- 1889-1951. -- Tractatus logico-philosophicus.Logic, Symbolic and mathematical. Language and languages -- Philosophy.

BC141 Logic of chance. Probability

BC141.C3 1962
Carnap, Rudolf, 1891-1970.
Logical foundations of probability.   Chicago] University of Chicago Press [1962] 613 p.
62-052505   164
Probabilities.

BC141.G55 2000
Gillies, Donald,
Philosophical theories of probability/ Donald Gillies. London; Routledge , 2000.
00-029113   121/.63 21   041518276X
Probabilities.

BC141.H33 2001
Hacking, Ian.
An introduction to probability and inductive logic/ Ian Hacking. Cambridge, U.K.; Cambridge University Press, 2001. xvii, 302 p.
00-045503   160 21   0521775019
Probabilities. Induction (Logic)

BC141.H83 1959
Huff, Darrell.
How to take a chance. Illustrated by Irving Geis. New York, W. W. Norton [1959] 173 p.
58-013953   123.3   0393002632
Chance.

BC141.J44 1992
Jeffrey, Richard C.
Probability and the art of judgment/ Richard Jeffrey. Cambridge [England]; Cambridge University Press, 1992. xi, 244 p.
91-034257   121/.63 20   0521397707
Probabilities. Judgment.

BC141.K4 1979
Keynes, John Maynard,
A treatise on probability/ by John Maynard Keynes. 1st AMS ed. New York: AMS Press, 1979. xi, 466 p.
75-041163   519.2   0404145639
Probabilities. Probabilities -- Bibliography.

BC141.K9
Kyburg, Henry Ely, 1928-
Probability and the logic of rational belief. Middletown, Conn., Wesleyan University Press [1961] 346 p.
61-011615   164
Probabilities.   Logic,   Symbolic   and mathematical.

BC141.L4713 1998
Lestienne, Remy.
The creative power of chance/ Remy Lestienne; translated from the French by E.C. Neher. Urbana: University of Illinois Press, c1998. 202 p.
97-045250   123/.3   0252023862
Chance.

BC141.W4 1982
Weatherford, Roy, 1943-
Philosophical foundations of probability theory/ Roy Weatherford. London; Routledge & K. Paul, 1982. xi, 282 p.
81-022730   121/.63   0710090021
Probabilities.

BC145 Deontic logic

BC145.F67 1989
Forrester, James W.
Why you should: the pragmatics of deontic speech/ James W. Forrester. Hanover, NH: Published for Brown University Press, c1989. x, 246 p.
88-040111   160   0874514533
Deontic logic. Pragmatics.

BC171 Special topics — Truth and error. Certitude

BC171.G76 1992
Grover, Dorothy,
A prosentential theory of truth/ Dorothy Grover. Princeton, N.J.: Princeton University Press, c1992. xii, 288 p.
91-036788   121 20   0691073996
Truth.   Language   and   languages   -- Philosophy. Proposition (Logic)

BC171.K55 1992
Kirkham, Richard L.
Theories of truth: a critical introduction/ Richard L. Kirkham. Cambridge, Mass.: MIT Press, c1992. xi, 401 p.
91-042394   121   0262111675
Truth.

BC171.M65
Moody, Ernest A. 1903-
Truth and consequence in mediaeval logic. Amsterdam, North-Holland Pub. Co., 1953. 113 p.
53-004268   160
Truth. Logic, Medieval.

BC171.S38 1994
Schum, David A.
The evidential foundations of probabilistic reasoning/ David A. Schum. New York: Wiley, c1994. xviii, 545 p.
93-035633   121/.65   047157936X
Evidence. Inference. Probabilities.

BC171.T76 1999
Truth/ edited by Simon Blackburn and Keith Simmons. Oxford; Oxford University Press, 1999. vi, 406 p.
99-019787   121 21   0198752512
Truth.

BC173 Special topics — Proof

BC173.C66 1983
The Concept of evidence/ edited by Peter Achinstein. Oxford [Oxfordshire]; Oxford University Press, 1983. 182 p.
83-008266   121/.65   0198750625
Evidence. Logic.

BC175 Special topics — Fallacies

BC175.F35 1995
Fallacies: classical and contemporary readings/ edited by Hans V. Hansen and Robert C. Pinto. University Park, Pa.: Pennsylvania State University Press, c1995. xi, 356 p.
94-020973   165   0271014164
Fallacies (Logic)

BC175.K25 1988
Kahane, Howard,
Logic and contemporary rhetoric: the use of reason in everyday life/ Howard Kahane. 5th ed. Belmont, Calif.: Wadsworth Pub. Co., c1988. xvi, 346 p.
87-031719   160 19   0534090184
Fallacies (Logic) Reasoning. Judgment (Logic)

BC175.W322 1999
Walton, Douglas N.
Appeal to popular opinion/ Douglas Walton. University Park, Pa.: Pennsylvania State University Press, c1999. 289 p.
98-031384   168   0271018186
Appeal to popular opinion (Logical fallacy)

BC175.W355 2000
Walton, Douglas N.
Scare tactics: arguments that appeal to fear and threats/ by Douglas Walton. Dordrecht [Netherlands]; Kluwer Academic Publishers, xv, 218 p.
00-061299 160 21 0792365437
Appeal to force (Logical fallacy)

BC177 Special topics — Reasoning, argumentation, etc.

BC177.A43 1982
Advances in argumentation theory and research/ edited by J. Robert Cox & Charles Arthur Willard. Carbondale: Published for the American Forensic Association, c1982. xlvii, 421 p.
82-005496 001.54 0809310503
Reasoning.

BC177.C64 1998
Cogan, Robert,
Critical thinking: step by step/ Robert Cogan. Lanham, Md.: University Press of America, c1998. 381 p.
98-005370 160 21 0761810676
Reasoning. Critical thinking.

BC177.C765 1996
Crosswhite, James.
The rhetoric of reason: writing and the attractions of agrument/ James Crosswhite. Madison, Wis.: University of Wisconsin Press, c1996. xi, 329 p.
95-044286 168 20 0299149544
Reasoning. Logic.

BC177.F57 1988
Fisher, Alec.
The logic of real arguments/ Alec Fisher. Cambridge [England]; Cambridge University Press, 1988. xi, 190 p.
87-031178 168 0521308496
Reasoning.

BC177.H65 1987
Hollis, Martin.
The cunning of reason/ Martin Hollis. Cambridge [Cambridgeshire]; Cambridge University Press, 1987. viii, 222 p.
87-014630 128/.3 0521248795
Reason.

BC177.K38 1998
Kelley, David,
The art of reasoning/ David Kelley. 3rd expanded ed. New York: W.W. Norton, c1998. xviii, 582 p.
97-025896 160 21 0393972135
Reasoning. Logic.

BC177.L83 1994
Luckhardt, C. Grant, 1943-
How to do things with logic/ C. Grant Luckhardt, William Bechtel. Hillsdale, N.J.: L. Erlbaum Associates, 1994. xi, 263 p.
93-034138 160 0805800751
Reasoning. Logic.

BC177.N69 1993
Nozick, Robert.
The nature of rationality/ Robert Nozick. Princeton, N.J.: Princeton University Press, c1993. xvi, 226 p.
92-046660 128/.3 0691074240
Reasoning. Reason.

BC177.P395
Perelman, Chaïm.
The new rhetoric and the humanities: essays on rhetoric and its applications/ Ch. Perelman; with an introd. by Harold Zyskind. Dordrecht, Holland; D. Reidel Pub. Co., c1979. xxiii, 174 p.
79-019797 160 9027710198
Reasoning. Rhetoric.

BC177.P48 1991
Philosophy and AI: essays at the interface/ edited by Robert Cummins and John Pollock. Cambridge, Mass.: MIT Press, c1991. xi, 304 p.
91-016817 128/.3 0262031809
Reasoning. Artificial intelligence. Computers.

BC177.P599 1995
Pollock, John L.
Cognitive carpentry: a blueprint for how to build a person/ John L. Pollock. Cambridge, Mass.: MIT Press, c1995. xiii, 377 p.
94-048106 006.3/3 20 0262161524
Pollock, John L. How to build a person. Reasoning. Cognition. Artificial intelligence -- Philosophy. Machine learning.

BC177.R345 1990
Regal, Philip J.
The anatomy of judgment/ Philip J. Regal. Minneapolis: University of Minnesota Press, c1990. xii, 368 p.
89-020374 128/.3 0816618240
Reasoning. Judgment. Methodology.

BC177.S64 1998
Smith, P. Christopher.
The hermeneutics of original argument: demonstration, dialectic, rhetoric/ P. Christopher Smith. Evanston, IL: Northwestern University Press, c1998. xii, 364 p.
98-003028 121/.686 0810116073
Heidegger, Martin, -- 1889-1976.Rhetoric -- History. Reasoning -- History.

BC177.T59 1984
Toulmin, Stephen Edelston.
An introduction to reasoning/ Stephen Toulmin, Richard Rieke, Allan Janik. New York: Macmillan; c1984. ix, 435 p.
83-016196 160 0024211605
Reasoning.

BC177.T6 1958
Toulmin, Stephen Edelston.
The uses of argument. Cambridge [Eng.] University Press, 1958. vi, 264 p.
58-002813 160
Logic. Reasoning.

BC177.W315 1997
Walton, Douglas N.
Appeal to expert opinion: arguments from authority/ Douglas Walton. University Park, Pa.: Pennsylvania State University Press, c1997. xiv, 281 p.
96-039773 160 0271016949
Reasoning. Authority. Fallacies (Logic)

BC177.W3215 1996
Walton, Douglas N.
Arguments from ignorance/ Douglas Walton. University Park, Pa.: Pennsylvania State University Press, c1996. xii, 313 p.
94-045436 160 0271014741
Reasoning. Ignorance (Theory of knowledge) Burden of proof.

BC177.W322 1991
Walton, Douglas N.
Begging the question: circular reasoning as a tactic of argumentation/ Douglas N. Walton. New York: Greenwood Press, 1991. xv, 340 p.
90-024984 165 0313275963
Reasoning. Fallacies (Logic)

BC177.W324 1989
Walton, Douglas N.
Informal logic: a handbook for critical argumentation/ Douglas N. Walton. Cambridge; Cambridge University Press, 1989. xiii, 292 p.
88-030762 168 0521370329
Logic. Reasoning.

BC177.W3255 1999
Walton, Douglas N.
One-sided arguments: a dialectical analysis of bias/ Douglas Walton. Albany, NY: State University of New York Press, c1999. xix, 295 p.
99-015100 168 0791442675
Reasoning. Prejudice.

BC177.W544 1989
Willard, Charles Arthur.
A theory of argumentation/ Charles Arthur Willard. Tuscaloosa: University of Alabama Press, c1989. viii, 324 p.
88-027742 168 0817304274
Reasoning.

BC181 Special topics — Propositions. Prediction. Judgment

BC181.E67 2001
Epstein, Richard L., 1947-
Predicate logic: the semantic foundations of logic. / Richard L. Epstein. Belmont, CA: Wadsworth Thomson Learning, c2001. 412 p.
00-687819   160   0534558461
Logic. Predicate (Logic) Logic, Symbolic and mathematical.

BC181.G58 1965
Goodman, Nelson.
Fact, fiction, and forecast. Indianapolis, Bobbs-Merrill [1965] xii, 128 p.
65-017597   160
Forecasting. Science -- Philosophy. Logic.

BC181.H34 2000
Halpern, Paul, 1961-
The pursuit of destiny: a history of prediction/ Paul Halpern. Cambridge, MA: Perseus Pub., 2000 xxii, 250 p.
00-105201   0738200956
Forecasting. Prediction (Logic) Prediction theory -- History.

BC181.J6613
Jouvenel, Bertrand de, 1903-
The art of conjecture. Translated from the French by Nikita Lary. New York, Basic Books [1967] xii, 307 p.
67-012649   133.32
Prediction (Logic)

BC181.P58
Pole, David.
Conditions of rational inquiry; a study in the philosophy of value. [London] University of London, Athlone Press, 1961. 229 p.
61-019430
Judgment (Logic) Judgment (Ethics) Knowledge, Theory of.

BC181.P75 1988
Propositions and attitudes/ edited by Nathan Salmon and Scott Soames. Oxford; Oxford University Press, 1988. 282 p.
88-009862   160 19   0198750927
Proposition (Logic) Belief and doubt. Knowledge, Theory of.

BC181.R5 1990
Richard, Mark.
Propositional attitudes: an essay on thoughts and how we ascribe them/ Mark Richard. Cambridge [England]; New York: Cambridge University Press, 1990. ix, 275 p.
89-035543   160   0521381266
Proposition (Logic) Cognition. Attitude (Psychology)

BC199-199.2 Special topics — Other special topics, A-Z

BC199.A26 J67 1994
Abductive inference: computation, philosophy, technology/ edited by John R. Josephson, Susan G. Josephson. Cambridge; Cambridge University Press, 1994. viii, 306 p.
93-016027   160 20   0521434610
Abduction (Logic) Inference. Knowledge, Theory of.

BC199.C5.L56 1998
Lingis, Alphonso, 1933-
The imperative/ Alphonso Lingis. Bloomington, Ind.: Indiana University Press, c1998. 234 p.
98-020003   128   025333442X
Kant, Immanuel, -- 1724-1804.Perception (Philosophy) Commands (Logic)

BC199.C55 B89 2002
Buzaglo, Meir,
The logic of concept expansion/ Meir Buzaglo. Cambridge, U.K.; Cambridge University Press, 2002. xi, 182 p.
2001-037558   160 21   052180762X
Logic. Concepts.

BC199.C56 C655 1985
Conditionals: from philosophy to computer science/ edited by G. Crocco, L. Fariñas del Cerro, and A. Herzig. Oxford: Clarendon Press; viii, 368 p.
96-160574   160 20   0198538618
Conditionals (Logic) Language and languages -- Philosophy. Language and logic. Logic.

BC199.C56.J33 1987
Jackson, Frank, 1943-
Conditionals/ Frank Jackson. Oxford, UK; B. Blackwell, 1987. vi, 148 p.
87-000844   160   0631146210
Conditionals (Logic)

BC199.C56 J34 1998
Jackson, Frank,
Mind, method, and conditionals: selected essays/ Frank Jackson. London; Routledge, 1998. viii, 284 p.
97-050010   199/.94 21   0415165741
Conditionals (Logic) Philosophy of mind. Methodology.

BC199.C56 S26 2003
Sanford, David H.,
If P, then Q: conditionals and the foundations of reasoning/ David H. Sanford. 2nd ed. London; Routledge, 2003.
2002-036920   160 21   0415283698
Conditionals (Logic)

BC199.I4.B74 1988
Brennan, Andrew.
Conditions of identity: a study in identity and survival/ Andrew Brennan. Oxford [Oxfordshire]: Clarendon Press; 1988. ix, 375 p.
87-028237   110   0198249748
Identity. Metaphysics. Identity (Psychology)

BC199.I4.S33 1996
Schechtman, Marya, 1960-
The constitution of selves/ Marya Schechtman. Ithaca, NY: Cornell University Press, 1996. xi, 169 p.
96-016537   126   0801431670
Identity. Self. Self-knowledge, Theory of.

BC199.I4.W55 1989
Williams, Christopher John Fards.
What is identity?/ C.J.F. Williams. Oxford: Clarendon Press; 1989. xx, 207 p.
89-009285   160   0198248083
Identity.

BC199.I5.A5 1957a
Anscombe, G. E. M.
Intention. Ithaca, N. Y., Cornell University Press [1957] 93 p.
58-001550
Intention (Logic)

BC199.M6.B65 1993
Boolos, George.
The logic of provability/ George Boolos. Cambridge [England]; Cambridge University Press, 1993. xxxvi, 275 p.
92-043610   160   0521433428
Modality (Logic) Proof theory.

BC199.M6.C47
Chellas, Brian F.
Modal logic: an introduction/ Brian F. Chellas. Cambridge [Eng.]; Cambridge University Press, [1980] xii, 295 p.
76-047197   160   0521224764
Modality (Logic)

BC199.M6 H85 1996
Hughes, G. E.
A new introduction to modal logic/ G.E. Hughes and M.J. Cresswell. London; Routledge, 1996. x, 421 p.
95-014728   160 20   0415126002
Modality (Logic)

BC199.M6.K66 1986
Konyndyk, Kenneth.
Introductory modal logic/ Kenneth Konyndyk. Notre Dame, Ind.: University of Notre Dame Press, c1986. x, 133 p.
85-041007   160   0268011591
Modality (Logic)

BC199.M6.L54
Linsky, Leonard.
Reference and modality; edited by Leonard Linsky. London, Oxford University Press, 1971. 177 p.
72-595855   160   019875017X
Modality (Logic) Description (Philosophy)

BC199.M6 P7 2003
Prior, A. N.
Papers on time and tense/ Arthur N. Prior. [2nd ed.]/ edited by Per Hasle ... [et al.]. Oxford; Oxford University Press, 2003. ix, 331 p.
2002-029796   160 21   0199256071
Modality (Logic) Tense (Logic)

BC199.N3.M33 1989
McCulloch, Gregory.
The game of the name: introducing logic, language, and mind/ Gregory McCulloch. Oxford: Clarendon Press; 1989. xvi, 320 p.
88-037246   146/.4   0198750870
Names. Analysis (Philosophy) Cognitive science.

BC199.N4 B73 2001
Brann, Eva T. H.
The ways of naysaying: no, not, nothing, and nonbeing/ Eva Brann. Lanham, Md.: Rowman & Littlefield Publishers, c2001. xviii, 249 p.
00-062638   160   0742512282
Negation (Logic) Nonbeing. Nothing (Philosophy)

BC199.P2.E75 1998
Erickson, Glenn W., 1951-
Dictionary of paradox/ Glenn W. Erickson, John A. Fossa. Lanham, MD: University Press of America, c1998. 220 p.
98-010526   165   0761810668
Paradox -- Dictionaries.

BC199.P2.K35 1988
Kainz, Howard P.
Paradox, dialectic, and system: a contemporary reconstruction of the Hegelian problematic/ Howard P. Kainz. University Park: Pennsylvania State University Press, c1988. ix, 137 p.
86-043036   142   0271004991
Hegel, Georg Wilhelm Friedrich, -- 1770-1831.Paradox. Dialectic.

BC199.P2 S25 1995
Sainsbury, R. M.
Paradoxes/ R.M. Sainsbury. 2nd ed. Cambridge; Cambridge University Press, 1995. x, 165 p.
94-039587   165 20   0521483476
Paradox.

BC199.Q4.B44
Belnap, Nuel D., 1930-
The logic of questions and answers/ Nuel D. Belnap, Jr., Thomas B. Steel, Jr. New Haven: Yale University Press, 1976. vi, 209 p.
75-027761   160   0300019629
Question (Logic) Question-answering systems. Formal languages.

BC199.2.S56 1993
Simmons, Keith.
Universality and the liar: an essay on truth and the diagonal argument/ Keith Simmons. Cambridge; Cambridge University Press, 1993. xii, 229 p.
92-028986   165   0521430690
Liar paradox. Universals (Philosophy)

BD Speculative philosophy

BD21-23 General philosophical works — Introduction to philosophy — 1801-

BD21.A38 1995
Almond, Brenda.
Exploring philosophy: the philosophical quest/ Brenda Almond. Oxford [England]; Blackwell, c1995.
94-029551   100   0631194851
Philosophy -- Introductions.

BD21.A86 1998
Aspenson, Steven Scott, 1961-
The philosopher's tool kit/ Steven Scott Aspenson. Armonk, N.Y.: M.E. Sharpe, c1998. xvii, 125 p.
97-016070   101   0765602172
Philosophy -- Introductions.

BD21.B47 1999
Blackburn, Simon.
Think: a compelling introduction to philosophy/ Simon Blackburn. Oxford; Oxford University Press, 1999. vii, 312 p.
00-265286   100   0192100246
Philosophy.

BD21.C656 1996
Cooper, David Edward.
World philosophies: an historical introduction/ David E. Cooper. Oxford, UK; Blackwell, 1996. vi, 527 p.
95-005864   109   0631188665
Philosophy -- Introductions. Philosophy -- History.

BD21.D36 1989
Danto, Arthur Coleman, 1924-
Connections to the world: the basic concepts of philosophy/ Arthur C. Danto. New York: Harper & Row, c1989. xvii, 281 p.
88-045571   100   006015960X
Philosophy -- Introductions. Philosophy, Modern -- 20th century.

BD21.D7 1968
Drake, Durant, 1878-1933.
Invitation to philosophy. New York, Greenwood Press [1968, c1933] xxvi, 537 p.
69-013887   110
Philosophy -- Introductions.

BD21.K55
Klausner, Neal W.
Philosophy, the study of alternative beliefs [by] Neal W. Klausner [and] Paul G. Kuntz. New York, Macmillan [1961] 674 p.
61-005948   100
Philosophy -- Introductions.

BD21.N38 1999
Navia, Luis E.
The adventure of philosophy/ Luis E. Navia. Westport, Conn.: Greenwood Press, c1999. ix, 160 p.
99-014838   100   0313309760
Philosophy -- Introductions.

BD21.P44 1996
Phillips, D. Z.
Introducing philosophy: the challenge of scepticism/ D.Z. Phillips. Oxford; Blackwell, 1996. xiii, 206 p.
95-036644   100   0631200401
Philosophy -- Introductions. Skepticism.

BD21.P468 1995
Philosophy: a guide through the subject/ edited by A.C. Grayling. Oxford; Oxford University Press, 1995. vi, 677 p.
95-223633   100 20   0198751575
Philosophy.

BD21.P469 1998
Philosophy 2: further through the subject/ edited by A.C. Grayling. Oxford; Oxford University Press, 1998. viii, 869 p.
99-203968   100 21   0198751788
Philosophy.

BD21.P475 2003
Philosophy for the 21st century: a comprehensive reader/ edited by Steven M. Cahn; associate editors, Delia Graff ... [et al.]. New York: Oxford University Press, 2003. x, 854 p.
2002-029007   100 21   0195147928
Philosophy -- Introductions.

BD21.P48 2002
Philosophy: the quest for truth/ [edited by] Louis P. Pojman. 5th ed. New York: Oxford University Press, c2002. xvi, 622 p.
2002-278350   100 21   0195156242
Philosophy -- Introductions.

BD21.P483 1998
Philosophy then and now/ edited by N. Scott Arnold, Theodore M. Benditt, George Graham. Malden, Mass.: Blackwell Publishers, 1998. xii, 604 p.
97-047396   100   1557867410
Philosophy -- Introductions.

BD21.P485 1989
Pinchin, Calvin.
Issues in philosophy/ Calvin Pinchin. Savage, Md.: Barnes & Noble Books, 1990. ix, 366 p.
89-035658   100   0389208701
Philosophy -- Introductions.

BD21.R8 1959
Russell, Bertrand, 1872-1970.
The problems of philosophy. New York, Oxford University Press, 1959. 167 p.
59-016125   110
Philosophy -- Introductions. Metaphysics. Knowledge, Theory of.

BD21.T35 1999
Teichman, Jenny.
Philosophy: a beginner's guide/ Jenny Teichman & Katherine C. Evans. 3rd ed. Oxford, UK; Blackwell Publishers, 1999. ix, 274 p.
99-019756   100 21   063121321X
Philosophy -- Introductions.

BD21.T7
Trueblood, Elton, 1900-
General philosophy. New York, Harper & Row [1963] 370 p.
63-011292   102
Philosophy -- Introductions.

BD21.W36 2001
Washburn, Phil.
Philosophical dilemmas: a pro and con introduction to the major questions/ Phil Washburn. New York: Oxford University Press, 2001. xxiii, 439 p.
00-039934   100   0195134966
Philosophy -- Introductions.

BD21.W4
Weiss, Paul, 1901-
Reality/ Paul Weiss. Princeton, N. J.: Princeton University Press; 1938.
39-003540   110
Reality.

BD21.W43 1996
Western philosophy: an anthology/ edited by John Cottingham. Oxford, OX, UK; Blackwell Publishers, xxiii, 626 p.
95-042829   190 20   0631186271
Philosophy -- Introductions.

BD21.W64
Wolff, Robert Paul.
About philosophy/ Robert Paul Wolff. Englewood Cliffs, N.J.: Prentice-Hall, c1976. xiv, 305 p.
75-015739   100   0130008362
Philosophy -- Introductions.

BD22.M37 1989
Maritain, Jacques,
An introduction to philosophy/ Jacques Maritain; with a new foreword by Stephen J. Vicchio. Westminster, Md.: Christian Classics, 1989. xxiii, 191 p.
89-061354   100 20   087061164X
Philosophy -- Introductions.

BD23.H412
Heidegger, Martin, 1889-1976.
What is philosophy? Translated with an introd. by William Kluback and Jean T. Wilde. [New York] Twayne Publishers [1958] 97 p.
58-002869
Philosophy -- Introductions.

BD23.J313 1951a
Jaspers, Karl, 1883-1969.
Way to wisdom, an introduction to philosophy; translated by Ralph Manheim. New Haven, Yale University Press, 1951. 208 p.
51-013957   100
Philosophy -- Introductions.

BD31 General philosophical works — Elementary textbooks. Outlines, syllabi, etc. — Polyglot

BD31.P56 2001
Phillips, Christopher, 1959 July 15-
Socrates cafe: a fresh taste of philosophy/ Christopher Phillips. New York: W.W. Norton, c2001. 232 p.
00-062211   100   0393049566
Philosophy.

BD31.R32 1969
Rader, Melvin Miller,
The enduring questions; main problems of philosophy [by] Melvin Rader. 2d ed. New York, Holt, Rinehart and Winston [1969] xi, 838 p.
71-077813   190/.8   0030809762
Philosophy.

BD41 General philosophical works — Addresses, essays, lectures

BD41.W5
Whitehead, Alfred North, 1861-1947.
The function of reason, by Alfred North Whitehead ... Louis Clark Vanuxem foundation lectures delivered at Princeton university, March 1929. Princeton, Princeton university press, 1929. 72 p.
30-002482
Reason.

BD111-118 Metaphysics — General works, treatises, and advanced textbooks — 1801-

BD111.B39 1989
Benardete, Jose A.
Metaphysics: the logical approach/ Jose A. Benardete. Oxford; Oxford University Press, 1989. x, 210 p.
88-009933   110   0192192175
Metaphysics.

BD111.B57 2002
The Blackwell guide to metaphysics/ edited by Richard M. Gale. Oxford, UK; Blackwell Publishers, 2002. vi, 348 p.
2002-066443   110 21   0631221212
Metaphysics.

BD111.B8 1969
Bradley, F. H. 1846-1924.
Appearance and reality: a metaphysical essay, by F. H. Bradley. London, Oxford U.P., 1969. xxvi, 570 p.
79-405526   110   0198811500
Metaphysics. Reality. Knowledge, Theory of.

BD111.C584 1990
Coburn, Robert C.
The strangeness of the ordinary: problems and issues in contemporary metaphysics/ Robert C. Coburn. Savage, Md.: Rowman & Littlefield, c1990. xiii, 179 p.
89-028058   110
Metaphysics.

BD111.C624 1984
Comfort, Alex, 1920-
Reality and empathy: physics, mind, and science in the 21st century/ Alex Comfort. Albany: State University of New York Press, c1984. xxi, 272 p.
83-009318   110   0873957628
Metaphysics. Science -- Philosophy. Intuition.

BD111.F29 1996
Ferre, Frederick.
Being and value: toward a constructive postmodern metaphysics/ Frederick Ferre. Albany: State University of New York Press, c1996. xviii, 406 p.
95-004239   121/.8   0791427552
Postmodernism. Metaphysics -- History. Metaphysics.

BD111.H42 2000
Heidegger, Martin, 1889-1976.
Introduction to metaphysics/ Martin Heidegger; new translation by Gregory Fried and Richard Polt. New Haven: Yale University Press, c2000. xxx, 254 p.
99-088479   110   0300083270
Metaphysics.

BD111.L43 1988
Lemos, Ramon M., 1927-
Metaphysical investigations/ Ramon M. Lemos. Rutherford, [N.J.]: Fairleigh Dickinson University Press; c1988. 290 p.
86-046324   110   0838633072
Metaphysics.

BD111.M3
Martin, William Oliver.
Metaphysics and ideology. Milwaukee, Marquette University Press, 1959. 87 p.
59-009870   110
Metaphysics. Ideology.

BD111.M45 1991
Mathews, Freya, 1949-
The ecological self/ Freya Mathews. London: Routledge, 1991. x, 192 p.
90-039277   0415052521
Metaphysics. Cosmology. Physics -- Philosophy.

BD111.M55 1999
Metaphysics: an anthology/ edited by Jaegwon Kim and Ernest Sosa. Malden, Mass.: Blackwell Publishers, 1999. xi, 676 p.
98-008538   110 21   063120279X
Metaphysics.

BD111.M564 1993
Metaphysics as foundation: essays in honor of Ivor Leclerc/ edited by Paul A. Bogaard and Gordon Treash. Albany, NY: State University of New York Press, c1993. xi, 358 p.
91-043054   110   0791412571
Whitehead, Alfred North, -- 1861-1947.Metaphysics.

BD111.M67 1992
Morris, Michael (Michael Rowl
The good and the true/ Michael Morris. Oxford: Clarendon Press; 1992. 336 p.
92-000462   110   0198239440
Metaphysics. Scientism. Content (Psychology)

BD111.P38 1966
Pepper, Stephen Coburn, 1891-
World hypotheses, a study in evidence, by Stephen C. Pepper. Berkeley and Los Angeles, University of California press, 1966 [1942]
42-037134   110
Metaphysics.

BD111.S575 1995
Smith, Quentin, 1952-
Time, change, and freedom: an introduction to metaphysics/ Quentin Smith and L. Nathan Oaklander. London; Routledge, 1995. vi, 218 p.
94-034474   110   0415102480
Metaphysics. Time. Change.

BD111.S7
Stace, W. T. 1886-
The nature of the world; an essay in phenomenalist metaphysics, by W.T. Stace. Princeton, Princeton university press; 1940. vi, 262 p.
40-008303   110
Metaphysics. Phenomenology.

BD111.S78
Strawson, P. F.
Individuals, an essay in descriptive metaphysics. London, Methuen [1959] 255 p.
59-001521   110
Metaphysics.

BD111.T3
Taylor, Richard, 1919-
Metaphysics. Englewood Cliffs, N.J., Prentice-Hall [1963] 109 p.
63-011699   110
Metaphysics.

BD111.U7
Urban, Wilbur Marshall, 1873-
The intelligible world; metaphysics and value, by Wilbur Marshall Urban. London, G. Allen & Unwin; 1929. 479 p.
29-019466
Metaphysics. Values. Philosophy, Modern.

BD111.V38 2002
Van Inwagen, Peter.
Metaphysics/ Peter van Inwagen. 2nd ed. Cambridge, MA: Westview Press, 2002. xiv, 235 p.
2002-002981   110 21   0813390559
Metaphysics.

BD111.V67 1995
Voss, Sarah, 1945-
What number is God?: metaphors, metaphysics, metamathematics, and the nature of things/ by Sarah Voss. Albany, N.Y.: State University of New York Press, 1995. xviii, 214 p.
94-018260   110   0791424170
Metaphysics. Mathematics -- Philosophy.

BD111.W56 1990
Wood, Robert E., 1934-
A path into metaphysics: phenomenological, hermeneutical, and dialogical studies/ Robert E. Wood. Albany: State University of New York Press, c1990. xviii, 387 p.
89-038073   110   079140305X
Metaphysics. Phenomenology.

BD112.B42 1955
Bergson, Henri, 1859-1941.
An introduction to metaphysics. Authorized translation by T. E. Hulme; with an introd. by Thomas A. Goudge. New York, Liberal Arts Press, [c1955] 62 p.
49-003135   110   0672601710
Metaphysics.

BD112.S22 1990
Schuon, Frithjof, 1907-
To have a center/ Frithjof Schuon. Bloomington, Ind.: World Wisdom Books, c1990. viii, 184 p.
90-038811   110   0941532097
Metaphysics. Human beings. Religion -- Philosophy.

BD118.R8.B42 1952
Berdiaev, Nikolai, 1874-1948.
The beginning and the end. [Translated from the Russian by R. M. French] London, G. Bles, 1952. 256 p.
52-002650   110
Metaphysics. Eschatology.

BD131 Metaphysics — Elementary textbooks. Outlines, syllabi, etc.

BD131.L83 2001
Loux, Michael J.
Metaphysics: a contemporary introduction/ Michael J. Loux. 2nd ed. New York: Routledge, 2001.
2001-031996   110 21   0415261074
Metaphysics.

BD143 Epistemology. Theory of knowledge — Collected works (nonserial)

BD143.S95
Swartz, Robert J.
Perceiving, sensing, and knowing; a book of readings from twentieth-century sources in the philosophy of perception, edited, with an introd. by Robert J. Swartz. Garden City, N.Y., Anchor Books, 1965. xxii, 538 p.
65-014024   121.082
Knowledge, Theory of.

BD143.T48 1993
The Theory of knowledge: classical and contemporary readings/ [compiled and edited by] Louis P. Pojman. Belmont, Calif.: Wadsworth Pub. Co., c1993. xii, 556 p.
92-012263   121 20   053417826X
Knowledge, Theory of.

BD161-162 Epistemology. Theory of knowledge — General works — 1801-

BD161.A47 1998
Almeder, Robert F.
Harmless naturalism: the limits of science and the nature of philosophy/ Robert Almeder. Chicago: Open Court, c1998. xii, 235 p.
97-053307   146   0812693795
Knowledge, Theory of. Naturalism. Scientism.

BD161.A783 2002
Audi, Robert,
Epistemology: a contemporary introduction to the theory of knowledge / Robert Audi. 2nd ed. London; Routledge, 2002.
2002-068748   121 21   0415281091
Knowledge, Theory of.

BD161.B459 2000
Brook, Andrew.
Knowledge and mind: a philosophical introduction/ Andrew Brook and Robert J. Stainton. Cambridge, Mass.: MIT Press, 2000. xiv, 253 p.
99-038797   121   0262024756
Knowledge, Theory of. Philosophy of mind.

BD161.B465 1999
The Blackwell guide to epistemology/ edited by John Greco and Ernest Sosa. Malden, Mass.: Blackwell, 1999. ix, 464 p.
98-023967 121 21 0631202919
Knowledge, Theory of.

BD161.B53
Boas, George, 1891-
The inquiring mind. La Salle, Ill., Open Court Pub. Co., 1959. 428 p.
58-006815 121
Knowledge, Theory of.

BD161.C352 1992
Carruthers, Peter, 1952-
Human knowledge and human nature: a new introduction to an ancient debate/ Peter Carruthers. Oxford [England]; Oxford University Press, 1992. viii, 199 p.
91-023735 121 019875101X
Knowledge, Theory of. Innate ideas (Philosophy) Empiricism.

BD161.C355 1999
Cavell, Stanley,
The claim of reason: Wittgenstein, skepticism, morality, and tragedy / Stanley Cavell. New York: Oxford University Press, 1999. xxvi, 511 p.
98-031557 121 21 019513107X
Wittgenstein, Ludwig, 1889-1951. Knowledge, Theory of. Skepticism. Ethics.

BD161.C47
Chisholm, Roderick M.
Perceiving: a philosophical study. Ithaca, Cornell University Press [1957] 203 p.
58-000028 121
Knowledge, Theory of.

BD161.C633 1992
Cohen, L. Jonathan
An essay on belief and acceptance/ L. Jonathan Cohen. Oxford: Clarendon Press; 1992. x, 163 p.
92-008704 121/.6 0198242948
Knowledge, Theory of. Belief and doubt. Philosophy of mind.

BD161.D4
Dewey, John, 1859-1952.
The quest for certainty: a study of the relation of knowledge and action, by John Dewey. New York, Minton, Balch, 1929.
29-023500
Thought and thinking. Science -- Philosophy. Knowledge, Theory of.

BD161.E6 1990
Epistemology/ edited by Stephen Everson. Cambridge [England]; Cambridge University Press, 1990. viii, 288 p.
89-007116 121/.0938 0521341612
Knowledge, Theory of -- History. Philosophy, Ancient.

BD161.E86 1987
Evolutionary epistemology, rationality, and the sociology of knowledge / edited by Gerard Radnitzky and W.W. Bartley III; with contributions by Sir Karl Popper ... [et al.]. La Salle [Ill.]: Open Court, c1987. xiv, 475 p.
86-023589 121 19 0812690397
Knowledge, Theory of. Knowledge, Sociology of. Evolution -- Philosophy. Biology -- Philosophy. Physics -- Philosophy.

BD161.F39 1998
Ferre, Frederick.
Knowing and value: toward a constructive postmodern epistemology/ Frederick Ferre. Albany: State University of New York Press, c1998. xviii, 393 p.
98-014887 121 0791439895
Knowledge, Theory of. Postmodernism.

BD161.F565 2001
Foley, Richard.
Intellectual trust in oneself and others/ Richard Foley. Cambridge, UK; Cambridge University Press, 2001. x, 182 p.
00-065171 121/.6 21 0521793084
Knowledge, Theory of.

BD161.F57 1987
Foley, Richard.
The theory of epistemic rationality/ Richard Foley. Cambridge, Mass.: Harvard University Press, 1987. ix, 335 p.
86-031963 121/.6 0674882768
Knowledge, Theory of.

BD161.F58 1993
Foley, Richard.
Working without a net: a study of egocentric epistemology/ Richard Foley. New York: Oxford University Press, 1993. x, 214 p.
91-048108 121 0195076990
Descartes, Rene, -- 1596-1650. Knowledge, Theory of.

BD161.G64 1988
Goldman, Alan H., 1945-
Empirical knowledge/ Alan H. Goldman. Berkeley: University of California Press, c1988. xi, 409 p.
87-030143 121 0520062027
Knowledge, Theory of. Empiricism. Realism.

BD161.G74 1966a
Grene, Marjorie Glicksman, 1910-
The knower and the known [by] Marjorie Grene. New York, Basic Books [1966] 283 p.
66-012294 121
Knowledge, Theory of.

BD161.H45 1996
Hetherington, Stephen Cade.
Knowledge puzzles: an introduction to epistemology/ Stephen Cade Hetherington. Boulder, Colo.: Westview Press, 1996. xv, 193 p.
95-040996 121 0813324866
Knowledge, Theory of.

BD161.H537 1990
Historical foundations of cognitive science/ edited by J-C. Smith. Dordrecht; Kluwer Academic Publishers, c1990. xxiii, 303 p.
89-038208 128/.2/09 20 0792304519
Knowledge, Theory of -- History. Philosophy of mind -- History. Cognitive science -- History.

BD161.H85 2003
Human knowledge: classical and contemporary approaches/ edited by Paul K. Moser, Arnold vander Nat. 3rd ed. New York: Oxford University Press, 2003. ix, 582 p.
2002-728591 121 22 0195149661
Knowledge, Theory of.

BD161.H86 1995
Hundert, Edward M.
Lessons from an optical illusion: on nature and nurture, knowledge and values/ Edward M. Hundert. Cambridge, Mass.: Harvard University Press, 1995. xiv, 258 p.
94-037095 155.2/34/01 067452540X
Knowledge, Theory of. Values. Nature and nurture.

BD161.J6 1969
Joachim, Harold H. 1868-1938.
The nature of truth; an essay. New York, Greenwood Press [1969] 182 p.
69-013954 111.8/3
Knowledge, Theory of. Truth.

BD161.K53 1986
Kitchener, Richard F.,
Piaget's theory of knowledge: genetic epistemology & scientific reason/ Richard F. Kitchener. New Haven: Yale University Press, c1986. ix, 230 p.
85-026289 121/.092/4 19 0300035799
Piaget, Jean, 1896- -- Contributions in theory of knowledge. Knowledge, Theory of -- History -- 20th century. Genetic epistemology -- History -- 20th century.

BD161.K62 2002
Kornblith, Hilary.
Knowledge and its place in nature/ Hilary Kornblith. Oxford: Clarendon Press; x, 189 p.
2002-020000 121 21 0199246319
Knowledge, Theory of. Naturalism.

BD161.L32 1989
Landesman, Charles.
Color and consciousness: an essay in metaphysics/ Charles Landesman. Philadelphia: Temple University Press, 1989. xi, 135 p.
88-029442 111/.1 0877226164
Knowledge, Theory of. Metaphysics. Color (Philosophy)

BD161.L368 1990
Lehrer, Keith.
Theory of knowledge/ Keith Lehrer. Boulder: Westview Press, 1990. xii, 212 p.
89-037511 121 0813305705
Knowledge, Theory of.

BD161.L38 1956
Lewis, Clarence Irving, 1883-1964.
Mind and the world-order; outline of a theory of knowledge. New York, Dover Publication [1956, c1929] 446 p.
58-013364   121
Knowledge, Theory of.

BD161.M28
Malcolm, Norman, 1911-
Knowledge and certainty, essays and lectures. Englewood Cliffs, N.J., Prentice-Hall [1963] 244 p.
63-010529   121   0801491541
Knowledge, Theory of. Memory.

BD161.M283
Malcolm, Norman,
Thought and knowledge: essays/ by Norman Malcolm. Ithaca, N.Y.: Cornell University Press, 1977. 218 p.
76-025647   121   0801410746
Knowledge, Theory of.

BD161.M387 1995
McGrew, Timothy J., 1965-
The foundations of knowledge/ Timothy J. McGrew. Lanham, Md.: Littlefield Adams Books, 1995. xiv, 149 p.
95-020456   121   0822630427
Knowledge, Theory of.

BD161.M7 1928
Montague, William Pepperell, 1873-1953.
The ways of knowing; or, The methods of philosophy, by Wm. Pepperell Montague. London, G. Allen & Unwin ltd.; [1928]
32-000101   121
Knowledge, Theory of.

BD161.M848 1989
Moser, Paul K., 1957-
Knowledge and evidence/ Paul K. Moser. Cambridge; Cambridge University Press, 1989. xii, 285 p.
88-031570   121   0521370280
Knowledge, Theory of.

BD161.M8485 1998
Moser, Paul K., 1957-
The theory of knowledge: a thematic introduction/ Paul K. Moser, Dwayne H. Mulder, J.D. Trout. New York: Oxford University Press, 1998. x, 212 p.
96-052985   121   0195094654
Knowledge, Theory of.

BD161.M88
Murphy, Arthur Edward, 1901-1962.
The uses of reason. New York, Macmillan, 1943. vii, 346 p.
43-016321   121
Rationalism. Reality. Reason.

BD161.M89 1992
Musgrave, Alan.
Common sense, science, and scepticism: a historical introduction to the theory of knowledge/ Alan Musgrave. Cambridge; Cambridge University Press, 1993. xiv, 310 p.
92-012657   121   0521430402
Knowledge, Theory of.

BD161.N29 1993
Naturalizing epistemology/ edited by Hilary Kornblith. 2nd ed. Cambridge, Mass.: MIT Press, c1994. viii, 478 p.
93-023976   121 20   0262610906
Knowledge, Theory of. Naturalism.

BD161.O96 2002
The Oxford handbook of epistemology/ edited by Paul K. Moser. Oxford; Oxford University Press, 2002. x, 595 p.
2001-058016   121 21   0195130057
Knowledge, Theory of.

BD161.P43 2001
Perry, John, 1943-
Knowledge, possibility, and consciousness/ John Perry. Cambridge, Mass.: MIT Press, c2001. xvi, 221 p.
00-048959   128/.2   0262161990
Knowledge, Theory of.

BD161.P57 1993
Plantinga, Alvin.
Warrant and proper function/ Alvin Plantinga. New York: Oxford University Press, 1993. xii, 243 p.
92-000408   121/.6   0195078632
Knowledge, Theory of. Belief and doubt. Cognition.

BD161.P58 1993
Plantinga, Alvin.
Warrant: the current debate/ Alvin Plantinga. New York: Oxford University Press, 1993. xii, 228 p.
92-013183   121/.6   0195078616
Knowledge, Theory of. Belief and doubt.

BD161.P6 1994
Plotkin, H.C.
Darwin machines and the nature of knowledge/ Henry Plotkin. Cambridge, Mass.: Harvard University Press, 1994. xviii, 269 p.
93-039328   121   067419280X
Knowledge, Theory of. Evolution. Evolution (Biology)

BD161.P7245 1999
Pollock, John L.
Contemporary theories of knowledge/ John L. Pollock and Joseph Cruz. 2nd ed. Lanham, Md.: Rowman & Littlefield Publishers, c1999. xiv, 262 p.
99-012525   121 21   0847689379
Knowledge, Theory of. Philosophy, Modern -- 20th century.

BD161.P75
Prichard, Harold Arthur, 1871-
Knowledge and perception; essays and lectures. Oxford, Clarendon Press, 1950. 214 p.
50-007803   121
Perception. Knowledge, Theory of.

BD161.R468 1990
Rescher, Nicholas.
Baffling phenomena: and other studies in the philosophy of knowledge and valuation/ Nicholas Rescher. Savage, Md.: Rowman & Littlefield, c1991. 223 p.
89-048469   121   0847676382
Knowledge, Theory of. Values.

BD161.R483 2001
Resurrecting old-fashioned foundationalism/ edited by Michael R. DePaul. Lanham, Md.: Rowman & Littlefield, c2001. xiii, 93 p.
00-059059   121 21   0847692892
Knowledge, Theory of.

BD161.R78
Russell, Bertrand, 1872-1970.
Human knowledge, its scope and limits. New York, Simon and Schuster, 1948. xvi, 524 p.
48-011754   121
Knowledge, Theory of.

BD161.S647 1991
Sosa, Ernest.
Knowledge in perspective: selected essays in epistemology/ Ernest Sosa. Cambridge [England]; Cambridge University Press, 1991. xi, 298 p.
90-044708   121   0521356288
Knowledge, Theory of.

BD161.S67
Stace, W. T. 1886-
The theory of knowledge and existence, by W. T. Stace ... Oxford, The Clarendon press, 1932. xii, 455 p.
33-004368   121
Knowledge, Theory of. Metaphysics.

BD161.S685 1990
Stich, Stephen P.
The fragmentation of reason: preface to a pragmatic theory of cognitive evaluation/ Stephen P. Stich. Cambridge, Mass.: MIT Press, c1990. x, 181 p.
89-039165   121   0262192934
Knowledge, Theory of.

BD161.U7
Urban, Wilbur Marshall, 1873-
Beyond realism and idealism. London, Allen & Unwin [1949] 266 p.
50-004197   121
Knowledge, Theory of. Realism. Idealism.

BD161.W47 1999
Williams, Michael,
Groundless belief: an essay on the possibility of epistemology: with a new preface and afterword/ Michael Williams. Princeton, NJ: Princeton University Press, 1999.
99-017411   121 21   0691009074
Knowledge, Theory of.

BD161.W49 1991
Williams, Michael, 1947 July 6--
Unnatural doubts: epistemological realism and the basis of scepticism/ Michael Williams. Oxford, UK; B. Blackwell, 1991. xxiii, 386 p.
91-014349   121/.2   0631162518
Knowledge, Theory of. Skepticism.

BD161.Y65 1996
Yolton, John W.
Perception & reality: a history from Descartes to Kant/ John W. Yolton. Ithaca, NY: Cornell University Press, 1996. xi, 240 p.
95-049162   121/.3   0801432278
Descartes, Rene, -- 1596-1650. Kant, Immanuel, -- 1724-1804. Knowledge, Theory of. Philosophy, Modern -- 18th century. Philosophy, Modern -- 17th century.

BD162.M273 1959
Maritain, Jacques, 1882-1973.
The degrees of knowledge. Newly translated from the 4th French ed. under the supervision of Gerald B. Phelan. New York, Scribner [1959] xix, 476 p.
59-012892   121
Knowledge, Theory of. Metaphysics.

BD162.M43 1962
Meyerson, Emile, 1859-1933.
Identity & reality. Authorized translation by Kate Loewenberg. New York, Dover Publications [1962] 495 p.
62-053523   121
Reality. Knowledge, Theory of.

BD171 Epistemology. Theory of knowledge — Truth. Error. Certitude, etc.

BD171.A24 1984
Adler, Mortimer Jerome,
Six great ideas: truth, goodness, beauty, liberty, equality, justice: ideas we judge by, ideas we act on/ Mortimer J. Adler. 1st Collier Books ed. New York: Collier Books; 1984, xii, 243 p.
83-018888   111/.8 19   0020720203
Truth. Good and evil. Aesthetics. Liberty. Equality. Justice (Philosophy)

BD171.A3855 1993
Allen, Barry, 1957-
Truth in philosophy/ Barry Allen. Cambridge, Mass.: Harvard University Press, 1993. xi, 230 p.
92-035722   121   0674910907
Truth.

BD171.A42 1996
Alston, William P.
A realist conception of truth/ William P. Alston. Ithaca, N.Y.: Cornell University Press, 1996. xii, 274 p.
95-031251   121   0801431875
Truth. Realism. Knowledge, Theory of.

BD171.J59 1992
Johnson, Lawrence E.
Focusing on truth/ Lawrence E. Johnson. London; Routledge, 1992. 279 p.
91-035743   121   0415072522
Truth. Truth -- Correspondence theory. Truth -- Coherence theory.

BD171.L87 1998
Lynch, Michael P. 1966-
Truth in context: an essay on pluralism and objectivity/ Michael P. Lynch. Cambridge, Mass.: MIT Press, c1998. x, 184 p.
98-018000   121   026212212X
Truth. Pluralism. Objectivity.

BD171.P875
Putnam, Hilary.
Reason, truth, and history/ Hilary Putnam. Cambridge [Cambridgeshire]; Cambridge University Press, 1981. xii, 222 p.
81-006126   121   0521230357
Truth. Rationalism. Mind and body.

BD171.R8 1994
Rue, Loyal D.
By the grace of guile: the role of deception in natural history and human affairs/ Loyal Rue. New York: Oxford University Press, 1994. viii, 359 p.
93-032877   302/.1   0195075080
Deception.

BD171.S325 1995
Schmitt, Frederick F., 1951-
Truth: a primer/ Frederick F. Schmitt. Boulder, CO: Westview Press, 1995. xi, 251 p.
95-003422   121   0813320003
Truth -- Correspondence theory. Pragmatism. Realism.

BD171.T45 2000
Thagard, Paul.
Coherence in thought and action/ Paul Thagard. Cambridge, Mass.: MIT Press, c2000. xiv, 312 p.
00-035503   121   0262201313
Truth -- Coherence theory.

BD171.T69 1999
Trundle, Robert C., 1943-
From physics to politics: the metaphysical foundations of modern philosophy/ Robert C. Trundle, Jr.; with a foreword by Peter A. Redpath. New Brunswick, N.J.: Transaction Publishers, c1999. xiv, 190 p.
98-054820   121   1560004118
Truth. Ideology. Philosophy, Modern.

BD171.W28 1989
Walker, Ralph Charles Sutherland.
The coherence theory of truth: realism, anti-realism, idealism/ Ralph C.S. Walker. London; Routledge, 1989. xi, 247 p.
88-018282   121   0415018684
Truth -- Coherence theory.

BD171.W44 1993
Weissman, David, 1936-
Truth's debt to value/ David Weissman. New Haven: Yale University Press, c1993. xi, 355 p.
92-043608   121   0300054254
Truth. Values.

BD175 Epistemology. Theory of knowledge — Epistemology and sociology. Sociology of knowledge

BD175.A85 1989
Ashmore, Malcolm.
The reflexive thesis: wrighting sociology of scientific knowledge/ Malcolm Ashmore; foreword by Steve Woolgar. Chicago: University of Chicago Press, 1989. xxix, 287 p.
89-004728   121 19   0226029689
Knowledge, Sociology of. Self-knowledge, Theory of.

BD175.B34 1994
Bailey, Leon, 1952-
Critical theory and the sociology of knowledge: a comparative study in the theory of ideology/ Leon Bailey. New York: P. Lang, c1994. xii, 215 p.
93-006953   140   0820419885
Knowledge, Sociology of. Critical theory. Ideology.

BD175.B4
Berger, Peter L.
The social construction of reality; a treatise in the sociology of knowledge, by Peter L. Berger and Thomas Luckmann. Garden City, N.Y., Doubleday, 1966. vii, 203 p.
66-014925   301.01
Knowledge, Sociology of.

BD175.B68 1999
Bowker, Geoffrey C.
Sorting things out: classification and its consequences/ Geoffrey C. Bowker, Susan Leigh Star. Cambridge, Mass.: MIT Press, c1999. xii, 377 p.
99-026894   001/.01/2   0262024616
Knowledge, Sociology of. Classification.

BD175.B86 2000
Burke, Peter.
A social history of knowledge: from Gutenberg to Diderot/ Peter Burke. Cambridge, UK; Polity Press, 2000. vii, 268 p.
00-039973   306.4/2/0903   0745624847
Knowledge, Sociology of -- History.

BD175.C565 1998
Collins, Randall, 1941-
The sociology of philosophies: a global theory of intellectual change/ Randall Collins. Cambridge, Mass.: Belknap Press of Harvard University Press, 1998. xix, 1098 p.
97-018446   306.4/2/09   0674816471
Knowledge, Sociology of. Philosophy -- History. Comparative civilization.

BD175.C68 1989
Coulter, Jeff.
Mind in action/ Jeff Coulter. Atlantic Highlands, NJ: Humanities Press International, c1989. vii, 158 p.
89-011106   302   0391036564
Knowledge, Sociology of.

BD175.F834 1992
Fuchs, Stephan, 1956-
The professional quest for truth: a social theory of science and knowledge/ Stephan Fuchs. Albany: State University of New York Press, c1992. xviii, 254 p.
91-003095   306.4/5   0791409236
Knowledge, Sociology of. Science -- Social aspects.

BD175.F85 2002
Fuller, Steve,
Social epistemology/ Steve Fuller. 2nd ed. Bloomington: Indiana University Press, c2002. xxxi, 314 p.
2001-045723   001 21   0253215153
Social epistemology. Knowledge, Sociology of.

BD175.G64 1999
Goldman, Alvin I.,
Knowledge in a social world/ Alvin I. Goldman. Oxford: Clarendon Press; xiii, 407 p.
98-043283   121 21   0198238207
Social epistemology.

BD175.H28 1998
Haack, Susan.
Manifesto of a passionate moderate: unfashionable essays/ Susan Haack. Chicago: University of Chicago Press, c1998. x, 223 p.
98-022658   121   0226311368
Knowledge, Sociology of. Knowledge, Theory of. Science -- Philosophy.

BD175.H29 1999
Hacking, Ian.
The social construction of what?/ Ian Hacking. Cambridge, Mass: Harvard University Press, 1999. x, 261 p.
98-046140   121   067481200X
Knowledge, Sociology of.

BD175.H65
Horowitz, Irving Louis.
Philosophy, science, and the sociology of knowledge. With a foreword by Robert S. Cohen. Springfield, Ill., Thomas [1961] 169 p.
60-015850   121
Knowledge, Sociology of.

BD175.L66 1989
Longhurst, Brian, 1956-
Karl Mannheim and the contemporary sociology of knowledge/ Brian Longhurst. New York: St. Martin's Press, 1989. xii, 202 p.
88-004627   306/.42/0924   0312020171
Mannheim, Karl, -- 1893-1947 -- Contributions in sociology of knowledge.Knowledge, Sociology of -- History -- 20th century.

BD175.M31513 1986
Mannheim, Karl,
Conservatism: a contribution to the sociology of knowledge/ by Karl Mannheim; edited and introduced by David Kettler, Volker Meja, and Nico Stehr; translated by David Kettler and Volker Meja from a first draft by Elizabeth R. King. London; Routledge & Kegan Paul, 1986. vii, 256 p.
85-019354   306/.42 19   0710203381
Knowledge, Sociology of. Conservatism.

BD175.S43 1995
Searle, John R.
The construction of social reality/ John R. Searle. New York: Free Press, c1995. xiii, 241 p.
94-041402   121   0029280451
Social epistemology. Philosophy of mind.

BD175.S623 1994
Socializing epistemology: the social dimensions of knowledge/ edited by Frederick F. Schmitt. Lanham, Md.: Rowman & Littlefield Publishers, c1994. 315 p.
94-011232   121   0847679586
Social epistemology.

BD175.5 Epistemology. Theory of knowledge — Epistemology and sociology. Sociology of knowledge — Special topics, A-Z

BD175.5.M84 D33 1998
Dallmayr, Fred R.
Alternative visions: paths in the global village/ Fred Dallmayr. Lanham, Md.: Rowman & Littlefield, c1998. xii, 307 p.
97-029035   303.48/2/01 21   0847687686
Multiculturalism. Intercultural communication. Philosophy, Comparative. East and West. Civilization, Modern -- 20th century.

BD175.5.M84.D35 1996
Dallmayr, Fred R. 1928-
Beyond orientalism: essays on cross-cultural encounter/ Fred Dallmayr. Albany: State University of New York Press, c1996. xxii, 277 p.
96-012033   303.48/2/01   0791430693
Multiculturalism. Intercultural communication. Philosophy, Comparative.

BD175.5.M84 D48 1996
Devine, Philip E.,
Human diversity and the culture wars: a philosophical perspective on contemporary cultural conflict/ Philip E. Devine. Westport, Conn.: Praeger, 1996. xix, 192 p.
96-015319   306/.0973 20   0275952053
Multiculturalism. Political correctness. Culture conflict -- United States. United States -- Civilization -- 20th century.

BD175.5.P65.C46 1992
Choi, Jung Min.
The politics and philosophy of political correctness/ Jung Min Choi and John W. Murphy. Westport, Conn.: Praeger, 1992. xiv, 168 p.
92-019834   320.5   0275942864
Political correctness.United States -- Politics and government -- 1989-1993.

BD175.5.P65.F75 1995
Friedman, Marilyn, 1945-
Political correctness: for and against/ Marilyn Friedman and Jan Narveson. Lanham, Md.: Rowman & Littlefield, c1995. viii, 153 p.
94-033880   306/.0973   0847679853
Political correctness. Feminist theory.

BD176 Epistemology. Theory of knowledge — Epistemology and ethics. Intellectual virtues

BD176.V57 2001
Virtue epistemology: essays on epistemic virtue and responsibility/ edited by Abrol Fairweather & Linda Zagzebski. Oxford; Oxford University Press, 2001. ix, 251 p.
00-061152   121 21   019514077X
Virtue epistemology.

BD176.Z34 1996
Zagzebski, Linda Trinkaus, 1946-
Virtues of the mind: an inquiry into the nature of virtue and the ethical foundations of knowledge/ Linda Trinkaus Zagzebski. New York, NY, USA: Cambridge University Press, 1996. xvi, 365 p.
95-026531   121   0521570603
Knowledge, Theory of. Virtue. Ethics.

BD177 Epistemology. Theory of knowledge — Epistemology and evolution

BD177.W85 1990
Wuketits, Franz M.
Evolutionary epistemology and its implications for humankind/ Franz M. Wuketits. State University Plaza, Albany, N.Y.: State University of New York, c1990. xi, 262 p.
89-036315   121   0791402851
Evolution. Knowledge, Theory of.

BD181 Epistemology. Theory of knowledge — Origins and sources of knowledge

BD181.C23 1992
Campbell, Richard,
Truth and historicity/ Richard Campbell. Oxford: Clarendon Press; 1992. xi, 463 p.
92-000983   121/.09   0198239270
Truth. History -- Philosophy.

BD181.C48
Childe, V. Gordon 1892-1957.
Society and knowledge. New York, Harper [1956] 131 p.
55-010691   121
Knowledge, Theory of.

BD181.C59 1992
Coady, C. A. J.
Testimony: a philosophical study/ C.A.J. Coady. Oxford: Clarendon Press; 1992. x, 315 p.
91-026438   121   0198247869
Knowledge, Theory of. Witnesses. Other minds (Theory of knowledge)

BD181.L47
Lewis, Clarence Irving, 1883-1964.
An analysis of knowledge and valuation/ C. I. Lewis. La Salle, Ill.: Open Court, c1946. xxi, 568 p.
47-020878   121
Knowledge, Theory of. Values.

BD181.O3
Oakeshott, Michael Joseph.
Experience and its modes, by Michael Oakeshott... Cambridge [Eng.] The University press, 1933. viii, 359 p.
34-016688   121
Experience.

BD181.P43 1992
Peacocke, Christopher.
A study of concepts/ Christopher Peacocke. Cambridge, Mass.: MIT Press, c1992. xiii, 266 p.
91-046487   121/.4   0262161338
Concepts.

BD181.Q47 1994
Questions of evidence: proof, practice, and persuasion across the disciplines/ edited by James Chandler, Arnold I. Davidson, and Harry Harootunian. Chicago: University of Chicago Press, 1994. vii, 518 p.
94-012897   121/.65 20   0226100839
Evidence. Critical theory. Interdisciplinary research.

BD181.W384 1988
Weitz, Morris.
Theories of concepts: a history of the major philosophical tradition/ Morris Weitz. London; Routledge, 1988. xxi, 310 p.
87-031663   121/.4   0415001803
Concepts -- History.

BD181.7 Epistemology. Theory of knowledge — Memory

BD181.7.C33 2000
Casey, Edward S.,
Remembering: a phenomenological study/ Edward S. Casey. 2nd ed. Bloomington: Indiana University Press, c2000. xxiv, 362 p.
00-057231   128/.3 21   0253214122
Memory (Philosophy) Phenomenology.

BD181.7.D4713 1996
Derrida, Jacques.
Archive fever: a Freudian impression/ Jacques Derrida; translated by Eric Prenowitz. Chicago: University of Chicago Press, 1996. 113 p.
96-018568   153.1/2   0226143368
Freud, Sigmund, -- 1856-1939.Psychoanalysis. Memory (Philosophy)

BD182 Epistemology. Theory of knowledge — Criterion

BD182.A45 1993
Amico, Robert P., 1947-
The problem of criterion/ Robert P. Amico. Lanham, Md.: Rowman & Littlefield Publishers, c1993. xi, 156 p.
92-037597   121/.65   0847678180
Criterion (Theory of knowledge)

BD183 Epistemology. Theory of knowledge — Inquiry

BD183.B53 1998
Blachowicz, James, 1943-
Of two minds: the nature of inquiry/ James Blachowicz. Albany, NY: State University of New York Press, c1998. xv, 434 p.
97-013473   121/.6   0791436411
Inquiry (Theory of knowledge)

BD183.G55 1993
Gill, Jerry H.
Learning to learn: toward a philosophy of education/ Jerry H. Gill. Atlantic Highlands, N.J.: Humanities Press, 1993. x, 252 p.
92-013967   370/.1   0391037730
Inquiry (Theory of knowledge) Interdisciplinary approach to knowledge. Education -- Philosophy.

BD190 Epistemology. Theory of knowledge — Analogy

BD190.A6 1969
Anderson, James Francis,
The bond of being; an essay on analogy and existence, by James F. Anderson. New York, Greenwood Press [1969, c1949] xvi, 341 p.
77-091752   111   0837124352
Analogy.

BD190.H65 1995
Holyoak, Keith James, 1950-
Mental leaps: analogy in creative thought/ Keith J. Holyoak and Paul Thagard. Cambridge, Mass.: MIT Press, c1995. xiii, 320 p.
94-022734   169   0262082330
Analogy. Creative thinking.

BD201 Epistemology. Theory of knowledge — Limits of knowledge

BD201.H48 1991
Hetherington, Stephen Cade.
Epistemology's paradox: is a theory of knowledge possible?/ Stephen Cade Hetherington. Savage, Md.: Rowman & Littlefield, c1992. x, 234 p.
91-017930   121   0847676749
Knowledge, Theory of.

BD201.M37 1989
McGinn, Marie.
Sense and certainty: a dissolution of scepticism/ Marie McGinn. Oxford, UK; Blackwell, 1989. 166 p.
88-022207   149/.73   0631157867
Skepticism.

BD201.R47 1980
Rescher, Nicholas.
Scepticism, a critical reappraisal/ Nicholas Rescher. Totowa, N.J.: Rowman and Littlefield, 1980. xii, 265 p.
79-022990   149/.73   0847662403
Skepticism. Reasoning. Knowledge, Theory of.

BD201.S73 2000
Stern, Robert,
Transcendental arguments and scepticism: answering the question of justification/ Robert Stern. Oxford: Clarendon Press; x, 261 p.
00-031357   121/.2 21   0198250533
Skepticism. Transcendental logic. Justification (Theory of knowledge)

BD201.W54 1996
Whitman, Jeffrey P.
The power and value of philosophical skepticism/ Jeffrey P. Whitman. Lanham, Md.: Rowman & Littlefield Publishers, c1996. x, 110 p.
96-012527   149/.73   0847682323
Skepticism. Knowledge, Theory of.

BD201.W55 1966
Wisdom, John.
Other minds.   Oxford, Blackwell, 1965 viii, 265 p.
66-072161   121
Knowledge, Theory of. Mind and body.

BD209 Epistemology. Theory of knowledge — Authority

BD209.A9
Authority: a philosophical analysis/ edited by R. Baine Harris; with bibliography by Richard T. De George. University, Ala.: University of Alabama Press, c1976. vi, 173 p.
75-011666   301.15/52/01   0817366202
Authority. Authority -- Religious aspects.

BD212 Epistemology. Theory of knowledge — Justification

BD212.A47 1989
Alston, William P.
Epistemic justification: essays in the theory of knowledge/ William P. Alston. Ithaca: Cornell University Press, c1989. xi, 354 p.
89-042865   121   0801422574
Justification (Theory of knowledge)

BD212.G65 2002
Goldman, Alvin I.,
Pathways to knowledge: private and public/ Alvin I. Goldman. Oxford; Oxford University Press, 2002. xiv, 224 p.
2001-046411   121 21   0195138791
Justification (Theory of knowledge) Knowledge, Sociology of. Consciousness.

BD212.H38 1995
Hauptli, Bruce W., 1948-
The reasonableness of reason: explaining rationality naturalistically/ Bruce W. Hauptli. Chicago, Ill.: Open Court, c1995. x, 276 p.
95-014893   121/.3   0812692837
Reason. Justification (Theory of knowledge) Naturalism.

BD212.5 Epistemology. Theory of knowledge — Verification. Empirical verification. Verifiability

BD212.5.M57 1995
Misak, C. J.
Verificationism: its history and prospects/ C.J. Misak. London; Routledge, 1995. xvii, 254 p.
95-007728   111/.8   0415125979
Verification (Empiricism)

BD214 Epistemology. Theory of knowledge — Senses and sensation

BD214.A57 1993
Alston, William P.
The reliability of sense perception/ William P. Alston. Ithaca, N.Y.: Cornell University Press, 1993. x, 148 p.
92-054964   121/.3   0801428629
Senses and sensation. Belief and doubt. Knowledge, Theory of.

BD214.H54 1991
Hill, Christopher S.
Sensations: a defense of type materialism/ Christopher S. Hill. Cambridge [England]; Cambridge University Press, 1991. ix, 253 p.
90-015019   128/.3   0521394236
Senses and sensation. Knowledge, Theory of.

BD214.5 Epistemology. Theory of knowledge — Body. Somatic aspects

BD214.5.S66 1989
Sorri, Mari.
A post-modern epistemology: language, truth, and body/ Mari Sorri & Jerry H. Gill. Lewiston, N.Y., USA: E. Mellen Press, c1989. 214 p.
89-012434   121   0889463247
Knowledge, Theory of. Body, Human (Philosophy) Mind and body.

BD215 Epistemology. Theory of knowledge — Belief. Faith

BD215.A97 1990
Austin, David F., 1952-
What's the meaning of "this"?: a puzzle about demonstrative belief/ David F. Austin. Ithaca: Cornell University Press, 1990. xvii, 172 p.
89-022110   121/.6   0801424097
Belief and doubt. Proposition (Logic)

BD215.B27 1987
Baker, Lynne Rudder, 1944-
Saving belief: a critique of physicalism/ Lynne Rudder Baker. Princeton, N.J.: Princeton University Press, c1987. xii, 177 p.
87-025926   121/.6   0691073201
Belief and doubt.

BD215.B67 1997
Botwinick, Aryeh.
Skepticism, belief, and the modern: Maimonides to Nietzsche/ Aryeh Botwinick. Ithaca, N.Y.: Cornell University Press, 1997. x, 249 p.
97-019770   190   0801432081
Maimonides, Moses, -- 1135-1204. Hobbes, Thomas, -- 1588-1679. Nietzsche, Friedrich Wilhelm, -- 1844-1900. Liberalism. Belief and doubt. Monotheism.

BD215.C825 1992
Crimmins, Mark.
Talk about beliefs/ Mark Crimmins. Cambridge, Mass.: MIT Press, c1992. xi, 214 p.
91-031795   121/.6   026203185X
Belief and doubt. Semantics (Philosophy)

BD215.D3 1958
D'Arcy, Martin Cyril, 1888-1976.
The nature of belief. St. Louis, Herder c1958. 236 p.
58-004618   121
Newman, John Henry, -- 1801-1890 -- Essay in aid of a grammar of assent. Faith. Belief and doubt. Knowledge, Theory of.

BD215.E43 1979
Ellis, B. D. 1929-
Rational belief systems/ Brian Ellis. Totowa, N.J.: Rowman and Littlefield, 1979. ix, 118 p.
78-011988   121/.6   0847661083
Belief and doubt. Logic. Reasoning.

BD215.H439 1994
Helm, Paul.
Belief policies/ Paul Helm. Cambridge; Cambridge University Press, 1994. xiii, 226 p.
93-032409   121/.6   052146028X
Belief and doubt.

BD215.L45 1991
Levi, Isaac, 1930-
The fixation of belief and its undoing: changing beliefs through inquiry/ Isaac Levi. Cambridge; Cambridge University Press, 1991. 192 p.
91-014207   121/.6   0521412668
Belief and doubt. Probabilities. Epistemics.

BD215.L92 1988
Lycan, William G.
Judgement and justification/ William G. Lycan. Cambridge [Cambridgeshire]; Cambridge University Press, 1988. xiv, 236 p.
87-012490   121/.6   0521340470
Belief and doubt. Justification (Theory of knowledge)

BD215.P513 1975
Pieper, Josef, 1904-
Belief and faith: a philosophical tract/ by Josef Pieper; translated from the German by Richard and Clara Winston. Westport, Conn.: Greenwood Press, 1975, c1963. xi, 106 p.
75-031841   121/.6   0837184908
Belief and doubt. Faith and reason.

BD215.P7
Price, H. H. 1899-
Belief: the Gifford lectures delivered at the University of Aberdeen in 1960, by H. H. Price. London, Allen & Unwin; 1969. 495 p.
76-390002   121/.6   0041210093
Belief and doubt -- Addresses, essays, lectures.

BD215.S28 1997
Sayre, Kenneth M., 1928-
Belief and knowledge: mapping the cognitive landscape/ Kenneth M. Sayre. Lanham, Md.: Rowman & Littlefield, c1997. xvi, 311 p.
97-014921   121/.6   0847684725
Knowledge, Theory of. Belief and doubt.

BD215.S34 1991
Schmitt, Frederick F., 1951-
Knowledge and belief/ Frederick F. Schmitt. London; Routledge, 1992. x, 278 p.
91-030982   121/.6   0415033179
Belief and doubt. Skepticism. Justification (Theory of knowledge)

BD216 Epistemology. Theory of knowledge — Hope

BD216.S43 2001
Shade, Patrick, 1965-
Habits of hope: a pragmatic theory/ Patrick Shade. Nashville: Vanderbilt University Press, 2001. xv, 238 p.
00-010465   128   0826513611
Hope. Pragmatism. Philosophy, American -- 20th century.

BD220 Epistemology. Theory of knowledge — Objectivity

BD220.B87 1998
Butchvarov, Panayot, 1933-
Skepticism about the external world/ Panayot Butchvarov. New York: Oxford University Press, 1998. viii, 184 p.
97-014104   121/.2   0195117190
Skepticism. Realism.

BD220.M67 1993
Moser, Paul K., 1957-
Philosophy after objectivity: making sense in perspective/ Paul K. Moser. New York: Oxford University Press, 1993. xii, 267 p.
92-038864   121   0195081099
Objectivity. Realism. Relativity.

BD220.R49 1997
Rescher, Nicholas.
Objectivity: the obligations of impersonal reason/ Nicholas Rescher. Notre Dame, Ind.: University of Notre Dame Press, c1997. ix, 230 p.
96-026431   149/.7   0268037019
Objectivity.

BD220.S2 1982
Scheffler, Israel.
Science and subjectivity/ Israel Scheffler. 2nd ed. Indianapolis, Ind.: Hackett Pub. Co., 1982. xii, 166 p.
81-085414   121 19   0915145308
Objectivity. Knowledge, Theory of. Science -- Philosophy.

BD221 Epistemology. Theory of knowledge — Relativity of knowledge

BD221.C285
Cassirer, Ernst, 1874-1945.
Substance and function, and Einstein's theory of relativity, by Ernst Cassirer; authorized translation by William Curtis Swabey, PH.D., and Marie Collins Swabey, PH.D. Chicago, The Open court publishing company, 1923.
23-014107
Relativity (Physics) Substance (Philosophy) Knowledge, Theory of.

BD221.H37 1992
Harris, James F.
Against relativism: a philosophical defense of method/ James F. Harris. La Salle, Ill.: Open Court, c1992. xvi, 228 p.
92-021019   149 20   0812692020
Relativity. Knowledge, Theory of. Methodology.

BD221.M33 1991
Margolis, Joseph, 1924-
The truth about relativism/ Joseph Margolis. Oxford UK; Cambridge USA: B. Blackwell, 1991. xvi, 224 p.
91-007535   149   0631179119
Protagoras.Relativity.

BD223 Epistemology. Theory of knowledge — Relativity of knowledge — Subject

BD223.L56 1989
Lingis, Alphonso, 1933-
Deathbound subjectivity/ Alphonso Lingis. Bloomington: Indiana University Press, c1989. 211 p.
88-045450   126   025331660X
Subject (Philosophy) Death.

BD223.M37 1995
Mapping the subject: geographies of cultural transformation/ edited by Steve Pile and Nigel Thrift. London; Routledge, 1995. xi, 414 p.
94-023747   302/.1   0415102251
Subject (Philosophy) Power (Philosophy) Identity.

BD223.W49 1991
Who comes after the subject?/ edited by Eduardo Cadava, Peter Connor, Jean-Luc Nancy. New York: Routledge, 1991. vii, 258 p.
90-020555   126   0415903599
Subject (Philosophy)

BD232 Epistemology. Theory of knowledge — Value. Worth

BD232.A48 1993
Anderson, Elizabeth, 1959-
Value in ethics and economics/ Elizabeth Anderson. Cambridge, Mass.: Harvard University Press, 1993. xiv, 245 p.
93-000365   121/.8   0674931890
Values. Value. Reason.

BD232.B595 1995
Bok, Sissela.
Common values/ Sissela Bok. Columbia, Mo.: University of Missouri Press, c1995. xi, 130 p.
95-025333   170   0826210384
Values. Ethics. Social values.

BD232.G38 1990
Gaus, Gerald F.
Value and justification: the foundations of liberal theory/ Gerald F. Gaus. Cambridge [England]; Cambridge University Press, 1990. xviii, 540 p.
89-027088   121/.8   0521375258
Values. Ethics. Emotions (Philosophy)

BD232.G63
Gotshalk, Dilman Walter, 1901-
Patterns of good and evil; a value analysis. Urbana, University of Illinois Press, 1963. xiv, 138 p.
63-017047   121.8
Values.

BD232.G667 1996
Griffin, James, 1933-
Value judgement: improving our ethical beliefs/
James Griffin. Oxford: Clarendon Press; c1996.
xii, 180 p.
96-010751   170/.42   0198235534
Values.

BD232.H25
Hall, Everett Wesley.
Our knowledge of fact and value. Introd. by E.
M. Adams. Chapel Hill, University of North
Carolina Press [1961] 220 p.
61-016130   121.8
Values. Knowledge, Theory of.

BD232.H26 1952
Hall, Everett Wesley.
What is value?: An essay in philosophical
analysis. New York: Humanities Press, [1961,
1952]. xiii, 255 p.
54-000675
Values.

BD232.H296 1989
Hans, James S., 1950-
The question of value: thinking through
Nietzsche, Heidegger, and Freud/ James S.
Hans. Carbondale: Southern Illinois University
Press, c1989. xiv, 204 p.
88-018451   121/.8   0809315068
Nietzsche, Friedrich Wilhelm, -- 1844-1900 --
Influence. Heidegger, Martin, -- 1889-1976 --
Influence. Freud, Sigmund, -- 1856-1939 --
Influence. Values.

BD232.K6 1966
Kohler, Wolfgang, 1887-
The place of value in a world of facts. New
York, New American Library [c1966] 320 p.
67-001672
Science -- Philosophy. Worth.

BD232.L398 1995
Lemos, Ramon M., 1927-
The nature of value: axiological investigations/
Ramon M. Lemos. Gainesville: University Press
of Florida, c1995. xiii, 220 p.
95-001079   121/.8   0813013666
Values.

BD232.L42 1970
Lepley, Ray, 1903-
Value; a cooperative inquiry.   New York,
Columbia University Press [1949] 487 p.
49-050256   121/.8   083713904X
Dewey, John, -- 1859-1952.Values.

BD232.M34
Maslow, Abraham H.
New knowledge in human values. Foreword by
Pitirim A. Sorokin. New York, Harper [1959]
268 p.
58-011051   121.8082
Worth.

BD232.N47 1989
Nerlich, Graham, 1929-
Values and valuing: speculations on the ethical
life of persons/ Graham Nerlich. Oxford;
Clarendon Press, 1989. 217 p.
90-124768   170   0198248474
Values. Ethics.

BD232.P27
Parker, DeWitt Henry, 1885-1949.
The philosophy of value; with a pref. by William
K. Frankena. Ann Arbor, University of Michigan
Press [1957] 272 p.
57-005142   121
Values.

BD232.P45 1950
Perry, Ralph Barton, 1876-1957.
General theory of value, its meaning and basic
principles construed in terms of interest.
Cambridge, Harvard University Press, 1950
[c1926] xvii, 702 p.
51-008984   121
Worth. Philosophy, Modern.

BD232.T33
Taylor, Paul W.
Normative   discourse/   Paul   W.   Taylor.
Englewood Cliffs, N.J.: Prentice-Hall, 1961.
xvii, 360 p.
61-011822   121.8
Values. Judgment.

BD232.W53 1998
Wiggins, David.
Needs, values, truth: essays in the philosophy of
value/ David   Wiggins. 3rd ed. Oxford:
Clarendon Press; xii, 398 p.
98-215665   121 21   0198237197
Values.

BD236 Epistemology. Theory of knowledge — Comparison. Resemblance. Identity

BD236.B3813 1994
Baudrillard, Jean.
Simulacra and simulation/ by Jean Baudrillard;
translated by Sheila   Faria Glaser. Ann Arbor:
University of Michigan Press, c1994. 164 p.
94-038393   194 20   0472065211
Resemblance (Philosophy) Reality.

BD236.G35 1998
Gallois, Andre.
Occasions of identity: a study in the metaphysics
of persistence, change, and sameness/ Andre
Gallois. Oxford: Clarendon Press; 1998. xiii,
296 p.
97-024226   111/.82   0198237448
Identity. Change.

BD236.H413 1969
Heidegger, Martin, 1889-1976.
Identity and difference. Translated and with an
introd. by Joan Stambaugh. New York, Harper &
Row [1969] 146 p.
69-017025   111
Identity. Metaphysics.

BD236.I42 1995
The identity in question/ edited by John
Rajchman. New York: Routledge, 1995. xiii,
295 p.
94-024832   306 20   0415906180
Identity. Political science -- Philosophy.
Culture -- Philosophy. Critical theory.
Nationalism. Philosophy, Modern -- 20th
century.

BD236.O27 1993
Oderberg, David S.
The metaphysics of identity over time/ David S.
Oderberg. New York: St. Martin's Press, 1993.
ix, 228 p.
93-023788   111/.82   0312102089
Identity. Continuity.

BD236.W53 1980
Wiggins, David.
Sameness and substance/ David Wiggins.
Cambridge, Mass.: Harvard University Press,
1980. xi, 238 p.
79-025134   110   0674785959
Identity. Individuation (Philosophy) Essence
(Philosophy)   Conceptualism.   Substance
(Philosophy)

BD237 Epistemology. Theory of knowledge — Explanation

BD237.R83 1990
Ruben, David-Hillel.
Explaining explanation/ David-Hillel Ruben.
London; Routledge, 1990. xi, 265 p.
91-100577   121/.4   0415032695
Explanation.

BD241 Methodology — General works — 1801-

BD241.B33 1978
Bauman, Zygmunt.
Hermeneutics and social science/ Zygmunt
Bauman. New York: Columbia University Press,
1978. 263 p.
78-000877   300/.1   0231045468
Hermeneutics. Social sciences.

BD241.B78 1992
Bruns, Gerald L.
Hermeneutics, ancient and modern/ Gerald L.
Bruns. New Haven: Yale University Press,
c1992. xii, 318 p.
92-014839   121/.68   0300054505
Hermeneutics -- History.

BD241.B785 2000
Bryant, Rebecca, 1970-
Discovery and decision: exploring the metaphysics and epistemology of scientific classification/ Rebecca Bryant. Madison [N.J.]: Fairleigh Dickinson University Press, c2000. 131 p.
00-037169 001/.01/2 0838638767
Classification of sciences. Metaphysics. Knowledge, Theory of.

BD241.B79 1988
Bubner, Rüdiger,
Essays in hermeneutics and critical theory/ by Rüdiger Bubner; translated by Eric Matthews. New York: Columbia University Press, 1988. viii, 262 p.
87-013156 120 19 0231057040
Hermeneutics. Ethics. Critical theory.

BD241.C65
Costello, Harry Todd, 1885-
Josiah Royce's seminar, 1913-1914: as recorded in the notebooks of Harry T. Costello. Edited by Grover Smith. With an essay on the philosophy of Royce by Richard Hocking. New Brunswick, N. J., Rutgers University Press [1963] 209 p.
62-018949
Royce, Josiah, -- 1855-1916.Methodology.

BD241.C76 1991
Crusius, Timothy W., 1950-
A teacher's introduction to philosophical hermeneutics/ Timothy W. Crusius. Urbana, Ill.: National Council of Teachers in English, c1991. xiv, 103 p.
91-034817 121/.68/0248 0814150160
Hermeneutics. Rhetoric -- Philosophy.

BD241.F4213 1996
Ferraris, Maurizio,
History of hermeneutics/ Maurizio Ferraris; translated by Luca Somigli. Atlantic Highlands, N.J.: Humanities Press, 1996. xxi, 358 p.
95-035119 121/.68 20 0391039318
Hermeneutics.

BD241.G313 1989
Gadamer, Hans Georg,
Truth and method/ Hans-Georg Gadamer. 2nd rev. ed./ translation revised by Joel Weinsheimer and Donald G. New York: Crossroad, 1989. xxxviii, 594 p.
88-009666 121 19 0826404014
Humanities -- Methodology. Hermeneutics. Aesthetics.

BD241.G34 1991
Gadamer and hermeneutics/ edited with an introduction by Hugh J. Silverman. New York; London: 1991. 332 p.
90-025404 121/.68 20 0415903742
Gadamer, Hans Georg, 1900- Hermeneutics. Philosophy, Modern -- 20th century.

BD241.G48 1960
Gilbert, Neal Ward.
Renaissance concepts of method. New York, Columbia University Press, 1960. 255 p.
60-006638 112
Philosophy, Renaissance. Methodology.

BD241.G65 1988
Goodman, Nelson.
Reconceptions in philosophy and other arts and sciences/ Nelson Goodman, Catherine Z. Elgin. Indianapolis: Hackett Pub. Co., c1988. xiv, 174 p.
87-031330 101 0872200523
Methodology. Aesthetics. Symbolism.

BD241.G69513 1994
Grondin, Jean.
Introduction to philosophical hermeneutics/ Jean Grondin; foreword by Hans-Georg Gadamer; translated by Joel Weinsheimer. New Haven: Yale University Press, c1994. xv, 231 p.
94-012360 121/.68 0300059698
Hermeneutics -- History.

BD241.H355 1990
The Hermeneutic tradition: from Ast to Ricoeur/ edited by Gayle L. Ormiston and Alan D. Schrift. Albany, NY: State University of New York Press, c1990. xii, 380 p.
89-004173 121/.68 0791401367
Hermeneutics.

BD241.H375 1988
Hermeneutics versus science?: three German views: essays/ by H.-G. Gadamer, E.K. Specht, W. Stegmuller; translated, edited, and introduced by John M. Connolly and Thomas Keutner. Notre Dame, Ind.: University of Notre Dame Press, c1988. viii, 176 p.
87-040346 121/.68 0268010846
Hermeneutics. Science -- Philosophy. Meaning (Philosophy)

BD241.K6413 1996
Kogler, Hans-Herbert,
The power of dialogue: critical hermeneutics after Gadamer and Foucault/ Hans Herbert Kogler; translated by Paul Hendrickson. Cambridge, Mass.: MIT Press, c1996. ix, 322 p.
96-021484 121/.68 0262112167
Gadamer, Hans Georg, -- 1900- -- Contributions in hermeneutics. Foucault, Michel -- Contributions in hermeneutics. Hermeneutics -- History -- 20th century.

BD241.M25 1988
Madison, Gary Brent.
The hermeneutics of postmodernity: figures and themes/ G.B. Madison. Bloomington: Indiana University Press, c1988. xvi, 206 p.
87-046089 121/.68 0253321905
Hermeneutics. Phenomenology.

BD241.M3
Martin, William Oliver
The order and integration of knowledge [by] William Oliver Martin. Ann Arbor, University of Michigan Press [1957] viii, 355 p.
56-011320 112
Methodology.

BD241.P65 1962
Popper, Karl Raimund, 1902-
Conjectures and refutations; the growth of scientific knowledge, by Karl R. Popper. New York, Basic Books [c1962] xi, 412 p.
63-011566 112 0710065078
Knowledge, Theory of. Science -- Methodology. Methodology.

BD241.R484
Ricœur, Paul.
Hermeneutics and the human sciences: essays on language, action, and interpretation/ Paul Ricoeur; edited, translated, and introduced by John B. Thompson. Cambridge [Eng.]; Cambridge University Press; viii, 314 p.
80-041546 101 19 0521280028
Hermeneutics. Social sciences -- Philosophy.

BD241.R594 1998
Robinson, Guy, 1927-
Philosophy and mystification: a reflection on nonsense and clarity/ Guy Robinson. London; Routledge, 1998. ix, 299 p.
97-018223 101 0415178517
Methodology. Philosophy.

BD241.R65
Rosenberg, Jay F.
The practice of philosophy: a handbook for beginners/ Jay F. Rosenberg. Englewood Cliffs, N.J.: Prentice-Hall, c1978. xii, 111 p.
77-013424 101/.8 013687178X
Methodology. Philosophy -- Introductions.

BD241.T46 1992
Thiselton, Anthony C.
New horizons in hermeneutics/ Anthony C. Thiselton. Grand Rapids, Mich.: Zondervan Pub. House, c1992. xii, 703 p.
91-040572 220.6/01 0310515904
Hermeneutics.

BD241.T5813 1982
Todorov, Tzvetan, 1939-
Symbolism and interpretation/ Tzvetan Todorov; translated by Catherine Porter. Ithaca, N.Y.: Cornell University Press, c1982. 175 p.
82-005078 001.54 0801412692
Hermeneutics. Symbolism. Structural linguistics.

BD241.T7 1990
Transforming the hermeneutic context: from Nietzsche to Nancy/ edited by Gayle L. Ormiston and Alan D. Schrift. Albany, NY: State University of New York Press, c1990. xii, 306 p.
89-004172 121/.68 0791401340
Hermeneutics.

BD241.V24513 1997
Vattimo, Gianni, 1936-
Beyond interpretation: the meaning of hermeneutics for philosophy/ Gianni Vattimo; translated by David Webb. Stanford, Calif.: Stanford University Press, 1997. x, 129 p.
96-071016   121/.686   0804729921
Hermeneutics.

BD241.W343 1990
Wallulis, Jerald, 1947-
The hermeneutics of life history: personal achievement and history in Gadamer, Habermas, and Erikson/ Jerald Wallulis. Evanston, Ill.: Northwestern University Press, 1990. xv, 158 p.
90-049019   128/.5   0810109670
Gadamer, Hans Georg, -- 1900- Habermas, Jurgen. Erikson, Erik H. -- (Erik Homburger), -- 1902- Hermeneutics. Biography. Psychoanalysis and philosophy.

BD241.W345 1987
Walzer, Michael.
Interpretation and social criticism/ Michael Walzer. Cambridge, Mass.: Harvard University Press, 1987. viii, 96 p.
86-014997   300/.1 19   0674459709
Hermeneutics. Ethics. Social sciences -- Philosophy.

BD241.W44 1991
Weinsheimer, Joel.
Philosophical hermeneutics and literary theory/ Joel Weinsheimer. New Haven: Yale University Press, c1991. xiii, 173 p.
90-039159   121/.68/092   0300047851
Gadamer, Hans Georg, -- 1900- -- Contributions in hermeneutics.Hermeneutics. Literature -- Philosophy.

BD255 Methodology — Interdisciplinary approach to knowledge

BD255.J68
Journal of interdisciplinary studies. Santa Monica, CA: Institute for Interdisciplinary Research, [c1989-]
89-656301   001/.05
Interdisciplinary approach to knowledge -- Periodicals. Religion and civilization -- Periodicals. Ethics -- Periodicals.

BD255.K538 1996
Klein, Julie Thompson.
Crossing boundaries: knowledge, disciplinarities, and interdisciplinarities/ Julie Thompson Klein. Charlottesville, Va.: University Press of Virginia, 1996. x, 281 p.
96-007615   001.2 20   0813916798
Interdisciplinary approach to knowledge.

BD255.K54 1990
Klein, Julie Thompson.
Interdisciplinarity: history, theory, and practice/ Julie Thompson Klein. Detroit: Wayne State University Press, 1990. 331 p.
89-035166   001   0814320872
Interdisciplinary approach to knowledge.

BD260 Methodology — Heuristic

BD260.M68 1990
Moustakas, Clark E.
Heuristic research: design, methodology, and applications/ Clark Moustakas. Newbury Park: Sage Publications, c1990. 130 p.
90-034596   001.4/2   0803938810
Heuristic. Problem solving.

BD300 Ontology — General works — Early through 1800

BD300.W93.R6 1961a
Robson, J. A. 1930-
Wyclif and the Oxford schools; the relation of the "Summa de ente" to scholastic debates at Oxford in the later fourteenth century. Cambridge, University Press, 1961. xiii, 268 p.
61-016171   149.73
Wycliffe, John, -- d. 1384. -- Summa de ente.Scholasticism.

BD311 Ontology — General works — 1801-

BD311.B494 1993
Bigwood, Carol, 1957-
Earth muse: feminism, nature, and art/ Carol Bigwood. Philadelphia: Temple University Press, 1993. xi, 375 p.
92-020270   111/.082   0877229864
Ontology. Femininity (Philosophy) Feminist theory.

BD311.J66 1998
Jones, Judith A., 1963-
Intensity: an essay in Whiteheadian ontology/ Judith A. Jones. Nashville, Tenn.: Vanderbilt University Press, 1998. xiv, 247 p.
97-021240   111/.092   082651300X
Whitehead, Alfred North, -- 1861-1947.Ontology. Process philosophy.

BD311.N36 1993
Nancy, Jean-Luc.
The birth to presence/ Jean-Luc Nancy; translated by Brian Holmes & others. Stanford, Calif.: Stanford University Press, 1993. x, 423 p.
92-030596   110 20   0804721890
Ontology. Criticism.

BD311.R67 1989
Ross, Stephen David.
Inexhaustibility and human being: an essay on locality/ Stephen David Ross. New York: Fordham University Press, 1989. xiii, 330 p.
88-082222   128   0823212238
Ontology. Finite, The. Knowledge, Theory of.

BD311.V35 1990
Van Inwagen, Peter.
Material beings/ Peter van Inwagen. Ithaca, N.Y.: Cornell University Press, 1990. viii, 299 p.
90-055125   111   0801419697
Ontology. Identity.

BD311.W54 1995
Wilber, Ken.
Sex, ecology, spirituality: the spirit of evolution/ Ken Wilber. Boston: Shambhala; 1995. xi, 831 p.
94-003701   110   1570620725
Cosmology. Consciousness. Evolution (Philosophy)

BD331 Ontology — Being. Nature of reality. Substance. First philosophy

BD331.F428 1989
Ferguson, Harvie.
The science of pleasure: cosmos and psyche in the bourgeois world view/ Harvie Ferguson. London; Routledge, 1990. x, 364 p.
89-032956   303.3/72/08622   0415028930
Cosmology -- History. Science -- History. Psychology -- History.

BD331.G273 1998
Gangadean, Ashok K.,
Between worlds: the emergence of global reason/ Ashok K. Gangadean. New York: Peter Lang, c1998. xlii, 386 p.
96-033952   110 20   0820424900
First philosophy. Reason. Ontology. Logic. Language and languages -- Philosophy.

BD331.G65
Goodman, Nelson.
Ways of worldmaking/ Nelson Goodman. Indianapolis,: Hackett Pub. Co., c1978. x, 142 p.
78-056364   191   0915144522
Reality -- Addresses, essays, lectures. Style (Philosophy) -- Addresses, essays, lectures. Facts (Philosophy) -- Addresses, essays, lectures.

BD331.H334
Hartmann, Nicolai, 1882-1951
New ways of ontlogy; translated by Reinhard C. Kuhn. Chicago, H. Regnery Co., 1953 [1952] 145 p.
53-005776
Ontology.

BD331.H4313
Heidegger, Martin, 1889-1976.
An introduction to metaphysics. Translated by
Ralph Manheim. New Haven, Yale University
Press, 1959. xi, 214 p.
59-006796　111　0300017405
Ontology.

BD331.K3 1967
Kattsoff, Louis Osgood, 1908-
Logic and the nature of reality.　The Hague,
Martinus Nijhoff, 1967. 247 p.
74-570252　111
Reality. Logic.

BD331.L45813 1998
Levinas, Emmanuel.
Of God who comes to mind/ Emmanuel Levinas;
translated by Bettina Bergo. Stanford, Calif.:
Stanford University Press, 1998. xv, 211 p.
97-049446　212　0804730938
God. Ontology.

BD331.M87 1990
Munitz, Milton Karl, 1913-
The question of reality/ Milton K. Munitz.
Princeton, N.J.: Princeton University Press,
c1990. x, 212 p.
89-010210　111　0691073627
Reality. Creation. Truth.

BD331.P7 1970
Pratt, James Bissett,
Matter and spirit; a study of mind and body in
their relation to the　spiritual life.　Westport,
Conn., Greenwood Press [1970, c1922] ix,
232 p.
71-106723　128　0837135486
Mind and body. Dualism.

BD331.S3
Santayana, George, 1863-1952.
The realm of essence. Book first of Realms, of
being, by George Santayana. London, Constable
and company, ltd., 1928. xxiii, 183 p.
28-012886
Ontology.

BD331.S33
Santayana, George, 1863-1952.
The realm of matter. Book second of Realms of
being, by George Santayana. London, Constable,
1930. xv, 209 p.
30-027103　111
Matter.

BD331.S82
Streatfeild, D., 1909-
Persephone, a study of two worlds.　London,
Routledge and Paul [1959] v, 367 p.
61-001495
Consciousness. Dreams. Psychoanalysis.

BD331.T68
Toms, Eric.
Being, negation, and logic. Oxford, Blackwell,
1962. 124 p.
63-001687
Negation (Logic) Ontology.

BD331.W866 1992
Woolley, Benjamin.
Virtual worlds: a journey in hype and
hyperreality/ Benjamin Woolley. Oxford, UK;
Blackwell, 1992. viii, 274 p.
92-007617　306.4/6　0631182144
*Reality. Virtual reality. Knowledge, Sociology
of.*

BD348 Ontology — Perspective

BD348.C35 1997
Calhoun, Laurie.
Philosophy unmasked: a skeptic's critique/
Laurie Calhoun. Lawrence, Kan.: University
Press of Kansas, c1997. xi, 212 p.
97-001484　101　0700608338
*Philosophy.　Perspective　(Philosophy)
Absolute, The.*

BD348.H37 2001
Harries, Karsten.
Infinity and perspective/ Karsten Harries.
Cambridge, Mass.: MIT Press, c2001. xii, 380 p.
00-048034　190　0262082926
*Nicholas, -- of Cusa, Cardinal, -- 1401-1464.
Alberti, Leon Battista, -- 1404-1472.
Perspective (Philosophy) -- History. Infinite --
History.*

BD372 Ontology — Becoming. Process

BD372.E55 1991
Emmet, Dorothy Mary, 1904-
The passage of nature/ Dorothy Emmet.
Philadelphia: Temple University Press, c1992.
xi, 137 p.
91-017064　146/.7　0877228965
Process philosophy. Metaphysics.

BD372.M67 1990
Morris, Randall C., 1955-
Process philosophy and political ideology: the
social and political thought of Alfred North
Whitehead and Charles Hartshorne/ Randall C.
Morris. Albany: State University of New York
Press, c1991. xii, 289 p.
89-049229　320/.01　0791404153
*Whitehead, Alfred North, -- 1861-1947 --
Political and social views. Hartshorne, Charles,
-- 1897- -- Political and social views. Process
philosophy. Political science.*

BD372.R47 1996
Rescher, Nicholas.
Process metaphysics: an introduction to process
philosophy/ Nicholas Rescher. Albany: State
University of New York Press, c1996. vii, 213 p.
95-008784　146/.7　0791428176
Process philosophy.

BD372.R475 2000
Rescher, Nicholas.
Process philosophy: a survey of basic issues/
Nicholas Rescher. [Pittsburgh]: University of
Pittsburgh Press, c2000. 144 p.
00-011647　146/.7　0822941422
Process philosophy.

BD373 Ontology — Change

BD373.B96 2001
Bynum, Caroline Walker.
Metamorphosis and identity/ Caroline Walker
Bynum. New York: Zone Books; 280 p.
00-047316　126 21　1890951226
*Change.　Metamorphosis.　Identity
(Philosophical concept)*

BD373.P58 1990
Pivcevic, Edo.
Change and selves/ Edo Pivcevic. Oxford
[England]: Clarendon Press; 1990. vii, 151 p.
89-039350　116　0198242492
Change. Self (Philosophy)

BD390 Ontology — Division

BD390.H57 1993
Hirsch, Eli, 1938-
Dividing reality/ Eli Hirsch. New York: Oxford
University Press, 1993. xv, 247 p.
92-036251　111　0195057546
Division (Philosophy)

BD394 Ontology — Unity and plurality

BD394.I52 1994
Individuation and identity in early modern
philosophy: Descartes to Kant/ Kenneth F.
Barber and Jorge J.E. Gracia, editors. Albany:
State University of New York Press, c1994. vi,
275 p.
93-038028　111/.82　0791419673
*Individuation　(Philosophy)　--　History.
Identity. Philosophy, Modern.*

BD396 Ontology — Whole and parts (Philosophy). "Ganzheit"

BD396.B32 1995
Bacon, John, 1940-
Universals and property instances: the alphabet
of being/ John Bacon. Oxford; Blackwell, 1995.
xiv, 159 p.
94-028779　111　0631196293
*Whole and parts (Philosophy) Individuation
(Philosophy) Metaphysics.*

BD399 Ontology — Holes

BD399.C37 1994
Casati, Roberto, 1961-
Holes and other superficialities/ Roberto Casati, Achille C. Varzi. Cambridge, Mass.: MIT Press, c1994. x, 253 p.
93-027886   117   0262032112
Holes.

BD411 Ontology — Finite and infinite

BD411.I53
Infinity and continuity in ancient and medieval thought/ edited by Norman Kretzmann. Ithaca, N.Y.: Cornell University Press, 1982. 367 p.
81-015209   111/.6   080141444X
Infinite -- History. Continuity -- History. Philosophy, Medieval.

BD411.M59 1990
Moore, A. W., 1956-
The infinite/ A.W. Moore. London; Routledge, 1990. xii, 268 p.
89-010458   111/.6   0415033071
Infinite.

BD418 Ontology — Mind — Early works through 1800

BD418.W45 1991
White, Stephen L., 1948-
The unity of the self/ Stephen L. White. Cambridge, Mass.: MIT Press, c1991. xii, 424 p.
90-029869   126   026223162X
Philosophy of mind. Self (Philosophy) Identity (Psychology)

BD418.3 Ontology — Mind — 1801-

BD418.3.G88 2000
Guttenplan, Samuel D.
Mind's landscape: an introduction to the philosophy of mind/ Samuel Guttenplan. Malden, Mass.: Blackwell Publishers, 2000. viii, 358 p.
00-022955   128/.2   063120217X
Philosophy of mind.

BD418.3.B35 1995
Baker, Lynne Rudder, 1944-
Explaining attitudes: a practical approach to the mind/ Lynne Rudder Baker. Cambridge; Cambridge University Press, 1995. xi, 246 p.
94-016693   128/.2   0521420539
Philosophy of mind. Attitude (Psychology)

BD418.3.B57 2003
The Blackwell guide to philosophy of mind/ edited by Stephen P. Stich and Ted A. Warfield. Malden, MA: Blackwell Pub., 2003.
2002-071221   128/.2 21   0631217754
Philosophy of mind.

BD418.3.B64 1994
Thought as a system/ David Bohm. London; Routledge, 1994. xvii, 250 p.
93-046728   128/.2 20   0415110300
Philosophy of mind. Knowledge, Theory of.

BD418.3.B72 1996
Braddon-Mitchell, David.
The philosophy of mind and cognition/ David Braddon-Mitchell and Frank Jackson. Oxford, OX, UK; Blackwell Publishers, xiii, 293 p.
95-053332   128/.2 20   0631191682
Philosophy of mind.

BD418.3.C43 1996
Chalmers, David John, 1966-
The conscious mind: in search of a fundamental theory/ David J. Chalmers. New York: Oxford University Press, 1996. xvii, 414 p.
95-036036   128/.2   0195105532
Philosophy of mind. Consciousness. Mind and body.

BD418.3.C435 2002
Chalmers, David John,
Philosophy of mind: classical and contemporary readings/ David J. Chalmers. New York: Oxford University Press, 2002. xii, 675 p.
2002-072403   128/.2 21   019514581X
Philosophy of mind.

BD418.3.C473 1998
Churchland, Paul M., 1942-
On the contrary: critical essays, 1987-1997/ Paul M. Churchland and Patricia S. Churchland. Cambridge, Mass.: MIT Press, c1998. xii, 349 p.
97-040386   128/.2   0262032546
Philosophy of mind. Science -- Philosophy.

BD418.3.C53 1997
Clark, Andy, 1957-
Being there: putting brain, body, and world together again/ Andy Clark. Cambridge, Mass.: MIT Press, c1997. xix, 269 p.
96-011817   153   0262032406
Philosophy of mind. Mind and body. Cognitive science.

BD418.3.D46 1998
Dennett, Daniel Clement.
Brainchildren: essays on designing minds/ Daniel C. Dennett. Cambridge, Mass.: MIT Press, c1998. ix, 418 p.
97-009440   128/.2   0262041669
Philosophy of mind. Artificial intelligence. Animal intelligence.

BD418.3.D74 1995
Dretske, Fred I.
Naturalizing the mind/ Fred Dretske. Cambridge, Mass.: MIT Press, c1995. xvi, 208 p.
95-002229   128/.2   0262041499
Philosophy of mind.

BD418.3.F627 2000
Fodor, Jerry A.
The mind doesn't work that way: the scope and limits of computational psychology/ Jerry Fodor. Cambridge, Mass.: MIT Press, c2000. 126 p.
99-089687   153   0262062127
Cognitive science. Philosophy of mind. Nativism (Psychology)

BD418.3.F63 1990
Fodor, Jerry A.
A theory of content and other essays/ Jerry A. Fodor. Cambridge, Mass.: MIT Press, c1990. xii, 270 p.
89-028523   128/.2   0262061309
Philosophy of mind. Content (Psychology) Mental representation.

BD418.3.F67 1991
Foster, John, 1941 May 5-
The immaterial self: a defence of the Cartesian dualist conception of the mind/ John Foster. London; Routledge, c1991. ix, 298 p.
90-026357   128/.2   0415029899
Descartes, Rene, -- 1596-1650 -- Contributions in dualist doctrine of mindDualism. Mind and body. Philosophy of mind.

BD418.3.G75 1998
Griffin, David Ray, 1939-
Unsnarling the world-knot: consciousness, freedom, and the mind-body problem/ David Ray Griffin. Berkeley, Calif.: University of California Press, c1998. xv, 266 p.
97-008390   128/.2   0520209443
Philosophy of mind. Consciousness. Mind and body.

BD418.3.H37 1996
Hardcastle, Valerie Gray.
How to build a theory in cognitive science/ Valerie Gray Hardcastle. Albany: State University of New York Press, c1996. x, 249 p.
95-046981   128/.2   0791428850
Philosophy of mind. Philosophy and cognitive science. Functionalism (Psychology)

BD418.3.H375 1999
Hasker, William, 1935-
The emergent self/ William Hasker. Ithaca, N.Y.: Cornell University Press, 1999. xi, 240 p.
99-026814   128/.2   0801436524
Philosophy of mind. Mind and body.

BD418.3.H38 1998
Haugeland, John, 1945-
Having thought: essays in the metaphysics of mind/ John Haugeland. Cambridge, Mass.: Harvard University Press, 1998. 390 p.
97-044542   128/.2   0674382331
Philosophy of mind.

BD418.3.K53 1998
Kim, Jaegwon.
Mind in a physical world: an essay on the mind-body problem and mental causation/ Jaegwon Kim. Cambridge, Mass.: MIT Press, c1998. viii, 146 p.
98-024346   128/.2   0262112345
Philosophy of mind. Mind and body. Causation.

BD418.3.K54 1996
Kim, Jaegwon.
Philosophy of mind/ Jaegwon Kim. Boulder, Col.: Westview Press, 1996. xii, 258 p.
96-166594   128/.2   0813307759
Philosophy of mind.

BD418.3.L35 1999
Lakoff, George.
Philosophy in the flesh: the embodied mind and its challenge to Western thought/ George Lakoff and Mark Johnson. New York: Basic Books, c1999. xiv, 624 p.
98-037113   128   0465056733
Philosophy of mind. Cognitive science.

BD418.3.L44 1990
Lehrer, Keith.
Metamind/ Keith Lehrer. Oxford [England]: Clarendon Press; viii, 313 p.
89-037494   128/.2 20   0198248504
Philosophy of mind. Metacognition.

BD418.3.L69 2000
Lowe, E. J.
An introduction to the philosophy of mind/ E.J. Lowe. Cambridge, U.K.; Cambridge University Press, 2000. xiii, 318 p.
99-021498   128/.2   0521652855
Philosophy of mind.

BD418.3.M36 1995
McClamrock, Ronald Albert.
Existential cognition: computational minds in the world/ Ron McClamrock. Chicago: University of Chicago Press, 1995. ix, 205 p.
93-048967   128/.2   0226556417
Philosophy of mind. Philosophy and cognitive science. Knowledge, Theory of.

BD418.3.M37 1994
McDowell, John Henry.
Mind and world/ John McDowell. Cambridge, Mass.: Harvard University Press, 1994. x, 191 p.
93-044418   121/.4   0674576098
Philosophy of mind. Knowledge, Theory of. Concepts.

BD418.3.M45 1993
Mental causation/ edited by John Heil and Alfred Mele. Oxford: Clarendon Press; 1993. x, 342 p.
92-022764   128/.2   0198239297
Philosophy of mind. Mind and body. Causation.

BD418.3.N45 1996
Nelkin, Norton.
Consciousness and the origins of thought/ Norton Nelkin. Cambridge [England]; Cambridge University Press, 1996. xv, 341 p.
95-046968   128/.2   0521564093
Philosophy of mind. Consciousness.

BD418.3.O34 1997
O'Hear, Anthony.
Beyond evolution: human nature and the limits of evolutionary explanation/ Anthony O'Hear. Oxford: Clarendon Press; 1997. viii, 220 p.
97-229482   128   0198242549
Philosophy of mind. Philosophical anthropology. Evolution.

BD418.3.O42 1995
Olafson, Frederick A.
What is a human being?: a Heideggerian view/ Frederick A. Olafson. Cambridge; Cambridge University Press, 1995. vii, 262 p.
94-034854   128   0521473950
Heidegger, Martin, -- 1889-1976.Philosophy of mind. Humanism -- 20th century.

BD418.3.P65 1998
Pols, Edward.
Mind regained/ Edward Pols. Ithaca, N.Y.: Cornell University Press, c1998. x, 151 p.
98-009482   128/.2   0801435315
Philosophy of mind. Causation.

BD418.3.P75 1991
Priest, Stephen.
Theories of the mind/ Stephen Priest. Boston: Houghton Mifflin, c1991. xii, 233 p.
91-048100   128/.2   0395623383
Philosophy of mind.

BD418.3.R33 1994
Rachlin, Howard, 1935-
Behavior and mind: the roots of modern psychology/ Howard Rachlin. New York: Oxford University Press, 1994. viii, 163 p.
92-047398   128/.2   0195079795
Philosophy of mind. Psychology and philosophy. Behaviorism.

BD418.3.R78 1999
Rowlands, Mark.
The body in mind: understanding cognitive processes/ Mark Rowlands. Cambridge, U.K.; Cambridge University Press, 1999. x, 270 p.
98-045620   128/.2   052165274X
Philosophy of mind. Mind and body. Cognition.

BD418.3.S34 1997
Scheffler, Israel.
Symbolic worlds: art, science, language, ritual/ Israel Scheffler. Cambridge [England]; Cambridge University Press, 1997. viii, 214 p.
96-021483   121/.68 20   0521564255
Philosophy of mind. Symbolism. Science -- Philosophy. Language and languages -- Philosophy.

BD418.3.S42 1998
Searle, John R.
Mind, language, and society: philosophy in the real world/ John R. Searle. New York, NY: Basic Books, c1998. x, 175 p.
99-187320   128/.2   0465045197
Philosophy of mind.. Sociology -- Philosophy. Language and languages -- Philosophy.

BD418.3.S43 1992
Searle, John R.
The rediscovery of the mind/ John R. Searle. Cambridge, Mass.: MIT Press, c1992. xv, 270 p.
92-012747   128/.2 20   026269154X
Philosophy of mind. Consciousness.

BD418.3.S5 1990
Sharpe, R. A.
Making the human mind/ R.A. Sharpe. London; Routledge, 1990. vii, 134 p.
90-032963   128/.2   0415047676
Philosophy of mind.

BD418.3.S74 1997
Steward, Helen.
The ontology of mind: events, processes, and states/ Helen Steward. Oxford: Clarendon Press; 1997. viii, 276 p.
96-052313   128.2   0198240988
Philosophy of mind.

BD418.3.S75 1996
Stich, Stephen P.
Deconstructing the mind/ Stephen P. Stich. New York: Oxford University Press, 1996. viii, 222 p.
95-042096   128/.2   0195100816
Philosophy of mind. Mental representation. Cognitive science.

BD418.3.T35 1991
Tallis, Raymond.
The explicit animal: a defence of human consciousness/ Raymond Tallis. Basingstoke [England]: Macmillan Academic and Professional, 1991. ix, 297 p.
92-138510   128/.2   0333546148
Philosophy of mind. Consciousness.

BD418.3.T87 1991
Turbayne, Colin Murray.
Metaphors for the mind: the creative mind and its origins/ Colin Murray Turbayne. Columbia, S.C.: University of South Carolina Press, c1991. xv, 133 p.
90-038182   128/.2   0872496996
Philosophy of mind -- History. Metaphor -- History.

BD418.3.W54 1995
Wilson, Robert A.
Cartesian psychology and physical minds: individualism and the sciences of the mind/ Robert A. Wilson. Cambridge; Cambridge University Press, 1995. xii, 273 p.
94-036307   128/.2   0521474027
Philosophy of mind. Individualism. Human behavior.

BD418.3.W65 1993
Wollheim, Richard, 1923-
The mind and its depths/ Richard Wollheim. Cambridge, Mass.: Harvard University Press, 1993. x, 214 p.
92-012738   128/.2   067457611X
Philosophy of mind. Arts -- Psychological aspects. Psychoanalysis.

BD418.8 Ontology — Mind — Artificial life

BD418.8.B63 1996
The philosophy of artificial life/ edited by Margaret A. Boden. Oxford; Oxford University Press, 1996. viii, 405 p.
95-043389   113/.8   0198751540
Artificial life.

BD421 Ontology — The soul. Spirit. Immortality, etc. — General works

BD421.F54 2000
Flew, Antony, 1923-
Merely mortal?: can you survive your own death?/ Antony Flew. Amherst, N.Y.: Prometheus Books, 2000. xviii, 200 p.
00-045842   129   1573928410
Immortality   (Philosophy)   Identity (Psychology) Parapsychology.

BD421.F76 1999
From soul to self/ edited by M. James C. Crabbe. London; Routledge, 1999. xi, 158 p.
98-041840   128/.1 21   0415171180
Soul -- History of doctrines. Self (Philosophy) -- History.

BD421.M58
Montagu, Ashley, 1905-
Immortality.   New York, Grove Press [c1955] 72 p.
55-005109   218
Immortality.

BD431 Ontology — Life — 1801-

BD431.B242 1969
Baker, Herschel Clay, 1914-
The wars of truth; studies in the decay of Christian humanism in the earlier seventeenth century.   Gloucester, Mass., P. Smith, 1969 [c1952] xi, 390 p.
73-010679   128
Man (Theology) Theology, Doctrinal -- History -- 17th century.

BD431.B77
Brinton, Crane, 1898-1968.
The fate of man, edited with introductions and postscript, by Crane Brinton. New York, G. Braziller, 1961. 532 p.
61-008477   128.3
Man.

BD431.E94 2002
The every day life reader/ edited by Ben Highmore. London; Routledge, 2002.
2001-044194   306 21   041523025X
Life. Civilization, Modern -- 20th century. Culture -- Philosophy.

BD431.F85 1988
Fulghum, Robert.
All I really need to know I learned in kindergarten: uncommon thoughts on common things/ Robert Fulghum. 1st ed. New York: Villard Books, 1988. ix, 196 p.
88-040144   128 19
Life.

BD431.J48
Jonas, Hans, 1903-
The phenomenon of life: toward a philosophical biology; [essays.   New York, Harper & Row [1966] x, 303 p.
66-015037   110
Life.

BD431.L36513 1991
Lefebvre, Henri, 1905-
Critique of everyday life/ Henri Lefebvre; translated by John Moore; with a preface by Michel Trebitsch. London; Verso, [1991-   ] v. 1
91-020747   194   0860913406
Life. Philosophy, Marxist.

BD431.L42 1940
Lin, Yutang, 1895-
The importance of living. New York, J. Day Co. [1940] xvi, 459 p.
40-009459

BD431.M69
Montagu, Ashley, 1905-
The biosocial nature of man.   New York, Grove Press [1956] 123 p.
56-008055   136
Social psychology. Man.

BD431.M897
Mumford, Lewis, 1895-
The conduct of life.   New York, Harcourt, Brace [1951] ix, 342 p.
51-012387   128
Life. Conduct of life.

BD431.N32
Nagel, Thomas,
Mortal questions/ Thomas Nagel. Cambridge [Eng.]; Cambridge University Press, 1979. xiii, 213 p.
78-058797   170   0521223601
Life -- Addresses, essays, lectures. Ethics -- Addresses, essays, lectures.

BD431.P5
Phenix, Philip Henry, 1915-
Realms of meaning; a philosophy of the curriculum for general education. New York, McGraw-Hill [1964] xiv, 391 p.
63-023114   375.0001
Semantics   (Philosophy)   Education, Humanistic.

BD431.P533 2001
Philosophy and everyday life/ edited by Laura Duhan Kaplan. New York: Seven Bridges Press, [2001] ix, 255 p.
00-012509   100 21   1889119679
Life.

BD431.S2753
Scheler, Max, 1874-1928.
Man's place in nature. Translated, and with an introd. by Hans Meyerhoff. Boston, Beacon Press [1961] xxxv, 105 p.
61-006417   128
Mind and body. Man. Soul.

BD431.S578 1992
Singer, Irving.
Meaning in life: the creation of value/ Irving Singer. New York: Free Press, c1992. xiii, 158 p.
91-029401   128   002928905X
Life. Meaning (Philosophy)

BD431.T19
Temkin, Owsei, 1902-
Respect for life in medicine, philosophy, and the law/ Owsei Temkin, William K. Frankena, Sanford H. Kadish. Baltimore: Johns Hopkins University Press, c1977. ix, 107 p.
76-047366   179/.7   0801819423
Life. Medical ethics.

BD431.U5
Ulich, Robert, 1890-
The human career; a philosophy of self-transcendence.   New York, Harper [c1955] xii, 255 p.
54-012159   128
Life.

BD435 Ontology — Life — General special

BD435.A23 1988
Abelson, Raziel.
Lawless mind/ Raziel Abelson. Philadelphia: Temple University Press, 1988. xix, 209 p.
88-012358   146/.6   0877225796
Mechanism (Philosophy) Mind and body. Human beings.

BD435.E38
Eiseley, Loren C.,
Man, time, and prophecy [by] Loren Eiseley. [1st ed.] New York, Harcourt, Brace & World [1966] 39 p.
67-001433   128
Human beings.

BD435.G46 1998
Gillan, Garth, 1939-
Rising from the ruins: reason, being, and the good after Auschwitz/ Garth Jackson Gillan. Albany: State University of New York Press, c1998. xi, 140 p.
97-035889   128   0791437337
Life. Reason. Ontology.

BD435.K37 2000
Kekes, John.
Pluralism in philosophy: changing the subject/ John Kekes. Ithaca, N.Y.: Cornell University Press, 2000. ix, 225 p.
00-009351　147/.4　0801438055
Life. Pluralism.

BD435.L52 1955a
Lindbergh, Anne Morrow, 1906-
Gift from the sea. [New York] Pantheon [1955] 127 p.
57-004637
Life.

BD436 Ontology — Love

BD436.B47 1987
Bergmann, Martin S., 1913-
The anatomy of loving: the story of man's quest to know what love is/ Martin S. Bergmann. New York: Columbia University Press, 1987. xii, 302 p.
86-031743　155.3　0231064861
Love -- History.

BD436.B76 1987
Brown, Robert, 1920-
Analyzing love/ Robert Brown. Cambridge; Cambridge University Press, 1987. viii, 133 p.
87-009342　128/.3　0521340381
Love.

BD436.D3713 1997
Aragona, Tullia d', ca. 1510-1556
Dialogue on the infinity of love/ by Tullia d'Aragona; edited and translated by Rinaldina Russell and Bruce Merry; introduction and notes by Rinaldina Russell. Chicago: University of Chicago Press, 1997. 114 p.
96-028841　128/.4　0226136388
Love -- Early works to 1800.

BD436.D54 1998
Dilman, Ilham.
Love: its forms, dimensions, and paradoxes/ Ilham Dilman. New York, N.Y.: St. Martin's Press, 1998. xxi, 239 p.
98-023463　128/.46　0312216432
Love.

BD436.G55 1991
Gilbert, Paul, 1942-
Human relationships: a philosophical introduction/ Paul Gilbert. Oxford UK; B. Blackwell, 1991. vi, 164 p.
91-012475　177/.6　0631171576
Love. Friendship. Social sciences -- Philosophy.

BD436.J64 2001
Johnson, Rolf M.
Three faces of love/ Rolf M. Johnson. DeKalb, Ill.: Northern Illinois University Press, c2001. x, 208 p.
00-037996　128/.46　0875802702
Love.

BD436.L68 1997
Love analyzed/ edited by Roger E. Lamb. Boulder, Colo.: Westview Press, 1997. xvii, 267 p.
96-038902　128/.4 20　0813332230
Love.

BD436.M8
Murry, John Middleton, 1889-1957.
Love, freedom, and society. London, J. Cape [1957] 253 p.
57-003641　128
Lawrence, D. H. -- (David Herbert), -- 1885-1930. Schweitzer, Albert, -- 1875-1965. Love.

BD436.S44 1995
Sexual love and western morality: a philosophical anthology/ edited, and with introductions by D.P. Verene. 2nd ed. Boston: Jones and Bartlett, c1995. xxiii, 312 p.
94-040478　176 20　086720964X
Love. Sexual ethics.

BD436.S5 1984
Singer, Irving.
The nature of love/ Irving Singer. Chicago: University of Chicago Press, 1984-1987. 3 v.
84-002554　128　0226760944
Love.

BD436.S54 1989
Sircello, Guy.
Love and beauty/ by Guy Sircello. Princeton, N.J.: Princeton University Press, c1989. vi, 253 p.
88-014005　128　069107335X
Love. Aesthetics.

BD436.S59 1990
Soble, Alan.
The structure of love/ Alan Soble. New Haven: Yale University Press, c1990. xiv, 374 p.
89-016571　128/.4　0300045662
Love.

BD436.S6 1988
Solomon, Robert C.
About love: reinventing romance for our times/ Robert C. Solomon. New York: Simon and Schuster, c1988. 349 p.
87-028863　128/.4　0671623680
Love.

BD436.W34 1997
Wagoner, Bob, 1930-
The meanings of love: an introduction to philosophy of love/ Robert E. Wagoner. Westport, Conn.: Praeger, 1997. viii, 149 p.
96-037115　128/.46　0275958396
Love. Love -- History.

BD438 Ontology — Power

BD438.F76 1992
Froman, Lewis A. 1935-
Language and power/ Creel Froman. Atlantic Highlands, N.J.: Humanities Press, 1992-1996. v. 1-4
91-023768　149/.94　0391037331
Power (Philosophy) Metaphysics. Language and languages -- Political aspects.

BD438.M63 1987
Morriss, Peter.
Power: a philosophical analysis/ Peter Morriss. New York: St. Martin's Press, 1987. 266 p.
87-009837　303.3/01　0312009437
Power (Philosophy)

BD438.S25 1966
Sampson, Ronald Victor.
The psychology of power [by] Ronald V. Sampson. New York, Pantheon Books [1966, c1965] 247 p.
66-010771　158.2
Control (Psychology)

BD438.5 Ontology — Self

BD438.5.C85 1997
Culture and self: philosophical and religious perspectives, East and West/ edited by Douglas Allen, with the assistance of Ashok Malhotra. Boulder, Colo.: Westview Press, 1997. xv, 184 p.
97-008093　126/.09 21　0813326745
Self (Philosophy) -- Comparative studies. Religion and culture. East and West.

BD438.5.S37 1997
Schrag, Calvin O.
The self after postmodernity/ Calvin O. Schrag. New Haven, CT: Yale University Press, c1997. xiv, 155 p.
96-038600　126　0300068425
Self (Philosophy) Postmodernism.

BD439 Ontology — Self-deception

BD439.B37 1997
Barnes, Annette.
Seeing through self-deception/ Annette Barnes. Cambridge; Cambridge University Press, 1997. x, 182 p.
97-020457　128/.3　0521620147
Self-deception.

BD439.P47 1988
Perspectives on self-deception/ edited by Brian P. McLaughlin and Amelie Oksenberg Rorty. Berkeley: University of California Press, c1988. vi, 558 p.
87-027471　128/.3　0520052080
Self-deception.

BD443 Ontology — Birth

BD443.A66 1991
Applewhite, E. J.
Paradise mislaid: birth, death & the human predicament of being biological/ E.J. Applewhite. New York: St. Martin's Press, 1991. xii, 480 p.
90-027309 128 0312059442
Birth (Philosophy) Life. Death.

BD444 Ontology — Death — General works

BD444.A93 1995
Awareness of mortality/ edited by Jeffrey Kauffman. Amityville, N.Y.: Baywood Pub. Co., c1995. 228 p.
95-007706 128/.5 20 0895031736
Death.

BD444.D42 1998
Dollimore, Jonathan.
Death, desire, and loss in Western culture/ Jonathan Dollimore. New York: Routledge, 1998. xxxii, 384 p.
98-004041 128/.5 0415921740
Death. Lust. Loss (Psychology)

BD444.D46513 1993
Derrida, Jacques.
Aporias: dying--awaiting (one another at) the "limits of truth" (mourir--s'attendre aux "limites de la verite")/ Jacques Derrida; translated by Thomas Dutoit. Stanford, Calif.: Stanford University Press, 1993. x, 87 p.
93-029865 128/.5 0804722331
Death. Contradiction. Belief and doubt.

BD444.F415
Feifel, Herman,
The meaning of death. New York, Blakiston Division, McGraw-Hill, 1959. 351 p.
59-015049 128.5
Terminal care. Death.

BD444.F44 1992
Feldman, Fred, 1941-
Confrontations with the reaper: a philosophical study of the nature and value of death/ Fred Feldman. New York: Oxford University Press, 1992. xiv, 249 p.
91-003640 128/.5 0195071026
Death. Life. Abortion.

BD444.K34 1989
Kapleau, Philip,
The wheel of life and death: a practical and spiritual guide/ Philip Kapleau. 1st ed. New York: Doubleday, 1989. xxv, 370 p.
88-025751 291.2/3 19
Death. Karma. Reincarnation.

BD444.M429 1993
The Metaphysics of death/ edited, with an introduction, by John Martin Fischer. Stanford, Calif.: Stanford University Press, 1993. xiv, 423 p.
92-036933 128/.5 20 0804721041
Death.

BD444.M65 1988
Momeyer, Richard W., 1942-
Confronting death/ Richard W. Momeyer. Bloomington: Indiana University Press, c1988. xviii, 184 p.
87-045439 179/.7 0253314038
Death. Right to die.

BD444.T47 2001
Terkel, Studs,
Will the circle be unbroken?: reflections on death, rebirth, and hunger for a faith/ Studs Terkel. New York: New Press: 2001. xxiv, 407 p.
2001-030781 128/.5 21 1565846923
Death. Death -- Religious aspects.

BD445 Ontology — Death — Suicide

BD445.C36 1988
Campbell, Robert.
Ending lives/ Robert Campbell, Diane Collinson. Oxford, UK; B. Blackwell, 1988. xviii, 203 p.
87-029366 179/.7 0631153292
Suicide. Euthanasia.

BD445.S93
Suicide, the philosophical issues/ edited by M. Pabst Battin and David J. Mayo. New York: St. Martin's Press, c1980. viii, 292 p.
79-027372 179/.7 0312775318
Suicide -- Addresses, essays, lectures.

BD450 Ontology — Philosophical anthropology

BD450.A4525 1986
Ainsworth-Land, George T.,
Grow or die: the unifying principle of transformation/ George T. Ainsworth-Land. Reissued ed., 1st ed. New York: Wiley, c1986. xviii, 267 p.
86-005522 116 19 0471829714
Human beings. Evolution. Growth.

BD450.A4725 1997
Allen, Prudence.
The concept of woman: the Aristotelian revolution, 750 BC-AD 1250/ Prudence Allen. Grand Rapids, Mich.: W.B. Eerdmans Pub., 1997. xxiv, 583 p.
96-009102 305.4/01 20 0802842704
Femininity (Philosophy) -- History. Women -- History. Sex -- History.

BD450.A4727 1992
Allen, R. T., 1941-
The education of autonomous man/ R.T. Allen. Aldershot, Hants, England; Avebury, c1992. vi, 82 p.
92-002446 128 185628381X
Human beings. Autonomy (Philosophy)

BD450.A69 2000
Archer, Margaret Scotford.
Being human: the problem of agency/ Margaret S. Archer. Cambridge, U.K.; Cambridge University Press, 2000. x, 323 p.
00-031287 128 21 0521795648
Agent (Philosophy) Philosophical anthropology.

BD450.B39
Becker, Ernest.
The birth and death of meaning; a perspective in psychiatry and anthropology. New York, Free Press [1962] 210 p.
62-015359 128/.3
Philosophical anthropology. Human behavior. Psychiatry.

BD450.B436 1998
Bermudez, Jose Luis.
The paradox of self-consciousness/ Jose Luis Bermudez. Cambridge, Mass.: MIT Press, c1998. xiv, 338 p.
97-040757 0262024411
Self (Philosophy) Self-consciousness. Thought and thinking.

BD450.B438 1995
Berofsky, Bernard.
Liberation from self: a theory of personal autonomy/ Bernard Berofsky. Cambridge; Cambridge University Press, 1995. ix, 270 p.
95-011441 128 0521480450
Self (Philosophy) Free will and determinism.

BD450.B526 1995
Bloom, Howard K., 1943-
The Lucifer principle: a scientific expedition into the forces of history/ Howard Bloom. New York: Atlantic Monthly Press, c1995. xii, 466 p.
94-011464 128 0871135329
Human beings. Evolution. History -- Philosophy.

BD450.B539 1994
Bock, Kenneth Elliott, 1916-
Human nature mythology/ Kenneth Bock. Urbana: University of Illinois Press, c1994. 138 p.
93-024318 128 0252020723
Philosophical anthropology -- History. Free will and determinism -- History.

BD450.B64
Bourke, Vernon Joseph, 1907-
Will in Western thought; an historico-critical survey. New York, Sheed and Ward [1964] vi, 247 p.
64-013569 128
Will.

BD450.B653 2002
Bronowski, Jacob,
The identity of man/ Jacob Bronowski. Amherst, N.Y.: Prometheus Books, 2002. xi, 107 p.
2002-031842   128 21   1591020255
Philosophical anthropology. Science -- Philosophy. Self (Philosophy)

BD450.C23 1988
Callinicos, Alex.
Making history: agency, structure, and change in social theory/ Alex Callinicos. Ithaca, N.Y.: Cornell University Press, 1988. viii, 275 p.
87-047766   128/.4   0801421217
Marx, Karl, -- 1818-1883.Agent (Philosophy) Act (Philosophy) Structuralism.

BD450.C244 1984
Campbell, Keith,
Body and mind/ by Keith Campbell. 2nd ed. Notre Dame, Ind.: University of Notre Dame Press, 1984. vi, 168 p.
84-013082   128/.2 19   0268006733
Mind and body.

BD450.C4715 1988
Champlin, T. S.
Reflexive paradoxes/ T.S. Champlin. London; Routledge, 1988. viii, 235 p.
89-163318   126   0415000831
Self (Philosophy) Paradox. Self-knowledge, Theory of.

BD450.C5413 1998
Cioran, E. M.
A short history of decay/ E.M. Cioran; translated from the French by Richard Howard. 1st Arcade paperback ed. New York: Arcade Pub.: 181 p.
98-021994   128 21   1559704640
Human beings. Life. Philosophy.

BD450.C626 1992
Constructions of the self/ edited by George Levine. New Brunswick, N.J.: Rutgers University Press, c1992. viii, 300 p.
91-027274   126   0813517729
Self (Philosophy) Self.

BD450.D65 1989
Doran, Kevin.
What is a person: the concept and the implications for ethics/ Kevin Doran. Lewiston, NY, USA: E. Mellen Press, c1989. ix, 179 p.
89-033546   126   0889461406
Philosophical anthropology. Man (Christian theology) Agent (Philosophy)

BD450.D87 2001
Dupré, John.
Human nature and the limits of science/ John Dupré. Oxford: Clarendon Press; x, 201 p.
2002-277430   128 21   0199248060
Human beings -- Philosophy. Science -- Philosophy. Genetic psychology. Rational choice theory.

BD450.F43 1991
Feminist ethics/ edited by Claudia Card. Lawrence, Kan.: University Press of Kansas, c1991. viii, 300 p.
91-006753   170/.82 20   0700604839
Femininity (Philosophy) -- History. Feminism -- Moral and ethical aspects. Social ethics.

BD450.F535 2002
Flanagan, Owen J.
The problem of the soul: two visions of mind and how to reconcile them/ Owen Flanagan. New York: Basic Books, 2002.
2002-023233   128 21   0465024602
Philosophical anthropology. Philosophy of mind. Naturalism.

BD450.F78 1968
Fromm, Erich,
The nature of man; readings selected, edited, and furnished with an introductory essay by Erich Fromm and Ramón Xirau. New York, Macmillan [1968] vi, 343 p.
68-008951   128/.08
Philosophical anthropology.

BD450.F7825
Fromm, Erich,
On disobedience and other essays/ by Erich Fromm. New York: Seabury Press, 1981. 135 p.
81-002260   128 19
Human beings. Civilization, Modern -- 1950- Alienation (Social psychology)

BD450.G317 1990
Gans, Eric Lawrence, 1941-
Science and faith: the anthropology of revelation/ Eric Gans. Savage, Md.: Rowman & Littlefield, c1990. viii, 129 p.
90-042472   215   0847676595
Philosophical anthropology. Language and languages -- Origin. Revelation.

BD450.G4455 1989
Gender/body/knowledge: feminist reconstructions of being and knowing/ edited by Alison M. Jaggar and Susan R. Bordo. New Brunswick, N.J.: Rutgers University Press, 1989. vi, 376 p.
88-018370   110   0813513782
Body, Human. Sex role. Knowledge, Theory of.

BD450.H855 1991
Human beings/ edited by David Cockburn. Cambridge [England]; New York: c1991. iv, 277 p.
91-017597   128 20   0521422450
Human beings. Identity. Mind-brain identity theory.

BD450.J2413 1991
Jacques, Francis.
Difference and subjectivity: dialogue and personal identity/ Francis Jacques; translated by Andrew Rothwell. New Haven: Yale University Press, c1991. xxix, 374 p.
90-046661   126 20   0300048300
Philosophical anthropology. Individual differences. Subjectivity. Interpersonal communication. Interpersonal relations.

BD450.K368 1986
Keller, Catherine,
From a broken web: separation, sexism, and self/ Catherine Keller. Boston: Beacon Press, c1986. xii, 277 p.
86-047508   126 19   0807067326
Self (Philosophy) Self. Women -- Psychology. Women in literature.

BD450.L65 1996
Lowe, E. J.
Subjects of experience/ E.J. Lowe. Cambridge [England]; Cambridge University Press, 1996. x, 209 p.
95-015748   126   0521475031
Agent (Philosophy) Self (Philosophy) Subject (Philosophy)

BD450.M345 1990
McCall, Catherine.
Concepts of person: an analysis of concepts of person, self, and human being/ Catherine McCall. Aldershot, Hants, England: Avebury; c1990. viii, 202 p.
90-046794   126   185628039X
Agent (Philosophy) Self (Philosophy) Identity.

BD450.M863 1988
Munro, Donald J.
Images of human nature: a Sung portrait/ Donald J. Munro. Princeton, N.J.: Princeton University Press, c1988. xi, 322 p.
88-012661   128/.092/4   0691073309
Chu, Hsi, -- 1130-1200.Philosophical anthropology -- History. Neo-Confucianism.

BD450.N635 1989
Noonan, Harold W.
Personal identity/ Harold W. Noonan. London; Routledge, 1989. ix, 262 p.
88-026422   126   0415033659
Identity. Mind and body. Self.

BD450.O376 1997
O'Hara, Mary L. 1923-
The logic of human personality: an onto-logical account/ Mary L. O'Hara. Atlantic Highlands, N.J.: Humanities Press, 1997. xi, 149 p.
96-039586   126   0391040227
Agent (Philosophy) -- History. Personality -- Philosophy -- History.

BD450.O46 1997
Olson, Eric T. 1963-
The human animal: personal identity without psychology/ Eric T. Olson. New York: Oxford University Press, 1997. x, 189 p.
96-007018 128 0195105060
Human beings. Identity. Philosophy of mind.

BD450.O72 1987
Organ, Troy Wilson.
Philosophy and the self: East and West/ Troy Wilson Organ. Selinsgrove [Pa.]: Susquehanna University Press; c1987. 239 p.
86-062506 126 0941664805
Self (Philosophy)

BD450.P57 1970
Platt, John Rader, 1918-
Perception and change; projections for survival. Essays by John Platt. Ann Arbor, University of Michigan Press [1970] 178 p.
70-124450 301.2/4 0472731009
Philosophical anthropology. Change. Perception.

BD450.P75 2000
Psyche and soma: physicians and metaphysicians on the mind-body problem from Antiquity to Enlightenment/ edited by John P. Wright and Paul Potter. Oxford: Clarendon Press; xii, 298 p.
99-057195 128/.2 21 0198238401
Mind and body -- History.

BD450.R4448 1997
Rewriting the self: histories from the Renaissance to the present/ edited by Roy Porter. London; Routledge, 1997. xii, 283 p.
96-015698 126/.09 20 0415142806
Self (Philosophy) -- History. Self (Philosophy) in literature -- History. Identity (Psychology) -- History.

BD450.R6538 1998
Rovane, Carol A. 1955-
The bounds of agency: an essay in revisionary metaphysics/ Carol Rovane. Princeton, N.J.: Princeton University Press, c1998. viii, 260 p.
97-017514 126 0691017166
Agent (Philosophy) Self (Philosophy) Subject (Philosophy)

BD450.S46
Shoemaker, Sydney.
Self-knowledge and self-identity. Ithaca, N.Y., Cornell University Press [1963] 264 p.
63-013910 126
Self. Self-knowledge, Theory of. Personality (Theory of knowledge)

BD450.S747 1996
Stein, Edward, 1965-
Without good reason: the rationality debate in philosophy and cognitive science/ Edward Stein. Oxford: Clarendon Press; 1996. viii, 296 p.
95-032650 128/.3 0198235747
Human beings. Reason. Philosophy of mind.

BD450.S818 2000
The study of human nature: a reader/ edited by Leslie Stevenson. 2nd ed. New York: Oxford University Press, 2000. vi, 330 p.
98-032001 128 21 0195127153
Philosophical anthropology. Man (Theology) Behaviorism (Psychology)

BD450.T266 1989
Taylor, Charles, 1931-
Sources of the self: the making of the modern identity/ Charles Taylor. Cambridge, Mass.: Harvard University Press, 1989. xii, 601 p.
88-037229 126 0674824253
Self (Philosophy) Civilization, Modern. Philosophical anthropology.

BD450.T39 1988
Technologies of the self: a seminar with Michel Foucault/ edited by Luther H. Martin, Huck Gutman, Patrick H. Hutton. Amherst: University of Massachusetts Press, 1988. 166 p.
87-010756 126 0870235923
Foucault, Michel -- Contributions in concept of the self. Self (Philosophy)

BD450.T56 1995
Tilley, Allen.
Plots of time: an inquiry into history, myth, and meaning/ Allen Tilley. Gainesville: University Press of Florida, c1995. xi, 128 p.
94-048704 128 0813013577
Philosophical anthropology. Myth.

BD450.T668 1999
Trigg, Roger.
Ideas of human nature: an historical introduction/ Roger Trigg. 2nd ed. Oxford, UK; Blackwell Publishers, 1999. viii, 216 p.
99-030907 128 21 0631214062
Philosophical anthropology -- History.

BD450.U46 1990
Unger, Peter K.
Identity, consciousness, and value/ Peter Unger. New York: Oxford University Press, 1990. xiv, 344 p.
89-028758 126 0195054016
Identity. Consciousness. Values.

BD450.W3 1972
Watts, Alan,
The book; on the taboo against knowing who you are [by] Alan Watts. New York, Vintage Books [1972, c1966] x, 146 p.
72-004715 128/.3 0394718534
Self. Self-knowledge, Theory of.

BD450.Y8213 1987
Yuasa, Yasuo.
The body: toward an Eastern mind-body theory/ Yuasa Yasuo; edited by Thomas P. Kasulis; translated by Nagatomo Shigenori, Thomas P. Kasulis. Albany: State University of New York Press, c1987. vii, 256 p.
86-022994 128/.2 0887064698
Mind and body -- Japan. Body, Human (Philosophy) -- Japan. Philosophy, Japanese.

BD495-495.5 Cosmology —
History — By period

BD495.A5
Ancient cosmologies/ edited by Carmen Blacker and Michael Loewe; with contributions by J. M. Plumley ... [et al.]. London: Allen and Unwin, 1975. 270 p.
76-363037 523.1/01 0041000382
Cosmology, Ancient -- Addresses, essays, lectures.

BD495.F87 1987
Furley, David J.
The Greek cosmologists/ David Furley. Cambridge; Cambridge University Press, [1987-] v. 1
86-026384 113/.0938 0521333288
Cosmology, Ancient.

BD495.5.S5513 1996
Simek, Rudolf, 1954-
Heaven and earth in the Middle Ages: the physical world before Columbus/ Rudolf Simek; translated by Angela Hall. Woodbridge, Suffolk; Boydell Press, 1996. xii, 164 p.
96-033259 523.1/09/02 0851156088
Cosmology, Medieval.

BD511-518 Cosmology —
General works — 1801-

BD511.B34 1988
Barrow, John D.,
The anthropic cosmological principle/ John D. Barrow and Frank J. Tipler; with a foreword by John A. Wheeler. Oxford [England]; Oxford University Press, 1988, c1986. xx, 706 p.
87-028148 113 19 0192821474
Anthropic principle. Human beings. Intellect. Life on other planets. Science -- Philosophy.

BD511.J35 1989
Jaki, Stanley L.
God and the cosmologists/ Stanley L. Jaki. Washington, D.C.: Regnery Gateway; c1989. xi, 286 p.
89-029186 113 0895267497
Cosmology. Physics -- Religious aspects -- Christianity.

BD511.K67
Koyre, Alexandre, 1892-1964.
From the closed world to the infinite universe. Baltimore, Johns Hopkins Press [1957] 313 p.
57-007080 113
Cosmology.

BD511.M18 1994
McCall, Storrs.
A model of the universe: space-time, probability, and decision/ Storrs McCall. Oxford: Clarendon press; c1994. x, 328 p.
93-005378 113 0198240538
Cosmology. Metaphysics. Space and time.

BD511.M8 1981
Munitz, Milton Karl,
Space, time, and creation: philosophical aspects of scientific cosmology/ Milton K. Munitz. 2nd ed. New York: Dover Publications, 1981. viii, 184 p.
81-068277   113 19   048624220X
Cosmology.

BD511.M85 1996
Murphy, Nancey C.
On the moral nature of the universe: theology, cosmology, and ethics/ Nancey Murphy and George F.R. Ellis. Minneapolis, Minn.: Fortress Press, 1996. xvi, 268 p.
96-038384   149/.2   0800629833
Cosmology. Ethics. Theology.

BD511.P38
Pendergast, Richard J.
Cosmos [by] Richard J. Pendergast. New York, Fordham University Press, 1973. xiii, 207 p.
72-082897   113   0823209555
Cosmology. Evolution. Good and evil.

BD511.S37 1992
Schrempp, Gregory Allen,
Magical arrows: the Maori, the Greeks, and the folklore of the universe/ Gregory Schrempp; foreword by Marshall Sahlins. Madison, Wis.: University of Wisconsin Press, c1992. xviii, 217 p.
91-033076   113/.09 20   029913234X
Zeno, of Elea. Cosmology. Cosmology, Ancient. Mythology, Maori. Maori (New Zealand people) -- Social life and customs.

BD511.S5 1961
Singh, Jagjit, 1912-
Great ideas and theories of modern cosmology. New York, Dover Publications [1961] 276 p.
62-000239   113
Cosmology.

BD511.W5 1978
Whitehead, Alfred North, 1861-1947.
Process and reality: an essay in cosmology/ by Alfred North Whitehead. New York: Free Press, 1978, c1929. xxxi, 413 p.
77-090011   113   0029345804
Cosmology -- Addresses, essays, lectures. Science -- Philosophy -- Addresses, essays, lectures. Organism (Philosophy) -- Addresses, essays, lectures.

BD511.W515.S5
Sherburne, Donald W.
A key to Whitehead's Process and reality. Edited by Donald W. Sherburne. New York, Macmillian [c1966] viii, 263 p.
66-013269   113
Whitehead, Alfred North, -- 1861-1947. -- Process and reality.

BD518.D8.W5413 1982
Wildiers, N. M., 1904-
The theologian and his universe: theology and cosmology from the Middle Ages to the present/ N. Max Wildiers [translated from the Dutch by Paul Dunphy]. New York: Seabury Press, 1982. viii, 289 p.
82-003257   261.5/5   0816405336
Cosmology -- History. Theology -- History. Religion and science -- History.

BD523 Cosmology — Addresses, essays, lectures

BD523.H67
Hoyle, Fred,
Man in the universe.   New York, Columbia University Press, 1966. 81 p.
66-017067   100.8
Cosmology. Philosophical anthropology.

BD541 Cosmology — Teleology. Causation. Final cause. Design and purpose — General works

BD541.B85 1979
Bunge, Mario Augusto.
Causality and modern science/ by Mario Bunge. New York: Dover Publications, 1979. xxx, 394 p.
78-074117   122   0486237281
Causation. Determinism (Philosophy) Science -- Philosophy.

BD541.C63 1988
Contemporary science and natural explanation: commonsense conceptions of causality/ Denis J. Hilton, editor. New York: New York University Press, 1988. xii, 244 p.
87-011142   122   081473443X
Causation. Explanation.

BD541.D46 1998
Denton, Michael.
Nature's destiny: how the laws of biology reveal purpose in the universe/ Michael J. Denton. New York: Free Press, c1998. xix, 454 p.
98-003295   124 21   0684845091
Teleology. Cosmology. Philosophical anthropology.

BD541.E95 1994
Evidence of purpose: scientists discover the creator/ edited by John Marks Templeton. New York: Continuum, 1994. 212 p.
94-013472   124   0826406491
Teleology. Causation. Religion and science.

BD541.F35 1990
Fales, Evan, 1943-
Causation and universals/ Evan Fales. London; Routledge, 1990. xxii, 362 p.
89-010902   110   0415044383
Causation. Universals (Philosophy) Realism.

BD541.G63 2003
God and design: the teleological argument and modern science/ [edited by] Neil A. Manson. London; Routledge, 2003.
2002-027548   212/.1 21   0415263441
Teleology. Religion and science.

BD541.H78 1989
Humphreys, Paul.
The chances of explanation: causal explanation in the social, medical, and physical sciences/ Paul Humphreys. Princeton, N.J.: Princeton University Press, c1989. x, 170 p.
89-010269   122   0691073538
Causation. Chance.

BD541.N33 1993
Causation in early modern philosophy: Cartesianism, occasionalism, and preestablished harmony/ edited by Steven Nadler. University Park, Pa.: Pennsylvania State University Press, c1993. x, 219 p.
91-046809   122/.09/032   0271008636
Causation -- History. Philosophy, Modern -- 17th century.

BD541.O84 1992
Owens, David
Causes and coincidences/ David Owens. Cambridge [England]; Cambridge University Press, 1992. xii, 188 p.
91-030562   122   0521416507
Causation. Coincidence.

BD541.P43 2000
Pearl, Judea.
Causality: models, reasoning, and inference/ Judea Pearl. Cambridge, U.K.; Cambridge University Press, 2000. xvi, 384 p.
99-042108   122   0521773628
Causation. Probabilities.

BD541.T66 1987
Tooley, Michael, 1941-
Causation: a realist approach/ Michael Tooley. Oxford [Oxfordshire]: Clarendon Press; 1987. xiii, 360 p.
87-028130   122   0198249624
Causation. Realism.

BD553 Cosmology — Teleology. Causation. Final cause. Design and purpose — Mechanism. Mechanical theories of the universe

BD553.F25 1986
Faber, Roger J., 1931-
Clockwork garden: on the mechanistic reduction of living things/ Roger J. Faber. Amherst: University of Massachusetts Press, 1986. xii, 268 p.
85-028408   113/.8   0870235214
Mechanism (Philosophy) Mind and body. Quantum theory.

BD555 Cosmology — Teleology. Causation. Final cause. Design and purpose — Theism

BD555.C57 2000
Conway, David, 1947-
The rediscovery of wisdom: from here to antiquity in quest of Sophia/ David Conway. New York: St. Martin's Press, 2000. x, 196 p.
00-023818   100   0312234066
Theism. Philosophy. Philosophy and religion.

BD555.P87 1990
Prevost, Robert
Probability and theistic explanation/ Robert Prevost. Oxford: Clarendon Press; 1990. 195 p.
90-033121   211/.3   0198267355
Theism. Religion -- Philosophy. God.

BD555.V76 1999
Vroman, A. J.
On God, space & time/ Akiva Jaap Vroman. New Brunswick, N.J.: Transaction Publishers, c1999. xii, 251 p.
98-040493   181/.3   1560003979
Theism. Space and time. God (Judaism) -- History of doctrines.

BD573 Cosmology — Teleology. Causation. Final cause. Design and purpose — Philosophy of religion

BD573.B4
Beck, Lewis White.
Six secular philosophers. New York, Harper [1960] 126 p.
60-011769   190
Philosophy and religion. Secularism.

BD573.H29
Hartshorne, Charles, 1897-
The logic of perfection, and other essays in neoclassical metaphysics. LaSalle, Ill., Open Court Pub. Co. [1962] xvi, 335 p.
61-011286   111
God -- Proof, Ontological. Religion -- Philosophy. Philosophy.

BD573.H4513 1999
Heyde, Ludwig,
The weight of finitude: on the philosophical question of God/ by Ludwig Heyde; translated by Alexander Harmsen and William Desmond; foreword by William Desmond. Albany: State University of New York Press, c1999. xviii, 176 p.
99-017957   211 21   0791442667
God. Religion -- Philosophy.

BD573.R44 1999
Referring to God: Jewish and Christian philosophical and theological perspectives/ edited by Paul Helm. New York: St. Martin's Press, 1999. ix, 175 p.
99-016644   211   0312226950
God. Philosophy, Jewish. Philosophy and religion.

BD581 Cosmology — Teleology. Causation. Final cause. Design and purpose — Philosophy of nature

BD581.A75 1983
Armstrong, D. M. 1926-
What is a law of nature?/ D.M. Armstrong. Cambridge [Cambridgeshire]; Cambridge University Press, 1983. x, 180 p.
83-005130   113   0521253438
Philosophy of nature.

BD581.C665 1992
The Concept of nature/ edited by John Torrance. Oxford [England]: Clarendon Press; 1992. xii, 186 p.
92-018125   210   0198522762
Philosophy of nature -- History. Nature.

BD581.C76 2002
Crosby, Donald A.
A religion of nature/ Donald A. Crosby. Albany, NY: State University of New York Press, c2002. xii, 200 p.
2002-017734   113 21   0791454541
Philosophy of nature.

BD581.G55 1997
Grange, Joseph, 1940-
Nature: an environmental cosmology/ Joseph Grange. Albany: State University of New York Press, c1997. xviii, 272 p.
96-041494   113   0791433471
Philosophy of nature. Environmental ethics.

BD581.H573 1995
Hogan, Linda.
Dwellings: a spiritual history of the living world/ Linda Hogan. 1st ed. New York: W.W. Norton, c1995. 159 p.
95-001725   113 20   0393037843
Philosophy of nature.

BD581.K54 1984
Kohak, Erazim V.,
The embers and the stars: a philosophical inquiry into the moral sense of nature/ Erazim Kohak. Chicago: University of Chicago Press, 1984. xiii, 269 p.
83-017889   113   0226450228
Philosophical anthropology. Philosophy of nature. Ethics.

BD581.K597 2000
Kowalewski, David.
Deep power: the political ecology of wilderness and civilization/ David Kowalewski. Commack, NY: Nova Science Publishers, c2000. xvii, 149 p.
99-056806   179/.1 21   1560727691
Philosophy of nature. Civilization -- Philosophy. Human ecology -- Philosophy. Political ecology.

BD581.N48 1989
Neville, Robert C.
Recovery of the measure: interpretation and nature/ Robert Cummings Neville. Albany, N.Y.: State University of New York Press, c1989. xiii, 369 p.
89-011441   133   0791400980
Philosophy of nature. Hermeneutics. Metaphysics.

BD581.R59 2003
Roach, Catherine M.,
Mother/nature: popular culture and environmental ethics/ Catherine M. Roach. Bloomington, IN: Indiana University Press, c2002. xvi, 221 p.
2002-007644   304.2 21   0253215625
Philosophy of nature. Ecology -- Philosophy. Popular culture. Environmental ethics.

BD581.S67 1995
Soper, Kate.
What is nature?/ Kate Soper. Oxford; Blackwell, 1995. x, 289 p.
94-046739   113   0631188894
Philosophy of nature. Nature and nurture. Environmental ethics.

BD581.V27 1989
Van Fraassen, Bas C., 1941-
Laws and symmetry/ Bas C. van Fraassen. Oxford; Oxford University Press, 1989. xv, 395 p.
89-030366   113   0198248113
Philosophy of nature. Necessity (Philosophy) Symmetry.

BD581.V57 1996
Vogel, Steven,
Against nature: the concept of nature in critical theory/ Steven Vogel. Albany: State University of New York Press, c1996. vi, 225 p.
95-041253   113/.09/04 20   0791430464
Philosophy of nature. Critical theory.

BD581.W476 1996
Wilson, Edward Osborne, 1929-
In search of nature/ Edward O. Wilson. Washington, D.C.: Island Press, c1996. x, 214 p.
96-011226   113   1559632151
Philosophy of nature. Human beings. Human ecology -- Philosophy.

BD591-595 Cosmology — Teleology. Causation. Final cause. Design and purpose — Cause and effect

BD591.C26 1993
Causation/ edited by Ernest Sosa and Michael Tooley. Oxford; Oxford University Press, 1993. viii, 252 p.
92-028442   122 20   0198750943
Causation.

BD591.W74
Wright, G. H. von 1916-
Causality and determinism.   New York, Columbia University Press, 1974. xxi, 143 p.
74-011030   122   0231037589
Causation. Free will and determinism.

BD595.C65 2001
Combs, Allan,
Synchronicity: through the eyes of science, myth, and the trickster/ Allan Combs and Mark Holland. [3rd ed.]. New York: Marlowe, [2001] xxxix, 184 p.
2001-271527   123 21   1569245991
Coincidence.   Science -- Philosophy. Mythology.

BD595.H33 1990
Hacking, Ian.
The taming of chance/ Ian Hacking. Cambridge [England]; Cambridge University Press, 1990. xiii, 264 p.
89-036411   123/.3   0521380146
Chance. Necessity (Philosophy)

BD595.R47 1995
Rescher, Nicholas.
Luck: the brilliant randomness of everyday life/ Nicholas Rescher. 1st ed. New York: Farrar, Straus and Giroux, 1995. ix, 237 p.
95-017421   123/.3 20   0374194289
Chance. Fortune. Fate and fatalism.

BD621 Cosmology — Space, time, matter and motion — Space

BD621.C35 1999
Casati, Roberto,
Parts and places: the structures of spatial representation/ Roberto   Casati, Achille C. Varzi. Cambridge, Mass.: MIT Press, c1999. viii, 238 p.
98-051512   114 21   026203266X
Space and time.

BD621.C66 1991
Concepts of space, ancient and modern/ edited by Kapila Vatsyayan. New Delhi: Indira Gandhi National Centre for the Arts: 1991. xxiv, 665 p.
91-906348   114   8170172527
Space and time -- Congresses. Space (Art) -- Congresses. Sacred space -- Congresses.

BD621.L4813 1991
Lefebvre, Henri, 1905-
The production of space/ Henri Lefebvre; translated by Donald Nicholson-Smith. Oxford, OX, UK; Blackwell, 1991. 454 p.
90-021058   115   0631140484
Space and time.

BD632 Cosmology — Space, time, matter and motion — Space and time

BD632.C48 1993
Christensen, F. M.
Space-like time: consequences of, alternatives to, and arguments regarding the theory that time is like space/ F.M. Christensen. Toronto; University of Toronto Press, c1993. xii, 316 p.
94-103981   115   0802028160
Space and time.

BD632.N45 1994
Nerlich, Graham,
The shape of space/ Graham Nerlich. 2nd ed. Cambridge; Cambridge University Press, c1994. xv, 290 p.
93-028935   114 20   0521456452
Space and time. Relation (Philosophy) Science -- Philosophy.

BD632.R39 1991
Ray, Christopher, 1951-
Time, space, and philosophy/ Christopher Ray. London; Routledge, 1991. xi, 268 p.
90-024118   115   0415032210
Space and time.

BD632.R413
Reichenbach, Hans, 1891-1953.
The philosophy of space & time. Translated by Maria Reichenbach and John Freund. With introductory remarks by Rudolf Carnap. New York, Dover Publications [1958] 295 p.
58-007082   113
Space and time. Relativity (Physics)

BD632.S645 1998
Strobach, Nico.
The moment of change: a systematic history in the philosophy of space   and time/ by Nico Strobach.   Dordrecht;   Kluwer   Academic Publishers, c1998. xii, 302 p.
98-022288   115 21   0792351207
Space and time -- History.

BD632.T78 1991
Trusted, Jennifer.
Physics and metaphysics: theories of space and time/ Jennifer Trusted. London; Routledge, 1991. xii, 210 p.
90-046821   113   0415059488
Space and time -- History. Philosophy and science -- History. Religion and science -- History.

BD638 Cosmology — Space, time, matter and motion — Time. Beginning

BD638.B7 1999
Brand, Stewart.
The clock of the long now: time and responsibility/ Stewart brand. 1st ed. New York: Basic Books, c1999. 190 p.
99-219976   115 21   046504512X
Time. Responsibility. Strategic planning.

BD638.C48 1991
Chronotypes: the construction of time/ edited by John Bender and David E. Wellbery. Stanford, Calif.: Stanford University Press, 1991. xi, 257 p.
90-026967   115   0804719101
Time.

BD638.C63 1997
Cockburn, David, 1949-
Other times: philosophical perspectives on past, present,   and   future/   David   Cockburn. Cambridge; Cambridge University Press, 1997. xiv, 355 p.
96-050077   115   0521592143
Time. Tense (Logic)

BD638.E42 1992
Elias, Norbert.
Time: an essay/ Norbert Elias; translated in part from the German by Edmund Jephcott. Oxford, UK; B. Blackwell, c1992. 216 p.
91-032598   115   0631157980
Time.

BD638.F33 2002
Fagg, Lawrence W.,
The becoming of time: integrating physical and religious time/ by Lawrence W. Fagg. Durham , NC: Duke University Press, 2002.
2002-013819   115 21   0822331446
Time. Time -- Religious aspects.

BD638.F68 1999
Fraser, J. T. 1923-
Time, conflict, and human values/ J. T. Fraser. Urbana: University of Illinois Press, c1999. 306 p.
98-058033   115   0252024761
Time. Values. Conflict (Psychology)

BD638.F69 1987
Fraser, J. T. 1923-
Time, the familiar stranger/ J.T. Fraser. Amherst: University of Massachusetts Press, 1987. xiii, 389 p.
87-010865   529   0870235761
Time.

BD638.F7
Fraser, J. T. 1923-
The voices of time; a cooperative survey of man's views of time as expressed by the sciences and by the humanities, edited by J. T. Fraser. New York, G. Braziller [1966] xxv, 710 p.
65-019326   115
Time.

BD638.H277 1988
Harris, Errol E.
The reality of time/ Errol E. Harris. Albany: State University of New York Press, c1988. xii, 204 p.
88-002136   115   088706860X
Time.

BD638.L4 1957
Lewis, Wyndham, 1882-1957.
Time and Western man. Boston, Beacon Press [1957] 469 p.
57-009207   115
Spengler, Oswald, -- 1880-1936. -- Untergang des Abendlandes.Literature, Modern -- History and criticism. Time. Civilization -- History.

BD638.L83 1989
Lucas, J. R. 1929-
The future: an essay on God, temporality, and truth/ J.R. Lucas. Oxford, UK; Basil Blackwell, 1989. x, 245 p.
88-027541   115   0631166599
God. Truth. Time.

BD638.M38 1990
McInerney, Peter K.
Time and experience/ Peter K. McInerney. Philadelphia: Temple University Press, 1991. vii, 283 p.
90-032383   115   0877227527
Time. Experience.

BD638.P73 1996
Price, Huw, 1953-
Time's arrow & Archimedes' point: new directions for the physics of time/ Huw Price. New York: Oxford University Press, 1996. xiii, 306 p.
95-025508   523.1   0195100956
Time. Physics -- Philosophy.

BD638.Q47 1998
Questions of time and tense/ edited by Robin Le Poidevin. Oxford: Clarendon Press; 1998. xii, 293 p.
98-028486   115   0198236956
Time.

BD638.R4 1974
Reitmeister, Louis Aaron,
A philosophy of time.   Westport, Conn., Greenwood Press [1974, c1962] 452 p.
72-010699   115   0837166187
Time.

BD638.S43 1987
Seddon, Keith, 1956-
Time: a philosophical treatment/ Keith Seddon. London; Croom Helm, c1987. 166 p.
87-003607   115   0709954247
Time.

BD638.S64 1993
Smith, Quentin, 1952-
Language and time/ Quentin Smith. New York: Oxford University Press, 1993. ix, 262 p.
92-037004   115   0195082273
Time. Language and languages -- Philosophy.

BD638.S67 1983
Sorabji, Richard.
Time, creation, and the continuum: theories in antiquity and the early middle ages/ Richard Sorabji. Ithaca, N.Y.: Cornell University Press, 1983. xviii, 473 p.
82-048714   115   0801415934
Time. Creation. Continuity.

BD638.S76 2001
Steiner, George, 1929-
Grammars of creation: originating in the Gifford Lectures for 1990/ George Steiner. New Haven: Yale University Press, 2001. 344 p.
00-061448   116   0300088639
Beginning -- Miscellanea. Creation -- Miscellanea. Creative ability -- Miscellanea.

BD638.T66 2000
Tooley, Michael,
Time, tense, and causation/ Michael Tooley. Oxford: Clarendon Press;
00-056651   115 21   0198250746
Time. Causation.

BD638.T67 1983
Toulmin, Stephen Edelston.
The discovery of time/ Stephen Toulmin, June Goodfield. New York: Octagon Books, 1983, c1965. 280 p., [8] p. of plates:
83-013112   901 19   0882548689
Time. Cosmology -- History.

BD638.Z48 2003
Zerubavel, Eviatar.
Time maps: collective memory and the social shape of the past/ Eviatar Zerubavel. Chicago, Ill.: University of Chicago Press, c2003. xii, 180 p.
2002-012327   304.2/3 21   0226981525
Time. History -- Philosophy. Civilization -- Philosophy.

BD646 Cosmology — Space, time, matter and motion — Structure of matter. Atomism, etc.

BD646.W5
Whyte, Lancelot Law, 1896-1972.
Essay on atomism, from Democritus to 1960. Middletown, Conn., Wesleyan University Press [1961] 108 p.
61-014236   146.5
Atomism.

BD648 Cosmology — Space, time, matter and motion — Matter and form. Hylomorphism

BD648.B66
Boulding, Kenneth Ewart, 1910-
The image; knowledge in life and society. Ann Arbor, University of Michigan Press [1956] 175 p.
56-009720   110
Form (Philosophy)

BD648.W47 1970
Whyte, Lancelot Law, 1896-1972.
Accent on form; an anticipation of the science of tomorrow. New York Harper, [1954] 198 p.
54-006036   110
Form (Philosophy) Science -- Philosophy.

BD701 Cosmology — Miscellaneous speculations. Curiosa, etc.

BD701.E383 1959
Eliade, Mircea, 1907-
Cosmos and history; the myth of the eternal return. Translated from the French by Willard R. Trask. New York, Harper [1959] 176 p.
59-006648   113
Religion. Myth. History (Theology)

BD701.H37 1991
Harris, Errol E.
Cosmos and anthropos: a philosophical interpretation of the anthropic cosmological principle/ Errol E. Harris. Atlantic Highlands, N.J.: Humanities Press International, 1991. ix, 194 p.
90-037036   113   0391036947
Anthropic principle. Evolution. Human beings.

BD701.N38 1998
The necessity of friction/ edited by Nordal Akerman. Boulder, Colo.: WestviewPress, 1998. viii, 320 p.
97-022525   110   0813334349
Friction. Life.

BH Aesthetics

BH21 Collected works (nonserial) — Polyglot

BH21.C3
Carritt, E. F. 1876-1964.
Philosophies of beauty from Socrates to Robert Bridges, being the sources of aesthetic theory. Selected and edited by E. F. Carritt... Oxford, The Clarendon Press, 1931. xxi, 334 p.
32-003577   701
Aesthetics.

BH21.L4
Levich, Marvin,
Aesthetics and the philosophy of criticism. New York, Random House [c1963] 649 p.
62-016202
Aesthetics. Criticism.

BH21.R3 1979
Rader, Melvin Miller, 1903-
A modern book of esthetics: an anthology/ edited with introd. and notes by Melvin Rader. New York: Holt, Rinehart and Winston, c1979. 563 p.
78-016041   111.8/5   0030193311
Aesthetics -- Addresses, essays, lectures.

BH21.R4 1960
Read, Herbert Edward, 1893-1968.
The forms of things unknown; essays towards an aesthetic philosophy. New York, Horizon Press, 1960. 248 p.
60-014683   111.85
Aesthetics.

BH21.S4
Sesonske, Alexander.
What is art? Aesthetic theory from Plato to Tolstoy. New York, Oxford University Press, 1965. xvi, 428 p.
65-012469   111.85082
Aesthetics.

BH21.V55
Vivas, Eliseo,
The problems of aesthetics, a book of readings, edited by Eliseo Vivas and Murray Krieger. New York, Rinehart [1953] 639 p.
52-014017   701.17
Aesthetics.

BH39 Philosophy. Methodology. Relation to other topics

BH39.A57 1990
Anderson, Richard L.,
Calliope's sisters: a comparative study of philosophies of art/ Richard L. Anderson. Englewood Cliffs, N.J.: Prentice Hall, c1990. xv, 320 p.
89-008389   701/.17 20   0131554255
Aesthetics -- Comparative studies.

BH39.A685 2003
Art and essence/ edited by Stephen Davies and Ananta Ch. Sukla. Westport, CT: Greenwood Pub. Group, 2003.
2002-190813   111/.85 21   0275977668
Aesthetics. Art -- Philosophy.

BH39.A69 1984
Art and its significance: an anthology of aesthetic theory/ edited by Stephen David Ross. Albany: State University of New York Press, c1984. x, 574 p.
83-009683   701/.1/7   0873957644
Aesthetics. Art -- Philosophy.

BH39.A695 2002
Art and morality/ edited by José Luis Bermúdez and Sebastian Gardner. London; Routledge, 2002.
2002-068196   111/.85 21   0415192528
Aesthetics. Ethics. Art -- Moral and ethical aspects.

BH39.B35313 1993
Barilli, Renato.
A course on aesthetics/ Renato Barilli; translated by Karen E. Pinkus. Minneapolis: University of Minnesota Press, c1993. xiii, 170 p.
93-021779   111/.85   0816621187
Aesthetics.

BH39.B393 2000
Berger, Karol, 1947-
A theory of art/ Karol Berger. New York: Oxford University Press, 2000. xii, 287 p.
98-047060   700/.1   0195128605
Arts -- Philosophy. Aesthetics. Poetics.

BH39.B3945 1991
Berleant, Arnold, 1932-
Art and engagement/ Arnold Berleant. Philadelphia: Temple University Press, 1991. xvii, 259 p.
90-039920   111/.85   0877227977
Aesthetics. Engagement (Philosophy)

BH39.B6
Boas, George, 1891-
A primer for critics, by George Boas. Baltimore, The Johns Hopkins press, 1937. viii, 153 p.
37-003836   701
Aesthetics. Criticism.

BH39.C376 1999
Carroll, Noel
Philosophy of art: a contemporary introduction/ Noel Carroll. London; Routledge, 1999. ix, 273 p.
99-025928   111/.85   0415159636
Art -- Philosophy. Aesthetics.

BH39.C62 1995
The Columbia dictionary of modern literary and cultural criticism/ Joseph Childers and Gary Hentzi, general editors. New York: Columbia University Press, c1995. xii, 362 p.
94-042535   001.3/03   0231072422
Criticism -- Dictionaries. Humanities -- Philosophy -- Dictionaries. Social sciences -- Philosophy -- Dictionaries.

BH39.C67 1990
Cothey, A. L. 1951-
The nature of art/ A.L. Cothey. London; Routledge, 1990. xi, 201 p.
90-032935   701/.17   0415033578
Aesthetics. Art -- Philosophy.

BH39.D349 1998
Danto, Arthur Coleman,
Beyond the brillo box: the visual arts in post-historical perspective / Arthur C. Danto. Berkeley: University of California Press, [1998]. x, 263 p.
98-015100   111/.85 21   0520216741
Aesthetics.

BH39.D35 1986
Danto, Arthur Coleman,
The philosophical disenfranchisement of art/ Arthur C. Danto. New York: Columbia University Press, 1986. xvi, 216 p.
86-002260   700/.1 19   0231063644
Aesthetics. Art -- Philosophy.

BH39.D36
Danto, Arthur Coleman, 1924-
The transfiguration of the commonplace: a philosophy of art/ Arthur C. Danto. Cambridge, Mass.: Harvard University Press, 1981. x, 212 p.
80-018700   700/.1   0674903455
Aesthetics. Art -- Philosophy.

BH39.D4513 1987
Derrida, Jacques.
The truth in painting/ Jacques Derrida; translated by Geoff Bennington and Ian McLeod. Chicago: University of Chicago Press, 1987. xiv, 386 p.
86-030914   701/.1/7   0226143244
Aesthetics.

BH39.D48
Dickie, George, 1926-
Aesthetics; an introduction.   [Indianapolis] Pegasus [c1971] x, 200 p.
72-128659   111.8/5
Aesthetics. Aesthetics, Modern -- 20th century.

BH39.D493 1988
Dickie, George, 1926-
Evaluating art/ George Dickie. Philadelphia: Temple University Press, 1988. x, 193 p.
88-029541   111/.85   0877225974
Aesthetics.

BH39.D494 1996
Dickie, George, 1926-
Introduction to aesthetics: an analytic approach/ George Dickie. New York: Oxford University Press, 1997. x, 189 p.
96-026825   111/.85
Aesthetics.

BH39.D52 2000
Differential aesthetics: art practices, philosophy and feminist understandings/ edited by Penny Florence, Nicola Foster. Aldershot, Hants, England; Ashgate, c2000. xx, 360 p.
00-134813   111/.85 21   075461493X
Aesthetics. Art -- Philosophy. Feminist theory. Feminism and the arts.

BH39.D555 1993
Dipert, Randall R.
Artifacts, art works, and agency/ Randall R. Dipert. Philadelphia: Temple University Press, 1993. xx, 273 p.
92-009344   111/.85   0877229902
Aesthetics. Act (Philosophy)

BH39.D56 1992
Dissanayake, Ellen.
Homo aestheticus: where art comes from and why/ Ellen Dissanayake. New York: Free Press; c1992. xxii, 297 p.
91-045335   701/.17   0029078857
Aesthetics.

BH39.D68 1996
Douglas, Mary.
Thought styles: critical essays on good taste/ Mary Douglas. London; Sage Publications, 1996. xvii, 222 p.
96-067253   121/.8 21   0803976569
Aesthetics. Values. Cognitive styles. Reasoning.

BH39.E26 1989
Eaton, Marcia Muelder, 1938-
Aesthetics and the good life/ Marcia Muelder Eaton. Rutherford [N.J.]: Fairleigh Dickinson University Press; c1989. 209 p.
87-046420   111/.85   0838633366
Aesthetics.

BH39.E265 2001
Eaton, Marcia Muelder, 1938-
Merit, aesthetic and ethical/ Marcia Muelder Eaton. Oxford; Oxford University Press, 2001. vi, 252 p.
00-028555   111/.85   0195140249
Aesthetics. Ethics. Art -- Moral and ethical aspects.

BH39.E29213 1989
Eco, Umberto.
The open work/ Umberto Eco; translated by Anna Cancogni; with an introduction by David Robey. Cambridge, Mass.: Harvard University Press, 1989. xxxii, 285 p.
88-021399   111/.85   0674639758
Joyce, James, -- 1882-1941 -- Criticism and interpretation. Wiener, Norbert, -- 1894-1964. Aesthetics. Poetry. Semiotics.

BH39.E54 1998
Elkins, James, 1955-
On pictures and the words that fail them/ James Elkins. Cambridge; Cambridge University Press, c1998. xix, 326 p.
97-027900   121/.68   0521571081
Pictures. Image (Philosophy) Interpretation (Philosophy)

BH39.G5815 1995
Goldman, Alan H., 1945-
Aesthetic value/ Alan H. Goldman. Boulder, Colo.: Westview Press, 1995. ix, 198 p.
95-017025   111/.85   0813320186
Aesthetics. Values.

BH39.H787 1987
Huer, Jon.
Art, beauty, and pornography: a journey through American culture/ Jon Huer. Buffalo, N.Y.: Prometheus Books, 1987. 239 p.
87-002472   700/.1   0879753978
Aesthetics. Pornography.

BH39.K575 1997
Kivy, Peter.
Philosophies of arts: an essay in differences/ Peter Kivy. Cambridge; Cambridge University Press, 1997. xi, 242 p.
96-037698   700/.1   0521591783
Arts -- Philosophy. Aesthetics, Modern. Arts -- Philosophy -- History.

BH39.K69 1987
Krukowski, Lucian, 1929-
Art and concept: a philosophical study/ Lucian Krukowski. Amherst: University of Massachusetts Press, 1987. xi, 127 p.
87-005012   701   087023563X
Aesthetics.

BH39.L495 1996
Levinson, Jerrold.
The pleasures of aesthetics: philosophical essays/ Jerrold Levinson. Ithaca, NY: Cornell University Press, 1996. xiv, 312 p.
95-043808   111/.85   0801430593
Aesthetics.

BH39.L5595 2000
Liu, Kang, 1955-
Aesthetics and Marxism: Chinese aesthetic Marxists and their Western contemporaries/ Kang Liu. Durham: Duke University Press, 2000. xvi, 230 p.
99-043220   111/.85/09   0822324253
Aesthetics. Culture. Philosophy, Marxist -- China.

BH39.L8313 2000
Luhmann, Niklas.
Art as a social system/ Niklas Luhmann; translated by Eva M. Knodt. Stanford, Calif.: Stanford University Press, 2000. 422 p.
00-041050   306.4/7   0804739064
Aesthetics. Art and society.

BH39.L95 1997
Lyas, Colin.
Aesthetics/ Colin Lyas. London; UCL Press, 1997. xii, 239 p.
97-196486   111/.85   1857286782
Aesthetics. Art -- Philosophy.

BH39.M385 1998
Manns, James W.
Aesthetics/ James W. Manns. Armonk, N.Y.: M.E. Sharpe, c1998. xiii, 190 p.
97-021723   111/.85   1563249537
Aesthetics.

BH39.M394 1978
Margolis, Joseph, 1924-
Philosophy looks at the arts: contemporary readings in aesthetics/ edited by Joseph Margolis. Philadelphia: Temple University Press, 1978. ix, 481 p.
77-095028   111.8/5   0877221235
Aesthetics. Art -- Philosophy. Hermeneutics.

BH39.M618
Morawski, Stefan.
Inquiries into the fundamentals of aesthetics. Cambridge, Mass., MIT Press [1974] xviii, 408 p.
74-006123   111.8/5   0262130963
Aesthetics.

BH39.M6227 1997
Mortensen, Preben, 1957-
Art in the social order: the making of the modern conception of art/ Preben Mortensen. Albany: State University of New York Press, c1997. ix, 213 p.
96-015473   701   0791432777
Aesthetics. Aesthetics, Modern -- 18th century.

BH39.M83
Munro, Thomas, 1897-
Toward science in aesthetics; selected essays. New York, Liberal Arts Press, 1956. xv, 371 p.
56-003418   701.7
Aesthetics. Art -- Philosophy.

BH39.N2713 1996
Nancy, Jean-Luc.
The muses/ Jean-Luc Nancy; translated by Peggy Kamuf. Stanford, Calif.: Stanford University Press, 1996. 118 p.
96-010880   701   0804727805
Aesthetics. Arts. Art -- Philosophy.

BH39.O8 1953
Osborne, Harold, 1905-
Theory of beauty; an introduction to aesthetics.
New York, Philosophical Library [1953] 220 p.
53-001197   701.17
Aesthetics.

BH39.R5
Righter, William.
Logic and criticism. New York, Chilmark Press;
[1963] ix, 148 p.
64-010087   801.9
Criticism. Aesthetics.

BH39.S5256 1992
Shusterman, Richard.
Pragmatist aesthetics: living beauty, rethinking
art/ Richard Shusterman. Oxford, UK; B.
Blackwell, 1992. xii, 324 p.
91-013980   111/.85   0631164456
Aesthetics. Pragmatism.

BH39.S634 1982
Sparshott, Francis Edward, 1926-
The theory of the arts/ Francis Sparshott.
Princeton, N.J.: Princeton University Press,
c1982. xiii, 726 p.
82-005333   700/.1   0691072663
Arts -- Philosophy. Aesthetics.

BH39.S913 1987
Summers, David, 1941-
The judgment of sense: Renaissance naturalism
and the rise of aesthestics/ David Summers.
Cambridge; Cambridge University Press, 1987.
xiii, 365 p.
86-009538   111/.85   0521326753
*Aesthetics.   Naturalism.   Perception
(Philosophy)*

BH39.T395 1993
Taubes, Timothy.
Art & philosophy/ Timothy Taubes. Buffalo,
N.Y.: Prometheus Books, 1993. 121 p.
93-036085   111/.85   0879758651
*Art -- Philosophy. Aesthetics, Modern -- 20th
century.*

BH39.T87 1992
Turner, Frederick, 1943-
Beauty: the value of values/ Frederick Turner.
Charlottesville: University Press of Virginia,
1991. 140 p.
91-022536   111/.85   0813913578
Aesthetics. Values.

BH39.W375 1992
Wegener, Charles.
The discipline of taste and feeling/ Charles
Wegener. Chicago: University of Chicago Press,
1992. xi, 224 p.
91-044410   111/.85   0226878937
Aesthetics.

BH39.W64 1980
Wollheim, Richard, 1923-
Art and its objects: with six supplementary
essays/   Richard   Wollheim.   Cambridge;
Cambridge University Press, 1980. xv, 270 p.
79-020790   700/.1   0521228980
Aesthetics -- Addresses, essays, lectures.

BH39.Z444 1997
Zemach, Eddy M.
Real beauty/ Eddy M. Zemach. University Park,
Pa.: Pennsylvania State University Press, c1997.
xi, 222 p.
96-023182   111/.85   0271016388
Aesthetics.

BH41 Philosophy. Methodology. Relation to other topics — Special methods

BH41.B45
Bennett, Tony.
Formalism   and   Marxism/   Tony   Bennett.
London: Methuen, 1979. xii, 200 p.
80-473608   801/.95   0416708706
*Communist aesthetics. Formalism (Literary
analysis) Criticism.*

BH41.E4
Elton, William
Aesthetics and language; essays by W. B. Gallie
[and others] New York, Philosophical Library
[1954] vi, 186 p.
54-012049   701.17
Aesthetics.

BH56 Dictionaries. Encyclopedias

BH56.C65 1992
A Companion to aesthetics/ edited by David E.
Cooper; advisory editors, Joseph Margolis and
Crispin Sartwell. Oxford, OX, UK; Blackwell
Reference, 1992. xiii, 466 p.
92-038691   111/.85/03 20   0631178015
Aesthetics -- Encyclopedias.

BH56.E53 1998
Encyclopedia of aesthetics/ Michael Kelly,
editor in chief. New York: Oxford University
Press, 1998. 4 v.
98-018741   111/.85/03   0195113071
Aesthetics -- Encyclopedias.

BH81 History

BH81.B4 1966
Beardsley, Monroe C.
Aesthetics from classical Greece to the present;
a short history [by] Monroe C. Beardsley. New
York, Macmillan [1966] 414 p.
65-024765   111.85
Aesthetics -- History.

BH81.G5 1953
Gilbert, Katharine (Everett) 1886-1952.
A history of esthetics, by Katharine Everett
Gilbert and Helmut Kuhn. Bloomington, Indiana
University Press, 1953. xxi, 613 p.
53-007022   701.17
Aesthetics -- History.

BH81.K3
Kallen, Horace Meyer, 1882-1974.
Art and freedom; a historical and biographical
interpretation of the relations between the ideas
of beauty, use, and freedom in western
civilization from the Greeks to the present day
[by] Horace M. Kallen. New York, Duell, Sloan
and Pearce [1942] 2 v.
43-000399   701.17   083712249X
*Aesthetics -- History. Art -- Philosophy --
History. Literature -- Esthetics.*

BH81.W66 1999
Wood, Robert E., 1934-
Placing aesthetics: reflections on the philosophic
tradition/ Robert E. Wood. Athens, OH: Ohio
University Press, c1999. xvi, 413 p.
99-027142   111/.85/09   0821412809
Aesthetics -- History.

BH91 History — Ancient — General works

BH91.H32 1969
Harrison, Jane Ellen, 1850-1928.
Ancient art and ritual. New York, Greenwood
Press [1969, c1951] 256 p.
69-013924   291/.3   0837119812
Art, Primitive. Ritual. Aesthetics.

BH131 History — Medieval

BH131.M67 1990
Morrison, Karl Frederick.
History as a visual art in the twelfth-century
renaissance/ Karl F. Morrison. Princeton, N.J.:
Princeton University Press, c1990. xxvi, 262 p.
90-008251   111/.85/09409021   0691055823
*Aesthetics,   Medieval.   Historiography.
Cognition.*

BH151 History — Modern

BH151.B47 1992
Bernstein, J. M.
The fate of art: aesthetic alienation from Kant to Derrida and Adorno/ J.M. Bernstein. University Park, Pa.: Pennsylvania State University Press, c1992. x, 292 p.
91-035215   111/.85   0271008385
Kant, Immanuel, -- 1724-1804 -- Aesthetics. Heidegger, Martin, -- 1889-1976 -- Aesthetics. Derrida, Jacques -- Aesthetics. Aesthetics, Modern.

BH151.E2 1990
Eagleton, Terry, 1943-
The ideology of the aesthetics/ Terry Eagleton. Oxford, UK; Blackwell, 1990. 426 p.
89-035824   111/.85/0903   0631163018
Aesthetics, Modern.

BH151.S3313 2000
Schaeffer, Jean-Marie.
Art of the modern age: philosophy of art from Kant to Heidegger/ Jean-Marie Schaeffer; translated by Steven Rendall, with a foreword by Arthur C. Danto. Princeton, N.J.:   Princeton University Press, c2000. xvii, 352 p.
99-038862   111/.85/0903   0691016690
Aesthetics, Modern. Art -- Philosophy.

BH151.T36 1993
Taminiaux, Jacques, 1928-
Poetics, speculation, and judgment: the shadow of the work of art from Kant to phenomenology/ Jacques Taminiaux; translated and edited by Michael Gendre. Albany: State University of New York Press, c1993. viii, 191 p.
92-035025   111/.85/0903   0791415473
Aesthetics, Modern -- 18th century. Aesthetics, Modern -- 19th century. Aesthetics, Modern -- 20th century.

BH181-183 History — Modern — 18th century

BH181.D53 1996
Dickie, George, 1926-
The century of taste: the philosophical odyssey of taste in the eighteenth century/ George Dickie. New York: Oxford University Press, 1996. xii, 156 p.
94-049131   111/.85/09033   0195096800
Aesthetics, Modern -- 18th century.

BH181.M36 1990
McCormick, Peter
Modernity, aesthetics, and the bounds of art/ Peter J. McCormick. Ithaca: Cornell University Press, 1990. xiii, 349 p.
89-071309   111/.85   0801424526
Aesthetics, Modern -- 18th century. Aesthetics, Modern -- 20th century.

BH181.W66 1994
Woodmansee, Martha.
The author, art, and the market: rereading the history of aesthetics / Martha Woodmansee. New York: Columbia University Press, c1994. xv, 200 p.
93-035564   111/.85 20   0231080603
Aesthetics, Modern -- 18th century. Aesthetics, Comparative. Popular culture.

BH183.K313 1960
Kant, Immanuel, 1724-1804.
Observations on the feeling of the beautiful and sublime. Translated by John T. Goldthwait. Berkeley, University of California Press, 1960. 124 p.
60-014379   111.85   0520074041
Aesthetics

BH191 History — Modern — 19th century

BH191.K78 1992
Krukowski, Lucian, 1929-
Aesthetic legacies/ Lucian Krukowski. Philadelphia: Temple University Press, 1992. xiv, 245 p.
92-019307   111/.85/09034   0877229724
Kant, Immanuel, -- 1724-1804 -- Aesthetics. Schopenhauer, Arthur, -- 1788-1860 -- Aesthetics. Hegel, Georg Wilhelm Friedrich, -- 1770-1831 -- Aesthetics. Aesthetics, Modern -- 19th century. Aesthetics, Modern -- 20th century. Modernism (Aesthetics)

BH201-205 History — Modern — 20th century

BH201.A395 1999
Agamben, Giorgio, 1942-
Potentialities: collected essays in philosophy/ Giorgio Agamben; edited and translated with an introduction by Daniel Heller-Roazen. Stanford, Calif.: Stanford University Press, 1999. x, 307 p.
99-039449   195   0804732779
Aesthetics, Modern -- 20th century. Language and languages -- Philosophy. History -- Philosophy.

BH201.A63 1989
Analytic aesthetics/ [edited by] Richard Shusterman. Oxford, UK; B. Blackwell, 1989. viii, 198 p.
88-023338   111/.85   0631162534
Aesthetics, Modern -- 20th century. Analysis (Philosophy) Arts -- Philosophy.

BH201.A74 2001
Arguing about art: contemporary philosophical debates/ edited by Alex Neill and Aaron Ridley. 2nd ed. London; Routledge, 2001.
2001-049059   111/.85 21   0415237394
Aesthetics, Modern.

BH201.B4 1981
Beardsley, Monroe C.
Aesthetics, problems in the philosophy of criticism/ Monroe C.   Beardsley. 2d ed. Indianapolis: Hackett Pub. Co., c1981. lxiv, 614 p.
80-028899   111/.85 19   0915145081
Aesthetics.

BH201.C28
Carritt, E. F. 1876-1964.
An introduction to aesthetics.   London, Hutchinson's University Library [1949] 151 p.
50-001040   701.17
Aesthetics.

BH201.C29 1949
Carritt, E. F. 1876-1964.
The theory of beauty.   London, Methuen [1949] viii, 344 p.
50-012450   701.17
Aesthetics.

BH201.G55
Gilson, Etienne, 1884-1978.
The arts of the beautiful [by] Etienne Gilson. New York, Scribner [1965] 189 p.
65-014767   111.85
Aesthetics.

BH201.H29 1996
Harrison, Thomas J., 1955-
1910, the emancipation of dissonance/ Thomas Harrison. Berkeley: University of California Press, c1996. xii, 264 p.
95-025990   111/.85   0520200438
Michelstaedter, Carlo, -- 1887-1910. Aesthetics, Modern -- 20th century. Expressionism. Anxiety. Europe -- Intellectual life -- 20th century.

BH201.N32 1978
Nahm, Milton Charles, 1903-
The artist as creator: an essay of human freedom/ by Milton C. Nahm. [Ann Arbor: University Microfilms International, [1978] c1956. xi, 352 p.
78-007316   701/.17   0835703177
Aesthetics. Creation (Literary, artistic, etc.) Art -- Philosophy.

BH201.O5 1948
Ogden, C. K. 1889-1957.
The Foundations of aesthetics/ I.A. Richards, C.K. Ogden, James Wood. New York: Lear Publishers, [1948] 92 p.
49-004778
Aesthetics

BH201.P4 1970
Pepper, Stephen Coburn, 1891-
Aesthetic quality; a contextualistic theory of beauty, by Stephen C. Pepper. Westport, Conn., Greenwood Press [1970, c1965] ix, 255 p.
79-110052   111.8/5   083714437X
Aesthetics.

BH201.P42
Pepper, Stephen Coburn, 1891-
The basis of criticism in the arts, by Stephen C. Pepper ... Cambridge, Mass., Harvard University Press, 1945.
45-005598   701.18
Aesthetics. Criticism.

BH201.R28
Rader, Melvin Miller, 1903-
Art and human values/ Melvin Rader, Bertram Jessup; with a foreword by Virgil C. Aldrich. Englewood Cliffs, N.J.: Prentice-Hall, c1976. x, 406 p.
75-022486   111.8/5   0130468215
Aesthetics. Values. Art -- Philosophy.

BH201.R4 1973
Reid, Louis Arnaud,
A study in aesthetics.   Westport, Conn., Greenwood Press [1973] 415 p.
70-114546   111.8/5   0837147948
Aesthetics.

BH201.S49 1992
Sim, Stuart.
Beyond aesthetics: confrontations with poststructuralism and postmodernism/ Sim Stuart. Toronto; University of Toronto Press, 1992. ix, 181 p.
93-108505   111/.85/0904   0802029515
Derrida, Jacques. Lyotard, Jean Francois. Postmodernism. Aesthetics, Modern -- 20th century. Poststructuralism.

BH201.S6
Sparshott, Francis Edward
The structure of aesthetics. Toronto, University of Toronto Press, [c1963]. xiii, 471 p.
64-000966
Art -- Philosophy. Aesthetics.

BH202.F63 1948
Focillon, Henri, 1881-1943.
The life of forms in art. New York, Wittenborn [1948] x, 94 p.
48-005278   701.17
Art.

BH202.G4713 1999
Genette, Gerard, 1930-
The aesthetic relation/ Gerard Genette; translated by G.M. Goshgarian. Ithaca, N.Y.: Cornell University Press, 1999. xi, 243 p.
99-031406   111/.85   0801435110
Aesthetics, Modern -- 20th century. Art -- Philosophy.

BH205.O713 1968
Ortega y Gasset, Jose, 1883-1955.
The dehumanization of art; and other essays on art, culture, and literature. Princeton, N.J., Princeton University Press, 1968 [c1948] 204 p.
68-008963   700/.1
Aesthetics. Fiction.

BH221 By region or country, A-Z

BH221.A65 B3413 1998
Behrens-Abouseif, Doris.
Beauty in Arabic culture/ by Doris Behrens-Abouseif. Princeton, NJ: Markus Wiener, 1998.
98-043118   111/.85/09174927   21
1558761993
Aesthetics, Arab. Civilization, Arab. Civilization, Islamic.

BH221.C6.L5 1994
Li, Tse-hou.
The path of beauty: a study of Chinese aesthetics/ Li Zehou; translated by Gong Lizeng. Hong Kong; Oxford University Press, 1994. 244 p.
93-048191   700/.951   019586526X
Aesthetics, Chinese.

BH221.C6.W33 1997
Wang, Ban, 1957-
The sublime figure of history: aesthetics and politics in twentieth-century China/ Ban Wang. Stanford, Calif.: Stanford University Press, c1997. ix, 312 p.
96-048432   111/.85/09510904   0804728461
Aesthetics, Chinese -- 20th century. Aesthetics, Modern -- 20th century. Arts, Chinese -- 20th century. China -- Civilization -- 20th century.

BH221.E853 B47 2002
Bernheimer, Charles,
Decadent subjects: the idea of decadence in art, literature, philosophy, and culture of the fin de siècle in Europe/ Charles Bernheimer; edited by T. Jefferson Kline and Naomi Schor. Baltimore, Md.: Johns Hopkins University Press, 2002. xviii, 227 p.
2001-050319   111.85/09409034   21
0801867401
Aesthetics, European -- 19th century. Degeneration -- History -- 19th century. Decadence (Literary movement) Decadence in art.

BH221.F8.A53 1984
Anderson, Mary R., 1937-
Art in a desacralized world: nineteenth century France and England/ Mary R. Anderson. Lanham, MD: University Press of America, c1984. x, 174 p.
84-013081   801/.93   081914147X
Aesthetics, French -- 19th century. Aesthetics, British -- 19th century.

BH221.G3 C57 2003
Classic and romantic German aesthetics/ edited by J.M. Bernstein. Cambridge, UK; Cambridge University Press, 2003. xli, 311 p.
2003-271174   0521001110
Aesthetics, German. Arts, Classical -- Aesthetics. Arts, Classical -- Philosophy.

BH221.G3.G47 1984
German aesthetic and literary criticism. edited and introduced by David Simpson. Cambridge [Cambridgeshire]; Cambridge University Press, 1984. x, 294 p.
83-015320   111/.85   0521236304
Aesthetics, German -- 18th century. Aesthetics, German -- 19th century. Criticism -- Germany -- History -- 18th century.

BH221.G32.M37 1996
Martin, Nicholas.
Nietzsche and Schiller: untimely aesthetics/ Nicholas Martin. Oxford: Clarendon Press; 1996. xi, 219 p.
95-040307   111/.85/0922   0198159137
Nietzsche, Friedrich Wilhelm, -- 1844-1900. -- Geburt der Tragodie. Schiller, Friedrich, -- 1759-1805. -- Uber die asthetische Erziehung des Menschen in einer Reihe von Briefen. Aesthetics, German -- 18th century. Aesthetics, German -- 19th century.

BH221.G33 B68 2003
Bowie, Andrew,
Aesthetics and subjectivity: from Kant to Nietzsche/ Andrew Bowie. 2nd ed., completely re-written and updated. Manchester, UK; Manchester University Press, 2003.
2002-045163   111/.85/094309033   21
0719057388
Aesthetics, German -- 18th century. Aesthetics, German -- 19th century. Aesthetics, Modern -- 18th century. Aesthetics, Modern -- 19th century. Subjectivity.

BH221.G34.W37413 1989
Ferretti, Silvia.
Cassirer, Panofsky, and Warburg: symbol, art, and history/ Silvia Ferretti; translated by Richard Pierce. New Haven: Yale University Press, c1989. xix, 282 p.
89-030836   111/.85   0300045166
Warburg, Aby, -- 1866-1929. Cassirer, Ernst, -- 1874-1945. Panofsky, Erwin, -- 1892-1968. Aesthetics, German. Aesthetics, Modern -- 19th century. Aesthetics, Modern -- 20th century.

BH221.G7.B36
Bate, Walter Jackson, 1918-
From classic to romantic; premises of taste in eighteenth-century England, by Walter Jackson Bate. Cambridge, Harvard University Press, 1946.
46-002976   701.17
Classicism. Romanticism -- England. Aesthetics -- History.

BH221.G72.H5
Hipple, Walter John.
The beautiful, the sublime, & the picturesque in eighteenth-century British aesthetic theory. Carbondale, Southern Illinois University Press, 1957. vi, 390 p.
57-009535   701.17
Aesthetics -- History. Sublime, The.

BH221.G72.P38 1989
Paulson, Ronald.
Breaking and remaking: aesthetic practice in England, 1700-1820/ Ronald Paulson. New Brunswick: Rutgers University Press, c1989. xiv, 363 p.
89-030375   700/.1 0813514398
Arts -- England -- History -- 18th century. Arts -- England -- History -- 19th century. Aesthetics, British -- 18th century.

BH221.I53.P33 1977
Pandit, Sneh.
An approach to the Indian theory of art and aesthetics/ Sneh Pandit. New Delhi: Sterling Publishers; c1977. vii, 148 p.
77-905389   111.8/5 0842610057
Aesthetics, Indic.

BH221.J3 H57 2001
A history of modern Japanese aesthetics/ translated and edited by Michael F. Marra. onolulu: University of Hawai i Press, c2001. x, 398 p.
00-062950   111/.85/0952 21 0824823990
Aesthetics, Japanese -- 19th century. Aesthetics, Japanese -- 20th century.

BH221.J3 I95
Izutsu, Toshihiko,
The theory of beauty in the classical aesthetics of Japan/ Toshihiko and Toyo Izutsu. The Hague; Martinus Nijhoff Publishers; x, 167 p.
80-016994   111/.85 9024723817
Aesthetics, Japanese.

BH221.J3 J37 1995
Japanese aesthetics and culture: a reader/ edited by Nancy G. Hume. Albany, N.Y.: State University of New York Press, c1995. xx, 378 p.
94-012715   111/.85/0952 20 0791424006
Aesthetics, Japanese. Arts, Japanese -- Philosophy.

BH221.J3 J374 2000
Japanese hermeneutics: current debates on aesthetics and interpretation/ edited by Michael F. Marra. Honolulu, HI: University of Hawai'i Press, 2002. xi, 247 p.
2001-040663   111/.85/0952 21 0824824571
Aesthetics, Japanese. Hermeneutics. Japanese literature -- History and criticism.

BH221.J3 K67 1994
Koren, Leonard,
Wabi-sabi for artists, designers, poets & philosophers/ Leonard Koren. Berkeley, Calif.: Stone Bridge Press, 1994. 94 p.
94-002537   111/.85/0952 20 1880656124
Aesthetics, Japanese.

BH221.J3 M36 1999
Marra, Michele.
Modern Japanese aesthetics: a reader/ Michele Marra. Honolulu: University of Hawai i Press, c1999. x, 322 p.
99-027949   111/.85/0952 21 0824821734
Aesthetics, Japanese -- 19th century. Aesthetics, Japanese -- 20th century.

BH221.R93.W47
West, James D.
Russian symbolism; a study of Vyacheslav Ivanov and the Russian symbolist aesthetic. London, Methuen [1970] vii, 250 p.
79-139834   891.7/09/003 0416193501
Ivanov, V. I. -- (Viacheslav Ivanovich), -- 1866-1949.Aesthetics, Russian -- 20th century. Symbolism in art.

BH301 Special topics, A-Z

BH301.A7.B45 1996
Bell-Villada, Gene H., 1941-
Art for art's sake & literary life: how politics and markets helped shape the ideology & culture of aestheticism, 1790-1990/ Gene H. Bell-Villada. Lincoln: University of Nebraska Press, c1996. x, 340 p.
95-031648   700/.9 0803212607
Art for art's sake (Movement) Aestheticism (Literature)

BH301.A94.B8313 1984
Burger, Peter.
Theory of the avant-garde/ Peter Burger; translation from the German by Michael Shaw; foreword by Jochen Schulte-Sasse. Minneapolis: University of Minnesota Press, c1984. lv, 135 p.
83-010549   111/.85 0816610681
Avant-garde (Aesthetics)

BH301.C7.M38
McFadden, George, 1916-
Discovering the comic/ George McFadden. Princeton, N.J.: Princeton University Press, c1982. 268 p.
81-015825   809/.917 0691064962
Comic, The.

BH301.C7.S9 1970
Swabey, Marie Taylor (Collins) 1891-
Comic laughter, a philosophical essay, by Marie Collins Swabey. [Hamden, Conn.] Archon Books, 1970 [c1961] vi, 251 p.
78-113019   152.4 020800825X
Comic, The. Laughter.

BH301.C84.B37 1990
Battersby, Christine, 1946-
Gender and genius: towards a feminist aesthetics/ Christine Battersby. Bloomington: Indiana University Press, 1989. viii, 192 p.
89-046346   111/.85/082 0253311268
Creation (Literary, artistic, etc.) Genius. Feminist theory.

BH301.C84.B65 1998
Bohm, David.
On creativity/ David Bohm; edited by Lee Nichol. London; Routledge, 1998. xxiv, 125 p.
97-029460   153.3/5 0415173957
Creation (Literary, artistic, etc.) Creative ability in science. Creation in art.

BH301.C84.C66 1981
The Concept of creativity in science and art/ edited by Denis Dutton and Michael Krausz. The Hague; M. Nijhoff; 1981. 212 p.
81-004001   128/.3 902472418X
Creation (Literary, artistic, etc.) Creative ability in science. Creative thinking.

BH301.E9 P36 2001
Pan, David, 1963-
Primitive renaissance: rethinking German expressionism/ David Pan. Lincoln: University of Nebraska Press, c2001. 239 p.
00-062028   111/.85/0943 0803237278
Aesthetics. Expressionism. Primitivism -- Germany. Germany -- Intellectual life -- 20th century.

BH301.L3 A66 1996
Appleton, Jay.
The experience of landscape/ Jay Appleton. Rev. ed. Chichester; Wiley, c1996. xiv, 282 p.
96-001681   700/.1 20 047196235X
Landscape. Landscape in art.

BH301.L3.O3
Ogden, Henry Vining Seton, 1905-
English taste in landscape in the seventeenth century, by Henry V. S. Ogden and Margaret S. Ogden. Ann Arbor, University of Michigan Press, 1955. xi, 224 p.
55-008649   704.943
Nature (Aesthetics) Landscape. Landscape painting -- England. England -- Civilization.

BH301.L3 W8 1995
Wu, Jiahua,
A comparative study of landscape aesthetics: landscape morphology/ Jiahua Wu. Lewiston, N.Y.: Edwin Mellen Press, c1995. xxix, 450 p.
94-040516   704.9/436/01 20 0773491317
Landscape. Nature (Aesthetics) Landscape -- Great Britain. Landscape -- China. Aesthetics, British. Aesthetics, Chinese.

BH301.M54.A57 1983
The Anti-aesthetic: essays on postmodern culture/ edited by Hal Foster. Port Townsend, Wash.: Bay Press, 1983. xvi, 159 p.
83-070650   909.82 094192002X
Modernism (Aesthetics) Civilization, Modern -- 1950-

BH301.M54.B47 1994
Berman, Art, 1938-
Preface to modernism/ Art Berman. Urbana: University of Illinois Press, c1994. xii, 354 p.
93-036653   190 0252021037
Modernism (Aesthetics) Philosophy, Modern -- 19th century. Philosophy, Modern -- 20th century.

BH301.M54.C34 1987
Calinescu, Matei.
Five faces of modernity: modernism, avant-garde, decadence, kitsch, postmodernism/ by Matei Calinescu. Durham: Duke University Press, 1987. xii, 395 p.
86-032756 111/.85 082230726X
Kitsch. Decadence in literature. Modernism (Aesthetics)

BH301.M54.L37 1990
Larsen, Neil.
Modernism and hegemony: a materialist critique of aesthetic agencies/ Neil Larsen; foreword by Jaime Concha. Minneapolis: University of Minnesota Press, c1990. xlvi, 125 p.
89-030475 111/.85/0904 0816617848
Modernism (Art) Ideology. Aesthetics, Modern -- 20th century.

BH301.M54.M44 1985
Megill, Allan.
Prophets of extremity: Nietzsche, Heidegger, Foucault, Derrida/ Allan Megill. Berkeley: University of California Press, c1985. xxiii, 399 p.
84-008518 190 0520052390
Nietzsche, Friedrich Wilhelm, -- 1844-1900. Heidegger, Martin, -- 1889-1976. Foucault, Michel. Modernism (Aesthetics) Philosophy, Modern -- 19th century. Philosophy, Modern -- 20th century.

BH301.N3.B37 1995
Barrow, John D., 1952-
The artful universe/ John D. Barrow. Oxford: Clarendon Press; 1995. x, 274 p.
95-010805 111/.85 0198539967
Nature (Aesthetics) Philosophy of nature.

BH301.N3.H555 1996
Hildebrandt, Stefan.
The parsimonious universe: shape and form in the natural world/ Stefan Hildebrandt, Anthony Tromba. New York: Copernicus, c1996. xiii, 330 p.
95-019692 117 0387979913
Nature (Aesthetics) Form (Philosophy) Motion.

BH301.N3.T47 1983
Thacker, Christopher.
The wildness pleases: the origins of romanticism/ by Christopher Thacker. London: Croom Helm; 1983. vi, 282 p.
82-010769 111/.85 0312879601
Nature (Aesthetics)

BH301.P45.S74 1990
Stephan, Michael, 1948-
A transformational theory of aesthetics/ Michael Stephan. London; Routledge, 1990. xii, 242 p.
89-070164 111/.85 0415041961
Aesthetics -- Psychological aspects.

BH301.P78.S34 1992
Schenk, Ronald, 1944-
The soul of beauty: a psychological investigation of appearance/ Ronald Schenk. Lewisburg [Pa.]: Bucknell University Press; c1992. 176 p.
91-055125 150/.1 0838752144
Aesthetics -- Psychological aspects -- History. Psychology and philosophy -- History.

BH301.R47.W35 1990
Walton, Kendall L., 1939-
Mimesis as make-believe: on the foundations of the representational arts/ Kendall L. Walton. Cambridge, Mass.: Harvard University Press, 1990. xiv, 450 p.
89-039455 111/.85 0674576195
Aesthetics. Representation (Philosophy) Mimesis in literature.

BH301.S7B83 2000
Budick, Sanford, 1942-
The Western theory of tradition: terms and paradigms of the cultural sublime/ Sanford Budick. New Haven: Yale University Press, c2000. xxii, 293 p.
99-086678 111/.85 0300081510
Sublime, The -- History. Tradition (Philosophy) -- History. Civilization, Western -- History.

BH301.S7.D4 1989
De Bolla, Peter, 1957-
The discourse of the sublime: readings in history, aesthetics, and the subject/ Peter de Bolla. Oxford [England]; B. Blackwell, 1989. vii, 324 p.
88-024253 126/.09/033 0631161732
Sublime, The -- History -- 18th century. Aesthetics, British -- 18th century. Individualism -- History -- 18th century.

BH301.S7.M6 1960
Monk, Samuel Holt.
The sublime; a study of critical theories in XVIII-century England. With a new pref. by the author. [Ann Arbor] University of Michigan Press [1960] 250 p.
60-063909 111.85
Sublime, The. Aesthetics, British -- 18th century. Criticism -- Great Britain -- History -- 18th century.

BH301.S7.W44
Weiskel, Thomas.
The romantic sublime: studies in the structure and psychology of transcendence/ Thomas Weiskel. Baltimore: Johns Hopkins University Press, c1976. xi, 220 p.
75-036932 128/.3 0801817706
Sublime, The. Transcendence (Philosophy) Romanticism.

BH301.S75.F6 1960
Fowlie, Wallace, 1908-
Age of surrealism. Bloomington, Indiana University Press [1960] 215 p.
60-008309 709.04
Surrealism.

BH301.S75.N33
Nadeau, Maurice.
The history of surrealism. Translated from the French by Richard Howard. With an introd. by Roger Shattuck. New York, Macmillan [1965] 351 p.
65-023834 709.04
Surrealism. Arts, Modern -- 20th century.

BH301.T7.G67 2001
Gordon, Paul, 1951-
Tragedy after Nietzsche: rapturous superabundance/ Paul Gordon. Urbana: University of Illinois Press, c2001. 162 p.
99-050656 128 0252025741
Nietzsche, Friedrich Wilhelm, -- 1844-1900. -- Geburt der Tragodie.Tragic, The.

BH301.T7 P45 2000
Philosophy and tragedy/ edited by Miguel de Beistegui and Simon Sparks. London; Routledge, 2000. ix, 246 p.
99-028329 128 21 0415191424
Tragic, The -- History -- 19th century. Philosophy, German -- 19th century. Tragic, The -- History -- 20th century. Philosophy, German -- 20th century.

BH301.T7.T72 1993
Tragedy and philosophy/ edited by N. Georgopoulos. New York: St. Martin's Press, 1993. x, 221 p.
92-037143 111/.85 0312089384
Tragic, The.

BH301.T77.R36 1997
Rapaport, Herman, 1947-
Is there truth in art?/ Herman Rapaport. Ithaca: Cornell University Press, 1997. xvii, 221 p.
96-028088 111/.85 0801432758
Truth (Aesthetics) Truth.

BJ10-1725 Ethics

BJ10 Societies — International societies and movements, A-Z

BJ10.M6 H567 1962
Howard, Peter,
Frank Buchman's secret. [1st American ed.] Garden City, N.Y., Doubleday [1962, c1961] 142 p.
62-015095 248/.25
Buchman, Frank Nathan Daniel, 1878-1961. Moral re-armament.

BJ10.M6.H63 1951b
Howard, Peter, 1908-1965.
The world rebuilt, the true story of Frank Buchman and the men and women of moral re-armament. London, Blandford Press [1951] 232 p.
51-001609   248/.25/0924
Buchman, Frank Nathan Daniel, -- 1878-1961.Moral re-armament. Moral re-armament -- Biography.

BJ21 Collected works (nonserial) — Polyglot

BJ21.F4
Feinberg, Joel,
Moral concepts; edited by Joel Feinberg. London, Oxford U.P., 1969. vi, 184 p.
78-459821   170/.8   0199750129
Ethics -- Addresses, essays, lectures.

BJ21.F6
Foot, Philippa.
Theories of ethics; edited by Philippa Foot. London, Oxford U.P., 1967. 188 p.
68-074186   171/.08
Ethics.

BJ21.G38
Gauthier, David P.,
Morality and rational self-interest. Edited by David P. Gauthier. Englewood Cliffs, N.J., Prentice-Hall [1970] viii, 184 p.
78-113847   171/.5   0136008909
Ethics -- Addresses, essays, lectures. Rationalism -- Addresses, essays, lectures. Egoism -- Addresses, essays, lectures.

BJ21.H8
Hudson, W. D.
The is-ought question: a collection of papers on the central problems in moral philosophy, edited by W. D. Hudson. London, Macmillan, 1969. 271 p.
74-444093   170/.8   0333101782
Ethics -- Addresses, essays, lectures.

BJ21.M28
Margolis, Joseph, 1924-
Contemporary ethical theory; a book of readings, [edited] by Joseph Margolis. New York, Random House [1966] viii, 536 p.
66-026073   170.8
Ethics.

BJ21.M58
Moral development and behavior: theory, research, and social issues/ Thomas Lickona, editor, consulting editors, Gilbert Geis, Lawrence Kohlberg. New York: Holt, Rinehart and Winston, c1976. xiv, 430 p.
75-029471   170   0030028116
Ethics -- Addresses, essays, lectures. Social ethics -- Addresses, essays, lectures. Moral education -- Addresses, essays, lectures.

BJ21.M83
Murphy, Jeffrie G.,
An introduction to moral and social philosophy; basic readings in theory and practice. Edited by Jeffrie G. Murphy. Belmont, Calif., Wadsworth Pub. Co. [1973] xi, 528 p.
72-091356   170/.8   0534002404
Ethics. Social history -- 20th century.

BJ21.P33
Pahel, Kenneth,
Readings in contemporary ethical theory. Edited by Kenneth Pahel & Marvin Schiller. Englewood Cliffs, N.J., Prentice-Hall [1970] ix, 572 p.
78-087265   170/.8   0137558198
Ethics.

BJ21.R62 1991
Roth, John K.
Ethics, an annotated bibliography/ John K. Roth, with the assistance of Teresa A. Gonsalves ... [et al.]. Pasadena, Calif.: Salem Press, c1991. xiii, 169 p.
90-048585   016.17   0893566624
Ethics -- Abstracts.

BJ21.S4 1970
Sellars, Wilfrid,
Readings in ethical theory, edited by Wilfrid Sellars [and] John Hospers. New York, Appleton-Century-Crofts [1970] x, 786 p.
75-107425   170/.8   039079550X
Ethics.

BJ37 Philosophy. Methodology. Relation to other topics

BJ37.A3
Adams, E. M. 1919-
Ethical naturalism and the modern world-view/ by E.M. Adams. Chapel Hill: University of North Carolina Press, c1960. xii, 229 p.
60-004135   170
Ethics. Naturalism.

BJ37.B27 1990
Barden, Garrett.
After principles/ Garrett Barden. Notre Dame: University of Notre Dame Press, c1990. x, 160 p.
89-040743   170   0268006261
Ethics. Conduct of life. Tradition (Philosophy)

BJ37.B43 1998
Beckwith, Francis.
Relativism: feet firmly planted in mid-air/ Francis J. Beckwith and Gregory Koukl. Grand Rapids, Mich.: Baker Books, c1998. 188 p.
98-017425   171/.7 21   0801058066
Ethical relativism.

BJ37.B77
Brandt, Richard B.
Ethical theory; the problems of normative and critical ethics. Englewood Cliffs, N.J., Prentice-Hall, 1959. 538 p.
59-010075   170
Ethics.

BJ37.M23 1990
MacIntyre, Alasdair C.
Three rival versions of moral enquiry: encyclopaedia, genealogy, and tradition: being Gifford lectures delivered in the University of Edinburgh in 1988/ by Alasdair MacIntyre. Notre Dame, Ind.: University of Notre Dame Press, c1990. x, 241 p.
89-029275   170/.9/034   0268018715
Aristotle -- Ethics. Augustine, -- Saint, Bishop of Hippo -- Ethics. Thomas, -- Aquinas, Saint, -- 1225?-1274 -- Ethics. Ethics -- Methodology. Thomists. Ethics -- Study and Teaching.

BJ37.M24
Mackie, J. L.
Ethics: inventing right and wrong/ [by] J. L. Mackie. Harmondsworth; Penguin, 1977. 249 p.
78-300959   170   0140219579
Ethics.

BJ37.M818 1990
Moral expertise: studies in practical and professional ethics/ edited by Don MacNiven. London; Routledge, 1990. xix, 231 p.
88-026814   174 19   0415035767
Ethics. Professional ethics.

BJ37.P7
Prior, Arthur N.
Logic and the basis of ethics. Oxford, Clarendon Press, 1949. xi, 111 p.
50-001527   170
Ethics.

BJ37.S35 1990
Scott, Charles E.
The question of ethics: Nietzsche, Foucault, Heidegger/ Charles E. Scott. Bloomington: Indiana University Press, c1990. xii, 225 p.
89-046341   170   0253351235
Nietzsche, Friedrich Wilhelm, -- 1844-1900 -- Ethics. Foucault, Michel -- Ethics. Heidegger, Martin, -- 1889-1976 -- Ethics. Ethics, Modern -- 20th century. Ethics -- Methodology.

BJ37.T55 1999
Timmons, Mark,
Morality without foundations: a defense of ethical contextualism/ Mark Timmons. New York: Oxford University Press, 1999. viii, 269 p.
97-026312   170/.42 21   019511731X
Ethics. Naturalism.

BJ37.V4
Veatch, Henry Babcock.
Rational man; a modern interpretation of Aristotelian ethics. Bloomington, Indiana University Press [1962] 226 p.
62-016161   170   0253200717
Aristotle.Ethics.

BJ42 Philosophy. Methodology. Relation to other topics — Relation to rhetoric

BJ42.L48 1998
Levine, Peter, 1967-
Living without philosophy: on narrative, rhetoric, and morality/ Peter Levine. Albany, N.Y.: State University of New York Press, c1998. xi, 292 p.
98-007524   170   079143897X
Ethics. Description (Rhetoric)

BJ43 Philosophy. Methodology. Relation to other topics — Relation to logic

BJ43.B55 1961
Blanshard, Brand, 1892-1987.
Reason and goodness.   London, G. Allen & Unwin. [1961] 451 p.
61-003548   170
Ethics. Reason.

BJ43.S8
Stevenson, Charles L. 1908-
Ethics and language, by Charles L. Stevenson ... New Haven, Yale University Press; 1944. xi, 338 p.
45-001043   171
Meaning (Psychology) Judgment (Logic) Ethics.

BJ43.T47 1999
Thomson, Anne.
Critical reasoning in ethics: a practical introduction/ Anne Thomson. London; Routledge, 1999. vii, 214 p.
98-031830   170   0415171849
Ethics. Social ethics. Logic.

BJ43.T6
Toulmin, Stephen Edelston.
An examination of the place of reason in ethics. Cambridge [Eng.] University Press, 1950. xiv, 228 p.
51-005171   170
Reason. Ethics.

BJ44 Philosophy. Methodology. Relation to other topics — Relation to language

BJ44.L36 1991
Lang, Berel.
Writing and the moral self/ Berel Lang. New York: Routledge, 1991. ix, 182 p.
90-025234   808/.001   0415902959
Language and ethics. English language -- Philosophy. Style (Philosophy)

BJ45 Philosophy. Methodology. Relation to other topics — Relation to psychology. Morale

BJ45.C4313 2000
Changeux, Jean-Pierre.
What makes us think?: a neuroscientist and a philosopher argue about ethics, human nature, and the brain/ Jean-Pierre Changeux and Paul Ricoeur; translated by M.B. DeBevoise. Princeton, N.J.: Princeton University Press, c2000. x, 335 p.
00-024827   153   0691009406
Changeux, Jean-Pierre -- Interviews. Ricoeur, Paul -- Interviews.   Ethics. Neuroscientists -- France -- Interviews. Neuropsychology.

BJ45.F53 1991
Flanagan, Owen J.
Varieties of moral personality: ethics and psychological realism/ Owen Flanagan. Cambridge, Mass.: Harvard University Press, 1991. xiv, 393 p.
90-039222   170/.1/9   0674932188
Ethics. Psychology and philosophy.

BJ45.F7
Fromm, Erich, 1900-
Man for himself, an inquiry into the psychology of ethics.   New York, Rinehart [1947] xiv, 254 p.
47-012365   171
Humanistic ethics.

BJ45.H7
Holt, Edwin B. 1873-1946.
The Freudian wish and its place in ethics, by Edwin B. Holt. New York, H. Holt and company, 1915.
16-002010
Freud, Sigmund, -- 1856-1939.Psychology. Ethics.

BJ45.I34 1990
Identity, character, and morality: essays in moral psychology/ edited by Owen Flanagan and Amelie Oksenberg Rorty. Cambridge, Mass.: MIT Press, c1990. vii, 487 p.
90-034927   170   0262061155
Ethics Psychology and philosophy.

BJ45.M67 1993
The Moral self/ edited by Gil G. Noam and Thomas E. Wren in cooperation with Gertrud Nunner-Winkler and Wolfgang Edelstein. Cambridge, Mass.: MIT Press, c1993. xi, 400 p.
92-021501   170   0262140527
Ethics. Moral development. Psychology and philosophy.

BJ45.W35 1991
Wallwork, Ernest.
Psychoanalysis and ethics/ Ernest Wallwork. New Haven: Yale University Press, c1991. 344 p.
91-015276   171   0300048785
Freud, Sigmund, -- 1856-1939 -- Ethics.Psychoanalysis and philosophy. Ethics.

BJ45.5 Philosophy. Methodology. Relation to other topics — Relation to cognitive science. Philosophy of mind

BJ45.5.M56 1996
Mind and morals: essays on cognitive science and ethics/ edited by Larry May, Marilyn Friedman, and Andy Clark. Cambridge, Mass.: MIT Press, c1996. x, 315 p.
95-022361   170   026213313X
Cognitive science -- Moral and ethical aspects. Cognitive science. Ethics.

BJ46 Philosophy. Methodology. Relation to other topics — Relation to aesthetics (Art, literature, etc.)

BJ46.H37 1999
Harpham, Geoffrey Galt, 1946-
Shadows of ethics: criticism and the just society/ Geoffrey Galt Harpham. Durham, NC: Duke University Press, 1999. xiv, 282 p.
98-055943   170   0822323001
Ethics, Modern. Criticism.

BJ46.M34 1997
McGinn, Colin, 1950-
Ethics, evil, and fiction/ Colin McGinn. Oxford: Clarendon Press; 1997. x, 186 p.
97-004157   170   0198237162
Ethics. Ethics in literature.

BJ46.N87 1990
Nussbaum, Martha Craven,
Love's knowledge: essays on philosophy and literature/ Martha C. Nussbaum. New York: Oxford University Press, 1990. xiv, 403 p.
89-039728   170 20   0195054571
Ethics. Literature and morals. Philosophy in literature.

BJ47 Philosophy. Methodology. Relation to other topics — Relation to religion and the supernatural

BJ47.E84 1992
Ethics, religion, and the good society: new directions in a pluralistic world/ Joseph Runzo, editor. 1st ed. Louisville, Ky.: Westminster/John Knox Press, c1992. xxiii, 200 p.
91-048260   291.5 20   0664252850
Religion and ethics. Religious pluralism. Religions.

BJ47.G74 1988
Green, Ronald Michael.
Religion and moral reason: a new method for comparative study/ Ronald M. Green. New York: Oxford University Press, 1988. xvi, 278 p.
87-015230   291.5   0195043405
Religion and ethics. Revelation. Reason.

BJ47.L5 1934
Lippmann, Walter, 1889-1974.
A preface to morals. New York, The Macmillan company, 1934. viii, 348 p.
37-005080
Ethics. Philosophy and religion.

BJ51 Philosophy. Methodology. Relation to other topics — Relation to history and sociology

BJ51.S57 1981
Singer, Peter, 1946-
The expanding circle: ethics and sociobiology/ Peter Singer. New York: Farrar, Straus & Giroux, 1981. xii, 190 p.
80-020718   170/.42   0374234965
Ethics. Sociobiology.

BJ52 Philosophy. Methodology. Relation to other topics — Relation to anthropology and culture

BJ52.C66 1999
Cook, John W.
Morality and cultural differences/ John W. Cook. New York: Oxford University Press, 1999. x, 204 p.
98-027685   171/.7 21   0195126793
Ethics. Anthropology. Ethical relativism.

BJ52.M66 1997
Moody-Adams, Michele M.
Fieldwork in familiar places: morality, culture, and philosophy/ Michele M. Moody-Adams. Cambridge, Mass.: Harvard University Press, 1997. x, 260 p.
97-012694   170/.42 21   0674299531
Ethics. Anthropology. Ethical relativism. Female gang members.

BJ52.5 Philosophy. Methodology. Relation to other topics — Relation to agriculture

BJ52.5.E84 1991
Ethics and agriculture: an anthology on current issues in world context/ edited by Charles V. Blatz. Moscow, Idaho: University of Idaho Press, 1991. x, 674 p.
91-011713   174/.963 20   0893011347
Agriculture -- Moral and ethical aspects.

BJ52.5.L48 1995
Lehman, Hugh.
Rationality and ethics in agriculture/ Hugh Lehman. Moscow, Idaho: University of Idaho Press, 1995. xi, 228 p.
94-045942   174/.963   0893011797
Agriculture -- Moral and ethical aspects. Rationalism.

BJ52.5.T539 1998
Thompson, Paul B., 1951-
Agricultural ethics: research, teaching, and public policy/ Paul B. Thompson. Ames: Iowa State University Press, 1998. xi, 239 p.
97-045232   174/.963   0813828066
Agriculture -- Moral and ethical aspects.

BJ55 Philosophy. Methodology. Relation to other topics — Relation to law and politics

BJ55.G73 2000
Gr^ciâc, Joseph.
Ethics and political theory/ Joseph Gr^ciâc. Lanham, Md.: University Press of America, c2000. vi, 251 p.
99-047772   172 21   0761815392
Political ethics.

BJ55.L53 1987
Liberty, equality, and law: selected Tanner lectures on moral philosophy/ John Rawls ... [et al.]; Sterling M. McMurrin, editor. Salt Lake City: University of Utah Press, 1987. x, 205 p.
86-028300   340/.11 19   0874802717
Law and ethics. Law -- Philosophy. Liberty. Equality. Self-control.

BJ55.L95 1984
Lyons, David, 1935-
Ethics and the rule of law/ David Lyons. Cambridge [Cambridgeshire]; Cambridge University Press, 1984. x, 229 p.
83-007687   174/.3   0521257859
Law and ethics.

BJ55.P67 1997
Posner, Richard A.
The problematics of moral and legal theory/ Richard A. Posner. Cambridge, Mass.: Belknap Press of Harvard University Press, 1999. x, 320 p.
98-029596   170   0674707710
Law and ethics. Sociological jurisprudence.

BJ55.R44 1997
Reed, Donald R. C.
Following Kohlberg: liberalism and the practice of democratic community/ Donald R.C. Reed. Notre Dame, Ind.: University of Notre Dame Press, c1997. xv, 280 p.
97-021491   170/.92   0268028516
Kohlberg, Lawrence, -- 1927-Ethics. Political ethics. Moral development.

BJ55.T46 1990
Thomson, Judith Jarvis.
The realm of rights/ Judith Jarvis Thomson. Cambridge, Mass.: Harvard University Press, 1990. viii, 383 p.
90-031045   170   0674749480
Law and ethics.

BJ57 Philosophy. Methodology. Relation to other topics — Relation to science

BJ57.D35 1998
Daleiden, Joseph L.
The science of morality: the individual, community, and future generations/ Joseph L. Daleiden. Amherst, N.Y.: Prometheus Books, 1998. 534 p.
98-007119   170   1573922250
Ethics. Science -- Moral and ethical aspects.

BJ57.S34 1989
Scientists and their responsibility/ William R. Shea and Beat Sitter, editors. Canton, MA: Watson Pub. International, 1989. xii, 348 p.
89-005249   174/.95   0881350540
Science and ethics.

BJ58 Philosophy. Methodology. Relation to other topics — Relation to biology

BJ58.A43 1987
Alexander, Richard D.
The biology of moral systems/ Richard D. Alexander. Hawthorne, N.Y.: A. de Gruyter, c1987. xx, 301 p.
86-025897   171/.7 19   0202011747
Ethics. Bioethics. Arms race -- Moral and ethical aspects.

BJ63 Dictionaries. Encyclopedias

BJ63.D53 1996
Dictionary of ethics, theology, and society/ edited by Paul Barry Clarke and Andrew Linzey. London; Routledge, 1996. xxxiii, 926 p.
95-238078   170/.3 21   0415062128
Ethics -- Dictionaries. Social ethics -- Dictionaries. Theology -- Dictionaries.

BJ63.E44 1998
Encyclopedia of applied ethics/ [editor-in-chief, Ruth Chadwick]. San Diego: Academic Press, c1998. 4 v.
97-074395   170/.3   0122270657
Applied ethics -- Encyclopedias.

BJ63.E45 2001
Encyclopedia of ethics/ Lawrence C. Becker and Charlotte B. Becker, editors. 2nd ed. New York: Routledge, 2001. 3 v. (xxxv, 1977 p.);
2001-019657   170/.3 21   0415936756
Ethics -- Encyclopedias.

BJ63.E46 1999
Encyclopedia of ethics/ Susan Neiburg Terkel, consulting editor; R. Shannon Duval, editor. New York: Facts On File, c1999. xvi, 302 p.
98-039932   170/.3   0816033110
Ethics -- Encyclopedias.

BJ63.F4
Ferm, Vergilius Ture Anselm, 1896-1974.
Encyclopedia of morals. New York, Philosophical Library [1956] x, 682 p.
56-058813   170.3
Ethics -- Dictionaries.

BJ63.H47 1996
Hester, Joseph P.
Encyclopedia of values and ethics /Joseph P. Hester. Santa Barbara, Calif.: ABC-CLIO, c1996. xiii, 376 p.
96-036928   170/.3   087436857X
Ethics -- Encyclopedias. Values -- Encyclopedias.

BJ63.M3
Macquarrie, John.
Dictionary of Christian ethics, edited by John Macquarrie. Philadelphia, Westminster Press [1967] viii, 366 p.
67-017412   241/.03
Ethics -- Dictionaries. Christian ethics -- Dictionaries.

BJ66 Study and teaching. Research — General works

BJ66.N37 2002
Nash, Robert J.
"Real world" ethics: frameworks for educators and human service professionals/ Robert J. Nash; foreword by Jonas F. Soltis. 2nd ed. New York: Teachers College Press, c2002. xii, 224 p.
2002-024575   170/.71 21   0807742562
Applied ethics -- Study and teaching. Ethics -- Study and teaching. Professional ethics -- Study and teaching.

BJ69 Comparative ethics

BJ69.A5 1998
An, Ok-Sun,
Compassion and benevolence: a comparative study of early Buddhist and classical Confucian ethics/ Ok-Sun An. New York: Peter Lang, 1998. x, 180 p.
97-005219   294.3/5 21   0820438014
Ethics, Comparative. Buddhist ethics. Confucian ethics. Compassion -- Religious aspects -- Buddhism. Benevolence.

BJ71 History — General works — Polyglot

BJ71.A84 1997
Ashby, Warren, 1920-
A comprehensive history of western ethics: what do we believe?/ Warren Ashby; edited with a foreword by W. Allen Ashby. Amherst, N.Y.: Prometheus Books, 1997.
97-008613   170/.9   1573921521
Ethics -- History.

BJ71.B69 1959
Brinton, Crane, 1898-1968.
A history of Western morals. New York, Harcourt, Brace [1959] 504 p.
59-006426   170/.9
Moral conditions. Ethics -- History.

BJ71.E84 1989
Ethics in the history of western philosophy/ edited by Robert J. Cavalier, James Gouinlock, and James P. Sterba. New York: St. Martin's Press, 1989. xiii, 434 p.
88-018182   170/.9   0312021453
Ethics -- History.

BJ71.K75
Krook, Dorothea.
Three traditions of moral thought. Cambridge [Eng.] University Press, 1959. xiii, 354 p.
59-004821
Ethics -- History. Love.

BJ71.M3 1998
MacIntyre, Alasdair C.
A short history of ethics: a history of moral philosophy from the Homeric Age to the twentieth century/ Alasdair MacIntyre. Notre Dame, Ind.: University of Notre Dame Press, 1998. xxii, 280 p.
97-022280   170/.9   026801759X
Ethics -- History.

BJ71.M35
Markun, Leo, 1901-
Mrs. Grundy: a history of four centuries of morals intended to illuminate present problems in Great Britain and the United States/ by Leo Markun. New York; D. Appleton and Company, 1930. xii, 665 p.
30-013518   170.9
Ethics -- History. Great Britain -- Moral conditions. United States -- Moral conditions.

BJ71.M5 1977
Mencken, H. L. 1880-1956.
Treatise on right and wrong/ H. L. Mencken. New York: Octagon Books, 1977, c1934. viii, 331 p.
76-054778   170/.9   0374955794
Ethics -- History. Ethics.

BJ71.S55 1960
Sidgwick, Henry, 1838-1900.
Outlines of the history of ethics for English readers/ by Henry Sidgwick; with an additional chapter by Alban G. Widgery. Boston: Beacon Press, 1960. xxvi, 342 p.
60-050661   170.9
Ethics -- History.

BJ72 History —
General works — French

BJ72.M313
Maritain, Jacques, 1882-1973.
Moral philosophy; an historical and critical survey of the great systems.   New York, Scribner [1964] xii, 468 p.
64-014663   170.9
Ethics -- History.

BJ78 History —
General works — Other, A-Z

BJ78.D3.L613 1997
Logstrup, K. E. 1905-
The ethical demand/ Knud Ejler Logstrup. Notre Dame, Ind.: University of Notre Dame Press, c1997. xxxviii, 300 p.
96-026430   170   0268009341
Ethics.

BJ101-214 History —
By period — Ancient

BJ101.F4
Ferguson, John, 1921-
Moral values in the ancient world.   London, Methuen [1958] 256 p.
59-000133   170.901
Ethics -- History.

BJ101.H35
Harkness, Georgia Elma, 1891-1974.
The sources of Western morality, from primitive society through the beginnings of Christianity. New York, Scribner, 1954. 257 p.
54-010370   170.901
Ethics -- History.

BJ117.B76 1991
Brokaw, Cynthia Joanne.
The ledgers of merit and demerit: social change and moral order in late imperial China/ Cynthia J. Brokaw. Princeton, N.J.: Princeton University Press, c1991. x, 287 p.
90-009059   170/.951/09031   0691055432
Ethics -- China -- History -- 16th century. Ethics -- China -- History -- 17th century. Moral education -- China -- History. China -- Social conditions -- 960-1644.

BJ117.C83 1998
Cua, A. S. 1932-
Moral vision and tradition: essays in Chinese ethics/ A. S. Cua. Washington, D.C.: Catholic University of America Press, c1998. xiii, 357 p.
96-053933   171   0813208904
Ethics, Chinese. Philosophy, Confucian. Philosophy, Chinese.

BJ117.E2
Eberhard, Wolfram, 1909-
Guilt and sin in traditional China.   Berkeley, University of California Press, 1967. 141 p.
67-012297   170/.951
Ethics -- China. Guilt. Guilt and culture -- China.

BJ117.I8 1993
Ivanhoe, P. J.
Confucian moral self cultivation/ Philip J. Ivanhoe. New York: P. Lang, c1993. xii, 115 p.
93-024085   171   0820422002
Ethics -- China. Philosophy, Confucian.

BJ117.I83 2002
Ivanhoe, P. J.
Ethics in the Confucian tradition: the thought of Mengzi and Wang Yangming/ Philip J. Ivanhoe. 2nd ed. Indianapolis: Hackett, c2002. xvii, 243 p.
2001-051550   170/.92/251 21   0872205975
Mencius -- Contributions in Confucius ethics. Wang, Yangming, 1472-1529 -- Contributions in Confucius ethics. Confucian ethics.

BJ117.R64 1993
Roetz, Heiner, 1950-
Confucian ethics of the axial age: a reconstruction under the aspect of the breakthrough toward postconventional thinking/ Heiner Roetz. Albany, NY: State University of New York Press, c1993. xiii, 373 p.
92-039938   170/.931   0791416496
Confucian ethics -- History.

BJ117.S87 1998
Svarverud, Rune.
Methods of the way: early Chinese ethical thought/ by Rune   Svarverud. Leiden; Brill, c1998. xvi, 430 p.
98-015905   170/.931 21   9004110100
Chia, I, 200-168 B.C. Hsin shu. Ethics -- China.

BJ117.T44 1988
T ien, Ju-k ang.
Male anxiety and female chastity: a comparative study of Chinese ethical values in Ming-Ch ing times/ by T ien Ju-K ang. Leiden; Brill, 1988. xiii, 172 p.
87-027639   303.3/72 19   9004083618
Ethics -- China. Chastity. Anxiety. China -- Social conditions -- 960-1644.

BJ122.C7 1989
Coward, Harold G.
Hindu ethics: purity, abortion, and euthanasia/ Harold G. Coward, Julius J. Lipner, Katherine K. Young. Albany: State University of New York Press, c1989. 139 p.
87-018075   294.5/48697   0887067638
Hindu ethics. Body, Human -- Religious aspects -- Hinduism. Abortion -- Religious aspects -- Hinduism.

BJ122.H6 1968
Hopkins, Edward Washburn, 1857-1932.
Ethics of India.   Port Washington, N.Y., Kennikat Press [1968, c1924] xiv, 265 p.
68-015828   294.5/48
Hindu ethics.

BJ122.J55 1989
Jhingran, Saral, 1939-
Aspects of Hindu morality/ Saral Jhingran. Delhi: Motilal Banarsidass Publishers, 1989. xvii, 241 p.
89-903053   294.5/48   8120805747
Hindu ethics.

BJ132.B7 1934
Breasted, James Henry, 1865-1935.
Dawn of conscience, by James Henry Breasted. New York, C. Scribner's sons, 1934.
34-007122   170.932
Ethics, Egyptian. Ethics, Jewish.   Egypt -- Civilization. Egypt -- Religion -- History.

BJ161.A2.O3 1969
Oakeley, Hilda Diana, 1867-
Greek ethical thought from Homer to the Stoics. Boston, Beacon Press, 1950. 226 p.
52-008223
English literature -- Translations from Greek. Ethics -- Greece. Greek literature -- Translations into English.

BJ161.B78 1996
Bryant, Joseph M.,
Moral codes and social structure in ancient Greece: a sociology of Greek ethics from Homer to the Epicureans and Stoics/ Joseph M. Bryant. Albany, N.Y.: State University of New York Press, c1996. xv, 575 p.
95-040573   938 20   0791430421
Ethics, Ancient. Knowledge, Sociology of. Epicureans (Greek philosophy) Greece -- Social life and customs. Greece -- Intellectual life -- To 146 B.C. Greece -- Social conditions -- To 146 B.C.

BJ161.C66 1999
Cooper, John M.
Reason and emotion: essays on ancient moral psychology and ethical theory/ John M. Cooper. Princeton, N.J.: Princeton University Press, c1999. xvi, 588 p.
98-011851   170/.938 21   069105875X
Plato -- Ethics. Aristotle -- Ethics. Ethics, Ancient.

BJ161.E84 1998
Ethics/ edited by Stephen Everson. Cambridge
[England]; Cambridge University Press, 1998.
300 p.
97-008899   170/.938   0521381614
Ethics, Ancient.

BJ161.P72 1990
Prior, William J.
Virtue and knowledge: an introduction to ancient
Greek ethics/ William J. Prior. London;
Routledge, 1991. 240 p.
89-049680   170/.938   0415024706
Ethics -- Greece.

BJ171.H35.A56 1993
Annas, Julia.
The morality of happiness/ Julia Annas. New
York: Oxford University Press, 1993. x, 502 p.
92-037003   170/.938   019507999X
Happiness. Ethics, Ancient.

BJ171.R4.A3
Adkins, A. W. H.
Merit and responsibility; a study in Greek
values. Oxford, Clarendon Press, 1960. xiv,
380 p.
60-000811   170.938
Responsibility. Ethics, Greek.

BJ171.V55 H87 2001
Hurka, Thomas,
Virtue, vice, and value/ Thomas Hurka. Oxford;
Oxford University Press, c2001. ix, 272 p.
00-022588   179/.9 21   0195137167
Virtue.

BJ192.N87 2001
Nussbaum, Martha Craven,
The fragility of goodness: luck and ethics in
Greek tragedy and   philosophy/ Martha C.
Nussbaum. Rev. ed. Cambridge, U.K.;
Cambridge University Press, 2001. xliv, 544 p.
00-062128   170/.938 21   0521794722
*Ethics -- Greece -- History. Greek drama
(Tragedy) -- History and criticism. Fortune in
literature. Ethics, Ancient, in literature.*

BJ214.S4 E73
Seneca, Lucius Annaeus,
Letters from a Stoic.Epistulae morales ad
Lucilium [by] Seneca; selected and translated
[from the Latin], with an introduction, by Robin
Campbell. Harmondsworth, Penguin, 1969.
254 p.
70-459637   188   0140442103
*Ethics--Early works to 1800. Conduct of life--
Early works to 1800.*

BJ255 History — By period — Medieval

BJ255.T5.M35 1992
McInerny, Ralph M.
Aquinas on human action: a theory of practice/
Ralph McInerny. Washington, D.C.: Catholic
University of America Press, c1992. ix, 244 p.
90-027754   170   0813207460
*Thomas, -- Aquinas, Saint, -- 1225?-
1274.Human acts -- History of doctrines --
Middle Ages, 600-1500. Act (Philosophy)*

BJ271-285 History — By period — Renaissance

BJ271.S77 1992
Struever, Nancy S.
Theory as practice: ethical inquiry in the
Renaissance/ Nancy S. Struever. Chicago:
University of Chicago Press, c1992. xiii, 246 p.
91-020446   170/.94/09023   0226777421
*Ethics,   Renaissance.   Philosophy,
Renaissance.*

BJ285.B69 1991
Boyle, Robert, 1627-1691.
The early essays and ethics of Robert Boyle/
edited and annotated with an introduction by
John T. Harwood. Carbondale: Southern Illinois
University Press, c1991. lxix, 330 p.
90-048968   170   080931522X
Ethics, Modern -- 17th century.

BJ301-971 History — By period — Modern (1700-   )

BJ301.P66 1991
Poole, Ross, 1938-
Morality and modernity/ Ross Poole. London;
Routledge, 1991. xii, 196 p.
90-039730   170/.9/03   0415036003
Ethics, Modern. Liberalism.

BJ311.N67 1995
Norton, Robert Edward, 1960-
The beautiful soul: aesthetic morality in the
eighteenth century/ Robert E. Norton. Ithaca:
Cornell University Press, 1995. xi, 314 p.
94-037298   170/.9/033   080143050X
*Ethics, Modern -- 18th century. Aesthetics,
Modern -- 18th century. Soul.*

BJ319.B28 1993
Bauman, Zygmunt.
Postmodern ethics/ Zygmunt Bauman. Oxford,
UK; Blackwell, 1993. vi, 255 p.
93-016048   170 20   063118693X
*Ethics,   Modern   --   20th   century.
Postmodernism.*

BJ319.D37 1984
Darwin, Marx, and Freud: their influence on
moral theory/ edited by Arthur L. Caplan and
Bruce Jennings. New York: Plenum Press,
c1984. xxvii, 230 p.
84-001909   170/.92/2 19   0306415305
*Darwin, Charles, 1809-1882 -- Ethics. Marx,
Karl, 1818-1883 -- Ethics. Freud, Sigmund,
1856-1939 -- Influence. Ethics, Modern -- 20th
century.*

BJ319.D47 1993
DePaul, Michael R. 1954-
Balance and refinement: beyond coherence
methods of moral inquiry/ Michael R. DePaul.
London; Routledge, 1993. xii, 245 p.
92-010800   170/.42   0415042208
Ethics, Modern -- 20th century.

BJ319.E7854 1999
The ethics of postmodernity: current trends in
continental thought/ edited by Gary B. Madison
and   Marty   Fairbairn.   Evanston,   Ill.:
Northwestern University Press, c1999. viii,
266 p.
99-021665   170/.9/045 21   0810113759
*Ethics,   Modern   --   20th   century.
Postmodernism.*

BJ319.H25 1987
Hall, Robert T. 1938-
Emile Durkheim: ethics and the sociology of
morals/ Robert T. Hall. New York: Greenwood
Press, 1987. xiv, 234 p.
87-010713   303.3/72   0313258473
*Durkheim,   Emile,   --   1858-1917   --
Contributions in ethics.Ethics, Modern -- 20th
century.*

BJ319.H276 1993
Hannaford, Robert V., 1929-
Moral anatomy and moral reasoning/ Robert V.
Hannaford. Lawrence, Kan.: University Press of
Kansas, c1993. x, 197 p.
93-018648   171/.3   0700606076
*Ethics,   Modern   --   20th   century.   Self
(Philosophy) Reasoning.*

BJ319.H5
Hill, Thomas English.
Contemporary ethical theories.   New York,
Macmillan, 1950. xii, 368 p.
50-008616
Ethics.

BJ319.W3 1978
Warnock, Mary.
Ethics since 1900/ [by] Mary Warnock. Oxford;
Oxford University Press, 1978. ix, 150 p.
79-311024   170/.9/04   0192891081
Ethics, Modern -- 20th century.

BJ352.C66 1999
Cooper, James F., 1935-
Knights of the brush: the Hudson River School and the moral landscape/ James F. Cooper; foreword by Frederick Turner. New York: Hudson Hills Press, c1999. 109 p.
99-016549 758/.1/0973 1555951805
  Values -- United States -- History. Hudson River school of landscape painting.

BJ352.M39 2000
McDowell, Banks.
Ethics and excuses: the crisis in professional responsibility/ Banks McDowell. Westport, Conn.: Quorum Books, 2000. ix, 169 p.
99-462239 174 1567203868
  Ethics -- United States. Responsibility -- United States. Excuses.

BJ352.Q56 1991
Quinby, Lee, 1946-
Freedom, Foucault, and the subject of America/ Lee Quinby. Boston: Northeastern University Press, c1991. xii, 201 p.
91-009577 170/.973 1555531083
  Foucault, Michel.Liberty -- History. Ethics -- United States -- History.

BJ352.S56
Smith, Wilson.
Professors & public ethics; studies of Northern moral philosophers before the Civil War. Ithaca, N.Y., Published for the American Historical Association, [1956] vii, 244 p.
57-013532 170.973
  Ethics -- History -- United States.

BJ352.W65 2001
Wolfe, Alan,
Moral freedom: the impossible idea that defines the way we live now/ Alan Wolfe. 1st ed. New York: W.W. Norton, c2001. 256 p.
00-051969 170/.973 21 0393048438
  Ethics -- United States -- Public opinion. Public opinion -- United States.

BJ354.A42.R4
Aiken, Henry David, 1912-
Reason and conduct; new bearings in moral philosophy. New York, Knopf, 1962. 375 p.
62-012564 171
  Ethics.

BJ414.D873.B37 1998
Barber, Michael D., 1949-
Ethical hermeneutics: rationality in Enrique Dussel's Philosophy of liberation/ by Michael Barber. New York: Fordham University Press, 1998. xxiii, 184 p.
96-037190 199/.8 0823217035
  Dussel, Enrique D. -- Ethics. Levinas, Emmanuel. Ethics, Modern -- 20th century. Social ethics. Hermeneutics.

BJ601.R3
Raphael, D. D. 1916-
British moralists, 1650-1800; selected and edited with comparative notes and analytical index by D. D. Raphael. Oxford, Clarendon P., 1969. 2 v.
77-411471 170/.941/09032 0198750099
  Ethics.

BJ604.P7.T47
Thomas, David Oswald.
The honest mind: the thought and work of Richard Price/ D. O. Thomas. Oxford: Clarendon Press, 1977. xvi, 366 p.
77-374313 192 0198245718
  Price, Richard, -- 1723-1791.

BJ604.S5.S36
Schneewind, J. B. 1930-
Sidgwick's ethics and Victorian moral philosophy/ by J. B. Schneewind. Oxford; Clarendon Press, 1977. xvi, 465 p.
78-301054 170/.92/4 0198245521
  Sidgwick, Henry, -- 1838-1900.Ethics -- England -- History.

BJ703.D44.M38 1995
May, Todd, 1955-
The moral theory of poststructuralism/ Todd May. University Park, Pa.: Pennsylvania State University Press, c1995. 152 p.
94-045435 170/.944 0271014687
  Foucault, Michel -- Ethics. Deleuze, Gilles -- Ethics. Lyotard, Jean Francois -- Ethics. Ethics -- France. Ethics, Modern -- 20th century. Poststructuralism.

BJ966.M3 1984
Madsen, Richard, 1941-
Morality and power in a Chinese village/ Richard Madsen. Berkeley: University of California Press, c1984. xvi, 283 p.
83-004887 170/.951 0520047974
  Ethics -- China -- History -- 20th century. Confucianism. China -- Politics and government -- 1949-

BJ970.C37 2001
Carter, Robert Edgar,
Encounter with enlightenment: a study of Japanese ethics/ Robert E. Carter; foreword by Yuasa Yasuo. Albany, NY: State University of New York Press, c2001. xxxiii, 258 p.
00-046356 170/.952 21 0791450171
  Ethics -- Japan. Enlightenment -- Japan.

BJ971.B8 B56 1994
Blomberg, Catharina.
The heart of the warrior: origins and religious background of the Samurai system in feudal Japan/ Catharnia Blomberg. Sandgate, Folkestone, Kent: Japan Library, 1994. xiii, 226 p.
93-190707 170/.44/0952 20 1873410131
  Bushido. Samurai -- Conduct of life.

BJ971.B8.Y333313
Mishima, Yukio, 1925-1970.
The way of the samurai: Yukio Mishima on Hagakure in modern life/ [by Yukio Mishima]; translated by Kathryn N. Sparling. New York: Basic Books, c1977. x, 166 p.
75-036381 170/.952 0465090893
  Yamamoto, Tsunetomo, -- 1659-1719. -- Hagakure.Bushido.

BJ971.S5 S29 1993
Sawada, Janine Anderson,
Confucian values and popular Zen: Sekimon shingaku in eighteenth-century Japan/ Janine Anderson Sawada. Honolulu: University of Hawaii Press, c1993. xi, 256 p.
92-045047 299/.56 20 0824814142
  Shingaku. Confucianism -- Japan -- History -- 18th century.

BJ1005-1031 General works, treatises, and textbooks — English — General works

BJ1005.H8 1957
Hume, David,
An inquiry concerning the principles of morals; with a supplement: A dialogue. New York, Liberal Arts Press [1957] lxiv, 158 p.
57-001076
  Ethics. [from old catalog]

BJ1005.S59
Smith, Adam, 1723-1790.
Adam Smith's moral and political philosophy; edited with an introd. by Herbert W. Schneider. New York, Hafner, 1948. xxviii, 484 p.
49-001022 170
  Ethics. Economics.

BJ1008.B8 1962b
Bradley, F. H. 1846-1924.
Ethical studies/ by F.H. Bradley. Oxford: Clarendon Press; [1962, c1927] xvi, 344 p.
94-151540 0198810393
  Ethics.

BJ1008.S5 1981
Sidgwick, Henry, 1838-1900.
The methods of ethics/ Henry Sidgwick; foreword by John Rawls. Indianapolis: Hackett Pub. Co., 1981. xxxviii, 528 p.
81-085772 170 0915145294
  Ethics.

BJ1011.B45
Binkley, Luther John, 1925-
Contemporary ethical theories/ by Luther J. Binkley. New York: Philosophical Library, 1961. 203 p.
61-010605 171
  Ethics.

BJ1011.C27
Carritt, E. F. 1876-1964.
Ethical and political thinking. Oxford [Eng.]
Clarendon Press, 1947. xx, 186 p.
47-007789   170
Ethics. Political ethics.

BJ1011.E84
Ewing, A. C. 1899-
Second thoughts in moral philosophy.   New
York, Macmillan [1959] 190 p.
59-065060
Ethics.

BJ1011 .F57 1957
Fite, Warner, 1867-1955.
The examined life; an adventure in moral
philosophy.   Bloomington, Indiana University
Press [1957] x, 276 p.
57-007879   170
Ethics.

BJ1011.H48
Hill, Thomas English.
Ethics in theory and practice.   New York,
Crowell, 1956. 431 p.
56-007455   170
Ethics.

BJ1011.M69
Montefiore, Alan.
A modern introduction to moral philosophy.
London, Routledge and Paul [1958] 213 p.
59-024410
Ethics.

BJ1011.M7 1966
Moore, G. E. 1873-1958.
Ethics, by G.E. Moore. London, Oxford U.P.,
1966. 137 p.
67-073816   170
Ethics.

BJ1011.R75
Ross, W. D. 1877-
Foundations of ethics; the Gifford lectures
delivered in the University of Aberdeen, 1935-6,
by Sir W. David Ross ... Oxford, The Clarendon
Press, 1939. xvi, 328 p.
40-004299   170
Ethics.

BJ1011.T18 1937
Taylor, A. E. 1869-1945.
The faith of a moralist; Gifford lectures
delivered in the University of St. Andrews,
1926-1928, by A. E. Taylor London, Macmillan
and co., limited, 1937. 2 v. in 1
37-023815
Natural theology. Philosophy and religion.
Ethics.

BJ1012.A29 1991
Adler, Mortimer Jerome, 1902-
Desires, right & wrong: the ethics of enough/
Mortimer J. Adler. New York: Macmillan;
c1991. 200 p.
91-016382   170   0025002813
Ethics. Desire (Philosophy)

BJ1012.A45 2000
Almeder, Robert F.
Human happiness and morality: a brief
introduction to ethics/ Robert Almeder.
Amherst, N.Y.: Prometheus Books, 2000. 212 p.
99-048053   170   1573927597
Ethics. Happiness.

BJ1012.A66 1988
Applied ethics and ethical theory/ edited by
David M. Rosenthal and Fadlou Shehadi;
foreword by Margaret P. Battin and Leslie P.
Francis. Salt Lake City: University of Utah
Press, 1988. xxii, 325 p.
88-014304   170   087480289X
Applied ethics. Ethics. Social ethics.

BJ1012.A85 1987
Attfield, Robin.
A theory of value and obligation/ Robin Attfield.
London; Croom Helm, c1987. x, 262 p.
87-008928   171/.2   0709905726
Ethics. Values. Duty.

BJ1012.A93 1997
Audi, Robert,
Moral knowledge and ethical character/ Robert
Audi. New York: Oxford University Press, 1997.
xi, 304 p.
96-036703   170/.42 21   0195114698
Ethics.

BJ1012.B45 1992
Benhabib, Seyla.
Situating the self: gender, community, and
postmodernism in contemporary ethics/ Seyla
Benhabib. New York: Routledge, 1992. viii,
266 p.
91-045826   170   041590546X
Ethics.   Liberalism   --   Philosophy.
Communication -- Moral and ethical aspects.

BJ1012.B47 1998
Bernstein, Mark H.,
On moral considerability: an essay on who
morally matters/ Mark H. Bernstein. New York:
Oxford University Press, 1998. 189 p.
97-052259   179/.1 21   0195123913
Ethics. Animal welfare -- Moral and ethical
aspects.

BJ1012.B62 1996
Brandt, Richard B.
Facts, values, and morality/ Richard B. Brandt.
Cambridge [England]; Cambridge University
Press, 1996. vii, 319 p.
96-003301   170   0521578272
Ethics.

BJ1012.B63
Brandt, Richard B.
A theory of the good and the right/ Richard B.
Brandt. Oxford: Clarendon Press; 1979. xiii,
362 p.
78-040647   171/.5   0198245505
Ethics.

BJ1012.B676 1989
Brink, David Owen, 1958-
Moral realism and the foundations of ethics/
David O. Brink.   Cambridge;   Cambridge
University Press, 1989. xii, 340 p.
88-016179   170   0521350808
Ethics. Realism.

BJ1012.B737 1996
Brown, Montague, 1952-
The quest for moral foundations: an introduction
to ethics/ Montague Brown. Washington, D.C.:
Georgetown University Press, 1996. xiv, 173 p.
95-042088   170   0878406026
Ethics.

BJ1012.B76 1989
Butchvarov, Panayot, 1933-
Skepticism in ethics/ Panayot Butchvarov.
Bloomington: Indiana University Press, c1989.
viii, 225 p.
88-045103   170   0253353211
Ethics. Skepticism.

BJ1012.B97 1999
Byrne, Peter,
The philosophical and theological foundations of
ethics: an introduction to moral theory and its
relation to religious belief/ Peter Byrne. 2nd ed.
New York: St. Martin's Press, 1999. xii, 197 p.
98-043030   170 21   0312220006
Ethics. Religion and ethics.

BJ1012.C316 1993
Caputo, John D.
Against ethics: contributions to a poetics of
obligation   with   constant   reference   to
deconstruction/ John D. Caputo. Bloomington,
Ind.: Indiana University Press, c1993. 292 p.
92-041567   170 20   0253208165
Ethics.

BJ1012.C3 1967
Campbell, Charles Arthur.
In defence of free will, with other philosophical
essays, by C. A. Campbell. London, Allen &
Unwin, 1967. 277 p.
67-091696   170
Ethics -- Addresses, essays, lectures.
Knowledge, Theory of -- Addresses, essays,
lectures.

BJ1012.C58 1984
Clark, Stephen R. L.
The moral status of animals/ Stephen R.L. Clark.
Oxford; Oxford University Press, 1984, c1977.
xii, 221 p.
83-026819   179/.3 19   0192830406
Ethics. Animal welfare -- Moral and ethical
aspects.

BJ1012.C62 1991
A Companion to ethics/ edited by Peter Singer.
Oxford, UK; Blackwell Reference, 1991. xxii,
565 p.
90-023456   170   0631162119
Ethics. Social ethics.

BJ1012.C669 1993
Cooper, David Edward.
Value pluralism and ethical choice/ David Cooper. New York: St. Martin's Press, c1993. x, 214 p.
92-050008   170   0312068433
Ethics.

BJ1012.C87 1993
Curtler, Hugh Mercer.
Ethical argument: critical thinking in ethics/ Hugh Mercer Curtler. 1st ed. New York: Paragon House, 1993. xxiii, 150 p.
91-044764   170 20   1557785139
Ethics. Critical thinking. Decision making -- Moral and ethical aspects.

BJ1012.D263 1993
Dancy, Jonathan.
Moral reasons/ Jonathan Dancy. Oxford [England]; Blackwell , 1993. xiii, 274 p.
92-021888   170   0631177752
Ethics.

BJ1012.D325 1997
Darwall, Stephen L.,
Moral discourse and practice: some philosophical approaches/ Stephen Darwall, Allan Gibbard, Peter Railton. New York: Oxford University Press, 1997. x, 422 p.
95-051121   170 20   019509669X
Ethics.

BJ1012.D4
De George, Richard T.,
Ethics and society; original essays on contemporary moral problems, by Henry David Aiken [and others] Edited by Richard T. De George. Garden City, N.Y., Anchor Books, 1966. viii, 217 p.
66-017410   170
Ethics -- Addresses, essays, lectures.

BJ1012.D455 2000
Devine, Philip E., 1944-
Natural law ethics/ Philip E. Devine. Westport, Conn.: Greenwood Press, 2000. xiii, 202 p.
99-025006   171/.2   0313307024
Ethics. Natural law.

BJ1012.D57
Donagan, Alan.
The theory of morality/ Alan Donagan. Chicago: University of Chicago Press, 1977. xvi, 278 p.
76-025634   170   0226155668
Ethics.

BJ1012.E85 1988
Essays on moral realism/ edited by Geoffrey Sayre-McCord. Ithaca, N.Y.: Cornell University Press, 1988. xiii, 317 p.
88-047753   170/.42   0801495415
Ethics.

BJ1012.E883 1987
Ethical principles and practice/ edited by John Howie. Carbondale: Southern Illinois University Press, c1987. xvii, 171 p.
86-033897   170   080931410X
Ethics. Social ethics.

BJ1012.E88344 1998
Ethical theory/ edited by James Rachels. Oxford; Oxford University Press, 1998. 578 p.
97-041148   170 21   0198751931
Ethics. Ethics, Modern -- 20th century.

BJ1012.E8937 2000
Ethics: classical Western texts in feminist and multicultural perspectives/ edited by James P. Sterba. New York: Oxford University Press, 2000. v, 570 p.
99-022801   170 21   0195127269
Ethics. Feminist ethics. Ethics, Comparative.

BJ1012.E8957 1998
Ethics: the classic readings/ edited by David E. Cooper; advisory editors, Robert L. Arrington, James Rachels. Malden, Mass.: Blackwell Publishers, 1998. 287 p.
97-008622   170 21   0631206337
Ethics.

BJ1012.F42 1992
Feinberg, Joel,
Freedom and fulfillment: philosophical essays/ Joel Feinberg. Princeton, N.J.: Princeton University Press, c1992. xvi, 358 p.
91-046753   170 20   0691074127
Ethics. Social ethics.

BJ1012.F57 1978
Foot, Philippa.
Virtues and vices and other essays in moral philosophy/ Philippa Foot. Berkeley: University of California Press, 1978. xiv, 207 p.
78-054794   170   0520036867
Ethics.

BJ1012.F74
Fried, Charles, 1935-
Right and wrong/ Charles Fried. Cambridge, Mass.: Harvard University Press, 1978. x, 226 p.
77-016479   170   0674769058
Ethics. Right and wrong.

BJ1012.F85 1990
Fumerton, Richard A., 1949-
Reason and morality: a defense of the egocentric perspective/ Richard A. Fumerton. Ithaca: Cornell University Press, 1990. xiii, 247 p.
89-038801   170/.42   080142366X
Ethics. Reason.

BJ1012.G44 1996
Gensler, Harry J., 1945-
Formal ethics/ Harry J. Gensler. London; Routledge, 1996. viii, 213 p.
95-038892   170   0415130654
Ethics. Social ethics.

BJ1012.G45 1998
Gert, Bernard, 1934-
Morality: its nature and justification/ Bernard Gert. New York: Oxford University Press, 1998. xiv, 408 p.
97-031586   171/.2   0195122550
Ethics.

BJ1012.G47
Gewirth, Alan.
Reason and morality/ Alan Gewirth. Chicago: University of Chicago Press, 1978. xii, 393 p.
77-013911   170   0226288757
Ethics.

BJ1012.G53 1990
Gibbard, Allan.
Wise choices, apt feelings: a theory of normative judgment/ Allan Gibbard. Cambridge, Mass.: Harvard University Press, 1990. x, 346 p.
89-028705   170/.42   0674953770
Ethics. Judgment (Logic)

BJ1012.G655 1992
The Good life and the human good/ edited by Ellen Frankel Paul, Fred D. Miller, Jr., and Jeffrey Paul. Cambridge, England; Cambridge University Press, xiv, 211 p.
92-013361   170 20   0521437598
Ethics. Social ethics.

BJ1012.G665 1993
Gouinlock, James.
Rediscovering the moral life: philosophy and human practice/ James Gouinlock. Buffalo, N.Y.: Prometheus Books, 1993. 344 p.
93-005169   170   0879758155
Ethics.

BJ1012.G75 1986
Griffin, James, 1933-
Well-being: its meaning, measurement, and moral importance/ James Griffin. Oxford [Oxfordshire]: Clarendon Press, 1986. xii, 412 p.
86-028475   170   0198249039
Ethics.

BJ1012.H285 1988
Hardin, Russell, 1940-
Morality within the limits of reason/ Russell Hardin. Chicago: University of Chicago Press, 1988. xx, 234 p.
88-001172   171/.5   0226316181
Ethics. Social ethics. Utilitarianism.

BJ1012.H3
Hare, R. M.
Freedom and reason. Oxford, Clarendon Press, 1963. 228 p.
63-001450   170
Ethics.

BJ1012.H31352 1997
Hare, R. M.
Sorting out ethics/ by R.M. Hare. Oxford: Clarendon Press; c1997. vii, 191 p.
97-008001   170   0198237278
Ethics.

BJ1012.H316 1996
Harman, Gilbert.
Moral relativism and moral objectivity/ Gilbert Harman, Judith Jarvis Thomson. Cambridge, Mass., USA: Blackwell, 1996. x, 225 p.
95-012472   171/.7   0631192093
Ethics. Ethical relativism. Objectivity.

BJ1012.H317
Harman, Gilbert.
The nature of morality: an introduction to ethics/ Gilbert Harman. New York: Oxford University Press, 1977. xiii, 165 p.
76-029806   160   0195021428
Ethics.

BJ1012.H347 1997
Hauerwas, Stanley, 1940-
Christians among the virtues: theological conversations with ancient and modern ethics/ Stanley Hauerwas, Charles Pinches. Notre Dame, Ind.: University of Notre Dame Press, c1997. xvii, 230 p.
96-026432   241/.4   0268008175
Aristotle. -- Nicomachean ethics.Ethics. Christian ethics. Virtues.

BJ1012.H45 1988
Heller, Agnes.
General ethics/ Agnes Heller. Oxford [Oxfordshire]; B. Blackwell, 1988. 202 p.
87-020880   170   063115888X
Ethics.

BJ1012.H46 1990
Heller, Agnes.
A philosophy of morals/ Agnes Heller. Oxford, UK; B. Blackwell, 1990. xiv, 245 p.
89-037500   170   0631170839
Ethics.

BJ1012.J64 1989
Johnston, Paul, 1962-
Wittgenstein and moral philosophy/ Paul Johnston. London; Routledge, 1989. x, 244 p.
88-026816   192   0415001552
Wittgenstein, Ludwig, -- 1889-1951 -- Influence.Ethics.

BJ1012.K244 1998
Kagan, Shelly.
Normative ethics/ Shelly Kagan. Boulder, Colo.: Westview Press, c1998. xi, 337 p.
97-030631   170/.44   0813308453
Ethics.

BJ1012.K274 1993
Kane, Robert, 1938-
Through the moral maze: searching for absolute values in a pluralistic world/ Robert Kane. New York, N.Y.: Paragon House, 1994. x, 251 p.
92-036927   170   1557786011
Ethics. Values. Respect for persons.

BJ1012.K4 1988
Kekes, John.
The examined life/ John Kekes. Lewisburg: Bucknell University Press; c1988. 201 p.
87-048006   171/.3   0838751326
Ethics. Life.

BJ1012.L34 1987
Larmore, Charles E.
Patterns of moral complexity/ Charles E. Larmore. Cambridge; Cambridge University Press, 1987. xv, 193 p.
86-017014   170 19   0521338913
Ethics.

BJ1012.L43 1992
Lee, Donald C.
Toward a sound world order: a multidimensional, hierarchical ethical theory/ Donald C. Lee. Westport, Conn.: Greenwood Press, 1992. xv, 219 p.
91-040942   170   0313279039
Ethics.

BJ1012.L47 1987
Letwin, Oliver, 1956-
Ethics, emotion and the unity of the self/ Oliver Letwin. London; Croom Helm, c1987. x, 132 p.
87-024306   126   0709941102
Ethics. Emotions. Self.

BJ1012.L67 1992
Louden, Robert B., 1953-
Morality and moral theory: a reappraisal and reaffirmation/ Robert B. Louden. New York: Oxford University Press, 1992. x, 230 p.
91-021428   170   019507145X
Ethics.

BJ1012.M318 1994
McGrath, Elizabeth Z.
The art of ethics: a psychology of ethical beliefs/ Elizabeth Z. McGrath. Chicago: Loyola University Press, c1994. xi, 163 p.
93-036798   170/.1   0829407537
Ethics. Psychology.

BJ1012.M325 1984
MacIntyre, Alasdair C.
After virtue: a study in moral theory/ by Alasdair MacIntyre. Notre Dame, Ind.: University of Notre Dame Press, 1984. xi, 286 p.
83-040601   170/.42   0268006105
Ethics. Virtues. Virtue.

BJ1012.M326 1999
MacIntyre, Alasdair C.
Dependent rational animals: why human beings need the virtues/ Alasdair MacIntyre. Chicago, Ill.: Open Court, c1999. xiii, 172 p.
99-011357   170   0812693973
Ethics. Virtues.

BJ1012.M42 1988
McNaughton, David,
Moral vision: an introduction to ethics/ David McNaughton. Oxford, UK; B. Blackwell, 1988. viii, 214 p.
88-005101   170 19   0631159452
Ethics.

BJ1012.M5 1984
Midgley, Mary, 1919-
Animals and why they matter/ Mary Midgley. Athens: University of Georgia Press, 1984, c1983. 158 p.
83-017933   179/.3   0820307041
Ethics. Social ethics. Social contract.

BJ1012.M52
Midgley, Mary, 1919-
Heart and mind: the varieties of moral experience/ Mary Midgley. New York: St. Martin's Press, c1981. x, 176 p.
81-082751   170   0312365888
Ethics -- Addresses, essays, lectures.

BJ1012.M54 1992
Miller, Richard W., 1945-
Moral differences: truth, justice, and conscience in a world of conflict/ Richard W. Miller. Princeton, N.J.: Princeton University Press, c1992. ix, 396 p.
91-040205   170   0691074097
Ethics. Truth. Justice.

BJ1012.M633 1996
Moral knowledge?: new readings in moral epistemology/ [edited by] Walter Sinnott-Armstrong, Mark Timmons. New York: Oxford University Press, 1996. vi, 342 p.
95-044287   170 20   019508988X
Ethics.

BJ1012.M88 1982
Murphy, Jeffrie G.
Evolution, morality, and the meaning of life/ Jeffrie G. Murphy. Totowa, N.J.: Rowman and Littlefield, 1982. xii, 158 p.
82-009782   171   084767147X
Ethics. Evolution. Sociobiology.

BJ1012.N48 1987
Neville, Robert C.
The Puritan smile: a look toward moral reflection/ by Robert Cummings Neville. Albany: State University of New York Press, c1987. xi, 248 p.
86-030162   170   0887065422
Ethics.

BJ1012.O34 2000
Oderberg, David S.
Moral theory: a non-consequentialist approach/ David S. Oderberg. Oxford; Blackwell Publishers, 2000. xiii, 197 p.
99-045661   171/.2   0631219021
Ethics.

BJ1012.P454 2001
Peterson, Anna Lisa,
Being human: ethics, environment, and our place
in the world/ Anna L. Peterson. Berkeley:
University of California Press, c2001. x, 289 p.
00-055170   179/.1 21   0520226550
Ethics. Environmental ethics.

BJ1012.P455 1994
Philips, Michael, 1942-
Between universalism and skepticism: ethics as
social artifact/ Michael Philips. New York:
Oxford University Press, 1994. viii, 213 p.
93-024722   171/.7   0195086465
Ethics.

BJ1012.P633 1991
Platts, Mark de Bretton, 1947-
Moral realities: an essay in philosophical
psychology/ Mark de Bretton Platts. London;
Routledge, 1991. viii, 232 p.
90-044550   170   0415058929
Ethics. Desire (Philosophy) Values.

BJ1012.Q56 1993
Quinn, Warren,
Morality and action/ Warren Quinn. Cambridge
[England]; Cambridge University Press, xii,
255 p.
93-002769   170 20   0521446961
Ethics. Act (Philosophy)

BJ1012.R3485 1993
Rationality, justice and the social contract:
themes from Morals by agreement/ edited by
David Gauthier and Robert Sugden. Ann Arbor:
University of Michigan Press, c1993. ix, 201 p.
93-016233   171 20   0472103946
Gauthier, David P. Morals by agreement.
Ethics. Social contract. Reason. Justice.

BJ1012.S34 1992
Scheffler, Samuel, 1951-
Human morality/ Samuel Scheffler. New York:
Oxford University Press, 1992. 150 p.
91-035625   170   0195074483
Ethics.

BJ1012.S346 1995
Schmidtz, David.
Rational choice and moral agency/ David
Schmidtz. Princeton, N.J.: Princeton University
Press, c1995. xii, 283 p.
94-019059   170/.42   069103401X
Ethics. Rationalism.

BJ1012.S485 1997
Singer, Peter,
How are we to live?: ethics in an age of self-
interest/ Peter Singer. Oxford: Oxford
University Press, 1997.
97-019760   170/.44 21   0192892959
Ethics. Social ethics. Self-interest.

BJ1012.S5165 1992
Slote, Michael A.
From morality to virtue/ Michael Slote. New
York: Oxford University Press, 1992. xx, 267 p.
91-038853   170   0195075625
   Kant, Immanuel, -- 1724-1804 --
Ethics.Virtue. Ethics. Common sense.

BJ1012.S525 2000
Smith, Tara, 1961-
Viable values: a study of life as the root and
reward of morality/ Tara Smith. Lanham, Md.:
Rowman & Littlefield, c2000. ix, 205 p.
99-045671   171/.9   0847697606
   Ethics. Life -- Moral and ethical aspects.

BJ1012.S53 1991
Smith, Tony, 1951-
The role of ethics in social theory: essays from a
Habermasian perspective/ Tony Smith. Albany:
State University of New York Press, c1991. xiii,
246 p.
90-040194   170   0791406520
   Habermas, Jurgen.Social ethics. Ethics.

BJ1012.S545 1992
Snare, Francis.
The nature of moral thinking/ Francis Snare.
London; Routledge, 1992. vi, 187 p.
91-030981   170   0415047080
   Ethics. Ethical relativism. Subjectivity.

BJ1012.S58 2000
Sorell, Tom.
Moral theory and anomaly/ Tom Sorell. Malden,
Ma.: Blackwell Publishers, 2000. xii, 218 p.
99-016128   170   0631218335
   Ethics. Applied ethics.

BJ1012.S595 1988
Sprigge, Timothy L. S.
The rational foundations of ethics/ T.L.S.
Sprigge. London; Routledge & Kegan Paul,
1988, c1987. x, 283 p.
87-012894   171/.5   0710207050
   Ethics.

BJ1012.S69 2001
Sterba, James P.
Three challenges to ethics: environmentalism,
feminism, and multiculturalism/ James P. Sterba.
New York: Oxford University Press, 2001. vi,
153 p.
99-054881   170   0195124758
   Ethics. Feminist ethics. Multiculturalism.

BJ1012.S8 1975
Stevenson, Charles L. 1908-
Facts and values: studies in ethical analysis/ by
Charles L. Stevenson. Westport, Conn.:
Greenwood Press, 1975, c1963. xi, 244 p.
75-014601   170   0837182123
   Ethics. Semantics (Philosophy)

BJ1012.S848 1988
Stout, Jeffrey.
Ethics after Babel: the languages of morals and
their discontents/ Jeffrey Stout. Boston: Beacon
Press, c1988. xiv, 338 p.
87-042847   170   0807014028
   Ethics.

BJ1012.T37 2000
Taylor, Richard,
Good and evil/ Richard Taylor. Rev. ed.
Amherst, N.Y.: Prometheus Books, 2000. 336 p.
99-044712   171/.3 21   157392752X
   Ethics. Good and evil.

BJ1012.T46 1987
Theron, Stephen, 1939-
Morals as founded on natural law: the existence
of moral truths and what is required for this
existence/ Stephen Theron. Frankfurt am Main;
P. Lang, c1987. 218 p.
87-004055   171/.2   3820496858
   Ethics. Conscience. Natural law.

BJ1012.T545 2001
Thomson, Judith Jarvis.
Goodness & advice/ Judith Jarvis Thomson;
[comments by] Philip Fisher ... [et al.]; edited
and introduced by Amy Gutmann. Princeton,
N.J.: Princeton University Press, c2001. xvi,
188 p.
00-048322   170   0691086737
   Ethics. Consequentialism (Ethics)

BJ1012.V66 1997
Von Dohlen, Richard F.
Culture war and ethical theory/ Richard F. Von
Dohlen. Lanham [Md.]: University Press of
America, 1997. vii, 148 p.
96-046342   171   0761806164
   Rawls, John, -- 1921- MacIntyre, Alasdair C.
Culture conflict -- Moral and ethical aspects.
Culture conflict -- United States -- History --
20th century. United States -- Moral conditions.
United States -- Intellectual life -- 20th century.

BJ1012.W447 2001
Weston, Anthony, 1954-
A 21st century ethical toolbox/ Anthony Weston.
New York: Oxford University Press, 2001. ix,
406 p.
00-036327   170   0195130405
   Ethics. Applied ethics.

BJ1012.W5375 1993
Wilson, James Q.
The moral sense/ James Q. Wilson. New York:
Free Press; c1993. xviii, 313 p.
93-018520   171/.2   0029354056
   Ethics. Moral development. Social ethics.

BJ1012.W97 1990
Wyschogrod, Edith.
Saints and postmodernism: revisioning moral
philosophy/ Edith Wyschogrod. Chicago:
University of Chicago Press, c1990. xxvii,
298 p.
90-036721   170   0226920429
   Ethics. Postmodernism. Altruism.

BJ1025.D5 1957
Dewey, John, 1859-1952.
Outlines of a critical theory of ethics. New York, Hillary House, 1957. viii, 253 p.
57-004521   170
Ethics.

BJ1025.D53 1960
Dewey, John, 1859-1952.
Theory of the moral life. With an introd. by Arnold Isenberg. New York: Holt, Rinehart and Winston [1960] 179 p.
60-009060   170
Ethics.

BJ1025.F18 1989
Fagothey, Austin,
Fagothey's Right & reason: ethics in theory and practice/ Milton A. Gonsalves. 9th ed. Columbus: Merrill Pub. Co., c1989. xi, 611 p.
88-080956   170 19   0675209145
Ethics.

BJ1025.H3
Hare, R. M.
The language of morals. Oxford [Eng.] Clarendon Press, 1952. 202 p.
52-004801   170
Ethics.

BJ1025.H66
Hospers, John, 1918-
Human conduct; an introduction to the problems of ethics. New York, Harcourt, Brace & World [1961] 600 p.
61-011838   171
Ethics.

BJ1025.M665 2004
The moral life: an introductory reader in ethics and literature/ [edited by] Louis P. Pojman. 2nd ed. New York: Oxford University Press, 2004.
2002-193073   170 21   0195166086
Ethics.

BJ1025.M67 2002
Morality and moral controversies: readings in moral, social, and political philosophy/ John Arthur, editor. 6th ed. Upper Saddle River, N.J.: Prentice Hall, c2002. xii, 655 p.
2001-036836   170 21   013034155X
Ethics. Social problems.

BJ1031.A48 2002
Alternative conceptions of civil society/ edited by Simone Chambers and Will Kymlicka. Princeton, N.J.: Princeton University Press, c2002. vi, 237 p.
2001-036262   172 21   0691087962
Ethics. Social ethics. Pluralism (Social sciences)

BJ1031.A65 1999
Applbaum, Arthur Isak.
Ethics for adversaries: the morality of roles in public and professional life/ Arthur Isak Applbaum. Princeton, N.J.: Princeton University Press, c1999. xii, 273 p.
98-032010   172 21   0691007128
Ethics. Professional ethics. Political ethics. Adversary system (Law)

BJ1031.A77 1989
Arrington, Robert L., 1938-
Rationalism, realism, and relativism: perspectives in contemporary moral epistemology/ Robert L. Arrington. Ithaca: Cornell University Press, 1989. 321 p.
89-042874   171   0801423023
Ethics. Ethics, Modern -- 20th century. Knowledge, Theory of.

BJ1031.B65 1994
Blum, Lawrence A.
Moral perception and particularity/ Lawrence A. Blum. Cambridge [England]; Cambridge University Press, 1994. ix, 273 p.
93-025284   170   0521430283
Ethics. Psychology.

BJ1031.B74 1987
Brown, Les, 1914-
Conservation and practical morality: challenges to education and reform/ Les Brown. New York: St. Martins [sic] Press, 1987. ix, 222 p.
86-001795   170   0312162723
Ethics. Social ethics. Conservation of natural resources -- Moral and ethical aspects.

BJ1031.C67 1990
Cortese, Anthony Joseph Paul.
Ethnic ethics: the restructuring of moral theory/ Anthony J. Cortese. Albany: State University of New York Press, c1990. 197 p.
89-039656   170/.89   0791402797
Ethics. Ethnicity. Pluralism (Social sciences)

BJ1031.D67 1990
Dore, Clement, 1930-
Moral scepticism/ Clement Dore. New York: St. Martin's Press, 1991. x, 137 p.
90-043530   170/.42   0312053495
Ethics. Skepticism.

BJ1031.E83 1997
Ethics and practical reason/ edited by Garrett Cullity and Berys Gaut. Oxford: Clarendon Press; viii, 421 p.
97-015977   170 21   0198236697
Ethics -- Congresses. Practical reason -- Congresses.

BJ1031.F56 1994
Fleischacker, Samuel.
The ethics of culture/ Samuel Fleischacker. Ithaca: Cornell University Press, 1994. xii, 260 p.
94-006106   170   0801429919
Culture -- Moral and ethical aspects. Multiculturalism -- Moral and ethical aspects. Ethical relativism.

BJ1031.G376 1994
Garner, Richard, 1936-
Beyond morality/ Richard Garner. Philadelphia: Temple University Press, 1994. xiii, 404 p.
93-007399   170   1566390761
Ethics. Religion and ethics.

BJ1031.G65 1988
Goldman, Alan H., 1945-
Moral knowledge/ Alan H. Goldman. London; Routledge, 1988. ix, 224 p.
88-015720   170   0415013100
Hobbes, Thomas, -- 1588-1679 -- Ethics. Hume, David, -- 1711-1776 -- Ethics. Kant, Immanuel, -- 1724-1804 -- Ethics. Ethics. Realism. Emotivism.

BJ1031.H755 2000
Hooker, Brad, 1957-
Ideal code, real world: a rule-consequentialist theory of morality/ Brad Hooker. Oxford: Clarendon Press; 2000. xiii, 213 p.
00-057113   171/.5   019825069X
Consequentialism (Ethics) Rules (Philosophy)

BJ1031.I58 1995
Introducing applied ethics/ edited by Brenda Almond. Oxford, UK; Blackwell, 1995.
94-033508   170 20   063119391X
Applied ethics.

BJ1031.J644 1993
Johnson, Mark, 1949-
Moral imagination: implications of cognitive science for ethics/ Mark Johnson. Chicago: University of Chicago Press, 1993. xiv, 287 p.
92-029896   171/.2   0226401685
Ethics. Imagination -- Moral and ethical aspects.

BJ1031.K23 1995
Kahane, Howard, 1928-
Contract ethics: evolutionary biology and the moral sentiments/ Howard Kahane. Lanham, Md.: Rowman & Littlefield, c1995. xiii, 151 p.
95-033953   171/.7   0847681173
Ethics. Contracts -- Moral and ethical aspects. Ethics, Evolutionary.

BJ1031.K24 1993
Kekes, John.
The morality of pluralism/ John Kekes. Princeton, N.J.: Princeton University Press, c1993. xii, 227 p.
92-040492   171/.7   0691032300
Pluralism. Values. Ethics.

BJ1031.L59 1997
Loewy, Erich H.
Moral strangers, moral acquaintance, and moral friends: connectedness and its conditions/ Erich H. Loewy. Albany, N.Y.: State University of New York Press, c1997. xii, 251 p.
96-002444   170   0791431312
Ethics. Suffering -- Moral and ethical aspects.

BJ1031.M29 1992
Manning, Rita C.
Speaking from the heart: a feminist perspective on ethics/ Rita C. Manning. Lanham, Md.: Rowman & Littlefield, c1992. xvi, 183 p.
91-044434   170/.82   0847677338
Ethics. Caring. Feminism.

BJ1031.M312 1996
Margolis, Joseph, 1924-
Life without principles: reconciling theory and practice / Joseph Margolis. Cambridge, MA: Blackwell Publishers, 1996. ix, 262 p.
95-036405   170   0631195025
Ethics. Theory (Philosophy) Practice (Philosophy)

BJ1031.M354 1990
McShea, Robert J.
Morality and human nature: a new route to ethical theory/ Robert J. McShea. Philadelphia: Temple University Press, 1990. vii, 291 p.
90-032382   171/.2   0877227357
Ethics. Human beings. Philosophical anthropology.

BJ1031.M63 1998
Modeling rationality, morality, and evolution/ edited by Peter A. Danielson. New York: Oxford University Press, 1998. 463 p.
98-027140   110 21   0195125509
Ethics. Rational choice theory. Ethics, Evolutionary. Prisoner's dilemma game.

BJ1031.M665 1996
Moral dilemmas and moral theory/ edited by H.E. Mason. New York: Oxford University Press, 1996. 246 p.
95-016122   170   0195096819
Ethics. Dilemma. Decision making -- Moral and ethical aspects.

BJ1031.O34 2000
Oderberg, David S.
Applied ethics: a non-consequentialist approach/ David S. Oderberg. Oxford; Blackwell Publishers, 2000.
99-045660   170   0631219048
Applied ethics. Ethical problems.

BJ1031.O94 2003
The Oxford handbook of practical ethics/ edited by Hugh LaFollette. Oxford; Oxford University Press, 2003. xvii, 772 p.
2002-070167   170 21   0198241054
Applied ethics. Ethics.

BJ1031.S368 1996
Scott, Charles E.
On the advantages and disadvantages of ethics and politics/ Charles E. Scott. Bloomington: Indiana University Press, c1996. xii, 216 p.
95-053713   170   0253330734
Ethics. Political science -- Philosophy. Philosophy, Modern -- 19th century.

BJ1031.S37 1990
Scott, G. E., 1931-
Moral personhood: an essay in the philosophy of moral psychology/ G.E. Scott. Albany, N.Y.: State University of New York Press, c1990. xvi, 202 p.
89-039221   170   0791403211
Ethics. Self (Philosophy)

BJ1031.S42 1991
Seidler, Victor J., 1945-
The moral limits of modernity: love, inequality, and oppression/ Victor J. Seidler. New York: St. Martin's Press, 1991. xiv, 250 p.
90-045271   170   031205596X
Ethics. Love. Social justice.

BJ1031.S55 1988
Sinnott-Armstrong, Walter, 1955-
Moral dilemmas/ Walter Sinnott-Armstrong. Oxford, UK; B. Blackwell, 1988. viii, 264 p.
87-029908   170   0631157085
Ethics. Dilemma.

BJ1031.S64 1995
Smith, Michael
The moral problem/ Michael Smith. Oxford, UK; Blackwell, 1995. xiii, 226 p.
94-006156   170 20   0631192468
Ethics. Rationalism.

BJ1031.S75 1997
Stevens, Edward, 1928-
Developing moral imagination: case studies in practical morality/ Edward Stevens. Kansas City, MO: Sheed & Ward, c1997. xiv, 256 p.
97-033535   170   1556129785
Ethical problems. Applied ethics.

BJ1031.S86 1987
Sumner, L. W.
The moral foundation of rights/ L.W. Sumner. Oxford [Oxfordshire]: Clarendon Press; 1987. x, 224 p.
87-005640   172   0198247516
Ethics

BJ1031.T54 1994
Tierney, Nathan L., 1953-
Imagination and ethical ideals: prospects for a unified philosophical and psychological understanding/ Nathan L. Tierney. Albany: State University of New York Press, c1994. x, 184 p.
93-037146   170   0791420477
Ethics. Imagination (Philosophy)

BJ1031.T77 1989
Tuan, Yi-fu, 1930-
Morality and imagination: paradoxes of progress/ Yi-fu Tuan. Madison, Wis.: University of Wisconsin Press, c1989. xi, 209 p.
88-040445   170   0299120600
Ethics. Social ethics. Imagination -- Moral and ethical aspects.

BJ1031.W29 1996
Wallace, James D., 1937-
Ethical norms, particular cases/ James D. Wallace. Ithaca, N.Y.: Cornell University Press, 1996. xi, 171 p.
96-005043   171/.2   0801432138
Ethics. Practice (Philosophy) Authority.

BJ1031.W65 1984
Wong, David B.
Moral relativity/ David B. Wong. Berkeley: University of California Press, c1984. xii, 248 p.
83-018073   170/.42   0520049764
Ethical relativism.

BJ1063 General works, treatises, and textbooks — French and Belgian — General works

BJ1063.B382
Beauvoir, Simone de, 1908-
The ethics of ambiguity; tr. from the French by Bernard Frechtman. New York, Philosophical Library [1948] 163 p.
49-008287
Ethics.

BJ1114 General works, treatises, and textbooks — German — General works

BJ1114.B5713 1989
Bittner, Rudiger, 1945-
What reason demands/ Rudiger Bittner; translated by Theodore Talbot. Cambridge [England]; Cambridge University Press, 1989. ix, 198 p.
88-020340   170   0521352150
Ethics.

BJ1114.S5413 1989
Spaemann, Robert.
Basic moral concepts/ Robert Spaemann; translated by T.J. Armstrong. London; Routledge, 1989. viii, 99 p.
89-003493   170   0415041600
Ethics.

BJ1114.Z8713 1990
The moral domain: essays in the ongoing discussion between philosophy and the social sciences/ edited by Thomas E. Wren, in cooperation with Wolfgang Edelstein and Gertrud Nunner-Winkler. Cambridge, Mass.: MIT Press, c1990. xxix, 414 p.
89-035726   170   0262231476
Kohlberg, Lawrence, -- 1927- Habermas, Jurgen. Moral development. Ethics. Psychology -- Philosophy.

BJ1125 General works, treatises, and textbooks — German — General special

BJ1125.K8713 1998
Küng, Hans,
A global ethic for global politics and economics/ Hans Küng. New York: Oxford University Press, 1998. xvii, 315 p.
97-030562   170 21   0195122283
Ethics. World politics -- 1989- International economic relations. International economic relations -- Religious aspects. Religion and international affairs.

BJ1188 Religious ethics. The ethics of the religions — General works

BJ1188.E825 1999
Ethics and world religions: cross-cultural case studies/ Regina Wentzel Wolfe, Christine E. Gudorf, editors. Maryknoll, N.Y.: Orbis Books, c1999. ix, 419 p.
99-017423   291.5 21   1570752400
Religious ethics -- Case studies. Ethical problems.

BJ1188.E96 1998
Explorations in global ethics: comparative religious ethics and interreligious dialogue/ edited by Sumner B. Twiss and Bruce Grelle. Boulder, CO: Westview Press, 1998.
98-009706   291.5   0813328810
Religious ethics -- Comparative studies. Religions -- Relations.

BJ1188.F37 1993
Fasching, Darrell J., 1944-
The ethical challenge of Auschwitz and Hiroshima: Apocalypse or Utopia?/ Darrell J. Fasching. Albany: State University of New York Press, c1993. xvi, 366 p.
92-008118   241/.62   0791413756
Religious ethics. Human rights -- Religious aspects. Technology -- Moral and ethical aspects.

BJ1188.K44 1989
Kellenberger, James.
God-relationships with and without God/ J. Kellenberger. New York: St. Martin's Press, 1989. xi, 176 p.
89-036308   291.5   0312036612
Religious ethics. Religious pluralism.

BJ1188.L57 1978
Little, David, 1933-
Comparative religious ethics/ David Little, Sumner B. Twiss. New York: Harper & Row, c1978. xi, 266 p.
76-010003   291.5   0060652543
Religious ethics -- Comparative studies.

BJ1188.Z56 2001
Zinbarg, Edward D.
Faith, morals, and money: what the world's religions tell us about money in the marketplace/ Edward D. Zinbarg. New York: Continuum, 2001. 182 p.
2001-032566   291.5/64 21   0826413420
Religious ethics. Business ethics -- Religious aspects.

BJ1190 Religious ethics. The ethics of the religions — Christian ethics — Collected works (nonserial)

BJ1190.P67 1995
Porter, Jean, 1955-
Moral action and Christian ethics/ Jean Porter. Cambridge [England]; Cambridge University Press, 1995. xvi, 235 p.
94-018230   241   0521443296
Christian ethics.

BJ1212-1253 Religious ethics. The ethics of the religions — Christian ethics — History

BJ1212.M43 1993
Meeks, Wayne A.
The origins of Christian morality: the first two centuries/ Wayne A. Meeks. New Haven: Yale University Press, c1993. x, 275 p.
93-010226   241/.09/015   0300056400
Ethics in the Bible. Christian ethics -- History -- Early church, ca. 30-600. Sociology, Biblical.

BJ1217.P67 1990
Porter, Jean, 1955-
The recovery of virtue: the relevance of Aquinas for Christian ethics/ Jean Porter. Louisville, Ky.: Westminster/J. Knox Press, c1990. 208 p.
90-032954   241/.042/092   0664219241
Thomas, -- Aquinas, Saint, -- 1225?-1274 -- Contributions in Christian ethics. Christian ethics -- History -- Middle Ages, 600-1500. Virtues -- History.

BJ1231.B45 1987
Being and doing: Paul Tillich as ethicist/ edited by John J. Carey. Macon, GA: Mercer, c1987. x, 222 p.
87-031355   170/.92/4   0865542856
Tillich, Paul, -- 1886-1965 -- Contributions in ethics. Christian ethics -- History -- 20th century. Ethics, Modern -- 20th century.

BJ1231.L66 1982
Long, Edward Le Roy.
A survey of recent Christian ethics/ Edward LeRoy Long, Jr. New York: Oxford University Press, 1982. xi, 215 p.
82-002099   241/.09/048   0195031598
Christian ethics -- History -- 20th century.

BJ1231.R3
Ramsey, Paul.
Nine modern moralists. Englewood Cliffs, N.J., Prentice-Hall [1962] 271 p.
62-013729   241/.09/03
Christian ethics. Natural law.

BJ1231.S45 1997
Siker, Jeffrey S.
Scripture and ethics: twentieth-century portraits/ Jeffrey S. Siker. New York: Oxford University Press, 1997. 294 p.
96-008899   241   0195101049
Christian ethics -- Methodology. Ethics in the Bible. Christian ethics -- History -- 20th century.

BJ1231.S6
Spencer, Frederick Augustus Morland.
The ethics of the gospel/ by Frederick A. M. Spencer. London, G. Allen & Unwin Ltd. [1925] 255, [1] p.
26-007196
Christian ethics.

BJ1231.W42 1998
Webster, J. B. 1955-
Barth's moral theology: human action in Barth's thought/ John Webster. Grand Rapids, Mich.: W.B. Eerdmans Pub., 1998. ix, 223 p.
98-204435   241/.092   0802838588
Barth, Karl, -- 1886-1968 -- Contributions in Christian ethics. Christian ethics -- Reformed authors.

BJ1241.H38
Hauerwas, Stanley, 1940-
Vision and virtue; essays in Christian ethical reflection. Notre Dame, Ind., Fides Publishers [1974] ix, 264 p.
74-009712   241   0819004855
Christian ethics.

BJ1241.L4
Lehmann, Paul Louis, 1906-
Ethics in a Christian context. New York, Harper & Row [1963] 384 p.
63-011545   241
Christian ethics.

BJ1241.M83 1998
Mudge, Lewis Seymour.
The church as moral community: ecclesiology and ethics in ecumenical debate/ Lewis S. Mudge. New York: Continuum; c1998. 192 p.
98-015081   241   0826410480
Christian ethics. Church.

BJ1249.B42 1998
Bernardin, Joseph Louis, 1928-
A moral vision for America/ Joseph Cardinal Bernardin; edited by John P. Langan. Washington, D.C.: Georgetown University Press, c1998. xi, 176 p.
97-037973   241/.042   0878406751
Christian ethics -- Catholic authors. United States -- Moral conditions.

BJ1249.B87 1989
Burtchaell, James Tunstead.
The giving and taking of life: essays ethical/ James Tunstead Burtchaell. Notre Dame, Ind.: University of Notre Dame Press, c1989. xi, 324 p.
89-040023 241/.042 0268010188
Christian ethics -- Catholic authors. Life and death, Power over -- Religious aspects -- Catholic Church.

BJ1249.C8173 1996
Curran, Charles E.
History and contemporary issues: studies in moral theology/ Charles E. Curran. New York: Continuum, 1996. 275 p.
96-026514 241/.042 20 082640944X
Christian ethics -- Catholic authors. Church and social problems -- Catholic Church.

BJ1249.C83 1988
Curran, Charles E.
Tensions in moral theology/ Charles E. Curran. Notre Dame, IN: University of Notre Dame Press, c1988. vii, 214 p.
87-040622 241/.042 0268018669
Christian ethics -- Catholic authors. Sex -- Religious aspects -- Catholic Church. Church and social problems -- Catholic Church.

BJ1249.H36
Haring, Bernhard, 1912-
Free and faithful in Christ: moral theology for clergy and laity/ Bernhard Haring. New York: Seabury Press, 1978-1981. 3 v.
78-012253 241/.042 0816403988
Christian ethics -- Catholic authors.

BJ1249.H578 2002
Hollenbach, David.
The common good and Christian ethics/ David Hollenbach. Cambridge, UK; Cambridge University Press, 2002. xvi, 269 p.
2002-073786 241/.042 21 0521894514
Christian ethics -- Catholic authors. Common good -- Religious aspects -- Christianity.

BJ1249.M1644 1987
Mahoney, John, 1931-
The making of moral theology: a study of the Roman Catholic tradition/ John Mahoney. Oxford, OX: Clarendon Press; 1987. xxv, 357 p.
86-019188 241/.042 0198264526
Christian ethics -- History.

BJ1249.M713 1990
Moser, Antonio.
Moral theology: dead ends and alternatives/ Antonio Moser, Bernardino Leers; translated from the Portuguese by Paul Burns. Maryknoll, N.Y.: Orbis Books, 1990. xvi, 240 p.
90-187473 241/.042 0883446804
Christian ethics -- Catholic authors.

BJ1249.O37 1995
O'Keefe, Mark,
Becoming good, becoming holy: on the relationship of Christian ethics and spirituality/ Mark O'Keefe. New York: Paulist Press, c1995. vi, 185 p.
95-016977 241/.042 20 0809135930
Christian ethics -- Catholic authors. Spirituality -- Catholic Church.

BJ1251.B43
Bennett, John Coleman,
The radical imperative: from theology to social ethics/ by John C. Bennett. Philadelphia: Westminster Press, [1975] 208 p.
75-015538 241 066420824X
Christian ethics. Social ethics.

BJ1251.B87 1999
Burtness, James H.
Consequences: morality, ethics, and the future/ James H. Burtness. Minneapolis: Fortress Press, c1999. ix, 173 p.
99-017002 241 0800630920
Christian ethics.

BJ1251.C246 2001
The Cambridge companion to Christian ethics/ [edited by] Robin Gill. Cambridge, U.K.; Cambridge University Press, 2001. xv, 290 p.
00-031181 241 21 0521779189
Christian ethics.

BJ1251.C498 1996
Christian ethics: problems and prospects/ edited by Lisa Sowle Cahill and James F. Childress. Cleveland, Ohio: Pilgrim Press, 1996. xi, 399 p.
96-039058 241 21 0829811362
Christian ethics. Religious ethics. Social ethics.

BJ1251.F55 C6
Cox, Harvey Gallagher,
The situation ethics debate, edited with an introd. by Harvey Cox. Philadelphia, Westminster Press [1968] 285 p.
68-011991 241
Fletcher, Joseph F. Situation ethics. Situation ethics.

BJ1251.F67 1990
Ford, S. Dennis, 1947-
Sins of omission: a primer on moral indifference/ S. Dennis Ford. Minneapolis: Fortress Press, c1990. 128 p.
89-039163 241/.3 0800624017
Christian ethics. Indifferentism (Ethics) Apathy -- Religious aspects -- Christianity.

BJ1251.G8765 1996
Gustafson, James M.
Intersections: science, theology, and ethics/ James M. Gustafson. Cleveland, Ohio: Pilgrim Press, 1996. xxi, 174 p.
96-028322 241 20 0829811370
Christian ethics. Religion and science. Medical ethics.

BJ1251.H325
Hauerwas, Stanley, 1940-
A community of character: toward a constructive Christian social ethic/ Stanley Hauerwas. Notre Dame, Ind.: University of Notre Dame Press, c1981. x, 298 p.
80-053072 241 0268007330
Christian ethics. Social ethics.

BJ1251.H326 2001
Hauerwas, Stanley,
The Hauerwas reader/ Stanley Hauerwas; edited by John Berkman and Michael Cartwright. Durham, NC: Duke University Press, 2001. xiii, 729 p.
00-047709 241/.0404 21 0822326914
Christian ethics.

BJ1251.I54 1970
Inge, William Ralph, 1860-1954.
Christian ethics and modern problems. Westport, Conn., Greenwood Press [1970] ix, 427 p.
72-104283 261 0837139600
Christian ethics. Social problems.

BJ1251.K52 2001
Kirkpatrick, Frank G.
The ethics of community/ Frank G. Kirkpatrick. Oxford; Blackwell, 2001. xiv, 183 p.
00-009969 241/.62 0631216820
Christian ethics. Community -- Moral and ethical aspects. Social ethics.

BJ1251.L34 1991
Layman, Charles S., 1950-
The shape of the good: Christian reflections on the foundations of ethics/ C. Stephen Layman. Notre Dame: University of Notre Dame Press, c1991. ix, 243 p.
90-050977 241 0268017395
Christian ethics.

BJ1251.L4 1943a
Lewis, Clive Staples,
Christian behaviour, New York, The Macmillan company, 1943. 3 p.
43-015459
Christian ethics. [from old catalog]

BJ1251.M487 1991
Meilaender, Gilbert, 1946-
Faith and faithfulness: basic themes in Christian ethics/ Gilbert Meilaender. Notre Dame: University of Notre Dame Press, c1991. xii, 211 p.
90-050966 241 0268009821
Christian ethics. Faith. Man (Christian theology)

BJ1251.M49 1987
Meilaender, Gilbert, 1946-
The limits of love: some theological explorations/ Gilbert Meilaender. University Park: Pennsylvania State University Press, c1987. 156 p.
87-042548 241 0271006110
Christian ethics. Sexual ethics. Medical ethics.

BJ1251.N5
Niebuhr, Reinhold, 1892-1971.
An interpretation of Christian ethics, by Reinhold Niebuhr. New York, Harper & Brothers, 1935. 244 p.
35-027444   171.1
Love -- Religious aspects -- Christianity. Christian ethics.

BJ1251.N52 1963
Niebuhr, H. Richard 1894-1962.
The responsible self; an essay in Christian moral philosophy. With an introd. by James M. Gustafson. New York, Harper & Row [1963] 183 p.
63-015955   171.1
Christian ethics.

BJ1251.N523.T75 1993
Trimiew, Darryl M., 1952-
Voices of the silenced: the responsible self in a marginalized community/ Darryl M. Trimiew. Cleveland, Ohio: Pilgrim Press, 1993. xix, 139 p.
93-019178   241/.04   0829809627
Niebuhr, H. Richard -- (Helmut Richard), -- 1894-1962. -- Responsible self. Turner, Henry McNeal, -- 1834-1915. Wells-Barnett, Ida B., -- 1862-1931. Christian ethics. Responsibility. Marginality, Social -- Moral and ethical aspects.

BJ1251.R284 1994
Ramsey, Paul.
The essential Paul Ramsey: a collection/ edited by William Werpehowski and Stephen D. Crocco. New Haven: Yale University Press, c1994. xxv, 272 p.
93-035449   241/.092   0300058152
Christian ethics.

BJ1251.T47
Tillich, Paul, 1886-1965.
Morality and beyond. New York, Harper & Row [c1963] 95 p.
63-018280   171.1
Christian ethics.

BJ1253.B3513
Barth, Karl, 1886-1968.
Ethics/ Karl Barth; edited by Dietrich Braun; translated by Geoffrey W. Bromiley. New York: Seabury Press, 1981. x, 534 p.
80-029327   241   0816404844
Christian ethics -- Reformed authors -- Addresses, essays, lectures.

BJ1253.B615 1955a
Bonhoeffer, Dietrich, 1906-1945.
Ethics. Edited by Eberhard Bethge. [Translated by Neville Horton Smith] New York, Macmillan, 1955. xii, 340 p.
55-012644   171.1
Christian ethics.

BJ1275 Religious ethics.
The ethics of the religions — Christian ethics — General special

BJ1275.C33 1988
Cannon, Katie G.
Black womanist ethics/ Katie G. Cannon. Atlanta, Ga.: Scholars Press, c1988. x, 183 p.
87-038120   241/.08996073 19   155540216X
Christian ethics -- United States. Feminist ethics -- United States. Afro-American women -- Conduct of life.

BJ1275.C76 1992
Cronin, Kieran.
Rights and Christian ethics/ by Kieran Cronin. Cambridge [England]; Cambridge University Press, 1992. xxi, 324 p.
92-003126   241/.622   0521418895
Christian ethics. Human rights.

BJ1275.F47 1998
Fergusson, David.
Community, liberalism, and Christian ethics/ David Fergusson. Cambridge; Cambridge University Press, 1998. xii, 219 p.
97-047493   241 21   0521496780
Christian ethics -- Reformed authors. Communitarianism.

BJ1275.G35 1995
Gardner, E. Clinton
Justice and Christian ethics/ E. Clinton Gardner. Cambridge; Cambridge University Press, 1995. xiv, 179 p.
94-042267   241/.622 20   052149639X
Christian ethics. Justice.

BJ1275.G55 1999
Gill, Robin.
Churchgoing and Christian ethics/ Robin Gill. Cambridge, U.K.; Cambridge University Press, 1999. xi, 277 p.
98-053583   241/.0941 21   0521578280
Christian ethics -- Great Britain -- Public opinion. Christians -- Great Britain -- Attitudes. Church attendance -- Great Britain. Public opinion -- Great Britain.

BJ1275.G63 2000
God and globalization/ edited by Max L. Stackhouse with Peter Paris. Harrisburg, Pa.: Trinity Press International, c2000-c2001 v. 1-2
00-020203   261.8   156338311X
Christian ethics. Globalization -- Moral and ethical aspects. Globalization -- Religious aspects -- Christianity.

BJ1275.H24 1996
Hare, J. E., 1949-
The moral gap: Kantian ethics, human limits, and God's assistance/ John E. Hare. Oxford: Clarendon Press; 1996. x, 292 p.
95-041862   241   0198263813
Kant, Immanuel, -- 1724-1804 -- Ethics. Christian ethics. Ethics, Modern. Human beings.

BJ1275.H49 2000
Hicks, Douglas A.
Inequality and Christian ethics/ Douglas A. Hicks. Cambridge, U.K.; Cambridge University Press, c2000. xxii, 287 p.
99-087146   241   0521772532
Christian ethics. Equality -- Religious aspects -- Christianity.

BJ1275.M34 1994
Mackey, James Patrick.
Power and Christian ethics/ James P. Mackey. Cambridge [England]; Cambridge University Press, 1994. ix, 241 p.
93-008053   241   0521415950
Christian ethics. Power (Christian theology)

BJ1275.M365 1994
Markham, Ian S.
Plurality and Christian ethics/ by Ian S. Markham. Cambridge; Cambridge University Press, 1994. xiv, 225 p.
93-022811   241/.62   0521453283
Christian ethics -- United States. Pluralism (Social sciences) -- United States.

BJ1275.W42 1989
Welch, Sharon D.
A feminist ethic of risk/ Sharon D. Welch. Minneapolis: Fortress Press, c1990. ix, 206 p.
89-032986   241/.082   0800623398
Christian ethics. Feminist ethics. Social ethics.

BJ1278 Religious ethics.
The ethics of the religions — Christian ethics — Special, A-Z

BJ1278.F45 P37 1996
Parsons, Susan Frank.
Feminism and Christian ethics/ Susan Frank Parsons. New York: Cambridge University Press, 1996. xvii, 279 p.
95-013211   241/.082 20   0521468205
Christian ethics. Feminist ethics. Feminist theology.

BJ1278.P73.H35 1998
Hallett, Garth.
Priorities and Christian ethics/ Garth L. Hallett. Cambridge; Cambridge University Press, 1998. xiii, 202 p.
97-041080   241   0521623510
Christian ethics. Priority (Philosophy)

BJ1278.5 Religious ethics. The ethics of the religions — Christian ethics — Ethical philosophers, A-Z

BJ1278.5.T48.B73 1997
Bradley, Denis J. M., 1943-
Aquinas on the twofold human good: reason and human happiness in Aquinas's moral science/ Denis J.M. Bradley. Washington, D.C.: Catholic University of America Press, c1997. xiv, 610 p.
96-008286   171/.2/092   0813208610
Thomas, -- Aquinas, Saint, -- 1225?-1274 -- Ethics. Aristotle. -- Nicomachean ethics. Ethics, Medieval. Man (Christian theology) -- History of doctrines -- Middle Ages, 600-1500. Human beings.

BJ1279 Religious ethics. The ethics of the religions — Jewish ethics — Collected works (nonserial)

BJ1279.T48 1990
This I believe: documents of American Jewish life/ Jacob Rader Marcus [compiler]. Northvale, N.J.: J. Aronson, c1990. xxi, 277 p.
90-033814   296.3/85   0876687826
Ethics, Jewish. Wills, Ethical. Jews -- United States -- Biography -- Sources.

BJ1285 Religious ethics. The ethics of the religions — Jewish ethics — By period

BJ1285.A53 1994
Amsel, Nachum.
The Jewish encyclopedia of moral and ethical issues/ Nachum Amsel. Northvale, N.J.: J. Aronson, c1994. ix, 505 p.
94-002484   296.3/85   1568211740
Ethics, Jewish. Judaism -- 20th century. Judaism -- Doctrines.

BJ1285.C65 1995
Contemporary Jewish ethics and morality: a reader/ edited by Elliot N. Dorff, Louis E. Newman. New York: Oxford University Press, 1995. xiii, 468 p.
94-012180   296.3/85 20   0195090667
Ethics, Jewish. Jewish law -- Moral and ethical aspects. Judaism and social problems. Medicine -- Religious aspects -- Judaism. Judaism -- 20th century.

BJ1285.N49 1998
Newman, Louis E.
Past imperatives: studies in the history and theory of Jewish ethics / Louis E. Newman. Albany, N.Y.: State University of New York Press, c1998. xiii, 283 p.
97-038798   296.3/6 21   0791438686
Ethics, Jewish -- Philosophy. Jewish law -- Philosophy. Judaism -- Doctrines Bioethics.

BJ1285.W87 1994
Wurzburger, Walter S.
Ethics of responsibility: pluralistic approaches to covenantal ethics / Walter S. Wurzburger. 1st ed. Philadelphia: Jewish Publication Society, 1994. xii, 156 p.
93-047414   296.3/85 20   0827605145
Ethics, Jewish. Orthodox Judaism -- Doctrines.

BJ1287 Religious ethics. The ethics of the religions — Jewish ethics — Ethical philosophers, A-Z

BJ1287.A155.S54 2000
Sherwin, Byron L.
Jewish ethics for the twenty-first century: living in the image of God/ Byron L. Sherwin; with a foreword by Louis Jacobs. Syracuse, N.Y.: Syracuse University Press, 2000. xxvi, 203 p.
99-041320   296.3/6   0815628560
Ethics, Jewish. Bioethics -- Religious aspects -- Judaism.

BJ1289 Religious ethics. The ethics of the religions — Buddhist ethics

BJ1289.B835 1991
Buddhist ethics and modern society: an international symposium/ edited by Charles Wei-hsun Fu and Sandra A. Wawrytko; foreword by Sheng-Yen. New York: Greenwood Press, 1991. xxvii, 442 p.
91-008237   294.3/5   0313276285
Buddhist ethics -- Congresses. Buddhism -- Social aspects -- Congresses. Buddhism -- Doctrines -- Congresses.

BJ1289.H37 2000
Harvey, Peter
An introduction to Buddhist ethics: foundations, values, and issues/ Peter Harvey. Cambridge, UK; Cambridge University Press, 2000. xx, 478 p.
99-027718   294.3/5 21   0521553946
Buddhist ethics.

BJ1289.K44 1992
Keown, Damien, 1951-
The nature of Buddhist ethics/ Damien Keown. New York: St. Martin's Press, 1992. xi, 269 p.
91-047931   294.3/5   0312079052
Buddhist ethics.

BJ1289.K6513 1998
Kon-sprul Blo-gros-mtha-yas, 1813-1899.
Buddhist ethics/ Jamgon Kongtrul Lodro Taye; translated and edited by the International Translation Committee. Ithaca, N.Y.: Snow Lion Publications, c1998. 564 p.
97-033450   294.3/5   1559390662
Buddhist ethics. Buddhism -- China -- Tibet.

BJ1291 Religious ethics. The ethics of the religions — Islamic ethics

BJ1291.C66 2000
Cook, M. A.
Commanding right and forbidding wrong in Islamic thought / Michael Cook. Cambridge, UK; Cambridge University Press, 2000. xvii, 702 p.
99-054807   297.5 21   0521661749
Islamic ethics. Religious life -- Sh⁻i ah. Religious life -- Islam. Islam -- Doctrines.

BJ1291.F28 1991
Fakhry, Majid.
Ethical theories in Islam/ by Majid Fakhry. Leiden; E.J. Brill, 1991. x, 230 p.
90-042390   297/.5   9004093001
Islamic ethics. Philosophy, Islamic.

BJ1292 Religious ethics. The ethics of the religions — Islamic ethics — Special classes, groups, etc., A-Z

BJ1292.W6.T4713 1990
Thanvi, Ashraf Ali.
Perfecting women: Maulana Ashraf Ali Thanawi's Bihishti zewar: a partial translation with commentary/ Barbara Daly Metcalf. Berkeley: University of California Press, c1990. xv, 436 p.
89-030552   297/.448/024042   0520064917
Muslim women -- Conduct of life. Islam-- Customs and practices.

BJ1298 Evolutionary and genetic ethics — History

BJ1298.B73 1994
Bradie, Michael.
The secret chain: evolution and ethics/ by Michael Bradie. Albany: State University of New York Press, c1994. xiii, 198 p.
93-047679   171/.7   0791421058
Ethics, Evolutionary -- History. Evolution (Biology) -- Moral and ethical aspects.

BJ1298.F37 1994
Farber, Paul Lawrence, 1944-
The temptations of evolutionary ethics/ Paul Lawrence Farber. Berkeley: University of California Press, c1994. xii, 210 p.
94-005507   171/.7   0520087739
Ethics, Evolutionary -- History.

BJ1311 Evolutionary and genetic ethics — General works — 1861-

BJ1311.A66 1998
Arnhart, Larry, 1949-
Darwinian natural right: the biological ethics of human nature/ Larry Arnhart. Albany, NY: State University of New York Press, c1998. xvi, 332 p.
97-049287   171/.7   0791436934
Ethics, Evolutionary.

BJ1311.B5 1999
Biology and the foundation of ethics/ edited by Jane Maienschein, Michael Ruse. Cambridge, UK; Cambridge University Press, 1999. viii, 336 p.
98-030711   171/.7   0521551005
Bioethics. Ethics, Evolutionary.

BJ1311.B53 2000
Blackburn, Simon.
Ruling passions: a theory of practical reasoning/ Simon Blackburn. Oxford; Oxford University Press, 2000.
00-056647   171/.2 21   0199241392
Ethics, Evolutionary.

BJ1311.E96 1993
Evolutionary ethics/ edited by Matthew H. Nitecki and Doris V. Nitecki. Albany: State University of New York Press, c1993. x, 368 p.
92-047270   170/.9   079141499X
Ethics, Evolutionary.

BJ1311.H6 1951
Hobhouse, Leonard Trelawney, 1864-1928.
Morals in evolution; a study in comparative ethics. With a new introd. by Morris Ginsberg. London, Chapman & Hall, 1951. iiv, 648 p.
51-011288   171.7
Ethics, Evolutionary.

BJ1311.H64 2000
Hocutt, Max.
Grounded ethics: the empirical bases of normative judgements/ Max Hocutt. New Brunswick, N.J.: Transaction Publishers, c2000. xvi, 347 p.
00-034403   171/.7   0765800268
Ethics, Evolutionary. Normativity (Ethics)

BJ1311.H8 1971
Huxley, Thomas Henry, 1825-1895.
Touchstone for ethics, 1893-1943 [by] Thomas H. Huxley and Julian Huxley. Freeport, N.Y., Books for Libraries Press [1971, c1947] viii, 257 p.
74-156661   171/.7   0836924029
Ethics, Evolutionary.

BJ1311.P48 1995
Petrinovich, Lewis F.
Human evolution, reproduction, and morality/ Lewis Petrinovich. New York: Plenum Press, c1995. xvi, 339 p.
95-006514   176   0306449390
Ethics, Evolutionary. Human evolution -- Moral and ethical aspects. Human reproduction -- Moral and ethical aspects.

BJ1311.R65 1998
Rolston, Holmes, 1932-
Genes, genesis, and God: values and their origins in natural and human history/ Holmes Rolston III. Cambridge, U.K.; Cambridge University Press, 1998. xvi, 400 p.
98-020715   171/.7   052164108X
Ethics, Evolutionary. Religion. Values.

BJ1311.R68 1998
Rottschaefer, William A. 1933-
The biology and psychology of moral agency/ William A. Rottschaefer. Cambridge [England]; Cambridge University Press, 1998. xi, 293 p.
97-008764   171/.7   0521592658
Ethics, Evolutionary.

BJ1311.W16 1961
Waddington, Conrad Hal, 1905-
The ethical animal.   New York, Atheneum, 1961. 231 p.
61-012788   171.7
Ethics, Evolutionary.

BJ1311.W5 1924
Westermarck, Edward Alexander, 1862-1939.
The origin and development of the moral ideas, by Edward Westermarck. London, Macmillan and co., limited, 1924-26. 2 v.
31-013900   170.9
Ethics. Ethics -- History. Primitive societies.

BJ1311.W9
Wylie, Philip, 1902-1971.
An essay on morals. New York, Rinehart & company, inc. [1947] xvi, 204 p.
47-001685   170
Ethics, Evolutionary.

BJ1360 Humanist ethics

BJ1360.A33 1997
Adams, E. M.
A society fit for human beings/ E.M. Adams. Albany: State University of New York Press, c1997. xxii, 269 p.
96-052316   144 21   0791435245
Humanistic ethics. Civilization, Modern -- 1950- Civilization -- Philosophy.

BJ1360.G72 2003
Grayling, A. C.
Life, sex, and ideas: the good life without God/ A.C. Grayling. Oxford; Oxford University Press, 2003. xiv, 236 p.
2002-035834   171/.2 21   0195162528
Humanistic ethics.

BJ1388 Socialist ethics

BJ1388.S74 1990
Socialism and morality/ edited by David McLellan and Sean Sayers. New York: St. Martin's Press, 1990. x, 176 p.
89-038412   171/.7 20   0312037015
Socialist ethics.

BJ1390 Communist ethics (20th century)

BJ1390.L79 1988
Lukes, Steven.
Marxism and morality/ Steven Lukes. Oxford [England]; Oxford University Press, 1988. xiii, 163 p.
87-015292   171/.7 19   0192820745
Marx, Karl, 1818-1883 -- Ethics. Engels, Friedrich, 1820-1895 -- Ethics. Communist ethics -- History.

BJ1390.M277 2001
Marxism's ethical thinkers/ edited by Lawrence Wilde. Houndmills, Basingstoke, Hampshire; Palgrave, 2001. viii, 203 p.
2001-034803   171/.7 21   0333778073
Communist ethics.

BJ1390.N465 1989
Nielsen, Kai, 1926-
Marxism and the moral point of view: morality, ideology, and historical materialism/ Kai Nielsen. Boulder, Colo.: Westview Press, 1989. vii, 302 p.
88-014146   171/.7   0813306531
Communist ethics.

BJ1395 Feminist ethics

BJ1395.B45 1993
Bell, Linda A.
Rethinking ethics in the midst of violence: a feminist approach to freedom/ Linda A. Bell; with a foreword by Claudia Card. Lanham, Md.: Rowman & Littlefield Publishers, c1993. xxii, 296 p.
93-002697   170/.82 20   0847678458
Feminist ethics. Violence -- Moral and ethical aspects.

BJ1395.F446 1997
Feminist ethics and social policy/ edited by
Patrice DiQuinzio and Iris Marion Young.
Bloomington: Indiana University Press, c1997.
xv, 302 p.
96-053431 170/.82 0253332966
*Feminist ethics.United States -- Social policy
-- 1993-*

BJ1395.K64 1998
Koehn, Daryl, 1955-
Rethinking feminist ethics: care, trust and
empathy/ Daryl Koehn. London; Routledge,
1998. viii, 215 p.
97-052282 170/.82 0415180325
Feminist ethics. Caring. Dialogue.

BJ1395.M48 1994
Meyers, Diana T.
Subjection & subjectivity: psychoanalytic
feminism & moral philosophy/ Diana Tietjens
Meyers. New York: Routledge, 1994. x, 199 p.
94-020584 176/.082 0415904714
*Feminist ethics. Psychoanalysis and feminism.
Subjectivity.*

BJ1395.W55 1995
Willett, Cynthia, 1956-
Maternal ethics and other slave moralities/
Cynthia Willett. New York: Routledge, 1995. x,
218 p.
95-035111 170/.82 0415912091
Feminist ethics. Feminist theory.

BJ1400-1401 Special topics — Good and evil — General works

BJ1400.T4813 1995
Thomas, Aquinas, Saint 1225?-1274.
On evil/ St. Thomas Aquinas; translated by Jean
T. Oesterle. Notre Dame, Ind.: University of
Notre Dame Press, 1995. xxii, 547 p.
94-044961 111/.84 0268037000
*Good and evil -- Early works to 1800. Sin --
Early works to 1800.*

BJ1401.A435 1999
Adams, Marilyn McCord.
Horrendous evils and the goodness of God/
Marilyn McCord Adams. Ithaca, N.Y.: Cornell
University Press, 1999. xi, 220 p.
98-031382 231/.8 21 0801436117
Good and evil. Theodicy.

BJ1401.A53 1994
Anders, Timothy.
The evolution of evil: an inquiry into the
ultimate origins of human suffering/ Timothy
Anders. Chicago: Open Court, c1994. xv, 381 p.
94-038539 155.7 0812691741
*Good and evil. Evolution -- Moral and ethical
aspects.*

BJ1401.A67 1985
The Anthropology of evil/ edited by David
Parkin. Oxford [Oxfordshire]; B. Blackwell,
1985. 283 p.
84-020344 291.5 19 0631137173
Good and evil. Human beings.

BJ1401.B45 1991
Being and goodness: the concept of the good in
metaphysics and philosophical theology/ edited
by Scott MacDonald. Ithaca, N.Y.: Cornell
University Press, 1991. ix, 328 p.
90-055197 111/.84 0801423120
*Good and evil. Metaphysics. Philosophical
theology.*

BJ1401.B58 1999
Blumenthal, David R.
The banality of good and evil: moral lessons
from the Shoah and Jewish tradition/ David R.
Blumenthal; foreword by James W. Fowler.
Washington, D.C.: Georgetown University
Press, c1999. viii, 326 p.
98-043090 296.3/6 0878407154
*Good and evil (Judaism) Holocaust, Jewish
(1939-1945) -- Moral and ethical aspects.
Government, Resistance to -- Religious aspects -
- Judaism.*

BJ1401.E77 1982
Evans, G. R.
Augustine on evil/ G.R. Evans. Cambridge
[Cambridgeshire]; Cambridge University Press,
1982. xiv, 198 p.
81-021793 241/.092/4 0521245265
*Augustine, -- Saint, Bishop of Hippo.Good
and evil -- History.*

BJ1401.G35 1990
Gaita, Raimond, 1946-
Good and evil: an absolute conception/ Raimond
Gaita. New York: St. Martin's Press, 1991. ix,
340 p.
90-042731 216 0312053223
Good and evil.

BJ1401.H4 1976
Hebblethwaite, Brian.
Evil, suffering, and religion/ Brian
Hebblethwaite. New York: Hawthorn Books,
1976. vii, 115 p.
76-015424 291.2 0801524385
*Good and evil. Suffering -- Religious aspects.
Theodicy.*

BJ1401.K38 1993
Katz, Fred E., 1927-
Ordinary people and extraordinary evil: a report
on the beguilings of evil/ Fred E. Katz. Albany:
State University of New York Press, c1993. xii,
154 p.
92-015578 170 0791414418
*Good and evil -- Case studies. Good and evil -
- Psychological aspects.*

BJ1401.L35 1995
Leaman, Oliver.
Evil and suffering in Jewish philosophy/ Oliver
Leaman. Cambridge; Cambridge University
Press, 1995. xiii, 257 p.
94-033186 296.3/11 0521417244
*Suffering -- Religious aspects -- Judaism.
Judaism -- Doctrines. Philosophy, Jewish.*

BJ1401.L4
Lewis, C. S. 1898-1963.
The great divorce, by C. S. Lewis. New York,
The Macmillan company, 1946.
46-001417 237
Good and evil.

BJ1401.M52 1984
Midgley, Mary, 1919-
Wickedness: a philosophical essay/ Mary
Midgley. London; Routledge & Kegan Paul,
1984. viii, 224 p.
84-003257 170 071009759X
Good and evil.

BJ1401.N45 2002
Neiman, Susan.
Evil in modern thought: an alternative history of
philosophy/ Susan Neiman. Princeton, N.J.:
Princeton University Press, c2002. xii, 358 p.
2002-070374 170 21 0691096082
*Good and evil -- History. Philosophy,
Modern.*

BJ1401.N63 1989
Noddings, Nel.
Women and evil/ Nel Noddings. Berkeley:
University of California Press, c1989. ix, 284 p.
88-008000 170/.88042 0520065700
Good and evil. Women. Feminism.

BJ1401.O35
O'Flaherty, Wendy Doniger.
The origins of evil in Hindu mythology/ Wendy
Doniger O'Flaherty. Berkeley: University of
California Press, c1976. xi, 411 p.
75-040664 294.5/2 0520031636
Good and evil (Hinduism)

BJ1401.O66 1996
Oppenheimer, Paul.
Evil and the demonic: a new theory of
monstrous behavior/ Paul Oppenheimer. New
York: New York University Press, 1996. xii,
237 p.
96-022374 111/.84 0814761933
Good and evil. Demonology.

BJ1401.P93 1991
Pybus, Elizabeth, 1944-
Human goodness: generosity and courage/
Elizabeth Pybus. London: Harvester Wheatsheaf,
1991. x, 149 p.
91-190666 179/.9 0710812272
Good and evil. Courage. Ethics.

BJ1401.R48 2001
Rethinking evil: contemporary perspectives/ edited by María Pía Lara. Berkeley: University of California Press, c2001. vii, 307 p.
2001-041450 170 21 0520226348
Good and evil.

BJ1401.S77
Sparshott, Francis Edward, 1926-
An enquiry into goodness, and related concepts; with some remarks on the nature and scope of such enquiries. [Chicago] University of Chicago Press [1958] 304 p.
58-001392 179.9
Good and evil.

BJ1401.S83 1993
Stewart, Melville Y.
The greater-good defence: an essay on the rationality of faith/ Melville Y. Stewart. New York: St. Martin's Press, 1993. xi, 202 p.
92-006281 216 0312080956
Good and evil. Religion -- Philosophy. Free will and determinism.

BJ1401.W45 1999
Weisberger, A. M., 1957-
Suffering belief: evil and the Anglo-American defense of theism/ A.M. Weisberger. New York: P. Lang, c1999. xv, 244 p.
98-008243 214 0820439754
Good and evil.

BJ1401.W7 1963
Wright, G. H. von 1916-
The varieties of goodness. London, Routledge & K. Paul; [1963] 222 p.
63-005625 111.84
Good and evil. Ethics.

BJ1406 Special topics — Good and evil — Origin of evil. Depravity of human nature

BJ1406.A44 1997
Alford, C. Fred.
What evil means to us/ C. Fred Alford. Ithaca: Cornell University Press, 1997. xi, 185 p.
97-010437 111/.84 0801434300
Good and evil.

BJ1406.B7713
Buber, Martin, 1878-1965.
Good and evil, two interpretations: I. right and wrong. [Translated by Ronald Gregor Smith] II. Images of good and evil. [Translated by Michael Bullock] New York, Scribner, 1953. 143 p.
53-008318 111.84
Good and evil -- Biblical teaching.

BJ1406.E95 1998
Evil and suffering/ edited by Jacob Neusner. Cleveland, Ohio: Pilgrim Press, 1998. x, 165 p.
98-036235 291.2/118 21 0829812490
Good and evil -- Comparative studies. Suffering -- Religious aspects -- Comparative studies.

BJ1406.J6
Joad, C. E. M. 1891-1953.
God and evil, by C. E. M. Joad. London, Faber and Faber limited [1942] 363 p.
43-008433 111.84
Good and evil. Theism. Religion and science.

BJ1406.K56 2002
Kimball, Charles.
When religion becomes evil/ Charles Kimball. 1st ed. [San Francisco, Calif.]: HarperSanFrancisco, c2002. xi, 240 p.
2002-068903 291.2/118 21 0060506539
Good and evil -- Comparative studies. Religions.

BJ1406.S82 1988
Suchocki, Marjorie.
The end of evil: process eschatology in historical context/ Marjorie Hewitt Suchocki. Albany: State University of New York Press, c1988. ix, 182 p.
87-019834 216 0887067239
Good and evil. Free will and determinism. Finite, The.

BJ1406.W37 1995
Watson, Lyall.
Dark nature: a natural history of evil/ Lyall Watson. New York: HarperCollinsPublishers, c1995. xvi, 318 p.
96-001663 111/.84 0060176881
Good and evil. Philosophy of nature. Human beings.

BJ1408.5 Special topics — Good and evil — Moral judgment

BJ1408.5.C65 1987
Colby, Anne, 1946-
The measurement of moral judgment/ Anne Colby and Lawrence Kohlberg in collaboration with Anat Abrahami ... [et al.]. Cambridge [Cambridgeshire]; Cambridge University Press, 1987. 2 v.
86-028401 155.2 052132565X
Judgment (Ethics)

BJ1408.5.M52 1991
Midgley, Mary, 1919-
Can't we make moral judgements?/ Mary Midgley. New York: St. Martin's Press, 1991. viii, 167 p.
90-026426 170 0312061293
Judgment (Ethics)

BJ1408.5.T47 1995
Thomas, R. Murray
Classifying reactions to wrongdoing: taxonomies of misdeeds, sanctions, and aims of sanctions/ R. Murray Thomas. Westport, Conn.: Greenwood Press, 1995. x, 218 p.
95-016270 170 20 0313297177
Judgment (Ethics) Reasoning. Discipline.

BJ1408.5.T48 1993
Thomas, R. Murray 1921-
What wrongdoers deserve: the moral reasoning behind responses to misconduct/ R. Murray Thomas and Ann Diver-Stamnes. Westport, Conn.: Greenwood Press, 1993. ix, 172 p.
93-009322 172/.2 0313286302
Justice (Philosophy) -- Public opinion. Judgment (Ethics) -- Public opinion. Punishment -- Public opinion.

BJ1408.5.V48 1994
Vetlesen, Arne Johan, 1960-
Perception, empathy, and judgment: an inquiry into the preconditions of moral performance/ Arne Johan Vetlesen. University Park, Pa.: Pennsylvania State University Press, c1994. xii, 391 p.
92-043991 170 0271010568
Judgment (Ethics) Empathy.

BJ1409 Special topics — Pain and suffering

BJ1409.L64 1991
Loewy, Erich H.
Suffering and the beneficent community: beyond libertarianism/ Erich H. Loewy; foreword by David C. Thomasma. Albany: State University of New York Press, c1991. xviii, 139 p.
90-046087 171/.7 0791407454
Suffering -- Moral and ethical aspects. Ethics. Libertarianism.

BJ1409.M28 1999
Mayerfeld, Jamie.
Suffering and moral responsibility/ Jamie Mayerfeld. New York; Oxford University Press, 1999. xiii, 237 p.
98-019813 179 0195115996
Suffering -- Moral and ethical aspects. Responsibility.

BJ1409.P67 2000
Portmann, John.
When bad things happen to other people/ John Portmann. New York: Routledge, 2000. xxi, 242 p.
99-026106 248.4 0415923344
Suffering -- Moral and ethical aspects. Pleasure -- Moral and ethical aspects. Sympathy -- Moral and ethical aspects.

BJ1409.S35 1985
Scarry, Elaine.
The body in pain: the making and unmaking of the world/ Elaine Scarry. New York: Oxford University Press, 1985. vii, 385 p.
85-015585 128 19 0195036018
Pain. War. Torture.

BJ1411 Special topics — Right and wrong — 1801-

BJ1411.S36 1998
Scanlon, Thomas.
What we owe to each other/ T.M. Scanlon. Cambridge, Mass.: Belknap Press of Harvard University Press, 1998. ix, 420 p.
98-023318   170   0674950895
Right and wrong. Judgment (Ethics)

BJ1418.5 Special topics — Appropriateness

BJ1418.5.H65 1998
Holland, Nancy J.
The madwoman's reason: the concept of the appropriate in ethical thought/ Nancy J. Holland. University Park, Pa.: Pennsylvania State University Press, 1998. xxxi, 119 p.
97-033170   170/.42   0271017708
Appropriateness (Ethics)

BJ1419 Special topics — Decision making

BJ1419.H87 1989
Hurley, S. L.
Natural reasons: personality and polity/ S.L. Hurley. New York: Oxford University Press, 1989. xii, 462 p.
88-037967   170   0195056159
Decision making -- Moral and ethical aspects. Jurisprudence.

BJ1421 Special topics — Truth and falsehood. Lying — General works

BJ1421.B335 1991
Bailey, F. G.
The prevalence of deceit/ F.G. Bailey. Ithaca, N.Y.: Cornell University Press, 1991. xxii, 143 p.
90-042148   177/.3   0801425425
Truthfulness and falsehood.

BJ1421.B64
Bok, Sissela.
Lying: moral choice in public and private life/ by Sissela Bok. New York: Pantheon Books, c1978. xxii, 326 p.
77-088779   177/.3   0394413700
Truthfulness and falsehood.

BJ1421.P74 2001
Press, Bill,
Spin this!: all the ways we don't tell the truth/ Bill Press; foreword by Bill Maher. New York: Pocket Books, c2001. xxvi, 245 p.
2001-052386   177/.3 21   0743442679
Truthfulness and falsehood -- United States. Presidents -- United States -- Professional ethics.

BJ1429.5 Special topics — Secrecy

BJ1429.5.B64 1983
Bok, Sissela.
Secrets: on the ethics of concealment and revelation/ Sissela Bok. New York: Pantheon Books, [1983] c1982. xviii, 332 p.
82-047891   177   0394515811
Secrecy -- Moral and ethical aspects.

BJ1431 Special topics — Compromise. Tolerance. Toleration — Polyglot

BJ1431.B46 1990
Benjamin, Martin.
Splitting the difference: compromise and integrity in ethics and politics/ Martin Benjamin. Lawrence, Kan.: University Press of Kansas, c1990. x, 195 p.
89-039224   170   0700604146
Compromise (Ethics) Integrity.

BJ1431.F68 1992
Fotion, N.
Toleration/ Nick Fotion and Gerard Elfstrom. Tuscaloosa: University of Alabama Press, c1992. x, 204 p.
91-046331   179/.9   0817305815
Toleration.

BJ1431.N67 1996
Norton, David L.
Imagination, understanding, and the virtue of liberality/ by David L. Norton. Lanham, Md.: Rowman & Littlefield, c1996. xvi, 122 p.
95-038510   179/.9   0847681270
Toleration. Empathy. Imagination (Philosophy)

BJ1431.O24 2001
Oberdiek, Hans, 1937-
Tolerance: between forbearance and acceptance/ Hans Oberdiek. Lanham, Md.: Rowman & Littlefield Publishers, c2001. ix, 182 p.
00-069043   179/.9   0847687856
Toleration.

BJ1431.T64 1996
Toleration: an elusive virtue/ edited by David Heyd. Princeton, NJ: Princeton University Press, c1996. 242 p.
95-034037   179/.9 20   069104371X
Toleration.

BJ1431.W6 1969
Wolff, Robert Paul.
A critique of pure tolerance [by] Robert Paul Wolff, Barrington Moore, Jr. [and] Herbert Marcuse. Boston, Beacon Press [1969] vi, 123 p.
73-010908   179/.9
Toleration.

BJ1441 Special topics — Casuistry — Polyglot

BJ1441.J66 1988
Jonsen, Albert R.
The abuse of casuistry: a history of moral reasoning/ Albert R. Jonsen, Stephen Toulmin. Berkeley: University of California Press, c1988. ix, 420 p.
87-014307   171/.6   0520060636
Casuistry.

BJ1451 Special topics — Duty. Obligation. Responsibility. Supererogation — English and American

BJ1451.B47 1987
Berofsky, Bernard.
Freedom from necessity: the metaphysical basis of responsibility/ Bernard Berofsky. London; Routledge & Kegan Paul, 1987. viii, 231 p.
87-012869   123/.5   0710209983
Responsibility. Necessity (Philosophy) Free will and determinism.

BJ1451.F43
Feinberg, Joel, 1926-
Doing & deserving; essays in the theory of responsibility, by Joel Feinberg. Princeton, N.J., Princeton University Press, 1970. xi, 299 p.
78-113000   170   0691071705
Responsibility -- Addresses, essays, lectures.

BJ1451.F57 1998
Fischer, John Martin, 1952-
Responsibility and control: a theory of moral responsibility/ John Martin Fischer, Mark Ravizza. Cambridge; Cambridge University Press, 1998. viii, 277 p.
97-008646   170   0521480558
Responsibility. Law -- Philosophy.

BJ1451.H87 2003
Hurley, S. L.
Justice, luck, and knowledge/ S.L. Hurley. Cambridge, Mass.: Harvard University Press, 2003. viii, 341 p.
2002-038824   172 21   0674010299
Responsibility. Distributive justice. Fortune -- Moral and ethical aspects.

BJ1451.M36 1992
May, Larry.
Sharing responsibility/ Larry May. Chicago: University of Chicago Press, c1992. x, 204 p.
92-012658   170   0226511685
Responsibility. Social ethics. Social groups -- Moral and ethical aspects.

BJ1451.M649 1996
Moran, Gabriel.
A grammar of responsibility/ by Gabriel Moran. New York: Crossroad Pub. Co., 1996. 253 p.
95-054001   170   0824515544
Responsibility.

BJ1451.M65
Morris, Herbert, 1928-
Freedom and responsibility: Stanford, Calif., Stanford University Press, 1961. 547 p.
61-008469
Liability (Law). Jurisprudence. Responsibility.

BJ1451.P7
Prichard, Harold Arthur, 1871-1947.
Moral obligation; essays and lectures. Oxford, Clarendon Press, 1949. 200 p.
50-003474   171
Duty.

BJ1451.R47 1987
Responsibility, character, and the emotions: new essays in moral psychology/ edited by Ferdinand Schoeman. Cambridge [Cambridgeshire]; Cambridge University Press, 1987. ix, 358 p.
87-017768   170   0521327202
Responsibility. Character. Emotions -- Moral and ethical aspects.

BJ1451.S9 1989
Swinburne, Richard.
Responsibility and atonement/ Richard Swinburne. Oxford [England]: Clarendon Press; 1989. 213 p.
88-034613   241   0198248393
Responsibility. Atonement.

BJ1451.W27 1994
Wallace, R. Jay.
Responsibility and the moral sentiments/ R. Jay Wallace. Cambridge, Mass.: Harvard University Press, 1994. xii, 275 p.
94-017255   170   0674766229
Responsibility. Agent (Philosophy) Social ethics.

BJ1453 Special topics — Duty. Obligation. Responsibility. Supererogation — German

BJ1453.I49 1983
Ingarden, Roman, 1893-
Man and value/ Roman Ingarden; translation by Arthur Szylewicz. Washington, D.C.: Catholic University of America Press; c1983. 184 p.
83-015245   170   0813205921
Responsibility. Human beings. Values.

BJ1453.J6613 1984
Jonas, Hans, 1903-
The imperative of responsibility: in search of an ethics for the technological age/ Hans Jonas; translated by Hans Jonas, with the collaboration of David Herr. Chicago: University of Chicago Press, 1984. xii, 255 p.
83-018249   170/.42   0226405966
Responsibility. Technology -- Moral and ethical aspects. Ethics.

BJ1460-1461 Special topics — Freedom of the Will. Necessitarianism — General works

BJ1460.D55 1999
Dilman, çIlham.
Free will: an historical and philosophical introduction/ Ilham Dilman. London; Routledge, 1999. viii, 273 p.
98-035363   123/.5/09 21   0415200563
Free will and determinism -- History.

BJ1460.L8 1957a
Luther, Martin, 1483-1546.
Martin Luther on the bondage of the will. A new translation of De servo arbitrio (1525) Martin Luther's reply to Erasmus of Rotterdam, by J. I. Packer and O. R. Johnston. [Westwood, N. J.] Revell [1957] 322 p.
58-008660   234.9
Erasmus, Desiderius, -- d. 1536. Free will and determinism.

BJ1460.L85.M23
McSorley, Harry J.
Luther: right or wrong? An ecumenical-theological study of Luther's major work, The bondage of the will, by Harry J. McSorley. New York, Newman Press [1968, c1969] xvii, 398 p.
68-059159   123
Luther, Martin, -- 1483-1546. -- De servo arbitrio. Free will and determinism.

BJ1461.A34 1995
Agents, causes, and events: essays on indeterminism and free will/ edited by Timothy O'Connor. New York: Oxford University Press, 1995. x, 274 p.
94-013498   123/.5 20   0195091574
Free will and determinism.

BJ1461.B47
Berofsky, Bernard,
Free will and determinism. New York, Harper & Row [1966] x, 379 p.
66-011261   123
Free will and determinism.

BJ1461.B64 1998
Bok, Hilary, 1959-
Freedom and responsibility/ Hilary Bok. Princeton, N.J.: Princeton University Press, c1998. 220 p.
98-021288   123/.5   069101566X
Free will and determinism. Responsibility.

BJ1461.B69 1989
Breer, Paul E.
The spontaneous self: viable alternatives to free will/ Paul Breer. Cambridge, Mass.: Institute For Naturalistic Philosophy, c1989. ix, 308 p.
89-084648   123/.5   0962358908
Free will and determinism.

BJ1461.D426 1984
Dennett, Daniel Clement.
Elbow room: the varieties of free will worth wanting/ Daniel C. Dennett. Cambridge, Mass.: MIT Press, c1984. x, 200 p.
84-009709   123.5 19   0262540428
Free will and determinism.

BJ1461.D67 1991
Double, Richard.
The non-reality of free will/ Richard Double. New York: Oxford University Press, 1991. xi, 247 p.
90-033531   123/.5   0195064976
Free will and determinism.

BJ1461.F3 1960
Farrer, Austin Marsden.
The freedom of the will/ by Auatin Farrer. New York: Scribner, c1960. 330 p.
60-008116   123
Free will and determinism.

BJ1461.F49 1994
Fischer, John Martin, 1952-
The metaphysics of free will: an essay on control/ John Martin Fischer. Cambridge, Mass.: Blackwell, 1994. ix, 273 p.
93-051073   123/.5   1557861552
Free will and determinism. Responsibility. Agent (Philosophy)

BJ1461.F74 2001
The Oxford handbook of free will/ edited by Robert Kane. Oxford; Oxford University Press, 2001. xvii, 638 p.
00-052872   123/.5 21   0195133366
Free will and determinism. Philosophy, Modern -- 20th century. Ethics, Modern -- 20th century.

BJ1461.F75 2003
Free will/ edited by Gary Watson. 2nd ed. Oxford; Oxford University Press, 2003. vi, 462 p.
2002-192455   123/.5 21   019925494X
Free will and determinism.

BJ1461.G67 1990
Gosling, J. C. B.
Weakness of the will/ Justin Gosling. London; Routledge, 1990. ix, 221 p.
89-049681   128/.3   0415034353
Will -- History. Ethics -- History. Self-control -- Moral and ethical aspects -- History.

BJ1461.H26 1998
Haji, Ishtiyaque.
Moral appraisability: puzzles, proposals, and perplexities/ Ishtiyaque Haji. New York: Oxford University Press, 1998. xii, 272 p.
96-040432   170   0195114744
Ethics. Free will and determinism. Responsibility.

BJ1461.H27
Hampshire, Stuart, 1914-
Freedom of the individual. New York, Harper & Row [1965] 112 p.
65-014682   123
Free will and determinism.

BJ1461.H57 2002
Honderich, Ted.
How free are you?: the determinism problem/ Ted Honderich. 2nd ed. Oxford; Oxford University Press, 2002. 176 p.
2002-024214   123/.5 21   0199251975
Free will and determinism. Philosophy of mind.

BJ1461.L4
Lehrer, Keith,
Freedom and determinism. [Contributors]: Roderick M. Chisholm [and others] New York, Random House [1966] 207 p.
66-010536   123
Free will and determinism.

BJ1461.L8
Luther and Erasmus: Free will and salvation. Philadelphia, Westminster Press [1969] xiv, 348 p.
76-079870   234/.9   0664220177
Free will and determinism.

BJ1461.M4
Melden, A. I. 1910-
Free action. London, Routledge & Paul; [1961] 226 p.
62-005762   159.1
Free will and determinism.

BJ1461.N37 1992
Nathan, N. M. L.
Will and world: a study in metaphysics/ N.M.L. Nathan. Oxford; Clarendon Press; 1992. x, 171 p.
91-024031   123/.5   0198239548
Will. Free will and determinism.

BJ1461.N4 1957
New York University Institute of Philosophy, 1957.
Determinism and freedom in the age of modern science: a philosophical symposium/ ed. by Sidney Hook. New York, New York University Press, 1958. 247 p.
58-005042
Free will and determinism

BJ1461.O35
Ofstad, Harald, 1920-
An inquiry into the freedom of descision. Oslo, Norwegian Universities Press; [c1961] 391 p.
62-003987
Free will and determinism. Decision-making (Ethics)

BJ1461.P55 1996
Pink, Thomas.
The psychology of freedom/ Thomas Pink. Cambridge; Cambridge University Press, 1996. x, 284 p.
95-051644   128/.3   0521555043
Free will and determinism. Decision making.

BJ1461.S77 1986
Strawson, Galen.
Freedom and belief/ Galen Strawson. Oxford [Oxfordshire]: Clarendon Press; 1986. xiv, 339 p.
86-017941   123/.5   0198249381
Free will and determinism.

BJ1461.W55 1993
White, Morton Gabriel, 1917-
The question of free will: a holistic view/ Morton White. Princeton, N.J.: Princeton University Press, c1993. x, 137 p.
93-007104   123/.5   069103317X
Free will and determinism.

BJ1461.W64 1990
Wolf, Susan R.
Freedom within reason/ Susan Wolf. New York: Oxford University Press, 1990. xii, 162 p.
89-077306   123/.5   0195056167
Free will and determinism. Ethics. Reason.

BJ1468.5 Special topics — Freedom of the Will. Necessitarianism — General special

BJ1468.5.C43 1988
Charlton, William, 1935-
Weakness of will/ William Charlton. Oxford, UK; B. Blackwell, 1988. 196 p.
87-035575   128/.3   0631157581
Will.

BJ1468.5.D68 1996
Double, Richard.
Metaphilosophy and free will/ Richard Double. New York: Oxford University Press, 1996. 176 p.
95-050082   123/.5   0195107624
Free will and determinism. Methodology.

BJ1469 Special topics — Power over life and death

BJ1469.G46 2002
Gennaro, Rocco J.
A dialogue on ethical issues of life and death/ Rocco J. Gennaro. Lanham, MD: University Press of America, 2002.
2002-020136   179.7 21   0761822372
Life and death, Power over.

BJ1470 Special topics — Self-realization

BJ1470.C75 1999
Critto, Adolfo.
Overcoming modern confusion: consistency and choice/ Adolfo Critto. Lanham, MD: University Press of America, 1999.
99-018632   170/.42   0761813608
Self-realization. Cognitive consistency. Integration (Theory of knowledge)

BJ1470.G48 1998
Gewirth, Alan.
Self-fulfillment/ Alan Gewirth. Princeton, N.J.: Princeton University Press, c1998. x, 235 p.
98-005127   171/.3   0691059764
Self-realization.

BJ1470.N68
Norton, David L.
Personal destinies: a philosophy of ethical individualism/ by David L. Norton. Princeton, N.J.: Princeton University Press, c1976. xiv, 398 p.
76-003011   170/.202   0691072159
Self-realization. Social ethics.

BJ1471 Special topics — Conscience

BJ1471.A468 1982
Amato, Joseph Anthony.
Guilt and gratitude: a study of the origins of contemporary conscience/ Joseph Anthony Amato II; foreword by Thaddeus C. Radzialowski. Westport, Conn.: Greenwood Press, c1982. xxv, 218 p.
81-006991   170/.42   0313229465
Conscience. Guilt. Gratitude.

BJ1471.H93 2001
Hyde, Michael J., 1950-
The call of conscience: Heidegger and Levinas, rhetoric and the euthanasia debate/ Michael J. Hyde. Columbia: University of South Carolina Press, c2001. xvii, 300 p.
00-011421   170   1570033889
Heidegger, Martin, -- 1889-1976 -- Contributions in concept of conscience. Levinas, Emmanuel -- Contributions in concept of conscience. Conscience. Rhetoric -- Moral and ethical aspects. Euthanasia

BJ1471.S69 2000
Stilwell, Barbara M.
Right vs. wrong--: raising a child with a conscience/ Barbara M. Stilwell, Matthew R. Galvin, S. Mark Kopta. Bloomington: Indiana University Press, c2000. xiii, 235 p.
99-054311   649/.7   0253337097
Conscience. Moral development. Moral education (Elementary)

BJ1471.5 Special topics — Guilt

BJ1471.5.G74 1995
Greenspan, Patricia S., 1944-
Practical guilt: moral dilemmas, emotions, and social norms/ P.S. Greenspan. New York: Oxford University Press, 1995. xii, 246 p.
93-040067   128/.3   0195087623
Guilt. Emotions (Philosophy) Social norms.

BJ1473 Special topics — Emotivism

BJ1473.O24 1991
Oakley, Justin, 1960-
Morality and the emotions/ Justin Oakley. London; Routledge, 1992. x, 253 p.
91-009497   170/.1/9   0415056616
Emotions -- Moral and ethical aspects.

BJ1474 Special topics — Altruism and egotism. Self-interest and egoism

BJ1474.M74 1996
Monroe, Kristen R., 1946-
The heart of altruism: perceptions of a common humanity/ Kristen Renwick Monroe. Princeton, N.J.: Princeton University Press, c1996. xix, 292 p.
95-039585   171/.8   0691043558
Altruism.

BJ1474.O39 1995
Oliner, Pearl M.
Toward a caring society: ideas into action / Pearl M. Oliner and Samuel P. Oliner. Westport, Conn.: Praeger, 1995. x, 240 p.
95-003339   171/.8   0275951987
Altruism. Caring. Helping behavior.

BJ1474.O85 1999
Ozinga, James R.
Altruism/ James R. Ozinga. Westport, Conn.: Praeger, 1999. xvii, 174 p.
99-022137   171/.8   0275967352
Altruism.

BJ1474.P3
Palmer, George Herbert, 1842-1933.
Altruism; its nature and varieties; the Ely lectures for 1917-18, by George Herbert Palmer. New York, C. Scribner's Sons, 1919.
19-004094
Altruism.

BJ1474.S43 1999
Shaver, Robert, 1961-
Rational egoism: a selective and critical history/ Robert Shaver. Cambridge, U.K.; Cambridge University Press, 1999. xii, 162 p.
98-017212   171/.9   0521632536
Hobbes, Thomas, -- 1588-1679 -- Ethics.
Sidgwick, Henry, -- 1838-1900 -- Ethics.
Egoism.

BJ1474.S65
Sorokin, Pitirim Aleksandrovich, 1889-1968.
Altruistic love; a study of American "good neighbors" and Christian saints. Boston, Beacon Press, 1950. vii, 253 p.
50-008042   171.8
Altruism. Saints.

BJ1474.S69 2002
Sorokin, Pitirim Aleksandrovich,
The ways and power of love: types, factors, and techniques of moral transformation/ Pitirim A. Sorokin; introduction by Stephen G. Post. Timeless classic pbk. ed. Philadelphia: Templeton Foundation Press, 2002. xxviii, 552 p.
2001-058134   171/.8 21   1890151866
Altruism. Love.

BJ1474.V36 1994
Van Ingen, John Frederick, 1945-
Why be moral?: the egoistic challenge/ John van Ingen. New York: P. Lang, c1994. viii, 192 p.
93-036873   171/.9   0820423572
Egoism.

BJ1474.5 Special topics — Exploitation

BJ1474.5.W47 1996
Wertheimer, Alan.
Exploitation/ Alan Wertheimer. Princeton, N.J.: Princeton University Press, c1996. xiv, 316 p.
95-052898   170   0691027420
Exploitation.

BJ1475 Special topics — Sympathy. Compassion. Caring

BJ1475.C53 1997
Clark, Candace.
Misery and company: sympathy in everyday life/ Candace Clark. Chicago: University of Chicago Press, 1997. xii, 316 p.
96-034946   177/.7 20   0226107566
Sympathy.

BJ1475.C57 1996
Clement, Grace.
Care, autonomy, and justice: feminism and the ethic of care/ Grace Clement. Boulder, Colo.: Westview Press, 1996. viii, 135 p.
96-008449   177/.7   0813325374
Caring. Autonomy (Philosophy) Justice (Philosophy)

BJ1475.C75 1994
The Crisis of care: affirming and restoring caring practices in the helping professions/ edited by Susan S. Phillips and Patricia Benner. Washington, D.C.: Georgetown University Press, 1994. xi, 190 p.
94-009702   174   0878405585
Caring. Helping behavior. Professional ethics.

BJ1475.N62 1984
Noddings, Nel.
Caring, a feminine approach to ethics & moral education/ Nel Noddings. Berkeley: University of California Press, c1984. xi, 216 p.
83-018223   170   0520050436
Caring -- Moral and ethical aspects. Feminist ethics. Women -- Psychology.

BJ1476 Special topics — Forgiveness. Pardon

BJ1476.F67 2001
Forgiveness and reconciliation: religion, public policy & conflict transformation/ edited by Raymond G. Helmick & Rodney L. Petersen. Philadelphia: Templeton Foundation Press, c2001. xxvii, 440 p.
2001-027132   291.2/2   1890151491
Forgiveness. Forgiveness -- Religious aspects. Reconciliation -- Religious aspects.

BJ1476.G685 2002
Govier, Trudy.
Forgiveness and revenge/ Trudy Govier. London; Routledge, 2002.
2002-021327   179/.9 21   0415278562
Forgiveness. Revenge.

BJ1476.H33 1991
Haber, Joram Graf.
Forgiveness: a philosophical study/ Joram Graf Haber. Savage, MD: Rowman & Littlefield Publishers, c1991. xi, 146 p.
91-017869   179/.9   0847676714
Forgiveness.

BJ1476.M87 1988
Murphy, Jeffrie G.
Forgiveness and mercy/ Jeffrie G. Murphy and Jean Hampton. Cambridge; Cambridge University Press, 1988. xii, 194 p.
88-009502   179/.9   0521361281
Forgiveness. Hate. Mercy.

BJ1477 Special topics — Optimism and pessimism

BJ1477.S2 1925
Saltus, Edgar, 1855-1921.
The anatomy of negation/ Edgar E. Saltus. New York: Brentano's, [1925] vii, 225 p.
25-012636
Skepticism. Pessimism.

BJ1481 Special topics — Happiness and joy — General works

BJ1481.A68 1996
Aristotle, Kant, and the Stoics: rethinking happiness and duty/ edited by Stephen Engstrom, Jennifer Whiting. Cambridge; Cambridge University Press, 1996. ix, 310 p.
95-025299　170 20　0521553121
Aristotle -- Contributions in ethics -- Congresses. Kant, Immanuel, 1724-1804 -- Ethics -- Congresses. Happiness -- Congresses. Duty -- Congresses. Stoics -- Congresses.

BJ1481.G626 1999
The good life/ edited, with introductions, by Charles Guignon. Indianapolis, Ind.: Hackett Pub., c1999. xv, 325 p.
98-050831　170 21　0872204383
Happiness. Conduct of life.

BJ1481.G636 1982
Gosling, J. C. B.
The Greeks on pleasure/ J.C.B. Gosling and C.C.W. Taylor. Oxford [Oxfordshire]: Clarendon Press; 1982. xiii, 497 p.
82-007940　128　0198246668
Pleasure. Philosophy, Ancient.

BJ1481.H83 1996
Hudson, Deal Wyatt.
Happiness and the limits of satisfaction: Deal W. Hudson. Lanham, Md.: Rowman & Littlefield, c1996. xxi, 218 p.
95-042149　170　0847681394
Happiness.

BJ1481.I5 1995
In pursuit of happiness/ edited by Leroy S. Rouner. Notre Dame, Ind.: University of Notre Dame Press, c1995. xv, 176 p.
95-016518　170　0268011745
Happiness.

BJ1481.J65
Jones, Howard Mumford, 1892-
The pursuit of happiness. Cambridge, Harvard University Press, 1953. xi, 168 p.
52-012265　171.4
Happiness.

BJ1481.M16
MacIver, Robert M. 1882-1970.
Pursuit of happiness; a philosophy for modern living. New York, Simon and Schuster, 1955. 182 p.
55-010289　171.4
Happiness.

BJ1481.P56 2000
Potkay, Adam, 1961-
The passion for happiness: Samuel Johnson and David Hume/ Adam Potkay. Ithaca, NY: Cornell University Press, c2000. xv, 241 p.
99-052777　170　080143727X
Johnson, Samuel, -- 1696-1772 -- Contributions in concept of happiness. Hume, David, -- 1711-1776 -- Contributions in concept of happiness. Happiness -- History -- 18th century.

BJ1481.P6 1974
Powys, John Cowper, 1872-1963.
The art of happiness/ by John Cowper Powys. London (131 Kings Rd., S.W.3): Village Press, 1974. 45 p.
75-300274　128/.3　090424721X
Happiness.

BJ1481.R75 1971
Russell, Bertrand, 1872-1970.
The conquest of happiness.　New York, Liveright, [1971, c1930] 249 p.
74-149626　131.3　0871400510
Happiness.

BJ1490 Special topics — Revenge

BJ1490.B58 2002
Blumenfeld, Laura.
Revenge: a story of hope/ Laura Blumenfeld. New York: Simon & Schuster, c2002. 382 p., [8] p. of plates:
2002-017552　　　364.15/2/095694　21
0684853167
Blumenfeld, Laura. Revenge. Arab-Israeli conflict -- Personal narratives, American. Arab-Israeli conflict -- Personal narratives, Jewish.

BJ1490.F74 2001
French, Peter A.
The virtues of vengeance/ Peter A. French. Lawrence, Kan.: University Press of Kansas, c2001. xii, 248 p.
00-049959　179　0700610766
Revenge. Ethics.

BJ1491 Special topics — Hedonism and asceticism. Renunciation

BJ1491.L48 1989
Levy, Zeev.
David Baumgardt and ethical hedonism/ Ze'ev Levy. Hoboken, NJ: Ktav Pub. House, 1989. ix, 248 p.
88-024160　171/.4/0924　0881253049
Baumgardt, David, -- 1890-1963 -- Ethics.Hedonism -- History -- 20th century. Philosophy, Jewish -- History -- 20th century.

BJ1498 Special topics — Active vs. meditative life — Work. Labor and idleness. Leisure

BJ1498.M87 1981
Murphy, James Frederick, 1943-
Concepts of leisure/ James F. Murphy. Englewood Cliffs, NJ: Prentice-Hall, c1981. xi, 210 p.
80-022349　790/.01/35　013166512X
Leisure.

BJ1499 Special topics — Active vs. meditative life — Other topics, A-Z

BJ1499.S65 C65 2002
Colegate, Isabel.
A pelican in the wilderness: hermits, solitaries and recluses/ by Isabel Colegate. Washington, D.C.: Counterpoint, 2002.
2001-047242　291.4/47 21　1582431213
Hermits. Solitude.

BJ1500 Special topics — Other special topics in ethics, A-Z

BJ1500.B47 B46 2001
Ben-Yehuda, Nachman.
Betrayals and treason: violations of trust and loyalty/ Nachman Ben-Yehuda. Boulder, Colo.: Westview Press, 2001. xii, 401 p.
00-043985　179/.8 21　0813397766
Betrayal. Treason.

BJ1500.T78 H37 2002
Hardin, Russell,
Trust and trustworthiness/ Russell Hardin. New York: Russell Sage Foundation, c2002. xxi, 234 p.
2001-040817　179/.9 21　0871543427
Trust. Reliability. Interpersonal relations.

BJ1500.W44 1999
What do we deserve?: a reader on justice and desert/ Louis P. Pojman, Owen McLeod, editors. New York: Oxford University Press, 1999. ix, 317 p.
97-046362　170 21　0195122186
Merit (Ethics)

BJ1520 Individual ethics. Character. Virtue — General works — Early through 1800

BJ1520.E3
Edwards, Jonathan, 1703-1758.
The nature of true virtue. With a foreword by William K. Frankena. [Ann Arbor] University of Michigan Press [1960] xiii, 107 p.
60-001751   170
Virtue.

BJ1520.M4 1988
Mandeville, Bernard,
The fable of the bees, or, Private vices, publick benefits/ by Bernard Mandeville; with a commentary, critical, historical, and explanatory/ by F.B. Kaye. Indianapolis: Liberty Classics, 1988. 2 v.
88-000646   170 19   0865970777
Ethics -- Early works to 1800. Virtue -- Early works to 1800. Charity-schools -- Early works to 1800.

BJ1521 Individual ethics. Character. Virtue — General works — 1801-

BJ1521.H83 1996
How should one live?: essays on the virtues/ edited by Roger Crisp. Oxford: Clarendon Press; 1996. viii, 263 p.
95-025349   179/.9   0198240589
Virtue. Ethics.

BJ1521.K87 1991
Kupperman, Joel.
Character/ Joel J. Kupperman. New York: Oxford University Press, 1991. vi, 193 p.
90-026463   170   019506870X
Character. Ethics.

BJ1531 Individual ethics. Character. Virtue — General special

BJ1531.C28 1996
Card, Claudia.
The unnatural lottery: character and moral luck/ Claudia Card. Philadelphia, PA: Temple University Press, c1996. xiv, 212 p.
96-001316   170 20   1566394538
Character. Fortune. Feminist theory. Philosophy.

BJ1531.C66 1995
The content of America's character: recovering civic virtue/ edited by Don E. Eberly; foreword by George Gallup, Jr. Lanham: Madison Books: xv, 352 p.
95-008944   170/.973 20   1568330553
Character. Values -- Political aspects -- United States. United States -- Politics and government -- 1993-2001.

BJ1531.K72 1991
Kvanvig, Jonathan L.
The intellectual virtues and the life of the mind: on the place of the virtues in epistemology/ Jonathan L. Kvanvig. Savage, Md.: Rowman & Littlefield Publishers, c1992. xii, 198 p.
91-023775   121   0847676935
Virtues. Knowledge, Theory of.

BJ1531.V57 1997
Virtue ethics/ edited by Daniel Statman. Washington, D.C.: Georgetown University Press, 1997. viii, 306 p.
97-013008   179/.9 21   0878402217
Virtue. Ethics.

BJ1531.Y42 1990
Yearley, Lee H.
Mencius and Aquinas: theories of virtue and conceptions of courage/ Lee H. Yearley. Albany, N.Y.: State University of New York Press, c1990. xiv, 280 p.
89-077407   170/.92/2   0791404315
Mencius -- Ethics. Thomas, -- Aquinas, Saint, -- 1225?-1274 -- Ethics. Courage. Virtue. Virtues.

BJ1533 Individual ethics. Character. Virtue — Special virtues, A-Z

BJ1533.C8.T5
Tillich, Paul, 1886-1965.
The courage to be. New Haven, Yale University Press, 1952. 197 p.
52-009261   179.6
Courage. Ontology. Anxiety.

BJ1533.D49.M45 1995
Mele, Alfred R., 1951-
Autonomous agents: from self-control to autonomy/ Alfred R. Mele. New york: Oxford University Press, 1995. viii, 271 p.
94-032890   128/.3   0195094549
Self-control. Autonomy (Philosophy)

BJ1533.F2.B7
Braithwaite, Richard Bevan.
Theory of games as a tool for the moral philosopher. An inaugural lecture delivered in Cambridge on 2 December 1954. Cambridge [Eng.] University Press, 1955. 75 p.
56-000087   179.9
Fairness. Games of strategy (Mathematics)

BJ1533.F2 F56 2001
Finkel, Norman J.
Not fair!: the typology of commonsense unfairness/ Norman J. Finkel. 1st ed. Washington, DC: American Psychological Association, c2001. xv, 335 p.
00-068943   170 21   1557987521
Fairness.

BJ1533.F8.F75 1993
Friedman, Marilyn, 1945-
What are friends for?: feminist perspectives on personal relationships and moral theory/ Marilyn Friedman. Ithaca, NY: Cornell University Press, 1993. xi, 276 p.
93-025812   177/.6   0801427215
Friendship -- Moral and ethical aspects. Interpersonal relations -- Moral and ethical aspects. Caring.

BJ1533.H8 F33 1998
The faces of honor: sex, shame, and violence in colonial Latin America/ edited by Lyman L. Johnson and Sonya Lipsett-Rivera. 1st ed. Albuquerque, NM: University of New Mexico Press, c1998. x, 240 p.
98-018974   306/.098 21   0826319068
Honor -- Latin America -- History. Latin America -- Social life and customs.

BJ1533.H8.N84 1993
Nye, Robert A.
Masculinity and male codes of honor in modern France/ Robert A. Nye. New York: Oxford University Press, 1993. ix, 316 p.
92-022151   305.31/0944/0903   0195046498
Honor -- France -- History. Men -- France -- Conduct of life -- History. Masculinity -- France -- History. France -- Social life and customs.

BJ1533.H8 W66 2001
Woodruff, Paul,
Reverence: renewing a forgotten virtue/ Paul Woodruff. Oxford; Oxford University Press, 2001. 248 p.
2001-036135   170 21   0195147782
Honor. Respect.

BJ1533.H93.R53 1992
Richards, Norvin, 1943-
Humility/ Norvin Richards. Philadelphia: Temple University Press, 1992. xvi, 224 p.
92-003110   179/.9   0877229279
Humility.

BJ1533.I58.B32 1996
Babbitt, Susan E.
Impossible dreams: rationality, integrity, and moral imagination/ Susan E. Babbitt. Boulder, Colo.: Westview Press, 1996. xii, 242 p.
95-045757   170   0813326397
Integrity. Reason. Imagination.

BJ1533.J9 O64 2000
O'Neill, Onora, 1941-
Bounds of justice/ Onora O'Neill, Cambridge, U.K.; Cambridge University Press, 2000. ix, 219 p.
99-056414   172/.2   052144232X
Justice.

BJ1533.L8.F54 1993
Fletcher, George P.
Loyalty: an essay on the morality of relationships/ George P. Fletcher. New York: Oxford University Press, 1993. xii, 211 p.
92-000460   179/.9   0195070267
Loyalty.

BJ1533.L8.R6 1908a
Royce, Josiah, 1855-1916.
The philosophy of loyalty. New York, Hafner
Pub. Co., 1971 [c1908] xiii, 409 p.
76-153586   179/.9
Loyalty.

BJ1533.P36.H87 1993
Hurka, Thomas, 1952-
Perfectionism/ Thomas Hurka. New York:
Oxford University Press, 1993. xi, 222 p.
92-036601   171/.3   0195080149
Perfection -- Moral and ethical aspects.

BJ1533.R4 A34 1998
Abel, Richard L.
Speaking respect, respecting speech/ Richard L.
Abel. Chicago: University of Chicago Press,
c1998. x, 380 p.
97-030778   179.7 21   0226000567
*Respect. Respect for persons. Hate speech.
Speech perception. Freedom of speech. Social
problems.*

BJ1533.R42.H37 1997
Harris, George W.
Dignity and vulnerability: strength and quality
of character/ George W. Harris. Berkeley:
University of California Press, c1997. x, 148 p.
96-048497   649/.1   0520208439
*Respect for persons -- History. Character --
History. Dignity -- History.*

BJ1533.R42 K85 1995
Kultgen, John H.
Autonomy and intervention: parentalism in the
caring life/ John Kultgen. New York: Oxford
University Press, 1995. xiii, 262 p.
94-005588   177/.7 20   0195085310
*Respect for persons. Caring. Parentalism --
Moral and ethical aspects. Autonomy
(Philosophy) Community life. Involuntary
treatment -- Moral and ethical aspects.*

BJ1533.R42.L39 1999
Lawrence-Lightfoot, Sara, 1944-
Respect: an exploration/ Sara Lawrence-
Lightfoot. Reading, Mass.: Perseus Books,
c1999. xi, 243 p.
98-089427   179/.9   073820093X
Respect. Self-esteem. Respect for persons.

BJ1533.S3 D54 1995
Dignity, character, and self-respect/ edited, and
with an introduction by Robin S. Dillon. New
York: Routledge, 1995. x, 326 p.
94-020565   179/.9 20   0415907098
Self-esteem.

BJ1533.S3.I5 1972
Jewish Theological Seminary of America.
Integrity and compromise; problems of public
and private conscience, edited by Robert M.
MacIver. Freeport, N.Y., Books for Libraries
Press [1972, c1957] 150 p.
74-167367   170   0836926560
Self-esteem. Compromise (Ethics)

BJ1535 Individual ethics. Character. Virtue — Vices — Special vices, A-Z

BJ1535.A6.S33
Scheler, Max, 1874-1928.
Ressentiment. Edited with an introd. by Lewis
A. Coser. Translated by William W. Holdheim.
[New York] Free Press of Glencoe [1961] 201 p.
60-012185   157.3   0805203702
Anger. Values.

BJ1535.G6.G66 1994
Good gossip/ edited by Robert F. Goodman,
Aaron Ben-Ze'ev. Lawrence, Kan.: University
Press of Kansas, c1994. vi, 215 p.
93-046229   177/.2   0700606696
*Gossip. Interpersonal communication.
Interpersonal relations.*

BJ1535.S4.C65 1991
Collier, James Lincoln, 1928-
The rise of selfishness in America/ James
Lincoln Collier. New York: Oxford University
Press, 1991. ix, 308 p.
90-021127   302.5/4   0195052773
*Selfishness -- History -- 20th century.United
States -- Moral conditions -- History -- 20th
century.*

BJ1550-1581.2 Individual ethics. Character. Virtue — Practical and applied ethics. Conduct of life, etc. — General works

BJ1550.D48513 1991
Dhuoda.
Handbook for William: a Carolingian woman's
counsel for her son/ by Dhuoda; translated and
with an introduction by Carol Neel. Lincoln:
University of Nebraska Press, c1991. xxviii,
152 p.
90-043359   170/.835/1   0803216866
*Conduct of life -- Early works to 1900.
Teenage boys -- Conduct of life -- Early works to
1800.*

BJ1581.2.K45 1986
Keyes, Ken.
Handbook to higher consciousness/ Ken Keyes,
Jr. 7th ed. Coos Bay, Or.: Ken Keyes College,
[1986], c1975. xvi, 215 p., [2] p. of plates:
86-027785   158/.1 19   0960068880
Conduct of life.

BJ1581.2.O2
Oakeshott, Michael Joseph, 1901-
On human conduct/ by Michael Oakeshott.
Oxford [Eng.]: Clarendon Press, 1975. x, 329 p.
75-323711   320/.01   0198271956
*Conduct of life. Social contract. Europe --
Politics and government -- 1492-1648.*

BJ1595 Individual ethics. Character. Virtue — Practical and applied ethics. Conduct of life, etc. — General special

BJ1595.N37 1998
Nehamas, Alexander, 1946-
The art of living: Socratic reflections from Plato
to Foucault/ Alexander Nehamas. Berkeley:
University of California Press, c1998. xi, 283 p.
97-025834   190   0520211731
*Socrates.Conduct of life. Philosophers --
Conduct of life.*

BJ1595.5 Individual ethics. Character. Virtue — Practical and applied ethics. Conduct of life, etc. — Philosophical counseling

BJ1595.5.R23 2001
Raabe, Peter B, 1949-
Philosophical counseling: theory and practice/
Peter B. Raabe. Westport, Conn.: Praeger, 2001.
xxii, 303 p.
00-032377   100   0275970566
Philosophical counseling.

BJ1601-1604 Individual ethics. Character. Virtue — Practical and applied ethics. Conduct of life, etc. — The "gentlemen," the courtier, etc.

BJ1601.C2
Cady, Edwin Harrison.
The gentleman in America; a literary study in
American culture. [Syracuse, N.Y.] Syracuse
Univ. Press [1949] 232 p.
49-010671   810.9
*Conduct of life. American literature -- History
and criticism. United States -- Civilization.*

BJ1604.C33 B87 1996
Burke, Peter.
The fortunes of the Courtier: the European
reception of Castiglione's Cortegiano/ Peter
Burke. University Park: Pennsylvania State
University Press, 1996. x, 210 p., [8] p. of
plates:
95-017617   170/.44 20   0271015179
*Castiglione, Baldassarre, conte, 1478-1529.
Libro del cortegiano. Courts and courtiers.
Courtesy.*

BJ1604.C37 1967
Castiglione, Baldassarre, 1478-1529.
The book of the courtier. Translated and with an
introd. by George Bull. Baltimore, Penguin
Books [1967] 361 p.
68-001599   170/.44
Courts and courtiers. Courtesy.

BJ1611-1611.2 Individual ethics. Character. Virtue — Practical and applied ethics. Conduct of life, etc. — Success

BJ1611.D36 1997
Decker, Jeffrey Louis.
Made in America: self-styled success from Horatio Alger to Oprah Winfrey/ Jeffrey Louis Decker. Minneapolis: University of Minnesota Press, c1997. xxix, 170 p.
97-019568   302/.14/0973   0816630208
Success -- United States -- History.

BJ1611.H824
Huber, Richard M.
The American idea of success [by] Richard M. Huber. New York, McGraw-Hill [1971] x, 563 p.
76-167555   131.3   0070308357
Success -- United States -- History. Success in popular culture -- United States -- History.

BJ1611.2.D45 1996
DeVitis, Joseph L.
The success ethic, education, and the American dream/ Joseph L. DeVitis and John Martin Rich. Albany: State University of New York Press, c1996. xii, 227 p.
96-003227   170/.973   0791429938
Success. Conduct of life. Ethics.

BJ1611.2.K55 1996
Kilmer, Paulette D., 1949-
The fear of sinking: the American success formula in the Gilded Age/ Paulette D. Kilmer. Knoxville: University of Tennessee Press, [1996] xvi, 230 p.
95-041826   302/.14/097309034   0870499394
Success in popular culture -- United States -- History -- 19th century.United States -- Social life and customs -- 1865-1918.

BJ1611.2.S43 1989
Shames, Laurence.
The hunger for more: searching for values in an age of greed/ by Laurence Shames. New York, NY: Times Books, c1989. xi, 291 p.
88-029473   178   0812916565
Success. Wealth -- Moral and ethical aspects.

BJ1631 Individual ethics. Character. Virtue — Practical and applied ethics. Conduct of life, etc. — Ethics for children

BJ1631.D66 1995
Dosick, Wayne D.,
Golden rules: the ten ethical values parents need to teach their children/ Wayne Dosick. 1st ed. [San Francisco]: HarpersSanFrancisco, c1995. viii, 221 p.
94-037098   649/.7 20   0062512498
Children -- Conduct of life. Children -- Religious life. Child rearing -- Moral and ethical aspects. Moral education. Moral development.

BJ1631.L452
Leaf, Munro, 1905-
How to behave and why.   Philadelphia, Lippincott [1946] 55 p.
46-008358   170
Ethics -- Juvenile literature. Children -- Conduct of life. Ethics.

BJ1671 Individual ethics. Character. Virtue — Practical and applied ethics. Conduct of life, etc. — Ethics for young men and young women

BJ1671.C53 1973
Chesterfield, Philip Dormer Stanhope, 1694-1773.
Letters to his son and others. Introd. by R. K. Root. London, Dent; [1973] xix, 314 p.
74-152924   170/.202   0460008234
Chesterfield, Philip Dormer Stanhope, -- Earl of, -- 1694-1773 -- Correspondence.Young men -- Conduct of life -- Early works to 1800. Statesmen -- Great Britain -- Correspondence. Authors, English -- 18th century -- Correspondence.

BJ1725 Ethics of social groups, classes, etc. — Professional ethics

BJ1725.B33 1994
Beabout, Gregory R.,
Applied professional ethics: a developmental approach for use with case studies/ Gregory R. Beabout, Daryl J. Wennemann. Lanham: University Press of America, c1994. xi, 175 p.
93-039775   174 20   0819193747
Professional ethics. Moral development.

BJ1725.C66 2001
Conflict of interest in the professions/ edited by Michael Davis, Andrew Stark. Oxford; Oxford University Press, 2001. viii, 355 p.
2001-021983   174 21   019512863X
Professional ethics. Conflict of interests.

BJ1725.H35 1996
Harris, Nigel G. E., 1940-
Professional codes of conduct in the United Kingdom: a directory/ Nigel G.E. Harris. London; Mansell, 1996. 438 p.
95-031458   174/.0941   072012235X
Professional ethics -- Great Britain. Trade associations -- Great Britain -- Directories.

BJ1725.K84 1988
Kultgen, John H.
Ethics and professionalism/ John Kultgen. Philadelphia: University of Pennsylvania Press, 1988. xii, 394 p.
87-026569   174   0812280946
Professional ethics.

BJ1725.M35 1996
May, Larry.
The socially responsive self: social theory and professional ethics/ Larry May. Chicago: University of Chicago Press, c1996. xii, 209 p.
96-014866   174 20   0226511723
Professional ethics. Responsibility -- Social aspects.

BJ1725.M67 1994
Moral development in the professions: psychology and applied ethics/ edited by James R. Rest, Darcia Narvaez. Hillsdale, N.J.: L. Erlbaum Associates, 1994. xii, 233 p.
94-011072   174   0805815384
Professional ethics. Moral development. Moral education.

BJ1725.M68 1990
Mount, Eric.
Professional ethics in context: institutions, images, and empathy/ Eric Mount, Jr. Louisville, Ky.: Westminster/J. Knox Press, c1990. 176 p.
90-033574   174   0664251439
Professional ethics.

BJ1725.S85 1995
Sullivan, William M.
Work and integrity: the crisis and promise of professionalism in America/ William M. Sullivan. New York: HarperBusiness, c1995. xix, 268 p.
94-037870   174   0887307272
Professional ethics -- United States. Professions -- United States. Professional socialization -- United States.

BJ1725.W45 1994
Welch, Don, 1947-
Conflicting agendas: personal morality in institutional settings/ D. Don Welch. Cleveland, Ohio: Pilgrim Press, 1994. 195 p.
94-006912   174   0829810013
Professional ethics. Corporate culture. Individualism.

BJ1853-2122 Social usages. Etiquette

BJ1853 General works — American — General works

BJ1853.C23 1999
Caldwell, Mark.
A short history of rudeness: manners, morals, and misbehavior in modern America/ Mark Caldwell. 1st ed. New York: Picador USA, 1999. 274 p.
99-022051   395/.0973 21   0312204329
Etiquette -- United States -- History. United States -- Social life and customs.

BJ1853.F62 2000
Foster, Gwendolyn Audrey.
Troping the body: gender, etiquette, and performance/ Gwendolyn Audrey Foster. Carbondale: Southern Illinois University Press, c2000. xii, 148 p.
99-038549   395/.01   0809322862
Etiquette. Man-woman relationships.

BJ1853.P6 1969b
Post, Emily, 1873-1960.
Etiquette. New York, Funk & Wagnalls [1968, c1969] xi, 721 p.
68-055996   395
Etiquette.

BJ1853.P6 1997
Post, Peggy,
Emily Post's Etiquette. 16th ed./ Peggy Post. New York, NY: HarperCollins Publishers, c1997. xvii, 845 p.
96-043427   395 20   0062701754
Etiquette.

BJ1853.R65
Roosevelt, Eleanor, 1884-1962.
Eleanor Roosevelt's Book of common sense etiquette. New York: Macmillan, 1962. 591 p.
62-019687   395
Etiquette.

BJ2007 General works — Other languages, A-Z

BJ2007.J3.J3
Japanese etiquette. Tokyo.
61-018778   395.0952
Etiquette -- Japan.

BJ2010 Religious etiquette — General works

BJ2010.M34 1996
How to be a perfect stranger: a guide to etiquette in other people's religious ceremonies/ edited by Arthur J. Magida. Woodstock, Vt.: Jewish Lights Pub., c1996-c1997 v. 1-2
95-037474   291.3/8   1879045397
Religious etiquette -- United States. United States -- Religion -- 20th century.

BJ2021 Etiquette of entertaining. Duties of host and hostess. Hospitality — General works — Polyglot

BJ2021.H42 1990
Heal, Felicity.
Hospitality in early modern England/ Felicity Heal. Oxford [England]: Clarendon Press; 1990. x, 452 p.
89-070937   177/.1/09420903   0198217633
Hospitality -- England -- History.England -- Social life and customs.

BJ2041 Etiquette of entertaining. Duties of host and hostess. Hospitality — Table etiquette

BJ2041.V57 1991
Visser, Margaret.
The rituals of dinner: the origins, evolution, eccentricities, and meaning of table manners/ Margaret Visser. 1st American ed. New York: Grove Weidenfeld, 1991. xiii, 432 p.
90-027181   395/.54/09 20   0802111165
Table etiquette. Table etiquette -- History.

BJ2071 Etiquette of entertaining. Duties of host and hostess. Hospitality — Etiquette of special occasions — Funerals

BJ2071.P47 2000
The perfect stranger's guide to funerals and grieving practices: a guide to etiquette in other people's religious ceremonies/ edited by Stuart M. Matlins. Woodstock, Vt.: Skylight Paths Pub., c2000. 229 p.
00-059574   395.2/3 21   1893361209
Religious etiquette -- United States. United States -- Religion -- 20th century.

BJ2121 Etiquette of conversation — 1801- — Polyglot

BJ2121.P74 1972
Prochnow, Herbert Victor, 1897-
1001 ways to improve your conversation & speeches [by] Herbert V. Prochnow. Westport, Conn., Greenwood Press [1972, c1952] viii, 341 p.
70-109301   808.5   0837138442
Conversation. English language -- Errors of usage. Quotations, English.

BL Religions. Mythology. Rationalism

BL21 Religion — Congresses

BL21.R39513 1998
Religion/ edited by Jacques Derrida and Gianni Vattimo. Stanford, CA: Stanford University Press, 1998. x, 211 p.
98-060374   200   0804734860
Religion -- Congresses.

BL21.W8.S43 1995
Seager, Richard Hughes.
The World's Parliament of Religions: the East/West encounter, Chicago, 1893/ Richard Hughes Seager. Bloomington: Indiana University Press, c1995. xxxi, 208 p.
94-005510   291.1/72/09034   0253351375
Religions -- Relations. East and West -- History -- 19th century. Liberalism (Religion) -- United States -- History -- 19th century. United States -- Religion -- 19th century.

BL25 Religion — Collected works — Several authors

BL25.H5 1930
Tagore, Rabindranath, 1861-1941.
The religion of man/ Rabindranath Tagore. New York, Macmillan, 1931. 244 p.
31-006500
Religion.

BL25.L4 no. 4
Wach, Joachim, 1898-1955.
A comparative study of religions. Edited with an introd. by Joseph M. Kitagawa. New York, Columbia University Press, 1968. 231 p.
58-009237   290
Religions.

BL31 Religion — Dictionaries. Encyclopedias

BL31.A24 1989
The perennial dictionary of world religions/ Keith Crim, general editor; Roger A. Bullard, Larry D. Shinn, associate editors. 1st Harper & Row pbk. ed. San Francisco: Harper & Row, 1989, c1981. xviii, 830 p.
89-045260   291/.03 19   006061613X
Religions--Dictionaries.

BL31.C67 1994
The Continuum dictionary of religion/ edited by Michael Pye. New York: Continuum, 1994. xiii, 319 p.
93-036623   200/.3   0826406394
Religion -- Dictionaries. Religions -- Dictionaries. Religion -- Study and teaching -- Dictionaries.

BL31.C75 1998
Critical terms for religious studies/ edited by Mark C. Taylor. Chicago: University of Chicago Press, 1998. v, 423 p.
97-052257   210/.1/4   0226791564
Religion -- Terminology.

BL31.D53 1994
Larousse dictionary of beliefs and religions/ editor, Rosemary Goring; consultant editor, Frank Whaling. Edinburgh; Larousse, 1994. xii, 605 p.
94-191416   200/.3 20   0752350005
Religion -- Dictionaries. Religions -- Dictionaries.

BL31.E46 1987
The Encyclopedia of religion/ [editor in chief, Mircea Eliade; editors, Charles J. Adams ... et al.]. New York: Macmillan, c1987. 16 v
86-005432   291/.03/21 19
Religion--Encyclopedias.

BL31.H37 1995
The HarperCollins dictionary of religion/ general editor, Jonathan Z. Smith; associate editor, William Scott Green; area editors, Jorunn Jacobsen Buckley ... [et al.]; with the American Academy of Religion. San Francisco: HarperSanFrancisco, c1995. xxviii, 1154 p.
95-037024   200/.3   0060675152
Religion -- Dictionaries. Religions -- Dictionaries.

BL31.H498 1993
Hexham, Irving.
Concise dictionary of religion/ Irving Hexham. Downers Grove, Ill.: InterVarsity Press, c1993. 245 p.
93-018089   200/.3 20   0830814043
Religions -- Dictionaries.

BL31.M47 1999
Merriam-Webster's encyclopedia of world religions; Wendy Doniger, consulting editor. Springfield, Mass.: Merriam-Webster, c1999. xvii, 1181 p.
99-033147   200/.3   0877790442
Religion -- Encyclopedias.

BL35 Religion — Directories

BL35.W67
World guide to religious and spiritual organizations/ edited by Union of International Associations. Munchen; K.G. Saur, [1996-]
98-652619
Religious institutions -- Directories. Religion -- Societies, etc. -- Directories.

BL37 Religion — Computer network resources

BL37.B73 2001
Brasher, Brenda E., 1952-
Give me that online religion/ Brenda E. Brasher. San Francisco: Jossey-Bass, c2001. xii, 203 p.
00-011190   025.06/2   078794579X
Religion -- Computer network resources. Internet -- Religious aspects. Cyberspace -- Religious aspects.

BL41 Religion — Study of comparative religion. Historiography. Methodology

BL41.C75 1998
The craft of religious studies/ edited by Jon R. Stone. New York: St. Martin's Press, Scholarly and Reference Division, 1998. xv, 335 p.
97-022903   291   0312177275
Religion -- Methodology.

BL41.C86 1999
Cunningham, Graham.
Religion and magic: approaches and theories/ Graham Cunningham. New York: New York University Press, 1999. xv, 126 p.
98-043421   200/.7   0814715877
Religion -- Study and teaching. Magic -- Study and teaching.

BL41.E5
Eliade, Mircea, 1907-
The history of religions; essays in methodology. Edited by Mircea Eliade and Joseph M. Kitagawa. With a pref. by Jerald C. Brauer. [Chicago] University of Chicago Press [1959] xi, 163 p.
59-011621   290.82
Religion -- Study and teaching.

BL41.M35 1997
McCutcheon, Russell T., 1961-
Manufacturing religion: the discourse on sui generis religion and the politics of nostalgia/ Russell T. McCutcheon. New York: Oxford University Press, 1997. xiii, 249 p.
96-022755   200/.72   0195105036
Religion -- Study and teaching -- Methodology.

BL41.P69 1987
Preus, James S. 1933-
Explaining religion: criticism and theory from Bodin to Freud/ J. Samuel Preus. New Haven: Yale University Press, c1987. xxi, 231 p.
86-032418   200/.7   0300038224
Religion -- Study and teaching -- History.

BL41.W33 1988
Wach, Joachim, 1898-1955.
Essays in the history of religions/ Joachim Wach; edited by Joseph M. Kitagawa and Gregory D. Alles. New York: Macmillan; c1988. xxii, 202 p.
87-017187   291/.09   0029335205
Religion -- Study and teaching. Religion and sociology.

BL41.W47 1999
Wiebe, Donald, 1943-
The politics of religious studies: the continuing conflict with theology in the academy/ Donald Wiebe. New York: St. Martin's Press, 1998. xx, 332 p.
98-041099   200/.71   0312176961
Religion -- Study and teaching.

BL42 Religion — Religious education — General works

BL42.E75 2000
Erricker, Clive.
Reconstructing religious, spiritual, and moral education/ Clive Erricker and Jane Erricker. London; Routledge, 2000. xiv, 210 p.
00-022587   291.7/5   0415189462
Religious education. Moral education.

BL42.P37 2000
Parks, Sharon Daloz, 1942-
Big questions, worthy dreams: mentoring young adults in their search for meaning, purpose, and faith/ Sharon Daloz Parks. San Francisco, Calif.: Jossey-Bass, c2000. xiv, 261 p.
00-009170   261.8/34242   0787941719
Religious education of young people. Young adults -- Religious life. Faith development.

BL43 Religion — Biography of students and historians, A-Z

BL43.E4.C38 1993
Cave, David.
Mircea Eliade's vision for a new humanism/ David Cave. New York: Oxford University Press, 1993. x, 218 p.
91-039810 291/.092 0195074343
Eliade, Mircea, -- 1907-Humanism -- 20th century. Religion. Human beings.

BL43.E4.O47 1992
Olson, Carl.
The theology and philosophy of Eliade: a search for the centre/ Carl Olson. New York: St Martin's Press, 1992. xiii, 218 p.
92-004275 291/.092 0312079060
Eliade, Mircea, -- 1907-

BL48 Religion — General works

BL48.B585 2002
Bolle, Kees W.
The enticement of religion/ Kees W. Bolle. Notre Dame, Ind.: University of Notre Dame Press, c2002. xiii, 330 p.
2002-012295 200 21 026802765X
Religion.

BL48.C325 1988
Campbell, Joseph, 1904-
An open life: Joseph Campbell in conversation with Michael Toms/ foreword by Jean Erdman Campbell; selected and edited by John M. Maher and Dennie Briggs. Burdett, N.Y.: Published for the Paul Brunton Philosophic Foundation by Larson Publications, c1988. 137 p.
88-051185 291.1/3 0943914477
Campbell, Joseph, -- 1904- -- Interviews.Religion. Myth.

BL48.C5 1925a
Chesterton, G. K.
The everlasting man, G.K. Chesterton ... New York, Dodd, Mead & Company, 1925. 344 p.
25-023426
Religion. Christianity and other religions.

BL48.C5535 1993
Clarke, Peter B.
Religion defined and explained/ Peter B. Clarke and Peter Byrne. New York, N.Y.: St. Martin's Press, 1993. ix, 216 p.
92-042691 200 0312094728
Religion.

BL48.D4
Dewey, John, 1859-1952.
A common faith [by] John Dewey. New Haven, Yale University Press, 1934. 87 p.
34-027264 201
Religion.

BL48.D67 1970b
Douglas, Mary.
Natural symbols; explorations in cosmology [by] Mary Douglas. New York, Pantheon Books [1970] xvii, 177 p.
77-110128 301.5/8
Body, Human -- Religious aspects. Body, Human -- Mythology. Symbolism.

BL48.E3813
Eliade, Mircea,
A history of religious ideas/ Mircea Eliade; translated from the French by Willard R. Trask. Chicago: University of Chicago Press, c1978-c1985. 3 v.
77-016784 291 0226204006
Religion -- History. Religions -- History.

BL48.E413
Eliade, Mircea,
The sacred and the profane; the nature of religion. Translated from the French by Willard R. Trask. [1st American ed.] New York, Harcourt, Brace [1959] 256 p.
58-010904 290
Religion.

BL48.G83 2000
Guide to the study of religion/ edited by Willi Braun and Russell T. McCutcheon. New York: Cassell, 2000. xii, 560 p.
99-030537 200/.71 0304701750
Religion.

BL48.H45 1989
Hick, John.
An interpretation of religion: human responses to the transcendent/ John Hick. New Haven: Yale University Press, 1989. xv, 412 p.
88-050863 200 0300042485
Religion. Religion -- Philosophy. Religions.

BL48.H475 1999
Hinde, Robert A.
Why gods persist: a scientific approach to religion/ Robert A. Hinde. London; Routledge, 1999. vi, 288 p.
98-049646 200 0415208254
Religion.

BL48.S591 1996
Smart, Ninian 1927-
Dimensions of the sacred: an anatomy of the world's beliefs/ Ninian Smart. Berkeley: University of California Press, c1996. xxviii, 331 p.
96-020663 291.2 0520207777
Religion.

BL48.S724 1987
Stark, Rodney.
A theory of religion/ Rodney Stark, William Sims Bainbridge. New York: P. Lang, c1987. 386 p.
87-004222 200/.1 0820403563
Religion.

BL48.W313 1993
Webb, Stephen H., 1961-
Blessed excess: religion and the hyperbolic imagination/ Stephen H. Webb. Albany: State University of New York Press, c1993. xviii, 203 p.
92-006298 200/.14 0791413578
Religion. Hyperbole.

BL48.W35
Whitehead, Alfred North, 1861-1947.
Religion in the making; Lowell lectures, 1926, by Alfred North Whitehead ... New York, The Macmillan Company, 1926. 160 p.
26-015643
Religion.

BL50 Religion — Addresses, essays, lectures

BL50.A85 1993
Asad, Talal.
Genealogies of religion: discipline and reasons of power in Christianity and Islam/ Talal Asad. Baltimore: Johns Hopkins University Press, c1993. 335 p.
93-021831 306.6 20 0801846323
Rushdie, Salman. Religion. Civilization, Christian. Civilization, Islamic.

BL50.E46
Eliade, Mircea, 1907-
The quest; history and meaning in religion. Chicago, University of Chicago Press [1969] 180 p.
69-019059 200/.9
Religion.

BL50.J35 1982
James, William, 1842-1910.
Essays in religion and morality/ William James; [Frederick H. Burkhardt, general editor; Fredson Bowers, textual editor; Ignas K. Skrupskelis, associate editor; introduction by John J. McDermott]. Cambridge, Mass.: Harvard University Press, 1982. xxviii, 345 p.
81-007040 200 0674267354
Religion -- Addresses, essays, lectures. Ethics -- Addresses, essays, lectures.

BL50.T69 1979
Toynbee, Arnold Joseph, 1889-1975.
An historian's approach to religion/ Arnold Toynbee. Oxford; Oxford University Press, 1979. xiii, 340 p.
78-040535 200 0192152602
Religion. Civilization, Western -- History.

BL51 Religion — Philosophy of religion. Philosophy and religion

BL51.A83 1998
Aslan, Adnan.
Religious pluralism in Christian and Islamic philosophy: the thought of John Hick and Seyyed Hossein Nasr/ Adnan Aslan. Richmond, England: Curzon, 1998. xiv, 290 p.
98-220276   291.1/72   0700710256
Hick, John. Nasr, Seyyed Hossein. Religious pluralism -- Islam. Religion -- Philosophy. Religious pluralism -- Christianity.

BL51.B238 1990
Banner, Michael C.
The justification of science and the rationality of religious belief/ Michael C. Banner. Oxford [England]: Clarendon Press; 1990. x, 196 p.
89-022852   121/.7   0198248210
Religion -- Philosophy. Science -- Philosophy.

BL51.B554 2000
Bhaskar, Roy, 1944-
From east to west: odyssey of a soul/ Roy Bhaskar. London; Routledge, 2000. x, 157 p.
99-087584   181/.4   0415233240
Religion -- Philosophy. Critical realism. Philosophy, Comparative.

BL51.B584513
Bloch, Ernst, 1885-
Man on his own; essays in the philosophy of religion. Translated by E. B. Ashton. [New York] Herder and Herder [1970] 240 p.
79-087749   200/.1
Religion -- Philosophy -- Addresses, essays, lectures.

BL51.B6487 2000
Brainard, F. Samuel, 1943-
Reality and mystical experience/ F. Samuel Brainard. University Park, Pa.: Pennsylvania State University Press, c2000. xiii, 295 p.
98-054922   291.4/22   0271019379
Religion -- Philosophy. Mysticism -- Comparative studies.

BL51.B82 1957
Buber, Martin, 1878-1965.
Eclipse of God; studies in the relation between religion and philosophy. New York, Harper [1957, c1952] 152 p.
61-000678   201
Religion -- Philosophy. Philosophy and religion.

BL51.C325 2001
Caputo, John D.
On religion/ John D. Caputo. New York: Routledge, 2001.
00-062807   200 21   041523333X
Religion -- Philosophy.

BL51.C634 1996
A companion to the philosophy of religion/ edited by Philip L. Quinn & Charles Taliaferro. Oxford, UK; Blackwell, 1997. vi, 639 p.
96-011495   210   0631191534
Religion -- Philosophy.

BL51.E954 1992
Experience of the sacred: readings in the phenomenology of religion/ Sumner B. Twiss and Walter H. Conser, Jr., editors. Hanover, N.H.: University Press of New England, c1992. x, 294 p.
92-053867   291   0874515300
Religion -- Philosophy. Phenomenology.

BL51.G625 2000
Gier, Nicholas F., 1944-
Spiritual Titanism: Indian, Chinese, and Western perspectives/ Nicholas F. Gier. Albany, NY: State University of New York Press, c2000. xxvi, 302 p.
99-038494   291.2/13   0791445275
Religion -- Philosophy. Superman (Philosophical concept) Philosophy, Comparative.

BL51.G69 1989
Godlove, Terry F.
Religion, interpretation, and diversity of belief: the framework model from Kant to Durkheim to Davidson/ Terry F. Godlove, Jr. Cambridge [England]; Cambridge University Press, 1989. xii, 207 p.
88-037093   200/.1   0521361796
Religion -- Philosophy -- History.

BL51.H3 2001
Hammer, Olav.
Claiming knowledge: strategies of epistemology from theosophy to the new age/ by Olav Hammer. Leiden; Brill, 2001. xviii, 547 p.
00-050801   299/.93   9004120165
Knowledge, Theory of (Religion) Postmodernism -- Religious aspects. Theosophy.

BL51.H336 2000
Hart, William D., 1957-
Edward Said and the religious effects of culture/ William D. Hart. Cambridge, U.K.; Cambridge University Press, 2000. xiii, 236 p.
99-036183   306.6/092   0521770521
Said, Edward W. -- Contributions in philosophy of religion. Said, Edward W. -- Contributions in the concept of secularism. Religion -- Philosophy. Secularism.

BL51.H455 2000
Helm, Paul.
Faith with reason/ Paul Helm. New York: Oxford University Press, 2000. xvi, 185 p.
00-020587   210   0198238452
Faith and reason. Religion -- Philosophy.

BL51.H4695 1993
Herder, Johann Gottfried, 1744-1803.
Against pure reason: writings on religion, language, and history/ Johann Gottfried Herder; translated, edited, and with an introduction by Marcia Bunge. Minneapolis: Fortress Press, c1993. xx, 264 p.
92-000360   200   0800632125
Religion -- Philosophy -- Early works to 1800. Theology -- Early works to 1800. History (Theology) -- Early works to 1800.

BL51.H476
Heschel, Abraham Joshua, 1907-1972.
Man is not alone; a philosophy of religion. New York, Farrar, Straus & Young, 1951. 305 p.
51-009992   201
Religion -- Philosophy. Judaism.

BL51.H494
Hick, John.
Philosophy of religion. Englewood Cliffs, N.J., Prentice-Hall [1963] 111 p.
63-010528   201
Religion -- Philosophy.

BL51.H963 1976
Hume, David, 1711-1776.
The natural history of religion/ by David Hume; edited by A. Wayne Colver, and Dialogues concerning natural religion/ by David Hume; edited by John Valdimir Price. Oxford [Eng.]: Clarendon Press, 1976. 299 p.
77-354407   210   0198243790
Religion -- Philosophy. Natural theology -- Early works to 1900.

BL51.H98
Huxley, Aldous, 1894-1963.
The perennial philosophy/ by Aldous Huxley. New York; Harper & Brothers [1945] xi, 312 p.
45-008579   201
Religion -- Philosophy. Philosophy and religion.

BL51.J353
Jaspers, Karl, 1883-1969.
Myth and Christianity; an inquiry into the possibility of religion without myth, by Karl Jaspers and Rudolf Bultmann. New York, Noonday Press [1958] 116 p.
58-008951   201
Bultmann, Rudolf Karl, -- 1884-1976.Demythologization.

BL51.K48713 1985
Kierkegaard, Soren, 1813-1855.
Philosophical fragments, Johannes Climacus/ by Soren Kierkegaard; edited and translated with introduction and notes by Howard V. Hong and Edna H. Hong. Princeton, N.J.: Princeton University Press, c1985. xxii, 371 p.
85-003420   201   0691072736
Religion -- Philosophy.

BL51.M226 2001
McKim, Robert.
Religious ambiguity and religious diversity/
Robert McKim. Oxford; Oxford University
Press, 2001. xv, 280 p.
99-044714 200 0195128354
Religion — Philosophy. Hidden God.
Religious pluralism.

BL51.M62 1969
Mill, John Stuart, 1806-1873.
Three essays on religion. New York,
Greenwood Press [1969] xi, 302 p.
69-013997 200/.1 0837119863
Berkeley, George, -- 1685-1753.Religion --
Philosophy. Nature. Theism.

BL51.P3449 1995
Penelhum, Terence, 1929-
Reason and religious faith/ Terence Penelhum.
Boulder, Colo.: Westview Press, 1995. x, 166 p.
95-002902 210 0813320356
Religion -- Philosophy. Faith. Faith and
reason.

BL51.R43225 1995
Ricoeur, Paul.
Figuring the sacred: religion, narrative, and
imagination/ Paul Ricoeur; translated by David
Pellauer; edited by Mark I. Wallace.
Minneapolis: Fortress Press, c1995. viii, 340 p.
95-005454 200 0800628942
Storytelling. Storytelling -- Religious aspects -
- Christianity. Hermeneutics.

BL51.R598
Roth, Robert J.
American religious philosophy [by] Robert J.
Roth. New York, Harcourt, Brace & World
[1967] vi, 211 p.
67-018540 200/.1
Religion -- Philosophy. Philosophy,
American. Religious thought -- United States.

BL51.S49 1990
Sharma, Arvind.
A Hindu perspective on the philosophy of
religion/ Arvind Sharma. New York: St. Martin's
Press, 1991. ix, 180 p.
90-043340 200/.1 0312053037
Religion -- Philosophy. Philosophy, Hindu.

BL51.T58
Tillich, Paul, 1886-1965.
What is religion? Edited and with an introd. by
James Luther Adams. New York, Harper & Row
[1969] 191 p.
69-017014 200.1
Religion -- Philosophy.

BL51.T65 1998
Trigg, Roger.
Rationality and religion: does faith need
reason?/ Roger Trigg. Oxford; Blackwell, 1998.
vi, 226 p.
97-038754 210 0631197478
Religion -- Philosophy.

BL53 Religion — Psychology of religion. Religious experience — Periodicals. Societies. Serials

BL53.C42 1988
Chapman, J. Harley, 1940-
Jung's three theories of religious experience/ J.
Harley Chapman. Lewiston, NY: Edwin Mellen
Press, c1988. 178 p.
87-020465 291.4/2 0889462453
Jung, C. G. -- (Carl Gustav), -- 1875-1961 --
Contributions in concept of religious
experience.Experience (Religion) -- History of
doctrines -- 20th century.

BL53.D47
The Dialogue between theology and psychology,
by LeRoy Aden [and others] Edited by Peter
Homans. Chicago, University of Chicago Press
[1968] x, 295 p.
68-016698 200/.19
Psychology, Religious.

BL53.F67 1962
Freud, Sigmund, 1856-1939.
The future of an illusion/ Sigmund Freud;
translated by W.D. Robson-Scott. London:
Hogarth Press: 1962. x, 59 p.
82-179739 201/.9
Psychology, Religious. Religion.
Psychotherapy.

BL53.H378
Heisig, James W., 1944-
Imago Dei: a study of C. G. Jung's psychology
of religion/ James W. Heisig. Lewisburg [Pa.]:
Bucknell University Press, c1979. 253 p.
77-074405 200/.1/9 0838720765
Jung, C. G. -- (Carl Gustav), -- 1875-
1961.Psychology, Religious -- History.

BL53.H557 1991
Hitchcock, John L., 1936-
The web of the universe: Jung, the "new
physics" and human spirituality/ by John
Hitchcock. New York: Paulist Press, 1991. ix,
243 p.
91-024868 150.19/54 0809132672
Jung, C. G. -- (Carl Gustav), -- 1875-
1961.Psychology, Religious. Physics -- Religious
aspects. Spirituality.

BL53.J36 2002
James, William,
The varieties of religious experience: a study in
human nature: being the Gifford lectures on
natural religion delivered at Edinburgh in 1901-
1902/ by William James. Mineola, N.Y.: Dover
Publications, 2002. x, 534 p.
2002-019222 291.4/2 21 0486421643
Experience (Religion) Psychology, Religious.
Religion.

BL53.J8
Jung, C. G. 1875-1961.
Psychology and religion, by Carl Gustav Jung.
New Haven, Yale university press; 1938. 131 p.
38-027254 201
Psychology, Religious. Symbolism.

BL53.M38
Maslow, Abraham H.
Religions, values, and peak-experiences, by
Abraham H. Maslow. Columbus, Ohio State
University Press [1964] xx, 123 p.
64-023886 201.6
Psychology, Religious. Peak experiences.

BL53.P228 1997
Pargament, Kenneth I. 1950-
The psychology of religion and coping: theory,
research, practice/ Kenneth I. Pargament. New
York: Guilford Press, c1997. xii, 548 p.
97-009599 200/.1/9 1572302143
Psychology, Religious. Adjustment
(Psychology) -- Religious aspects.

BL53.R435 1992
Religion and mental health/ edited by John F.
Schumaker. New York: Oxford University Press,
1992. viii, 320 p.
92-003775 291.1/78322 20 0195069854
Psychology, Religious. Mental health --
Religious aspects.

BL53.T38 1999
Taves, Ann, 1952-
Fits, trances, & visions: experiencing religion
and explaining experience from Wesley to
James/ Ann Taves. Princeton, N.J.: Princeton
University Press, c1999. xii, 449 p.
99-029754 291.4/2
Experience (Religion) -- History -- 18th
century. Psychology, Religious -- History -- 18th
century. Methodism -- History -- 18th century.

BL60 Religion — Religion and sociology

BL60.A53 1999
Aldridge, Alan
Religion in the contemporary world: a
sociological introduction/ Alan Aldridge.
Cambridge, UK; Polity Press, 1999. 232 p.
99-026047 306.6 0745620825
Religion and sociology.

BL60.B53 2001
The Blackwell companion to sociology of
religion/ edited by Richard K. Fenn. Oxford,
UK; Blackwell Publishers, 2001. xx, 485 p.
00-060791 306.6 063121240X
Religion and sociology.

BL60.C375 1994
Casanova, Jose.
Public religions in the modern world/ Jose
Casanova. Chicago: University of Chicago
Press, 1994. x, 320 p.
93-037485   306.6   0226095347
Religion and sociology.

BL60.R4216 1998
Religion in a changing world: comparative
studies in sociology/ edited by Madeleine
Cousineau. Westport, Conn.: Praeger, 1998. xv,
235 p.
98-015658   306.6   0275960781
Religion and sociology.

BL60.W433
Weber, Max, 1864-1920.
The sociology of religion. Translated by
Ephraim Fischoff. Introd. by Talcott Parsons.
Boston, Beacon Press [1963] lxvii, 304 p.
62-016644   290
Religion and sociology.

BL60.W543
Wilson, Bryan R.
Religion in sociological perspective/ Bryan
Wilson. New York: Oxford University Press,
1982. vii, 187 p.
81-016829   306/.6   0198266634
Religion and sociology.

BL60.W87 1987
Wuthnow, Robert.
Meaning and moral order: explorations in
cultural analysis/ Robert Wuthnow. Berkeley:
University of California Press, c1987. xiii,
435 p.
86-014668   306   0520059506
*Religion and sociology. Sociology. Social
ethics.*

BL65 Religion —
Religion in relation to other
subjects, A-Z

BL65.A4.C65 1998
Coleman, Earle Jerome.
Creativity and spirituality: bonds between art
and religion/ Earle J. Coleman. Albany: State
University of New York Press, c1998. xx, 237 p.
97-019143   291.1/75   0791436993
Art and religion.

BL65.A4.M35 1990
Martin, James Alfred, 1917-
Beauty and holiness: the dialogue between
aesthetics and religion/ James Alfred Martin, Jr.
Princeton, N.J.: Princeton University Press,
c1990. ix, 222 p.
89-012835   200/.1   0691073570
*Aesthetics -- Religious aspects. Art and
religion.*

BL65.A46.K64 1995
Koenig, Harold George.
Research on religion and aging: an annotated
bibliography/ compiled by Harold G. Koenig.
Westport, Conn.: Greenwood Press, 1995. xviii,
172 p.
94-044350   200/.84/6   0313294275
*Aging -- Religious aspects -- Abstracts. Aging
-- Religious aspects -- Indexes. Aging --
Religious aspects -- Bibliography.*

BL65.C45.B35 1998
Bald, Margaret.
Literature suppressed on religious grounds/
Margaret Bald; introduction by Ken
Wachsberger; foreword by Siobhan Dowd. New
York, NY: Facts on File, c1998. xxii, 362 p.
97-043638   016.098/11   0816033064
*Censorship -- Religious aspects. Censorship -
- Religious aspects -- Christianity. Prohibited
books -- Bibliography.*

BL65.C8 H95 2002
Hymes. Robert P.
Way and byway: Taoism, local religion, and
models of divinity in Sung and modern China/
Robert Hymes. Berkeley: University of
California Press, 2002.
2001-041451   299/.51 21   0520207599
*Religion and culture -- China. Taoism. Gods,
Chinese. China -- Religious life and customs.*

BL65.C8.R454 1998
Religion, modernity, and postmodernity/ edited
by Paul Heelas, with the assistance of David
Martin and Paul Morris. Oxford, UK; Blackwell
Publishers, 1998. vi, 338 p.
97-029586   200   0631198474
*Religion and culture. Postmodernism --
Religious aspects -- 20th century. Religion --
History -- 20th century.*

BL65.C8.S26 1996
Sanneh, Lamin O.
Religion and the variety of culture: a study in
origin and practice/ Lamin Sanneh. Valley
Forge, Pa.: Trinity Press International, c1996.
viii, 87 p.
96-008088   291.1/7   1563381664
Religion and culture. Christianity and culture.

BL65.D67.B85 1994
Bulkeley, Kelly, 1962-
The wilderness of dreams: exploring the
religious meanings of dreams in modern Western
culture/ Kelly Bulkeley. Albany: State
University of New York Press, c1994. xiii,
309 p.
93-009484   291.4/2   079141745X
*Dreams -- Religious aspects. Dream
interpretation.*

BL65.H64.S53 1998
Shallenberger, David, 1950-
Reclaiming the spirit: gay men and lesbians
come to terms with religion/ David
Shallenberger. New Brunswick, N.J.: Rutgers
University Press, c1998. x, 281 p.
97-024856   200/.86/64   0813524881
*Gays -- Religious life. Gays -- Interviews.
Homosexuality -- Religious aspects.*

BL65.H78.L47 2000
Lerner, Natan.
Religion, beliefs, and international human rights/
Natan Lerner. Maryknoll, N.Y.: Orbis Books,
c2000. xii, 183 p.
99-086309   323.44/2/09   1570753016
*Human rights -- Religious aspects. Religion
and international affairs.*

BL65.H78.P47 1998
Perry, Michael J.
The idea of human rights: four inquiries/
Michael J. Perry. New York: Oxford University
Press, 1998. 162 p.
97-012764   323/.01   0195116364
*Human rights -- Religious aspects. Human
rights -- Philosophy.*

BL65.L33 R446 2000
Religion, law, and freedom: a global
perspective/ edited by Joel Thierstein and Yahya
R. Kamalipour; foreword by Cees J. Hamelink.
Westport, Conn.: Praeger, 2000. xxiv, 242 p.
99-088506   291.1/772   0275964523
Religion and law. Freedom of information.

BL65.M4 A83 1995
Avalos, Hector.
Illness and health care in the ancient Near East:
the role of the temple in Greece, Mesopotamia,
and Israel/ Hector Avalos. Atlanta, Ga.: Scholars
Press, c1995. xxv, 463 p.
95-000190   306.4/61 20   0788500988
*Healing -- Religious aspects -- Comparative
studies. Healing in the Bible. Temples -- Greece.
Temples -- Iraq. Temples -- Palestine. Greece --
Religion. Iraq -- Religion. Israel -- Religion.*

BL65.M4.H43 1989
Healing and restoring: health and medicine in
the world's religious traditions/ edited by
Lawrence E. Sullivan. New York: Macmillan;
[1989] xx, 468 p.
89-030298   291.1/75   0029237912
*Religion and Medicine. Mental Healing.
Health -- Religious aspects.*

BL65.M4 K646 2001
Koenig, Harold George.
Handbook of religion and health/ Harold G.
Koenig, Michael E. McCullough, David B.
Larson. Oxford; Oxford University Press, 2001.
xii, 712 p.
99-054710   291.1/78321   0195118669
Health -- Religious aspects.

BL65.M4.T35 1991
Temkin, Owsei, 1902-
Hippocrates in a world of pagans and Christians/ Owsei Temkin. Baltimore: Johns Hopkins University Press, c1991. xiv, 315 p.
90-045564   610/.9/015   0801840902
Hippocrates.Medicine -- Religious aspects -- History. Paganism -- History. Spiritual healing -- History.

BL65.P7.C37 2000
Carter, Stephen L., 1954
God's name in vain: the wrongs and rights of religion in politics/ Stephen L. Carter. New York: Basic Books, 2000. x, 248 p.
00-033741   322/.1/0973   0465008860
Religion and politics. Religion and state.

BL65.P7.E43 1995 vol. 4
Elazar, Daniel Judah.
Covenant and civil society: the constitutional matrix of modern democracy/ Daniel J. Elazar. New Brunswick, NJ: Transaction, 1998. x, 404 p.
97-049240   301   1560003111
Civil society -- History. Covenants -- Political aspects -- History. Democracy -- History.

BL65.P7.E53 1998
The encyclopedia of politics and religion/ Robert Wuthnow, editor in chief. Washington, D.C.: Congressional Quarterly, c1998. 2 v.
98-029879   322/.1/03   156802164X
Religion and politics -- Encyclopedias.

BL65.P7.H38 1994
Haynes, Jeffrey.
Religion in Third World politics/ Jeff Haynes. Boulder, CO: Lynne Rienner, c1994. ix, 166 p.
93-011091   322/.1/09124   1555874568
Religion and politics -- Developing countries. Christianity -- Developing countries -- 20th century. Islam -- Developing countries -- 20th century. Developing countries -- Religion.

BL65.P7.O34 1993
Oakeshott, Michael Joseph, 1901-
Religion, politics, and the moral life/ Michael Oakeshott; edited by Timothy Fuller. New Haven: Yale University Press, 1993. viii, 166 p.
93-001607   291.1/77   0300056435
Religion and politics. Religion and ethics. Political science -- Philosophy.

BL65.P7.R35 1998
Ramet, Sabrina P., 1949-
Nihil obstat: religion, politics, and social change in East-Central Europe and Russia/ Sabrina Petra Ramet. Durham, NC: Duke University Press, 1998. xi, 424 p.
97-023350   322/.1/09470904   0822320568
Religion and politics -- Europe, Eastern -- History -- 20th century. Christianity and politics -- Europe, Eastern -- History -- 20th century. Communism and religion -- Europe, Eastern -- History. Europe, Eastern -- Religion -- 20th century. Europe, Eastern -- Church history -- 20th century.

BL65.P7 R427 1989
Religion and political behavior in the United States/ edited by Ted G. Jelen. New York: Praeger, 1989. xvi, 308 p.
88-032186   322/.1/0973 19   0275930890
Religion and politics -- United States.

BL65.P7.S74 1987
Spirit matters: the worldwide impact of religion on contemporary politics/ edited by Richard L. Rubenstein; with an introduction by Huston Smith. New York: Paragon House Publishers, c1987. xxvii, 384 p.
86-025172   291.1/77   0887022030
Religion and politics -- History -- 20th century. World politics -- 1945-

BL65.P73.T38 2000
Taylor, Victor E.
Para/inquiry: postmodern religion and cultue/ Victor E. Taylor. London; Routledge, 2000. xi, 145 p.
99-020816   149/.97   0415189020
Postmodernism -- Religious aspects.

BL65.S62.A66 2000
Appleby, R. Scott, 1956-
The ambivalence of the sacred: religion, violence, and reconciliation/ R. Scott Appleby. Lanham, MD: Rowman & Littlefield Publishers, c2000. xiii, 429 p.
99-032597   291.1/7873   0847685543
Social conflict -- Religious aspects. Peace -- Religious aspects.

BL65.V44.B47 1998
Berry, Rynn.
Food for the Gods: vegetarianism and the world's religions/ by Rynn Berry. New York: Pythagorean, 1998.
97-029810   291.5/693   0962616923
Vegetarianism -- Religious aspects.

BL65.V55.E55 1997
Ellis, Marc H.
Unholy alliance: religion and atrocity in our time/ Marc H. Ellis. Minneapolis, MN: Fortress Press, c1997. xviii, 214 p.
96-042502   291.5/697   0800630807
Violence -- Religious aspects. Atrocities -- History -- 20th century.

BL65.V55.H33 2000
Hall, John R., 1960-
Apocalypse observed: religious movements, and violence in North America, Europe, and Japan/ John R. Hall with Philip D. Schuyler and Sylvaine Trinh. London; Routledge, 2000. xi, 228 p.
99-039629   306.6   0415192765
Violence -- Religious aspects -- Case studies. Nativistic movements -- History.

BL65.V55.J84 2000
Juergensmeyer, Mark.
Terror in the mind of God: the global rise of religious violence/ Mark Juergensmeyer. Berkeley: University of California Press, c2000. xv, 316 p.
99-030466   291.1/78331   0520223012
Violence -- Religious aspects.

BL65.W2.E74 1996
The ethics of war and peace: religious and secular perspectives/ edited by Terry Nardin. Princeton, N.J.: Princeton University Press, c1996. x, 286 p.
95-000691   172/.42   0691037132
War -- Religious aspects -- Comparative studies -- Congresses. War -- Moral and ethical aspects -- Congresses. Peace -- Religious aspects -- Comparative studies -- Congresses.

BL70 Religion — Sacred books (General) — Collected works

BL70.S56 2001
Snodgrass, Mary Ellen.
Encyclopedia of world scriptures/ Mary Ellen Snodgrass. Jefferson, N.C.: McFarland, c2001. ix, 302 p.
2001-037057   291.8/2/03 21   0786410051
Sacred books -- Encyclopedias.

BL71 Religion — Sacred books (General) — History and criticism

BL71.R48 1989
Rethinking scripture: essays from a comparative perspective/ Miriam Levering, editor. Albany: State University of New York Press, c1989. ix, 276 p.
87-009919   291.8/2   0887066135
Sacred books -- History and criticism.

BL71.5 Religion — Biography — History and criticism

BL71.5.L45 2000
Leigh, David J.
Circuitous journeys: modern spiritual autobiography/ by David J. Leigh. New York: Fordham University Press, 2000. xvi, 259 p.
99-087373   291.4/092/2   0823219933
Spiritual biography -- History and criticism. Autobiography -- Religious aspects.

BL72 Religion — Biography — Collective

BL72.B68 1993
Bowden, Henry Warner.
Dictionary of American religious biography/ Henry Warner Bowden. Westport, Conn.: Greenwood Press, 1993. ix, 686 p.
92-035524   209/.2/2   0313278253
Religious biography -- United States -- Dictionaries.United States -- Biography -- Dictionaries.

BL72.I58 1994
International biographical dictionary of religion: an encyclopedia of more than 4,000 leading personalities/   Union   of   International Associations, Brussels; edited by Jon C. Jenkins; assisted by Cécile Vanden Bloock. München: Saur, 1994. xviii, 385 p.
94-180647   200/.92/2 B 20   3598111002
Religious biography -- Dictionaries.

BL72.L48 1999
Lewis, James R.
Peculiar prophets: a biographical dictionary of new religions/ by James R. Lewis. 1st ed. St. Paul, Minn.: Paragon House, 1999. xiii, 400 p.
99-021563   200/.92/2 B 21   1557787689
Religious biography -- Dictionaries. Cults -- Dictionaries. Sects -- Dictionaries.

BL72.M33 1996
Macquarrie, John.
Mediators between human and divine: from Moses to Muhammad/ John Macquarrie. New York: Continuum, 1996. viii, 171 p.
95-050680   291.6   0826408877
Religious biography. Religions.

BL72.R58 2001
The rivers of paradise: Moses, Buddha, Confucius, Jesus, and Muhammad as religious founders/ edited by David Noel Freedman and Michael J. McClymond; foreword by Hans Kung. Grand Rapids, Mich.: W.B. Eerdmans, c2001. ix, 702 p.
00-063665   291.6/3   0802845401
Religious biography. Religions.

BL72.S76 1996
Storr, Anthony.
Feet of clay: saints, sinners, and madmen: a study of gurus/ Anthony Storr. New York: Free Press, c1996. xvii, 253 p.
96-011884   291.6/1   0684828189
Gurus -- Biography. Spiritual biography. Cults -- Biography.

BL72.W54 1992
Who's who of world religions/ editor, John R. Hinnells. New York: Simon & Schuster, c1992. xvi, 560 p.
91-036866   200/.92/2   0139529462
Religious biography -- Dictionaries. Religions -- Bibliography.

BL72.W54 1996
Who's who of religions/ edited by John R. Hinnells. London; Penguin Books, 1996. xvi, 560 p.
96-220871   200/.92/2 B 21   0140513493
Religious biography -- Dictionaries.

BL72.W88 2001
Wuthnow, Robert.
Creative spirituality: the way of the artist/ Robert Wuthnow. Berkeley: University of California Press, c2001. x, 309 p.
00-046704   291.1/75   0520225007
Spiritual biography -- United States. Artists -- Religious life -- United States. Arts and religion -- United States.

BL73 Religion — Biography — Individual, A-Z

BL73.W55 A3 1999
Wilber, Ken.
One taste: the journals of Ken Wilber. 1st ed. Boston: Shambhala, 1999. viii,386 p.
98-022970   191 B 21   1570623872
Wilber, Ken -- Diaries. Spiritual biography -- United States. Spiritual life.

BL74 Religion — Religions of the world — Collected works

BL74.E4 1967
Eliade, Mircea, 1907-
From primitives to Zen; a thematic sourcebook of the history of religions. New York, Harper & Row [1967] xxv, 644 p.
66-020775   291/.09
Religions -- History -- Sources.

BL80-80.2 Religion — Religions of the world — General works

BL80.E513
Eliade, Mircea, 1907-
Patterns in comparative religion. Translated by Rosemary Sheed. New York, Sheed & Ward [1958] xv, 484 p.
58-005885   291
Religions.

BL80.2.B385 1993
Beit-Hallahmi, Benjamin.
The illustrated encyclopedia of active new religions, sects, and cults/ Benjamin Beit-Hallahmi. New York: Rosen Pub. Group, 1993. 341 p.
93-018928   291.9/03   0823915050
Religions -- Encyclopedias.

BL80.2.C596 1996
Contemporary religious ideas: bibliographic essays/ G. Edward Lundin, Anne H. Lundin [editors].   Englewood,   Colo.:   Libraries Unlimited, 1996. xxxiv, 538 p.
95-024234   016.291   0872876799
Religions.   Religions   --   Bibliography. Religions -- Study and teaching.

BL80.2.E47 1998
World religions.   New York: Macmillan Reference USA, 1998. xii, 782 p.
98-201984   200/.3 21   0028649214
Religions -- Encyclopedias.

BL80.2.E76 2002
Esposito, John L.
World religions today/ John L. Esposito, Darrell J. Fasching, Todd Lewis. New York: Oxford University Press, 2002. xi, 562 p.
2001-053093   291 21   0195102533
Religions.

BL80.2.H275 1996
A new handbook of living religions/ edited by John R. Hinnells. Cambridge, Mass.: Blackwell Publishers, 1997.
96-013842   291   0631182756
Religions.

BL80.2.L463 1996
Levinson, David, 1947-
Religion: a cross-cultural encyclopedia/ David Levinson. Santa Barbara, Calif.: ABC-CLIO, c1996. xx, 288 p.
96-045172   200/.3   0874368650
Religions -- Encyclopedias.

BL80.2.L464 2000
Levinson, David, 1947-
The Wilson chronology of the world's religions/ David Levinson; with contributions by John Bowman ... [et al.]. New York: H.W. Wilson Co., c2000. xi, 688 p.
99-052362   200/.2/02   0824209788
Religion -- History -- Chronology.

BL80.2.L83 2001
Ludwig, Theodore M.
The sacred paths: understanding the religions of the world/ Theodore M. Ludwig. 3rd ed. Upper Saddle River, N.J.: Prentice Hall, c2001. xii, 564 p.
99-037756   291 21   013025682X
Religions.

BL80.2.R448 1993
Religious traditions of the world: a journey through Africa, Mesoamerica, North America, Judaism,   Christianity,   Islam,   Hinduism, Buddhism, China, and Japan/ edited by H. Byron Earhart. 1st ed. [San Francisco, Calif.]: HarperSanFrancisco, c1993. xx, 1204 p.
91-055481   291 20   006062115X
Religions.

BL80.2.R86 1998
Ruland, Vernon.
Imagining the sacred: soundings in world religions/ Vernon Ruland. Maryknoll, N.Y.: Orbis Books, c1998. vii, 309 p.
98-028478   291   1570752095
Religions.

BL80.2.S593 1981
Smart, Ninian, 1927-
Beyond ideology: religion and the future of Western civilization/ Ninian Smart. San Francisco: Harper & Row, c1981. 350 p.
81-047429   291.1/7   0060674024
Religions -- Addresses, essays, lectures. Ideology -- Addresses, essays, lectures. Secularism -- Addresses, essays, lectures.

BL80.2.S645 1991
Smith, Huston.
The world's religions: our great wisdom traditions/ Huston Smith. [San Francisco]: HarperSanFrancisco, c1991. xvi, 399 p.
90-056449   291 20   0062508113
Religions.

BL80.2.S6455 1994
Smith, Huston.
The illustrated world's religions: a guide to our wisdom traditions/ Huston Smith. 1st ed. [San Francisco]: HarperSanFrancisco, c1994. 255 p.
93-024107   291 20   0060674539
Religions.

BL80.2.W656 1997
World religions: an introduction for students/ Jeaneane Fowler ... [et al.]. Portland, Or.: Sussex Academic Press, 1997. xi, 431 p.
97-034865   291   1898723486
Religions.

BL85 Religion — Religions of the world — General special

BL85.M72 1999
Morreall, John, 1947-
Comedy, tragedy, and religion/ John Morreall. Albany, NY: State University of New York Press, c1999. ix, 177 p.
98-051495   200   0791442055
Religions -- Miscellanea. Tragic, The -- Religious aspects. Comic, The -- Religious aspects

BL85.P325 1997
Parker, Philip M., 1960-
Religious cultures of the world: a statistical reference/ Philip M. Parker. Westport, Conn.: Greenwood Press, 1997. viii, 144 p.
96-043833   200/.21   0313297681
Religions -- Statistics. Demographic surveys.

BL85.R375 1989
Religious issues and interreligious dialogues: an analysis and sourcebook of developments since 1945/ edited by Charles Wei-hsun Fu and Gerhard E. Spiegler. New York: Greenwood Press, 1989. x, 693 p.
88-021398   291.1/72/0904   0313232393
Religions. Religions -- Relations.

BL96-98 Religion — Religions of the world — History. By period

BL96.G3 1961
Gaster, Theodor Herzl, 1906-
Thespis; ritual, myth, and drama in the ancient Near East. Foreword by Gilbert Murray. Garden City, N.Y., Doubleday, 1961. 515 p.
61-007650   291.1/3
Rites and ceremonies -- Middle East. Mythology. Religious drama -- History and criticism. Middle East -- Religion.

BL98.R43 1987
Religious resurgence: contemporary cases in Islam, Christianity, and Judaism/ edited by Richard T. Antoun and Mary Elaine Hegland. Syracuse, N.Y.: Syracuse University Press, 1987. xiii, 269 p.
87-010225   291   0815624093
Religion -- History -- 20th century. Religions -- History -- 20th century.

BL99 Religion — Religions of the world — Liberalism (Religion)

BL99.R45 1987
Reines, Alvin Jay, 1926-
Polydoxy: explorations in a philosophy of liberal religion/ Alvin J. Reines. Buffalo, N.Y.: Prometheus Books, c1987. 219 p.
87-002259   291/.01   0879753994
Liberalism (Religion) Reform Judaism. Judaism -- 20th century.

BL182 Religion — Natural theology — General works

BL182.T35 1994
Taliaferro, Charles.
Consciousness and the mind of God/ Charles Taliaferro. Cambridge [England]; Cambridge University Press, 1994. viii, 349 p.
93-042897   212/.1   0521461731
God -- Proof. Dualism. Materialism.

BL200 Religion — Natural theology — Theism

BL200.F65 1996
Forrest, Peter, 1948-
God without the supernatural: a defense of scientific theism/ Peter Forrest. Ithaca, NY: Cornell University Press, c1996. ix, 256 p.
96-001044   211/.3   0801432553
Theism. Religion and science.

BL205-215 Religion — Natural theology — Nature and attributes of Deity

BL205.M34 1970
Mbiti, John S.
Concepts of God in Africa [by] John S. Mbiti. New York, Praeger Publishers [1970] xv, 348 p.
78-095360   299/.6
God.Africa -- Religion.

BL215.G88 1993
Guthrie, Stewart, 1941-
Faces in the clouds: a new theory of religion/ Stewart Elliott Guthrie. New York: Oxford University Press, 1993. x, 290 p.
92-009498   211   0195069013
Anthropomorphism. Religion -- Controversial literature.

BL221 Religion — Natural theology — Monotheism

BL221.N52
Niebuhr, H. Richard 1894-1962.
Radical monotheism and Western culture, with supplementary essays. New York, Harper [1960] 144 p.
60-011784   211.3
Civilization, Western. Monotheism.

BL225-226 Religion — Natural theology — Creation. Theory of the earth

BL225.G75 1958
Graves, Robert, 1895-
Adam's rib, and other anomalous elements in the Hebrew creation myth; a new view. With wood engravings by James Metcalf. New York, T. Yoseloff [1958, c1955] 72 p.
58-008030   213
Creation in art. Creation.

BL226.W45 1989
Weigle, Marta.
Creation and procreation: feminist reflections on mythologies of cosmogony and parturition/ Marta Weigle. Philadelphia: University of Pennsylvania Press, c1989. xiv, 292 p.
89-040401   291.2/4/082   0812280962
Creation. Human reproduction -- Mythology. Women -- Mythology.

BL238 Religion — Natural theology — Fundamentalism

BL238.A76 2000
Armstrong, Karen, 1944-
The battle for God/ Karen Armstrong. New York: Alfred A. Knopf, 2000. xvi, 442 p.
99-034022 200/.9 0679435972
Religious fundamentalism. Orthodox Judaism -- Israel -- History. Islamic fundamentalism -- History.

BL238.E63 2001
Encyclopedia of fundamentalism/ Brenda E. Brasher, editor. New York: Routledge, 2001. xviii, 558 p.
2001-019951 200/.9/0403 21 0415922445
Fundamentalism -- Encyclopedias.

BL238.F83 1991 vol. 1
Fundamentalisms observed/ edited by Martin E. Marty and R. Scott Appleby; a study conducted by the American Academy of Arts and Sciences. Chicago: University of Chicago Press, 1991. xvi, 872 p.
90-024894 291/.09/04 s 0226508773
Religious fundamentalism -- Comparative studies.

BL238.F83 1991 vol. 4
Accounting for fundamentalisms: the dynamic character of movements/ edited by Martin E. Marty and R. Scott Appleby; sponsored by the American Academy of Arts and Sciences. Chicago: University of Chicago Press, 1994. ix, 852 p.
93-036621 291/.09/04 s 0226508854
Religious fundamentalism.

BL238.F83 1991 vol. 5
Fundamentalisms comprehended/ edited by Martin E. Marty and R. Scott Appleby. Chicago: University of Chicago Press, 1995. x, 522 p.
94-045338 291/.09/04 s 0226508870
Religious fundamentalism. Religion and sociology. Religions.

BL238.K4613 1994
Kepel, Gilles.
The revenge of God: the resurgence of Islam, Christianity, and Judaism in the modern world/ Gilles Kepel; translated by Alan Braley. University Park, Pa.: Pennsylvania State University Press, 1994. 215 p.
93-036094 291/.09/04 0271013133
Islam -- Mediterranean Region -- History -- 20th century. Religious fundamentalism -- History. Protestant churches -- United States -- History -- 20th century. Europe -- Church history -- 20th century. United States -- Church history -- 20th century. Mediterranean Region -- Religion.

BL238.N54 1993
Nielsen, Niels Christian, 1921-
Fundamentalism, mythos, and world religions/ Niels C. Nielsen, Jr. Albany: State University of New York Press, c1993. ix, 186 p.
92-037601 200/.9/04 0791416534
Religious fundamentalism -- Comparative studies. Myth. Religions.

BL238.Q47 1996
Questioning the secular state: the worldwide resurgence of religion in politics/ edited by David Westerlund. New York: St. Martin's Press, c1996. xii, 428 p.
95-019152 200/.9/045 0312125224
Religious fundamentalism -- Case studies. Secularism -- Case studies. Religion and politics -- Case studies.

BL240-263 Religion — Natural theology — Religion and science

BL240.R8
Russell, Bertrand, 1872-1970.
Religion and science, Bertrand Russell. London, Butterworth, [1935] 255 p.
36-018962
Religion and science. Religion and science -- 1926-1945.

BL240.2.B368 1990
Barbour, Ian G.
Religion in an age of science/ Ian G. Barbour. San Francisco: Harper & Row, c1990. xv, 297 p.
89-045552 291.1/75 0060603836
Religion and science.

BL240.2.C75 1990
Critical issues in modern religion/ Roger A. Johnson ... [et al.]. 2nd ed. Englewood Cliffs, N.J.: Prentice Hall, c1990. viii, 436 p.
89-027217 200/.1 20 0131939963
Religion and science. Religion.

BL240.2.F45 1995
Ferguson, Kitty.
The fire in the equations: science, religion, and the search for God/ Kitty Ferguson. Grand Rapids, Mich.: W.B. Eerdmans Pub. Co., 1995. 307 p.
95-019181 261.5/5 0802838057
Religion and science. God -- Proof, Cosmological. Knowledge, Theory of.

BL240.2.G68 1999
Gould, Stephen Jay.
Rocks of ages: science and religion in the fullness of life/ Stephen Jay Gould. New York: Ballantine Pub. Group, 1999. viii, 241 p.
98-031335 291.1/75 0345430093
Religion and science.

BL240.2.J547 1995
Johnson, George,
Fire in the mind: science, faith, and the search for order/ George Johnson. 1st ed. New York: Knopf, 1995. 379 p.
94-038382 215 20 0679411925
Johnson, George, 1952 Jan. 20- Religion and science. Tewa philosophy. Science -- Philosophy. New Mexico -- Description and travel.

BL240.2.M413 1999
McGrath, Alister E., 1953-
Science & religion: an introduction/ Alister E. McGrath. Oxford, UK; Blackwell Publishers, 1999. xii, 250 p.
98-023477 0631208410
Religion and science.

BL240.2.R335 2001
Ratzsch, Delvin Lee, 1945-
Nature, design, and science: the status of design in natural science/ Del Ratzsch. Albany: State University of New York Press, c2001. x, 220 p.
00-049647 215 0791448932
Religion and science. God -- Proof, Teleological.

BL240.2.R36 1998
Raymo, Chet.
Skeptics and true believers: the exhilarating connection between science and religion/ Chet Raymo. New York: Walker and Co., 1998. 288 p.
98-014647 215 0802713386
Religion and science.

BL240.2.R366 2002
Barbour, Ian G.
Nature, human nature, and God/ Ian G. Barbour. Minneapolis, MN: Fortress Press, c2002. x, 170 p.
2002-510046 291.1/75 21 0800634772
Religion and science. Man (Christian theology) Philosophical anthropology.

BL240.2.R43 1996
Religion & science: history, method, dialogue/ edited by W. Mark Richardson and Wesley J. Wildman. New York: Routledge, 1996. xx, 450 p.
95-047045 261.5/5 0415916666
Religion and science. Religion and science -- History. Religion and science -- Methodology.

BL240.2.R48 1998
Rethinking theology and science: six models for the current dialogue/ edited by Niels Henrik Gregersen and J. Wentzel van Huyssteen. Grand Rapids, Mich.: William B. Eerdmans Pub., c1998. viii, 240 p.
98-015995 291.1/75 0802844642
Religion and science. Knowledge, Theory of.

BL240.2.S3245 2000
Science and religion in search of cosmic purpose/ edited by John F. Haught; contributors, Francisco J. Ayala ... [et al.]. Washington, D.C.: Georgetown University Press, c2000. xvi, 137 p.
99-036843   291.1/75   0878407693
Religion and science -- Congresses. Teleology -- Congresses.

BL240.2.S545 2000
Shermer, Michael.
How we believe: the search for God in an age of science/ Michael Shermer. New York: W.H. Freeman, c2000. xvii, 302 p.
99-040406   215   071673561X
Religion and science. Faith and reason.

BL240.2.S635 2001
Smith, Huston.
Why religion matters: the fate of the human spirit in an age of disbelief/ Huston Smith. New York, N.Y.: HarperCollins, c2001. xiv, 290 p.
00-058188   200   0060670991
Religion and science.

BL240.3.E43 2003
Encyclopedia of science and religion/ J. Wentzel Vrede van Huyssteen,   editor in chief. New York: Macmillan Reference, 2003.
2002-152471   291.1/75 21   0028657063
Religion and science -- Encyclopedias.

BL241.C588 1995
Cosmic beginnings and human ends: where science and religion meet/ edited by Clifford N. Matthews, Roy Abraham Varghese. Chicago and LaSalle, Ill.: Open Court, c1995. ix, 433 p.
94-023845   291.1/75   0812692691
Religion and science -- Congresses. Cosmogony -- Congresses. Cosmology -- Congresses.

BL245.B77 1991
Brooke, John Hedley.
Science   and   religion: some   historical perspectives/ John Hedley Brooke. Cambridge; Cambridge University Press, 1991. x, 422 p.
90-048909   291.1/75   0521239613
Religion and science -- History.

BL245.C66 1998
Conkin, Paul Keith.
When all the gods trembled: Darwinism, Scopes, and American intellectuals/ Paul K. Conkin. Lanham, Md.: Rowman & Littlefield Publishers, c1998. xi, 185 p.
98-027694   291.1/75   0847690636
Scopes, John Thomas -- Trials, litigation, etc. Darwin, Charles, -- 1809-1882. Religion and science -- United States -- History -- 20th century. Human evolution -- Religious aspects -- Christianity -- History -- 20th century. United States -- Religion -- 1901-1945. United States -- Intellectual life -- 20th century.

BL245.G55 1997
Gilbert, James Burkhart.
Redeeming culture: American religion in an age of science/ James Gilbert. Chicago, IL: University of Chicago Press, c1997. viii, 407 p.
96-047973   306.4/5/09730904   0226293203
Religion and science -- United States -- History -- 20th century. Religion and culture -- United States -- History -- 20th century. United States -- Religion -- 20th century. United States -- Intellectual life -- 20th century.

BL245.H36 2000
Hazen, Craig James.
The village enlightenment in America: popular religion and science in the nineteenth century/ Craig James Hazen. Urbana: University of Illinois Press, c2000. 194 p.
99-006336   291.1/75   0252025121
Pratt, Orson, -- 1811-1881. Hare, Robert, -- 1781-1858. Quimby, P. P. -- (Phineas Parkhurst), -- 1802-1866. Religion and science -- History -- 19th century.

BL245.P45 1993
Pelikan, Jaroslav Jan, 1923-
Christianity   and   classical   culture: the metamorphosis of natural theology in the Christian encounter with Hellenism/ Jaroslav Pelikan. New Haven: Yale University Press, c1993. xvi, 368 p.
92-042407   210/.939/34   0300055544
Macrina, -- the Younger, Saint, -- ca. 330-379 or 80.Cappadocian Fathers. Natural theology -- History of doctrines -- Early church, ca. 30-600. Christianity and culture -- History -- Early church, ca. 30-600.

BL255.C38 1996
Cavanaugh, Michael, 1944-
Biotheology: a new synthesis of science and religion/ Michael Cavanaugh; foreword by Loyal Rue. Lanham, Md.: Univeristy Press of America, c1996. xxvi, 334 p.
95-033439   215   0761801049
Biology -- Religious aspects. Evolution -- Religious aspects. Ethics.

BL256.K57 1995
Klass, Morton, 1927-
Ordered   universes: approaches   to   the anthropology of religion/ Morton Klass. Boulder: Westview Press, c1995. xiv, 177 p.
94-041434   306.6   0813312132
Religion. Ethnology -- Religious aspects. Religions.

BL263.C774 1993
Corey, Michael Anthony, 1957-
Back to Darwin: the scientific case for Deistic evolution/   M.A.   Corey.   Lanham,   Md.: University Press of America, c1993.
93-034539   213   0819193062
Evolution -- Religious aspects. Evolution (Biology) Deism.

BL263.C776 2000
Corey, Michael Anthony, 1957-
Evolution and the problem of natural evil/ Michael A. Corey. Lanham, Md.: University Press of America, c2000. x, 367 p.
00-047921   215/.7   0761818111
Evolution (Biology) -- Religious aspects. Theodicy.

BL303 Religion — The myth. Comparative mythology — Dictionaries

BL303.C67 1989
Cotterell, Arthur.
The Macmillan illustrated encyclopedia of myths & legends/ Arthur Cotterell. New York: Macmillan, c1989. 260 p.
89-008282   291.1/3/03   0025801813
Mythology -- Dictionaries. Legends -- Dictionaries.

BL303.M45 1988
Mercatante, Anthony S.
The Facts on File encyclopedia of world mythology and legend/ Anthony S. Mercatante. New York: Facts on File, c1988. xviii, 807 p.
84-021218   291.1/3/0321   0816010498
Mythology -- Dictionaries. Folklore -- Dictionaries.

BL303.6 Religion — The myth. Comparative mythology — Biography

BL303.6.C35.A3 1990
Campbell, Joseph, 1904-
The hero's journey: the world of Joseph Campbell: Joseph Campbell on his life and work/ edited and with an introduction by Phil Cousineau; foreword by Stuart L. Brown, executive editor. San Francisco: Harper & Row, c1990. xxix, 255 p.
89-045561   291.1/3/092   006250102X
Campbell,   Joseph,   --   1904-   -- Interviews.Mythologists -- United States -- Interviews. Mythology. Heroes.

BL304 Religion — The myth. Comparative mythology — Myth. The nature of myth

BL304.C36 1988
Campbell, Joseph, 1904-
The power of myth/ Joseph Campbell, with Bill Moyers; Betty Sue Flowers, editor. New York: Doubleday, c1988. xix, 231 p.
88-004218   291.1/3   0385247745
Campbell,   Joseph,   --   1904-   -- Interviews.Myth. Religion historians -- United States -- Interviews.

BL304.D54 1998
Doniger, Wendy.
The implied spider: politics & theology in myth/
Wendy Doniger. New York: Columbia
University Press, c1998. x, 200 p.
97-026476   291.1/3/01   0231111703
Myth -- Study and teaching -- Methodology.
Mythology -- Study and teaching --
Methodology.

BL304.D55 1988
Doniger, Wendy.
Other peoples' myths: the cave of echoes/
Wendy Doniger O'Flaherty. New York:
Macmillan; c1988. x, 225 p.
88-018723   291.1/3   0028960416
Myth. Storytelling -- Religious aspects.
Religion.

BL304.D58 2000
Doty, William G., 1939-
Mythography: the study of myths and rituals/
William G. Doty. Tuscaloosa: University of
Alabama Press, c2000. xxi, 577 p.
99-006781   291.1/3   0817310061
Myth -- Study and teaching. Ritual -- Study
and teaching. Myth and ritual school.

BL304.S54 1997
Sienkewicz, Thomas J.
Theories of myth: an annotated bibliography/
Thomas J. Sienkewicz. Lanham, Md.: Scarecrow
Press; 1997. xi, 227 p.
97-025078   016.3982   0810833883
Myth -- Indexes. Myth -- Bibliography.

BL310-311 Religion — The myth. Comparative mythology — General works

BL310.F715 1936
Frazer, James George,
Aftermath; a supplement to The golden bough,
by Sir James George Frazer ... London,
Macmillan and Co., 1936. xx, 494 p.
37-002300
Mythology. Religion. Magic. Superstition.

BL310.F72 1951
Frazer, James George,
The golden bough; a study in magic and
religion. Abridged ed. New York, Macmillan,
1951 [c1950] xvi, 864 p.
52-009265   291
Mythology. Religion. Magic. Superstition.

BL310.G853
Larousse encyclopedia of mythology. With an
introd. by Robert Graves. [Translated by Richard
Aldington and Delano Ames, and rev. by a panel
of editorial advisers from the Larousse
mythologie generale, edited by Felix Guirand]
New York, Prometheus Press, 1959. viii, 500 p.
59-011019   290
Mythology. Folklore.

BL311.C276
Campbell, Joseph,
Occidental mythology/ Joseph Campbell.
Harmondsworth, Eng.; Penguin Books, 1976,
c1964. x, 564 p.
76-023179   291/.13   0140043063
Mythology.

BL311.P46 1999
Philip, Neil.
Annotated guides, myths & legends/ Neil Philip.
New York: DK Pub., 1999. 128 p.
98-048836   291.1/3   0789441179
Mythology. Legends.

BL313 Religion — The myth. Comparative mythology — General special

BL313.C28 1949
Campbell, Joseph,
The hero with a thousand faces.   [New York]
Pantheon Books [1949] xxiii, 416 p.
49-008590   291
Mythology. Psychoanalysis.

BL313.J83 1963
Jung, C. G.   1875-1961
Essays on a science of mythology; the myths of
the divine child and the divine maiden, by C. G.
Jung and C. Kerenyi. Translated by R. F. C.
Hull. New York, Harper & Row [1963] viii,
200 p.
63-003824   291.13
Mythology. Psychoanalysis.

BL313.R3 1952
Rank, Otto,   1884-1939.
The myth of the birth of the hero; a
psychological interpretation of mythology,
translated by F. Robbins and Smith Ely Jelliffe.
New York, R. Brunner, 1952. 100 p.
52-009509   290
Psychology, Pathological. Heroes.
Mythology.

BL325 Religion — The myth. Comparative mythology — Topics in comparative mythology, A-Z

BL325.C7.C64 1993
Cohn, Norman Rufus Colin.
Cosmos, chaos, and the world to come: the
ancient roots of apocalyptic faith/ Norman Cohn.
New Haven: Yale University Press, 1993. 271 p.
93-001294   291.2/4   0300055986
Creation -- Comparative studies. Cosmogony
-- Comparative studies. Eschatology --
Comparative studies.

BL325.F4.C54 2000
Cleary, Thomas.
Twilight goddess: spiritual feminism and
feminine spirituality/ Thomas Cleary & Sartaz
Aziz. Boston: Shambhala, 2000.
00-021870   291.2/114   1570624992
Goddess religion. Women and religion.

BL325.F4.K53 1997
Knapp, Bettina Liebowitz 1926-
Women in myth/ Bettina L. Knapp. Albany, NY:
State University of New York Press, c1997. xxii,
270 p.
96-031315   291.1/3/082   0791431630
Women -- Mythology. Women and religion.

BL325.F4 L44 1994
Leeming, David Adams,
Goddess: myths of the female divine/ David
Leeming and Jake Page. New York: Oxford
University Press, 1994. xiv, 189 p.
94-018604   291.2/114 20   0195086392
Femininity of God -- Legends. Goddesses --
Legends. Goddess religion.

BL325.K5 F7 1978
Frankfort, Henri,
Kingship and the gods: a study of ancient Near
Eastern religion as the integration of society &
nature/ Henri Frankfort; with a new pref. by
Samuel Noah Kramer. Phoenix ed. Chicago:
University of Chicago Press, c1978. xxiii, 444 p.
78-105541   299/.3/1   0226260119
Kings and rulers -- Religious aspects. Assyro-
Babylonian religion. Egypt -- Religion. Egypt --
Kings and rulers -- Religious aspects.

BL325.S42.D65 1999
Doniger, Wendy.
Splitting the difference: gender and myth in
ancient Greece and India/ Wendy Doniger.
Chicago: University of Chicago Press, 1999. xi,
376 p.
98-047996   291.1/78343   0226156400
Sex -- Mythology -- Comparative studies.
Mythology, Greek. Mythology, Hindu.

BL380 Religion — Classification of religions — Ethnic

BL380.I56 2000
Indigenous religions: a companion/ edited by
Graham Harvey. London; Cassell, 2000. xii,
302 p.
99-041462   299   0304704482
Indigenous peoples -- Religion.

BL435 Religion — Religious doctrines (General) — Nature worship

BL435.A53 1998
Andrews, Tamra.
Legends of the earth, sea, and sky: an encyclopedia of nature myths/ Tamra Andrews. Santa Barbara, Calif.: ABC-CLIO, c1998. xiii, 322 p.
98-040603   291.2/12/03   0874369630
Nature -- Mythology -- Encyclopedias.

BL435.G74 1992
Greene, Mott T., 1945-
Natural knowledge in preclassical antiquity/ Mott T. Greene. Baltimore: Johns Hopkins University Press, c1992. xix, 182 p.
91-026952   121/.093   0801842921
Hesiod. -- Theogony.Science, Ancient. Myth. Mythology, Classical.

BL439.5-447 Religion — Religious doctrines (General) — Nature worship

BL439.5.A55 1986
Animal sacrifices: religious perspectives on the use of animals in science/ edited by Tom Regan. Philadelphia: Temple University Press, 1986. xii, 270 p.
85-022093   291.5/694 19   0877224110
Animal experimentation -- Religious aspects. Animal experimentation -- Moral and ethical aspects. Animals -- Religious aspects.

BL447.B47 1990
Bernbaum, Edwin.
Sacred mountains of the world/ Edwin Bernbaum. San Francisco: Sierra Club Books, c1990. xxiii, 291 p.
90-008038   291.3/5/09143 20   0871567121
Mountains -- Religious aspects.

BL458 Religion — Religious doctrines (General) — Woman in comparative religion

BL458.E53 1999
Encyclopedia of women and world religion/ edited by Serinity Young. New York: Macmillan Reference USA, c1999. 2 v.
98-039292   200/.82   0028646088
Women and religion -- Encyclopedias.

BL458.F455 1999
Feminism and world religions/ Arvind Sharma and Katherine K. Young, editors. Albany, N.Y.: State University of New York Press, c1999. x, 333 p.
98-010509   291.1/783442   0791440230
Women and religion. Feminism -- Religious aspects. Religions.

BL458.H35 1996
Hampson, Margaret Daphne.
After Christianity/ Daphne Hampson. Valley Forge, Pa.: Trinity Press International, 1996. x, 326 p.
96-045179   230   1563381966
Women and religion. Christianity -- Controversial literature. Feminism -- Religious aspects -- Christianity.

BL458.P36 1997
Paper, Jordan D.
Through the earth darkly: female spirituality in comparative perspective/ by Jordan Paper; with Elizabeth Aijin-Tettey ... [et al.]; foreword by Rita Gross; afterword by Catherine Keller. New York: Continuum, 1997. xxi, 290 p.
97-023307   200/.82 21   0826410502
Women and religion.

BL458.P88 1997
Puttick, Elizabeth, 1952-
Women in new religions: insearch of community, sexuality, and spiritual power/ Elizabeth Puttick; foreword by Ursula King; consultant editor, Jo Campling. New York: St. Martin's Press, 1997. xii, 282 p.
96-046619   291/.046/082   0312172591
Women and religion. Sects -- History -- 20th century. Cults -- History -- 20th century.

BL458.S45 1994
Sered, Susan Starr.
Priestess, mother, sacred sister: religions dominated by women/ Susan Starr Sered. New York: Oxford University Press, 1994. 330 p.
93-035557   200/.82   0195083954
Women and religion -- Cross-cultural studies. Women -- Religious life -- Cross-cultural studies.

BL458.W572 1985
Womanguides: readings toward a feminist theology/ [compiled by] Rosemary Radford Ruether. Boston: Beacon Press, c1985. xii, 274 p.
84-014508   291.8/088042   0807012025
Feminist theology. Women and religion. Feminism -- Religious aspects.

BL473 Religion — Religious doctrines (General) — God. Gods

BL473.C67 2000
Coulter, Charles Russell, d. 1997.
Encyclopedia of ancient deities/ by Charles Russell Coulter and Patricia Turner. Jefferson, N.C.: McFarland, c2000. x, 597 p.
97-040330   291.2/11/03   0786403179
Gods -- Encyclopedias.

BL473.J67 1993
Jordan, Michael.
Encyclopedia of gods: over 2,500 deities of the world/ Michael Jordan. New York: Facts on File, c1993. xi, 337 p.
92-046762   291.2/11   0816029091
Gods -- Encyclopedias.

BL473.5 Religion — Religious doctrines (General) — Goddesses

BL473.5.A66 1993
Ann, Martha.
Goddesses in world mythology/ Martha Ann, Dorothy Myers Imel. Santa Barbara, Calif.: ABC-CLIO, c1993. xx, 655 p.
93-031496   291.2/114/03 20   0874367158
Goddesses -- Dictionaries. Mythology -- Dictionaries.

BL473.5.G33 1989
Gadon, Elinor W., 1925-
The once and future goddess: a symbol for our time/ Elinor W. Gadon. New York: Harper & Row, c1989. xv, 405 p.
89-045399   291.2/114   0062503464
Goddesses.

BL475.5 Religion — Religious doctrines (General) — Revelation

BL475.5.W37 1994
Ward, Keith, 1938-
Religion and revelation: a theology of revelation in the world's religions/ Keith Ward. Oxford: Clarendon Press; 1994. 350 p.
93-046985   291.2/11   0198264666
Revelation -- Comparative studies.

BL477 Religion — Religious doctrines (General) — Angels. Good spirits

BL477.G87 1996
Guiley, Rosemary.
Encyclopedia of angels/ Rosemary Ellen Guiley. New York, NY: Facts on File, c1996. ix, 214 p.
96-012009   291.2/15/03   0816029881
Angels -- Dictionaries.

BL477.L45 1996
Lewis, James R.
Angels, A to Z/ James R. Lewis and Evelyn Dorothy Oliver; Kelle S. Sisung, editor; foreword by Andy Lakey. New York: Gale Research, c1996. xxiv, 485 p.
95-035403   291.2/15/03   0787604895
Angels -- Dictionaries.

BL488 Religion — Religious doctrines (General) — Saints

BL488.S32 1988
Sainthood: its manifestations in world religions/ edited by Richard Kieckhefer and George D. Bond. Berkeley: University of California Press, c1988. xii, 263 p.
88-006963   291.6/1   0520051548
Saints -- Comparative studies.

BL501 Religions — Eschatology — Apocalypticism. Apocalyptic literature

BL501.E53 1998
The encyclopedia of apocalypticism. New York: Continuum, 1998. 3 v.
97-046016   291.2/3   0826410715
Apocalyptic literature -- Comparative studies. End of the world -- Comparative studies.

BL503.2 Religion — Eschatology — Millennialism

BL503.2.W47 2000
Wessinger, Catherine Lowman.
How the millennium comes violently: from Jonestown to Heaven's Gate/ Catherine Wessinger; foreword by Jayne Seminare Docherty. New York: Seven Bridges Press, c2000. xiii, 305 p.
99-039978   291.2/3   1889119245
Millennialism -- Case studies. Violence -- Religious aspects -- Case studies.

BL504 Religion — Eschatology — Death

BL504.C76 1995
A cross-cultural look at death, dying, and religion/ edited by Joan K. Parry and Angela Shen Ryan. Chicago: Nelson-Hall Publishers, c1995. xxvi, 251 p.
94-042941   291.2/3 20   0830413332
Death -- Religious aspects -- Comparative studies. Death -- Cross-cultural studies.

BL504.D33 1991b
Death and afterlife: perspectives of world religions/ edited by Hiroshi Obayashi. New York: Greenwood Press, 1992. xxii, 209 p.
91-017855   291.2/3   0313279063
Death -- Religious aspects -- Comparative studies. Future life -- Comparative studies.

BL504.I3 2001
If I should die/ edited by Leroy S. Rouner. Notre Dame, Ind.: University of Notre Dame Press, c2001. xvii, 192 p.
00-011593   291.2/3   0268031606
Death -- Religious aspects. Immortality (Philosophy)

BL530 Religion — Eschatology — Immortality

BL530.R68 1968
Royce, Josiah, 1855-1916.
The conception of immortality. New York, Greenwood Press, 1968 [c1900] 91 p.
68-019293   236/.22
Immortality -- Addresses, essays, lectures. Individuality -- Addresses, essays, lectures.

BL535 Religion — Eschatology — Future life

BL535.K8613 1984
Kung, Hans, 1928-
Eternal life?: life after death as a medical, philosophical, and theological problem/ Hans Kung; translated by Edward Quinn. Garden City, N.Y.: Doubleday, 1984. xvi, 271 p.
82-045112   236/.2   0385182074
Jesus Christ -- Resurrection.Death -- Religious aspects -- Christianity. Resurrection. Future life -- Christianity.

BL570 Religion — Worship. Cultus — Sacrifice. Offerings. Vows

BL570.H813
Hubert, Henri,
Sacrifice: its nature and function.   [Chicago] University of Chicago Press [1964] 165 p.
64-012260
Sacrifice.

BL580-581 Religion — Worship. Cultus — Sacred places

BL580.B76 1997
Brockman, Norbert C.,
Encyclopedia of sacred places/ Norbert C. Brockman. Santa Barbara, Calif.: ABC-CLIO, c1997. xxii, 342 p.
96-053652   291.3/5/03 21   0874368308
Sacred space -- Encyclopedias.

BL580.S25 1998
Sacred space: shrine, city, land/ edited by Benjamin Z. Kedar and R.J. Zwi Werblowsky. New York, N.Y.: New York University Press, 1998. 348 p.
97-023137   291.3/5   0814746802
Sacred space -- Congresses.

BL580.W55 1996
Wilson, Colin, 1931-
The atlas of holy places & sacred sites/ Colin Wilson. New York: DK Pub., 1996. 192 p.
96-005632   291.3/5/09   0789410516
Sacred space -- Guidebooks. Shrines -- Guidebooks.

BL581.U6
Snodgrass, Mary Ellen.
Religious sites in America: a dictionary/ Mary Ellen Snodgrass. Santa Barbara, Calif.: ABC-CLIO, c2000. xvii, 508 p.
00-010425   291.3/5/0973   1576071545
Sacred space -- United States -- Encyclopedias.United States -- Religion -- Encyclopedias.

BL600-610 Religion — Worship. Cultus — Rites and ceremonies. Ritual, cult, symbolism

BL600.B46 1992
Bell, Catherine M.,
Ritual theory, ritual practice/ Catherine Bell. New York: Oxford University Press, 1992. x, 270 p.
91-016816   291.3/8 20   0195069234
Ritual. Anthropology -- Methodology.

BL600.G5413
Girard, René,
Violence and the sacred/ Rene Girard; translated by Patrick Gregory. Baltimore: Johns Hopkins University Press, c1977. vii, 333 p.
77-004539   291.3/4   0801819636
Rites and ceremonies. Sacrifice.

BL600.G74 1995
Grimes, Ronald L.,
Beginnings in ritual studies/ Ronald L. Grimes. Rev. ed. Columbia, S.C.: University of South Carolina Press, c1995. xxviii, 299 p.
94-018722   291.3/8 20   1570030014
Ritual.

BL600.M35
May, Rollo,
Symbolism in religion and literature. New York, G. Braziller, 1960. 253 p.
59-008842   246
Symbolism. Symbolism in literature.

BL600.R37 1999
Rappaport, Roy A.
Holiness and humanity: ritual in the making of religious life/ Roy A. Rappaport. Cambridge; Cambridge University Press, 1999.
98-024494   291.3/8   0521228735
Ritual. Religion.

BL603.E45 1985
Eliade, Mircea,
Symbolism, the sacred, and the arts/ Mircea Eliade; edited by Diane Apostolos-Cappadona. New York: Crossroad, 1985. xxi, 185 p.
85-014037   291.1/75 19   0824507231
Symbolism. Arts and religion.

BL603.L5413 1991
Liungman, Carl G., 1938-
Dictionary of symbols/ Carl G. Liungman. Santa Barbara, Calif.: ABC-CLIO, c1991. ix, 596 p.
91-036657   302.2/22   0874366100
Signs and symbols. Picture-writing.

BL604.B64 R45 1995
Religious reflections on the human body/ edited
by Jane Marie Law. Bloomington: Indiana
University Press, c1995. xiv, 314 p.
94-004436   291.2/2 20   0253209021
Body, Human -- Religious aspects.

BL610.B87 1987
Burkert, Walter, 1931-
Ancient mystery cults/ Walter Burkert.
Cambridge, Mass.: Harvard University Press,
1987. ix, 181 p.
87-008379   291/.093   0674033868
*Mysteries, Religious.Greece -- Religion. Rome
-- Religion.*

BL624 Religion — Religious life — General works

BL624.A43 2001
Alexander, Hanan A., 1953-
Reclaiming goodness: education and the
spiritual quest/ Hanan A. Alexander. Notre
Dame, Ind.: University of Notre Dame Press,
c2001. xix, 268 p.
00-010905   291.4   0268040036
Spiritual life. Moral education.

BL624.E93 1993
Evans, Donald D.
Spirituality and human nature/ Donald Evans.
Albany: State University of New York Press,
c1993. x, 314 p.
91-044693   291.4   0791412792
Spirituality. Psychology, Religious.

BL624.W66 2001
Wolman, Richard.
Thinking with your soul: spiritual intelligence
and why it matters/ Richard N. Wolman. New
York: Harmony Books, c2001. xii, 288 p.
00-044846   291.4   0609605488
Spiritual life. Multiple intelligences.

BL625 Religion — Religious life — Asceticism. Mysticism

BL625.A836 1995
Asceticism/ edited by Vincent L. Wimbush,
Richard Valantasis. New York, N.Y.: Oxford
University Press, 1995. 638 p.
94-017642   291.4/47   0195085353
Asceticism -- Congresses.

BL625.I5 1948
Inge, William Ralph, 1860-1954.
Mysticism in religion. Chicago, University of
Chicago Press [1948] 168 p.
48-008494
Mysticism.

BL625.I56 1998
The innate capacity: mysticism, psychology, and
philosophy/ edited by Robert K.C. Forman. New
York: Oxford University Press, 1998. xiv, 245 p.
97-001585   291.4/22   0195116976
*Mysticism -- Psychology. Mysticism --
Comparative studies.*

BL625.K37 2000
Mysticism and sacred Scripture/ edited by
Steven T. Katz. Oxford [England]; Oxford
University Press, 2000. ix, 260 p.
99-028187   291.4/22   0195097033
Mysticism. Sacred books.

BL625.S61513 2001
Solle, Dorothee.
The silent cry: mysticism and resistance/
Dorothee Soelle; translated by Barbara and
Martin Rumscheidt. Minneapolis: Fortress Press,
c2001. ix, 325 p.
00-067713   291.4/22   0800632664
Mysticism.

BL625.T43 1999
Teasdale, Wayne.
The mystic heart: discovering a universal
spirituality in the world's religions/ Wayne
Teasdale; foreword by His Holiness the Dalai
Lama; preface by Beatrice Bruteau. Novato,
Calif: New World Library, 1999. xxi, 292 p.
99-041879   291.4/22   1577311027
Mysticism. Religions.

BL625.5-625.7 Religion — Religious life — Special classes of persons

BL625.5.C64 1990
Coles, Robert.
The spiritual life of children/ Robert Coles.
Boston: Houghton Mifflin, 1990. xix, 358 p.
90-040097   291.4/083   0395559995
Children -- Religious life.

BL625.6.F36 2000
Family, religion, and social change in diverse
societies/ edited by Sharon K. Houseknecht,
Jerry G. Pankhurst. New York: Oxford
University Press, 2000. xiv, 395 p.
98-049893   306.6/911783585 21   0195131185
Family -- Religious life. Religion and culture.

BL625.7.E45 1993
Eller, Cynthia.
Living in the lap of the Goddess: the feminist
spirituality movement in America/ Cynthia Eller.
New York: Crossroad, 1993. xii, 276 p.
93-003928   299/.93   0824512456
*Women -- United States -- Religious life.
Feminism -- Religious aspects. Goddess religion
-- United States. United States -- Religion --
1960-*

BL625.7.G63 1991
The Goddess celebrates: an anthology of
women's rituals/ edited by   Diane Stein.
Freedom, CA: Crossing Press, c1991. 259 p.
90-028925   291.3/8/082 20   089594460X
*Women -- Religious life. Women and religion.
Rites and ceremonies.*

BL626.3-626.5 Religion — Religious life — Other special topics

BL626.3.S47 1994
Sessions, William Lad.
The concept of faith: a philosophical
investigation/ William Lad Sessions. Ithaca:
Cornell University Press, 1994. x, 298 p.
93-030546   234/.2   0801428734
Faith -- Comparative studies.

BL626.5.S65 1997
Smith, Lacey Baldwin, 1922-
Fools, martyrs, traitors: the story of martyrdom
in the Western world/ Lacey Baldwin Smith.
New York: Alfred A. Knopf, 1997. ix, 433 p.
96-038582   179/.7   0679451242
*Martyrdom -- History. Martyrs -- Biography.
Traitors -- Biography.*

BL631 Religion — Religious organization — Monasticism and religious orders

BL631.E63 2000
Encyclopedia of monasticism/ editor, William
M. Johnston; photo editor, Claire Renkin.
Chicago; Fitzroy Dearborn, c2000. 2 v.
00-712518   291.6/57/03   1579580904
*Monasticism and religious orders --
Encyclopedias. Monasticism and religious
orders, Buddhist -- Encyclopedias.*

BL632.5 Religion — Religious organization — Communities and institutions

BL632.5.U5.G37 1998
Gatherings in diaspora: religious communities
and the new immigration/ edited by R. Stephen
Warner and Judith G. Wittner. Philadelphia, PA:
Temple University Press, c1998. 409 p.
97-038147   305.6/0973   1566396131
*Religious communities -- United States. South
Asians -- United States. Immigrants -- Religious
life -- United States.*

BL633 Religion — Prophets and prophecy

BL633.O24 1997
Oakes, Len.
Prophetic charisma: the psychology of revolutionary religious personalities/ Len Oakes; with a foreword by Sarah Hamilton-Byrne. Syracuse, N.Y.: Syracuse University Press, 1997. xiii, 246 p.
97-020929   291.6/1/019   0815627009
Prophets — Psychology. Charisma (Personality trait) Cults — Psychology.

BL639.5 Religion — Apostasy

BL639.5.P64 1998
The politics of religious apostasy: the role of apostates in the transformation of religious movements/ edited by David G. Bromley. Westport, Conn.: Praeger, 1998. viii, 244 p.
97-034747   306.6/9142   0275955087
Apostasy.

BL640 Religion — Religious liberty

BL640.R45 1999
Religious toleration: "the variety of rites" from Cyrus to Defoe/ edited by John Christian Laursen. New York: St. Martin's Press, 1999. xx, 252 p.
99-012813   323.44/2/09   0312222335
Religious tolerance — History.

BL689-980 Religion — History and principles of religion — European. Occidental

BL689.D68 2000
Dowden, Ken, 1950-
European paganism: the realities of cult from antiquity to the Middle Ages/ Ken Dowden. London; Routledge, 2000. xix, 367 p.
99-028007   200/.94   0415120314
Paganism — Europe — History.Europe — Religion.

BL689.J66 1995
Jones, Prudence.
A history of pagan Europe/ Prudence Jones and Nigel Pennick. London; Routledge, 1995. xv, 262 p.
94-021101   200/.94   0415091365
Paganism — History. Mythology, European. Goddess religion. Europe — Religion.

BL690.M38 1981
McLeod, Hugh.
Religion and the people of Western Europe, 1789-1970/ Hugh McLeod. Oxford; Oxford University Press, 1981. 169 p.
82-112525   274/.08   0192158325
Europe — Religion.

BL690.R46 2000
Religions of late antiquity in practice/ Richard Valantasis, editor. Princeton, N.J.: Princeton University Press, c2000. xvi, 511 p.
99-049325   200/.9/015   0691057508
Religions — History. Church history — Primitive and early church, ca. 30-600. Europe — Religion.

BL715.B445 1991
Bell, Robert E.
Women of classical mythology: a biographical dictionary/ Robert E. Bell. Santa Barbara, Calif.: ABC-CLIO, c1991. xii, 462 p.
91-026649   292.1/3/082   0874365813
Mythology, Classical — Biography — Dictionaries. Goddesses — Dictionaries. Women — Mythology — Biography — Dictionaries.

BL715.H4713 1994
The Chiron dictionary of Greek & Roman mythology: gods and goddesses, heroes, places, and events of antiquity/ translated by Elizabeth Burr. Wilmette, Ill.: Chiron, c1994. v, 312 p.
93-043989   292.1/3/03   0933029829
Mythology, Classical — Dictionaries.

BL715.R66 1997
Room, Adrian.
Who's who in classical mythology/ Adrian Room. Lincolnwood, Ill.: NTC Pub. Group, c1997. 341 p.
96-026181   292.1/3/03 20   084425469X
Mythology, Classical — Dictionaries.

BL722.T75 2001
Tripolitis, Antonia,
Religions of the Hellenistic-Roman age/ Antonia Tripolitis. Grand Rapids, Mich.: W.B. Eerdmans, c2002. x, 165 p.
2001-040380   200/.938 21   080284913X
Greece — Religion. Rome — Religion.

BL723.M67 2003
Morford, Mark P. O.,
Classical mythology/ Mark P.O. Morford, Robert J. Lenardon. 7th ed. New York: Oxford University Press, 2003. xvii, 778 p.
2002-025270   292.1/3 21   0195153448
Mythology, Classical.

BL781.G65 1957
Graves, Robert, 1895-
The Greek myths. New York, G. Braziller, 1957. 2 v. in 1.
57-004984   292
Mythology, Greek.

BL782.S5713 2000
Sissa, Giulia, 1954-
The daily life of the Greek gods/ Guilia Sissa and Marcel Detienne; translated by Janet Lloyd. Stanford, Calif.: Stanford University Press, c2000. xi, 287 p.
99-087856   292.2/11   0804736138
Homer. — Iliad.Gods, Greek. Mythology, Greek. Greece — Social life and customs.

BL782.V4713 1988
Veyne, Paul,
Did the Greeks believe in their myths?: an essay on the constitutive imagination/ Paul Veyne; translated by Paula Wissing. Chicago: University of Chicago Press, 1988. xii, 161 p.
87-025536   292/.13 19   0226854345
Mythology, Greek.

BL785.H4 1955
Harrison, Jane Ellen,
Prolegomena to the study of Greek religion. [3d ed.] New York, Meridian Books, 1955. xxii, 682 p.
55-009705   292
Mythology, Greek. Cultus, Greek. Mysteries, Religious. Greece — Religion.

BL795.H6.C65 1997
Conner, Randy P.
Cassell's encyclopedia of queer myth, symbol, and spirit: gay, lesbian, bisexual, and transgender lore/ Randy P. Conner, David Hatfield Sparks, Mariya Sparks; foreword by Gloria E. Anzaldua. London; Cassell, 1997. xiii, 382 p.
97-185203   0304337609
Homosexuality — Mythology — Encyclopedias. Homosexuality — Religious aspects — Encyclopedias. Homosexuality in art — Encyclopedias.

BL798.A35 1996
Adkins, Lesley.
Dictionary of Roman religion/ Lesley Adkins & Roy A. Adkins. New York: Facts on File, c1996. xvi, 288 p.
95-008355   292.07/03   0816030057
Rome — Religion — Dictionaries.

BL802.B43 1998
Beard, Mary.
Religions of Rome/ Mary Beard, John North, Simon Price. Cambridge; Cambridge University Press, 1998. 2 v.
97-021302   200/.937/6   0521304016
Rome — Religion.

BL805.F56 1997
Finn, Thomas M. 1927-
From death to rebirth: ritual and conversion in antiquity/ Thomas M. Finn. New York; Paulist Press, 1997. v, 286 p.
97-001341   291.4/2   0809136899
Conversion — Comparative studies. Conversion — Christianity — History of doctrines — Early church, ca. 30-600. Proselytes and proselyting, Jewish. Rome — Religion.

BL805.T8713 1996
Turcan, Robert.
The cults of the Roman Empire/ Robert Turcan; translated by Antonia Neville. Cambridge, Mass.: Blackwell Publishers, 1996. xiii, 399 p.
96-007500   292.9   0631200460
Cults -- Rome.Rome -- Religion.

BL820.C5.S63 1996
Spaeth, Barbette Stanley.
The Roman goddess Ceres/ Barbette Stanley Spaeth. Austin: University of Texas Press, 1996. xvi, 256 p.
95-013112   292.2/114   0292776926
Ceres (Roman deity)Rome -- Religion.

BL860.L56 2001
Lindow, John.
Handbook of Norse mythology/ John Lindow. Santa Barbara, Calif.: ABC-CLIO, 2001. xv, 365 p.
2001-001351   293/.13   1576072177
Mythology, Norse.

BL900.E45 1992
Ellis, Peter Berresford.
Dictionary of Celtic mythology/ Peter Berresford Ellis. Santa Barbara: ABC-CLIO, c1992. viii, 232 p.
92-000872   299/.16   0874366097
Mythology, Celtic -- Dictionaries.

BL930.D58 1998
Dixon-Kennedy, Mike, 1958-
Encyclopedia of Russian & Slavic myth and legend/ Mike Dixon-Kennedy. Santa Barbara, Calif.: ABC-CLIO, c1998. xiv, 375 p.
98-020330   398.2/0947   1576070638
Mythology, Slavic -- Juvenile literature. Mythology, Slavic. Mythology -- Encyclopedias.

BL940.S65.C36 1989
Candle in the wind: religion in the Soviet Union/ edited by Eugene B. Shirley, Jr. and Michael Rowe; foreword by Richard Schifter. Washington, D.C.: Ethics and Public Policy Center, c1989. xxvii, 328 p.
89-001277   291/.0947   0896331350
Religion and state -- Soviet Union. Persecution -- Soviet Union. Soviet Union -- Religion.

BL980.I7 J47 2000
Jestice, Phyllis G.
Encyclopedia of Irish spirituality/ Phyllis G. Jestice; photographs by Kate O'Day. Santa Barbara, Calif.: ABC-CLIO, c2000. xiv, 416 p.
00-011297   200/.9415/03   1576071464
Religion -- Ireland -- Encyclopedias.

BL980.R8.A9
Aspects of religion in the Soviet Union, 1917-1967. Edited by Richard H. Marshall, Jr. Associate editors: Thomas E. Bird and Andrew Q. Blane. Chicago, University of Chicago Press [1971] xv, 489 p.
70-115874   200/.947   0226507009
Soviet Union -- Religion.

BL1005 Religion — History and principles of religion — Asian. Oriental — Dictionaries. Encyclopedias

BL1005.L46 2001
Leeming, David Adams, 1937-
A dictionary of Asian mythology/ David Leeming. New York, N.Y.: Oxford University Press, 2001. v, 232 p.
00-062389   291.1/3/09503   0195120523
Mythology, Asian -- Dictionaries -- Polyglot. Dictionaries, Polyglot. Asia -- Religion -- Dictionaries -- Polyglot.

BL1005.L4813 1989
The encyclopedia of Eastern philosophy and religion: Buddhism, Hinduism, Taoism, Zen/ Ingrid Fischer-Schreiber [et al.]; editors, Stephan Schuhmacher, Gert Woerner; translators, Michael H. Kohn, Karen Ready, Werner Wünsche. 1st ed. Boston: Shambhala, 1989. xv, 468 p.
88-015837   291/.095 19   087773433X
Religions -- Dictionaries. Philosophy, Asian -- Dictionaries. Asia -- Religion -- Dictionaries.

BL1032 Religion — History and principles of religions — Asian. Oriental — General works

BL1032.E38 1996
Eastern wisdom: an illustrated guide to the religions and philosophies of the East/ C. Scott Littleton, general editor. 1st American ed. New York: Henry Holt, 1996. 176 p.
95-038082   291/.095 20   080504647X
Philosophy, Asian. Asia -- Religion.

BL1035 Religion — History and principles of religions — Asian. Oriental — Addresses, essays, lectures

BL1035.I43 1998
Images, miracles, and authority in Asian religious traditions/ edited by Richard H. Davis. Boulder, Colo.: Westview Press, 1998. 239 p.
98-009211   291.3/7/095   0813334632
Idols and images -- Asia -- Worship. Miracles. Asia -- Religion.

BL1055-1060 Religion — History and principles of religions — Asian. Oriental — By region

BL1055.S68 2000
The South Asian religious diaspora in Britain, Canada, and the United States/ edited by Harold Coward, John R. Hinnells, and Raymond Brady Williams. Albany, NY: State University of New York Press, c2000. viii, 319 p.
99-039476   200/.89/914   0791445097
South Asians -- Great Britain -- Religion. South Asians -- Canada -- Religion. South Asians -- United States -- Religion. South Asia -- Emigration and immigration. South Asia -- Religion.

BL1060.L44 1991
Leick, Gwendolyn, 1951-
A dictionary of ancient Near Eastern mythology/ Gwendolyn Leick. London; Routledge, 1991. xiii, 199 p.
90-039713   299/.2   0415007623
Mythology, Oriental -- Dictionaries. Mythology, Assyro-Babylonian -- Dictionaries.

BL1105-2370 Religion — History and principles of religions — Asian. Oriental — By religion

BL1105.S78 1984
Stutley, Margaret, 1917-
Harper's dictionary of Hinduism: its mythology, folklore, philosophy, literature, and history/ Margaret and James Stutley. San Francisco: Harper & Row, 1984, c1977. xx, 372 p.
76-009999   294.5/03/21   0060677678
Hinduism -- Dictionaries -- Sanskrit. Sanskrit language -- Dictionaries -- English.

BL1105.S85 1997
Sullivan, Bruce M., 1951-
Historical dictionary of Hinduism/ Bruce M. Sullivan. Lanham, Md.: Scarecrow Press, 1997. xvii, 345 p.
97-011325   294.5/03   0810833271
Hinduism -- Dictionaries.

BL1112.7.M35 1998
Mahony, William K.
The artful universe: an introduction to the Vedic religious imagination/ William K. Mahony. Albany: State University of New York Press, c1998. xii, 325 p.
97-009205   294.5/921046   0791435792
Hinduism.

BL1124.52.E5 1996
Upaniòsads/ translated from the original Sanskrit by Patrick Olivelle. Oxford; Oxford University Press, 1996. lx, 446 p.
95-031976   294.5/9218 20   0192822926

BL1130.A4.B84
The Bhagavadgita in the Mahabharata: text and translation/ J. A. B. van Buitenen. Chicago: University of Chicago Press, c1981. xii, 176 p.
79-013021 294/.5/924 0226846601

BL1135.P6213
Classical Hindu mythology: a reader in the Sanskrit Puranas/ edited and translated by Cornelia Dimmitt and J. A. B. van Buitenen. Philadelphia: Temple University Press, c1978. xiii, 373 p.
77-092643 294.5/925 0877221170

BL1138.62.E5 1988
The Bhagavad Gīta: a new translation with commentary/ David White. New York: P. Lang, c1988. 246 p.
88-009723 294.5/924 19 0820405272
International Society for Krishna Consciousness.

BL1138.62.E5 1994
The Bhagavad Gita/ translated with an introduction and notes by W.J. Johnson. Oxford: Oxford University Press, 1994. xxiii, 95 p.
93-040558 294.5/924 20 0192829521

BL1139.22.E54 1984
Valmiki.
The Ramayana of Valmiki: an epic of ancient India/ introduction and translation by Robert P. Goldman; annotation by Robert Goldman and Sally J. Sutherland. Princeton, N.J.: Princeton University Press, c1984-c1986 v. 1-2
82-061364 294.5/922 0691065616

BL1150.F85 1992
Fuller, C. J. 1949-
The camphor flame: popular Hinduism and society in India / C.J. Fuller. Princeton, N.J.: Princeton University Press, c1992. xii, 306 p.
91-028619 294.5/0954 0691074046
Hinduism -- India. Religion and sociology -- India. India -- Social life and customs. India -- Religious life and customs.

BL1150.K43 1971
Keith, Arthur Berriedale, 1879-1944.
The religion and philosophy of the Veda and Upanishads. Westport, Conn., Greenwood Press [1971] 2 v.
71-109969 294/.1 0837144752
Philosophy, Hindu.India -- Religion.

BL1151.3.S53 1998
Sharma, Arvind.
The concept of universal religion in modern Hindu thought/ Arvind Sharma. New York, N.Y.: St. Martin's Press, 1998. viii, 173 p.
98-022843 294.5/2 0312216475
Hinduism -- History -- 20th century. Hinduism -- Relations. Religions (Proposed, universal, etc.)

BL1151.3.S93 1993
Subramuniya,
Dancing with Siva: Hinduism's contemporary catechism = Sibena saha nartanam: sanatanadharmaprasnottarm/ Sivaya Subramuniyaswami. Concord, Calif.: Himalayan Academy, c1993. 2 v.
92-073040 294.5/513
Hinduism -- Catechisms. Saivism -- Catechisms.

BL1152.3.B37 1989
Basham, A. L.
The origins and development of classical Hinduism/ A.L. Basham; edited and annotated by Kenneth G. Zysk. Boston: Beacon Press, c1989. xix, 159 p.
88-043314 294.5/0901 0807073008
Hinduism -- History.

BL1153.5.F68 1997
Fowler, Jeaneane D.
Hinduism: beliefs and practices/ Jeaneane Fowler. Brighton; Sussex Academic Press, 1997. xii, 162 p.
97-159424 294.5 1898723605
Hinduism.

BL1175.T47
Das, Shukavak.
Hindu encounter with modernity: Kedarnath Dutta Bhaktivinode, Vaishnava theologian/ Shukavak N. Dasa. Los Angeles: SRI, 1999. xix, 348 p.
97-002565 294.5/512/092 188975630X
Thakkura, Bhaktibinoda.Chaitnya (Sect) -- Doctrines. Hinduism -- India -- Bengal. Bengal (India) -- Religion -- 19th century.

BL1202.B494 2002
Bhaskarananda,
The essentials of Hinduism: a comprehensive overview of the world's oldest religion/ by Swami Bhaskarananda. 2nd ed. Seattle, WA: Viveka Press, c2002. xviii, 234 p.
2001-091048 1884852041
Hinduism.

BL1202.C4713 1991
Chakravarti, Sitansu S.,
Hinduism, a way of life/ Sitansu S. Chakravarti. Delhi: Motilal Banarsidass Publishers, 1991. 104 p.
91-906162 294.5 20 8120808991
Hinduism.

BL1202.K56 1994
Klostermaier, Klaus K., 1933-
A survey of Hinduism/ Klaus K. Klostermaier. Albany: State University of New York Press, c1994. xii, 715 p.
93-046778 294.5 0791421090
Hinduism.

BL1202.K564 2000
Knott, Kim.
Hinduism: a very short introduction/ Kim Knott. Oxford: Oxford University Press, 2000. 140 p.
98-010944 294.5 21 0192853414
Hinduism.

BL1202.L56 1994
Lipner, Julius.
Hindus: their religious beliefs and practices/ Julius Lipner. London; Routledge, 1994. xiii, 375 p.
93-003813 0415051819
Hinduism.

BL1202.S385 1996
Sharma, Arvind.
Hinduism for our times/ Arvind Sharma. Delhi; Oxford University Press, 1996. 116 p.
96-900196 294.5 0195637496
Hinduism.

BL1202.S39 1993
Shearer, Alistair.
The Hindu vision: forms of the formless/ Alistair Shearer. New York: Thames and Hudson, c1993. 96 p.
93-060423 294.5/37 20 0500810435
Hinduism. Art, Hindu. Hindu symbolism.

BL1205.E25 1998
Eck, Diana L.
Darsán: seeing the divine image in India/ Diana L. Eck. 3rd ed. New York: Columbia University Press, c1998. 115 p.
99-192162 0231112653
Hinduism. Gods, Hindu. Hindu symbolism.

BL1205.V5 1977
Vitsaxis, Basile.
Hindu epics, myths, and legends in popular illustrations/ by Vassilis G. Vitsaxis; with a foreword by A. L. Basham. Delhi: Oxford University Press, 1977. xii, 98 p.
78-106720
Legends, Hindu -- Illustrations. Prints -- India. Mythology, Hindu -- Illustrations.

BL1212.72.H47 1991
Herman, A. L.
A brief introduction to Hinduism: religion, philosophy, and ways of liberation/ A.L. Herman. Boulder, Colo.: Westview Press, c1991. xxi, 181 p.
90-025262 294.5 0813381096
Hinduism -- Doctrines -- History. Philosophy, Hindu -- History. Hinduism -- History.

BL1214.32.B53
Prentiss, Karen Pechilis.
The embodiment of bhakti/ Karen Pechilis Prentiss. New York: Oxford University Press, c1999. xi, 265 p.
98-045874 294.5/4 0195128133
Bhakti -- History. Hindu literature -- History and criticism. Bakhti in literature.

BL1215.N34 H56 2000
Hinduism and ecology: the intersection of earth, sky, and water/ edited by Christopher Key Chapple and Mary Evelyn Tucker. Cambridge, MA: Distributed by Harvard University Press for the Center for the Study of World Religions Harvard Divinity School,, c2000. xlix, 600 p.
00-059665 294.5/178362 0945454252
Ecology -- Religious aspects -- Hinduism. Nature -- Religious aspects -- Hinduism. Natural history -- India.

BL1215.N34.P86 1998
Purifying the earthly body of God: religion and ecology in Hindu India/ edited by Lance E. Nelson. Albany, N.Y.: State University of New York Press, c1998. ix, 366 p.
97-050608 294.5/178362 0791439232
Human ecology -- Religious aspects -- Hinduism. Hinduism -- Doctrines. Human ecology -- India.

BL1215.P65 H36 1999
Hansen, Thomas Blom, 1958-
The saffron wave: democracy and Hindu nationalism in modern India/ Thomas Blom Hansen. Princeton, NJ: Princeton University Press, 1999. vi, 293 p.
98-033355 294.5/5/0954 0691006709
Hinduism and politics -- India. Nationalism -- Religious aspects -- Hinduism. India -- Politics and government -- 1977-

BL1215.P65 M35 1996
McKean, Lise.
Divine enterprise: Gurus and the Hindu Nationalist Movement/ Lise McKean. Chicago: University of Chicago Press, 1996. xviii, 361 p.
95-024600 294.5/177/0954 20 0226560104
Hinduism and politics -- India. Nationalism -- Religious aspects -- Hinduism. Gurus -- India. Hinduism -- Social aspects -- India.

BL1216.2.D48 1996
Devi: goddesses of India/ edited by John S. Hawley and Donna M. Wulff. Berkeley: University of California Press, c1996. xii, 352 p.
95-046773 294.5/2114 0520200578
Goddesses, Hindu.

BL1216.2.G63 1996
Gods of flesh, gods of stone: the embodiment of divinity in India/ edited by Joanne Punzo Waghorne and Norman Cutler in association with Vasudha Narayanan. New York: Columbia University Press, 1996. vi, 208 p.
96-028517 294.5/211 20 0231107773
Gods, Hindu. Idols and images -- India -- Worship.

BL1218.S62 1996
Smith, David 1944-
The dance of Siva: religion, art and poetry in South Indai/ David Smith. Cambridge; Cambridge University Press, 1996. xii, 301 p.
95-035644 294.5/513/095482 0521482348
Umapati Civacariyar, -- 14th cent.Siva (Hindu deity)

BL1218.2.T4813 1989
Poems to Siva: the hymns of the Tamil saints/ Indira Viswanathan Peterson. Princeton, N.J.: Princeton University Press, c1989. xvi, 382 p.
88-022470 294.5/43 0691067678
Siva (Hindu deity) -- Prayer-books and devotions -- English. Saivism -- Prayer-books and devotions -- English. Siva (Hindu deity) -- Prayer-books and devotions -- Tamil -- History and criticism.

BL1220.S5 1981
Singer, Milton B.,
Krishna, myths, rites, and attitudes/ edited by Milton Singer; with a foreword by Daniel H. H. Ingalls. Westport, Conn.: Greenwood Press, 1981, c1966. xvii, 277 p.
80-029194 294.5/211 0313228221
Krishna (Hindu deity)

BL1225.K3 C35 1999
Caldwell, Sarah.
Oh terrifying mother: sexuality, violence, and worship of the goddess K͞aòli/ Sarah Caldwell. New Delhi; Oxford University Press, 1999. xiv, 320 p.
99-952752 294.5/2114 21 019564462X
K͞alī (Hindu deity) -- Cult -- India. Sex -- Religious aspects -- Hinduism.

BL1225.L3.K86 1997
Kumar, P. Pratap, 1952-
The goddess Laksmi: the divine consort in South Indian Vaisnava tradition/ P. Pratap Kumar. Atlanta, Ga.: Scholars Press, c1997. x, 186 p.
97-021914 294.5/2114 0788501984
Lakshmi (Hindu deity)

BL1226.85.M54
Miller, David M.,
Hindu monastic life: the monks and monasteries of Bhubaneswar/ by David M. Miller and Dorothy C. Wertz. Montreal: McGill-Queen's University Press, 1976. xv, 228 p.
76-373803 294.5/6/5 0773501908
Monastic and religious life (Hinduism) -- India -- Bhubaneswar. Monasteries, Hindu -- India -- Bhubaneswar.

BL1237.46.R64 1992
Roles and rituals for Hindu women/ edited by Julia Leslie. Rutherford: Fairleigh Dickinson University Press, c1991. xviii, 267 p.
91-018883 294.5/082 0838634753
Hindu women -- Religious life. Hindu women -- Social life and customs. Hindu women -- History.

BL1238.52.F47 1997
Feuerstein, Georg.
The Shambhala encyclopedia of yoga/ Georg Feuerstein. Boston, Mass.: Shambhala Publications, 1997. xxi, 357 p.
96-042066 181/.45/03 1570621373
Yoga -- Dictionaries.

BL1238.56.K86.J86 1996
Jung, C. G. 1875-1961.
The psychology of Kundalini yoga: notes of the seminar given in 1932 by C.G. Jung/ edited by Sonu Shamdasani. Princeton, N.J.: Princeton University Press, c1996. xlvi, 128 p.
95-044198 294.5/43 0691021279
Kundalini -- Psychology.

BL1241.56.W47 1996
White, David Gordon.
The alchemical body: Siddha traditions in medieval India/ David Gordon White. Chicago: University of Chicago Press, 1996. xviii, 596 p.
96-016977 294.5/514 0226894975
Siddhas. Alchemy -- Religious aspects -- Tantrism. Yoga, Hatha.

BL1255.D3.J67
Jordens, J. T. F.
Dayananda Sarasvati, his life and ideas/ J. T. F. Jordens. Delhi: Oxford University Press, 1978. xvii, 368 p.
79-111204 294.5/6/4 0195609956
Dayananda Sarasvati, -- Swami, -- 1824-1883.

BL1281.1547.L38 1999
Lawrence, David Peter, 1959-
Rediscovering God with transcendental argument: a contemporary interpretation of monistic Kashmiri Saiva philosophy/ David Peter Lawrence. Albany, N.Y.: State University of New York Press, c1999. xvii, 306 p.
98-038219 181/.4 0791440575
Utpala, -- fl. 900-950. Abhinavagupta, -- Rajanaka. Kashmir Saivism -- Doctrines. Philosophy, Hindu.

BL1281.24.C54 1997
Chekki, Danesh A.
Religion and social system of the Virasaiva community/ Dan A. Chekki. Westport, Conn.: Greenwood Press, 1997. xiv, 148 p.
96-029950 294.5/513 0313302510
Lingayats. Lingayats -- Social aspects.

BL1285.392.P87.C37 1999
Case, Margaret H.
Seeing Krishna/ the religious world of a Brahmin family in Vrindaban/ Margaret H. Case. New York: Oxford University Press, 2000. xi, 167 p.
98-053863 294.5/512/09542 0195130103
Purusottama Gosvami, -- Maharaj. Goswami, Shrivatsa. Religious life -- Chaitanya (Sect)Vrindavan (India) -- Religious life and customs.

BL1285.832.V75.B76 1989
Brooks, Charles R., 1946-
The Hare Krishnas in India/ Charles R. Brooks. Princeton, N.J.: Princeton University Press, c1989. x, 265 p.
88-022655 294.5/512 0691031355
Vrindavan (India) -- Religion.

BL1285.835.U6.S55 1987
Shinn, Larry D., 1942-
The dark lord: cult images and the Hare Krishnas in America/ Larry D. Shinn. Philadelphia: Westminster Press, c1987. 204 p.
86-032480   294.5/51   0664241700
Hare Krishnas -- United States.

BL1351.2.D86 1992
Dundas, Paul, 1952-
The Jains/ Paul Dundas. London; Routledge, 1992. x, 276 p.
92-000237   294.4   0415051835
Jainism. Jains.

BL1356.C67 2001
Cort, John E., 1953-
Jains in the world: religious values and ideology in India/ John E. Cort. New York: Oxford University Press, 2001. xii, 267 p.
99-028440   294.4   0195132343
Jainism -- Doctrines. Religious life -- Jainism.

BL1411.B3.E6 1957
Bardo thodol.
The Tibetan book of the dead; or, The after-death experiences on the Bardo plane, according to Lama Kazi Dawa-Samdup's English rendering, by W. Y. Evans-Wentz. With a psychological commentary by C. G. Jung, introducing foreword by Lama Anagarika Govinda, and foreword by John Woodruffe [i. e. Woodroffe] London, Oxford University Press [1965] lxxxiv, 249 p.
57-003183   294.32
Luther, Martin -- Theology. Heresies and heretics. Reformation.

BL1416.A7 M33
Aâsvaghoòsa.
The awakening of faith, attributed to Aâsvaghosha. Translated, with commentary, by Yoshito S. Hakeda. New York, Columbia University Press, 1967. xi, 128 p.
67-013778   294.3/42042 21

BL1442.Z4.S76
Suzuki, Daisetz Teitaro, 1870-1966.
The essentials of Zen Buddhism, selected from the writings of Daisetz T. Suzuki. Edited, and with an introd., by Bernard Phillips. New York, Dutton, 1962. 544 p.
61-005041   294.329
Zen Buddhism.

BL1470.F623
Foucher, A. 1865-1952.
The life of the Buddha, according to the ancient texts and monuments of India. Abridged translation by Simone Brangier Boas. Middletown, Conn., Wesleyan University Press [1963] xiv, 272 p.
63-017795   294.3
Gautama Buddha.

BL1478.6.S9 1970
Suzuki, Shunryu.
Zen mind, beginner's mind. Edited by Trudy Dixon. With an introd. by Richard Baker. [1st ed.] New York, Walker/Weatherhill [1970] 134 p.
70-123326   294.3/4/43   0802724334
Meditation -- Zen Buddhism. Zen Buddhism.

BL1483.S82 1963
Suzuki, Daisetz Teitaro, 1870-1966.
Outlines of Mahayana Buddhism. Prefatory essay by Alan Watts. New York, Schocken Books [1963] xxix, 383 p.
63-018394   294.32
Mahayana Buddhism.

BL1493.H413 1964
Herrigel, Eugen,
Zen/ Eugen Herrigel; translated by R.F.C. Hull. New York: McGraw-Hill, [1964] 109, 124 p.
64-056163   294.329
Zen Buddhism. Archery.

BL1571.C53 1998
Clark, Peter, 1957-
Zoroastrianism: an introduction to an ancient faith/ Peter Clark. Portland, OR: Sussex Academic Press, 1998. xv, 204 p.
98-027763   295   1898723788
Zoroastrianism.

BL1620.M36 1990
McCall, Henrietta.
Mesopotamian myths/ Henrietta McCall. 1st University of Texas Press ed. Austin: University of Texas Press, 1990. 80 p.
90-083365   299/.21 20   0292751303
Mythology, Assyro-Babylonian.

BL1620.M98 1989
Myths from Mesopotamia: creation, the flood, Gilgamesh, and others/ translated with an introduction and notes by Stephanie Dalley. Oxford [England]; Oxford University Press, 1989. xix, 337 p.
89-003108   299/.21   0198143974
Mythology, Assyro-Babylonian.

BL1685.S74 1996
Stetkevych, Jaroslav.
Muhammad and the golden bough: reconstructing Arabian myth/ Jaroslav Stetkevych. Bloomington: Indiana University Press, c1996. xi, 169 p.
96-012390   299/.27   0253332087
Muhammad, -- Prophet, -- d. 632 -- Legends.Mythology, Arab. Thamud (Arabian people) Mythology -- Comparative studies.

BL1802.C548 1993
Ching, Julia.
Chinese religions/ Julia Ching. Maryknoll, New York: Orbis Books, 1993. xv, 275 p.
93-002896   291/.095   0883448769
China -- Religion -- History.

BL1802.C59413 1991
Religion under socialism in China/ Luo Zhufeng, editor; translated by Donald E. MacInnis and Zheng Xi'an; with an introduction by Donald E. MacInnis; with a foreword by K.H. Ting. Armonk, N.Y.: M.E. Sharpe, c1991. xxiii, 254 p.
90-033534   291/.0951/09045   0873326091
Communism and religion.China -- Religion -- 20th century.

BL1802.D38 2001
Davis, Edward L.
Society and the supernatural in Song China/ Edward L. Davis. Honolulu: University of Hawai'i Press, c2001. 355 p.
00-064893   299/.51 21   0824823982
China -- Religious life and customs. China -- History -- Sung dynasty, 960-1279.

BL1802.D43 1998
Dean, Kenneth,
Lord of the three in one: the spread of a cult in Southeast China/ Kenneth Dean. Princeton, N.J.: Princeton University Press, c1998. xii, 406 p.
97-046181   299/.51 21   0691028818
Lin, Chao-en, 1517-1598.Cults--China--Fujian Sheng--History. Confucianism--China--Rituals. Buddhism--China--Rituals.

BL1802.F48 1992
Feuchtwang, Stephan.
The imperial metaphor: popular religion in China/ Stephan Feuchtwang. London; Routledge, 1992. ix, 214 p.
91-010825   299/.51   0415021464
China -- Religious life and customs. Taiwan -- Religious life and customs. China -- Religion.

BL1802.H35 1990
Hansen, Valerie,
Changing gods in medieval China, 1127-1276/ Valerie Hansen. Princeton, N.J.: Princeton University Press, c1990. xii, 256 p.
88-026895   299/.51/09021 19   0691055599
Cults--China--History--To 1500.

BL1802.M29 1989
MacInnis, Donald E.
Religion in China today: policy and practice/ Donald E. MacInnis. Maryknoll, N.Y.: Orbis Books, c1989. xviii, 458 p.
89-038900   291/.0951/09048   0883445948
China -- Religion -- 20th century.

BL1802.O93 1999
Overmyer, Daniel L.,
Precious volumes: an introduction to Chinese sectarian scriptures from the sixteenth and seventeenth centuries/ Daniel L. Overmyer. Cambridge, Mass.: Published by the Harvard University Asia Center: xi, 444 p.
99-019188   299/.51 21   067469838X
Religious literature, Chinese--History and criticism. Chinese literature--Ming dynasty, 1368-1644--History and criticism. Chinese literature--Ch'ing dynasty, 1644-1912--History and criticism.

BL1802.P37 1995
Paper, Jordan D.
The spirits are drunk: comparative approaches to Chinese religion/ Jordan Paper. Albany, N.Y.: State University of New York Press, c1995. xx, 315 p.
94-009954 299/.51 0791423158
China -- Religion.

BL1802.P65 1998
Poo, Mu-chou.
In search of personal welfare: a view of ancient Chinese religion/ Mu-chou Poo. Albany: State University of New York Press, c1998. xiii, 331 p.
97-019197 299/.51/0901 21 0791436306
China -- Religion. China -- Religious life and customs. China -- Civilization.

BL1802.R43 1996
Religions of China in practice/ Donald S. Lopez, Jr., editor. Princeton, N.J.: Princeton University Press, c1996. xvi, 499 p.
95-041332 0691021430
China -- Religion.

BL1802.R45 1993
Religion and society in Tang and Sung China/ edited by Patricia Buckley Ebrey and Peter N. Gregory. Honolulu: University of Hawaii Press, c1993. xv, 379 p.
93-020371 200/.951/09021 20 0824815300

BL1802.T5 1996
Thompson, Laurence G.
Chinese religion: an introduction/ Laurence G. Thompson. 5th ed. Belmont: Wadsworth Pub. Co., c1996. xxiv, 182 p.
95-010344 299/.51 20 0534255361
China -- Religion.

BL1812.G63 K37 1995
Katz, Paul R.,
Demon hordes and burning boats: the cult of Marshal Wen in late Imperial Chekiang/ Paul R. Katz. Albany: State University of New York Press, c1995. xviii, 261 p.
95-015323 299/.51 20 0791426629
Marshal Wen (Chinese deity) Zhejiang Sheng (China) -- Religious life and customs.

BL1812.G63 S74 2001
Stevens, Keith G.,
Chinese mythological Gods/ Keith G. Stevens. Oxford; Oxford University Press, 2001. vi, 82 p., [16] p. of plates:
2001-051004 299/.51 21 0195919904
Gods, Chinese. China -- Religious life and customs.

BL1812.P45.M49 1991
Meyer, Jeffrey F.
The dragons of Tiananmen: Beijing as a sacred city/ Jeffrey F. Meyer. Columbia, S.C.: University of South Carolina Press, c1991. xii, 208 p.
90-029120 299/.51235/0951156 0872497399
Sacred space -- China -- Beijing.China -- Religion. Beijing (China) -- Religion.

BL1812.R57 L35 1998
Lam, Joseph Sui Ching.
State sacrifices and music in Ming China: orthodoxy, creativity, and expressiveness/ Joseph S.C. Lam. Albany: State University of New York Press, c1998. xvi, 205 p.
97-036909 299/.51238 21 0791437051
Rites and ceremonies -- China. Sacrifice -- China. Music -- Religious aspects. China -- History -- Ming dynasty, 1368-1644.

BL1825.B57 1993
Birrell, Anne.
Chinese mythology: an introduction/ Anne Birrell; with a foreword by Yuan Ko. Baltimore: Johns Hopkins University Press, c1993. xix, 322 p.
93-014738 299/.51 0801845955
Mythology, Chinese. Tales -- China.

BL1825.B573 2000
Birrell, Anne.
Chinese myths/ Anne Birrell. 1st University of Texas Press ed. Austin: University of Texas Press: 80 p.
00-039296 299/.51 21 0292708793
Mythology, Chinese.

BL1825.P37 1996
Porter, Deborah Lynn.
From deluge to discourse: myth, history, and the generation of Chinese fiction/ Deborah Lynn Porter. Albany, N.Y.: State University of New York Press, 1996. xviii, 284 p.
95-041456 895.1/31 20 0791430340
Mythology, Chinese. Legends -- China. Chinese fiction -- History and criticism.

BL1829.C5
Chai, Chu.
The sacred books of Confucius, and other Confucian classics. Edited ans translated by Chu Chai and Winberg Chai. New Hyde Park, N. Y., University Books [1965] 384 p.
65-022805 181.09512
Confucianism -- Sacred books.

BL1830.I23.L4 1964
I ching; Book of changes. Translated by James Legge. Edited with introd. and study guide by Ch'u Chai with Winberg Chai. New Hyde Park, N.Y., University Books [c1964] ci, 448 p.
64-025866 895.18

BL1830.W67 1991
Worldly wisdom: Confucian teachings of the Ming Dynasty/ translated and edited by J.C. Cleary. 1st ed. Boston: Shambhala; xxv, 172 p.
90-042220 181/.112 20 0877736014
Confucianism. Philosophy, Confucian.

BL1840.N56 1996
Nivison, David S.
The ways of Confucianism: investigations in Chinese philosophy/ David S. Nivison; edited with an introduction by Bryan W. Van Norden. Chicago: Open Court, c1996. xiv, 339 p.
96-039050 181/.112 20 081269340X
Confucianism. Philosophy, Chinese.

BL1842.C85 1999
Culture and the state in late Chosæon Korea/ JaHyun Kim Haboush & Martina Deuchler, editors. Cambridge, Mass.: Harvard University Asia Center, 1999. x, 304 p.
99-024738 951.9/02 21 067417982X
Confucianism and state--Korea--History. Neo-Confucianism--Korea.

BL1842.P33 1996
Palais, James B., 1934-
Confucian statecraft and Korean Institutions: Yu Hyongwon and the late Choson Dynasty/ James B. Palais. Seattle: University of Washington Press, 1996.
94-035259 320.9519/09/032 0295974559
Yu, Hyong-won, -- 1622-1673 -- Pangye surok.Confucianism and state -- Korea. Sirhak school. Korea -- Politics and government -- 1392-1910.

BL1844.A78.C64 1998
Confucianism and the family/ edited by Walter H. Slote and George A. De Vos. Albany, N.Y.: State University of New York Press, c1998. xiv, 391 p.
97-026846 299/.5121783585 0791437353
Confucianism -- Asia. Family -- Asia. Asia -- Social life and customs

BL1852.D43 1991
De Bary, William Theodore,
The trouble with Confucianism/ Wm. Theodore De Bary. Cambridge, Mass.; Harvard University Press, xiv, 132 p.
91-013249 181/.112 20 067491015X
Confucianism. Neo-Confucianism.

BL1852.N48 2000
Neville, Robert C.
Boston Confucianism: portable tradition in the late-modern world/ Robert Cummings Neville. Albany, N.Y.: State University of New York Press, 2000. xxxv, 258 p.
00-020624 181/.112 21 0791447189
Tu, Wei-ming -- Views on Confucianism. Confucianism. Philosophy, Comparative. East and West.

BL1852.T39 1990
Taylor, Rodney Leon, 1944-
The religious dimensions of Confucianism/ Rodney L. Taylor. Albany: State University of New York Press, c1990. xiii, 198 p.
89-021724 299/.215 0791403114
Confucianism. Confucianism -- Relations -- Buddhism. Buddhism -- Relations -- Confucianism.

BL1852.T8 1993
Tu, Wei-ming.
Way, learning, and politics: essays on the Confucian intellectual/ Tu Wei-ming. Albany: State University of New York Press, c1993. xix, 202 p.
93-018447 181/.112 20 079141776X
Confucianism. Confucian ethics.

BL1852.Y36 2000
Yao, Hsin-chung.
An introduction to Confucianism/ Xinzhong Yao. New York: Cambridge University Press, 2000. xviii, 344 p.
99-021094 181/.112 0521643120
Confucianism.

BL1852.Z48 1999
Zhang, Wei-Bin,
Confucianism and modernization: industrialization and democratization of the Confucian regions/ Wei-Bin Zhang. New York: St. Martin's Press, 1999. ix, 229 p.
99-011856 181/.112 21 0312224117
Confucianism. Philosophers--China.

BL1853.O44 2002
Oldstone-Moore, Jennifer.
Confucianism: origins, beliefs, practices, holy texts, sacred places / Jennifer Oldstone-Moore. Oxford; Oxford University Press, 2002. 112 p.
2002-072269 299/.512 21 0195219082
Confucianism.

BL1853.R48 2002
Rethinking confucianism: past and present in China, Japan, Korea, and Vietnam/ edited by Benjamin A. Elman, John B. Duncan and Herman Ooms. Los Angeles: UCLA Asian Pacific Monograph Series, 2002.
2002-017309 181/.112 21 1883191068
Confucianism.

BL1858.O5 2002
On sacred grounds: culture, society, politics, and the formation of the cult of Confucius/ Thomas A. Wilson, editor. Cambridge, Mass.: Harvard University Asia Center: xiv, 424 p.
2002-027570 299/.512 21 0674009614
Confucianism -- Rituals.

BL1900.C46.E5 1998
Chuang-tzu.
The essential Chuang Tzu/ translated from the Chinese by Sam Hamill and J.P. Seaton. Boston: Shambhala Publications, 1998. xx, 170 p.
97-038797 299.51482 1570623368

BL1900.C576 E77 1996
Essays on skepticism, relativism and ethics in the Zhuangzi/ edited by Paul Kjellberg and Philip J. Ivanhoe. New York: State University of New York Press, c1996. xx, 240 p.
95-019688 181/.114 20 0791428923
Zhuangzi. Skepticism.

BL1900.C576 H63 2001
Höchsmann, Hyun.
On Chuang Tzu/ Hyun Höchsmann. Belmont, CA: Wadsworth/Thomson Learning, c2001. 96 p.
2001-269845 181/.114 21 0534583717
Zhuangzi.

BL1900.C576 L5863 1994
Liu, Xiaogan,
Classifying the Zhuangzi chapters/ Liu Xiaogan; [translated by William E. Savage]. Ann Arbor, Mich.: Center for Chinese Studies, University of Michigan, xxii, 217 p.
93-050079 299/.51482 20 089264107X
Zhuangzi. Nanhua jing. Laozi. Dao de jing.

BL1900.C576 W34 1998
Wandering at ease in the Zhuangzi/ edited by Roger T. Ames. Albany: State University of New York Press, c1998. viii, 239 p.
97-043323 299/.51482 21 0791439224
Zhuangzi. Nanhua jing.

BL1900.H7965.K64 1991
Kohn, Livia, 1956-
Taoist mystical philosophy: the scripture of western ascension/ Livia Kohn. Albany: State University of New York Press, c1991. xvi, 345 p.
90-034598 299/.51482 0791405427
Taoism. Mysticism -- Taoism. Philosophy, Taoist.

BL1900.H824 E5 1994
Ames, Roger T.,
The art of rulership: a study of ancient Chinese political thought/ Roger T. Ames; foreword by Harold D. Roth. Albany: State University of New York Press, c1994. xxv, 277 p.
93-045477 320/.01 20 0791420620
Huai-nan tzu, d. 122 B.C. Huai-nan tzu. 9. Chu shu hsün. Political science -- China -- History.

BL1900.H825 V35 2001
Vankeerberghen, Griet,
The Huainanzi and Liu An's claim to moral authority/ Griet Vankeerberghen. Albany, NY: State University of New York Press, c2001. viii, 225 p.
00-054796 181/.114 21 0791451488
Liu, An d. 122 B.C.

BL1900.L26 E513 1999
Laozi.
The classic of the way and virtue: a new translation of the Tao-te ching of Laozi as interpreted by Wang Bi/ translated by Richard John Lynn. New York: Columbia University Press, c1999. 244 p.
98-044394 299/.51482 21 0231105800

BL1900.L26.E5 2000
Lao-tzu.
Lao Tzu's Tao Te Ching: a translation of the startling new documents found at Guodian/ Robert G. Henricks. New York: Columbia University Press, c2000. x, 241 p.
99-037496 299/.51482 0231118163

BL1900.L35 C5439 2000
Cheng, David Hong.
On Lao tzu = [Tao]/ David Hong Cheng. Belmont, CA: Wadsworth/Thomson Learning, c2000. 93 p.
00-698381 299/.51482 21 0534576095
Laozi. Dao de jing. Taoism.

BL1900.L35 L32 1994
LaFargue, Michael.
Tao and method: a reasoned approach to the Tao Te Ching/ Michael LaFargue. Albany: State University of New York Press, c1994. xvi, 642 p.
93-050081 299/.51482 20 0791416011
Laozi. Dao de jing.Philosophy, Chinese--To 221 B.C.

BL1900.L35.L3755 1998
Lao-tzu and the Tao-te-ching/ edited by Livia Kohn and Michael LaFargue. Albany, N.Y.: State University of New York Press, c1998. xii, 330 p.
97-007857 299/.51482 0791435997
Lao-tzu. -- Tao te ching. Lao-tzu. Taoism.

BL1900.L35 R46 1999
Religious and philosophical aspects of the Laozi/ edited by Mark Csikszentmihalyi and Philip J. Ivanhoe. Albany: State University of New York Press, c1999. xi, 276 p.
98-046708 299/.51482 21 0791441121
Laozi. Dao de jing.Taoism--China. Philosophy, Taoist.

BL1900.L35 R628 2001
Roberts, Moss,
Dao de jing: the book of the way/ translation and commentary by Moss Roberts. Berkeley: University of California Press, c2001. ix, 226 p.
2001-005077 299/.51482 21 0520205553
Laozi. Dao de jing.

BL1900.L35 W29 2000
Wagner, Rudolf G.
The craft of a Chinese commentator: Wang Bi on the Laozi/ Rudolf G. Wagner. Albany, NY: State University of New York Press, c2000. ix, 361 p.
99-040511 299/.51482 21 0791443957
Laozi. Dao de jing. Wang, Bi, 226-249. Laozi dao de jing zhu.

BL1900.L88 E52 1997
Harmonizing yin and yang: the Dragon-tiger classic/ translated and with an introduction by Eva Wong. 1st ed. Boston: Shambhala, 1997. vi, 146 p.
97-002435 299/.51482 21 1570623066
Taoism -- Sacred books. Alchemy -- Religious aspects -- Taoism. Yin-yang.

BL1900.N45 R67 1999
Roth, Harold David.
Original Tao: inward training (nei-yeh) and the foundations of Taoist mysticism/ Harold D. Roth. New York: Columbia University Press, c1999. xv, 275 p.
99-020737 299/.51482 21 0231115644
Philosophy, Taoist. Meditation -- Taoism.

BL1910.C63 1993
Cleary, Thomas F.,
The essential Tao: an initiation into the heart of Taoism through the authentic Tao te ching and the inner teachings of Chuang-Tzu/ translated and presented by Thomas Cleary. 1st HarperCollins paperback ed. [San Francisco]: HarperSanFrancisco, 1993. 168 p.
91-055283   299/.51482 20   0062501623
Laozi. Dao de jing. Zhuangzi. Nanhua jing. Taoism.

BL1910.K64 1993
Kohn, Livia,
The Taoist experience: an anthology/ Livia Kohn. Albany, N.Y.: State University of New York Press, c1993. vii, 391 p.
92-032933   299/.514 20   0791415805
Taoism--China.

BL1910.R63 1997
Robinet, Isabelle.
Taoism: growth of a religion/ Isabelle Robinet; translated by Phyllis Brooks. Stanford, Calif.: Stanford University Press, c1997. xx, 296 p.
96-030127   299/.514/09   0804728380
Taoism -- History.

BL1910.W66 1997
Wong, Eva,
The Shambhala guide to Taoism/ Eva Wong. 1st ed. Boston: Shambhala, c1997. x, 268 p.
96-014960   299/.514 20   1570621691
Taoism -- China -- History. Taoism.

BL1920.B45 1991
Belyea, Charles.
Dragon's play: a new Taoist transmission of the complete experience of human life/ Charles Belyea and Steven Tainer; illustrations by Xiao-Lun Lin. 1st ed. Berkeley: Great Circle Lifeworks, c1991. xi, 196 p.
91-072597   0962930814
Taoism.

BL1920.C55 2000
Clarke, J. J. 1937-
The Tao of the West: Western transformations of Taoist thought/ J.J. Clarke. London; Routledge, 2000. xii, 270 p.
00-701296   299/.514   0415206197
Taoism -- Europe -- History. East and West.

BL1920.S2813 1993
Schipper, Kristofer Marinus.
The Taoist body/ Kristofer Schipper; translated by Karen C. Duval; foreword by Norman Girardot. Berkeley: University of California Press, c1993. xx, 273 p.
93-028999   299/.514   0520054881
Taoism.

BL1920.T33 1999
The Taoist classics: the collected translations of Thomas Cleary. Boston: Shambhala, 1999. 4 v.
99-027951   299/.51482   1570624852
Taoism.

BL1923.B57
Blofeld, John Eaton Calthrope,
Gateway to wisdom: Taoist and Buddhist contemplative and healing yogas adapted for Western students of the way/ by John Blofeld. Boulder, Colo.: Shambhala; x, 214 p.
79-067685   294.3/4/43 19   0394738780
Meditation -- Taoism. Meditation -- Buddhism. Yoga. Tao.

BL1923.E84 1998
Eskildsen, Stephen, 1963-
Asceticism in early taoist religion/ Stephen Eskildsen. Albany: State University of New York Press, c1998. vii, 229 p.
97-050629   299/.514447   0791439550
Asceticism -- Taoism. Taoism.

BL1923.L78 1991
Lü, Tung-pin,
The secret of the golden flower: the classic Chinese book of life/ translated, with introduction, notes, and commentary, by Thomas Cleary. 1st ed. [San Francisco, Calif.]: HarperSanFrancisco, c1991. 154 p.
90-055796   299/.5144 20   0062501844
Spiritual life--Taoism. Spiritual life--Buddhism.

BL1923.P37 1998
Pas, Julian F.
Historical dictionary of Taoism/ Julian F. Pas, in cooperation with Man Kam Leung. Lanham, Md.: Scarecrow Press, 1998. xliii, 414 p.
97-025780   299/.514/03   0810833697
Taoism -- History -- Dictionaries.

BL1923.R6313 1993
Robinet, Isabelle.
Taoist meditation: the Mao-shan tradition of great purity/ Isabelle Robinet; translated by Julian F. Pas and Norman J. Girardot; with a foreword by Norman J. Girardot, and a new afterword by Isabelle Robinet. Albany, NY: State University of New York Press, c1993. xxix, 285 p.
92-023086   299/.51443 20   0791413608
Meditation -- Taoism.

BL1923.S44 1990
Seven Taoist masters: a folk novel of China/ translated by Eva Wong. 1st ed. Boston: Shambhala; xxiii, 178 p.
89-043307   299/.5144 20   0877735441
Spiritual life -- Taoism.

BL1923.S48 1996
The Shambhala dictionary of Taoism/ Ingrid Fischer-Schreiber; translated by Werner Wünsche. 1st ed. Boston: Shambhala, 1996. xiv, 235 p.
95-025358   299/.514/03 20   1570622035
Taoism--Dictionaries.

BL1930.K58 1998
Kohn, Livia,
God of the Dao: Lord Lao in history and myth/ Livia Kohn. Ann Arbor: Center for the Chinese Studies, University of Michigan, xiii, 390 p.
98-037907   299/.5142113 21   0892641339
Laozi. Taoism -- Relations.

BL1940.K93 D435 1993
Deng, Ming-Dao.
Chronicles of Tao: the secret life of a Taoist master/ Deng Ming-Dao. 1st HarperCollins paperback ed. San Francisco: HarperSanFrancisco, 1993. 467 p.
92-056409   299/.514/092 B 20   0062502190
Kwan, Saihung. Taoists--China--Biography.

BL1941.5.J84 K37 1999
Katz, Paul R.,
Images of the immortal: the cult of Lü Dongbin at the Palace of Eternal Joy/ Paul R. Katz. Honolulu, HI: University of Hawai'i Press, 1999. xvi, 309 p.
99-031640   299/.51 21   082482170X
Lü, Dongbin, b. 798. Taoism.

BL1942.85.W45 K56 1994
Kleeman, Terry F.,
A god's own tale: the Book of transformations of Wenchang, the Divine Lord of Zitong/ Terry F. Kleeman. Albany: State University of New York Press, c1994. xv, 335 p.
93-034016   299/.51482 20   0791420027
Wenchang (Taoist deity)

BL1945.T5.T815
Tucci, Giuseppe, 1894-
The religions of Tibet/ Giuseppe Tucci; translated from the German and Italian by Geoffrey Samuel. Berkeley: University of California Press, c1980. xii, 340 p.
80-110768   294.3/923   0520038568
Tibet (China) -- Religion.

BL1950.S5 E4 1990
Elliott, Alan J. A.
Chinese spirit-medium cults in Singapore/ Alan J.A. Elliott. London; Athlone Press, 1990. 179 p.
90-035762   299/.51/095957 20   0485195143
Chinese--Singapore--Religious life. Spiritualism--Singapore.

BL2001.2.P22 1990
Padhi, Bibhu, 1951-
Indian philosophy and religion: a reader's guide/ Bibhu Padhi, Minakshi Padhi. Jefferson, N.C.: McFarland & Co., c1990. x, 413 p.
89-042745   181/.4   0899504469
Philosophy, Indic. India -- Religion.

BL2001.2.R384 1995
Religions of India in practice/ Donald S. Lopez, Jr., Editor. Princeton, N.J.: Princeton University Press, c1995. xvi, 655 p.
94-034695   294   0691043256
India -- Religion.

BL2003.L37 1995
Larson, Gerald James.
India's agony over religion/ Gerald James Larson. Albany, N.Y.: State University of New York Press, c1995. xiv, 393 p.
94-018318   291.1/72/0954   0791424111
Civil religion -- India. Religion and state -- India. India -- Religion.

BL2015.N26.V44 1994
Veer, Peter van der.
Religious nationalism: Hindus and Muslims in India/ Peter Van der Veer. Berkeley, CA: University of California Press, 1994. xvi, 247 p.
93-028079   320.5/5/0954   0520083776
Nationalism -- Religious aspects. Nationalism -- Religious aspects -- Hinduism. Nationalism -- Religious aspects -- Islam.

BL2018.M319 1989
McLeod, W. H.
Who is a Sikh?: the problem of Sikh identity/ W.H. McLeod. Oxford: Clarendon Press; 1989. viii, 140 p.
89-002936   294.6   0198265484
Sikhs. Sikhism.

BL2018.M38 1995
McLeod, W. H.
Historical dictionary of Sikhism/ W.H. McLeod. Lanham, Md.: Scarecrow Press, 1995. xi, 322 p.
95-015853   294.6/03 20   0810830353
Sikhism -- Dictionaries.

BL2032.S45.O77
Ortner, Sherry B., 1941-
Sherpas through their rituals/ Sherry B. Ortner. Cambridge; Cambridge University Press, 1978. xii, 195 p.
76-062582   294.3/4/3   0521215366
Sherpa (Nepalese people) -- Religion. Buddhism -- Doctrines -- Himalaya Mountains Region.

BL2123.N43.S35 1997
Schiller, Anne
Small sacrifices: religious change and cultural identity among the Ngaju of Indonesia/ Anne Schiller. New York: Oxford University Press, 1997. xii, 178 p.
96-020913   299/.92   019509557X
Ngaju (Indonesian people) -- Religion.

BL2202.K49 1987
Kitagawa, Joseph Mitsuo, 1915-
On understanding Japanese religion/ Joseph M. Kitagawa. Princeton, N.J.: Princeton University Press, c1987. xxxi, 343 p.
87-002795   291/.0952   0691073139
Japan -- Religion.

BL2202.R43 1993
Reader, Ian,
Japanese religions: past and present/ Ian Reader, Esben Andreason [sic], Finn Stefánsson. Honolulu: University of Hawaii Press, c1993. 189 p.
93-002725   200/.952 20   0824815467
Japan -- Religion.

BL2203.D37 1992
Davis, Winston Bradley.
Japanese religion and society: paradigms of structure and change/ Winston Davis. Albany: State University of New York Press, c1992. x, 327 p.
90-024745   306.6/0952   079140840X
Religion and sociology -- Japan. Japan -- Religion.

BL2207.5.R45 1993
Religion and society in modern Japan: selected readings/ edited by Mark R. Mullins, Shimazono Susumu, Paul L. Swanson. Berkeley, Calif.: Asian Humanities Press, c1993. x, 310 p.
93-023877   306.6/0952 20   0895819368
Religion and sociology -- Japan. Japan -- Religion -- 1868-1912. Japan -- Religion -- 20th century.

BL2209.J36 1994
Japanese new religions in the West/ edited by Peter B. Clarke & Jeffrey Somers. Sandgate, Folkestone, Kent, [Eng.]: Japan Library, 1994. ix, 167 p.
94-221238   299/.56   1873410247
Japan -- Religion -- 1945-

BL2209.R42 1990
Reader, Ian, 1949-
Religion in contemporary Japan/ by Ian Reader. Honolulu: University of Hawaii Press, c1991. xv, 277 p.
90-038407   291/.0952   0824813537
Japan -- Religion -- 1945-

BL2211.I5.S69 1999
Smyers, Karen Ann, 1954-
The fox and the jewel: shared and private meanings in contemporary Japanese inari worship/ Karen A. Smyers. Honolulu: University of Hawaii Press, c1999. viii, 271 p.
98-034604   299/.561211   0824820584
Inari. Foxes -- Religious aspects. Cults -- Japan.

BL2211.R44.R43 1998
Reader, Ian, 1949-
Practically religious: worldly benefits and the common religion of Japan/ Ian Reader and George J. Tanabe, Jr. Honolulu: University of Hawaii Press, c1998. xii, 303 p.
98-004192   200/.952   0824820657
Reward (Theology) Reward (Buddhism) Reward (Shinto) Japan -- Religious life and customs.

BL2211.R5.C47 1995
Ceremony and ritual in Japan: religious practices in an industrialized society/ edited by Jan van Bremen and D.P. Martinez. London; Routledge, 1995. xii, 268 p.
94-026158   291/.0952   0415116635
Rites and ceremonies -- Japan. Japan -- Religious life and customs.

BL2216.1.P53 2002
Picken, Stuart D. B.
Historical dictionary of Shinto/ Stuart D. B. Picken. Lanham, Md.: Scarecrow Press, 2002. xxxiv, 285 p.
2001-020061   299/.561/03 21   0810840162
Shinto -- Dictionaries -- Japanese. Japanese language -- Dictionaries.

BL2220.N45 2000
Nelson, John K.
Enduring identities: the guise of Shinto in contemporary Japan/ John K. Nelson. Honolulu: University of Hawai'i Press, c2000. ix, 324 p.
99-044520   299/.561   0824821203
Shinto. Shinto shrines.

BL2220.P47 1994
Picken, Stuart D. B.
Essentials of Shinto: an analytical guide to principal teachings/ Stuart D.B. Picken. Westport, Conn.: Greenwood Press, 1994. xxxiii, 400 p.
93-040619   299/.5612   0313264317
Shinto.

BL2225.N2552.S883 1996
Nelson, John K.
A year in the life of a Shinto shrine/ John K. Nelson. Seattle: University of Washington Press, 1996. viii, 286 p.
95-023257   299/.56135/095224   0295974990
Religious life -- Shinto. Shinto -- Customs and practices.

BL2225.N32 K423 1992
Grapard, Allan G.
The protocol of the gods: a study of the Kasuga cult in Japanese history/ Allan G. Grapard. Berkeley: University of California Press, c1992. xiv, 295 p.
92-016300   299/.561/0952184 20   0520070976
Shinto -- Relations -- Buddhism. Buddhism -- Relations -- Shinto.

BL2270.S26 2000
Sanasarian, Eliz.
Religious minorities in Iran/ Eliz Sanasarian. Cambridge; Cambridge University Press, 2000. xix, 228 p.
99-032293   305.6/0955   0521770734
Religious minorities -- Iran. Religion and state -- Iran. Religious tolerance -- Iran. Iran -- Politics and government -- 1979-1997.

BL2370.A5.M8 1963
Munro, N.
Ainu creed and cult. Edited with a pref. and an additional chapter by B.Z. Seligman. Introd. by H. Watanabe. New York, Columbia University Press, 1963 [c1962] 182 p.
63-007510   299.46
Ainu -- Religion.

BL2370.S5.H85 1996
Humphrey, Caroline.
Shamans and elders: experience, knowledge and power among the Daur Mongols/ Caroline Humphrey with Urgunge Onon. Oxford, New York: Clarendon Press, 1996. x, 396 p.
96-230468   299/.42   0198279418
Shamanism -- China -- Manchuria. Dagur (Chinese people) -- Rites and ceremonies. Dagur (Chinese people) -- Religion. Manchuria (China) -- Religious life and customs.

BL2370.S5 K43 2000
Kehoe, Alice Beck,
Shamans and religion: an anthropological exploration in critical   thinking/ Alice Beck Kehoe. Prospect Heights, Ill.: Waveland Press, c2000. viii, 125 p.
2001-268737   291.1/44 21   1577661621
Shamanism. Shamans. Ethnology--Religious aspects.

BL2370.S5 S525 1988
Shaman's path: healing, personal growth & empowerment/ compiled &   edited by Gary Doore. 1st ed. Boston: Shambhala: xii, 236 p.
87-032233   291.6/2 19   0877734321
Shamanism. Shamans. Healing -- Religious aspects.

BL2400-2490 Religion — History and principles of religions — African

BL2400.M383 1991
Mbiti, John S.
Introduction to African religion/ John S. Mbiti. 2nd rev. ed. Oxford [England]; Heinemann Educational 216 p.
91-028675   299/.6 20   0435940023
Africa -- Religion.

BL2400.N485 1998
New trends and developments in African religions/ edited by Peter B. Clarke. Westport, Conn.: Greenwood Press, 1998. xii, 309 p.
97-032006   299/.6   031330128X
Blacks -- Religion.

BL2400.S24 2000
Scheub, Harold.
A dictionary of African mythology: the mythmaker as storyteller/ Harold Scheub. Oxford; Oxford University Press, 2000. xiii, 368 p.
99-035035   299/.62/03   0195124561
Mythology, African -- Dictionaries.

BL2400.Z2813
Zahan, Dominique.
The religion, spirituality, and thought of traditional Africa/ Dominique Zahan; translated by Kate Ezra Martin and Lawrence M. Martin. Chicago: University of Chicago Press, 1979. 180 p.
78-023525   299/.6   0226977773
Africa -- Religion.

BL2428.M47 1995
Mercatante, Anthony S.
Who's who in Egyptian mythology/ Anthony S. Mercatante; edited and revised by Robert Steven Bianchi; illustrated by Anthony S. Mercatante. Lanham, MD: Scarecrow Press, 1995. xxi, 231 p.
94-038889   299/.31   0810829673
Mythology, Egyptian -- Dictionaries.

BL2441.2.R35 1991
Religion in ancient Egypt: gods, myths, and personal practice/ edited by Byron E. Shafer; contributors, John Baines, Leonard H. Lesko, David P. Silverman. Ithaca: Cornell University Press, 1991. xiv, 217 p.
90-040874   299/.31   0801425506
Cosmogony, Egyptian -- Congresses. Egypt -- Religion -- Congresses.

BL2443.H6613 1999
Hornung, Erik.
Akhenaten and the religion of light/ Erik Hornung; translated from the German by David Lorton. Ithaca: Cornell University Press, 1999. xii, 146 p.
99-016166   299/.31   0801436583
Akhenaton, -- King of Egypt. Sun worship -- Egypt. Egypt -- Religion.

BL2450.G6.M4413 1996
Meeks, Dimitri.
Daily life of the Egyptian gods/ Dimitri Meeks, Christine Favard-Meeks; translated from the French by G.M. Goshgarian. Ithaca: Cornell University Press, 1996. vii, 249 p.
96-007984   299/.31   0801431158
Gods, Egyptian. Egypt -- Religion.

BL2462.5.A375 2000
African spirituality: forms, meanings, and expressions/ edited by Jacob K. Olupona. New York: Crossroad, c2000. xxxvi, 476 p.
00-010546   200/.89/96   0824507940
Spirituality -- Africa. Africa -- Religious life and customs.

BL2462.5.E53 2001
The encyclopedia of African and African-American religions/ Stephen D. Glazier, editor. New York: Routledge, 2000. xx, 452 p.
00-059136   299/.6/03   0415922453
African Americans -- Religion -- Encyclopedias. Blacks -- America -- Religion -- Encyclopedias. Africa, Sub-Saharan -- Religion -- Encyclopedias. America -- Religion -- Encyclopedias.

BL2462.5.M36 1990
Mbiti, John S.
African religions & philosophy/ John S. Mbiti. 2nd rev. and enl. ed. Oxford; Heinemann, 1990. xiv, 288 p.
89-048596   299/.6 20   0435895915
Philosophy, African. Africa, Sub-Saharan -- Religion.

BL2470.N5.F35 1998
Falola, Toyin.
Violence in Nigeria: the crisis of religious politics and secular ideologies/ Toyin Falola. Rochester, NY: University of Rochester Press, 1998. xxi, 386 p.
97-047488   291.1/72/09669   1580460186
Religion and politics -- Nigeria -- History -- 20th century. Violence -- Religious aspects -- History -- 20th century. Violence -- Nigeria -- History -- 20th century. Nigeria -- Politics and government -- 1960-

BL2470.S6.C45 1991
Chidester, David.
Religions of South Africa/ David Chidester. London; Routledge, 1992. xvi, 286 p.
91-003329   291/.0968   041504779X
South Africa -- Religion.

BL2480.C45 1991
Fardon, Richard.
Between God, the dead and the wild: Chamba interpretations of religion and ritual/ Richard Fardon.   Washington,   D.C.:   Smithsonian Institution Press, c1990. xvii, 252 p.
90-063714   1560980443
Chamba (African people) -- Religion.

BL2480.M32
Masquelier, Adeline Marie, 1960-
Prayer has spoiled everything: possession, power, and identity in an Islamic town of Niger/ Adeline Masquelier. Durham, NC: Duke University Press, 2001. xix, 348 p.
00-047696   299/.37   0822326337
Mawri (African people) -- Niger -- Dogondoutchi -- Religion. Bori (Cult) -- Niger -- Dogondoutchi. Dogondoutchi (Niger) -- Religion.

BL2490.D37 1998
Davis, Rod, 1946-
American voudou: journey into a hidden world/ by Rod Davis. Denton, Tex.: University of North Texas Press, 1998. xvii, 392 p.
98-021264   299/.675/0973   1574410490
Voodooism -- United States. Hoodoo (Cult)

BL2490.L26 1989
Laguerre, Michel S.
Voodoo and politics in Haiti/ Michel S. Laguerre. New York: St. Martin's Press, 1989. ix, 152 p.
88-018181   299/.67 19   031202066X
Voodooism -- Haiti. Religion and politics -- Haiti. Haiti -- Religion. Haiti -- Politics and government.

BL2490.L27
Laguerre, Michel S.
Voodoo heritage/ Michel S. Laguerre; foreword by Vera Rubin. Beverly Hills, Calif.: Sage Publications, c1980. 231 p.
79-025318   299/.67   0803914032
Voodooism -- Haiti.

BL2490.M453 1959a
Métraux, Alfred,
Voodoo in Haiti. Translated by Hugo Charteris.
[London] A. Deutsch [1959] 400 p.
60-000970   133.4
Voodooism. Folklore -- Haiti.

BL2490.M87 1994
Murphy, Joseph M., 1951-
Working the spirit: ceremonies of the African
diaspora/ Joseph M. Murphy. Boston: Beacon
Press, c1994. xiii, 263 p.
93-003929   200/.89/96   0807012203
*Afro-Americans -- Religion. Blacks -- Latin
America -- Religion. Voodooism.*

BL2490.R45 2001
Reinventing religions: syncretism and
transformation in Africa and the Americas/
edited by Sidney M. Greenfield and Andre
Droogers. Lanham, Md.: Rowman & Littlefield,
c2001. 232 p.
00-059199   200/.89/96   0847688526
*Blacks -- Religion -- Congresses. Syncretism
(Religion) -- Africa, Sub-Saharan -- Congresses.
Syncretism (Religion) -- Latin America --
Congresses.*

BL2520-2590 Religion — History and principles of religions — American

BL2520.M55 1997
Millennium, messiahs, and mayhem:
contemporary apocalyptic movements/ edited by
Thomas Robbins and Susan J. Palmer. New
York: Routledge, 1997. 334 p.
97-012408   291.2/3   0415916488
*Millennialism -- North America -- History --
20th century. End of the world -- History of
doctrines -- 20th century. Violence -- Religious
aspects -- History of doctrines -- 20th century.
North America -- Religion -- 20th century.*

BL2525.A4 1990
Albanese, Catherine L.
Nature religion in America: from the Algonkian
Indians to the New Age/ Catherine L. Albanese.
Chicago: University of Chicago Press, 1990. xvi,
267 p.
89-039561   291.2/12/0973   0226011453
*Nature worship -- United States --
History. United States -- Religion.*

BL2525.A85 1999
Asian religions in America: a documentary
history/ edited by Thomas A. Tweed, Stephen
Prothero. New York: Oxford University Press,
1999. xvi, 416 p.
98-017674   200/.973   0195113381
*United States -- Religion -- Sources. Asia --
Religion -- Sources.*

BL2525.B45 1998
Benowitz, June Melby.
Encyclopedia of American women and religion/
June Melby Benowitz. Santa Barbara, Calif.:
ABC-CLIO, c1998. xi, 466 p.
98-025706   200/.82/0973   0874368871
*Women and religion -- United States --
Biography -- Encyclopedias. United States --
Religion -- Encyclopedias. United States --
Biography -- Encyclopedias.*

BL2525.C65 2000
Contemporary American religion/ Wade Clark
Roof, editor in chief. New York: Macmillan
Reference USA, c2000. 2 v.
99-046712   200/.973/03   0028649265
United States -- Religion -- Encyclopedias.

BL2525.C68 1999
Corbett, Michael, 1943-
Politics and religion in the United States/
Michael Corbett, Julia Mitchell Corbett. New
York: Garland Pub., 1999. xix, 460 p.
98-019364   322/.1/0973   081533141X
Religion and politics -- United States.

BL2525.D43 1994
Dean, William D.
The religious critic in American culture/ William
Dean. Albany: State University of New York
Press, c1994. xxiii, 256 p.
93-042683   200/.973 20   0791421147
*Religious thought -- United States -- 20th
century. Religion and culture -- United States --
History -- 20th century. United States --
Civilization -- 20th century. United States --
Religion -- 1945- United States -- Religion --
1901-1945. United States -- Intellectual life --
20th century. United States -- History --
Philosophy. United States -- Moral conditions.*

BL2525.E35 2001
Eck, Diana L.
A new religious America: how a "Christian
country" has now become the world's most
religiously diverse nation/ Diana L. Eck. San
Francisco: HarperSanFrancisco, 2001. xii, 404 p.
2001-016884   200/.92   0060621583
United States -- Religion.

BL2525.E415 2000
Eisenach, Eldon J.
The next religious establishment: national
identity and political theology in post-Protestant
America/ Eldon J. Eisenach. cLanham, Md.:
Rowman & Littlefield Publishers, c2000. xii,
177 p.
99-056786   322/.1/0973   0847696189
*Religion and politics -- United States. Church
and state -- United States. Nationalism --
Religious aspects. United States -- Religion.*

BL2525.E52 1999
Encyclopedia of religion in American politics/
edited by Jeffrey D. Schultz, John G. West, Jr.
and Iain MacLean; foreword by Helen Thomas.
Phoenix, Ariz.: Oryx Press, 1999. xxxii, 389 p.
98-047223   322/.1/097303   1573561304
*Religion and politics -- United States --
Encyclopedias. United States -- Religion --
Encyclopedias.*

BL2525.E53 1988
Encyclopedia of the American religious
experience: studies of traditions and
movements/ Charles H. Lippy and Peter W.
Williams, editors. New York: Scribner, c1988.
3 v.
87-004781   291/.0973 19   0684180626
*United States -- Religion -- Encyclopedias.
North America -- Religion -- Encyclopedias.*

BL2525.G625 2001
God in the details: American religion in popular
culture/ edited by Eric Michael Mazur, Kate
McCarthy. New York: Routledge, 2000.
00-035309   306/.0973   0415925630
*Popular culture -- United States. United States
-- Religion -- 1960-*

BL2525.H36 2000
Hammond, Phillip E.
The dynamics of religious organizations: The
extravasation of the sacred and other essays/
Phillip E. Hammond. Oxford; Oxford University
Press, 2000. xii, 197 p.
00-025845   291.6/5/0973   0198297629
*Religious institutions -- United States --
Sociological aspects. Religion and sociology --
United States. United States -- Religion.*

BL2525.H47 1983
Herberg, Will.
Protestant, Catholic, Jew: an essay in American
religious sociology/ Will Herberg; with a new
introduction by Martin E. Marty. Chicago:
University of Chicago Press, 1983, c1960. xvi,
309 p.
83-009120   306.6   0226327345
*United States -- Religion -- 1945-1960. United
States -- Civilization -- 1945-*

BL2525.H65 1995
Hofrenning, Daniel J. B.
In Washington but not of it: the prophetic
politics of religious lobbyists/ Daniel J.B.
Hofrenning. Philadelphia: Temple University
Press, 1995. x, 246 p.
94-049061   324/.4/0882   1566393035
*Religion and politics -- United States --
History -- 20th century. Lobbying -- United
States. United States -- Religion -- 20th century.
United States -- Politics and government -- 20th
century.*

BL2525.J46 2000
Jenkins, Philip, 1952-
Mystics and messiahs: cults and new religions in American history/ Philip Jenkins. Oxford; Oxford University Press, 2000. 294 p.
99-028732   200/.973   0195127447
Cults -- United States -- History -- 20th century. United States -- Religion -- 20th century.

BL2525.K67 2001
Korean Americans and their religions: pilgrims and missionaries from a different shore/ edited by Ho-Youn Kwon, Kwang Chung Kim, and R. Stephen Warner. University Park, Pa.: Pennsylvania State University Press, c2001. 307 p.
00-037452   200/.89/957073   0271020725
Korean Americans -- Religion. Korean Americans -- Ethnic identity. United States -- Church history -- 20th century. United States -- Religion -- 20th century.

BL2525.L486 1998
Lewis, James R.
Cults in America: a reference handbook/ James R. Lewis. Santa Barbara, Calif.: ABC-CLIO, c1998. xii, 232 p.
98-029089   291   157607031X
Cults -- United States. Sects -- United States. United States -- Religion.

BL2525.L49 2002
The encyclopedia of cults, sects, and new religions/ [edited by] James R. Lewis. 2nd ed. Amherst, N.Y.: Prometheus Books, 2002. 951 p.
2002-019180   200/.3 21   1573928887
Cults -- United States -- Encyclopedias. Sects -- United States -- Encyclopedias. United States -- Religion -- Encyclopedias.

BL2525.L55 1996
Lindley, Susan Hill, 1945-
You have stept out of your place: a history of women and religion in America/ Susan Hill Lindley. Louisville, Ky.: Westminster John Knox Press, c1996. xi, 500 p.
96-000541   277.3/0082   0664220819
Women and religion -- United States -- History. United States -- Religion.

BL2525.L566 1996
Lippy, Charles H.
Modern American popular religion: a critical assessment and annotated bibliography/ Charles H. Lippy. Westport, Conn.: Greenwood Press, 1996. xiv, 250 p.
95-046009   200/.973 20   0313277869
United States -- Religion -- 1960- -- Abstracts. United States -- Religious life and customs -- Abstracts. United States -- Religion -- 1960- -- Indexes. United States -- Religious life and customs -- Indexes.

BL2525.L567 2000
Lippy, Charles H.
Pluralism comes of age: American religious culture in the twentieth century/ Charles H. Lippy. Armonk, N.Y.: M.E. Sharpe, c2000. x, 250 p.
99-088431   291.1/72/0973   0765601508
Religious pluralism -- United States -- History of doctrines -- 20th century. United States -- Religion -- 20th century.

BL2525.M39 1999
Mazur, Eric Michael.
The Americanization of religious minorities: confronting the constitutional order/ Eric Michael Mazur. Baltimore: Johns Hopkins University Press, 1999. xxvi, 196 p.
99-024616   305.6/0973   0801862205
Religious minorities -- United States. Religion and law -- United States. Freedom of religion -- United States.

BL2525.M425 1995
Mead, Frank Spencer,
Handbook of denominations in the United States/ Frank S. Mead. New 10th ed./ revised by Samuel S. Hill. Nashville, Tenn.: Abingdon Press, c1995. 352 p.
95-038528   291/.0973 20   0687014786
Sects--United States--Dictionaries.

BL2525.M449 1999
Melton, J. Gordon.
Encyclopedia of American religions/ J. Gordon Melton. 6th ed. Detroit: Gale Research, c1999. xxiv, 1243 p.
00-702484   200/.973 21   0810384175
Sects -- United States. Cults -- United States. Sects -- United States -- Directories. Cults -- United States -- Directories. United States -- Religion.

BL2525.M45 1992
Melton J. Gordon.
Encyclopedic handbook of cults in America/ by J. Gordon Melton. Rev. and updated ed. New York: Garland Pub., 1992. xv, 407 p.
92-011540   291/.0973 20   0815311400
Cults -- United States. Sects -- United States. Cults -- History and criticism. United States -- Religion.

BL2525.M67 1994
Moore, R. Laurence 1940-
Selling God: American religion in the marketplace of culture/ R. Laurence Moore. New York: Oxford University Press, 1994. 317 p.
93-019624   200/.973   0195082281
Religion and culture -- United States. United States -- Religion -- Economic aspects.

BL2525.N38
National directory of churches, synagogues, and other houses of worship. Detroit: Washington, D.C.: London: Gale Research, Inc., [c1994-]
93-649999   200/.25/73 20
Religious institutions--United States--Directories.

BL2525.Q44 2001
Queen, Edward L.
Encyclopedia of American religious history/ Edward L. Queen II, Stephen R. Prothero, and Gardiner H. Shattuck, Jr.; foreword by Martin E. Marty, editorial adviser; book producer, Marie A. Cantlon. Rev. ed. New York: Facts on File, c2001. 2 v.
00-069512   200/.973/03 21   0816043353
Religious biography -- United States -- Encyclopedias. United States -- Religion -- Encyclopedias.

BL2525.R4613 2000
Religion and popular culture in America/ edited by Bruce David Forbes and Jeffrey H. Mahan. Berkeley, Calif.: University of California Press, c2000. xi, 324 p.
99-032106   291.1/7/0973   0520213246
Popular culture -- Religious aspects. Religion and culture -- United States. United States -- Religion -- 1960-

BL2525.R4616 2000
Religion and the new immigrants: continuities and adaptations in immigrant congregations/ edited by Helen Rose Ebaugh and Janet Saltzman Chafetz. Walnut Creek, CA: AltaMira Press, 2000.
99-059895   200/.86/91097641411   0742503895
Immigrants -- Religious life -- United States. United States -- Emigration and immigration -- Religious aspects.

BL2525.R4623 2000
Religion and the new republic: faith in the founding of America/ edited by James H. Hutson. Lanham, Md.: Rowman & Littlefield Publishers, 2000. viii, 213 p.
99-026705   200/.973/09033   084769433X
Church and State -- United States -- History -- 18th century. Church and state -- United States -- History -- 19th century. United States -- Religion -- 19th century. United States -- Religion -- To 1800.

BL2525.R654 1999
Roof, Wade Clark.
Spiritual marketplace: baby boomers and the remaking of American religion/ Wade Clark Roof. Princeton, N.J .: Princeton University Press, c1999. x, 367 p.
99-022825   200/.973/09045   0691016593
Baby boom generation -- Religious life. United States -- Religion -- 1960-

BL2525.R68 1997
Roth, John K.
Private needs, public selves: talk about religion in America/ John K. Roth. Urbana: University of Illinois Press, c1997. xx, 262 p.
97-004613   200/.973   0252019334
United States -- Religion -- 20th century. United States -- Religion.

BL2525.S23 1998
Sacred companies: organizational aspects of religion and religious aspects of organizations/ edited by N.J. Demerath III ... [et al.]. New York: Oxford University Press, 1998. xxiv, 410 p.
96-021167   291.6/5/0973   0195113225
Religious institutions -- United States.United States -- Religious life and customs.

BL2525.S44 1998
Segers, Mary C.
A wall of separation?: debating the public role of religion/ Mary C. Segers and Ted G. Jelen; introduction by Clarke E. Cochran. Lanham, MD: Rowman & Littlefield Publishers, c1998. xx, 191 p.
98-023173   322/.1/0973   0847683877
Church and state -- United States. Religion and politics -- United States. United States -- Religion.

BL2525.S58 1998
Sects, cults, and spiritual communities: a sociological analysis/ edited by William W. Zellner and Marc Petrowsky. Westport, Conn.: Praeger, 1998. x, 182 p.
97-032995   306.6/0973   0275958604
Cults -- United States -- History -- 20th century. Religion and sociology -- Case studies. United States -- Religion -- 1960-

BL2525.T84 1989
Twentieth-century shapers of American popular religion/ edited by Charles H. Lippy. New York: Greenwood Press, 1989. xxv, 494 p.
88-015487   291/.092/2 B 19   0313253560
Religious biography -- United States. United States -- Religion -- 20th century.

BL2525.W35 2003
Wald, Kenneth D.
Religion and politics in the United States/ Kenneth D. Wald. 4th ed. Lanham, Md.: Rowman & Littlefield, c2003.
2002-151628   322/.1/0973 21   0742518418
Religion and politics -- United States -- History -- 20th century. United States -- Religion -- 1960- United States -- Politics and government -- 1981-1989.

BL2525.W85 1998
Wuthnow, Robert.
After heaven: spirituality in America since the 1950s/ Robert Wuthnow. Berkeley: University of California Press, c1998. ix, 277 p.
97-045121   200/.973/09045   0520213963
United States -- Religion -- 20th century.

BL2525.W88 1988
Wuthnow, Robert.
The restructuring of American religion: society and faith since World War II/ Robert Wuthnow. Princeton, N.J.: Princeton University Press, c1988. xiv, 374 p.
87-025903   306/.6/0973   0691077592
United States -- Religion -- 1945-

BL2525.Z47 1997
Zepp, Ira G.
The new religious image of urban America: the shopping mall as ceremonial center/ Ira G. Zepp, Jr.; with a foreword and introduction by David Carrasco. 2nd ed. Niwot, Colo.: University Press of Colorado, c1997. xv, 212 p.
96-051780   291.3/5 21   0870814362
Shopping malls -- Religious aspects. Shopping malls -- United States. United States -- Religion -- 1960-

BL2527.D33.E35 2000
Eiesland, Nancy L., 1964-
A particular place: urban restructuring and religious ecology in a southern exurb/ Nancy L. Eiesland. New Brunswick, NJ: Rutgers University Press, c2000. xiv, 254 p.
99-015069   306.6/09758/223   0813527376
Ethnology -- Georgia -- Dacula. Ethnology -- Religious aspects. Dacula (Ga.) -- Religious life and customs.

BL2527.W18 M49 2001
Meyer, Jeffrey F.
Myths in stone: religious dimensions of Washington, D.C./ Jeffrey F. Meyer. Berkeley, CA: University of California Press, 2001.
00-020172   975.3   0520214811
Sacred space -- Washington (D.C.)Washington (D.C.) -- Religion.

BL2530.H3 D38 1985
Davis, Wade.
The serpent and the rainbow/ Wade Davis. New York: Simon and Schuster, c1985. 297 p.
85-022114   299/.65 19   0671502476
Davis, Wade. Zombiism -- Haiti. Bizango (Cult) Tetrodotoxin -- Physiological effect. Datura stramonium. Pharmacopoeias -- Haiti. Haiti -- Description and travel. Haiti -- Religious life and customs. Haiti -- Social life and customs.

BL2530.H3.D48 1992
Desmangles, Leslie Gerald.
The Faces of the gods: vodou and Roman Catholicism in Haiti/ Leslie G. Desmangles. Chapel Hill, NC: The University of North Carolina Press, c1992. xiii, 218 p.
92-053625   299/.67   0807820598
Voodooism -- Haiti.Haiti -- Religion.

BL2530.U6.S53
Shupe, Anson D.
The new vigilantes: deprogrammers, anti-cultists, and the new religions/ Anson D. Shupe, Jr. and David G. Bromley; foreword by Joseph R. Gusfield. Beverly Hills: Sage Publications, c1980. 267 p.
80-023276   306/.6   080391542X
Cults -- United States. Deprogramming -- United States.

BL2530.U6.W87
Wuthnow, Robert.
Experimentation in American religion: the new mysticisms and their implications for the churches/ Robert Wuthnow. Berkeley: University of California Press, c1978. x, 221 p.
77-071068   200/.973   0520034465
Cults -- United States. Christianity and other religions. United States -- Religion -- 1945-1960. United States -- Religion -- 1960-

BL2532.R37 B57 1986
Bishton, Derek.
Black heart man/ Derek Bishton. London: Chatto & Windus, 1986. 135 p.
86-234877   299/.67 19   0701127953
Rastafari movement.

BL2532.R37.C47 1994
Chevannes, Barry.
Rastafari: roots and ideology/ Barry Chevannes. Syracuse, N.Y.: Syracuse University Press, 1994. xiv, 298 p.
94-018608   299/.67   081562638X
Rastafari movement -- Jamaica -- Kingston -- History. Dreadlocks -- History. Kingston (Jamaica) -- Religion.

BL2532.R37.M84 1990
Mulvaney, Rebekah Michele.
Rastafari and reggae: a dictionary and sourcebook/ Rebekah Michele Mulvaney; bibliography by Carlos I.H. Nelson; illustrations by Barbara Boyle. New York: Greenwood Press, 1990. xvi, 253 p.
90-003591   299/.67   0313260710
Rastafari movement -- Dictionaries. Reggae music -- Dictionaries. Rastafari movement -- Bibliography.

BL2532.S3.B73 1993
Brandon, George, 1947-
Santeria from Africa to the new world: the dead sell memories/ George Brandon. Bloomington: Indiana University Press, c1993. x, 206 p.
92-024251   299/.67   0253312574
Santeria.

BL2532.S3 G66
González-Wippler, Migene.
Santería; African magic in Latin America. New York, Julian Press [1973] 181 p.
73-082439   299/.6   0870970550
Santeria.

BL2532.S3 M87 1988
Murphy, Joseph M.,
Santería: an African religion in America/ Joseph M. Murphy. Boston: Beacon Press, c1988. xi, 189 p.
87-042845   299/.67 19   0807010146
Santeria.

BL2565.S23 1997
Sacred possessions: Vodou, Santeria, Obeah, and the Caribbean/ edited by Margarite Fernandez Olmos and Lizabeth Paravisini-Gebert. New Brunswick, N.J.: Rutgers University Press, c1997. viii, 312 p.
96-018145   299/.6/09729   0813523605
Blacks -- Caribbean Area -- Religion.Caribbean Area -- Religion.

BL2590.P5.S25 1987
Sallnow, Michael J., 1949-
Pilgrims of the Andes: regional cults in Cusco/ Michael J. Sallnow. Washington, D.C.: Smithsonian Institution Press, c1987. xiii, 351 p.
87-043043   263/.042/8537   0874748267
Pilgrims and pilgrimages -- Peru -- Cuzco (Dept.) Shrines -- Peru -- Cuzco (Dept.) Cults -- Peru -- Cuzco (Dept.) Cuzco (Peru: Dept.) -- Religious life and customs.

BL2615-2620 Religion — History and principles of religions — Pacific Ocean islands. Pacific Area

BL2615.G7 1956
Grey, George, 1812-1898.
Polynesian mythology, and ancient traditional history of the Maori as told by their priests and chiefs. Christchurch] Whitcombe and Tombs, 1956. 250 p.
57-041672
Mythology, Polynesian. Legends -- New Zealand.

BL2620.M4.C37 1990
Cargo cults and millenarian movements: transoceanic comparisons of new religious movements/ edited by G.W. Trompf. Berlin; Mouton de Gruyter, 1990. xvii, 456 p.
89-028140   291/.046   0899256015
Cargo cults. Millennialism -- Comparative studies. Adventists -- Comparative studies.

BL2620.N45.R45 1989
The Religious imagination in New Guinea/ edited by Gilbert Herdt and Michele Stephen. New Brunswick: Rutgers University Press, c1989. vi, 262 p.
89-030376   299/.92   0813514576
Imagination -- Religious aspects.New Guinea -- Religion.

BL2747.3 Rationalism — Special theories — Atheism

BL2747.3.B83 1987
Buckley, Michael J.
At the origins of modern atheism/ Michael J. Buckley. New Haven: Yale University Press, c1987. viii, 445 p.
86-028248   211/.8/0903   0300037198
Atheism -- History -- Modern period, 1500-

BL2747.3.M3313 1990
Martin, Michael, 1932 Feb. 3--
Atheism: a philosophical justification/ Michael Martin. Philadelphia: Temple University Press, 1990. xiii, 541 p.
89-033121   211/.8   0877226423
Atheism.

BL2747.3.V58 1999
Vitz, Paul C.,
Faith of the fatherless: the psychology of atheism/ Paul C. Vitz. Dallas: Spence Pub. Co., c1999. xv, 174 p.
99-016667   211/.8/019 21   1890626120
Atheism -- Psychology. Atheists -- Psychology -- Case studies. Theists -- Psychology -- Case studies. Father and child -- Religious aspects.

BL2747.4 Rationalism — Special theories — Deism

BL2747.4.W33 1992
Walters, Kerry S.
The American deists: voices of reason and dissent in the early republic/ Kerry S. Walters. Lawrence, Kan.: University Press of Kansas, c1992. x, 394 p.
92-002827   211/.5/097309033   0700605401
Deism. Deism -- United States -- History -- 18th century.

BL2747.8 Rationalism — Special theories — Secularism

BL2747.8.B78 2002
Bruce, Steve,
God is dead: secularization in the West/ Steve Bruce. Malden, MA: Blackwell Pub., 2002. xv, 269 p.
2001-004195   200/.9182/1 21   0631232745
Secularism.

BL2747.8.D28 1998
Davison, Andrew, 1962-
Secularism and revivalism in Turkey: a hermeneutic reconsideration/ Andrew Davison. New Haven: Yale University Press, c1998. viii, 270 p.
97-049379   322/.1/09561   0300069367
Secularism -- Turkey -- History -- 20th century. Islam and state -- Turkey -- History -- 20th century. Turkey -- Religion -- 20th century.

BL2757 Rationalism — History — By period

BL2757.T87 1985
Turner, James, 1946-
Without God, without creed: the origins of unbelief in America/ James Turner. Baltimore: Johns Hopkins University Press, c1985. xviii, 316 p.
84-015397   211/.8/0973   080182494X
Irreligion -- History. Irreligion -- United States -- History.

BL2760 Rationalism — History — By region or country

BL2760.P4
Persons, Stow, 1913-
Free religion, an American faith. New Haven, Yale University Press [c1947] 168 p.
47-005568   211
Unitarianism -- History. Humanism, Religious. Free thought -- History.

BL2775 Rationalism — Works by agnostics, atheists, freethinkers, etc. — General works

BL2775.M3983 1964
Marx, Karl, 1818-1883.
On religion [by] Karl Marx and Friedrich Engels. Introd. by Reinhold Niebuhr. New York, Schocken Books [1964] 382 p.
64-015219   201
Religion -- Controversial literature.

BL2780 Rationalism — Works by agnostics, atheists, freethinkers, etc. — Addresses, essays, lectures

BL2780.R87 1957
Russell, Bertrand, 1872-1970.
Why I am not a Christian, and other essays on religion and related subjects. Edited, with an appendix on the "Bertrand Russell case," by Paul Edwards. New York, Simon and Schuster, 1957. 266 p.
57-010982   211
Free thought.

BL2785 Rationalism — Biography — Collective

BL2785.W55 2000
Who's who in hell: handbook and international directory for humanists, freethinkers, rationalists, and non-theists/ compiled by Warren Allen Smith. New York: Barricade Books, 2000. xii, 1237 p.
99-055376   211/.6/0922   1569801584
Rationalists -- Biography -- Dictionaries. Atheists -- Biography -- Dicitonaries.

BM Judaism

BM40 Collected works — Several authors

BM40.J86 1982
The Judaic tradition: texts/ edited and introduced by Nahum N. Glatzer. Rev. ed. with new introd. New York, N.Y.: Behrman House, 1982, c1969. xviii, 838 p.
82-012956   296.1 19   0874413443
Judaism--History--Sources. Holocaust, Jewish (1939-1945)--Influence. Zionism--Philosophy.

BM40.M58
Modern Jewish thought; selected issues, 1889-1966. New introd. by Louis Jacobs. New York, Arno Press, 1973. 1 v.
73-002221   296   0405052839
Judaism--Addresses, essays, lectures.

BM42 Collected works — Several authors — Addresses, essays, lectures

BM42.B54 2000
The Blackwell companion to Judaism/ edited by Jacob Neusner, Alan J. Avery-Peck. Malden, MA: Blackwell Publishers, 2000. xv, 553 p.
00-021874   296   1577180585
Judaism.

BM43 Collected works — Several authors — Extracts from several authors

BM43.G69 1996
Great Jewish quotations/ selected and annotated by Alfred J. Kolatch. Middle Village, N.Y.: Jonathan David Publishers, c1996. x, 612 p.
93-038747   296 20   0824603699
Judaism -- Quotations, maxims, etc. Jews -- Quotations.

BM43.S78
Studies in Jewish thought: an anthology of German Jewish scholarship / selected, edited, and introduced by Alfred Jospe. Detroit: Wayne State University Press, 1981. 434 p.
80-029338   296 19   081431676X
Mendelssohn, Moses, 1729-1786 -- Addresses, essays, lectures. Judaism -- History -- Addresses, essays, lectures. Judaism -- Doctrines -- Addresses, essays, lectures.

BM45 Collected works — Individual authors

BM45.B8
Buber, Martin, 1878-1965.
Mamre, essays in religion by Martin Buber, translated by Greta Hort. Melbourne and London, Melbourne University Press, 1946. xiii, 190 p.
46-007913   296
Judaism. Hasidism.

BM50 Dictionaries. Encyclopedias

BM50.D525 1996
Dictionary of Judaism in the biblical period: 450 B.C.E. to 600 C.E. / Jacob Neusner, editor in chief; William Scott Green, editor. New York: Macmillan Library Reference, c1996. 2 v.
95-031543   296/.09/01 20   0028972899
Judaism -- History -- Post-exilic period, 586 B.C.-210 A.D. -- Dictionaries. Judaism -- History -- Talmudic period, 10-425 -- Dictionaries. Rabbinical literature -- Dictionaries.

BM50.E47 2001
Eisenberg, Joyce.
JPS dictionary of Jewish words/ by Joyce Eisenberg and Ellen Scolnic. Philadelphia, PA: Jewish Publication Society, 2001. xxi, 202 p.
2001-029218   296/.03   0827607237
Judaism -- Terminology. Hebrew language -- Terms and phrases.

BM50.E634 1999
The encyclopedia of Judaism/ edited by Jacob Neusner, Alan J. Avery-Peck, William Scott Green. New York: Continuum, 1999. 3 v.
99-034729   296/.03 21   0826411770
Judaism -- Encyclopedias.

BM50.E634 1999 Suppl
Encyclopedia of Judaism. edited by Jacob Neusner, Alan J. Avery-Peck, and William Scott Green. New York: Continuum International Pub. Group, [2002-] v. <4 >
2002-014145   296/.03 21   0826414605
Judaism -- Encyclopedias.

BM50.J28 1995
Jacobs, Louis.
The Jewish religion: a companion/ Louis Jacobs. Oxford; Oxford University Press, 1995. 641 p.
95-003203   296/.03 20   0198264631
Judaism -- Dictionaries. Judaism -- Essence, genius, nature.

BM50.O94 1997
The Oxford dictionary of the Jewish religion/ editors in chief R.J. Zwi Werblowsky, Geoffrey Wigoder. New York: Oxford University Press, 1997 xviii, 764 p.
96-045517   296/.03   0195086058
Judaism -- Dictionaries.

BM50.R43 2000
Reader's guide to Judaism/ editor, Michael Terry. Chicago; Fitzroy Dearborn, 2000. xxv, 718 p.
2001-274119   296/.03   1579581390
Judaism -- Encyclopedias.

BM50.S65 1998
Solomon, Norman,
Historical dictionary of Judaism/ Norman Solomon. Lanham, MD: Scarecrow Press, 1998. viii, 521 p.
98-004182   296/.03 21   0810834979
Judaism -- Dictionaries. Jews -- Biography -- Dictionaries.

BM71 Study and teaching — General special

BM71.A33 2000
Academic approaches to teaching Jewish studies/ edited by Zev Garber. Lanham, Md.: University Press of America, c2000. xvi, 332 p.
99-048952   296/.071/1   076181552X
Judaism -- Study and teaching (Higher)

BM71.C64 2000
Cohen, Norman J.
The way into Torah/ Norman J. Cohen. Woodstock, VT: Jewish Lights Pub., 2000. xv, 145 p.
00-023563   296.6/8   1580230288
Talmud Torah (Judaism) Tradition (Judaism) Judaism -- Study and teaching (Continuing education)

BM157 History — General special

BM157.P47 1982
Peters, F. E.
Children of Abraham: Judaism, Christianity, Islam/ F.E. Peters. Princeton, N.J.: Princeton University Press, c1982. xi, 225 p.
81-047941   291   0691072671
Judaism -- History. Christianity. Islam -- History.

BM175-177 History — By period — Ancient

BM175.Q6 M34 2002
Magness, Jodi.
The archaeology of Qumran and the Dead Sea Scrolls/ Jodi Magness. Grand Rapids, MI.: William B. Eerdmans Pub., c2002. x, 238
2002-067924 296.1/55 21 0802845894
Qumran community. Excavations (Archaeology) -- West Bank. Qumran Site (West Bank)

BM176.C614 1999
Cohen, Shaye J. D.
The beginnings of Jewishness: boundaries, varieties, uncertainties/ Shaye J.D. Cohen. Berkeley: University of California Press, c1999. xiii, 426 p.
98-039899 296/.09/014 0520211413
Judaism -- History -- Post-exilic period, 586 B.C.-210 A.D. Jews -- Identity -- History -- To 1500 A.D. Proselytes and proselyting, Jewish -- History -- To 1500 A.D.

BM176.F37 1956
Farmer, William Reuben.
Maccabees, Zealots, and Josephus; an inquiry into Jewish nationalism in the Greco-Roman period. New York, Columbia University Press, 1956. 239 p.
56-007364
Josephus, Flavius.Judaism -- History -- Post-exilic period, 586 B.C.-210 A.D. Jewish nationalism. Maccabees.

BM176.G82
Guignebert, Charles,
The Jewish world in the time of Jesus, by Ch. Guignebert. Translated from the French by S.H. Hooke. London, K. Paul, Trench, Trubner & Co., 1939. xiv, 288 p.
39-008534
Jews -- History -- 586 B.C.-70 A.D.

BM176.S26
Sandmel, Samuel.
Judaism and Christian beginnings/ Samuel Sandmel. New York: Oxford University Press, 1978. xvii, 510 p.
77-077609 296/.09 0195022815
Judaism -- History -- Post-exilic period, 586 B.C.-210 A.D. Christianity -- Origin.

BM176.T49 1998
Texts and traditions: a source reader for the study of Second Temple and rabbinic Judaism/ compiled, edited, and introduced by Lawrence H. Schiffman. Hoboken, NJ: KTAV Pub. House, 1998. xxvi, 777 p.
97-035800 296/.09/014 0881254347
Judaism -- History -- Post-exilic period, 586 B.C.-210 A.D. -- Sources. Judaism -- History -- Talmudic period, 10-425 -- Sources. Jews -- History -- 586 B.C.-70 A.D. -- Sources.

BM177.N474 1988
Neusner, Jacob, 1932-
Judaism and its social metaphors: Israel in the history of Jewish thought/ Jacob Neusner. Cambridge [England]; Cambridge University Press, 1989. xiv, 258 p.
88-017057 296.3 0521354714
Judaism -- History -- Talmudic period, 10-425. Rabbinical literature -- History and criticism. Sociology, Jewish.

BM194-198 History — By period — Modern

BM194.S67 1996
Sorkin, David Jan.
Moses Mendelssohn and the religious enlightenment/ David Sorkin. Berkeley, Calif.: University of California Press, c1996. xxv, 214 p.
95-023910 296.3/092 0520202619
Mendelssohn, Moses, -- 1729-1786.Haskalah -- Germany. Jews -- Emancipation -- Germany. Germany -- Ethnic relations.

BM195.C64 1996
Cohn-Sherbok, Dan.
Modern Judaism/ Dan Cohn-Sherbok. New York, N.Y.: St. Martin's Press, 1996. xv, 260 p.
96-012368 296/.09/03 0312161883
Judaism -- History -- Modern period, 1750- Jewish sects -- History -- 19th century. Jewish sects -- History -- 20th century.

BM197.M48 1988
Meyer, Michael A.
Response to modernity: a history of the Reform Movement in Judaism/ Michael A. Meyer. New York: Oxford University Press, 1988. xvi, 494 p.
87-020354 296.8/346/09 019505167X
Reform Judaism -- History.

BM197.5.J48 2000
Jews in the center: conservative synagogues and their members/ edited by Jack Wertheimer. New Brunswick, NJ: Rutgers University Press, c2000. xii, 407 p.
99-045701 296.8/342/0973 0813528216
Conservative Judaism -- United States. Judaism -- 20th century. Jews -- United States -- Social life and customs.

BM198.B7783
Buber, Martin, 1878-1965.
Tales of the Hasidim [tr. by Olga Marx] New York, Schocken Books [1947-48] 2 v.
47-002952 296
Hasidim -- Legends. Hasidic parables.

BM198.I32 1995
Idel, Moshe, 1947-
Hasidism: between ecstasy and magic/ by Moshe Idel. Albany: State University of New York Press, c1995. x, 438 p.
92-047504 296.8/332/09 0791417336
Hasidism -- History. Mysticism -- Judaism -- History. Cabala -- History.

BM205-229 History — By region or country — North America

BM205.C62 2000
Cohen, Steven Martin.
The Jew within: self, family, and community in America/ Steven M. Cohen and Arnold M. Eisen. Bloomington: Indiana University Press, 2000. x, 242 p.
00-037000 296/.0973/09051 0253337828
Judaism -- United States. Jewish way of life. Jewish families -- United States -- Religious life.

BM205.D27 1989
Danzger, Murray Herbert.
Returning to tradition: the contemporary revival of Orthodox Judaism/ M. Herbert Danzger. New Haven: Yale University Press, c1989. x, 374 p.
88-027735 296.8/32/095694 0300039476
Orthodox Judaism -- United States -- History -- 20th century. Orthodox Judaism -- Israel -- History -- 20th century. Jews -- Return to Orthodox Judaism.

BM205.K38 1998
Karp, Abraham J.
Jewish continuity in America: creative survival in a free society/ Abraham J. Karp. Tuscaloosa: University of Alabama Press, c1998. xii, 301 p.
98-008951 296/.0973 0817309233
Judaism -- United States -- History. Judaism -- History -- Modern period, 1750- Rabbis -- United States.

BM205.O45 1996
Olitzky, Kerry M.
The American synagogue: a historical dictionary and sourcebook/ Kerry M. Olitzky; Marc Lee Raphael, advisory editor. Westport, Conn.: Greenwood Press, 1996. xiii, 409 p.
95-049681 296.6/5/0973 0313288569
Synagogues -- United States -- Dictionaries. Synagogues -- Canada -- Dictionaries. Judaism -- United States -- History.

BM205.W46 1993
Wertheimer, Jack.
A people divided: Judaism in contemporary America/ Jack Wertheimer. New York, NY: BasicBooks, c1993. xix, 267 p.
92-054514 296./0973/0904 0465001653
Judaism -- United States. Judaism -- 20th century. Jews -- United States -- Identity.

BM229.T67
Diamond, Etan.
And I will dwell in their midst: Orthodox Jews in suburbia/ by Etan Diamond. Chapel Hill, NC: University of North Carolina Press, c2000. xx, 215 p.
00-029880 296.8/32/0971354091733 080782576X
Orthodox Judaism -- Ontario -- Toronto Suburban Area. Jews -- Ontario -- Toronto Suburban Area -- Social life and customs. Toronto Suburban Area (Ont.) -- Religious life and customs.

BM376 History —
By region or country — Europe

BM376.H8.K3813 1998
Katz, Jacob, 1904-
A house divided: orthodoxy and schism in nineteenth-century Central European Jewry/ Jacob Katz; translated by Ziporah Brody. Hanover, NH: University Press, c1998. x, 339 p.
97-036812   296.8/32/094309034   0874517966
Orthodox Judaism -- Relations -- Nontraditional Jews. Orthodox Judaism -- Hungary -- History -- 19th century. Orthodox Judaism -- Germany -- History -- 19th century.

BM390 History —
By region or country — Asia

BM390.C62 2000
Cohen, Asher, 1936-
Israel and the politics of Jewish identity: the secular-religious impasse/ Asher Cohen and Bernard Susser. Baltimore, Md.: Johns Hopkins University Press, 2000. xiv, 167 p.
99-089238   320.95694   0801863457
Judaism and state -- Israel. Religion and politics -- Israel. Orthodox Judaism -- Israel -- Relations -- Nontraditional Jews. Israel -- Politics and government.

BM390.S5112 2000
Sharkansky, Ira.
The politics of religion and the religion of politics: looking at Israel/ Ira Sharkansky. Lanham, MD.: Lexington Books, 2000. xi, 161 p.
99-086513   296.3/82/095694   0739101099
Judaism -- Israel. Religion and politics -- Israel. Orthodox Judaism -- Israel -- Israel -- Politics and government.

BM440 History —
By region or country — Africa

BM440.M8.B44 1998
Ben-Ami, Issachar.
Saint veneration among the Jews in Morocco/ Issachar Ben-Ami. Detroit: Wayne State University Press, c1998. 388 p.
97-015878   296.6/1/0964   0814321984
Zaddikim -- Morocco. Judaism -- Morocco.

BM485 Pre-Talmudic
Jewish literature
(non-Biblical) —
History and criticism

BM485.L57 1984 vol. 2
Jewish writings of the Second Temple period: Apocrypha, Pseudepigrapha, Qumran, sectarian writings, Philo, Josephus/ edited by Michael E. Stone. Assen, Netherlands: Van Gorcum; 1984. xxiii, 697 p.
83-048926   296.1 s   0800606035
Jewish religious literature -- History and criticism. Judaism -- History -- Post-exilic period, 586 B.C.-210 A.D. -- Sources.

BM487 Pre-Talmudic Jewish
literature (non-Biblical) —
Special texts or groups of texts —
Dead Sea scrolls

BM487.E53 2000
Encyclopedia of the Dead Sea scrolls/ Lawrence H. Schiffman, James C. VanderKam, editors in chief. New York, N.Y.: Oxford University Press, 2000. 2 v.
99-055300   296.1/55/03   0195084500
Dead Sea scrolls -- Encyclopedias.

BM487.G65 1995
Golb, Norman.
Who wrote the Dead Sea scrolls?: the search for the secret of Qumran/ Norman Golb. New York: Scribner, c1995. xvi, 446 p.
94-023295   296.1/55   002544395X
Judaism -- History -- Post-exilic period, 586 B.C.-210 A.D. -- Sources.

BM487.K63 2000
Knohl, Israel.
The Messiah before Jesus: the suffering servant of the Dead Sea Scrolls/ Israel Knohl; translated by David Maisel. Berkeley: University of California Press, c2000. xiv, 145 p.
00-037404   296.3/36   0520215923
Jesus Christ -- Messiahship. Servant of Jehovah. Christianity -- Origin.

BM487.S453 1998
Shanks, Hershel.
The mystery and meaning of the Dead Sea scrolls/ Hershel Shanks. New York: Random House, 1998. xxi, 246 p.
97-029391   296.1/55   0679457577
Dead Sea scrolls.

BM496.5 Sources of Jewish
religion. Rabbinical literature —
Works about the sources —
Treatises

BM496.5.N4826 1989
Neusner, Jacob, 1932-
Translating the classics of Judaism: in theory and in practice/ by Jacob Neusner. Atlanta, Ga.: Scholars Press, c1989. xix, 158 p.
89-006281   296.1/205   1555403530
Rabbinical literature -- Translations into English -- History and criticism. Rabbinical literature -- Translating.

BM501-504.2 Sources of Jewish
religion. Rabbinical literature —
Talmudic literature —
Babylonian Talmud

BM501.K72 1990
Kraemer, David Charles.
The mind of the Talmud: an intellectual history of the Bavli/ David Kraemer. New York: Oxford University Press, 1990. xiv, 217 p.
89-022953   296.1/2506   0195062906
Jewish law -- Interpretation and construction.

BM501.15.B3313 1988
Bader, Gershom,
The encyclopedia of Talmudic sages/ Gershom Bader; translated by Solomon Katz. Northvale, N.J.: Jason Aronson, c1988. xii, 876 p.
87-033465   296.1/2/00922 19   0876689039
Rabbis -- Biography.

BM503.B47 1998
Berger, Michael S.
Rabbinic authority/ Michael S. Berger. New York: Oxford University Press, 1998. xii, 226 p.
97-036779   296.1/2/00922   0195122690
Tannaim. Amoraim. Rabbis -- Office.

BM504.R657 2000
Rosen, Jonathan, 1963-
The Talmud and the Internet: a journey between worlds/ Jonathan Rosen. New York: Farrar, Straus and Giroux, 2000. 132 p.
99-085987   296.1/206   0374272387
Internet -- Religious aspects.

BM504.2.K688 1996
Kraemer, David Charles.
Reading the rabbis: the Talmud as literature/ David Kraemer. New York: Oxford University Press, 1996. x, 165 p.
95-020715   296.1/25066   0195096231
Talmud -- Criticism, interpretation, etc. Talmud as literature.

BM514 Sources of Jewish religion. Rabbinical literature — Midrash — Works about the Midrash

BM514.G65 1988
Goldin, Judah, 1914-
Studies in Midrash and related literature/ Judah Goldin; edited by Barry L. Eichler and Jeffrey H. Tigay. Philadelphia: Jewish Publication Society, 1988. xx, 419 p.
86-031136   296.1/4   0827602774
Midrash -- History and criticism. Aggada -- History and criticism. Judaism -- Essence, genius, nature.

BM516.5 Sources of Jewish religion. Rabbinical literature — Midrash — Aggada

BM516.5.R83 1999
Rubenstein, Jeffrey L.
Talmudic stories: narrative art, composition, and culture/ Jeffrey L. Rubenstein. Baltimore: Johns Hopkins University Press, c1999. xvi, 435 p.
99-010877   296.1/27606   0801861462
Aggada -- History and criticism. Narration in rabbinical literature. Rabbinical literature -- Translations into English.

BM520.5 Sources of Jewish religion. Rabbinical literature — Halacha — History

BM520.5.G67 1990
Gordis, Robert, 1908-
The dynamics of Judaism: a study of Jewish law/ Robert Gordis. Bloomington: Indiana University Press, 1990.
88-045502   296.1/8   0253326028
Jewish law -- History. Judaism -- Essence, genius, nature.

BM520.6 Sources of Jewish religion. Rabbinical literature — Halacha — Philosophy

BM520.6.N69 1998
Novak, David, 1941-
Natural law in Judaism/ David Novak. Cambridge; Cambridge University Press, 1998. xii, 210 p.
97-050609   296.3/6   052163170X
Jewish law -- Philosophy. Natural law. Ethics, Jewish.

BM525 Sources of Jewish religion. Rabbinical literature — Cabala — Sources

BM525.A52 M37 1983
Zohar, the book of enlightenment/ translation and introduction by Daniel Chanan Matt; preface by Arthur Green. New York: Paulist Press, c1983. xvi, 320 p.
83-082145   296.1/6 19   0809123878
Cabala -- Early works to 1800.

BM525.A59.G55 2001
Giller, Pinchas, 1953-
Reading the Zohar: the sacred text of the Kabbalah/ Pinchas Giller. New York: Oxford University Press, 2001. xviii, 246 p.
99-029413   296.1/62   0195118499
Cabala.

BM525.C65413 1994
Cordovero, Moses ben Jacob, 1522-1570.
Moses Cordovero's introduction to Kabbalah: an annotated translation of his Or neerav/ by Ira Robinson. New York: Michael Scharf Pub. Trust of Yeshiva Univ. Press, 1994. xxxiv, 238 p.
93-045501   296.1/6   0881254398
Cabala -- Early works to 1800.

BM526 Sources of Jewish religion. Rabbinical literature — Cabala — History and criticism

BM526.S36413 1991
Scholem, Gershom Gerhard, 1897-
On the mystical shape of the godhead: basic concepts in the Kabbalah/ Gershom Scholem; translated from the German by Joachim Neugroschel; edited and revised, according to the 1976 Hebrew edition, with the author's emendations, by Jonathan Chipman; foreword by Joseph Dan. New York: Schoken Books; c1991. 328 p.
90-052543   296.1/6   0805240829
Cabala -- History. God (Judaism) Transmigration -- Judaism.

BM526.S93 1996
Swartz, Michael D.
Scholastic magic: ritual and revelation in early Jewish mysticism/ Michael D. Swartz. Princeton, NJ: Princeton University Press, c1996. x, 263 p.
96-033720   296.1 20   0691010986
Mysticism -- Judaism -- History. Magic, Jewish. Rabbis -- Prayer-books and devotions. Intercessory prayer -- Judaism.

BM530 Sources of Jewish religion. Rabbinical literature — Myths and legends — General works

BM530.L457 1993
Liebes, Yehuda.
Studies in Jewish myth and Jewish messianism/ Yehuda Liebes; translated from the Hebrew by Batya Stein. Albany: State University of New York Press, c1993. ix, 226 p.
91-036470   296.1/6   0791411931
Nahman, -- of Bratslav, -- 1772-1811. -- Tikun ha-kelali.Messiah -- Judaism. Sabbathaians. Mythology, Jewish.

BM534 Relation of Judaism to special subject fields — Religions — General works

BM534.F45 1993
Feldman, Louis H.
Jew and Gentile in the ancient world: attitudes and interactions from Alexander to Justinian/ Louis H. Feldman. Princeton, N.J.: Princeton University Press, c1993. xii, 679 p.
92-011952   296.3/872/09015   069107416X
Judaism -- Relations. Jews -- Public opinion -- History. Jews -- History -- 586 B.C.-70 A.D.

BM535 Relation of Judaism to special subject fields — Religions — Christianity. Jews and Christianity

BM535.B2
Baeck, Leo, 1873-1956.
Judaism and Christianity; essays, translated with an introd. by Walter Kaufmann. Philadelphia, Jewish publication Society of America, 1958. 292 p.
58-008991   296
Judaism -- Influence. Judaism -- Relations -- Christianity. Christianity and other religions -- Judaism.

BM535.C5775 2000
Christianity in Jewish terms/ editors by Tikva Frymer-Kensky ... [et al.]. Boulder, CO: Westview Press, 2000. xxii, 438 p.
00-044773   296.3/96   0813337801
Judaism -- Relations -- Christianity. Christianity and other religions -- Judaism. Judaism (Christian theology)

BM535.C6 1971
Cohen, Arthur Allen, 1928-
The myth of the Judeo-Christian tradition, and other dissenting essays [by] Arthur A. Cohen. New York, Schocken Books [1971] xx, 223 p.
77-152766   296.3/87/2   0805202935
Judaism -- Relations -- Christianity. Christianity and other religions -- Judaism.

BM535.G33 1983
Gager, John G.
The origins of anti-semitism: attitudes toward Judaism in pagan and Christian antiquity/ John G. Gager. New York: Oxford University Press, 1983. viii, 312 p.
82-024523   296.3/872   0195033167
Paul, -- the Apostle, Saint -- Views on Judaism.Christianity and antisemitism. Judaism -- Relations -- Christianity. Christianity and other religions -- Judaism.

BM535.J465 1990
Jewish perspectives on Christianity: Leo Baeck, Martin Buber, Franz Rosenzweig, Will Herberg, and Abraham J. Heschel/ edited by Fritz A. Rothschild. New York: Crossroad, 1990. x, 363 p.
90-001670   296.3/872   0824509374
Judaism -- Relations -- Christianity. Christianity and other religions -- Judaism. Judaism -- 20th century.

BM535.L76 1990
Lubarsky, Sandra B., 1954-
Tolerance and transformation: Jewish approaches to religious pluralism/ Sandra B. Lubarsky. Cincinnati: Hebrew Union College Press; c1990. x, 149 p.
90-004206   296.3/872   0878205047
Judaism -- Relations -- Christianity. Christianity and other religions -- Judaism. Judaism -- 20th century.

BM535.O2413 1984
Oberman, Heiko Augustinus.
The roots of anti-Semitism in the age of Renaissance and Reformation/ Heiko A. Oberman; translated by James I. Porter. Philadelphia: Fortress Press, c1984. xi, 163 p.
83-005695   261.2/6   0800607090
Luther, Martin, -- 1483-1546 -- Views on Judaism.Reformation. Renaissance. Christianity and antisemitism -- History -- 16th century.

BM535.U53 1988
Unanswered questions: theological views of Jewish-Catholic relations/ edited by Roger Brooks. Notre Dame, Ind.: University of Notre Dame Press, c1988. x, 224 p.
87-040353   261.2/6   0268019177
Judaism -- Relations -- Catholic Church.

BM536 Relation of Judaism to special subject fields — Religions — Other religions, A-Z

BM536.G7
Hellenism in the land of Israel/ John J. Collins, Gregory E. Sterling, editors. Notre Dame, IN: University of Notre Dame, 2001. ix, 343 p.
00-055988   296/.0933/09014   0268030510
Judaism -- Relations -- Greek. Jews -- Civilization -- Greek influences. Hellenism. Greece -- Religion.

BM538 Relation of Judaism to special subject fields — Other, A-Z

BM538.A7.B55 2000
Bland, Kalman P., 1942-
The artless Jew: medieval and modern affirmations and denials of the visual/ by Kalman P. Bland. Princeton, NJ: Princeton University Press, 2000. 233 p.
99-044922   296.4/6/09   0691010439
Judaism and art -- History of doctrines. Art, Jewish. Jewish aesthetics.

BM538.H43.D68 1998
Dorff, Elliot N.
Matters of life and death: a Jewish approach to modern medical ethics/ Elliot N. Dorff. Philadelphia: Jewish Publication Society, 1998. xix, 456 p.
97-036295   296.3/642   0827606478
Medicine -- Religious aspects -- Judaism. Health -- Religious aspects -- Judaism. Medical laws and legislation (Jewish law)

BM538.H85.T67 2000
Torah of the earth: exploring 4,000 years of ecology in Jewish thought/ edited by Arthur Waskow. Woodstock, Vt.: Jewish Lights Pub., c2000. 2 v.
00-008696   296.3/8   1580230865
Human ecology -- Religious aspects -- Judaism. Nature -- Religious aspects -- Judaism. Human ecology -- Israel.

BM538.P3.H6613 1994
Homolka, Walter.
The gate to perfection: the idea of peace in Jewish thought/ Walter H. Homolka, Albert H. Friedlander; with a preface by Elie Wiesel. Providence: Berghahn Books, 1994. xv, 128 p.
94-022783   296.3/87873   1571810188
Peace -- Religious aspects -- Judaism.

BM538.S3.F57 1997
Fisch, Menachem.
Rational rabbis: science and Talmudic culture/ Menachem Fisch. Bloomington: Indiana University Press, c1997. xxii, 263 p.
97-007349   296.3/75   0253333164
Talmud Torah (Judaism) Judaism and science.

BM545 General works on the principles of Judaism — Early to 1800 — Maimonides. Moses ben Maimon

BM545.A45T9 1972
Moses ben Maimon, 1135-1204.
A Maimonides reader, edited, with introductions and notes, by Isadore Twersky. New York, Behrman House [1972] xvii, 494 p.
76-160818   296.3   0874412005
Judaism -- Works to 1900.

BM560 General works on the principles of Judaism — Modern works — 1801-1950

BM560.H46
Heschel, Abraham Joshua, 1907-1972.
God in search of man: a philosophy of Judaism. New York: Jewish Publication Society of America, 1955. 437 p.
55-011188   296   0374513317
Judaism. Religion -- Philosophy.

BM565 General works on the principles of Judaism — Modern works — General special

BM565.L54 1990
Liebman, Charles S.
Two worlds of Judaism: the Israeli and American experiences/ Charles S. Liebman and Steven M. Cohen. New Haven: Yale University Press, c1990. xi, 202 p.
89-028457   296/.095694/09045   0300047266
Judaism -- 20th century. Judaism -- Israel. Judaism -- United States.

BM565.M63 2001
Morgan, Michael L., 1944-
Interim Judaism: Jewish thought in a century of crisis/ Michael L. Morgan. Bloomington: Indiana University Press, c2001. 146 p.
00-063465   296.3/09/04   0253338565
Judaism -- 20th century. Judaism -- United States. Revelation (Jewish theology)

BM601 Dogmatic Judaism — General works — 1951-2000

BM601.B623.R48 2000
Reviewing the covenant: Eugene Borowitz and the postmodern revival of Jewish theology/ edited by Peter Ochs with Eugene Borowitz; including responses by Yudit Kornberg Greenberg ... [et al.]. Albany: State University of New York Press, c2000. ix, 214 p.
99-037866   296.3   079144533X
Borowitz, Eugene B. -- Renewing the covenant.Judaism -- 20th century. Commandments (Judaism) -- History of doctrines -- 20th century. Covenants -- Religious aspects -- Judaism -- History of doctrines -- 20th century.

BM601.T48 1989
Three faiths--one God: a Jewish, Christian, Muslim encounter/ edited by John Hick and Edmund S. Meltzer; foreword by John David Maguire. Albany: State University of New York Press, c1989. xiv, 240 p.
88-038014   291.2   0791400425
Judaism -- Doctrines. Theology, Doctrinal. Islam -- Doctrines.

BM610 Dogmatic Judaism — Conception of God

BM610.G53 2000
Gillman, Neil.
The way into encountering God in Judaism/ Neil Gillman. Woodstock, Vt.: Jewish Lights, c2000. xix, 205 p.
00-011769   296.3/11   1580230253
  God (Judaism) God (Judaism) -- History of doctrines.

BM610.S38 2000
Seeskin, Kenneth, 1947-
Searching for a distant God: the legacy of Maimonides/ Kenneth Seeskin. New York: Oxford University Press, 2000. xii, 252 p.
98-037882   296.3/11/092   019512846X
  Maimonides, Moses, -- 1135-1204 -- Contributions in the doctrine of God.God (Judaism) -- History of doctrines. Philosophy, Jewish.

BM612.5 Dogmatic Judaism — Covenants. Covenant theology

BM612.5.B74 1989
Breslauer, S. Daniel.
Covenant and community in modern Judaism/ S. Daniel Breslauer. New York: Greenwood Press, 1989. xi, 126 p.
88-024631   296.3/11   0313266050
  Covenants -- Religious aspects -- Judaism -- History of doctrines. Judaism -- History -- Modern period, 1750-

BM615 Dogmatic Judaism — Messiah — General works

BM615.E87 1992
Essential papers on messianic movements and personalities in Jewish history/ edited by Marc Saperstein. New York: New York University Press, c1992. xii, 580 p.
92-003350   296.8 20   0814779433
  Jewish messianic movements -- History.

BM620 Dogmatic Judaism — Messiah — Attitude toward Jesus Christ

BM620.B213 2001
Ben-Chorin, Schalom.
Brother Jesus: the Nazarene through Jewish eyes/ Schalom Ben-Chorin; translated and edited by Jared S. Klein and Max Reinhart. Athens, GA: University of Georgia Press, c2001. xiv, 252 p.
00-045136   232.9/06   0820322563
  Jesus Christ -- Jewish interpretations.

BM627 Dogmatic Judaism — Man

BM627.B44 1979
Belkin, Samuel.
In His image: the Jewish philosophy of man as expressed in rabbinic tradition/ by Samuel Belkin. Westport, Conn.: Greenwood Press, 1979, c1960. 290 p.
78-010192   296.3/8   0313212341
  Man (Jewish theology)

BM627.F83 2000
Fuchs, Lawrence H.
Beyond patriarchy: Jewish fathers and families/ Lawrence H. Fuchs. Hanover: Published by University Press of New England, Brandeis University Press, c2000. xi, 216 p.
00-008426   306.85/8/089924   0874519411
  Patriarchy -- Religious aspects -- Judaism. Jewish families -- Conduct of life -- History. Patriarchy -- History.

BM635.7 Dogmatic Judaism — Eschatology. Future life — Transmigration

BM635.7.S65 2000
Spitz, Elie Kaplan, 1954-
Does the soul survive?: a Jewish journey to belief in afterlife, past lives, & living with purpose/ Elie Kaplan Spitz; foreword by Brian L. Weiss. Woodstock, Vt.: Jewish Lights Publishing, c2000. xxv, 245 p.
00-009624   296.3/3   1580230946
  Transmigration -- Judaism. Soul (Judaism)

BM645 Dogmatic Judaism — Other topics, A-Z

BM645.H43.W75 2000
Wright, J. Edward.
The early history of heaven/ J. Edward Wright. New York: Oxford University Press, c2000. xviii, 318 p.
98-049461   291.2/3   019513009X
  Heaven -- Judaism -- History of doctrines. Heaven -- Christianity -- History of doctrines -- Early church, ca. 30-600. Heaven -- Comparative studies.

BM645.H6.E43 1990
Ellis, Marc H.
Beyond innocence and redemption: confronting the Holocaust and Israeli power: creating a moral future for the Jewish people/ Marc H. Ellis. San Francisco: Harper & Row, c1990. xvi, 214 p.
89-045954   296.3   0060622156
  Holocaust (Jewish theology) Jewish-Arab relations -- Religious aspects -- Judaism. Judaism and social problems. Israel -- Moral conditions.

BM645.H85.G66 1998
Goodman, Lenn Evan, 1944-
Judaism, human rights, and human values/ Lenn E. Goodman. New York: Oxford University Press, c1998. xxi, 202 p.
97-036235   296.3/82   0195118340
  Mill, John Stuart, -- 1806-1873. -- On liberty.Human rights -- Philosophy. Human rights -- Religious aspects -- Judaism. Liberty.

BM645.P67 N64 2002
Noegel, Scott B.
Historical dictionary of prophets in Islam and Judaism/ Scott B. Noegel, Brannon M. Wheeler. Lanham, MD: Scarecrow, 2002. xxxvii, 522 p.
2002-022372   296/.092/2 B 21   0810843056
  Prophecy -- Judaism -- Dictionaries. Prophecy -- Islam -- Dictionaries. Prophecy -- Dictionaries. Prophets -- Biography -- Dictionaries.

BM652 Practical Judaism — Priests, rabbis, etc. — Office of the rabbi

BM652.S26 1993
Schwarzfuchs, Simon.
A concise history of the rabbinate/ Simon Schwarzfuchs. Oxford, UK; B. Blackwell, 1993. xii, 179 p.
92-042506   296.6/1   0631161325
  Rabbis -- Office -- History. Rabbinical seminaries -- History.

BM653 Practical Judaism — Congregations. Synagogues — Organization and administration

BM653.L38 2000
Levine, Lee I.
The ancient synagogue: the first thousand years/ Lee I. Levine. New Haven: Yale University Press, c2000. xvi, 748 p.
98-052667   296.6/5/0901   0300074751
  Synagogues -- History -- To 1500. Judaism -- History -- Post-exilic period, 586 B.C.-210 A.D. Judaism -- History -- Talmudic period, 10-425.

BM656 Practical Judaism — Forms of worship — General works

BM656.K713
Kraus, Hans-Joachim.
Worship in Israel: a cultic history of the Old Testament/ by Hans-Joachim Kraus; translated by Geoffrey Buswell. Richmond: John Knox Press, 1966. xi, 246 p.
65-016432   296.4
  Worship (Judaism)

BM660 Practical Judaism — Liturgy and ritual — General works

BM660.E513 1993
Elbogen, Ismar, 1874-1943.
Jewish liturgy: a comprehensive history/ by Ismar Elbogen; translated by Raymond P. Scheindlin. Philadelphia: Jewish Publication Society; c1993. xxi, 501 p.
93-018401   296.4   0827604459
Judaism -- Liturgy -- History.

BM660.O43 2000
Olitzky, Kerry M.
An encyclopedia of American synagogue ritual/ Kerry M. Olitzky; Marc Lee Raphael, advisory editor. Westport, Conn.: Greenwood Press, 2000. xxiv, 160 p.
99-054418   296.4/5/097303   0313308144
Judaism -- Liturgy -- Encyclopedias. Judaism -- Liturgy -- History -- Encyclopedias. Judaism -- United States -- Encyclopedias.

BM705 Practical Judaism — Rites and customs — Berit milah (Circumcision)

BM705.H63 1996
Hoffman, Lawrence A., 1942-
Covenant of blood: circumcision and gender in rabbinic Judaism/ Lawrence A. Hoffman. Chicago: University of Chicago Press, 1996. 256 p.
95-016067   296.4/422   0226347834
Berit milah -- History. Blood -- Religious aspects -- Judaism. Women in rabbinical literature.

BM712 Practical Judaism — Rites and customs — Funeral rites. Mourning customs

BM712.H45 2001
Heilman, Samuel C.
When a Jew dies: the ethnography of a bereaved son/ Samuel C. Heilman. Berkeley: University of California Press, c2001. 271 p.
00-053210   296.4/45   0520219651
Jewish mourning customs. Bereavement -- Social aspects. Bereavement -- Religious aspects -- Judaism.

BM712.L3 2000
Lamm, Maurice.
The Jewish way in death and mourning/ by Maurice Lamm. Middle Village, NY: Jonathan David Publishers, 1999. xvii, 318 p.
99-088942   294.4/45   0824604237
Jewish mourning customs.

BM723 Practical Judaism — Jewish way of life. Spiritual life. Mysticism. Personal religion — General works

BM723.C64 1994
Cohn-Sherbok, Dan.
Jewish & Christian mysticism: an introduction/ Dan Cohn-Sherbok & Lavinia Cohn-Sherbok. New York: Continuum, 1994. viii, 186 p.
94-079113   248.2/2   0826406955
Mysticism -- Judaism -- History. Mysticism -- History.

BM723.H33 1998
Hanson, Kenneth, 1953-
Kabbalah: three thousand years of mystic tradition/ Kenneth Hanson. Tulsa, Okla.: Council Oak Books, c1998. 270 p.
98-036441   296.1/6   1571780726
Mysticism -- Judaism -- History. Cabala -- History.

BM723.S35 1961
Scholem, Gershom Gerhard,
Major trends in Jewish mysticism. New York, Schocken Books [1961, c1954] 460 p.
61-008991   296.833
Mysticism -- Judaism. Cabala -- History.

BM723.S665 2000
Sonsino, Rifat, 1938-
Six Jewish spiritual paths: a rationalist looks at spirituality/ Rifat Sonsino. Woodstock, Vt.: Jewish Lights Publishing, c2000. ix, 180 p.
00-010650   296.7   1580230954
Spiritual life -- Judaism. Jewish way of life.

BM726 Practical Judaism — Jewish way of life. Spiritual life. Mysticism. Personal religion — Religious duties

BM726.B49 1999
Berkovic, Sally.
Straight talk: my dilemma as an Orthodox Jewish woman/ Sally Berkovic. Hoboken, NJ: KTAV Pub. House, c1999. 254 p.
99-026775   296.8/32/082   0881256617
Berkovic, Sally -- Religion. Orthodox Judaism. Women in Judaism.

BM729 Practical Judaism — Other special topics, A-Z

BM729.W6.A29 1999
Adler, Rachel.
Engendering Judaism: an inclusive theology and ethics/ Rachel Adler. Boston: Beacon Press, 1999.
99-025989   296.3/082   0807036196
Feminism -- Religious aspects -- Judaism. Judaism -- Doctrines. Women in Judaism.

BM729.W6 G445 1994
Gender & Jewish studies: a curriculum guide/ Judith R. Baskin and Shelly Tenenbaum, [editors]. New York: Biblio Press, 1994. 163 p.
93-074870   296/.082 20   0930395190
Women in Judaism -- Outlines, syllabi, etc. Women in Judaism -- Bibliography. Jewish women -- Outlines, syllabi, etc. Jewish women -- Bibliography. Universities and colleges -- United States -- Curricula. Women's studies -- United States -- Curricula.

BM729.W6.G73
Greenberg, Blu, 1936-
On women & Judaism: a view from tradition/ Blu Greenberg. Philadelphia: Jewish Publication Society of America, 1981. xi, 178 p.
81-011779   296.3/878344   0827601956
Women in Judaism -- Addresses, essays, lectures.

BM729.W6 J49 1991
Jewish women in historical perspective/ edited by Judith R. Baskin. Detroit: Wayne State University Press, c1991. 300 p.
91-010491   296/.082 20   0814320910
Women in Judaism. Jewish women -- History. Jewish women -- Religious life.

BM729.W6.M67 1998
Morris, Bonnie J., 1961-
Lubavitcher women in America: identity and activism in the postwar era/ Bonnie J. Morris. Albany: State University of New York Press, c1998. x, 186 p.
97-028021   296.8/3322/0820973   079143799X
Women in Judaism -- United States. Chabad -- United States. Jewish women -- Religious life -- United States. Crown Heights (New York, N.Y.) -- Religious life and customs.

BM729.W6 P55 1990
Plaskow, Judith.
Standing again at Sinai: Judaism from a feminist perspective/ Judith Plaskow. 1st ed. San Francisco: Harper & Row, c1990. xix, 282 p.
89-045559   296/.082 20   0060666838
Women in Judaism. Feminism -- Religious aspects -- Judaism.

BM750 Biography — Collective

BM750.N33 1988
Nadell, Pamela Susan.
Conservative Judaism in America: a biographical dictionary and sourcebook/ Pamela S. Nadell. New York: Greenwood Press, 1988. xvi, 409 p.
87-031782   296.8/342/0922   0313242054
Conservative Judaism -- United States. Jews -- United States -- Biography -- Dictionaries.

BM750.R39 1993
Reform Judaism in America: a biographical dictionary and sourcebook/ edited by Kerry M. Olitzky, Lance J. Sussman, and Malcolm H. Stern. Westport, Conn.: Greenwood Press, 1993. xxxi, 347 p.
92-025794   296.8/346/0973   0313246289
Jews -- United States -- Biography -- Dictionaries. Reform Judaism -- United States.

BM750.S395 1996
Sherman, Moshe D.
Orthodox Judaism in America: a biographical dictionary and sourcebook/ Moshe D. Sherman. Westport, Conn.: Greenwood Press, 1996. x, 291 p.
95-020932   296.8/32/092273   0313243166
Orthodox Judaism -- United States -- History. Jews -- United States -- Biography.

BM755 Biography — Individual, A-Z

BM755.G4.H47 1998
Heschel, Susannah.
Abraham Geiger and the Jewish Jesus/ Susannah Heschel. Chicago: University of Chicago Press, 1998. xii, 317 p.
97-027313   296/.092   0226329585
Geiger, Abraham, -- 1810-1874. Jesus Christ -- Jewish interpretations. Jewish scholars -- Germany -- Biography. Rabbis -- Germany -- Biography.

BM755.H37.M66 1989
Moore, Donald J.
The human and the holy: the spirituality of Abraham Joshua Heschel/ Donald J. Moore. New York: Fordham University Press, 1989. viii, 215 p.
89-080461   296.3/092   0823212351
Heschel, Abraham Joshua, -- 1907-1972.

BM755.K66.R285 1995
Rabbi Abraham Isaac Kook and Jewish spirituality/ edited by Lawrence J. Kaplan and David Shatz. New York: New York University Press, c1995. xiii, 346 p.
94-017494   296.8/32/092   0814746527
Kook, Abraham Isaac, -- 1865-1935.Orthodox Judaism -- History -- 20th century. Religious Zionism.

BM755.S295.B5
Biale, David, 1949-
Gershom Scholem: Kabbalah and counter-history/ David Biale. Cambridge, Mass.: Harvard University Press, 1979. vi, 279 p.
78-023620   296.7/1   0674363302
Scholem, Gershom Gerhard, -- 1897-Jewish scholars -- Germany -- Biography. Jewish scholars -- Israel -- Biography. Mysticism -- Judaism -- Historiography.

BM755.S544.Z56 1997
Abba Hillel Silver and American Zionism/ edited by Mark A. Raider, Jonathan D. Sarna, and Ronald W. Zweig. London; Frank Cass, 1997. 127 p.
97-026840   320.54/095694   0714648248
Silver, Abba Hillel, -- 1893-1963. Ben-Gurion, David, -- 1886-1973. Zionists -- United States -- Biography. Zionism -- United States -- History. Rabbis -- Ohio -- Cleveland -- Biography.

BP Islam. Bahai Faith. Theosophy, etc.

BP40 Islam — Dictionaries. Encyclopedias

BP40.H8 1982
Hughes, Thomas Patrick,
Dictionary of Islam: being a cyclopaedia of the doctrines, rites, ceremonies, and customs, together with the technical and theological terms of the Muhammadan religion/ by Thomas Patrick Hughes. New Delhi, India: Cosmo Publications, 1982. vii, 750 p.
83-125349   297/.03/21 19
Islam -- Dictionaries.

BP40.M83 1996
The Muslim almanac: a reference work on the history, faith, culture, and peoples of Islam/ Azim A. Nanji, editor. Detroit, MI: Gale Research, c1996. xxxv, 581 p.
95-017324   297   081038924X
Islam.Islamic countries.

BP40.N48 1992
Netton, Ian Richard.
A popular dictionary of Islam/ Ian Richard Netton. Atlantic Highlands, NJ: Humanities Press International, 1992. 279 p.
92-013600   297/.03 20   0391037560
Islam -- Dictionaries.

BP40.O95 2003
The Oxford dictionary of Islam/ John L. Esposito, editor in chief. New York: Oxford University Press, 2003. xviii, 359 p.
2002-030261   297/.03 21   0195125584
Islam -- Dictionaries.

BP50 Islam — History — General works

BP50.A33 2001
Adamec, Ludwig W.
Historical dictionary of Islam/ Ludwig W. Adamec. Lanham, Md.: Scarecrow Press, 2001. xxxiii, 417 p.
00-050470   297/.03 21   0810839628
Islam -- History -- Dictionaries.

BP50.A69 2000
Armstrong, Karen, 1944-
Islam: a short history/ Karen Armstrong. New York: Modern Library, 2000. xxxiv, 222 p.
00-025285   297/.09   0679640401
Islam -- History.Islamic Empire -- History.

BP50.J46 1999
Jenkins, Everett,
The Muslim diaspora: a comprehensive reference to the spread of Islam in Asia, Africa, Europe, and the Americas/ by Everett Jenkins, Jr. Jefferson, N.C.: McFarland, [1999]- v. <1-2 >
98-049332   297/.09 21   0786404310
Islam -- History.

BP52 Islam — History — General special

BP52.A35 1988
Ahmed, Akbar S.
Discovering Islam: making sense of Muslim history and society/ Akbar S. Ahmed. London; Routledge & K. Paul, 1988. x, 251 p.
87-004967   297/.09   0710210493
Islam -- History. Islam -- Essence, genius, nature. Islam -- 20th century.

BP55-60 Islam — History — By period

BP55.B57 2002
Bloom, Jonathan
Islam: a thousand years of faith and power/ Jonathan Bloom and Sheila Blair. New York: TV Books, c2000. 268 p.
00-023449   297/.09   157500092X
Islam -- History.Islamic Empire -- History.

BP60.D38 1998
Davidson, Lawrence, 1945-
Islamic fundamentalism/ Lawrence Davidson. Westport, Conn.: Greenwood Press, c1998. xxi, 186 p.
97-037511   320.5/5/0917671   0313299781
Islamic fundamentalism. Islam -- 20th century.

BP60.E84 1999
Esposito, John L.
The Islamic threat: myth or reality?/ John L.
Esposito. 3rd ed. New York: Oxford University
Press, 1999. xvi, 328 p.
99-028443 327.4017/671 21 0195130766
*Islam -- 20th century. Islamic countries --
Relations -- Europe. Europe -- Relations --
Islamic countries.*

BP60.H8 1998
Huband, Mark.
Warriors of the Prophet: the struggle for Islam/
Mark Huband. Boulder, Colo.: Westview Press,
1998.
98-012261 320.5/5/0917671 0813327806
*Islamic fundamentalism. Terrorism --
Religious aspects -- Islam. Terrorism -- Islamic
countries -- History -- 20th century.*

BP60.I82 1996
Islamic fundamentalism/ edited by Abdel Salam
Sidahmed, Anoushiravan Ehteshami. Boulder,
Colo.: Westview Press, 1996. xiv, 284 p.
96-016463 322/.1/0917671 20 0813324300
*Islamic fundamentalism. Islamic countries --
Politics and government.*

BP60.M36 1999
Mawsilili, Ahmad.
Historical dictionary of Islamic fundamentalist
movements in the Arab world, Iran, and Turkey/
Ahmad S. Moussalli. Lanham, Md.: Scarecrow
Press, 1999. xxviii, 401 p.
98-045879 297/.09 0810836092
*Islamic fundamentalism -- Arab countries --
History -- Dictionaries. Islamic fundamentalism
-- Middle East -- History -- Dictionaries. Islamic
fundamentalism -- Turkey -- History --
Dictionaries.*

BP60.M55 2002
Modernist Islam, 1840-1940: a sourcebook/
edited by Charles Kurzman. Oxford; Oxford
University Press, 2002. xi, 389 p.
2002-022046 297/.09/04 21 0195154681
*Islamic renewal -- History -- 19th century.
Islamic renewal -- History -- 20th century.
Islamic countries -- Intellectual life -- 19th
century. Islamic countries -- Intellectual life --
20th century.*

BP60.P56 1994
Pioneers of Islamic revival/ edited by Ali
Rahnema. London; Zed Books, 1994 viii, 279 p.
94-032598 297/.2/0922 20 1856492540
Islamic renewal.

BP60.P64 1997
Political Islam: revolution, radicalism, or
reform?/ edited by John L. Esposito. Boulder,
Colo.: Lynne Rienner Publishers, 1997. vi,
281 p.
96-038160 320.5/5/0917671 155587262X
*Islam and politics.Islamic countries -- Politics
and government.*

BP63-67 Islam — History — By continent and country

BP63.A34.K54 1998
Khalid, Adeeb, 1964-
The politics of Muslim cultural reform: jadidism
in Central Asia/ Adeeb Khalid. Berkeley:
University of California Press, c1998. xx, 335 p.
98-004189 958/.04 0520213556
*Islam -- Asia, Central. Islam and politics --
Asia, Central. Islam and state -- Asia, Central.
Asia, Central -- Politics and government.*

BP63.A34 R65 2000
Ro'i, Yaacov.
Islam in the Soviet Union: from the second
World War to Gorbachev/ by Yaacov Roi. New
York: Columbia University Press, 2000.
99-041848 297/.0947/09045 0231119542
*Islam -- Former Soviet republics -- 20th
century. Islam -- Russia (Federation) -- 20th
century.*

BP63.A4.A7247 1997
Ghadbian, Najib.
Democratization and the Islamist challenge in
the Arab world/ Najib Ghadbian. Boulder, Colo.:
Westview Press, 1997. xv, 171 p.
97-000411 320.917/4927/009048
0813327849
*Islam and politics -- Arab countries. Islam
and state -- Arab countries. Islam -- 20th
century. Arab countries -- politics and
government -- 1945-*

BP63.A4.D45 1985
Dekmejian, R. Hrair, 1933-
Islam in revolution: fundamentalism in the Arab
world/ R. Hrair Dekmejian. Syracuse, N.Y.:
Syracuse University Press, 1985. 249 p.
84-026766 322/.1/09174927 0815623291
*Islamic fundamentalism -- Arab countries --
History -- 20th century.*

BP63.A4 M533 1998
Esposito, John L.
Islam and politics/ John L. Esposito. 4th ed.
Syracuse, N.Y.: Syracuse University Press,
1998. xxii, 393 p.
97-051941 320.917/671 21 0815627742
*Islam and politics -- Middle East. Islam and
politics -- Africa, North. Political science --
Middle East -- History. Political science --
Africa, North -- History. Middle East -- Politics
and government. Africa, North -- Politics and
government.*

BP63.A65.F35 1997
Faksh, Mahmud A.
The future of Islam in the Middle East:
fundamentalism in Egypt, Algeria, and Saudi
Arabia/ Mahmud A. Faksh. Westport, Conn.:
Praeger, 1997. xvi, 132 p.
96-009564 297/.0956/09049 0275951286
*Islamic fundamentalism -- Arab countries --
History -- 20th century.*

BP63.I5 F43 1995
Federspiel, Howard M.
A dictionary of Indonesian Islam/ by Howard M.
Federspiel. Athens, Ohio: Ohio University,
Center for International Studies, xxx, 297 p.
94-040777 297/.09598 20 0896801829
*Islam -- Indonesia -- Dictionaries. Indonesian
language -- Dictionaries -- English. Islam --
Dictionaries.*

BP63.I5 H44 2000
Hefner, Robert W., 1952-
Civil Islam: Muslims and democratization in
Indonesia/ Robert W. Hefner. Princeton, NJ:
Princeton University Press, 2000. xxiv, 286 p.
00-020486 322/.1/09598 0691050465
*Islam and politics -- Indonesia. Democracy --
Religious aspects -- Islam. Islam and state --
Indonesia. Indonesia -- Politics and government
-- 1966-1998. Indonesia -- Politics and
government -- 1998-*

BP63.P2.M348 1996
Malik, Jamal.
Colonialization of Islam: dissolution of
traditional institutions in Pakistan/ Jamal Malik.
New Delhi: Manohar, 1996. xiv, 359 p.
96-903921 297.2/7/095491 8173041482
*Islam and state -- Pakistan.Pakistan --
Politics and government.*

BP63.P32.W47413 1994
Abu `Amr, Ziyad.
Islamic fundamentalism in the West Bank and
Gaza: Muslim Brotherhood and Islamic Jihad/
Ziad Abu-Amr. Bloomington: Indiana University
Press, 1994. xvii, 169 p.
93-028504 322.4/2/0956953 0253208661
*Islam and politics -- Gaza Strip. Islam and
politics -- West Bank. Gaza Strip -- Politics and
government. West Bank -- Politics and
government.*

BP63.S95 C66 1990
Commins, David Dean.
Islamic reform: politics and social change in late
Ottoman Syria/ David Dean Commins. New
York: Oxford University Press, 1990. viii, 199 p.
89-016211 956.91/03 20 0195061039
*Islam -- Syria -- History -- 19th century. Islam
-- Syria -- History -- 20th century.*

BP63.T8.M44 1990
Mehmet, Ozay.
Islamic identity and development: studies of the
Islamic periphery/ Ozay Mehmet. London;
Routledge, c1990. ix, 259 p.
90-008353 297/.1978/09561 0415043867
*Islam -- Turkey. Islam -- Malaysia. Islam and
state -- Turkey. Malaysia -- Economic policy.
Turkey -- Economic policy.*

BP64.A1 H57 1994
Hiskett, M.
The course of Islam in Africa/ Mervyn Hiskett.
Edinburgh: Edinburgh University Press, c1994.
ix, 218 p.
95-168334 297/.096 20 0748604618
Islam -- Africa -- History.

BP64.A1 H62 2000
The History of Islam in Africa/ edited by Nehemia Levtzion & Randall L. Pouwels. Athens: Ohio University Press, 2000. x, 591 p.
99-027729   297/.096 21   0821412973
Islam -- Africa -- History.

BP64.A37 Q56 2003
Quinn, Charlotte A.
Pride, faith, and fear: Islam in Sub-Saharan Africa/ Charlotte A. Quinn and Frederick Quinn. Oxford; Oxford University Press, 2003. vi, 175 p.
2002-019044   297/.0967 21   0195063864
Islam -- Africa, Sub-Saharan -- History -- 20th century. Islam and state -- Africa, Sub-Saharan. Religion and state -- Africa, Sub-Saharan. Africa, Sub-Saharan -- Religion.

BP64.A4 N6423 1994
Fluehr-Lobban, Carolyn.
Islamic society in practice/ Carolyn Fluehr-Lobban. Gainesville: University Press of Florida, c1994. x, 191 p.
94-013713   297/.0962 20   0813013194
Islam -- Africa, North. Islam. Islam -- Egypt. Islam -- Tunisia. Africa, North -- Religious life and customs. Sudan -- Religious life and customs. Egypt -- Religious life and customs. Tunisia -- Religious life and customs.

BP64.A4.N677 1997
Shahin, Emad Eldin, 1957-
Political ascent: contemporary Islamic movements in North Africa/ Emad Eldin Shahin. Boulder, Colo.: Westview Press, 1997. xii, 275 p.
96-046801   320.5/5/0961   081332775X
Islam -- Africa, North -- History -- 20th century. Islam and politics -- Africa, North. Africa, North -- Politics and government.

BP64.A4.W367 1997
Sanneh, Lamin O.
The crown and the turban: Muslims and West African pluralism/ Lamin Sanneh. Boulder, Colo.: Westview Press, 1997. xiii, 290 p.
96-035598   297/.0966   0813330580
Islam -- Africa, West.

BP64.N6.L65 1997
Loimeier, Roman.
Islamic reform and political change in northern Nigeria/ Roman Loimeier. Evanston, Ill.: Northwestern University Press, 1997. xxvi, 415 p.
96-047274   322/.1/0966909045   0810113465
Islam -- Nigeria -- History -- 20th century. Islam and politics -- Nigeria. Nigeria -- Politics and government -- 1993-

BP65.G7.K4713 1997
Kepel, Gilles.
Allah in the West: Islamic movements in America and Europe/ Gilles Kepel; translated by Susan Milner. Stanford, Calif.: Stanford University Press, 1997. 273 p.
95-072624   297/.09182/1   0804727511
Islam -- Great Britain. Islam -- France. Black Muslims.

BP67.A1.I78
Islam in America. Olympia, WA: Olduvai Humanities Library, c1994-c1997. 3 v.
94-648610   297/.0973/05 20
Islam -- North America -- Abstracts -- Periodicals. Muslims -- North America -- Abstracts -- Periodicals.

BP67.A1.I82 1992
Islam in North America: a sourcebook/ edited by Michael A. Koszegi and J. Gordon Melton. New York: Garland Pub., 1992. xxii, 414 p.
92-017794   297/.0973   081530918X
Islam -- North America -- Handbooks, manuals, etc. Islam -- United States -- Handbooks, manuals, etc.

BP67.A1.M34 1996
Making Muslim space in North America and Europe/ edited by Barbara Daly Metcalf. Berkeley: University of California Press, c1996. xix, 264 p.
95-043429   297/.3   0520204034
Muslims -- North America. Muslims -- Europe.

BP67.U6 M86 1994
Muslim communities in North America/ edited by Yvonne Yazbeck Haddad and Jane Idleman Smith. Albany, N.Y.: State University of New York Press, c1994. xxx, 545 p.
93-036564   297/.0973 20   0791420205
Islam -- United States.

BP67.U6 M87 1991
The Muslims of America/ edited by Yvonne Yazbeck Haddad. New York: Oxford University Press, 1991. x, 249 p.
90-044510   297/.0973 20   0195067282
Islam -- United States. Muslims -- United States.

BP70 Islam — Biography — Collective

BP70.E86 2001
Esposito, John L.
Makers of contemporary Islam/ John L. Esposito, John O. Voll. New York: Oxford University Press, 2001. 257 p.
00-056674   297.2/092/2 B 21   0195141288
Scholars, Muslim -- Islamic countries -- Biography. Intellectuals -- Islamic countries -- Biography. Islam and secularism -- Islamic countries. Islam -- 20th century.

BP75-80 Islam — Biography — Individual

BP75.B477 2000
The Biography of Muhammad: the issue of the sources/ edited by Harald Motzki. Boston, MA: Brill, 2000. xvi, 330 p.
99-041850   297.6/3   9004115137
Muhammad, -- Prophet, -- d. 632 -- Biography. Muhammad, -- Prophet, -- d. 632 -- Biography -- Sources.

BP75.I25 1997
Ibn Hisham, Abd al-Malik, d. 834.
The life of Muhammad: a translation of Ishaq's Sirat rasul Allah/ with introduction and notes by A. Guillaume. Karachi; Oxford University Press, 1997. xlvii, 813 p.
98-115611   297.6/3   0195778286
Muhammad, -- Prophet, -- d. 632.Muslims -- Saudi Arabia -- Biography.

BP75.I53 2001
Inamdar, Subhash C.
Muhammad and the rise of Islam: the creation of group identity/ Subhash C. Inamdar. Madison, Conn.: Psychosocial Press, c2001. xix, 266 p.
00-045723   297.6/3   1887841288
Muhammad, -- Prophet, -- d. 632 -- Biography.Ummah (Islam) Civilization, Islamic -- History. Islamic Empire -- History.

BP75.P4 1994
Peters, F. E.
Muhammad and the origins of Islam/ F.E. Peters. Albany: State University of New York Press, c1994. xiii, 334 p.
93-010568   297.63   0791418758
Muhammad, -- Prophet, -- d. 632.

BP75.P45 1996
Phipps, William E., 1930-
Muhammad and Jesus: a comparison of the prophets and their teachings/ William E. Phipps. New York, NY: Continuum, 1996. 304 p.
94-036176   297.63   0826409148
Muhammad, -- Prophet, -- d. 632. Jesus Christ. Islam -- Relations -- Christianity. Christianity and other religions -- Islam.

BP80.A52.S64 1994
Spellberg, D. A.
Politics, gender, and the Islamic past: The Legacy of Aisha bint Abi Bakr/ D.A. Spellberg. New York: Columbia University Press, c1994. x, 243 p.
94-025025   297/.64   0231079982
Aishah, -- ca. 614-678. Muhammad, -- Prophet, -- d. 632 -- Family. Muslim women. Women, Muslim -- Saudi Arabia -- Biography.

BP80.M34.N37 1996
Nasr, Seyyed Vali Reza, 1960-
Mawdudi and the making of Islamic revivalism/ Seyyed Vali Reza Nasr. New York: Oxford University Press, 1996. viii, 222 p.
95-000201   297/.1977/092   0195096959
Maudoodi, Syed Abul Ala, -- d1903-1979.Muslims -- Pakistan -- Biography. Muslims -- India -- Biography.

BP80.Q86.M68 1992
Moussalli, Ahmad S.
Radical Islamic fundamentalism: the ideological and political discourse of Sayyid Qutb/ Ahmad S. Moussalli. Beirut: American University of Beirut, c1992. 262 p.
93-115586   297/.1977/092
Qutb, Sayyid, -- 1903-1966.Islamic fundamentalism -- Egypt. Islam -- 20th century.

BP89 Islam — Islamic literature. Islamic authors — History and criticism

BP89.E75 1998
Erickson, John D.
Islam and postcolonial narrative/ John Erickson. Cambridge; Cambridge University Press, 1998. xiii, 202 p.
98-226792   809/.8917671   0521594235
Muslim authors -- 20th century. Literature, modern -- 20th century. European literature -- Islamic influences.

BP109-133 Islam — Sacred books — Koran

BP109.P5 1997
The meaning of the glorious Koran: an explanatory translation/ by Mohammed Marmaduke Pickthall. New York: Meridian, 1997.
97-006717   297.1/22521 21   0452011809

BP110.J4 2000
The Koran: selected suras/ translated from the Arabic by Arthur Jeffery. Mineola, NY: Dover Publications, 2000. 231 p.
56-000998   297.1/22521 21   0486414256

BP130.D73 2000
Draz, Mohammad Abd Allah.
Introduction to the Quran/ M.A. Draz. New York: I.B. Tauris Publishers, 2000. xi, 164 p.
2001-266289   297.1/2261 21   186064421X

BP130.4.C66 2000
Cook, M. A.
The Koran, a very short introduction/ Michael Cook. Oxford; Oxford University Press, 2000. 162 p.
99-057686   297.1/2261 21   0192853449

BP130.4.S43 1999
Approaching the Quran: the early revelations/ introduced and translated by Michael Sells. Ashland, OR: White Cloud Press, 1999. 219 p.
99-013401   297.1/2261   1883991307
Koran -- Commentaries. Sells, Michael Anthony.

BP133.E53 2001
Encyclopaedia of the Qur¯an/ Jane Dammen McAuliffe, general editor. Leiden: Brill, 2001- <2002 > v. <1-2 >
2002-265705   297.1/22/03 21   9004120351

BP133.K37 1983
Kassis, Hanna E.
A concordance of the Quran/ Hanna E. Kassis; foreword by Fazlur Rahman. Berkeley: University of California Press, c1983. xxxix, 1444 p.
82-040100   297/.1225/21 19   0520044096

BP133.M57 1987
Mir, Mustansir, 1949-
Dictionary of Quranic terms and concepts/ Mustansir Mir. New York: Garland Pub., 1987. xiv, 244 p.
87-012103   297/.122/0321   0824085469
Koran -- Dictionaries.

BP134 Islam — Sacred books — Koran

BP134.P745 W48 2001
Wheeler, Brannon M.,
Prophets in the Quran: an introduction to the Quran and muslim exegesis/ selected and translated by Brannon M. Wheeler. New York: Continuum, 2002.
2001-028582   297.1/222 21   0826449573
Prophets in the Koran. Koran stories.

BP135-135.8 Islam — Sacred books — Hadith literature. Traditions. Sunna

BP135.B79 1994
Burton, John,
An introduction to the òHad¯ith/ John Burton. Edinburgh: Edinburgh University Press, c1994. xxvi, 210 p.
94-134831   297/.124061 20   0748603506
Hadith -- Introductions.

BP135.8.W67 M4713 1991
Mernissi, Fatima.
The veil and the male elite: a feminist interpretation of women's rights in Islam/ Fatima Mernissi; translated by Mary Jo Lakeland. Reading, Mass.: Addison-Wesley Pub. Co., c1991. xi, 228 p.
90-047404   297/.12408 20   0201523213
Muòhammad, Prophet, d. 632 -- Views on women. Women in the Hadith. Women in Islam.

BP161 Islam — General works on Islam. Treatises — 1801-1950

BP161.G5713
Goldziher, Ignac, 1850-1921.
Introduction to Islamic theology and law/ by Ignaz Goldziher; translated by Andras and Ruth Hamori; with an introd. and additional notes by Bernard Lewis. Princeton, N.J.: Princeton University Press, c1981. xv, 302 p.
80-007523   297   0691072574
Islam.

BP161.2 Islam — General works on Islam. Treatises — 1951-2000

BP161.2.D46 1994
Denny, Frederick Mathewson.
An introduction to Islam/ Frederick Mathewson Denny. 2nd ed. New York: Macmillan Pub. Co., c1994. xv, 405 p.
92-039701   297 20   0023285192
Islam.

BP161.2.F3 2000
Farah, Caesar E.
Islam: beliefs and observances/ Caesar E. Farah. 6th ed. Hauppauge, NY: Barron's Educational Series, 2000. 468 p.
99-073279   297 21   0764112058
Islam.

BP161.2.I882 1984
Islam: the religious and political life of a world community/ edited by Marjorie Kelly. New York: Praeger, 1984. xii, 321 p.
84-013307   909/.097671   0030010888
Islam. Islam and politics. Islamic countries -- History.

BP161.2.M78 1994
Murata, Sachiko,
The vision of Islam/ by Sachiko Murata and William C. Chittick. New York: Paragon House, c1994. xxxix, 368 p.
94-016064   297 20   1557785163
Islam.

BP161.2.R43 1994
A Reader on classical Islam/ [edited by] F.E. Peters. Princeton, N.J.: Princeton University Press, c1994. xiii, 420 p.
93-014595   297 20   0691000409
Islam.

BP161.2.R53 1990
Rippin, Andrew, 1950-
Muslims: their religious beliefs and practices/ Andrew Rippin. London; Routledge, 1990-1993. 2 v.
89-010442   297   0415045185
Islam.

BP161.2.Z46 2000
Zepp, Ira G.
A Muslim primer: beginner's guide to Islam/ Ira G. Zepp, Jr.; foreword by Sayyid Muhammad Syeed. 2nd ed. Fayetteville: University of Arkansas Press, 2000. xxxvii, 218 p.
00-008610   297 21
Islam. Islam -- Doctrines.

BP163 Islam — General special

BP163.A417 1991
Akhtar, Shabbir, 1960-
A faith for all seasons: Islam and the challenge of the modern world/ Shabbir Akhtar. Chicago: I.R. Dee, c1990. 251 p.
90-024786　297　0929587545
Islam -- 20th century.

BP163.A69613 1994
Arkoun, Mohammed.
Rethinking Islam: common questions, uncommon answers/ Mohammed Arkoun; translated and edited by Robert D. Lee. Boulder: Westview Press, 1994. xv, 139 p.
94-002485　297　0813384745
Islam -- 20th century.

BP163.I77313 2000
The Islamic world and the West: an introduction to political cultures and international relations/ edited by Kai Hafez; with a foreword by Mohammed Arkoun and Udo Steinbach; translated from the German by Mary Ann Kenny. Leiden; Brill, 2000. xvi, 246 p.
99-086056　327/.0917/671　9004116516
Islam -- 20th century. Islam and politics. Islamic countries -- Relations -- Europe. Europe -- Relations -- Islamic countries.

BP163.K3813 1990
Kasravi, Ahmad, 1890 or 91-19
On Islam; and, Shi`ism/ Ahmad Kasravi; translated from the Persian by M.R. Ghanoonparvar; with an introductory essay and bibliographical note by M.A. Jazayery. Costa Mesa, CA: Mazda Publishers, 1990. x, 209 p.
90-005897　297　0939214393
Islam -- 20th century. Shi`ah.

BP163.M4713 1992
Mernissi, Fatima.
Islam and democracy: fear of the modern world/ Fatima Mernissi; translated by Mary Jo Lakeland. Reading, Mass.: Addison-Wesley Pub. Co., [1992] 195 p.
92-014666　909/.0974927　0201608839
Islam -- 20th century. Civilization, Arab -- 20th century.

BP169 Islam — Works against Islam and the Koran

BP169.Q47 2000
The quest for the historical Muhammad/ edited and translated by Ibn Warraq. Amherst, N.Y.: Prometheus Books, 2000. 554 p.
99-054420　297.6/3　1573927872
Muhammad, -- Prophet, -- d. 632.Islam -- Controversial literature.

BP172 Islam — Relation of Islam to other religions — Relation to Christianity

BP172.A736 2002
Armour, Rollin S.
Islam, Christianity, and the West: a troubled history/ Rollin Armour, Sr. Maryknoll, N. Y.: Orbis Books, c2002. xv, 197 p.
2001-008228　261.2/7/09 21　1570754071
Islam -- Relations -- Christianity. Christianity and other religions -- Islam. Islam -- History. Islamic countries -- Relations -- Europe. Europe -- Relations -- Islamic countries.

BP172.B8613 1997
Busse, Heribert.
Islam, Judaism and Christianity: the theological and historical affilliations/ Heribert Busse; translated from German by Allison Brown. Princeton, N.J.: Markus Wiener Publishers, 1997.
97-040190　297.2/8　1558761438
Islam -- Relations -- Christianity. Islam -- Relations -- Judaism. Christianity and other religions -- Islam.

BP172.C6413 1997
Courbage, Youssef.
Christians and Jews under Islam/ Youssef Courbage and Philippe Fargues; translated by Judy Mabro. London; Tauris, 1997. xiii, 242 p.
95-062310　305.6/0917671　1860640133
Islam -- Relations -- Christianity. Christianity and other religions -- Islam. Islam -- Relations -- Judaism.

BP172.M396 1996
Medieval Christian perceptions of Islam: a book of essays/ edited by John Victor Tolan. New York: Garland Pub., 1996. xxi, 414 p.
94-005298　261.2/7/09　0815314264
Islam -- Relations -- Christianity. Christianity and other religions -- Islam. Religious thought -- Middle Ages, 600-1500.

BP172.S53 1997
Siddiqui, Ataullah.
Christian-Muslim dialogue in the twentieth century/ Ataullah Siddiqui. New York: St. Martin's Press, 1997. xviii, 248 p.
96-017954　297/.1972　0333673581
Islam -- Relations -- Christianity. Christianity and other religions -- Islam.

BP173 Islam — Relation of Islam to other religions — Other, A-Z

BP173.J8.J83 2000
Judaism and Islam in practice: a sourcebook/ [edited by] Jacob Neusner, Tamara Sonn, and Jonathan E. Brockopp. London; Routledge, 2000. xi, 241 p.
99-034708　296.3/97　0415216737
Judaism -- Relations -- Islam -- Sources. Islam -- Relations -- Judaism -- Sources. Jewish law -- Sources.

BP173.25 Islam — Islamic sociology — General works

BP173.25.C49 1998
Choudhury, Masudul Alam, 1948-
Studies in Islamic social sciences/ Masudul Alam Choudhury; with a foreword by Johan Saravanamutta Abdullah; and a chapter by B.N. Ghosh ... [et al.]. New York, N.Y.: St. Martin's Press, 1998. xx, 252 p.
97-003011　297.2/7　0312175167
Islam and the social sciences. Sociology, Islamic. Islam -- Social aspects.

BP173.25.G44 1998
Gellner, Ernest.
Muslim society/ Ernest Gellner. Cambridge; Cambridge University Press, 1981. ix, 267 p.
80-041103　909/.097671 19　0521221609
Sociology, Islamic. Islam -- Africa, North. Africa, North -- Social conditions.

BP173.25.M39 1999
Max Weber & Islam/ edited by Toby E. Huff and Wolfgang Schluchter editors. New Brunswick, NJ: Transaction, c1999. viii, 332 p.
99-024272　306.6/97/092　1560004002
Weber, Max, -- 1864-1920.Sociology, Islamic.

BP173.4 Islam — Islamic sociology — Women

BP173.4.I73 1998
Islam, gender, & social change/ edited by Yvonne Yazbeck Haddad, & John L. Esposito. New York: Oxford University Press, 1998. xxviii, 259 p.
97-002845　297/.082　019511356X
Women in Islam. Muslim women -- Social conditions. Sex role -- Religious aspects -- Islam.

BP173.6 Islam —
Islam and the state

BP173.6.B47 2000
Between the state and Islam/ edited by Charles E. Butterworth, I. William Zartman. New York: Cambridge University Press, 2000. ix, 256 p.
00-034257   322/.1/0917671   0521783526
Islam and state -- Islamic countries. Islam and politics -- Islamic countries. Islamic countries -- Politics and government.

BP173.7 Islam —
Islam and politics

BP173.7.M38 1999
Mawsilili, Ahmad.
Moderate and radical Islamic fundamentalism: the quest for modernity, legitimacy, and the Islamic state/ Ahmad S. Moussalli. Gainesville: University Press of Florida, c1999. 249 p.
98-036151   297.2/72   0813016584
Islam and politics. Islamic fundamentalism. Islam and state.

BP182 Islam —
The practice of Islam —
Jihad (Holy War)

BP182.F5 1999
Firestone, Reuven,
Jih‾ad: the origin of holy war in Islam/ Reuven Firestone. New York: Oxford University Press, 1999. xi, 195 p.
98-036384   297.7/2/09 21   0195154940
Jihad -- History. War -- Religious aspects -- Islam.

BP182.P48 1996
Peters, Rudolph.
Jihad in classical and modern Islam: a reader/ by Rudolph Peters. Princeton: Markus Wiener, c1996. ix, 204 p.
95-020943   297/.72   155876108X
Jihad. Islam -- Doctrines.

BP185 Islam —
The practice of Islam —
Religious functionaries. Polity.
Government. Ulama

BP185.Z36 2002
Zaman, Muhammad Qasim.
The ulama in contemporary Islam: custodians of change/ Muhammad Zaman Qasim. Princeton, NJ: Princeton University Press, c2002. xv, 293 p.
2002-020127   297.6/1 21   0691096805
Ulama. Scholars, Muslim.

BP187.3 Islam —
The practice of Islam —
Shrines, sacred places, etc.

BP187.3.P475 1994
Peters, F. E.
The Hajj: the Muslim pilgrimage to Mecca and the holy places/ F.E. Peters. Princeton, N.J.: Princeton University Press, 1994. xxiv, 399 p.
93-047292   297/.55   0691021201
Muslim pilgrims and pilgrimages -- Saudi Arabia -- Mecca -- History.

BP188.8-189.7 Islam —
The practice of Islam —
Islamic religious life
(Descriptive works)

BP188.8.E3.H64 1995
Hoffman, Valerie J. 1954-
Sufism, mystics, and saints in modern Egypt/ Valerie J. Hoffman. Columbia, S.C.: University of South Carolina Press, c1995. xix, 461 p.
95-004373   297/.4/0962   1570030553
Sufism -- Egypt.

BP188.8.M6.C67 1998
Cornell, Vincent J.
Realm of the saint: power and authority in Moroccan Sufism/ by Vincent J. Cornell. Austin: University of Texas Press, 1998. xliv, 398 p.
97-032878   297.4/0964   029271209X
Sufism -- Morocco.Morocco -- Religious life and customs.

BP188.9.R53 1998
Ridgeon, Lloyd V. J.
Aziz Nasafi/ Lloyd V.J. Ridgeon. Richmond: Curzon, 1998. xiv, 234 p.
98-189785   297.4/092   0700710132
Nasafi, Aziz al-Din ibn Muhammad, -- 13th cent.Sufism. Religious life -- Islam.

BP189.26.I2623.C47 1998
Chittick, William C.
The self-disclosure of God: principles of Ibn al-Arabi's cosmology/ William C. Chittick. Albany: State University of New York Press, c1998. xl, 483 p.
97-030521   297/.4   0791434036
Ibn al-Arabi, -- 1165-1240. -- Futuhat al-Makkiyah.God (Islam) -- Early works to 1800. Islamic cosmology -- Early works to 1800. Sufism -- Early works to 1800.

BP189.7.S5.J64 1996
Johansen, Julian.
Sufism and Islamic reform in Egypt: the battle for Islamic tradition/ Julian Johansen. Oxford: Clarendon Press; 1996. 323 p.
95-024660   297/.4   0198267576
Shadhiliyah -- Egypt.

BP190.5 Islam —
Topics not otherwise
provided, A-Z

BP190.5.S35.H69 2000
Howe, Marvine.
Turkey today: a nation divided over Islam's revival/ Marvine Howe. Boulder, CO: Westview Press, 2000. xv, 310 p.
00-024978   322/.1/09561   081333764X
Islam and secularism -- Turkey. Islam and state -- Turkey.

BP190.5.S35 I85 2000
Islam and secularism in the Middle East/ Azzam Tamimi, John L. Esposito, editors. New York: New York University Press, c2000. ix, 214 p.
00-036065   322/.1/0956 21   0814782612
Islam and secularism -- Middle East. Islam and politics -- Middle East. Middle East -- Politics and government -- 1979-

BP190.5.T78 G66 2002
Goodman, Lenn Evan,
Islamic humanism/ Lenn E. Goodman. New York: Oxford University Press, 2002.
2002-071525   297.2/6 21   0195135806
Islam and humanism. Islam and social problems. Human rights -- Religious aspects -- Islam. Philosophy, Islamic.

BP192.7-193.5 Islam —
Branches, sects, and
modifications — Shiites

BP192.7.I4.P56 1992
Pinault, David.
The Shiites: ritual and popular piety in a Muslim community/ David Pinault. New York: St. Martin's Press, 1992. xiii, 210 p.
92-005210   297/.82/095484   0312079532
Shiah -- India -- Hyderabad. Shiah. Hyderabad (India) -- Religious life

BP192.7.I7.W55 1992
Wiley, Joyce N.
The Islamic movement of Iraqi Shi'as/ Joyce N. Wiley. Boulder, Colo.: Lynne Rienner Publishers, 1992. ix, 193 p.
91-029921   297/.82/09567   1555872727
Shiah -- Iraq -- History -- 20th century. Islam and politics -- Iraq. Iraq -- Politics and government.

BP193.5.R5313 1995
Richard, Yann.
Shiite Islam: polity, ideology, and creed/ Yann Richard. Cambridge, Mass.: Blackwell, 1995.
94-015820   297/.2042   1557864691
Shiah.

BP194.18 Islam — Branches, sects, and modifications — Shiites

BP194.18.C383 2002
Bill, James A.
Roman Catholics & Shi i Muslims: prayer, passion & politics/ James A. Bill & John Alden Williams. Chapel Hill: University of North Carolina Press, c2002. x, 194 p.
2001-053233   261.2/7 21   0807826898
Sh¯i ah -- Relations -- Catholic Church. Catholic Church -- Relations -- Sh¯i ah. Islam -- Relations -- Catholic Church.

BP195 Islam — Branches, sects, and modifications — Other (to 1900), A-Z

BP195.I8.M43 1996
Mediaeval Ismaili history and thought/ edited by Farhad Daftary. New York, N.Y.: Cambridge University Press, 1996. xviii, 331 p.
95-021159   297/.822/0902   052145140X
Ismailites -- History.

BP223 Islam — Branches, sects, and modifications — Other, 1900-

BP223.Z8.E434 1999
Evanzz, Karl.
The messenger: the rise and fall of Elijah Muhammad/ Karl Evanzz. New York: Pantheon Books, c1999. xv, 667 p.
99-011826   297.8/7/092   067944260X
Elijah Muhammad, -- 1897-Black Muslims -- Biography. Afro-Americans -- Biography.

BP223.Z8.L5733339 1998
DeCaro, Louis A., 1957-
Malcolm and the cross: the Nation of Islam, Malcolm X, and christianity / Louis A. DeCaro, Jr. New York and London: New York University Press, c1998. xv, 270 p.
98-019687   297.8/7   0814718604
X, Malcolm, -- 1925-1965 -- Religion.Black Muslims. Afro-Americans -- Religion. Islam -- Relations -- Christianity.

BP223.Z8.L5772 1994
Sales, William W.
From civil rights to Black liberation: Malcolm X and the Organization of Afro-American Unity/ William W. Sales, Jr. Boston, Mass.: South End Press, c1994. viii, 247 p.
94-008691   320.5/4/092   0896084817
X, Malcolm, -- 1925-1965.

BP223.Z8 L5776 1994
Strickland, William,
Malcolm X, make it plain/ text by William Strickland; oral histories selected and edited by Cheryll Y. Greene; with the Malcolm X Documentary   Production   Team;   picture research by Michele McKenzie. New York: Viking, 1994. viii, 245 p.
93-006297   320.5/4/092 B 20   067084893X
X, Malcolm, 1925-1965 -- Pictorial works. X, Malcolm, 1925-1965. Black Muslims -- Biography. Afro-Americans -- Biography.

BP327 Bahai Faith — Dictionaries. Encyclopedias

BP327.A33 1998
Adamson, Hugh C.
Historical dictionary of the Baha'i Faith/ Hugh C. Adamson and Philip Hainsworth. Lanham, Md.: Scarecrow Press, 1998. ix, 504 p.
97-002610   297.9/3/03   0810833530
Bahai Faith -- History -- Dictionaries.

BP573 Theosophy — Special topics, A-Z

BP573.F46 D59 2001
Dixon, Joy,
Divine feminine: theosophy and feminism in England/ Joy Dixon. Baltimore, Md.: Johns Hopkins University Press, c2001. xix, 293 p.
00-009881   299/.934/0820941   21
0801864992
Feminism -- Religious aspects -- Theosophical Society (Great Britain) Feminism -- England -- History.

BP585 Theosophy — Biography — Individual, A-Z

BP585.B6.C73 1993
Cranston, S. L.
HPB: the extraordinary life and influence of Helena Blavatsky, founder of the modern Theosophical movement/ Sylvia Cranston. New York: G.P. Putnam's Sons, c1993. xxiii, 648 p.
92-005910   299/.934/092   0874776880
Blavatsky, H. P. -- (Helena Petrovna), -- 1831-1891.Theosophists   --   Biography. Theosophy -- History.

BP601 Other beliefs and movements — Dictionaries

BP601.C47 2001
Chryssides, George D.,
Historical   dictionary   of   new   religious movements/ George D.   Chryssides. Lanham, Md.: Scarecrow Press, 2001. xxxi, 515 p.
2001-034196   291/.046 21   0810840952
Cults -- Dictionaries. Cults -- History -- Dictionaries.

BP603 Other beliefs and movements — General works

BP603.B37 2001
Barrett, David V.
The new believers: a survey of sects, cults, and alternative religions/ David V. Barrett. London; New York, N.Y.: Cassell; Sterling Pub., 2001. 544 p.
2001-347660
Cults. Sects. Religions.

BP605 Other beliefs and movements — Works. By movement, A-Z

BP605.B72.T33 1995
Tabor, James D., 1946-
Why Waco?: cults and the battle for religious freedom in America/ James D. Tabor and Eugene V. Gallagher. Berkeley: University of California Press, c1995. xiv, 252 p.
95-003553   299/.93   0520201868
Koresh, David, -- 1959-1993.Waco Branch Davidian Disaster, Tex., 1993. Cults -- United States.

BP605.C38 C48 2000
Chancellor, James D.
Life in the family: an oral history of the Children of God/ James D. Chancellor; with a foreword by William Sims Bainbridge. New York: Syracuse University Press, 2000. xxiii, 291 p.
00-022544   289.9   0815606451
Children of God (Movement)

BP605.G94.G4613 1996
Gurdjieff: essays and reflections on the man and his teaching/ edited by Jacob Needleman and George Baker; associate editor, Mary Stein. New York: Continuum, 1996. xiv, 450 p.
96-003612   197   0826408001
Gurdjieff, Georges Ivanovitch, -- 1872-1949.

BP605.N48.H36 1998
Hanegraaff, Wouter J.
New Age religion and Western culture: esotericism in the mirror of secular thought/ by Wouter J. Hanegraaff. Albany, NY: State University of New York Press, c1998. xiii, 580 p.
97-037707   299/.93   0791438546
New Age movement. Occultism.

BP605.N48.Y67 1995
York, Michael, 1939-
The emerging network: a sociology of the New Age and neo-pagan movements/ Michael York. Lanham, Md.: Rowman & Littlefield, c1995. xvii, 372 p.
94-043545   306.6/9993   0847680002
New Age movement. New Age movement -- Great Britain. New Age movement -- United States. Great Britain -- Religion -- 20th century. United States -- Religion -- 1960-

BP605.O88.M48 2000
Metraux, Daniel Alfred.
Aum Shinrikyo's impact on Japanese society/ Daniel A. Metraux. Lewiston, N.Y.: Edwin Mellen Press, c2000. viii, 165 p.
00-035520   299/.93   0773477667
Oumu Shinrikyō (Religious organization) -- Social aspects -- Japan.

BP605.S2.W34 1977
Wallis, Roy.
The road to total freedom: a sociological analysis of scientology/ Roy Wallis. New York: Columbia University Press, 1977, c1976. xiv, 282 p.
76-027273   131/.35   0231042000
Scientology.

BQ Buddhism

BQ128 Encyclopedias (General)

BQ128.E62 2003
Encyclopedia of Buddhism/ edited by Robert E. Buswell, Jr. New York: Macmillan, USA, 2003.
2003-009965   294.3/03 21   0028657209
Buddhism -- Encyclopedias.

BQ130 Buddhism — Dictionaries (General)

BQ130.N9 1983
Nyanatiloka,
Buddhist dictionary: Manual of Buddhist terms and doctrines/ by Nyanatiloka. New York: AMS Press, [1983] v, 189 p.
77-087508   294.3/42/0321 19   0404168469
Buddhism -- Dictionaries -- Pali. Pali language -- Dictionaries -- English.

BQ130.P74 1993
Prebish, Charles S.
Historical dictionary of Buddhism/ by Charles S. Prebish. Metuchen, N.J.: Scarecrow Press, 1993. xxxiii, 387 p.
93-004247   294.3/03   0810826984
Buddhism -- Dictionaries -- Polyglot. Dictionaries, Polyglot. Buddhism -- Bibliography.

BQ266 History — General works — 1946-

BQ266.M48 2002
Mitchell, Donald W.
Buddhism: introducing the Buddhist experience/ Donald W. Mitchell. New York: Oxford University Press, 2002. xvi, 368 p.
2001-053126   294.3 21   0195139526
Buddhism -- History.

BQ266.R43 1994
Reat, N. Ross, 1951-
Buddhism: a history/ by Noble Ross Reat. Berkeley, Calif.: Asian Humanities Press, c1994. xi, 376 p.
93-001792   294.3/09   0875730019
Buddhism -- History.

BQ270 History — General special

BQ270.B83 1999
Buddhism and politics in twentieth-century Asia/ edited by Ian Harris. London; Pinter, 1999.
98-043860   294.3/377/0950904   1855675986
Buddhism and politics -- Asia -- History -- 20th century.Asia -- Politics and government -- 20th century.

BQ336-704 History — By region or country — Asia

BQ336.C66x 1983
Conze, Edward, 1904-
Buddhist thought in India: three phases of Buddhist philosophy/ by Edward Conze. London; Allen & Unwin, 1983. 302 p.
84-673618   0042941288
Buddhism -- India. Philosophy, Buddhist. Mahayana Buddhism.

BQ400.H542 F65 2002
Föllmi, Olivier,
Buddhist Himalayas/ photographs by Olivier & Danielle Föllmi & Matthieu Ricard; with a contribution by the Dalai Lama. New York: Harry N. Abrams, Inc., 2002.
2002-008849   294.3/095496 21   0810934892
Buddhism -- Himalaya Mountains Region -- Pictorial works. Buddhism -- China -- Tibet -- Pictorial works.

BQ626.B83 2001
The Buddhist world-view/ editors, Raghwendhra Pratap Singh, George F. McLean. Faridabad: Om Publications, 2001. 152 p.
99-953936   8186867317
Buddhism--China--History. Buddhism--Relations--Hinduism. Buddhism--Influence.

BQ632.B83 1992
Buddhist studies in the People's Republic of China, 1990-1991/ translated and edited by Michael R. Saso. Honolulu: Tendai Education Foundation: viii, 143 p.
2002-319191   0824814649
Zhuangzi.Buddhism--China. Zen Buddhism--China. Buddhism--China--Doctrines--History.

BQ632.W75 1990
Wright, Arthur F.,
Studies in Chinese Buddhism/ Arthur F. Wright; edited by Robert M. Somers. New Haven: Yale University Press, c1990. xii, 204 p.
89-022604   294.3/0951 20   0300047177
Buddhism--China--History.

BQ636.T75713 1985
Tsukamoto, Zenryu, 1898-
A history of early Chinese Buddhism: from its introduction to the death of Hui-yuan/ by Zenryu Tsukamoto; translated from the Japanese by Leon Hurvitz. Tokyo; Kodansha International: 1985. 2 v.
83-048873   294.3/0931   0870116355
Buddhism -- China -- History -- To 581 A.D.

BQ638.G4713 1995
Gernet, Jacques.
Buddhism in Chinese society: an economic history from the fifth to the tenth centuries/ Jacques Gernet; translated by Franciscus Verellen. New York: Columbia University Press, c1995. xvii, 441 p.
94-042484   294.3/0951/09021 20   0231073801
Buddhism--China--History--581-960. Buddhism--Economic aspects--China.

BQ640.D86 1996
Dunnell, Ruth W.,
The great state of white and high: Buddhism and state formation in eleventh-century Xia/ Ruth W. Dunnell. Honolulu: University of Hawai'i Press, c1996. xxv, 278 p.
95-031978   322/.1/09517509021 20   0824817192
Buddhism -- China -- History -- 960-1644. Buddhism and state -- China. China -- History -- Xi xia dynasty, 1038-1227. Tangut (Chinese people) -- History.

BQ647.W44
Welch, Holmes.
Buddhism under Mao. Cambridge, Mass., Harvard University Press, 1972. xviii, 666 p.
72-078428   294.3/0951   0674085655
Buddhism -- China.

BQ661.A87 1991
Assimilation of Buddhism in Korea: religious maturity and innovation in the Silla Dynasty/ edited by Lewis R. Lancaster and C.S. Yu. Berkeley, Calif.: Asian Humanities Press, c1991. viii, 250 p.
91-014079   294.3/09519/09021   0895818787
Buddhism -- Korea -- History -- To 935.

BQ687.R48 1998
Re-visioning "Kamakura" Buddhism/ edited by Richard K. Payne. Honolulu: University of Hawaii Press, c1998. viii, 280 p.
98-009375   294.3/0952/0902   082482024X
Buddhism -- Japan -- History -- 1185-1600.

BQ693.K48 1990
Ketelaar, James Edward,
Of heretics and martyrs in Meiji Japan: Buddhism and its persecution / James Edward Ketelaar. Princeton, N.J.: Princeton University Press, c1990. xiv, 285 p.
90-030100   294.3/0952/09034   20   0691055998
Buddhism--Japan--History--1868-1945. Buddhists--Persecutions--Japan. Buddhism--Social aspects--Japan.

BQ704.B38 1994
Batchelor, Stephen.
The awakening of the west: the encounter of Buddhism and Western culture/ Stephen Batchelor. Berkeley, Calif.: Parallax Press, c1994. xvi, 416 p.
94-008016   294.3/09182/1   0938077686
Buddhism -- Europe -- History. Buddhism -- Study and teaching -- Europe -- History.

BQ724-736 History — By region or country — America

BQ724.E64 2000
Engaged Buddhism in the west/ Christopher S. Queen, editor. Boston, Mass.: Wisdom Publications, 2000. xi, 544 p.
99-036870   294.3/37   0861711599
Buddhism -- Social aspects -- North America -- History. Buddhism -- Social aspects -- United States -- History. Buddhism -- Social aspects -- Europe -- History.

BQ732.P736 1999
Prebish, Charles S.
Luminous passage: the practice and study of Buddhism in America/ Charles S. Prebish. Berkeley: University of California Press, c1999. xi, 334 p.
98-020767   294.3/0973   0520216962
Buddhism -- United States. Buddhism -- Canada.

BQ734.S44 2000
Sherrill, Martha.
The Buddha from Brooklyn/ Martha Sherrill. New York: Random House, 2000. xix, 392 p.
99-045346   294.3/923/0973   0679452753
Ahkon Norbu Lhamo -- Jetsunma.Buddhist women -- United States. Buddhism -- Social aspects -- United States.

BQ736.F33 1998
The faces of Buddhism in America/ edited by Charles S. Prebish and Kenneth K. Tanaka. Berkeley: University of California Press, c1998. viii, 370 p.
97-038769   294.3/0973   0520204603
Buddhism -- United States.

BQ882 Biography — Individual — Gautama Buddha

BQ882.A76 2001
Armstrong, Karen,
Buddha/ Karen Armstrong. New York: Viking, 2001. xxix, 205 p.
00-043808   294.3/63 B 21   0670891932
Gautama Buddha.

BQ882.T45 2000
Thomas, E. J. 1869-
The life of Buddha as legend and history/ by Edward J. Thomas. Mineola, N.Y.: Dover Publications, 2000.
99-088879   294.3/63   048641132X
Gautama Buddha. Gautama Buddha -- Legends. Christianity and other religions -- Buddhism.

BQ944-988 Biography — Individual — Other individuals

BQ944.M47 A3 2000
Cameron, Sharon.
Beautiful work: a meditation on pain/ Sharon Cameron. Durham, NC: Duke Univeristy Press, 2000. vi, 121 p.
99-059146   818/.5403   082232508X
Cameron, Sharon.Spiritual biography -- United States. Pain -- Religious aspects -- Buddhism. Literary historians -- United States -- Biography.

BQ962.U33.W75 1998
Wright, Dale S.
Philosophical meditations on Zen Buddhism/ Dale S. Wright. New York: Cambridge University Press, 1998. xv, 227 p.
97-038793   294.3/927   0521590108
Huang-po, -- d. 850.Zen Buddhism -- Doctrines.

BQ966.I32965.A3 1998
Jigs-med-glin-pa Ran-byun-rdo-rje, 1729 or 30-17
Apparitions of the self: the secret autobiographies of a Tibetan visionary: a translation and study of Jigme Lingpa's Dancing moon in the water and Dakki's grand secret-talk/ Janet Gyatso. Princeton, N.J.: Princeton University Press, c1998. xxiv, 360 p.
97-010191   294.3/923/092   0691011109
Jigs-med-glin-pa Ran-byun-rdo-rje, -- 1729 or 30-1798.Lamas -- China -- Tibet -- Biography.

BQ988.U9.C47 1999
Chadwick, David, 1945-
Crooked cucumber: the life and Zen teaching of Shunryu Suzuki/ David Chadwick. New York: Broadway Books, c1999. xvi, 432 p.
98-046707   294.3/927/092   0767901045
Suzuki, Shunryu, -- 1904-Priests, Zen -- Japan -- Biography. Priests, Zen -- United States -- Biography.

BQ1012 Buddhist literature — Collections. Collected works — English

BQ1012.B83 1995
Buddhism in practice/ Donald S. Lopez, Jr., editor. Princeton, N.J.: Princeton University Press, c1995. xvi, 608 p.
94-048201   294.3 20   0691044414
Buddhist literature -- Translations into English.

BQ2025-3080 Tripi.taka (Canonical literature) — By version — Divisions not limited to a particular linguistic version

BQ2025.H853 T36 1990
Tanaka, Kenneth Kenichi.
The dawn of Chinese pure land Buddhist doctrine: Ching-ying Hui-yuan's Commentary on the Visualization sutra/ Kenneth K. Tanaka. Albany: State University of New York Press, c1990. xxiv, 304 p.
89-021685   294.3/85 20   0791402983
Hui-yüan, 523-592. Kuan wu liang shou ching i shu. Pure Land Buddhism -- China -- Doctrines -- History.

BQ2052.E5 W38 1993
The Lotus Sutra/ translated by Burton Watson. New York: Columbia University Press, 1993. xxix, 359 p.
92-038410   294.3/82 20   023108160X

BQ2057.L66 1989
The Lotus Sutra in Japanese culture/ edited by
George J. Tanabe, Jr. and Willa Jane Tanabe.
Honolulu: University of Hawaii Press, c1989. x,
239 p.
88-036735   294.3/85 19   0824811984
*Japan -- Civilization -- Buddhist influences --
Congresses.*

BQ3080.A2522
Asanga.
Abhidharmasamuccaya = the compendium of the
higher teaching (philosophy)/ by Asanga;
originally translated into French and annotated
by Walpola Rahula; English version from the
French by Sara Boin-Webb. Fremont, CA: Asian
Humanities Press, c2000. xxvii, 327 p.
00-060590   294.3/85   0895819414

BQ4012 General works — 1946- — English

BQ4012.L65 2001
Lopez, Donald S., 1952-
The story of Buddhism: a concise guide to its
history and teachings/ Donald S. Lopez, Jr. [San
Francisco]: HarperSanFrancisco, c2001. xii,
275 p.
00-054263   294.3/09   0060699760
Buddhism.

BQ4012.W67 1991
The World of Buddhism: Buddhist monks and
nuns in society and culture / texts by Richard
Gombrich ... [et al.]; edited by Heinz Bechert
and Richard Gombrich. 1st pbk. ed. London:
Thames and Hudson, 1991. 308 p.
91-065147   0500276285
Buddhism.

BQ4015 General works — 1946- — German

BQ4015.D8413 1994
Dumoulin, Heinrich.
Understanding Buddhism: key themes/ Heinrich
Dumoulin; translated and adapted from the
German by Joseph O'Leary. 1st ed. New York:
Weatherill, 1994. vi, 173 p.
93-029191   294.3 20   083480297X
Buddhism.

BQ4090 Doctrinal and systematic Buddhism — History — General works

BQ4090.K36 1992
Kalupahana, David J., 1933-
A history of Buddhist philosophy: continuities
and discontinuities/ David J. Kalupahana.
Honolulu: University of Hawaii Press, c1992.
xvi, 304 p.
91-037326   181/.043   0824814029
*Buddhism -- Doctrines -- History. Philosophy,
Buddhist -- History.*

BQ4440 Doctrinal and systematic Buddhism — Special doctrines — Theory of knowledge. Buddhist epistemology

BQ4440.B53 2000
Bhatt, S. R. 1939-
Buddhist epistemology/ S.R. Bhatt and Anu
Mehrotra; foreword by the Dalai Lama.
Westport, Conn.: Greenwood Press, 2000. x,
140 p.
99-044513   121/.088/2943   0313310874
*Dignaga,   5th   cent.
Nyayamukha.Knowledge, Theory of (Buddhism)
Buddhist logic.*

BQ4485-4490 Doctrinal and systematic Buddhism — Special doctrines — Eschatology

BQ4485.N39 2001
Nawang Gehlek,
Good life, good death: Tibetan wisdom on
reincarnation/ Rimpoche Nawang Gehlek; with
Gini Alhadeff and Mark Magill; foreword by His
Holiness the Dalai Lama. New York: Riverhead
Books, 2001. xxii, 184 p.
2001-041625   294.3/4237 21   1573221961
*Reincarnation -- Buddhism. Death --
Religious aspects -- Buddhism. Future life --
Buddhism. Buddhism -- China -- Tibet --
Doctrines.*

BQ4485.O24 2002
Obeyesekere, Gananath.
Imagining karma: ethical transformation in
Amerindian, Buddhist, and Greek rebirth/
Gananath Obeyesekere. Berkeley: University of
California Press, 2002. xxix, 448 p.
2001-008252   291.2/37 21   0520232437
*Reincarnation -- Buddhism. Reincarnation --
Comparative studies. Religious ethics --
Comparative studies.*

BQ4485.T45 1994
Teiser, Stephen F.
The scripture on the ten kings and the making of
purgatory in medieval Chinese Buddhism/
Stephen F. Teiser. Honolulu, HI: University of
Hawaii Press, c1994. xxiii, 340 p.
94-002531   294.3/423 20   0824815874
*Eschatology, Buddhist. Hell--Buddhism.
Buddhism--China--Doctrines.*

BQ4490.K3713 1993
Karma-gliçn-pa,
The Tibetan book of the dead: the great book of
natural liberation through understanding in the
between/ composed by Padma Sambhava;
discovered by Karma Lingpa; translated by
Robert A.F. Thurman. New York, N.Y.: Bantam
Books, 1993. xxii, 278 p.
93-002891   294.3/423 20   0553370901
*Karma-gliçn-pa, 14th cent. Bar do thos grol.
Intermediate state -- Buddhism -- Early works to
1800. Death -- Religious aspects -- Buddhism --
Early works to 1800. Funeral rites and
ceremonies, Buddhist -- Early works to 1800.*

BQ4490.K373 C83 2002
Cuevas, Bryan J.,
The hidden history of the Tibetan book of the
dead/ Bryan J. Cuevas. New York: Oxford
University Press, c2003.
2002-027400   294.3/423 21   0195154134
*Karma-gliçn-pa, 14th cent. Bar do thos grol-
-Criticism,   Textual.Intermediate   state--
Buddhism. Death--Religious aspects--Buddhism.
Funeral rites and ceremonies, Buddhist--China--
Tibet.*

BQ4570 Doctrinal and systematic Buddhism — Special topics (nondoctrinal) and relations to special subjects, A-Z

BQ4570.A7 C86 2001
Cultural intersections in later Chinese
Buddhism/ edited by Marsha Weidner.
Honolulu: University of Hawai'i Press, c2001.
ix, 234 p.
2001-017125   294.3/437/0951   21
0824823087
Buddhism and art--China.

BQ4570.E23.D35 1998
De Silva, Padmasiri, 1933-
Environmental philosophy and ethics in
Buddhism/ Padmasiri de Silva; foreword by
Alastair S. Gunn. New York: St. Martin's Press,
1998. xviii, 194 p.
97-045495   294.3/378362   0312213166
*Human ecology -- Religious aspects --
Buddhism. Buddhism -- Social aspects. Buddhist
ethics.*

BQ4570.H85.H9 1989
Hyers, M. Conrad.
The laughing Buddha: Zen and the comic spirit/
Conrad Hyers. Wolfeboro, N.H.: Longwood
Academic, c1989. 195 p.
89-002592   294.3/927   089341560X
*Zen Buddhism -- Doctrines. Wit and humor --
Religious aspects -- Zen Buddhism.*

BQ4570.I55.H47 1999
Hershock, Peter D.
Reinventing the wheel: a Buddhist response to the information age/ Peter D. Hershock. Albany, N.Y.: State University of New York Press, c1999. xvii, 309 p.
98-046706 294.3/375 0791442314
Information technology -- Religious aspects -- Buddhism. Buddhism -- Social aspects. Buddhism -- Doctrines.

BQ4570.P76.R83 1996
Rubin, Jeffrey B.
Psychotherapy and Buddhism: toward an integration/ Jeffrey B. Rubin. New York: Plenum Press, c1996. xiv, 207 p.
96-034822 294.3/375 0306454416
Psychotherapy -- Religious aspects -- Buddhism. Buddhism -- Psychology.

BQ4570.S48 B83 1992
Buddhism, sexuality, and gender/ edited by José Ignacio Cabezón. Albany, NY: State University of New York Press, c1992. xix, 241 p.
90-046557 294.3/378344 20 0791407586
Sex -- Religious aspects -- Buddhism. Woman (Buddhism) Buddhism -- Doctrines.

BQ4570.S48.F3813 1998
Faure, Bernard.
The red thread: Buddhist approaches to sexuality/ Bernard Faure. Princeton, N.J.: Princeton University Press, c1998. vi, 338 p.
98-016645 294.3/37857 0691059985
Sex -- Religious aspects -- Buddhism. Buddhism -- Social aspects.

BQ4570.S6.G76 1998
Gross, Rita M.
Soaring and settling: Buddhist perspectives on contemporary social and religious issues/ Rita M. Gross. New York: Continuum, 1998. xiii, 238 p.
98-030086 294.3/37 0826411134
Buddhism -- Social aspects. Feminism -- Religious aspects -- Buddhism. Woman (Buddhism)

BQ4570.W6.W66 2000
Women's Buddhism, Buddhism's women: tradition, revision, renewal/ edited by Ellison Banks Findly. Boston: Wisdom Publications, c2000. xii, 498 p.
99-088200 294.3/082 0861711653
Buddhist women. Women in Buddhism. Buddhist nuns.

BQ5075 Practice of Buddhism. Forms of worship — Altar, liturgical objects, ornaments, memorials, etc. — Special objects, A-Z

BQ5075.P73 W44 2000
The wheel of great compassion: the practice of the prayer wheel in Tibetan Buddhism/ edited and introduced by Lorne Ladner; with translations by Lama Thubten Zopa Rinpoche ... [et al.]; foreword by Lama Thubten Zopa Rinpoche. Boston, MA: Wisdom Publications, c2000. xxii, 134 p.
00-043822 294.3/437 0861711742
Prayer wheels. Spiritual life -- Buddhism.

BQ5115 Practice of Buddhism. Forms of worship — Symbols and symbolism — By region or country, A-Z

BQ5115.C5 L4813 1996
Levenson, Claude B.
Symbols of Tibetan Buddhism/ text by Claude B. Levenson; photographs by Laziz Hamani; foreword by Dalai Lama; [translated by Nissim Marshall]. Paris: Editions Assouline, 1996. 127 p.
98-129633 294.3/437/09515 21 2908228866
Buddhist art and symbolism -- China -- Tibet. Spiritual life -- Buddhism. Buddhism -- China -- Tibet -- Rituals. Tibet (China) -- Religious life and customs.

BQ5125 Practice of Buddhism. Forms of worship — Symbols and symbolism — Special symbols, A-Z

BQ5125.M3.B7313 1997
Brauen, Martin.
The Mandala: sacred circle in Tibetan Buddhism/ Martin Brauen; translated by Martin Willson; with photographs by Peter Nebel and Doro Rothlisberger. Boston: Shambhala; 1997. 151 p.
96-035056 294.3/437 1570622965
Mandala (Buddhism)

BQ5125.M3.T46 1999
Ten Grotenhuis, Elizabeth.
Japanese mandalas: representations of sacred geography/ Elizabeth ten Grotenhuis. Honolulu: University of Hawai'i Press, 1999. x, 227 p.
98-024304 294.3/437 0824820002
Mandala (Buddhism) Buddhist art and symbolism -- Japan.

BQ5125.S8 S66 1985
Snodgrass, Adrian.
The symbolism of the stupa/ Adrian Snodgrass. Ithaca, N.Y.: Southeast Asia Program, Cornell University, 1985. v, 407 p.
85-192873 726/.143 19 0877277001
St̄upas. Buddhist art and symbolism.

BQ5630 Practice of Buddhism. Forms of worship — Religious life — Devotion. Meditation

BQ5630.V5.V64 1999
Voices of insight/ edited by Sharon Salzberg. Boston: Shambhala, c1999. xiii, 281 p.
99-023692 294.3/444 1570623988
Vipasyana (Buddhism) Compassion (Buddhism) Theravada Buddhism.

BQ6160 Monasticism and monastic life. Sa.mgha (Order) — By region or country, A-Z

BQ6160.C6 K54 1997
Kieschnick, John,
The eminent monk: Buddhist ideals in medieval Chinese hagiography/ John Kieschnick. Honolulu: University of Hawai'i Press, c1997. vii, 218 p.
97-005496 294.3/657/0922 21 0824818415
Monastic and religious life (Buddhism) -- China -- History. Buddhist monks -- China. Priests, Buddhist -- China. Religious biography -- China -- History and criticism..

BQ6331 Monasteries. Temples. Shrines. St-upas. Sites, etc. — By region or country — Asia

BQ6331.T332 T43
Thakur, Laxman S.
Buddhism in the western Himalaya: a study of the Tabo monastery. New Delhi; Oxford: Oxford University Press, c2001. xxi, 333 p.
2001-273495
Tabo Monastery (Tabo, India). Buddhist art and symbolism -- India -- Tabo. Buddhist antiquities -- India -- Tabo.

BQ7676-7590 Modifications, schools, etc. — Tibetan Buddhism (Lamaism) — History

BQ7576.K37 2000
Kapstein, Matthew.
The Tibetan assimilation of Buddhism: conversion, contestation, and memory/ Matthew T. Kapstein. Oxford; Oxford University Press, 2000. xx, 316 p.
99-033551 294.3/923/09 21 0195131223
Buddhism -- China -- Tiber -- History.

BQ7590.B84 1998
Buddhism in contemporary Tibet: religious revival and cultural identity/ edited by Melvyn C. Goldstein and Matthew T. Kapstein; with a foreword by Orville Schell. Berkeley: University of California Press, c1998. x, 207 p.
97-026851   294.3/923/0951509048
0520211308
Buddhism -- China -- Tibet -- History -- 20th century.Tibet (China) -- Religion -- 20th century.

BQ7604 Modifications, schools, etc. — Tibetan Buddhism (Lamaism) — General works

BQ7604.L66 1998
Lopez, Donald S., 1952-
Prisoners of Shangri-La: Tibetan Buddhism and the West/ Donald S. Lopez, Jr. Chicago: University of Chicago Press, 1998. x, 283 p.
97-041202   294.3/923   0226493105
Buddhism -- China -- Tibet.

BQ7604.P69 1995
Powers, John, 1957-
Introduction to Tibetan Buddhism/ John Powers. Ithaca, N.Y., USA: Snow Lion Publications, 1995. 501 p.
93-039500   294.3/923   155939028X
Buddhism -- China -- Tibet.Tibet (China) -- Religion.

BQ7604.T47 1987
Thondup, Tulku
Buddhist civilization in Tibet/ Tulku Thondup Rinpoche. New York: Routledge & Kegan Paul, 1987. 117 p.
87-004493   294.3/923/09515   0710210876
Buddhism -- China -- Tibet.

BQ7610 Modifications, schools, etc. — Tibetan Buddhism (Lamaism) — General special

BQ7610.C36 2002
Campbell, June.
Traveller in space: gender, identity, and Tibetan Buddhism/ June Campbell. Rev. ed. London; Continuum, c2002. xix, 236 p.
2001-047209   294.3/923/082 21   0826457193
Campbell, June.Women in Buddhism--China--Tibet. Woman (Buddhism) Women--China--Tibet.

BQ7620 Modifications, schools, etc. — Tibetan Buddhism (Lamaism) — Lamaist literature

BQ7620.R45 1997
Religions of Tibet in practice/ Donald S. Lopez, Jr., editor. Princeton, N.J.: Princeton University Press, c1997. x, 560 p.
96-031592   294.3/923   0691011842
Buddhism -- China -- Tibet. Buddhist literature, Tibetan -- Translations into English. Tibet (China) -- Religion.

BQ7634 Modifications, schools, etc. — Tibetan Buddhism (Lamaism) — Doctrine

BQ7634.R39 2000
Ray, Reginald A.
Indestructible truth: the living spirituality of Tibetan Buddhism/ Reginald A. Ray. Boston: Shambhala Publications, 2000. x, 495 p.
00-030128   294.3/923   1570621667
Spiritual life -- Buddhism. Buddhism -- Doctrines.

BQ7662.4 Modifications, schools, etc. — Tibetan Buddhism (Lamaism) — Special branches of Tibetan Buddhism

BQ7662.4.B783 2000
Bstan-dzin-rgya-mtsho, 1935-
Dzogchen: the heart essence of the great perfection: Dzogchen teachings given in the West/ by His Holiness the Dalai Lama; translated by Geshe Thupten Jinpa and Richard Barron (Chokyi Nyima); edited by Patrick Gaffney. Ithaca, NY: Snow Lion Publications, c2000. 271 p.
00-010505   155939157X
Rdzogs-chen (Rnin-ma-pa)

BQ7935-7950 Modifications, schools, etc. — Tibetan Buddhism (Lamaism) — Biography

BQ7935.B774 A93 1995
Bstan-í dzin-ryga-mtsho,
Awakening the mind, lightening the heart/ by His Holiness, the Dalai Lama. 1st ed. [San Francisco]: HarperSanFrancisco, c1995. xv, 238 p.
95-011538   294.3/42 20   0060616881
Spiritual life -- Buddhism. Buddhism -- China -- Tibet -- Doctrines.

BQ7935.B774 M39 2000
Bstan-dzin-rgya-mtsho, 1935-
The meaning of life: Buddhist perspectives on cause & effect/ Tenzin Gyatso, the Fourteenth Dalai Lama; translated and edited by Jeffrey Hopkins. Boston, MA: Wisdom Publications, c2000. viii, 148 p.
00-043485   294.3/42   0861711734
Causation (Buddhism) Karma. Religious life -- Buddhism.

BQ7950.T754.B9338 1998
Wallace, B. Alan.
The bridge of quiescence: experiencing Tibetan Buddhist meditation/ B. Alan Wallace; foreword by H.H. the Dalai Lama. Chicago: Open Court, c1998. xvi, 336 p.
97-041697   294.3/4435   0812693604
Tson-kha-pa Blo-bzan-grags-pa, -- 1357-1419. -- Byan chub lam gyi rim pa chun ba.Lam-rim. Meditation -- Buddhism.

BQ8149 Modifications, schools, etc. — Special modifications, sects, etc. — Hoss-o (Faxiang)

BQ8149.H787
Bernstein, Richard, 1944-
Ultimate journey: retracing the path of an ancient buddhist monk who crossed Asia in search of enlightenment/ Richard Bernstein. New York: A.A. Knopf, 2001. 352 p.
2001-267521   294.3/92   0375400095
Xuanzang, -- ca. 596-664.Priests, Buddhist -- China -- Biography.Silk Road -- Description and travel.

BQ8349-8409 Modifications, schools, etc. — Special modifications, sects, etc. — Nichiren

BQ8349.N573 E5 1990
Nichiren, 1222-1282
Selected writings of Nichiren/ translated by Burton Watson and others;   edited with an introduction by Philip B. Yampolsky. New York: Columbia University Press, c1990. xi, 508
90-001367   294.3/928 20   0231072600
Nichiren (Sect)--Doctrines--Early works to 1800.

BQ8409.D53 1983
A Dictionary of Buddhist terms and concepts. 1st ed. Tokyo: Nichiren Shoshu International Center, 1983. xvii, 579 p.
83-217692   294.3/928/0321 19   4888720142
Nichiren Sh¯osh¯u -- Dictionaries. Nichiren Sh¯osh¯u -- Dictionaries -- Japanese. Buddhism -- Dictionaries. Buddhism -- Dictionaries -- Japanese. Japanese language -- Dictionaries -- English.

BQ8672-8718.6 Modifications, schools, etc. — Special modifications, sects, etc. — Pure Land Buddhism

BQ8672.H23 1999
Haar, B. J. ter
The White Lotus teachings in Chinese religious history/ B.J. ter Haar. Honolulu: University of Hawai'i Press, c1999. ix, 343 p.
99-012375   294.3/926 21   0824822188
White lotus (Sect)--History. Buddhism--Social aspects--China.

BQ8715.4.A53 1998
Andreasen, Esben.
Popular Buddhism in Japan: Shin Buddhist religion & culture/ Esben Andreasen. Honolulu: University of Hawaii Press, c1998. xiv, 199 p.
97-033209   294.3/926   0824820274
Shin (Sect)

BQ8718.6.T68 2000
Toward a contemporary understanding of Pure Land Buddhism: creating a Shin Buddhist theology in a religiously plural world/ edited by Dennis Hirota. Albany, N.Y.: State University of New York Press, c2000. ix, 257 p.
99-040513   294.3/926   0791445291
Shin (Sect) -- Doctrines. Pure Land Buddhism -- Doctrines.

BQ8915-8965.4 Modifications, schools, etc. — Special modifications, sects, etc. — Tantric Buddhism (Vajray-ana Buddhism)

BQ8915.S53 1994
Shaw, Miranda Eberle, 1954-
Passionate enlightenment: women in Tantric Buddhism/ Miranda Shaw. Princeton, N.J.: Princeton University Press, c1994. xiii, 291 p.
93-031407   294.3/925/082   0691033803
Women in Tantric Buddhism -- India.

BQ8965.4.R3513
Rambach, Pierre,
The secret message of tantric Buddhism/ Pierre Rambach; [translated   from the French by Barbara Bray]. New York: Rizzoli International Publications, 1979. 169 p.
78-058701   294.3/925/0952   0847801926
Shingon (Sect) Tantric Buddhism -- Japan.

BQ9262.3-9294.4 Modifications, schools, etc. — Special modifications, sects, etc. — Zen Buddhism

BQ9262.3.D85513 1988
Dumoulin, Heinrich.
Zen Buddhism: a history/ Heinrich Dumoulin; translated by James W. Heisig and Paul Knitter. New York: Macmillan; c1988-c1990. 2 v.
87-034834   294.3/927/09   002908220X
Zen Buddhism -- History.

BQ9262.9.C5.F37813 1997
Faure, Bernard.
The will to orthodoxy: a critical genealogy of Northern Chan Buddhism/ Bernard Faure. Stanford, Calif.: Stanford University Press, 1997. xii, 289 p.
97-009658   294.3/927/0951   0804728658
Shen-hsiu.Zen Buddhism -- China -- History.

BQ9262.9.C5 N39 1995
Nan, Huai-chin.
The story of Chinese Zen/ by Nan Huai-chin; translated by Thomas Cleary. 1st ed. Boston: C.E. Tuttle, c1995. ix, 258 p.
95-023255   294.3/927/0951 20   0804830509
Zen Buddhism--China. Buddhism--China--History.

BQ9268.6.O46 2000
Olson, Carl.
Zen and the art of postmodern philosophy: two paths of liberation from the representational mode of thinking/ Carl Olson. Albany: State University of New York Press, c2000. xii, 309 p.
99-058390   181/.043   0791446530
Zen Buddhism -- Philosophy. Postmodernism -- Religious aspects -- Zen Buddhism.

BQ9294.4.J3 C64
Collcutt, Martin,
Five Mountains: the Rinzai Zen monastic institution in medieval Japan / Martin Collcutt. Cambridge, Mass.: Published by Council on East Asian Studies, xxi, 399 p.
80-023316   294.3/657/0952 19   0674304977
Monasticism and religious orders, Zen--Japan. Monastic and religious life (Zen Buddhism)--Japan.

BQ9294.4.J3 V3613 1999
Van de Wetering, Janwillem,
The empty mirror: experiences in a Japanese Zen monastery / Janwillem van de Wetering. 1st ed. New York: St. Martin's Griffin, 1999.
99-014023   294.3/657/092 B 21   0312207743
Moanastic and religious life (Zen Buddhism)--Japan.

BQ9294.4.U6
Maguire, Jack, 1945-
Waking up: a week inside a Zen monastery/ Jack Maguire; foreword by John Daido Loori. Woodstock, Vt.: SkyLight Paths Pub., c2000. xviii, 189 p.
00-010977   294.3/927   1893361136
Monastic and religious life (Zen Buddhism) -- United States.

BR Christianity

BR50 Collected works — General — Single volumes. Festschriften

BR50.B63 1990
Bonhoeffer, Dietrich, 1906-1945.
A testament to freedom: the essential writings of Dietrich Bonhoeffer/ edited by Geffrey B. Kelly and F. Burton Nelson. [San Francisco, Calif.]: HarperSanFrancisco, c1990. xxii, 579 p.
89-045514   230/.044   0060608137
Theology.

BR53 Collected works — General — Selections (Several authors)

BR53.C38 2001
Christian literature: an anthology/ edited by Alister E. McGrath. Oxford, UK; Blackwell Publishers, 2001. xx, 796 p.
00-023646   230 21   0631216065
Christianity. Christian literature, English.

BR53.F6
Forell, George Wolfgang,
Christian social teachings; a reader in Christian social ethics from the Bible to the present. Compiled and edited by George W. Forell. Garden City, N.Y., Anchor Books, 1966. xx, 491 p.
66-021010   261/.08
Christian literature. Sociology, Christian.

BR53.M4 1986
Medieval women's visionary literature/ [edited by] Elizabeth Alvilda Petroff. New York: Oxford University Press, 1986. xii, 402 p.
85-013717   270 19   019503712X
Christian literature -- Women authors. Christian biography -- Europe. Women -- Europe -- Biography. Spiritual life -- Christianity -- History of doctrines -- Middle Ages,

BR60 Collected works — Early Christian literature. Fathers of the Church, etc. — Collections of several authors

BR60.A5 1950
The Ante-Nicene Fathers; translations of the writings of the Fathers down to A. D. 325. Alexander Roberts and James Donaldson, editors. Grand Rapids, W. B. Eerdmans Pub. Co., [1950-]
52-008705
Christian literature, Early. Christian literature, Early -- Bibliography.

BR60.A62.G713 1964
The Apostolic Fathers; a new translation and commentary. [Edited by Robert M. Grant] New York, T. Nelson [1964-68] 6 v.
64-011546   281.1
Christian literature, Early.

BR60.F3.G74 1998
Gregory, Thaumaturgus, Saint, ca. 213-ca. 2
St. Gregory Thaumaturgus: life and works/ translated by Michael Slusser. Washington, D.C.: The Catholic University of America Press, c1998. xix, 199 p.
97-049907   270 s   0813200989

BR60.F3.I27 1999
Iberian fathers: Pacian of Barcelona and Orosius of Braga: [writings]/ translated by Craig L. Hanson. Washington, D.C.: Catholic University of America Press, c1999. x, 192 p.
98-016992   270 s   0813200997
Theology -- Early works to 1800. Apologetics -- Early works to 1800.

BR65 Collected works — Early Christian literature. Fathers of the Church, etc. — Individual authors

BR65.A5.E53 1990
Augustine, Saint, Bishop of Hippo.
The works of Saint Augustine: a translation for the 21st century/ translation and notes, Edmund Hill; editor, John E. Rotelle. Brooklyn, N.Y.: New City Press, c1990-c1996
89-028878   270.2   1565480554
Theology -- Early works to 1800.

BR65.A6 E5 2001b
Augustine,
The confessions/ Augustine; translated and edited by Philip Burton; with an introduction by Robin Lane Fox. New York: A.A. Knopf, 2001. li, 370 p.
2001-029345   270.2/092 B 21   0375411739
Augustine, Saint, Bishop of Hippo.Christian saints--Algeria--Hippo (Extinct city)--Biography.

BR65.A62.T78 1999
Troup, Calvin L., 1961-
Temporality, eternity, and wisdom: the rhetoric of Augustine's Confessions/ Calvin L. Troup. Columbia, S. C.: University of South Carolina Press c1999. xii, 199 p.
98-058083   270/.2/092
Augustine, -- Saint, Bishop of Hippo. -- Confessions.Eternity. Time.

BR65.A9.A83 2000
Augustine and his critics: essays in honour of Gerald Bonner/ edited by Robert Dodaro and George Lawless. London; Routledge, 2000. xiii, 273 p.
99-034141   230/.14/092   0415200628
Augustine, -- Saint, Bishop of Hippo.

BR65.L26.D54 2000
Digeser, Elizabeth DePalma, 1959-
The making of a Christian empire: Lactantius & Rome/ Elizabeth DePalma Digeser. Ithaca, N.Y.: Cornell University Press, 2000. xv, 199 p.
99-016168   270.1/092   0801435943
Lactantius, -- ca. 240-ca. 320 -- Divinae institutiones. Lactantius, -- ca. 240-ca. 320 -- Influence. Church history -- Primitive and early church, ca. 30-600.Rome -- History -- Empire, 284-476. Rome -- Civilization.

BR66.5-67.2 Collected works — Early Christian literature. Fathers of the Church, etc. — History and criticism

BR66.5.L4813 2000
Dictionary of early Christian literature/ edited by Siegmar Dopp and Wilhelm Geerlings; translated from the German by Matthew O'Connell. New York: Crossroad Publishing Co., c2000. xvi, 621 p.
00-010545   270.1/03   0824518055
Christian literature, Early -- Dictionaries.

BR66.5.D53 1998
A dictionary of early Christian beliefs: a reference guide to more than 700 topics discussed by the Early Church Fathers/ David Bercot, editor. Peabody, Mass.: Hendrickson Publishers, c1998. xx, 704 p.
98-008259   270.1 21   1565633571
Fathers of the Church -- Dictionaries. Theology -- Dictionaries. Fathers of the Church -- Quotations. Theology -- Quotations, maxims, etc.

BR66.5.D5813 1991
Encyclopedia of the early church/ produced by the Institutum Patristicum Augustinianum and edited by Angelo Di Berardino; translated from the Italian by Adrian Walford; with a foreword and bibliographic amendments by W.H.C. Frend. New York: Oxford University Press, 1992. 2 v.
91-023934   270.1/03   0195208927
Christian literature, Early -- Dictionaries -- Italian. Church history -- Primitive and early church, ca. 30-600 -- Dictionaries -- Italian.

BR67.2.H35 2000
Haines-Eitzen, Kim.
Guardians of letters: literacy, power, and the transmitters of early Christian literature/ Kim Haines-Eitzen. Oxford; Oxford University Press, 2000. x, 212 p.
00-021072   270.1   0195135644
Christian literature, Early -- Rome -- History and criticism. Transmission of texts -- Rome. Scribes -- Rome.

BR67.2.G35 1995
Gamble, Harry Y., 1941-
Books and readers in the early church: a history of early Christian texts/ Harry Y. Gamble. New Haven: Yale University Press, c1995. xii, 337 p.
94-024351   002/.08/8211   0300060246
Christian literature, Early -- Publication and distribution -- Rome. Books -- Rome -- History -- To 400. Books -- Rome -- History -- 400-1400.

BR85 Collected works — Writers, 19th-20th centuries — Individual authors

BR85.L484
Lewis, C. S. 1898-1963.
God in the dock; essays on theology and ethics, by C. S. Lewis. Edited by Walter Hooper. Grand Rapids, Eerdmans [1970] 346 p.
70-129851   201
Theology.

BR85.N615 1996
Niebuhr, H. Richard 1894-1962.
Theology, history, and culture: major unpublished writings/ H. Richard Niebuhr; edited by William Stacy Johnson; foreword by Richard R. Niebuhr. New Haven: Yale University Press, c1996. xxxvii, 236 p.
95-022557   230   0300063709
Theology.

BR85.T3313 1971
Teilhard de Chardin, Pierre.
Christianity and evolution. Translated by Rene Hague. New York, Harcourt Brace Jovanovich [1971] 255 p.
78-162798   201/.1   015117850X
Theology -- Addresses, essays, lectures.

BR95 Encyclopedias. Dictionaries

BR95.B575 2000
Biographical dictionary of Christian theologians/ edited by Patrick W. Carey and Joseph T. Lienhard. Westport, Conn.: Greenwood Press, 2000. xiv, 589 p.
99-022143   230/.092/2   0313296499
Theologians -- Biography -- Dictionaries.

BR95.B58 1993
The Blackwell encyclopedia of modern Christian thought/ edited by Alister McGrath. Oxford [England]; Blackwell, 1993. xiii, 701 p.
93-012925   230/.09/03   0631168966
Theology -- History -- 18th century -- Encyclopedias. Theology -- History -- 19th century -- Encyclopedias. Theology -- History -- 20th century -- Encyclopedias.

BR95.B65 1991
Bowden, John.
Who's who in theology: from the first century to the present/ John Bowden. New York: Crossroad, 1992. viii, 152 p.
91-018978   230/.092/2 B 20   0824511506
Abelard, Peter, 1079-1142. Zwingli, Ulrich, 1484-1531. Theologians -- Dictionaries. Theology -- Dictionaries.

BR95.D46 1986
The Dictionary of Bible and religion/ William H. Gentz, editor. Nashville: Abingdon, c1986. 1147 p.
85-015011   203/.21 19   0687107571
Theology -- Dictionaries. Religion -- Dictionaries. Religions -- Dictionaries.

BR95.D486 2000
Dictionary of Third World theologies/ Virginia Fabella and R.S. Sugirtharajah, editors. Maryknoll, N.Y.: Orbis Books, c2000. xxiii, 261 p.
00-021887   230/.09172/4   1570752346
Christianity -- Dictionaries. Christianity -- Developing countries -- Dictionaries. Theology -- Dictionaries.

BR95.E87 2001
Evangelical dictionary of theology/ edited by Walter A. Elwell. 2nd ed. Grand Rapids, Mich.: Baker Academic; 1312 p.
2001-272311   230/.04624/03 21
Theology -- Dictionaries.

BR95.E8913 1999
The encyclopedia of Christianity/ editors, Erwin Fahlbusch ... [et al.]; translator and English-language editor, Geoffrey W. Bromiley; statistical editor, David B. Barrett; foreword, Jaroslav Pelikan. Grand Rapids, Mich.: Wm. B. Eerdmans; [1999-   ] v. 1
98-045953   230/.003   0802824137
Christianity -- Encyclopedias.

BR95.N35 2001
Nelson's new Christian dictionary: the authoritative resource on the Christian world/ George T. Kurian, editor. Nashville, Tenn.: Thomas Nelson Pubs., c2001. xviii, 983 p.
2001-275024   230/.003 21   0785243003
Christianity -- Dictionaries.

BR95.N395 1991
New 20th-century encyclopedia of religious knowledge/ edited by J.D. Douglas; consulting editors, Robert G. Clouse ... [et al.]. 2nd ed. Grand Rapids, Mich.: Baker Book House, c1991. xv, 896 p.
90-029129   230/.03 20   0801030021
Theology -- History -- 20th century -- Encyclopedias. Theology -- Encyclopedias.

BR95.O25 1991
O'Collins, Gerald.
A concise dictionary of theology/ by Gerald O'Collins and Edward G. Farrugia. New York: Paulist Press, c1991. 268 p.
91-007187   230/.03 20   0809132354
Theology -- Dictionaries.

BR95.O82 2000
The concise Oxford dictionary of the Christian Church/ [edited by] E.A. Livingstone. Oxford [England]; Oxford University Press, 2000. viii, 643 p.
2001-266596   270/.03   0192800574
Theology -- Dictionaries.

BR95.O94 2000
The Oxford companion to Christian thought/ edited by Adrian Hastings, Alistair Mason, and Hugh Pyper; with Ingrid Lawrie and Cecily Bennett. Oxford; Oxford University Press, 2000. xxviii, 777 p.
2001-267818   230/.03   0198600240
Theology -- Dictionaries.

BR99 Ecclesiastical geography — Dictionaries

BR99.74
Veith, Gene Edward, 1951-
Christians in a .com world: getting connected without being consumed/ Gene Edward Veith, Jr. and Christopher L. Stamper. Wheaton, Ill.: Crossway, c2000. 190 p.
00-009617   261.5   1581342187
Internet x Religious aspects -- Christianity. Cyberspace -- Religious aspects -- Christianity.

BR100 Philosophy of Christianity. Philosophy and Christianity

BR100.A49 1998
Anderson, Victor, 1955-
Pragmatic theology: negotiating the intersections of an American philosophy of religion and public theology/ Victor Anderson. Albany, N.Y.: State University of New York Press, c1998. xiv, 172 p.
97-012086   261.5/1/0973   0791436373
Philosophy and religion. Pragmatism. Religion -- Philosophy.

BR100.K5216.K53
Kierkegaard's Fear and trembling: critical appraisals/ edited by Robert L. Perkins. University: University of Alabama Press, c1981. xii, 251 p.
79-016984   198/.9   0817300287
Kierkegaard, Soren, -- 1813-1855. -- Frygt og baeven -- Addresses, essays, lectures.Christianity -- Philosophy -- Addresses, essays, lectures. Sin -- Addresses, essays, lectures.

BR100.K52 1941
Kierkegaard, Søren,
Fear and trembling, a dialectical lyric, by S. Kierkegaard, translated, with introduction and notes, by Walter Lowrie. Princeton, Princeton university press, 1941. xxviii, 208 p.
42-002194   198.9
Christianity -- Philosophy.

BR100.P53 1988
Philosophy and the Christian faith/ Thomas V. Morris, editor. Notre Dame, Ind.: University of Notre Dame Press, c1988. xiv, 300 p.
87-040618   230/.01   0268015708
Christianity -- Philosophy.

BR100.S754 1994
Stead, Christopher.
Philosophy in Christian antiquity/ Christopher Stead. Cambridge; Cambridge University Press, 1994. xi, 261 p.
94-005960   189   0521465532
Christianity -- Philosophy -- History. Philosophy, Ancient. Theology, Doctrinal -- History -- Early church, ca. 30-600.

BR100.T53
Tillich, Paul, 1886-1965.
Biblical religion and the search for ultimate reality. [Chicago] University of Chicago Press [1955] 84 p.
55-005149   201
Christianity -- Philosophy.

BR102 Biography of Christian philosophers

BR102.A1.G63 1994
God and the philosophers: the reconciliation of faith and reason/ edited by Thomas V. Morris. New York: Oxford University Press, 1994. vii, 285 p.
93-038656   210/.92/2   0195088220
Christian philosophers -- United States -- Biography. Philosophers, Jewish -- United States -- Biography. Philosophy and religion.

BR115 Christianity in relation to special subjects, A-Z

BR115.A8.K47 2000
Kessler, Herbert L., 1941-
Spiritual seeing: picturing God's invisibility in medieval art/ Herbert L. Kessler. Philadelphia: University of Pennsylvania Press, c2000. xiii, 265 p.
00-029939   246/.1   0812235606
Christian art and symbolism -- Medieval, 500-1500. Image (Theology) -- History of doctrines -- Middle Ages, 600-1500.

BR115.C3.S43 1999
Sedgwick, P. H. 1948-
The market economy and Christian ethics/ Peter H. Sedgwick. Cambridge, U.K.; Cambridge University Press, 1999. xii, 325 p.
98-053577   261.8/5   052147048X
Capitalism -- Religious aspects -- Christianity. Capitalism -- Moral and ethical aspects. Christian ethics -- Anglican authors.

BR115.C3 W413 2002b
Weber, Max,
The Protestant ethic and the "spirit" of capitalism and other writings / by Max Weber; edited, translated, and with an introduction by Peter Baehr and Gordon C. Wells. New York: Penguin Books, 2002. lxxii, 392 p.
2001-133065   306.6 21   0140439218
Capitalism -- Religious aspects -- Protestant churches. Protestant work ethic.

BR115.C8.C85 1988
Culture and Christianity: the dialectics of transformation/ edited by George R. Saunders. New York: Greenwood Press, 1988. xiii, 217 p.
88-005651   261   0313261180
Christianity and culture.

BR115.C8.S37 1988
Scriven, Charles.
The transformation of culture: Christian social ethics after H. Richard Niebuhr/ Charles Scriven; foreword by James W. McClendon, Jr. Scottdale, Pa.: Herald Press, c1988. 224 p.
87-033935   241   0836131010
Niebuhr, H. Richard -- (Helmut Richard), -- 1894-1962. -- Christ and culture.Christianity and culture. Anabaptists. Social ethics -- History -- 20th century.

BR115.C8.W43 1998
Wells, David F.
Losing our virtue: why the church must recover its moral vision/ David F. Wells. Grand Rapids, Mich.: W.B. Eerdmans Pub., c1998. xii, 228 p.
97-032963   241/.0973   0802838278
Christianity and culture -- United States. Christianity -- United States -- 20th century. Christian ethics. United States -- Moral conditions.

BR115.E3.K45 1999
King, Paul G., 1940-
Liberating nature: theology and economics in a new order/ Paul G. King and David O. Woodyard. Cleveland, Ohio: Pilgrim Press, 1999. xiii, 146 p.
98-045512   261.8/5   0829813179
Economics -- Religious aspects -- Christianity. Human ecology -- Religious aspects -- Christianity.

BR115.E3.M315 2001
McFague, Sallie.
Life abundant: rethinking theology and economy for a planet in peril/ Sallie McFague. Minneapolis: Fortress Press, c2001. xiv, 251 p.
00-057274   261.8   0800632699
Economics -- Religious aspects -- Christianity. Human ecology -- Religious aspects -- Christianity.

BR115.E3.W33 2000
Walsh, Andrew D., 1965-
Religion, economics, and public policy: ironies, tragedies, and absurdities of the contemporary culture wars/ Andrew D. Walsh. Westport, Conn.: Praeger, 2000. xi, 156 p.
99-088505   261.8/5   0275966119
Economics -- Religious aspects -- Christianity -- History -- 20th century.United States -- Economic policy.

BR115.H5.D4 1988
Dean, William D.
History making history: the new historicism in American religious thought/ William Dean. Albany: State University of New York Press, c1988. xiv, 175 p.
88-009745   200/.973   0887068928
History (Theology) -- History of doctrines -- 20th century. Historicism -- History -- 20th century. Religious thought -- United States -- History -- 20th century.

BR115.H6.H38 1996
Hartman, Keith, 1966-
Congregations in conflict: the battle over homosexuality/ Keith Hartman. New Brunswick, N.J.: Rutgers University Press, c1996. xii, 195 p.
95-008754   261.8/35766/0973   0813522293
Homosexuality -- Religious aspects -- Christianity. Gay men -- Religious life -- United States. Lesbians -- Religious life -- United States.

BR115.H6 W38 1999
Waun, Maurine C.
More than welcome: learning to embrace gay, lesbian, bisexual, and transgendered persons in the church/ Maurine C. Waun. St. Louis, Mo.: Chalice Press, c1999. xiii, 153 p.
98-043562   261.8/35766 21   0827223250
Homosexuality -- Religious aspects -- Christianity. Christian gays.

BR115.J8.B76
Brown, Robert McAfee, 1920-
Theology in a new key: responding to liberation themes/ Robert McAfee Brown. Philadelphia: Westminster Press, c1978. 212 p.
78-006494   261.8   0664242049
Christianity and justice. Mission of the church. Liberation theology.

BR115.J8.F67 1997
Forrester, Duncan B., 1933-
Christian justice and public policy/ Duncan B. Forrester. Cambridge, U.K.; Cambridge University Press, 1997. xiv, 274 p.
96-048229   261.8   0521554314
Christianity and justice. Church and social problems. Christianity and politics.

BR115.K55.M66 1999
Monod, Paul Kleber.
The power of kings: monarchy and religion in Europe, 1589-1715/ Paul Kleber Monod. New Haven, Conn.: Yale University Press, c1999. x, 417 p.
99-017815   321/.6/0940903   0300078102
Kings and rulers -- Religious aspects -- Christianity -- History.Europe -- Politics and government -- 1517-1648. Europe -- Politics and government -- 1648-1715. Europe -- Kings and rulers -- History.

BR115.N87 S23 2000
Sack, Daniel.
Whitebread Protestants: food and religion in American culture/ Daniel Sack. 1st ed. New York: St. Martin's Press, 2000. x, 262 p.
00-030899   261 21   0312217315
Food--Religious aspects--Christianity--History of doctrines--19th Protestants--United States--History--19th century. Food--Religious aspects--Christianity--History of doctrines--20th

BR115.P7 B656 2001
Bolt, John, 1947-
A free church, a holy nation: Abraham Kuyper's American public theology/ John Bolt. Grand Rapids, Mich.: W.B. Eerdmans, c2000. xxv, 502 p.
00-063607   261.8/092   0802842542
Kuyper, Abraham, -- 1837-1920.Christianity and politics -- United States.

BR115.P7.C689 1992
Craig, Robert H. 1942-
Religion and radical politics: an alternative Christian tradition in the United States/ Robert H. Craig. Philadelphia: Temple University Press, 1992. vii, 307 p.
91-046652   261.7/0973   0877229732
Christianity and politics -- History.United States -- Social conditions. United States -- Politics and government.

BR115.P7.M5444 1992
Moen, Matthew C., 1958-
The transformation of the Christian Right/
Matthew C. Moen. Tuscaloosa: University of
Alabama Press, c1992. x, 209 p.
91-031447　322/.1/097309048　0817305742
　*Christianity and politics -- History -- 20th
century. Christians -- United States -- Political
activity. Fundamentalism -- History -- 20th
century. United States -- Politics and
government -- 1977-1981. United States --
Politics and government -- 1981-1989.*

BR115.P7.R4338 1997
Religion and contemporary liberalism/ edited by
Paul J. Weithman. Notre Dame, Ind.: University
of Notre Dame Press, 1997. viii, 315 p.
97-001806　261.7　0268016585
　Christianity and politics. Liberalism.

BR115.P7.S514 1995
Shriver, Donald W.
An ethic for enemies: forgiveness in politics/
Donald W. Shriver, Jr. New York: Oxford
University Press, 1995. xi, 284 p.
94-014773　172　0195091051
　*Christianity and politics. Forgiveness --
Religious aspects -- Christianity. Civil society.
United States -- Politics and government -- 20th
century.*

BR115.P7.T475 1996
Thiemann, Ronald F.
Religion in public life: a dilemma for
democracy/ Ronald F. Thiemann. Washington,
D.C.: Georgetown University Press, c1996. xiii,
186 p.
95-042085　322/.1/0973　0878406093
　*Democracy -- Religious aspects --
Christianity. Religion and state -- United States.
Religion and politics -- United States. United
States -- Politics and government. United States
-- Politics and government -- 1993- United
States -- Religion.*

BR115.T42.N63 1997
Noble, David F.
The religion of technology: the divinity of man
and the spirit of invention/ David Noble. New
York: A.A. Knopf: 1997. x, 273 p.
96-048019　261.5/6　0679425640
　*Technology -- Religious aspects --
Christianity. Religion and science. Presence of
God.*

BR115.W2.R25
Ramsey, Paul.
War and the Christian conscience; how shall
modern war be conducted justly? Durham, N.C.,
Published for the Lilly Endowment Research
Program in Christianity and Politics by Duke
University Press, 1961. 331 p.
61-010666　261.63
　War -- Religious aspects.

BR115.W6.M45413 1999
Moltmann, Jurgen.
God for a secular society: the public relevance
of theology/ Jurgen Moltmann. Minneapolis:
Fortress Press, 1999. xi, 292 p.
99-019747　261.7　0800631846
　Church and the world. Theology, Doctrinal.

BR117 Literary history (General): Christian literature — General works

BR117.C48 1988
Christian spirituality: the essential guide to the
most influential spiritual writings of the
Christian tradition/ edited by Frank N. Magill
and Ian P. McGreal. 1st ed. San Francisco:
Harper & Row, c1988. xix, 694 p.
87-045713　200 19　0060653736
　Christian literature -- History and criticism.

BR118 Christian theology — General works

BR118.F75 1992
Frei, Hans W.
Types of Christian theology/ Hans W. Frei;
edited by George Hunsinger and William C.
Placher. New Haven: Yale University Press,
c1992. xi, 180 p.
91-034427　230/.01　0300051042
　Theology -- Methodology -- History.

BR118.L69 1993
Lowe, Walter James, 1940-
Theology and difference: the wound of reason/
Walter Lowe. Bloomington: Indiana University
Press, c1993. xiii, 181 p.
92-026531　209/.04　0253336112
　*Theology -- Methodology. Theology.
Theodicy.*

BR118.P72 2000
Practical theology: perspectives from the plains/
edited by Michael G. Lawler & Gail S. Risch.
Omaha, Neb.: Creighton University Press,
c2000. x, 294 p.
00-020116　230　1881871371
　Theology.

BR120 General works on Christianity — Treatises — Early through 1800

BR120.L62
Locke, John, 1632-1704.
The reasonableness of Christianity, with A
discourse of miracles, and part of A third letter
concerning toleration. Edited, abridged, and
introduced by I. T. Ramsey. Stanford, Calif.,
Stanford University Press [1958] 102 p.
58-008595
　*Christianity -- 17th cent. Philosophy and
religion.*

BR121 General works on Christianity — Treatises — 1801-1950

BR121.B2455 1957
Barth, Karl, 1886-1968.
The word of God and the word of man.
Translated with a new foreword by Douglas
Horton. New York, Harper [1957] vii, 327 p.
57-007531　230.04
　Christianity. Christianity -- 20th century.

BR121.C5 1909a
Chesterton, G. K. 1874-1936.
Orthodoxy, by Gilbert K. Chesterton. London,
John Lane; 1909.
44-032773
　*Chesterton, G. K. -- (Gilbert Keith), -- 1874-
1936.Christianity -- Essence, genius, nature.
Apologetics.*

BR123 General works on Christianity — Addresses, essays, etc. (separates)

BR123.L482
Lewis, C. S. 1898-1963.
The case for Christianity, by C. S. Lewis.
Published in England under the title "Broadcast
talks." New York, The Macmillan company,
1943.
44-019997　230
　Christianity. Ethics.

BR123.L484 1952
Lewis, C. S. 1898-1963.
Mere Christianity; a revised and enlarged
edition, with a new introduction of the three
books, The case for christianity, Christian
behaviour, and Beyond personality. New York,
Macmillan, 1952. 175 p.
52-014321　230
　Christianity.

BR123.N53
Niebuhr, Reinhold, 1892-1971.
The godly and the ungodly; essays on the religious and secular dimensions of modern life. London, Faber and Faber [1959, c1958] x, 150 p.
66-002142
Christianity -- Addressses, essays, lectures.

BR123.T54
Tillich, Paul, 1886-1965.
The future of religions. Edited by Jerald C. Brauer. New York, Harper & Row [1966] 94 p.
66-015864   230.0924
Tillich, Paul, -- 1886-1965.Christianity -- 20th century.

BR124 General works on Christianity — Personal opinions

BR124.D68 1998
The Doubleday Christian quotation collection/ compiled by Hannah Ward and Jennifer Wild. 1st ed. in the U.S. New York: Doubleday, 1998. viii, 502 p.
97-048809   270 21   0385489943
Christianity -- Quotations, maxims, etc.

BR124.H49 1999
Heyward, Carter.
Saving Jesus from those who are right: rethinking what it means to be Christian/ Carter Heyward. Minneapolis: Fortress Press, c1999. xviii, 275 p.
99-037663   232   0800629663
Jesus Christ -- Person and offices.Christianity -- Miscellanea. Liberalism (Religion)

BR125 General works on Christianity — Pamphlets, etc.

BR125.L67 1982
Lewis, C. S.
The screwtape letters; with, Screwtape proposes a toast/ C.S. Lewis. Rev. ed. New York: Macmillan, 1982. xv, 172 p.
82-017262   248.4 19
Christianity -- 20th century.

BR127 Relation of Christianity to other religious and philosophical systems — General works

BR127.C66 1988
Cox, Harvey Gallagher.
Many mansions: a Christian's encounter with other faiths/ Harvey Cox. Boston: Beacon Press, c1988. 216 p.
88-047656   261.2   0807012084
Cox, Harvey Gallagher.Christianity and other religions.

BR127.T56
Tillich, Paul, 1886-1965.
Christianity and the encounter of the world religions. New York, Columbia University Press, 1963. viii, 97 p.
63-007508   290
Christianity and other religions.

BR127.T6
Toynbee, Arnold Joseph, 1889-1975.
Christianity among the religions of the world. New York, Scribner [1957] 116 p.
57-012066   290
Christianity and other religions. Religions.

BR128 Relation of Christianity to other religious and philosophical systems — Special, A-Z

BR128.B8.C465 1987
The Christ and the Bodhisattva/ edited by Donald S. Lopez, Jr., and Steven C. Rockefeller. Albany: State University of New York Press, c1987. viii, 274 p.
86-014356   261.2/43   0887064019
Christianity and other religions -- Buddhism - - Congresses. Buddhism -- Relations -- Christianity -- Congresses.

BR128.H5.H42 1990
Healy, Kathleen.
Christ as common ground: a study of Christianity and Hinduism/ Kathleen Healy; foreward [sic] by Bede Griffiths. Pittsburgh, Pa.: Duquesne University Press, c1990. xiv, 218 p.
90-034260   261.2/45/0954   0820702277
Christianity and other religions -- Hinduism. Hinduism -- Relations -- Christianaity.

BR128.H8.C48 1995
Christian humanism: international perspectives/ edited by Richard P. Francis and Jane E. Francis. New York: P. Lang, c1995. xvi, 452 p.
93-006955   144   0820421650
Christianity and religious humanism -- Congresses.

BR128.R7.C58 1990
Chuvin, Pierre.
A chronicle of the last pagans/ Pierre Chuvin; translated by B.A. Archer. Cambridge, Mass.: Harvard University Press, 1990. 188 p.
89-020091   292/.009/015   0674129709
Paganism -- Rome. Church history -- Primitive and early church, ca. 30-600. Christianity and other religions. Rome -- Civilization.

BR129 Sources of Christianity. Origins — General works

BR129.C44 1992
Christianity and rabbinic Judaism: a parallel history of their origins and early development/ edited by Hershel Shanks. Washington, D.C.: Biblical Archaeology Society, c1992. xxii, 380 p.
92-039396   261.2/6/09015   1880317036
Christianity -- Origin. Church history -- Primitive and early church, ca. 30-600. Judaism -- History -- Talmudic period, 10-425.

BR129.F56 1983
Schussler Fiorenza, Elisabeth, 1938-
In memory of her: a feminist theological reconstruction of Christian origins/ Elisabeth Schussler Fiorenza. New York: Crossroad, 1983. xxv, 357 p.
82-019896   270.1/0842   0824504933
Women in Christianity -- History -- Early church, ca. 30-600. Christianity -- Origin.

BR132 Christian antiquities. Archaeology. Museums — Other

BR132.F74 1996
Frend, W. H. C.
The archaeology of early Christianity: a history/ William H.C. Frend. Minneapolis: Fortress Press, 1996. xix, 412 p.
95-049242   270.1   080062811X
Christian antiquities -- Study and teaching -- History. Christian antiquities. Excavations (Archaeology)

BR138 Historiography. Methodology — General works

BR138.B69 1995
Bradley, James E.,
Church history: an introduction to research, reference works, and methods/ James E. Bradley and Richard A. Muller. Grand Rapids, Mich.: Eerdmans, c1995. xvi, 236 p.
94-040617   270/.072 20   0802808263
Church history -- Study and teaching. Church history -- Historiography. Church history -- Bibliography. Church history -- Reference books.

BR145 History — General works — 1801-1950

BR145.L28
Latourette, Kenneth Scott,
A history of Christianity/ Kenneth Scott Latourette. 1st ed. New York: Harper, [1953] xxvii, 1516 p.
53-005004   270
Church history.

BR145.W34 1985
Walker, Williston, 1860-1922.
A history of the Christian church/ by Williston Walker and Richard A. Norris, David W. Lotz, Robert T. Handy. New York: Scribner, c1985. xii, 756 p.
84-023614   270   0684184176
Church history.

BR145.2 History — General works — 1951-2000

BR145.2.C42 1996
Chadwick, Owen.
A history of Christianity/ by Owen Chadwick. 1st U.S. ed. New York: St. Martin's Press, c1996. 304 p.
96-002631   270 20   0312138075
Church history.

BR145.2.E26 1997
Edwards, David Lawrence.
Christianity: the first two thousand years/ David L. Edwards. Maryknoll, N.Y.: Orbis Books, 1997. viii, 664 p.
97-024093   270   1570751609
Church history.

BR145.2.G65 1996
González, Justo L.
Church history: an essential guide/ Justo L. González. Nashville: Abingdon Press, c1996. 95 p.
96-020588   270 20   0687016118
Church history.

BR145.2.H37 1999
A world history of Christianity/ edited by Adrian Hastings. Grand Rapids, Mich.: W.B. Eerdmans, c1999. xiv, 594 p.
98-042984   270 21   0802824420
Church history.

BR145.2.O86 1990
The Oxford illustrated history of Christianity/ edited by John McManners. Oxford; Oxford University Press, 1990. xi, 724 p.
90-030280   270 20   0198229283
Church history. Church history -- Pictorial works.

BR145.3 History — General works — 2001-

BR145.3.I78 2001
Irvin, Dale T.,
History of the world Christian movement/ Dale T. Irvin, Scott W. Sunquist. Maryknoll, N.Y.: Orbis Books, [2001-] v. <1- >
2001-041424   270 21   1570753962
Church history.

BR148 History — General special

BR148.R85 1988
Rowland, Christopher, 1947-
Radical Christianity: a reading of recovery/ Christopher Rowland. Maryknoll, N.Y.: Orbis Books, c1988. vi, 199 p.
88-012402   270   0883443708
Church history. Christian sects -- History. Church and social problems -- History.

BR149 History — Outlines, syllabi, tables, etc.

BR149.G66 1990
Gross, Ernie.
This day in religion/ by Ernie Gross. New York, N.Y.: Neal-Schuman Publishers, c1990. v, 294 p.
90-147534   270/.02/02 20   1555700454
Church history -- Chronology.

BR150 History — Popular works

BR150.I58 1995
Introduction to the history of Christianity/ organizing editor, Tim Dowley; consulting editors, John H.Y. Briggs, Robert Linder, David F. Wright. 1st Fortress Press ed. Minneapolis: Fortress Press, 1995. 688 p.
95-160819   270 20   0800629353
Church history. Church history -- Chronology -- Charts, diagrams, etc.

BR157 History — Christian denominations. Sects (General)

BR157.C36 1996
Campbell, Ted.
Christian confessions: a historical introduction/ Ted A. Campbell. Louisville, Ky.: Westminster John Knox Press, c1996. xxi, 336 p.
95-046675   230/.09   0664256503
Christian sects. Theology, Doctrinal -- Comparative studies. Creeds -- Comparative studies.

BR157.W67 2001
World Christian encyclopedia: a comparative survey of churches and religions in the modern world/ David B. Barrett, George T. Kurian, Todd M. Johnson. 2nd ed. Oxford; Oxford University Press, 2001. 2 v.
99-057323   230/.003 21   019510319X
Christianity. Christian sects. Ecclesiastical geography. Christianity -- Statistics.

BR158 History — Jewish Christians

BR158.C645 2000
Cohn-Sherbok, Dan.
Messianic Judaism/ Dan Cohn-Sherbok. London; Cassell, 2000.
99-050300   289.9   0304701327
Jewish Christians. Missions to Jews -- History. Jewish Christians -- History.

BR160.3-270 History — By period — Early and medieval

BR160.3.H37 1999
Hargis, Jeffrey W., 1961-
Against the Christians: the rise of early anti-Christian polemic/ Jeffrey W. Hargis. New York: Peter Lang, c1999. 172 p.
98-025584   270.1   0820441562
Christianity -- Controversial literature. Philosophy, Ancient. Christianity and other religions -- Roman. Rome -- Religion.

BR162.2.B76 1995
Brown, Peter Robert Lamont.
The rise of Western Christendom: triumph and diversity, 200-1000 A.D/ Peter Brown. Cambridge, Mass.: Blackwell, 1995.
95-011589   274   1557861366
Church history -- Primitive and early church, ca. 30-600. Church history -- Middle Ages, 600-1500. Civilization, Medieval.

BR162.2.E53 1997
Encyclopedia of early Christianity/ editor, Everett Ferguson; associate editors, Michael P. McHugh, Frederick W. Norris. New York: Garland Pub., 1997. 2 v.
96-036865 270.1/03 0815316631
Church history -- Primitive and early church, ca. 30-600 -- Encyclopedias.

BR165.B712 1995
Brox, Norbert, 1935-
A concise history of the early church/ Norbert Brox. New York: Continuum, 1995. viii, 184 p.
94-045256 270.1 0826407927
Church history -- Primitive and early church, ca. 30-600.

BR165.C48 1968b
Chadwick, Henry, 1920-
The early church. Grand Rapids, Mich., Eerdmans [1968, c1967] 304 p.
72-004670 270.1
Church history -- Primitive and early church, ca. 30-600.

BR166.M44 1983
Meeks, Wayne A.
The first urban Christians: the social world of the Apostle Paul/ Wayne A. Meeks. New Haven: Yale University Press, c1983. x, 299 p.
82-008447 270.1 0300028768
Paul, -- The Apostle, Saint.Sociology, Christian -- History -- Early church, ca. 30-600.

BR166.S58 1999
Snyder, Graydon F.
Inculturation of the Jesus tradition: the impact of Jesus on Jewish and Roman cultures/ Graydon F. Snyder. Harrisburg, Pa.: Trinity Press International, c1999. x, 247 p.
99-029803 232.9/04 1563382954
Christianity and culture -- History -- Early church, ca. 30-600. Jews -- Civilization -- Christian influences. Rome -- Civilization -- Christian influences.

BR166.S75 1996
Stark, Rodney.
The rise of Christianity: a sociologist reconsiders history/ Rodney Stark. Princeton, N.J.: Princeton University Press, c1996. xiv, 246 p.
95-044197 306.6/701 0691027498
Church history -- Primitive and early church, ca. 30-600. Sociology, Christian -- History -- Early church, ca. 30-600.

BR170.C55 1993
Church and state in the early church/ edited with introductions by Everett Ferguson. New York: Garland, 1993. xiii, 415 p.
92-041857 261.7/09/015 20 0815310676
Church history -- Primitive and early church, ca. 30-600. Persecution -- History -- Early church, ca. 30-600. Church and state.

BR170.M33 1997
MacMullen, Ramsay, 1928-
Christianity and paganism in the fourth to eighth centuries/ Ramsay MacMullen. New Haven, Conn.: Yale University Press, c1997. vi, 282 p.
97-007786 270.2 0300071485
Church history -- Primitive and early church, ca. 30-600. Paganism -- Relations -- Christianity. Christianity and culture -- History -- Early church, ca. 30-600. Rome -- Religion -- Relations -- Christianity.

BR185.E38 1996
Edwards, Douglas R.
Religion & power: pagans, Jews, and Christians in the Greek East/ Douglas R. Edwards. New York: Oxford University Press, 1996. x, 234 p.
95-035320 291/.093 019508263X
Church history -- Primitive and early church, ca. 30-600. Christianity and other religions -- Greek. Christianity and other religions -- Roman. Middle East -- Religion. Rome -- Religion.

BR190.M47 1997
Merdinger, J. E. 1952-
Rome and the African church in the time of Augustine/ J.E. Merdinger. New Haven: Yale University Press, c1997. xvi, 267 p.
96-020999 276.1/02 0300040172
Popes -- Primacy -- History of doctrines -- Early church, ca. 30-600.Africa, North -- Church history.

BR195.A89.K38 1996
Kaufman, Peter Iver.
Church, book, and bishop: conflict and authority in early Latin Christianity/ Peter Iver Kaufman. Boulder, Colo.: Westview Press, 1996. ix, 166 p.
96-005047 262/.8/09015 0813318165
Church -- Authority -- History of doctrines -- Early church, ca. 30-600. Episcopacy -- History of doctrines -- Early church, ca. 30-600. Councils and synods -- Rome -- History.

BR195.C45.B76 1988
Brown, Peter Robert Lamont.
The body and society: men, women, and sexual renunciation in early Christianity/ Peter Brown. New York: Columbia University Press, 1988. xx, 504 p.
87-030941 253/.2 0231061005
Celibacy -- Christianity -- History of doctrines -- Early church, ca. 30-600. Virginity -- Religious aspects -- Christianity -- History of doctrines -- Early church, ca. 30-600. Sex -- Religious aspects -- Christianity -- History of doctrines -- Early church, ca. 30-600.

BR195.W6.S3613 1995
Schottroff, Luise.
Lydia's impatient sisters: a feminist social history of early Christianity/ Luise Schottroff; translated by Barbara and Martin Rumscheidt. Louisville, Ky.: Westminster John Knox Press, c1995. xvi, 298 p.
95-020339 270.1/082 066422072X
Women in Christianity -- History -- Early church, ca. 30-600. Feminist theology.

BR195.W6.W58 1988
Witherington, Ben, 1951-
Women in the earliest churches/ Ben Witherington III. Cambridge; Cambridge University Press, 1988. xiii, 300 p.
87-024916 270.1/088042 0521346487
Women in Christianity -- History -- Early church, ca. 30-600. Women in the Bible.

BR203.R87 1994
Russell, James C.
The Germanization of early medieval Christianity: a sociohistorical approach to religious transformation/ James C. Russell. New York: Oxford University Press, 1994. ix, 258 p.
92-013182 274.3/02 0195076966
Sociology, Christian -- History -- Early church, ca. 30-600. Social history -- Medieval, 500-1500. Germanic peoples -- Religion.

BR219.M37 1990
Markus, R. A. 1924-
The end of ancient Christianity/ R.A. Markus. Cambridge [England]; Cambridge University Press, 1990. xvii, 258 p.
89-077196 270.2 0521327164
Church history -- Primitive and early church, ca. 30-600. Spirituality -- History of doctrines. Theology -- History -- Early church, ca. 30-600.

BR252.B7313 1994
Bredero, Adriaan Hendrik.
Christendom and Christianity in the Middle Ages: the relations between religion, church, and society/ Adriaan H. Bredero; translated by Reinder Bruinsma. Grand Rapids, Mich.: W.B. Eerdmans, c1994. xiii, 402 p.
91-037168 270.4 0802836925
Church history -- Middle Ages, 600-1500.

BR253.B96 1987
Bynum, Caroline Walker.
Holy feast and holy fast: the religious significance of food to medieval women/ Caroline Walker Bynum. Berkeley: University of California Press, c1987. xvi, 444 p.
85-028896 248.4/6 19 0520057228
Food -- Religious aspects -- Christianity -- History of doctrines -- Middle Women -- History -- Middle Ages, 500-1500. Social history -- Medieval, 500-1500. Food habits -- History -- To 1500.

BR270.M64 1989
Morris, Colin, 1928-
The papal monarchy: the Western church from 1050 to 1250/ Colin Morris. Oxford [England]: Clarendon Press; 1989. xvii, 673 p.
88-018984 282/.09/02 0198269072
Church history -- Middle Ages, 600-1500. Papacy -- History -- To 1309. Church and state -- Europe -- History.

BR270.O9
Ozment, Steven E.
The age of reform (1250-1550): an intellectual and religious history of late medieval and Reformation Europe/ Steven Ozment. New Haven: Yale University Press, 1980. xii, 458 p.
79-024162   274   0300024770
Church history -- Middle Ages, 600-1500. Reformation. Theology, Doctrinal -- History -- Middle Ages, 600-1500.

BR290-479 History — By period — Modern period

BR290.T73 1999
Tracy, James D.
Europe's reformations, 1450-1650/ James D. Tracy. Lanham: Rowman & Littlefield, c1999. xvii, 387 p.
99-034167   274/.06   0847688348
Reformation.Europe -- Church history -- 15th century. Europe -- Church history -- Modern period, 1500-

BR302.8.H55 2000
Hillerbrand, Hans Joachim.
Historical dictionary of the Reformation and Counter-Reformation/ Hans J. Hillerbrand. Lanham, MD: Scarecrow Press, 2000. xxxvii, 265 p.
99-026815   270.6   0810836734
Reformation -- Dictionaries. Counter-Reformation -- Dictionaries.

BR302.8.O93 1996
The Oxford encyclopedia of the Reformation/ Hans J. Hillerbrand, editor in chief. New York: Oxford University Press, 1996. 4 v.
95-024520   270.6/03   0195064933
Reformation -- Encyclopedias. Reformation -- Biography -- Encyclopedias. Theology, Doctrinal -- Europe -- History -- 16th century -- Encyclopedias. Europe -- Church history -- 16th century -- Encyclopedias.

BR305.2.C35 1991
Cameron, Euan.
The European Reformation/ Euan Cameron. Oxford: Clarendon Press; xiv, 564 p.
90-047890   274/.06 20   0198730934
Reformation -- Europe.

BR305.2.H5 1964
Hillerbrand, Hans Joachim,
The Reformation; a narrative history related by contemporary observers and participants [edited by] Hans J. Hillerbrand. New York, Harper & Row [1964] 495 p.
64-015480   270.6082
Reformation.

BR305.2.L486 1996
Lindberg, Carter, 1937-
The European reformations/ Carter Lindberg. Oxford, OX, UK; Blackwell Publishers, 1996. xv, 444 p.
95-022971   274/.06   1557865744
Reformation. Church history -- 15th century. Counter-Reformation.

BR305.2.M35 2001
Matheson, Peter.
The imaginative world of the Reformation/ Peter Matheson. 1st Fortress Press ed. Minneapolis, MN: Fortress Press, 2001. xiii, 153 p.
2001-270891   274/.06 21   0800632915
Reformation.

BR305.2.P48 2000
The Reformation world/ edited by Andrew Pettegree. London; Routledge, 2000. xvi, 576 p.
99-035295   274/.06   0415163579
Reformation.Europe -- Church history -- 16th century.

BR307.G74 1999
Gregory, Brad S. 1963-
Salvation at stake: Christian martyrdom in early modern Europe/ Brad S. Gregory. Cambridge, Mass.: Harvard University Press, 1999. xvi, 528 p.
99-029379   273.6   0674785517
Christian martyrs -- Europe -- History -- 16th century. Martyrdom (Christianity) -- History of doctrines -- 16th century. Reformation.

BR307.H643
Holl, Karl, 1866-1926.
The cultural significance of the Reformation. Introd. by Wilhelm Pauck. Translated by Karl and Barbara Hertz and John H. Lichtblau. New York, Meridian Books [1959] 191 p.
59-007188   270.6
Reformation.

BR307.S464 1994
Scribner, Robert W.
For the sake of simple folk: popular propaganda for the German Reformation/ R.W. Scribner. Oxford: Clarendon Press;
94-009048   274.3/06 20   0198203268
Reformation -- Germany. Propaganda, German. Christian art and symbolism -- Germany -- Renaissance, 1450-1600. Illustrated books -- Germany. Illustrated books -- Germany -- History -- 15th and 16th centuries Christian literature, German -- History and criticism.

BR315.S83 2001
Steinmetz, David Curtis.
Reformers in the wings: from Geiler von Kaysersberg to Theodore Beza/ David C. Steinmetz. New York: Oxford University Press 2000. xi, 200 p.
99-048788   270.6/092/2   0195130472
Reformation -- Biography.

BR325.B69513 1990
Brendler, Gerhard.
Martin Luther: theology and revolution/ Gerhard Brendler; translated by Claude R. Foster, Jr. New York: Oxford University Press, 1991. 383 p.
88-038881   284.1/092/4   0195051122
Luther, Martin, -- 1483-1546.Reformation -- Germany -- Biography.

BR325.O2713 1989
Oberman, Heiko Augustinus.
Luther: man between God and the Devil/ Heiko A. Oberman; translated by Eileen Walliser-Schwarzbart. New Haven: Yale University Press, c1989. xx, 380 p.
89-005747   284.1/092   0300037945
Luther, Martin, -- 1483-1546.Reformation -- Germany. Reformation -- Germany -- Biography. Germany -- Church history -- 16th century.

BR331.E5.W6
Luther, Martin, 1483-1546.
Reformation writings of Martin Luther/ translated with introduction and note from the definitive Weimar edition by Bertram Lee Woolf. New York: Philosophical Library, [c1953]
53-008176   208.1
Reformation.

BR331.E5 1989a
Luther, Martin, 1483-1546.
Martin Luther's basic theological writings/ edited by Timothy F. Lull; foreword by Jaroslav Pelikan. Minneapolis: Fortress Press, c1989. xix, 755 p.
89-034201   230/.41   0800623274
Theology -- Early works to 1800.

BR333.3.L88 2002
Luther on women: a sourcebook/ edited and translated by Susan C. Karant-Nunn, Merry E. Wiesner. Cambridge, UK; Cambridge University Press, 2002.
2002-031241   261.8/344/092 21   0521658845
Luther, Martin, 1483-1546. Women -- Religious aspects -- Christianity -- History of doctrines -- 16th

BR336.A33. 1962
Melanchthon, Philipp, 1497-1560.
Selected writings/ Translated by Charles Leander Hill. Edited by Elmer Ellsworth Flack and Lowell J. Satre. Minneapolis: Augsburg Pub. House, [1962] 190 p.
62-009092   230.41
Theology -- 16th century.

BR346.A24
Zwingli, Ulrich, 1484-1531.
Zwingli and Bullinger; selected translations with introductions and notes by G. W. Bromiley. Philadelphia, Westminster Press [1953] 364 p.
53-001533   270.6
Theology -- 16th century.

BR346.S74 1992
Stephens, W. P.
Zwingli: an introduction to his thought/ W.P. Stephens. Oxford [England]: Clarendon Press; 1992. xiii, 174 p.
91-038083   230/.42/092   0198263295
Zwingli, Ulrich, -- 1484-1531.

BR350.E7.R86 1989
Rummel, Erika, 1942-
Erasmus and his Catholic critics/ Erika Rummel. Nieuwkoop: De Graaf, 1989. 2 v.
89-208398   199/.492   9060044010
Erasmus, Desiderius, -- d. 1536 -- Adversaries.

BR350.S78.B72 1997
Brady, Thomas A.
The politics of the Reformation in Germany: Jacob Sturm (1489-1553) of Strasbourg/ Thomas A. Brady, Jr. Atlantic Highlands, N.J.: Humanities Press, 1997. xiii, 280 p.
96-026855   944/.38353028/092   0391040049
Sturm, Jakob, -- 1489-1553.Reformation -- France -- Strasbourg -- Biography. Reformation -- Germany. Germany -- Church history -- 16th century. Strasbourg (France) -- Biography. Strasbourg (France) -- Church history -- 16th century.

BR350.T8.M6
Mozley, James Frederic, 1887-
William Tyndale, by J. F. Mozley, M.A. New York, Alec R. Allenson, Inc., [1937]
38-004874   922.342
Tyndale, William, -- d. 1536.

BR355.P36.C47 1996
Chrisman, Miriam Usher.
Conflicting visions of reform: German lay propaganda pamphlets, 1519-1530/ Miriam Usher Chrisman. Atlantic Highlands, N.J.: Humanities Press, 1996. xiii, 288 p.
95-008888   274.3/06   039103944X
Reformation -- Germany -- Pamphlets. Laity -- Germany -- History -- 16th century. Laity -- Germany -- Religious life. Germany -- History -- 1517-1648 -- Pamphlets.

BR375.D52 1968
Dickens, A. G. 1910-
The Reformation in England, to the accession of Elizabeth I, edited by A.G. Dickens and Dorothy Carr. New York, St. Martin's Press, 1968 [c1967] vii, 167 p.
67-029568   270.6/0942
Reformation -- England -- Sources.

BR375.E53 1998
England's long reformation, 1500-1800/ edited by Nicholas Tyacke. London; UCL Press, 1998. xii, 347 p.
98-120310   274.2/06 21   1857287568
Reformation -- England. England -- Church history -- 16th century. England -- Church history -- 17th century. England -- Church history -- 18th century.

BR377.S64 1990
Solt, Leo F. 1921-
Church and state in early modern England, 1509-1640/ Leo F. Solt. New York: Oxford University Press, 1990. xii, 272 p.
89-015999   322/.1/0942   0195059794
Church and state -- England -- History -- 16th century. Church and state -- England -- History -- 17th century. England -- Church history -- 16th century. England -- Church history -- 17th century.

BR377.T48 1997
Thomas, Keith,
Religion and the decline of magic: studies in popular beliefs in sixteenth and seventeenth century England/ Keith Thomas. New York: Oxford University Press, 1997. xviii, 716 p.
97-002365   133/.0942/09031 21   0195213602
Occultism -- England -- History -- 16th century. Occultism -- England -- History -- 17th century. England -- Religious life and customs.

BR400.S29 1995
The Scandinavian Reformation: from evangelical movement to institutionalisation of reform/ edited by Ole Peter Grell. Cambridge; Cambridge University Press, 1995. xi, 218 p.
94-014116   274.8/06   0521441625
Reformation -- Scandinavia.Scandinavia -- Church history -- 16th century.

BR420.P7.F6 1971
Fox, Paul, b. 1874.
The reformation in Poland; some social and economic aspects. Westport, Conn., Greenwood Press [1971] viii, 153 p.
71-104272   943.8/02   0837139244
Reformation -- Poland.Poland -- Social conditions. Poland -- Economic conditions.

BR430.W7 1982
Wright, A. D.
The counter-reformation: Catholic Europe and the non-Christian world/ A.D. Wright. New York: St. Martin's Press, 1982. 344 p.
82-003210   270.6   0312170211
Counter-Reformation.

BR450.C48 1995
Church and state in the modern age: a documentary history/ edited by J.F. Maclear. New York: Oxford University Press, 1995. xviii, 510 p.
94-030051   322/.1/0903   0195086813
Church and state -- History -- 17th century -- Sources. Church and state -- History -- 18th century -- Sources. Church and state -- History -- 19th century -- Sources.

BR477.M34 1996
McLeod, Hugh.
Piety and poverty: working-class religion in Berlin, London, and New York, 1870-1914/ Hugh McLeod. New York: Holmes & Meier, 1996. xxx, 264 p.
94-036428   270.81/08/624   0841913560
Working class -- Germany -- Berlin -- Religious life. Working class -- England -- London -- Religious life. Working class -- New York (State) -- New York -- Religious life. Berlin (Germany) -- Religion -- 19th century. London (England) -- Religion -- 19th century. New York (N.Y.) -- Religion -- 19th century.

BR479.T5
Tillich, Paul, 1886-1965.
The religious situation/ by Paul Tillich; translated by H. Richard Niebuhr. New York: Meridian Books, 1956, c1932. 219 p.
56-009242
Sociology, Christian. Religious thought -- 20th century.

BR500 History — By region or country — Groups of countries not in a particular geographic area

BR500.L54 1992
Lippy, Charles H.
Christianity comes to the Americas, 1492-1776/ Charles H. Lippy, Robert Choquette, Stafford Poole. New York, N.Y.: Paragon House, 1992. xi, 400 p.
91-015675   277   1557782342
America -- Church history.

BR515-645 History — By region or country — America

BR515.C665 1995
Concise dictionary of Christianity in America/ coordinating editor, Daniel G. Reid; consulting editors, Robert D. Linder, Bruce L. Shelley, Harry S. Stout; Abridging editor, Craig A. Noll. Downers Grove, Ill.: InterVarsity Press, c1995. 378 p.
95-040444   277.3/003 20   0830814469
Christianity -- United States -- Dictionaries. United States -- Church history -- Dictionaries.

BR515.E53 1997
Encyclopedia of religious controversies in the United States/ edited by George H. Shriver and Bill J. Leonard. Westport, Conn.: Greenwood Press, 1997. xii, 542 p.
97-008781   273/.9/0973   031329691X
Church controversies -- Encyclopedias.United States -- Church history -- Encyclopedias. United States -- Religion -- Encyclopedias.

BR515.F56 1992
Finke, Roger, 1954-
The churching of America, 1776-1990: winners and losers in our religious economy/ Roger Finke and Rodney Stark. New Brunswick, N.J.: Rutgers University Press, c1992. xiv, 328 p.
91-045908   277.3/08   0813518377
Sociology, Christian -- United States.United States -- Church history.

BR515.H334 1992
Hammond, Phillip E.
The Protestant presence in twentieth-century America: religion and political culture/ Phillip E. Hammond. Albany: State University of New York Press, c1992. vii, 199 p.
91-031731   280/.4/09730904   0791411214
Protestant churches -- United States -- History -- 20th century. Christianity and politics -- History -- 20th century. Christianity and culture -- History -- 20th century. United States -- Church history -- 20th century.

BR515.M324 1984
Marty, Martin E.,
Pilgrims in their own land: 500 years of religion in America/ Martin E. Marty. 1st ed. Boston: Little, Brown, c1984. xii, 500 p.
84-000821   291/.0973 19   0316548677
United States -- Church history. United States -- Religion.

BR515.M35 1995
McDannell, Colleen.
Material Christianity: religion and popular culture in America/ Colleen McDannell. New Haven: Yale University Press, 1995. x, 312 p.
95-018066   246/.0973   0300064403
Religious articles -- United States. Christianity -- United States. United States -- Religious life and customs.

BR515.N49 2000
Newman, William M.
Atlas of American religion: the denominational era, 1776-1990/ William M. Newman, Peter L. Halvorson. Walnut Creek, CA: AltaMira Press, c2000. 176 p.
99-006320   277.3/08/0223   0761990577
Christian sects -- United States -- History.United States -- Church history. United States -- Religion -- History.

BR515.W648 1981
Women and religion in America/ [edited by] Rosemary Radford Ruether, Rosemary Skinner Keller. San Francisco: Harper & Row, c1981-c1986 v. 1-3
80-008346   280/.088042   0060668296
Women in Christianity -- United States -- History. Women in Judaism -- United States -- History. United States -- Religion.

BR516.B795 1997
The bully pulpit: the politics of Protestant clergy/ James L. Guth ... [et al.]. Lawrence, Kan.: University Press of Kansas, c1997. xi, 221 p.
97-035918   261.7/0973   0700608680
Protestant churches -- United States -- Clergy -- Political activity -- History -- 20th century. Christianity and politics -- United States -- History -- 20th century.

BR516.H2 1998
Hammond, Phillip E.
With liberty for all: freedom of religion in the United States/ Phillip E. Hammond. Louisville, Ky.: Westminster John Knox Press, c1998. xvi, 128 p.
97-028819   323.44/2/0973   0664257682
Freedom of religion -- United States.United States -- Religion.

BR516.H78 1988
Hutcheson, Richard G., 1921-
God in the White House: how religion has changed the modern presidency/ Richard G. Hutcheson, Jr. New York: Macmillan; c1988. xiii, 267 p.
88-002968   322/.1/0973   0025577603
Freedom of religion -- United States -- History -- 20th century. Presidents -- United States -- Religion. Church and state -- United States -- History -- 20th century. United States -- Church history -- 20th century.

BR516.K66 1996
Kramnick, Isaac.
The godless constitution: the case against religious correctness/ Isaac Kramnick and R. Laurence Moore. New York: Norton, c1996. 191 p.
95-020735   322/.1/0973   0393039617
Church and state -- United States. Freedom of religion -- United States.

BR516.N59 1998
Noonan, John Thomas, 1926-
The lustre of our country: the American experience of religious freedom/ John T. Noonan, Jr. Berkeley: University of California Press, c1998. 436 p.
97-049327   323.44/2/0973   0520209974
Freedom of religion -- United States -- History.United States -- Church history.

BR516.R34 1990
Religion and American politics: from the colonial period to the 1980s/ edited by Mark A. Noll. New York: Oxford University Press, 1990. xiii, 401 p.
88-037117   322/.1/0973   0195058801
Church and state -- United States -- History. Christianity and politics -- History. United States -- Religion. United States -- Politics and government.

BR516.R364 1994
Religion, public life, and the American polity/ edited by Luis E. Lugo. Knoxville: University of Tennessee Press, c1994. xvi, 269 p.
93-038721   200/.973   0870498304
Church and state -- United States. Freedom of religion -- United States. United States -- Politics and government. United States -- Religion.

BR516.5.C65 1997
Conkin, Paul Keith.
American originals: homemade varieties of Christianity/ Paul K. Conkin. Chapel Hill: University of North Carolina Press, c1997. xv, 336 p.
96-035270   280/.0973   0807823422
Christian sects -- United States.

BR516.5.M56 1998
Minority faiths and the American Protestant mainstream/ edited by Jonathan D. Sarna. Urbana: University of Illinois Press, c1998. x, 377 p.
97-004617   200/.973   0252022939
Protestant churches -- United States -- Influence. Christian sects -- United States. Religious pluralism -- United States. United States -- Religion.

BR517.S76 1993
Stone, Jon R.,
A guide to the end of the world: popular eschatology in America/ by Jon R. Stone. New York: Garland Pub., 1993. xi, 329 p.
92-035100   236/.9 20   0815313128
Millennialism -- United States -- History. Millennialism -- United States -- Bibliography. United States -- Church history. United States -- Church history -- Bibliography.

BR517.V47 1985
Vidich, Arthur J.
American sociology: worldly rejections of religion and their directions/ Arthur J. Vidich and Stanford M. Lyman. New Haven: Yale University Press, c1985. xiii, 380 p.
84-002268   301/.0973   0300030371
Sociology, Christian -- United States.

BR520.H323 1994
Hall, Timothy D., 1955-
Contested boundaries: itinerancy and the reshaping of the Colonial American religious world/ Timothy D. Hall. Durham: Duke University Press, 1994. x, 196 p.
94-017145   277.3/07   0822315114
Great Awakening. Itinerancy (Church polity) -- History of doctrines -- 18th century. Circuit riders -- United States -- History -- 18th century.

BR520.M36 1982
Marini, Stephen A., 1946-
Radical sects of revolutionary New England/ Stephen A. Marini. Cambridge, Mass.: Harvard University Press, 1982. 213 p.
81-006913   289   0674746252
Christian sects -- New England.New England -- Church history.

BR525.C37
Carter, Paul Allen, 1926-
The spiritual crisis of the gilded age [by] Paul A. Carter. DeKalb, Northern Illinois University Press, 1971. xiii, 295 p.
72-156938   209/.73   0875800262
United States -- Religion -- 19th century.

BR525.H37 1989
Hatch, Nathan O.
The democratization of American Christianity/ Nathan O. Hatch. New Haven: Yale University Press, c1989. xiv, 312 p.
89-005439   277.3/081   0300044704
Democracy -- Religious aspects -- Christianity -- History of doctrines -- 19th century. United States -- Church history -- 19th century.

BR525.R35 1998
Re-forming the center: American Protestantism, 1900 to the present/ edited by Douglas Jacobsen and William Vance Trollinger, Jr. Grand Rapids, Mich.: W.B. Eerdmans Pub., c1998. xvi, 492 p.
98-006059   280/.4/09730904   0802842984
Protestantism -- 20th century. Protestant churches -- United States -- History -- 20th century. Liberalism (Religion) -- Protestant churches -- History -- 20th century. United States -- Church history -- 20th century.

BR526.B47 1989
Between the times: the travail of the Protestant establishment in America, 1900-1960/ edited by William R. Hutchison. Cambridge [England]; Cambridge University Press, 1989. xvii, 322 p.
89-031134   280/.4/0973   0521361680
Protestant churches -- United States -- History -- 20th century. Sociology, Christian -- United States -- History -- 20th century. United States -- Church history -- 20th century.

BR526.B58 1992
Boyer, Paul S.
When time shall be no more: prophecy belief in modern American culture/ Paul Boyer. Cambridge, Mass.: Belknap Press of Harvard University Press, 1992. xiv, 468 p.
91-045302   231.7/45/0973   067495128X
Millennialism -- United States. Twentieth century -- Forecasts. Prophecy (Christianity) United States -- Religious life and customs. United States -- Religion -- 1945-

BR526.F33 1988
Falling from the faith: causes and consequences of religious apostasy/ edited by David G. Bromley. Newbury Park, Calif.: Sage Publications, c1988. 266 p.
87-019281   262/.8   0803931883
Ex-church members -- United States. Apostasy -- Christianity. Religion and sociology -- United States. United States -- Church history -- 20th century.

BR526.G63 1995
God at the grass roots: the Christian right in the 1994 elections/ edited by Mark J. Rozell and Clyde Wilcox. Lanham, Md.: Rowman & Littlefield Publishers, Inc., c1995. ix, 274 p.
95-030671   324.973/0929/0882   0847680975
Conservatism -- Religious aspects -- Christianity -- History -- 20th century. Elections -- United States. United States -- Politics and government -- 1993- United States -- Church history -- 20th century.

BR526.H25 1992
Hammond, Phillip E.
Religion and personal autonomy: the third disestablishment in America/ Phillip E. Hammond. Columbia, SC: University of South Carolina Press, c1992. xv, 219 p.
91-046356   261.8/34/0973   0872498204
Sociology, Christian -- United States -- History -- 20th century. United States -- Religion -- 1960-

BR526.H64 1994
Hoge, Dean R., 1937-
Vanishing boundaries: the religion of mainline Protestant baby boomers/ Dean R. Hoge, Benton Johnson, Donald A. Luidens. Louisville, Ky.: Westminster/John Knox Press, c1994. viii, 254 p.
93-031968   280/.4/097309045   0664254926
Liberalism (Religion) -- Protestant churches. Protestant churches -- United States -- History -- 20th century. Baby boom generation -- Religious life. United States -- Church history -- 20th century.

BR526.H83 1994
Hudnut-Beumler, James David.
Looking for God in the suburbs: the religion of the American dream and its critics, 1945-1965/ James Hudnut-Beumler. New Brunswick, N.J.: Rutgers University Press, c1994. xi, 229 p.
93-041778   277.3/0825   0813520835
Religion and culture -- United States. Suburban churches -- United States. United States -- Church history -- 20th century. United States -- Religion -- 1945-1960. United States -- Religion -- 1960-

BR526.M27 2000
McCarraher, Eugene.
Christian critics: religion and the impasse in modern American social thought/ Eugene McCarraher. Ithaca, NY: Cornell University Press, 2000. xi, 241 p.
00-037679   261.8/0973/0904   0801434734
United States -- Church history -- 20th century.

BR526.M35
Marty, Martin E.,
The new shape of American religion. New York, Harper [1959] 180 p.
59-010336   209.73
Christianity -- United States. Protestant churches -- United States.

BR526.M554 1997
Miller, Donald E. 1946-
Reinventing American Protestantism: Christianity in the new millennium/ Donald E. Miller. Berkeley, Calif.: University of California Press, c1997. ix, 253 p.
96-035140   280/.4/097301   0520209389
Protestant churches -- United States -- Forecasting. Calvary Chapel movement. Protestant churches -- California, Southern -- Case studies. California, Southern -- Religious life and customs. United States -- Church history -- 20th century.

BR526.O57 1996
Oldfield, Duane Murray.
The right and the righteous: the Christian Right confronts the Republican Party/ Duane Murray Oldfield. Lanham: Rowman & Littlefield, c1996. x, 281 p.
96-014647   322/.1/097309045   0847681904
Christianity and politics -- United States -- History -- 20th century. Conservatism -- Religious aspects -- Christianity -- History -- 20th century. Conservatism -- United States -- History -- 20th century. United States -- Politics and government -- 1945-1989. United States -- Politics and government -- 1989- United States -- Church history -- 20th century.

BR526.U88 1995
Utter, Glenn H.
The religious right: a reference handbook/ Glenn H. Utter and John W. Storey. Santa Barbara, Calif.: ABC-CLIO, c1995. xiv, 298 p.
95-044344   277.3/0825   0874367786
Conservatism -- Religious aspects -- Christianity -- History -- 20th century. Conservatism -- Religious aspects -- Christianity -- History -- 20th century -- Study and teaching. Christianity and politics -- History -- 20th century. United States -- Politics and government -- 20th century. United States -- Politics and government -- 20th century -- Study and teaching. United States -- Church history -- 20th century.

BR526.W33 1997
Watson, Justin, 1957-
The Christian Coalition: dreams of restoration, demands for recognition/ Justin Watson. New York: St. Martin's Press, 1997. 292 p.
97-011578   320.5/5/0973   0312172362
Conservatism -- Religious aspects -- Christianity -- History -- 20th century. Conservatism -- United States -- History -- 20th century. Evangelicalism -- Political aspects -- United States. United States -- Church history -- 20th century. United States -- Politics and government -- 1989-

BR526.W53 1996
Wilcox, Clyde, 1953-
Onward Christian soldiers?: the religious right in American politics/ Clyde Wilcox. Boulder, Colo.: Westview Press, 1996. xii, 180 p.
96-022561　261.7/0973　0813326966
　Christianity and politics -- United States -- History -- 20th century. Conservatism -- Religious aspects -- Christianity -- History -- 20th century. Conservatism -- United States -- History -- 20th century. United States -- Politics and government -- 1945-1989. United States -- Politics and government -- 1989- United States -- Church history -- 20th century.

BR526.W58 1993
Witten, Marsha Grace.
All is forgiven: the secular message in American Protestantism/ Marsha G. Witten. Princeton, N.J.: Princeton University Press, c1993. ix, 179 p.
93-004048　251/.00973　0691032807
　Protestant churches -- United States -- Doctrines -- History -- 20th century. Secularization (Theology) -- History of doctrines -- 19th century. Preaching -- United States -- History -- 20th century. United States -- Church history -- 20th century.

BR526.W65 1997
Wojcik, Daniel.
The end of the world as we know it: faith, fatalism, and apocalypse in America/ Daniel Wojcik. New York: New York University Press, c1997. ix, 281 p.
97-004781　001.9　0814792839
　Millennialism -- United States -- History -- 20th century. End of the world -- History of doctrines -- 20th century. United States -- Religion -- 1960-

BR526.W88 1993
Wuthnow, Robert.
Christianity in the twenty-first century: reflections on the challenges ahead/ Robert Wuthnow. New York: Oxford University Press, 1993. viii, 251 p.
92-028689　277.3/08　0195079574
　Christianity -- United States. Twenty-first century -- Forecasts.

BR535.H47 1997
Heyrman, Christine Leigh.
Southern cross: the beginnings of the Bible Belt/ Christine Leigh Heyrman. New York: A.A. Knopf: 1997. xi, 336 p.
97-006354　277.5/081　0679446389
　Evangelicalism -- Southern States -- History.Southern States -- Church history.

BR535.H5 1999
Hill, Samuel S.
Southern churches in crisis revisited/ Samuel S. Hill. Tuscaloosa: University of Alabama Press, 1999. lxix, 234 p.
98-058067　280/.4/0975　0817309799
　Protestant churches -- Southern States.Southern States -- Church history.

BR535.M38 1995
McCauley, Deborah Vansau, 1954-
Appalachian mountain religion: a history/ Deborah Vansau McCauley. Urbana: University of Illinois Press, c1995. xiv, 551 p.
94-018247　277.4/08　0252021290
　Christian sects -- Appalachian Region -- History.Appalachian Region -- Religious life and customs.

BR535.S76 1998
Stowell, Daniel W.
Rebuilding Zion: the religious reconstruction of the South, 1863-1877/ Daniel W. Stowell. New York: Oxford University Press, 1998. viii, 278 p.
97-010589　277.5/081　0195101944
　Reconstruction.United States -- History -- Civil War, 1861-1865 -- Religious aspects -- Protestant churches. Southern States -- Church history -- 19th century.

BR555.M4 P47 1991
Pestana, Carla Gardina.
Quakers and Baptists in colonial Massachusetts/ Carla Gardina Pestana. Cambridge [England]; Cambridge University Press, 1991. xii, 197 p.
90-028973　286/.13744 21　0521411114
　Society of Friends -- Massachusetts -- History. Baptists -- Massachusetts -- History. Church and state -- Massachusetts -- History. Massachusetts -- Church history. Massachusetts -- History -- Colonial period, ca. 1600-1775.

BR560.P86
Schantz, Mark S. 1955-
Piety in Providence: class dimensions of religious experience in antebellum Rhode Island/ Mark S. Schantz. Ithaca: Cornell University Press, 2000. xiii, 280 p.
00-022674　274.5/2081　0801429528
　Religion and social status -- Rhode Island -- Providence -- History -- 19th century.Providence (R.I.) -- Church history -- 19th century.

BR563.C45.Y36 1999
Yang, Fenggang.
Chinese Christians in America: conversion, assimilation, and adhesive identities/ Fenggang Yang. University Park, Pa.: Pennsylvania State University Press, c1999. x, 238 p.
98-037365　280/.4/0899510753　0271019166
　Chinese Americans -- Religion -- Case studies.

BR563.E27.W55 1996
Williams, Raymond Brady.
Christian pluralism in the United States: the Indian immigrant experience/ by Raymond Brady Williams. New York: Cambridge University Press, 1996. xii, 303 p.
95-051450　277.3/082/089914　0521570166
　East Indians -- United States -- Religion.United States -- Church history -- 20th century. India -- Emigration and immigration -- Religious aspects -- Christianity. United States -- Emigration and immigration -- Religious aspects -- Christianity.

BR563.H57.D53 1998
Diaz-Stevens, Ana Maria, 1942-
Recognizing the Latino resurgence in U.S. religion: the Emmaus papadigm/ Ana Maria Diaz-Stevens, Anthony M. Stevens-Arroyo. Boulder, Colo.: Westview Press, 1998. xxi, 272 p.
97-035173　277.3/0829/08968　0813325099
　Hispanic Americans -- Religion.

BR563.H57.I82 1993
Isasi-Diaz, Ada Maria.
En la lucha = In the struggle: a Hispanic women's liberation theology/ Ada Maria Isasi-Diaz. Minneapolis: Fortress Press, c1993. xxi, 226 p.
93-009220　230/.082　0800626109
　Hispanic American women -- Religious life. Mujerista theology. Christianity and culture.

BR563.N4 A354 1994
African-American Christianity: essays in history/ edited by Paul E. Johnson. Berkeley: University of California Press, c1994. xi, 189 p.
93-003895　277.3/0089/96073　20 0520075943
　African Americans -- Religion. African American churches -- History. United States -- Religion.

BR563.N4.A359 1999
African American religious history: a documentary witness/ [edited by] Milton C. Sernett. Durham, NC: Duke University Press, 1999. x, 595 p.
99-016287　200/.89/96073　0822324261
　Afro-Americans -- Religion.

BR563.N4.B34 1992
Baer, Hans A., 1944-
African-American religion in the twentieth century: varieties of protest and accommodation/ Hans A. Baer and Merrill Singer. Knoxville: University of Tennessee Press, c1992. xxiii, 265 p.
91-040209　277.3/082/08996073　0870497464
　Afro-Americans -- Religion.

BR563.N4.B573 1998
Black religion after the Million Man March: voices on the future/ edited by Garth Kasimu Baker-Fletcher. Maryknoll, N.Y.: Orbis Books, c1998. vi, 170 p.
97-032791　277.3/0829/08996073 1570751595
　Afro-American men -- Religious life. Afro-Americans -- Religion.

BR563.N4.B574 1998
Black religious leadership from the slave community to the Million Man March: flames of fire/ edited by Felton O. Best. Lewiston, NY: Edwin Mellen Press, c1998. 262 p.
98-007594　277.3/08/08996073　0773483454
　Afro-Americans -- Religion. Afro-American clergy -- History. Afro-Americans -- Social conditions.

BR563.N4.B67 2001
Bridges, Flora Wilson, 1948-
Resurrection song: African-American spirituality/ Flora Wilson Bridges. Maryknoll, N.Y.: Orbis Books, c2001. xi, 195 p.
00-068808 200/.89/96073 1570753598
African Americans -- Religion. Spirituality -- United States.

BR563.N4 D57 1995
Directory of African American religious bodies: a compendium by the Howard University School of Divinity/ edited by Wardell J. Payne; prepared under the auspices of the Research Center on Black Religious Bodies, Howard University School of Divinity, Washington, D.C. 2nd ed. Washington, D.C.: Howard University Press, 1995. xxiv, 382 p.
95-010152 280/.089/96073 20 0882581856
African American churches -- Directories. African Americans -- Religion. African American scholars -- Directories. Religious institutions -- United States -- Directories.

BR563.N4.E53 1993
Encyclopedia of African American religions/ edited by Larry G. Murphy, J. Gordon Melton, Gary L. Ward. New York: Garland Pub., 1993. lxxvi, 926 p.
93-007224 200/.89/96073 0815305001
Afro-Americans -- Religion -- Encyclopedias. Afro-American churches -- Encyclopedias. United States -- Religion -- Encyclopedias.

BR563.N4.F74 1998
Frey, Sylvia R., 1935-
Come shouting to Zion: African American Protestantism in the American South and British Caribbean to 1830/ Sylvia R. Frey and Betty Wood. Chapel Hill: University of North Carolina Press, c1998. xiv, 285 p.
97-021477 277.5/07/08996073 0807823759
Afro-Americans -- Southern States -- Religion. Blacks -- Caribbean Area -- Religion.

BR563.N4.G54 2001
Gilkes, Cheryl.
If it wasn't for the women--: Black women's experience and womanist culture in church and community/ Cheryl Townsend Gilkes. Maryknoll, N.Y.: Orbis Books, c2001. viii, 253 p.
00-047863 277.3/0082 1570753431
African American women -- Religious life. African American women political activists. Womanist theology.

BR563.N4.H56 2000
Hinson, Glenn.
Fire in my bones: transcendence and the Holy Spirit in African American gospel/ Glenn Hinson in collaboration with saints from a host of churches; photographs by Roland L. Freeman. Philadelphia, Pa.: University of Pennsylvania Press, c2000. x, 408 p.
99-036613 306.6/64/008996073 0812235282
Afro-American public worship. Experience (Religion) Afro-Americans -- Religion.

BR563.N4.M37 2000
McQueen, Clyde, 1926-
Black churches in Texas: a guide to historic congregations/ Clyde McQueen; introduction by William E. Montgomery. College Station: Texas A&M University Press, c2000. xxiv, 253 p.
99-045373 277.64/08/08996073 0890969027
Afro-American churches -- Texas -- History.

BR563.N4.S474 1997
Sernett, Milton C., 1942-
Bound for the promised land: African American religion and the great migration/ Milton C. Sernett. Durham, NC: Duke University Press, 1997. x, 345 p.
97-006537   277.3/0821/08996073
0822319845
Afro-Americans -- Religion. Afro-Americans -- Migrations -- History -- 20th century. Migration, Internal -- United States -- History -- 20th century. United States -- Church history -- 20th century.

BR563.N4.S79 1998
The stones that the builders rejected: the development of ethical leadership from the Black church tradition/ edited and with an introduction by Walter Earl Fluker. Harrisburg, Pa.: Trinity Press, c1998. xii, 115 p.
97-049922   277.3/0829/08996073
1563382350
Afro-Americans -- Religion. Leadership -- Religious aspects. Leadership -- Moral and ethical aspects -- United States.

BR563.N4.S97 1989
Swift, David Everett, 1914-
Black prophets of justice: activist clergy before the Civil War/ David E. Swift. Baton Rouge: Louisiana State University Press, c1989. xv, 384 p.
88-030327 285/.108996073 0807114618
Afro-American clergy -- Biography. Afro-American clergy -- Political activity. Afro-American Presbyterians -- Biography. United States -- Race relations.

BR563.N4.T39 1998
Terrell, JoAnne Marie.
Power in the blood?: the cross in the African American experience/ JoAnne Marie Terrell. Maryknoll, N.Y.: Orbis Books, c1998. xi, 187 p.
98-027278 232/.4/08996073 1570752168
Afro-Americans -- Religion. Holy cross -- History of doctrines. Womanist theology.

BR600.C26 1990
Candelaria, Michael R.
Popular religion and liberation: the dilemma of liberation theology/ Michael R. Candelaria. Albany: State University of New York Press, c1990. xiv, 194 p.
89-004573 282/.8 0791402290
Liberation theology. Latin America -- Religious life and customs.

BR600.M4 1966
Mecham, John Lloyd, 1893-
Church and state in Latin America; a history of politicoecclesiastical relations, by J. Lloyd Mecham. Chapel Hill, University of North Carolina Press [1966] viii, 465 p.
66-015511 261.7098
Church and state -- Latin America.

BR615.T65.V36 1998
Vanderwood, Paul J.
The power of God against the guns of government: religious upheaval in Mexico at the turn of the nineteenth century/ Paul J. Vanderwood. Stanford, Calif.: Stanford University Press, c1998. xi, 409 p.
97-032506 972/.16 0804730385
Urrea, Teresa. Government, Resistance to -- Mexico -- Tomochic -- History -- 19th century. Church and state -- Mexico -- Tomochic. Tomochic (Mexico) -- History -- 19th century. Tomochic (Mexico) -- Religion. Tomochic (Mexico) -- Church history -- 19th century.

BR620.B48 1994
Berryman, Phillip.
Stubborn hope: religion, politics, and revolution in Central America/ Phillip Berryman. Maryknoll, N.Y.: Orbis Books; c1994. viii, 276 p.
94-002253 277.28/0828 0883449625
Christians -- Central America -- Political activity. Church and social problems -- Central America -- History -- 20th century. Social conflict -- Central America -- History -- 20th century. Central America -- Politics and government -- 1979-

BR625.N5.L35 1988
Lancaster, Roger N.
Thanks to God and the revolution: popular religion and class consciousness in the new Nicaragua/ Roger N. Lancaster. New York: Columbia University Press, 1988. xxi, 244 p.
88-004960 277.285/082 0231067305
Christianity -- Nicaragua. Social classes -- Nicaragua -- History -- 20th century. Communism and religion -- History -- 20th century. Nicaragua -- Politics and government -- 1979-1990.

BR645.C9.K57 1989
Kirk, John M., 1951-
Between God and the party: religion and politics in revolutionary Cuba/ John M. Kirk. Tampa: University of South Florida Press, c1989. xxi, 231 p.
87-016006 322/.1 081300909X
Church and state -- Cuba -- History -- 20th century. Cuba -- Church history. Cuba -- Politics and government -- 1959-

BR735-1027 History —
By region or country — Europe

BR735.M66 1984
Monter, E. William.
Ritual, myth, and magic in early modern Europe/ William Monter. Athens, Ohio: Ohio University Press, 1984, c1983. 184 p.
83-043136　274/.06　0821407627
Superstition -- History. Religious tolerance -- Europe -- History. Europe -- Church history.

BR738.6.R26 1987
Ramet, Sabrina P., 1949-
Cross and commissar: the politics of religion in Eastern Europe and the USSR/ Pedro Ramet. Bloomington: Indiana University Press, c1987. x, 244 p.
86-046165　322/.1/0947　0253315751
Church and state -- Communist countries -- History. Church and state -- Soviet Union -- History -- 20th century. Communism and Christianity -- Europe, Eastern -- History -- 20th century. Europe, Eastern -- Church history. Soviet Union -- Church history.

BR742.D84 1992
Duffy, Eamon.
The stripping of the altars: traditional religion in England, c.1400-c.1580/ Eamon Duffy. New Haven, CT: Yale University Press, 1992. xii, 654 p.
92-050579　274.2/05　0300053428
Reformation -- England. Anglican Communion -- England -- History -- 16th century. England -- Religious life and customs. England -- Church history -- 16th century.

BR744.N67
Norman, Edward R.
Church and society in England 1770-1970: a historical study/ by E. R. Norman. Oxford: Clarendon Press, 1976. 507 p.
76-377182　261　0198264356
Sociology, Christian -- England -- History.

BR745.H37 1993
Harvey, Margaret
England, Rome, and the papacy, 1417-1464: the study of a relationship/ Margaret Harvey. Manchester; Manchester University Press; c1993. viii, 295 p.
92-029774　282/.42/09024　0719034590
Church history -- Middle Ages, 600-1500. Papacy -- History. England -- Church history -- 1066-1485.

BR750.S83 1989
Swanson, R. N.
Church and society in late medieval England/ R.N. Swanson. Oxford, UK; Blackwell, 1989. xii, 427 p.
88-031863　282/.42　0631146598
Church history -- Middle Ages, 600-1500. Social history -- Medieval, 500-1500. England -- Church history -- 1066-1485. England -- Social conditions -- 1066-1485.

BR754.C6.G57 1989
Gleason, John B.
John Colet/ John B. Gleason. Berkeley: University of California Press, c1989. xiii, 416 p.
88-032907　230/.2/0924　0520065107
Colet, John, -- 1467?-1519.

BR755.G54
Gilbert, Alan D.
Religion and society in industrial England: church, chapel, and social change, 1740-1914/ Alan D. Gilbert. London; Longman, 1976. ix, 251 p.
76-360904　301.5/8/0942　0582483220
Sociology, Christian -- England.England -- Religion.

BR756.D665 1994
Doran, Susan.
Elizabeth I and religion, 1558-1603/ Susan Doran. London; Routledge, 1994. xiv, 73 p.
93-019320　274.2/06 20　0415073529
Elizabeth I, Queen of England, 1533-1603 -- Religion. Reformation -- England. England -- Church history -- 16th century. England -- Church history -- 17th century. Great Britain -- History -- Elizabeth, 1558-1603.

BR756.M45 1998
Marsh, Christopher, 1964-
Popular religion in sixteenth-century England: holding their peace/ Christopher Marsh. New York: St. Martin's Press, 1998. viii, 258 p.
97-030787　274.2/06　0312210930
England -- Religious life and customs. England -- Church history -- 16th century.

BR756.M55 1995
Milton, Anthony.
Catholic and Reformed: the Roman and Protestant churches in English Protestant thought, 1600-1640/ Anthony Milton. Cambridge [England]; Cambridge University Press, 1995. xvi, 599 p.
93-046984　274.2/06　0521401410
Anglican Communion -- Relations -- Catholic Church. Anglican Communion -- Relations -- Reformed Church. England -- Church history -- 17th century.

BR758.B76 1990
Brown, Richard, 1948-
Church and state in modern Britain, 1700-1850/ Richard Brown. London [England]; Routledge, 1991. xiii, 571 p.
90-031958　941.07　0415011221
Church and state -- Great Britain -- History -- 18th century. Church and state -- Great Britain -- History -- 19th century. Great Britain -- Church history -- 18th century. Great Britain -- Politics and government -- 18th century. Great Britain -- Politics and government -- 19th century.

BR759.M27 1987
Machin, G. I. T.
Politics and the churches in Great Britain, 1869 to 1921/ G.I.T. Machin. Oxford [Oxfordshire]: Clarendon Press; 1987. x, 376 p.
87-001620　322/.1/0941　0198201060
Church and state -- Great Britain -- History -- 19th century. Church and state -- Great Britain -- History -- 20th century. Great Britain -- Church history -- 19th century. Great Britain -- Church history -- 20th century. Great Britain -- Politics and government -- 1837-1901.

BR759.M37 1996
McLeod, Hugh.
Religion and society in England, 1850-1914/ Hugh McLeod. New York: St. Martin's Press, 1996. viii, 267 p.
95-031702　274.2/08　0312157983
Christianity -- England -- 19th century. Christianity -- England -- 20th century. England -- Social conditions.

BR759.P388 1992
Paz, D. G.
Popular anti-Catholicism in Mid-Victorian England/ D.G. Paz. Stanford, Calif.: Stanford University Press, 1992. 332 p.
92-026730　305.6/2042/09034　0804719845
Anti-Catholicism -- England -- History -- 19th century.England -- Church history -- 19th century.

BR763.K46.Y38 1994
Yates, Nigel.
Religion and society in Kent, 1640-1914/ Nigel Yates, Robert Hume, Paul Hastings. Woodbridge, Suffolk, UK; Boydell Press; 1994. 244 p.
94-014000　942.2/3　0851155561
Church and state -- England -- Kent -- History.Kent (England) -- Social conditions. Kent (England) -- Church history.

BR828.A4.M37 1996
Marnef, Guido.
Antwerp in the age of Reformation: underground Protestantism in a commercial metropolis, 1550-1577/ Guido Marnef; translated by J.C. Grayson. Baltimore: Johns Hopkins University Press, 1996. xv, 304 p.
95-004836　274.93/22206　0801851696
Reformation -- Belgium -- Antwerp.Antwerp (Belgium) -- Church history -- 16th century.

BR856.B398 1996
Bergen, Doris L.
Twisted cross: the German Christian movement in the Third Reich/ by Doris L. Bergen. Chapel Hill: University of North Carolina Press, c1996. xiii, 341 p.
95-017954　261.7/0943/09043　0807845604
German-Christian movement -- History.Germany -- Church history -- 1933-1945.

BR874.M55 2000
Miller, Maureen C. 1959-
The bishop's palace: architecture and authority in medieval Italy/ Maureen C. Miller. Ithaca, N.Y.: Cornell University Press, 2000. xv, 307 p.
00-022380 262/.12245/0902 0801435358
Bishops -- Dwellings -- Italy. Palaces -- Italy. Italy -- Church history -- 476-1400.

BR877.F74.G5613
Ginzburg, Carlo.
The cheese and the worms: the cosmos of a sixteenth-century miller/ Carlo Ginzburg; translated by John and Anne Tedeschi. Baltimore: Johns Hopkins University Press, 1980. xxvii, 177 p.
79-003654 273/.6 0801823366
Scandella, Domenico, -- 1532-1601.Heretics, Christian -- Italy -- Udine (Province) Heresies, Christian -- History -- Modern period, 1500- Peasantry -- Italy -- Udine (Province) -- History -- 16th century. Udine (Italy: Province) -- Religious life and customs. Udine (Italy: Province) -- Civilization. Udine (Italy: Province) -- Church history.

BR932.C4513
Chyĕzĭhevs§kyæi, Dmytro,
Russian intellectual history/ Dmitrij Tschizewskij; translated by John C. Osborne; edited by Martin P. Rice. Ann Arbor: Ardis, c1978. 283 p.
78-110675 001.2/0947 0882332198
Soviet Union -- Religion. Soviet Union -- Church history. Soviet Union -- Intellectual life.

BR936.C49 1989
Christianity and Russian culture in Soviet society/ edited by Nicolai N. Petro. Boulder: Westview Press, 1989. xi, 244 p.
89-049774 274.7/.082 0813377420
Christianity -- Soviet Union. Christianity and culture. Church and state -- Soviet Union -- History. Soviet Union -- Church history. Soviet Union -- Civilization.

BR952.K58132000
Kloczowski, Jerzy.
A history of Polish Christianity/ Jerzy Kloczowski. Cambridge, UK; Cambridge University Press, 2000. xxxviii, 385 p.
99-056878 274.38 0521364299
Poland -- Church history.

BR987.M67.B83 1996
Buckser, Andrew, 1964-
Communities of faith: sectarianism, identity, and social change on a Danish island/ Andrew Buckser. Providence: Berghahn Books, 1996. xxiv, 264 p.
96-025652 274.89/5 1571810420
Christian sects -- Denmark -- Mors. Sociology, Christian -- Denmark -- Mors. Secularism. Mors (Denmark) Mors (Denmark) -- Church history.

BR1024.S79 2000
Stocking, Rachel L.
Bishops, councils, and consensus in the Visigothic Kingdom, 589-633/ Rachel L. Stocking. Ann Arbor: University of Michigan Press, c2000. viii, 217 p.
99-050877 274.6/02 0472111337
Church and state -- Spain -- History -- To 1500. Visigoths -- Spain -- History. Spain -- Church history. Spain -- History -- Gothic period, 414-711.

BR1065-1307 History — By region or country — Asia. The Orient

BR1065.D52 2001
A dictionary of Asian christianity/ edited by Scott Sunquist; associate editors, David Wu Chu Sing and John Chew Hiang Chea. Grand Rapids, MI: W.B. Eerdmans, 2001. xliii, 937 p.
2001-033224 275/.003 080283776X
Christianity -- Asia -- Dictionaries.

BR1065.M63 1992
Moffett, Samuel H.
A history of Christianity in Asia/ Samuel Hugh Moffett. [San Francisco, Calif.]: HarperSanFrancisco, [c1992-] v. 1
91-055085 275 0060657790
Asia -- Church history.

BR1067.A7 C74 1991
Cragg, Kenneth.
The Arab Christian: a history in the Middle East/ Kenneth Cragg. 1st ed. Louisville, Ky.: Westminster/John Knox Press, c1991. 336 p.
91-015206 275.6/0089/927 20 0664219454
Christians -- Arab countries -- History. Arabs -- Religion. Arab countries -- Church history.

BR1287.D86 2001
Dunch, Ryan, 1962-
Fuzhou Protestants and the making of a modern China, 1857-1927/ Ryan Dunch. New Haven: Yale University Press, c2001. xxi, 293 p.
00-011311 280/.4/0951245 0300080506
Protestant churches -- China -- Fuzhou Region (Fujian Sheng) -- History -- 19th century. Christianity and politics -- China -- Fuzhou Region (Fujian Sheng) -- History -- 19th century. Protestant churches -- China -- Fuzhou Region (Fujian Sheng) -- History -- 20th century. Fuzhou Region (Fujian Sheng, China) -- Church history -- 19th century. Fuzhou Region (Fujian Sheng, China) -- Church history -- 20th century.

BR1305.J37 1996
Japan and Christianity: impacts and responses/ edited by John Breen and Mark Williams. Houndmills, Basingstoke [England]: Macmillan Press; 1996. xiii, 189 p.
95-017862 275.2 0333589386
Japan -- Church history. Japan -- Civilization -- Christian influences.

BR1307.M85 1998
Mullins, Mark.
Christianity made in Japan: a study of indigenous movements/ Mark R. Mullins. Honolulu: University of Hawai'i Press, c1998. x, 277 p.
98-035083 275.2 0824821149
Christian sects -- Japan. Christianity and culture -- Japan. Japan -- Church history.

BR1360-1450 History — By region or country — Africa

BR1360.A526
African Christianity: patterns of religious continuity/ edited by George Bond, Walton Johnson, Sheila S. Walker. New York: Academic Press, c1979. xvi, 175 p.
79-051668 289.9 0121134504
Christianity -- Africa -- Addresses, essays, lectures. Christian sects -- Africa -- Addresses, essays, lectures. Africa -- Church history -- Addresses, essays, lectures.

BR1360.I75 1995
Isichei, Elizabeth Allo.
A history of Christianity in Africa: from antiquity to the present/ Elizabeth Isichei. Grand Rapids, Mich.: W.B. Eerdmans Pub. Co.; 1995. xi, 420 p.
94-046617 276 0802808433
Christianity -- Africa.Africa -- Church history.

BR1367.H94.M39 1999
Maxwell, David
Christians and chiefs in Zimbabwe: a social history of the Hwesa people/ David Maxwell. Westport, Conn.: Praeger, 1999. x, 291 p.
98-054355 276.891 0275966267
Hwesa (African people) -- Religion. Christianity and culture -- Zimbabwe -- Hwesaland -- History. Hwesaland (Zimbabwe) -- Kings and rulers -- Religious aspects. Hwesaland (Zimbabwe) -- Church history.

BR1430.G54 1998
Gifford, Paul, 1944-
African Christianity: its public role/ Paul Gifford. Bloomington: Indiana University Press, 1998. viii, 368 p.
98-005333 276.7/0829 0253334179
Christianity -- Africa, Sub-Saharan. Church and state -- Africa, Sub-Saharan

BR1430.W45 1996
Weigert, Stephen L.
Traditional religion and guerrilla warfare in modern Africa/ Stephen L. Weigert. Houndmills, Basingstoke, Hampshire: Macmillan Press; 1996. ix, 151 p.
95-020245 960.3/2 0333637984
Guerrilla warfare -- Africa, Sub-Saharan.Africa, Sub-Saharan -- History -- 1884-1960 Africa, Sub-Saharan -- History -- 1960- Africa, Sub-Saharan -- Religion.

BR1440.E27 1999
East African expressions of Christianity/ edited by Thomas Spear & Isaria N. Kimambo. Oxford: James Currey; 1999. xi, 340 p.
98-032021   276.76   0852557574
Christianity -- Africa, East.

BR1450.B67 1998
Borer, Tristan Anne, 1965-
Challenging the state: churches as political actors in South Africa, 1980-1994/ Tristan Anne Borer. Notre Dame, Ind.: University of Notre Dame Press, c1998. xx, 289 p.
98-018608   261.7/0968/09048   0268008299
Christianity and politics -- South Africa -- History -- 20th century.South Africa -- Church history -- 20th century. South Africa -- Politics and government -- 1978-1989. South Africa -- Politics and government -- 1989-1994.

BR1450.G73 1995
Graybill, Lyn S.
Religion and resistance politics in South Africa/ Lyn S.Graybill. Westport, Conn.: Praeger, 1995. 157 p.
95-013895   322/.1/0968   0275951413
Religion and politics -- South Africa. South Africa -- Politics and government -- 20th century. Blacks -- South Africa -- Politics and government.

BR1603 Persecution. Martyrs — History — Early Christians under the Roman Empire

BR1603.A1 M87
Musurillo, Herbert,
The acts of the Christian martyrs; introduction, texts and   translations by Herbert Musurillo. Oxford, Clarendon Press, 1972. lxxiii, 379 p.
72-177389   272/.1/0922 B   0198268068
Martyrs. Persecution -- History -- Early church, ca. 30-600.

BR1640 Movements transcending geographical and denominational lines and theological disciplines — Evangelicalism — Periodicals. Societies, etc.

BR1640.B35 2002
Balmer, Randall Herbert.
The encyclopedia of evangelicalism/ Randall Balmer. 1st ed. Louisville, Ky.: Westminster John Knox Press, c2002. viii, 654 p.
2001-026902   270.8/2/03 21   0664224091
Evangelicalism   --   Encyclopedias. Evangelicalism   --   United   States   -- Encyclopedias.

BR1640.S27 2000
Sargeant, Kimon Howland, 1964-
Seeker churches: promoting traditional religion in a nontraditional way/ Kimon Howland Sargeant. cNew Brunswick, N.J.: Rutgers University Press, c2000. xi, 252 p.
99-049852   280/.4/097309049   0813527864
Evangelicalism -- United States. Church renewal.

BR1641 Movements transcending geographical and denominational lines and theological disciplines — Evangelicalism — Relations with other religions, denominations, etc.

BR1641.J83.R38 1991
Rausch, David A.
Communities in conflict: evangelicals and Jews/ David A. Rausch. Philadelphia: Trinity Press International, 1991. x, 204 p.
91-024449   261.2/6   1563380293
Evangelicalism -- Relations -- Judaism. Judaism -- Relations -- Evangelicalism. United States -- Religion -- 1960-

BR1642 Movements transcending geographical and denominational lines and theological disciplines — Evangelicalism — By region or country, A-Z

BR1642.A357
Freston, Paul.
Evangelicals and politics in Asia, Africa, and Latin America/ Paul Freston. Cambridge; Cambridge University Press, 2001. xiii, 344 p.
00-063098   322/.1/0882044   0521800412
Evangelicalism -- Political aspects -- Africa, Sub-Saharan. Christianity and politics -- Africa, Sub-Saharan. Evangelicalism -- Political aspects -- Asia.

BR1642.L29.S76 1990
Stoll, David, 1952-
Is Latin America turning Protestant?: the politics of Evangelical growth/ David Stoll. Berkeley: University of California Press, c1990. xxi, 424 p.
89-004790   280/.4/098   0520064992
Evangelicalism -- Latin America -- History -- 20th century.Latin America -- Church history -- 20th century.

BR1642.U5.B35 1989
Balmer, Randall Herbert.
Mine eyes have seen the glory: a journey into the evangelical subculture in America/ Randall Balmer. New York: Oxford University Press, 1989. xii, 246 p.
88-034315   277.3/0828   0195051173
Evangelicalism -- United States -- History -- 20th century. Fundamentalism -- History -- 20th century. Pentecostals -- United States -- History. United States -- Church history -- 20th century.

BR1642.U5.B78 1988
Bruce, Steve, 1954-
The rise and fall of the new Christian right: conservative Protestant politics in America, 1978-1988/ Steve Bruce. Oxford: Clarendon Press; 1988. 210 p.
88-019786   320.5/5/0973   0198275919
Evangelicalism -- United States -- History -- 20th century. Fundamentalism -- History -- 20th century. Conservatism -- United States -- History -- 20th century. United States -- Politics and government -- 1977-1981. United States -- Politics and government -- 1981-1989. United States -- Church history -- 20th century.

BR1642.U5.D52 1998
Diamond, Sara.
Not by politics alone: the enduring influence of the Christian Right/ Sara Diamond. New York: Guilford Press, c1998. xiv, 280 p.
98-024502   322.4/4/0973   1572303859
Evangelicalism -- Political aspects -- United States -- History -- 20th century. Conservatism -- Religious aspects -- Christianity -- History -- 20th century. Christianity and politics -- United States -- History -- 20th century.

BR1642.U5.K56 1997
Kintz, Linda, 1945-
Between Jesus and the market: the emotions that matter in right-wing America/ Linda Kintz. Durham, N.C.: Duke University Press, 1997. 313 p.
96-049941   320.5/5/097309049   0822319594
Evangelicalism -- Political aspects -- United States -- History -- 20th century. Conservatism -- Religious aspects -- Christianity -- History -- 20th century. Christianity and politics -- United States -- History -- 20th century.

BR1642.U5.M46 1996
Menendez, Albert J.
Evangelicals at the ballot box/ Albert J. Menendez. Amherst, NY: Prometheus Books, 1996. 340 p.
96-022931   324.973/00882   1573920932
Evangelicalism -- United States. Christian sects -- United States -- Political activity. Christianity and politics.

BR1642.U5.M64 1989
Moen, Matthew C., 1958-
The Christian Right and Congress/ Matthew C. Moen. Tuscaloosa: University of Alabama Press, c1989. xi, 234 p.
88-034010   328.73/078   0817304452
Fundamentalism -- History -- 20th century. Christianity and politics -- History -- 20th century. Evangelicalism -- United States -- History -- 20th century. United States -- Politics and government -- 1981-1989. United States -- Church history -- 20th century.

BR1642.U5.S456 1996
Shibley, Mark A., 1961-
Resurgent Evangelicalism in the United States: mapping cultural change since 1970/ Mark A. Shibley. Columbia, S.C.: University of South Carolina Press, c1996. x, 156 p.
95-050218   280/.4/097309045   1570031061
Evangelicalism -- United States -- History -- 20th century. United States -- Church history -- 20th century.

BR1642.U5.S623 2000
Smith, Christian 1960-
Christian America?: what evangelicals really want/ Christian Smith. Berkeley: University of California Press, c2000. x, 257 p.
99-048340   277.3/0829   0520220412
Evangelicalism -- United States -- History -- 20th century. Christianity and culture -- United States -- History -- 20th century. Christianity and politics -- United States -- History -- 20th century.

BR1642.U5.V38 1991
The Variety of American evangelicalism/ edited by Donald W. Dayton and Robert K. Johnston. Knoxville: University of Tennessee Press, 1991. vi, 285 p.
90-036516   277.3/082   087049659X
Evangelicalism -- United States. United States -- Church history.

BR1644 Movements transcending geographical and denominational lines and theological disciplines — Pentecostalism. Charismatic Movement — General works

BR1644.L44 1996
Lehmann, David.
Struggle for the spirit: religious transformation and popular culture in Brazil and Latin America/ David Lehmann. Cambridge, Mass: Polity Press, 1996. xiv, 244 p.
96-026914   278/.0825   0745617840
Pentecostalism -- LatinAmerica. Pentecostalism -- Brazil. Brazil -- Church history. Latin America -- Church history.

BR1644.S46 2000
Shaull, Richard.
Pentecostalism and the future of the Christian churches: promises, limitations, challenges/ Richard Shaull and Waldo Cesar. Grand Rapids, Mich.: W.B. Eerdmans Pub., 2000. xiv, 236 p.
00-027983   270.8/3   0802846661
Pentecostalism.

BR1644.5 Movements transcending geographical and denominational lines and theological disciplines — Pentecostalism. Charismatic Movement — By region or country, A-Z

BR1644.5.J25 A97 1997
Austin-Broos, Diane J.
Jamaica genesis: religion and the politics of moral orders/ Diane J. Austin-Broos. Chicago: University of Chicago Press, 1997. xxiii, 304 p.
96-039540   289.9/4/097292 21   0226032868
Pentecostal churches -- Jamaica. Sociology, Christian -- Jamaica. Jamaica -- Church history -- 20th century. Jamaica -- Religious life and customs.

BR1644.5.L29.P68 1997
Power, politics, and Pentecostals in Latin America/ edited by Edward L. Cleary and Hannah W. Stewart-Gambino. Boulder, Colo.: Westview Press, 1997. vii, 261 p.
96-039896   280/.4/098   081332128X
Pentecostal churches -- Latin America. Christianity and politics -- Latin America -- History -- 20th century. Latin America -- Church history -- 20th century. Latin America -- Politics and government -- 1980-

BR1644.5.U6.G75 1997
Griffith, R. Marie 1967-
God's daughters: evangelical women and the power of submission/ R. Marie Griffith. Berkeley: University of California Press, c1997. xi, 275 p.
97-004931   267/.43   0520207645
Pentecostal women -- United States -- History -- 20th century. Women's prayer groups -- Christianity -- History -- 20th century. Evangelicalism -- United States -- History -- 20th century.

BR1644.5.U6.L68 1996
Loveland, Anne C., 1938-
American Evangelicals and the U.S. military, 1942-1993/ Anne C. Loveland. Baton Rouge: Louisiana State University Press, c1996. xiv, 356 p.
96-026309   277.3/0825/088355   080712091X
Evangelicalism -- United States -- History -- 20th century. United States -- Armed Forces -- Religious life. United States -- Military policy. United States -- Church history -- 20th century.

BR1644.5.U6.P46 1999
Pentecostal currents in American Protestantism/ edited by Edith L. Blumhofer, Russell P. Spittler, and Grant A. Wacker. Urbana: University of Illinois Press, c1999. xiii, 273 p.
98-025395   280/.4/0973   0252024508
Pentecostalism -- United States. Pentecostal churches -- United States.

BR1644.5.U6 W33 2001
Wacker, Grant,
Heaven below: early Pentecostals and American culture/ Grant Wacker. Cambridge, Mass.: Harvard University Press, 2001. xiii, 364 p.
00-054221   289.9/4/097309041   21   067400499X
Pentecostalism -- United States -- History -- 20th century. Pentecostal churches -- United States -- History -- 20th century. United States -- Church history -- 20th century.

BR1661 Movements transcending geographical and denominational lines and theological disciplines — Primitivism

BR1661.P75 1995
The primitive church in the modern world/ edited by Richard T. Hughes. Urbana: University of Illinois Press, c1995. xviii, 229 p.
95-005366   270.8   0252021940
Primitivism -- Religious aspects -- Christianity.

BR1690 Biography — Religious biographies and confessions as a subject of study

BR1690.M59 2001
Moody, Joycelyn, 1957-
Sentimental confessions: spiritual narratives of nineteenth-century African American women/ Joycelyn Moody. Athens: University of Georgia Press, c2001. xvi, 208 p.
00-029925   277.3/081/082   0820322369
Afro-American women authors -- Religious life. Afro-American women authors -- Biography -- History and criticism. Christian biography -- United States -- History and criticism.

BR1700.2-1700.3 Biography — Collective — General

BR1700.2.C64 1998
Cohn-Sherbok, Lavinia.
Who's who in Christianity/ Lavinia Cohn-Sherbok. London; Routledge, 1998. xvi, 361 p.
97-022310   270/.092/2 B 21   0415135834
Christian biography -- Dictionaries.

BR1700.3.D53 2001
Dictionary of Christian biography/ edited by Michael Walsh. Collegeville, Minn.: Liturgical Press, 2001. xiv, 1250 p.
2002-283697   270/.092/2 B 21   0826452639
Christian biography -- Dictionaries.

BR1706 Biography — Collective — Lives of the Fathers of the Church (General)

BR1706.C313 1969
Campenhausen, Hans, 1903-
The fathers of the Latin Church. Translated by Manfred Hoffman. Stanford, Calif., Stanford University Press [1969, c1964] vii, 328 p.
76-075260   270.1/092/2
Fathers of the Church, Latin -- Biography.

BR1720 Biography — Individual biography — Early Christian biography to ca. 600, A-Z

BR1720.A9.B7 1967b
Brown, Peter Robert Lamont.
Augustine of Hippo; a biography, by Peter Brown. Berkeley, University of California Press, 1967. 463 p.
67-013137   270.2/0924
Augustine, -- Saint, Bishop of Hippo.

BR1720.C5.K45 1995
Kelly, J. N. D.
Golden mouth: the story of John Chrysostom-- ascetic, preacher, bishop/ J.N.D. Kelly. Ithaca, N.Y.: Cornell University Press, 1995. x, 310 p.
95-001444   270.2/092   0801431891
John Chrysostom, -- Saint, -- d. 407.Christian saints -- Turkey -- Biography.

BR1720.O7.C7613 1989
Crouzel, Henri.
Origen/ Henri Crouzel; translated by A.S. Worrall. San Francisco: Harper & Row, c1989. xvi, 278 p.
88-045985   270.1/092/4   0060616326
Origen.Theology, Doctrinal -- History -- Early church, ca. 30-600.

BS The Bible

BS12 General — Texts and versions — Early versions

BS12 1957.L3
The Holy Bible from ancient Eastern manuscripts. Containing the Old and New Testaments, translated from the Peshitta, the authorized Bible of the church of the East, by George M. Lamsa. Philadelphia, A. J. Holman Co. [1957] xix, 1243 p.
57-012183   0879810262

BS186-195 General — Texts and versions — Modern texts and versions

BS186.M33 2001
McGrath, Alister E., 1953-
In the beginning: the story of the King James Bible and how it changed a nation, a language, and a culture/ Alister E. McGrath. New York: Doubleday, c2001. x, 340 p.
00-060348   220.5/2038   038549890X
Bible. English -- Versions -- Authorized. Bible. English -- History.

BS191.A1 1965.N412
The Oxford annotated Bible, with the Apocrypha. Revised standard version. With an introductory article, The number, order, and names of the books of the Bible. Edited by Herbert G. May [and] Bruce M. Metzger. New York, Oxford University Press, 1965. 1 v.
65-023646   220.5204

BS192.A1 1970.L6
The New English Bible with the Apocrypha. London, Oxford U.P., 1970. xxi, 336 p.
75-498997   220.52   019180004X

BS192.16 1989.N48 1989b
The Revised English Bible: with the Apocrypha. [Oxford, England]: Oxford University Press; 1989. xvii, 828 p.
88-035277   220.5/2062   0195294084

BS195.J4 1966
The Jerusalem Bible. General editor: Alexander Jones. Garden City, N.Y., Doubleday, 1966. xvi, 1547 p.
66-024278   220.5204

BS195.N375 1999
The new Jerusalem Bible: standard edition. 1st Doubleday standard ed. New York: Doubleday, 1999. 1406 p.
97-045913   220.5/2072 21   0385493207

BS417 General — Works about the Bible — Reference handbooks. Manuals, helps

BS417.N448 1993
Nelson's complete book of Bible maps & charts: Old and New Testaments. Nashville: T. Nelson Publishers, c1993. 504 p.
93-001734   220.9/022/3   0840783558
Bible -- Handbooks, manuals, etc. Bible -- Geography -- Maps.

BS425 General — Works about the Bible — Concordances

BS425.E4 1984
Ellison, John W.
Nelson's complete concordance of the Revised Standard version Bible/ compiled under the supervision of John W. Ellison. 2nd ed. Nashville: T. Nelson Publishers, c1984. 1136 p.
84-027256   220.5/20423 19   0840749546

BS425.K645 1991
Kohlenberger, John R.
The NRSV concordance unabridged: including the Apocryphal/Deuterocanonical books/ John R. Kohlenberger III. Grand Rapids, Mich.: Zondervan, c1991. xiv, 1483 p.
91-012197   220.5/20433   0310539102
Bible -- Concordances, English -- New Revised Standard.

BS425.W48 1988
Whitaker, Richard E.
The Eerdmans analytical concordance to the Revised Standard Version of the Bible/ compiled by Richard E. Whitaker; with James E. Goehring and research personnel of the Institute for Antiquity and Christianity. Grand Rapids, Mich.: Eerdmans, c1988. xiv, 1548 p.
88-019217   220.5/20423 19   080282403X
Hebrew language -- Glossaries, vocabularies, etc. Greek language, Biblical -- Glossaries, vocabularies, etc. Latin language -- Glossaries, vocabularies, etc.

BS425.Y7 1955
Young, Robert,
Analytical concordance to the Bible on an entirely new plan containing about 311,000 references, subdivided under the Hebrew and Greek originals, with the literal meaning and pronunciation of each; designed for the simplest reader of the English Bible Also index lexicons to the Old and New Testaments, being a guide to parallel passages and a complete list of Scripture proper names showing their modern pronunciation. 22d American ed., rev. by Wm. B. Stevenson. To which is added a New York, Funk & Wagnalls [1955] ix, 1090 p.
55-005338   220.2
Hebrew language -- Dictionaries -- English. Greek language, Biblical -- Dictionaries -- English. Palestine -- Antiquities.

BS432 General — Works about the Bible — Topical indexes, analyses, digests

BS432.D34 1992
Day, A. Colin.
Roget's thesaurus of the Bible/ A. Colin Day. San Francisco: HarperSan Francisco, c1992. 927 p.
92-053896   220.3   0060617721
Bible -- Indexes.

BS440 General — Works about the Bible — Dictionaries. Glossaries. Encyclopedias

BS440.A54 1992
The Anchor Bible dictionary/ David Noel Freedman, editor-in-chief; associate editors, Gary A. Herion, David F. Graf, John David Pleins; managing editor, Astrid B. Beck. New York: Doubleday, c1992. 6 v.
91-008385   220.3   0385193513
Bible -- Dictionaries.

BS440.B73 1996
Browning, W. R. F.
A dictionary of the Bible/ W.R.F. Browning; consultant editors, Richard Coggins, Graham N. Stanton. Oxford; New York: 1996. xv, 412 p.
96-013033   220.3 20   0192116916

BS440.E44 2000
Eerdmans dictionary of the Bible/ David Noel Freedman, editor-in-chief; Allen C. Myers, associate editor; Astrid B. Beck, managing editor. Grand Rapids, Mich.: W.B. Eerdmans, 2000. xxxiii, 1425 p.
00-056124   220.3 21   0802824005
Bible -- Dictionaries.

BS440.H69 1991
Holman Bible dictionary: with summary definitions and explanatory articles on every Bible subject, introductions and teaching outlines for each Bible book, in-depth theological articles, plus internal maps, charts, illustrations, scale reconstruction general editor Trent C. Butler. Nashville, Tenn.: Holman Bible Publishers, c1991. xx, 1450 p.
91-199677   220.3 20   1558190538

BS440.I63
The Interpreter's dictionary of the Bible; an illustrated encyclopedia identifying and explaining all proper names and significant terms and subjects in the Holy Scriptures, including the Apocrypha, [Editorial board: George Arthur Buttrick, dictionary editor, and others] New York, Abingdon Press [1962] 4 v.
62-009387   220.3
Bible -- Dictionaries.

BS440.M434 1993
The Oxford companion to the Bible/ edited by Bruce M. Metzger, Michael D. Coogan. New York: Oxford University Press, 1993. xxi, 874 p.
93-019315   220.3 20   0195046455

BS440.N42 1996
New Bible dictionary/ organizing editor (first edition), J.D. Douglas; revision editor (second edition), N. Hillyer. 3rd ed./ revision editor (third edition), D.R.W. Wood; consulting Leicester, England; InterVarsity Press, xix, 1298 p.
96-024002   220.3 20   0830814396

BS440.N437 2000
New dictionary of biblical theology/ editors, T. Desmond Alexander, Brian S. Rosner. Leicester, England: Inter-Varsity Press; xx, 866 p.
00-047156   230/.041/03 21   085111976X

BS440.N44 1987
The New international dictionary of the Bible/ J.D. Douglas, revising editor, Merrill C. Tenney, general editor. Pictorial ed. Grand Rapids, MI, U.S.A.: Regency Reference Library, Zondervan Pub. xix, 1162 p.
87-002220   220.3 19   0310331900

BS440.O94 2001
The Oxford guide to ideas & issues of the Bible/ edited by Bruce M. Metzger, Michael D. Coogan. Oxford: Oxford University Press, c2001. xxi, 585 p.
2001-037039   220.3 21   0195149173

BS445-480 General — Works about the Bible — Introductory works

BS445.O94 2001
The Oxford illustrated history of the Bible/ edited by John Rogerson. Oxford; Oxford University Press, 2001. xvi, 395 p.
2001-272513   220/.09 21   0198601182

BS449.C37 1998
Carson, D. A.
The inclusive-language debate: a plea for realism/ D.A. Carson. Grand Rapids, MI: Baker Books, c1998. 221 p.
98-023473   220.5/2/001   080105835X
Nonsexist language -- Religious aspects -- Christianity.

BS455.G55 2000
Gilmore, Alec.
A dictionary of the English Bible and its origins/ Alec Gilmore. Sheffield: Sheffield Academic Press, c2000. 192 p.
2002-489513   220.52003   1841270687
Bible. English -- Dictionaries. Bible. English -- History.

BS455.T55 1999
Thuesen, Peter Johannes, 1971-
In discordance with the Scriptures: American Protestant battles over translating the Bible/ Peter J. Thuesen. New York: Oxford University Press, 1999. xi, 238 p.
99-024447   220.5/2/00973   0195127366
Protestant churches -- United States -- Doctrines. Bible -- United States -- History.

BS465.B74 1997
Brenneman, James E., 1954-
Canons in conflict: negotiating texts in true and false prophecy/ James E. Brenneman. New York: Oxford University Press, 1997. xvii, 228 p.
96-027946   220.1/2   0195109090
Prophecy. Canon (Literature)

BS475.2.A155 2000
Aageson, James W., 1947-
In the beginning: critical concepts for the study of the Bible/ Jamew W. Aageson. Boulder, CO: Westview Press, 2000. xii, 153 p.
99-087540   220.6/1   0813366194
Bible -- Introductions.

BS475.2.B69 1998
Bowker, John Westerdale.
The complete Bible handbook/ John Bowker. New York: DK Pub., 1998. 544 p.
98-004478   220.6/1   0789435683
Bible -- Introductions.

BS475.2.C26 1997
The Cambridge companion to the Bible/ Howard Clark Kee ... [et al.]. Cambridge; Cambridge University Press, 1997. vi, 616 p.
96-043914   220.9   0521343690
Bible -- Introductions. Bible -- History of contemporary events. Bible -- History of Biblical events.

BS475.3.F36 2001
Fant, Clyde E.
An introduction to the Bible/ Clyde E. Fant, Donald W. Musser, Mitchell G. Reddish. Rev. ed. Nashville: Abingdon Press, c2001. 472 p.
2001-045139   220.6/1 21   0687084563

BS476.V34 1998
Vanhoozer, Kevin J.
Is there a meaning in this text?: the Bible, the reader, and the morality of literary knowledge/ Kevin J. Vanhoozer. Grand Rapids, Mich.: Zondervan, c1998. 496 p.
98-012627   220.6/01   0310211565
Hermeneutics.

BS480.C6 1957
Coleridge, Samuel Taylor, 1772-1834.
Confessions of an inquiring spirit. Edited with an introductory note by H. StJ. Hart. Stanford, Calif., Stanford University Press [1957] 120 p.
57-009372   220.13*
Lessing, Gotthold Ephraim, -- 1729-1781.

BS480.L347 1992
Lane Fox, Robin, 1946-
The unauthorized version: truth and fiction in the Bible/ Robin Lane Fox. New York: Knopf: 1992. 478 p.
91-058553   220.6/7   0394573986
Bible -- Evidences, authority, etc. Bible -- Controversial literature.

BS491.2 General — Works about the Bible — Commentaries

BS491.2.H37 2000
The HarperCollins Bible commentary/ general editor, James L. Mays; associate editors, Beverly R. Gaventa ... [et al.]; with the Society of Biblical Literature. San Francisco: HarperSanFrancisco, c2000. xxvi, 1203 p.
00-020818   220.7   0060655488
Bible -- Commentaries.

BS491.2.I57
The Interpreter's one volume commentary on the Bible: introd. and commentary for each book of the Bible including the Apocrypha, with general articles. Edited by Charles M. Laymon. Nashville, Abingdon Press [1971] xiv, 1386 p.
71-144392   220.7   0687192994
Bible -- Commentaries.

BS491.2.N484 1994
The New Interpreter's Bible: general articles & introduction, commentary, & reflections for each book of the Bible, including the Apocryphal/Deuterocanonical books. Nashville: Abingdon Press, [c1994-] v. <1-2, 4, 5, 7-9, 12>
94-021092   220.7/7 20   0687278147

BS491.2.W66 1992
The Women's Bible commentary/ Carol A. Newsom and Sharon H. Ringe, editors. London: SPCK; 1992. xix, 396 p.
91-044831   220.7/082   028104581X
Women -- Middle East -- History. Women -- Rome -- History.

BS500-521.8 General — Works about the Bible — Criticism and interpretation

BS500.B33 1991
Barlow, Philip L.
Mormons and the Bible: the place of the Latter-Day Saints in American religion/ Philip L. Barlow. New York: Oxford University Press, 1991. xxix, 251 p.
90-036034   220/.08/8283   0195062337
Mormon Church -- Doctrines -- History.

BS500.S46 1994
Shuger, Debora K., 1953-
The Renaissance Bible: scholarship, sacrifice, and subjectivity/ Debora Kuller Shuger. Berkeley: University of California Press, c1994. xv, 297 p.
93-005892   220/.094/09024   0520084802
European literature -- 17th century. Christianity and literature. European literature -- Renaissance, 1450-1600.

BS511.2.C35 1998
The Cambridge companion to biblical interpretation/ edited by John Barton. Cambridge; Cambridge University Press, 1998. xv, 338 p.
97-027945   220.6/1   0521481449
Bible -- Criticism, interpretation, etc.

BS511.2.L24 1998
Lacocque, Andre.
Thinking biblically: exegetical and hermeneutical studies/ Andre LaCocque and Paul Ricoeur; translated by David Pellauer. Chicago: University of Chicago Press, c1998. xix, 441 p.
97-044091   221.6   0226713377
Bible. O.T. -- Criticism, interpretation, etc. Bible. O.T. -- Hermeneutics.

BS521.4.I97 2002
The IVP women's Bible commentary/ edited by Catherine Clark Kroeger & Mary J. Evans. Downers Grove, Ill.: InterVarsity Press, c2002. xxxvii, 874 p.
2001-039360   220.7/82 21   083081437X

BS521.4.S45 1996
Selvidge, Marla J., 1948-
Notorious voices: feminist biblical interpretation, 1500-1920/ Marla J. Selvidge. New York: Continuum, c1996. x, 246 p.
94-033899   220.6/082   1557786305
Women in Christianity -- History.

BS521.8.A53 2001
Aichele, George.
The control of biblical meaning: canon as semiotic mechanism/ George Aichele. Harrisburg, Pa.: Trinity Press International, c2001. xi, 259 p.
00-062853   220.1/2   1563383330
Semiotics -- Religious aspects -- Christianity.

BS535-537 General — Works about the Bible — The Bible as literature

BS535.A57 1991
Alter, Robert.
The world of biblical literature/ Robert Alter. [New York]: BasicBooks, c1992. xii, 225 p.
91-055462   809/.93522   0465092551
Bible as literature.

BS535.L54 1987
The literary guide to the Bible/ edited by Robert Alter and Frank Kermode. Cambridge, Mass.: Belknap Press of Harvard University Press, 1987. 678 p.
86-032172   809/.93522 19
Bible as literature.

BS535.P75 1996
Prickett, Stephen.
Origins of narrative: the romantic appropriation of the Bible/ Stephen Prickett. Cambridge [England]; Cambridge University Press, 1996. xvi, 288 p.
95-021587   220/.09/033   0521445434
Bible and literature. Romanticism.

BS537.K67 1988
Kort, Wesley A.
Story, text, and scripture: literary interests in biblical narrative/ Wesley A. Kort. University Park: Pennsylvania State University Press, c1988. xii, 159 p.
87-042549   220.6/6   0271006102
Narration in the Bible. Bible as literature.

BS537.W54 2000
Wiersbe, Warren W.
Index of biblical images: similes, metaphors, and symbols in Scripture: based on the text of the New International Version of the Bible/ Warren W. Wiersbe. Grand Rapids, Mich.: Baker Books, c2000. 127 p.
00-710334   016.2206/4   0801091071
Symbolism in the Bible -- Indexes.

BS544 General — Works about the Bible — God in the Bible

BS544.M64 1983
Mollenkott, Virginia R.
The divine feminine: the biblical imagery of God as female/ Virginia Ramey Mollenkott. New York, NY: Crossroad Pub. Co., 1983. 119 p.
82-023542   220.6/4   0824505654
Femininity of God -- Biblical teaching.

BS570-580 General — Works about the Bible — Men, women, and children of the Bible

BS570.C645 2001
New international encyclopedia of Bible characters: the complete who's who in the Bible/ Paul D. Gardner, editor. Grand Rapids, Mich.: ZondervanPublishingHouse, [2001], c1995. xiii, 688 p.
00-140138   220.9/2/03 B 21   0310240077

BS570.O94 2001
The Oxford guide to people & places of the Bible/ edited by Bruce M. Metzger, Michael D. Coogan. Oxford, New York: Oxford University Press, c2001. xxii, 374 p.
00-066900   220.9/03   0195146417
Bible -- Biography -- Encyclopedias. Bible -- Geography -- Encyclopedias.

BS575.W593 2000
Women in scripture: a dictionary of named and unnamed women in the Hebrew Bible, the Apocryphal/Deuterocanonical books, and the New Testament/ Carol Meyers, general editor; Toni Craven and Ross S. Kraemer, associate editors. Boston: Houghton Mifflin, 2000. xv, 592 p.
99-089577   220.9/2/082   0395709369
Women in the Bible -- Indexes. Women in the Bible -- Biography -- Dictionaries.

BS580.D3.M37 2000
McKenzie, Steven L., 1953-
King David: a biography/ Steven L. McKenzie. New York: Oxford University Press, 2000. viii, 232 p.
99-044315   222.4/092   0195132734
David, -- King of Israel.

BS580.E85.N67 1999
Norris, Pamela.
Eve: a biography/ Pamela Norris. New York: New York University Press, 1999. xvi, 496 p.
99-034540   222/.11092   0814758126
Eve -- (Biblical figure)

BS580.M6.B8 1958
Buber, Martin, 1878-1965.
Moses; the revelation and the covenant. New York, Harper [1958] 226 p.
58-005216   221.92
Moses.

BS580.M6.F7 1939
Freud, Sigmund, 1856-1939.
Moses and monotheism [by] Sigmund Freud; translated from the German by Katherine Jones. [London] The Hogarth press and the Institute of psycho-analysis, 1939. 223 p.
39-015290   221.92
Moses -- (Biblical leader)Monotheism. Jews -- Religion -- Relations -- Egyptian. Psychology, Religious.

BS580.M6.Y47 1991
Yerushalmi, Yosef Hayim, 1932-
Freud's Moses: Judaism terminable and interminable/ Yosef Hayim Yerushalmi. New Haven: Yale University Press, c1991. xix, 159 p.
90-023859   222/.1092   0300049218
Freud, Sigmund, -- 1856-1939. -- Mann Moses und die monotheistische Religion. Moses -- (Biblical leader) Freud, Sigmund, -- 1856-1939. Monotheism. Psychology, Religious. Judaism -- History.

BS585 General — Works about the Bible — Study and teaching

BS585.N67 2000
Norton, David.
A history of the English Bible as literature/ David Norton. Cambridge, U.K.; Cambridge University Press, 2000. xii, 484 p.
99-016897   809/.93522   0521771404
Bible as literature.

BS621-661 General — Works about the Bible — Auxiliary topics

BS621.C6415 1976
Cornfeld, Gaalyahu, 1902-
Archaeology of the Bible: book by book/ Gaalyah Cornfeld; David Noel Freedman, consulting editor. New York: Harper & Row, c1976. 334 p.
76-009979   220.9/3   0060615842
Bible -- Antiquities.

BS621.H56 1998
Hoerth, Alfred J.
Archaeology and the Old Testament/ Alfred J. Hoerth. Grand Rapids, Mich.: Baker Books, c1998. 447 p.
98-023086   221.9/3   0801011299
Bible. O.T. -- Antiquities. Bible. O.T. -- History of Biblical events.

BS621.L37 2000
Laughlin, John C. H. 1942-
Archaeology and the Bible/ John C.H. Laughlin. London; Routledge, 2000. x, 196 p.
99-019503   220.9/3   0415159938
Middle East -- Antiquities.

BS630.O96 1984
Oxford Bible atlas/ edited by Herbert G. May; with the assistance of G.N.S. Hunt; in consultation with R.W. Hamilton. New York: Oxford University Press, 1984. 144 p.
84-010052   220.9/1   0191434523
Bible -- Geography. Bible -- Geography -- Maps.

BS630.R37 1989
Rasmussen, Carl.
Zondervan NIV atlas of the Bible/ Carl G. Rasmussen; maps by Carta, Jerusalem. Grand Rapids, Mich.: Regency Reference Library, c1989. 256 p.
89-008506   220.9/1 20   0310251605

BS635.G73 1997
Gordon, Cyrus Herzl, 1908-
The Bible and the ancient Near East/ Cyrus H. Gordon and Gary A. Rendsburg. New York: W.W. Norton & Co., c1997. 345 p.
96-037110   221.9/5   0393039420
Bible. O.T. -- History of contemporary events.

BS635.2.P67 1998
Porter, J. R.
The illustrated guide to the Bible/ J.R. Porter. New York: Oxford University Press, 1998. 288 p.
98-006535   220.6/1 21
Jews -- Civilization -- To 70 A.D. Palestine -- Civilization.

BS637.2.F5 1998
Finegan, Jack,
Handbook of biblical chronology: principles of time reckoning in the ancient world and problems of chronology in the Bible/ Jack Finegan. Rev. ed. Peabody, Mass.: Hendrickson Publishers, c1998. xxxvii, 426 p.
95-030873   220.9 20   1565631439

BS650.S35 1997
Schroeder, Gerald L.
The science of God: the convergence of scientific and biblical wisdom/ Gerald Schroeder. New York: Free Press, c1997. xii, 226 p.
97-014978   261.5/5   0684837366
Bible and science.

BS651.C6926 1994
The Creation hypothesis: scientific evidence for an intelligent designer/ J.P. Moreland, editor; foreword by Phillip E. Johnson. Downers Grove, Ill.: InterVarsity Press, c1994. 335 p.
93-042724   231.7/65 20   0830816984
Creationism. God -- Proof, Cosmological. Naturalism. Religion and science.

BS651.E84 1990
Eve, Raymond A., 1946-
The creationist movement in modern America/ Raymond A. Eve, Francis B. Harrold. Boston: Twayne Publishers, 1990. xii, 234 p.
90-040090   306.6/31765   0805797416
Creationism. Evolution.

BS651.M3976 1993
McKown, Delos Banning.
The mythmaker's magic: behind the illusion of "creation science"/ by Delos B. McKown. Buffalo, N.Y.: Prometheus Books, 1993. 180 p.
92-034549   231.7/65   0879757701
Creationism. Religion and science -- United States.

BS651.T59 1994
Toumey, Christopher P., 1949-
God's own scientists: creationists in a secular world/ Christopher P. Toumey. New Brunswick, N.J.: Rutgers University Press, c1994. xi, 289 p.
93-024241   306.6/31765   0813520436
Creationism -- United States. Creationism -- North Carolina. United States -- Church history -- 20th century. North Carolina -- Church history.

BS658.R93 1998
Ryan, William B. F.
Noah's flood: the new scientific discoveries about the event that changed history/ William Ryan and Walter Pitman; illustrations by Anastasia Sotiropoulos; maps by William Haxby. New York: Simon & Schuster, c1998. 319 p.
98-045384   930/.2   0684810522
Deluge.

BS661.O94 1996
Overholt, Thomas W., 1935-
Cultural anthropology and the Old Testament/
by Thomas Overholt. Minneapolis: Fortress
Press, c1996. ix, 116 p.
95-043457   221.6/7   0800628896
Ethnology in the Bible.

BS665 General — Works about the Bible — Auxiliary topics

BS665.Z64 1982
Zohary, Michael,
Plants of the Bible: a complete handbook to all
the plants with 200 full-color plates taken in the
natural habitat/ Michael Zohary. London;
Cambridge University Press, 1982. 223 p.
82-004535   220.8/582 19   0521249260
Plants in the Bible.

BS680 General — Works about the Bible — Topics (not otherwise provided for), A-Z

BS680.G57 D53 1999
Dictionary of deities and demons in the Bible
DDD/ Karel van der Toorn, Bob Becking, Pieter
W. van der Horst, editors. 2nd extensively rev.
ed. Leiden; Brill; 1999. xxxviii, 960 p.
98-042505   220.3 21   0802824919
*Gods   in   the   Bible   --   Dictionaries.
Demonology in the Bible -- Dictionaries.*

BS680.W7.M87 1998
Murphy, Cullen.
The Word according to Eve: women and the
Bible in ancient times and our own/ Cullen
Murphy. Boston: Houghton Mifflin, 1998. xiii,
302 p.
98-018015   220.8/3054   0395701139
Bible and feminism.

BS895 Old Testament — Texts and versions — Modern texts and versions of the Old Testament

BS895.J4 1985
Tanakh = [Tanakh]: a new translation of the
Holy Scriptures according to the traditional
Hebrew text.   Philadelphia: Jewish Publication
Society, 1985. xxvi, 1624 p.
85-010006   221.5/2   0827602529

BS1140.2 Old Testament — Works about the Old Testament — Introductory works

BS1140.2.C64 1990
Coggins, R. J., 1929-
Introducing the Old Testament/ R.J. Coggins.
Oxford [England]; Oxford University Press,
1990. xi, 165 p.
89-035933   221.6/1   0192132547
Bible. O.T. -- Introductions.

BS1140.2.C73 1989
Creating the Old Testament: the emergence of
the Hebrew Bible/ edited by Stephen Bigger.
Oxford, UK; B. Blackwell, 1989. xx, 364 p.
89-030938   221.6/1   0631159096
Bible. O.T. -- Introductions.

BS1140.2.S2
Sandmel, Samuel.
The Hebrew Scriptures; an introduction to their
literature and religious ideas.   New York, Knopf,
1963. 552 p.
62-019580   221.6
Bible. O.T. -- Introductions.

BS1160-1188 Old Testament — Works about the Old Testament — Criticism and interpretation

BS1160.H43 1985
The Hebrew Bible and its modern interpreters/
edited by Douglas A. Knight and Gene M.
Tucker. Chico, Calif.: Scholars Press, c1985.
xxvii, 516 p.
84-025936   221.6/09/04   0891307842
*Bible. O.T. -- Criticism, interpretation, etc. --
History -- 20th century.*

BS1171.2.A45
Alter, Robert.
The art of Biblical narrative/ Robert Alter. New
York: Basic Books, c1981. xii, 195 p.
80-068958   221.4/4   0465004245
Narration in the Bible.

BS1171.2.C77 1998
Cross, Frank Moore.
From epic to canon: history and literature in
ancient Israel/ Frank Moore Cross. Baltimore:
Johns Hopkins University press, c1998. xv,
262 p.
98-007322   221.6   0801859824
Judaism -- History -- To 70 A.D.

BS1174.2.B3713 1998
Steck, Odil Hannes.
Old Testament exegesis: a guide to the
methodology/ by Odil Hannes Steck; translated
by James D. Nogalski. Atlanta, Ga.: Scholars
Press, c1998. xxiv, 202 p.
98-020955   221.6/01   0788504657
*Bible. O.T. -- Criticism, interpretation, etc. --
Methodology.*

BS1180.C66 1996
The context of Scripture/ editor, William W.
Hallo; associate editor, K.L. Younger. Leiden;
Brill, [1997-] v. <1- >
96-048987   220.9/5 21   9004106189
*Middle Eastern literature -- Relation to the
Old Testament. Middle Eastern literature --
Translations into English.*

BS1180.D66 2001
Dever, William G.
What did the biblical writers know, and when
did they know it?: what archaeology can tell us
about the reality of ancient Israel/ William G.
Dever. Grand Rapids, Mich.: Eerdmans Pub.
Co., c2001. xiii, 313 p.
00-067678   220.9/5   0802847943
*Jews -- History -- 1200-953 B.C. Jews --
History -- 953-586 B.C.*

BS1186.F36 1990
Fackenheim, Emil L.
The Jewish Bible after the Holocaust: a re-
reading/ Emil L. Fackenheim. Bloomington:
Indiana University Press, c1990. xi, 122 p.
90-005170   221.6   0253320976
*Holocaust (Jewish theology) Holocaust
(Christian theology)*

BS1188.S33 2000
Sacred text, secular times: the Hebrew Bible in
the modern world/ Leonard Jay Greenspoon,
editor. Omaha, Neb.: Creighton University
Press, 1999.
99-037241   221.6   1881871320
*Bible. O.T. -- Criticism, interpretation, etc. --
Congresses.*

BS1192 Old Testament — Works about the Old Testament — Addresses, essays, lectures on the Old Testament (General)

BS1192.B8
Buber, Martin, 1878-1965.
On the Bible; eighteen studies. Edited by Nahum
N. Glatzer. New York, Schocken Books [1968]
vi, 247 p.
68-016653   221
Bible. O.T. -- Addresses, essays, lectures.

BS1192.6 Old Testament — Works about the Old Testament — God in the Old Testament

BS1192.6.Y34 1996
Gerstenberger, Erhard.
Yahweh--the patriarch: ancient images of God
and feminist theology/ Erhard S. Gerstenberger;
translated by Frederick J. Gaiser. Minneapolis:
Fortress Press, 1996. xv, 168 p.
96-018044   231/.1   0800628438
*God -- Biblical teaching. Masculinity of God -
- Biblical teaching. Patriarchy -- Biblical
teaching.*

BS1197 Old Testament — Works about the Old Testament — Auxiliary topics

BS1197.B756 1995
Brettler, Marc Zvi.
The creation of history in Ancient Israel/ Marc Zvi Brettler. London; Routledge, 1995. xv, 254 p.
94-039144   221.6/7   0415118603
Jews — History — To 70 A.D. — Historiography. Bible as literature.

BS1199 Old Testament — Works about the Old Testament — Topics (not otherwise provided for), A-Z

BS1199.G63.G65 1998
Goldenberg, Robert.
The nations that know thee not: ancient Jewish attitudes towards other religions/ Robert Goldenberg. New York: New York University Press, c1998. xi, 214 p.
97-033898   296.3/9/0901   0814731074
Gods — Biblical teaching. Judaism — Relations — Paganism. Paganism — Relations — Judaism.

BS1199.S59
Olyan, Saul M.
Rites and rank: hierarchy in biblical representations of cult/ Saul M. Olyan. Princeton, N.J.: Princeton University Press, c2000. xii, 190 p.
99-045170   221.6   0691029482
Worship in the Bible. Social stratification in the Bible.

BS1199.S6.P54 2001
Pleins, J. David.
The social visions of the Hebrew Bible: a theological introduction/ J. David Pleins. Louisville, Ky.: Westminster John Knox c2000. xii, 592 p.
00-040810   221.6   0664221750
Sociology, Biblical.

BS1199.W7
Fuchs, Esther, 1953-
Sexual politics in the biblical narrative: reading the Hebrew Bible as a woman/ Esther Fuchs. Sheffield, England: Sheffield Academic Press, c2000. 244 p.
00-421396   221.6/082   1841271381
Man-woman relationships in the Bible. Women in the Bible.

BS1223-1335.52 Old Testament — Special parts of the Old Testament — Historical books

BS1223. 1990
The book of J/ translated from the Hebrew by David Rosenberg; interpreted by Harold Bloom. New York: Grove Weidenfeld, c1990. 340 p.
90-037391   222/.105209   0802110509
J document (Biblical criticism)

BS1225.2.H32 1997
Halivni, David.
Revelation restored: divine writ and critical responses/ David Weiss Halivni. Boulder, Colo.: Westview Press, 1997. xxiii, 114 p.
97-008573   222/.101   0813333466
Bible. O.T. Pentateuch — Canon. Bible. O.T. Pentateuch — Criticism, interpretation, etc., Jewish. Bible. O.T. Pentateuch — Hermeneutics.

BS1225.2.M33 1993
McDowell, Josh.
Evidence that demands a verdict: historical evidences for the Christian faith/ Josh McDowell. Nashville, Tenn.: T. Nelson, [c1993-] v. <2 >
93-024923   220.6/01 20   0840743793
Documentary hypothesis (Pentateuchal criticism)

BS1225.5.P37 2000
Pardes, Ilana.
The biography of ancient Israel: national narratives in the Bible/ Ilana Pardes. Berkeley: University of California Press, c2000. xi, 211 p.
99-027865   296.3/1172   0520211103
Bible as literature. Jewish nationalism.

BS1235.3.E87 1999
Eve and Adam: Jewish, Christian, and Muslim readings on Genesis and gender/ edited by Kristen E. Kvam, Linda S. Schearing, and Valarie H. Ziegler. Bloomington: Indiana University Press, 1999. xviii, 515 p.
98-039873   222/.1106/09   025333490X
Eve — (Biblical figure) Adam — (Biblical figure) Feminism — Religious aspects — Judaism. Feminism — Religious aspects — Christianity. Feminism — Religious aspects — Islam.

BS1285.2.F74 2000
Freedman, David Noel, 1922-
The nine commandments: uncovering a hidden pattern of crime and punishment in the Hebrew Bible/ David Noel Freedman; with Jeffrey C. Geoghegan and Michael M. Homan; edited by Astrid B. Beck. New York: Doubleday, 2000. xvii, 217 p.
00-029492   222/.1606   0385499868
Crime in the Bible.

BS1286.S94 2001
Sweeney, Marvin A. 1953-
King Josiah of Judah: the lost messiah of Israel/ Marvin A. Sweeney. Oxford; Oxford University Press, 2001. xvi, 350 p.
99-037745   222/.54092   0195133242
Josiah, — King of Judah.Jews — History — To 586 B.C. — Historiography. Deuteronomistic history (Biblical criticism)

BS1323.A48 1999
The David story: a translation with commentary of 1 and 2 Samuel/ Robert Alter. New York: W.W. Norton, c1999. xxxvii, 410 p.
99-021116   222/.4077   0393048039
Bible. O.T. Samuel — Commentaries.

BS1335.52.Z56 2001
Ziolkowski, Eric Jozef, 1958-
Evil children in religion, literature, and art/ Eric Ziolkowski. New York: Palgrave, 2001. xvii, 253 p.
2001-021946   700/.452054   0333918959
Elisha — (Biblical prophet)Children in the Bible. Children in literature. Children in art.

BS1430.2 Old Testament — Special parts of the Old Testament — Poetical books. Old Testament lyrics. Songs, hymns, etc.

BS1430.2.H85 1999
Hunter, Alastair G.
Psalms/ Alastair G. Hunter. London; Routledge, 1999. xiii, 298 p.
98-054242   223/.206   0415127696
Bible. O.T. Psalms — Criticism, interpretation, etc.

BS1515.2 Old Testament — Special parts of the Old Testament — Prophetic books. The Prophets

BS1515.2.S35 1996
Sawyer, John F. A.
The fifth gospel: Isaiah in the history of Christianity/ John F.A. Sawyer. New York: Cambridge University Press, 1996. xvii, 281 p.
95-022281   224/.106/09   0521440076
Bible. O.T. Isaiah — Criticism, interpretation, etc. — History.

BS1692 Old Testament — Special parts of the Old Testament — Apocrypha and apocryphal books

BS1692.1957
The Apocrypha, Revised standard version of the Old Testament. Translated from the Greek and Latin tongues, being the version set forth A.D. 1611, rev. A.D. 1894, compared with the most ancient authorities and rev. A.D. 1957. New York, Nelson, 1957. 250 p.
57-010132   229

BS2025-2095 New Testament — Texts and versions — Modern texts and versions of the New Testament

BS2025.1962.W4
The New Testament octapla; eight English versions of the New Testament in the Tyndale-King James tradition. Edited by Luther A. Weigle. New York, T. Nelson [1962] xvi, 1489 p.
62-010331   225.5
Bible. N.T. English -- Versions.

BS2095.P5
The New Testament in modern English. Translated by J. B. Phillips. New York, Macmillan, 1958. 575 p.
58-010922   225.52

BS2320-2331 New Testament — Works about the New Testament — Introductory works

BS2320.T7613 2000
Trobisch, David.
The first edition of the New Testament/ David Trobisch. Oxford; Oxford University Press, 2000. viii, 175 p.
99-048733   225.1/2   0195112407
Bible. N.T. -- Canon. Bible. N.T. -- Publication and distribution -- Rome.

BS2325.E47 1993
Ehrman, Bart D.
The Orthodox corruption of scripture: the effect of early Christological controversies on the text of the New Testament/ Bart D. Ehrman. New York: Oxford University Press, 1993. xiii, 314 p.
92-028607   225/.06   0195080785
Jesus Christ -- History of doctrines -- Early church, ca. 30-600.Heresies, Christian -- History -- Early church, ca. 30-600.

BS2325.V3213 1991
Vaganay, Leon, b. 1882.
An introduction to New Testament textual criticism/ Leon Vaganay; translated into English by Jenny Heimerdinger. Cambridge; Cambridge University Press, 1991. xxiv, 227 p.
90-027539   225.4/8   0521364337
Bible. N.T. -- Criticism, Textual.

BS2330.2.B73 1998
Branick, Vincent P.
Understanding the New Testament and its message: an introduction/ by Vincent P. Branick. New York: Paulist Press, c1998. 412 p.
97-047026   225.6/1   0809137801
Bible. N.T. -- Introductions.

BS2330.2.E36 2000
Ehrman, Bart D.
The New Testament: a historical introduction to the early Christian writings/ Bart D. Ehrman. 2nd ed. New York: Oxford University Press, 2000. xxvi, 465 p.
99-022360   225.6/7 21   0195126394

BS2330.2.P46 1982
Perrin, Norman.
The New Testament, an introduction: proclamation and parenesis, myth and history/ Norman Perrin, Dennis C. Duling. New York: Harcourt Brace Jovanovich, c1982. xx, 516 p.
82-080524   225.6/1   0155657267
Bible. N.T. -- Introductions.

BS2331.T83 1987
Tuckett, C. M.
Reading the New Testament: methods of interpretation/ Christopher Tuckett. Philadelphia: Fortress Press, 1987. 200 p.
86-046429   225.6/01   0800620585
Bible. N.T. -- Hermeneutics.

BS2361.2-2379 New Testament — Works about the New Testament — Criticism and interpretation

BS2361.2.M13 1995
Mack, Burton L.
Who wrote the New Testament?: the making of the Christian myth/ Burton L. Mack. San Francisco, Ca.: HarperSan Francisco, c1995. ix, 326 p.
95-008937   225.6   0060655178
Christianity -- Origin.

BS2361.2.P47
Petersen, Norman R., 1933-
Literary criticism for New Testament critics/ by Norman R. Petersen. Philadelphia: Fortress Press, c1978. 92 p.
77-015241   225.6/1   0800604652
Bible. N.T. -- Criticism, interpretation, etc.

BS2379.S43 1993
Searching the Scriptures/ Elisabeth Schussler Fiorenza with the assistance of Shelly Matthews. New York: Crossroad, 1993-1994. 2 v.
93-031336   220.6/082   0824513819
Women in Christianity -- History -- Early church, ca. 30-600.

BS2395 New Testament — Works about the New Testament — Addresses, essays, etc. on the New Testament in general

BS2395.B83 1984
Bultmann, Rudolf Karl, 1884-1976.
New Testament and mythology and other basic writings/ Rudolf Bultmann; selected, edited, and translated by Schubert M. Ogden. Philadelphia: Fortress Press, c1984. x, 168 p.
84-047912   225.6/8   0800607279
Demythologization.

BS2397 New Testament — Works about the New Testament — Theology of the New Testament

BS2397.C35 1994
Caird, G. B. 1917-
New Testament theology/ G.B. Caird; completed and edited by L.D. Hurst. Oxford: Clarendon Press; 1994. xix, 498 p.
93-036971   230   019826660X
Bible. N.T. -- Theology.

BS2398 New Testament — Works about the New Testament — God in the New Testament

BS2398.G66 2001
Goodwin, Mark.
Paul, apostle of the living God: kerygma and conversion in 2 Corinthians/ Mark J. Goodwin. Harrisburg, Pa.: Trinity Press International, c2001. ix, 261 p.
00-052744   227/.306   1563383187
God -- Biblical teaching.

BS2398.W75 1992
Wright, N. T.
Christian origins and the question of God/ N.T. Wright. Minneapolis: Fortress Press, 1992-1996 v. 1-2
92-019348   225.6   0800626818
God -- History of doctrines -- Early church, ca. 30-600. God -- Biblical teaching. Christianity -- Origin.

BS2407 New Testament — Works about the New Testament — Auxiliary topics

BS2407.K37 1983
Kee, Howard Clark.
Understanding the New Testament/ Howard Clark Kee. Englewood Cliffs, N.J.: Prentice-Hall, c1983. viii, 408 p.
82-016482   225.6/1   0139365915
Bible. N.T. -- History of Biblical events. Bible. N.T. -- Introductions.

BS2417 New Testament — Works about the New Testament — The teachings of Jesus

BS2417.E8.S67 1999
Spohn, William C.
Go and do likewise: Jesus and ethics/ William C. Spohn. New York: Continuum, 1999. x, 227 p.
98-040778   241   0826411185
Jesus Christ -- Ethics.Christian ethics.

BS2485-2520 New Testament — Works about the New Testament — Men, women, and children of the New Testament

BS2485.J36 2000
Jansen, Katherine Ludwig, 1957-
The making of the Magdalen: preaching and popular devotion in the later Middle Ages/ Katherine Ludwig Jansen. Princeton, N.J.: Princeton University Press, c2000. xiii, 389 p.
99-045174   274/.05   0691058504
Mary Magdalene, -- Saint -- Cult -- Italy -- History -- Middle Ages, 600-1500. Mary Magdalene, -- Saint -- Cult -- France -- Provence -- History -- Middle Ages, 600-1500. Women in Christianity -- Italy -- History -- To 1500. Preaching -- Italy -- History -- Middle Ages, 600-1500. Preaching -- France -- Provence -- History -- Middle Ages, 600-1500. Italy -- Church history. Provence (France) -- Church history.

BS2506.M855 1996
Murphy-O'Connor, J. 1935-
Paul: a critical life/ Jerome Murphy-O'Connor. Oxford: Clarendon Press; 1996. xvi, 416 p.
95-049173   225.9/2   0198267495
Paul, -- the Apostle, Saint.Christian saints -- Turkey -- Tarsus -- Biography. Apostles -- Biography.

BS2506.R595 1998
Roetzel, Calvin J.
Paul: the man and the myth/ Calvin J. Roetzel. Columbia, S.C.: University of South Carolina Press, c1998. xii, 269 p.
98-025446   225.9/2   1570032645
Paul, -- the Apostle, Saint.Apostles -- Biography. Christian saints -- Biography.

BS2506.W54 1997
Wilson, A. N., 1950-
Paul: the mind of the Apostle/ A.N. Wilson. New York: W.W. Norton & Co., 1997. 273 p.
96-047834   225.9/   0393040666
Paul, -- the Apostle, Saint.Apostles -- Biography.

BS2520.P55.W76 2000
Wroe, Ann.
Pontius Pilate: the biography of an invented man/ Ann Wroe. New York: Random House, c2000. xv, 412 p.
99-043000   226/.092   0375503056
Pilate, Pontius, -- 1st cent.

BS2545 New Testament — Works about the New Testament — Topics (not otherwise provided for), A-Z

BS2545.J44.C64 1988
Cohen, Norman M., 1950-
Jewish Bible personages in the New Testament/ Norman M. Cohen. Lanham, MD: University Press of America, c1989. xii, 163 p.
88-031249   225/.089924   0819172529
Jews in the New Testament.

BS2545.S36.P34 1988
Pagels, Elaine H., 1943-
Adam, Eve, and the serpent/ Elaine Pagels. New York: Random House, c1988. xxviii, 189 p.
87-043227   241/.66/09015   0394521404
Sex -- Biblical teaching. Sex -- Religious aspects -- Christianity -- History of doctrines -- Early church, ca. 30-600.

BS2545.S55.H37 1998
Hanson, K. C.
Palestine in the time of Jesus: social structures and social conflicts/ K.C. Hanson and Douglas E. Oakman. Minneapolis: Fortress Press, c1998. xx, 235 p.
98-018073   225.9/5   080062808X
Sociology, Biblical. Jews -- Social life and customs -- To 70 A.D. Palestine -- Social life and customs -- To 70 A.D.

BS2553-2615.5 New Testament — Special parts of the New Testament — Gospels

BS2553.B33 2002
The New Covenant, commonly called the New Testament. and Apocalypse/ Willis Barnstone, newly translated from the Greek and informed Semitic sources. New York: Riverhead Books, 2002.
2001-019102   225.5/209 21   1573221821

BS2553.P5 1958
The Gospels, translated into modern English, by J.B. Phillips. New York, Macmillan, 1958. ix, 252 p.
57-014426   226

BS2555.2.D53 1992
Dictionary of Jesus and the Gospels/ editors, Joel B. Green, Scot McKnight; consulting editor, I. Howard Marshall. Downers Grove, Ill.: InterVarsity Press, c1992. xxv, 933 p.
91-032382   226/.03 20   0851106463
Bible. N.T. Gospels -- Criticism, interpretation
,   *etc. -- Dictionaries.*

BS2555.2.H46 2000
Hengel, Martin.
The four Gospels and the one Gospel of Jesus Christ: an investigation of the collection and origin of the Canonical Gospels/ Martin Hengel; [translated by John Bowden from the German]. Harrisburg, Pa.: Trinity Press International, 2000. xii, 354 p.
00-029911   226/.066   1563383004
Bible. N.T. Gospels -- Canonical criticism.

BS2555.2.K567 2000
Kloppenborg, John S., 1951-
Excavating Q: the history and setting of the sayings gospel/ John S. Kloppenborg Verbin. Minneapolis: Fortress Press, 2000. xii, 546 p.
99-046058   226/.066   080062601X
Q hypothesis (Synoptics criticism)

BS2555.3.B7633 1994
Brown, Raymond Edward.
The death of the Messiah: from Gethsemane to the grave: a commentary on the Passion narratives in the four Gospels/ by Raymond E. Brown. New York: Doubleday, c1994. 2 v.
93-009241   226/.07   0385193963
Passion narratives (Gospels)

BS2555.5.D62 1980
Documents for the study of the Gospels/ [edited by] David R. Cartlidge, David L. Dungan. Philadelphia: Fortress Press, 1980. 298 p.
79-021341   226/.06
Rome -- Religion.

BS2555.5.M66 1989
Moore, Stephen D., 1954-
Literary criticism and the Gospels: the theoretical challenge/ Stephen D. Moore. New Haven: Yale University Press, c1989. xxii, 226 p.
89-030951   226/.066   0300045255
Narration (Rhetoric) Bible as literature. Deconstruction.

BS2555.6.H4.P55 2000
Pilch, John J.
Healing in the New Testament: insights from medical and Mediterranean anthropology/ John J. Pilch. Minneapolis: Fortress Press, c2000. xiii, 180 p.
99-033004   261.8/321/09015   0800631781
Healing in the Bible. Medical anthropology. Health -- Religious aspects -- Christianity -- History of doctrines -- Early church, ca. 30-600.

BS2585.2.P48 2000
Peterson, Dwight N.
The origins of Mark: the Markan community in current debate/ by Dwight N. Peterson. Leiden; Brill, 2000. 220 p.
00-041376   226.3/06   9004117555
Bible. N.T. Mark -- Criticism, interpretation, etc.

BS2585.5.M33 2000
MacDonald, Dennis Ronald, 1946-
The Homeric epics and the Gospel of Mark/ Dennis R. MacDonald. New Haven: Yale University Press, c2000. viii, 262 p.
99-046344   226.3/066   0300080123
Homer. -- Iliad. Homer. -- Odyssey. Greek literature -- Relation to the New Testament.

BS2615.2.C364 1996
Carmichael, Calum M.
The story of Creation: its origin and its interpretation in Philo and the Fourth Gospel/ Calum M. Carmichael. Ithaca: Cornell University Press, 1996. xii, 136 p.
96-006131   220.6   0801432618
Philo, -- of Alexandria.Creation -- Biblical teaching.

BS2615.3.S313 1980
Schnackenburg, Rudolf, 1914-
The Gospel according to St. John/ Rudolf Schnackenburg; [this translation by Cecily Hastings ... et al.] New York: Seabury Press, [1980-]
79-067156   226/.5/07   0816412103
Bible. N.T. John -- Commentaries.

BS2615.5.H38 1996
Hawkin, David J.
The Johannine world: reflections on the theology of the Fourth Gospel and contemporary society/ David J. Hawkin. Albany: State University of New York Press, c1996. xiv, 183 p.
95-046390   226.5/06   0791430650
Church and the world -- Biblical teaching.

BS2650.2-2675.5 New Testament — Special parts of the New Testament — Epistles

BS2650.5.P38 1990
Paul and the legacies of Paul/ edited by William S. Babcock. Dallas: Southern Methodist University Press, 1990. xxviii, 426 p.
89-078490   225.9/2   0870743058
Paul, -- the Apostle, Saint -- Congresses. Paul, -- the Apostle, Saint -- Influence -- Congresses.   Theology -- History -- Early church, ca. 30-600 -- Congresses.

BS2651.D66 1997
Donaldson, Terence L.
Paul and the gentiles: remapping the Apostle's convictional world/ Terence L. Donaldson. Minneapolis, Minn.: Fortress Press, 1997. xviii, 409 p.
97-000202   225.9/2   0800629930
Paul, -- the Apostle, Saint.Gentiles in the New Testament.

BS2651.D84 1998
Dunn, James D. G., 1939-
The theology of Paul the Apostle/ James D.G. Dunn. Grand Rapids, Mich.: W.B. Eerdmans Pub., c1998. xxxvi, 808 p.
97-023189   227/.092   0802838448
Paul, -- the Apostle, Saint.

BS2655.C36.T76 1994
Trobisch, David.
Paul's letter collection: tracing the origins/ David Trobisch; foreword by Gerd Theissen. Minneapolis: Fortress Press, c1994. xi, 107 p.
94-004746   227/.066   0800625978
Bible. N.T. Epistles of Paul -- Canon. Bible. N.T. Epistles of Paul -- Criticism, interpretation, etc.

BS2655.J4 G34 2000
Gager, John G.
Reinventing Paul/ John G. Gager. Oxford; Oxford University Press 2000. x, 198 p.
99-045706   225.9/2   0195134745
Paul, -- the Apostle, Saint -- Views on Judaism.Christianity and other religions -- Judaism. Judaism -- Relations -- Christianity.

BS2675.2.F87 1999
Furnish, Victor Paul.
The theology of the first letter to the Corinthians/ Victor Paul Furnish. Cambridge, U.K.; Cambridge University Press, 1999. xix, 167 p.
98-035136   227/.206   0521352525
Bible. N.T. Corinthians, 1st -- Criticism, interpretation, etc. Bible. N.T. Corinthians, 1st -- Theology.

BS2675.5.W56 2001
Winter, Bruce W.
After Paul left Corinth: the influence of secular ethics and social change/ Bruce W. Winter. Grand Rapids, Mich.: W.B. Eerdmans, c2001. xvi, 344 p.
00-052150   227/.2067   0802848982
Ethics -- Greece -- Corinth -- History. Ethics in the Bible.   Corinth (Greece) -- Social conditions. Corinth (Greece) -- Social life and customs.

BS2832-2851 New Testament — Special parts of the New Testament — New Testament apocryphal books

BS2832.A2 1993
The Apocryphal New Testament: a collection of apocryphal Christian literature in an English translation/ [edited by] J.K. Elliott. Oxford: Clarendon Press; xxv, 747 p.
92-038129   229/.9205208 20   0198261829
Apocryphal books (New Testament) Apocryphal books (New Testament) -- Criticism, interpretation, etc.

BS2851.J46 2001
Jenkins, Philip, 1952-
Hidden Gospels: how the search for Jesus lost its way/ Philip Jenkins. New York: Oxford University Press, 2001. 260 p.
00-040641   229/.8   0195135091
Apocryphal Gospels. Christianity -- Origin.

BT Doctrinal theology

BT10 Collected works — Several authors

BT10.K5
Kimmel, William Breyfogel, 1908-
Dimensions of faith; contemporary prophetic Protestant theology. [By] Karl Barth [and others] edited by William Kimmel and Geoffrey Clive. With a foreword by James Luther Adams. New York, Twayne Publishers [1960] 507 p.
60-008551   230.082
Theology, Doctrinal

BT21.2 Doctrine and dogma — History — General works

BT21.2.D53 2000
The dictionary of historical theology/ general editor, Trevor A. Hart; consulting editors, Richard Bauckham ... [et al.]. Carlisle, Cumbria, U.K.: Paternoster Press; c2000. xx, 599 p.
00-045323   230/.09   1842270028
Theology, Doctrinal -- History -- Encyclopedias.

BT21.2.P42
Pelikan, Jaroslav Jan, 1923-
The Christian tradition; a history of the development of doctrine [by] Jaroslav Pelikan. Chicago, University of Chicago Press 1971-1989 v. 1-5
79-142042   230   0226653706
Theology, Doctrinal -- History.

BT21.2.T5 1968
Tillich, Paul, 1886-1965.
A history of Christian thought.   New York, Harper & Row [1968] xvii, 300 p.
68-017592   230/.09
Theology, Doctrinal -- History.

BT24-28 Doctrine and dogma — History — By period

BT24.H85 1994
Hultgren, Arland J.
The rise of normative Christianity/ Arland J. Hultgren. Minneapolis: Fortress Press, c1994. xiii, 210 p.
93-014307   270.1   0800626451
Christianity -- Origin. Theology -- History -- Early church, ca. 30-600. Church history -- Primitive and early church, ca. 30-600.

BT25.W63
Wolfson, Harry Austryn, 1887-
The philosophy of the Church fathers. Cambridge, Harvard University Press [1970-]
70-119077   230   0674665511

Theology, Doctrinal -- History -- Early church, ca. 30-600. Incarnation -- History of doctrines. Trinity -- History of doctrines -- Early church, ca. 30-600.

BT26.M37 1988
McGrath, Alister E., 1953-
Reformation thought: an introduction/ Alister E. McGrath. Oxford OX, UK; Blackwell, 1988. x, 212 p.
87-037951   270.6   0631158022

Theology, Doctrinal -- History -- 16th century. Reformation.

BT28.B75 1987
Brown, David, 1948 July 1-
Continental philosophy and modern theology: an engagement/ David Brown. Oxford, UK; Blackwell, 1987. xii, 250 p.
87-011817   230   0631157344

Theology, Doctrinal -- History -- 19th century. Theology, Doctrinal -- History -- 20th century. Philosophy, Modern -- 19th century.

BT28.G754 1989
Griffin, David Ray, 1939-
Varieties of postmodern theology/ David Ray Griffin, William A. Beardslee, Joe Holland. Albany: State University of New York Press, c1989. xiv, 164 p.
88-013923   230/.09/04   0791400506

Theology, Doctrinal -- History -- 20th century. Postmodernism -- Religious aspects -- Christianity.

BT28.M247 1987
Mackey, James Patrick.
Modern theology: a sense of direction/ James P. Mackey. Oxford; Oxford University Press, 1987. 200 p.
86-023770   230/.09/04   0192192205

Jesus Christ -- Person and offices. Christianity -- Philosophy. Theology.

BT28.N48 1996
A new handbook of Christian theologians/ Donald W. Musser and Joseph L. Price, editors. Nashville: Abingdon Press, c1996. 523 p.
96-012801   230/.092/2 B 20   0687278031

Theology, Doctrinal -- History -- 20th century. Theologians -- Biography.

BT28.T5
Tillich, Paul, 1886-1965.
Perspectives on 19th and 20th century Protestant theology. Edited and with an introd. by Carl E. Braaten. New York, Harper & Row [1967] xxiv, 252 p.
67-011507   230/.4

Protestant churches -- Doctrines -- History. Theology, Doctrinal -- History -- 19th century. Theology, Doctrinal -- History -- 20th century.

BT30 Doctrine and dogma — History — By region or country, A-Z

BT30.A438.Y68 1993
Young, Josiah U.
African theology: a critical analysis and annotated bibliography/ Josiah U. Young III. Westport, Conn.: Greenwood Press, 1993. xii, 257 p.
92-038979   230/.0967   0313264872

Theology, Doctrinal -- Africa, Sub-Saharan -- History -- 20th century. Theology, Doctrinal -- Africa, Sub-Saharan -- History -- 20th century -- Bibliography. Africa, Sub-Saharan -- Religion. Africa, Sub-Saharan -- Religion -- Bibliography.

BT30.U6.F33 1982
Fackre, Gabriel J.
The Religious Right and Christian faith/ by Gabriel Fackre. Grand Rapids, Mich.: Eerdmans, c1982. xiii, 126 p.
82-002488   230/.044   080283566X

Falwell, Jerry. Theology, Doctrinal -- United States -- History -- 20th century. Fundamentalism -- History -- 20th century. Christianity and politics -- History -- 20th century.

BT40 Philosophy. Philosophical theology — General works

BT40.M5
Mitchell, Basil.
Faith and logic; Oxford essays in philosophical theology. Boston, Beacon Press [1957] v, 222 p.
57-002513   230.01

Christianity -- Philosophy.

BT65 Doctrinal, dogmatic, systematic theology — Introductions. Prolegomena, etc.

BT65.B313
Barth, Karl, 1886-1968.
Evangelical theology, an introduction. Translated by Grover Foley. New York, Holt, Rinehart and Winston [1963] xiii, 206 p.
63-007268   230

Theology, Doctrinal.

BT65.N48 1991
Neville, Robert C.
A theology primer/ Robert Cummings Neville. Albany: State University of New York Press, c1991. xxix, 221 p.
90-019636   230   0791408493

Theology, Doctrinal.

BT75 Doctrinal, dogmatic, systematic theology — Formal treatises — 1801-1950

BT75.B283 1975
Barth, Karl, 1886-1968.
Church dogmatics/ by Karl Barth; editors, G. W. Bromiley, T. F. Torrance; [translator, G. W. Bromiley]. Edinburgh: T. & T. Clark, [1975-]
78-315267   230   0567090132

Theology, Doctrinal.

BT75.2 Doctrinal, dogmatic, systematic theology — Formal treatises — 1951-2000

BT75.2.R3313
Rahner, Karl, 1904-
Foundations of Christian faith: an introduction to the idea of Christianity/ Karl Rahner; translated by William V. Dych. New York: Seabury Press, 1978. xv, 470 p.
77-013336   230/.2   0816403546

Catholic Church -- Doctrines.

BT77 Doctrinal, dogmatic, systematic theology — Popular works

BT77.K79 1994
Kung, Hans, 1928-
Great Christian thinkers/ Hans Kung. New York: Continuum, c1994. 235 p.
94-000883   230/.092/2   0826406432

Theologians. Theology -- Introductions.

BT78 Doctrinal, dogmatic, systematic theology — General special

BT78.B3 1963
Barth, Karl, 1886-1968.
God in action. Introd. by Elmer G. Homrighausen. Translated by E. G. Homrighausen and Karl J. Ernst. Manhasset, N.Y., Round Table Press; distributed by Channel Press, 1963. 143 p.
63-015798   230.4

Dialectical theology. Theology, Doctrinal

BT78.F36 2001
Fenn, Richard K.
Time exposure: the personal experience of time in secular societies/ Richard K. Fenn. Oxford; Oxford University Press, 2001. viii, 166 p.
00-020716   261   0195139534

Time -- Religious aspects -- Christianity -- History of doctrines. Time -- Social aspects -- History. Secularization -- History.

BT78.K8613 1988
Kung, Hans, 1928-
Theology for the third millennium: an ecumenical view/ Hans Kung; translated by Peter Heinegg New York: Doubleday, 1988 xvi, 316 p.
87-029621 230 0385244983
Ecumenical movement Christianity and other religions Theology -- Methodology

BT78.R48 2001
Rieger, Joerg.
God and the excluded: visions and blind spots in contemporary theology/ Joerg Rieger. Minneapolis: Fortress Press, c2001. xi, 241 p.
00-044253 230/.01 0800632540
Theology, Doctrinal. Marginality, Social -- Religious aspects -- Christianity.

BT78.W585 1993
Williamson, Clark M.
A guest in the house of Israel: post-Holocaust church theology/ Clark M. Williamson. Louisville, Ky.: Westminster/John Knox Press, c1993. viii, 344 p.
93-003261 231.7/6 0664254543
Theology, Doctrinal -- 20th century. Judaism (Christian theology) Holocaust, Jewish (1939-1945) -- Influence.

BT80 Doctrinal, dogmatic, systematic theology — Addresses, essays, sermons, etc.

BT80.P3413 1983
Pannenberg, Wolfhart, 1928-
Basic questions in theology: collected essays/ Wolfhart Pannenberg; translated by George H. Kehm. Philadelphia: Westminster Press, 1983, c1970 2 v.
82-015984 230/.044 0664244661
Theology, Doctrinal -- Addresses, essays, lectures.

BT82.2 Doctrinal, dogmatic, systematic theology — Schools of thought affecting doctrine and dogma (19th-20th centuries) — Fundamentalism

BT82.2.H36 2000
Harding, Susan Friend.
The book of Jerry Falwell: fundamentalist language and politics/ Susan Friend Harding. Princeton, N.J.: Princeton University Press, c2000. xvi, 336 p.
99-045172 280/.4/097309048 0691059896
Falwell, Jerry -- Language. Falwell, Jerry -- Oratory. Fundamentalism. Language and languages -- Religious aspects -- Christianity.

BT82.2.M39 1991
Marsden, George M., 1939-
Understanding fundamentalism and evangelicalism/ George M. Marsden. Grand Rapids, Mich.: W.B. Eerdmans, c1991. x, 208 p.
90-022212 277.3/082 0802805396
Machen, J. Gresham -- (John Gresham), -- 1881-1937.Evangelicalism -- United States -- History. Fundamentalism -- History.

BT82.2.W54 1992
Wilcox, Clyde, 1953-
God's warriors: the Christian right in twentieth-century America/ Clyde Wilcox. Baltimore: Johns Hopkins University Press, c1992. xx, 249 p.
91-015849 322/.1/09730904 0801842638
Fundamentalism. Christianity and politics -- History -- 20th century. United States -- Politics and government -- 20th century.

BT82.7 Doctrinal, dogmatic, systematic theology — Schools of thought affecting doctrine and dogma (19th-20th centuries) — Black theology

BT82.7.H663 2000
Hopkins, Dwight N.
Down, up, and over: slave religion and Black theology/ Dwight N. Hopkins. Minneapolis, MN: Fortress Press, c2000. xii, 300 p.
99-054737 230/.089/96073 0800627237
Black theology.

BT82.7.M38 1998
Matthews, Donald Henry, 1952-
Honoring the ancestors: an African cultural interpretation of Black religion and literature/ Donald H. Matthews. New York: Oxford University Press, 1998. xiii, 171 p.
97-001140 230/.089/96073 0195091043
Black theology. Afro-Americans -- Religion. Spirituals (Songs) -- History and criticism.

BT83 Doctrinal, dogmatic, systematic theology — Schools of thought affecting doctrine and dogma (19th-20th centuries) — Dialectical theology

BT83.B613 1962a
Bonhoeffer, Dietrich, 1906-1945.
Act and being. Translated by Bernard Noble. Introd. by Ernst Wolf. New York, Harper [1962, c1961] 192 p.
62-007951 230
Dialectical theology. Act (Philosophy)

BT83.55 Doctrinal, dogmatic, systematic theology — Schools of thought affecting doctrine and dogma (19th-20th centuries) — Feminist theology

BT83.55.C35 2002
The Cambridge companion to feminist theology/ edited by Susan Frank Parsons. Cambridge, UK; Cambridge University Press, 2002. xviii, 268 p.
2002-073700 230/.082 21 0521663806
Feminist theology.

BT83.55.C48 1989
Chopp, Rebecca S., 1952-
The power to speak: feminism, language, God/ Rebecca S. Chopp. New York: Crossroad, 1989. 167 p.
89-033953 230/.082 0824509404
Feminist theology. Word of God (Theology) Nonsexist language -- Religious aspects -- Christianity.

BT83.55.G34 2000
Gagne, Laurie Brands, 1951-
The uses of darkness: women's underworld journeys, ancient and modern/ Laurie Brands Gagne. Notre Dame, Ind.: University of Notre Dame Press, c2000. xiii, 223 p.
00-009069 230/.082 0268043051
Feminist theology. Christian women -- Religious life.

BT83.55.G73 2000
Greene-McCreight, Kathryn, 1961-
Feminist reconstruction of Christian doctrine: narrative analysis and appraisal/ Kathryn Greene-McCreight. New York: Oxford University Press, 2000. vi, 175 p.
99-019374 230/.082 0195128621
Feminist theology.

BT83.55.H64 1995
Hogan, Linda.
From women's experience to feminist theology/ Linda Hogan. Sheffield, England: Sheffield Academic Press, c1995. 192 p.
96-143759 230/.082 1850755205
Feminist theology.

BT83.55.M27 1994
Martin, Francis, 1930-
The feminist question: feminist theology in the light of Christian tradition/ Francis Martin. Grand Rapids, Mich.: W.B. Eerdmans Pub. Co., c1994. xviii, 461 p.
94-032318 230/.082 0802807941
Women -- Religious aspects -- Christianity. Women in Christianity. Feminist theology.

BT83.55.W55 1993
Williams, Delores S.
Sisters in the wilderness: the challenge of womanist God-talk/ Delores S. Williams. Maryknoll, N.Y.: Orbis Books, c1993. xvi, 287 p.
93-010654   230/.082 20   088344772X
Feminist theology. Black theology. Afro-American women -- Religious life.

BT83.57 Doctrinal, dogmatic, systematic theology — Schools of thought affecting doctrine and dogma (19th-20th centuries) — Liberation theology

BT83.57.B59613 1987
Boff, Leonardo.
Introducing liberation theology/ Leonardo Boff, Clodovis Boff; translated from the Portuguese by Paul Burns. Maryknoll, N.Y.: Orbis Books, c1987. xi, 99 p.
87-005672   230/.2   0883445751
Liberation theology.

BT83.57.C68 2000
Connor, Kimberly Rae, 1957-
Imagining grace: liberating theologies in the slave narrative tradition/ Kimberly Rae Connor. Urbana: University of Illinois Press, c2000. xi, 311 p.
99-006615   230/.089/96073   025202530X
Liberation theology -- United States. Slaves' writings, American -- History and criticism.

BT83.57.L69 1996
Lowy, Michael, 1938-
The war of gods: religion and politics in Latin America/ Michael Lowy. New York: Verso, 1996. 163 p.
96-012017   261.7/098   1859849075
Liberation theology. Church and state -- Latin America. Church and social problems -- Latin America.

BT83.57.L95 1991
Lynch, Edward A.
Religion and politics in Latin America: liberation theology and Christian democracy/ Edward A. Lynch. New York: Praeger, 1991. xi, 200 p.
90-048694   261.7/098   0275937747
Liberation theology. Christian democracy -- Latin America. Christianity and politics.

BT83.57.S64 1991
Smith, Christian 1960-
The emergence of liberation theology: radical religion and social movement theory/ Christian Smith. Chicago: University of Chicago Press, c1991. xiv, 300 p.
90-026575   306.6/3028   0226764095
Liberation theology. Sociology, Christian (Catholic)

BT83.7 Doctrinal, dogmatic, systematic theology — Schools of thought affecting doctrine and dogma (19th-20th centuries) — Secularization

BT83.7.H64 1998
Hoedemaker, L. A.
Secularization and mission: a theological essay/ Bert Hoedemaker. Harrisburg, Pa.: Trinity Press International; c1998. x, 82 p.
97-041099   266/.001   1563382245
Secularization (Theology) Missions -- Theory.

BT84 Doctrinal, dogmatic, systematic theology — Schools of thought affecting doctrine and dogma (19th-20th centuries) — Existentialism

BT84.P37 1999
Pattison, George, 1950-
Anxious angels: a retrospective view of religious existentialism/ George Pattison. New York: St. Martin's Press, 1999. xv, 285 p.
98-030657   230/.046   0312220111
Christianity and existentialism -- History.

BT88 Authority — General works

BT88.T35 1978
Tavard, George H. 1922-
Holy Writ or Holy Church: the crisis of the Protestant Reformation/ George H. Tavard. Westport, Conn.: Greenwood Press, 1978, c1959. x, 250 p.
78-017085   230   0313205841
Authority -- Religious aspects -- Christianity - - History of doctrines. Protestant churches -- Relations -- Catholic Church.

BT91 Authority — Church. Teaching office of the Church

BT91.R36 1995
Rankin, David 1952-
Tertullian and the church/ by David Rankin. Cambridge; Cambridge University Press, 1995. xvii, 229 p.
94-024375   262/.013/092   0521480671
Tertullian, -- ca. 160-ca. 230. Church -- Authority -- History of doctrines -- Early church, ca. 30-600. Montanism.

BT93 Judaism — General works

BT93.L63 2000
Locke, Hubert G.
Learning from history: a Black Christian's perspective on the Holocaust/ Hubert Locke. Westport, Conn.: Greenwood Press, 2000. xv, 128 p.
00-022304   231.7/6   0313315698
Holocaust (Christian theology) Blacks -- Social conditions.

BT93.M35 1992
Manuel, Frank Edward.
The broken staff: Judaism through Christian eyes/ Frank E. Manuel. Cambridge, Mass.: Harvard University Press, 1992. ix, 363 p.
91-028520   261.2/6/094   0674083709
Judaism (Christian theology) -- History of doctrines. Judaism -- Relations -- Christianity. Christianity and other religions -- Judaism.

BT93.S35 1996
Soulen, R. Kendall, 1959-
The God of Israel and Christian theology/ R. Kendall Soulen. Minneapolis: Fortress Press, c1996. xii, 195 p.
95-046692   231.7/6   0800628837
Judaism (Christian theology) -- History of doctrines. Christianity and other religions -- Judaism. Judaism -- Relations -- Christianity.

BT93.8 Palestine in Christianity. Palestinian liberation and Christianity

BT93.8.W55 1992
Wilken, Robert Louis, 1936-
The land called holy: Palestine in Christian history and thought/ Robert L. Wilken. New Haven: Yale University Press, c1992. xvi, 355 p.
92-015258   263/.0425694   0300054912
Palestine in Christianity.Palestine -- Church history.

BT96.2 Divine law. Moral government — General works — 1951-2000

BT96.2.H34 1995
Hall, Douglas John, 1928-
God and the nations/ Douglas John Hall, Rosemary Radford Ruether. Minneapolis, MN: Fortress Press, c1995. 110 p.
95-005197   231.7/6   0800629000
Providence and government of God. Nationalism -- Religious aspects -- Christianity. Church and the world.

BT98 God — History of doctrines concerning God

BT98.A65 1993
Armstrong, Karen, 1944-
A history of God: the 4000-year quest of Judaism, Christianity, and Islam/ by Karen Armstrong. New York: A.A. Knopf: 1993. xxiii, 460 p.
92-038318   291.2/11   0679426000
God -- Comparative studies. God -- Biblical teaching. God -- History of doctrines.

BT102 God — General works — 1951-2000

BT102.A46 1991
Alston, William P.
Perceiving God: the epistemology of religious experience/ William P. Alston. Ithaca, N.Y.: Cornell University Press, 1991. xii, 320 p.
91-055068   248.2/01   0801425972
God -- Knowableness. Experience (Religion) Knowledge, Theory of (Religion)

BT102.G747 1995
Grigg, Richard, 1955-
When God becomes goddess: the transformation of American religion/ Richard Grigg. New York: Continuum, 1995. 155 p.
95-020444   231/.0973/0904   0826408648
God -- History of doctrines -- 20th century. Christianity -- United States -- 20th century. Feminist theology.

BT102.J647 1987
Jones, Major J., 1918-
The color of God: the concept of God in Afro-American thought/ by Major J. Jones. Macon, GA: Mercer, c1987. xi, 124 p.
87-018449   231/.08996073   0865542740
God. God -- History of doctrines. Black theology. United States -- Religion.

BT102.M3
Maritain, Jacques, 1882-1973.
Man's approach to God.   Latrobe, Pa.: Archabbey Press, [1960] 53 p.
61-002276   231
God -- Knowableness.

BT102.O29 1998
O'Connor, David, 1949-
God and inscrutable evil: in defense of theism and atheism/ David O'Connor. Lanham, Md.: Rowman & Littlefield, 1998. xiii, 273 p.
97-034277   231   0847687635
God -- Proof. Good and evil. Atheism.

BT102.S68 2000
Clayton, Philip, 1956-
The problem of God in modern thought/ Clayton. Grand Rapids, Mich.: W.B. Eerdmans Pub., c2000. xv, 516 p.
00-023129   212   0802838855
God. Philosophy, Modern.

BT103 God — General works — 2001-

BT103.S37 2002
Schrag, Calvin O.
God as otherwise than being: toward a semantics of the gift/ Calvin O. Schrag. Evanston, Ill.: Northwestern University Press, 2002. xvi, 157 p.
2002-002168   211 21   0810119234
God. Ontology. Postmodernism.

BT111.2 God — Doctrine of the Trinity — General works

BT111.2.M613 1981
Moltmann, Jurgen.
The Trinity and the kingdom: the doctrine of God/ Jurgen Moltmann; [translated by Margaret Kohl]. San Francisco: Harper & Row, c1981. xvi, 256 p.
80-008352   231/.044   0060659068
Trinity. Kingdom of God.

BT121.2 God — Holy Spirit. The Paraclete — General works

BT121.2.W32 1996
Wallace, Mark I., 1956-
Fragments of the spirit: nature, violence, and the renewal of creation/ Mark I. Wallace. New York: Continuum, 1996. xii, 237 p.
95-049441   231/.3
Holy Spirit. Spirit. Violence -- Religious aspects -- Christianity.

BT123 God — Holy Spirit. The Paraclete — Other

BT123.H6513 1998
Holl, Adolf.
The left hand of God: a biography of the Holy Spirit/ Adolf Holl; translated from the German by John Cullen. New York: Doubleday, c1998. xi, 352 p.
98-017994   231/.3   0385492847
Holy Spirit.

BT153 God — Divine attributes — Individual attributes

BT153.S8.R67 1997
Ross, Ellen M., 1959-
The grief of God: images of the suffering Jesus in late medieval England/ Ellen M. Ross. New York: Oxford University Press, 1997. xiii, 200 p.
96-005502   232.96   019510451X
Jesus Christ -- Crucifixion -- Art.God -- Mercy -- History of doctrines -- Middle Ages, 600-1500. Suffering of God -- History of doctrines -- Middle Ages, 600-1500. Christian art and symbolism -- Medieval, 500-1500 -- England. England -- Church history -- 1066-1485.

BT160 God — Theodicy. Vindication of the justice of God — General works

BT160.R57 1997
Rodin, R. Scott, 1957-
Evil and theodicy in the theology of Karl Barth/ R. Scott Rodin. New York: P. Lang, c1997. x, 310 p.
96-030661   231/.8/092   0820434965
Barth, Karl, -- 1886-1968 -- Contributions in doctrine of theodicy.Theodicy -- History of doctrines -- 20th century.

BT198 Christology — History of Christological doctrines and study

BT198.A48 1997
Altizer, Thomas J. J.
The contemporary Jesus/ Thomas J.J. Altizer. Albany, N.Y.: State University of New York Press, c1997. xxvii, 225 p.
96-039269   232   0791433757
Jesus Christ -- History of doctrines. Jesus Christ -- History of doctrines -- 20th century. Jesus Christ -- Influence.

BT198.C32 1997
Carrell, Peter R.
Jesus and the angels: angelology and the christology of the Apocalypse of John/ Peter R. Carrell. Cambridge; Cambridge University Press, 1997. xxii, 270 p.
96-047526   232/.09/015   0521590116
Jesus Christ -- History of doctrines -- Early church, ca. 30-600.Angels -- History of doctrines -- Early church, ca. 30-600.

BT198.D25 1991
Dahl, Nils Alstrup.
Jesus the Christ: the historical origins of christological doctrine/ Nils Alstrup Dahl; edited by Donald H. Juel. Minneapolis: Fortress Press, c1991. 249 p.
90-044551   232/.09/015   0800624580
Jesus Christ -- History of doctrines -- Early church, ca. 30-600.

BT198.J643 1998
Jonge, Marinus de, 1925-
God's final envoy: early Christology and Jesus' own view of his mission/ Marinus de Jonge. Grand Rapids, Mich.: W.B. Eerdmans Pub., c1998. x, 166 p.
98-025620   232/.09/015   0802844820
Jesus Christ -- History of doctrines -- Early church, ca. 30-600. Jesus Christ -- Person and offices -- Biblical teaching.

BT198.M295 1990
Macquarrie, John.
Jesus Christ in modern thought/ John Macquarrie. London: SCM Press; 1990. x, 454 p.
90-031831   232/.09   0334024579
Jesus Christ -- History of doctrines. Jesus Christ -- Person and offices.

BT198.P44 1985
Pelikan, Jaroslav Jan, 1923-
Jesus through the centuries: his place in the history of culture/ Jaroslav Pelikan. New Haven [Conn.]: Yale University Press, c1985. xvi, 270 p.
85-002428   232.9/04   0300034962
Jesus Christ -- History of doctrines. Jesus Christ -- Influence.

BT201 Christology —
General works.
The person of Jesus — 1801-1950

BT201.S263
Santayana, George, 1863-1952.
The idea of Christ in the Gospels; or, God in man, a critical essay by George Santayana. New York, C. Scribner's sons, 1946. 266 p.
46-025109   232
Jesus Christ -- Person and offices.

BT202 Christology —
General works.
The person of Jesus — 1951-2000

BT202.B5313
Boff, Leonardo.
Jesus Christ liberator: a critical Christology for our time/ Leonardo Boff; translated by Patrick Hughes. Maryknoll, N.Y.: Orbis Books, c1978. xii, 323 p.
78-000969   232   0883442361
Jesus Christ -- Person and offices.

BT202.F695 2000
Freeman, Laurence.
Jesus, the teacher within/ Laurence Freeman. New York: Continuum, c2000. 271 p.
99-056233   232   0826412238
Jesus Christ -- Person and offices.

BT202.H24 1999
Haight, Roger.
Jesus, symbol of God/ Roger Haight. Maryknoll, N.Y.: Orbis Books, c1999. xiv, 505 p.
98-049921   232   1570752478
Jesus Christ -- Person and offices.

BT202.J43613 1984
Faces of Jesus: Latin American christologies/ edited by Jose Miguez Bonino; translated from the Spanish by Robert R. Barr. Maryknoll, N.Y.: Orbis Books, c1984. vi, 186 p.
83-019375   232/.098   0883441292
Jesus Christ -- Person and offices. Theology, Doctrinal -- Latin America -- History -- 20th century.

BT202.O313 1995
O'Collins, Gerald.
Christology: a biblical, historical, and systematic study of Jesus/ Gerald O'Collins. Oxford; Oxford University Press, 1995. ix, 333 p.
94-032210   232   0198755015
Jesus Christ -- Person and offices. Jesus Christ -- History of doctrines.

BT203 Christology —
General works.
The person of Jesus — 2001-

BT203.J47 2001
Jesus then & now: images of Jesus in history and Christology/ edited by Marvin Meyer and Charles Hughes. Harrisburg, Pa.: Trinity Press International, c2001. viii, 294 p.
00-064838   232/.8   1563383446
Jesus Christ -- Person and offices.

BT205 Christology —
General special

BT205.E83 1996
Evans, C. Stephen.
The historical Christ and the Jesus of faith: the incarnational narrative as history/ C. Stephen Evans. Oxford: Clarendon Press; 1996. xi, 386 p.
95-041328   232.9/08   0198263821
Jesus Christ -- Person and offices -- Biblical teaching. Jesus Christ -- Historicity. Incarnation -- Biblical teaching. Atonement -- Biblical teaching.

BT220 Christology —
Natures of Christ — Humanity

BT220.R34 1997
Rae, Murray.
Kierkegaard's vision of the Incarnation: by faith transformed/ Murray A. Rae. Oxford: Clarendon Press; 1997. xii, 267 p.
97-025131   232/.1   0198269404
Kierkegaard, Soren, -- 1813-1855. Repentance -- Christianity -- History of doctrines -- 19th century. Faith -- History of doctrines -- 19th century. Incarnation -- History of doctrines -- 19th century.

BT265.2 Christology —
Offices of Christ — Priestly office

BT265.2.B37 2001
Bartlett, Anthony W.
Cross purposes: the violent grammar of Christian atonement/ Anthony W. Bartlett. Harrisburg, Pa.: Trinity Press International, c2001. vii, 277 p.
00-066316   232/.3   1563383365
Atonement. Violence -- Religious aspects -- Christianity.

BT297 Christology —
Life of Christ —
Sources of biography

BT297.T4713 1998
Theissen, Gerd.
The historical Jesus: a comprehensive guide/ Gerd Theissen and Annette Merz; [translated by John Bowden from the German]. Minneapolis: Fortress Press, 1998. xxix, 642 p.
98-016181   232.9/08   0800631234
Jesus Christ -- Biography -- Sources. Jesus Christ -- Historicity.

BT297.V36 2000
Van Voorst, Robert E.
Jesus outside the New Testament: an introduction to the ancient evidence/ Robert E. Van Voorst. Grand Rapids, Mich.: W.B. Eerdmans Pub., c2000. xiv, 248 p.
99-086146   232.9/08   0802843689
Jesus Christ -- Biography -- Sources. Jesus Christ -- Historicity.

BT301.2 Christology —
Life of Christ — Biographies

BT301.2.C76 1991
Crossan, John Dominic.
The historical Jesus: the life of a Mediterranean Jewish peasant/ John Dominic Crossan. [San Francisco]: HarperSanFrancisco, c1991. xxxiv, 506 p.
90-056451   232.9/01   0060616075
Jesus Christ -- Biography. Jesus Christ -- Biography -- History and criticism. Jesus Christ.

BT301.2.C77 1994
Crossan, John Dominic.
Jesus: a revolutionary biography/ John Dominic Crossan. [San Francisco]: HarperSanFrancisco, c1994. xiv, 209 p.
93-024685   232.9/01   006061661X
Jesus Christ -- Biography. Jesus Christ -- Historicity.

BT301.2.S254 1993
Sanders, E. P.
The historical figure of Jesus/ E.P. Sanders. 1st ed. London: Allen Lane: 1993. xiii, 337 p.
94-136152   0713990597
Jesus Christ -- Biography. Jesus Christ -- Biography -- Sources. Jesus Christ -- Historicity.

BT303.2 Christology — Life of Christ — Historicity of Christ

BT303.2.H49 2000
The historical Jesus through Catholic and Jewish eyes/ edited by Leonard Greenspoon, Dennis Hamm, Bryan F. LeBeau. Harrisburg, Pa.: Trinity Press International, c2000. xviii, 171 p.
00-037413   232.9/08   1563383225
Jesus Christ -- Historicity. Jesus Christ -- Jewish interpretations.

BT303.2.S33 2000
Schussler Fiorenza, Elisabeth, 1938-
Jesus and the politics of interpretation/ Elisabeth Schussler Fiorenza. New York: Continuum, 2000. xi, 180 p.
00-056986   232.9/08   0826412734
Jesus Christ -- Historicity -- History of doctrines.Feminist theology.

BT303.2.B586 1994
Borg, Marcus J.
Jesus in contemporary scholarship/ Marcus J. Borg. Valley Forge, Pa.: Trinity Press International, c1994. xiii, 209 p.
94-018255   232/.09/048   1563380943
Jesus Christ -- Historicity. Jesus Christ -- Biography -- History and criticism.

BT303.2.D753 1998
Drews, Arthur, 1865-1935.
The Christ myth/ Arthur Drews; translated from the third edition (revised and enlarged) by C. Delisle Burns. Amherst, N.Y.: Prometheus Books, 1998. 304 p.
97-046443   232.9/08   1573921904
Jesus Christ -- Historicity.

BT303.2 .J47 2000
Jesus two thousand years later/ edited by James H. Charlesworth and Walter P. Weaver. Harrisburg, Pa.: Trinity Press International, c2000. xi, 130 p.
99-053669   232.9/08   1563383039
Jesus Christ -- Historicity. Jesus Christ -- Biography -- History and criticism.

BT303.2.K435 2000
Keck, Leander E.
Who is Jesus?: history in perfect tense/ Leander E. Keck. Columbia, S.C.: University of South Carolina Press, c2000. x, 207 p.
99-050778   232.9/08   1570033382
Jesus Christ -- Historicity.

BT303.2.P75 2000
Price, Robert M., 1954-
Deconstructing Jesus/ Robert M. Price. Amherst, N.Y.: Prometheus Books, 2000. 284 p.
99-048140   232   1573927589
Jesus Christ -- Historicity.Church history -- Primitive and early church, ca. 30-600.

BT306 Christology — Life of Christ — Words of Christ. Sayings

BT306.C76 1983
Crossan, John Dominic.
In fragments: the aphorisms of Jesus/ John Dominic Crossan. San Francisco: Harper & Row, c1983. x, 389 p.
83-047719   232.9/54   0060616083
Jesus Christ -- Words.Aphorisms and apothegms.

BT309 Christology — Life of Christ — Occult, astrological interpretations

BT309.G68
Graves, Robert, 1895-
King Jesus, by Robert Graves. New York, Creative Age Press, inc. [1946] viii, 424 p.
46-007142   232.993
Jesus Christ -- Fiction.

BT375.2-468 Christology — Life of Christ — Special topics

BT375.2.H78 2000
Hultgren, Arland J.
The parables of Jesus: a commentary/ Arland J. Hultgren. Grand Rapids, Mich.: W.B. Eerdmans, c2000. xxix, 522 p.
00-037140   226.8/07   0802844758
Jesus Christ -- Parables.

BT375.2.C85 1995
Culbertson, Philip Leroy, 1944-
A word fitly spoken: context, transmission, and adoption of the parables of Jesus/ Philip L. Culbertson. Albany: State University of New York Press, c1995. xvi, 390 p.
94-009989   226.8/066   0791423115
Jesus Christ -- Parables.

BT380.B66 1959
Bonhoeffer, Dietrich, 1906-1945.
The cost of discipleship. [Translated from the German by R. H. Fuller, with some revision by Irmgard Booth] New York, Macmillan [1959] 285 p.
60-000677   226.2
Sermon on the mount.

BT380.2.W54 2001
Wierzbicka, Anna.
What did Jesus mean?: explaining the Sermon on the Mount and the parables in simple and universal human concepts/ Anna Wierzbicka. Oxford; Oxford University Press, 2001. xiv, 509 p.
00-021159   226.8/06   0195137329
Jesus Christ -- Parables.Semantics.

BT431.5.C76 1995
Crossan, John Dominic.
Who killed Jesus?: exposing the roots of anti-semitism in the Gospel story of the death of Jesus/ John Dominic Crossan. [San Francisco]: HarperSanFrancisco, c1995. xii, 238 p.
94-040200   232.96   006061479X
Jesus Christ -- Passion -- Role of Jews -- History of doctrines. Jesus Christ -- Resurrection -- History of doctrines. Passion narratives (Gospels) Christianity and antisemitism -- History.

BT456.R6713 1987
Rosse, Gerard.
The cry of Jesus on the cross: a biblical and theological study/ Gerard Rosse; translated by Stephen Wentworth Arndt. New York: Paulist Press, c1987. x, 145 p.
87-027392   232.9/635   0809129221
Jesus Christ -- Seven last words. Jesus Christ -- Person and offices.

BT468.L49 2001
Lewis, Alan E. 1944-
Between cross and Resurrection: a theology of Holy Saturday/ Alan E. Lewis. Grand Rapids, Mich.: W.B. Eerdmans, c2001. xiii, 477 p.
00-069197   242/.35   0802847021
Jesus Christ -- Three days in the tomb.Holy Saturday.

BT587 Christology — Relics — Special, A-Z

BT587.S4.W515 1998
Wilson, Ian, 1941-
The blood and the shroud: new evidence that the world's most sacred relic is real/ Ian Wilson. New York: Free Press, c1998. xvi, 333 p.
98-144693   232.96/6   0684853590
Holy Shroud.

BT590 Christology — Topics (not otherwise provided for), A-Z

BT590.J8 C45 2000
Chilton, Bruce.
Rabbi Jesus: an intimate biography/ by Bruce Chilton. New York: Doubleday, 2000. xxii, 330 p.
00-031548   232.9/01   038549792X
Jesus Christ -- Jewishness.

BT590.P9.M55 1997
Miller, John W., 1926-
Jesus at thirty: a psychological and historical portrait/ John W. Miller. Minneapolis: Fortress Press, c1997. ix, 177 p.
97-023723   232.9/01   0800631072
Jesus Christ -- Psychology.

BT610 Mary, Mother of Jesus Christ. Mariology — Theology — History of doctrines

BT610.P45 1996
Pelikan, Jaroslav Jan, 1923-
Mary through the centuries: her place in the history of culture/ Jaroslav Pelikan. New Haven: Yale University Press, c1996. x, 267 p.
96-024726   232.91   0300069510
Mary, -- Blessed Virgin, Saint -- History of doctrines. Mary, -- Blessed Virgin, Saint -- Theology.

BT650 Mary, Mother of Jesus Christ. Mariology — Miracles. Apparitions. Shrines, sanctuaries, images, processions, etc. — General works

BT650.Z56 1991
Zimdars-Swartz, Sandra, 1949-
Encountering Mary: from La Salette to Medjugorje/ Sandra L. Zimdars-Swartz. Princeton, N.J.: Princeton University Press, c1991. xv, 342 p.
90-046215   232.91/7/09034   0691073716
Mary, -- Blessed Virgin, Saint -- Apparitions and miracles -- History -- 19th century. Mary, -- Blessed Virgin, Saint -- Apparitions and miracles -- History -- 20th century.

BT660 Mary, Mother of Jesus Christ. Mariology — Miracles. Apparitions. Shrines, sanctuaries, images, processions, etc. — Special

BT660.G8.P66 1995
Poole, Stafford.
Our Lady of Guadalupe: the origins and sources of a Mexican national symbol, 1531-1797/ by Stafford Poole. Tuscon: University of Arizona Press, c1995. xi, 325 p.
94-018724   232.91/7/097253   0816515263
Guadalupe, Our Lady of -- History.Mexico -- Religious life and customs.

BT695.5 Creation — General works

BT695.5.C49 2000
Christianity and ecology: seeking the well-being of earth and humans/ edited by Dieter T. Hessel and Rosemary Radford Ruether. Cambridge, Mass.: Distributed by Harvard University Press for the Harvard University Center for the Study of World Religions,
vinity School, c2000. xlvii, 720 p.
99-044576   261.8/362   0945454198
Human ecology -- Religious aspects -- Christianity.

BT695.5.D78 2000
Drummy, Michael F.
Being and earth: Paul Tillich's theology of nature/ Michael F. Drummy. Lanham, Md.: University Press of America, c2000. xiv, 185 p.
00-056369   230/.092   0761817913
Tillich, Paul, -- 1886-1965 -- Contributions in doctrine of nature.Nature -- Religious aspects -- Christianity.

BT695.5.G68 1995
Gottfried, Robert R.
Economics, ecology, and the roots of Western faith: perspectives from the garden/ Robert R. Gottfried. Lanham, Md.: Rowman & Littlefield, c1995. viii, 165 p.
95-014492   261.8/362   0847680169
Human ecology -- Religious aspects -- Christianity. Economics -- Religious aspects -- Christianity.

BT695.5.S27 1997
Scharper, Stephen B.
Redeeming the time: a political theology of the environment/ Stephen Bede Scharper. New York: Continuum, 1997. 240 p.
96-053591   261.8/32   0826409350
Ecology -- Religious aspects -- Christianity.

BT695.5.S68 1988
Sorrell, Roger D.
St. Francis of Assisi and nature: tradition and innovation in Western   Christian attitudes toward the environment/ Roger D. Sorrell. New York: Oxford University Press, 1988. viii, 204 p.
85-010135   231.7 19   0195053222
Francis, of Assisi, Saint, 1182-1226 -- Views on nature. Nature -- Religious aspects -- Christianity -- History of doctrines -- Middle

BT695.5.S75 1997
Stoll, Mark, 1954-
Protestantism, capitalism, and nature in America/ Mark Stoll. Albuquerque: University of New Mexico Press, c1997. xii, 276 p.
96-025351   261.8/362/0973   0826317804
Nature -- Religious aspects -- Christianity. Human ecology -- Religious aspects -- Protestant churches. Protestant churches -- United States -- Doctrines.

BT701-701.2 Creation — Man. Doctrinal anthropology — General works

BT701.N5213 1996
Niebuhr, Reinhold, 1892-1971.
The nature and destiny of man: a Christian interpretation/ Reinhold Niebuhr; introduction by Robin W. Lovin. Louisville, Ky.: Westminster John Knox Press, c1996. 2 v.
96-032259   233   0664257097
Man (Christian theology)

BT701.2.C2955 1988
Carr, Anne E.
A search for wisdom and spirit: Thomas Merton's theology of the self/ Anne E. Carr. Notre Dame, Ind.: University of Notre Dame Press, c1988. xii, 171 p.
87-040352   233/.092/4   0268017271
Merton, Thomas, -- 1915-1968 -- Contributions in theology of the self.Man (Christian theology) -- History of doctrines -- 20th century. Self -- History -- 20th century.

BT701.2.E47 2000
Elshtain, Jean Bethke, 1941-
Who are we?: critical reflections and hopeful possibilities/ Jean Bethke Elshtain. Grand Rapids, Mich.: W.B. Eerdmans Pub. Co., c2000. xvii, 178 p.
99-462191   261   080283888X
Bonhoeffer, Dietrich, -- 1906-1945. John Paul -- II, -- Pope, -- 1920- Man (Christian theology)

BT703.5 Creation — Man. Doctrinal anthropology — Men

BT703.5.M46 1996
Men's bodies, men's gods: male identities in a (post-) Christian culture/ edited by Bjorn Krondorfer. New York: New York University Press, c1996. xviii, 324 p.
95-032466   233/.5/081   0814746683
Men (Christian theology) Body, Human -- Religious aspects -- Christianity. Men (Christian theology) -- History of doctrines.

BT704 Creation — Man — Woman

BT704.M355 1999
Manning, Christel.
God gave us the right: conservative Catholic, Evangelical Protestant, and Orthodox Jewish women grapple with feminism/ Christel J. Manning. New Brunswick, N.J.: Rutgers University Press, c1999. xi, 283 p.
98-008500   305.48/6/0973   0813525985
Feminism -- Religious aspects -- Christianity. Conservatism -- Religious aspects -- Christianity. Christian women -- Religious life -- United States.

BT704.R835 1998
Ruether, Rosemary Radford.
Women and redemption: a theological history/ Rosemary Radford Ruether. Minneapolis, MN: Fortress Press, c1998. xi, 366 p.
98-011783   230/.082   0800629450
Women -- Religious aspects -- Christianity -- History of doctrines. Redemption -- History of doctrines. Feminist theology.

BT707.7 Creation — Man. Doctrinal anthropology — Family

BT707.7 .C35 2000
Cahill, Lisa Sowle.
Family: a Christian social perspective/ Lisa Sowle Cahill. Minneapolis: Fortress Press, c2000. xiv, 170 p.
00-056182   261.8/3585   0800632524
Family -- Religious aspects -- Christianity. Sociology, Christian -- United States. Family -- Religious aspects -- Catholic Church.

BT707.7.G73 2000
Grant, Brian W., 1939-
The social structure of Christian families: a historical perspective/ Brian W. Grant. St. Louis, Mo.: Chalice Press, c2000. vii, 189 p.
00-008624   261.8/3585/09   0827234465
Family -- Religious aspects -- Christianity -- History of doctrines.

BT707.7.R84 2000
Ruether, Rosemary Radford.
Christianity and the making of the modern family/ Rosemary Radford Ruether. Boston: Beacon Press, c2000. 294 p.
00-008448   261.8/3585/09   0807054046
Family -- Religious aspects -- Christianity -- History of doctrines. Family -- History.

BT708 Creation — Man. Doctrinal anthropology — Sex

BT708.C283 1996
Cahill, Lisa Sowle.
Sex, gender, and Christian ethics/ Lisa Sowle Cahill. Cambridge; Cambridge University Press, 1996. xvii, 327 p.
95-048156   241/.66   0521440114
Sex -- Religious aspects -- Christianity. Sex role -- Religious aspects -- Christianity. Christian ethics.

BT712 Creation — Man. Doctrinal anthropology — Evolution

BT712.H38 2000
Haught, John F.
God after Darwin: a theology of evolution/ John F. Haught. Boulder, Colo.: Westview Press, 2000. xiii, 221 p.
99-032621   231.7/652   0813367239
Evolution -- Religious aspects -- Christianity.

BT715 Creation — Man. Doctrinal anthropology — Sin

BT715.K5313 1941
Kierkegaard, Soren, 1813-1855.
The sickness unto death, by S. Kierkegaard, translated with an introduction, by Walter Lowrie. Princeton, Princeton University Press, 1941. xix, 231 p.
42-000895   233.2
Sin. Despair.

BT732.7 Creation — Man. Doctrinal anthropology — Man in health and sickness

BT732.7.I55 1997
Inbody, Tyron.
The transforming God: an interpretation of suffering and evil/ Tyron Inbody. Louisville, Ky.: Westminster John Knox Press, c1997. 233 p.
96-037844   231/.8   0664257119
Suffering -- Religious aspects -- Christianity. Theodicy.

BT732.7.S53 1994
Sia, Marian F.
From suffering to God: exploring our images of God in the light of suffering/ Marian F. Sia and Santiago Sia. New York: St. Martin's Press, 1994. xii, 207 p.
94-025373   231/.8   0333616383
Suffering -- Religious aspects -- Christianity. Theodicy. Image of God.

BT734.2 Creation — Man. Doctrinal anthropology — Man and race

BT734.2.E48 2000
Emerson, Michael O., 1965-
Divided by faith: evangelical religion and the problem of race in America/ Michael O. Emerson, Christian Smith. Oxford; Oxford University Press, 2000. x, 212 p.
00-036743   261.8/348/00973   0195131401
Race relations -- Religious aspects -- Christianity. Evangelicalism -- United States. United States -- Race relations.

BT736.15-736.2 Creation — Man. Doctrinal anthropology — Man and state

BT736.15.H8313 1996
Huber, Wolfgang, 1942-
Violence: the unrelenting assault on human dignity/ Wolfgang Huber; translated by Ruth C.L. Gritsch; foreword by Daniel Berrigan. Minneapolis: Fortress Press, 1996. xvii, 157 p.
96-026623   241/.697   0800628586
Violence -- Religious aspects -- Christianity. Man (Christian theology)

BT736.15.K57 2001
Kirk-Duggan, Cheryl A.
Refiner's fire: a religious engagement with violence/ Cheryl A. Kirk-Duggan. Minneapolis, MN: Fortress Press, 2000. xvii, 206 p.
00-046267   241/.697   0800632532
Violence -- Religious aspects -- Christianity.

BT736.2.J64 1997
Johnson, James Turner.
The holy war idea in western and Islamic traditions/ James Turner Johnson. University Park, Pa.: Pennsylvania State University Press, c1997. ix, 185 p.
96-025660   297/.7   0271016329
War -- Religious aspects -- Christianity. War -- Religious aspects -- Islam. Jihad.

BT736.2.S65 1987
Stevenson, William R.
Christian love and just war: moral paradox and political life in St. Augustine and his modern interpreters/ William R. Stevenson, Jr. Macon, GA: Mercer University Press, c1987. xv, 166 p.
87-015376   241/.6242   0865542724
Augustine, -- Saint, Bishop of Hippo -- Contributions in just war doctrine. Ramsey, Paul. Niebuhr, Reinhold, -- 1892-1971. Just war doctrine -- History of doctrines -- Early church, ca. 30-600.

BT738-738.15 Creation — Man. Doctrinal anthropology — Man and society. Christian sociology

BT738.S394 1994
Scott, Peter, 1961-
Theology, ideology, and liberation: towards a liberative theology/ Peter Scott. Cambridge; Cambridge University Press, 1994. xiv, 272 p.
93-051059   230/.046   0521464765
Sociology, Christian. Idolatry. Ideology -- Religious aspects -- Christianity.

BT738.15.P85 2000
Pullen, L. Larry, 1947-
Christian ethics and U.S. foreign policy: the Helsinki accords and human rights/ L. Larry Pullen. Lanham, Md.: Lexington Books, c2000. x, 187 p.
99-087954   241/.624   0739101102
Human rights -- Religious aspects -- Christianity. Christianity and international affairs. Christian ethics. United States -- Foreign relations -- Moral and ethical aspects.

BT741.2 Creation — Man. Doctrinal anthropology — Natural and spiritual body. The soul

BT741.2.B95 1990
Bynum, Caroline Walker.
Fragmentation and redemption: essays on gender and the human body in Medieval religion/ Caroline Walker Bynum. New York: Zone Books; 426 p.
90-012451   233/.5 20   0942299639
Body, Human -- Religious aspects -- Christianity -- History of doctrines Sex role -- Religious aspects -- Christianity -- History of doctrines -- Middle Women -- Religious aspects -- Christianity -- History of doctrines -- Middle Women in Christianity -- History.

BT746 Creation — Animals — General works

BT746.A55 1988
Animals and Christianity: a book of readings/ edited by Andrew Linzey and Tom Regan. New York: Crossroads, 1988. xviii, 210 p.
88-016181   241/.693 19   0824509021
Animals -- Religious aspects -- Christianity.

BT746.A555 1998
Animals on the agenda: questions about animals for theology and ethics/ edited by Andrew Linzey and Dorothy Yamamoto. Illini books ed. Urbana: University of Illinois Press, 1998. xx, 297 p.
98-007118   241/.693 21   0252067614
Animals -- Religious aspects -- Christianity. Animal welfare -- Religious aspects -- Christianity.

BT749 Creation — Vegetarianism

BT749.Y68 1999
Young, Richard A., 1944-
Is God a vegetarian?: Christianity, vegetarianism, and animal rights/ Richard Alan Young; with a foreword by Carol J. Adams. Chicago: Open Court, c1999. xx, 187 p.
98-027827   241/.693   0812693930
Vegetarianism -- Religious aspects -- Christianity. Animal rights -- Religious aspects -- Christianity. Vegetarianism -- Biblical teaching.

BT771-771.2 Salvation. Soteriology — Faith. Faith and works — General works

BT771.T54 1958
Tillich, Paul, 1886-1965.
Dynamics of faith. New York, Harper [1958, c1957] 134 p.
58-010150   234.2
Faith.

BT771.2.N54 1989
Niebuhr, H. Richard 1894-1962.
Faith on earth: an inquiry into the structure of human faith/ by H. Richard Niebuhr; edited by Richard R. Niebuhr. New Haven, CT: Yale University Press, c1989. xiii, 123 p.
89-030178   234/.2   0300043155
Faith.

BT810 Salvation. Soteriology — Freedom. Autonomy. Predestination and Free will. Election. Effectual calling. Reprobation — General works

BT810.E63
Erasmus, Desiderius, d. 1536.
Discourse on free will [by] Erasmus [and] Luther. Translated and edited by Ernst F. Winter. New York, Ungar [1961] xiii, 138 p.
60-053363   234.9
Free will and determinism.

BT819.5 Eschatology. Last things — History

BT819.5.H55 2001
Hill, Charles E. 1956-
Regnum caelorum: patterns of millennial thought in early Christianity/ Charles E. Hill. Grand Rapids, Mich.: W.B. Eerdmans Pub. Co., c2001. xx, 324 p.
00-067688   236/.09/015   0802846343
Eschatology -- History of doctrines -- Early church, ca. 30-600. Millennium -- History of doctrines -- Early church, ca. 30-600.

BT821.2 Eschatology. Last things — General works — 1951-2000

BT821.2.M6313 1967b
Moltmann, Jurgen.
Theology of hope; on the ground and the implications of a Christian eschatology. New York, Harper & Row [1967] 342 p.
67-021550   236
Hope -- Religious aspects -- Christianity. Eschatology.

BT825 Eschatology. Last things — Death — General works

BT825.C45 1996
The Center for Bioethics and Human Dignity presents Dignity and dying: a Christian appraisal/ edited by John F. Kilner, Arlene B. Miller, and Edmund D. Pellegrino. [Carlisle, U.K.]: Paternoster Press; [1996] x, 256 p.
96-002784   241/.697   0802842321
Death -- Religious aspects -- Christianity. Terminal care -- Religious aspects -- Christianity. Church work with the terminally ill.

BT836.2 Eschatology. Last things — Hades. Sheol. Hell. Future punishment — General works

BT836.2.B47 1993
Bernstein, Alan E.
The formation of hell: death and retribution in the ancient and early Christian worlds/ Alan E. Bernstein. Ithaca: Cornell University Press, 1993. xiii, 392 p.
93-008308   291.2/3   0801428939
Hell -- Christianity -- History of doctrines -- Early church, ca. 30-600. Hell -- Comparative studies. Hell -- Biblical teaching. Rome -- Religion.

BT872 Eschatology. Last things — Resurrection — General works

BT872.B96 1995
Bynum, Caroline Walker.
The Resurrection of the body in Western Christianity, 200-1336/ Caroline Walker Bynum. New York: Columbia University Press, c1995. xx, 368 p.
94-017299   236/.8/09   023108126X
Resurrection -- History of doctrines -- Early church, ca. 30-600. Resurrection -- History of doctrines -- Middle Ages, 600-1500. Body, Human -- Religious aspects -- Christianity -- History of doctrines -- Early church, ca. 30-600.

BT876 Eschatology. Last things — End of the age. End of the world — General works

BT876.K95 1998
Kyle, Richard G.
The last days are here again: a history of the end times/ Richard Kyle. Grand Rapids, Mich.: Baker Books, c1998. 255 p.
98-013574   236/.9/09   0801058090
End of the world -- History of doctrines.

BT885 Eschatology. Last things — End of the age. End of the world — Second Coming of Christ. Second Advent. Parousia

BT885.A65
Apocalyptic spirituality: treatises and letters of Lactantius, Adso of Montier-en-Der, Joachim of Fiore, the Franciscan spirituals, Savonarola/ translation and introd. by Bernard McGinn; pref. by Marjorie Reeves. New York: Paulist Press, c1979. xviii, 334 p.
79-090834   236   0809103052
Second Advent -- Early works to 1800. Antichrist -- Early works to 1800. Apocalyptic literature -- Early works to 1800.

BT891 Eschatology. Last things — End of the age. End of the world — Millennium. Chiliasm. Premillennialism. Postmillennialism

BT891.E53 2000
Encyclopedia of millennialism and millennial movements/ Richard A. Landes, editor. New York: Routledge, 2000. xii, 478 p.
99-052373   306/.1   0415922461
Millennialism -- Encyclopedias.

BT921 Future state. Future life — Immortality — General works

BT921.L167 1965
Lamont, Corliss, 1902-
The illusion of immortality/ Corliss Lamont; introduction by John Dewey. New York: Continuum, 1990. xiii, 303 p.
65-025140   129.6   0804463778
Immortality.

BT972 Invisible world — Saints — Communion of saints

BT972.J57 1998
Johnson, Elizabeth A., 1941-
Friends of God and prophets: a feminist theological reading of the communion of saints/ Elizabeth A. Johnson. New York: Continuum, 1998. ix, 306 p.
97-046452   262/.73/082   0826410782
Communion of saints. Feminist theology.

BT985 Invisible world — Antichrist

BT985.M29 1994
McGinn, Bernard, 1937-
Antichrist: two thousand years of the human fascination with evil/ Bernard McGinn. [San Francisco, CA]: HarperSanFrancisco, c1994. xiii, 369 p.
94-014396   236   0060655437
Antichrist -- History of doctrines.

BT990 Creeds, confessions, covenants, etc. — General works

BT990.C64 2003
Creeds & confessions of faith in the Christian tradition/ edited by Jaroslav Pelikan and Valerie Hotchkiss. New Haven: Yale University Press, c2003.
2003-043067   238 21   0300093918
Creeds. Creeds -- History and criticism.

BT990.E58 1988
The encyclopedia of American religions, religious creeds: a compilation of more than 450 creeds, confessions, statements of faith, and summaries of doctrine of religious and spiritual groups in the J. Gordon Melton, editor. Detroit, Mich.: Gale Research Co., c1988-c1994. 2 v.
87-030384   291.2/0973   0810321327
Creeds.

BT1102 Apologetics. Evidences of Christianity — General works — 1951-2000

BT1102.G42 1999
Geisler, Norman L.
Baker encyclopedia of Christian apologetics/ Norman L. Geisler. Grand Rapids, Mich.: Baker Books, c1999. vii, 841 p.
98-008735   239/.03   0801021510
Apologetics -- Encyclopedias.

BT1102.P57 2000
Plantinga, Alvin.
Warranted Christian belief/ Alvin Plantinga. New York: Oxford University Press, 2000. xx, 508 p.
98-054362   230/.01   0195131932
Apologetics. Christianity -- Philosophy. Faith and reason -- Christianity.

BT1117 Apologetics. Evidences of Christianity — History — By period

BT1117.S55 1995
Sims, John
Missionaries to the skeptics: Christian apologists for the twentieth century: C.S. Lewis, Edward John Carnell, and Reinhold Niebuhr/ John A. Sims. Macon, Ga.: Mercer University Press, c1995. vii, 234 p.
95-041832   239/.0092/2   0865544964
Lewis, C. S. -- (Clive Staples), -- 1898-1963. Carnell, Edward John, -- 1919-1967. Niebuhr, Reinhold, -- 1892-1971. Apologetics -- History -- 20th century.

BT1180 Apologetics. Evidences of Christianity — Against opponents of Christianity — Diests

BT1180.M34 2000
McDermott, Gerald R.
Jonathan Edwards confronts the gods: Christian theology, Enlightenment religion, and non-Christian faiths/ Gerald R. McDermott. New York: Oxford University Press, 2000. xii, 245 p.
99-026834   239/.7   0195132742
Edwards, Jonathan, -- 1703-1758 -- Contributions in relations of Christianity and other religions. Edwards, Jonathan, -- 1703-1758 -- Contributions in theology of revelation. Apologetics -- United States -- History -- 18th century. Christianity and other religions -- History -- 18th century. Deism -- History -- 18th century.

BT1319-1410 History of specific doctrines and movements. Heresies and schisms — By period — Early to the Reformation, 1517

BT1319.F5313 1998
Fichtenau, Heinrich.
Heretics and scholars in the High Middle Ages, 1000-1200/ Heinrich Fichtenau; translated by Denise A. Kaiser. University Park, Pa.: Pennsylvania State University Press, c1998. viii, 403 p.
97-033622   272/.6   0271017651
Heresies, Christian -- History -- Middle Ages, 600-1500. Rationalism -- History. Europe -- Church history -- 600-1500.

BT1319.L35 2002
Lambert, Malcolm.
Medieval heresy: popular movements from the Gregorian reform to the Reformation/ Malcolm Lambert. 3rd ed. Oxford, UK; Blackwell Pub., 2002. vi, 491 p.
2001-043102   273/.6 21   0631222766
Heresies, Christian -- History -- Middle Ages, 600-1500.

BT1350.W55 1996
Wiles, Maurice F.
Archetypal heresy: Arianism through the centuries/ Maurice Wiles. Oxford: Clarendon Press; 1996. vii, 204 p.
95-052481   273/.4   0198269277
Arianism -- History.

BT1390.F5513 1990
Filoramo, Giovanni.
A history of Gnosticism/ Giovanni Filoramo; translated by Anthony Alcock. Oxford, UK; B. Blackwell, 1990. xxi, 269 p.
89-027513   299/.932 20
Gnosticism.

BT1390.P4513 1990
Petrement, Simone.
A separate God: the Christian origins of gnosticism/ Simone Petrement; translated by Carol Harrison. [San Francisco]: HarperSanFrancisco, c1990. viii, 542 p.
89-045551   273/.1   0060665017
Gnosticism.

BT1390.R7713 1983
Rudolph, Kurt.
Gnosis: the nature and history of gnosticism/ Kurt Rudolph; translation edited by Robert McLachlan Wilson. San Francisco: Harper & Row, 1983. xii, 411 p.
81-047437   299/.932   0060670177
Gnosticism.

BT1410.B43 2000
BeDuhn, Jason.
The Manichaean body: in discipline and ritual/ Jason David BeDuhn. Baltimore: Johns Hopkins University Press, 2000. xiv, 354 p.
99-045879   299/.932   0801862701
Manichaeism -- Discipline -- History. Manichaeism -- Rituals -- History.

BV Practical theology

BV5 Worship (Public and private) — History — General works

BV5.L36 1997
Lang, Bernhard, 1946-
Sacred games: a history of Christian worship/ Bernhard Lang. New Haven: Yale University Press, c1997. xiii, 527 p.
97-060406   264/.009   0300069324
Public worship -- Christianity -- History. Ritual -- History.

BV6 Worship (Public and private) — History — By period

BV6.C8413 1978
Cullmann, Oscar.
Early Christian worship/ Oscar Cullmann; [translation by A. Stewart Todd and James B. Torrance.] Philadelphia: Westminster Press, [1978] c1953. 126 p.
78-006636   264/.009   0664242200
Worship -- History -- Early church, ca. 30-600. Sabbath. Sacraments -- Biblical teaching.

BV55 Worship (Public and private) — Times and seasons. The Church year — Feast days

BV55.P275 1999
Passover and Easter: origin and history to modern times/ edited by Paul F. Bradshaw and Lawrence A. Hoffman. Notre Dame, Ind.: University of Notre Dame Press, c1999. vii, 252 p.
98-041342   263/.93/09   0268038570
Easter -- History. Passover -- History. Judaism -- Relations -- Christianity.

BV111 Worship (Public and private) — Times and seasons. he Church year — Lord's Day. Sunday. Sabbath

BV111.M35 2000
McCrossen, Alexis.
Holy day, holiday: the American Sunday/ Alexis McCrossen. Ithaca: Cornell University Press, 2000. xiii, 209 p.
99-055042   263/.3/0973   0801434173
Sunday -- History of doctrines -- 19th century. Weekly rest-day -- United States -- History -- 19th century. Rest -- Religious aspects -- Christianity -- History of doctrines -- 19th century.

BV150 Worship (Public and private) — Christian symbols and symbolism — General works

BV150.A66 1994
Apostolos-Cappadona, Diane.
Dictionary of Christian art/ Diane Apostolos-Cappadona. New York: Continuum, 1994. 376 p.
94-034345   246/.03   082640779X
Christian art and symbolism -- Encyclopedias.

BV210 Worship (Public and private) — Prayer — General works. Nature, obligation, etc.

BV210.B333
Barth, Karl, 1886-1968.
Prayer according to the catechisms of the Reformation; stenographic records of three seminars, adapted by A. Roulin. Translated by Sara F. Terrien. Philadelphia, Westminster Press [1952] 78 p.
52-009381   264.1
Lord's prayer. Prayer.

BV245 Worship (Public and private) — Prayer — Prayers

BV245.D65
Donne, John, 1572-1631.
Prayers; selected and edited from the earliest sources, with an essay on Donne's idea of prayer, by Herbert H. Umbach. New York, Bookman Associates [1951] 109 p.
51-005368
Prayers. Prayer.

BV312-313 Worship (Public and private) — Hymnology — History and criticism

BV312.A56 2002
An annotated anthology of hymns/ edited with commentary by J.R. Watson; with a foreword by Timothy Dudley-Smith. Oxford; Oxford University Press, 2002. xvii, 452 p.
2002-070139   264/.23 21   0198269730
Hymns, English -- History and criticism.

BV312.W38 1997
Watson, J. R. 1934-
The English hymn: a critical and historical study/ J.R. Watson. Oxford: Clarendon Press; 1997. x, 552 p.
96-043077   264/.2/0942   0198267622
Hymns, English -- History and criticism.

BV313.S64 1992
Spencer, Jon Michael.
Black hymnody: a hymnological history of the African-American church/ Jon Michael Spencer. Knoxville: University of Tennessee Press, c1992. xiii, 242 p.
91-031896   264/.2/08996073   0870497456
Afro-American churches -- Hymns -- History and criticism. Afro-Americans -- Religion. Hymns, English -- United States -- History and criticism.

BV598 Ecclesiastical theology — The Church — History of doctrines concerning the Church

BV598.K425 1995
Kee, Howard Clark.
Who are the people of God?: early Christian models of community/ Howard Clark Kee. New Haven: Yale University Press, c1995. vii, 280 p.
94-013883   270.1   0300059523
People of God -- History of doctrines -- Early church, ca. 30-600. Church -- History of doctrines -- Early church, ca. 30-600. Christianity -- Origin.

BV600.2 Ecclesiastical theology — The Church — General works

BV600.2.E94 1994
Evans, G. R.
The Church and the churches: toward an ecumenical ecclesiology/ G.R. Evans. Cambridge; Cambridge University Press, 1994. xvi, 329 p.
93-042441   262/.001/1   052146286X
Church.

BV629-630.2 Ecclesiastical theology — Special aspects of Church institutions (General) — Church and state

BV629.W62213 1995
William, of Ockham, ca. 1285-ca.
A letter to the Friars Minor, and other writings/ William of Ockham; edited by Arthur Stephen McGrade and John Kilcullen; translated by John Kilcullen. Cambridge [England]; Cambridge University Press, 1995. xl, 390 p.
94-043248   322/.1/09023   0521352436
Poverty -- Religious aspects -- Catholic Church. Church and state. Popes -- Primacy. Holy Roman Empire -- Kings and rulers.

BV630.A1.E33 1954
Ehler, Sidney Z.
Church and state through the centuries: a collection of historic documents with commentaries/ translated and edited by Sidney Z. Ehler and John B. Morrall. Westminster, Md.: Burns & Oates, 1954. xii, 625 p.
55-000327
Church and state -- History -- Sources.

BV630.2.M595 1997
Monsma, Stephen V., 1936-
The challenge of pluralism: church and state in five democracies/ by Stephen V. Monsma and J. Christopher Soper. Lanham, Md.: Rowman & Littlefield, c1997. x, 228 p.
97-009791   322/.1/0904   0847685683
Church and state -- History -- 20th century. Democracy -- Religious aspects -- Christianity -- History -- 20th century. Religious pluralism -- Christianity -- History -- 20th century.

BV639 Ecclesiastical theology — Special aspects of Church institutions (General) — The Church and special classes, A-Z

BV639.P6.L48 1989
Levi, Werner, 1912-
From alms to liberation: the Catholic Church, the theologians, poverty, and politics/ Werner Levi. New York: Praeger, 1989. vi, 175 p.
88-029009   261.8/325   0275931714
Church work with the poor -- Catholic Church. Liberation theology.

BV639.W7.D28
Daly, Mary, 1928-
The church and the second sex. New York, Harper & Row [1968] 187 p.
68-011737   261
Women in Christianity.

BV639.W7.R36 1998
Ranft, Patricia.
Women and spiritual equality in Christian tradition/ Patricia Ranft. New York: St. Martin's Press, 1998. xii, 307 p.
97-050397   270/.082   0312159110
Women in Christianity -- History. Spirituality -- History of doctrines. Equality -- Religious aspects -- Christianity -- History of doctrines.

BV648 Ecclesiastical theology — Church polity — History

BV648.B83 1992
Burtchaell, James Tunstead.
From synagogue to church: public services and offices in the earliest Christian communities/ James Tunstead Burtchaell. Cambridge; Cambridge University Press, 1992. xviii, 375 p.
91-036390   262/.1/09015   0521418925
Church polity -- History -- Early church, ca. 30-600. Pastoral theology -- History. Synagogues -- Organization and administration -- History.

BV652.95 Ecclesiastical theology — Mass media and telecommunication in religion — General works

BV652.95.R43 1996
Religion and mass media: audiences and adaptations/ [editors] Daniel A. Stout, Judith M. Buddenbaum. Thousand Oaks, Calif.: Sage Publications, c1996. 294 p.
95-041786   291.1/75   0803971737
Mass media -- Religious aspects -- Christianity. Mass media in religion.

BV652.97 Ecclesiastical theology — Mass media and telecommunication in religion — By region or country, A-Z

BV652.97.U6.R43 2000
Readings on religion as news/ edited by Judith M. Buddenbaum and Debra L. Mason. Ames: Iowa State University Press, 2000. xx, 501 p.
99-047158   070.4/49200973   0813829267
Mass media in religion -- United States -- Influence. Mass media in religion -- United States. Christianity and culture -- United States.

BV656-656.3 Ecclesiastical theology — Mass media and telecommunication in religion — Religious broadcasting

BV656.A66 2000
Apostolidis, Paul, 1965-
Stations of the Cross: Adorno and Christian right radio/ Paul Apostolidis. Durham, NC: Duke University Press, 2000. x, 273 p.
99-087368   261/.06/073   0822325047
Conservatism -- Religious aspects -- Christianity -- Case studies. Radio in religion -- United States -- Case studies. Christianity and politics -- United States -- History -- 20th century. United States -- Church history -- 20th century.

BV656.M45 1997
Melton, J. Gordon.
Prime-time religion: an encyclopedia of religious broadcasting/ by J. Gordon Melton, Phillip Charles Lucas, Jon R. Stone. Phoenix, Ariz.: Oryx Press, 1997. xvii, 413 p.
96-039495   269/.26/03   0897749022
Religious broadcasting -- Christianity -- Encyclopedias. Religious broadcasting -- Islam -- Encyclopedias. Religious broadcasting -- Encyclopedias.

BV656.3.H66 1988
Hoover, Stewart M.
Mass media religion: the social sources of the electronic church/ Stewart M. Hoover. Newbury Park, Calif.: Sage Publications, c1988. 251 p.
87-036859   269/.2 19   0803929951
Television in religion -- United States. Evangelicalism -- United States -- History -- 20th century. United States -- Church history -- 20th century.

BV656.3.S385 1991
Schultze, Quentin J. 1952-
Televangelism and American culture: the business of popular religion/ Quentin J. Schultze. Grand Rapids, Mich.: Baker Book House, c1991. 264 p.
90-049378   269/.26/0973   0801083192
Television in religion -- United States. Religious broadcasting -- Christianity. Popular culture -- United States. United States -- Church history -- 20th century.

BV676 Ecclesiastical theology — Ministry. Clergy. Religious vocations — Kinds of ministries

BV676.S34 1996
Schmidt, Frederick W.
A still small voice: women, ordination, and the church/ Frederick W. Schmidt, Jr.; with a foreword by Betty Bone Schiess. Syracuse, N.Y.: Syracuse University Press, 1996. xv, 194 p.
95-019950   262/.14/082   0815626835
Women clergy -- United States -- History -- 20th century. Christian sects -- United States -- Controversial literature.

BV676.W556 1998
Women preachers and prophets through two millennia of Christianity/ edited by Beverly Mayne Kienzle and Pamela J. Walker. Berkeley: University of California Press, c1998. xxii, 362 p.
97-030743   270/.082 21   0520209222
Women clergy -- History. Women evangelists -- History. Sex role -- Religious aspects -- Christianity -- History. Women in Christianity -- History.

BV960 Ecclesiastical theology — Religious societies, associations, etc. — Religious societies of men, brotherhoods, etc.

BV960.P76 2000
The Promise Keepers: essays on masculinity and Christianity/ edited by Dane S. Claussen. Jefferson, N.C.: McFarland, c2000. xvi, 336 p.
99-038799   267/.23   078640700X
Promise Keepers (Organization)

BV1393 Ecclesiastical theology — Religious societies, associations, etc. — Religious societies of women

BV1393.B58.W45 1997
Weisenfeld, Judith.
African American women and Christian activism: New York's Black YWCA, 1905-1945/ Judith Weisenfeld. Cambridge, Mass.: Harvard University Press, 1997. viii, 231 p.
97-021901   267/.597471/0996073 0674689739
Church work with Afro-Americans -- New York (State) -- New York. Young women -- New York (State) -- New York -- Religious life.

BV1461 Ecclesiastical theology — Religious education (General) — Dictionaries

BV1461.H37 1990
Harper's encyclopedia of religious education/ general editors, Iris V. Cully, Kendig Brubaker Cully. San Francisco: Harper & Row, c1990. xxiii, 717 p.
89-045392   268/.03   0006061656
Christian education -- Encyclopedias.

BV1464 Ecclesiastical theology — Religious education (General) — Theory, philosophy, etc.

BV1464.V45 1998
Ven, J. A. van der, 1940-
Formation of the moral self/ Johannes A. van der Ven. Grand Rapids, Mich.: W.B. Eerdmans, c1998. xiii, 410 p.
98-022514   268/.01   0802844391
Christian education -- Theory. Moral education. Moral development.

BV1475.2-1478 Ecclesiastical theology — Religious education (General) — By age group

BV1475.2.S776 1998
Stonehouse, Catherine.
Joining children on the spiritual journey: nurturing a life of faith/ Catherine Stonehouse. Grand Rapids, Mich.: Baker Books, c1998. 237 p.
97-048468   268/.432   0801058074
Christian education of children.

BV1478.J89 2000
Jussen, Bernhard.
Spiritual kinship as social practice: godparenthood and adoption in the early Middle Ages/ Bernhard Jussen; translated by Pamela Selwyn. Newark, Del.: University of Delaware Press; c2000. 362 p.
99-041732   306.83   0874136326
Sponsors -- Europe -- History. Social history -- Medieval, 500-1500. Adoption -- Europe -- History -- To 1500.

BV1478.L96 1986
Lynch, Joseph H.,
Godparents and kinship in early medieval Europe/ Joseph H. Lynch. Princeton, N.J.: Princeton University Press, 1986. xiv, 378 p.
85-043297   234/.161 19   0691054665
Sponsors -- Europe -- History. Social history -- Medieval, 500-1500. Kinship -- Europe -- History.

BV1534 Ecclesiastical theology — Religious education (General) — Special kinds of schools for religious education

BV1534.A76 2000
Armstrong-Hansche, Melissa.
Workshop rotation: a new model for Sunday School/ Melissa Armstrong-Hansche and Neil MacQueen. Louisville, Ky.: Geneva Press, c2000. 94 p.
99-046804   268/.6   0664501109
Christian education -- Teaching methods. Sunday schools.

BV2063 Missions — General and foreign — General special

BV2063.M626 1999
Montgomery, Robert L.
Introduction to the sociology of missions/ Robert L. Montgomery. Westport, Conn.: Praeger, 1999. xxi, 183 p.
99-016057   306.6/66   0275966917
Missions -- Sociological aspects.

BV2240 Missions — Special churches — Catholic Church

BV2240.N7.D75 1998
Dries, Angelyn.
The missionary movement in American Catholic history/ Angelyn Dries. Maryknoll, N.Y.: Orbis Books, c1998. xviii, 398 p.
97-032083   266/.273   1570751676
Missions -- North America -- History. Immigrants -- North America -- Religious life.

BV2370-2521 Missions — Special churches — Protestant churches

BV2370.A7.W674 1994
Wosh, Peter J.
Spreading the word: the Bible business in nineteenth-century America/ Peter J. Wosh. Ithaca: Cornell University Press, 1994. xii, 271 p.
93-043880   267/.13/0973   0801429285
United States -- Social conditions. United States -- Economic conditions.

BV2521.M37 1989
Martin, Sandy Dwayne.
Black Baptists and African missions: the origins of a movement, 1880-1915/ Sandy D. Martin. Macon, Ga.: Mercer, c1989. xii, 242 p.
89-039041   266/.6166/08996073   0865543534
Afro-American Baptists -- Missions -- Africa, West. Missions -- Africa, West. Africa, West -- Church history.

BV2610 Missions — Special types of missions — Work of women

BV2610.R63 1996
Robert, Dana Lee.
American women in mission: a social history of their thought and practice/ Dana L. Robert. Macon, Ga.: Mercer University Press, c1996. xxii, 444 p.
97-006439   266/.02373/0082   0865545499
Women in missionary work -- United States -- History. Women missionaries -- United States -- History. Missionaries' spouses -- United States -- History.

BV2788-2831 Missions — Missions in individual countries — America

BV2788.H56.Y64 1995
Yohn, Susan M.   1958-
A contest of faiths: missionary women and pluralism in the American Southwest/ Susan M. Yohn. Ithaca: Cornell University Press, 1995. xi, 266 p.
94-039195   266/.51789   0801429641
Women missionaries -- New Mexico. Presbyterian women -- New Mexico. Pluralism (Social sciences) -- New Mexico. New Mexico -- Church history -- 19th century. New Mexico -- Church history -- 20th century.

BV2831.N47 1995
The new Latin American mission history/ edited by Erick Langer and Robert H. Jackson. Lincoln: University of Nebraska Press, c1995. xviii, 212 p.
94-043080   266/.28   0803229119
Indians -- Missions -- Latin America -- History. Evangelistic work -- Latin America. Latin America -- Church history.

BV2900 Missions — Missions in individual countries — Europe

BV2900.C4313 1997
Chatellier, Louis.
The religion of the poor: rural missions in Europe and the formation of modern Catholicism, c.1500-c.1800/ Louis Chatellier; translated by Brian Pearce. Cambridge, U.K.; Cambridge University Press; 1997. xiii, 246 p.
96-045552   266/.24   0521562015
Church work with the poor -- Europe -- History. Church work with the poor -- Catholic Church -- History. Europe -- Church history. Europe -- Religious life and customs.

BV3202-3415 Missions — Missions in individual countries — Asia. The Orient. The East

BV3202.M55.D58 1999
Kreiger, Barbara.
Divine expectations: an American woman in 19th-century Palestine/ Barbara Kreiger with Shalom Goldman. Athens, Ohio: Ohio University Press, c1999. xvii, 199 p.
99-028478   266/.0092   0821412949
Minor, Clorinda. Missionaries -- Palestine -- Biography. Adventists -- Palestine -- Biography. Missionaries -- United States -- Biography.

BV3255.T3
Hudson, D. Dennis.
Protestant origins in India: Tamil Evangelical Christians, 1706-1835/ D. Dennis Hudson. Grand Rapids, Mich: William B. Eerdmans Pub.; 2000. xi, 220 p.
00-026467   266/.00954/8   0802847218
Tamil (Indic people) -- Missions -- History Protestant Churches -- Missions -- India, South -- History. Protestants -- India, South -- History. India, South -- Church history.

BV3415.L35 1967
Latourette, Kenneth Scott, 1884-1968.
A history of Christian missions in China. New York, Russell & Russell [1967] xii, 930 p.
66-024721   266/.023/0951
Missions -- China.

BV3415.V37 1977
Varg, Paul A.
Missionaries, Chinese, and diplomats; the American Protestant missionary movement in China, 1890-1952. Princeton, N.J., Princeton University Press, 1958. 335 p.
58-007134   275.1
Missions -- China -- History. China -- Relations -- United States. United States -- Relations -- China.

BV3520-3625 Missions — Missions in individual countries — Africa

BV3520.G72 1991
Gray, Richard, 1929-
Black Christians and White missionaries/ Richard Gray. New Haven: Yale University Press, 1990. viii, 134 p.
90-040030   276.7   0300049102
Missions -- Africa, Sub-Saharan. Africa, Sub-Saharan -- Religion. Africa, Sub-Saharan -- Church history.

BV3625.N5
Peel, J. D. Y. 1941-
Religious encounter and the making of the Yoruba/ J.D.Y. Peel. Bloomington, IN: Indiana University Press, c2000. xi, 420 p.
00-037031 266/.009669/09034 0253337941
Missions -- Nigeria -- History -- 19th century. Christianity and culture -- Nigeria -- History -- 19th century. Yoruba (African people) -- Religion. Nigeria -- Church history -- 19th century.

BV3700 Missions — Biography — Collective

BV3700.B56 1997
Biographical dictionary of Christian missions/ edited by Gerald H. Anderson. New York: Macmillan Reference USA, 1997. xxvi, 845 p.
96-049922 266/.0092/2 0028646045
Missionaries -- Biography -- Dictionaries.

BV3773 Evangelism. Revivals — History of revivals and evangelistic work

BV3773.K73 1999
Krapohl, Robert H.
The evangelicals: a historical, thematic, and biographical guide/ Robert H. Krapohl and Charles H. Lippy. Westport, Conn.: Greenwood Press, c1999. xii, 336 p.
98-030499 280/.4/0973 0313301034
Evangelical work -- United States -- History.

BV3773.N65 2001
Noll, Mark A., 1946-
American evangelical Christianity: an introduction/ Mark A. Noll. Oxford; Blackwell Publishers, c2001. vii, 320 p.
00-010082 277.3/082 0631219994
Evangelicalism -- United States.

BV3774-3775 Evangelism. Revivals — History of revivals and evangelistic work — America. United States

BV3774.K4 C65 1991
Conkin, Paul Keith.
Cane Ridge, America's Pentecost/ Paul K. Conkin. Madison, Wis.: University of Wisconsin Press, c1990. xi, 186 p.
90-050081 269/.24/09769423 20 0299127249
Revivals -- Kentucky -- Bourbon County -- History -- 19th century. Bourbon County (Ky.) -- Church history -- 19th century.

BV3775.B2.S38 1998
Sutton, William R., 1949-
Journeymen for Jesus: Evangelical artisans confront capitalism in Jacksonian Baltimore/ William R. Sutton. University Park, Pa.: Pennsylvania State University Press, c1998. xvi, 351 p.
97-049128 305.5/62/097527109034 0271017724
Evangelicalism -- Maryland -- Baltimore -- History -- 19th century. Artisans -- Religious life -- Maryland -- Baltimore -- History -- 19th century. Capitalism -- Religious aspects -- Protestant churches -- History -- 19th century. Baltimore (Md.) -- Church history -- 19th century.

BV3777 Evangelism. Revivals — History of revivals and evangelistic work — Other regions or countries, A-Z

BV3777.E9.W37 1992
Ward, W. Reginald
The Protestant evangelical awakening/ W.R. Ward. Cambridge [England]; Cambridge University Press, 1992. xviii, 370 p.
91-023665 280/.4/09409033 0521414911
Revivals -- Europe -- History -- 18th century. Protestant churches -- Europe -- History -- 18th century. Europe -- Church history -- 18th century.

BV3785 Evangelism. Revivals — Biography and memoirs of evangelists — Individual, A-Z

BV3785.G69.P597 1979
Pollock, John Charles.
Billy Graham, evangelist to the world: an authorized biography of the decisive years/ John Pollock. San Francisco: Harper & Row, c1979. x, 324 p.
76-062949 269/.2/0924 0060666919
Graham, Billy, -- 1918-Evangelists -- United States -- Biography.

BV3785.S8.B75 1992
Bruns, Roger.
Preacher: Billy Sunday and big-time American evangelism/ Roger A. Bruns. New York: W.W. Norton, c1992. 351 p.
91-027418 269/.2/092 0393030881
Sunday, Billy, -- 1862-1935.Evangelists -- United States -- Biography. Revivals -- United States -- History -- 20th century. United States -- Religious life and customs.

BV3785.S84.S43 1999
Seaman, Ann Rowe.
Swaggart: an unauthorized biography of an American evangelist/ Ann Rowe Seaman. New York: Continuum, c1999. 438 p.
99-032595 269/.2/092 0826411177
Swaggart, Jimmy.Evangelists -- United States -- Biography.

BV3798 Evangelism. Revivals — Camp meetings — General works

BV3798.B76 1992
Brown, Kenneth O., 1943-
Holy ground: a study of the American camp meeting/ by Kenneth O. Brown. New York: Garland, 1992. xvi, 254 p.
92-009742 269/.24/0973 0824048377
Camp-meetings -- United States -- History. Camp-meetings -- United States -- Bibliography. United States -- Church history. United States -- Church history -- Bibliography.

BV4011.5 Pastoral theology — Special — Ethics and etiquette

BV4011.5.B38 1990
Battin, M. Pabst.
Ethics in the sanctuary: examining the practices of organized religion/ Margaret P. Battin. New Haven: Yale University Press, c1990. xiii, 291 p.
89-029675 174/.1 0300045476
Clergy -- United States -- Professional ethics. Religious and ecclesiastical institutions -- Moral and ethical aspects. Religious and ecclesiastical institutions -- Employees -- Professional ethics.

BV4030-4070 Pastoral theology — Education — Training for the ordained ministry

BV4030.C46 1995
Cherry, Conrad, 1937-
Hurrying toward Zion: universities, divinity schools, and American Protestantism/ Conrad Cherry. Bloomington: Indiana University Press, c1995. xiii, 373 p.
95-003526 207/.73 0253329280
Protestant theological seminaries -- United States -- History -- 19th century. Protestant theological seminaries -- United States -- History -- 20th century.

BV4070.G48
Breyer, Chloe.
The close: a young woman's first year at seminary/ Chloe Breyer. New York: Basic Books, c2000. xix, 256 p.
00-034296 230/.07/337471 0465007147
Breyer, Chloe.Women seminarians -- United States. Seminarians -- United States.

BV4208 Pastoral theology — Preaching. Homiletics — History

BV4208.U6.L57 1995
Lischer, Richard.
The preacher King: Martin Luther King, Jr. and the word that moved America/ Richard Lischer. New York: Oxford University Press, 1995. xiv, 344 p.
94-030029   251/.0092   0195087798
King, Martin Luther, -- Jr., -- 1929-1968. King, Martin Luther, -- Jr., -- 1929-1968 -- Oratory. Sermons, American -- Afro-American authors. Preaching.

BV4208.U6.M68 1989
Mott, Wesley T.
The strains of eloquence: Emerson and his sermons/ Wesley T. Mott. University Park: Pennsylvania State University Press, c1989.
88-028123   252/.08   0271006609
Emerson, Ralph Waldo, -- 1803-1882 -- Contributions in preaching.Sermons, American -- History and criticism. Unitarian Universalist churches -- Sermons -- History and criticism.

BV4253-4316 Pastoral theology — Preaching. Homiletics — Sermons

BV4253.T58
Tillich, Paul, 1886-1965.
The new being. New York, Scribner, 1955. 179 p.
55-007198   252.04
Sermons, American.

BV4316.P7.B33
Barth, Karl, 1886-1968.
Deliverance to the captives. translated by Marguerite Wieser. New York, Harper [1961] 160 p.
61-007333   252
Prisons -- Sermons.

BV4327 Pastoral theology — Other pastoral offices — Relations to the state

BV4327.J45 1993
Jelen, Ted G.
The political world of the clergy/ Ted G. Jelen. Westport, Conn.: Praeger, 1993. xii, 169 p.
92-037526   323/.042/0882   0275939049
Clergy -- United States -- Political activity. Christianity and politics.   United States -- Church history -- 20th century.

BV4392.5 Pastoral theology — Personal life of the clergy — Sexual behavior

BV4392.5.B45 1998
Benyei, Candace Reed.
Understanding clergy misconduct in religious systems: scapegoating, family secrets, and the abuse of power/ Candace R. Benyei. New York: Haworth Pastoral Press, c1998. xv, 197 p.
97-037001   262/.1   0789004518
Sexual misconduct by clergy.

BV4445-4466 Pastoral theology — Practical church work. Social work. Work of the layman — Church work with special classes

BV4445.R36 1999
Ramsey, Janet L.
Spiritual resiliency in older women: models of strength for challenges through the life span/ Janet L. Ramsey, Rosemary Blieszner. Thousand Oaks: Sage Publications, c1999. xii, 180 p.
98-040299   261.8/3426   0761912762
Aged women -- Religious life -- United States -- Case studies. Aged women -- Religious life -- Germany -- Case studies. Church work with the aged.

BV4466.C63 1993
Coutin, Susan Bibler.
The culture of protest: religious activism and the U.S. sanctuary movement/ Susan Bibler Coutin. Boulder: Westview Press, 1993. xiv, 250 p.
92-045553   261.8/32   0813315530
Sanctuary movement. Refugees -- Central America.

BV4490 Practical religion. The Christian life — History

BV4490.B96 1982
Bynum, Caroline Walker.
Jesus as mother: studies in the spirituality of the High Middle Ages / Caroline Walker Bynum. Berkeley: University of California Press, c1982. xiv, 279 p.
81-013137   255 19   0520041941
Spiritual life -- Christianity -- History of doctrines -- Middle Ages, Monastic and religious life -- History -- Middle Ages, 600-1500. God -- Motherhood -- History of doctrines -- Middle Ages, 600-1500.

BV4490.C48 1987
Christian spirituality: high Middle Ages and Reformation/ edited by Jill Raitt in collaboration with Bernard McGinn and John Meyendorff. New York: Crossroad, 1987. xxiii, 479 p.
86-029212   248/.09/02 19   0824507657
Spiritual life -- Christianity -- History of doctrines -- Middle Ages, Spiritual life -- Christianity -- History of doctrines -- 16th century.

BV4495 Practical religion. The Christian life — Collections

BV4495.P513 1954
Early Fathers from the Philokalia: together with some writings of St. Abba Dorotheus, St. Isaac of Syria, and St. Gregory Palamas/ selected and translated from the Russian text Dobrotolubiye by E. Kadloubovsky and G.E.H. Palmer. London [England]: Faber and Faber, 1954. 421 p.
54-003934   248   0571037941
Spiritual life -- Orthodox Eastern authors. Christian literature, Early.

BV4501.2 Practical religion. The Christian life — General works — English

BV4501.2.C297 1988
Carl Jung and Christian spirituality/ Robert L. Moore, editor. New York: Paulist Press, c1988. xii, 252 p.
87-037480   201/.9   0809129507
Jung, C. G. -- (Carl Gustav), -- 1875-1961.Spiritual life -- Christianity.

BV4501.2.T269 1996
Taylor, Brian C., 1951-
Setting the gospel free: experiential faith and contemplative practice/ Brian C. Taylor. New York: Continuum, 1996. 156 p.
96-008813   248.4   0826409385
Spiritual life -- Christianity.

BV4509 Practical religion. The Christian life — General works — Other languages, A-Z

BV4509.L2.E833
Erasmus, Desiderius, 1466-1536.
The enchiridion. Translated and edited by Raymond Himelick. Bloomington, Indiana University Press [1963] 222 p.
63-016615   248.4
Christian life -- Middle Ages.

BV4515 Practical religion.
The Christian life —
Stories, allegories, emblems, etc.
— Early through 1950

BV4515.L37 1959
Lewis, C. S. 1898-1963.
The pilgrim's regress; an allegorical apology for Christianity, reason, and romanticism. Grand Rapids, Eerdmans [1959? c1943] 199 p.
59-006953   823.912
Pilgrims and pilgrimages -- Fiction.

BV4529.17 Practical religion.
The Christian life —
Religious works for special classes of persons — Parents

BV4529.17.E24 1999
The faith factor in fatherhood: renewing the sacred vocation of fathering/ edited by Don E. Eberly. Lanham, Md.: Lexington Books, c1999. xvi, 331 p.
99-037771   261.8/358742/0973   0739100793
Fatherhood -- Religious aspects -- Christianity. Church work with men -- United States.

BV4596 Practical religion.
The Christian life —
Religious works for special classes of persons — Other, A-Z

BV4596.A25.M36 1995
Manlowe, Jennifer L., 1963-
Faith born of seduction: sexual trauma, body image, and religion/ Jennifer L. Manlowe. New York: New York University Press, c1995. xiii, 225 p.
95-016206   261.8/32   0814755178
Adult child sexual abuse victims -- United States -- Religious life. Incest -- Religious aspects -- Christianity. Women -- Mental health -- United States.

BV4626 Practical religion.
The Christian life —
Moral theology — Sins and vices

BV4626.W55 1999
Wicked pleasures: meditations on the seven "deadly" sins/ edited by Robert C. Solomon. Lanham, Md.: Rowman & Littlefield, c1999. vii, 166 p.
98-027047   241/.3   0847692507
Deadly sins.

BV4630-4647 Practical religion.
The Christian life —
Moral theology — Virtues

BV4630.T473 1998
Thomas, Aquinas, Saint, 1225?-1274.
Disputed questions on virtue/ Thomas Aquinas; translated with a preface by Ralph McInerny. South Bend, Ind,: St. Augustine's Press, 1998. xix, 140 p.
98-020702   179/.9   1890318205
Virtue -- Early works to 1800.

BV4639.A6513 1995
Arendt, Hannah.
Love and Saint Augustine/ Hannah Arendt; edited and with an interpretive essay by Joanna Vecchiarelli Scott and Judith Chelius Stark. Chicago: University of Chicago Press, 1996. xx, 233 p.
95-012866   177/.7/092   0226025969
Augustine, -- Saint, Bishop of Hippo. Love -- Religious aspects -- Christianity -- History of doctrines -- Early church, ca. 30-600.

BV4639.G67 1990
Graham, Gordon, 1949 July 15-
The idea of Christian charity: a critique of some contemporary conceptions/ Gordon Graham. Notre Dame: University of Notre Dame Press, c1990. xiv, 190 p.
89-029257   241/.4   0268011672
Charity.

BV4647.L56
Schmidt, Leigh Eric.
Hearing things: religion, illusion, and the American enlightenment/ Leigh Eric Schmidt. Camnbridge, Mass.: Harvard University Press, 2000. xiii, 318 p.
00-038930   277.3/07   0674003039
Listening -- Religious aspects -- Christianity -- History of doctrines -- 18th century. Piety -- History -- 18th century. Enlightenment -- United States. United States -- Church history -- 18th century. United States -- Church history -- 19th century.

BV4647.P5
Tait, L. Gordon.
The piety of John Witherspoon: pew, pulpit, and public forum/ L. Gordon Tait. Louisville, Ky.: Geneva Press, c2001. xxiii, 256 p.
00-039312   285/.1/092   0664501338
Witherspoon, John, -- 1723-1794. Piety -- History of doctrines -- 18th century.

BV4740 Practical religion.
The Christian life —
Moral theology — Vocation. Calling

BV4740.G65 1988
Goldman, Harvey, 1946-
Max Weber and Thomas Mann: calling and the shaping of the self/ Harvey Goldman. Berkeley: University of California Press, c1988. xi, 284 p.
88-001327   126   0520062795
Weber, Max, -- 1864-1920. Mann, Thomas, -- 1875-1955. National characteristics, German. Vocation -- Christianity. Personality.

BV4811 Practical religion.
The Christian life —
Works of meditation and devotion — Selections for daily reading

BV4811.M578 1998
Morgan, Robert J., 1952-
From this verse: 365 Sscriptures that changed the world/ by Robert J. Morgan. Nashville, Tenn.: T. Nelson Publishers, c1998. 1 v.
98-015633   242/.2   0785213937
Devotional calendars.

BV4817 Practical religion.
The Christian life —
Works of meditation and devotion — General works

BV4817.W42
Weil, Simone, 1909-1943.
Waiting on God. [Translated from the French by Emma Craufurd] London, Routledge and K. Paul [1952] ix, 169 p.
65-007275   248
God -- Worship and love.

BV4831-4836 Practical religion.
The Christian life —
Works of meditation and devotion — Devotional works of individual authors

BV4831.J8 1978
Julian, of Norwich, b. 1343.
Showings/ Julian of Norwich; translated from the critical text, with an introd., by Edmund Colledge and James Walsh; pref. by Jean Leclercq. New York: Paulist Press, c1978. 369 p.
77-090953   242   080910234X
Devotional literature, English (Middle)

BV4836.K4813 1989
Kierkegaard, Soren, 1813-1855.
The laughter is on my side: an imaginative introduction to Kierkegaard/ edited by Roger Poole and Henrik Stangerup; preface and headnotes by Roger Poole. Princeton, N.J.: Princeton University Press, c1989. 245 p.
89-003943   198/.9   0691073619
Meditations.

BV4930-4935 Practical religion. The Christian life — Conversion literature — Religious experience. Conversion

BV4930.H65 1992
Holte, James Craig.
The conversion experience in America: a sourcebook on religious conversion autobiography/ James Craig Holte. New York: Greenwood Press, 1992. xiv, 228 p.
91-032173   291.4/2   0313266808
Converts -- United States -- Biography.

BV4930.P38 1998
Payne, Rodger M.
The self and the sacred: conversion and autobiography in early American Protestantism/ Rodger M. Payne. Knoxville: University of Tennessee Press, c1998. 123 p.
97-045426   248.2/4/097309033   1572330155
Converts -- United States -- Biography -- History and criticism. Christian biography -- United States -- History and criticism. Autobiography -- Religious aspects -- Christianity -- History -- 18th century.

BV4935.T37.A33
Tarrants, Thomas A.
The conversion of a Klansman: the story of a former Ku Klux Klan terrorist/ Thomas A. Tarrants III. Garden City, N.Y.: Doubleday, 1979. x, 130 p.
78-074713   248/.2   0385149263
Tarrants, Thomas A.Converts -- United States -- Biography.

BV5039 Practical religion. The Christian life — Asceticism — General works

BV5039.G7.S913
Symeon, the New Theologian, Saint, 949-1022.
The discourses/ Symeon the New Theologian; translation by C.J. de Catanzaro; introd. by George Maloney; pref. by Basile Krivocheine. New York: Paulist Press, c1980. xvii, 396 p.
80-082414   248.4/8140942   0809102927
Asceticism -- History -- Middle Ages, 600-1500. Spiritual life -- Christianity -- Early works to 1800.

BV5053-5067 Practical religion. The Christian life — Asceticism — External aids

BV5053.E474 1998
Empereur, James L.
Spiritual direction and the gay person/ James L. Empereur. New York: Continuum, 1998. xii, 180 p.
98-020738   259/.086/64   082641107X
Spiritual direction. Gays -- Pastoral counseling of. Church work with gays.

BV5067.D38 1993
Davidson, Linda Kay.
Pilgrimage in the Middle Ages: a research guide/ Linda Kay Davidson, Maryjane Dunn-Wood. New York: Garland, 1993. xiv, 480 p.
92-027624   248.4/63/0902   0824072219
Christian pilgrims and pilgrimages -- History -- Bibliography. Church history -- Middle Ages, 600-1500 -- Bibliography. Travel, Medieval -- Bibliography.

BV5075-5077 Practical religion. The Christian life — Mysticism — History

BV5075.B8 1968
Butler, Edward Cuthbert, 1858-1934.
Western mysticism; the teaching of Augustine, Gregory, and Bernard on contemplation and the contemplative life. New York, Barnes & Noble [1968, c1967] lxxii, 242 p.
68-006959   248.2/2
Augustine, -- Saint, Bishop of Hippo. Bernard, -- of Clairvaux, Saint, -- 1090 or 91-1153. Gregory -- I, -- Pope, -- ca. 540-604. Contemplation. Mysticism -- History -- Middle Ages, 600-1500.

BV5075.M37 1994
McGinn, Bernard,
The presence of God: a history of Western Christian mysticism/ by Bernard McGinn. New York: Crossroad, 1991-<1998 > v. <1-3 >
91-023931   248.2/2 20   0824511212
Mysticism -- History.

BV5075.M45 1994
Meister Eckhart and the Beguine mystics: Hadewijch of Brabant, Mechthild of Magdeburg, and Marguerite Porete/ edited by Bernard McGinn. New York: Continuum, 1994. 166 p.
94-013185   248.2/2/09409022   0826406815
Mechthild, -- of Magdeburg, -- ca. 1212-ca. 1282 -- Influence. Porete, Marguerite, -- ca. 1250-1310 -- Influence. Hadewijch, -- 13th cent. -- Influence. Mysticism -- History -- Middle Ages, 600-1500. Mysticism -- Catholic Church -- History. Beguines.

BV5077.E85.F87 1996
Furlong, Monica.
Visions and longings: medieval women mystics/ Monica Furlong. Boston, MA: Shambhala, 1996. 248 p.
95-048804   248.2/2/09224   157062125X
Women mystics -- Europe. Mysticism. Mysticism -- Europe -- History -- Middles Ages, 600-1500.

BV5077.G3 D48 2000
Deutsche Mystik im abendländischen Zusammenhang: neu erschlossene Texte, neue methodische Ansätze, neue theoretische Konzepte: Kolloquium, Kloster Fischingen 1998/ herausgegeben von Walter Haug und Wolfram Schneider-Lastin. Tübingen: Niemeyer, 2000. xii, 814 p.
2001-338922   3484640146
Mysticism--Germany--Congresses. Mystics--Germany--Congresses.

BV5077.G7.K58
Knowles, David, 1896-
The English mystical tradition. New York, Harper [1961] 197 p.
61-007343   248.220942
Mysticism -- Great Britain.

BV5077.S7.P52
Peers, E. Allison 1891-1952.
Studies of the Spanish mystics. London, S.P.C.K.; [1951-]
57-022935   149.3
Mysticism -- Spain. Spanish literature -- History and criticism.

BV5080-5082 Practical religion. The Christian life — Mysticism — General works

BV5080.B7.W413 1978
Bohme, Jakob, 1575-1624.
The way to Christ/ Jacob Boehme; translation and introd. by Peter Erb; pref. by Winfried Zeller. New York: Paulist Press, c1978. xviii, 307 p.
77-095117   248/.22   0809102374
Mysticism -- History.

BV5080.E45.E43 1958a
Eckhart, Meister, d. 1327.
Treatises and sermons. Selected and translated from Latin and German with an introd. and notes by James M. Clark and John V. Skinner. New York, Harper [1958] 267 p.
58-012934   189.5
Eckhart, -- Meister, -- d. 1327.Mysticism -- Middle Ages.

BV5080.J64213 1989
John of the Cross, 1542-1591.
St. John of the Cross (San Juan de la Cruz): alchemist of the soul: his life, his poetry (bilingual), his prose/ text, new edited translations by Antonio T. de Nicolas; foreword by Seyyed Hossein Nasr. New York: Paragon House, 1989. xxi, 260 p.
89-030265 248.2/2 1557780277
Mysticism -- Early works to 1800.

BV5081.U55 1930
Underhill, Evelyn, 1875-1941.
Mysticism; a study in the nature and development of man's spiritual consciousness, by Evelyn Underhill... New York, E. P. Dutton and company, inc. [1930]
31-026805 149.3
Mysticism.

BV5082.U5
Underhill, Evelyn, 1875-1941.
The essentials of mysticism and other essays, by Evelyn Underhill. London & Toronto, J. M. Dent & sons ltd.; vii, 245 p.
21-001752
Mysticism.

BV5083 Practical religion. The Christian life — Mysticism — General special. Psychology. etc.

BV5083.B29 1997
Barnard, G. William 1955-
Exploring unseen worlds: William James and the philosophy of mysticism/ G. William Barnard. Albany: State University of New York Press, c1997. xiv, 422 p.
96-013103 291.4/22/092 0791432238
James, William, -- 1842-1910 -- Contributions in study of mysticism.Mysticism -- Comparative studies. Mysticism -- Psychology.

BV5083.J36 1995
Jantzen, Grace.
Power, gender, and Christian mysticism/ Grace M. Jantzen. Cambridge; Cambridge University Press, 1995. xvii, 384 p.
94-044562 248.2/2/082 0521473764
Mysticism. Women mystics. Sex -- Religious aspects -- Christianity.

BV5095 Practical religion. The Christian life — Mysticism — Biography

BV5095.A1.B69 1998
Bruneau, Marie-Florine.
Women mystics confront the modern world: Marie de l'Incarnation (1599-1672) and Madame Guyon (1648-1717)/ Marie-Florine Bruneau. Albany: State University of New York Press, c1998. x, 279 p.
97-019144 248.2/2/0922 0791436616
Marie de l'Incarnation, -- mere, -- 1599-1672. Guyon, Jeanne Marie Bouvier de La Motte, -- 1648-1717. Mysticism -- History -- 17th century. Women mystics -- Biography.

BV5095.B7.H3 1958
Hartmann, Franz, d. 1912.
Personal Christianity; the doctrines of Jacob Boehme. New York, F. Ungar Pub. Co. [1957 or 8] 336 p.
57-012318 149.3
Bohme, Jakob, -- 1575-1624.

BV5095.H55.B44 1992
Beer, Frances.
Women and mystical experience in the Middle Ages/ Frances Beer. Woodbridge, Suffolk, UK: Boydell Press, 1992. 174 p.
92-015362 170 085115302X
Hildegard, -- Saint, -- 1098-1179. Mechthild, -- of Magdeburg, -- ca. 1212-ca. 1282. Julian, -- of Norwich, -- b. 1343. Women mystics -- Biography. Mysticism -- History -- Middle Ages, 600-1500.

BV5095.J3.M63 1995
Mommaers, Paul, 1935-
Mysticism, Buddhist and Christian: encounters with Jan van Ruusbroec/ Paul Mommaers & Jan van Bragt. New York: Crossroad, 1995. v, 302 p.
94-031692 248.2/2 0824514556
Ruusbroec, Jan van, -- 1293-1381.Christianity and other religions -- Buddhism. Mysticism -- History -- Middle Ages, 600-1500. Buddhism -- Relations -- Christianity.

BX Christian denominations

BX6 Church unity. Ecumenical movement. Interdenominational cooperation — Societies. Associations, conferences, etc. — Other, A-Z

BX6.W78.B4 1979
Bell, G. K. A. 1883-1958.
The kingship of Christ: the story of the World Council of Churches/ by G. K. A. Bell. Westport, Conn.: Greenwood Press, 1979. 181 p.
78-010482 262/.001 0313211213
Ecumenical movement -- History.

BX6.3 Church unity. Ecumenical movement. Interdenominational cooperation — Dictionaries. Encyclopedias

BX6.3.V36 1994
Van der Bent, A. J.
Historical dictionary of ecumenical Christianity/ Ans Joachim van der Bent. Metuchen, N.J.: Scarecrow Press, 1994. xxiii, 599 p.
94-000494 270.8/2/03 0810828537
Ecumenical movement -- Dictionaries. Ecumenists -- Biography -- Dictionaries. Christian union -- Dictionaries.

BX8.2 Church unity. Ecumenical movement. Interdenominational cooperation — General works — 1951-2000

BX8.2.F6813 1985
Fries, Heinrich.
Unity of the churches--an actual possibility/ Heinrich Fries and Karl Rahner; translated by Ruth C.L. Gritsch and Eric W. Gritsch. Philadelphia: Fortress Press; c1985. xi, 146 p.
84-048481 262/.0011 0800618203
Christian union.

BX230 Orthodox Eastern Church — Dictionaries. Encyclopedias

BX230.P76 1996
Prokurat, Michael, 1950-
Historical dictionary of the Orthodox Church/ by Michael Prokurat, Alexander Golitzin, Michael D. Peterson. Lanham, Md.: Scarecrow Press, 1996. xvii, 439 p.
95-037165　281.9/09　0810830817
Orthodox Eastern Church -- History -- Dictionaries. Orthodox Eastern Church -- Dictionaries.

BX290 Orthodox Eastern Church — History — General works

BX290.M413
Meyendorff, John, 1926-
The Orthodox Church, its past and its role in the world today. Trans. from the French by John Chapin. New York, Pantheon Books [1962] 244 p.
62-014260　281.9
Orthodox Eastern Church -- History.

BX300-310 Orthodox Eastern Church — History — By period

BX300.R86
Runciman, Steven, 1903-
The Byzantine theocracy/ Steven Runciman. Cambridge; Cambridge University Press, 1977. viii, 197 p.
76-047405　274.95　0521214017
Church and state -- Byzantine Empire -- History.

BX310.C58 2000
Clark, Victoria.
Why angels fall: a journey through Orthodox Europe from Byzantium to Kosovo/ Victoria Clark. New York: St. Martin's Press, 2000. xviii, 460 p.
00-711570　281.9/4　0312233965
Clark, Victoria -- Journeys -- Europe.Europe -- Church history.

BX310.S29 1993
Seeking God: the recovery of religious identity in Orthodox Russia, Ukraine, and Georgia/ edited by Stephen K. Batalden. DeKalb: Northern Illinois University Press, 1993. 299 p.
93-016553　281.9/47 20　0875801781
Russia (Federation) -- Religious life and customs. Ukraine -- Religious life and customs. Georgia (Republic) -- Religious life and customs.

BX320.2 Orthodox Eastern Church — General works. Doctrine, etc. — 1951-2000

BX320.2.C66 1982
Constantelos, Demetrios J.
Understanding the Greek Orthodox Church: its faith, history, and practice/ Demetrios J. Constantelos. New York, N.Y.: Seabury Press, 1982. xiii, 178 p.
81-021313　281.9/3　0816405158
Orthodox Eastern Church. Orthodoxos Ekkˉesia tˉes Hellados.

BX410 Orthodox Eastern Church — Divisions of the Church — Patriarchates of the East. Melchites

BX410.R8
Runciman, Steven, 1903-
The Great Church in captivity: a study of the Patriarchate of Constantinople from the eve of the Turkish conquest to the Greek War of Independence. London, Cambridge U.P., 1968. x, 455 p.
68-029330　281.9　0521071887
Constantinople (Ecumenical patriarchate) -- History. Constantinople (Ecumenical patriarchate) -- Relations.

BX492-493 Orthodox Eastern Church — Divisions of the Church — Russian Church

BX492.P67 1984
Pospielovsky, Dimitry, 1935-
The Russian church under the Soviet regime, 1917-1982/ Dimitry Pospielovsky. Crestwood, N.Y.: St. Vladimir's Seminary Press, 1984. 2 v.
84-005336　281.9/3　0881410152
Soviet Union -- Church history.

BX493.K33 1998
Kaariainen, Kimmo.
Religion in Russia after the collapse of communism: religious renaissance or secular state/ Kimmo Kaariainen. Lewiston, NY: E. Mellen Press, c1998. v, 201 p.
98-030155　200/.947/09049　0773482830
Russia (Federation) -- Religion.

BX735 Orthodox Eastern Church — Divisions of the Church — Orthodox Church in other regions or countries

BX735.F57 1995
FitzGerald, Thomas E., 1947-
The Orthodox Church/ Thomas E. FitzGerald. Westport, Conn.: Greenwood Press, c1995. xiii, 240 p.
94-021685　281.9/73　0313262810
Orthodox (Orthodox Eastern Church) -- United States -- Biography -- Dictionaries.

BX810 Catholic Church — Societies. Confraternities, etc. — Individual societies, sodalities, etc.

BX810.C393.A76 1987
Aronica, Michele Teresa.
Beyond charismatic leadership: the New York Catholic Worker Movement/ by Michele Teresa Aronica. New Brunswick, U.S.A.: Transaction Books, c1987. xi, 197 p.
87-010163　267/.1827471　0887381685
Maurin, Peter. Day, Dorothy, -- 1897-1980. Catholic Worker Movement.

BX819.3 Catholic Church — Personal prelatures — Individual prelatures, A-Z

BX819.3.O68.E7413 1995
Estruch, Juan, 1943-
Saints and schemers: Opus Dei and its paradoxes/ Joan Estruch; translated by Elizabeth Ladd Glick. New York: Oxford University Press, 1995. xviii, 302 p.
94-037014　306.6/67182　0195082516
Religion and sociology -- Spain.

BX825-830 Catholic Church — Councils — General and Ecumenical councils

BX825.B45 2002
Bellitto, Christopher M.
The general councils: a history of the twenty-one general councils from Nicaea to Vatican II/ Christopher M. Bellitto. New York: Paulist Press, c2002. xi, 156 p.
2002-005890　262/.52 21　0809140195
Councils and synods, Ecumenical.

BX825.H8
Hughes, Philip, 1895-1967.
The church in crisis: a history of the general councils, 325-1870. Garden City, N.Y., Hanover House [1961] 384 p.
61-006511　270
Councils and synods, Ecumenical.

BX830 1545.A3.S35

Canons and decrees of the Council of Trent/ original text with English translation by H.J. Schroeder. St. Louis, Mo.: B. Herder Book Co., 1960. xxxiii, 608 p.
41-021651   270.6

BX830 1962 .A3.G3

The documents of Vatican II. Introductions and commentaries by Catholic bishops and experts. Responses by Protestant and Orthodox scholars. Walter M. Abbott, general editor. Joseph Gallagher, translation editor. New York, Guild Press [1966] xxi, 794 p.
66-020201   262.5

BX841 Catholic Church — Dictionaries. Encyclopedias

BX841.N44 2003

New Catholic encyclopedia. 2nd ed. Detroit: Thomson/Gale; 15 v.
2002-000924   282/.03 21   0787640042

BX860 Catholic Church — Documents — Collections

BX860.A36 1956
Catholic Church.

The papal encyclicals in their historical context, by Anne Fremantle. With an introd. by Gustave Weigel. [New York] New American Library [1956] 317 p.
56-011328   262.8
Encyclicals, Papal.

BX932 Catholic Church — Study and teaching — Education of the laity

BX932.M36 1992
McNamara, Patrick H.

Conscience first, tradition second: a study of young American Catholics/ Patrick H. McNamara. Albany: State University of New York Press, c1992. xviii, 221 p.
90-022768   282/.73/0835   0791408132
Catholic high school students -- United States -- Religious life. Catholic high school students -- United States -- Attitudes. Catholic high school students -- United States -- Longitudinal studies.

BX945.2-945.3 Catholic Church — History — General works

BX945.2.C65 1997
Collinge, William J.,

Historical dictionary of Catholicism/ William J. Collinge. Lanham, Md.: Scarecrow Press, 1997. xx, 551 p.
96-030421   282/.03 20   081083233X
Church history -- Dictionaries.

BX945.3.K86 2001
Kung, Hans, 1928-

The Catholic Church: a short history/ Hans Kung; translated by John Bowden. New York: Modern Library, 2001. xxv, 221 p.
00-067568   282/.09   0679640924
Catholic Church -- History.

BX953-958 Catholic Church — History — History of the Papacy

BX953.G5
Giles, Edward

Documents illustrating papal authority, A.D. 96-454. London, S.P.C.K., 1952. xxi, 344 p.
53-008048   262.13
Papacy -- History -- Sources. Church history -- Primitive and early church -- Sources. Christian literature.

BX955.2.E53 1999

Encyclopedia of the Vatican and papacy/ edited by Frank J. Coppa. Westport, Conn.: Greenwood Press, 1999. viii, 483 p.
98-015328   262/.13/09   0313289174
Popes -- Biography -- Encyclopedias. Papacy -- History -- Encyclopedias. Councils and synods, Ecumenical -- Encyclopedias.

BX955.2.L35 1999
La Due, William J.

The chair of Saint Peter: a history of the papacy/ William J. La Due. Maryknoll, N.Y.: Orbis Books, c1999. x, 374 p.
98-050146   262/.13/09   1570752494
Papacy -- History.

BX958.F2.B6813 2001
Boureau, Alain.

The myth of Pope Joan/ Alain Boureau; translated by Lydia G. Cochrane. Chicago: University of Chicago Press, 2001. x, 385 p.
00-011154   262/.13   0226067440
Joan (Legendary Pope) Popes -- Legends. Women in Christianity -- History -- Middle Ages, 600-1500.

BX970-1396 Catholic Church — History — By period

BX970.R48
Richards, Jeffrey.

The popes and the papacy in the early Middle Ages, 476-752/ Jeffrey Richards. London; Routledge & Kegan Paul, 1979. viii, 422 p.
78-041023   262/.13/09021   0710000987
Papacy -- History -- To 1309.Europe -- Church history -- 600-1500.

BX1187.A4 1969
Catholic Church.

The correspondence of Pope Gregory VII; selected letters from the Registrum. Translated with an introd. by Ephraim Emerton. New York, Norton [1969, c1932] xxxi, 212 p.
70-008470   262/.13/0924
Gregory -- VII, -- Pope, -- ca. 1015-1085 -- Correspondence.Popes -- Correspondence.

BX1261.H3
Hales, E. E. Y. 1908-

Revolution and Papacy, 1769-1846. Hanover House, 1960. 320 p.
60-013527   282
Church history -- 18th century. Church history -- 19th century.

BX1270.R413
Renouard, Yves.

The Avignon papacy, 1305-1403. Translated by Denis Bethell. [Hamden, Conn.] Archon Books, 1970. 157 p.
70-021164   262/.13/09023   0208011560
Papacy -- History -- 1309-1378. Church history -- Middle Ages, 600-1500.

BX1361.C45
Chadwick, Owen.

The Popes and European revolution/ Owen Chadwick. Oxford: Clarendon Press; 1981. ix, 646 p.
80-040673   262/.13/09033   0198269196
Papacy -- History -- 1566-1799. Papacy -- History -- 19th century. Europe -- Politics and government -- 18th century. Europe -- Politics and government -- 1789-1900.

BX1378.P49 2000
Phayer, Michael, 1935-

The Catholic Church and the Holocaust, 1930-1965/ Michael Phayer. Bloomington: Indiana University Press, c2000. xviii, 301 p.
99-087415   282/.09/044   0253337259
Pius -- XII, -- Pope, -- 1876-1958 -- Relations with Jews.Judaism -- Relations -- Catholic Church. Holocaust, Jewish (1939-1945) World War, 1939-1945 -- Religious aspects -- Catholic Church.

BX1378.5.B67 2000
Boniecki, Adam.

The making of the Pope of the millenium: kalendarium of life of Karol Wojtyla/ Adam Boniecki. Stockbridge, Mass.: Marian Press, 2000. 938 p.
00-102005   0944203493
John Paul -- II, -- Pope, -- 1920-Popes -- Biography.

BX1378.5.S56 2001
Simpson, Peter.

On Karol Wojtyla/ Peter Simpson. Australia; Wadsworth, c2001. 93 p.
2001-271152   199/.438 21   053458375X
John Paul II, Pope, 1920-

BX1386.C58 1998
Coppa, Frank J.
The modern papacy since 1789/ Frank J. Coppa.
London; Longman, 1998. viii, 296 p.
98-018988   262/.13/09034   0582096294
   *Papacy -- History -- 1799-1870. Papacy --
History -- 19th century. Papacy -- History --
20th century.*

BX1390.M63 1990
Modern Catholicism: Vatican II and after/ edited
by Adrian Hastings. London: SPCK; 1991.
473 p.
90-040624   282/.09/045   0195206576
   *Catholic Church -- History -- 1965- Vatican
Council (2nd: 1962-1965) Catholic Church --
Doctrines -- History -- 20th century.*

BX1390.00S86 2000
Stourton, Edward.
Absolute truth: the struggle for meaning in
today's Catholic Church/ by Edward Stourton.
New York: TV Books, 2000.
00-032563   282/.09/045   1575001489
   Catholic Church -- History -- 1965-

BX1390.W67 1988
World Catholicism in transition/ edited by
Thomas M. Gannon. New York: Macmillan;
c1988. xiv, 402 p.
88-001644   282/.09/04   002911280X
   Catholic Church -- History -- 1965-

BX1396.C39 2000
Catholicism contending with modernity: Roman
Catholic modernism and anti-modernism in
historical context/ edited by Darrell Jodock.
Cambridge, U.K.; Cambridge University Press,
2000. xiv, 345 p.
99-034666   273/.9   0521770718
   *Modernism (Christian theology) -- Catholic
Church -- History.*

BX1404-1417 Catholic Church —
History —
By region or country —
North America

BX1404.T68
Toward Vatican III: The work that needs to be
done/ edited by David Tracy with Hans Kung
and Johann B. Metz. Nijmegen, Holland:
Concilium; 1978. xi, 333 p.
77-028606   262/.5/2   0816403791
   *Church renewal -- Catholic Church --
Congresses.*

BX1405.G46 2001
Gender identities in American Catholicism/
Paula Kane, James Kenneally, Karen Kennelly,
editors. Maryknoll, N.Y.: Orbis Books, c2001.
xxxi, 287 p.
2001-053124   282/.73/082 21   1570753601
   *Women in the Catholic Church -- United
States -- History -- Sources. United States --
Church history -- Sources.*

BX1406.2.B75 1992
Briggs, Kenneth A.
Holy Siege: the year that shook Catholic
America/ Kenneth A. Briggs. [San Francisco,
Calif.]: Harper San Francisco, c1992. x, 594 p.
91-058156   282/.73/09048   0060610581
   *United States -- Church history -- 20th
century.*

BX1406.2.B865 1992
Burns, Gene, 1958-
The frontiers of Catholicism: the politics of
ideology in a liberal world/ Gene Burns.
Berkeley: University of California Press, c1992.
xiii, 304 p.
91-046039   282/.73   0520077172
   Ideology -- Religious aspects -- Christianity.

BX1406.2.D42 1987
Deedy, John G.
American Catholicism: and now where?/ John
Deedy. New York: Plenum Press, c1987. xviii,
309 p.
87-012765   282/.73   0306427060
   *United States -- Church history -- 20th
century.*

BX1406.2.E53 1997
The encyclopedia of American Catholic history/
edited by Michael   Glazier and Thomas J.
Shelley. Collegeville, Minn.: Liturgical Press,
c1997. xi, 1567 p.
97-041221   282/.73/03 21   0814659195
   *United States -- Church history --
Encyclopedias.*

BX1406.2.F74 2000
Froehle, Bryan.
The Catholic Church today/ Bryan T. Froehle,
Mary L. Gautier. Maryknoll, N.Y.: Orbis Books,
[c2000-   ] v. 1
00-037483   282/.73/09051   1570752729
   *United States -- Church history -- 20th
century -- Statistics.*

BX1406.2.G45 1999
Gillis, Chester, 1951-
Roman Catholicism in America/ Chester Gillis.
New York: Columbia University Press, c1999. x,
365 p.
99-017945   282/.73   0231108702
   United States -- Church history.

BX1406.2.G58 1987
Gleason, Philip.
Keeping the faith/ American Catholicism, past
and present/ Philip Gleason. Notre Dame, Ind.:
University of Notre Dame Press, c1987. vii,
285 p.
86-040579   282/.73   026801227X
   United States -- Church history.

BX1406.2.W55 1996
Wilkes, Paul,
The good enough Catholic: a guide for the
perplexed/ Paul Wilkes. 1st ed. New York:
Ballantine Books, 1996. xxiii, 354 p.
96-038528   248.4/82 20   0345395433
   *Catholics -- United States -- Religion.
Catholics -- United States -- Social life and
customs.*

BX1406.2.Z6513 1999
Zoller, Michael.
Washington and Rome: Catholicism in American
culture/ Michael Zoller; translated by Steven
Rendall and Albert Wimmer. Notre Dame, IN:
University of Notre Dame Press, c1999. xii,
278 p.
98-003011   282/.73   0268019525
   United States -- Church history.

BX1407.I45.L57 1989
Liptak, Dolores Ann.
Immigrants and their Church/ Dolores Liptak.
New York: Macmillan; c1989. xviii, 221 p.
88-018109   282/.73   0029192315
   *Immigrants   --   United   States   --
Religion. United   States   --   Emigration   and
immigration. United States -- Church history.*

BX1407.P24.A44 1996
American Catholic pacifism: the influence of
Dorothy Day and the Catholic Worker
movement/ edited by Anne Klejment and Nancy
L. Roberts. Westport, Conn.: Praeger, 1996. x,
198 p.
96-016264   261.8/73/08822   027594784X
   *Day, Dorothy, -- 1897-1980. Pacifism --
Religious aspects -- Catholic Church -- History
of doctrines -- 20th century. Catholic Worker
Movement. United States -- Church history --
20th century.*

BX1407.P63.G45 1994
Gelm, Richard J.
Politics and religious authority: American
Catholics since the Second Vatican Council/
Richard J. Gelm. Westport, Conn.: Greenwood
Press, 1994. xiii, 151 p.
93-001650   282/.73/09045   0313289034
   *Catholics -- United States -- Attitudes. Church
-- Authority -- History of doctrines -- 20th
century. Christianity and politics -- Catholic
Church -- History -- 20th century. United States
-- Church history -- 20th century.*

BX1407.W65.K43 1990
Kenneally, James Joseph, 1929-
The history of American Catholic women/ James
J. Kenneally. New York: Crossroad, 1990. x,
286 p.
89-077880   282/.082   0824510097
   *Catholic women -- United States -- History.
Women in the Catholic Church -- United States -
- History. United States -- Church history.*

BX1417.B6 O36 1998
O'Connor, Thomas H., 1922-
Boston Catholics: a history of the church and its people/ Thomas H. O'Connor. Boston: Northeastern University Press, c1998. xvi, 357 p.
98-018996   282/.744   1555533590
Boston (Mass.) -- Church history.

BX1442.2-1484.2 Catholic Church — History — By region or country — Latin America

BX1442.2.K57 1992
Kirk, John M., 1951-
Politics and the Catholic church in Nicaragua/ John M. Kirk; foreword by Phillip Berryman. Gainesville, FL: University Press of Florida, c1992. xiii, 246 p.
92-005131   282/.7285   0813011388
Church and state -- Nicaragua -- History.Nicaragua -- Politics and government. Nicaragua -- Church history.

BX1446.2.P47 1997
Peterson, Anna Lisa, 1963-
Martyrdom and the politics of religion: progressive Catholicism in El Salvador's civil war/ Anna L. Peterson. Albany: State University of New York Press, c1997. xxiv, 211 p.
96-000367   282/.7284/09047   0791431819
Martyrdom.El Salvador -- Politics and government -- 1979-1992. El Salvador -- Church history -- 20th century.

BX1462.2.B84 1995
Burdick, Michael A., 1953-
For God and the fatherland: religion and politics in Argentina/ Michael A. Burdick. Albany: State University of New York Press, c1995 xi, 283 p.
95-003597   322/.1/09820904   0791427439
Church and state -- Argentina -- History -- 20th century. Church and state -- Catholic Church -- History -- 20th century. Argentina -- Church history -- 20th century. Argentina -- Politics and government.

BX1466.2.S48 2000
Serbin, Ken.
Secret dialogues: church-state relations, torture, and social justice in authoritarian Brazil/ Kenneth P. Serbin. Pittsburgh, Pa.: University of Pittsburgh Press, c2000. xx, 312 p.
00-009649   981.06/3   0822941236
Church and state -- Catholic Church -- History -- 20th century. Church and state -- Brazil -- History -- 20th century. Brazil -- Politics and government -- 1964-1985.

BX1484.2.P46 1995
Pena, Milagros, 1955-
Theologies and liberation in Peru: the role of ideas in social movements/ Milagros Pena. Philadelphia: Temple University Press, 1995. xii, 222 p.
94-036758   282/.85/09045   1566392942
Christianity and politics -- Catholic Church -- History -- 20th century. Liberation theology -- History. Peru -- Church history -- 20th century. Peru -- History -- 1968-1980. Peru -- History -- 1980-

BX1490-1584 Catholic Church — History — By region or country — Europe

BX1490.C4613 1989
Chatellier, Louis.
The Europe of the devout: the Catholic reformation and the formation of a new society/ Louis Chatellier; translated by Jean Birrell. Cambridge [England]; Cambridge University Press; 1989. xiv, 270 p.
88-036549   282/.4   0521363330
Sociology, Christian -- Europe.Europe -- Religious life and customs.

BX1504.U57 E44 2001
Elliott, Marianne,
The Catholics of Ulster: a history/ Marianne Elliott. New York: Basic Books, 2001.
54-722   282/.416 21   046501903X
Catholic Church -- Ulster (Northern Ireland and Ireland) -- History. Ulster (Northern Ireland and Ireland) -- Church history.

BX1530.2.W37 2000
Warner, Carolyn M., 1961-
Confessions of an interest group: the Catholic Church and political parties in Europe/ Carolyn M. Warner. Princeton, N.J.: Princeton University Press, c2000. xvi, 249 p.
99-041741   324/.088/22   0691010269
Christianity and politics -- Catholic Church -- History -- 20th century. Christian democratic parties -- France -- History -- 20th century. Christian democratic parties -- Italy -- History -- 20th century. France -- Church history -- 1945- Italy -- Church history -- 20th century. Germany -- Church history -- 1945-

BX1536.D54 1988
Dietrich, Donald J., 1941-
Catholic citizens in the Third Reich: psychosocial principles and moral reasoning/ Donald J. Dietrich. New Brunswick, U.S.A.: Transaction Books, c1988. xii, 356 p.
86-019344   282/.43   0887381316
Catholics -- Germany -- History -- 20th century. Church and state -- Germany -- History -- 1933-1945. Germany -- Church history -- 1933-1945.

BX1583.P29 1984
Payne, Stanley G.
Spanish catholicism: an historical overview/ Stanley G. Payne. Madison, Wis.: University of Wisconsin Press, 1984. xiii, 263 p.
83-025946   282/.46   0299098001
Spain -- Religious life and customs. Spain -- Church history.

BX1584.H66 2000
Homza, Lu Ann, 1958-
Religious authority in the Spanish Renaissance/ Lu Ann Homza. Baltimore: Johns Hopkins University Press, 2000 xxiii, 312 p.
99-032726   274.6/06   0801862434
Authority -- Religious aspects -- Catholic Church -- History of doctrines -- 16th century. Renaissance -- Spain. Spain -- Church history -- 16th century.

BX1656-1668 Catholic Church — History — By region or country — Asia

BX1656.S38
Schumacher, John N.
Readings in Philippine church history/ John N. Schumacher. Quezon City: Loyola School of Theology, Ateneo de Manila University, 1979. xi, 428 p.
81-185342   282/.599
Philippines -- Church history -- Sources.

BX1665.M29 1998
Madsen, Richard, 1941-
China's Catholics: tragedy and hope in an emerging civil society/ Richard Madsen. Berkeley: University of California Press, c1998. xiii, 183 p.
97-050613   282/.51/09045   0520213262
Catholic Church -- China.

BX1668.T4513 1996
The beginning of heaven and earth: the sacred book of Japan's hidden Christians/ translated and annotated by Christal Whelan. Honolulu: University of Hawaii Press, c1996. xii, 135 p.
96-012374   275.2/08   0824818067
Crypto-Christians -- Japan.Japan -- Church history.

BX1735 Catholic Church — History — History of the Inquisition

BX1735.C84 1991
Cultural encounters: the impact of the Inquisition in Spain and the New World/ edited by Mary Elizabeth Perry and Anne J. Cruz. Berkeley: University of California Press, c1991. xvi, 288 p.
90-022450   272/.2 20   0520070984
Inquisition -- Spain -- Congresses. Inquisition -- Mexico -- Congresses. Indians of Mexico -- Congresses.

BX1735.K312 1998
Kamen, Henry Arthur Francis.
The Spanish Inquisition: a historical revision/
Henry Kamen. New Haven: Yale University
Press, 1998. xii, 369 p.
97-032451 272/.2/0946 0300075227
Inquisition -- Spain.Spain -- Church history.

BX1735.W59 1999
Women in the Inquisition: Spain and the New
World/ edited by Mary E. Giles. Baltimore:
Johns Hopkins University Press, c1999. ix,
402 p.
98-003998 272/.2/082 080185931X
Inquisition -- Spain. Inquisition -- Mexico.
Women in the Catholic Church -- Spain --
History.

BX1745.5 Catholic Church —
Theology. Doctrine. Dogmatics —
Dictionaries. Encyclopedias

BX1745.5.L4913 1995
Handbook of Catholic theology/ edited by
Wolfgang Beinert, Francis Schussler Fiorenza.
New York: Crossroad, 1995. xiv, 783 p.
95-001216 230/.2/03 0824514238
Theology, Doctrinal -- Dictionaries.

BX1746 Catholic Church —
Theology. Doctrine. Dogmatics —
The nature of the Church in
Catholic theology

BX1746.H37 1995
Harmer, Catherine M.
Religious life in the 21st century: a
contemporary journey into Canaan/ Catherine M.
Harmer. Mystic, CT: Twenty-Third Publications,
c1995. 136 p.
95-060063 255/.001/12 0896226514
Church and the world. Christianity --
Forecasting.

BX1746.K7913 1990
Kung, Hans, 1928-
Reforming the Church today: keeping hope
alive/ Hans Kung; translated by Peter Heinegg
with Francis McDonagh ... [et al.] New York:
Crossroad, 1990 vi, 198 p.
90-038590 282/.09/045 0824510453
Church renewal -- Catholic Church Church

BX1747 Catholic Church —
Theology. Doctrine. Dogmatics —
History of Catholic doctrines

BX1747.K47 1990
Ker, I. T.
Newman on being a Christian/ Ian Ker. Notre
Dame, Ind.: University of Notre Dame Press,
c1990. x, 187 p.
89-040752 230/.2 026801468X
Newman, John Henry, -- 1801-1890.

BX1747.5 Catholic Church —
Theology. Doctrine. Dogmatics —
Collections of doctrinal decisions,
opinions, sources, etc.

BX1747.5.R66 1998
Rome has spoken: a guide to forgotten papal
statements and how they have changed through
the centuries/ Maureen Fiedler and Linda
Rabben, editors. New York: Crossroad, c1998.
xi, 243 p.
98-019447 262.9/1 0824517741
Church and social problems -- Catholic
Church -- Papal doctrines.

BX1751.2 Catholic Church —
Theology. Doctrine. Dogmatics —
General works

BX1751.2.B223 1984
Badia, Leonard F.
Basic Catholic beliefs for today: the Creed
explained/ by Leonard F. Badia. New York:
Alba House, c1984. 170 p.
84-014632 230/.2 0818904690
Catholic Church -- Doctrines.

BX1753 Catholic Church —
Theology. Doctrine. Dogmatics —
General special

BX1753.C86 1982
Curran, Charles E.
American Catholic social ethics: twentieth-
century approaches/ Charles E. Curran. Notre
Dame: University of Notre Dame Press, c1982.
x, 353 p.
82-004829 261.8/0973 0268006032
Sociology, Christian (Catholic) -- History of
doctrines -- 20th century. Christian ethics --
History of doctrines -- 20th century. Social
ethics -- History -- 20th century.

BX1754 Catholic Church —
Theology. Doctrine. Dogmatics —
Popular works

BX1754.G697 2000
Greeley, Andrew M., 1928-
The Catholic imagination/ Andrew Greeley.
Berkeley: University of California Press, c2000.
213 p.
99-033945 282 0520220854
Theology, Doctrinal -- Popular works.

BX1758.2 Catholic Church —
Moral theology. Casuistry.
Cases of conscience, etc. —
General works

BX1758.2.H32
Haring, Bernhard, 1912-
Toward a Christian moral theology [by] Bernard
Haring. [Notre Dame, Ind.] University of Notre
Dame Press, 1966. viii, 230 p.
66-015502 248.482
Christian ethics -- Catholic authors.

BX1765.2 Catholic Church —
Controversial works against the
Catholic Church —
General works

BX1765.2.P4
Pelikan, Jaroslav Jan, 1923-
The riddle of Roman Catholicism. New York,
Abingdon Press [1959] 272 p.
59-010367 282
Protestant churches -- Relations -- Catholic
Church. Catholic Church -- Doctrinal and
controversial works -- Protestant authors.
Catholic Church -- Relations -- Protestant
churches.

BX1765.2.W54 2000
Wills, Garry, 1934-
Papal sin: structures of deceit/ Garry Wills. New
York: Doubleday, 2000. viii, 326 p.
99-054851 262/.13 0385494106
Papacy.

BX1766 Catholic Church —
Controversial works against the
Catholic Church —
Anti-Catholicism. Anti-Papism

BX1766.B74 1998
Brewer, John D.
Anti-Catholicism in Northern Ireland, 1600-
1997: the mote and the beam/ John D. Brewer,
with Gareth I. Higgins. New York: St. Martin's
Press, 1998. xi, 248 p.
98-028305 305.6/20416 0312217382
Anti-Catholicism -- Northern Ireland --
History.Northern Ireland -- Religion. Northern
Ireland -- Politics and government.

BX1787 Catholic Church — Catholic Church and other churches — Participation in inter-faith movements

BX1787.R86 1992
Ruokanen, Miikka.
The Catholic doctrine of non-Christian religions: according to the Second Vatican Council/ by Miikka Ruokanen. Leiden; E.J. Brill, 1992. 169 p.
91-046332   261.2   9004095179
Christianity and other religions.

BX1793 Catholic Church — Catholic Church and the state — Catholic viewpoint on political theory, world politics, international relations, etc.

BX1793.C37 1993
Catholic social thought and the new world order: building on one hundred years/ Oliver F. Williams and John W. Houck, editors. Notre Dame, Ind.: University of Notre Dame Press, c1993. xiv, 383 p.
92-056866   261.8/08/822   0268007977
Catholic Church and world politics — Congresses. Sociology, Christian (Catholic) — Congresses. Church and social problems — Catholic Church — Congresses.

BX1793.S75 1999
Stiltner, Brian, 1966-
Religion and the common good: Catholic contributions to building community in a liberal society/ Brian Stiltner. Lanham, Md.: Rowman & Littlefield, c1999. viii, 203 p.
99-019013   261.8/088/22   0847694356
Christianity and politics — Catholic Church. Common good — Religious aspects — Catholic Church. Liberalism — Religious aspects — Catholic Church.

BX1795 Catholic Church — Other special topics, A-Z

BX1795.E27.P75 1990
Private virtue and public policy: Catholic thought and national life/ edited by James Finn. New Brunswick, U.S.A.: Transaction Publishers, c1990. x, 141 p.
89-030457   261.8/5/0973   0887383068
Sociology, Christian (Catholic) Economics — Religious aspects — Catholic Church. United States — Economic conditions — 1945-

BX1795.H66.S65 1994
Smith, Richard L. 1950-
AIDS, gays, and the American Catholic Church/ Richard L. Smith; foreword by Robert N. Bellah. Cleveland, Ohio: Pilgrim Press, 1994. xiv, 168 p.
94-003396   261.8/35766/08822   0829810110
AIDS (Disease) — Religious aspects — Catholic Church. Homosexuality — Religious aspects — Catholic Church.

BX1795.J87.B65 1998
Bokenkotter, Thomas S.
Church and revolution: Catholics in the struggle of democracy and social justice/ Thomas Bokenkotter. New York: Image Books, c1998. x, 580 p.
97-049429   261.8/088/22   0385487541
Democracy — Religious aspects — Catholic Church — History — 19th century. Democracy — Religious aspects — Catholic Church — History — 20th century. Christianity and justice — Catholic Church — History — 19th century.

BX1795.S48.M66 2000
Moore, Gareth.
The body in context: sex and catholicism/ Gareth Moore. — London: Continuum, 2001, c1992. xi, 242 p.
241   0826453562
Sex — Religious aspects — Catholic Church.

BX1912.9 Catholic Church — Government and organization of the Catholic Church — Priests. Deacons. Spiritual directors

BX1912.9.J46 1996
Jenkins, Philip, 1952-
Pedophiles and priests: anatomy of a contemporary crisis/ Philip Jenkins. New York: Oxford University Press, 1996. ix, 214 p.
95-045625   362.7/6   0195095650
Child sexual abuse by clergy — United States.

BX1920 Catholic Church — Government and organization of the Catholic Church — Laymen. Parish councils

BX1920.C258
Callahan, Daniel J.
The mind of the Catholic layman. New York, Scribner [1963] xiii, 208 p.
63-017937
Laity — Catholic Church.

BX1969 Catholic Church — Forms of worship. Catholic practice

BX1969.C37 1989
Carroll, Michael P., 1944-
Catholic cults and devotions: a psychological inquiry/ Michael P. Carroll. Kingston [Ont.]: McGill-Queen's University Press, c1989. 230 p.
89-187376   248.4/6/08822   0773506934
Catholic Church — Customs and practices — Psychological aspects. Catholic Church — Controversial literature.

BX1999.85 Catholic Church — Liturgy and ritual — Special liturgical books

BX1999.85.A3.D876 1996
Milfull, Inge B.
The hymns of the Anglo-Saxon church: a study and edition of the Durham Hymnal/ Inge B. Milfull. New York: Cambridge University Press, 1996. x, 500 p.
95-051247   264/.2   0521462525
Hymns, Latin (Medieval and modern) — England — Durham. Hymns, Latin (Medieval and modern) — England — Durham — History and criticism. Manuscripts, Latin (Medieval and modern) — England — Durham. Durham (England) — Church history.

BX2157 Catholic Church — Liturgy and ritual — Devotion to the Sacred Heart (or Hearts)

BX2157.J57 2000
Jonas, Raymond Anthony.
France and the cult of the Sacred Heart: an epic tale for modern times/ Raymond Jonas. Berkeley: University of California Press, c2000. xv, 208 p.
99-058920   232   0520221362
Sacred Heart, Devotion to — History of doctrines.France — Church history.

BX2170 Catholic Church — Liturgy and ritual — Other special devotions

BX2170.D5 M375 1994
McLaughlin, Megan,
Consorting with saints: prayer for the dead in early Medieval France / Megan McLaughlin. Ithaca: Cornell University Press, 1994. x, 306 p.
93-034803   264/.020985/094409021 20
0801426480
Dead -- Religious aspects -- Catholic Church -- History of doctrines -- Middle Death -- Religious aspects -- Christianity -- History of doctrines -- Middle Funeral rites and ceremonies -- France -- History. Mourning customs -- France. France -- Church history -- To 987.

BX2179 Catholic Church — Meditations. Devotional readings. Spiritual exercises, etc. — Meditations by the saints

BX2179.F8.I54 1992
Francis, de Sales, Saint, 1567-1622.
Introduction to the devout life/ St. Francis de Sales; edited and abridged by Charles Dollen. New York: Alba House, c1992. xx, 185 p.
92-010914   248.4/82   0818906340
Meditations -- Early works to 1800.

BX2179.L7.E5 1978
Ignatius, of Loyola, Saint, 1491-1556.
The spiritual exercises of St. Ignatius: a literal translation and a contemporary reading/ David L. Fleming. St. Louis: Institute of Jesuit Sources, 1978. xxiv, 244 p.
77-093429   248.3   0912422327
Spiritual exercises.

BX2200 Catholic Church — Sacraments of the Catholic Church — General works

BX2200.M355
Martos, Joseph, 1943-
Doors to the sacred: a historical introduction to sacraments in the Catholic Church/ Joseph Martos. Garden City, N.Y.: Doubleday, 1981. xiii, 531 p.
80-000626   234/.16   038515738X
Sacraments -- Catholic Church -- History of doctrines.

BX2203 Catholic Church — Sacraments of the Catholic Church — General special

BX2203.R65 1998
Ross, Susan A.
Extravagant affections: a feminist sacramental theology/ Susan A. Ross. New York: Continuum, 1998. 240 p.
98-025997   234/.16/082   0826410839
Feminist theology. Sacraments -- Catholic Church.

BX2215.2 Catholic Church — Sacraments of the Catholic Church — Special sacraments

BX2215.2.B33 1979
Balasuriya, Tissa.
The Eucharist and human liberation/ Tissa Balasuriya. Maryknoll, N.Y.: Orbis Books, 1979, c1977. xiii, 171 p.
78-009160   234/.163   0883441187
Lord's Supper -- Catholic Church.

BX2320.5 Catholic Church — Shrines. Holy places — By region or country, A-Z

BX2320.5.E85.N65 1989
Nolan, Mary Lee.
Christian pilgrimage in modern Western Europe/ Mary Lee Nolan & Sidney Nolan. Chapel Hill: University of North Carolina Press, c1989. xix, 422 p.
88-014364   263/.042/4   0807818143
Christian pilgrims and pilgrimages -- Europe. Christian shrines -- Europe. Europe -- Religious life and customs.

BX2320.5.G7
Morrison, Susan Signe, 1959-
Women pilgrims in late medieval England: private piety and public performance/ Susan Signe Morrison. London; Routledge, c2000. xii, 194 p.
99-087891   263/.04242/082   0415221803
Christian pilgrims and pilgrimages -- England -- History. Christian women -- Religious life -- England -- History. Church history -- Middle Ages, 600-1500.

BX2330 Catholic Church — Saints. Hagiology — Canonization. Beatification

BX2330.V3813 1997
Vauchez, André.
Sainthood in the later Middle Ages/ André Vauchez; translated by Jean Birrell. Cambridge; Cambridge University Press, c1997. xxvii, 645 p.
96-006461   235/.2/0902 20   0521445590
Canonization. Christian saints -- Cult -- History -- To 1500. Europe -- Religious life and customs.

BX2333 Catholic Church — Saints. Hagiology — Cultus. Relics

BX2333.B74
Brown, Peter Robert Lamont.
The cult of the saints: its rise and function in Latin Christianity/ Peter Brown. Chicago: University of Chicago Press, c1981. xv, 187 p.
80-011210   270.2   0226076210
Christian saints -- Cult -- History -- Addresses, essays, lectures.

BX2347.72-2347.8 Catholic Church — Practical religion — Church work. Social service

BX2347.72.N5.S23 1997
Sabia, Debra, 1957-
Contradiction and conflict: the popular church in Nicaragua/ Debra Sabia. Tuscaloosa: University of Alabama Press, c1997. x, 239 p.
96-046304   282/.7285/09048   0817308733
Basic Christian communities -- Nicaragua -- History. Socialism and Catholic Church -- Nicaragua -- History -- 20th century. Nicaragua -- Politics and government -- 1979-1990. Nicaragua -- Politics and government -- 1990- Nicaragua -- Church history -- 20th century.

BX2347.8.A52.K683 1994
Kowalewski, Mark R., 1957-
All things to all people: the Catholic Church confronts the AIDS crisis/ Mark R. Kowalewski. Albany: State University of New York Press, c1994. ix, 167 p.
93-037730   261.8/321969792   0791417778
AIDS (Disease) -- Religious aspects -- Catholic Church. AIDS (Disease) -- Patients -- Religious life. California -- Church history -- 20th century. Los Angeles (Calif.) -- Church history -- 20th century.

BX2347.8.P66.B76 1997
Brown, Dorothy M. 1932-
The poor belong to us: Catholic charities and American welfare/ Dorothy M. Brown, Elizabeth McKeown. Cambridge, Mass.: Harvard University Press, 1997. viii, 284 p.
97-025736   361.7/5/08822   0674689739
Church work with the poor -- Catholic Church -- History. Church work with the poor -- United States -- History. Public welfare -- United States -- History. United States -- Church history -- 19th century. United States -- Church history -- 20th century. United States -- Social conditions.

BX2347.8.W6.R43 1992
Redmont, Jane.
Generous lives: American Catholic women today/ Jane Redmont. New York: W. Morrow and Co., c1992. 381 p.
92-007950   282/.092/273   0688067077
Women in the Catholic Church -- United States. Catholic women -- United States -- Biography.

BX2350 Catholic Church — Christian life — General works

BX2350.M535
Merton, Thomas, 1915-1968.
No man is an island.   New York, Harcourt, Brace [1955] 264 p.
55-007420   248
Spiritual life -- Catholic Church.

BX2432 Catholic Church — Monasticism. Religious orders — General works

BX2432.N513
Nigg, Walter, 1903-
Warriors of God; the great religious orders and their founders. Edited and translated from the German by Mary Ilford. New York, Knopf, 1959. 353 p.
59-005429   271
Monasticism and religious orders -- History. Monastic and religious life -- Biography.

BX2465-2613 Catholic Church — Monasticism. Religious orders — History

BX2465.B87 1993
Burton-Christie, Douglas.
The Word in the desert: scripture and the quest for holiness in early Christian monasticism/ Douglas Burton-Christie. New York: Oxford University Press, 1993. ix, 336 p.
91-004150   271/.00932   0195066146
Monasticism and religious orders -- Egypt -- History. Monasticism and religious orders -- History -- Early church, ca. 30-600. Egypt -- Church history.

BX2470.L413 1982
Leclercq, Jean, 1911-
The love of learning and the desire for God: a study of monastic culture/ Jean Leclercq; translated by Catharine Misrahi. New York: Fordham University Press, 1982. viii, 282 p.
82-242178   255   0823204073
Monasticism and religious orders -- History -- Middle Ages, 600-1500. Learning and scholarship -- History -- Medieval, 500-1500. Christian literature, Early -- History and criticism.

BX2525.T733
Aprile, Dianne.
Making a heart for God: a week inside a Catholic monastery/ Dianne Aprile; foreword by Patrick Hart. Woodstock, Vt.: SkyLight Paths Pub., c2000. xiv, 197 p.
00-011792   255/.125   1893361144
Monastic and religious life.

BX2590.C66 1996
Constable, Giles.
The reformation of the twelfth century/ Giles Constable. Cambridge; Cambridge University Press, 1996. xx, 411 p.
96-013516   282/.4/09021   0521305144
Monasticism and religious orders -- Europe -- History -- Middle Ages, 600-1500. Church history -- 12th century. Europe -- Church history -- 600-1500.

BX2592.K57 1963
Knowles, David,
The monastic order in England; a history of its development from the times of St. Dunstan to the Fourth Lateran Council, 940-1216. 2d ed. Cambridge [Eng.] University Press, 1963. xxi, 780 p.
64-000029   271.00942
Monasticism and religious orders -- England.

BX2592.L64 1996
Logan, F. Donald.
Runaway religious in medieval England, c. 1240-1540/ F. Donald Logan. Cambridge; Cambridge University Press, 1996. xix, 301 p.
95-031970   271/.00942/0902   0521475023
Monasticism and religious orders -- England. Monasticism and religious orders -- History -- Middle Ages, 600-1500. England -- Church history -- 1066-1485.

BX2613.P68 1997
Potts, Cassandra, 1958-
Monastic revival and regional identity in early Normandy/ Cassandra Potts. Woodbridge, Suffolk, UK; Boydell Press, 1997. xi, 170 p.
97-012256   271/.00944/20902   0851157025
Monasticism and religious orders -- France -- Normandy -- History -- Middle Ages, 600-1500.Normandy (France) -- Church history.

BX2820 Catholic Church — Monasticism. Religious orders — Special classes of religious orders

BX2820.L38 1994
Lawrence, C. H. 1921-
The friars: the impact of the early mendicant movement on Western society/ C.H. Lawrence. London; Longman, 1994. x, 245 p.
93-025750   271/.0604/0902   0582056330
Friars -- Europe -- History.Europe -- Church history -- 600-1500.

BX3653-3742 Catholic Church — Monasticism. Religious orders — Individual orders of men

BX3653.U6 H3 1998
Henderson, Alice Corbin,
Brothers of light: the Penitentes of the Southwest/ by Alice Corbin Henderson; illustrations by William Penhallow Henderson. Las Cruces, N.M.: Yucca Tree Press, 1998. 104 p.
98-060376   267/.242789 21   1881325237
Hermanos Penitentes.

BX3703.G813
Guibert, J. de.
The Jesuits: their spiritual doctrine and practice; a historical study/ William J. Young, translator. George E. Ganss, editor. Chicago: Institute of Jesuit Sources, 1964. xxv, 692 p.
64-021430   271.5
Ignatius, -- of Loyola, Saint, -- 1491-1556. Ignatius, -- of Loyola, Saint, -- 1491-1556 -- Exercitia spiritualia.

BX3706.2.M57 1981
Mitchell, David J., 1924-
The Jesuits, a history/ by David Mitchell. New York: F. Watts, 1981, c1980. 320 p.
80-025316   271/.53   0531099474
Jesuits -- History.

BX3742.A1.A53 1996
Alden, Dauril.
The making of an enterprise: the Society of Jesus in Portugal, its empire, and beyond, 1540-1750/ Dauril Alden. Stanford, Calif.: Stanford University Press, 1996. xxxi, 707 p.
94-004820   271/.530469   0804722714
Portugal -- Church history. Portugal -- Colonies -- Religion.

BX4210-4220 Catholic Church — Monasticism. Religious orders — Religious orders of women. Convents, etc.

BX4210.W65 1995
Women, the book, and the godly: selected proceedings of the St. Hilda's conference, 1993/ edited by Lesley Smith and Jane H.M. Taylor. Woodbridge, Suffolk, UK; D.S. Brewer, [1995-] v. <1-2 >
94-044978   271.9/0094 20   0859914798
Monastic and religious life of women -- History -- Middle Ages, 600-1500 Women -- Religious life -- History -- Congresses. Women -- Europe -- Education -- History -- Congresses.

BX4220.E85.V46 1997
Venarde, Bruce L., 1962-
Women's monasticism and medieval society: nunneries in France and England, 890-1215/ Bruce L. Venarde. Ithaca: Cornell University Press, 1997. xix, 243 p.
96-030260   271.9/00420902   0801432030
Convents -- Europe -- History. Monasticism and religious orders for women -- History -- Middle Ages, 600-1500.

BX4655.2-4682 Catholic Church — Biography and portraits — Collective

BX4655.2.S23 1983
Saints and their cults: studies in religious sociology, folklore, and history/ edited with introduction and annotated bibliography by Stephen Wilson. Cambridge [Cambridgeshire]; Cambridge University Press, xii, 435 p.
82-025296   270 19   0521249783
Christian saints -- Cult. Muslim saints -- Cult.

BX4656.5.S26 1996
Sandoval, Annette.
The directory of saints: a concise guide to patron saints/ Annette Sandoval. New York: Dutton, 1996. 308 p.
95-044252   282/.092/2   0525941541
Christian patron saints -- Biography -- Dictionaries. Christian saints -- Biography -- Dictionaries.

BX4659.G7.W56 1997
Winstead, Karen A. 1960-
Virgin martyrs: legends of sainthood in late medieval England/ Karen A. Winstead. Ithaca, N.Y.: Cornell University Press, 1997. x, 201 p.
97-009318   272/.082   0801433339
Christian women saints -- Biography -- History and criticism. Christian women martyrs -- Biography -- History and criticism. Virginity -- Religious aspects -- Christianity -- History of doctrines -- Middle Ages, 600-1500. England -- Church history -- 1066-1485. England -- Religious life and customs.

BX4662.C86 1980
Cunningham, Lawrence.
The meaning of saints/ Lawrence S. Cunningham. San Francisco, CA: Harper & Row, c1980. 186 p.
80-007754   235/.2   0060616490
Christian saints.

BX4668.A1.A44 1997
Allitt, Patrick.
Catholic converts: British and American intellectuals turn to Rome/ Patrick Allitt. Ithaca: Cornell University Press, 1997. xii, 343 p.
96-029989   248.2/42/0941   080142996X
Catholic converts -- United States -- History. Intellectuals -- Religious life -- United States -- History. Catholic converts -- Great Britain -- History.

BX4668.B67
Bouyer, Louis, 1913-
The spirit and forms of Protestantism/ by Louis Bouyer; translated by A.V. Littledale. Westminster, Md.: Newman Press, 1956. xi, 234 p.
56-010001   284
Protestantism. Catholic converts.

BX4668.D3.A33 1952
Day, Dorothy, 1897-1980.
The long loneliness: the autobiography of Dorothy Day. New York: Curtis Books, [1972], c1952 320 p.
94-133451
Day, Dorothy, -- 1897-1980. Catholic converts -- United States -- Biography.

BX4682.K58 1998
Kitchen, John, 1963-
Saints' lives and the rhetoric of gender: male and female in Merovingian hagiography/ John Kitchen. New York: Oxford University Press, 1998. xv, 255 p.
97-030893   270/.092/244   0195117220
Christian saints -- France -- History -- Study and teaching. Christian hagiography -- History. Sex role -- History of doctrines -- Middle Ages, 600-1500. France -- Church history -- to 987. France -- History -- to 987.

BX4700-4705 Catholic Church — Biography and portraits — Individual

BX4700.A58.S59 1990
Southern R. W. 1912-
Saint Anselm: a portrait in a landscape/ R.W. Southern. Cambridge; Cambridge University Press, 1990. xxix, 493 p.
89-007237   282/.092   0521362628
Anselm, -- Saint, Archbishop of Canterbury, -- 1033-1109. Christian saints -- England -- Biography.

BX4700.B3.C5 1971
Chapman, John, 1865-1933.
Saint Benedict and the sixth century. Westport, Conn., Greenwood Press [1971] vi, 239 p.
79-109719   271/.1/024   0837142091
Benedict, -- Saint, Abbot of Monte Cassino. Benedict, -- Saint, Abbot of Monte Cassino. -- Regula. Monasticism and religious orders -- History -- Middle Ages, 600-1500.

BX4700.B5.A413
Bernard, of Clairvaux, Saint, 1090 or 1-115
Letters. Newly translated by Bruno Scott James. Chicago, H. Regnery, 1953. xx, 530 p.
54-000671

BX4700.B7.A43 1940
Boniface, Saint, Archbishop of Mainz, 675-754.
The letters of Saint Boniface, translated with an introduction by Ephraim Emerton. New York, Columbia university press, 1940. 204 p.
40-033656
Boniface, -- Saint, Archbishop of Mainz, -- 675-754 -- Correspondence.

BX4700.C8.C6
Colgrave, Bertram.
Two lives of Saint Cuthbert; a life by an anonymous monk of Lindisfarne and Bede's prose life; texts, translation, and notes by Bertram Colgrave. Cambridge [Eng.] The University press, 1940. xiii, 375 p.
40-035359   922.142
Cuthbert, -- Saint, Bishop of Lindisfarne, -- ca. 635-687.

BX4700.F34.H85 1989
Humanism, reform, and the Reformation: the career of Bishop John Fisher/ edited by Brendan Bradshaw and Eamon Duffy. Cambridge; Cambridge University Press, 1989. 260 p.
88-004351   282/.092/4   0521340349
Fisher, John, -- Saint, -- 1469-1535 -- Congresses.

BX4700.F37
Green, Hannah.
Little saint/ Hannah Green. New York: Random House, c2000. 276 p.
99-023023   270.1/092   0394565959
Foy, -- Saint, -- ca. 290-303. Christian child saints -- France -- Conques -- Biography. Conques (Aveyron, France) -- Religious life and customs. France -- Religious life and customs.

BX4700.F6 H27 1977
Habig, Marion Alphonse,
St. Francis of Assisi: writings and early biographies: English omnibus of the sources for the life of St. Francis/ edited by Marion A. Habig; translations by Raphael Brown ... [et al.]. 3d rev. ed., including A new Fioretti/ by John R. H. Moorman. Chicago: Franciscan Herald Press, [1977] c1973. xx, 1904 p.
76-058903   271/.3/024 B   0819906581
Francis, of Assisi, Saint, 1182-1226. Christian saints -- Italy -- Assisi -- Biography. Assisi (Italy) -- Biography.

BX4700.F6.H595 2001
House, Adrian.
Francis of Assisi/ Adrian House; foreword by Karen Armstrong. New York: HiddenSpring, c2001. xv, 336 p.
00-044979   271/.302   1587680092
Francis, -- of Assisi, Saint, -- 1182-1226.Christian saints -- Italy -- Assisi -- Biography.Assisi (Italy) -- Biography.

BX4700.H5 A4 1994
Hildegard,
The letters of Hildegard of Bingen/ translated by Joseph L. Baird, Radd K. Ehrman. New York: Oxford University Press, 1994-<1998 > v. <1-2 >
93-033715   282/.092 B 20   0195089375
Hildegard, Saint, 1098-1179 -- Correspondence. Christian saints -- Germany -- Correspondence.

BX4700.H5.N48 1987
Newman, Barbara, 1953-
Sister of wisdom: St. Hildegard's theology of the feminine/ Barbara Newman. Berkeley: University of California Press, c1987. xx, 289 p.
86-016094   230/.2/0924   0520058100
Hildegard, -- Saint, -- 1098-1179.Women -- Religious aspects -- Christianity -- History of doctrines -- Middle Ages, 600-1500.

BX4700.J7.D56 1992
Dombrowski, Daniel A.
St. John of the Cross: an appreciation/ Daniel A. Dombrowski. Albany: State University of New York Press, c1992. viii, 223 p.
90-028577   271.7302   0791408876
John of the Cross, -- Saint, -- 1542-1591.Mysticism -- Catholic Church -- History -- 16th century. Mysticism -- Spain -- History -- 16th century.

BX4700.L7.M54 1992
Meissner, W. W. 1931-
Ignatius of Loyola: the psychology of a saint/ W.W. Meissner. New Haven: Yale University Press, c1992. xxix, 480 p.
92-001270   271/.5302   0300051565
Ignatius, -- of Loyola, Saint, -- 1491-1556 -- Psychology.Psychoanalysis and religion.

BX4700.T4.G76 1993
Gross, Francis L.
The making of a mystic: seasons in the life of Teresa of Avila/ Francis L. Gross, Jr. with Toni Perior Gross. Albany, NY: State University of New York Press, c1993. xx, 285 p.
92-012040   282/.092   0791414116
Teresa, -- of Avila, Saint, -- 1515-1582.Christian saints -- Spain -- Avila -- Biography.Avila (Spain) -- Biography.

BX4700.T4.M38 1999
Medwick, Cathleen, 1948-
Teresa of Avila: the progress of a soul/ Cathleen Medwick. New York: Knopf, 1999. xvii, 282 p.
99-018921   282/.092   0394547942
Teresa, -- of Avila, Saint, -- 1515-1582.Christian saints -- Spain -- Avila -- Biography.

BX4700.T6.O44 1997
O'Meara, Thomas F., 1935-
Thomas Aquinas theologian/ Thomas Franklin O'Meara. Notre Dame, Ind.: University of Notre Dame Press, c1997. xxi, 302 p.
96-026438   230/.2/092   0268018987
Thomas, -- Aquinas, Saint, -- 1225?-1274.

BX4705.A2.C57 1997
Clanchy, M. T.
Abelard: a medieval life/ M.T. Clanchy. Oxford, UK; Blackwell Publishers, 1997. xiii, 416 p.
97-033340   189/.4   0631205020
Abelard, Peter, -- 1079-1142.Theology -- History -- Middle Ages, 600-1500. Theologians -- France -- Biography.

BX4705.B3845.A294 1971
Berrigan, Daniel.
The geography of faith; conversations between Daniel Berrigan, when underground, and Robert Coles. Boston, Beacon Press [1971] 179 p.
70-159844   201.1   080700538X
Berrigan, Daniel.

BX4705.B3846.A3 1970
Berrigan, Philip.
Prison journals of a priest revolutionary. Compiled and edited by Vincent McGee. Introd. by Daniel Berrigan. New York, Holt, Rinehart and Winston [1970] xxii, 198 p.
77-102136   271/.79   0030845130
Berrigan, Philip.

BX4705.B545.C69 1988
Cox, Harvey Gallagher.
The silencing of Leonardo Boff: the Vatican and the future of world Christianity/ Harvey Cox. Oak Park, IL: Meyer-Stone Books, c1988. x, 208 p.
87-043277   262/.8   0940989352
Boff, Leonardo. Ratzinger, Joseph. Freedom of speech in the church.

BX4705.D283.M477 1994
Merriman, Brigid O'Shea, 1942-
Searching for Christ: the spirituality of Dorothy Day / Brigid O'Shea Merriman. Notre Dame: University of Notre Dame, c1994. xi, 333 p.
93-023827   248/.092   0268017506
Day, Dorothy, -- 1897-1980.Spirituality -- Catholic Church -- History of doctrines -- 20th century.

BX4705.E46
Burke, Kevin F.
The ground beneath the Cross: the theology of Ignacio Ellacuria/ Kevin F. Burke. Washington, D.C.: Georgetown University Press, c2000. xviii, 244 p.
99-038855   230/.2/092   0878407618
Ellacuria, Ignacio.

BX4705.G6226
Trapnell, Judson B., 1954-
Bede Griffiths: a life in dialogue/ Judson B. Trapnell; foreword by Kenneth Cracknell. Albany, NY: State University of New York Press, c2001. xvii, 279 p.
00-038767   271/.102   0791448711
Griffiths, Bede, -- 1906-

BX4705.H7645
Harline, Craig E.
A bishop's tale: Mathias Hovius among his flock in seventeenth-century Flanders/ Craig Harline and Eddy Put. New Haven: Yale University Press, c2000. x, 387 p.
00-036810   282/.092   0300083424
Hovius, Matthias, -- 1542-1620Counter-Reformation -- Belgium.Flanders (Belgium) -- Church history -- 17th century. Flanders (Belgium) -- Religious life and customs. Flanders (Belgium) -- Church history -- 16th century.

BX4705.K76.H3713 1998
Haring, Hermann, 1937-
Hans Kung: breaking through/ Hermann Haring. New York: Continuum, c1998. xv, 377 p.
98-027568   230/.2/092   0826411347
Kung, Hans, -- 1928-Theology.

BX4705.L16.B47 1987
Bergin, Joseph, 1948-
Cardinal de La Rochefoucauld: leadership and reform in the French Church/ Joseph Bergin. New Haven: Yale University Press, 1987. viii, 302 p.
87-014255   282/.092/4   0300041047
La Rochefoucauld, Francois de, -- 1558-1645.Cardinals -- France -- Biography. Counter-Reformation -- France. France -- Church history -- 16th century. France -- Church history -- 17th century.

BX4705.M542.C86 1999
Cunningham, Lawrence.
Thomas Merton and the monastic vision/ Lawrence S. Cunningham. Grand Rapids, Mich.: W.B. Eerdmans Pub., c1999. xii, 228 p.
99-034656   271/.12502   0802802222
Merton, Thomas, -- 1915-1968.Monks -- United States -- Biography. Monastic and religious life.

BX4705.M542.I53 1998
Inchausti, Robert, 1952-
Thomas Merton's American prophecy/ Robert Inchausti. Albany: State University of New York Press, c1998. x, 210 p.
97-019155   271/.12502   0791436357
Merton, Thomas, -- 1915-1968.Monks -- United States -- Biography.

BX4705.N5.A15
Newman, John Henry, 1801-1890.
Autobiographical writings; edited with introductions by Henry Tristram. New York, Sheed and Ward [1957] 338 p.
57-006045
Newman, John Henry, -- 1801-1890.

BX4705.N5.A3 1968
Newman, John Henry, 1801-1890.
Apologia pro vita sua. An authoritative text, basic texts of the Newman-Kingsley controversy, origin and reception of the Apologia [and] essays in criticism. Edited by David J. DeLaura. New York, Norton, [1968] xviii, 506 p.
67-016618   282/.092/4
Newman, John Henry, -- 1801-1890.Catholics -- England -- Biography.

BX4705.R287.L46 1995
Lennan, Richard.
The ecclesiology of Karl Rahner/ Richard Lennan. Oxford: Clarendon Press; 1995. vi, 289 p.
94-036057   262/.02/092   0198263589
Rahner, Karl, -- 1904-Church -- History of doctrines -- 20th century.

BX4705.R446.A34
Reynolds, Bede, 1892-
A rebel from riches: the autobiography of an unpremeditated monk/ Bede Reynolds (ne Kenyon L. Reynolds). Canfield, Ohio: Alba Books, [1975] 150 p.
74-027608   271/.1/024
Reynolds, Bede, -- 1892-Monks -- United States -- Biography.

BX4705.S814.U56 1994
The unnecessary problem of Edith Stein/ edited by Harry James Cargas. Lanham, Md.: University Press of America, c1994. 105 p.
94-027846   271/.97102   081918781X
Stein, Edith, -- 1891-1942.Judaism -- Relations -- Catholic Church.

BX4811 Protestantism — General works — 1951-2000

BX4811.B74
Brown, Robert McAfee, 1920-
The spirit of Protestantism/ Robert McAfee Brown. New York: Oxford University Press, c1965. xxx, 270 p.
61-008367   284
Protestantism.

BX4817 Protestantism — General special

BX4817.T53
Tillich, Paul, 1886-1965.
The Protestant era; tr., and with a concluding essay, by James Luther Adams. Chicago, Univ. of Chicago Press [1948] xxxi, 323 p.
48-006650   284
Protestantism.   Theology,   Doctrinal. Christianity -- Philosophy.

BX4827 Protestantism — Biography — Individual, A-Z

BX4827.B3.B86313
Busch, Eberhard, 1937-
Karl Barth: his life from letters and autobiographical texts/ Eberhard Busch; translated by John Bowden. Philadelphia: Fortress Press, c1976. xvii, 569 p.
76-015881   230/.044/092   0800604857
Barth, Karl, -- 1886-1968.Theologians -- Switzerland -- Basel -- Biography.Basel (Switzerland) -- Biography.

BX4827.B3.C26 2000
The Cambridge companion to Karl Barth/ [edited by] John Webster. New York: Cambridge University Press, 2000. xiii, 312 p.
99-056882   230/.044/092   0521584760
Barth, Karl, -- 1886-1968.

BX4827.B3.J64 1997
Johnson, William Stacy.
The mystery of God: Karl Barth and the postmodern foundations of theology/ William Stacy Johnson. Louisville, Ky.: Westminster John Knox Press, c1997. x, 217 p.
96-040011   230/.044/092   0664220940
Barth, Karl, -- 1886-1968.

BX4827.B57.C36 1999
The Cambridge companion to Dietrich Bonhoeffer/ edited by John W. de Gruchy. Cambridge; Cambridge University Press, 1999. xxvi, 281 p.
98-035990   230/.044/092   052158258X
Bonhoeffer, Dietrich, -- 1906-1945.

BX4827.C65.B87 1994
Burrow, Rufus, 1951-
James H. Cone and Black liberation theology/ by Rufus Burrow, Jr. Jefferson: McFarland & Co., c1994. xxi, 256 p.
93-041759   230/.092   0899509002
Cone, James H.Black theology -- History of doctrines. Liberation theology -- History of doctrines.

BX4827.K5.T5 1969
Thomte, Reidar.
Kierkegaard's philosophy of religion. New York, Greenwood Press [1969, c1948] viii, 228 p.
69-014116   201
Kierkegaard, Soren, -- 1813-1855.

BX4827.M6
Moltmann, Jurgen.
Experiences in theology: ways and forms of Christian theology/ Jurgen Moltmann. Minneapolis, MN: Fortress Press, 2000. xxiv, 392 p.
00-042697   230/.044/092 21   0800632672
Moltmann, Jurgen.

BX4827.N5.B76 1992
Brown, Charles C. 1938-
Niebuhr and his age: Reinhold Niebuhr's prophetic role in the twentieth century/ Charles C. Brown. Philadelphia: Trinity Press International, 1992. xiii, 317 p.
92-025356   230/.092   1563380420
Niebuhr, Reinhold, -- 1892-1971.Theologians -- United States -- Biography. Theology -- History -- 20th century.

BX4827.N5.G55 2001
Gilkey, Langdon Brown, 1919-
On Niebuhr: a theological study/ Langdon Gilkey. Chicago: University of Chicago Press, c2001. xiii, 261 p.
00-060728   230/.092   0226293416
Niebuhr, Reinhold, -- 1892-1971.Theology -- History -- 20th century.

BX4827.N5.L68 1995
Lovin, Robin W.
Reinhold Niebuhr and Christian realism/ Robin W. Lovin. Cambridge [England]; Cambridge University Press, 1995. x, 255 p.
94-006809   261.8/092   0521443636
Niebuhr, Reinhold, -- 1892-1971.Sociology, Christian -- History -- 20th century. Christianity and politics -- History -- 20th century. Christian ethics -- History -- 20th century.

BX4832.5 Protestantism — By region or country — America

BX4832.5.M37 1990
Martin, David, 1929-
Tongues of fire: the explosion of Protestantism in Latin America/ David Martin; with a foreword by Peter Berger. Oxford, UK; B. Blackwell, 1990. xiii, 352 p.
89-035839   306.6/804/098   063117186X
Protestant churches -- Latin America. Evangelicalism -- Latin America. Pentecostal churches -- Latin America. Latin America -- Church history.

BX4844 Protestantism — By region or country — Europe

BX4844.H66 1995
Hope, Nicholas.
German and Scandinavian Protestantism, 1700-1918/ Nicholas Hope. Oxford: Clarendon Press; 1995. xxvii, 685 p.
95-012091   280/.4/094309033   0198269234
Protestant churches -- Germany -- History. Protestant churches -- Scandinavia -- History. Lutheran Church -- Germany -- History. Germany -- Church history -- 18th century. Scandinavia -- Church history -- 18th century. Germany -- Church history -- 19th century.

BX4881.2-4917 Protestantism — Individual sects — Pre-Reformation

BX4881.2.A8313 1999
Audisio, Gabriel.
The Waldensian dissent: persecution and survival, c. 1170-c. 1570/ Gabriel Audisio; translated by Claire Davison. Cambridge, U.K.; Cambridge University Press, 1999. xiv, 234 p.
98-049526   273/.6   0521550297
Waldenses.

BX4891.2.B37 2000
Barber, Malcolm.
The Cathars in Languedoc/ Malcolm Barber. Essex; Pearson Education, 2000.
00-022125   273/.6   0582256623
Albigenses -- France -- Languedoc -- History.Languedoc (France) -- Church history.

BX4891.2.W457 2001
Weis, Ren., 1953-
The yellow cross: the story of the last Cathars, 1290-1329/ Renelp Weis. 1st American ed. New York Knopf, 2001. 399 p.
2001-088078
Albigenses -- History.

BX4901.2.A84 1984
Aston, Margaret.
Lollards and reformers: images and literacy in late medieval religion / Margaret Aston. London: Hambledon Press, 1984. xi, 355 p.
83-123679   284/.3 19   0907628184
Lollards. Literacy -- England. Reformation -- England. Church history -- Middle Ages, 600-1500. England -- Church history -- 1066-1485.

BX4901.2.M37 1995
McSheffrey, Shannon.
Gender and heresy: women and men in Lollard communities, 1420-1530/ Shannon McSheffrey. Philadelphia: University of Pennsylvania Press, c1995. xi, 253 p.
95-037249   284/.3   0812233107
Lollards. Heresies, Christian -- England -- History -- Middle Ages, 600-1500. Sex role -- Religious aspects -- Christianity -- Case studies. England -- Church history -- 1066-1485.

BX4905.W6 1966
Workman, Herbert B. b. 1862.
John Wyclif; a study of the English medieval church, by Herbert B. Workman. Hamden, Conn., Archon Books, 1966. 2 v. in 1.
66-014608   270.5
Wycliffe, John, -- d. 1384.Church history -- Middle Ages.

BX4917.S7 1966
Spinka, Matthew, 1890-1972.
John Hus and the Czech reform.   Hamden, Conn., Archon Books, 1966 [c1941] vii, 81 p.
66-018645   284.3
Hus, Jan, -- 1369?-1415.

BX4931.2-4946 Protestantism — Individual sects — Post-Reformation

BX4931.2.C57
Clasen, Claus Peter.
Anabaptism; a social history, 1525-1618: Switzerland, Austria, Moravia, South and Central Germany.   Ithaca, Cornell University Press [1972] xviii, 523 p.
78-037751   284/.3   080140696X
Anabaptists -- History.

BX4933.G3
Haude, Sigrun, 1959-
In the shadow of "savage wolves": Anabaptist Munster and the German Reformation during the 1530s/ Sigrun Haude. Boston: Humanities Press, c2000. xiii, 192 p.
99-087228   284/.3/09435609031   0391041002
Anabaptists -- Germany -- Westphalia -- Public opinion -- History -- 16th century. Public opinion -- Germany -- Westphalia -- History -- 16th century. Anabaptists -- Germany -- Munster in Westfalen -- History -- 16th century. Westphalia (Germany) -- Church history -- 16th century. Munster in Westfalen (Germany) -- Church history -- 16th century.

BX4946.M8.S35 1989
Scott, Tom, 1947-
Thomas Muntzer: theology and revolution in the German Reformation/ Tom Scott. New York: St. Martin's Press, 1989. xix, 203 p.
88-028183   284/.3/0924   031202679X
Munzer, Thomas, -- 1490 (ca.)-1525.

BX5013 Church of England — Societies. Institutions

BX5013.E3.W5
White, James F.
The Cambridge movement: the ecclesiologists and the Gothic revival.   Cambridge [Eng.] University Press, 1962. xii, 272 p.
62-052258   283
Church architecture -- Great Britain. Anglican church buildings.

BX5055.2 Church of England — History — General works

BX5055.2.K55 1995
Knight, Frances.
The nineteenth-century church and English society/ Frances Knight. Cambridge [England]; Cambridge University Press, 1995. xiii, 230 p.
95-007838   283/.42/09034   0521453356
Anglican Communion -- England -- History -- 19th century. England -- Church history -- 19th century. Church and state -- England.

BX5056 Church of England — History — General special

BX5056.M43 1988
Medhurst, Kenneth, 1938-
Church and politics in a secular age/ Kenneth Medhurst and George Moyser. Oxford: Clarendon Press; 1988. xvi, 392 p.
88-001821   283/.42   0198264542
Anglican Communion -- England -- History. Church and state -- England -- History. Christianity and politics -- Church of England -- History. Great Britain -- Politics and government. England -- Church history.

BX5071 Church of England — History — By period

BX5071.L34 1988
Lake, Peter.
Anglicans and Puritans?: Presbyterianism and English conformist   thought from Whitgift to Hooker/ Peter Lake. London; Unwin Hyman, 1988. 262 p.
87-009252   262 19   0049422073
Anglican Communion -- England -- Government -- History of doctrines -- 16th Presbyterianism -- History of doctrines -- 16th century. Puritans -- England -- History -- 16th century. England -- Church history -- 16th century.

BX5121 Church of England — Special parties and movements — High Church. Anglo-Catholicism

BX5121.R44 1996
Reed, John Shelton.
Glorious battle: the cultural politics of Victorian Anglo-Catholicism/   John   Shelton   Reed. Nashville: Vanderbilt University Press, c1996. xxix, 357 p.
95-052009   283/.42/09034   0826512747
Anglo-Catholicism -- England -- History -- 19th century.England -- Church history -- 19th century.

BX5173 Church of England — Government. organization. Discipline — The cathedral

BX5173.L44 1996
Lehmberg, Stanford E.
Cathedrals under siege: cathedrals in English society, 1600-1700/ Stanford E. Lehmberg. University Park, Pa.: Pennsylvania State University Press, c1996. xxx, 270 p.
95-007502   262/.3/094209032   0271014946
Cathedrals -- England -- History -- 17th century. Anglican Communion -- England -- History -- 17th century.   England -- Church history -- 17th century.

BX5182.3 Church of England — Government. organization. Discipline — Women

BX5182.3.H43 1988
Heeney, Brian, 1933-1983.
The women's movement in the Church of England, 1850-1930/ Brian Heeney. Oxford [England]: Clarendon Press; 1988. xi, 144 p.
87-029804   283/.42/088042   0198226713
Women in the Anglican Communion -- England -- History -- 19th century. Women in the Anglican Communion -- England -- History - - 20th century. Feminism -- Religious aspects -- Church of England -- History of doctrines -- 19th century. England -- Church history -- 19th century. England -- Church history -- 20th century.

BX5195 Church of England — Cathedrals, churches, etc., in England and Wales — Individual churches, etc. By place, A-Z, or by name if nonurban

BX5195.N5575.N67 1996
Norwich Cathedral: church, city, and diocese, 1096-1996/ edited by Ian Atherton ... [et al.]. London; Hambledon Press, 1996. xvi, 784 p.
95-049426   293/.42615   1852851341
Norwich (England) -- Church history.

BX5199 Church of England — Biography — Individual, A-Z

BX5199.K3.G75 1987
Griffin, John R.
John Keble, saint of Anglicanism/ John R. Griffin. Macon, Ga.: Mercer University Press, c1987. viii, 122 p.
86-031210   283/.3   086554249X
Keble, John, -- 1792-1866.Anglican Communion -- England -- Clergy -- Biography. Oxford movement -- England -- History. England -- Church history -- 19th century.

BX5199.L53.C8
Cunningham, Richard B.
C. S. Lewis, defender of the faith, by Richard B. Cunningham. Philadelphia, Westminster Press [1967] 223 p.
67-019299   239/.00924
Lewis, C. S. -- (Clive Staples), -- 1898-1963 -- Religion.Christian literature, English -- History and criticism. Apologetics.

BX5199.L53.P55 1998
The pilgrim's guide: C.S. Lewis and the art of witness/ edited by David Mills. Grand Rapids, Mich.: William B. Eerdmans Pub., c1998. xviii, 297 p.
98-022482   230/.092   0802837778
Lewis, C. S. -- (Clive Staples), -- 1898-1963 -- Religion.Christian literature, English -- History and criticism.

BX5199.M3.Y68 1992
Young, David.
F. D. Maurice and Unitarianism/ David Young. Oxford: Clarendoan Press; 1992. xi, 305 p.
92-020341   283/.092   0198263392
Maurice, Frederick Denison, -- 1805-1872 -- Views on Unitarianism.Unitarianism -- England -- Doctrines -- History -- 19th century. Anglican Communion -- Doctrines -- History -- 19th century.

BX5203.2 Church of England — Dissent and nonconformity — General works. Histories

BX5203.2.R65 1960
Routley, Erik.
English religious dissent.   Cambridge [Eng.] University Press, 1960. 213 p.
60-051970   274.2
Dissenters -- England.

BX5203.2.W67 1994
The World of rural dissenters: 1520-1725/ edited by Margaret Spufford. Cambridge; Cambridge University Press, 1995. xx, 459 p.
93-022979   280.4/0942/091734   20
0521410614
Dissenters, Religious -- England -- History -- 16th century. Dissenters, Religious -- England -- History -- 17th century. Dissenters, Religious -- England -- History -- 18th century. England -- Church history -- 16th century. England -- Church history -- 17th century. England -- Church history -- 18th century. England -- Rural conditions.

BX5880 Episcopal Church. Protestant Episcopal Church in the United States of America — History — General works

BX5880.A33 1969
Addison, James Thayer, 1887-
The Episcopal Church in the United States, 1789-1931. [Hamden, Conn.] Archon Books, 1969 [c1951] xii, 400 p.
69-015786   283/.73   0208007415
Episcopal Church -- History.

BX5881 Episcopal Church. Protestant Episcopal Church in the United States of America — History — By period

BX5881.W65 1984
Woolverton, John Frederick, 1926-
Colonial Anglicanism in North America/ by John Frederick Woolverton. Detroit: Wayne State University Press, 1984. 331 p.
83-027400   283/.73   0814317553
United States -- Church history -- To 1775.

BX5925 Episcopal Church. Protestant Episcopal Church in the United States of America — Movements and parties

BX5925.B84 1995
Butler, Diana Hochstedt, 1959-
Standing against the whirlwind: evangelical Episcopalians in nineteenth-century America/ Diana Hochstedt Butler. New York: Oxford University Press, 1995. xiii, 270 p.
93-034323   283/.73   0195085426
Evangelicalism -- Episcopal Church -- History -- 19th century. Interdenominational cooperation -- United States -- History -- 19th century.

BX5979 Episcopal Church. Protestant Episcopal Church in the United States of America — Afro-Americans and the Episcopal Church

BX5979.S53 2000
Shattuck, Gardiner H.
Episcopalians and race: Civil War to civil rights/ Gardiner H. Shattuck, Jr. Lexington, Ky.: University Press of Kentucky, 2000. xiii, 298 p.
99-041357   261.8/348/00973   0813121493
Race relations -- Religious aspects -- Episcopal Church -- History -- 20th century. Race relations -- Religious aspects -- Episcopal Church -- History -- 19th century. United States -- Race relations -- History -- 19th century. United States -- Race relations -- History -- 19th century.

BX5980 Episcopal Church. Protestant Episcopal Church in the United States of America — Individual churches — United States

BX5980.C6768 W55 1999
Willoughby, Lynn,
A power for good: the history of Trinity Parish, Columbus, Georgia/ Lynn Willoughby; with photographs by Mike Culpepper. Columbus, Ga.: Trinity Episcopal Church with Smyth & Helwys, 1999.
99-045016   283/.758473 21   1573123099
Trinity Episcopal Church (Columbus, Ga.) -- History.

BX6065 Reformed Episcopal Church — History — General works

BX6065.G84 1994
Guelzo, Allen C.
For the union of Evangelical Christendom: the irony of the Reformed Episcopalians/ Allen C. Guelzo. University Park, Pa.: Pennsylvania State University Press, c1994. xi, 404 p.
93-002305   283/.3   0271010029
Evangelicalism -- Episcopal Church. Evangelicalism -- United States -- History. Anglican Communion -- United States -- History.

BX6115 Other Protestant denominations — Adventists. "Millerites" — History

BX6115.V36 1999
Vance, Laura Lee.
Seventh-Day Adventism in crisis: gender and sectarian change in an emerging religion/ Laura L. Vance. Urbana: University of Illinois Press, c1999. x, 261 p.
98-019765   286.7/32/09   0252024346
Seventh-Day Adventists -- History. Adventists -- History. Sabbatarians -- History.

BX6154 Other Protestant denominations — Adventists. "Millerites" — Individual branches of Adventists

BX6154.M624 2001
Morgan, Douglas, 1955-
Adventism and the American republic: the public involvement of a major apocalyptic movement/ Douglas Morgan; with a foreword by Martin L. Marty. Knoxville: University of Tennessee Press, c2001. xvi, 269 p.
00-010101   286.7/73   1572331119
Seventh-Day Adventists -- Doctrines. Church and state -- United States.

BX6196 Other Protestant denominations — Arminians. Remonstrants. Remonstrantsche. Broederschap — Biography

BX6196.B28 1985
Bangs, Carl, 1922-
Arminius: a study in the Dutch Reformation/ Carl Bangs. Grand Rapids, Mich.: F. Asbury Press, c1985. 388 p.
85-006050   284/.9/0924   0310294819
Arminius, Jacobus, -- 1560-1609. Reformed Church -- Netherlands -- Clergy -- Biography. Theologians -- Netherlands -- Biography.

BX6198 Other Protestant denominations — Arminians - Baptists

BX6198.A74.P65 1989
Poloma, Margaret M.
The Assemblies of God at the crossroads: charisma and institutional dilemmas/ Margaret M. Poloma. Knoxville: University of Tennessee Press, c1989. xxi, 309 p.
88-013761   289.9   0870496077
Pentecostal churches -- United States.

BX6211 Baptists — Dictionaries. Encyclopedias

BX6211.B73 1999
Brackney, William H.
Historical dictionary of the Baptists/ William H. Brackney. Lanham, Md.: Scarecrow Press, 1999. xxxii, 494 p.
99-021023   286/.03   0810836521
Baptists -- Dictionaries.

BX6211.D53 1994
Dictionary of Baptists in America/ editor, Bill J. Leonard. Downers Grove, Ill.: InterVarsity Press, c1994. xviii, 298 p.
94-031573   286/.0973 20   0830814477
Baptists -- United States -- Dictionaries.

BX6239-6241 Baptists — History — By region or country

BX6239.J87 1994
Juster, Susan.
Disorderly women: sexual politics & Evangelicalism in revolutionary New England/ Susan Juster. Ithaca, N.Y.: Cornell University Press, 1994. x, 224 p.
94-191656   286/.082   0801427320
Baptist women -- New England -- History -- 18th century. Baptists -- New England -- History -- 18th century. Sex role -- Religious aspects -- Christianity -- History of doctrines -- 18th century. New England -- Church history -- 18th century.

BX6241.H37 1997
Harvey, Paul, 1961-
Redeeming the South: religious cultures and racial identities among Southern Baptists, 1865-1925/ Paul Harvey. Chapel Hill: University of North Carolina Press, c1997. x, 330 p.
96-032882   286/.175/089   0807823244
Afro-American Baptists -- Southern States -- History -- 19th century. Afro-American Baptists -- Southern States -- History -- 20th century. Baptists -- Southern States -- History -- 19th century. Southern States -- Church history -- 20th century. Southern States -- Race relations. Southern States -- Church history -- 19th century.

BX6449 Baptists — Individual branches, conventions, associations, etc. — Afro-American Baptists

BX6449.K56.A3
King, Martin Luther, 1899-1984.
Daddy King: an autobiography/ Martin Luther King, Sr., with Clayton Riley; foreword by Benjamin E. Mays; introd. by Andrew J. Young. New York: Morrow, 1980. 215 p.
80-017411   286/.133/0924   0688036996
King, Martin Luther, -- 1899-1984. Baptists -- Clergy -- Biography. Clergy -- Georgia -- Atlanta -- Biography. Atlanta (Ga.) -- Biography.

BX6462.3-6462.7 Baptists — Individual branches, conventions, associations, etc. — Southern Baptist Convention

BX6462.3.S68 1993
Southern Baptists observed: multiple perspectives on a changing denomination/ edited by Nancy Tatom Ammerman. Knoxville: University of Tennessee Press, c1993. 362 p.
92-018725   286/.132   0870497693
Baptists -- United States -- History -- 1965- United States -- Church history -- 20th century.

BX6462.7.C67 1995
Copeland, E. Luther, 1916-
The Southern Baptist Convention and the judgement of history: the taint of an original sin/ E. Luther Copeland. Lanham, MD: University Press of America, c1995. xvii, 179 p.
95-012894   286/.132   0819199346
Racism -- Religious aspects -- Southern Baptist Convention. Sexism -- Religious aspects -- Southern Baptist Convention. Baptists -- United States -- History. United States -- Church history.

BX6462.7.R66 1989
Rosenberg, Ellen MacGilvra, 1929-
The Southern Baptists: a subculture in transition/ Ellen M. Rosenberg. Knoxville: University of Tennessee Press, c1989. xiii, 240 p.
88-031610   305.6/61   0870495984
Sociology, Christian (Baptist) Baptists -- United States. Conservatism -- United States -- History -- 20th century. Southern States -- Religious life and customs. Southern States -- Social conditions.

BX6495 Baptists — Biography — Individual, A-Z

BX6495.F68.M54 1985
Miller, Robert Moats.
Harry Emerson Fosdick: preacher, pastor, prophet/ Robert Moats Miller. New York: Oxford University Press, 1985. xvi, 608 p.
84-007168   286/.1/0924   0195035127
Fosdick, Harry Emerson, -- 1878-1969.Baptists -- United States -- Clergy -- Biography.

BX6600 Catholic Apostolic Church - Christadelphians

BX6600.C373.O46 1982
Omoyajowo, J. Akinyele.
Cherubim and Seraphim: the history of an African independent church/ by J. Akinyele Omoyajowo. New York: NOK Publishers International, c1982. xvi, 256 p.
78-064624   289.9   0883570688
Nigeria -- Church history.

BX6666 Christadelphians. Brothers of Christ — History — By region or country

BX6666.L56 1989
Lippy, Charles H.
The Christadelphians in North America/ Charles H. Lippy. Lewiston, NY, USA: Edwin Mellen Press, c1989. v, 336 p.
89-034071   289.9   0889466475
Christadelphians -- North America.

BX6931 Christian Science — History — General and the United States

BX6931.K54 1994
Knee, Stuart E.
Christian Science in the age of Mary Baker Eddy/ Stuart E. Knee. Westport, Conn.: Greenwood Press, 1994. xii, 158 p.
93-037506   289.5/09/034   0313283605
Eddy, Mary Baker, -- 1821-1910.Christian Science -- United States -- History -- 19th century. Christian Scientists -- United States -- Biography. United States -- Church history -- 19th century.

BX6943 Christian Science — General works — By others

BX6943.P4
Peel, Robert, 1909-
Christian Science: its encounter with American culture. New York, Holt [1958] 239 p.
58-008542   289.5
Christian Science. Transcendentalism (New England)

BX6950 Christian Science — Christian Science healing

BX6950.P44 1988
Peel, Robert, 1909-
Health and medicine in the Christian Science tradition: principle, practice, and challenge/ Robert Peel. New York: Crossroad, 1988 ix, 154 p.
88-020266   261.5/6   0824508955
Health -- Religious aspects -- Christian Science. Medicine -- Religious aspects -- Christian Science. Christian Science -- Doctrines.

BX6995 Christian Science — Biography — Individual

BX6995.G49 1998
Gill, Gillian.
Mary Baker Eddy/ Gillian Gill. Reading, Mass.: Perseus Books, c1998. xxxv, 713 p.
98-086397   289.5/092   0738200425
Eddy, Mary Baker, -- 1821-1910.Christian Scientists -- United States -- Biography. Christian Science -- History.

BX6995.T46 1994
Thomas, Robert David,
"With bleeding footsteps": Mary Baker Eddy's path to religious leadership/ Robert David Thomas. 1st ed. New York: Distributed by Random House, 1994. xvii, 363 p.
92-039053   289.5/092 B 20   0679414959
Eddy, Mary Baker, 1821-1910. Christian Scientists -- United States -- Biography. Christian Science -- United States -- History.

BX7032 Church of God (Cleveland, Tenn.) — Periodicals, societies, directories, yearbooks

BX7032.C662 1990
Crews, Mickey, 1950-
The Church of God: a social history/ Mickey Crews. Knoxville: University of Tennessee Press, c1990. xvi, 252 p.
89-038121   289.9   0870496344
Pentecostal churches -- United States -- History.

BX7066.5 Church of South India

BX7066.5.Z8.A934 2000
Harper, Susan Billington.
In the shadow of the Mahatma: Bishop V.S. Azariah and the travails of Christianity in British India/ Susan Billington Harper. Grand Rapids, Mich.: W.B. Eerdmans Pub. Co., c2000. xix, 462 p.
99-049030   283/.092   0802846793
Azariah, Vedanayagam Samuel, -- Bishop, -- 1874-1945.India, South -- Church history -- 20th century.

BX7075 Churches of Christ — Periodicals, societies, directories, yearbooks

BX7075.H84 1996
Hughes, Richard T. 1943-
Reviving the ancient faith: the story of Churches of Christ in America/ Richard T. Hughes. Grand Rapids, Mich.: W.B. Eerdmans Pub. Co., c1996. xiii, 448 p.
95-047321   286.6/3   0802840868
Churches of Christ -- History.United States -- Church history.

BX7077 Churches of Christ — Doctrines, creeds, catechisms, liturgy, ritual, sacraments, government, discipline, membership

BX7077.Z8.H354 2000
Harrell, David Edwin.
The Churches of Christ in the twentieth century: Homer Hailey's personal journey of faith/ David Edwin Harrell, Jr. Tuscaloosa: University of Alabama Press, c2000. xvii, 472 p.
99-006566   286.6/092   0817310088
Hailey, Homer, -- 1903-Churches of Christ -- Clergy -- Biography. Churches of Christ -- History -- 20th century.

BX7148-7176 Congregationalism — History — By region or country

BX7148.M4.C66 1999
Cooper, James F. 1955-
Tenacious of their liberties: the Congregationalists in colonial Massachusetts/ James F. Cooper, Jr. New York: Oxford University Press, 1999. viii, 282 p.
97-042441   285.8/744/09032   0195113608
Congregational churches -- Massachusetts -- History -- 17th century. Congregational churches -- Massachusetts -- History -- 18th century. Congregational churches -- Massachusetts -- Government. Massachusetts -- Church history -- 17th century. Massachusetts -- Church history -- 18th century.

BX7176.T46 1999
Thorne, Susan, 1958-
Congregational missions and the making of an imperial culture in nineteenth-century England/ Susan Thorne. Stanford, Calif.: Stanford University Press, 1999. 247 p.
98-051051   266/.02342/009034   0804730539
Congregational churches -- England -- History -- 19th century. Congregational churches -- Missions -- History -- 19th century. Imperialism -- History -- 19th century.

BX7252 Congregationalism — Special schools of doctrine — Other, A-Z

BX7252.N5.H57 1998
Hirrel, Leo P., 1952-
Children of wrath: New School Calvinism and antebellum reform/ Leo P. Hirrel. Lexington, Ky.: University Press of Kentucky, c1998. x, 248 p.
98-012157   285/.0973/09034   0813120616
New Haven theology. Calvinism -- United States -- History -- 19th century. Congregationalist churches -- United States -- History -- 19th century. United States -- Politics and government -- 1815-1861. United States -- Church history -- 19th century.

BX7260 Congregationalism — Biography — Individual, A-Z

BX7260.B31.F68 1999
Fox, Richard Wightman, 1945-
Trials of intimacy: love and loss in the Beecher-Tilton scandal/ Richard Wightman Fox. Chicago, IL: University of Chicago Press, c1999. xi, 419 p.
99-022120   285.8/092/2   0226259382
Beecher, Henry Ward, -- 1813-1887. Tilton, Elizabeth M. Richards, -- b. 1834. Tilton, Theodore, -- 1835-1907. Congregationalists -- New York -- Brooklyn -- Biography. Brooklyn (New York, N.Y.) -- Biography.

BX7260.C79.A4 2001
Cotton, John, 1584-1652.
The correspondence of John Cotton/ edited by Sargent Bush, Jr. Chapel Hill: Published for the Omohundro Institute of Early American History and Culture, Williamsburg, Virginia, by the University of North Carolina Press, c2001. xxvii, 548 p.
00-051204   285.8/092   0807826359
Cotton, John, -- 1584-1652 -- Correspondence.

BX7260.C79.Z5
Ziff, Larzer, 1927-
The career of John Cotton: Puritanism and the American experience. Princeton, N.J., Princeton University Press, 1962. 280 p.
62-007415   922.573
Cotton, John, -- 1584-1652.

BX7260.E3.C64 1995
Conforti, Joseph A.
Jonathan Edwards, religious tradition, and American culture/ by Joseph A. Conforti. Chapel Hill: University of North Carolina Press, c1995.
94-049526   285.8/092   0807822248
Edwards, Jonathan, -- 1703-1759 -- Influence. United States -- Civilization -- 19th century. United States -- Church history -- 19th century. United States -- Church history -- 20th century.

BX7260.E3.H59
Holmes, Stephen R.
God of grace and God of glory: an account of the theology of Jonathan Edwards/ Stephen R. Holmes. Grand Rapids, Mich.: William B. Eerdmans Pub. Co., 2001. xiv, 289 p.
2001-275342   230/.58/092   0802839142
Edwards, Jonathan, -- 1703-1758. Theology, Doctrinal -- United States -- History -- 18th century.

BX7260.E3.M33 1998
McClymond, Michael James, 1958-
Encounters with God: an approach to the theology of Jonathan Edwards/ Michael J. McClymond. New York: Oxford University Press, 1998. xii, 194 p.
97-009358   230/.58/092   0195118227
Edwards, Jonathan, -- 1703-1758.

BX7260.F47.H35 1996
Hambrick-Stowe, Charles E.
Charles G. Finney and the spirit of American Evangelicalism/ Charles E. Hambrick-Stowe. Grand Rapids, Mich.: W.B. Eerdmans Pub. Co., c1996. xvii, 317 p.
96-016697   285.8/092   0802801293
Finney, Charles Grandison, -- 1792-1875. Congregational churches -- United States -- Clergy -- Biography. Evangelists -- United States -- Biography. Revivals -- United States -- History -- 19th century.

BX7260.N49
Walker, Randi Jones.
Emma Newman, a frontier woman minister/ Randi Jones Walker. Syracuse, N.Y.: Syracuse University Press, 2000. xxi, 200 p.
00-034429   285.8/092   0815606745
Newman, Emma.

BX7343 Disciples of Christ. Campbellites. Christians — Biography — Individual, A-Z

BX7343.S3.W35 1999
Walter Scott: a nineteenth-century evangelical/ Mark G. Toulouse, editor. St. Louis, Mo.: Chalice Press, c1999. x, 150 p.
98-050821   286.6/092   0827242387
Scott, Walter, -- 1796-1861. Restoration movement (Christianity)

BX7350 Divine, Father (the man and his following)

BX7350.A4.W44 1983
Weisbrot, Robert.
Father Divine and the struggle for racial equality/ Robert Weisbrot. Urbana: University of Illinois Press, c1983. 241 p.
82-002644   299/.93   0252009738
Father Divine. Afro-Americans -- Civil rights. Race relations -- Religious aspects -- Christianity. United States -- Race relations.

BX7415 Dowieism. Christian Catholic Church — General works. History

BX7415.C66 1996
Cook, Philip L.
Zion City, Illinois: twentieth-century utopia/ Philip L. Cook. Syracuse, N.Y.: Syracuse University Press, 1996. xii, 283 p.
95-033571   277.3/21   0815626215
Dowie, John Alexander, -- 1847-1907. Utopias -- Illinois -- History -- 20th century. Christian communities -- Illinois -- History -- 20th century. Zion (Ill.) -- Church history.

BX7611 Friends. Society of Friends. Quakers — Dictionaries. Encyclopedias

BX7611.A23 2003
Abbott, Margery Post.
Historical dictionary of the Friends (Quakers)/ Margery Post Abbott, Mary Ellen Chijioke, Pink Dandelion. Lanham, Md.: Scarecrow Press, c2003.
2002-012989   289.6/03 21   0810844834
Society of Friends -- History -- Dictionaries.

BX7615 Friends. Society of Friends. Quakers — Collected works — Several authors

BX7615.W4
West, Jessamyn,
The Quaker reader. Selected and introduced by Jessamyn West. New York, Viking Press [1962] 522 p.
62-009147   289.6082
Society of Friends.

BX7631.2 Friends. Society of Friends. Quakers — History — General works

BX7631.2.T6
Tolles, Frederick Barnes, 1915-
Quakers and the Atlantic culture. New York, Macmillan, 1960. 160 p.
60-007085   289.6
Society of Friends -- History. Society of Friends -- Influence. United States -- Civilization.

BX7637-7639 Friends. Society of Friends. Quakers — History — By region or country

BX7637.H35 1988
Hamm, Thomas D.
The transformation of American Quakerism: Orthodox Friends, 1800-1907/ Thomas D. Hamm. Bloomington: Indiana University Press, c1988 xvii, 261 p.
86-046236   289.6/3   0253360048
Society of Friends -- United States -- History -- 19th century.

BX7639.W432001
Weddle, Meredith Baldwin, 1939-
Walking in the way of peace: Quaker pacifism in the seventeenth century/ Meredith Baldwin Weddle. Oxford; Oxford University Press, 2001. xiv, 348 p.
99-053089   261.8/73/088286   019513138X
Quakers -- New England -- History -- 17th century. Quakers -- England -- History -- 17th century. King Philip's War, 1675-1676 -- Religious aspects -- Society of Friends. New England -- Church history -- 17th century. England -- Church history -- 17th century.

BX7731.2 Friends. Society of Friends. Quakers — General works. Doctrine, etc. — 1951-2000

BX7731.2.B37 1988
Barbour, Hugh.
The Quakers/ Hugh Barbour and J. William Frost. New York: Greenwood Press, 1988. xiv, 407 p.
88-010240   289.6/73   0313228167
Society of Friends. Society of Friends -- United States. Quakers -- United States -- Biography.

BX7738 Friends. Society of Friends. Quakers — Spiritual life

BX7738.Q34 1984
Quaker spirituality: selected writings/ edited and introduced by Douglas V. Steere; preface by Elizabeth Gray Vining. New York: Paulist Press, c1984. xii, 334 p.
83-063537   248.4/896   0809103354
Spirituality -- Society of Friends -- Addresses, essays, lectures. Society of Friends -- Doctrines -- Addresses, essays, lectures.

BX7748 Friends. Society of Friends. Quakers — Other special topics, A-Z

BX7748.D43
Bradney, Anthony.
Living without law: an ethnography of Quaker decision-making, dispute avoidance, and dispute resolution/ Anthony Bradney and Fiona Cownie. Burlington, VT: Ashgate, 2000. vii, 187 p.
00-034841   262/.096   1855215551
Decision-making -- Religious aspects -- Society of Friends. Conflict management -- Religious aspects -- Society of Friends. Society of Friends -- Government.

BX7748.W64.M33 1992
Mack, Phyllis.
Visionary Women: ecstatic prophecy in seventeenth-century England/ Phyllis Mack. Berkeley: University of California Press, c1992. xiii, 465 p.
91-039580   289.6/42/082   0520078454
Quaker women -- England -- History -- 17th century. Prophecy (Christianity) -- History -- 17th century. Spirituality -- Society of Friends -- History -- 17th century.

BX7795 Friends. Society of Friends. Quakers — Biography — Individual, A-Z

BX7795.F7.I54 1994
Ingle, H. Larry 1936-
First among friends: George Fox and the creation of Quakerism/ H. Larry Ingle. New York: Oxford University Press, 1994. ix, 407 p.
93-007660   289.6/092   0195078039
Fox, George, -- 1624-1691.Quakers -- England -- Biography.

BX7795.F75.K86 1994
Kunze, Bonnelyn Young.
Margaret Fell and the rise of Quakerism/ Bonnelyn Young Kunze. Stanford, CA: Stanford University Press, 1994. xix, 327 p.
92-085445   289.6/092   0804721548
Fox, Margaret Askew Fell, -- 1614-1702.Society of Friends -- Great Britain -- History -- 17th century. Quakers -- Great Britain -- Biography. Women -- Religious life. Great Britain -- Social life and customs -- 17th century.

BX7800 Friends - German Baptist Brethren

BX7800.F864.A45 1987
Ammerman, Nancy Tatom, 1950-
Bible believers: fundamentalists in the modern world/ Nancy Tatom Ammerman. New Brunswick: Rutgers University Press, c1987. ix, 247 p.
86-029668   306/.6   081351231X
Fundamentalist churches -- United States -- Case studies.United States -- Church history -- 20th century.

BX7815 German Baptist Brethren. Church of the Brethren. "Dunkards" or "Dunkers" — History — General works

BX7815.B59 1995
Bowman, Carl F.
Brethren society: the cultural transformation of a "peculiar people"/ Carl F. Bowman. Baltimore, Md.: Johns Hopkins University Press, 1995. xii, 491 p.
94-019329   286/.5   0801849047
Sociology, Christian.

BX7990 German Reformed Church - Lutheran churches

BX7990.H6 H55 2001
Historical dictionary of the Holiness movement/ edited by William C. Kostlevy; Gari-Anne Patzwald, associate editor. Lanham, Md.: Scarecrow Press, 2001. xxvi, 307 p.
00-048239   270.8 21   0810839555
Holiness churches -- History -- Dictionaries.

BX8007 Lutheran churches — Dictionaries. Encyclopedias

BX8007.G37 2001
Gassmann, Günther.
Historical dictionary of Lutheranism/ Günther Gassmann; in cooperation with Duane H. Larson and Mark W. Oldenburg. Lanham, Md.: Scarecrow Press, 2001. xxiii, 420 p.
00-063745   284.1/03 21   0810839458
Lutheran Church -- Dictionaries. Lutheran Church -- History -- Dictionaries.

BX8009 Lutheran churches — Directories. Yearbooks. Almanacs. Calendars

BX8009.B33 1989
Bachmann, E. Theodore (Ernest Theod
Lutheran churches in the world: a handbook/ E. Theodore Bachmann and Mercia Brenne Bachmann; foreword by Gunnar Staalsett. Minneapolis: Augsburg, c1989. 631 p.
89-031064   284.1/09   0806623713
Lutheran Church -- Directories. Lutheran Church -- History.

BX8061 Lutheran churches — History — By region or country

BX8061.M7.T63 2000
Todd, Mary.
Authority vested: a story of identity and change in the Lutheran Church-Missouri Synod/ Mary Todd; [foreword by Martin E. Marty]. Grand Rapids, Mich.: W.B. Eerdmans Pub. Co., c2000. xvi, 336 p.
99-051879   284.1/322   080284457X
Authority -- Religious aspects -- Lutheran Church--Missouri Synod -- History of doctrines.

BX8063.7 Lutheran churches — Relations with other churches, A-Z

BX8063.7.C3
Hampson, Margaret Daphne.
Christian contradictions: the structures of Lutheran and Catholic thought/ Daphne Hampson. Cambridge, U.K.; Cambridge University Press, 2001. xi, 323 p.
00-041416   280/.042   0521450608
Lutheran Church -- Doctrines. Lutheran Church -- Relations -- Catholic Church.

BX8065.2 Lutheran churches — General works on Lutheranism. Doctrine, church government, etc. — 1951-2000

BX8065.2.G74
Gritsch, Eric W.
Lutheranism: the theological movement and its confessional writings/ Eric W. Gritsch and Robert W. Jenson. Philadelphia: Fortress Press, c1976. x, 214 p.
76-007869   230/.4/1   080060458X
Lutheran Church -- Doctrines -- History.

BX8080 Lutheran churches — Biography — Individual, A-Z

BX8080.B645.M3
Marty, Martin E., 1928-
The place of Bonhoeffer: problems and possibilities in his thought. Edited and introduced by Martin E. Marty, with Peter Berger [and others] New York, Association Press [1962] 224 p.
62-016875   193
Bonhoeffer, Dietrich, -- 1906-1945.

BX8080.N48.D3
Davidson, Clarissa Start.
God's man; the story of Pastor Niemoeller. New York, I. Washburn [1959] 242 p.
59-012256   922.443
Niemoller, Martin, -- 1801-

BX8116 Mennonites — History — By region or country

BX8116.B87 1998
Bush, Perry.
Two kingdoms, two loyalties: Mennonite pacifism in modern America/ Perry Bush. Baltimore, Md.: Johns Hopkins University Press, 1998. xii, 362 p.
97-044233   261.8/73/088287   0801858275
Mennonites -- United States -- History -- 20th century. Pacifism -- Religious aspects -- Mennonites -- History of doctrines -- 20th century.

BX8128 Mennonites — Special topics, A-Z

BX8128.E36.K73 1995
Kraybill, Donald B.
Amish enterprise: from plows to profits/ Donald B. Kraybill, Steven M. Nolt. Baltimore: Johns Hopkins University Press, c1995. xiv, 300 p.
95-001433   305.6/87074815   0801850622
Economics -- Religious aspects -- Amish -- History of doctrines -- 20th century. Amish -- Pennsylvania -- Lancaster Co. -- History -- 20th century. Lancaster County (Pa.) -- Church history -- 20th century. Lancaster County (Pa.) -- Economic conditions.

BX8128.P4
From the ground up: Mennonite contributions to international peacebuilding/ edited by Cynthia Sampson, John Paul Lederach. New York: Oxford University Press, 2000. xv, 316 p.
99-044848   261.8/73/088287   019513642X
Peace -- Religious aspects -- Mennonites -- Case studies. Mennonites -- Doctrines -- History.

BX8128.T45 U53 1996
Umble, Diane Zimmerman.
Holding the line: the telephone in Old Order Mennonite and Amish life / Diane Zimmerman Umble. Baltimore, Md.: Johns Hopkins University Press, 1996. xix, 192 p.
95-047049   384.6/08/8287 20   0801853125
Telephone -- Religious aspects -- Old Order Mennonites. Telephone -- Religious aspects -- Amish. Telephone -- Social aspects -- Pennsylvania -- Lancaster County. Amish -- Pennsylvania -- Lancaster County -- Customs and practices. Old Order Mennonites -- Pennsylvania -- Lancaster County -- Customs and Lancaster County (Pa.) -- Church history -- 20th century. Lancaster County (Pa.) -- Religious life and customs.

BX8129 Mennonites — Individual branches of Mennonites

BX8129.A6 S38
Schwieder, Elmer,
A peculiar people: Iowa's old order Amish/ Elmer Schwieder and Dorothy Schwieder. 1st ed. Ames: Iowa State University Press, 1975. ix, 188 p.
75-023420   977.7/0088287 19   0813801052
Amish -- Iowa. Iowa -- History.

BX8129.B63.O94 1996
Oved, Iaacov.
The witness of the brothers: a history of the Bruderhof/ Yaacov Oved. New Brunswick, N.J.: Transaction, c1996. viii, 342 p.
96-000574   289.7/3   1560002034
Hutterian Brethren -- History.

BX8129.B65.R83 2000
Rubin, Julius H.
The other side of joy: religious melancholy among the Bruderhof/ Julius H. Rubin. New York: Oxford University Press, 2000. xii, 264 p.
97-024740   289.7/3   0195119436
Hutterian Brethren -- Membership. Depression, Mental -- Religious aspects -- Christianity -- History of doctrines. Depression, Mental -- Epidemiology.

BX8129.B68.A6913 1998
Baum, Markus, 1963-
Against the wind: Eberhard Arnold and the Bruderhof/ Markus Baum; foreword by Jim Wallis; [translated and edited by the Bruderhof Communities]. Farmington, PA: Plough Pub. House, c1998. ix, 301 p.
98-005665   289.7/092   0874869536
Arnold, Eberhard, -- 1883-1935.Hutterian Brethren -- Germany -- Biography.

BX8129.O43
Lee, Daniel B.
Old Order Mennonites: rituals, beliefs, and community/ Daniel B. Lee. Chicago: Burnham, [2000] viii, 167 p.
00-033739   289.7/747   0830415734
Old Order Mennonites -- New York (State)New York (State) -- Religious life and customs.

BX8211 Methodism — Dictionaries. Encyclopedias

BX8211.H57 1996
Yrigoyen, Charles, 1937-
Historical dictionary of Methodism/ Charles Yrigoyen, Jr. and Susan E. Warrick. Lanham, Md.: Scarecrow Press, c1996. xxv, 299 p.
96-003558   287/.03   0810831406
Methodist Church -- Dictionaries. Methodist Church -- Biography -- Dictionaries.

BX8236 Methodism — History — By region or country

BX8236.A53 2000
Andrews, Dee.
The Methodists and revolutionary America, 1760-1800: the shaping of an evangelical culture/ Dee E. Andrews. Princeton, N.J.: Princeton University Press, c2000. xv, 367 p.
99-037485   287/.0973/09033   0691009589
Methodist Church -- United States -- History - - 18th century. Methodism -- History -- 18th century. United States -- Church history -- 18th century.

BX8337 Methodism — Services. Ritual. Liturgy

BX8337.T83 2001
Tucker, Karen B. Westerfield.
American Methodist worship/ Karen B. Westerfield Tucker. Oxford; Oxford University Press, 2001. xiv, 345 p.
99-049346   264/.07/00973 21   019512698X
Methodist Church--United States--Liturgy. Public worship.

BX8382.2 Methodism — Individual branches of Methodists — United Methodist Church (United States). Methodist Church (United States). Methodist Episcopal Church

BX8382.2.A4.K57 1996
Kirby, James E.
The Methodists/ James E. Kirby, Russell E. Richey, and Kenneth E. Rowe. Westport, Conn.: Greenwood Press, 1996. xv, 399 p.
96-000536   287/.6   0313220484
Methodist Church -- United States.

BX8443-8447 Methodism — Individual branches of Methodists — Black Methodists

BX8443.C36 1995
Campbell, James T.
Songs of Zion: the African Methodist Episcopal Church in the United States and South Africa/ James T. Campbell. New York: Oxford University Press, 1995. xv, 418 p.
94-019872   287/.83   0195078926
Afro-American Methodists -- Missions -- South Africa -- History. Missions, American -- South Africa -- History. Blacks -- Missions -- South Africa -- History. South Africa -- Church history.

BX8443.L58 2000
Little, Lawrence S.
Disciples of liberty: the African Methodist Episcopal Church in the age of imperialism, 1884-1916/ Lawrence S. Little. Knoxville: University of Tennessee Press, c2000. xvii, 246 p.
99-050910   287/.83   1572330856
Christianity and politics -- African Methodist Episcopal Church -- History. Imperialism -- History -- 19th century. Imperialism -- History -- 20th century.

BX8444.F6
Rivers, Larry E., 1950-
Laborers in the vineyard of the Lord: the beginnings of the AME Church in Florida, 1865-1895/ Larry Rivers and Canter Brown, Jr. Gainesville: University Press of Florida, c2001. xx, 244 p.
00-053658   287/.8759   0813018900
Florida -- Church history -- 19th century.

BX8447.S63 2000
Social protest thought in the African Methodist Episcopal Church, 1862-1939/ edited by Stephen W. Angell, Anthony B. Pinn. Knoxville: University of Tennessee Press, c2000. xxxi, 357 p.
99-006912   261.8/088/27   1572330651
Sociology, Christian (Methodist)

BX8476 Methodism — Methodist camp meetings — Individual, A-Z

BX8476.O2.M47 1999
Messenger, Troy.
Holy leisure: recreation and religion in God's square mile/ Troy Messenger. Minneapolis: University of Minnesota Press, c1999. xiv, 171 p.
98-051342   287/.674946   0816632537
Recreation -- Religious aspects -- Methodist Church -- History of doctrines. Recreation -- New Jersey -- Ocean Grove -- History. Ocean Grove (N.J.) -- Church history.

BX8495 Methodism — Biography — Individual, A-Z

BX8495.B754.B73 1994
Brasher, John Lawrence, 1947-
The sanctified South: John Lakin Brasher and the Holiness Movement/ J. Lawrence Brasher. Urbana: University of Illinois Press, c1994. xviii, 260 p.
93-013604   287/.6/092   0252020502
Brasher, John Lakin, -- 1868-1971.Methodist Church -- Southern States -- Clergy -- Biography. Holiness churches -- Southern States -- Clergy -- Biography. Southern States -- Church history -- 19th century. Southern States - - Church history -- 20th century.

BX8495.W5.A3 1987
Wesley, John, 1703-1791.
The journal of John Wesley: a selection/ edited with an introduction by Elisabeth Jay. Oxford; Oxford University Press, 1987. xxviii, 290 p.
87-001563   287/.092/4   0192122681
Wesley, John, -- 1703-1791 -- Diaries.Methodist Church -- Clergy -- Biography.

BX8525 Millennial Dawnists. Jehovah's Witnesses — Periodicals. Serials

BX8525.P48 2000
Peters, Shawn Francis, 1966-
Judging Jehovah's Witnesses: religious persecution and the dawn of the rights revolution/ Shawn Francis Peters. Lawrence, Kan.: University Press of Kansas, c2000. x, 342 p.
99-048616   289.9/2/0973   0700610081
Persecution -- United States -- History -- 20th century. Freedom of religion -- United States -- History -- 20th century.

BX8526 Millennial Dawnists. Jehovah's Witnesses — General works

BX8526.P46 1985
Penton, M. James, 1932-
Apocalypse delayed: the story of Jehovah's Witnesses/ M. James Penton. Toronto; University of Toronto Press, c1985. xvii, 400 p.
85-244517   289.9/2   0802025404
Jehovah's Witnesses.

BX8605.5 Mormons. Church of Jesus Christ of Latter-Day Saints — Dictionaries. Encyclopedias

BX8605.5.B588 1994
Bitton, Davis, 1930-
Historical dictionary of Mormonism/ by Davis Bitton. Metuchen, N.J.: Scarecrow Press, 1994. x, 338 p.
93-035972   289.3/03   0810827794
Mormon Church -- Dictionaries. Mormons -- Dictionaries.

BX8605.5.E62 1992
Encyclopedia of Mormonism/ edited by Daniel H. Ludlow. New York: Macmillan, c1992. 5 v.
91-034255   289.3/03 20   002904040X
Mormon Church -- Encyclopedias. Mormons -- Encyclopedias.

BX8611 Mormons. Church of Jesus Christ of Latter-Day Saints — History — General works

BX8611.S493 2000
Shipps, Jan, 1929-
Sojourner in the promised land: forty years among the Mormons/ Jan Shipps. Urbana: University of Illinois Press, c2000. xiii, 400 p.
00-008491   289.3/09   0252025903
Shipps, Jan, -- 1929-Mormon Church -- Study and teaching -- History. Mormon Church -- History.

BX8611.W4
West, Ray Benedict, 1908-
Kingdom of the saints; the story of Brigham Young and the Mormons. New York, Viking Press, 1957. 389 p.
57-006437   289.309
Young, Brigham, -- 1801-1877.Mormons and Mormonism -- History.

BX8623 Mormons. Church of Jesus Christ of Latter-Day Saints — Sources of Mormonism. The Sacred Books (Teachings of Joseph Smith) — Book of Mormon

BX8623. 1964
The Book of Mormon; an account written by the hand of Mormon upon plates taken from the plates of Nephi. Translated by Joseph Smith, Jr. Salt Lake City, Church of Jesus Christ of Latter-Day Saints, 1964 [c1963] 558 p.
72-008846   289.3/22

BX8628 Mormons. Church of Jesus Christ of Latter-Day Saints — Sources of Mormonism. The Sacred Books (Teachings of Joseph Smith) — Book of Doctrine and Covenants

BX8628.A3 1971
Smith, Joseph, 1805-1844.
The doctrine and covenants, of the Church of Jesus Christ of Latter-Day Saints, containing the revelations given to Joseph Smith, Jun., the prophet, for the building up of the Kingdom of God in the Divided into verses, with references, by Orson Pratt, Sen. Westport, Conn., Greenwood Press [1971] 503 p.
69-014082   289.3/2   083714101X
Mormon Church -- Doctrines.

BX8635.2 Mormons. Church of Jesus Christ of Latter-Day Saints — General treatises. Doctrines, etc. — 1951-2000

BX8635.2.H36
Hansen, Klaus J.
Mormonism and the American experience/ Klaus J. Hansen. Chicago: University of Chicago Press, c1981. xviii, 257 p.
80-019312   289.3/73   0226315525
Mormon Church -- History.

BX8637 Mormons. Church of Jesus Christ of Latter-Day Saints — Addresses, essays, lectures

BX8637.M67 2001
Mormons and Mormonism: an introduction to an American world religion/ edited by Eric A. Eliason. Urbana: University of Illinois Press, c2001. ix, 250 p.
00-008707   289.3   0252026098
Mormon Church.

BX8643 Mormons. Church of Jesus Christ of Latter-Day Saints — Special topics — Other, A-Z

BX8643.G63
Widmer, Kurt, 1962-
Mormonism and the nature of God: a theological evolution, 1830-1915/ Kurt Widmer; foreword by Irving Hexham. Jefferson, N.C.: McFarland, c2000. vi, 209 p.
00-025624   230/.93/09034   078640776X
Mormon Church -- Doctrines -- History -- 19th century. God -- History of doctrines -- 19th century.

BX8643.S25
Davies, Douglas James.
The Mormon culture of salvation: force, grace, and glory/ Douglas J. Davies. Aldershot, Hants, England; Ashgate, c2000. vii, 293 p.
00-029310   289.3   0754613283
Salvation. Mormon Church -- Doctrines.

BX8645 Mormons. Church of Jesus Christ of Latter-Day Saints — Controversial works against the Mormons — General works

BX8645.B45 2000
Bennett, John Cook,
The history of the saints, or, An exposé of Joe Smith and Mormonism/ John C. Bennett; introduction by Andrew F. Smith. 3rd ed. Urbana: University of Illinois Press, [2000] xlviii, 341 p.
99-087027   289.3 21   025202589X
Smith, Joseph, 1805-1844.Mormons--Controversial literature. Mormons--Illinois--Nauvoo--History--19th century.

BX8645.5 Mormons. Church of Jesus Christ of Latter-Day Saints — Controversial works against the Mormons — History and criticism

BX8645.5.G58 1997
Givens, Terryl.
The viper on the hearth: Mormons, myths, and the construction of heresy/ Terryl L. Givens. New York: Oxford University Press, 1997. x, 205 p.
96-011019   305.6/83   0195101839
Mormon Church -- Controversial literature -- History and criticism. American literature -- 19th century -- History and criticism.

BX8678 Mormons. Church of Jesus Christ of Latter-Day Saints — Individual branches or sects of Mormons — Reorganized Church of Jesus Christ of Latter-Day Saints

BX8678.S6.L38 1988
Launius, Roger D.
Joseph Smith III: pragmatic prophet/ Roger D. Launius. Urbana: University of Illinois Press, c1988. xii, 394 p.
87-035724   289.3/33/0924   0252015142
Smith, Joseph, -- 1832-1914.Mormons -- United States -- Biography. Mormon Church -- History.

BX8695 Mormons. Church of Jesus Christ of Latter-Day Saints — Biography — Individual, A-Z

BX8695.A77.A3 1998
Arrington, Leonard J.
Adventures of a church historian/ Leonard J. Arrington. Urbana: University of Illinois Press, c1998. 249 p.
97-033895   289.3/092   0252023811
Arrington, Leonard J.Mormons -- Biography. Mormon Church -- History.

BX8695.P68.A3 1998
Pratt, Louisa Barnes, 1802-1880.
The history of Louisa Barnes Pratt: being the autobiography of a Mormon missionary widow and pioneer/ edited by S. George Ellsworth. Logan, Utah: Utah State University Press, 1998. xxviii, 420 p.
98-025346   289.3/092   0874212529
Pratt, Louisa Barnes, -- 1802-1880.Mormons -- United States -- Biography. Frontier and pioneer life.

BX8695.Y7.A85 1985
Arrington, Leonard J.
Brigham Young: American Moses/ Leonard J. Arrington. New York: Knopf: 1985. xvii, 522 p.
84-048650   289.3/32/0924   0394510224
Young, Brigham, -- 1801-1877.Mormon Church -- Presidents -- Biography.

BX8712 New Jerusalem Church. New Church. Swedenborgianism — Collected works — Individual authors

BX8712.A8.Z73 1984
Swedenborg, Emanuel, 1688-1772.
The universal human and Soul-body interaction/ Emanuel Swedenborg; edited and translated by George F. Dole; introduction by Stephen Larsen; preface by Robert H. Kirven. New York: Paulist Press, c1984. xvi, 267 p.
84-060734   230/.94   0809125544
Body, Human -- Religious aspects. New Jerusalem Church -- Doctrines.

BX8748 New Jerusalem Church. New Church. Swedenborgianism — Biography — Individual

BX8748.B3913 2002
Benz, Ernst,
Emanuel Swedenborg: visionary savant in the age of reason/ by Ernst Benz; introduced and translated by Nicholas Goodrick-Clarke. West Chester, Pa.: Swedenborg Foundation, c2002. xxi, 536 p.
2002-001156   289/.4/092 B 21   0877851956
Swedenborg, Emanuel, 1688-1772.

BX8748.L3613 2000
Lamm, Martin, 1880-1950.
Emanuel Swedenborg: the development of his thought/ Martin Lamm; translated by Tomas Spiers and Anders Hallengren. West Chester, Pa.: Swedenborg Foundation, c2000. xxx, 354 p.
00-059537   289/.4/092   087785193X
Swedenborg, Emanuel, -- 1688-1772.

BX8762 Pentecostal churches — General works

BX8762.A45.B625 1997
Chesnut, R. Andrew.
Born again in Brazil: the Pentecostal boom and the pathogens of poverty/ R. Andrew Chesnut. New Brunswick, N.J.: Rutgers University Press, c1997. x, 203 p.
97-009191   289.9/4/098109049   0813524059
Pentecostal churches -- Brazil -- History -- 20th century. Spiritual healing -- Brazil -- History -- 20th century. Poor -- Brazil -- Religious life. Brazil -- Church history -- 20th century.

BX8762.5 Pentecostal churches — Afro-American Pentecostal Churches

BX8762.5.D87 1996
DuPree, Sherry Sherrod, 1946-
African-American Holiness Pentecostal movement: an annotated bibliography/ Sherry Sherrod DuPree. New York: Garland, 1996. lxvii, 650 p.
94-020225   016.2899/4/008996073   0824014499
Afro-American Pentecostal churches -- Abstracts. Afro-American Pentecostal churches -- Indexes. United States -- Church history -- Sources -- Abstracts. United States -- Church history -- Sources -- Indexes.

BX8770 Pentecostal churches — Individual branches — Mt. Calvary Holy Church of America

BX8770.A4.P37 1982
Paris, Arthur E., 1945-
Black Pentecostalism: Southern religion in an urban world/ Arthur E. Paris. Amherst: University of Massachusetts Press, 1982. vii, 183 p.
81-016169   289.9   087023353X
Afro-Americans -- Massachusetts -- Boston -- Religion.Boston (Mass.) -- Church history.

BX8935-8937 Presbyterianism. Calvinistic Methodism — History — By region or country

BX8935.B355 1993
Balmer, Randall Herbert.
The Presbyterians/ Randall Balmer and John R. Fitzmier. Westport, Conn.: Greenwood Press, c1993. xi, 274 p.
92-017840   285/.1   0313260842
Presbyterian Church — United States — History. Presbyterian Church — United States — Biography — Dictionaries.

BX8937.L65 1991
Longfield, Bradley J.
The Presbyterian controversy: fundamentalists, modernists, and moderates/ Bradley J. Longfield. New York: Oxford University Press, 1991. 333 p.
90-033625   285/.1/09042   0195064194
Modernist-fundamentalist controversy. Presbyterian Church — United States — History — 20th century.

BX9211 Presbyterianism. Calvinistic Methodism — Individual churches — United States

BX9211.C414.W48 1999
Wellman, James K.
The gold coast church and the ghetto: Christ and culture in mainline Protestantism/ James K. Wellman, Jr.; foreword by Martin E. Marty. Urbana: University of Illinois Press, c1999. xv, 257 p.
98-058127   285/.177311   0252024893
Protestant churches — United States — Case studies. Christianity and culture — United States — Case studies. Chicago (Ill.) — Church history.

BX9223-9225 Presbyterianism. Calvinistic Methodism — Biography — Individual

BX9223.M37 2000
Marshall, Rosalind Kay.
John Knox/ Rosalind K. Marshall. Edinburgh: Birlinn, 2000. xiii, 244 p.
2001-369156   1841580910
Knox, John, — ca. 1514-1572.

BX9225.C6243.A34 1977
Coffin, William Sloane.
Once to every man: a memoir/ William Sloane Coffin, Jr. New York: Atheneum, 1977. viii, 344 p.
77-076547   230/.5/10924   0689108117
Coffin, William Sloane.Presbyterian Church — United States — Clergy — Biography.

BX9225.M39.A4 2000
McDowell, Sally Campbell Preston, 1821-1895.
"If you love that lady don't marry her": the courtship letters of Sally McDowell and John Miller, 1854-1856/ edited by Thomas E. Buckley. Columbia: University of Missouri Press, c2000. xliv, 896 p.
00-023994   975.5/03/0922   0826212786
McDowell, Sally Campbell Preston, — 1821-1895 — Correspondence. Miller, John, — 1819-1895 — Correspondence. Presbyterian Church — Pennsylvania — Philadelphia — Clergy — Correspondence.

BX9322 Puritanism — General works. History. Puritan doctrine, government, etc. — 1951-2000

BX9322.D45 1989
Delbanco, Andrew, 1952-
The Puritan ordeal/ Andrew Delbanco. Cambridge, Mass.: Harvard University Press, 1989. ix, 306 p.
88-011218   285/.9/0973   0674740556
Puritans. Puritans — United States.

BX9334.2 Puritanism — By region or country — Great Britain. England

BX9334.2.P66 2000
Poole, Kristen.
Radical religion from Shakespeare to Milton: figures of nonconformity in early modern England/ Kristen Poole. Cambridge, U.K.; Cambridge University Press, 2000. xiii, 272 p.
99-037800   285/.9/0942   0052164047
Puritans — England — Controversial literature — History and criticism. Dissenters, Religious — England — Controversial literature — History and criticism.

BX9334.2.S68 1998
Spurr, John.
English Puritanism, 1603-1689/ John Spurr. New York: St. Martin's Press, 1998. x, 245 p.
98-004785   285/.9/094209032   031221426X
Puritans — England — History — 17th century.England — Church history — 17th century.

BX9354.2-9355 Puritanism — By region or country — America

BX9354.2.P67 1992
Porterfield, Amanda, 1947-
Female piety in Puritan New England: the emergence of religious humanism/ Amanda Porterfield. New York: Oxford University Press, 1992. x, 207 p.
91-008985   285/.9/082   0195068211
Puritans — New England. Women in Christianity — New England. Identification (Religion) — History of doctrines. New England — Church history.

BX9355.M4.P48 1997
Peterson, Mark A., 1960-
The price of redemption: the spiritual economy of Puritan New England/ Mark A. Peterson. Stanford, Calif.: Stanford University Press, 1997. ix, 325 p.
97-033712   285/.9/0974409032   0804729123
Puritans — Massachusetts — History. Spirituality — Puritans — History. Economics — Religious aspects — Puritans — History of doctrines. Boston (Mass.) — Church history. Westfield (Mass.) — Church history. Massachusetts — Church history — 17th century.

BX9406 Reformed or Calvinistic churches — Dictionaries. Encyclopedias

BX9406.E56 1992
Encyclopedia of the Reformed faith/ Donald K. McKim, editor: David F. Wright, consulting editor. Louisville, Ky.: Westminster/John Knox Press; 1992. xxiv, 414 p.
91-037540   284/.2/03   0664218822
Reformed Church — Encyclopedias. Presbyterian Church — Encyclopedias.

BX9410 Reformed or Calvinistic churches — Collected works — Individual authors

BX9410.B323
Barth, Karl, 1886-1968.
Community, state, and church; three essays. With an introd. by Will Herberg. Garden City, N.Y., Doubleday, 1960. 193 p.
60-013233   261.704
Theology. Reformed Church.

BX9415 Reformed or Calvinistic churches — History

BX9415.B46 1999
Benedetto, Robert, 1950-
Historical dictionary of Reformed Churches/ Robert Benedetto, Darrell L. Guder, Donald K. McKim. Lanham, Md.: Scarecrow Press, 1999. lii, 508 p.
98-050486   284/.2/09   0810836289
Reformed Church -- History -- Dictionaries.

BX9415.B47 2002
Benedict, Philip.
Christ's churches purely reformed: a social history of Calvinism/ Philip Benedict. New Haven: Yale University Press, c2002. xxvi, 670 p.
2002-002411   284/.24 21   0300088124
Calvinism -- Europe -- History.

BX9418 Reformed or Calvinistic churches — Biography — Individual

BX9418.B715 1988
Bouwsma, William James, 1923-
John Calvin: a sixteenth-century portrait/ William J. Bouwsma. New York: Oxford University Press, 1988. viii, 310 p.
87-012338   284/.2/0924   0195043944
Calvin, Jean, -- 1509-1564.

BX9418.C5913 2000
Cottret, Bernard.
Calvin: a biography/ Bernard Cottret; translated by M. Wallace McDonald. Grand Rapids, Mich.: W.B. Eerdmans Pub. Co.; 2000. xv, 376 p.
00-037142   284/.2/092   0802842895
Calvin, Jean, -- 1509-1564.Reformation -- Switzerland -- Geneva -- Biography. Reformed Church -- Switzerland -- Geneva -- Clergy -- Biography. Geneva (Switzerland) -- Biography. Geneva (Switzerland) -- Church history -- 16th century.

BX9418.M29 1990
McGrath, Alister E., 1953-
A life of John Calvin: a study in the shaping of Western culture/ Alister E. McGrath. Oxford, UK; B. Blackwell, 1990. xv, 332 p.
90-031240   284/.2/092   0631163980
Calvin, Jean, -- 1509-1564. Calvin, Jean, -- 1509-1564 -- Influence. Reformation -- Biography. Calvinism. Reformed Church -- Doctrines.

BX9418.T38 2000
Tavard, George H. 1922-
The starting point of Calvin's theology/ George H. Tavard. Grand Rapids, Mich.: W.B. Eerdmans, c2000. ix, 199 p.
00-035430   230/.42/092   0802847188
Calvin, Jean, -- 1509-1564. Psychopannychia. Calvin, Jean, -- 1509-1564. -- Institutio Christianae religionis. Reformed Church -- Doctrines. Theology, Doctrinal. Soul.

BX9422.2 Reformed or Calvinistic churches — General works on Reformed doctrine. Calvinism — 1951-2000

BX9422.2.G47
Gerrish, B. A. 1931-
Tradition and the modern world: reformed theology in the nineteenth century/ B. A. Gerrish. Chicago: University of Chicago Press, c1978. xii, 263 p.
78-004982   230   0226288668
Reformed Church -- Doctrines -- History -- 18th century. Theology, Doctrinal -- History -- 19th century.

BX9422.5 Reformed or Calvinistic churches — Addresses, essays, lectures

BX9422.5.C35 1994
Calvinism in Europe, 1540-1620/ edited by Andrew Pettegree, Alastair Duke, and Gillian Lewis. Cambridge; Cambridge University Press, 1994. xii, 283 p.
93-037383   284/.24/0903 20   0521432693
Calvinism -- Europe -- History -- Congresses.

BX9498-9593 Reformed or Calvinistic churches — By country — United States

BX9498.D87
Fabend, Firth Haring, 1937-
Zion on the Hudson: Dutch New York and New Jersey in the age of revivals/ Firth Haring Fabend. New Brunswick, N.J.: Rutgers University Press, c2000. xvi, 284 p.
99-043168   285.7/747/0893931   0813527716
Dutch Americans -- New York -- Religion. Dutch Americans -- New Jersey -- Religion. Reformed Church -- New York -- History -- 19th century. New York -- Church history -- 19th century. New Jersey -- Church history -- 19th century.

BX9543.P4.G46 1993
George, Carol V. R.
God's salesman: Norman Vincent Peale & the power of positive thinking/ Carol V.R. George. New York: Oxford University Press, 1993. xv, 271 p.
92-016176   285.7/092   0195074637
Peale, Norman Vincent, -- 1898-Reformed Church -- United States -- Clergy -- Biography. Peace of mind -- Religious aspects -- Christianity -- History of doctrines -- 20th century. Success -- Religious aspects -- Christianity -- History of doctrines -- 20th century.

BX9593.N4.W46 1997
Wentz, Richard E.
John Williamson Nevin: American theologian/ Richard E. Wentz. New York: Oxford University Press, 1997. viii, 169 p.
96-012652   230/.57/092   0195082435
Nevin, John Williamson, -- 1803-1886.Theologians -- United States -- Biography. Reformed Church -- United States -- Doctrines -- History -- 19th century. Mercersburg theology.

BX9715 Salvation Army — History — General works

BX9715.M87 1994
Murdoch, Norman H.
Origins of the Salvation Army/ Norman H. Murdoch. Knoxville: University of Tennessee Press, c1994. xii, 241 p.
94-009334   287.9/6/09   0870498584
Salvation Army -- History.

BX9718 Salvation Army — History — By region or country

BX9718.N7.W56 1999
Winston, Diane H., 1951-
Red-hot and righteous: the urban religion of the Salvation Army/ Diane Winston. Cambridge, Mass.: Harvard University Press, 1999. 290 p.
98-047842   287.9/6/097471   0674867068
Salvation Army -- New York (State) -- New York -- History.

BX9750 Schwenckfelder Church - Shakers — Segye Kidokkyo T'ongil Sillyong Hyophoe (Sun Myung Moon). Unification Church

BX9750.S44.C47 1990
Chryssides, George D., 1945-
The advent of Sun Myung Moon: the origins, beliefs, and practices of the Unification Church/ George D. Chryssides. New York: St. Martin's Press, 1991. xii, 230 p.
90-042732   289.9/6   0312053479
Moon, Sun Myung.

BX9765 Shakers. United Society of Believers. Millennial Church — History — General works

BX9765.D84 2000
Duffield, Holley Gene, 1934-
Historical dictionary of the Shakers/ Holley Gene Duffield. Lanham, Md.: Scarecrow Press, 2000. xxvi, 219 p.
99-038149   289/.8/03   0810836831
Shakers -- History -- Dictionaries. Shakers -- Biography -- Dictionaries.

BX9766 Shakers. United Society of Believers. Millennial Church — History — By region or country

BX9766.S74 1992
Stein, Stephen J., 1940-
The Shaker experience in America: a history of the United Society of Believers/ Stephen J. Stein. New Haven: Yale University Press, c1992. xx, 554 p.
91-030836   289/.8/0973   0300051395
Shakers -- United States -- History.

BX9831 Unitarianism — History — General works

BX9831.W49 1945
Wilbur, Earl Morse, 1866-1956.
A history of Unitarianism. Cambridge, Harvard University Press, 1945-19. 2 v.
45-003134   288.09
Unitarian Universalist churches -- History. Socinianism.

BX9833 Unitarianism — History — By region or country

BX9833.A273 1989
American Unitarianism, 1805-1865/ edited by Conrad Edick Wright. Boston: Massachusetts Historical Society: c1989. xiii, 272 p.
88-013445   288/.73   1555530478
Unitarianism -- United States -- History -- 19th century -- Congresses.United States -- Church history -- 19th century -- Congresses.

BX9833.R63 1985
Robinson, David, 1947-
The Unitarians and the universalists/ David Robinson. Westport, Conn.: Greenwood Press, 1985. xiii, 368 p.
84-009031   288/.73   0313209464
Unitarianism -- United States -- History. Universalists -- United States -- History. Liberalism (Religion) -- United States -- History.

BX9869 Unitarianism — Biography — Individual, A-Z

BX9869.P3 G76 2002
Grodzins, Dean.
American heretic: Theodore Parker and transcendentalism/ Dean Grodzins. Chapel Hill: University of North Carolina Press, c2002. xiii, 631 p.
2002-003832   289.1/092 B 21   080782710X
Parker,   Theodore,   1810-1860. Transcendentalism.

BX9869.P8.S36 1997
Schofield, Robert E.
The enlightenment of Joseph Priestley: a study of his life and work from 1733 to 1773/ Robert E. Schofield. University Park, Pa.: Pennsylvania State University Press, c1997. xii, 305 p.
96-054484   540/.92   0271016620
Priestley,   Joseph,   --   1733-1804. Unitarian churches -- Clergy -- Biography. Chemists -- Biography.

__INDEXES__

Rudolph, Kurt. BT1390.R7713 1983

Rue, Loyal D. BD171.R8 1994

Ruether, Rosemary Radford. BT704.R835 1998
  BT707.7.R84 2000

Ruland, Vernon. BL80.2.R86 1998

Rummel, Erika. BR350.E7.R86 1989

Runciman, Steven. BX300.R86
  BX410.R8

Runes, Dagobert D. B51.8.R8

Ruokanen, Miikka. BX1787.R86 1992

Russell, Bertrand. B72.R8
  B72.R83 1959a
  B1649.R91.C37
  B1649.R91.E38
  B1649.R91 1983
  B1649.R93.B4
  B1649.R93.E8
  B1649.R93.L6
  B1649.R93.O9 1927a
  B1649.R93.U49
  B1649.R96.O8 1929
  BD21.R8 1959
  BD161.R78
  BJ1481.R75 1971
  BL240.R8
  BL2780.R87 1957

Russell, James C. BR203.R87 1994

Rutherford, R. B. B583.R88 1989

Ryan, Alan. B1649.R94.R93 1988

Ryan, William B. F. BS658.R93 1998

Ryder, John. B851.R93 1999

Ryle, Gilbert. B393.R9

Sabia, Debra. BX2347.72.N5.S23 1997

Sack, Daniel. BR115.N87 S23 2000

Saenz, Mario. B1008.L53.S24 1999

Saher, P. J. B799.S32 1970

Sainsbury, R. M. BC135.S14 1991
  BC199.P2 S25 1995

Salerno, Joseph. B3245.F24 S24 2001

Sales, William W. BP223.Z8.L5772 1994

Sallis, John,1938-. B395.S23 1996

Sallis, John. B3313.G43.S24 1991

Sallnow, Michael J. BL2590.P5.S25 1987

Salmon, Merrilee H. BC71.S25 1995

Salmon, Wesley C. BC108.S2 1984

Saltus, Edgar. BJ1477.S2 1925

Salvan, Jacques Leon. B2430.S34.S3

Samburský, Samuel. B528.S25

Sampson, Ronald Victor. BD438.S25 1966

Samuelson, Norbert Max. B157.C65.S25 1994

Sanasarian, Eliz. BL2270.S26 2000

Sanders, E. P. BT301.2.S254 1993

Sandmel, Samuel. B689.Z7 S28
  BM176.S26
  BS1140.2.S2

Sandoval, Annette. BX4656.5.S26 1996

Sanford, David H. BC199.C56 S26 2003

Sanneh, Lamin O. BL65.C8.S26 1996
  BP64.A4.W367 1997

Santas, Gerasimos Xenophon. B398.L9.S26 1988

Santayana, George. B945.S21 C59 1995
  B945.S21.C6
  B945.S21 E3 1936
  B945.S2 1986 vol. 1
  B945.S2 1986 vol. 5
  B945.S23.D5 1957
  B945.S23 L7 1998
  B945.S23.R38
  B945.S23.R4
  B945.S23.R42 1972
  B2528.E3.S3
  BD331.S3
  BD331.S33
  BT201.S263

Sargeant, Kimon Howland. BR1640.S27 2000

Sartre, Jean Paul. B819.S32
  B2430.S32.E53
  B2430.S33.C3213 1992
  B2430.S33.V4713 1992
  B2430.S33 C713 1991

Sarup, Madan. B831.2.S27 1993

Sassi, Maria Michela. B187.M25 S2713 2001

Sawada, Janine Anderson. BJ971.S5 S29 1993

Sawyer, John F. A. BS1515.2.S35 1996

Sayre, Kenneth M. B395.S28 1995
  BD215.S28 1997

Scaltsas, T. B434.S32 1994

Scanlon, Thomas. BJ1411.S36 1998

Scarry, Elaine. BJ1409.S35 1985

Schaeffer, Jean-Marie. BH151.S3313 2000

Schantz, Mark S. BR560.P86

Scharfstein, Ben-Ami. B105.I533 S33 1993
  B799.S37 1998

Scharper, Stephen B. BT695.5.S27 1997

Schechtman, Marya. BC199.I4.S33 1996

American philosophy in the twentieth century; a sourcebook from pragmatism to philosophical analysis, / B934.K8 1966

American philosophy today, and other philosophical studies / B945.R454 R37 1994

American philosophy: the early schools / B865.R5 1958

American pragmatists; selected writings, The / B832.K6

American religious philosophy / BL51.R598

American sociology: worldly rejections of religion and their directions / BR517.V47 1985

American synagogue: a historical dictionary and sourcebook, The / BM205.O45 1996

American transcendentalism and Asian religions / B905.V47 1993

American Unitarianism, 1805-1865 / BX9833.A273 1989

American voudou: journey into a hidden world / BL2490.D37 1998

American women in mission: a social history of their thought and practice / BV2610.R63 1996

Americanization of religious minorities: confronting the constitutional order, The / BL2525.M39 1999

Amish enterprise: from plows to profits / BX8128.E36.K73 1995

Anabaptism; a social history, 1525-1618: Switzerland, Austria, Moravia, South and Central Germany / BX4931.2.C57

Analysis of knowledge and valuation, An / BD181.L47

Analytic aesthetics / BH201.A63 1989

Analytic philosophy: an anthology / B808.5.A52 2001

Analytic tradition: meaning, thought, and knowledge, The / B808.5.A532 1990

Analytical concordance to the Bible on an entirely new plan containing about 311,000 references, subdivided under the Hebrew and Greek originals, with the literal meaning and pronunciation of each; designed for the simplest reader of the English Bible / BS425.Y7 1955

Analytical philosophy / BC6.B8

Analyzing love / BD436.B76 1987

Anatomy of judgment, The / BC177.R345 1990

Anatomy of loving: the story of man's quest to know what love is, The / BD436.B47 1987

Anatomy of negation, The / BJ1477.S2 1925

Anaximander in context: new studies in the origins of Greek philosophy / B208.Z7 C68 2003

Anchor Bible dictionary, The / BS440.A54 1992

Ancient art and ritual / BH91.H32 1969

Ancient concepts of philosophy / B178.J67 1990

Ancient cosmologies / BD495.A5

Ancient formal logic / BC28.B58

Ancient mystery cults / BL610.B87 1987

Ancient synagogue: the first thousand years, The / BM653.L38 2000

Ancient women philosophers, 600 B.C.-500 A.D / B105.W6 A53 1987

Ancients and the moderns: rethinking modernity, The / B791.R77 1989

And I will dwell in their midst: Orthodox Jews in suburbia / BM229.T67

Angels, A to Z / BL477.L45 1996

Anglicans and Puritans?: Presbyterianism and English conformist thought from Whitgift to Hooker / BX5071.L34 1988

Animal minds and human morals: the origins of the Western debate / B187.M55.S67 1993

Animal others: on ethics, ontology, and animal life / B105.A55 A55 1999

Animal sacrifices: religious perspectives on the use of animals in science / BL439.5.A55 1986

Animals and Christianity: a book of readings / BT746.A55 1988

Animals and why they matter / BJ1012.M5 1984

Animals on the agenda: questions about animals for theology and ethics / BT746.A555 1998

Annotated anthology of hymns, An / BV312.A56 2002

Annotated guides, myths & legends / BL311.P46 1999

Ante-Nicene Fathers; translations of the writings of the Fathers down to A. D. 325, The / BR60.A5 1950

Anthropic cosmological principle, The / BD511.B34 1988

Anthropology of evil, The / BJ1401.A67 1985

Anti-aesthetic: essays on postmodern culture, The / BH301.M54.A57 1983

Anti-Catholicism in Northern Ireland, 1600-1997: the mote and the beam / BX1766.B74 1998

Antichrist: two thousand years of the human fascination with evil / BT985.M29 1994

Antisthenes of Athens: setting the world aright / B293.A34

Antwerp in the age of Reformation: underground Protestantism in a commercial metropolis, 1550-1577 / BR828.A4.M37 1996

Anxious angels: a retrospective view of religious existentialism / BT84.P37 1999

Apocalypse delayed: the story of Jehovah's Witnesses / BX8526.P46 1985

Apocalypse observed: religious movements, and violence in North America, Europe, and Japan / BL65.V55.H33 2000

Apocalyptic spirituality: treatises and letters of Lactantius, Adso of Montier-en-Der, Joachim of Fiore, the Franciscan spirituals, Savonarola / BT885.A65

Apocrypha, The / BS1692.1957

Apocryphal New Testament: a collection of apocryphal Christian literature in an English translation, The / BS2832.A2 1993

Apologia pro vita sua. An authoritative text, basic texts of the Newman-Kingsley controversy, origin and reception of the Apologia [and] essays in criticism / BX4705.N5.A3 1968

Blackwell guide to epistemology, The / BD161.B465 1999

Blackwell guide to metaphysics, The / BD111.B57 2002

Blackwell guide to philosophy of mind, The / BD418.3.B57 2003

Blackwell guide to the modern philosophers: from Descartes to Nietzsche, The / B791.B57 2000

Blaise Pascal: the life and work of a realist / B1903.M63 1976

Blessed excess: religion and the hyperbolic imagination / BL48.W313 1993

Blood and the shroud: new evidence that the world's most sacred relic is real, The / BT587.S4.W515 1998

Bodies of resistance: new phenomenologies of politics, agency, and culture / B829.5.B63 2001

Body and mind / BD450.C244 1984

Body and society: men, women, and sexual renunciation in early Christianity, The / BR195.C45.B76 1988

Body in context: sex and catholicism, The / BX1795.S48.M66 2000

Body in mind: understanding cognitive processes, The / BD418.3.R78 1999

Body in pain: the making and unmaking of the world, The / BJ1409.S35 1985

Body in the mind: the bodily basis of meaning, imagination, and reason, The / B105.M4 J64 1987

Body, self-cultivation, and ki-energy, The / B127.C49 Y83 1993

Body: classic and contemporary readings, The / B105.B64 B64 1999

Body: toward an Eastern mind-body theory, The / BD450.Y8213 1987

Boethius, the consolations of music, logic, theology, and philosophy / B659.Z7.C45

Bond of being; an essay on analogy and existence, The / BD190.A6 1969

Book of J, The / BS1223. 1990

Book of Jerry Falwell: fundamentalist language and politics, The / BT82.2.H36 2000

Book of Mormon; an account, The / BX8623. 1964

Book of the courtier, The / BJ1604.C37 1967

Book; on the taboo against knowing who you are, The / BD450.W3 1972

Books and readers in the early church: a history of early Christian texts / BR67.2.G35 1995

Born again in Brazil: the Pentecostal boom and the pathogens of poverty / BX8762.A45.B625 1997

Boston Catholics: a history of the church and its people / BX1417.B6 O36 1998

Boston Confucianism: portable tradition in the late-modern world / BL1852.N48 2000

Bottle in the sea / B945.G83.B6

Bound for the promised land: African American religion and the great migration / BR563.N4.S474 1997

Bound to act: models of action, dramas of inaction / B105.A35.W33 1999

Bounds of agency: an essay in revisionary metaphysics, The / BD450.R6538 1998

Bounds of justice / BJ1533.J9 O64 2000

Bounds of logic: a generalized viewpoint, The / BC71.S47 1991

Brahma sutra, the philosophy of spiritual life, The / B132.V3.B2 1960

Brain mystery light and dark: the rhythm and harmony of consciousness / B808.9.K49 1999

Brainchildren: essays on designing minds / BD418.3.D46 1998

Brave new world of the enlightenment, The / B2621.B68

Breaking and remaking: aesthetic practice in England, 1700-1820 / BH221.G72.P38 1989

Brethren society: the cultural transformation of a "peculiar people" / BX7815.B59 1995

Bridge of quiescence: experiencing Tibetan Buddhist meditation, The / BQ7950.T754.B9338 1998

Brief history of western philosophy, A / B72.K44 1998

Brief introduction to Hinduism: religion, philosophy, and ways of liberation, A / BL1212.72.H47 1991

Brief introduction to Islamic philosophy, A / B741.L42 2001

Brigham Young: American Moses / BX8695.Y7.A85 1985

British moralists, 1650-1800; / BJ601.R3

Broken staff: Judaism through Christian eyes, The / BT93.M35 1992

Brother Jesus: the Nazarene through Jewish eyes / BM620.B213 2001

Brothers of light: the Penitentes of the Southwest / BX3653.U6 H3 1998

Buddha / BQ882.A76 2001

Buddha from Brooklyn, The / BQ734.S44 2000

Buddhism and politics in twentieth-century Asia / BQ270.B83 1999

Buddhism in Chinese society: an economic history from the fifth to the tenth centuries / BQ638.G4713 1995

Buddhism in contemporary Tibet: religious revival and cultural identity / BQ7590.B84 1998

Buddhism in practice / BQ1012.B83 1995

Buddhism in the western Himalaya: a study of the Tabo monastery / BQ6331.T332 T43

Buddhism under Mao / BQ647.W44

Buddhism, sexuality, and gender / BQ4570.S48 B83 1992

Buddhism: a history / BQ266.R43 1994

Buddhism: introducing the Buddhist experience / BQ266.M48 2002

Buddhist civilization in Tibet / BQ7604.T47 1987

Buddhist dictionary: Manual of Buddhist terms and doctrines / BQ130.N9 1983

Buddhist epistemology / BQ4440.B53 2000

Buddhist ethics / BJ1289.K6513 1998

Buddhist ethics and modern society: an international symposium / BJ1289.B835 1991

Buddhist Himalayas / BQ400.H542 F65 2002

Buddhist studies in the People's Republic of China, 1990-1991 / BQ632.B83 1992

Buddhist thought in India: three phases of Buddhist philosophy / BQ336.C66x 1983

Buddhist world-view, The / BQ626.B83 2001

Bully pulpit: the politics of Protestant clergy, The / BR516.B795 1997

By the grace of guile: the role of deception in natural history and human affairs / BD171.R8 1994

Byzantine theocracy, The / BX300.R86

C. S. Lewis, defender of the faith, / BX5199.L53.C8

Caliban's reason: introducing Afro-Carribean philosophy / B1028.P34 2000

Call of conscience: Heidegger and Levinas, rhetoric and the euthanasia debate, The / BJ1471.H93 2001

Calliope's sisters: a comparative study of philosophies of art / BH39.A57 1990

Calvin: a biography / BX9418.C5913 2000

Calvinism in Europe, 1540-1620 / BX9422.5.C35 1994

Cambridge companion to Aquinas, The / B765.T54 C29 1993

Cambridge companion to Aristotle, The / B485.C35 1995

Cambridge companion to biblical interpretation, The / BS511.2.C35 1998

Cambridge companion to Christian ethics, The / BJ1251.C246 2001

Cambridge companion to Dietrich Bonhoeffer, The / BX4827.B57.C36 1999

Cambridge companion to early Greek philosophy, The / B188.C35 1999

Cambridge companion to feminist theology, The / BT83.55.C35 2002

Cambridge companion to German idealism, The / B2745.C36 2000

Cambridge companion to Hegel, The / B2948.C28 1993

Cambridge companion to Heidegger, The / B3279.H49.C25 1993

Cambridge companion to Hobbes, The / B1247.C26 1996

Cambridge companion to Husserl, The / B3279.H94.C28 1995

Cambridge companion to Karl Barth, The / BX4827.B3 C26 2000

Cambridge companion to Malebranche, The / B1897.S368 2000

Cambridge companion to Mill, The / B1607.C25 1998

Cambridge companion to Ockham, The / B765.O34.C36 1999

Cambridge companion to Plato, The / B395.C28 1992

Cambridge companion to Plotinus, The / B693.Z7 C36 1996

Cambridge companion to Schopenhauer, The / B3148.C36 1999

Cambridge companion to the Bible, The / BS475.2.C26 1997

Cambridge companion to William James, The / B945.J21.P87 1997

Cambridge companion to Wittgenstein, The / B3376.W564.C345 1996

Cambridge dictionary of philosophy, The / B41.C35 1999

Cambridge history of Hellenistic philosophy, The / B171.C36 1999

Cambridge history of seventeenth-century philosophy, The / B801.C35 1998

Cambridge movement: the ecclesiologists and the Gothic revival, The / BX5013.E3.W5

Cambridge Platonists; a study, The / B1133.C2 P6 1971

Camera obscura: of ideology / B823.3.K613 1999

Camphor flame: popular Hinduism and society in India, The / BL1150.F85 1992

Candle in the wind: religion in the Soviet Union / BL940.S65.C36 1989

Cane Ridge, America's Pentecost / BV3774.K4 C65 1991

Canons and decrees of the Council of Trent / BX830 1545.A3.S35

Canons in conflict: negotiating texts in true and false prophecy / BS465.B74 1997

Can't we make moral judgements? / BJ1408.5.M52 1991

Cardinal de La Rochefoucauld: leadership and reform in the French Church / BX4705.L16.B47 1987

Care, autonomy, and justice: feminism and the ethic of care / BJ1475.C57 1996

Career of John Cotton: Puritanism and the American experience, The / BX7260.C79.Z5

Cargo cults and millenarian movements: transoceanic comparisons of new religious movements / BL2620.M4.C37 1990

Caring, a feminine approach to ethics & moral education / BJ1475.N62 1984

Carl Jung and Christian spirituality / BV4501.2.C297 1988

Carnap's construction of the world: the Aufbau and the emergence of logical empiricism / B945.C163.L6336 1998

Cartesian psychology and physical minds: individualism and the sciences of the mind / BD418.3.W54 1995

Case for Christianity, The / BR123.L482

Case for freedom: Machiavellian humanism, A / B785.M24.D36 1997

Cassell's encyclopedia of queer myth, symbol, and spirit: gay, lesbian, bisexual, and transgender lore / BL795.H6.C65 1997

Cassirer, Panofsky, and Warburg: symbol, art, and history / BH221.G34.W37413 1989

Cults in America: a reference handbook / BL2525.L486 1998

Cults of the Roman Empire, The / BL805.T8713 1996

Cultural anthropology and the Old Testament / BS661.O94 1996

Cultural encounters: the impact of the Inquisition in Spain and the New World / BX1735.C84 1991

Cultural intersections in later Chinese Buddhism / BQ4570.A7 C86 2001

Cultural significance of the Reformation, The / BR307.H643

Cultural software: a theory of ideology / B823.3.B25 1998

Culture and Christianity: the dialectics of transformation / BR115.C8.C85 1988

Culture and cultural entities: toward a new unity of science / B29.M3673 1984

Culture and modernity: East-West philosophic perspectives / B59.C84 1991

Culture and self: philosophical and religious perspectives, East and West / BD438.5.C85 1997

Culture and the state in late Chosæon Korea / BL1842.C85 1999

Culture of protest: religious activism and the U.S. sanctuary movement, The / BV4466.C63 1993

Culture war and ethical theory / BJ1012.V66 1997

Cumulative index to Kierkegaard's writings / B4375.K54 2000

Cunning of reason, The / BC177.H65 1987

Cynics: the cynic movement in antiquity and its legacy, The / B508.C94 1996

Daddy King: an autobiography / BX6449.K56.A3

Daily life of the Egyptian gods / BL2450.G6.M4413 1996

Daily life of the Greek gods, The / BL782.S5713 2000

Dance of Siva: religion, art and poetry in South Indai, The / BL1218.S62 1996

Dancing with Siva: Hinduism's contemporary catechism = Sibena saha nartanam: sanatanadharmaprasnottarm / BL1151.3.S93 1993

Dao de jing: the book of the way / BL1900.L35 R628 2001

Daoist identity: history, lineage, and ritual / B127.T3 D36 2002

Daoist theory of Chinese thought: a philosophical interpretation, A / B126.H277 1992

Dark lord: cult images and the Hare Krishnas in America, The / BL1285.835.U6.S55 1987

Dark nature: a natural history of evil / BJ1406.W37 1995

Dark riddle: Hegel, Nietzsche, and the Jews / B2949.J84.Y68 1998

Darkness and the light: a philosopher reflects upon his fortunate career and those who made it possible, The / B945.H354.A3 1990

Darsán: seeing the divine image in India / BL1205.E25 1998

Darwin machines and the nature of knowledge / BD161.P6 1994

Darwin, Marx, and Freud: their influence on moral theory / BJ319.D37 1984

Darwinian natural right: the biological ethics of human nature / BJ1311.A66 1998

Darwinism in philosophy, social science, and policy / B828.2.R66 2000

David Baumgardt and ethical hedonism / BJ1491.L48 1989

David Hume and the problem of reason: recovering the human sciences / B1499.R4.D35 1990

David Hume's theory of mind / B1499.M47.F55 1990

David story: a translation with commentary of 1 and 2 Samuel, The / BS1323.A48 1999

Dawn of Chinese pure land Buddhist doctrine: Ching-ying Hui-yuan's Commentary on the Visualization sutra, The / BQ2025.H853 T36 1990

Dawn of conscience, / BJ132.B7 1934

Dayananda Sarasvati, his life and ideas / BL1255.D3.J67

Dead Philosophers' Cafe: an exchange of letters for children and adults, The / B105.C45.K1513 2000

Death and afterlife: perspectives of world religions / BL504.D33 1991b

Death and life of philosophy, The / B52.G74 1999

Death of Socrates and the life of philosophy: an interpretation of Plato's Phaedo, The / B379.A87 1995

Death of the Messiah: from Gethsemane to the grave: a commentary on the Passion narratives in the four Gospels, The / BS2555.3.B7633 1994

Death, desire, and loss in Western culture / BD444.D42 1998

Deathbound subjectivity / BD223.L56 1989

Decadent subjects: the idea of decadence in art, literature, philosophy, and culture of the fin de siècle in Europe / BH221.E853 B47 2002

Deconstructing Jesus / BT303.2.P75 2000

Deconstructing the mind / BD418.3.S75 1996

Deconstruction as analytic philosophy / B2430.D484.W475 2000

Deconstruction in a nutshell: a conversation with Jacques Derrida / B809.6.D46 1997

Deduction / BC71.J53 1991

Deep power: the political ecology of wilderness and civilization / BD581.K597 2000

Degrees of knowledge, The / BD162.M273 1959

Dehumanization of art; and other essays on art, culture, and literature, The / BH205.O713 1968

Deleuzism: a metacommentary / Ian Buchanan / B2430.D454.B83 2000

Deliverance to the captives / BV4316.P7.B33

Democratic philosophy and the politics of knowledge / B65.P43 1996

Democratization and the Islamist challenge in the Arab world / BP63.A4.A7247 1997

Five faces of modernity: modernism, avant-garde, decadence, kitsch, postmodernism / BH301.M54.C34 1987

Five great philosophies of life, The / B505.H75

Five Mountains: the Rinzai Zen monastic institution in medieval Japan / BQ9294.4.J3 C64

Fixation of belief and its undoing: changing beliefs through inquiry, The / BD215.L45 1991

Fly and the fly-bottle; encounters with British intellectuals / B1111.M4

Focusing on truth / BD171.J59 1992

Fodor: language, mind, and philosophy / B945.F634 C35 2002

Following Kohlberg: liberalism and the practice of democratic community / BJ55.R44 1997

Food for the Gods: vegetarianism and the world's religions / BL65.V44.B47 1998

Fools, martyrs, traitors: the story of martyrdom in the Western world / BL626.5.S65 1997

For a philosophy of freedom and strife: politics, aesthetics, metaphysics / B3240.F493.F8713 1998

For God and the fatherland: religion and politics in Argentina / BX1462.2.B84 1995

For the sake of simple folk: popular propaganda for the German Reformation / BR307.S464 1994

For the union of Evangelical Christendom: the irony of the Reformed Episcopalians / BX6065.G84 1994

Forgetting of air in Martin Heidegger, The / B3279.H49.I7513 1999

Forgiveness and mercy / BJ1476.M87 1988

Forgiveness and reconciliation: religion, public policy & conflict transformation / BJ1476.F67 2001

Forgiveness and revenge / BJ1476.G685 2002

Forgiveness: a philosophical study / BJ1476.H33 1991

Formal ethics / BJ1012.G44 1996

Formal logic / BC108.P8 1962

Formal logic: its scope and limits / BC71.J38 1981

Formal methods; an introduction to symbolic logic and to the study of effective operations in arithmetic and logic / BC135.B45

Formalism and Marxism / BH41.B45

Formation of hell: death and retribution in the ancient and early Christian worlds, The / BT836.2.B47 1993

Formation of the moral self / BV1464.V45 1998

Forms of things unknown; essays towards an aesthetic philosophy, The / BH21.R4 1960

Fortunes of the Courtier: the European reception of Castiglione's Cortegiano, The / BJ1604.C33 B87 1996

Foucault and religion: spiritual corporality and political spirituality / B2430.F724.C365 1999

Foucault: an introduction / B2430.F724.F5713 1992

Foucault: historian or philosopher? / B2430.F724.O43 1989

Foundations of aesthetics, The / BH201.O5 1948

Foundations of Christian faith: an introduction to the idea of Christianity / BT75.2.R3313

Foundations of ethics; the Gifford lectures delivered in the University of Aberdeen, 1935-6, / BJ1011.R75

Foundations of Kierkegaard's vision of community: religion, ethics, and politics in Kierkegaard / B4378.E8.F68 1992

Foundations of knowledge, The / BD161.M387 1995

Foundations of philosophical semantics, The / B820.P58 1984

Four Gospels and the one Gospel of Jesus Christ: an investigation of the collection and origin of the Canonical Gospels, The / BS2555.2.H46 2000

Four modern philosophers: Carnap, Wittgenstein, Heidegger, Sartre / B3279.H49.N33

Four political treatises of the Yellow Emperor: original Mawangdui texts with complete English translations and an introduction, The / B126.C4466 1998

Four views of time in ancient philosophy / B187.T55.C3

Fox and the jewel: shared and private meanings in contemporary Japanese inari worship, The / BL2211.I5.S69 1999

Fragile "we": ethical implications of Heidegger's Being and Time, The / B3279.H48.S489 1994

Fragility of goodness: luck and ethics in Greek tragedy and philosophy, The / BJ192.N87 2001

Fragmentation and redemption: essays on gender and the human body in Medieval religion / BT741.2.B95 1990

Fragmentation of reason: preface to a pragmatic theory of cognitive evaluation, The / BD161.S685 1990

Fragments of the spirit: nature, violence, and the renewal of creation / BT121.2.W32 1996

Frame of order: an outline of Elizabethan belief taken from treatises of the late sixteenth century, The / B776.E5.W5 1976

France and the cult of the Sacred Heart: an epic tale for modern times / BX2157.J57 2000

Francis Bacon / B1197.Z34 1998

Francis Bacon, the first statesman of science / B1198.C7

Francis Bacon: the history of a character assassination / B1197.M47 1996

Francis Bacon's idea of science and the maker's knowledge tradition / B1198.P44 1988

Francis of Assisi / BX4700.F6.H595 2001

Frank Buchman's secret / BJ10.M6 H567 1962

Free action / BJ1461.M4

Free and faithful in Christ: moral theology for clergy and laity / BJ1249.H36

Free church, a holy nation: Abraham Kuyper's American public theology, A / BR115.P7 B656 2001

Free religion, an American faith / BL2760.P4

Free will / BJ1461.F75 2003

Free will and determinism / BJ1461.B47

Free will: an historical and philosophical introduction / BJ1460.D55 1999

Freedom and belief / BJ1461.S77 1986

Freedom and determinism / BJ1461.L4

Freedom and fulfillment: philosophical essays / BJ1012.F42 1992

Freedom and reason / BJ1012.H3

Freedom and responsibility / BJ1461.B64 1998

Freedom and responsibility: / BJ1451.M65

Freedom from necessity: the metaphysical basis of responsibility / BJ1451.B47 1987

Freedom of the individual / BJ1461.H27

Freedom of the will, The / BJ1461.F3 1960

Freedom within reason / BJ1461.W64 1990

Freedom, Foucault, and the subject of America / BJ352.Q56 1991

Frege: a critical introduction / B3245.F24.N66 2001

Frege's logical theory / B3245.F24.S7

French free-thought from Gassendi to Voltaire, / B1815.S68 1969

French philosophy in the twentieth century / B2421.G88 2001

Freudian wish and its place in ethics, The / BJ45.H7

Freud's Moses: Judaism terminable and interminable / BS580.M6.Y47 1991

Friars: the impact of the early mendicant movement on Western society, The / BX2820.L38 1994

Friends of God and prophets: a feminist theological reading of the communion of saints / BT972.J57 1998

Friendship and moral education: twin pillars of philosophy for children / B105.C45 R44 1999

From a broken web: separation, sexism, and self / BD450.K368 1986

From a logical point of view; 9 logico-philosophical essays / BC71.Q48 1963

From Africa to Zen: an invitation to world philosophy / B73.F76 1993

From alms to liberation: the Catholic Church, the theologians, poverty, and politics / BV639.P6.L48 1989

From civil rights to Black liberation: Malcolm X and the Organization of Afro-American Unity / BP223.Z8.L5772 1994

From classic to romantic; premises of taste in eighteenth-century England, / BH221.G7.B36

From death to rebirth: ritual and conversion in antiquity / BL805.F56 1997

From deluge to discourse: myth, history, and the generation of Chinese fiction / BL1825.P37 1996

From Descartes to Hume: continental metaphysics and the development of modern philosophy / B801.L63

From east to west: odyssey of a soul / BL51.B554 2000

From epic to canon: history and literature in ancient Israel / BS1171.2.C77 1998

From Hegel to Marx: studies in the intellectual development of Karl Marx / B3305.M74.H6 1994

From Marx to Hegel / B809.8.L499

From metaphysics to ethics: a defence of conceptual analysis / B808.5.J33 1998

From morality to virtue / BJ1012.S5165 1992

From Nietzsche to Wittgenstein: the problem of truth and nihilism in the modern world / B828.3.M27 1989

From physics to politics: the metaphysical foundations of modern philosophy / BD171.T69 1999

From Platonism to Neoplatonism / B517.M4

From primitives to Zen; a thematic sourcebook of the history of religions / BL74.E4 1967

From religion to philosophy; a study in the origins of western speculation / B188.C6 1957

From soul to self / BD421.F76 1999

From suffering to God: exploring our images of God in the light of suffering / BT732.7.S53 1994

From synagogue to church: public services and offices in the earliest Christian communities / BV648.B83 1992

From text to action / B2430.R553.D813 1991

From the closed world to the infinite universe / BD511.K67

From the ground up: Mennonite contributions to international peacebuilding / BX8128.P4

From this verse: 365 Sscriptures that changed the world / BV4811.M578 1998

From women's experience to feminist theology / BT83.55.H64 1995

Frontiers of Catholicism: the politics of ideology in a liberal world, The / BX1406.2.B865 1992

Function of reason, The / BD41.W5

Fundamentalism, mythos, and world religions / BL238.N54 1993

Fundamentalisms comprehended / BL238.F83 1991 vol. 5

Fundamentalisms observed / BL238.F83 1991 vol. 1

Fundamentals of yoga; a handbook of theory, practice, and application / B132.Y6.M5

Further reflections on things at hand: a reader / B128.C53 H7513 1991

Future of an illusion, The / BL53.F67 1962

Future of Islam in the Middle East: fundamentalism in Egypt, Algeria, and Saudi Arabia, The / BP63.A65.F35 1997

Future of religions, The / BR123.T54

Future: an essay on God, temporality, and truth, The / BD638.L83 1989

Fuzhou Protestants and the making of a modern China, 1857-1927 / BR1287.D86 2001

Fuzzy thinking: the new science of fuzzy logic / BC108.K59 1993

G.E. Moore / B1647.M74.B35 1990

Gadamer and hermeneutics / BD241.G34 1991

Game of the name: introducing logic, language, and mind, The / BC199.N3.M33 1989

Gate to perfection: the idea of peace in Jewish thought, The / BM538.P3.H6613 1994

Gateway to wisdom: Taoist and Buddhist contemplative and healing yogas adapted for Western students of the way / BL1923.B57

Gatherings in diaspora: religious communities and the new immigration / BL632.5.U5.G37 1998

Gender & Jewish studies: a curriculum guide / BM729.W6 G445 1994

Gender and genius: towards a feminist aesthetics / BH301.C84.B37 1990

Gender and heresy: women and men in Lollard communities, 1420-1530 / BX4901.2.M37 1995

Gender identities in American Catholicism / BX1405.G46 2001

Gender/body/knowledge: feminist reconstructions of being and knowing / BD450.G4455 1989

Genealogies of religion: discipline and reasons of power in Christianity and Islam / BL50.A85 1993

Genealogy of the way: the construction and uses of the Confucian tradition in late imperial China / B5233.C6 W55 1995

General councils: a history of the twenty-one general councils from Nicaea to Vatican II, The / BX825.B45 2002

General ethics / BJ1012.H45 1988

General philosophy / BD21.T7

General theory of value, its meaning and basic principles construed in terms of interest / BD232.P45 1950

Generous lives: American Catholic women today / BX2347.8.W6.R43 1992

Genes, genesis, and God: values and their origins in natural and human history / BJ1311.R65 1998

Genres in dialogue: Plato and the construct of philosophy / B395.N54 1996

Gentleman in America; a literary study in American culture, The / BJ1601.C2

Genuine individuals and genuine communities: a Roycean public philosophy / B945.R64.K44 1997

Geography of faith; conversations between Daniel Berrigan, when underground, and Robert Coles, The / BX4705.B3845.A294 1971

George Grant and the subversion of modernity: art, philosophy, politics, religion, and education / B995.G724 G45 1996

George Santayana, literary philosopher / B945.S24 S56 2000

George Sylvester Morris: his philosophical career and theistic idealism / B945.M54.J6 1948a

German aesthetic and literary criticism / BH221.G3.G47 1984

German and Scandinavian Protestantism, 1700-1918 / BX4844.H66 1995

German dictionary of philosophical terms = Wörterbuch philosophischer Fachbegriffe Englisch / B43.W29 1997

German philosophy and politics / B2741.D5

German philosophy: an introduction / B2521.R63 1988

Germanization of early medieval Christianity: a sociohistorical approach to religious transformation, The / BR203.R87 1994

Gershom Scholem: Kabbalah and counter-history / BM755.S295.B5

Gift from the sea / BD435.L52 1955a

Gift of death, The / B2430.D483.D6613 1995

Gilles Deleuze: vitalism and multiplicity / B2430.D454.M35 1998

Give me that online religion / BL37.B73 2001

Giving and taking of life: essays ethical, The / BJ1249.B87 1989

Global ethic for global politics and economics, A / BJ1125.K8713 1998

Glorious battle: the cultural politics of Victorian Anglo-Catholicism / BX5121.R44 1996

Gnosis: the nature and history of gnosticism / BT1390.R7713 1983

Go and do likewise: Jesus and ethics / BS2417.E8.S67 1999

God after Darwin: a theology of evolution / BT712.H38 2000

God and design: the teleological argument and modern science / BD541.G63 2003

God and evil, / BJ1406.J6

God and globalization / BJ1275.G63 2000

God and Greek philosophy: studies in the early history of natural theology / B398.G6 G47 1994

God and inscrutable evil: in defense of theism and atheism / BT102.O29 1998

God and the cosmologists / BD511.J35 1989

God and the excluded: visions and blind spots in contemporary theology / BT78.R48 2001

God and the nations / BT96.2.H34 1995

God and the philosophers: the reconciliation of faith and reason / BR102.A1.G63 1994

God as otherwise than being: toward a semantics of the gift / BT103.S37 2002

God at the grass roots: the Christian right in the 1994 elections / BR526.G63 1995

God for a secular society: the public relevance of theology / BR115.W6.M45413 1999

God gave us the right: conservative Catholic, Evangelical Protestant, and Orthodox Jewish women grapple with feminism / BT704.M355 1999

God in action / BT78.B3 1963

God in search of man: a philosophy of Judaism / BM560.H46

God in the details: American religion in popular culture / BL2525.G625 2001

God in the dock; essays on theology and ethics, / BR85.L484

God in the White House: how religion has changed the modern presidency / BR516.H78 1988

God is dead: secularization in the West / BL2747.8.B78 2002

God of grace and God of glory: an account of the theology of Jonathan Edwards / BX7260.E3.H59

God of Israel and Christian theology, The / BT93.S35 1996

Hurrying toward Zion: universities, divinity schools, and American Protestantism / BV4030.C46 1995

Husserl and the search for certitude / B3279.H94.K64

Hymns of the Anglo-Saxon church: a study and edition of the Durham Hymnal, The / BX1999.85.A3.D876 1996

I and Thou / B3213.B83I213 1970

I ching; Book of changes / BL1830.I23.L4 1964

I think, therefore I laugh: the flip side of philosophy / BC71.P38 2000

Iberian fathers: Pacian of Barcelona and Orosius of Braga: [writings] / BR60.F3.I27 1999

Ibn 'Arabi and modern thought: the history of taking metaphysics seriously / B753.I24 C58 2002

Idea into image: essays on ancient Egyptian thought / B141.H6713 1992

Idea of Christ in the Gospels; or, God in man, a critical essay, The / BT201.S263

Idea of Christian charity: a critique of some contemporary conceptions, The / BV4639.G67 1990

Idea of freedom, The / B105.L45.A3

Idea of human rights: four inquiries, The / BL65.H78.P47 1998

Idea of the good in Platonic-Aristotelian philosophy, The / B398.E8 G2913 1986

Idea of the postmodern: a history, The / B831.2.B47 1995

Ideal code, real world: a rule-consequentialist theory of morality / BJ1031.H755 2000

Idealism as modernism: Hegelian variations / B823.P55 1997

Idealism: a critical survey / B823.E8 1974

Ideals and illusions: on reconstruction and deconstruction in contemporary critical theory / B809.3.M33 1991

Ideas of human nature: an historical introduction / BD450.T668 1999

Ideas: general introduction to pure phenomenology / B3279.H972i

Identity & reality / BD162.M43 1962

Identity and difference / BD236.H413 1969

Identity in question, The / BD236.I42 1995

Identity of liberation in Latin American thought: Latin American historicism and the phenomenology of Leopoldo Zea, The / B1008.L53.S24 1999

Identity of man, The / BD450.B653 2002

Identity, character, and morality: essays in moral psychology / BJ45.I34 1990

Identity, consciousness, and value / BD450.U46 1990

Ideological dilemmas: a social psychology of everyday thinking / B823.3.I285 1988

Ideology of the aesthetics, The / BH151.E2 1990

Idler and his works, and other essays, The / B945.S21.C6

If I should die / BL504.I3 2001

If it wasn't for the women--: Black women's experience and womanist culture in church and community / BR563.N4.G54 2001

If P, then Q: conditionals and the foundations of reasoning / BC199.C56 S26 2003

Ignatius of Loyola: the psychology of a saint / BX4700.L7.M54 1992

Illness and health care in the ancient Near East: the role of the temple in Greece, Mesopotamia, and Israel / BL65.M4 A83 1995

Illusion of immortality, The / BT921.L167 1965

Illusion of the epoch; Marxism-Leninism as a philosophical creed, The / B809.8.A32 1957

Illustrated encyclopedia of active new religions, sects, and cults, The / BL80.2.B385 1993

Illustrated guide to the Bible, The / BS635.2.P67 1998

Illustrated world's religions: a guide to our wisdom traditions, The / BL80.2.S6455 1994

Image; knowledge in life and society, The / BD648.B66

Images of human nature: a Sung portrait / BD450.M863 1988

Images of the immortal: the cult of Lü Dongbin at the Palace of Eternal Joy / BL1941.5.J84 K37 1999

Images, miracles, and authority in Asian religious traditions / BL1035.I43 1998

Imagination and ethical ideals: prospects for a unified philosophical and psychological understanding / BJ1031.T54 1994

Imagination, understanding, and the virtue of liberality / BJ1431.N67 1996

Imaginative world of the Reformation, The / BR305.2.M35 2001

Imagining grace: liberating theologies in the slave narrative tradition / BT83.57.C68 2000

Imagining karma: ethical transformation in Amerindian, Buddhist, and Greek rebirth / BQ4485.O24 2002

Imagining the sacred: soundings in world religions / BL80.2.R86 1998

Imago Dei: a study of C. G. Jung's psychology of religion / BL53.H378

Immanuel Kant reader, An / B2758 .B5

Immanuel Kant's moral theory / B2799.E8.S83 1989

Immaterial self: a defence of the Cartesian dualist conception of the mind, The / BD418.3.F67 1991

Immigrants and their Church / BX1407.I45.L57 1989

Immortal longings: versions of transcending humanity / B56.K47 1997

Immortality / BD421.M58

imone Weil and the intellect of grace / B2430.W474.F54 1999

Imperative of responsibility: in search of an ethics for the technological age, The / BJ1453.J6613 1984

Imperative, The / BC199.C5.L56 1998

Imperial metaphor: popular religion in China, The / BL1802.F48 1992

Implications of induction, The / BC91.C63

Japanese religion and society: paradigms of structure and change / BL2203.D37 1992

Japanese religions: past and present / BL2202.R43 1993

Jean-Paul Sartre and the politics of reason: a theory of history / B2430.S34.D63 1993

Jean-Paul Sartre: politics and culture in Postwar France / B2430.S34.S369 1999

Jean-Paul Sartre: the existentialist ethic / B2430.S34.G7

Jerusalem Bible, The / BS195.J4 1966

Jesuits, a history, The / BX3706.2.M57 1981

Jesuits: their spiritual doctrine and practice; a historical study, The / BX3703.G813

Jesus and the angels: angelology and the christology of the Apocalypse of John / BT198.C32 1997

Jesus and the politics of interpretation / BT303.2.S33 2000

Jesus as mother: studies in the spirituality of the High Middle Ages / BV4490.B96 1982

Jesus at thirty: a psychological and historical portrait / BT590.P9.M55 1997

Jesus Christ in modern thought / BT198.M295 1990

Jesus Christ liberator: a critical Christology for our time / BT202.B5313

Jesus in contemporary scholarship / BT303.2.B586 1994

Jesus outside the New Testament: an introduction to the ancient evidence / BT297.V36 2000

Jesus the Christ: the historical origins of christological doctrine / BT198.D25 1991

Jesus then & now: images of Jesus in history and Christology / BT203.J47 2001

Jesus through the centuries: his place in the history of culture / BT198.P44 1985

Jesus two thousand years later / BT303.2 .J47 2000

Jesus, symbol of God / BT202.H24 1999

Jesus, the teacher within / BT202.F695 2000

Jesus: a revolutionary biography / BT301.2.C77 1994

Jew and Gentile in the ancient world: attitudes and interactions from Alexander to Justinian / BM534.F45 1993

Jew within: self, family, and community in America, The / BM205.C62 2000

Jewish & Christian mysticism: an introduction / BM723.C64 1994

Jewish and Islamic philosophy: crosspollinations in the classic age / B755.G66 1999

Jewish Bible after the Holocaust: a re-reading, The / BS1186.F36 1990

Jewish Bible personages in the New Testament / BS2545.J44.C64 1988

Jewish continuity in America: creative survival in a free society / BM205.K38 1998

Jewish encyclopedia of moral and ethical issues, The / BJ1285.A53 1994

Jewish ethics for the twenty-first century: living in the image of God / BJ1287.A155.S54 2000

Jewish liturgy: a comprehensive history / BM660.E513 1993

Jewish perspectives on Christianity: Leo Baeck, Martin Buber, Franz Rosenzweig, Will Herberg, and Abraham J. Heschel / BM535.J465 1990

Jewish religion: a companion, The / BM50.J28 1995

Jewish way in death and mourning, The / BM712.L3 2000

Jewish women in historical perspective / BM729.W6 J49 1991

Jewish world in the time of Jesus, The / BM176.G82

Jewish writings of the Second Temple period: Apocrypha, Pseudepigrapha, Qumran, sectarian writings, Philo, Josephus / BM485.L57 1984 vol. 2

Jews in the center: conservative synagogues and their members / BM197.5.J48 2000

Jews in the Hellenistic world: Philo / B689.Z7.W54 1989

Jih⁻ad: the origin of holy war in Islam / BP182.F5 1999

Jihad in classical and modern Islam: a reader / BP182.P48 1996

Johannine world: reflections on the theology of the Fourth Gospel and contemporary society, The / BS2615.5.H38 1996

John Calvin: a sixteenth-century portrait / BX9418.B715 1988

John Colet / BR754.C6.G57 1989

John Dewey and Arthur F. Bentley: a philosophical correspondence, 1932-1951 / B945.D44.A43

John Dewey and self-realization / B945.D44.R6 1963

John Dewey and the lessons of art / B945.D4.J33 1998

John Dewey in perspective / B945.D44.G4

John Dewey, an intellectual portrait / B945.D44.H47 1971

John Dewey: rethinking our time / B945.D4.B65 1998

John Hus and the Czech reform / BX4917.S7 1966

John Keble, saint of Anglicanism / BX5199.K3.G75 1987

John Knox / BX9223.M37 2000

John Locke and the ethics of belief / B1298.R4.W65 1996

John Locke and the way of ideas, / B1297.Y6 1968

John Scottus Eriugena / B765.J34.C33 2000

John Stuart Mill: a mind at large / B1607.A95

John Williamson Nevin: American theologian / BX9593.N4.W46 1997

John Wyclif; a study of the English medieval church, / BX4905.W6 1966

Joining children on the spiritual journey: nurturing a life of faith / BV1475.2.S776 1998

Jonathan Edwards confronts the gods: Christian theology, Enlightenment religion, and non-Christian faiths / BT1180.M34 2000

Jonathan Edwards, religious tradition, and American culture / BX7260.E3.C64 1995

Joseph Smith III: pragmatic prophet / BX8678.S6.L38 1988

Josiah Royce: selected writings / B945.R61 1988

Liberation from self: a theory of personal autonomy / BD450.B438 1995

Liberty, equality, and law: selected Tanner lectures on moral philosophy / BJ55.L53 1987

Life abundant: rethinking theology and economy for a planet in peril / BR115.E3.M315 2001

Life and thought of Josiah Royce, The / John Clendenning, The / B945.R64 C54 1999

Life and writings of Giambattista Vico, The / B3583.A3

Life in the family: an oral history of the Children of God / BP605.C38 C48 2000

Life of Bertrand Russell, The / B1649.R94.C55 1976

Life of Buddha as legend and history, The / BQ882.T45 2000

Life of David Hume, The / B1497.M65 1980

Life of forms in art, The / BH202.F63 1948

Life of Ibn Sina; a critical edition and annotated translation, The / B751.A5 S5 1974

Life of John Calvin: a study in the shaping of Western culture, A / BX9418.M29 1990

Life of John Stuart Mill, The / B1606.P3

Life of Muhammad: a translation of Ishaq's Sirat rasul Allah, The / BP75.I25 1997

Life of reason, The / B945.S23 L7 1998

Life of reason; Hobbes, Locke, Bolingbroke, The / B1131.J3

Life of the Buddha, according to the ancient texts and monuments of India, The / BL1470.F623

Life of the mind, The / B29.A73

Life— scientific philosophy: phenomenology of life and the sciences of life / B3279.H94.A129 Vol.59,etc

Life without principles: reconciling theory and practice / BJ1031.M312 1996

Life, sex, and ideas: the good life without God / BJ1360.G72 2003

Limits of love: some theological explorations, The / BJ1251.M49 1987

Limits of reason, The / B53.B56

Literary criticism and the Gospels: the theoretical challenge / BS2555.5.M66 1989

Literary criticism for New Testament critics / BS2361.2.P47

Literary essays / B3209.B751.J67213 1998

Literary guide to the Bible, The / BS535.L54 1987

Literate experience: the work of knowing in seventeenth-century English writing / B1133.K56 B37 2002

Literature suppressed on religious grounds / BL65.C45.B35 1998

Little saint / BX4700.F37

Lives of Michel Foucault: a biography, The / B2430.F724.M327 1993

Lives of the mind: the use and abuse of intelligence from Hegel to Wodehouse / B791.K535 2002

Living across and through skins: transactional bodies, pragmatism, and feminism / B105.B64 S85 2001

Living in the lap of the Goddess: the feminist spirituality movement in America / BL625.7.E45 1993

Living thoughts of Kierkegaard, The / B4372.E5.A8

Living without law: an ethnography of Quaker decision-making, dispute avoidance, and dispute resolution / BX7748.D43

Living without philosophy: on narrative, rhetoric, and morality / BJ42.L48 1998

Locke and French materialism / B1925.M25.Y64 1991

Locke dictionary, A / B1297.Y64 1993

Logic / BC108.S2 1984

Logic and contemporary rhetoric: the use of reason in everyday life / BC175.K25 1988

Logic and criticism / BH39.R5

Logic and knowledge; essays, 1901-1950 / B1649.R93.L6

Logic and language (first series): essays / BC71.E67 1978

Logic and nature / BC108.S9 1955

Logic and other nonsense: the case of Anselm and his God / B765.A84.B46 1993

Logic and philosophy: an integrated introduction / BC51.B664 1993

Logic and philosophy; selected readings / BC6.I8

Logic and rhetoric in England, 1500-1700 / BC38.H6 1961

Logic and the basis of ethics / BJ37.P7

Logic and the nature of reality / BD331.K3 1967

Logic and the philosophy of language / BC60.L64 1988

Logic book, The / BC135.B435

Logic for mathematicians / BC135.R58 1978

Logic of concept expansion, The / BC199.C55 B89 2002

Logic of human personality: an onto-logical account, The / BD450.O376 1997

Logic of induction, The / BC99.P65.M6713 1988

Logic of perfection, and other essays in neoclassical metaphysics, The / BD573.H29

Logic of provability, The / BC199.M6.B65 1993

Logic of questions and answers, The / BC199.Q4.B44

Logic of real arguments, The / BC177.F57 1988

Logic of society: a philosophical study, The / B63.A3

Logic of the history of ideas, The / B822.B48 1999

Logic of the sciences and the humanities, The / BC71.N6

Logic primer / BC108.A543 2001

Logic with trees: an introduction to symbolic logic / BC135.H68 1997

Logic without metaphysics, and other essays in the philosophy of science / BC50.N23

Logic, logic, and logic / BC51.B58 1998

Logic, semantics, metamathematics: papers from 1923 to 1938 / BC135.T35 1983

Logic, the theory of inquiry, / BC50.D43

Logical basis of metaphysics, The / BC51.D85 1991

Logical empiricism: historical & contemporary perspectives / B824.6.L6225 2003

Logical essays / B945.R63.L6

Logical forms: an introduction to philosophical logic / BC135.S14 1991

Logical foundations of probability / BC141.C3 1962

Logical properties: identity, existence, predication, necessity, truth / BC71.M36 2000

Logical syntax of language, The / BC135.C323

Logical thinking / BC108.P89

Logics of disintegration: post-structuralist thought and the claims of critical theory / B841.4.D49 1987

Lollards and reformers: images and literacy in late medieval religion / BX4901.2.A84 1984

Long loneliness: the autobiography of Dorothy Day, The / BX4668.D3.A33 1952

Looking for God in the suburbs: the religion of the American dream and its critics, 1945-1965 / BR526.H83 1994

Lord of the three in one: the spread of a cult in Southeast China / BL1802.D43 1998

Losing our virtue: why the church must recover its moral vision / BR115.C8.W43 1998

Lost world of Thomas Jefferson: with a new preface, The / B878.B6 1993

Lotus Sutra in Japanese culture, The / BQ2057.L66 1989

Lotus Sutra, The / BQ2052.E5 W38 1993

Love analyzed / BD436.L68 1997

Love and beauty / BD436.S54 1989

Love and Saint Augustine / BV4639.A6513 1995

Love of learning and the desire for God: a study of monastic culture, The / BX2470.L413 1982

Love, freedom, and society / BD436.M8

Love: its forms, dimensions, and paradoxes / BD436.D54 1998

Love's knowledge: essays on philosophy and literature / BJ46.N87 1990

Loyalty: an essay on the morality of relationships / BJ1533.L8.F54 1993

Lu Hsiang shan ... a twelfth century Chinese idealist philosopher, / B128.L83.H8 1944

Lubavitcher women in America: identity and activism in the postwar era / BM729.W6.M67 1998

Lucifer principle: a scientific expedition into the forces of history, The / BD450.B526 1995

Luck: the brilliant randomness of everyday life / BD595.R47 1995

Lucretius and scientific thought / B577.L64.W5

Ludwig Feuerbach and the outcome of classical German philosophy, / B2973.E5 1934a

Ludwig Wittgenstein, a memoir / B3376.W564.M2 1958

Luminous passage: the practice and study of Buddhism in America / BQ732.P736 1999

Lustre of our country: the American experience of religious freedom, The / BR516.N59 1998

Luther and Erasmus: Free will and salvation / BJ1461.L8

Luther on women: a sourcebook / BR333.3.L88 2002

Luther: man between God and the Devil / BR325.O2713 1989

Luther: right or wrong? An ecumenical-theological study of Luther's major work, The bondage of the will, / BJ1460.L85.M23

Lutheran churches in the world: a handbook / BX8009.B33 1989

Lutheranism: the theological movement and its confessional writings / BX8065.2.G74

Lydia's impatient sisters: a feminist social history of early Christianity / BR195.W6.S3613 1995

Lying: moral choice in public and private life / BJ1421.B64

Lyotard: towards a postmodern philosophy / B2430.L964W55 1998

Lyotard: writing the event / B2430.L964.B46 1988

Maccabees, Zealots, and Josephus; an inquiry into Jewish nationalism in the Greco-Roman period / BM176.F37 1956

Machiavelli and us / B785.M24.A48 1999

Macmillan illustrated encyclopedia of myths & legends, The / BL303.C67 1989

Made in America: self-styled success from Horatio Alger to Oprah Winfrey / BJ1611.D36 1997

Madwoman's reason: the concept of the appropriate in ethical thought, The / BJ1418.5.H65 1998

Magical arrows: the Maori, the Greeks, and the folklore of the universe / BD511.S37 1992

Maimonides and St. Thomas on the limits of reason / B759.M34 D62 1995

Maimonides' ethics: the encounter of philosophic and religious morality / B759.M34.W45 1991

Maimonides on Judaism and the Jewish people / B759.M34.K44 1991

Maimonides reader, A / BM545.A45T9 1972

Major trends in Jewish mysticism / BM723.S35 1961

Major trends in Mexican philosophy / B1016.M413

Makers of contemporary Islam / BP70.E86 2001

Making a heart for God: a week inside a Catholic monastery / BX2525.T733

Making a necessity of virtue: Aristotle and Kant on virtue / B491.E7 S44 1997

Making history: agency, structure, and change in social theory / BD450.C23 1988

Making Muslim space in North America and Europe / BP67.A1.M34 1996

Making of a Christian empire: Lactantius & Rome, The / BR65.L26.D54 2000

Making of a mystic: seasons in the life of Teresa of Avila, The / BX4700.T4.G76 1993

Making of a philosopher: my insider's journey through twentieth century philosophy, The / B804.M355 2001

Making of an enterprise: the Society of Jesus in Portugal, its empire, and beyond, 1540-1750, The / BX3742.A1.A53 1996

Modernism as a philosophical problem: on the dissatisfactions of European high culture / B803.P57 1999

Modernist Islam, 1840-1940: a sourcebook / BP60.M55 2002

Modernity and the hegemony of vision / B846.M63 1993

Modernity, aesthetics, and the bounds of art / BH181.M36 1990

Modes of scepticism: ancient texts and modern interpretations, The / B837.A55 1985

Modes of thought, / B1674.W37.M6

Moment of change: a systematic history in the philosophy of space and time, The / BD632.S645 1998

Monastic order in England; a history of its development from the times of St. Dunstan to the Fourth Lateran Council, 940-1216, The / BX2592.K57 1963

Monastic revival and regional identity in early Normandy / BX2613.P68 1997

Moral action and Christian ethics / BJ1190.P67 1995

Moral anatomy and moral reasoning / BJ319.H276 1993

Moral and political philosophy of David Hume, The / B1498.S8

Moral appraisability: puzzles, proposals, and perplexities / BJ1461.H26 1998

Moral codes and social structure in ancient Greece: a sociology of Greek ethics from Homer to the Epicureans and Stoics / BJ161.B78 1996

Moral concepts; / BJ21.F4

Moral development and behavior: theory, research, and social issues / BJ21.M58

Moral development in the professions: psychology and applied ethics / BJ1725.M67 1994

Moral differences: truth, justice, and conscience in a world of conflict / BJ1012.M54 1992

Moral dilemmas / BJ1031.S55 1988

Moral dilemmas and moral theory / BJ1031.M665 1996

Moral discourse and practice: some philosophical approaches / BJ1012.D325 1997

Moral domain: essays in the ongoing discussion between philosophy and the social sciences, The / BJ1114.Z8713 1990

Moral expertise: studies in practical and professional ethics / BJ37.M818 1990

Moral foundation of rights, The / BJ1031.S86 1987

Moral freedom: the impossible idea that defines the way we live now / BJ352.W65 2001

Moral gap: Kantian ethics, human limits, and God's assistance, The / BJ1275.H24 1996

Moral imagination: implications of cognitive science for ethics / BJ1031.J644 1993

Moral knowledge / BJ1031.G65 1988

Moral knowledge and ethical character / BJ1012.A93 1997

Moral knowledge?: new readings in moral epistemology / BJ1012.M633 1996

Moral law; Kant's Groundwork of the metaphysic of morals, The / B2766.E6.P3 1967

Moral life: an introductory reader in ethics and literature, The / BJ1025.M665 2004

Moral limits of modernity: love, inequality, and oppression, The / BJ1031.S42 1991

Moral obligation; essays and lectures / BJ1451.P7

Moral perception and particularity / BJ1031.B65 1994

Moral personhood: an essay in the philosophy of moral psychology / BJ1031.S37 1990

Moral philosophy; an historical and critical survey of the great systems / BJ72.M313

Moral problem, The / BJ1031.S64 1995

Moral progress: a process critique of MacIntyre / B1647.M124.B45 2000

Moral realism and the foundations of ethics / BJ1012.B676 1989

Moral realities: an essay in philosophical psychology / BJ1012.P633 1991

Moral reasons / BJ1012.D263 1993

Moral relativism and moral objectivity / BJ1012.H316 1996

Moral relativity / BJ1031.W65 1984

Moral scepticism / BJ1031.D67 1990

Moral self, The / BJ45.M67 1993

Moral sense, The / BJ1012.W5375 1993

Moral status of animals, The / BJ1012.C58 1984

Moral strangers, moral acquaintance, and moral friends: connectedness and its conditions / BJ1031.L59 1997

Moral theology: dead ends and alternatives / BJ1249.M713 1990

Moral theory and anomaly / BJ1012.S58 2000

Moral theory of poststructuralism, The / BJ703.D44.M38 1995

Moral theory: a non-consequentialist approach / BJ1012.O34 2000

Moral values in the ancient world / BJ101.F4

Moral vision and tradition: essays in Chinese ethics / BJ117.C83 1998

Moral vision for America, A / BJ1249.B42 1998

Moral vision: an introduction to ethics / BJ1012.M42 1988

Moral writings of John Dewey, The / B945.D41 G68 1994

Morality and action / BJ1012.Q56 1993

Morality and beyond / BJ1251.T47

Morality and cultural differences / BJ52.C66 1999

Morality and human nature: a new route to ethical theory / BJ1031.M354 1990

Morality and imagination: paradoxes of progress / BJ1031.T77 1989

Morality and modernity / BJ301.P66 1991

Morality and moral controversies: readings in moral, social, and political philosophy / BJ1025.M67 2002

On Augustine/ B655.Z7 K29 2001

On authority and revelation: The book on Adler, or A Cycle of ethico-religious essays / B4351.A34.K5

On Bentham and Coleridge / B1574.B34.M5 1951

On Brentano / B3212.Z7 V45 2000

On Carnap / B945.C164 M39 2002

On Chinese body thinking: a cultural hermeneutic / B5231.W846 1997

On Chuang Tzu / BL1900.C576 H63 2001

On creativity / BH301.C84.B65 1998

On de Beauvoir / B2430.B344 S36 2000

On Derrida / B2430.D484 H34 2002

On disobedience and other essays / BD450.F7825

On evil / BJ1400.T4813 1995

On experience, nature, and freedom; representative selections / B945.D41.B4

On Fodor / B945.F634 P74 2001

On Frege / B3245.F24 S24 2001

On Gandhi / B133.G4 G78 2001

On God, space & time / BD555.V76 1999

On Heidegger / B3279.H49 J34 2000

On history / B2799.H7.B43

On human conduct / BJ1581.2.O2

On Husserl / B3279.H94 V45 2000

On Islam; and, Shi`ism / BP163.K3813 1990

On Karol Wojtyla / BX1378.5.S56 2001

On Kripke / B945.K794 P74 2003

On Lao tzu = [Tao] / BL1900.L35 C5439 2000

On Locke / B1296.T46 2001

On Marx / B809.8.L4734 2001

On Mead / B945.M464 D48 2002

On Mill / B1607.A53 2000

On moral considerability: an essay on who morally matters / BJ1012.B47 1998

On Niebuhr: a theological study / BX4827.N5.G55 2001

On Nietzsche / B3317.B41513 1992

On phenomenology and social relations; selected writings / B829.5.S38 1970

On pictures and the words that fail them / BH39.E54 1998

On Quine / B945.Q54 N45 2000

On religion / BL2775.M3983 1964

On religion / BL51.C325 2001

On Ricoeur / B2430.R554 M85 2002

On Rousseau / B2137.S34 2001

On Russell / B1649.R94 O34 2000

On sacred grounds: culture, society, politics, and the formation of the cult of Confucius / BL1858.O5 2002

On Sartre / B2430.S34 K337 2000

On the advantages and disadvantages of ethics and politics / BJ1031.S368 1996

On the basis of morality / B3114.E5.P3

On the Bible; eighteen studies / BS1192.B8

On the contrary: critical essays, 1987-1997 / BD418.3.C473 1998

On the moral nature of the universe: theology, cosmology, and ethics / BD511.M85 1996

On the mystical shape of the godhead: basic concepts in the Kabbalah / BM526.S36413 1991

On the pragmatics of communication / B831.5.H33 1998

On transforming philosophy: a metaphilosophical inquiry / B945.N533.O6 1995

On understanding Japanese religion / BL2202.K49 1987

On what we know we don't know: explanation, theory, linguistics, and how questions shape them / B29.B7442 1992

On Wittgenstein / B3376.W564 H56 2000

On women & Judaism: a view from tradition / BM729.W6.G73

Once and future goddess: a symbol for our time, The / BL473.5.G33 1989

Once to every man: a memoir / BX9225.C6243.A34 1977

One hundred twentieth-century philosophers / B804.O55 1998

One taste: the journals of Ken Wilber / BL73.W55 A3 1999

One thousand years of philosophy: from Ramanuja to Wittgenstein / B72.H317 2000

One-sided arguments: a dialectical analysis of bias / BC177.W3255 1999

Ontology of mind: events, processes, and states, The / BD418.3.S74 1997

Onward Christian soldiers?: the religious right in American politics / BR526.W53 1996

Open society and its enemies, The / B63.P6 1950

Open work, The / BH39.E29213 1989

Opening of vision: nihilism and the postmodern situation, The / B828.3.L39 1988

Order and integration of knowledge, The / BD241.M3

Ordered universes: approaches to the anthropology of religion / BL256.K57 1995

Ordinary people and extraordinary evil: a report on the beguilings of evil / BJ1401.K38 1993

Oriental philosophies / B121.K56 1985

Origen / BR1720.O7.C7613 1989

Origin and authority in seventeenth-century England: Bacon, Milton, Butler / B1131.S65 1994

Origin and development of the moral ideas, The / BJ1311.W5 1924

Original Tao: inward training (nei-yeh) and the foundations of Taoist mysticism / BL1900.N45 R67 1999

Origins and development of classical Hinduism, The / BL1152.3.B37 1989

Origins of analytical philosophy / B808.5.D86 1994

Origins of anti-semitism: attitudes toward Judaism in pagan and Christian antiquity, The / BM535.G33 1983

Origins of Christian morality: the first two centuries, The / BJ1212.M43 1993

Poems to Siva: the hymns of the Tamil saints / BL1218.2.T4813 1989

Poetics, speculation, and judgment: the shadow of the work of art from Kant to phenomenology / BH151.T36 1993

Poetry and philosophy; a study in the thought of John Stuart Mill / B1607.W65

Political ascent: contemporary Islamic movements in North Africa / BP64.A4.N677 1997

Political correctness: for and against / BD175.5.P65.F75 1995

Political Islam: revolution, radicalism, or reform? / BP60.P64 1997

Political uses of ideology, The / B823.5.D78

Political world of the clergy, The / BV4327.J45 1993

Politics and excellence: the political philosophy of Alfarabi / B753.F34 G35 1990

Politics and philosophy of political correctness, The / BD175.5.P65.C46 1992

Politics and religion in the United States / BL2525.C68 1999

Politics and religious authority: American Catholics since the Second Vatican Council / BX1407.P63.G45 1994

Politics and the Catholic church in Nicaragua / BX1442.2.K57 1992

Politics and the churches in Great Britain, 1869 to 1921 / BR759.M27 1987

Politics of friendship / B2430.D483.P6613 1997

Politics of Muslim cultural reform: jadidism in Central Asia, The / BP63.A34.K54 1998

Politics of religion and the religion of politics: looking at Israel, The / BM390.S5112 2000

Politics of religious apostasy: the role of apostates in the transformation of religious movements, The / BL639.5.P64 1998

Politics of religious studies: the continuing conflict with theology in the academy, The / BL41.W47 1999

Politics of skepticism in the ancients, Montaigne, Hume, and Kant, The / B837.L38 1992

Politics of the Reformation in Germany: Jacob Sturm (1489-1553) of Strasbourg, The / BR350.S78.B72 1997

Politics, gender, and the Islamic past: The Legacy of Aisha bint Abi Bakr / BP80.A52.S64 1994

Politics, law, and morality: essays / B4262.E5.W69 2000

Polydoxy: explorations in a philosophy of liberal religion / BL99.R45 1987

Polynesian mythology, / BL2615.G7 1956

Pontius Pilate: the biography of an invented man / BS2520.P55.W76 2000

Poor belong to us: Catholic charities and American welfare, The / BX2347.8.P66.B76 1997

Popes and European revolution, The / BX1361.C45

Popes and the papacy in the early Middle Ages, 476-752, The / BX970.R48

Popper's Open society after fifty years: the continuing relevance of Karl Popper / B63.P62 1999

Popular anti-Catholicism in Mid-Victorian England / BR759.P388 1992

Popular Buddhism in Japan: Shin Buddhist religion & culture / BQ8715.4.A53 1998

Popular dictionary of Islam, A / BP40.N48 1992

Popular religion and liberation: the dilemma of liberation theology / BR600.C26 1990

Popular religion in sixteenth-century England: holding their peace / BR756.M45 1998

Portable age of reason reader, The / B802.B7

Portable Nietzsche;, The / B3312.E52.K3

Portrait of Aristotle, A / B485.G595

Portraits of American continental philosophers / B935.P66 1999

Positivism in Latin America, 1850-1900: Are order and progress reconcilable? / B1008.P6 W66

Possibility of naturalism: a philosophical critique of the contemporary human sciences, The / B828.2.B44 1998

Possible experience: understanding Kant's Critique of pure reason / B2779.C54 1999

Posterior analytics / B441.A5 B37 1994

Post-modern epistemology: language, truth, and body, A / BD214.5.S66 1989

Postmodern ethics / BJ319.B28 1993

Postmodernism and the New Enlightenment / B831.2.M48 1999

Postmodernism rightly understood: the return to realism in American thought / B944.P67.L38 1999

Postmodernism: a reader / B831.2.P675 1993

Postmodernism: the key figures / B831.2.P683 2002

Potentialities: collected essays in philosophy / BH201.A395 1999

Power and Christian ethics / BJ1275.M34 1994

Power and value of philosophical skepticism, The / BD201.W54 1996

Power for good: the history of Trinity Parish, Columbus, Georgia, A / BX5980.C6768 W55 1999

Power in the blood?: the cross in the African American experience / BR563.N4.T39 1998

Power of consciousness and the force of circumstances in Sartre's philosophy, The / B2430.S34.B87 1990

Power of dialogue: critical hermeneutics after Gadamer and Foucault, The / BD241.K6413 1996

Power of God against the guns of government: religious upheaval in Mexico at the turn of the nineteenth century, The / BR615.T65.V36 1998

Power of kings: monarchy and religion in Europe, 1589-1715, The / BR115.K55.M66 1999

Power of myth, The / BL304.C36 1988

Power to speak: feminism, language, God, The / BT83.55.C48 1989

Power, gender, and Christian mysticism / BV5083.J36 1995

Power, politics, and Pentecostals in Latin America / BR1644.5.L29.P68 1997

Power: a philosophical analysis / BD438.M63 1987

Powers of the rational: science, technology, and the future of thought / B2430.J283.P8513 1994

Practical guilt: moral dilemmas, emotions, and social norms / BJ1471.5.G74 1995

Practical logic / BC71.B3

Practical logic: an antidote for uncritical thinking / BC108.B27 1998

Practical reasoning / B105.A35.A93 1989

Practical reasoning: goal-driven, knowledge-based, action-guiding argumentation / B105.A35.W34 1989

Practical theology: perspectives from the plains / BR118.P72 2000

Practically religious: worldly benefits and the common religion of Japan / BL2211.R44.R43 1998

Practice of philosophy: a handbook for beginners, The / BD241.R65

Pragmatic mind: explorations in the psychology of belief, The / B832.B36 1997

Pragmatic theology: negotiating the intersections of an American philosophy of religion and public theology / BR100.A49 1998

Pragmatism and feminism: reweaving the social fabric / B832.S45 1996

Pragmatism and other writings / B945.J21 2000

Pragmatism, a new name for some old ways of thinking; The meaning of truth, a sequel to Pragmatism / B832.J2 1978

Pragmatism, and four essays from The meaning of truth / B832.J2 1955

Pragmatist aesthetics: living beauty, rethinking art / BH39.S5256 1992

Pragmatist's progress?: Richard Rorty and American intellectual history, A / B945.R524.P73 2000

Praise of theory: speeches and essays / B3248.G343.L6313 1998

Prayer according to the catechisms of the Reformation; / BV210.B333

Prayer has spoiled everything: possession, power, and identity in an Islamic town of Niger / BL2480.M32

Prayers; selected and edited from the earliest sources, with an essay on Donne's idea of prayer, / BV245.D65

Preacher King: Martin Luther King, Jr. And the word that moved America, The / BV4208.U6.L57 1995

Preacher: Billy Sunday and big-time American evangelism / BV3785.S8.B75 1992

Precious volumes: an introduction to Chinese sectarian scriptures from the sixteenth and seventeenth centuries / BL1802.O93 1999

Predicate logic: the semantic foundations of logic. / BC181.E67 2001

Preface to logic, A / BC71.C63 1977

Preface to modernism / BH301.M54.B47 1994

Preface to morals., A / BJ47.L5 1934

Preface to Sartre, A / B2430.S34.L24

Preferring justice: rationality, self-transformation, and the sense of justice / B105.J87.C38 1998

Pre-Platonic philosophers, The / B187.5.N5413 2001

Presbyterian controversy: fundamentalists, modernists, and moderates, The / BX8937.L65 1991

Presbyterians, The / BX8935.B355 1993

Presence of God: a history of Western Christian mysticism, The / BV5075.M37 1994

Presence of Stoicism in medieval thought, The / B528.V4 1983

Present philosophical tendencies; a critical survey of naturalism, idealism, pragmatism, and realism, / B804.P3 1955

Presocratic philosophers, The / B188.B34 1982

Presocratic philosophers: a critical history with a selection of texts, The / B188.K5 1983

Prevalence of deceit, The / BJ1421.B335 1991

Price of redemption: the spiritual economy of Puritan New England, The / BX9355.M4.P48 1997

Pride, faith, and fear: Islam in Sub-Saharan Africa / BP64.A37 Q56 2003

Priestess, mother, sacred sister: religions dominated by women / BL458.S45 1994

Primacy of perception, and other essays on phenomenological psychology, the philosophy of art, history, and politics, The / B2430.M378.E5 1964

Primal roots of American philosophy: pragmatism, phenomenology, and Native American thought, The / B893.W55 2000

Primer for critics, A / BH39.B6

Prime-time religion: an encyclopedia of religious broadcasting / BV656.M45 1997

Primitive church in the modern world, The / BR1661.P75 1995

Primitive renaissance: rethinking German expressionism / BH301.E9 P36 2001

Princess and the philosopher: letters of Elisabeth of the Palatine to Rene Descartes, The / B1873.N93 1999

Principle and practicality: essays in Neo-Confucianism and practical learning / B127.N4.P74

Principles and proofs: Aristotle's theory of demonstrative science / B441.M525 1992

Principles of human knowledge, and Three dialogues between Hylas and Philonous, The / B1331.T8 1963

Principles of mathematical logic, / BC135.H514

Principles of the philosophy of the future / B2971.G7.E52

Priorities and Christian ethics / BJ1278.P73.H35 1998

Prison journals of a priest revolutionary / BX4705.B3846.A3 1970

Prisoners of Shangri-La: Tibetan Buddhism and the West / BQ7604.L66 1998

Private needs, public selves: talk about religion in America / BL2525.R68 1997

Private virtue and public policy: Catholic thought and national life / BX1795.E27.P75 1990

Reality and mystical experience / BL51.B6487 2000

Reality of time, The / BD638.H277 1988

Realm of essence. Book first of Realms, of being, The / BD331.S3

Realm of matter. Book second of Realms of being, The / BD331.S33

Realm of rights, The / BJ55.T46 1990

Realm of spirit and the realm of Caesar;, The / B4238.B43.T83 1953

Realm of spirit. Book fourth of Realms of being, The / B945.S23.R38

Realm of the saint: power and authority in Moroccan Sufism / BP188.8.M6.C67 1998

Realm of truth. Book third of Realms of being, The / B945.S23.R4

Realms of being / B945.S23.R42 1972

Realms of meaning; a philosophy of the curriculum for general education / BD431.P5

Reason and anti-reason in our time / B3279.J33.V453

Reason and conduct; new bearings in moral philosophy / BJ354.A42.R4

Reason and emotion: essays on ancient moral psychology and ethical theory / BJ161.C66 1999

Reason and goodness / BJ43.B55 1961

Reason and morality / BJ1012.G47

Reason and morality: a defense of the egocentric perspective / BJ1012.F85 1990

Reason and religious faith / BL51.P3449 1995

Reason in the age of science / B29.G17 1982

Reason, truth, and history / BD171.P875

Reasonableness of Christianity, with A discourse of miracles, and part of A third letter concerning toleration, The / BR120.L62

Reasonableness of reason: explaining rationality naturalistically, The / BD212.H38 1995

Reasoning after revelation: dialogues in postmodern Jewish philosophy / B5802.P67.K46 1998

Rebel from riches: the autobiography of an unpremeditated monk, A / BX4705.R446.A34

Rebuilding Zion: the religious reconstruction of the South, 1863-1877 / BR535.S76 1998

Recent American philosophy; studies of ten representative thinkers, / B893.R4 1964

Reclaiming goodness: education and the spiritual quest / BL624.A43 2001

Reclaiming reality: a critical introduction to contemporary philosophy / B804.B48 1989

Reclaiming the spirit: gay men and lesbians come to terms with religion / BL65.H64.S53 1998

Recluse of Loyang: Shao Yung and the moral evolution of early Sung thought, The / B128.S514.W93 1996

Recognizing the Latino resurgence in U.S. religion: the Emmaus papadigm / BR563.H57.D53 1998

Recollection and experience: Plato's theory of learning and its successors / B398.L3 S36 1995

Reconceiving experience: a solution to a problem inherited from Descartes / B945.K393.R43 1996

Reconceptions in philosophy and other arts and sciences / BD241.G65 1988

Reconstructing religious, spiritual, and moral education / BL42.E75 2000

Recovery of the measure: interpretation and nature / BD581.N48 1989

Recovery of virtue: the relevance of Aquinas for Christian ethics, The / BJ1217.P67 1990

Red thread: Buddhist approaches to sexuality, The / BQ4570.S48.F3813 1998

Redeeming culture: American religion in an age of science / BL245.G55 1997

Redeeming the South: religious cultures and racial identities among Southern Baptists, 1865-1925 / BX6241.H37 1997

Redeeming the time: a political theology of the environment / BT695.5.S27 1997

Red-hot and righteous: the urban religion of the Salvation Army / BX9718.N7.W56 1999

Rediscovering God with transcendental argument: a contemporary interpretation of monistic Kashmiri Saiva philosophy / BL1281.1547.L38 1999

Rediscovering the moral life: philosophy and human practice / BJ1012.G665 1993

Rediscovery of the mind, The / BD418.3.S43 1992

Rediscovery of wisdom: from here to antiquity in quest of Sophia, The / BD555.C57 2000

Reduction and givenness: investigations of Husserl, Heidegger, and phenomenology / B3279.H49.M27413 1998

Reference and generality: an examination of some medieval and modern theories / BC71.G34 1980

Reference and modality; / BC199.M6.L54

Referring to God: Jewish and Christian philosophical and theological perspectives / BD573.R44 1999

Refiner's fire: a religious engagement with violence / BT736.15.K57 2001

Reflections on Jesus and Socrates: word and silence / B317.G66 1996

Reflections on the problem of relevance / B105.R3S34 1970

Reflections on things at hand; the Neo-Confucian anthology / B125.C513

Reflexive paradoxes / BD450.C4715 1988

Reflexive thesis: wrighting sociology of scientific knowledge, The / BD175.A85 1989

Reform Judaism in America: a biographical dictionary and sourcebook / BM750.R39 1993

Reformation in England, to the accession of Elizabeth I, The / BR375.D52 1968

Reformation in Poland; some social and economic aspects, The / BR420.P7.F6 1971

Reformation of the twelfth century, The / BX2590.C66 1996

Reformation thought: an introduction / BT26.M37 1988

Reformation world, The / BR305.2.P48 2000

Reformation writings of Martin Luther / BR331.E5.W6

Reformation; a narrative history related by contemporary observers and participants, The / BR305.2.H5 1964

Reformers in the wings: from Geiler von Kaysersberg to Theodore Beza / BR315.S83 2001

Re-forming the center: American Protestantism, 1900 to the present / BR525.R35 1998

Reforming the Church today: keeping hope alive / BX1746.K7913 1990

Regnum caelorum: patterns of millennial thought in early Christianity / BT819.5.H55 2001

Rehabilitation of myth: Vico's New science, The / B3581.P73.M35 1992

Reinhold Niebuhr and Christian realism / BX4827.N5.L68 1995

Reinventing American Protestantism: Christianity in the new millennium / BR526.M554 1997

Reinventing Paul / BS2655.J4 G34 2000

Reinventing religions: syncretism and transformation in Africa and the Americas / BL2490.R45 2001

Reinventing the wheel: a Buddhist response to the information age / BQ4570.I55.H47 1999

Relativism: feet firmly planted in mid-air / BJ37.B43 1998

Relevance of Whitehead; philosophical essays in commemoration of the centenary of the birth of Alfred North Whitehead, The / B1674.W354.L38 1961

Reliability of sense perception, The / BD214.A57 1993

Religion & power: pagans, Jews, and Christians in the Greek East / BR185.E38 1996

Religion & science: history, method, dialogue / BL240.2.R43 1996

Religion / BL21.R39513 1998

Religion and American politics: from the colonial period to the 1980s / BR516.R34 1990

Religion and contemporary liberalism / BR115.P7.R4338 1997

Religion and magic: approaches and theories / BL41.C86 1999

Religion and mass media: audiences and adaptations / BV652.95.R43 1996

Religion and mental health / BL53.R435 1992

Religion and moral reason: a new method for comparative study / BJ47.G74 1988

Religion and personal autonomy: the third disestablishment in America / BR526.H25 1992

Religion and philosophy of the Veda and Upanishads, The / BL1150.K43 1971

Religion and political behavior in the United States / BL65.P7 R427 1989

Religion and politics in Latin America: liberation theology and Christian democracy / BT83.57.L95 1991

Religion and politics in the United States / BL2525.W35 2003

Religion and popular culture in America / BL2525.R4613 2000

Religion and radical politics: an alternative Christian tradition in the United States / BR115.P7.C689 1992

Religion and resistance politics in South Africa / BR1450.G73 1995

Religion and revelation: a theology of revelation in the world's religions / BL475.5.W37 1994

Religion and science, / BL240.R8

Religion and social system of the Virasaiva community / BL1281.24.C54 1997

Religion and society in England, 1850-1914 / BR759.M37 1996

Religion and society in industrial England: church, chapel, and social change, 1740-1914 / BR755.G54

Religion and society in Kent, 1640-1914 / BR763.K46.Y38 1994

Religion and society in modern Japan: selected readings / BL2207.5.R45 1993

Religion and society in Tang and Sung China / BL1802.R45 1993

Religion and the common good: Catholic contributions to building community in a liberal society / BX1793.S75 1999

Religion and the decline of magic: studies in popular beliefs in sixteenth and seventeenth century England / BR377.T48 1997

Religion and the new immigrants: continuities and adaptations in immigrant congregations / BL2525.R4616 2000

Religion and the new republic: faith in the founding of America / BL2525.R4623 2000

Religion and the people of Western Europe, 1789-1970 / BL690.M38 1981

Religion and the variety of culture: a study in origin and practice / BL65.C8.S26 1996

Religion defined and explained / BL48.C5535 1993

Religion in a changing world: comparative studies in sociology / BL60.R4216 1998

Religion in an age of science / BL240.2.B368 1990

Religion in ancient Egypt: gods, myths, and personal practice / BL2441.2.R35 1991

Religion in China today: policy and practice / BL1802.M29 1989

Religion in contemporary Japan / BL2209.R42 1990

Religion in public life: a dilemma for democracy / BR115.P7.T475 1996

Religion in Russia after the collapse of communism: religious renaissance or secular state / BX493.K33 1998

Religion in sociological perspective / BL60.W543

Religion in the contemporary world: a sociological introduction / BL60.A53 1999

Religion in the making; Lowell lectures, 1926, / BL48.W35

Religion in Third World politics / BL65.P7.H38 1994

Religion of man, The / BL25.H5 1930

Road to total freedom: a sociological analysis of scientology, The / BP605.S2.W34 1977

Robert Nozick / B945.N684 R63 2002

Rocks of ages: science and religion in the fullness of life / BL240.2.G68 1999

Roger Bacon and his search for a universal science; a reconsideration of the life and work of Roger Bacon in the light of his own stated purposes / B765.B24.E28 1970

Roger Bacon in life and legend, / B765.B24.W4 1974

Roget's thesaurus of the Bible / BS432.D34 1992

Role of ethics in social theory: essays from a Habermasian perspective, The / BJ1012.S53 1991

Roles and rituals for Hindu women / BL1237.46.R64 1992

Roman Catholicism in America / BX1406.2.G45 1999

Roman Catholics & Shi i Muslims: prayer, passion & politics / BP194.18.C383 2002

Roman goddess Ceres, The / BL820.C5.S63 1996

Roman mind; studies in the history of thought from Cicero to Marcus Aurelius, The / B505.C58 1968

Romantic sublime: studies in the structure and psychology of transcendence, The / BH301.S7.W44

Rome and the African church in the time of Augustine / BR190.M47 1997

Rome has spoken: a guide to forgotten papal statements and how they have changed through the centuries / BX1747.5.R66 1998

Roots of anti-Semitism in the age of Renaissance and Reformation, The / BM535.O2413 1984

Roots of power: animate form and gendered bodies, The / B105.B64 S48 1994

Rorty and his critics / B945.R524 R673 2000

Rousseau, a study of his thought / B2137.B7 1963

Routledge encyclopedia of philosophy / B51.R68 1998

Routledge philosophy guidebook to Berkeley and the Principles of human knowledge / B1334.F64 2001

Royce on the human self / B945.R64.C6

Royce's mature philosophy of religion / B945.R64 O657 1987

Ruling passions: a theory of practical reasoning / BJ1311.B53 2000

Runaway religious in medieval England, c. 1240-1540 / BX2592.L64 1996

Russian church under the Soviet regime, 1917-1982, The / BX492.P67 1984

Russian intellectual history / BR932.C4513

Russian philosophy / B4201.E3

Russian symbolism; a study of Vyacheslav Ivanov and the Russian symbolist aesthetic / BH221.R93.W47

Sacred and the profane; the nature of religion, The / BL48.E413

Sacred books of Confucius, and other Confucian classics, The / BL1829.C5

Sacred companies: organizational aspects of religion and religious aspects of organizations / BL2525.S23 1998

Sacred games: a history of Christian worship / BV5.L36 1997

Sacred mountains of the world / BL447.B47 1990

Sacred paths: understanding the religions of the world, The / BL80.2.L83 2001

Sacred possessions: Vodou, Santeria, Obeah, and the Caribbean / BL2565.S23 1997

Sacred space: shrine, city, land / BL580.S25 1998

Sacred text, secular times: the Hebrew Bible in the modern world / BS1188.S33 2000

Sacrifice: its nature and function / BL570.H813

Saffron wave: democracy and Hindu nationalism in modern India, The / BL1215.P65 H36 1999

Sage philosophy: indigenous thinkers and modern debate on African philosophy / B5377.S24 1990

Saint Anselm: a portrait in a landscape / BX4700.A58.S59 1990

Saint Benedict and the sixth century / BX4700.B3.C5 1971

Saint veneration among the Jews in Morocco / BM440.M8.B44 1998

Sainthood in the later Middle Ages / BX2330.V3813 1997

Sainthood: its manifestations in world religions / BL488.S32 1988

Saints and postmodernism: revisioning moral philosophy / BJ1012.W97 1990

Saints and schemers: Opus Dei and its paradoxes / BX819.3.O68.E7413 1995

Saints and their cults: studies in religious sociology, folklore, and history / BX4655.2.S23 1983

Saints' lives and the rhetoric of gender: male and female in Merovingian hagiography / BX4682.K58 1998

Salvation at stake: Christian martyrdom in early modern Europe / BR307.G74 1999

Sameness and substance / BD236.W53 1980

Sanctified South: John Lakin Brasher and the Holiness Movement, The / BX8495.B754.B73 1994

Santayana and the sense of beauty / B945.S24.A8

Santayana, pragmatism, and the spiritual life / B945.S24 L48 1992

Santayana: an examination of his philosophy / B945.S24 S65

Santeria from Africa to the new world: the dead sell memories / BL2532.S3.B73 1993

Santería: an African religion in America / BL2532.S3 M87 1988

Santería; African magic in Latin America / BL2532.S3 G66

Sartre and evil: guidelines for a struggle / B2430.S34.G63 1995

Sartre, life and works / B2430.S34.T52 1984

Sartre, romantic rationalist / B2430.S34.M8

Sartre: a life / B2430.S34.C5413 1987

Sartre's two ethics: from authenticity to integral humanity / B2430.S34.A753 1993

Sense and certainty: a dissolution of scepticism / BD201.M37 1989

Sense and non-sense / B2430.M379.S43

Sentimental confessions: spiritual narratives of nineteenth-century African American women / BR1690.M59 2001

Separate God: the Christian origins of gnosticism, A / BT1390.P4513 1990

Serpent and the rainbow, The / BL2530.H3 D38 1985

Setting the gospel free: experiential faith and contemplative practice / BV4501.2.T269 1996

Seven Taoist masters: a folk novel of China / BL1923.S44 1990

Seventh-Day Adventism in crisis: gender and sectarian change in an emerging religion / BX6115.V36 1999

Sex, ecology, spirituality: the spirit of evolution / BD311.W54 1995

Sex, gender, and Christian ethics / BT708.C283 1996

Sexual love and western morality: a philosophical anthology / BD436.S44 1995

Sexual politics in the biblical narrative: reading the Hebrew Bible as a woman / BS1199.W7

Shadows of ethics: criticism and the just society / BJ46.H37 1999

Shaker experience in America: a history of the United Society of Believers, The / BX9766.S74 1992

Shamans and elders: experience, knowledge and power among the Daur Mongols / BL2370.S5.H85 1996

Shamans and religion: an anthropological exploration in critical thinking / BL2370.S5 K43 2000

Shaman's path: healing, personal growth & empowerment / BL2370.S5 S525 1988

Shambhala dictionary of Taoism, The / BL1923.S48 1996

Shambhala encyclopedia of yoga, The / BL1238.52.F47 1997

Shambhala guide to Taoism, The / BL1910.W66 1997

Shape of ancient thought: comparative studies in Greek and Indian philosophies, The / B165.M22 2002

Shape of space, The / BD632.N45 1994

Shape of the good: Christian reflections on the foundations of ethics, The / BJ1251.L34 1991

Shape of the turtle: myth, art, and cosmos in early China, The / B126.A44 1991

Sharing responsibility / BJ1451.M36 1992

Sherpas through their rituals / BL2032.S45.O77

Shiite Islam: polity, ideology, and creed / BP193.5.R5313 1995

Shiites: ritual and popular piety in a Muslim community, The / BP192.7.I4.P56 1992

Short history of Chinese philosophy, A / B126.F42 1948

Short history of Confucian philosophy, A / B128.C8.L58 1979

Short history of decay, A / BD450.C5413 1998

Short history of ethics: a history of moral philosophy from the Homeric Age to the twentieth century, A / BJ71.M3 1998

Short history of modern philosophy: from Descartes to Wittgenstein, A / B791.S29 2001

Short history of philosophy, A / B72.S66 1996

Short history of rudeness: manners, morals, and misbehavior in modern America, A / BJ1853.C23 1999

Short history of Western philosophy, A / B82.H5613 1976b

Short introduction to Islamic philosophy, theology and mysticism, A / B741.F265 1997

Showings / BV4831.J8 1978

Sickness unto death, The / BT715.K5313 1941

Sidgwick's ethics and Victorian moral philosophy / BJ604.S5.S36

Significance of consciousness, The / B808.9.S54 1998

Signs, language, and behavior / B840.M6 1955

Silencing of Leonardo Boff: the Vatican and the future of world Christianity, The / BX4705.B545.C69 1988

Silent cry: mysticism and resistance, The / BL625.S61513 2001

Simone de Beauvoir writing the self: philosophy becomes autobiography / B2430.B344.P55 1999

Simone Weil: a life / B2430.W474.P4613

Simone Weil: portrait of a self-exiled Jew / B2430.W474.N48 1991

Simone Weil: the way of justice as compassion / B2430.W474.B434 1998

Simplicity and complexity: pondering literature, science, and painting / B105.S55.M47 1998

Simpsons and philosophy: the d'oh! Of Homer, The / B68.S55 2001

Simulacra and simulation / BD236.B3813 1994

Singer and his critics / B5704.S554.S56 1999

Sinism: a study of the evolution of the Chinese world-view / B126.C7 1975

Sins of omission: a primer on moral indifference / BJ1251.F67 1990

Sister of wisdom: St. Hildegard's theology of the feminine / BX4700.H5.N48 1987

Sisters in the wilderness: the challenge of womanist God-talk / BT83.55.W55 1993

Situating the self: gender, community, and postmodernism in contemporary ethics / BJ1012.B45 1992

Situation ethics debate, The / BJ1251.F55 C6

Situations and attitudes / B840.B37 1999

Six great ideas: truth, goodness, beauty, liberty, equality, justice: ideas we judge by, ideas we act on / BD171.A24 1984

Six great themes of western metaphysics and the end of the Middle Ages, The / B738.M47.H4513 1994

Six great thinkers: Socrates, St. Augustine, Lord Bacon, Rousseau, Coleridge, John Stuart Mill / B72.D4

Six Jewish spiritual paths: a rationalist looks at spirituality / BM723.S665 2000

Six secular philosophers / BD573.B4

Talk about beliefs / BD215.C825 1992

Talking philosophy: a wordbook / B49.S63 1990

Talmud and the Internet: a journey between worlds, The / BM504.R657 2000

Talmudic stories: narrative art, composition, and culture / BM516.5.R83 1999

Taming of chance, The / BD595.H33 1990

Tanakh = [Tanakh]: a new translation of the Holy Scriptures according to the traditional Hebrew text / BS895.J4 1985

Tao and method: a reasoned approach to the Tao Te Ching / BL1900.L35 L32 1994

Tao encounters the West: explorations in comparative philosophy, The / B127.C65.L495 1999

Tao of philosophy: the edited transcripts, The / B799.W34 1995

Tao of the West: Western transformations of Taoist thought, The / BL1920.C55 2000

Taoism: growth of a religion / BL1910.R63 1997

Taoist body, The / BL1920.S2813 1993

Taoist classics: the collected translations of Thomas Cleary, The / BL1920.T33 1999

Taoist experience: an anthology, The / BL1910.K64 1993

Taoist meditation: the Mao-shan tradition of great purity / BL1923.R6313 1993

Taoist mystical philosophy: the scripture of western ascension / BL1900.H7965.K64 1991

Teacher's introduction to philosophical hermeneutics, A / BD241.C76 1991

Teachings of the Tao: readings from the Taoist spiritual tradition / B127.T3 T43 1997

Tears and saints / B105.S79 C5613 1995

Technical methods in philosophy / BC135.P683 1990

Technologies of the self: a seminar with Michel Foucault / BD450.T39 1988

Technology, war, and fascism / B945.M298 1998 vol. 1

Televangelism and American culture: the business of popular religion / BV656.3.S385 1991

Temporality, eternity, and wisdom: the rhetoric of Augustine's Confessions / BR65.A62.T78 1999

Temptations of evolutionary ethics, The / BJ1298.F37 1994

Tenacious of their liberties: the Congregationalists in colonial Massachusetts / BX7148.M4.C66 1999

Tensions in moral theology / BJ1249.C83 1988

Teresa of Avila: the progress of a soul / BX4700.T4.M38 1999

Terror in the mind of God: the global rise of religious violence / BL65.V55.J84 2000

Tertullian and the church / BT91.R36 1995

Testament to freedom: the essential writings of Dietrich Bonhoeffer, A / BR50.B63 1990

Testimony: a philosophical study / BD181.C59 1992

Texts and dialogues / B2430.M3763.T49 1991

Texts and traditions: a source reader for the study of Second Temple and rabbinic Judaism / BM176.T49 1998

Thales to Dewey; a history of philosophy / B74.C56

Thanks to God and the revolution: popular religion and class consciousness in the new Nicaragua / BR625.N5.L35 1988

Theologian and his universe: theology and cosmology from the Middle Ages to the present, The / BD518.D8.W5413 1982

Theologies and liberation in Peru: the role of ideas in social movements / BX1484.2.P46 1995

Theology and difference: the wound of reason / BR118.L69 1993

Theology and philosophy of Eliade: a search for the centre, The / BL43.E4.O47 1992

Theology for the third millennium: an ecumenical view / BT78.K8613 1988

Theology in a new key: responding to liberation themes / BR115.J8.B76

Theology of hope; on the ground and the implications of a Christian eschatology / BT821.2.M6313 1967b

Theology of Paul the Apostle, The / BS2651.D84 1998

Theology of the first letter to the Corinthians, The / BS2675.2.F87 1999

Theology primer, A / BT65.N48 1991

Theology, history, and culture: major unpublished writings / BR85.N615 1996

Theology, ideology, and liberation: towards a liberative theology / BT738.S394 1994

Theories of concepts: a history of the major philosophical tradition / BD181.W384 1988

Theories of ethics; / BJ21.F6

Theories of myth: an annotated bibliography / BL304.S54 1997

Theories of the mind / BD418.3.P75 1991

Theories of truth: a critical introduction / BC171.K55 1992

Theory as practice: ethical inquiry in the Renaissance / BJ271.S77 1992

Theory of argumentation, A / BC177.W544 1989

Theory of art, A / BH39.B393 2000

Theory of beauty in the classical aesthetics of Japan, The / BH221.J3 I95

Theory of beauty, The / BH201.C29 1949

Theory of beauty; an introduction to aesthetics / BH39.O8 1953

Theory of content and other essays, A / BD418.3.F63 1990

Theory of epistemic rationality, The / BD161.F57 1987

Theory of games as a tool for the moral philosopher. An inaugural lecture delivered in Cambridge on 2 December 1954 / BJ1533.F2.B7

Theory of knowledge / BD161.L368 1990

Theory of knowledge and existence, The / BD161.S67

Theory of knowledge, The / B809.8.C68

Wheel of great compassion: the practice of the prayer wheel in Tibetan Buddhism, The / BQ5075.P73 W44 2000

Wheel of life and death: a practical and spiritual guide, The / BD444.K34 1989

When a Jew dies: the ethnography of a bereaved son / BM712.H45 2001

When all the gods trembled: Darwinism, Scopes, and American intellectuals / BL245.C66 1998

When bad things happen to other people / BJ1409.P67 2000

When God becomes goddess: the transformation of American religion / BT102.G747 1995

When religion becomes evil / BJ1406.K56 2002

When time shall be no more: prophecy belief in modern American culture / BR526.B58 1992

White Lotus teachings in Chinese religious history, The / BQ8672.H23 1999

Whitebread Protestants: food and religion in American culture / BR115.N87 S23 2000

Whiteheadian aesthetic; some implications of Whitehead's metaphysical speculation, A / B1674.W354.S45 1970

Whitehead's metaphysics of creativity / B1674.W354.W53 1990

Whitehead's theory of experience / B1674.W38.S5 1950

Whitehead's theory of reality / B1674.W354.J6 1962

Who are the people of God?: early Christian models of community / BV598.K425 1995

Who are we?: critical reflections and hopeful possibilities / BT701.2.E47 2000

Who comes after the subject? / BD223.W49 1991

Who is a Sikh?: the problem of Sikh identity / BL2018.M319 1989

Who is Jesus?: history in perfect tense / BT303.2.K435 2000

Who killed Jesus?: exposing the roots of anti-semitism in the Gospel story of the death of Jesus / BT431.5.C76 1995

Who wrote the Dead Sea scrolls?: the search for the secret of Qumran / BM487.G65 1995

Who wrote the New Testament?: the making of the Christian myth / BS2361.2.M13 1995

Who's who in Christianity / BR1700.2.C64 1998

Who's who in classical mythology / BL715.R66 1997

Who's who in Egyptian mythology / BL2428.M47 1995

Who's who in hell: handbook and international directory for humanists, freethinkers, rationalists, and non-theists / BL2785.W55 2000

Who's who in philosophy / B804.W52

Who's who in theology: from the first century to the present / BR95.B65 1991

Who's who of religions / BL72.W54 1996

Who's who of world religions / BL72.W54 1992

Why Althusser killed his wife: essays on discourse and violence / B831.2.F56 1996

Why angels fall: a journey through Orthodox Europe from Byzantium to Kosovo / BX310.C58 2000

Why be moral?: the egoistic challenge / BJ1474.V36 1994

Why gods persist: a scientific approach to religion / BL48.H475 1999

Why I am not a Christian, and other essays on religion and related subjects / BL2780.R87 1957

Why Nietzsche still?: reflections on drama, culture, politics / B3317.W456 2000

Why religion matters: the fate of the human spirit in an age of disbelief / BL240.2.S635 2001

Why Waco?: cults and the battle for religious freedom in America / BP605.B72.T33 1995

Why you should: the pragmatics of deontic speech / BC145.F67 1989

Whys of a philosophical scrivener, The / B29.G253 1983

Wicked pleasures: meditations on the seven "deadly" sins / BV4626.W55 1999

Wickedness: a philosophical essay / BJ1401.M52 1984

Wilderness of dreams: exploring the religious meanings of dreams in modern Western culture, The / BL65.D67.B85 1994

Wildness pleases: the origins of romanticism, The / BH301.N3.T47 1983

Will and world: a study in metaphysics / BJ1461.N37 1992

Will in Western thought; an historico-critical survey / BD450.B64

Will the circle be unbroken?: reflections on death, rebirth, and hunger for a faith / BD444.T47 2001

Will to orthodoxy: a critical genealogy of Northern Chan Buddhism, The / BQ9262.9.C5.F37813 1997

William James / B945 .J24 B39 1999

William James on radical empiricism and religion / B945.J24.B762000

William James: the essential writings / B945.J21 1984

William James's "Springs of delight": the return to life / B945.J24.O55 2001

William James's philosophy: a new perspective / B945.J24 F67 1982

William Tyndale, / BR350.T8.M6

Wilson chronology of the world's religions, The / BL80.2.L464 2000

Wisdom of Confucius, The / B128.C7.L5 1943

Wisdom of the West; a historical survey of Western philosophy in its social and political setting / B72.R83 1959a

Wise choices, apt feelings: a theory of normative judgment / BJ1012.G53 1990

Wit and wisdom of Albert Schweitzer;, The / B3329.S52.E5 1949

With liberty for all: freedom of religion in the United States / BR516.H2 1998

Without God, without creed: the origins of unbelief in America / BL2757.T87 1985

Without good reason: the rationality debate in philosophy and cognitive science / BD450.S747 1996

Witness of the brothers: a history of the Bruderhof, The / BX8129.B63.O94 1996

Witnessing: beyond recognition / B828.45.O55 2001

Wittgenstein / B3376.W564.H244 1999

Wittgenstein and Kierkegaard: religion, individuality, and philosophical method / B3376.W564.C74 1989

Wittgenstein and moral philosophy / BJ1012.J64 1989

Wittgenstein, empiricism, and language / B3376.W564.C65 2000

Wittgenstein, Frazer, and religion / B3376.W564.C57 1999

Wittgenstein: attention to particulars: essays in honour of Rush Rhees (1905-89) / B3376.W564.W5556 1989

Wittgenstein's city / B3376.W564.A64 1988

Wittgenstein's early philosophy: three sides of the mirror / B3376.W563.T7356 1990

Wittgenstein's later philosophy / B3376.W564.H295 1989

Wittgenstein's thought in transition / B3376.W564.J33 1998

Wittgenstein's Tractatus: a critical exposition of its main lines of thought / BC135.W52.S8 1981

Wittgenstein's Vienna revisited / B3376.W564.J364 2001

Womanguides: readings toward a feminist theology / BL458.W572 1985

Women and evil / BJ1401.N63 1989

Women and mystical experience in the Middle Ages / BV5095.H55.B44 1992

Women and redemption: a theological history / BT704.R835 1998

Women and religion in America / BR515.W648 1981

Women and spiritual equality in Christian tradition / BV639.W7.R36 1998

Women in myth / BL325.F4.K53 1997

Women in new religions: insearch of community, sexuality, and spiritual power / BL458.P88 1997

Women in scripture: a dictionary of named and unnamed women in the Hebrew Bible, the Apocryphal/Deuterocanonical books, and the New Testament / BS575.W593 2000

Women in the earliest churches / BR195.W6.W58 1988

Women in the Inquisition: Spain and the New World / BX1735.W59 1999

Women mystics confront the modern world: Marie de l'Incarnation (1599-1672) and Madame Guyon (1648-1717) / BV5095.A1.B69 1998

Women of classical mythology: a biographical dictionary / BL715.B445 1991

Women of color and philosophy: a critical reader / B105.W6 W64 2000

Women philosophers / B105.W6 W65 1996

Women pilgrims in late medieval England: private piety and public performance / BX2320.5.G7

Women preachers and prophets through two millennia of Christianity / BV676.W556 1998

Women, the book, and the godly: selected proceedings of the St. Hilda's conference, 1993 / BX4210.W65 1995

Women's Bible commentary, The / BS491.2.W66 1992

Women's Buddhism, Buddhism's women: tradition, revision, renewal / BQ4570.W6.W66 2000

Women's monasticism and medieval society: nunneries in France and England, 890-1215 / BX4220.E85.V46 1997

Women's movement in the Church of England, 1850-1930, The / BX5182.3.H43 1988

Word according to Eve: women and the Bible in ancient times and our own, The / BS680.W7.M87 1998

Word and object / B840.Q5

Word fitly spoken: context, transmission, and adoption of the parables of Jesus, A / BT375.2.C85 1995

Word in the desert: scripture and the quest for holiness in early Christian monasticism, The / BX2465.B87 1993

Word of God and the word of man, The / BR121.B2455 1957

Words of power: a feminist reading of the history of logic / BC57.N94 1990

Work and integrity: the crisis and promise of professionalism in America / BJ1725.S85 1995

Work of friendship: Rorty, his critics, and the project of solidarity, The / B945.R524.R68 1999

Working the spirit: ceremonies of the African diaspora / BL2490.M87 1994

Working without a net: a study of egocentric epistemology / BD161.F58 1993

Works of Francis Bacon, Baron of Verulam .., The / B1153. 1857

Works of Herbert Spencer, The / B1652.A2 1966

Works of Saint Augustine: a translation for the 21st century, The / BR65.A5.E53 1990

Workshop rotation: a new model for Sunday School / BV1534.A76 2000

World Catholicism in transition / BX1390.W67 1988

World Christian encyclopedia: a comparative survey of churches and religions in the modern world / BR157.W67 2001

World guide to religious and spiritual organizations / BL35.W67

World history of Christianity, A / BR145.2.H37 1999

World hypotheses, a study in evidence, / BD111.P38 1966

World of biblical literature, The / BS535.A57 1991

World of Buddhism: Buddhist monks and nuns in society and culture, The / BQ4012.W67 1991

World of Parmenides: essays on the Presocratic enlightenment, The / B187.5.P66 1998